A
BODY OF
DOCTRINAL DIVINITY

JOHN GILL, D.D.
1697-1771

A Body of Doctrinal Divinity;

OR
A SYSTEM OF EVANGELICAL TRUTHS,

DEDUCED FROM THE
SACRED SCRIPTURES.

BY JOHN GILL, D.D.

A NEW EDITION

The Baptist Standard Bearer, Inc.
NUMBER ONE IRON OAKS DRIVE • PARIS, ARKANSAS 72855

Thou hast given a *standard* to them that fear thee;
that it may be displayed because of the truth.
— *Psalm 60:4*

ADVERTISEMENT.

SHOULD the Public require any pledge in order to create a confidence in, or *preference* for, *this* Edition of Dr. GILL'S BODY OF DIVINITY; they are respectfully assured that it is a *verbatim* reprint of the *original, in 3 vols. quarto,* (which was published under the inspection of the Author's own eye,) without any abridgment, or the *least* alteration, excepting in a few instances, where *typographical* errors may have been discovered. The work has undergone a very careful revisal; and is therefore presented as the most correct Edition which has ever yet appeared.

The Publishers also flatter themselves, that the *excellent* Portrait of the venerable Doctor, together with the interesting Memoir of his Life and Writings, which accompany the book, will be found greatly to enhance its value, and raise it far above the level of *all* preceding editions.

London, June 1839.

*Reprinted
by*

THE BAPTIST STANDARD BEARER, INC.
No. 1 Iron Oaks Drive
Paris, Arkansas 72855
(501) 963-3831

THE WALDENSIAN EMBLEM
lux lucet in tenebris
"The Light Shineth in the Darkness"

ISBN #1-57978-887-4

CONTENTS.

INTRODUCTION xxiii

A BODY OF DOCTRINAL DIVINITY.

BOOK I.

OF GOD, HIS WORD, NAMES, NATURE, PERFECTIONS, AND PERSONS.

CHAP.	PAGE
1 Of the Being of God	1
2 Of the Holy Scriptures	11
3 Of the Names of God	25
4 Of the Nature of God	30
Of the Spirituality of God	31
Of the Simplicity of God	33
5 Of the Attributes of God	34
Of the Immutability of God	35
6 Of the Infinity of God	41
Of the Omnipresence of God	42
Of the Eternity of God	45
7 Of the Life of God	50
8 Of the Omnipotence of God	53
9 Of the Omniscience of God	58
10 Of the Wisdom of God	64
11 Of the Will of God, and its Sovereignty	70
12 Of the Love of God	78
13 Of the Grace of God	81
14 Of the Mercy of God	85
15 Of the Long-suffering of God	89
16 Of the Goodness of God	91
17 Of the Anger of God	95
Of the Wrath of God	97
18 Of the Hatred of God	99
19 Of the Joy of God	102
20 Of the Holiness of God	103
21 Of the Justice of God	106
22 Of the Veracity of God	110
23 Of the Faithfulness of God	113
24 Of the Sufficiency and Perfection of God	119
25 Of the Blessedness of God	122
26 Of the Unity of God	125
27 Of a Plurality in the Godhead	130
28 Of the Personal Relations in Deity	140
29 Of the Distinct Personality and Deity of the Father	160
30 Of the Distinct Personality and Deity of the Son	162
31 Of the Distinct Personality and Deity of the Holy Spirit	167

BOOK II.
OF THE ACTS AND WORKS OF GOD.

1 Of the Internal Acts of God, and of his Decrees in general	172
2 Of the Special Decrees of God, particularly of Election	176
3 Of the Rejection of some Angels, and some Men	192
4 Of the Union of the Elect to God	198
5 Of Adoption as an Immanent Act	201
Of Justification as an Immanent Act	203
6 Of the Everlasting Council	209
7 Of the Everlasting Covenant of Grace	214
8 Of the Part which the Father takes in the Covenant	219

CHAP.	PAGE
9 Of the Part which the Son takes in the Covenant	226
10 Of Christ as the Covenant Head of the Elect	227
11 Of Christ the Mediator of the Covenant	229
12 Of Christ the Surety of the Covenant	237
13 Of Christ the Testator of the Covenant	241
14 Of the Concern which the Spirit has in the Covenant	244
15 Of the Properties of the Covenant	247
16 Of the Complacency and Delight which the Divine Persons had in each other from Eternity	250

BOOK III.
OF THE EXTERNAL WORKS OF GOD.

1 Of Creation in General	256
2 Of the Creation of Angels	262
3 Of the Creation of Man	268
4 Of the Providence of God	277
5 Of the Confirmation of the Elect Angels, and Fall of the Non-elect	304
6 Of the Honour and Happiness of Man in Innocence	309
7 Of the Law given to Adam, and Covenant made with him	311
8 Of the Sin and Fall of our First Parents	317
9 Of the Nature, Aggravations, and Sad Effects of the sin of Man	321
10 Of the Imputation of Adam's sin to all his Posterity	324
11 Of the Corruption of Human Nature	330
12 Of Actual Sins, and Transgressions	337
13 Of the Punishment of Sin	341

BOOK IV.
OF THE ACTS OF THE GRACE OF GOD, TOWARDS, AND UPON HIS ELECT IN TIME.

1 Of the Manifestation, and Administration of the Covenant of Grace	345
2 Of the Covenant of Grace in the Patriarchal State	348
3 Of the Covenant of Grace under the Mosaic Dispensation	354
4 Of the Covenant of Grace in the times of David and the Prophets	357
5 Of the Abrogation of the Old Covenant	360
6 Of the Law of God	367
7 Of the Gospel	372

BOOK V.
OF THE GRACE OF CHRIST IN HIS STATES OF HUMILIATION AND EXALTATION, AND IN THE OFFICES EXERCISED BY HIM IN THEM.

1 Of the Incarnation of Christ	378
2 Of Christ's State of Humiliation	390
3 Of the Active Obedience of Christ	396
4 Of the Passive Obedience of Christ	401

CONTENTS.

CHAP.	PAGE.
5 Of the Burial of Christ	406
6 Of the Resurrection of Christ	410
7 Of the Ascension of Christ	415
8 Of the Session of Christ at the Right Hand of God	420
9 Of the Prophetic Office of Christ	424
10 Of the Priestly Office of Christ	427
11 Of the Intercession of Christ	431
12 Of Christ's Blessing his People as a Priest	435
13 Of the Kingly Office of Christ	439
14 Of the Spiritual Reign of Christ	448

BOOK VI.
OF THE BLESSINGS OF GRACE, AND THE DOCTRINES OF IT.

1 Of Redemption by Christ	454
2 Of the Causes of Redemption	457
3 Of the Objects of Redemption	461
4 Of Scriptures which seem to Favour Universal Redemption	467
5 Of the Satisfaction of Christ	475
6 Of Propitiation, Atonement, and Reconciliation	488
7 Of Pardon of Sin	493
8 Of Justification	501

CHAP.	PAGE
9 Of Adoption	518
10 Of the Liberty of the Sons of God	525
11 Of Regeneration	528
12 Of Effectual Calling	538
13 Of Conversion	545
14 Of Sanctification	552
15 Of the Perseverance of the Saints	559

BOOK VII.
OF THE FINAL STATE OF MAN.

1 Of the Death of the Body	579
2 Of the Immortality of the Soul	585
3 Of the Separate State of the Soul	593
4 Of the Resurrection of the Body	602
5 Of the Second Coming and Personal Appearance of Christ	615
6 Of the Conflagration of the Universe	625
7 Of the New Heavens and Earth, and their Inhabitants	636
8 Of the Millennium, or Personal Reign of Christ	643
9 Of the Last and General Judgment	667
10 Of the Final State of the Wicked	676
11 Of the Final State of the Saints in Heaven	686

Memoir of John Gill and Publisher's Foreword to our 1984 Edition are Appendices to "A Body of Practical Divinity".

INTRODUCTION.

HAVING completed an Exposition of the whole Bible, the Books both of the Old and of the New Testament; I considered with myself what would be best next to engage in for the further instruction of the people under my care; and my thoughts led me to enter upon a Scheme of Doctrinal and Practical Divinity, first the former and then the latter; the one being the foundation of the other, and both having a close connection with each other. Doctrine has an influence upon practice, especially evangelical doctrine, spiritually understood, affectionately embraced, and powerfully and feelingly experienced; so true is what the Apostle asserts, that the *Grace of God*, that is, the Doctrine of the Grace of God, *that bringeth Salvation*, the good news, the glad tidings of salvation by Christ, which is peculiar to Gospel Doctrine, *hath appeared to all men*, Gentiles as well as Jews, in the external ministry of the word; *teaching us*, to whom it comes with power and efficacy in the demonstration of the Spirit, *that denying ungodliness and worldly lusts, we should live soberly, righteously, and godly in this present world*, Tit. ii. 11, 12. Where there is not the doctrine of faith, the obedience of faith cannot be expected. Where there is not the doctrine of the Gospel, and men have not learned Christ, they live for the most part as if there was no God in the world, and give themselves up to work all sin with greediness. And on the other hand, doctrine without practice, or a mere theory and speculative knowledge of things, unless reduced to practice, is of no avail; such are only "vainly puffed up in their fleshly minds, profess to know God in word, but in works deny him, have a form of godliness without the power of it, a name to live but are dead." Doctrine and practice should go together; and in order both to know and do the will of God, instruction in doctrine and practice is necessary; and the one being first taught will lead on to the other. This method of instruction the Apostle Paul has pointed out to us in some of his Epistles, especially in the Epistle to the Ephesians; in which he first treats of Election, Predestination, Adoption, Acceptance in Christ, Redemption and Pardon of Sin, Regeneration and other doctrines of grace, and of the privileges of the Saints under the Gospel dispensation; and then enforces the several duties incumbent on them as men and Christians, respecting them in their several stations, in the church, in their families, and in the world. So the Apostle instructed Timothy, first to *teach* the wholesome words of our Lord Jesus, the doctrine that is according to godliness and productive of it, and then to *exhort* and press men to the duties of religion from evangelical motives and principles. And he also enjoined Titus to affirm the doctrines of the Gospel with constancy and certainty, to this end, "that they which have believed in God might be careful to maintain good works." 1. Tim. vi. 2, 3. Tit. iii. 8.

And now having finished my Scheme of Doctrinal Divinity, at the importunity of my friends I have been prevailed upon to publish it.

Systematical Divinity, I am sensible, is now become very unpopular. Formulas and articles of faith, creeds, confessions, catechisms, and summaries of divine truths, are greatly decried in our age; and yet, what art or science soever but has been reduced to a system? physic, metaphysic, logic, rhetoric, &c. Philosophy in general has had its several systems: not to take notice of the various sects and systems of philosophy in ancient times; in the last age, the Cartesian system of philosophy greatly obtained, as the Newtonian system now does. Astronomy in particular has been considered as a system; sometimes called the System of the Universe, and sometimes the Solar or Planetary System: the first that is known is what was brought by Pythagoras into Greece and Italy, and from him called the Pythagorean System; and which was followed by many of the first and ancient philosophers, though for many years it lay neglected; but has been of late ages revived, and now much in vogue: the next is the Ptolemaic System, advanced by Ptolemy; which places the earth in the centre of the universe, and makes the heavens, with the sun, moon, and stars, to revolve about it; and which was universally embraced for many hundred years, till the Pythagorean System was revived by Copernicus, two or three hundred years ago, called, from him, the Copernican System. In short, medicine, jurisprudence or law, and every art and science, are reduced to a system or body; which is no other than an assemblage or composition of the several doctrines or parts of a science; and why should Divinity, the most noble science,[1] be without a system? Evangelical truths are spread and scattered about in the sacred Scriptures; and to gather them together, and dispose of them in a regular orderly method, surely cannot be disagreeable; but must be useful, for the more clear and perspicuous understanding them, for the better retaining them in memory, and to shew the connection, harmony, and agreement of them. Accordingly, we find that Christian writers, in ancient times, attempted something of this nature; as the several formulas of faith, symbols, or creeds, made in the first three or four centuries of Christianity; the *Stromata* of Clemens of Alexandria; the four books of Principles, by Origen; the divine Institutions of Lactantius; the large Catechism of Gregory Nyssene; the Theology of Gregory Nazianzen; the Exposition of the Apostles' Symbol, by Ruffinus; and the Enchiridion of Austin, with many others that followed: and since the Reformation, we have had bodies or systems of divinity, and confessions of faith, better digested, and drawn up with greater accuracy and consistence; and which have been very serviceable to lead men into the knowledge of evangelical doctrine, and confirm them in it; as well as to shew the agreement and harmony of sound divines and churches, in the more principal parts of it: and even those who now cry out against systems, confessions, and creeds, their predecessors had those of their own; Arius had his creed; and the Socinians have their catechism, the Racovian Catechism; and the Remonstrants have published their confession of faith; not to take notice of the several Bodies of Divinity, published by Episcopius, Limborch, Curcellæus, and others. The Jews in imitation of the Christians, have reduced their theology to certain heads or articles of faith; the chief, if not the first that took this method, was the famous Maimonides, who comprised their religious tenets in *thirteen* articles: after him R. Joseph Alba reduced them to *three* classes, the Existence of God, the Law of Moses, and the Doctrine of Rewards and Punishments.

But what makes most for our purpose, and is worthy of our example, are the Scripture Compendiums or Systems of Doctrine and Duty. What a compendium or body of laws is the *Decalogue* or *Ten Commands*, drawn up and calculated more especially for the use of the Jews, and suited to their circumstances! a body of laws not to be equalled by the wisest legislators of Greece and Rome, Minos, Lycurgus, Zaleucus, and Numa; nor by the laws of the Twelve Roman Tables, for order and regularity, for clearness and perspicuity, for comprehensiveness and brevity; being divided into two tables, in the most perfect order; the first respecting the worship of God and the duties owing to him, and the other respecting men and the mutual duties they owe to each other. As prayer is a very principal and incumbent duty on men with respect to God, our Lord has given a very compendious directory, as to the matter of it, in what is commonly called the *Lord's Prayer;* which consists of petitions the most full, proper, and pertinent, and in the most regular order. And as to articles of faith or things to be believed, we have a creed, made mention of in Heb. vi. 1, 2. consisting of six articles; repentance from dead works, faith towards God, the doctrine of baptisms, and of laying on of hands, the resurrection of the dead, and eternal judgment. These are commonly thought to be so many articles of the Christian faith; but I rather think[2] they are so many articles of the Jewish Creed, embraced and professed by believers under the Jewish dispensation; since the Christian Hebrews are directed to consider them as the principles of the doctrine of Christ, as an introduction, and as leading on to it, and which were in some sense to be *left* and not *laid again;* they were not to stick and stop here, but to go on to perfection, by searching into and embracing doctrines more sublime and perfect, revealed in

---

[1] Quo enim et nobilior cæteris omnibus disciplinis est theologia, eo magis accurate sunt ejus dogmata noscenda, ac methodice etiam percipienda; Amesii Paraenesis ad Studios. Theolog.
[2] See my Exposition of Heb. vi. 1. 2.

the Gospel; at least they were not to be any longer instructed in the above articles in the manner they had been, but in a clearer manner, unattended with legal ceremonies, to view them and make use of them. Thus for instance, they, the believers, Christian Hebrews, were not to learn the doctrine of *repentance* from slain beasts or to signify it by them, as they had been used to do; for every sacrifice brought for sin, which they were no longer obliged to, was a tacit confession and an acknowledgment of sin, and that they repented of it, and deserved to die as the creature did; but now they were to exercise evangelical repentance in the view of a crucified Christ, and remission of sin by his blood: and whereas they had been taught to have *faith towards God*, as the God of Israel, they were now moreover to believe in Christ as the Son of God, the true Messiah, the Saviour of lost sinners, without the intervention of sacrifices. See John xiv. 1. The *doctrine of baptisms*, is to be understood of the divers baptisms, or bathings among the Jews, spoken of in Heb. ix. 10. which had a doctrine in them, teaching the cleansing virtue of the blood of Christ to wash in for sin and for uncleanness; which they were no more to learn in this way, but to apply immediately to the blood of Christ for it. And the doctrine of *laying on of hands* respects the laying on of the hands of the priests and people on the head of the sacrifices, which instructed in that great and evangelical truth, the transfer and imputation of sin to Christ, offered up in the room and stead of his people; and which was to be taught and learnt no longer in that manner, since Christ was now made sin for his people, and had had their sins imputed to him, which he had borne in his own body on the tree: and as for the doctrines of the *resurrection of the dead and eternal judgment*, they were such as distinguished Jews and Gentiles, which latter were greatly strangers to a future state; and though they were common to Jews and Christians, yet the believing Hebrews were not to rest in the knowledge they had of these, as enjoyed under the former dispensation; but to go on to perfection; and press forward towards a greater share of knowledge of them and of other more sublime doctrines; since life and immortality were brought to light by Christ in a clearer and brighter manner through the Gospel. But all that I mean by this is, that the principal doctrines of faith under the Jewish dispensation are reduced to a system, though to be improved and perfected under the gospel dispensation. Those articles were but few; though Gregory[3] observes, that according to the increase of times, the knowledge of saints increased, and the nearer they were to the coming of the Saviour the more fully they perceived the mysteries of salvation: and so the articles in the formulas and symbols of the first Christians were but few, suitable to the times in which they lived, and as opposite to the errors then broached; and which were increased by new errors that sprung up, which made an increase of articles necessary; otherwise the same articles of faith were believed by the ancients as by later posterity, as Aquinas concludes:[4] " Articles of faith," says he, " have increased by succession of times, not indeed, as to the substance, but as to the explanation and express profession of them; for what are explicitly and under a greater number believed by posterity, all the same were believed by the fathers before them, implicitly and under a lesser number." It is easy to observe, that the first summaries of faith recorded by the most ancient writers, went no further than the doctrine of the Trinity, or what concerns the Three Divine Persons; the doctrines of the heretics of the first ages being opposed to one or other of them: but when other heresies sprung up and other false doctrines were taught, it became necessary to add new articles, both to explain, defend, and secure truth, and to distinguish those who were sound in the faith of the Gospel from those that were not.

Mention is made in the New Testament of a *form of doctrine delivered*, and a *form of sound words* that had been *heard* and was to be *held fast*, and of a *proportion* or *analogy of faith*, according to which ministers were to prophesy or preach; the first of these is spoken of in Rom. vi. 17.—*But ye have obeyed from the heart that form of doctrine which was delivered to you;* which is not be understood of the Scriptures or written word delivered unto them; but of the Gospel and the doctrines of it preached by the apostle in the ministry of the word to the Romans, which they had yielded the obedience of faith unto, and which was τυπος, a *type*, or pattern, as the word is rendered, Heb. viii. 5. and an *example*, 1 Tim. iv. 12. according to which they were to conform

---

[3] Homil. 16. in Ezek. apud Aquin.
[4] Summa Theolog. Sec. sec. qu. i. artic. 7.

their faith and practice; and which in the next place referred to, 2 Tim. i. 13. is called ὑποτύπωσις, translated a *pattern*, 1 Eph. i. 16. a form exactly expressed, always to be had in view, to be attended to, and followed; and a delineation, such as a picture or the outlines of a portrait given by painters to their learners, always to be looked unto and imitated; and such a form the apostle proposed to Timothy, carefully to respect and give information of to others as a rule of faith and practice;[5] which cannot be understood of the Scriptures, though of what is agreeable to them; since it is what Timothy had heard of the apostle, either in his private conversation, or in his public ministry, even a set of Gospel doctrines collected out of the scriptures and confirmed by them, reduced into a system; and thus the apostle himself reduces his ministry to these two heads, *repentance towards God*, and *faith towards the Lord Jesus Christ*, Acts xx. 21. And a rich summary and glorious compendium and chain of Gospel truths does he deliver, Rom. viii. 30. worthy, as a form and pattern, to gospel ministers to attend unto, and according to it to regulate their ministrations. Once more, the apostle speaks of a *proportion* or an *analogy of faith*, in Rom. xii. 6. *Whether prophesy, let us prophesy according to the proportion of faith;* by which *faith* Calvin, on the text observes, are meant the first axioms of religion, to which whatsoever doctrine is not found to answer is convicted of falsehood. And so Piscator, upon the words, according *to the analogy of faith*, that is, so as that the interpretation of Scripture we bring is analogous to the articles of faith, that is, agreeing with them and consenting to them, and not repugnant; and Paræus on the text is more express: "*Analogy*," he says, "is not the same as *measure* (ver. 3.) for measure is of one thing measured, but analogy is between two things that are analogous; but the apostle seems to describe something more, namely, to prescribe a rule by which all prophesying is to be directed; therefore by *faith* others understand the rule of Scripture, and the axioms of faith, such as are comprehended in the Symbol of the Apostolic faith (or the Apostles' Creed) which have in them a manifest truth from the Scriptures. *Analogy* is the evident harmony of faith and consent of the heads (or articles) of faith, to which whatever agrees is true, and whatsoever disagrees is false and adulterate. This is the rule of all prophesying (or preaching;) therefore, according to the rule of the sacred Scripture and the Apostles' Creed, all interpretations, disputations, questions, and opinions in the church, are to be examined, that they may be conformable thereunto." And though what is now called the Apostles' Creed might not be composed by them, nor so early as their time; yet the substance of it was agreeable to their doctrine, and therefore called theirs; and there was a *regula fidei*, a rule of faith, very near it in words, received, embraced, and professed very early in the Christian church; which Tertullian[6] gives in these words, "The rule of faith is truly one, solely immoveable and irreformable (not to be corrected and mended;) namely, of believing in the only God Almighty, the maker of the world, and in his Son Jesus Christ, born of the virgin Mary, crucified under Pontius Pilate, raised from the dead on the third day, received into heaven, sitting now at the right hand of the Father, who will come to judge the quick and dead by or at the resurrection of the dead." And such a set of principles these, as or what are similar to them and accord with the word of God, may be called the analogy of faith. And a late writer[7] observes on the word *analogy;* "The analogy of faith, our divines call the sum of heavenly doctrine concerning articles of faith, taken out of such passages of Scripture, where, as in their proper place, they are treated of in clear and plain words." Upon the whole, it seems no ways incongruous with the sacred writings, but perfectly agreeable to them, that articles and heads of faith, or a summary of gospel truths, may be collected from them, to declare explicitly our belief of them, to strengthen the faith of others in them, to shew our agreement in them with other Christians in the principal

---

[5] Calvin on the passage has these words, "The apostle seems to me to command Timothy that he be tenacious of the doctrine he had learned, not only as to the substance, but as to the figure of the oration, (or form of speech or set of words used) for ὑποτύπωσις, the word used, is a lively expression of things as if presented to the eye. Paul knew how easy is a lapse or deflection from the pure doctrine, and therefore solicitously cautioned Timothy not to decline from the form of teaching he had received."

[6] De virgin. veland. c. l. vid. præscript. hæret. c. 13.

[7] Analogiam fidei nostrates dicunt summam cœlestis doctrinæ de articulis fidei e talibus scripturæ petitam locis, ubi claris et perspicuis verbis ac, seu in propria sede, de iis agitur, Stockii Clavis Ling. s. Nov. Test. p. 627.

parts of them, and to distinguish ourselves from those who oppose the faith once delivered to the saints.

It is strongly pleaded, that articles and confessions of faith, in which men are to agree, should be expressed in the bare words of the sacred Scriptures, and that nothing should be considered as a fundamental article that is matter of controversy : as to the latter, if that was admitted, there would be scarce any article left us at all to believe; for what is there almost that is believed, but what is controverted by some, nor any passage of Scripture brought in support of it, but the sense of it is called in question, or perverted? for as Clemens of Alexandria[a] says, " I do not think there is any scripture so happy as to be contradicted by none." As to the former, that we are to be tied up to the bare words of Scripture concerning any doctrine of faith delivered in them; though we ought to entertain the highest esteem of the words of Scripture, and have the greatest value for them, as being clothed with such majesty, and having such an energy in them, which the words that man's wisdom teacheth have not; yet our sense of them cannot be expressed but in words literally varying from them: and it should be settled what is meant by bare words of scripture, whether of the original text, Hebrew and Greek, or of any translation, as English, &c.; if the words of a translation, a man cannot be sure that this always does express the sense of scripture, especially in passages difficult and controverted; if of the original, then both he that makes the confession, and they to whom it is made, ought to understand Hebrew and Greek; and even every member of a church where a confession of faith is required in order to communion; and if this is to be made in the bare words of Scripture, be it in the words of a translation, without an explanation of their sense of them in other words, it might introduce into a Christian community all sorts of errors that can be named, which would be utterly inconsistent with its peace, concord, harmony, and union: moreover, to be obliged to express ourselves only in the words of Scripture, would be—1. To destroy all exposition and interpretation of Scripture; for without words different from, though agreeable to, the sacred Scriptures, we can never express our sense of them, nor explain them to others according to the sense we have entertained of them; and though no scripture is of private interpretation, or a man's own interpretation, so as to be obliging on others, yet by this means it will become of no interpretation at all, private or public, of a man's own or of others. It is indeed sometimes said that *Scripture is the best interpreter of Scripture*, and which in some respects is true; as when for the better understanding of a passage of Scripture, another more clear and explicit is set unto it and compared with it, and which serves to throw light on it and give a clearer discernment of it, and of its true sense; but then that light, discernment and sense, cannot be expressed but in words literally different from them both.—2. To be obliged to express ourselves about divine things in the bare words of Scripture, must tend to make the ministry and preaching of the word in a great measure useless; for then a minister of the word would have nothing else to do but to repeat or read some select passages of Scripture relating to any particular subject, or collect a string of them, which refer to the same subject, and deliver them without attempting any illustration of them, or making use of any reasonings from them, to explain or strengthen any point of doctrine contained in them; so that the people in common may as well, in a manner, stay at home and read the Scriptures in their private houses, as to attend on public ministrations. Surely the apostle Paul, when he "reasoned out of the Scriptures, opening and alledging that Christ must needs have suffered and risen again from the dead, and that this Jesus whom he preached was Christ," (Acts xvii. 2, 3.) must in these his reasonings, explanations, and allegations, use his own words; which though they accorded with the Scriptures, must literally vary from them out of which he reasoned, and by which he elucidated and confirmed his arguments concerning the Messiahship of Jesus, his suffering of death, and resurrection from the dead: and though he said no other as to substance than what Moses and the prophets said concerning Christ, yet in words different from theirs. According to this scheme all public ministrations must be at an end, as well as all writing in defence of truth and for the confutation of errors; yea—3. This must in a great measure cramp all religious conversation about divine things, if not destroy it. To what purpose is it for them that fear God to meet frequently and speak often one to another about the

[a] Stromat. l. 1. p. 277.

things of God, and truths of the Gospel, if they are not to make use of their own words to express their sense of these things by them? and how in this way can their Christian conferences be to mutual edification? how can they build up one another in their most holy faith? how can weaker and less experienced Christians receive any advantage from more knowing and stronger ones, if only they are to declare their sense of things in the bare words of Scripture?—4. Indeed, as Dr. Owen says,[9] if this is the case, as it would be unlawful to speak or write, otherwise than in the words of Scripture, so it would be unlawful to think or conceive in the mind any other than what the Scripture expresses: the whole of what he says on this subject is worth repeating; "To deny the liberty, yea, the necessity hereof, (that is, of making use of such words and expressions, as it may be, are not literally and formally contained in Scripture, but only are unto our conceptions and apprehensions expository of what is so contained) is to deny all interpretation of the Scripture, all endeavours to express the sense of the words of it unto the understandings of one another, which is in a word, to render the Scripture itself altogether useless; if it is unlawful for me to *speak* or *write*, what I conceive to be the sense of the words of Scripture and the nature of the thing signified and expressed by them, it is unlawful for me also to *think* or conceive in my mind, what is the sense of the words or nature of the things; which to say, is to make *brutes* of ourselves, and to frustrate the whole design of God in giving unto us the great privilege of his word."—5. In this way, the sentiments of one man in any point of religion cannot be distinguished from those of another, though diametrically opposite; so an Arian cannot be known from an Athanasian, both will say, in the words of Scripture, that Christ is the *great God*, the *true God*, and *over all God blessed for ever*; but without expressing themselves in their own words, their different sentiments will not be discerned; the one holding that Christ is a created God, of a like but not of the same substance with his Father; the other, that he is equal with him, of the same nature, substance, and glory: and he that believes the latter, surely it cannot be unlawful to express his belief of it in such words which declare the true sense of his mind. So a Sabellian or Unitarian, and a Trinitarian, will neither of them scruple to say in Scripture-terms what Christ says of himself and his Father, *I and my Father are one;* and yet the former holds, they are one in person or but one person; whereas the latter affirms, that they are one in nature and essence, but two distinct persons; and surely it must be lawful so to express himself, if this is the real sentiment of his mind. A Socinian and an Anti-socinian will join in saying that Christ the *Word is God,* and that he is the *only begotten of the Father,* and the *only begotten Son of God;* and yet the one maintains that he is only God by office, not by nature, and that he is the only begotten Son of God by office or by adoption; when the other believes that Christ is God by nature, and that he is the Son of the Father by natural and eternal generation, being begotten by him. It is necessary therefore they should make use of their own words to express their sentiments by, or how otherwise should it be known that they differ from one another? And indeed this seems to be the grand reason why it is urged with so much vehemence, by some, that only Scripture words and phrases should be made use of, that their erroneous tenets may not be detected and exposed; for, as a learned man has observed,[10] such as cavil at the formulas (of sound doctrine used by the orthodox) and plead they should be very short, and composed in the bare words of Scripture *eos aliquid monstri alere,* these nourish and cherish some monstrous notion, as the experience of all ages testify. And sometimes such persons take detached passages of Scripture from different places, and join them together, though they have no connection and agreement with each other; and such a method Irenæus [11] observes the ancient heretics took, who made use of passages of Scripture "that their figments might not seem to be without a testimony; but passed over the order and connection of the Scriptures, and loosened the parts of truth as much as in them lay;" and who fitly compares such to one who should take the effigy of a king made of jewels and precious stones by a skilful artific and loosen and separate them, and of them make the form of a dog or a fox.—6. It does not appear that those men who are so strenuous for the use of

---

[9] The Doctrine of the Trinity vindicated, p. 21.
[10] Witsius in Symbol. Exercitat. 2. s. 21. p. 21.
[11] Adv. Hæres. l. 1. c. 1. p. 33.

Scripture phrases only in articles of religion, have a greater value for the Scriptures than others; nay, not so much; for if we are to form a judgment of them by their sermons and writings, one would think they never read the Scriptures at all, or very little, since they make such an infrequent use of them; you shall scarcely hear a passage of Scripture quoted by them in a sermon, or produced by them in their writings; more frequently Seneca, Cicero, and others; and it looks as if they thought it very unpolite, and what might serve to disgrace their more refined writings, to fill their performances with them: and after all, it is easy to observe that these men, as the Arians formerly, and the Socinians more lately, carry on their cause, and endeavour to support it by making use of unscriptural words and phrases; and therefore it is not with a very good grace that such men, or those of the same cast with them, object to the use of words and phrases not syllabically expressed in Scripture; and the rather since the Arians were the first that began to make use of unscriptural phrases, as Athanasius affirms.[12] The Athanasians had as good a right to use the word ουοουσιος, as the Arians ομοιουσιος, and thereby explain their sense and defend their doctrine concerning the person of Christ, and his equality with God, against the latter, who introduced a phrase subversive of it; and the Calvinists have as good authority to make use of the word *satisfaction* in the doctrine of expiation of sin and atonement for it, as the Socinians and Remonstrants have for the use of the word *acceptilation*, whereby they seek to obscure and weaken it. Words and phrases though not literally expressed in scripture, yet if what is meant by them is to be found there, they may be lawfully made use of; as some respecting the doctrine of the Trinity; of these some are plainly expressed, which are used in treating of that doctrine, as *nature*, Gal. iv. 8. *Godhead*, Col. ii. 9. *Person*, the person of the Father, and the person of Christ, Heb. i. 3. 2 Cor. ii. 10. and iv. 6. and others clearly signified, as *essence*, by the name of God, *I am that I am*, Exod. iii. 14. the *unity* of divine persons in it, John x. 30. a *Trinity* of Persons in the unity of Essence, 1 John v. 7. the *generation* of the Son by and of the Father, Psalm ii. 7. John i. 14, 18. and others respecting some peculiar doctrines of revelation, concerning the state of men and the grace of Christ; as the *imputation of Adam's sin* to his posterity, Rom. v. 19. and the *imputation of righteousness*, i. e. of Christ's to them that believe, which is nearly syllabically expressed in Rom. iv. 6. and the *imputation* of sin to Christ, who *was made sin*, i. e. by imputation, 2 Cor. v. 21. And the *satisfaction* of Christ for sin, in all those places where it is signified that what Christ has done and suffered in the room and stead of his people is to the content of law and justice, and God is well pleased with it: and these are the principal words and phrases objected to, and which we shall not be prevailed upon to part with easily. And indeed, words and phrases, the use of which have long obtained in the churches of Christ, and the sense of them, is well known, and serve aptly to convey the sense of those that use them; it is unreasonable to require them to part with them, unless others, and those better words and phrases, are substituted in their room; and such as are proposed should not be easily admitted without strict examination; for there is oftentimes a good deal of truth in that saying, *qui fingit nova verba, nova gignit dogmata;* he that coins new words, coins new doctrines; which is notorious in the case of Arius; for not only Alexander,[13] his Bishop charged him with saying, without Scripture, and what was never said before, that God was not always a Father, but there was a time when he was not a Father; and that the Word was not always, but was made out of things that were not; and that there was a time when he was not a Son: but Eusebius,[14] a favourer of his, also owns that the inspired writings never used such phrases, το εξ ουκ οντων, και το, ην ποτε οτε ουκ ην, that Christ was *from non-entities*, from things that are not, *i. e.* was made out of nothing; and that *there was a time when he was not;* phrases, he says, they had never been used to.

The subject of the following Work being *Theology*, or what we call *Divinity*, it may be proper to consider the signification and use of the word, and from whence it has its rise. I say, what we call *Divinity;* for it seems to be a word, as to the use of it in this subject, peculiar to us; foreign writers never entitle their works of this kind, *Corpus* vel *systema* vel *medulla Divinitatis*, a body or system or marrow of Divinity; but *Corpus* vel

---

[12] Synod. Nicen. contr. hæres. Arian. decret. p. 417.
[13] Apud Socrat. Hist. l. 1. c. 6. vid. Sozomen. Hist. l. 1. c. 15.
[14] Apud Theodoret. Hist. l. 1. c. 12.

systema vel *medulla Theologiæ*, a body or system or marrow of Theology. The word *Divinitas*, from whence our word *Divinity* comes, is only used by Latin writers for Deity or Godhead; but since custom and use have long fixed the sense of the word among us, to signify, when used on this subject, a Treatise on the science of divine things, sacred truths, and christian doctrines, taken out of the scriptures; we need not scruple the use of it. The *Jews* seem to come nearest to us in the phrase which they use concerning it, calling it,[15] האלהית vel חכמת האלהות *a Science of Divinity*, or a *divine Science*; that is, a Science or doctrine concerning divine things; concerning God; concerning his divinity and things belonging to him; and which, in the main, is the same as to sense with the word *Theology*, as will be seen hereafter; and here, before we proceed any further, it may not be improper to observe, the distinction of the Jewish Theology, or the two parts into which they divide it. The first they call מעשה בראשית the work of Bereshith or the creation; for Bereshith being the first word in Gen. i. 1. *In the beginning God created*, they frequently use it to signify the whole work of the creation; so that this part of their Theology respects the creatures God has made, and the nature of them; whereby the invisible things of God, as the apostle says, are discerned, even his eternal power and Godhead; and this is their *physics* or *natural Theology*. The other branch is called מעשה מרכבה the *work of the chariot*,[16] which appellation is taken from the vision in Ezek. i. of the four living creatures in the form of a chariot, which is the more abstruse and mysterious part of their Theology; and may be called their *metaphysics* or *supernatural Theology*; and which treats of God, and of his divine attributes; of the Messiah; of Angels, and the souls of men; as in the Book of Zohar, and other cabalistic writings. But to go on.

Theology is a Greek word, and signifies a discourse concerning God and things belonging to him; it was first in use among the heathen poets and philosophers, and so the word *Theologue*. Lantantius says,[17] the most ancient writers of Greece were called *Theologues*; these were their poets who wrote of their Deities, and of the genealogies of them; Pherecydes is said to be the first that wrote of divine things; so Thales says,[18] in his letter to him, hence he had the name of *Theologue*;[19] though some make Museus the son of Eumolphus, the first of this sort;[20] others give the title to Orpheus. Pythagoras, the disciple of Pherecydes, has also this character; and Porphyry,[21] by way of eminence, calls him *the Theologue*; and who often in his writings speaks of the *Theologues*;[22] and this character was given to Plato; also Aristotle[23] makes mention of the *Theologues*, as distinct from naturalists, or the natural philosophers; and Cicero[24] also speaks of them, and seems to design by them the poets or the authors of mystic Theology. The Egyptians had their Theology,[25] which they communicated to Darius, the father of Xerxes; and so had the Magi and the Chaldeans; of whom Democritus is said to learn Theology and Astrology.[26] The priests of Delphos are called by Plutarch,[27] the *Theologues* of Delphos. It is from hence now that these words *Theology* and *Theologues* have been borrowed, and made use of by christian writers; and I see no impropriety in the use of them; nor should they be thought the worse of for their original, no more than other words which come from the same source; for though these words are used of false deities, and of persons that treat of them; it follows not but that they may be used, with great propriety, of discourses concerning the true God, and things belonging to him, and of those that discourse of them. The first among Christians that has the title of *Theologue*, or *Divine*, is St. John, the writer of the book of the Revelation; for so the inscription of the book runs "the Revelation of St. John the

---

[15] Vid. Buxtorf. Talmud. Lex. Col. 752.
[16] Vid. Maimon. præfat. ad More Nevochim, par. 1.
[17] De Ira c. 11.
[18] Apud. Laert. l. 1. in vita ejus.
[19] Ib. in vita Pherecydis.
[20] Ib. Proœm.
[21] De Abstinentia, l. 2. c. 36. et de antro Nympharum.
[22] De Abstinentia, l. 2. s. 43, 44, 47. et de antro Nympharum.
[23] Metaphysic. l. 12. c. 6. 10.
[24] De Divinatione, l. 3. c. 21. vid. Plato de Repub. l. 2. p. 605.
[25] Diodorus Sic. l. 1. p. 85.
[26] Laert. l. 9. in vita ejus.
[27] De defect. Orac. p. 417. vid. ib. 410, 436.

Divine." In the Complutensian edition, and so in the King of Spain's Bible, it is "the Revelation of the holy Apostle and Evangelist, John the Divine." Whether this word *Theologue* or *Divine*, was originally in the inscription of this book, I will not say; but this may be said, that Origen,[28] a very early christian writer, gives to John the title of the Divine, as it should seem from hence; and Athanasius,[29] in his account of the sacred writings, calls the book of the Revelation, "the Revelation of John the Divine;" and who also styles him, "John the Evangelist and Divine." These words *Theologue* and *Theology*, are to be met with frequently in the ancient Fathers, in following ages, and in all christian writers to the present times. Upon the whole, it appears that *Theology* or *Divinity*, as we call it, is no other than a science or doctrine concerning God, or a discoursing and treating of things relating to him; and that a *Theologue*, or a *Divine*, is one that understands, discourses, and treats of divine things; and perhaps the Evangelist John might have this title eminently given to him by the ancients, because of his writing concerning, and the record he bore to Christ, the λογος, the essential Word of God, to his proper Deity, divine Sonship, and distinct personality. Suidas[30] not only calls him the Divine and the Evangelist, but says, that he wrote *Theology*; by which he seems to mean the book of the Revelation, which book some have observed contains a complete body of Divinity. Here we are taught the divine authority and excellency of the sacred scriptures; that there is but one God, and that he only is to be worshipped, and not angels; that God is the Triune God; that there are three Persons in the Godhead, Father, Son, and Holy Spirit; that God is eternal, the Creator, and Preserver of all things; that Christ is truly God and truly man; that he is Prophet, Priest and King; that men are by nature wretched, blind, naked, poor, and miserable; that some of all nations are redeemed by the blood of the Lamb; and that they are justified and washed from their sins in his blood; the articles of the resurrection of the dead, the last judgment, the sad estate of the wicked, and the happiness of the saints may be observed in it.

And as we are upon this subject, it may not be amiss if we take a brief compendious view of the state of Theology; or if you please, Divinity, from the beginning of it to the present time. Theology may be considered either as *natural*, which is from the light of nature, and is attained unto through the use and exercise of it, or *supernatural*, which is come at by divine Revelation.

Natural Theology may be considered either as it was in Adam before the fall, or as in him and his posterity since the fall. Adam before the fall, had great knowledge of things divine as well as natural, moral and civil; he was created in the image of God, which image lay in knowledge, as well as in righteousness and holiness; before he came short of this glory, and lost this image, or at least was greatly impaired and obliterated in him by sin; he knew much of God, of his nature and attributes, of his mind and will, and the worship of him; he had knowledge of the persons in God, of a Trinity of persons who were concerned in the creation of all things, and in his own; and without which he could have had no true knowledge of God, nor have yielded the worship due to each divine person: not that all the knowledge he had was innate, or sprung from the light of nature within himself; but in it he was assisted, and it was capable of being increased by things without, as by symbols, the tree of life in the midst of the garden, &c. by positive precepts relating to the worship of God, and obedience to his will, as the prohibition to eat of the tree of knowledge of good and evil, the institution of marriage, &c. and through a constant and diligent contemplation of the works of creation: nor can we suppose him to be altogether without the benefit and advantage of divine Revelation; since he had such a near and immediate intercourse and converse with God himself: and some things he could not have known without it; as the creation of the world, the order and manner of it; his own formation out of the dust of the earth; and the formation of Eve from him, that she was flesh of his flesh, and bone of his bone, and was designed of God to be his wife, and an help-meet to him, and who should be the mother of all living; with other things respecting the worship of God, and the manner of it, and the covenant made with him as a federal head to all his posterity that

---

[28] Homil. 2. in Evangel. Joan. l. 1.
[29] Synops. s. Script. p. 65, 152.
[30] In voce Ιωαννης et in voce Νοννος.

should spring from him. These, with many other things, no doubt, Adam had immediate knowledge of from God himself.

But this kind of Theology appeared with a different aspect in Adam after his fall, and in his posterity; by sin his mind was greatly beclouded, and his understanding darkened; he lost much of his knowledge of God, and of his perfections, or he could never have imagined that going among the trees of the garden would hide him from the presence of God, and secure him from his justice. What a notion must he have of the omnipresence of God? and what also of his omniscience, when he attempted to palliate and cover his sin by the excuse he made? And he immediately lost his familiar intercourse with God, and communion with him, being drove out of the garden: and as for his posterity, descending from him by ordinary generation, they appear to be in the same case and circumstances, without God in the world, without any true knowledge of him, and fellowship with him; they appear to be in the image of the earthly and sinful Adam, and not to have the image of God upon them; they are alienated from the life of God, and their understandings darkened as to the knowledge of divine and spiritual things; and though there are some remains of the light of nature in them, by which something of God may be known by them, even his eternal power and Godhead, by considering the works of creation, or else be inexcusable; yet whatever they know of him in theory, which does not amount to a true knowledge of God, they are without a practical knowledge of him; they glorify him not as God, and serve the creature more than the Creator; yea, what knowledge they have of God is very dim and obscure; they are like persons in the dark, who grope about, if haply they may feel after him, and find him; and what ridiculous notions have they entertained of Deity? and what gods have they feigned for themselves? and have fallen into impiety and idolatry, polytheism and atheism: being without a divine Revelation, they are without the true knowledge of the worship of God; and therefore have introduced strange and absurd modes of worship; as well as are at a loss what methods to take to reconcile God, offended with them for their sins, when at any time sensible thereof; and what means and ways to make use of to recommend themselves to him; and therefore have gone into practices the most shocking and detestable. Being destitute of a divine Revelation, they can have no assurance that God will pardon sin and sinners; nor have they any knowledge of his way of justifying sinners by the righteousness of his Son; which are doctrines of pure Revelation: they can have no knowledge of Christ as Mediator, and of the way of peace and reconciliation, of life and salvation by him, and so can have no true knowledge of God in Christ; *for this is life eternal, to know the only true God, and Jesus Christ whom he has sent.* There is no saving knowledge of God without Christ; wherefore the light of nature is insufficient to salvation; for though by it men may arrive to the knowledge of a God as the Creator of all things, yet not to the knowledge of Christ as the Saviour of men; and without faith in him there can be no salvation: and though men may by means of it know in some instances what is displeasing to God, and what agreeable to him, what to be avoided, and what to be performed; in which knowledge they are yet deficient; reckoning such things to be no sins which are grievous ones, as fornication, polygamy, suicide, &c. yet even in the things they do know, they do not in their practice answer to their knowledge of them; and did they, they could not be saved by them; for if by obedience to the law of Moses none are justified and saved, then certainly not by obedience to the law and light of nature; none can be saved without faith in Christ, and his righteousness; there is no pardon but by his blood; no acceptance with God but through him: things that the light of nature leaves men strangers to. But of the weakness and insufficiency of natural Theology to instruct men in the knowledge of divine things, destitute of a divine revelation, perhaps more may be said hereafter, when the Theology of the Pagans may be observed.

Supernatural Theology, or what is by pure Revelation, may be next considered, in its original rise and progress; and as it has been improved and increased, or has met with checks and obstructions.

The state of this Theology may be considered as it was from the first appearance of it, after the fall of Adam, to the flood in the times of Noah, or throughout the old world. What gave rise unto it, and is the foundation of it, is what God pronounced to the serpent; *It* (the seed of the woman) *shall bruise thy head, and thou shalt bruise his heel:* these words contain the principal articles of Christian Theology; as the incarnation of the Messiah, the Saviour of men; who should be *the seed of the woman*, made of a woman, made flesh, and become a partaker of the flesh and blood of those he was to save: and this seems to be understood by our first parents; hence it is thought that Eve imagined that this illustrious person was born of her, when she brought forth her first-born, saying, *I have gotten a man the Lord*, as some choose to render the word; as Enos, the son of Seth, afterwards was expected to be the Redeemer of the world, according to the Cabalists;[31] and therefore was called *Enos, the man*, the famous excellent man; as they say. Likewise the sufferings and death of Christ in the human nature, by means of the serpent Satan; treading on whom, he, like a serpent, would turn himself, and bite his heel; wound him in his human nature, his inferior nature, called his heel, and so bring him to the dust of death. When the Messiah, by his sufferings and death, would *bruise* his *head*, confound his schemes, destroy his works; yea, destroy him himself, the devil, who had the power of death; and abolish that, and make an end of sin, the cause of it, by giving full satisfaction for it; and so save and deliver his people from all the sad effects of it, eternal wrath, ruin, and damnation. This kind of Theology received some further improvement, from the coats of skin the Lord God made and clothed our first parents with, an emblem of the justifying righteousness of Christ, and of the garments of salvation wrought out by his obedience, sufferings, and death; signified by slain beasts; and which God puts upon his people, and clothes them with, through his gracious act of imputation; and hence they are said to be *justified by blood:* and to which may be added the hieroglyphic of the cherubim and flaming sword, placed at the end of the garden, to observe or point at the tree of life; representing the prophets of the Old, and the apostles and ministers of the New Testament, being placed and appointed to shew unto men the way of salvation by Christ the tree of life. And what serves to throw more light on this evangelical Theology, are the sacrifices ordered to be offered up; and which were types of the sacrifice of Christ; and particularly that which was offered up by Abel, who, *by faith* in the sacrifice of Christ, *offered up a more excellent sacrifice than Cain;* which also was a lamb, the firstling of his flock, and pointed at the Lamb of God, who by his sacrifice takes away the sins of his people. Within this period of time, men seem to have increased in light, as to the worship of God, especially public worship; for in the times of Enos, the grandson of Adam, men *began to call upon the name of the Lord*. Prayer to God, and invocation of his name, were, no doubt, used before; but men increasing, and families becoming more numerous, they now met and joined together in carrying on social and public worship: and though there were corruptions in practice, within this period of time; wicked Cain, whose works were evil, and who set a bad example to his posterity, he and they lived together, separate from the posterity of Seth, indulging themselves in the gratification of sinful pleasures; and it is said, that in the times of Jared, some descended from the holy mountain, as it is called, to the company of Cain, in the valley, and mixed themselves with them, and took of their daughters for wives; from whence sprung a race of giants and wicked men, who were the cause of the flood. Lamech gave into the practice of bigamy; and Pseudo-Berosus says,[32] that Ham lived a very vicious and profligate life before the flood; yet there does not appear to have been any corruption in doctrine and worship, or any idolatry exercised. Some indeed have pretended[33] that in the days of Enos images were invented, to excite the minds of creatures to pray to God by them as mediators; but this is said without any foundation.

The next period of time in which supernatural Theology may be traced, is from the flood, in the times of Noah, to the giving of the law to Israel, in the times of Moses. Noah was instructed in it by his Father Lamech, who expected[34] great comfort from him; and, as some think, in spiritual as well as in civil things, Gen. v. 29. however, he instructed him in the true religion, as it was received from the first man, Adam; and it was taught by Noah, and the knowledge of it conveyed to his posterity, partly in the ministry of the word by him; for he was a *preacher of righteousness*, even of evangelical righteousness, *of the righteousness of faith;* of which he was an heir, and therefore no doubt preached the

[31] Reuchlin, Cabalæ. l. 1. p. 740.
[32] Antiq. l. 3. p. 25.
[33] Juchasin, fol. 134. 2. Shalshalet Hakabala, fol. 74. 2.
[34] Reuchlin. Ib.

same to others: and partly by the sacrifices he offered, which were of clean creatures he had knowledge of the distinction of; and which sacrifices were of a sweet savour to God, and were typical of the purity of Christ's sacrifice for sin, and of the acceptance of it to God, which is to him of a sweet smelling savour. Moreover, the waters of the flood, and the ark in which Noah and his family were preserved, were a type of an evangelical ordinance, the ordinance of baptism; which is an emblem of the death, burial, and resurrection of Christ; by which men are saved: for Noah and his family going into the ark, where, when the fountains of the great deep were broken up below, and the windows of heaven opened above, they were like persons covered in water, and immersed in it, and as persons buried; and when they came out of it, the water being carried off, it was like a resurrection, and as life from the dead; the *like figure*, or antitype *whereunto*, the Apostle says, *even baptism, doth also now save us, by the resurrection of Jesus Christ* signified thereby, 1 Pet. iii. 21. likewise the rainbow, the token of the covenant; which, though not the covenant of grace, yet of kindness and preservation; was an emblem of peace and reconciliation by Christ, the Mediator of the covenant of grace; and may assure of the everlasting love of God to his people, and of the immoveableness of the covenant of his peace with them, Isa. liv. 9, 10. In the line of Shem, the son of Noah, the knowledge of this kind of Theology was continued: Noah's blessing of him is thought by the Cabalists,[35] to contain his earnest desire that he might be the Redeemer of men. However, God was the Lord of Shem, known, owned, and professed by him; and he was the father of all the children of Eber. According to the Jews[36] Shem had a divinity-school, where the sons of Japhet, becoming proselytes, dwelt; and which continued to the times of Isaac; for he is reported to go thither to pray for Rebecca.[37] Eber also, according to them, had such a school; where Jacob[38] was a minister, servant, or disciple; and so had Abraham in the land of Canaan; and his three hundred trained servants are supposed to be his catechumens; and also in Haran, where Abraham, it is said,[39] taught and proselyted the men, and Sarah the women: however, this we are sure of, that he instructed and "commanded his children, and his household after him, to keep the way of the Lord, and to do justice and judgment," Gen. xviii. 19. Moreover, as the gospel was preached unto Abraham, Gal. iii. 8. there is no doubt but that he preached it to others; and as he had knowledge of the Messiah, who should spring from him, in whom all nations of the earth would be blessed, and who saw his day and was glad; so his grandson Jacob had a more clear and distinct view of him, as God's salvation, as the Shiloh, the peace-maker and prosperous one, who should come, before civil government was removed from the Jews; and when come, multitudes should be gathered to him, Gen. xlix. 10—18. Idolatry within this period first began among the builders of Babel: some say in the days of Serug;[40] it was embraced by the Zabians in Chaldea, and obtained in the family of Terah, the father of Abraham. The worship of the sun and moon prevailed in the times of Job, in Arabia; who lived about the time of the children of Israel being in Egypt, and a little before their coming out of it; who do not appear to have given into the idolatry of that people. As for Job and his three friends, it is plain they had great knowledge of God and divine things; of the perfections of God; of the impurity of human nature; of the insufficiency of man's righteousness to justify him before God; and of the doctrine of redemption and salvation by Christ, Job xiv. 4. and xxv. 4, 5. and xix. 25, 26. and xxxiii. 23, 24.

The next period is from the giving of the law to Israel, by the hand of Moses, to the times of David and the prophets; in which supernatural Theology was taught by types; as the passover, the manna, the brazen serpent, and other things; which were emblems of Christ and his grace, and salvation by him: and by the sacrifices instituted, particularly the daily sacrifice morning and evening, and the annual sacrifices on the day of atonement; which besides all others, were typical of, and led the faith of men to the expiation of sins, to be made by the sacrifice of Christ: the whole ceremonial law, all that related to the priests, their garments, and their work and office, had an

---

[35] Reuchlin. ut supra.
[36] Targum Jon. in Gen. ix. 27.
[37] Targ. Jerus. et Jon. in Gen. xxv. 22.
[38] Targ. Onk. et Jon. in Gen. xxv. 27.
[39] Bereshit Rabba, s. 39. fol. 35. 1.
[40] Suidas in voce Αβρααμ et in voce Σιρυχ.

evangelical signification; it was the Jews' gospel, and which led them to Christ, and to an acquaintance with the things of Christ; and to what make him, his grace and righteousness, necessary to salvation; as the evil nature of sin; the insufficiency of men to make atonement for it; to fulfil the law, and bring in a righteousness answerable to it: Moses wrote of Christ, of his prophetic, priestly, and kingly offices, either by type or prophecy: the song of Moses in Deut. xxxii. and of Hannah, 1 Sam. ii. very clearly speak of the perfections of God, of his works of providence and grace, and of the Messiah. According to the Jews, there was a divinity-school in the times of Samuel. Naioth in Ramah is interpreted[41] an house of doctrine, or school of instruction, of which Samuel was president; where he stood over the prophets, teaching and instructing them, 1 Sam. xix. 18, 19. Such schools there were in after-times, at Bethel, and Jericho and Gilgal; even in the times of Elijah and Elisha; where the sons or disciples of the prophets were trained up in the knowledge of divine things, 2 Kings ii. 3, 5. and iv. 38. in such a college or house of instruction, as the Targum, Huldah the prophetess dwelt at Jerusalem, 2 Kings xxii. 14. There were within this time some checks to the true knowledge and worship of God, by the idolatry of the calf at Sinai; of Baal-peor, on the borders of Moab; and of Baalim and Ashtaroth and other deities, after the death of Joshua, and in the times of the Judges.

The period from the times of David including them, to the Babylonish captivity, abounds with evangelic truths, and doctrines of supernatural Theology. The Psalms of David are full of spiritual and evangelic knowledge; many intimations are given of the sufferings and death of Christ, of his burial, resurrection from the dead, ascension to heaven, and session at the right hand of God; and on which many blessings of grace depend, which could never have been known but by divine revelation. And the prophets which followed him speak out still more clearly of the incarnation of Christ; point out the very place where he was to be born, and the country where he would preach the gospel, to the illumination of those that sat in darkness. They plainly describe him in his person, and offices, the sufferings he should undergo, and the circumstances of them, and benefits arising from them; they bear witness to the doctrines of pardon of sin through him, and justification by him; and of his bearing sin, and making satisfaction for it: in short, a scheme of evangelic truths may be deduced from the prophetic writings; and, indeed, the great apostle Paul himself said no other things than what the prophets did. There were some sad revolts from the true God, and his worship, within this compass of time, in the reigns of some of the kings of Israel and Judah; as the idolatry of the calves in the reign of Jeroboam, and others of the kings of Israel; and the idolatries committed in the times of Ahaz, Manasseh, and Amon, kings of Judah, which issued in the captivities of both people.

The period from the Babylonish captivity to the times of Christ, finish the Old Testament-dispensation. At the return of the Jews from captivity, who brought no idolatrous worship with them, there was a reformation made by Ezra and Nehemiah, with the prophets of their time; or who quickly followed, as Haggai, Zechariah, and Malachi; who all prophesied of Christ the Saviour, and of the salvation that should come by him; with the several blessings of it; and speak of his near approach, and point at the time of his coming, and the work he should do when come. But after the death of these prophets, and the Holy Spirit departed, and there was no more prophecy, supernatural Theology began greatly to decline; and the truths of revelation were neglected and despised; and the doctrines and traditions of men were preferred to the word of God, that was made of none effect by them. The sect of the Sadducees, a sort of free-thinkers, rose up; who said there was no resurrection, nor angel, nor spirit: and the sect of the Pharisees, a sort of free-willers, who set up traditions as the rule of men's worship, and which rose to an enormous bigness in the times of Christ, who severely inveighed against them; and which in after-times were compiled and put together in a volume, called, the *Misnah*, their *Traditional*, or Body of Traditions: and this, in course of time, occasioned a large work finished in Babylon and from thence called the *Babylonian Talmud;* which is their *Doctrinal*, or Body of Doctrine; full of fables, false glosses and interpretations of scriptures; and which is the foundation of the erroneous doctrines and practices of the Jews to this day.

[41] Targum in 1 Sam. xix. 19, 20.

And here I shall take leave to transcribe the interpretation of the vision in Zech. v. 6—11. given by that learned man George Eliezer Edzard,[42] it being very ingenious and uncommon, and much to our present purpose. This learned man observes that the preceding vision of the *flying roll*, describes the sad corruption of manners among the Jews, in the three or four former ages of the second temple; doctrine remaining pretty sound among them; which corruption of manners was punished by the incursions of the Lagidæ and Seleucidæ, kings of Egypt and Syria, into Judea, as the vision represents. The following vision of a woman sitting in an Ephah, and shut up in it, and then transported by two other women into the land of Shinah; he thus interprets: by the *woman*, who, by way of eminency, is called *wickedness;* is to be understood the impious and false doctrine devised by the Pharisees and Sadducees; and other corrupt doctors of the Jews in the latter times of the second temple, and handed down to posterity; compared to a woman, because it had nothing manly, nothing true, nothing solid in it; and moreover, caused its followers to commit spiritual fornication, and allured to it by its paints, flatteries, and prittle-prattle: and it is called *wickedness* because not only the less fundamentals, but the grand fundamentals, and principal articles of faith, concerning the mystery of the Trinity, the Deity of the Son of God, and of the Holy Spirit, the person and office of the Messiah, were sadly defiled by it; and in the room of them were substituted, traditions, precepts, and inventions of men; than which greater impiety cannot be thought of; and which issued in the contempt and rejection and crucifixion of the Messiah, sent as the Saviour of the world; and in the persecution of the preachers of the gospel, and putting a stop to the course of it, as much as could be; and which drew with it a train of other sins. The Ephah, he thinks, designs the whole body of the people of the Jews, throughout Judea, Samaria, and Galilee; which Ephah was first seen as *empty*, ver. 6. and this being a dry measure, with which wheat and such like things were measured, the food of the body, a proper type of the heavenly doctrine, the food of the soul: by the emptiness of the Ephah, is intimated, that sound doctrine, about the time of the Messiah's coming, would be banished out of Judea, and the neighbouring parts; and most of the inhabitants thereof would be destitute of the knowledge of the pure faith. And the wicked woman *sitting in the midst of the Ephah*, and filling it, not a corner of it, but the whole; and is represented not as lying prostrate, but sitting; denotes the total corruption of doctrine, its power and prevalence, throughout Judea, Samaria, and Galilee; obtaining in all places, synagogues, schools, and seats, and pulpits, and among all sorts of inhabitants; the few being crushed who professed the sound doctrine of the Trinity, and of the person and office of the Messiah. And whereas a *talent of lead* was seen *lifted up;* this signifies the divine decree concerning the destruction of the Jews and their polity by the Romans; which should be most surely executed on them, for their corruption of doctrine, and for sins that flowed from thence. The *lifting* up of the talent not only prefigured the near approach of the judgment, but the setting it before the eyes of the people, to be beheld through the ministry of Christ, and his apostles, before it was executed; that while there was hope, if it might be, some might be brought to repentance, and to the acknowledgment of the true Messiah; but this failing of success, the talent was *cast into the ephah*, and upon the woman in it, signifying the destruction of the Jews; of which the angel that talked with Zechariah the prophet, and who was no other than the Son of God, was the principal author; Vespasian, and the Roman army under him, being only ministers and instruments. Not that hereby the woman, or the corrupt doctrine, was wholly extinguished; but it was depressed, and weakened, and reduced, and was among a few only, great numbers of the doctors and disciples of it being slain, and many of both classes being exiled; the temple and city burnt, heretofore the chief seat of it, and the schools throughout Judea destroyed, in which it was propagated. But in process of time the Jews restored some schools in Palestine, as at Jabneh, Zippore, Cæsarea, and Tiberias, in the last of which R. Judah Hakkadosh compiled the *Misnah*, about *A. D.* 150. and after that came out the *Jerusalem Talmud*, *A. D.* 230. and after the death of the above Rabbi, his chief disciples went into Babylon, and carried with them the greatest part of the doctors and their scholars out of Palestine: so that doctrine by little and little disappeared in Judea, and entirely about the year 340, when R. Hillel died, the last

---

[42] Præfat. ad Annotat. in Tract. Beracot.

INTRODUCTION. xlix

of those promoted doctors in the land of Israel: and after this, scarce any thing was heard of the schools and wise men of Palestine; but schools continued in Babylon for many ages; and this is what is meant in the last part of the symbolic vision of Zechariah, by the Ephah being carried by two women into the land of Shinar, that is, Babylon. By these *two women* are meant the Misnic and Gemaristic doctors; the two heads of which were Raf and Samuel, who went into Babylon a little after the death of R. Judah, the saint, and carried the woman, false doctrine, along with them; these are said to have *wings like storks*, fit for long journeys, to fly with on high, and with swiftness, into remote parts; and fitly describes the above persons transporting their false doctrine into the remote parts of Babylon, far from Palestine; carrying great numbers from thence, which they did without weariness, and with as much celerity as they could: and *the wind* being *in their wings*, denotes the cheerfulness with which the Jewish Rabbins pursued their studies till they had finished their design, the Talmud, which they could not perfect without the impulse and help of an evil spirit, signified by the wind. And here in Babylon they *built an house* for their false doctrine, erected various schools, in which it was taught and propagated; and so it was *established* and *set on its own base*, and continued for 820 years or more. This is the sense which this learned man gives of the vision; on which I shall make no more remarks than I have done, by saying it is ingenious and uncommon, and suits with the subject I am upon, which introduced it, and opens the source of the corruption of doctrine among the Jews, and shews the continuance of it, and the means thereof.

Having traced supernatural theology, or divinity, to the times of Christ; let us a little look back upon the theology of the Pagans, before we proceed any further. At, or a little after, the building of Babel, and the dispersion of the people, idolatry began to appear; the knowledge of the true God was greatly lost, and the worship of him neglected. Some say this began in the days of Serug, but perhaps it might be earlier: the first objects of it seem to be the sun and moon; which it is certain obtained in the times of Job; and then their kings and heroes, whom they deified after death; and which at length issued in a multiplicity of gods throughout the several nations of the earth; and what of truth remained among them was disguised with fables; or, to use the apostle's phrase, they *changed the truth of God into a lie, and worshipped and served the creature more than the Creator;* their foolish hearts being darkened. The Theology of the Pagans, according to themselves, as Scævola[43] and Varro,[44] was of three sorts.—1. Mystic, or Fabulous, which belonged to the poets, and was sung by them.—2. Physic, or Natural; which belonged to the philosophers, and were studied by them.—3. Politic, or Civil, which belonged to princes, priests, and people; being instituted by the one, exercised by the other, and enjoined the people. The *first* of these may well be called Fabulous, as treating of the theogony and genealogy of their deities; in which they say such things as are unworthy of deity; ascribing to them thefts, murders, adulteries, and all manner of crimes; and therefore this kind of Theology is condemned by the wiser sort of heathens, as nugatory and scandalous; the writers of this sort of Theology were Sanchoniatho, the Phœnician; and of the Grecians, Orpheus, Hesiod, Pherecydes, &c. The *second* sort, called Physic, or Natural, was studied and taught by the philosophers; who, rejecting the multiplicity of gods introduced by the poets, brought their Theology to a more natural and rational form; and supposed that there was but one supreme God, which they commonly make to be the sun; at least as an emblem of him; but at too great a distance to mind the affairs of the world, and therefore devised certain demons, which they considered as mediators between the supreme God and man: and the doctrines of these demons to which the apostle is thought to allude in 1 Tim. iv. 1. were what the philosophers had a concern with, and who treat of their nature, office, and regard to men; as did Thales, Pythagoras, Plato, and the Stoics. The *third* part, called Politic, or Civil, was instituted by legislators, statesmen, and politicians: the first among the Romans was Numa Pompilius; this chiefly respected their gods, temples, altars, sacrifices, and rites of worship, and was properly their idolatry; the care of which belonged to the priests; and this was enjoined the common people, to keep them in obedience to the civil state. Thus things continued in the Gentile world, until the light of the

---

[43] Apud. Augustin. de Civ. Dei, l. 4. c. 27.
[44] Apud. Ib. l. 6. c. 5.

INTRODUCTION.

Gospel was sent among them: the times before that, were *times of ignorance*, as the apostle calls them; they were ignorant of the true God, and of the worship of him; and of the Messiah, and salvation by him: their state is truly described, Eph. ii. 12. that they were then *without Christ, aliens from the commonwealth of Israel, strangers from the covenants of promise, having no hope, and without God in the world*. And consequently, their Theology was insufficient for the salvation of them.

But to return to supernatural Theology, where we left it, having traced it to the times of Christ; at whose coming, and through whose ministry, and that of his forerunner, and of his apostles, it revived, and lift up its head, and appeared in all its purity, splendour, and glory. John, was a man sent from God to bear witness to the light that was just rising, even the Sun of righteousness, the Day-spring from on high; the great Light, that should lighten those that sat in darkness, with a supernatural light; he declared the kingdom of heaven, or Gospel dispensation, was at hand, and just ushering in; and preached the baptism of repentance for the remission of sin, and administered that Gospel ordinance. "God, who at sundry times, and in divers manners, had spoken to the fathers by the prophets, now spoke to men by his Son:" Christ, his only begotten Son, who lay in his bosom, came and declared him; who and what he was, and what was his mind and will. He brought the doctrines of grace and truth with him; and spoken such words of grace, truth and wisdom, as never man spake; his doctrine was not human, but divine; it was not his own as man, he received it from his Father, and delivered it to his apostles; who having a commission from him to preach it, and being qualified for it, with the gifts and graces of his Spirit in great abundance, they went into all the world, and preached the Gospel to every creature; and diffused the savour of his knowledge in every place; they had the deep things of God revealed unto them; things which could never have been discovered by the light of nature; nor were revealed in the law of Moses; things "which eye had not seen nor ear heard, nor ever entered into the heart of man;" which the reason of men could never have descried; "they spoke the wisdom of God in a mystery, even the hidden wisdom which God ordained before the world unto our glory." In the books of the New Testament are written, as with a sunbeam, those truths of pure revelation, the doctrines of a Trinity of divine Persons in the Godhead; of the eternal Sonship, distinct Personality and Deity of Christ, and of his several offices as Mediator; and of the distinct Personality and Deity of the Holy Spirit; and of his operations of grace upon the souls of men; of the everlasting and unchangeable love of the Three divine Persons to the elect; of the predestination of them to the adoption of children; and of their eternal election in Christ to grace and glory; of the covenant of grace made with them in Christ, and the blessings of it; of redemption by Christ, full pardon of sin through his blood, free justification from sin by his righteousness, and plenary satisfaction for it by his atoning sacrifice; of regeneration, or the new birth; effectual calling; conversion, and sanctification, by the efficacious grace of the Spirit; of the saints' final perseverance in grace to glory, of the resurrection from the dead, and of a future state of immortal life and happiness: all which are brought to light by the Gospel of Christ. And these are the sum and substance of supernatural Theology, and the glory of it. And whilst the apostles continued, and other ministers of the word raised up in their times, these doctrines were held fast, and held forth with great clearness and perspicuity; but, as the historian says,[45] after the holy company of the apostles had ended their lives, and that generation was gone, which was worthy to hear the divine wisdom, then a system of impious error took place, through the deceit of false teachers; false doctrine was attempted to be introduced, in opposition to the truth of the Gospel, which had been preached; not one of the apostles remaining to oppose it. The doctrines of divine revelation, Satan, by his emissaries, set himself against to undermine and destroy, were the doctrines of the Trinity; the Incarnation of Christ of a virgin; his proper Deity, as by some, and his real Humanity, as by others; his eternal Sonship, or his being begotten of the Father before all worlds. The school at Alexandria, from whence came several of the Christian doctors, as Pantænus, Clemens, Origen, &c. served very much to corrupt the simplicity of the Gospel; for though it mended the Platonic philosophy, it marred the Christian doctrine; and laid the foundation for Arianism and

---

[45] Egesippus apud Euseb. Hist. Eccl. l. 3. c. 32.

Pelagianism, which in aftertimes so greatly disturbed the church of God. As many of the fathers of the Christian Church were originally Pagans, they were better skilled in demolishing Paganism than in building up Christianity; and indeed they set themselves more to destroy the one than to illustrate and confirm the other: there was a purity in their lives, but a want of clearness, accuracy, and consistence in their doctrines; it would be endless to relate how much the Christian doctrine was obscured by the heretics that rose up in the latter part of the first century; and in the second, as well as after, by Sabellians, Photinians, Samosatenians, Arians, Eutychians, Nestorians, Macedonians, Pelagians, &c. though God was pleased to raise up instruments to stop their progress, and preserve the truth, and sometimes very eminent ones; as Athanasius against the Arians, and Austin against the Pelagians. The Gospel in its simplicity, through the power of divine grace attending it, made its way into the Gentile world, in these first centuries, with great success; and Paganism decreased before it; and which in the times of Constantine received a fatal blow in the Roman empire; and yet by degrees Pagan rites and ceremonies were introduced into the Christian church; and what with them, and errors in doctrine, and other things concurring, made way for the man of sin to appear; and that mystery of iniquity, which had been secretly working from the times of the apostles, to shew its head openly; and brought in the darkness of Popery upon almost all that bore the Christian name.

In the twelfth, thirteenth, and fourteenth centuries, flourished a set of men called *Schoolmen*; these framed a new sort of divinity, called from them *Scholastic Theology*; the first founder of which some make to be Damascene, among the Greeks; and others Lanfranc, Archbishop of Canterbury, among the Latins; though generally Peter Lombard is reckoned the father of these men; who was followed by our countryman Alexander Hales; and after him were Albertus Magnus, Bonaventure, and Thomas Aquinas; and after them Duns Scotus, Durandus, and others; their divinity was founded upon and confirmed by the philosophy of Aristotle; and that not understood by them, and wrongly interpreted to them; for as they could not read Aristotle in his own language, the Greek, they were beholden to the Arabic interpreters of him, who led them wrong. Their theology lay in contentious and litigious disputations; in thorny questions, and subtle distinctions; and their whole scheme was chiefly directed to support antichristianism, and the tenets of it; so that by their means popish darkness was the more increased, and Christian divinity was banished almost out of the world; and was only to be found among a few, among the Waldenses and Albigenses, and the inhabitants of the valleys of Piedmont, and some particular persons and their followers, as Wickliffe, John Huss, and Jerome of Prague; and so things continued till the reformation begun by Zuinglius and Luther, and carried on by others; by whose means evangelical light was spread through many nations in Europe; the doctrines of the apostles were revived, and supernatural Theology once more lift up its head; the reformed churches published their confessions of faith, and many eminent men wrote common places, and systems of divinity; in which they all agreed in the main, to support the doctrines of revelation; as of the Trinity, and the Deity of the divine Persons in it; those of predestination and eternal election in Christ, of redemption by him, pardon of sin by his blood, and justification by his righteousness.

But Satan, who envied the increasing light of the Gospel, soon began to bestir himself, and to play his old game which he had done with so much success in the first ages of Christianity; having been for a long time otherwise engaged, to nurse up the man of sin, and to bring him to the height of his impiety and tyranny, and to support him in it: and now as his kingdom was like to be shook, if not subverted, by the doctrines of the Reformation; he, I say, goes to his old work again; and revives the Sabellian and Photinian errors, by the Socinians in Poland; and the Pelagian errors, by the Arminians and Remonstrants in Holland; the pernicious influence of which has been spread in other countries; and, indeed, has drawn a veil over the glory of the Reformation, and the doctrines of it. And the doctrines of pure revelation are almost exploded; and some are endeavouring to bring us as fast as they can, into a state of paganism, only somewhat refined. It is a day of darkness and gloominess; a day of clouds and of thick darkness; the darkness is growing upon us, and night may be expected; though for our relief it is declared, " that at evening time it shall be light." Almost all the old heresies are revived, under a fond and foolish notion of new light;

when they are no other than what have been confuted over and over; and men please themselves that they are their own inventions, when they are the devices of Satan, with which he has deceived men once and again; and when men leave the sure Word, the only rule of faith and practice, and follow their own fancies, and the dictates of their carnal minds, they must needs go wrong, and fall into labyrinths, out of which they cannot find their way : "to the law, and to the testimony, if they speak not according to this word, it is because there is no light in them." Let us therefore search the Scriptures, to see whether doctrines advanced are according to them or not; which I fear are little attended to.

Upon the whole, as I suggested at the beginning of this Introduction, I have but little reason to think the following Work will meet with a favourable reception in general; yet, if it may be a means of preserving sacred Truths, of enlightening the minds of any into them, or of establishing them in them, I shall not be concerned at what evil treatment I may meet with from the adversaries of them; and be it as it may, I shall have the satisfaction of having done the best I can for the promoting TRUTH; and of bearing a testimony to it.

A BODY OF DOCTRINAL DIVINITY.

BOOK I.

OF GOD, HIS WORD, NAMES, NATURE, PERFECTIONS, AND PERSONS.

CHAP. I.

OF THE BEING OF GOD.

HAVING undertaken to write a System of Theology, or a Body of Doctrinal Divinity; and Theology being nothing else than a speaking of God, or a discoursing concerning him; his nature, names, perfections, and persons; his purposes, providences, ways, works, and word: I shall begin with the Being of God, and the proof and evidence of it; which is the foundation of all religion; for if there is no God, religion is a vain thing; and it matters not neither what we believe, nor what we do; since there is no superior Being to whom we are accountable for either faith or practice. Some, because the being of God is a first principle, which is not to be disputed; and because that there is one is a self-evident proposition, not to be disproved; have thought it should not be admitted as a matter of debate:[1] but since such is the malice of Satan, as to suggest the contrary to the minds of men; and such the badness of some wicked men as to listen to it, and imbibe it; and such the weakness of some good men as to be harrassed and distressed with doubts about it at times: it cannot be improper to endeavour to fortify our minds with reasons and arguments against such suggestions and insinuations. And my

First argument to prove the Being of a God, shall be taken from the general consent of men of all nations, in all ages of the world; among whom the belief of it has universally obtained; which it is not reasonable to suppose would have obtained, if it was not true. This has been observed by many heathen writers themselves. Aristotle says,[2] all men have a persuasion of Deity, or that there is a God. Cicero observes,[3] "There is no nation so wild and savage, whose minds are not imbued with the opinion of the gods; many entertain wrong notions of them; but all suppose and own the divine power and nature." And in another place[4] he says, "There is no animal besides man that has any knowledge of God; and of men there is no nation so untractable and fierce, although it may be ignorant what a God it should have, yet is not ignorant that one should be had." And again,[5] "It is the sense of all mankind, that it is *innate* in all, and is as it were, engraven on the mind, that there is a God; but what a one he his, in that they vary; but that he is, none denies." And to the same sense are the words[6] of Seneca, "There never was a nation so dissolute, and abandoned, so lawless and immoral, as to believe there is no God." So Ælianus[7] relates, "None of the barbarous nations ever fell into atheism, or doubted of the gods whether they were or no, or whether

---

[1] So Aristotle says, every problem and proposition is not to be disputed; they that doubt whether God is to be worshipped, and parents loved, are to be punished, and not disputed with. Topic. 1. 1. c. 9.
[2] De Cœlo, 1. 1. c. 3.
[3] Tusculan. Quæst. 1. 1. c. 13.
[4] De Legibus, 1. 1.
[5] De Natura Deorum, 1. 2.
[6] Ep. 117.
[7] Var. Hist. 1. 2. c. 31. So Plato de Legibus, 1. 10. p. 945.

they took care of human affairs or not; not the Indians, nor the Gauls, nor the Egyptians." And Plutarch[8] has these remarkable words, "If you go over the earth," says he, "you may find cities without walls, letters, kings, houses, wealth, and money, devoid of theatres and schools; but a city without temples and Gods, and where is no use of prayers, oaths, and oracles, nor sacrifices to obtain good or avert evil, no man ever saw." These things were observed and said, when the true knowledge of God was in a great measure lost, and idolatry prevailed; and yet even then, this was the general sense of mankind. In the first ages of the world, men universally believed in the true God, and worshipped him, as Adam and his sons, and their posterity, until the flood; nor does there appear any trace of idolatry before it, nor for some time after. The sins which caused that, and with which the world was filled, seem to be lewdness and uncleanness, rapine and violence. Some think the tower of Babel was built for an idolatrous use; and it may be that about that time idolatry was set up; as it is thought to have prevailed in the days of Serug: and it is very probable that when the greater part of the posterity of Noah's sons were dispersed throughout the earth, and settled in the distant parts of it; that as they were remote from those among whom the true worship of God was preserved; they, by degrees, lost sight of the true God, and forsook his worship; and this being the case, they began to worship the sun in his stead, and which led on to the worship of the moon, and the host of heaven; which seem to be the first objects of idolatry. This was as early as the times of Job, who plainly refers to it, chap. xxxi. 26, 27. And, indeed, when men had cast off the true object of worship, what more natural to substitute in his room than the sun, moon, and stars, which were above them, visible by them, and so glorious in themselves, and so beneficial to the earth and men on it? Hence the people of Israel were exhorted to take care that their eyes were not ensnared at the sight of them, to fall down and worship them; and which in after-times they did. Deut. iv. 19. 2 Kings xxi. 3. It appears also that men took very early to the deifying of their heroes after death, their kings, and great personages, either for their wisdom and knowledge, or for their courage and valour, and martial exploits, and other things; such were the Bel, or Belus, of the Babylonians; the Baal-peor of the Moabites; and the Moloch of the Phœnicians, and other Baalim lords, or kings, mentioned in the scriptures: and such were Saturn, Jupiter, Mars, Mercury, Hercules; and the rest of the rabble of the heathen deities; and indeed their Lares, and Penates, or household gods, were no other than the images of their deceased parents, or more remote ancestors, whose memory they revered; and in process of time their deities became very numerous; they had gods many and lords many: even with the Jews, when fallen into idolatry, their gods were according to the number of their cities, Jer. ii. 28. And as for the Gentiles, they worshipped almost every thing; not only the sun, moon, and stars; but the earth, fire, and water; and various sorts of animals, as oxen, goats, and swine, cats and dogs, the fishes of the rivers, the river-horse and the crocodile, those amphibious creatures; the fowls of the air, as the hawk, stork, and ibis; and even insects, the fly; yea, creeping things, as serpents, the beetle, &c.; as also vegetables, onions, and garlic; which occasioned the satirical poet[9] to say, *O sanctas gentes quibus hæc nascuntur in hortis, numina!* O holy nations, whose gods are born in their gardens! Nay some have worshipped the devil himself, as both in the East and West Indies;[10] and that for this reason, that he might not hurt them. Now though all this betrays the dreadful depravity of human nature; the wretched ignorance of mankind; and the sad stupidity men were sunk into; yet at the same time such shocking idolatry, in all the branches of it, is a full proof of the truth and force of my argument, that all men, in all ages and countries, have been possessed of the notion of a God; since, rather than to have no God, they have chosen false ones; so deeply rooted is a sense of Deity in the minds of all men.

I am sensible that to this it is objected, that there have been at different times, and in different countries, some particular persons[11] who have been reckoned atheists, deniers of the Being of a God. But some of these men were only deriders of the gods

---

[8] Adv. Colotem. Vol. II. p. 1125.
[9] Juvenal, Sat. 15. v. 10.
[10] Peter Martyr de Angleria. Decad. 1. l. 9. Vartoman. Navigat. l. 5. c. 12, 23. and l. 6. c. 16, 27.
[11] Plutarch. de Placitis Philosoph. l. 1. c. 7.

of their country; they mocked at them as unworthy of the name, as weak and insufficient to help them; as they reasonably might; just as Elijah mocked at Baal and his worshippers. Now the common people, because they so behaved towards their gods, looked upon them as atheists, as such who did not believe there was any God. Others were so accounted, because they excluded the gods from any concern with human affairs; they thought they were otherways employed, and that such things were below their notice, and not becoming their grandeur and dignity to regard; and had much the same sentiments as some of the Jews had, Ezek. ix. 9. Zeph. i. 12. But these men were not deniers of the existence of God, only of his providence as to the affairs of the world; and others have been rather practical than speculative atheists, as the fool in Psalm xiv. 1. who not only live as if there was no God; but wish in their hearts there was none, rather than believe there is none; that so they might take their fill of sin, without being accountable to a superior Being. The number of real speculative atheists have been very few, if any; some have boldly asserted their disbelief of a God; but it is a question whether their hearts and mouths have agreed; at least they have not been able to maintain their unbelief long[12] without some doubts and fears. And at most this only shows how much the reason of man may be debased, and how low it may sink when left to itself: these few instances are only particular exceptions to a general rule; which is not destroyed thereby, being contrary to the common sense of mankind; even as it is no sufficient objection to the definition of man, as a rational creature, that there is now and then an idiot born of his race, so not to the general belief of Deity, that there is now and then an atheist in the world.

It is further objected, that there have been whole nations in Africa and America, who have no notion of Deity. But this is what has not been sufficiently proved; it depends upon the testimonies of travellers, and what one affirms, another denies; so that nothing can with certainty be concluded from them. "I should rather question," says Herbert, Lord Cherbury,[13] "whether the light of the sun has shone on the remotest regions, than that the knowledge of the Supreme Being is hidden from them; since the sun is only conspicuous in its own sphere; but the Supreme Being is seen in every thing." Diodorus Siculus[14] says, a few of the Ethiopians were of opinion there was no God; though before he had represented them as the first and most religious of all nations, as attested by all antiquity. The Hottentots about the Cape of Good Hope have been instanced in, as without any knowledge of Deity: and certainly they are a most beastly and brutish people that can be named, and the most degenerate of the human species, and have survived the common instincts of humanity:[15] yet according to Mr. Kolben's account of them, published some years ago,[16] they appear to have some sense of a Supreme Being, and of inferior deities. They express a superstitious joy at new and full moons; and it is said they pray to a Being that dwells above; and offer sacrifice of the best things they have, with eyes lifted up to heaven.[17] And later discoveries of other nations, shew the contrary to what has been asserted of them; which assertions have arose either from want of intimate knowledge of them, and familiar acquaintance with them, or from their dissolute, wicked, and irreligious lives; when by conversing with them, it appears that they have a notion of the sun, or sky, or something or another being a sort of deity. Thus it has been observed of the Greenlanders,[18] that "they had neither a religion nor idolatrous worship; nor so much as any ceremonies to be perceived tending to it: hence the first missionaries entertained a supposition that there was not the least trace to be found among them of any conception of a divine Being, especially as they had no word to express him by. But when they came to understand their language better, they found quite the reverse to be true, from the notions they had, though very vague and various, concerning the soul, and concerning spirits; and also from their anxious solicitude about the state after death. And not only so, but they

---

[12] Plato observes, that no man that embraced this opinion from his youth, that there is no God, ever continued in it to old age. De Legibus, l. 10. p. 947.
[13] De Relig. Gent. c. 13. p. 225.
[14] Bibliothec. 1. 3. p. 148.
[15] See the Philosoph. Transac. Abridged. Vol. V. part 2. p. 154.
[16] See Dr. Watts's Strength and Weakness of human Reason, in Vol. II. of his works, p. 262, &c.
[17] See Ovington's Voyage to Surat, p. 489, 498. and Dampier's Voyages, Vol. I. p. 541.
[18] Crantz's History of Greenland, Vol. I. b. 3. ch. 5. p. 197, 198.

could plainly gather from a free dialogue they had with some perfectly wild Greenlanders, that their ancestors must have believed a supreme Being, and did render him some service; which their posterity neglected by little and little, the further they were removed from more wise and civilised nations; till at last they lost every just conception of the Deity; yet after all, it is manifest, that a faint idea of a divine Being lies concealed in the minds even of this people, because they directly assent, without any objection, to the doctrine of a God and his attributes." And as to what is concluded from the irreligious lives of the inhabitants of some nations, we need not be sent to Africa and America for such atheists as these; we have enough of them in our own nation; and I was just ready to say, we are a nation of atheists in this sense: and, indeed, all men in an unregenerate state, be they Jews or Gentiles, or live where they may, they are αθεοι, *atheists;* as the apostle calls them, Eph. ii. 12. they are "without God in the world, being alienated from the life of God," ch. iv. 18. otherwise there is such a general sense of Deity in mankind; and such a natural inclination to religion, of some sort or another, though ever so bad, that some have thought that man should rather be defined as a religious than a rational animal. I take no notice of the holy angels, who worship God continually; nor of the devils who believe there is one God and tremble; my argument being only concerned with men.

The *second* argument shall be taken from the law and light of nature, or from the general instinct in men, or impress of Deity on the mind of every man; that is, as soon as he begins to have the exercise of his rational powers, he thinks and speaks of God, and assents to the Being of a God. This follows upon the former, and is to be proved by it; for as Cicero [19] says, "The consent of all nations in any thing, is to be reckoned the law of nature." And since all nations agree in the belief of a Deity, that must be a part of the law of nature, inscribed on the heart of every man. Seneca[20] makes use of this to prove there is a God; "because," says he, "an opinion or sense of Deity, is *implanted* in the minds of all men." And so likewise Cicero, as observed before; and who calls them the notions of Deity *implanted* and *innate.* And whoever believes the Mosaic account of the creation of man, cannot doubt of this being his case, when first created; since he is said to be made *in the image, and after the likeness of God;* for the image of God surely could not be impressed upon him, without having the knowledge of him implanted in him; and though man by sinning has greatly come short of this image and glory of God, yet this light of nature is not wholly obscured, nor the law of nature entirely obliterated in him; there are some remains of it. There are some indeed among us, who deny there are any innate ideas in the minds of men, and particularly concerning God: but to such writers and reasoners I pay but little regard; when the inspired apostle assures us, that even the Gentiles, destitute of the law of Moses, have *the work of the law written in their hearts,* Rom. ii. 15. which as it regards duty to God, as well as man, necessarily supposes the knowledge of him; as well as of the difference between good and evil, as founded upon his nature and will: and though this light of nature is not sufficient to lead men in their present state, to a true spiritual and saving knowledge of God; yet it furnishes them with such a sense of him, as puts them upon seeking him; "if haply they may feel and grope after him and find him," Acts xvii. 27. These notices of a divine Being do not flow from the previous instructions of parents and others; but from a natural instinct; at most they are only drawn forth by instruction and teaching; "that there is a Deity," Velleius, the Epicurean says,[21] "nature itself has impressed the notion of on the minds of all men; for what nation, or sort of men," adds he, "that has not a certain anticipation of it without being taught it," or before taught it, as Julian[22] expresses it: nor do these notices take their rise from state-policy; or are the effects of that originally: if this was the case, if it was the contrivance of policitians to keep men in awe, and under subjection, it must be the contrivance of one man, or more united together. If of one, say, who is the man? in what age he lived, and where? and what is his name, or his son's name? If of more, say, when and where they existed? and who

---

[19] Ut supra.
[20] Ut supra.
[21] Apud Ciceron. de Natura Deorum, 1. 1.

[22] Apud Grotium de jure Belli, 1. 2. c. 20. s. 45. Annotat. in ibid. p. 334.

they were that met together? and where they formed this scheme? And let it be accounted for; if it can, that such a number of sage and wise men, who have been in the world; that no man should be able to get into the secret, and detect the fallacy and discover it, and free men from the imposition. Besides, these notices appeared before any scheme of politics was formed; or kings or civil magistrates were in being. Plato[23] has refuted this notion; and represents it as a very pestilent one, both in private and in public. Nor are these notices by tradition from one to another; since traditions are peculiar to certain people: the Jews had theirs, and so had the Gentiles; and particular nations among them had separate ones from each other; but these are common to all mankind: nor do they spring from a slavish fear and dread of punishment; for though it has been said,[24] that fear makes gods, or produces a notion of Deity; the contrary is true, that Deity produces fear, as will be seen in a following argument.

Under this head may be observed the *innate* desires of men after happiness, which are so boundless as not to be satisfied. Let a man have ever so great a compass of knowledge and understanding; or possess ever so large a portion of wealth and riches; or be indulged with the gratification of his senses to the highest degree; or enjoy all the pleasure the whole creation can afford him; yet after all, according to the wise man, the conclusion of the whole is, *all is vanity and vexation of spirit*, Eccles. i. 17. Now these desires are not in vain implanted, there must be an object answerable unto them; a perfect Being, which is no other than God; who is the first cause and last end of all things, of whom the Psalmist says, *Whom have I in heaven but thee? and there is none on earth my soul desires besides thee*, Ps. lxxiii. 25.

The *third* argument, proving the Being of God, shall be taken from the works of creation; concerning which the apostle says, *the invisible things of God, from the creation of the world, are clearly seen; being understood by the things that are made, even his eternal power and Godhead,* Rom. i. 20. Plutarch,[25] in answer to a question, Whence have men the knowledge of God? replies, "They first receive the knowledge of him from the beauty of things that appear; for nothing beautiful is made in vain, nor by chance, but wrought with some art: that the world is beautiful, is manifest from the figure, the colour, and magnitude of it; and from the variety of stars about the world." And these so clearly display the Being and power of God, as to leave the heathen without excuse, as the apostle observes; and as this, and other instances, shew. Most admirable was the reasoning of a wild Greenlander,[26] which he declared to a missionary to be the reasoning of his mind before his conversion; "It is true," said he to him, "we were ignorant heathens, and knew nothing of God, or a Saviour; and, indeed, who should tell us of him till you come? but thou must not imagine that no Greenlander thinks about these things. I myself have often thought: a *kajak* (a boat) with all its tackle and implements, does not grow into existence of itself; but must be made by the labour and ingenuity of man; and one that does not understand it would directly spoil it. Now the meanest bird has far more skill displayed in its structure, than the best *kajak;* and no man can make a bird: but there is still a far greater art shewn in the formation of a man, than of any other creature. Who was it that made him? I bethought me that he proceeded from his parents, and they from their parents; but some must have been the first parents; whence did they come? common report informs me, they grew out of the earth: but if so, why does it not still happen that men grow out of the earth? and from whence did this same earth itself, the sea, the sun, the moon, and stars, arise into existence? Certainly there must be some Being who made all these things; a Being that always was, and can never cease to be. He must be inexpressibly more mighty, knowing, and wise, than the wisest man. He must be very good too, because that every thing that he has made is good, useful, and necessary for us. Ah, did I but know him, how would I love him and honour him! But who has seen him? who has ever conversed with him? None of us poor men. Yet there may be men too that know something of him. O that I could but speak with such! therefore," said he, "as soon as ever I heard you speak of this great Being, I believed it directly, with all

---

[23] De Legibus, 1. 10. p. 948.
[24] Primus in orbe Deos fecit timor, Statii Thebaid. 1. 3. v. 661.
[25] De Placitis Philosoph. l. 1. c. 6. p. 879.
[26] Crantz's History of Greenland, ut supra.

my heart; because I had so long desired to hear it." A glaring proof this, that a supreme Being, the first cause of all things, is to be concluded from the works of creation. The notion of the eternity of the world has been imbibed by some heathens, but sufficiently confuted by others. And even Aristotle, to whom it is ascribed, asserts,[27] that "it was an ancient doctrine, and what all men received from their ancestors; that all things are of God, and consist by him." And those that believe the divine revelation, cannot admit of any other doctrine; but must explode the notion of the eternity of the world, and of its being of itself; since that assures us, that *in the beginning God created the heavens and the earth:* also that all things were made, *not of things which do appear,* but out of nothing, Gen. i. 1. Heb. xi. 3. for, be it, that the heavens and the earth were made out of a chaos, or out of pre-existent matter; it may be reasonably asked, out of what was that pre-existent matter made? the answer must be, out of nothing; since it was by creation, which is the production of something out of nothing: and which can never be performed by the creature; for out of nothing, nothing can be made by that. If therefore all things are originally produced out of nothing, it must be by one that is almighty, whom we rightly call God. No creature can produce itself; this involves such contradictions as can never be admitted; for then a creature must be before it was; as that which makes must be before that which is made: it must act and operate before it exists; and be and not be at one and the same time; which are such glaring contradictions, as sufficiently confute the creature's making itself; and therefore its being must be owing to another cause; even to God, the Creator; for between a creature and God, there is no medium: and if it could be thought or said, that the most excellent creatures, men, made themselves; besides the above contradictions, which would be implied, it might be asked, why did not they make themselves wiser and better; since it is certain they have knowledge of beings superior to them? and how is it that they know so little of themselves, either of their bodies or their souls, if both were made by them? and why are they not able to preserve themselves from a dissolution to which they are all subject? It may be further observed; that effects, which depend upon causes in subordination to one another, cannot be traced up *ad infinitum;*[28] but must be reduced to some first cause, where the inquiry must rest; and that first cause is God. Now here is an ample field to survey; which furnishes out a variety of objects, and all proofs of Deity. There is nothing in the whole creation the mind can contemplate, the eye look upon, or the hand lay hold on, but what proclaims the Being of God. When we look up to the heavens[29] above us; the surrounding atmosphere; the air in which we breathe, which compresses our earth, and keeps it together; the fluid ether, and spreading sky, bespangled with stars of light, and adorned with the two great luminaries, the sun and moon, especially the former, that inexhaustible fountain of light and heat; and under whose benign influences, so many things are brought forth on earth; whose circuit is from one end of the heaven to the other; and there is nothing hid from the heat thereof: when we consider its form, magnitude, and virtue; its proper distance from us, being not so near us as to scorch us; nor so remote as to be of no use to us; the motion given it at first, in which it has proceeded without stopping, but once as is supposed, in the days of Joshua; a motion it has had now almost six thousand years; the course it has steered, and steers, so that all parts of the earth, at one season or another, receive benefit by it; and the way it has been guided in, without varying or erring from it all this while. Whoever reflects on these things, must acknowledge it to be the work of an all-wise and almighty agent, we call God; and that it must be upheld, guided, and directed by his hand alone. When we take a view of the earth, of the whole terraqueous globe, hanging on nothing, like a ball in the air, poized with its own weight; the different parts of it, and all disposed for the use of man; stored with immense riches in the bowels of it, and stocked with inhabitants upon it; the various sorts of animals, of different forms and shapes, made, some for strength, some for swiftness, some for bearing burdens, and others for drawing carriages, some for food and others for clothing: the vast variety of the feathered tribes that cut the air; and the

---

[27] De Mundo, c. 6.
[28] αμφοτερως δε αδυνατον εις απειρον ιεναι, Aristot. Metaphysic. l. 2. c. 2.
[29] Quis est tam vecors, qui aut cum suspexerit in cœlum deos esse non sentiat, Cicero. Orat. 30. De Harusp. resp. So Plato de Legibus, l. 12. p. 999. Zaleucus apud Diodor. Sicul. l. 12. p. 84. Ed. Rhodoman.

innumerable kinds of fishes that swim the ocean. The consideration of all this will oblige us to say, *Lord, thou art God*, which hast made *the heaven, earth, and sea; and all that in them is*, Acts iv. 25. In short, there is not a shell in the ocean, nor a sand on the shore, nor a spire of grass in the field, nor any flower of different hue and smell in the garden, but what declare the Being of God: but especially our own composition is deserving of our notice; the fabric of the body, and the faculties of our souls. The body, its form and shape; whilst other animals look downwards to the earth, *os homini sublime dedit Deus*, as the poet says,[30] man has a lofty countenance given him, to behold the heavens, to lift up his face to the stars; and for what is this erect posture given him, but to adore his Creator? And it is remarkable that there is a natural instinct in men to lift up their hands and eyes to heaven, when either they have received any unexpected mercy, by way of thankfulness for it; or are in any great distress, as supplicating deliverance from it; which supposes a divine Being, to whom they owe the one, and from whom they expect the other. The several parts and members of the body are so framed and disposed, as to be subservient to one another; so that *the eye cannot say to the hand, I have no need of thee; nor the head to the feet, I have no need of you*. The same may be observed of the other members. The inward parts, which are weak and tender, and on which life much depends, were they exposed, would be liable to much danger and hurt; but these are *clothed with skin and flesh, and fenced with bones and sinews*; and every bone, and every nerve, and every muscle, are put in their proper places. All the organs of the senses, of sight, hearing, smelling, tasting, and feeling, are most wonderfully fitted for the purposes for which they are made. Galen, an ancient noted physician, being atheistically inclined, was convinced of his impiety by barely considering the admirable structure of the eye; its various humors, tunics, and provision for its defence and safety. The various operations performed in our bodies, many of which are done without our knowledge or will, are enough to raise the highest admiration in us: as the circulation of the blood through all parts of the body, in a very small space of time; the respiration of the lungs; the digestion of the food; the chylification of it; the mixing of the chyle with the blood; the nourishment thereby communicated; and which is sensibly perceived in the several parts of the body, and even in the more remote; which having been weakened and enfeebled by hunger, thirst, and labour, are in an instant revived and strengthened; and the accretion and growth of parts by all this. To which may be added other things worthy of notice; the faculty of speech, peculiar to man, and the organs of it; the features of their faces; and the shape of their bodies, which all differ from one another; the constant supply of animal spirits; the continuance of the vital heat, which outlasts fire itself; the slender threads and small fibres spread throughout the body, which hold and perform their office seventy or eighty years running: all which, when considered, will oblige us to say, with the inspired Psalmist, *I am fearfully and wonderfully made; marvellous are thy works; and that my soul knoweth right well*: and will lead us to ascribe this curious piece of workmanship to no other than to the divine Being, *the God of all flesh living*.[31]

But the soul of man, the more noble part of him, more fully discovers the original author of him;[32] being possessed of such powers and faculties that none but God could give: it is endowed with an *understanding*, capable of receiving and framing ideas of all things knowable, in matters natural, civil, and religious; and with *reason* to put these together, and compare them with each other, and discourse concerning them; infer one thing from another, and draw conclusions from them: and with *judgment*, by which it passes sentence on things it takes cognizance of, and reasons upon; and determines for itself what is right or wrong; and so either approves or disapproves: it has a *mind* susceptive of what is proposed unto it; it can, by instruction or study, learn any language; cultivate any art or science; and, with the help of some geographical principles, can travel over the globe, can be here and there at pleasure, in the four parts of the world;

---

[30] Ovid Metamorph. l. 1. fab. 2. v. 84, 85. Vid. Ciceronem de Natura Deorum, L 2. Hence the Greeks call man ανθρωπος, from his looking upwards, Lactant. de Orig. err. l. 2. c. 1.

[31] See an excellent treatise of Dr. Nieuwentyt, called, The Religious Philosopher; in which the Being and Perfections of God are demonstrated from the works of creation, in a very great variety of instances.

[32] So Plato proves the Being of God from the soul of man, de Legibus, p. 998.

and in a short time visit every city of note therein, and describe the situation of every country, with their religion, manners, customs, &c. it can reflect on things past, and has a foresight of, and can forecast and provide for things to come: it has a *will*, to accept or reject, to embrace or refuse, what is proposed unto it; with the greatest freedom of choice, and with the most absolute power and sovereignty: it has *affections*, of love and hatred, joy and grief, hope and fear, &c. according to the different objects it is conversant with. There is also the *conscience*, which is to a man as a thousand witnesses, for him or against him; which, if it performs its office as it should do, will accuse him when he does ill, and commend, or excuse him, when he does well; and from hence arise either peace of mind, or dread of punishment, in some shape or another, either here or hereafter: to which may be added the *memory*, which is a storehouse of collections of things thought to be most valuable and useful; where they are laid up, not in a confused, but orderly manner; so as to be called for and taken out upon occasion: here men of every character and profession lay up their several stores, to have recourse unto, and fetch out, as their case and circumstances may require. And besides this, there is the *fancy* or *imagination*, which can paint and describe to itself in a lively manner, objects presented to it, and it has entertained a conception of; yea, it can fancy and imagine things that never were, nor never will be: and to observe no more, there is the power of *invention;* which in some is more, in others less fertile; which, on a sudden, supplies with what is useful in case of an emergency. But above all, the *soul* of man is that wherein chiefly lay the image and likeness of God, when man was in his pure and innocent state; and though it is now sadly depraved by sin, yet it is capable of being renewed by the spirit of God, and of having the grace of God implanted in it, and is endowed with immortality, and cannot die: now to whom can such a noble and excellent creature as this owe its original? but to the divine Being, who may, with great propriety, be called, *the Father of spirits*, the Lord, the Jehovah, who *formeth the spirit of man within him.*

The *fourth* argument will be taken from the sustentation and government of the world; the provision made for the supply of creatures, and especially of man, and for his safety. As the world, as we have seen, is made by a divine Being, so by him it consists. Was there not such an almighty Being, "who upholds all things by the word of his power," they would sink and fall. Did he not bear up the pillars of the earth, they would tremble and shake, and not be able to bear its weight: the most stately, firm, and well-built palace, unless repaired and maintained, will fall to decay and ruin; and so the grand and magnificent building of this world would soon be dissolved, did not the divine agent that made it, keep it up: as he that built all things is God, so he that supports the fabric of the universe must be so too; no less than an almighty hand can preserve and continue it; and which has done it, without any visible appearance of age or decay, for almost six thousand years; and though there is such a vast number of creatures in the world, besides men, the beasts of the field, and "the cattle on a thousand hills," the fowls of the air, and the fishes of the sea; there is food provided for them all, and they have "every one their portion of meat in due season:" and as for man, he is richly provided for, with a plenty and variety of all good things; not only for necessity, but for delight; every man has a trade, business, and employment of life; or is put into such a situation and circumstances, that, with care, diligence, and industry, he may have enough for himself and family, and to spare: the earth produces a variety of things for food and drink for him; and of others for medicine, for the continuance of health, and restoration of it. And can all this be without the care, providence, and interposition of a wise and almighty Being? Can these ever be thought to be the effects of blind chance and fortune? Is it not plain and clear, that God hereby "has not left himself without a witness of his existence and providence, in that he does good to all his creatures, and gives rain from heaven, and fruitful seasons; filling men's hearts with food and gladness;" and continuing the certain and constant revolutions of "summer and winter, seedtime and harvest;" as well as night and day, cold and heat; all which have their peculiar usefulness and advantages to human life; and cannot be attributed to any thing else than the superintendency of the divine Being.

And as there is a provision made for the wants of men, so for their safety: were it not that God had put the fear of man upon the wild beasts of the field, and the dread of him in them, there would be no safety for him, especially in some parts of the world; and had he not put a natural instinct into them to avoid the habitations of men, and to resort to woods and deserts, and dwell in uninhabited places; to prowl about for their prey in the night, and in the morning return to their caves and dens, and lurking places; when men go forth to their work, they would be in the utmost danger of their lives: yea, were it not for the overruling providence of God, which governs the world, and restrains the lusts of men, *homo esset homini lupus;* "one man would be a wolf to another;" neither life nor property would be secure; but must fall a prey to the rapine and violence of powerful oppressors. Human laws, and civil magistracy, do something to restrain men, but not every thing; notwithstanding these, we see what outrages are committed: and how greater still would be their number, was it not for the interposition of divine providence: and even it is owing to a divine Being that there are human forms of government, and political schemes framed, and laws made for the better regulation of mankind, and these continued; for it is by him *kings reign, and princes decree justice:* and particularly, was it not for a divine agency, such is the rage and malice of Satan, and his principalities and powers, whose numbers fill the surrounding air; and who go about our earth like roaring lions, seeking whom they may devour; were they not chained by almighty power, and limited by the providence of God, the whole race of men would be destroyed by them, at least the godly among them.

The *fifth* argument may be taken from the uncommon heroic actions, prodigies, wonders, and miraculous things done in the world; which cannot be thought to be done without a superior and divine influence. Heroic actions, such as that of Abraham, who, with three hundred household-servants, pursued after, and engaged with four kings who had beaten five before, and recovered the goods they had taken away: of Shamgar, who fought with and killed six hundred Philistines with an ox-goad: and of Samson, who slew a thousand of them with the jaw-bone of an ass: of Jonathan, and his armour-bearer, who attacked and took a garrison of the same people, and threw a whole army of theirs into a panic and confusion; who had been for some time a terror to the whole land of Israel: and of David, a stripling, fighting with and conquering Goliath, a monstrous giant. These are scripture instances; and if scripture is only regarded as a common history; these merit our notice and credit, as any of the relations in profane history; in which are recorded the magnanimous actions of heroes, kings, and generals of armies; their wonderful successes, and amazing conquests; as of the Babylonians, Persians, Grecians, and Romans; which made such strange revolutions and changes in kingdoms and states; all which can never be supposed to be done without superior power, and the overruling, influencing providence of the divine Being; who inspired men to do things beyond their natural skill and courage; prodigies, strange and wonderful events; for which no natural cause can be assigned; such as the strange sights seen in the air, and voices heard in the temple, before the destruction of Jerusalem; with other things, related by Josephus,[33] and confirmed by Tacitus,[34] an heathen historian; to which might be added many others, which histories abound with: but besides these, things really miraculous have been wrought, such as are not only out of, and beyond the course of nature, but contrary to it, and to the settled laws of it; such as the miracles of Moses and the prophets, and of Christ and his apostles; which are recorded in the scriptures; and others in human writings; which are so well attested as oblige us to give credit to them: now, though these were not done to prove a divine Being; which needs them not; yet they necessarily suppose one, by whose power alone they are performed.

The *sixth* argument may be formed from the prophesies of contingent future events, and the exact fulfilment of them. This is what is challenged and required from heathen deities, to prove their right to such a character; as being what none but God can do: *Let them bring forth and shew us what shall happen: or declare us things for to come: shew the things that are to come hereafter; that we may know that ye are gods:*[35] which is what none but the true God can do, and has done; and which being done, proves there is a God, and one that is truly so; instances of which there are many in the sacred writings; prophesies which relate both to particular persons and to whole kingdoms and states; which

---

[33] De Bello Jud. l. 6. c. 5. s. 3.

[34] Hist. l. 5. c. 13.
[35] Isaiah xli. 21, 22.

have had their exact accomplishment: but not to insist on these, since those who are atheistically inclined, disbelieve the divine revelation; let it be observed, that the heathens have had their auguries, soothsayings, divinations, and oracles; by which pretensions have been made to foretel future events. That there is such a thing as divination, is said to be confirmed by the consent of all nations; and is explained of a presension and knowledge of future things:[36] now this being granted, it may be reasoned upon, that if there is a foretelling of future things, which certainly come to pass, there must be a God; since none but an omniscient Being can, with certainty, foretel what shall come to pass, which does not depend on necessary causes, and cannot be foreseen by the quickest sight, and sharpest wit, and sagacity of a creature.

The *seventh* argument may be urged from the fears of men, and the tortures of a guilty conscience, and the dread of a future state. Some are terribly affrighted at thunder and lightning, as Caligula, the Roman Emperor, used to be; who, at such times, would hide himself in, or under, his bed; and yet this man set himself up for a god. Now these fears and frights are not merely on account of the awful sound of the thunder, and the dreadful flashes of lightning; but because of the divine and tremendous Being who is supposed to send them: the Heathens were sensible that thunder is the voice of God, as the scriptures represent it, and therefore called their Jove, *Jupiter tonans;* "the thundering Jupiter." Many have been so terrified in their consciences on account of sin, that they could get no rest, nor enjoy peace any where, or by any means: as Cain, under the terrors of an evil conscience, fancied that "every one that found him would slay him:" and those wicked traitors, Catiline and Jugurtha: and those wicked emperors, those monsters in impiety, Tiberius and Nero,[37] and especially the latter, who was so tortured in his conscience, as if he was continually haunted by his mother's ghost, and by furies with burning torches: and Hobbes, our English atheist, as he was reckoned, was wont to be very uneasy when alone in the dark: and Epicurus, the philosopher, though he taught men to despise death, and out-brave it; yet, when he perceived that he himself was about to die, was most terribly frighted; and this has been the case of many others: bold and *strong spirits,* as atheistical persons love to be called, have been sometimes found to be very timorous and fearful. And, indeed, this is natural to all men, and which is proof of a superior Being. Thus a wild Greenlander[38] argued, before he had knowledge of the true God: "Man has an intelligent soul, is subject to no creature in the world; and yet man is afraid of the future state: who is it that he is afraid of there? That must be a great Spirit that has dominion over us. O did we but know him! O had we but him for our friend!" Now what do all these fears and tortures of conscience arise from, but from the guilt of sin, and a sense of a divine Being; who is above men, and will call them to an account for their sins, and take vengeance on them? And, indeed, the eternal punishment that will be inflicted on them, will greatly lie in the tortures of their conscience, which is the worm that will never die; and, in a sense of divine wrath, which is that fire that will never be quenched.

The *eighth* and last argument shall be taken from the judgments in the world; not only famine, sword, pestilence, earthquakes, &c. but such that have been inflicted on wicked men, atheistical persons, perjured ones, blasphemers, and the like. Not to take notice of the universal flood, which swept away a world of ungodly men; and of the burning of Sodom and Gomorrah, with other cities of the plain, by fire and brimstone from heaven; which yet are abundantly confirmed by the testimonies of heathen writers; nor of the awful instances in the New Testament, of Herod being smitten by an angel, and eaten of worms, and died, while the people was shouting him as a god, and he assented to their flattery; and of Ananias and Sapphira, being struck dead for lying unto God: besides these, there are innumerable instances of judgments, of the same or a like kind, in all ages and countries, recorded in the histories of them; and in our nation, and in our age, and within our knowledge; and who now can hear or read such awful judgments, and disbelieve the Being of God?

---

[36] Cicero de Divinatione, 1. 1. c. 1. et de Legibus, 1. 2.

[37] Sueton. Vita Tiberii, c. 67. et Nero. c. 34. Tacit. Annal. 1. 6. c. 6.
[38] Crantz's History of Greenland, ut supra.

CHAP. II.

OF THE HOLY SCRIPTURES.

As what I shall say hereafter concerning God, his essence, perfections, persons, works, and worship, and every thing relative to him, will be taken out of the sacred scriptures, and proved by them; it will be necessary, before I proceed any further, to secure the ground I go upon; and establish the divine authority of them; and shew that they are a perfect, plain, and sure rule to go by; and are the standard of faith and practice; and to be read constantly, studied diligently, and consulted with on all occasions.

By the Scriptures, I understand the books of the Old and of the New Testament. The books of the Old Testament, are the five books of Moses; Genesis, Exodus, Leviticus, Numbers, and Deuteronomy, sometimes called the Pentateuch; the historical books, Joshua, Judges, Ruth, the two books of Samuel, the two of Kings, the two of Chronicles, Ezra, Nehemiah, and Esther; the poetical books, Job, the Psalms, Proverbs, Ecclesiastes, and Solomon's Song; the prophetic books, the larger Prophets, Isaiah, Jeremiah, with the Lamentations, Ezekiel, and Daniel; the lesser Prophets, Hosea, Joel, Amos, Obadiah, Jonah, Micah, Nahum, Zephaniah, Haggai, Zechariah, and Malachi. The books of the New Testament, the four Evangelists, Matthew, Mark, Luke, and John, and the Acts of the Apostles; the fourteen Epistles of the Apostle Paul; one of James; two of Peter; three of John; one of Jude, and the Revelation. These books are commonly called Canonical Scripture, because they have been always received by the church into the canon, or rule of faith. The books of the Old Testament, by the Jewish church; with which entirely agree Josephus's account of them, and the catalogue of them brought from the East by Melito; and the books of both Testaments agree with the account which Origen gives of them in his time, and which have always been acknowledged by the christian church; and which testimony of both churches, respecting them, deserves our regard, and tends to corroborate their divine authority. Now these are the books which the apostle calls, *all Scripture*, or the whole of Scripture, said by him to be *given by inspiration of God:* which include not only the books of the Old Testament, which had been long in being in his time; but the books of the New Testament, which were all of them then written, excepting the book of the Revelation; since these words of his stand in an epistle supposed to be the last that was written by him; and however what is said by him is true of what might be written afterwards, for the uses he mentions, as well as before.

From these must be excluded, as un-canonical, the books that bear the name of Apocrypha; which are sometimes bound up with the Bible, to the great scandal and disgrace of it; for though there may be some things in them worthy to be read, as human writings; there is such a mixture of falsehood and impiety, that they cannot by any means be allowed to be placed upon an equality with the sacred scriptures. Likewise all such spurious books falsely ascribed to the apostles, or to some of the first christians; as, The Gospel of the Infancy of Jesus; The Constitutions of the Apostles; Hermes's Pastor, &c. which carry in them manifest marks of imposture. To which may be added, all human and unwritten traditions, pleaded for by the papists; and all dreams and visions, and pretended revelations and prophecies, delivered out in later ages, by enthusiastic persons. Blessed be God, we have a more sure word of prophecy to attend unto; concerning which, I shall,

I. Observe the *divine authority* of the Scriptures, or shew, that they are from God, or inspired by him; they lay in a claim to a divine original; and the claim is just, as will be seen. They are called the law, or doctrine of the Lord; the testimony of the Lord; the statutes of the Lord; the commandment of the Lord; the fear of the Lord; and the judgments of the Lord; by the Psalmist David, Psal. xix. 7, 8, 9. And the prophets frequently introduce their prophecies and discourses, by saying, *the word of the Lord came* to them; and with a, *thus saith the Lord*, Isa. i. 10. Jer. ii. 1, 2. And our Lord expressly calls the scripture the word of God, John x. 35. as it is also called, Heb. iv. 12. And which God "at sundry times, and in divers manners, spake by the prophets;" and by his Son, and his apostles, in later times, chap. i. 1, 2. And is represented as the oracles of God, and may be safely consulted and depended on; and according to which men are to speak, Rom. iii. 2. 1 Pet. i. 11. But before I proceed any further, in the proof of the divinity of the sacred Scriptures, I shall premise the following things.

First, That when we say that the Scriptures are the word of God, or that this word is of God; we do not mean that it was spoken with an articulate voice by him; or written immediately by the finger of God: the law of the Decalogue, or the Ten Commands, indeed, were articulately spoken by him, and the writing of them was the writing of God, Exod. xx. 1. and xxxi. 18. and xxxii. 15. in which he might set an example to his servants, in after times, to write what might be suggested to them by him; that it might remain to be read: it is enough, that they were bid to write what he delivered to them, as Moses and others were ordered to do, Deut. xxxi. 19. Jer. xxx. 2. Hab. ii. 2. Rev. i. 11, 19. and what was ordered by the Lord to be written, it is the same as if it was written by himself; and especially since the penmen wrote as they were directed, dictated and inspired by him, and "spake as they were moved by the Holy Ghost;" for they did not speak and write of their own head, and out of their own brains, nor according to their will, and when and what they pleased; but according to the will of God, and what he suggested to them, and when he inspired them, 2 Pet. i. 21.

Secondly, Not all that is contained in the scriptures is of God. Some are the words of others; yea, some are the speeches of Satan, and very bad ones too; as when he suggested that Job was not a sincere worshipper of God; and requested he might have leave to do an injury both to his property and to his person, Job i. 9, 10, 11. and ii. 4, 5, 6. So when he tempted our Lord, and moved him to cast himself down from the pinnacle of the temple, and destroy himself; and not succeeding in that, urged him to fall down and worship him, Matt. iv. 5, 9. But now the penman of these books, in which these speeches are, were moved and directed by the Lord to commit them to writing; so that though they themselves are not the word of God; yet that they are written, and are on record, is of God; and which was directed to, and done, to shew the malice, pride, blasphemy, and impiety, of that wicked spirit. There are also speeches of bad men, as of Cain, Pharaoh, and others, ordered to be written, to discover the more the corruption of human nature: and even of good men, as of Moses, David, Jonah, and particularly the friends of Job, and their long discourses, in which they said not that which was right of God, as Job did; and he himself did not say in every speech of his what was right of God; though he said more, and what was righter, than they did; and yet these speeches are on record, by divine order, to prove matters of fact, to shew the weaknesses and frailties of the best of men. Some of the writers of the scriptures, as Moses, and the historical ones, being eye and ear-witnesses of many things they wrote, could have wrote them of their own knowledge, and out of their own memories; and others they might take out of diaries, annals and journals, of their own and former times; yet in all they wrote, they were under the impulse and direction of God; what to leave, and what to take and insert into their writings, and transmit to posterity. So that all they wrote may be truly said to be by divine authority. In the writings and discourses of the apostle Paul, are several quotations out of heathen authors; one out of Aratus, when he was discoursing before the wise men at Athens; *as certain*, says he, *of your own poets have said, for we are also his offspring*, Acts xvii. 28. Another out of Menander; *Evil communications corrupt good manners*, 1 Cor. xv. 33. And another out of Epimenides, a poet of Crete, a testimony of his against the Cretians, who said they were, *always liars, evil beasts, slow bellies;* which were produced *ad hominum*, for greater conviction; and which he was directed to quote and write in his epistles and discourses, for that reason. So that though the words are not of God, yet that they were quoted and written, was of God.

Thirdly, Let it be observed, that not the matter of the Scriptures only, but the very words in which they are written are of God. Some who are not for organical inspiration, as they call it, think that the sacred writers were only furnished of God with matter, and had general ideas of things given them, and were left to clothe them with their own words, and to use their own style; which they suppose accounts for the difference of style to be observed in them: but if this was the case, as it sometimes is with men, that they have clear and satisfactory ideas of things in their own minds, and yet are at a loss for proper words to express and convey the sense of them to others; so it might be with the sacred writers, if words were not suggested to them, as well as matter; and then we should be left at an uncertainty about the real sense of the holy Spirit, if not led into a wrong one; it seems, therefore, most agreeable, that words also, as well as matter, were given by divine inspiration: and as for difference of style, as it was easy with God to direct to the use of proper words, so he could accommodate himself to the style such persons were wont to use, and which was natural to them, and agreeable to their genius and circumstances; and this may be confirmed from the testimonies of the writers themselves: says David, one of the writers of the Old Testament, *The Spirit of the Lord spake by me, and his word was in my tongue,* 2 Sam. xxiii. 2. And the apostle Paul speaks of himself, and other inspired apostles of the New Testament, *Which things,* says he, *we speak, not in the words which man's wisdom teacheth, but which the Holy Ghost teacheth,* 1 Cor. ii. 13. and it is *the writing,* or the word of God as written, that is, *by inspiration of God,* 2 Tim. iii. 16. But then,

Fourthly, This is to be understood of the Scriptures, as in the original languages in which they were written, and not of translations; unless it could be thought, that the translators of the Bible into the several languages of the nations into which it has been translated, were under the divine inspiration also in translating, and were directed of God to the use of words they have rendered the the original by; but this is not reasonable to suppose. The books of the Old Testament were written chiefly in the Hebrew language, unless some few passages in Jeremiah, Daniel, Ezra, and Esther, in the Chaldee language; and the New Testament in Greek: in which languages they can only be reckoned canonical and authentic; for this is like the charters and diplomas of princes; the wills or testaments of men; or any deeds made by them; only the original exemplar is authentic; and not translations, and transcriptions, and copies of them, though ever so perfect: and to the Bible, in its original languages, is every translation to be brought, and by it to be examined, tried, and judged, and to be corrected and amended: and if this was not the case, we should have no certain and infallible rule to go by; for it must be either all the translations together, or some one of them; not all of them, because they agree not in all things: not one; for then the contest would be between one nation and another which it should be, whether English, Dutch, French, &c. and could one be agreed upon, it could not be read and understood by all: so the papists, they plead for their vulgate Latin version; which has been decreed authentic by the council of Trent; though it abounds with innumerable errors and mistakes; nay, so far do they carry this affair, that they even assert that the Scriptures, in their originals, ought to submit to, and be corrected by their version; which is absurd and ridiculous. Let not now any be uneasy in their minds about translations on this account, because they are not upon an equality with the original text, and especially about our own; for as it has been the will of God, and appears absolutely necessary that so it should be, that the Bible should be translated into different languages, that all may read it, and some particularly may receive benefit by it; he has taken care, in his providence, to raise up men capable of such a performance, in various nations, and particularly in ours; for whenever a set of men have been engaged in this work, as were in our nation, men well skilled in the languages, and partakers of the grace of God; of sound principles, and of integrity and faithfulness, having the fear of God before their eyes; they have never failed of producing a translation worthy of acceptation; and in which, though they have mistook some words and phrases, and erred in some lesser and lighter matters; yet not so as to affect any momentous article of faith or practice; and therefore such translations as ours may be regarded as the rule of faith. And if any scruple should remain on the minds of any on this account, it will be sufficient to remove it, when it is observed, that the Scriptures, in our English translation, have been blessed of God, either by reading them in it, or by explaining them according to it, for the conversion, comfort, and edification of thousands and thousands. And the same may be said of all others, so far as they agree with the original, that they are the rule of faith and practice, and alike useful.

Here I cannot but observe the amazing ignorance and stupidity of some persons, who take it into their heads to decry learning and learned men; for what would they have done for a Bible, had it not been for them as instruments? and if they had it, so as to have been capable of reading it, God must have wrought a miracle for them; and continued that miracle in every nation, in every age, and to every individual; I mean the gift of tongues, in a supernatural way, as was bestowed upon the apostles on the day of Pentecost; which there is no reason in the world ever to have expected. Bless God, therefore, and be thankful that God has, in his providence, raised up such men to translate the Bible into the mother-tongue of every nation, and particularly into ours; and that he still continues to raise up such who are able to defend the translation made, against erroneous persons, and enemies of the truth; and to correct and amend it in lesser matters, in which it may have failed, and clear and illustrate it by their learned notes upon it. Having premised these things, I now proceed to prove the claim of the Scriptures to a divine authority, which may be evinced from the following things:

First, From the subject-matter of them. —1. In general there is nothing in them unworthy of God; nothing contrary to his truth and faithfulness, to his purity and holiness, to his wisdom and goodness, or to any of the perfections of his nature; there is no falsehood nor contradiction in them; they may with great propriety be called, as they are, *The Scriptures of truth*, and the *Word of truth*, Dan. x. 21. Eph. i. 13. There is nothing impious or impure, absurd or ridiculous in them; as in the Al-koran of Mahomet; which is stuffed with impurities and impieties, as well as with things foolish and absurd: or as in the Pagan treatises of their gods; which abound with tales of their murders, adulteries, and thefts; and the impure rites and ceremonies, and inhuman sacrifices used in the worship of them. But, 2. The things contained in the Scriptures are pure and holy; the holy Spirit dictated them, holy men spoke and wrote them, and they are justly called *holy Scriptures*, Rom. i. 2. and plainly shew they came from the holy God. The doctrines of them are holy; they are doctrines according to godliness, and tend to promote it; they teach and influence men to deny ungodliness and worldly lusts, and to live soberly, righteously, and godly: they are indeed, by some ignorant persons, charged with licentiousness; but the charge, as it is false, it is easily removed, by observing the nature of the doctrines, and the effects of them; the precepts the Scriptures enjoin, and the worship they require, are strictly holy; the law-part of them is *holy, just, and good*, Rom. vii. 12. It is holy in its own nature, and requires nothing but what is for the good of men, what is but a reasonable service to God, and what is just between man and man; it forbids whatever is evil, strikes at all sorts of sins, and sets them in a just light, exposes and condemns them. And hence it is that there is in natural men, whose carnal minds are enmity to God, such a backwardness, yea, an aversion to reading the Scriptures; because the doctrines and precepts of them are so pure and holy; they choose to read an idle romance, an impure novel, or any profane writings and histories, rather than the Bible; and from whence may be drawn no inconsiderable argument in favour of their being of God. The style of the Scriptures is pure and holy, chaste and clean, free from all levity and obscenity, and from every thing that might be offensive to the ear of the chaste and pious. And there are remarkable instances in the marginal readings of some passages in the Hebrew text, to prevent this; and care should be taken in all translations, to make use of language neat and clean; and keep up as much as may be, to the original purity of the Scriptures.—3. There are some things recorded in the Scriptures, which could never have been known but by revelation from God himself; as particularly, with respect to the creation of the world, and the original of mankind; that the world was made out of nothing; when made, how, and in what form and order, and how long it was in making; who were the first parents of mankind, when, how, and of what made; hence, without this revelation men have run into strange, absurd, and extravagant notions about these things. Yea, the Scriptures inform us what was done in eternity, which none but God himself could reveal, and make known to men; as the choice of men in Christ to everlasting salvation, which was from the beginning; not of their being, nor of their conversion, nor of time; but before time, or they or the earth were, even "before the foundation of the world," Eph. i. 4. And also the council held between the divine Persons, concerning the salvation of man; for as there was a consultation held about making him, so about saving him; which may be called the *council of peace*, Zech. vi. 13. When "God was in Christ reconciling the world unto himself," and the scheme of peace and reconciliation, and plan of salvation were formed and agreed upon: so the covenant of grace made with Christ from eternity, on the behalf of the chosen ones; whose "goings forth in it were of old, from everlasting; covenanting with his Father for them, and agreeing to be their Surety and Saviour; to become incarnate, and obey and suffer for them, and so work out the salvation of them; representing their persons and taking the charge and care of them, and of all blessings of grace given them, and of all promises made to them, in him, before the world began; in which covenant he was set up as Mediator, "from everlasting, or ever the earth was," Prov. viii. 22, 23. Mic. v. 2. 2 Tim. i. 9. Eph i. 3, 4. All which could never have been known unless God himself had revealed them.—4. There are some things recorded in the Scriptures as future, which God only could foreknow would be, and foretel with certainty that they should be; and which have accordingly come to pass, and proves the revelation to be of God. Some of them relate to particular persons, and contingent events; as Josiah, who was prophesied of by name, as to be born to the house of David, three or four hundred years before his birth, and what he should do; "offer up the idolatrous priests on Jeroboam's altar, and burn men's bones on it;" all which exactly came to pass, see 1 Kings xiii. 2. compared with 2 Kings xxiii. 17, 20. Cyrus, king of Persia, also was prophesied of by name, more than two hundred years before his birth, and what he should do; what conquests he should make, what immense riches he should possess; and that he should let the captive Jews go free, without price or reward, and give orders for the rebuilding their temple; all which was punctually fulfilled, Isa. xliv. 28. and xlv. 1, 2, 3, 13. see Ezra i. 1, 2, 3, 4. Others relate to kingdoms and states, and what should befal them; as the Egyptians, Moabites, Ammonites, Edomites, Assyrians, Babylonians, and others; of whose destruction Isaiah and Jeremiah prophesied, and who now are no more, have not so much as a name on earth: and particularly many things are foretold concerning the Jews; as their descent into Egypt, abode and bondage there, and coming from thence with great riches; which was made known to their great ancestor Abraham, before they were, Gen. xv. 14. see Exod. xii. 35, 40, 41. their captivity in Babylon, and return from thence after seventy years, Jer. xxix. 10, 11. see Dan. ix. 2. and all their miseries and afflictions in their last destruction, and present state, are prophetically described in Deut. xxviii. and their exact case, for about seventeen hundred years, is expressed in a few words; as well as their future conversion is prophesied of, Hos. iii. 4, 5. But especially the prophecies concerning Christ, are worthy of notice; his incarnation, and birth of a virgin; the place where he should be born; of what nation, tribe, and family; his sufferings and death, his burial, resurrection, ascension to heaven, and session at the right hand of God: all which are plainly pointed out in prophecy; and which, with many other things relating to him, have had their exact accomplishment in him. To which might be added, predictions of the calling of the Gentiles, by many of the prophets; and the abolition of paganism in the Roman empire; the rise, power, and ruin of antichrist; which are particularly spoken of in the book of the Revelation; great part of which prophetic book has been already fulfilled.—5. There are some things in the Scriptures, which, though not contrary to reason, yet are above the capacity of men ever to have made a discovery of; as the Trinity of persons in the Godhead; whose distinct mode of subsisting is mysterious to us; the eternal generation of the Son of God, which is ineffable by us; his incarnation and birth of a virgin, under the power of the Holy Ghost, which is wonderful and amazing; the union of the human nature to his divine person; which is, "without controversy, the great mystery of godliness:" the regeneration of men by the Spirit of God, and the manner of his operation on the souls of men; which, on hearing of, made a master of Israel say, "How can these things be?" and the resurrection of the same body at the last day, reckoned by the Gentiles incredible; and which things though revealed, are not to be accounted for upon the principles of nature and reason.—6. The things contained in the Scriptures, whether doctrines or facts, are harmonious; the doctrines, though delivered at sundry times, and in divers manners, are all of a piece; no yea and nay, no discord and disagreement among them; the two Testaments "are like two young roes that are twins;" to which some think they are compared in Cant. iv. 5. and vii. 3. and to the Cherubim over the mercy-seat, which were of one beaten piece, were exactly alike, and looked to one another, and both to the mercy-seat: a type of Christ, who is the foundation of the apostles and prophets, in which they unite, and both agree to lay; the apostle Paul said none other things than what Moses and the prophets did say should be. And as to historical facts, what seeming contradictions may be observed in any of them, are easily reconciled, with a little care, diligence, and study: and some of these arise from the carelessness of transcribers putting one word or letter for another; and even these instances are but few, and not very material; and which never affect any article of faith or practice: such care has divine providence taken of these peculiar and important writings, which with the harmony of them shew them to be of God.

Secondly, The style and manner in which the Scriptures are written, is a further evidence of their divine original; the majesty in which they appear, the authoritative manner in which they are delivered; not asking, but demanding, attention and assent unto them; and which commands reverence and acceptance of them; the figures used to engage hereunto are inimitable by creatures; and such as would be daring and presumptuous for any but God to use, with whom is terrible majesty; such as, *Hear, O heavens*, and *I will speak*, Deut. xxxii. 1. Isa. i. 2. the sublimity of the style is such as exceeds all other writings: Longinus, an heathen orator, who wrote *upon the Sublime*, admired some passages in the writings of Moses, particularly Gen. i. 3. That early composition, the book of Job, abounds with such strong and lofty expressions as are not to be found in human writings, especially the speeches Jehovah himself delivered out of the whirlwind, chap. xxxviii. xxxix. xl. and xli. the book of Psalms is full of bright figures and inimitable language, particularly see Psalm xviii. 7—15. and xxix. 3—10. and cxiii. 3—8. and cxxxix. 7—12. The prophecies of Isaiah are fraught with a rich treasure of divine elocution, which surpasses all that is to be met with in the writings of men; and it is remarkable, that in some of the inspired writers, who have been bred up in a rustic manner, are found some of the most grand images, and lively picturesques, and highest flights of language, as in Amos the herdman, chap. iv. 13. and ix. 2, 6.

Thirdly, Another argument for the divine authority of the Scriptures may be taken from the penmen and writers of them.— 1. Many of these were men of no education, in a low station of life, and were taken from the flock, or from the herd, or from their nets, or other mean employments; and what they wrote, both as to matter and manner, were above and beyond their ordinary capacities, and therefore must be of God; what they wrote could not be of themselves; but they "spake and wrote as they were moved by the Holy Ghost."— 2. They lived in different times and places, and were of different interests and capacities, and in different conditions and circumstances; and yet they were all of the same sentiment, they speak and write the same things, deliver out the same truths and doctrines, and enjoin the same moral duties of religion, and the same positive precepts, according to the different dispensations under which they were; and this shews that they were dictated, and influenced in all, by the same Spirit of God.—3. They were holy and good men, partakers of the grace of God; and therefore could never give into an imposture, nor deliver out a known lie, nor obtrude a falsehood upon the world.—4. They appear to be plain, honest, and faithful men; they conceal not their own failings and infirmities; so Moses published his own weaknesses and inadvertencies, and spared not the blemishes of his family; not of his more remote ancestor Levi, in the case of the Shechemites; nor of his immediate parents, their illegal marriage; nor of his favourite people the Israelites, their rebellion and obstinacy and idolatry: and the same may be observed of other inspired writers.—5. They were disinterested men; they sought not popular applause, nor worldly wealth, nor to aggrandize themselves and their families. Moses, when it was offered to him, by the Lord, to make of him a great nation, and cut off the people of Israel for their sins, refused it more than once; preferring the public good of that people to his own advantage; and though he was king in Jeshurun, he was not careful to have any of his posterity to succeed him in his office; and though the priesthood was conferred on Aaron his brother, and his sons, yet no other provision was made for his own family, than to attend the lower services of the tabernacle in common with the rest of his tribe: and of this disposition were the apostles of Christ, who left all, and followed him; and sought not the wealth of men, nor honour from them; but on the contrary, exposed themselves to reproach, poverty, vexation, and trouble; yea, to persecution, and death itself; which they would never have done, had they not been fully satisfied of their mission of God, and of their message from him; and therefore could not be deterred from speaking and writing in his name, by the terrors and menaces of men, and by all the afflictions, bonds, and persecution, and death in every shape, which awaited them. In short, the writers of the Scriptures seem to be men that neither could be imposed upon themselves, nor sought to impose on others; nor would it have been easy, had they been bad men, to have succeeded, had they attempted it.

Fourthly, Another argument may be drawn from the many wonderful effects the sacred writings, attended with a divine power and influence, have had upon the hearts and lives of men. Many have been converted from error, superstition, and idolatry, and from a vicious course of life, to embrace and profess the truth, and to live a holy life and conversation, upon reading the Scriptures, or hearing them explained; and even some of great natural parts and learning, who could not easily be prevailed upon to relinquish former tenets, and practices, had they not had full and clear conviction of them. This "Word of God has been quick and powerful, sharper than a two-edged sword;" it has pierced and penetrated into the recesses of the heart, and laid open the secrets of it; it has been the means of enlightening the mind, quickening the soul, regenerating and sanctifying the heart, and of producing faith, and every other grace in it, and of strengthening, comforting, and reviving the spirits of the people of God when in distress, by afflictions, or Satan's temptations; so that every good man has a testimony within himself of its divine authority; see 1 John v. 9, 10.

Fifthly, The testimony borne to the Scriptures by miracles, abundantly confirm the genuineness of them, and that they are of God; such as were done by Moses, and the prophets of the Old Testament, and by the apostles of the New; even such as are above, and contrary to the laws of nature, and are beyond the power of a creature to perform, and which only Omnipotence itself could work: now these God would never do to establish the character of impostors, or to confirm a lie; which yet he has done to witness the truth of divine revelation; see Mark xvi. 20. Heb. ii. 3, 4.

Sixthly, The hatred and opposition of men, and the enmity of devils, to them, afford no inconsiderable argument in favour of the divinity of them; for were they of men, they would not have such a disgust at them, and disapprobation of them, and make such opposition to them: by this are to be known the Spirit of truth, and the spirit of error; what is of the world, and merely human, is approved by the men of the world; but what is of God is rejected, 1 John iv. 5, 6. and if these writings were of Satan, and the work of forgery, imposture, and deceit, that wicked spirit would never have shewn such despite unto them, nor have taken such pains to tempt men, and prevail upon them not to read them; and to persuade others to use their utmost efforts to corrupt or destroy them, and root them out of the world.

Seventhly, The awful judgments of God on such who have despised them, and have endeavoured to destroy them, are no mean evidence that they are of God; who hereby has shewn his resentment of such conduct and behaviour; which might be illustrated by the instances of Antiochus Epiphanes, king of Syria, who cut to pieces the copies of the book of the law wherever he found them, and burnt them, and put to death all with whom they were, 1 Maccab. i. 59, 60. this man died of a violent disorder in his bowels, his body was covered with worms, his flesh flaked off, and was attended with an intolerable stench. 2 Maccab. ix. 5, 9. and of Dioclesian, the Roman emperor, who by an edict ordered all the sacred books to be burnt, that, if possible, he might root Christianity out of the world; and once fancied that he had done it; but when he found he had not accomplished his design, through madness and despair, in the height of his imperial glory, abdicated the empire, and retired to a private life, and at last poisoned himself: the one shewed a despite to the books of the Old Testament, the other more especially to the books of the New Testament; and both were highly resented by the divine Being, who hereby shewed himself the author of both. Many more instances might be produced, but these may suffice.

Eighthly, The antiquity and continuance of these writings may be improved into an argument in favour of them: Tertullian says, "That which is most ancient is most true." Men from the beginning had knowledge of God, and of the way of salvation, and in what manner God was to be worshipped; which could not be without a revelation; though for some time it was not delivered in writing. The antediluvian patriarchs had it, and so the postdiluvian ones, to the times of Moses; whose writings are the first, and are more ancient than any profane writings, by many hundreds of years; the most early of that sort extant, are the poems of Homer and Hesiod, who flourished about the times of Isaiah; and the divine writings have been preserved notwithstanding the malice of men and devils, some of them some thousands of years, when other writings are lost and perished.

To which may be added, that the Scriptures receive no small evidence of the authority of them, from the testimonies of many heathen writers agreeing with them, with respect to the chronology, geography, and history of them; as concerning the creation of the world, Noah's flood, the tower of Babel, the confusion of languages, the peopling the earth by the sons of Noah, the burning of Sodom and Gomorrah; with many other things respecting the people of Israel, their origin, laws, &c.[1] I go on to consider,

II. The *Perfection* of the Scriptures. When we assert the perfection of them, we do not mean that they contain a perfect account of all that God has done from the beginning of time, in the dispensations of his providence in the world, and in the distributions of his grace to the sons of men; though they relate much of the state and condition of the church of God in all ages, and as it will be to the end of time. Nor that they contain all the discourses, exhortations, admonitions, cautions, and counsels of the prophets, delivered to the people of Israel, in the several ages of time: nor all the sermons of the apostles, which they preached to the Jews, and among the Gentiles; nor are all that were said and done by our Lord Jesus Christ recorded in them; there were many signs done by him which are not written, which if they should be written, as the evangelist observes, *even the world itself could not contain the books that should be written,* John xx. 30. and xxi. 25. But then they relate all things necessary to salvation, every thing that ought to be believed and done; and are a complete, perfect standard of faith and practice: which may be proved,

First, From the Author of them, who is God; they are the word of God, and are "given by inspiration of God;" as is asserted in them, and has been clearly shown. Now since God is the author of them, who is a perfect Being, in whom is *no darkness at all;* not of ignorance, error, and imperfection; they coming from him, must be free from every thing of that kind; *he is a rock,* and *his work is perfect;* as his works of creation, providence, and redemption; so this work of the Scriptures.

Secondly, from the name they go by, a *Testament:* we commonly divide the Scriptures into the Books of the Old Testament, and the Books of the New Testament; and that there was a First and a Second Testament, an Old and a New one, is plainly intimated, Heb. ix. 15. Now a man's testament, or will, contains the whole of his will and pleasure, concerning the disposition of his estate to whomsoever he pleases, or it is not properly his will and testament; a man's testament, *if it be confirmed,* as the apostle observes, *no man disannulleth or addeth thereto,* Gal. iii. 15. Such the Scriptures are; they contain the whole will of God, about the disposition of the blessings of grace, and of the heavenly inheritance, to those who are appointed by him heirs; and being ratified and confirmed by the blood of Christ, are so sure and firm as not to be disannulled, and so perfect that nothing can be added thereunto.

Thirdly, From the epithet of *perfect* being expressly given unto them; *the law of the Lord is perfect,* Psalm xix. 7. which is to be understood, not of the Decalogue, or Ten Commands, but of the doctrine of the Lord, as the phrase signifies; even what was delivered in the sacred writings extant in the times of David; and if it was perfect then as to the substance of it, then much more must it appear so by the accession of the prophets, and the books of the New Testament since, in which there are plainer and clearer discoveries of the mind and will of God.

Fourthly, From the essential parts of them, the Law and Gospel; to which two heads the substance of them may be reduced: the Law is a perfect rule of duty; it contains what is the *good, acceptable,* and *perfect will of God,* Rom. xii. 2. What he would have done, or not done; the whole duty of man, both towards God and man; all is comprehended in these two commands, *Thou shalt love the Lord thy God with all thy heart,* &c. *and thou shalt love thy neighbour as thyself,* Matt. xxii. 37—40. The Gospel is the *perfect law,* or doctrine *of liberty,* the apostle James speaks of, chap. i. 25. which proclaims the glorious liberty of the children of God by Christ; and it is *perfect,* it treats of perfect things; of perfect justification by Christ; of full pardon of sin through his blood, and complete salvation in him; and contains a perfect plan of truth; every truth, "as it is in Jesus;" all

---

[1] See Gale's Court of the Gentiles.

the treasures of wisdom and knowledge: it is the whole, *or all the counsel of God*, concerning the spiritual and eternal salvation of men, Acts xx. 27.

Fifthly, From the integral parts of them; the Scriptures, containing all the books that were written by divine inspiration. The books of the Old Testament were complete and perfect in the times of Christ; not one was wanting, nor any mutilated and corrupted. The Jews, he says, have *Moses and the prophets;* and he himself, *beginning at Moses and all the prophets, expounded in all the scriptures, the things concerning himself,* Luke xvi. 24. and xxiv. 27. So that they had not only the five books of Moses, but *all* the prophets, and *all* the scriptures of the Old Testament: nay, he affirms, that *till heaven and earth pass, one jot, or one tittle, shall in no wise pass from the law till all be fulfilled,* Matt. v. 18. The Jews had *the oracles of God committed* to their care, Rom. iii. 2. and they have been faithful keepers of them, even some of them to superstition and scrupulous nicety, numbering not only the books and sections, but also the verses, and even the words and letters: and there never was nor now is, any reason to be given why they had corrupted, or would corrupt, any part of the Old Testament; on the coming of Christ it was not their interest to do it; and even before that it was translated into the Greek tongue, by which they would have been detected; and after the coming of Christ they could not do it if they would, copies of it being in the hands of christians; who were able to correct what they should corrupt, had they done it: and whatever attempts may have been made by any under the Christian name, to corrupt some copies of either Testament, they may be, and have been detected; or whatever mistakes may be made, through the carelessness of transcribers of copies, they are to be corrected by other copies, which God in his providence, has preserved; and, as it seems, for such purposes: so that we have a perfect canon, or rule of faith and practice. It is objected to the perfection of the books of the Old Testament, that the books of Nathan, Gad, and Iddo, the prophets mentioned therein, are lost; but then it should be proved that these were inspired writings, and, indeed that they are lost; they may be the same, as some think, with the books of Samuel, Kings, and Chronicles. And it is also objected to those of the New Testament, that there was an epistle from Laodicea, Col. iv. 16. and another to the Corinthians, distinct from those we have, 1 Cor. v. 9. neither of them now extant: as to the first, that is not an epistle *to* Laodicea, but *from* it; and may refer to one of the epistles, we have, written by the apostle Paul, when at that place: and as to that to the Corinthians, it does not appear to be another and distinct, but the same he was then writing: but admitting, for argument sake, though it is not to be granted, that some book or part of the inspired writings is lost; let it be proved, if it can, that any essential article of faith is lost with it; or that there is any such article of faith wanting in the books we have: if this cannot be proved, then, notwithstanding the pretended defect, we have still a perfect rule of faith; which is what is contended for.

Sixthly, This may be further evinced from the charge that is given, "not to add unto, nor diminish from, any part of the sacred writings, law or gospel:" this is strictly enjoined the Israelites to observe, with respect to the law, and the commandments of it, given them by Moses, Deut. iv. 2. and xii. 32. And with respect to the Gospel, the apostle Paul says, *Though we, or an angel from heaven, preach any other gospel unto you, than that which we have preached unto you—and ye have received, let him be accursed,* Gal. i. 8, 9. And the wise man, or Agur, says of the Scriptures in his time, *Every word of God is pure— add thou not unto his words.* And the apostle and evangelist John, closes the canon of the Scripture with these remarkable words, *If any man shall add unto these things, God shall add unto him the plagues that are written in this book; and if any man shall take away from the words of the book of this prophecy, God shall take away his part out of the book of life,* &c. Rev. xxii. 18, 19. Now if there is nothing superfluous in the Scriptures, to be taken from them; and nothing defective in them, which requires any addition to them; then they must be perfect.

Seventhly, This may be argued from the sufficiency of them to answer the ends and purposes for which they are written; as, *for doctrine, for reproof, for correction, and for instruction in righteousness,* (2 Tim. iii. 16.) they are sufficiently profitable and useful *for doctrine;* there is no spiritual truth, nor evangelical doctrine, but what they contain; they are called the *Scriptures of truth;* not only because they come from the God of truth, and whatsoever is in them is truth;

but they contain *all truth;* which the Spirit of God, the dictator of them, guides into, and that by means of them; (see Dan. x. 21. John xvi. 13.) every doctrine is to be confirmed and established by them: our Lord proved the things concerning himself, his person, office, sufferings, and death, by them, Luke xxiv. 25, 26, 27. the apostle Paul *reasoned out of the Scriptures,* in confirmation and defence of the doctrines he taught; *opening and alledging,* that is, from the Scriptures, *that Christ must needs have suffered and risen again from the dead; and that this Jesus is Christ,* whom he preached; and, indeed, he said *none other things than what Moses and the prophets did say* should be, and which he was able to prove from thence, Acts xvii. 2, 3. and xxvi. 22, 23. Every doctrine proposed by men, to the assent of others, is not immediately to be credited; but to be tried and proved, and judged of by the holy Scriptures, which are to be searched, as they were by the Beræans, to see whether those things be so or no; and being found agreeable to them, they are to be believed, and held fast; for *to the law and to the testimony; if men speak not according to this word, it is because there is no light in them.* Isa. viii. 20. See 1 John iv. 1. 1 Thess. v. 21. Acts xvii. 11. and these are serviceable *for reproof,* for the detection, confutation, and conviction of error: thus Christ confuted the error of the Sadducees by the Scriptures, Matt. xxii. 29, 30. and the apostles, with these, warred a good warfare; these were their spiritual weapons, the word of God is the sword of the Spirit, they used in fighting the good fight of faith, against false teachers; by sound doctrine, fetched from thence, they were able to convince and stop the mouths of gainsayers: there never was an error, or heresy, broached in the world yet, but what has been confuted by the Scriptures; and it is not possible that any one can arise in opposition to "the faith once delivered," but what may receive its refutation from thence. They are also of use *for correction,* of every sin, internal or external; of heart, lip, and life, secret or open; sins of omission or commission; all are forbidden, reproved, and condemned by the law of God; which says, *Thou shalt not covet,* nor do this, and that, and the other iniquity, Rom. vii. 7. and xiii. 9. And the Gospel agrees with the law herein; and what is contrary to the law, is to sound doctrine; the Gospel of the grace of God, teaches to "deny ungodliness and worldly lusts," 1 Tim. i. 9, 10, 11. Tit. ii. 11, 12. There is not a sin that can be named, but what the Scriptures inveigh against, forbid, and correct. And another end answered by them is, that they are *for instruction in righteousness,* in every moral duty of religion, and in every positive precept of God, according to the different dispensations; they instruct in every thing of a moral or positive nature, and direct to observe all that is commanded of God and Christ; and now writings by which all such ends are answered, must needs be perfect and complete.

The Scriptures are sufficient to *make a man of God perfect,* and *thoroughly furnish him unto all good works,* 2 Tim. iii. 17. Not a private good man only, but one in a public character and office; a prophet, a preacher, and minister of the word; in which sense the phrase is used both in the Old and New Testament, 1 Sam. ix. 6, 7. 1 Tim. vi. 11. An acquaintance with these fits him for the work of the ministry, and furnishes him with sound doctrine, to deliver out to the edification of others; by means of these he becomes "a scribe well instructed in the kingdom of God; and to be able to bring out of his treasure things new and old:" and if they are able to make such a man perfect, they must be perfect themselves.

Another use of the Scriptures, and an end to be, and which is, answered by them, is not only the learning and instruction of private men, as well as those of a public character; but to make them patient under afflictions, and comfort them in them, and give hope of deliverance out of them, as well as of eternal salvation hereafter; for the apostle says, *Whatsoever things were written aforetime, were written for our learning; that we, through patience and comfort of the Scriptures, might have hope,* Rom. xv. 4. Nor is there any afflictive circumstance a good man can come into, but there is a promise in the word of God suitable to him in it; and which may be a means of enlivening, cheering, and comforting him, Psalm cxix. 49, 50. yea, the scriptures are written to promote and increase the spiritual joy of God's people, and that that joy might be full, and therefore must be full and perfect themselves, 1 John, i. 3, 4.

Eightly, The Scriptures are able to make a man *wise unto salvation,* 2 Tim. iii. 15. One part of them being the gospel of salvation; which points out to men the way of salvation; gives an account of Christ, the author of it, and of the salvation itself wrought out by him; and describes the persons that have an interest in it, and shall enjoy it; and who, through the grace of God, are made wise enough to see their need of it, seek after it, and embrace it; for it is not barely by reading the word they become so wise; but through the Spirit of wisdom and revelation opening their eyes to see what is contained in it, and applying it to them; whereby the gospel becomes " the power of God unto salvation" to them. In short the Scriptures contain all things in them necessary to be believed unto salvation; and, indeed, they are written for this end, that men *might believe that Jesus is the Christ, the Son of God; and that believing*, they *might have life through his name*, John xx. 31. and hereby, under a divine influence and blessing, they come to have the knowledge of God and Christ, and of God in Christ; which is the beginning, earnest, and pledge of eternal life, John xvii. 3. I proceed,

III. To prove the *perspicuity* of the Scriptures; for since they are a rule of faith and practice, they should be clear and plain, as they are: not that they are all equally clear and plain; some parts of them, and some things in them, are dark and obscure; but then by comparing spiritual things with spiritual, or those more dark passages with those that are clearer, they may be plainly understood. Moreover, the light of the Scriptures has been a growing one; it was but dim under the dispensation of the law of Moses; it became more clear through the writings of the prophets; but most clear under the gospel dispensation; where, " as in a glass, we behold with open face, the glory of the Lord;" and of divine things: though in the gospel dispensation, and in such clear writings and epistles as those of the apostle Paul, who used *great plainness of speech*, there are some things *hard to be understood*, see 2 Cor. iii. 12—18. 2 Pet. iii. 16. And this is so ordered on purpose to remove all contempt and loathing of the Scriptures, and to humble the arrogance and pride of men, to engage reverence of them, and to excite attention to them, and to put men on searching them with close study, application, and prayer. Nor is every doctrine of the Scriptures expressed in so many words; as the doctrine of the Trinity of persons in the Godhead; the eternal generation of the Son of God, his incarnation and satisfaction, &c. but then the things themselves signified by them are clear and plain; and there are terms and phrases answerable to them; or they are to be deduced from thence by just and necessary consequences. Nor are the Scriptures clear and plain to every one that reads them; they are a sealed book, which neither learned nor unlearned men can understand and interpret without the Spirit of God, the dictator of them; the natural man, by the mere light of nature, and dint of reason, though he may understand the grammatical sense of words; yet he does not understand the meaning of them, at least in a spiritual way, with application to himself; and so far as he has any notion of them, he has a disgust and contempt of them, for the most part; yet they are so fully expressed and clearly revealed, that if the gospel is hid to any, it is to those that perish, who are left to the native darkness of their minds, and to be " blinded by the god of this world," that the glorious light of the gospel might not shine into them, see Isa. xxix. 11, 12. 1 Cor. ii. 14. 2 Cor. iv. 3, 4. But then the Scriptures are plain to them that have a spiritual understanding; who are spiritual men, and judge all things; "to whom it is given to know the mysteries of the kingdom." What are more clear and plain than the precepts of the law, commanding one thing to be done, and forbidding the doing of another? in what plain language are they expressed, *Thou shalt have no other gods before me*, &c. *Thou shalt not kill*, &c. And how clearly is asserted the great and fundamental doctrine of the gospel, "That salvation is alone by Jesus Christ, through the free grace of God; and not of the works of men?" and so every thing necessary of belief unto salvation. In short, as Gregory says,[2] they are like a full and deep river, in which the lamb may walk, and the elephant swim, in different places.

The perspicuity of the Scriptures may be argued, 1. From the author of them, God, as has been proved, who is *the Father of lights;* and therefore what comes from him must be light and clear, in whom is *no darkness at all*.—2. From the several parts of them, and what they are compared unto. The law, or legal part of them, is represented by things which are light, and give it; *The commandment is a lamp, and the law is light,* Prov. vi. 23. The commandments of the law, as before observed, are

---

[2] Præfat. in Job.

clearly expressed; and are a plain direction to men what to do, or shun; the same David says of the word of the Lord in general, and more explicitly, *Thy word is a lamp unto my feet, and a light unto my path*, Psalm cxix. 105. directing how to walk and act. The evangelical part of the Scriptures, or the gospel, is compared to a *glass*, in which may be clearly beheld, *the glory of the Lord;* of his person, offices, grace, and righteousness; and every one of the glorious truths and doctrines of it, 2 Cor. iii. 18. Hence the ministers of the word are called *the light of the world;* because by opening and explaining the Scriptures, they are instruments of enlightening men into the will of God, and the mysteries of his grace, Matt. v. 14.—3. From other testimonies of Scripture, particularly from Deut. xxx. 11—14. *For this commandment, which I command thee this day, is not hidden from thee; neither is it far off—it is not in heaven—neither is it beyond the sea—but the word is very nigh unto thee; in thy mouth, and in thy heart, that thou mayest do it.* And if it is not hidden, nor at a distance and inaccessible, then it must be open, and the knowledge of it to be come at; and this is to be understood, not only of the law of Moses, but more especially of the gospel, the word of faith, preached by the apostles, as the apostle Paul interprets it, Rom. x. 6, 7, 8. And the whole of Scripture is the *sure word of prophecy; whereunto* men *do well* to *take heed, as unto a light that shineth in a dark place:* and so the means of dispelling the darkness of ignorance, error, and unbelief; and of giving light all around, both with respect to doctrine and duty, see 2 Pet. i. 19.— 4. From exhortations to all sorts of people to read them, and who are commended for so doing. Not only the kings of Israel were to read the law of the Lord, but all that people in general; and there was a certain time of the year for them to assemble together to hear it read, men, women, children, and strangers; but if it was not plain and clear, and easy to be understood, it would have been to no purpose for them to attend it. Deut. xvii. 19. and xxxi. 11, 12, 13. Our Lord advises to "search the Scriptures;" which supposes them legible and intelligible, John v. 39. and the Beræans are commended as more noble than those of Thessalonica; because they searched the Scriptures daily, and compared what they heard with them; that they might know whether they were right or no, Acts. xvii. 11.

see Rev. i. 3.—5. From all sorts of persons being capable of reading them, and hearing them read, so as to understand them. Thus in the times of Nehemiah and Ezra, persons of every sex and age, who were at years of maturity, and had the exercise of their rational faculties, had the law read unto them, Neh. viii. 3. and Timothy, from a child knew the holy Scriptures, 2 Tim. iii. 15. believers, and regenerate persons of every rank and degree, have knowledge of them, whether fathers, young men, or little children, 1 John ii. 12, 13, 14. Nor is the public preaching of the word, and the necessity of it, to be objected to all this; since that is, as for conversion, so for greater edification and comfort, and for establishment in the truth, even though it is known; and besides, serves to lead into a larger knowledge of it, and is the ordinary means of guiding into it, and of arriving to a more perfect acquaintance with it, 1 Cor. xiv. 3. 2 Pet. i. 12. Acts viii. 30, 31. Eph. iv. 11, 12, 13. So that it may be concluded, upon the whole, that the Scriptures are

A sure, certain, and infallible rule to go by, with respect to things both to be believed and done: a rule they are, Gal. vi. 16. And since they are of divine authority, and are perfect and plain, they are a sure rule, and to be depended on; *The testimony of the Lord is sure*, Psalm xix. 7. and a *more sure word of prophecy* than all others whatever, 2 Peter i. 19. these are the witness of God, and therefore greater than man's; and to be believed before any human testimony, 1 John v. 9. yea, must be reckoned infallible, since they are the Scriptures of truth, and not only contain what is truth, and nothing but truth in them: but have a true, even a divine testimony bore unto them, and come from the God of truth, who cannot lie, Dan. x. 21. Tit. i. 2. They are the judge of all religious controversies, to which all are to be brought, and by them determined; according to these, spiritual men, who have their senses exercised, to discern between good and evil, try and judge all things. The Scripture is the best interpreter of Scripture, or the Spirit of God therein; nor are the church or its pastors, nor councils and popes, the infallible interpreters thereof; there is a private interpretation of Scripture, which every Christian may make, according to his ability and light; and there is a public one, by the preacher of the word; but both are subject to, and to be determined by the

Scripture itself, which is the only certain and infallible rule of faith and practice. And,

IV. There seems to be a real *necessity* of such a rule in the present state of things; and, indeed, a divine revelation was necessary to Adam, in a state of innocence; how, otherwise, should he have known any thing of the manner of his creation; of the state and condition in which he was created, after the image and in the likeness of God; the extent of his power and authority over the creation; by what means his animal life was to be supported; in what manner God was to be served and worshipped by him, especially the parts of positive and instituted worship, both as to matter, time, and place; and particularly the will of God, as to abstinence from eating of the fruit of the tree of knowledge of good and evil? And if our first parents stood in need of a divine revelation, as a rule and guide to them in their state of integrity; then much more we in our present state of ignorance and depravity. And after the fall, it was owing to divine revelation, that man had any knowledge of the way of his salvation, by the woman's seed; and of the appointment, nature, import, use, and end of sacrifices; and though this revelation was for a time unwritten, and was handed down by tradition to the patriarchs before the flood, and for some time after, whilst the lives of men were of a long continuance, and it required but few hands to transmit it from one to another; but when men's lives were shortened, and it was the pleasure of God to make further and clearer discoveries of his mind and will, and to frame new laws and rules of worship, in different dispensations; it seemed proper and necessary to commit them to writing, both that they might remain, and that they might be referred to in case of any doubt or difficulty about them; and particularly that the ends before mentioned might be answered by them, which it was intended should be; namely, the learning and instruction of men in matters of faith and practice, their peace, comfort, and edification, Rom. xv. 4. 2 Tim iii. 15, 16, 17. and the rather, since nothing else was, and nothing less than the Scriptures are, a sufficient rule and guide in matters of religion; even not the light of nature and reason, so much talked of, and so highly exalted; and since it has been set up as such against divine revelation, it may be proper to show the insufficiency of it. Now the light of nature or reason, is not to be taken in an abstract sense, or considered only in theory, what it has been, may be, or should be, but not subsisting in men or books; as such it can be no rule or guide at all to have recourse unto; and besides, reason in such sense is not opposed to revelation; there is nothing in revelation contrary to reason, though there are things above it, and of which it is not a competent judge, and therefore can be no guide in such matters; but it must be considered as it is in fact, and as it subsists, either in single individuals, or in whole bodies of men, and these unacquainted with, and unassisted by divine revelation; and then its sufficiency, or rather insufficiency, will soon appear. If it is considered as in individuals, it may easily be observed it is not alike in all, but differs, according to the circumstances of men, climate, constitution, education, &c. some have a greater share of it than others; and what is agreeable to the reason of one man, is not so to another; and therefore unless it was alike and equal in all, it can be no sure rule or guide to go by; let one of the most exalted genius, be pitched upon, one of the wisest and sagest philosophers of the Gentiles, that has studied nature most, and arrived to the highest pitch of reason and good sense; for instance, let Socrates be the man, who is sometimes magnified as *divine*, and in whom the light of nature and reason may be thought to be sublimated and raised to its highest pitch, in the Gentile world, without the help of revelation; and yet, as it was in him, it must be a very deficient rule of faith and practice; for though he asserted the unity of the divine Being, and is said to die a martyr for it; yet he was not clear of the heathenish notions of inferior deities, and of worship to be given them; for one of the last things spoken by him was, to desire his friends to fulfil a vow of his, to offer a cock to Esculapius, the god of health; and he is most grievously belied, if he was not guilty of the love of boys in an unnatural way; and besides, he himself bewails the weakness and darkness of human nature, and confessed the want of a guide. If the light of nature and reason be considered in large bodies of men, in whole nations, it will appear not to be the same in all. Some under the guidance of it have worshipped one sort of deities, and some others; have gone into different modes of worship, and devised different rites and ceremonies, and followed different customs and usages, and even differed in things of a moral nature: and as their forefathers, guided by this light, introduced and established the said things;

they, with all their observations, reflections, and reasonings on them, or increase of light, supposing they had any, were never able, by the light of nature and reason in them, to prevail over, and demolish such idolatry, and such profane and wicked practices that obtained among them; and the insufficiency thereof, as a rule and guide in religion, will further appear by considering the following particulars.

1. That there is a God may be known by the light of nature; but *who* and *what* he is, men, destitute of a divine revelation, have been at a loss about. Multitudes have gone into polytheism, and have embraced for gods almost every thing in and under the heavens; not only the sun, moon, and stars, and mortal men, they have deified; but various sorts of beasts, fishes, fowl, creeping things, and even forms of such that never existed: and some that have received the notion of a supreme Being, yet have also acknowledged a numerous train of inferior deities, and have worshipped the creature besides the Creator; whose folly is represented in a true and full light by the apostle, Rom. i. 19—25. and though the unity of the divine Being, is the voice of reason as well as of revelation; yet by the former, without the latter, we could have had no certain notion, if any at all, of three divine persons subsisting in the unity of the divine essence; and especially of the several parts they have taken in the economy of man's salvation; for as for what Plato and others have been supposed to say concerning a Trinity, it is very lame and imperfect, and what was borrowed from eastern tradition.

2. Though the light of nature may teach men that God, their Creator and Benefactor, is to be worshipped by them; and may direct them to some parts of worship, as to pray unto him for what they want, and praise him for what they have received; yet a perfect plan of worship, acceptable to God, could never have been formed according to that; and especially that part of it could not have been known which depends upon the arbitrary will of God, consists of positive precepts and institutions; hence the Gentiles, left to that, and without a divine revelation, have introduced modes of worship the most absurd and ridiculous, as well as cruel and bloody, even human sacrifices, and the slaughter of their own children, as well as the most shocking scenes of debauchery and uncleanness.

3. By the light of nature men may know that they are not in the same condition and circumstances they originally were; for when they consider things, they cannot imagine that they were made by a holy Being subject to such irregular passions and unruly lusts which now prevail in them; but in what state they were made, and how they fell from that estate, and came into the present depraved one, they know not; and still less how to get out of it, and to be cured of their irregularities: but divine revelation informs us how man was made upright, and like unto God: and by what means he fell from his uprightness into the sinful state he is in; and how he may be recovered from it, and brought out of it by the regenerating and sanctifying grace of the Spirit of God, and not otherwise.

4. Though, as the apostle says, the Gentiles without the law, *do by nature the things contained in the law;* and are *a law to themselves, which show the work of the law written on their hearts; their consciences also bearing witness, and their thoughts the meanwhile accusing, or else excusing one another,* Rom. ii. 14, 15. and so have some notion of the difference between moral good and evil; yet this is not so clear and extensive, but that some of the greatest moralists among them gave into the most notorious vices, and allowed of them, and recommended them; Chrysippus[3] allowed of incest; Plato[4] commended community of wives, Socrates a plurality of wives, and which he enforced by his own example;[5] Cicero[6] pleaded for fornication; the Stoics, a grave set of moralists, for the use of obscene words,[7] and recommended self-murder as becoming a wise man,[8] and as his duty to commit in some cases. So dim was this light of nature in things of a moral kind!

5. Though in many cases reason taught them that certain vices were disagreeable to God, and resented by him, and he was displeased with them, and would punish for them; and they were very desirous of appeasing him; but then how to reconcile him to them, and recommend themselves to his favour, they were quite ignorant; and therefore took the most shocking and detestable methods for it, as human sacrifices, and particularly burning their innocent

---

[3] Laertius in Vita ejus.
[4] Vid. Grotium in Eph. 5, 6.
[5] Laertius in Vita ejus.
[6] Orat. 34. pro Cœlio.

[7] Vid. Ciceron. Ep. 1. 9. ep. 22.
[8] Vid. Lips. Manuduct. Stoic. Philosoph. Dissert. 22. p. 365.

infants. But revelation shows us the more excellent way.

6. Men may, by the light of nature, have some notion of sin as an offence to God, and of their need of forgiveness from him; and from a general notion of his mercy and of some instances of kindness to them, may entertain some faint hope of the pardon of it; but then they cannot be certain of it from thence, or that even God will pardon sin at all, the sins of any man; and still less how this can be done consistent with his holiness and justice: but through divine revelation we come at a clear and certain knowledge of this doctrine, and of its consistence with the divine perfections.

7. The light of nature leaves men entirely without the knowledge of the way of salvation by the Son of God. And even without revelation, angels of themselves would not be able to know the way of saving sinful men, or how sinful men can be justified before God; wherefore, in order to know this, they "desire to look into it," 1 Pet. i. 12. Some have thought that Socrates had some notion of it; who is made to say,[9] " It is necessary to wait till some one teaches how to behave towards God and men:" but then this respects only a man's outward conduct, and not his salvation : nor does the philosopher seem to have any clear notion of the instructor, and of the means he should use to instruct, and still less of the certainty of his coming; and besides, the relator of this, Plato, might receive this as a tradition in the East, whither it is well known he travelled for knowledge. But the divine revelation gives an account of this glorious person, not merely as an instructor of men in the way of their duty, but as a Saviour of them from their sins; and in what way he has wrought out salvation, by his sacrifice, blood, and righteousness.

8. The light of nature is far from giving any clear and certain account of the immortality of the soul, the resurrection of the body, and a future state of happiness and misery : as for the immortality of the soul, the heathens rather wished it to be true than were fully satisfied of it; they that were for it made use of but mean arguments to prove it; and they themselves believed it only *fide dimidiata*, as Minutius Felix[10] expresses it, with a divided faith; they did, as it were, but half believe it; and as for the resurrection of the body, that was denied, as Tertullian says,[11] by every sect of the philosophers : and in what a low manner do they represent the happiness of the future state; by walking in pleasant fields, by sitting under fragrant bowers, and cooling shades, and by shelter from inclement weather; by viewing flowing fountains and purling streams; by carnal mirth, feasting, music, and dancing : and the misery of it, by being bound neck and heels together, or in chains, or fastened to rocks, and whipped by furies, with a scourge of serpents, or doomed to some laborious service. But not the least hint is given of the presence of God with the one, nor of his absence from the other; nor of any sensation of his love or wrath. Let us therefore bless God that we have a better rule and guide to go by; " a more sure word of prophecy to take heed unto :" let us have constant recourse unto it, as the standard of faith and practice ; and try every doctrine and practice by it, and believe and act as that directs us, and fetch every thing from it that may be for our good, and the glory of God.

CHAP. III.

OF THE NAMES OF GOD.

BEING about to treat of God, and of the things of God, it may be proper to begin with his names : the names of persons and things are usually the first that are known of them; and if these are not known, it cannot be thought that much, if any thing, is known of them; and where the name of God is not known, he himself cannot be known; and the rather the consideration of his name, or names, is worthy of regard, because they serve to lead into some knowledge of his nature and perfections; and therefore a proper introduction to such a subject. Indeed, properly speaking, since God is incomprehensible, he is not nominable; and being but one, he has no need of a name to distinguish him; and therefore Plato[1] says he has no name; and hence he commonly calls him το ον, *Ens, The Being*. So when Moses asked the Lord, what he should say to the children of Israel, should they ask the name of him that sent him to them, he bid him say, *I am that I am;* that is, The eternal Being, the Being of

---

[9] Plato in Alcibiad. 2. p. 459.
[10] Octav. p. 37.
[11] De Præscript. Hæret. c. 7. p. 232.

[1] ουδ' αρα ονομα εςιν αυτο, in Parmenide, p. 1120. Ed. Ficin. So Trismegistus apud Lactant. Institut. 1. 1. c. 6.

beings; which his name Jehovah is expressive of: nevertheless, there are names of God in the Scriptures taken from one or other of his attributes, which are worthy of consideration.

The names of God, as Zanchy[2] observes, some of them respect him as the subject, as Jehovah, Lord, God: others are predicates, what are spoken of him, or attributed to him, as holy, just, good, &c. Some respect the relation the divine Persons in the Godhead stand in to each other, as Father, Son, and Spirit: others the relation of God to the creatures; and which are properly said of him, and not them, as Creator, Preserver, Governor, &c. some are common to the Three divine persons, as Jehovah, God, Father, Spirit; and some peculiar to each, as the epithets of unbegotten, begotten, proceeding from the Father and the Son: some are figurative and metaphorical, taken from creatures to whom God is compared; and others are proper names, by which he either calls himself, or is called by the prophets and apostles, in the books of the Old and New Testament; which are what will be particularly considered.

1. *Elohim* is the first name of God we meet with in Scripture, and is translated God, Gen. i. 1. and is most frequently used throughout the whole Old Testament; sometimes, indeed, improperly of creatures, angels and men, and of false deities, Psalm viii. 5. and lxxxii. 1, 6. Jer. x. 11. but properly only of God.

Some derive this word from a root, which signifies to curse and swear; but as to the reasons why this name is given to the divine Being on that account, it is not agreed; some,[3] of late have given this as a reason, because the three divine Persons, as they in a shocking manner express it, bound themselves with an oath, under a curse, to redeem mankind; which, to say no worse of, is indecent and unworthy of the dignity and majesty of God, "who is blessed for evermore;" for to bind himself with an oath, and that under a conditional curse; which is no other than to imprecate a curse upon himself, if his oath and covenant are not fulfilled; is so harsh, if not something worse, as is not to be endured: and though Christ agreed to redeem men, and to be made a curse for them, that they might receive the blessing; yet he was not accursed through any failure of his oath and covenant; but on another account, being the Surety of his people; nor is he ever called Eloah on that account, and still less the other two persons: besides there are other and better reasons to be given for this name of the divine Being, supposing it to be taken from the word signifying as above; as, because he adjures and causes others to swear, and binds them with an oath to himself; in which sense the word is used of men, 1 Sam. xiv. 24. 1 Kings viii. 31. and is the business of judges; by which oath men are bound to God,[4] and not he to them; and so, according to the Jewish writers,[5] the word is expressive of God as a judge; in which they are followed by some learned men:[6] or, because he pronounces a man accursed who breaks his law, and neglects and despises the sacrifice and righteousness of Christ; so Cocceius:[7] or, because he is the object men must swear by, whenever they swear at all; see Deut. vi. 13. Isa. lxv. 16. Though this word Elohim cannot be derived from the word so signifying, because it has the immoveable and immutable ה, as appears from the point *mappick*, in its singular Eloah, and from the construction of it, which that word has not; and besides, that is never used of God when he is said to swear, but always another.

The word Elohim may be better derived from a word in the Arabic language, which signifies to *worship*, as is thought by many learned men;[8] and so is a fit name for God, who is the sole object of religious worship and adoration; not idols of gold, silver, &c. nor living men, nor persons deified after death, nor angels; but the Lord God only, Matt. iv. 10. It is a word of the plural number; and though it has a singular, which is sometimes used, yet it is most frequently in this form; and being joined with a verb singular, as in Gen. i. 1. it is thought[9] to denote a plurality of persons in the unity of the divine essence; and certain it is, that three persons, Father, Son and

---

[2] De Natura Dei, l. 1. c. 4.
[3] Called Hutchinsonians; see Catcott's Sermon, called The Supreme and Inferior Elahim, p. 8.
[4] Marckii Compend. Theolog. c. 4. s. 5. Mastrict. Theolog. 1. 2. c. 4. s. 9. Leigh's Critica Sacra in voce אלה.
[5] T. Bab. Yoma, fol. 87. 1. Sepher Cosri, par. 4. fol. 197. 2. Maimon. Moreh Nevochim. par. 2. c. 6.
[6] Lud. Capellus et alii.
[7] Lexic. col. 35.
[8] Stockii Clavis S. Ling. p. 61. Hottingeri Smegma Oriental. 1. 1. c. 8. p. 123. Schultens in Job i. 1. Noldius, No. 1093, Alting. Dissert. 4. de plural. Elohim, p. 177.
[9] Schindler. Lexic. Pentaglott. col. 78.

Spirit, appeared, and were concerned in the creation of all things, Gen. i. 1, 2, 3. Psalm xxxiii. 6.

2. Another name of God is *El;* and which may be observed in the word Beth-el, which signifies, *The house of God,* Gen. xii. 7, 8. Both the singular and plural, El Elim, the God of gods, are used in Dan. xi. 36. and the word is left untranslated in Matt. xxvii. 46. *Eli, Eli; my God, my God.* It is commonly rendered, by Junius and Tremellius, the strong or mighty God; an epithet that well agrees with the divine Being, Job ix. 4, 19. Psalm lxxxix 8, 13. and is one of the names of the Messiah, Isa. ix. 6. Hillerus[10] takes this to be a part of the word Eloah, the singular of Elohim; which according to him, signifies the first in essence; being the first and the last, the beginning and the end, Isa. xliv. 6. Rev. i. 8. it is expressive of the power of God.

3. The next name of God we meet with is *Elion,* the most high, Gen. xiv. 18, 19, 20, 22. So Christ is called *The son of the Highest,* and the Spirit, *the power of the Highest,* Luke i. 32, 35. and which name God has either from his habitation, the highest heavens; which is his palace, where he keeps his court, and which is his throne: in which high and holy place he, the high and lofty One, dwells, Isa. lvii. 15, and lxvi. 1. or from his superiority, power, and dominion over all creatures, over the highest personages on earth, and the highest angels in heaven, Psalm lxxxiii. 18. and xcvii. 9. see also Eccles. v. 8. or from the sublimity of his nature and essence, which is out of the reach of finite minds, and is incomprehensible, Job xi. 7, 8. This name was known among the Phœnicians, and is given to one of their deities, called Elioun, the most high;[11] it is expressive of the supremacy of God.

4. Another name of God is *Shaddai:* under this name God appeared to Abraham, Gen. xvii. 1. and to which reference is had, Exod. vi. 3. we translate it Almighty in both places, and in all others, particularly in the book of Job, where it is often mentioned; and it well agrees with him whose power is infinite and uncontrolable, and appears in the works of his hands, creation and providence. Some choose to render it *sufficient,* or *all-sufficient*[12] God; having a sufficiency in and of himself, and for himself, to make himself completely and infinitely happy; nor does he need, nor can he receive any thing from his creatures to add to his happiness; and he has a sufficiency for them; he can, and does, supply all the wants of his people, temporal and spiritual; "his grace is sufficient for them." Others render it *Nourisher;*[13] deriving it from a word which signifies *a breast;* that being what creatures nourish their young with; and is made mention of when this name of God is spoken of, Gen. xlix. 25. God not only fills men's hearts with food and gladness, but "he opens his hand, and satisfies the desire of all creatures, and gives them their meat in due season," Acts xiv. 17. Psalm cxlv. 15, 16. Hillerus [14] derives it from a word which signifies to *pour out,* or *shed;* and it well agrees with God, who pours forth, or sheds his blessings, in great plenty, on his creatures; and which flow from him as from a fountain; to which he is often compared: though others give a very different etymology of it; deriving it from a word [15] which signifies to *destroy;* to which there seems to be a beautiful allusion in Isaiah xiii. 6. "Destruction from Shaddai, the destroyer," who destroyed the whole world, Sodom and Gomorrah, the first-born of the Egyptians, and Pharaoh and his host: though God is so called, previous to most of these instances; indeed he is "the lawgiver, that is able to save and to destroy;" even to destroy body and soul in hell, with an everlasting destruction. And some render the word the *Darter,* or *Thunderer;*[16] whose darts are his thunderbolts, Job vi. 4. Psalm xviii. 13, 14. The heathens called their chief god, Jupiter, *Tonans, The Thunderer:* and, perhaps, from another etymology of this word before given, from שד a breast. Some of their deities are represented as full of breasts; so Ceres, Isis, and Diana. This name seems to be expressive of the all-sufficiency of God, and of the supply of his creatures from it.

5. Another of the names of God is, the Lord, or *God of hosts;* it is first mentioned in 1 Sam. i. 3, 11. but frequently afterwards; and is left untranslated in James v. 4. where the Lord is called, *the Lord of Sabaoth,* not *Sabbath* as it is sometimes

---

[10] Onomastic. Sacr. p. 254, 256.
[11] Sanchoniatho apud Euseb. Evangel. præpar. 1. 1. c. 10. p. 36.
[12] So Cocceius in Lex. col. 859. Jarchi in Gen. xvii. 1. Maimon. Moreh Nevochim par. 1. c. 63.
[13] Paschii Dissert. de Selah, p. 2. s. 6.
[14] Onomast. Sacr. p. 260, 261.
[15] שדד vastavit, Buxtorf.
[16] So Schmidt in Job vi. 4.

wrongly understood; and as if it was the same with *Lord of Sabbath*, Matt. xii. 8. for though the words are somewhat alike in sound, they are very different in sense; for *Sabbath* signifies *rest*, and *Sabaoth* hosts or *armies*: the Lord is the God of armies on earth, a man of war, expert in it; that teacheth men's hands to war, and their fingers to fight, and is the generalissimo of them, as he was particularly of the armies of Israel, as they are called, Exod. vii. 4. which he brought out of Egypt, and went at the head of them, and fought their battles for them; see Exod. xiv. 14. and xv. 3. and who gives success and victory on what side soever he takes: and he is the Lord of the hosts of the starry heavens; the sun, moon, and stars, called the host of heaven, Gen. ii. 1. 2 Kings xxi. 3. and xxiii. 5. and by this military term, because under the Lord they sometimes fight as the stars did against Sisera, Judges v. 20. and also of the airy heavens; and the locusts that fly there are his army, Joel ii. 7, 11. and the meteors, thunder and lightning, snow and hail, which are laid up by him against the day of battle and war, are the artillery he sometimes brings forth against the enemies of his people; as he did against the Egyptians and Canaanites, Job xxxviii 22, 23. Exod. ix. 23, 24, 25. Josh. x. 11. the angels also are the militia of heaven, and are called *the heavenly host*, Luke ii. 13. see 1 Kings xxii. 19. the place where the angels of God met Jacob, was called from thence Mahanaim, Gen. xxxii. 11, 12. two hosts or armies, one going before him and the other behind him; or the one on one side him and the other on the other, to guard him; hence they are said to *encamp* about them that fear the Lord, Psalm xxxiv. 7. These are the creatures of God by whom he is adored and served; they are at his command, and sometimes employed in a military way, to destroy his and his peoples' enemies; see 2 Kings xix. 35. This name is expressive of God's dominion over all his creatures, and the several armies of them.

6. Another name of God is *Adonai*, or *Adon*, Gen. xv. 2. and is commonly rendered Lord. Hence the Spanish word *don* for *lord*. God is so called, because he is the Lord of the whole earth, Zech. iv. 14.

Some [17] derive it from a word which signifies the basis, prop, or support of any thing.[18] So a king in the Greek language is called βασιλευς, because he is the basis and support of his people: and so God is the support of all his creatures; "he upholds all things by the word of his power;" he bears up the pillars of the earth; all men move and have their being in him; and "he upholds his saints with the right-hand of his righteousness;" and even his Son as man and mediator, Isa. xli. 10. and xlii. 1. Some think it has the signification of a judge;[19] "God is the judge of all the earth;" and is a righteous one, protects and defends good men, and takes vengeance on the wicked; and will judge the world in righteousness at the last day. Though perhaps, Hillerus [20] is rightest in rendering it *the Cause*, from which, and for which, all things are; as all things are made by the Lord, and for his will, pleasure, and glory, see Rom. xi, 36. Heb. ii. 10. Rev. iv. 11. Adon is used in the plural number of God, Mal. i. 6. and so Adonai is used of the Son, as well as of the Father, Psalm cxi. 1. and of the holy Spirit, Isa. vi. 8. compared with Acts xxviii. 25. Hence Adonis, with the heathens, the same with the sun, their chief deity, according to Macrobius,[21] by whom Bacchus is called [22] Ebon, or rather Edon; who, he says, is also the same with the sun.

7. The famous name of God is *Jehovah*; this is a name he takes to himself and claims it, Exod. vi. 3. Isa. xlii. 8. and is peculiar to him; his name alone is Jehovah, and incommunicable to another, Psalm lxxxiii. 18. because this name is predicated of God, as a necessary and self-existent being, as a learned Jew [23] observes, which no other is; for though it is sometimes spoken of another, yet not singly and properly, but with relation to him. So the church is called *Jehovah-shammah*, because of his presence with her, Ezek. xlviii. 35. The Jews, from a superstitious abuse of it, assert it to be ineffable, and not to be pronounced, and even not to be read and written, and therefore they substitute other names instead of it, as Adonai, and Elohim. This might arise, originally, from their very great awe and reverence of this name, according to Deut. xxviii. 58. but every

---

[17] Paschius in Dissert. de Selah, ut supra. Alsted. Lexic. Theolog. p. 82.
[18] אדני foundations, bases, Job xxxviii. 6. often rendered sockets in Exodus.
[19] A דן judicavit.

[20] Onomastic. Sacr. p. 258.
[21] Saturnal. 1. 1. c. 21.
[22] Ibid. c. 18.
[23] R. Joseph Albo in Sepher Ikkarim, 1. 2. c. 28.

name of God is reverend, and not to be taken in vain, nor used in common, nor with any degree of levity, Psalm cxi. 9. It is written with four letters only; hence the Jews call it *tetragrammaton*, and is very probably the τετρακτυς of the Pythagoreans, by which they swore; and it is remarkable, that the word for God is so written in almost all languages; denoting, it may be, that he is the God of the whole world; and ought to be served and worshipped, and his name to be great and had in reverence in the four quarters of it; it takes in all tenses, past, present, and to come:[24] the words of the evangelist John are a proper periphrasis of it; *which is, and which was, and which is to come*, Rev. i. 4. or, *shall be*, as in chap. xvi. 5. it comes from the root היה or הוה which signify, *to be*, and is expressive of the essence of God; of his necessary and self-existence, for God naturally and necessarily exists; which cannot be said of any other: creatures owe their being to the arbitrary will of God; and so might be, and might not be, as he pleased; but God exists in and of himself, he is a self-existent and independent Being, as he must needs be, since he is before all creatures, and therefore cannot have his being from them; and he is the cause of theirs, and therefore must be independent of them; and yet, when we say he is self-existent, it must not be understood as if he made himself; for though he exists, he is not made. He is the Being of beings; all creatures have their beings from him and in him, " the heavens, earth, and sea, and all that is in them;" he is the former and maker of all things; he is eminently *the Being*, and all in comparison of him are mere non-entities; *all nations*, and the inhabitants of them, *are as nothing before him; yea, less than nothing, and vanity,* Isa. xl. 17.

8. *Jah* is another name of God, which is mentioned in Psalm lxviii. 4. and cl. 6. Isa. xxvi. 4. though it may be only an abbreviation or contraction of the word Jehovah, and may signify the same; according to Cocceius,[25] it comes from יאת Jer. x. 7. and signifies *decency*, or what is meet and becoming.

9. *Ejeh* is a name God gave as a name of his to Moses, when he sent him to the children of Israel; and is translated *I AM that I AM*, Exod. iii. 13, 14. and may be rendered, *I shall be what I shall be*, and what I have been; so the Jews [26] interpret it; " I am he that was, I am he that is now, and I am he that is to come, or shall be." It seems to be of the same signification with Jehovah, and to be derived from the same word, and is expressive of the same things; of the being and existence of God, of his eternity and immutability, and of his faithfulness in performing his promises: our Lord has a manifest respect unto it, when he says, *Before Abraham was I AM*, John viii. 58. Hillerus [27] renders it *I remain*, that is, always the same.

10. The names of God in the New Testament are these two κυριος, and θεος, the one is usually rendered Lord and the other God. The first is derived either from κυρω, *to be,*[28] and signifies the same as Jehovah, to which it commonly answers, and denotes the essence or being of God; or from κυρος,[29] power and authority; and agrees with God, who has a sovereign power and authority over all creatures, having a property in them, by virtue of his creation of them; it is generally used of Christ, " who is Lord of all," Acts x. 36. 1 Cor. viii. 6. Eph. iv. 4. The etymology of θεος, God, is very different; as either from a word which signifies to *run*, or from one that signifies to *heat*, or from one that signifies to *see;* which seem to be calculated by the heathens for the sun, the object of their worship, applicable to it, for its constant course, being the fountain of light and heat, and seeing all things, as they affirm: though each of them may be applied to the true God, who runs to the assistance of his people in distress, 2 Chron. xvi. 9. Psal. xlvi. 1. is light itself, " the Father of lights, and a consuming fire," 1 John i. 5. Jam.i.17. Heb. xii. 29. and sees all men, their ways and works, and even their hearts, and the thoughts of them, Job xxxiv. 21, 22. 1 Sam. xvi. 7. Some derive it from a word which signifies *to dispose;* and which agrees with God, who disposes of, and orders all things " in the armies of the heavens, and among the inhabitants of the earth, according to the council of his will," and to answer the purposes of his own glory, and the good of his creatures. Though, perhaps, it may be best of all to derive it from a word which signifies *fear*,[30] and so describes God as the object of fear and reverence;

---

[24] Buxtorf. de Nomin. Dei, Heb. s. 10.
[25] Lexic. p. 283.
[26] Shemot Rabba, s. 3. fol. 93. 3.
[27] Onomast. Sacr. p. 248.
[28] κυρει, est, existit, Suidas: κυρω, sum, Scapula.
[29] κυρος, auctritas; κυριος, autoritatem habens, Scapula; so Philo, quis rer. divin. Hæres, p. 484.
[30] απο του θεειν, currere, so Plato in Cratylo, p. 273.

who is not only to be stood in awe of by all the inhabitants of the earth, Psal. xxxiii. 8. but more especially is to be feared with a godly fear by his saints, Psal. lxxxvii. 7. Heb. xii. 28. and fear sometimes takes in the whole worship of God, both internal and external; and so the true God in distinction from others, is called, *the fear*, that is, the God of Isaac, Gen. xxxi. 53. and רחלא *fear*, is sometimes used in the Targum[31] for the true God, as it sometimes is of idols.

From all these names of God we learn that God is the eternal, immutable, and almighty Being, the Being of beings, self-existent, and self-sufficient, and the object of religious worship and adoration.

CHAP. IV.

OF THE NATURE OF GOD.

THERE is a nature that belongs to every creature, which is difficult to understand; and so to God, the Creator, which is most difficult of all: that *Nature* may be predicated of God, is what the apostle suggests when he says, the Galatians, before conversion, served them, who, *by nature, were no gods*, Gal. iv. 8. which implies, that though the idols they had worshipped were not, yet there was one that was, by Nature, God; otherwise there would be an impropriety in denying it of them. Mention is also made of the *divine Nature*, 2 Pet. i. 4. which, indeed, is not the nature that is in God, but what is infused and implanted in men in regeneration; so called, not only because it is from God, as its author, but because it is the image of him, and bears a likeness and resemblance to him; but then there must be a nature in him to which this is similar, being "created, after him, in righteousness and true holiness;" or there would be no propriety in the denomination of it from him. This is what is called Divinity, Deity, or Godhead; which must not be thought to be "like to gold, silver, or stone, graven by art, or man's device;" or to be in the similitude of any creature, in a picture, painting, or sculpture; and which is to be seen and understood by the visible works of creation, and is what, "in all its perfection and fulness, dwells bodily in Christ," Acts xvii. 29. Rom. i. 20. Col. ii. 9. It is the same with the *form of God*, in which Christ is said to be, Phil. ii. 6. which designs not any external form, for God has no visible shape, but his internal Glory, excellency, nature, and perfections, in which "Christ is equal with him, and his fellow;" and he is not only the express image of him, but one with him; not merely of a like, but of the same nature; so that he that sees the one, sees the other. Essence, which is the same thing with nature, is ascribed to God; he is said to be *excellent* תושיה *in essence*, Isa. xxviii. 29. for so the words may be rendered, that is, he has the most excellent essence or being; this is contained in his names, *Jehovah*, and *I am that I am*, which are expressive of his essence or being, as has been observed; and we are required to believe that *he is*, that he has a being or essence, and does exist, Heb. xi. 6. and essence is that by which a person or thing is what it is, that is its nature; and with respect to God, it is the same with his *face*, which cannot be seen, Exod. xxxiii. 20, 23. that is, cannot be perceived, understood, and fully comprehended, especially in the present state; and, indeed, though in the future state saints will behold the face of God, and "see him face to face, and as he is," so far as they are capable of, yet it is impossible for a finite mind, in its most exalted state, to comprehend the infinite Nature and Being of God.

This nature is common to the three Persons in God, but not communicated from one to another; they each of them partake of it, and possess it as one undivided nature; they all enjoy it; it is not a part of it that is enjoyed by one, and a part of it by another, but the whole by each; as "all the fulness of the Godhead dwells in Christ," so in the holy Spirit; and of the Father, there will be no doubt; these equally subsist in the unity of the divine essence, and that without any derivation or communication of it from one to another. I know it is represented by some, who, otherwise, are sound in the doctrine of the Trinity, that the divine nature is communicated from the Father to the Son and Spirit, and that he is *fons Deitatis*, "the fountain of Deity;" which, I think, are unsafe phrases; since they seem to imply a priority in the Father to the other two persons; for he that communicates must,

---

Clem. Al. protrept. p. 15. vel αθειν, adurere, accendere, vel θιασθαι, cernere, vel a θω dispono; so Clem. Al. Stromat. in fine, Herodot. Euterpe, c. 52. vel a διος timor, Philo ut supra. These several etymologies may be seen in Zanchy de Natura Dei, 1. 1. c. 16. Alsted. Lexic. Theolog. p. 8.

[31] Targum Hierosol. in Deut. xxxii. 15.

at least in order of nature, and according to our conception of things, be prior to whom the communication is made; and that he has a superabundant plenitude of Deity in him, previous to this communication. It is better to say, that they are self-existent, and exist together in the same undivided essence; and jointly, equally, and as early one as the other, possess the same nature.

The nature of God is, indeed, incomprehensible by us; somewhat of it may be apprehended, but it cannot be fully comprehended; *Canst thou by searching find out God? Canst thou find out the Almighty unto perfection?* Job xi. 7. No: but then this does not forbid us searching and inquiring after him: though we cannot have adequate ideas of God, yet we should endeavour to get the best we can, and frame the best conceptions of him we are able; that so we may serve and worship him, honour and glorify him, in the best manner. *The world*, the heathen world, even the wisest in it, *by wisdom knew not God*, 1 Cor. i. 21. they knew, or might know, there was a God, but they did not know what he was, and so glorified him not as God. An heathen philosopher[1] being asked this question, what God was? required a day to think of it; when that was up, he asked a second, and still more time; and a reason of his dilatoriness being demanded of him, he replied, that the longer he considered of the question, the more obscure it was to him. Yet, somewhat of God, of his nature and perfections, may be known by the light of nature, Rom. i. 19, 20. and more by divine revelation; for though it may with propriety be said, *what is his name*, or nature, *if thou canst, tell?* Prov. xxx. 4. yet him whom the heathens *ignorantly worshipped*, the apostle Paul *declared* unto them, Acts xvii. 23. and though the Samaritans worshipped they knew not what, yet Christ declared to the woman of Samaria, what God, the object of spiritual worship, is; saying *God is a Spirit;* that is, he is of a spiritual nature, John iv. 22, 24. and this we may be sure is a true definition, description, and declaration of God, and of his nature; since this was given by the Son of God, who lay in his bosom, and perfectly knew his nature, as well as his will; see John i. 18. Matt. xi. 27. and by which we are taught,

1. That God is not a body, and that we are, in our conceptions of him, to remove every thing from him that is corporeal; for spirit, and body or flesh, are opposed to one another, Isa. xxxi. 3. Luke xxiv. 39. and yet there have been some, both ancients and moderns, atheistically inclined, who have asserted, that matter is God, and God is universal matter; and that the whole universe is God, and that extension is one of his attributes: and a sort of people called Anthropomorphites, who bore the christian name, ascribed an human body, and the parts of it, to God, in a proper sense, mistaking some passages of scripture; and the common people, among the papists, have no other notion of God, than of a grave old man: in this respect both Jews and Heathens have better notions; of the Jews, R. Joseph Albo,[2] Maimonides,[3] and others, deny that God is a body, or consists of bodily parts: and of heathens, Pythagoras,[4] Xenophanes,[5] Sallustius,[6] and others,[7] affirm God to be incorporeal; and the Stoics say, he has not an human form.[8] But if God was matter, which is inert, unactive, and motionless, he could not be the maker and mover of all things, as he is; *for in him we live, and move, and have our being,* Acts xvii. 28. Matter is without consciousness, is not capable of thinking, and without understanding, wisdom, and knowledge; and as it is not capable of acting, so much less of doing, such works as require contrivance, skill, wisdom, and knowledge, as the works of creation and providence; and therefore if God was matter, he could not be the Creator and Governor of the world; nor if a body, could he be omnipresent; a body is not every where, cannot be in two places at the same time; whereas God fills heaven and earth: and was he of so huge a body as to take up all space, there would be no room for other bodies, as there certainly is; nor would he be invisible; a body is to be seen and felt; but God is invisible and impalpable; "no man hath seen God at any time;" and if a body, he would not be the most perfect of beings, as he is, since angels, and the souls of men, being spirits, are more excellent than bodies.

---

[1] Simonides apud Cicero. de Natura Deor. 1. 1.
[2] Sepher Ikkarim, 1. 2. c. 6.
[3] Hilchot Yesude Hatorah, c. 1. s. 5, 6.
[4] Apud Lactant. de Ira, c. 11.
[5] Apud Clement. Stromat. 5. p. 601.
[6] De Diis et Mundo, c. 2.
[7] So Aristotle, Laert. 1. 5, in Vita ejus.
[8] Laert. 1. 7. in Vita Zeno.

It is no objection to this, that the parts of an human body are sometimes attributed to God; since these are to be understood of him not in a proper, but in an improper and figurative sense, and denote some act and action, or attribute of his; thus his *face* denotes his sight and presence, in which all things are, Gen. xix. 13. sometimes his favour and good will, and the manifestation of his love and grace, Psal. xxvii. 8. lxxx. 3. and sometimes his wrath and indignation against wicked men, Psal. xxxiv. 16. Rev. vi. 17. His *eyes* signify his omniscience and all-seeing providence; concerned both with good men, to protect and preserve them, and bestow good things on them; and with bad men, to destroy them, Prov. xv. 3. 2 Chron. xvi. 9. Amos ix. 8. His *ears*, his readiness to attend unto, and answer the requests of his people, and deliver them out of their troubles, Psal. xxxiv. 15. Isa. lix. 1. His *nose* and *nostrils*, his acceptance of the persons and sacrifices of men, Gen. viii. 21. or his disgust at them, anger with them, and non-acceptance of them, Deut. xxix. 20. Isa. lxv. 5. Psal. xviii. 8. His *mouth* is expressive of his commands, promises, threatenings, and prophecies delivered out by him, Lam. iii. 29. Isa. i. 20. Jer. xxiii. 16. His *arms* and *hands* signify his power, and the exertion of it, as in making the heavens and the earth, and in other actions of his, Psal. cii. 27. Job xxvi. 13. Psal. lxxxix. 13. and cxviii. 16. Deut. xxxiii. 27.

Nor is it any proof of corporeity in God, that a divine person has sometimes appeared in an human form; so one of the men that came to Abraham, in the plains of Mamre, was no other than the Lord omniscient and omnipotent, as the after discourse with him shews, Gen. xviii. 3. And the man that wrestled with Jacob till break of day, was a divine person, of which Jacob was sensible; and therefore called the place where he wrestled with him, *Peniel*, the face of God, Gen. xxxii. 24, 30. So he that appeared to Manoah, and his wife, Judg. xiii. 6, 10, 18. with other instances that might be mentioned. But then these were appearances of the Son of God in an human form, and were presages of his future incarnation; for as for the Father, no man ever saw his shape, John v. 37. and, it may be, the reason why the parts of an human body are so often ascribed to God, may be on account of Christ's incarnation, to prepare the minds of men for it, to inure them to ideas of it, to raise their expectation of it, and strengthen their faith in it; and the rather since these attributions were more frequent before the coming of Christ in the flesh, and very rarely used afterwards.

Nor will the formation of man in the image, and after the likeness of God, afford a sufficient argument to prove that there is something corporeal in God, seeing man has a soul or spirit, in which this image and likeness chiefly and principally lay; and which was originally created in righteousness and holiness, in wisdom and knowledge: and though he has a body also; yet, inasmuch as a body was prepared in the council and covenant of grace, from eternity, for the Son of God to assume in time; and in the book of God's eternal purposes, *all the members* of it *were written; which in continuance were fashioned, when as yet there was none of them*, Heb. x. 5. Psal. cxxxix. 16. God might, according to the idea of it in his eternal mind, form the body of the first man.

2. The description of God, as a Spirit, teaches us to ascribe to God all the excellencies to be found in spirits in a more eminent manner, and to consider them as transcendent and infinite in him. By spirits, I understand not subtilized bodies, extracted out of various things; nor the wind and air, so called because invisible, and very piercing and penetrating, though bodies, and very ponderous ones; nor the spirits of animals, which are material, die, and go downwards to the earth: but rational spirits, angels, and the souls of men; the former are called spirits, Zech. vi. 5. Heb. i. 13. and so are the latter, Job xxxii. 8. Heb. xii. 23. they are indeed created spirits, Psal. civ. 4. Zech. xii. 1. but God an uncreated one, and is the Creator of these, and therefore said to be, "the Father of spirits," Heb. xii. 9. These are creatures of time, and finite beings; made since the world was, and are not every where: but God is an eternal, infinite, and immense Spirit, from everlasting to everlasting; and whom "the heaven of heavens cannot contain;" yet there are some excellencies in spirits, which may lead more easily to conceive somewhat of God, and of his divine nature.

Spirits are immaterial, have no corporal parts, as flesh, blood, and bones, Luke xxiv. 39. and though eyes, hands, &c. are ascribed to God, yet not of flesh, Job x. 4. but such as express what is suitable to spiritual beings in the most exalted sense. Spirits are incorruptible; for having no matter about them, they are not liable to corruption; they are, indeed, capable of moral corruption, as appears from the angels that sinned, and from the depravity of the souls of men by the fall; but not of natural corruption: but God is not subject to corruption in any sense, and is therefore called the *incorruptible God*, Rom. i. 23. Spirits are immortal; angels die not, Luke xx. 36. the souls of men cannot be killed, Matt. x. 28. not consisting of parts, that are capable of being divided and separated, they cannot be brought to destruction. It is one of the characters of God, that he is *immortal*, yea, *only hath immortality;* and so more transcendently, and in a more eminent manner immortal than angels, and the souls of men; he has it of himself, and underivatively, and is the giver of it to others, 1 Tim. i. 17. and vi. 16. Spirits are invisible; it is a vulgar mistake that they are to be seen; who ever saw the soul of a man? or an angel, in its pure form? whenever they have made themselves visible, it has been by assuming another form, an human one. "God is invisible, and dwells in light, which no man can approach unto; whom no man hath seen, nor can see," 1 Tim. i. 17. and vi. 16. and therefore as no likeness and similitude of a spirit can be formed and taken, so none of God: who can tell of what colour, form and figure, shape and size, the soul of a man is? Nor can any describe the form and figure of an angel: as for the pictures, paintings, and sculptures of them, they are the fruit of mere fancy and imagination, and at most but emblematical: because angels have appeared in an human form, therefore they are painted as young men; and because of their quick dispatch, and swiftness, in doing the errands and messages they have been sent upon, wings are given them; but never was such a creature in real being, or ever seen in the whole world, in any age, as a young man with wings at his shoulders. So no likeness can be formed of God; no similitude was ever seen of him, and to whom can he be likened and compared? Deut. iv. 12. Isa. xl. 18. and xlvi. 5. Some of the Heathens[9] have acknowledged the invisibility of God, as a Spirit; and Aristotle[10] argues the invisibility of God, from the invisibility of the soul of man.

But besides these properties, there are others still more excellent in spirits, by which they approach nearer to God, and bear a greater resemblance to him, and serve to give us clearer ideas of his nature; they are living, active, endowed with understanding, will, and affections; they are lively, have a principle of life; angels are commonly thought to be the living creatures in Ezekiel's vision; however, they are such, and so the souls of men: the body of Adam, when first made, was a lifeless lump of clay; but when God breathed into him the breath of life, "he became a living soul," Gen. ii. 7. God is the living God, has life in and of himself, and gives life to all creatures that have it. Spirits are active, and can operate upon others, as the souls of men on their bodies; God is all act, *actus simplicissimus*, as he is sometimes styled, the most simple act; there is nothing passive in him, as matter, to be wrought upon; he works, and always works; and "all creatures live and move, and have their being in him," John v. 17. Acts xvii. 28. Spirits, angels, and the souls of men, are intelligent beings, have a faculty of understanding things natural and spiritual; the understanding of God is infinite, there is no searching of it; he understands himself, and all created beings, and their natures, Psal. cxlvii. 6. Isa. xl. 28. Spirits have the power of willing, they are voluntary agents; and God wills whatever he does, and does whatever he wills; his will is boundless, uncontrollable, and sovereign, Psal. cxv. 3. Dan. iv. 35. Spirits have the affections of love, mercy, pity, &c. God not only loves his creatures, but "is love itself," 1 John iv. 16. "His mercy is from everlasting to everlasting, on them that fear him;" and he pities them as a father pities his children, Psal. ciii. 13, 17.

3. God being a Spirit, we learn that he is a simple[11] and uncompounded Being, and does not consist of parts, as a body does; his spirituality involves his simplicity: some indeed consider this as an attribute of God; and his spirituality also: and, indeed, every attribute of God, is God himself, is his nature, and are only so many ways of considering it, or are so many displays of it. However, it is certain God is not composed of parts, in any sense; not in a *physical* sense, of essential parts, as matter and form, of which bodies consist: nor of integral

---

[9] Philemon et Orpheus apud Justin. de Monarch. p. 104, 105.
[10] De Mundo, c. 6. so Minutius Felix, in octavio, p. 35, 36.

[11] ἁπλοῦν τε εἶναι, καὶ πάντων ἥκιστα τῆς ἑαυτοῦ ἰδέας ἐκβαίνειν, is simple, and least of all departs from his own idea,—remains always simply in his own form. Plato de Republ. l. 2. p. 606.

parts, as soul and body, of which men consist: nor in a *metaphysical* sense, as of essence and existence, of act and power: nor in a *logical* sense, as of kind and difference, substance and accident; all which would argue imperfection, weakness, and mutability. If God was composed of parts he would not be *eternal*, and absolutely the first Being, since the composing parts would, at least, co-exist with him; besides, the composing parts, in our conception of them, would be prior to the compositum; as the body and soul of man, of which he is composed, are prior to his being a man: and, besides, there must be a composer, who puts the parts together, and therefore must be before what is composed of them: all which is inconsistent with the eternity of God: nor would he be *infinite* and *immense;* for either these parts are finite, or infinite; if finite, they can never compose an infinite Being; and if infinite, there must be more infinites than one, which implies a contradiction: nor would he be *independent;* for what is composed of parts, depends upon those parts, and the union of them, by which it is preserved: nor would he be *immutable,* unalterable, and immortal; since what consists of parts, and depends upon the union of them, is liable to alteration, and to be resolved into those parts again, and so be dissolved and come to destruction. In short, he would not be the most perfect of Beings; for as the more spiritual a being is, the more perfect it is; and so it is, the more simple and uncompounded it is: as even all things in nature are more noble, and more pure, the more free they are from composition and mixture.

Nor is the simplicity of God to be disproved by the Trinity of Persons in the Godhead; for though there are three distinct persons, there is but one nature and essence common to them all, and which is not parted and divided among them, but is jointly and equally possessed by them; nor do these persons really differ from the divine nature and essence, nor from one another, but by their distinct modes of subsisting; so that they only distinguish and modify, but do neither divide nor compose the divine nature: nor is it to be disproved by the decrees of God; the decrees of God are within himself, and, as it is commonly said, whatever is in God, is God, and so are no other than God himself, as to the act of decreeing, though not with respect to the things decreed; and though they are many and various, as to the objects of them, yet not in God, who, by one eternal act, in his infinite mind, has decreed every thing that has been, is, or shall be; and this is what Plato[12] means by ἐν καὶ πολλὰ, *one* and *many* in God; one, as to his essence; many, as to the ideas and decrees in it, which many are one: nor is it to be disproved by the attributes of God; for they are no other than God himself, and neither differ from one another, but with respect to their objects, and effects, and in our manner of conception of them; nor from the nature and essence of God; they are himself, and his nature; he is not only eternal, wise, good, loving, &c. but he is eternity itself, wisdom itself, goodness itself, love itself, &c. and these are not parts of his nature, but displays of the same undivided nature, and are different considerations of it, in which we view it; our minds being so weak as not to be able to conceive of God at once and together, and in the gross, but one thing after another, and the same in different lights, that we may better understand it: these several things, called attributes, which are one in God, are predicated of him, and ascribed to him distinctly, for helps to our finite understandings, and for the relief of our minds; and that we, with more facility and ease, might conceive of the nature of God, and take in more of him, as we can by parcels and piecemeals, than in the whole; and so, as a learned Jew[13] observes, all those attributes are only intellectual notions; by which are conceived the perfections that are in the essence of God, but in reality are nothing but his essence; and which attributes will be next considered.

CHAP. V.

OF THE ATTRIBUTES OF GOD IN GENERAL, AND OF HIS IMMUTABILITY IN PARTICULAR.

The attributes of God are variously distinguished by divines; some distinguish them into *negative* and *positive,* or affirmative: the negative are such as remove from him whatever is imperfect in

---

[12] In Philebo, p. 372, &c. et in Parmenide, p. 1110 &c.

[13] R. Joseph Albo in Sepher Ikkarim, l. 2. c. 8.

creatures; such are infinity, immutability, immortality, &c. which deny him to be finite, mutable, and mortal; and, indeed, it is easier to say what God is not, than what he is: the positive, or affirmative, are such as assert some perfection in God, which is in and of himself; and which in the creatures, in any measure, is from him, as wisdom, goodness, justice, holiness, &c. but the distinction is discarded by others; because in all negative attributes some positive excellency is found. Some distribute them into a *two-fold order*, first and second: attributes, or essential properties of the *first order*, declare the essence of God as in himself, such as his simplicity and perfection, infinity and immutability; and attributes, or essential properties of the *second order*, which though primarily and properly, and naturally, and infinitely, and in a more excellent manner are in God, than in creatures; yet secondarily, and in an analogical sense, are in them, there being some similitude of them in them, of which there is none of the former order in them; these are said to be life and immortality, blessedness and glory. Again, some are said to be *absolute*, and others *relative*: absolute ones are such as eternally agree with the essence of God, without respect to his creatures, and are expressed by his names, Jehovah, Jah, &c. relative ones are such as agree with him in time, with some certain respect to his creatures, and are expressed by his being their Creator, Governor, Preserver, Redeemer, &c. some are called *proper*, as those before mentioned; and others *figurative*, signified by the parts of the human body, and the affections of the mind, as observed in the preceding chapter: but the more commonly received distinction of the attributes of God, is, into the *communicable* and *incommunicable* ones; the incommunicable attributes of God, are such as there is no appearance or shadow of them in creatures; as independence, immutability, immensity, and eternity: communicable ones, are such as are common to God, with men; or, however, of which there is some resemblance in men, as goodness, holiness, justice, and wisdom; yet of these it may be said, that they are incommunicable, as they are in God, in whom they are infinite, and cannot, as such, be communicated to finite creatures: none but God is essentially, originally, underivatively, perfectly, and infinitely good, holy, just, and wise. But as God is defined a *Spirit* in scripture, as has been observed, I shall endeavour to sort the perfections and attributes of God in agreement with that: and with respect to his nature, as an uncreated Spirit, may be referred, besides his spirituality, and simplicity, already considered, his immutability, and infinity, which includes his immensity, or omnipresence, and eternity: and with respect to it as active, and operative, the life of God, and his omnipotence: and with respect to the faculties, as a rational spirit, particularly the understanding, to which may belong, his omniscience, and manifold wisdom; and the will, under which may be considered the acts of that, and the sovereignty of it; and the affections, to which may be reduced, the love, grace, mercy, hatred, anger, patience, and long suffering of God: and lastly, under the notions of qualities and virtues, may be considered, his goodness, holiness, justice, truth, and faithfulness; and, as the complement of the whole, his perfection or all-sufficiency, glory, and blessedness: and in this order I shall consider them. And begin with,

The *Immutability* of God; which arises from, and is closely connected with his spirituality and simplicity, or is what agrees with him, and is necessary to him as a spiritual, simple and uncompounded Being.[1]

Immutability is an attribute which God claims, and challenges as peculiar to himself; *I am the Lord, I change not*, Mal. iii. 6. Mutability belongs to creatures, immutability to God only; creatures change, but he does not: the heavens and the earth, which he has made, are not always the same; but "he is the same for ever:" the visible heavens are often changing; they are sometimes serene and clear, at other times covered with clouds and darkness, and filled with meteors, snow, rain, hail, &c. the face of the earth appears different at the various seasons of the year, and is particularly renewed every spring: it has undergone one great change by a flood, and will undergo another by fire; when that, and *the works that are therein, shall be burnt up; and the heavens*

---

[1] το θειον αμιταϐλητον αναγκαιον ειναι, Aristot. de Cœlo, l. 1. c. 9. παρ θεος αμεταϐλητος, Sallust. de Diis, c. 1. 2.

being on fire, shall be dissolved; and the elements shall melt with fervent heat; and *a new heavens,* and *a new earth,* shall succeed, 2 Pet. iii. 10, 12, 13. to which changeableness in them, the unchangeableness of God is opposed: *All of them shall wax old like a garment, as a vesture shalt thou change them, and they shall be changed; but thou art the same, and thy years shall have no end,* Psal. cii. 25, 26, 27. The sun in the firmament, that great luminary, and fountain of light and heat, in allusion to which, God is called *the Father of lights,* has its parallaxes, or various appearances, at morning, noon, and evening; it has its risings and settings; and never rises and sets at the same point in the heavens one day in the year, but always varies a little; it is sometimes under clouds, and in an eclipse; but *with God is no variableness,* παραλλαγη, or a parallax; the sun, at certain seasons of the year, passes from one tropic, and enters into another, as well as casts shades on the earth; but with God there is *no shadow of turning,* τροπης, of a trope, or tropic; there is no mutation nor turning in him, nor shadow of any, James i. 17. see Job xxiii. 13. the inhabitants of heaven and earth are changeable, even the most excellent of them, angels and men: angels in their original nature and state, were subject to change, as the apostasy of many of them have shewn; who have changed both state and place; they *kept not their first estate, but left their own habitation,* being obliged to the latter, because of the former; for sinning against God, they were hurled out of heaven, and *cast down to hell, and delivered into chains of darkness, to be reserved unto judgment,* Jude ver. 6. 2 Pet. ii. 4. the angels which stood when the rest fell, are now indeed become impeccable, and are firmly settled in their state of integrity; but then this is owing not to their own nature, but to the electing grace of God, in Christ, and to the confirming grace of Christ, their head, who is the *head of all principality and power,* 1 Tim. v. 21. Col. ii. 10. Man, *at his best estate,* his estate of innocence, and integrity, was *altogether vanity:* for though not sinful, yet being mutable, and left to the mutability of his will, which was his vanity, when tempted fell into sin; and though made upright, lost the rectitude of his nature; though made after the image of God, soon came short of that glory; and though he had dominion over the creatures, being in honour, he abode not long, but became like those he had the power over; and though placed in the most delightful and fruitful spot in all the globe, yet, rebelling against his Maker and Benefactor, was driven out from thence by him; and is now a creature subject to innumerable changes in life; diseases of various sorts seize his body, and change his beauty and his strength, and death at last turns him to corruption and dust; he is like the changeable grass of the field; flourishes a while, is then cut down, and withers away; but God and his *word endure for ever* the same, 1 Pet. i. 24, 25. good men are very mutable, both in their inward and outward estate: in spiritual affairs; in the frames of their minds, in the affections of their souls, in the exercise of grace, in their devotion and obedience to God, and worship of him: in temporal affairs; what an instance of mutability was Job, in his estate, in his family, and in his health and friends! well might he say, *changes and war are against me,* Job x. 17. and at length came to his great and last change, death; as all men must, even the best of men: indeed, in the future state, good men will be no more subject to change; their spirits will be made perfect, and sin no more, nor sorrow any more; and their bodies, when raised, will remain immortal, incorruptible, spiritual, powerful, and glorious; but this will be owing, not to themselves, but to the unchangeable grace and power of God: God only is in and of himself immutable; and he is unchangeable in his nature, perfections, and purposes, and in his love and affections to his people, and in his covenant, and the blessings and promises of it; and even in his threatenings.

1. In his nature and essence, being *simple,* and devoid of all composition, as has been proved: the more simple and free from mixture and composition any thing is, the less subject to change. Gold and silver, being the purest and freest of all metals from composition, are not so alterable as others: spirits, being uncompounded, and not consisting of parts, are not so changeable as bodies; and God, being an infinite and uncreated Spirit, and free from composition in every sense, is intirely and perfectly immutable: and since he is *eternal,* there can be no change of time with him; time doth not belong to him, only to a creature, which is the measure of its duration; and began when a creature began to be, and not before; but God is before all creatures; they being made by him, and so

before time; he was the same before the day was as now, and now as he was before; "even the same to-day, yesterday, and for ever:" though he is *the ancient of days*, he does not become older and older; he is no older now than he was millions of ages ago, nor will be millions of ages to come; his eternity is an everlasting and unchangeable *now; He is the same, and his years shall have no end*, Psal. cii. 27. see Heb. xiii. 8. and seeing he is *infinite, immense*, and *omnipresent;* there can be no change of place with him, for he *fills heaven and earth* with his presence; he is every where, and cannot change or move from place to place; when therefore he is said to *come down* on earth, or to *depart* from men, it is not to be understood of local motion, or change of place; but of some uncommon exertion of his power, and demonstration of his presence, or of the withdrawment of some benefit from them: but this will be considered more largely under the attribute of omnipresence, in its proper place. *God is the *most perfect* Being, and therefore can admit of no change in his nature, neither of increase nor decrease, of addition nor diminution; if he changes, it must be either for the better or the worse; if for the better, then he was imperfect before, and so not God: if for the worse, then he becomes imperfect; and the same follows: a like reasoning is used by Plato,[2] and by another ancient philosopher,[3] who asserts that God is good, impassible, and unchangeable; for whatsoever is changed, says he, is either for the better or the worse; if for the worse, it becomes bad; and if for the better, it was bad at first. Or if he changes from an infinitely perfect state, to another equally so, then there must be more infinites than one, which is a contradiction. ²Again, if any change is made in him, it must be either from somewhat within him, or from somewhat without him; if from within, he must consist of parts; there must be *another* and *another* in him; he must consist of act and power; there must be not only something active in him, to work upon him, but a passive power to be wrought upon; which is contrary to his simplicity, already established; for, as a Jew[4] well argues, what necessarily exists of itself, has no other cause by which it can be changed; nor that which changes, and that which is changed, cannot be together; for so there would be in it two, one which changes, and another which is changed, and so would be compound; which is inconsistent with the simplicity of God: if from somewhat without him, then there must be a superior to him, able to move and change him; but he is the most high God; there is none in heaven nor in earth above him; he is "God over all, blessed for ever."

Nor is the immutability of the divine nature to be disproved from the creation of the world, and all things in it; as when it is suggested, God, from a non-agent, became an agent, and acquired a new relation, that of a Creator, from whence mutability is argued: but it should be observed, that God had from all eternity the same creative power, and would have had, if he had never created any thing; and when he put it forth in time, it was according to his unchangeable will in eternity, and produced no change in him; the change was in the creatures made, not in him the Maker; and though a relation results from hence, and which is real in creatures, is only nominal in the Creator, and makes no change in his nature.

Nor is the unchangeableness of the divine nature to be disproved by the incarnation of Christ; for though he, a divine Person, possessed of the divine nature, was *made flesh*, or became man; the divine nature in him was not changed into the human nature, nor the human nature into the divine, nor a third nature made out of them both; was this the case, the divine nature would have been changeable; but so it was not; for as it has been commonly said, "Christ remained what he was, and assumed what he was not;" and what he assumed added nothing to his divine person; he was only *manifest in the flesh;* he neither received any perfection, nor imperfection, from the human nature; though that received dignity and honour by its union to him, and was adorned with the gifts and graces of the Spirit without measure, and is now advanced at the right hand of God. Nor was any change made in the divine nature by the sufferings of Christ; the divine nature is impassible, and is one reason why Christ assumed the human nature, that he might be capable of suffering and dying in the room and stead of his people; and though the Lord of life and

---

[2] De Republica, l. 2. p. 606.
[3] Sallustius de Diis et Mundo, c. 1.

[4] R. Joseph Albo in Sepher Ikkarim, l. 2. c. 5.

glory was crucified, and God purchased the church with his own blood, and the blood of Christ is called the blood of the Son of God; yet he was crucified in the human nature only, and his blood was shed in that, to which the divine person gave virtue and efficacy, through its union to it; but received no change by all this.

2. God is unchangeable in his perfections or attributes; which though they are the same with himself, his nature and essence, as has been observed; yet, considering them separately, they are helps to our better understanding of it, and serve particularly to illustrate the unchangeableness of it: thus, for instance, he is the same in his *power* as ever; though that has been displayed in various instances, in creation, providence, &c. it is not exhausted, nor in the least diminished; his hand is not shortened, his strength is everlasting, his power eternal, invariably the same: his *knowledge* is the same; his *understanding is infinite*, it can be neither increased nor lessened; the knowledge of angels and men increases gradually; but not so the knowledge of God, he knows no more now than he did from all eternity, he knew as much then as he does now; for he knows and sees all things together, and at once, in his vast eternal mind, and not one thing after another, as they appear in time; things past, present, and to come, are all beheld by him in one view; that is, which are so with respect to creatures, for with him there is no such consideration: his *goodness*, grace, and mercy, are immutable; though there has been such a profusion of his goodness to his creatures, and so many good and perfect gifts have been bestowed on them, it is still the same in him, without any abatement; he is abundant in it, and it endures continually the same: and so is his grace, which has been exceedingly abundant; he is as gracious and merciful as ever; "his mercy is from everlasting to everlasting, to them that fear him;" and his *faithfulness* he never suffers to fail; even though men believe not, he abides faithful; and the unbelief of men cannot make the faith or faithfulness of God without effect. And as he is *glorious* in *holiness*, that perfection never receives any tarnish, can never be sullied, but is always illustriously the same; there is no unrighteousness in God, he cannot change from holiness to unholiness, from righteousness to unrighteousness; he is the just one, that neither can nor will do iniquity; and so he is unchangeably good, and unchangeably happy, and immutable in every perfection.

3. God is unchangeable in his purposes and decrees, there is a purpose for every thing, and a time for that purpose; God has determined all that ever was, is, or shall be; all come to pass according to the counsel of his will, and all his decrees are unchangeable; they are like the laws of the Medes and Persians, and more unalterable than they were; they are the mountains of brass Zechariah saw in a vision, from whence proceed the providences of God, and the executioners of them, Zech. vi. 1. called *mountains* because of their immoveableness, and mountains of *brass* to denote their greater firmness and stability: immutability is expressly spoken of the counsel of God, Heb. vi. 17. the purposes of God are always carried into execution, they are never frustrated; it is not in the power of men and devils to disannul them; whatever devices and counter-workings to them may be framed and formed, they are of no avail; "the counsel of the Lord stands for ever." Psal. xxxiii. 11. Prov. xix. 21. and xxi. 30. Isa. xiv. 24, 27. and xlvi. 10. the purposes of God are *within* himself, Eph. i. 9. and what is in himself, is himself, and he can as soon cease to be, as to alter his mind, or change his counsels; and they are *eternal*, Eph. iii. 11. no new thoughts arise in his mind, no new resolutions are formed in his breast, no new decrees are made by him; his counsels are *of old*; and his purposes are called *counsels*, because designs wisely formed by men, are with consultation, and upon mature deliberation: and such are the decrees of God, they are made with the highest wisdom by him, who is wonderful in counsel, and excellent in working, and so are unchangeable: and besides, being *all-knowing*, he sees and declares the end from the beginning, and nothing unforeseen ever can appear to hinder the execution of his intentions and determinations; which is sometimes the case with men: and he is *able* to perform whatever he resolves upon; there is no lack of wisdom, nor of power in him, as often is in men; and he is *faithful* to himself, his purposes and decrees; his *counsels of old are faithfulness and truth;* or are truly and faithfully performed.

Nor is the immutability of the decrees of God to be disproved by his providences, which are many and various, unsearchable and past finding out, and which may seem to differ from, and clash with one another;

for all the changes in providence, whether with respect to the world in general, or with respect to individuals, are according to his unchangeable will. Job was a remarkable instance of changes in providence, and yet he was fully persuaded of the unchangeable will of God in them, and which he strongly expresses; *He is in one mind, and who can turn him? and what his soul desireth, even that he doth; for he performeth the thing that is appointed for me; and many such things are with him*, Job xxiii. 13, 14. Nor is it to be disproved by the different declarations of the will of God, what he would have observed and done, in the different dispensations of law and gospel. God, by Moses, ordered the children of Israel, to observe certain laws, rites, and ceremonies, until the time of reformation, and then there was a disannulling of them; the heavens and earth were shaken, that is, the whole Mosaic economy and dispensation, whereby these were removed and laid aside as useless, and other ordinances were fixed, to remain till Christ's second coming; but then the delivery of the one, and the time of their continuance, and the abolition of them, and the settling of the other gospel-ordinances to remain to the end of the world, were all according to the unchangeable will of God.

Nor is prayer any objection to the immutability of the divine will, which is not to be altered by it; for when the mind of God is not towards a people to do them good, it cannot be turned to them by the most fervent and importunate prayers of those who have the greatest interest in him, Jer. xv. 1. and when he bestows blessings on a praying people, it is not for the sake of their prayers, as if he was inclined and turned by them: but for his own sake, and of his own sovereign will and pleasure. Should it be said, to what purpose then is prayer? it is answered, this is the way and means God has appointed, for the communication of the blessings of his goodness to his people; for though he has purposed, provided, and promised them, yet he will be sought unto, to give them to them, and it is their duty and privilege to ask them of him; and when they are blessed with a spirit of prayer, it forebodes well, and looks as if God intended to bestow the good things asked; and which should be asked always with submission to the will of God, saying, *not my will, but thine be done.*

4. God is unchangeable in his love and affections to his people; "his love to them is from everlasting to everlasting, **without** any variation in his own heart, however different the manifestations of it may be to them; he ever rests in his love, and never alters, nothing can separate from it, he is love itself, and it is as unchangeable as himself, *the same to-day, yesterday, and for ever:* the fall made no difference in it, though the special objects of it fell with Adam, in his transgression, into the depths of sin and misery; this hindered not, but God continued his love, and manifested it in sending his Son to be the propitiation for their sins, and commended it, and gave a full proof and demonstration of it, in the delivery of Christ to death for them, even while they were yet sinners: nor does the sinful state and condition they were brought into, and continue in from their birth to their conversion, make any alteration in his love; but notwithstanding that, for the great love with which he loves them, "he quickens them when dead in trespasses and sins;" he looks upon them in all the impurity of their natural state, and says to them, *live;* and this time, as it is a time of life, it is a time of open love; see Eph. ii. 4, 5. Ezek. xvi. 6, 7, 8. Tit. iii. 3, 4, 5. Nor do the hidings of God's face from them after conversion, prove any change in his love to them; for though he hides his face from them, and forsakes them for a moment, in a little seeming wrath, to shew his resentment at their sins, to bring them to a sense of them, to humble them before him, and to cause them to seek his face and favour; yet with great mercies he gathers them again to himself, in the most tender manner, and with loving-kindness, has mercy on them; and, for the strengthening of their faith in his love, swears he will not be wroth with them; and declares his loving-kindness to be more immoveable than hills and mountains, Isa. liv. 7—10. Afflictions are no evidence of a change of affections to them; though he may thoroughly chastise them, and, as they may think, severely, yet he deals with them but as children; and, like Ephraim, they are his dear sons and daughters, and pleasant children, in whom he takes the utmost complacency and delight; chastenings are rather proofs of sonship, than arguments against it. God's rebukes of them are rebukes in love, and not in wrath and hot displeasure; though he visits their transgressions with a rod and stripes, he does not utterly, nor at all, take away his loving-kindness in Christ from them, Jer. xxxi.

18, 20. Heb. xii. 6, 7, 8. Rev. iii. 19. Psal. lxxxix. 32, 33. Nor is the unchangeableness of the love of God to his people to be disproved by his being said to be angry with them, and then to turn away his anger from them, Isa. xii. 1. for anger is not opposite to love. Jacob was angry with his beloved Rachel, and a father may be angry with his beloved child, and love him not the less. Wrath and hatred are opposed to love, which are never in the heart of God towards his beloved ones: besides, this is said after the manner of men, and according to our apprehension of things; the Lord doing somewhat similar to men when they are angry, who frown and turn away; and when God frowns in his providence, and deserts his people for awhile, they judge he is angry, when it only shews his displacency at their sins, but not at their persons; and then, when he smiles upon them again, and manifests his pardoning grace and mercy, they conclude he has turned himself from the fierceness of his anger, Psalm lxxxv. 2, 3.

5. God is unchangeable in his covenant of grace. This was made with Christ from everlasting, and stands fast with him; it is as immoveable as a rock, and can never be broken; the blessings of it are *sure mercies*, flow from the sovereign grace and mercy of God, and are sure and firm, being according to his unchangeable will, and are what he never repents of, nor revokes; and being once bestowed, are irreversible, and never taken away; such as are blessed with them are always blessed, and it is not in the power of men and devils to reverse them, Rom. xi. 29. and viii. 30. the promises of the covenant, which are gone out of his mouth and lips are unalterable; what has been said of purposes may be said of promises, that they were made before the world were, by God, that cannot lie, who is all-wise, all-knowing, and all-powerful, and faithful to perform them; and besides, "all the promises are yea and amen in Christ." Nay, even God is unchangeable in his threatenings, he watches to bring the evil he has threatened, as well as the good he has promised; and he assuredly performs the one as the other, Dan. ix. 14. see Isa. i. 20. Jer. xxiii. 20.

Nor is the unchangeableness of God in his word, whether in a way of promise or threatening, to be disproved by repentance being ascribed to him, which is to be taken in a limited sense, for in some sense it is absolutely denied of him, Numb. xxiii. 19.

1 Sam. xv. 29. When it is spoken of him, it is to be understood improperly and figuratively, after the manner of men, he doing like what men do, when they repent, that is, undo what they have done; as a potter, when he does not like a vessel he has made, breaks it to pieces: so when it repented God that he had made man on earth, and Saul king, Gen. vi. 6. 1 Sam. xv. 11. he destroyed man from off the earth, whom he had created; and took away the kingdom from Saul and his family, and gave it to another: in doing which he did not change his mind, but his operations and providences, and that according to his unchangeable will.

Nor is the immutability of God, in his promises and threatenings, to be disproved, by observing, that the promised good, and threatened evil, are not always done. For it should be considered, that what is promised or threatened, is either absolutely and unconditionally, or with a condition: now that any thing promised or threatened, absolutely and unconditionally, is not performed, must be denied; but if with a condition, and that condition not performed, the change will appear to be not in God, but in men: and in all such cases where God does not what he said he would do, a condition is either expressed or implied; see Jer. xviii. 8, 9, 10. Thus God promised that he would dwell in Zion, in Jerusalem, in the temple, and there should be his *rest for ever*, Psalm cxxxii. 13, 14. and the people of Israel should dwell in their land, and eat the good of it; but then it was provided they were obedient to God, and abode in his service and worship, and kept his laws and ordinances, Isa. i. 19. but they failing herein, he departed from them, and suffered them to be carried captive: in all which there was a change of his dispensations, but no change of his will. He threatened the Ninevites with the destruction of their city within forty days, that is, unless they repented: they did repent, and were saved from ruin, God repenting of what he had threatened; which, though a change of his outward conduct towards them, he threatened them with, was no change of his will; for both their repentance, and their deliverance, were according to his unchangeable will, Jonah iii. 4, 10. Nor is the case of Hezekiah any objection to the immutability of God; the outward declaration ordered to be made to him, was, that he should *die and not live;* as he must have done quickly, according to the nature of second causes, his disease being mortal; but the secret will of God was, that he should live *fifteen years* longer, as he did; which implies neither contradiction nor change: the outward declaration was made to humble Hezekiah, to set him a praying, and to make use of means: whereby the unchangeable will of God was accomplished.

CHAP. VI.

OF THE INFINITY OF GOD, HIS OMNIPRESENCE AND ETERNITY.

THE next attribute of God to be considered is, his *Infinity;* when we say that God is *infinite,* the meaning is, that he is unbounded and unlimited, unmeasurable or immense, unsearchable and not to be comprehended. This attribute chiefly respects and includes the *omnipresence* and *eternity* of God; these are the two branches of it; he is not bounded by space, and therefore is everywhere; and he is not bounded by time, so he is eternal:[1] and that he is in this sense infinite appears from his spirituality and simplicity, before established; he is not a body, consisting of parts; was he, he would be finite; for body, or matter, is a creature of time, and not eternal; and is limited to a certain place, and so not everywhere; but God is a *Spirit;* though this barely is not sufficient to prove him infinite; because there are finite spirits, as angels, and the souls of men; these are created spirits, and have a beginning, though they will have no end; which is owing not to themselves, but to the power of God, that supports them in their being; who could, if he would, annihilate them; and they are definitively in some place, and so, on all accounts, finite; but God is an uncreated Spirit; was before all time, so not bounded by it; and was before space or place were, and existed without it; and so not to be limited to it, and by it. He is the *first Being*, and from whom all others have their being; *Before him there was no God formed, neither shall there be after him;* yea, he is the *first* and the *last*, Isa. xliii. 10. and xliv. 6. and therefore there is none before him nor above him, to limit and restrain him: he is an *independent* Being; all creatures depend on him, but he depends on none; all things are *of* him, *through*

him, and *to* him, as the first cause and last end of them:[2] all creatures live, and move, and have their being in him; but not he in them: men, angels, good and bad, are checked and limited by him; but not he by them. He is *immutable;* this attribute has been already established; but if he changes place, or is moved from place to place, or is sometimes in one place, and sometimes in another, he would be mutable: and if he rose from non-existence into existence, or there is any end of his days, he would not be unchangeable; but he is the *same,* and his *years shall have no end:* immutability infers both omnipresence and eternity, the two branches of Infinity. We commonly say that sin is infinite, and the truest reason that can be given for it is, because God is the object of it; for as an act, it is finite, being the act of a finite creature; but with respect to the object against whom it is committed, it is infinite, and requires an infinite satisfaction; which none but an infinite person can give, and which Christ is in his divine nature, and so gave to his sufferings and death, in his human nature united to him, an infinite value and virtue, whereby justice had from them an infinite satisfaction.

God is infinite in all his attributes; and which are indeed, himself, his nature; as has been observed, and are separately considered by us, as a relief to our mind, and helps to our better understanding it; and, perhaps, by observing some of these distinctly, we may have a clearer idea of the infinity of God. His *understanding* is infinite, as is expressly said, Psalm cxlvii. 5. it reaches to, and comprehends all things that are, though ever so numerous; to the innumerable company of angels in the highest heavens; to the innumerable stars in the lower ones; to the innumerable inhabitants of the earth, men, and beasts, and fowl; and to the innumerable creatures that swim in the sea; yea, not only to all that are in being, but to all things possible to be made, which God could have made if he would; these he sees and knows in his eternal mind, so that there is *no searching of his understanding,* Isa. xl. 28. there is no end of it, and therefore infinite. The same may be said of his knowledge and wisdom, there is a βαθος, a *depth*, the apostle ascribes, to both; and which is not to

---

[1] το του απαντα απειρον θρονον και την απειριαν περιεχον τελος αιων εςιν, Aristot. de Cœlo, l. 1. c. 9.
[2] απειρον αρα το εν, ει μητε αρχην μητε τελευτην εχει,

Plato in Parmenide, p. 1117. nihil cum habeat extremum, infinitum sit necesse est, Cicero de Divinat. l. 2. c. 50.

be sounded by mortals, Rom. xi. 33. he is *a God of knowledge* or *knowledges*, of all things that are knowable, 1 Sam. ii. 3. he is the only and the all-wise God; and in comparison of him the wisdom of the wisest of creatures, the angels, is but folly, Job iv. 18. The *power* of God is infinite; with him nothing is impossible; his power has never been exerted to the uttermost; he that has made one world, could have made millions; there is no end of his power, and his making of that, proves his *eternal power*, that is, his infinite power; for nothing but infinite power could ever have made a world out of nothing, Rom. i. 20. Heb. xi. 3. His *goodness* is infinite, he is abundant in it, the earth is full of it, all creatures partake of it, and it endures continually; though there has been such a vast profusion of it from the beginning of the world, in all ages, it still abounds: there is no end of it, it is infinite, it is boundless; nor can there be any addition to it; it is infinitely perfect, *my goodness extends not to thee*, Psalm xvi. 2. God is infinite in his *purity, holiness,* and *justice:* there is none holy as he is; or pure and righteous, with him; in comparison of him, the most holy creatures are impure, and cover themselves before him, Job iv. 17, 18. Isa. vi. 2, 3. in short, he is infinitely perfect, and infinitely blessed and happy. We rightly give him titles and epithets of *immense* and *incomprehensible*, which belong to his infinity. He is *immense*, that is, unmeasurable; he measures all things, but is measured by none; who can take his dimensions? they are *as high as heaven, what canst thou do? deeper than hell, what canst thou know?* If the heavens above cannot be measured, and the foundations of the earth beneath cannot be searched out, how should he be measured or searched out to perfection that made all these? Job xi. 7, 8, 9. Jer. xxxi. 37. As there is an height, a depth, a length and breadth in the love of God, immeasurable, Eph. iii. 18. so there is in every attribute of God, and consequently in his nature; his immensity is his magnitude, and of his *greatness* it is said, that it is *unsearchable*, Psal. cxlv. 3. and therefore, upon the whole, must be *incomprehensible*; not only cannot be comprehended and circumscribed by space, or in place, *for the heaven of heavens cannot contain* him; but he is not to be comprehended by finite minds, that cannot conceive of him as he is; his omniscience is *too wonderful* for them, and *the thunder of his power who can understand?* Somewhat of him may be apprehended, but his nature and essence can never be comprehended, no not in a state of perfection; sooner may all the waters of the ocean be put into a nutshell, than that the infinite Being of God should be comprehended by angels or men, who are finite creatures; infinity is an attribute peculiar to God, and, as has been observed, its two chief branches are *omnipresence* and *eternity;* which will be next considered.

I. The *Omnipresence* of God, or his ubiquity, which, as it is included in his infinity, is a branch of it, and strictly connected with it, it must be strongly concluded from it; for if God is infinite, that is, unbounded with respect to space and place, then he must be everywhere; and this is to be proved from his power, which is everywhere: as appears, not only in the creation of all things, as the heaven, and the heaven of heavens, the earth, and the ends of them, and all that is in them; but in his providence, supporting and sustaining them; for not only the creatures have their being in him, and from him, and therefore he must be near them; but "he upholds all things by his power," they consist in him, he provides for them, and preserves them all; and which is the argument the apostle uses to prove that he is not far from them, Acts xvii. 27, 28. The omnipresence of God may be argued from the distributions of his goodness to all; to angels and glorified saints, who partake of his special favours; to all men on earth, to whom he does not leave himself without a witness of his kindness to them, giving them food and raiment, and all things richly to enjoy; he is present among them, and opens his hand and plentifully and liberally communicates to them: as well as from his universal government of the world by his wisdom; for his kingdom rules over all, the kingdom of nature and providence is his, and "he is the Governor among the nations." And as he is everywhere by his power and providence, so he is by his knowledge; all things are naked and open to him, being all before him, and he present with them; though he is in the highest heaven, he can see and judge through the dark clouds, and behold all the inhabitants of the world and their actions: and since these attributes of power, wisdom, and knowledge, are no other than his nature, or than himself, he must be everywhere by his essence;

and which is most clear from the omnipresence of the divine nature in Christ, who, as a divine person, was in heaven, when he, as man, was here on earth, John i. 18. and iii. 13. and, indeed, unless he was omnipresent, he could not be in whatsoever place two or three are gathered together in his name, or be in the midst of the candlesticks, the churches, or with his ministers, to the end of the world, Matt. xviii. 20. and xxviii. 29. for though this is to be understood of his gracious presence, yet unless he was omnipresent, this could not be vouchsafed to all the saints, and all the churches, in all ages, at different places, at the same time ; as when they are worshipping in different parts of the world ; as in Europe, so in America. Now if God, personally considered, or in any one of the divine Persons, is omnipresent, then God, essentially considered, must be so. The presence of God may be observed in a different manner; there is his glorious presence in heaven, where he, in a most eminent manner, displays the glory of his majesty to angels, and the spirits of just men made perfect ; and there is his powerful and providential presence with all his creatures, giving them being, and supporting them in it; and there is his gracious presence with good men, regenerating, sanctifying, comforting, and refreshing them; dwelling in them, carrying on his work of grace in them, to fit them for himself in glory; and all suppose his omnipresence : the heathens acknowledge this attribute; Anaxagoras calls him an infinite mind; and Pythagoras[3] defines him, a mind that is diffused throughout all the parts of the world, and goes through all nature; and Sallustius[4] observes, that he is not contained or comprehended in place. So the Jews say[5] the Shecinah, or divine Majesty, is everywhere; and they call God מקום, place, by an antiphrasis, as Buxtorf[6] observes, because he is illocal, who is not contained in any place, but gives place to all ; and so the Jews themselves say,[7] that he is the place of the world, but not the world his place, for he is without the world, and fills all worlds ; and they further say,[8] he is so called because in every place where the righteous are, he is with them ; or as Aben Ezra,[9] expresses it, because every place is full of his glory; agreeable to which Philo, the Jew,[10] says, αυτος ιαυτω τοπος he is place, full and sufficient to himself.

This attribute is most clearly expressed in several passages of Scripture, as particularly in Psalm cxxxix. 7—10. where the Psalmist asks, *Whither shall I go from thy Spirit ?* which, if it is to be understood of the third Person, the Spirit of the Father, and of the Son ; if there is no going from him, then not from them, since the same nature is in the one as in the other; if there is no going from God, personally considered, or as in any of the divine Persons, then not from him, as essentially considered : or by his Spirit may be meant himself, for " God is a Spirit," John iv. 24. He adds, *Or whither shall I flee from thy presence ?* not his gracious presence, for a good man would never seek to flee from that, nothing being more desirable to him ; nor is there any thing he more earnestly deprecates than to be cast away from it, Psalm iv. 6, 7. and li. 11. but his essential presence, which is everywhere ; it is in the Hebrew text *from thy face;* and face signifies the essence and nature of God, which is invisible and incomprehensible, Exod. xxxiii. 20. then the Psalmist goes on to enumerate all places that could be thought of to flee to, and yet God was there ; *If I ascend to heaven, thou art there :* could he by any means climb up to heaven, there God is in all the glory of his Majesty ; there is his palace, his habitation, and his throne. *If I make my bed in hell, behold thou art there :* whether the place where the wicked are turned, and the apostate angels cast ; there God is sustaining them in their being, pouring in his wrath into their consciences, and continuing the punishment inflicted on them : or whether the grave is meant, which is sometimes the sense of the word used, and is a bed to saints, Job xvii. 13. there God is watching over their dust, preserving it from being lost, in order to raise it up at the last day. *If I take the wings of the morning,* and fly as fast as the morning light, which soon reaches the furthest parts of the earth ; or as the rays of the sun,

---

[3] Ambo apud Lactant. de fals. relig. 1. 1. c. 5.
[4] De Diis, c. 2. Jovis omnia plena. Virgil. Bucolic. eclog. 3.
[5] T. Bab. Bava Bathra, fol. 25. 1.
[6] In rad. מקום.
[7] Vid. Baal Aruch in voce מקום.
[8] Pirke Eliezer, c. 35.
[9] Præfat. ad Comment. in lib. Esther.
[10] Leg. Allegor, 1. 1. p. 48.

which dart from east to west, at its rising, instantly; *and dwell in the uttermost parts of the sea;* in the most remote islands of it, or in the uttermost parts of the western shore; *even there shall thy hand lead me; and thy right-hand shall hold me:* there should he experience the providential goodness and special favour of God to him; who leads, guides, and upholds his people at the ends of the earth, where some of them sometimes are, and where they have his presence, Isa. xlv. 22. and xxiv. 16. see a like enumeration of places in Amos ix. 2, 3.[11] Another passage of Scripture, proving the Omnipresence of God, is in Isa. lxvi. 1. *Thus saith the Lord, the heaven is my throne, and the earth is my footstool.* So immense is he that he sits upon the one, and treads on the other: *Where is the house that ye build unto me?* or where can a house be built for him? what place can be found for him he is not possessed of, and does not dwell in already? Stephen, the proto-martyr, produces this to prove, *that the most High dwelleth not in temples made with hands;* that is, cannot be included in them, and limited to them, since he is everywhere, in heaven and in earth, Acts vii. 47—50. But nowhere is the Omnipresence of God more expressly declared than in Jer. xxiii. 23, 24. *Am I a God at hand, saith the Lord, and not afar off?* yea, he is both; he not only observes persons and things in heaven, which may be thought at hand, and near him; but persons and things on earth, and those at the greatest distance; he is as near to, and as present with the one as the other; and he sees and knows all that is done by them, as if he was at their elbow; and therefore adds, *Can any hide himself in secret places, that I shall not see him, saith the Lord?* As some might foolishly imagine, supposing him to be limited and confined to heaven above, and was not present to see what was done below; especially in the dark and distant places of the earth: *Do not I fill heaven and earth, saith the Lord?* not only with inhabitants, and with all things, the effects of his power and goodness; but with his nature and essence, which exceeds all bounds of place and space. Hence the Jews call God by the name of *Makom,* place; because he fills all places, and is contained in none; is illocal and infinite.

Nor is this to be disproved by other passages of Scripture, which may seem, at first sight, to discountenance or contradict it; not such as speak of men's departing and fleeing from his presence, as Cain and Jonah are said to do, Gen. iv. 16. Jonah i. 3. for Cain only went either from the place where he and the Lord had been conversing; or from the public place of worship, at the East of the garden of Eden, where were the symbol of the divine presence, an altar, where he and his brother had sacrificed. Jonah's fleeing, was withdrawing himself from the service of God, and declining to go on his errand; foolishly imagining, that, by going beyond sea, he should avoid being urged to his duty; but he soon found his mistake, and that God was everywhere, and could meet with him by sea and by land. Likewise, not such that represent God as descending from heaven; as at the building of Babel, at the cry of the sin of Sodom, and on mount Sinai, Gen. xi. 5, 7. and xviii. 21. Exod. xix. 18, 20. for these only denote some more than ordinary manifestations of his presence, or exertion of his power; as at Babel, by confounding the language; at Sodom, by destroying that, and the other cities; at Sinai, by giving the law out of the midst of fire, attended with thunder and lightning. Nor such as speak of the Lord not being with wicked men; particularly what Moses said to the disobedient Israelites, *The Lord is not among you;* and he *will not be with you,* Numb. xiv. 42, 43. which he might very truly say, since the ark of the covenant, the symbol of the divine presence, remained in the camp, and went not with them, ver. 44. nor had they any reason to believe that God, would be so with them, as to prosper and succeed them, when they acted contrary to his express command: nor is God ever in such sense with wicked men, as with good men; namely, by his gracious presence: but this hinders not, but that he is with them by his omnipresence and power, supporting them in their being. Nor such passages which relate the departure of God from men; as from Samson and Saul, Judg. xvi. 20. 1 Sam. xxviii. 15. since this only respects the withdrawment of uncommon bodily strength from the one; and wisdom and prudence, courage and greatness of soul from the

---

[11] Quo fugis Encelade, quascumque accesseris oras—sub Jove semper eris——Virgil.

other; leaving him to the fears, distractions, and confusions of his mind; without any hope of success in war: nor such portions of Scripture which express the desertions and distance of God from his people, and their desires that he would return to them, and not cast them away from his presence, Psalm x. 1. and lxxx. 14. and li. 1. since these only respect his gracious presence, the deprivation of that, and the return of it; the manifestations of his love and favour, and the withdrawment and renewal of them. And whereas it is urged against the omnipresence of God, that he is said to be in heaven, and that to be his habitation, and that men pray unto him as their Father in heaven, Psalm cxv. 3. Isa. lxiii. 15. Matt. v. 9. In what peculiar sense God may be said to be in heaven, has been observed already; nor is he ever said to be in heaven *only*, but in many places to be on earth also, and elsewhere; see Deut. iv. 39. Isa. lxvi. 1. though he is not contained in any place, as not on the earth, so neither can the heaven of heavens contain him, 1 Kings viii. 27. he was before there was any space or place; his nature, and so this attribute of omnipresence, were the same then as now: and should it be asked, Where did he dwell then? I answer, In himself, in his own immensity and eternity; see Isa. lvii. 15. The objection from the pollution of the divine Being, through sordid and filthy places, in which he must be if omnipresent, scarce deserves any regard, since bodies only touch them and are capable of being defiled by them; not spirits, even created ones, as angels, and the souls of men; as the angel in the filthy den of lions where Daniel was, was not; nor the souls of men that are in filthy bodies; much less God a pure, infinite, and uncreated Spirit, who can no more be affected by such means, than the sun is, by its rays striking on a dunghill.

II. The *Eternity* of God belongs to his infinity; for as he is not bounded by space, so neither by time, and therefore eternal. He is often called *the everlasting God*, and the *King eternal*, Gen. xxi. 31. Deut. xxxiii. 27. Isa. xl. 28. Jer. x. 10. Rom. xvi. 28. 1 Tim. i. 17. yea, eternity itself, 1 Sam. xv. 29. and is said to inhabit it, Isa. lvii. 15. These words, *eternal, everlasting*, and *for ever*, are sometimes used in an improper sense, as of things which are of a long duration, but limited, and have both a beginning and an end; as the everlasting possession of the land of Canaan, granted in the everlasting covenant of circumcision, and yet both are now at an end, Gen. xvii. 7, 8. the rites and ceremonies of the law of Moses are said to be ordinances and statutes for ever; and yet they were designed to continue but for a time, and have been long since abolished, Numb. x. 8. and xv. 15. and xviii. 8, 11, 19, 23. the temple built by Solomon is said to be a settled place for God to abide in for ever; yea, he himself says, that he would put his name in it for ever; and it should be his rest for ever; and yet it has been demolished long ago, 1 Kings viii. 13 and ix. 3. Psalm cxxxii. 14. the thrones of David and Solomon are said to be established for ever, and yet, if taken in a literal sense, they are no more; indeed, if understood spiritually, as David's Son and Antitype, his throne will be for ever and ever, 2 Sam. vii. 12, 16. the earth is said to abide, and not be removed for ever, Psalm civ. 5. Eccles. i. 4. yet both that and the heavens shall perish, though not as to substance, yet as to quality, form, figure, and present use. Sometimes this phrase *for ever*, only respects the year of jubilee, Exod. xxi. 6. and, at most, but during life, 1 Sam. i. 21.

Some creatures and things are said to be everlasting, and even eternal, which have a beginning, though they have no end; and this is what the schools call *æviternity*, as distinct from eternity: thus angels, and the souls of men, being creatures of God, have a beginning; though, being immaterial and immortal, shall never die. The happiness of the saints is called eternal glory, "an eternal weight of glory; eternal life; an eternal inheritance; an house eternal in the heavens," 1 Pet. v. 10. Tit. i. 2. 2 Cor. iv. 17. and v. 1. Heb. ix. 15. And the misery of the wicked is signified by suffering the vengeance of eternal fire, by everlasting fire, and everlasting punishment, Jude ver. 7. Matt. xxv. 41, 46. yet these have a beginning, though they will have no end; and so are improperly called eternal.

Eternity, properly so called, is that which is without beginning and end,[12] and is without succession, or does not proceed

---

[12] τα δ' αιδια, αγεννητα και αφθαρτα, Aristot. Ethic. 1. 6. c. 3.

in a succession of moments one after another; and is opposed to time, which has a beginning, goes on in a succession, and has an end: it is the measure of a creature's duration, and began when creatures began to be, and not before, and is proper to them, and not eternity, which only belongs to God. Thales being asked what God was, answered thus, what has neither beginning nor end,[13] which is eternity. A Jewish writer[14] defines it, "in which there is no former nor latter; nor order, nor succession of times; it being without motion." And which Boetius[15] expresses in a few words, "Eternity is the interminable or unbounded and perfect possession of life whole together." And is thus described, *Before the mountains were brought forth, or ever thou hadst formed the earth and the world, from everlasting to everlasting, thou art God*, Psalm xc. 2.

Eternity, in this sense, is peculiar to God; as he only hath immortality, so he only has eternity; which must be understood not of the Father, or first person only, but of the Son and Spirit also; who are, with the Father, the one God; and possess the same undivided nature; of which Eternity is an attribute. So the Son, though as to his human nature, was born in the fulness of time; yet as to his divine nature, *his goings forth* were *from of old, from everlasting*: and as Mediator, in his office-capacity, he was *set up from everlasting, or ever the earth was*, Mic. v. 2. Prov. viii. 23, 24. The Spirit of God was concerned in the creation of the heavens and the earth, and so must be before them; and which is the only idea we have of eternity, that it is before time and creatures were, Gen. i. 1, 2. Job xxvi. 13. Psalm xxxiii. 6. and, according to some, the Spirit is called, *the eternal Spirit*, Heb. ix. 14. Eternity is true of God, essentially considered, and in the sense explained, is to be proved; and that he is without beginning, without end, and without succession.

First, That he is without beginning, or from everlasting: this is put by way of interrogation, Hab. i. 12. not as a matter of doubt, but of certainty, and is strongly affirmed, Psalm xciii. 2. and may be proved.

1. From his nature and being; as from his *necessary self-existence*: the existence of God is not arbitrary, but necessary: if arbitrary, it must be from his own will, or from the will of another; not from his own will, which would suppose him in being already; and then he must be before he existed, and must be, and not be, at the same instant; which are such contradictions as cannot be endured: not from the will of another, for then that other would be both prior and superior to him, and so be God, and not he: it remains, therefore, that he necessarily existed; and if so, then he must be eternal; since there was none before him; nor can any reason be given why he should necessarily exist at such an instant, and not before. His eternity may be argued from a state of *non-existence* he must have been in, if not eternal; and if so, then there was an instant in which he was not; and if there was an instant in which he was not, then there was an instant in which there was no God; and if so, there may be one again in which he may cease to be; for that which once was not, may again not be; and this will bring us into the depth of atheism; unless it could be supposed, which is quite irrational, that there was a God before him, and that there will be one after him; but this is strongly denied by himself; *Before me there was no God formed; neither shall there be after me*, Isa. xliii. 10. The eternity of God may be inferred from his *immutability*, which has been already established: these two go together, and prove each other, Psalm cii. 27. they are both to be observed in the great name of God, Jehovah, which signifies, he is, and was, and is to come, and takes in all time; but he is bounded by none, and is eternally the same; for if he is not eternal, he must have passed from non-existence into being; and what can be a greater change, than to come out of nothing into being? Moreover, God is the most *perfect Being*; which he would not be, if not eternal; for not to be, or to have a beginning, is an imperfection; and it is an humbling consideration to man, a creature of time, that he is but *of yesterday*, Job viii. 9. And if God was not eternal, let his beginning be when it may, in comparison of an eternity past, it would be but as yesterday; which can never be admitted of. Add to this, that God is the *first Cause* of all things, and therefore

---

[13] τι το θειον, το μητε αρχην εχον, μητε τελευτην, Thales in Laert. 1. 1. Vita Thalet.
[14] R. Joseph Albo in Sepher Ikkarim, 1. 2. c. 18.
[15] Consolat. Philosoph. 1. 5. p. 137.

must be eternal: all wise and thoughtful men acknowledge a first Cause; and in their reasoning rise from one cause to another, until they arrive to a first Cause, and there stop, and which they truly call God; for otherwise there would be no subordination of causes: if there was not a first Cause, there would not be a second, nor a third, &c. but all would be first, and all eternal; and if God is the first Cause, then he is without a cause, and therefore must be eternal; hence he is so often called *the first and the last;* a phrase expressive of his eternity, Isa. xli. 4. and xliv. 6. and xlviii. 12. He is the *Creator* of all things, the heavens, earth, and sea, and all that in them are; and therefore must be before all things, as every artificer is before his work made by him; and if before all creatures, then before time, which begins with them, and therefore from eternity, since we can conceive of nothing before time but eternity.

2. The Eternity of God may be proved from his *attributes,* several of which are said to be eternal, or from everlasting: the *power* of God is expressly called his *eternal power;* and is proved to be so by the works of creation, to which it must be prior, Rom. i. 20. The *knowledge* God has of all things is from eternity; though the things known are in time, his knowledge of them is before time; *Known unto God are all his works from the beginning of the world,* απ' αιωνος, from eternity, Acts xv. 18. The *mercy* of God is eternal, it is said to be *from everlasting to everlasting* Psalm ciii. 17. And so the *love* of God, which is no other than himself, for *God is love,* 1 John iv. 16. his love to his Son, "the brightness of his glory, and the express image of his person," was from everlasting; before the earth, the hills, and mountains were formed, then was he by him, "as one brought up with him," his darling and delight, Prov. viii. 30. our Lord himself says, his Father loved him before the foundation of the world, John xvii. 24. and as early did he love his elect in him; for he loved them as he loved him, ver. 23. even with an everlasting love, a love which is both from everlasting and to everlasting, Jer. xxxi. 3.

3. That God is Eternal, may be argued from his purposes, counsels, and decrees; which are said to be *of old,* that is, from everlasting, Isa. xxv. 1. this is true of them in general; for no new purposes and resolutions rise up, or are framed by him in his mind; for then there would be something in him which was not before; which would imply mutability. Besides they are expressly said to be *eternal,* Eph. iii. 11. and if they are eternal, then God, in whom they are, and by whom they are formed, must be eternal also. In particular, the purpose of God, according to election, or his choice of men to everlasting life, is eternal; not only was before men had done any good or evil, Rom. ix. 11. but they were chosen by him *from the beginning,* 2 Thess. ii. 13. not from the beginning of the gospel coming to them, nor of their faith and conversion by it; but from the beginning of time, and before time, even *before the foundation of the world,* as is in so many words expressed, Eph. i. 4. wherefore God, that chose them to salvation, must be eternal. Christ is eminently called the elect of God, being as Man and Mediator, chosen out from among the people, Isa. xlii. 1. Psalm lxxxix. 19. and the appointment of him, to be the Redeemer and Saviour of men, or the preordination of him, to be the Lamb slain for the redemption of his people, was before the foundation of the world, 1 Pet. i. 20. and therefore God, that foreordained him thereunto, must be as early.

4. The Eternity of God may be concluded from the covenant of grace, styled an *everlasting covenant,* 2 Sam. xxiii. 5. not only because it will endure immoveable and unalterable for ever, but because it was from everlasting; for though it is sometimes called a new covenant, yet not because newly made, or only newly manifested; but because it is always new, and never waxes old. Christ, the Mediator of it, and with whom it was made, was set up from everlasting as such; and his goings forth in it, representing his people, and acting for them, were from of old, from everlasting, Prov. viii. 22, 23. Mic. v. 2. and he had a glory with God in it before the world began, John xvii. 5. there were blessings of goodness laid up in it, and with which Christ, the Mediator of it, was prevented; yea, the people of God were blessed with these spiritual blessings in Christ, as "they were chosen in him before the foundation of the world; and had grace given them in him before the world began," Eph. i. 3, 4. 2 Tim. i. 9. Promises also were made as early to Christ, and to them in him, into whose hands they were put, and in whom they are, yea and amen; particularly, eternal life was pro-

mised by God, that cannot lie, before the world was, Tit. i. 2. Now if there was a covenant made by God from everlasting, and Christ was set up by him so early, as the Mediator of it; and there were blessings of grace, and promises of grace, made by him before time was, then he must be from everlasting.

5. It may be proved from the works of God in time: all creatures are the works of his hands; all beings have their being from him; and time beginning with them, he that made them must be before all time, and therefore eternal; this is the argument used to prove the eternity of Christ, the Word, that he was in the beginning, that is, from eternity with God; "because all things were made by him, and that he is the first-born of every creature, and before all things, because all things are created by him, and by him do all things consist," John i. 1, 2, 3. Col. i. 15. 16, 17. and the same proves the eternity of God; for all things are from him, and so have a beginning; but he from whom they are, is from none, has no cause of his being, and therefore must be eternal. So creation is made a proof of his eternal power and Godhead, Rom. i. 20. creation proves his eternity, and his eternity proves his deity. Hence Thales said,[16] "the most ancient of Beings is God."

Secondly, That God is to everlasting, and without end, may be proved from his *spirituality* and *simplicity*, already established; what is mixed and compounded, and consists of parts, may be resolved into them again, and so be dissolved, as bodies may; but spirits, such as angels and the souls of men, being immaterial, are immortal, and continue for ever; and God being a Spirit, an infinite and uncreated one, simple, and uncompounded of parts, must much more be so; and therefore is called, *The incorruptible God*, Rom. i. 23. It may be argued from his *independency*, he is self-existent; the first Cause, and without any cause; he is the only Potentate, "God over all, blessed for ever," and dependant on none; there is none above him, nor superior to him, that can put an end to his being; nor can it be thought, he being in such a state of infinite happiness, would ever put an end to it himself. His eternity is to be proved from his *immutability*; for those, as before observed, infer one another. God is immutable, and therefore without end; for what can be a greater change than for a being not to be? Hence God is opposed to creatures, to mortal men, whose flesh is as grass, the most changeable and perishing of anything, and even to the heaven and the earth, they being such; but he is unchangeably the same; and so there is no end of his years, 1 Pet. ii. 24, 25. Psalm cii. 26, 27. This may be inferred from his *dominion* and government; he is, and sits King for ever; he is an everlasting King, his kingdom is an everlasting kingdom, and his dominion is from generation to generation, and will never end, Jer. x. 10. Psalm x. 16. and xxix. 10. Dan. iv. 3. and therefore he himself must be to everlasting. Moreover he is not only called the living God, Jer. x. 10. but is often said to *live for ever and ever*, Rev. iv. 9, 10. and x. 6. Hence his purposes and decrees are never frustrated, because he ever lives to bring them into execution: men take up resolutions, and form schemes, which, by reason, of death, are never executed; their purposes are broken, and their thoughts perish; but "the counsel of the Lord stands for ever; and the thoughts of his heart to all generations," Psalm xxxiii. 11. and therefore he himself must endure for ever: his promises are all fulfilled; not only because he is able and faithful to perform, but because he continues for ever to make them good; and therefore is said to "keep truth for ever," Psalm cxlvi. 6. His covenant is firm and sure; more immoveable than rocks and mountains; it stands fast, with Christ, for ever, and God commands it for ever; because he ever lives to keep it. His love is to everlasting, as well as from it; he rests in it; nothing can separate from it; and "with everlasting kindness he gathers his people, and has mercy on them;" and therefore must be for ever: his grace, mercy, and goodness, continually endure, and therefore he himself must; and "he will be the portion of his people for ever;" their everlasting ALL in ALL; and they shall reign and dwell with him for evermore. All which proves him to be without end.

Thirdly, The Eternity of God, or his being from everlasting to everlasting, is without succession, or any distinctions of time succeeding one another, as moments, minutes, hours, days, months, and years: the reasons are, because he existed before

---

[16] πρισβυτατον των οντων, θεος, αγεννητον γαρ, apud Laert. ut supra.

such were in being; *Before the day was, I am he,* Isa. xliii. 13. before there was a day, before the first day of the creation, before there were any days, consisting of so many hours, and these of so many minutes; and if his eternity past, may it be so called, was without successive duration, or without succeeding moments, and other distinctions of time, why not his duration through time, and to all eternity, in the same manner? Should it be said, that days and years are ascribed to God; it is true, they are; but it is in accommodation and condescension to our weak minds, which are not capable of conceiving of duration but as successive: and besides, those days and years ascribed to God are expressly said not to be as ours, Job x. 5. He is, indeed, called, *The Ancient of Days,* Dan. vii. 13. not ancient *in* days, or *through* them, as aged persons are said to be *in* years, and well stricken *in* them; not so God: the meaning is, that he is more ancient than days; he was before all days, and his duration is not to be measured by them. And it may be observed, that the differences and distinctions of time are together ascribed to God, and not as succeeding one another; he is *the same yesterday, to-day, and for ever;* these are all at once, and together with him; he is he *which is, and was, and is to come,* Heb. xiii. 8. Rev. i. 4. these meet together in his name, Jehovah;[17] and so in his nature he co-exists, with all the points of time, in time; but is unmoved and unaffected with any, as a rock in the rolling waves of the sea, or a tower in a torrent of gliding water; or as the gnomon or stile of a sundial, which has all the hours of the day surrounding it, and the sun, by it casts a shade upon them, points at and distinguishes them, but the stile stands firm and unmoved, and not affected thereby: hence it is that *one day is with the Lord as a thousand years; and a thousand years as one day,* 2 Pet. iii. 8. But if his duration was successive, or proceeded by succeeding moments, days, and years; one day would be but one day with him, and not a thousand; and a thousand days would answer to a thousand days, and not be as one only. Besides, if his duration was measured by a succession of moments, &c. then he would not be *immense, immutable,* and *perfect,* as he is: not *immense,* or unmeasurable, if to be measured by minutes, hours, days, months, and years; whereas, as he is not to be measured by space, so not by time: nor *immutable;* since he would be one minute what he was not before, even older, which cannot be said of God; for as a Jewish writer[18] well observes, it cannot be said of him, that he is older now than he was in the days of David, or when the world was created; for he is always, both before the world was made, and after it will cease to be; times make no change in him. Nor *perfect;* for if his duration was successive, there would be every moment something past and gone, lost and irrecoverable; and something to come not yet arrived to and obtained; and in other respects he must be imperfect: the *knowledge* of God proves him without successive duration. God knows all things, past, present, and to come, that is, which are so to us; not that they are so to him; these he knows at once, and all together, not one thing after another, as they successively come into being; all things are open and manifest to him at once and together, not only what are past and present, but he calls things that are not yet, as though they were; he sees and knows all in one view, in his all-comprehending mind: and as his knowledge is not successive, so not his duration. Moreover, in successive duration, there is an order of former and latter; there must be a beginning from whence every flux of time, every distinction proceeds; every moment and minute, has a beginning, from whence it is reckoned, so every hour, day, month, and year: but as it is said of Christ, with respect to his divine nature, so it is true of God, essentially considered, that he has *neither beginning of days, nor end of life,* Heb. vii. 3. In short, God is Eternity itself, and inhabits eternity; so he did before time, and without succession; so he does throughout time; and so he will to all eternity. The very heathens[19] themselves had a notion of their supreme God, as eternal: and this is the definition Thales gave of God; for being asked, What is God? answered, What has neither beginning nor end; and therefore calls

---

[17] Plato observes, that to a temporal being we say of it, "it is, and was, and will be;" but to the eternal Being, "τη το εςιν μονον, to him only it is," in Timæo, p. 1051.

[16] Joseph Albo in Sepher Ikkarim, fol. 66. 1.

[19] O pater, O hominum, ivumque æterna potestas Virgil. Æneid, 1. 10. v. 17. Alii Dii aliquando Dii non fuerunt, sed Jupiter ab æterno fuit Deus, Pompon. Sabin. in ibid. δικαιν εξ αιωνος ατερμονος εις ε-ερον αιωνα, Aristot. de Mundo, c. 7.

him, the most Ancient.[20] Sallustius[21] denied that the nature of God was made, because it always was.

CHAP. VII.

OF THE LIFE OF GOD.

HAVING considered the attributes of Simplicity, Immutability, Infinity, Omnipresence, and Eternity, which belong to God, as an uncreated, infinite, and eternal Spirit; and which distinguish him from all other Spirits; I shall now proceed to consider such as belong to him as an active and operative Spirit, as all spirits are, more or less; but he is infinitely so, being *actus, purus, et simplicissimus;* he is all act; and activity supposes life and operations; power, such as God performs, almighty power, or omnipotence; which are the attributes next to be considered; and first his *life.* Some think this is not a single perfection of God, but expressive of all the divine perfections: and, indeed, it is his nature and essence, it is himself; and so is every other attribute his nature, under different considerations, and as variously displayed; wherefore this may be treated of as a distinct attribute; and a very eminent and fundamental one it is; by which God exerts his nature and essence, and displays all his perfections.

And in order to apprehend somewhat of the life of God, for comprehend it we cannot, it may be necessary to consider life in the creatures, what that is; and by rising from the lowest degree of life to an higher, and from that to an higher still, we may form some idea of the life of God, though an inadequate one. Life is a principle in the creature by which it moves itself; what has motion has life, and what has not is without it; as long as a creature has any motion, it is supposed to have life; but when motionless, it is thought to be dead; the phrases, to move, and to have life, are synonymous, and express the same thing; see Gen. vii. 21, 22, 23. but it is not any kind of motion that can lay a claim to life; the sun, moon, and planets move, yet they are inanimate; so a dead carcass may be moved, though it cannot move; it is self-motion only that shews a creature to be alive, that is under a divine agency; for all creatures live and move and have their being in and of God; and hence it is that such who only seem to have self-motion, are, in an improper sense, said to live; as a fountain, flowing with water, is called living, Gen. xxvi. 19. to which the allusion is in Cant. iv. 15. Jer. ii. 13. John iv. 10. and water that is stagnated in pools and lakes, and remains unmoved, is dead. The lowest degree of real life is in vegetables, in herbs, plants, and trees; which are truly said to live, Ezek. xlvii. 7, 9. for though they have not a local motion, yet a motion of growth and increase; they become bigger and larger, and rise up to a greater height, and put forth leaves and fruit; which shews life. In animals there is an higher degree of life; in them there is the breath of life, which is common with the bodies of men, who live the same animal life with them; these are possessed of sensitive powers, of seeing, hearing, tasting, smelling, and feeling; and perform the common functions of life, eating, drinking, walking, &c. But neither of these sorts of life can assist us in our ideas of the life of God; there being nothing in theirs similar to his. There is an higher degree of life still, which is in rational creatures, angels, and the souls of men; by which they are capable not only of operating on bodies, on matter, without them, but of performing acts within themselves, by a self-motion, suitable to their nature as spirits, and rational ones; such as to understand, to will, to choose, and refuse; love, and hate, &c. which may be called the motions of the mind; as the first thoughts of, and inclinations to sin, are called, *motions*, Rom. vii. 5. And now these internal acts of the mind, which are good in angels or men, and shew a rational life in them, most resemble what is in God; who can, in, and of, and by himself, understand all things, will and decree whatever he pleases; and loves and hates what is agreeable or disagreeable to him, &c. But what comes nearest to the life of God, that we can conceive of, is that which is in regenerated persons, who have a principle of spiritual life, grace, and holiness, implanted in them, by the Spirit of God, and are made partakers of the divine nature, have Christ formed in them; "and they live, yet not they, but Christ lives in them;" and, by having such a principle of life wrought in them, they understand

---

[20] Laert. Vita Thalet. l. 1. p. 23, 24. Plutarch, Sept. Sap. Conviv. vol. 2. p. 153.

[21] De Diis, c. 2.

divine and spiritual things; they will that which is spiritually good, and do what is such; the Spirit of God working in them a disposition thereunto, and giving them power to perform; "being in Christ, and created in him unto good works," they perform vital spiritual acts, and live a life, a spiritual holy life, and which is called, *the life of God*, unconverted men are strangers to, Eph. iv. 18. Now this most resembles the life of God, especially as it will be perfect and eternal in a future state, though it comes abundantly short of what is in God; every imperfection in the life of angels and men, carried to its greatest height, must be removed from God; and every thing that is great and excellent must be ascribed to him; and as infinitely transcending what is in finite creatures. God is life essentially, life eternally, and life efficiently.

1. God is life *essentially*, it is his nature and essence, it is himself, it is in and of himself. The natural life of creatures is not in and of themselves; but is in God, and from him: the spiritual and eternal life of the saints is not in and of themselves; but is from God, "hid with Christ in God." But the life of God is in and of himself; *the Father has life in himself,* John v. 26. and so has the Son and Word of God, John i. 1, 4. and likewise the Spirit, called, therefore, *the spirit of life,* Rev. xi. 11. and what is true of all the Persons in the Godhead, they partaking of the same undivided nature and essence, and living the same life, is true of God, essentially considered. And as the life of God is *of himself,* it is independent; there is no cause from whence it is, or on which it depends. The natural and spiritual life of men is of God, depends on him; they live not so much their own life as another's; they have their life from God in every sense, and are supported in it by him; *he is thy life, and the length of thy days,* Deut. xxx. 20. But God lives his own life; which, as it is without a cause, has no dependence on any other. It does not arise from any composition of parts, and the union of them, as the life, even the natural life, of man does, who consists of soul and body; and his life is the result of the union of these, which when dissolved, it ceases; for *the body without,* or separate from, *the spirit,* or soul, *is dead,* James ii. 26. And the spiritual life of saints arises from the union of Christ and his Spirit, as a principle of life unto them; which, could it be dissolved, as it cannot, death would ensue, even death spiritual and eternal: but God is a Spirit, a simple and uncompounded Being; consists not of parts, from the union of which his life arises; and so his life is *infinite, eternal,* and *immutable,* as also *most perfect.* In the life of creatures, even in the highest degree, being finite and dependent, there is always something wanting; but in God there is none; he is *El-Shaddai,* God all-sufficient, blessed and happy in himself for evermore.

The Scriptures frequently speak of God as the *living God* both in the Old and New Testament, Deut. v. 26. Josh. iii. 10. Psal. xlii. 2. and lxxxiv. 2. Matt. xvi. 16. 2 Cor. vi. 16. who has life in himself, and gives life to all that have it; and not the Father only, but the Son of God also, is called the living God, Heb. iii. 12. and the Spirit is called the Spirit of the living God, 2 Cor. iii. 3. each person is the living God, and God, essentially considered, is so; and this title and epithet he has in opposition to, and contradistinction from, them that are not by nature God: the living God is opposed to idols, lifeless and motionless, Jer. x. 10. 5. 15, 16. Acts xiv. 15. 1 Thess. i. 9. he is distinguished by this essential attribute of his from the first objects of idolatrous worship, the sun, moon, and stars, which are inanimate; from heroes, kings, and emperors, deified after their death; which idolatry was very early; and worshipping them is called eating the sacrifices of the dead, Psalm cvi. 28. and from all images of wood, stone, brass, silver, and gold, which are dumb idols, and lifeless ones; see Psalm cxv. 4—7. And God is not only acknowledged to be the living God, and to live for ever and ever, by some of the greatest personages, and proudest monarchs that ever were upon earth, and who even had set up themselves for God, Dan. iv. 34. and vi. 26. but he asserts it of himself, which must be true, and may be depended on; *And lift up my hand, and say, I live for ever,* Deut. xxxii. 40. yea, it is an oath of his affirming the same, and it is the common form of swearing with him, *as I live, saith the Lord;* and which is very frequently used by him, see Numb. xiv. 28. and this is no other than swearing by his life, which is himself; "for when he could swear by no greater, he swore by himself," Heb. vi. 13. and so both men and angels swear by the living God; " by him that lives for ever and ever," Jer. v. 2. and xii. 16. Dan. xii. 7. Rev. x.

5, 6. which distinguishes him from, and prefers him to all other beings: and, indeed he is *most properly* said to live; the life of creatures is no life in comparison of his; especially the life of man: what is it? "it is but a vapour, that appears for a while, and then vanishes away," James iv. 14. But,

2. God is life *eternally*, without beginning, succession, or end; he is without beginning of life or end of days, and without any variableness; "the same to-day, yesterday, and for ever;" he that is the *true God*, is also *eternal life*, 1 John v. 20. It is indeed said of Christ, the Word and Son of God, that he is the *eternal life*, which was with *the Father* from eternity, before *manifested* unto men; and so lives from eternity to eternity; and, as before observed, what is true of God personally, is true of him essentially considered: he lived from eternity, and will live for ever and ever; as several of the above scripture-testimonies assure us; and which may be concluded from the *simplicity* of his nature: what consists of parts may be resolved into those parts again, and so cease to be; but God is a simple and uncompounded Being, as has been established; not consisting of parts, and so not capable of being reduced to them, or being dissolved, and therefore must live for ever: and from his *independency;* he has no cause prior to him, from whom he has received his life, or on whom it depends; there is none above him, superior to him, that can take away his life from him, as he can from his creatures, who are below him, and dependent on him; but he is above all, and dependent on none. Likewise from his *immutability;* there is no change, nor shadow of change, in him; and yet, if his life was not eternal, he must be subject to the greatest of changes, death; but *he is the same, and of his years there is no end,* Psalm cii. 27. The same arguments which prove his *eternity*, must prove also that he lives for ever; he *is the true God, the living God, and an everlasting King,* Jer. x. 10. he is called *immortal, eternal,* 1. Tim. i. 17. the very heathens have such a notion of Deity as immortal; nothing is more common with them than to call their gods, *the immortal ones*. God, says Socrates,[1] is, I think, the very species or idea of life, and if any thing else is immortal, and confessed by all that he cannot perish. Aristotle,[2] has this remarkable observation, "The energy, act, or operation of God, is immortality, this is everlasting life; wherefore there must needs be perpetual motion in God." And he reports,[3] that Alcmæon supposed that the soul was immortal, because it was like to the immortals. But our God, the true God, is he *who only hath immortality*, 1 Tim. vi. 16. that is, who hath it in and of himself, and gives it to others. Angels are immortal, they die not; but then this immortality is not of themselves, but of God, who supports and continues them in their being; for as he made them out of nothing, he could, if he would, annihilate them, and bring them to nothing again: the souls of men are immortal; they cannot be killed, nor do they die with their bodies; but then what has been said of angels may be said of them. The bodies of men, after the resurrection, are immortal; this mortal then puts on immortality, and always is clothed with it, and ever continues; but this is the gift of God, and the effect of his will and power; yea, even the bodies of the wicked are immortal, but not of themselves, it is even against their wills; they choose and seek for death, but cannot have it; their torments are endless, and the smoke of them ascends for ever and ever. God only has immortality in and of himself.

3. God is life *efficiently*, the source and spring, the author and giver of life to others; *With thee is the fountain of life,* Psalm xxxvi. 9. which he would not be, if he had not life in and of himself, essentially, originally, independently, most properly, and in the most perfect manner.

God is the author and giver of life, from the lowest to the highest degree of it. The vegetative life that is in herbs, plants, and trees, is from him, and supported by him; and he takes it away, when his spirit blows upon them, Gen. i. 11, 12. Isa. xl. 7. The animal life is owing to him; the life of all animals, of the fishes in the sea, the fowl of the air, and the beasts of the field; and he gives them life and breath; and when he takes it away, they die, and return to the dust, Gen. i. 20, 21, 24, 25. Acts xvii. 25. Psalm civ. 29. The rational life in angels and men, is from him; angels are made rational living spirits by him, and in him they consist: to men he grants life and favour, and his visitation preserves their spirit, and he is the God of their life, that gives it, and continues it,

---

[1] Apud Platon. in Phœdo, p. 79.
[2] De Cœlo, l. 2. c. 3.
[3] De Anima, l. 1. c. 2.

and takes it away at pleasure, Psalm xlii. 8. No creature can give real life; men may paint to the life, as we say, but they cannot give life: no man can make a living fly; he may as soon make a world.

The spiritual life that is in any of the sons of men, is from God. Men, in a state of unregeneracy, are dead, dead in a moral and spiritual sense: and whilst they are corporally alive, they are dead in trespasses and sins; and because of them dead as to their understanding of, will to, affection for what is morally and spiritually good; and their very living in sin is no other than death; nor can they quicken themselves; nothing can give what it has not; the resurrection of the dead, in a corporal sense, requires almighty power; and, in a spiritual sense, the exceeding greatness of God's power; so that it is not by might or power of man, but by the Spirit and Power of the living God. It is God, that of his rich mercy, and because of his great love, and by his almighty power, quickens men dead in sin, dead in law, and exposed unto eternal death; he speaks life into them, when he calls them by his grace, breathes into the dry bones the breath of life, and they live spiritually; a life of justification, through the righteousness of Christ, which is the justification of life, or adjudges and intitles them to eternal life; and a life of faith on Christ, and of holiness from him: they live in newness of life, soberly, righteously, and godly; which life is preserved in them, it springs up to everlasting life; it is hid and secured with Christ in God, is a never-dying one, and shall issue in eternal life; in which all the three Persons in the Godhead, are concerned, John v. 21, 25. and xi. 25. Rom. viii. 2.

Eternal life, so often spoken of in Scripture, as what the saints shall enjoy for evermore, is of God; it is what he has provided and prepared for them in his council and covenant: what they are fore-ordained unto in his purposes and decrees, and do most certainly enjoy; what he who cannot lie has promised to them before the world began, and which is his free gift, and flows from his free favour and good will, through Christ, Acts xiii. 48. Tit. i. 2. Rom. vi. 23. and in which the Son and Spirit have a concern; Christ came that his people might have it, and he gave his flesh for the life of them; it is put into his hands, and he has a power to dispose of it, and give it to his sheep; so that none of them shall perish, but have it, 1 John v. 12. John xvii. 2. and x. 28. And the Spirit, whose grace springs up to it, and issues in it; and he dwells in his people as the earnest of it, and works them up for it, and brings them into the full enjoyment of it. Now God must have life in the highest degree of it, as explained; even essentially, originally, infinitely, and perfectly; or he could never give life in every sense unto his creatures; and he must live for ever, to continue eternal life, particularly to his people, and preserve them in it.

CHAP. VIII.

OF THE OMNIPOTENCE OF GOD.

SOME of the names of God, in the Hebrew language, are thought to be derived from words which signify firmness and stability, strength and power; as Adonai, El, El-Shaddai, which latter is always rendered almighty, Gen. xvii. 1. Exod. vi. 3. and very frequently in the book of Job; and the Greek word παντοκρατωρ is used of God in the New Testament, and is translated almighty and omnipotent, Rev. 1. 8. and iv. 8. and xix. 6. and power is one of the names of God, Matt. xxvi. 64. compared with Heb. i. 3. the angel said to the Virgin Mary, *with God nothing shall be impossible*, Luke i. 37. and Epicharmus, the heathen, has the same expression;[1] and so Linus:[2] Omnipotence is essential to God, it is his nature; a weak Deity is an absurdity to the human mind: the very heathens suppose their gods to be omnipotent, though without reason; but we have reason sufficient to believe that the Lord our God, who is the true God, is Almighty; his operations abundantly prove it; though if he had never exerted his almighty power, nor declared it by any external visible works, it would have been the same in himself; for it being his nature and essence, was from eternity, before any such works were wrought, and will be when they shall be no more; and hence it is called, his *eternal power*, Rom. i. 20. and may be concluded from his being an uncreated eternal *Spirit*. All spirits are powerful, as their operations shew; we learn some-

---

[1] Apud Clement. Stromat. 1. 5. p. 597.

[2] ραδια παντα θεω τελισχι, και αδυνατον ουδεν, Linus.

what of their power from our own spirits or souls, which are endowed with the power and faculties of understanding, willing, reasoning, choosing and refusing, loving and hating, &c. and not only so, but are able to operate upon the body; and to quicken, move, direct and guide it to do whatever they please, and that that is capable of; and angelic spirits are more powerful still, they excel in strength, and are called mighty angels, Psalm ciii. 20. 2 Thess. i. 7. and have done very strange and surprising things; one of them slew in one night one hundred and eighty-five thousand men, in the Assyrian camp, 2 Kings xix. 35. and what then cannot God, the uncreated and infinite Spirit, do; who has endowed these with all their power, might, and strength? can less than omnipotence be ascribed to him? This may be inferred from his *infinity*. God is an infinite Being, and so is every perfection of his; his understanding is infinite, and such is his power; for, as a Jewish writer[3] argues, since power is attributed to God, it must be understood that it is infinite; for if it was finite, it might be conceived that there was a greater power than his; and so privation would fall on God; as if there was not in him the greater power that is to be conceived of. He is unlimited and unbounded, as to space, and so is omnipresent; and he is unlimited and unbounded as to time, and so is eternal; and he is unlimited and unbounded as to power, and so is omnipotent: to deny, or to call in question, his omnipotence, is to limit the holy one of Israel, which ought not to be done; this the Israelites are charged with, for distrusting his power to provide for them in the wilderness, Psalm lxxviii. 19, 20, 41. The omnipotence of God may be argued from his *independency;* all creatures depend on him, but he depends on none; there is no cause prior to him, nor any superior to him, or above him, that can control him; none, who, if his hand is stretched out, can turn it back, or stop it from proceeding to do what he will; none can stay his hand, or say unto him, what dost thou? "he does what he pleases in heaven and in earth," Dan. iv. 35. Moreover, this attribute of God may be confirmed by his *perfection;* God is a most perfect being; but that he would not be if any thing was wanting in him: want of power in a creature is an imperfection, and would be so in God, was that his case; but as he is great, his power is great; there is an exuberancy, an exceeding greatness of power in him, beyond all conception and expression; he is "able to do exceeding abundantly above all that we can ask or think," Eph. i. 19. and iii. 20. And this may be strengthened yet more by observing the *uselessness* of many other *perfections* without it; for what though he knows all things fit and proper to be done, for his own glory, and the good of his creatures, what does it signify, if he cannot do them? and though he may, in the most sovereign manner, will, determine, and decree, such and such things to be done; of what avail is it if he cannot carry his will, determinations, and decrees into execution? what dependance can there be upon his faithfulness in his promises, if he is not able also to perform? and of what use is his goodness, or an inclination and disposition in him to do good, if he cannot do it? or where is his justice in rendering to every man according to his works, if he cannot execute it? So that, upon the whole, it is a most certain truth, that *power belongs to God*, as the Psalmist says, Psalm lxii. 11. and to whom he ascribes it, even *power* and *might*, by which two words he expresses the greatness of power, superlative power, power in the highest degree, even omnipotence, 1 Chron. xxix. 12. and it may be observed, that in all the doxologies or ascriptions of glory to God, by angels and men, power or might is put into them, Rev. iv. 10, 11. and v. 13. and vii. 11, 12. And indeed it belongs to no other; it is peculiar to God: nor is it communicable to a creature; since that creature would then be God; for omnipotence is his nature; nor is it even communicable to the human nature of Christ, for the same reason; for though the human nature is united to a divine person, who is omnipotent, it does not become omnipotent thereby; though the two natures, divine and human, are closely united in Christ; yet the properties of each are distinct and peculiar; and it is easy to observe, that the human nature of Christ was subject to various infirmities, though sinless ones, and stood in need of help, strength, and deliverance; for which, as man, he prayed; and at last, he was crucified through weakness, Heb. iv. 15. Psalm xxii. 19, 20. 2 Cor. xiii. 4. And as for Matt. xxviii. 18.

---

[3] Joseph Albo in Sepher Ikkarim, fol. 68. 2.

CHAP. VIII. OF THE OMNIPOTENCE OF GOD.

that is said not of the attribute of divine power, which is not *given* him, but is natural to him, as a divine person, but of his authority over all, and their subjection to him as Mediator.

The power of God reaches to all things, and therefore is, with propriety, called Omnipotence; all things are possible with God, and nothing impossible; this is said by an angel, and confirmed by Christ, Luke i. 37. Mark xiv. 36. what is impossible with men is possible with God; what cannot be done according to the nature of things, the laws, rules, and course of nature, may be done by the God of nature, who is above these, and not bound by them, and sometimes acts contrary to them; as when he stopped the sun in its course, in the times of Joshua; made iron to swim by the hands of the prophet Elisha; and suffered not fire to burn in the furnace of Nebuchadnezzar, so that the three persons cast into it were not hurt by it, nor their clothes so much as singed, nor the smell of fire upon them: whereas, it is the nature of the sun to go on in its course, without stopping, nor can any creature stop it; and for ponderous bodies, as iron, to sink in water; and for fire to burn. There are some things, indeed, which God cannot do, and which the Scriptures express, as, that *he cannot deny himself*, 2 Tim. ii. 13. nor do any thing that is contrary to his being, his honour and glory, or subversive of it; thus, for instance, he cannot make another God, that would be contrary to himself, to the unity of his Being, and the declaration of his Word; *Hear, O Israel, the Lord our God is one Lord*, Deut. vi. 4. he cannot make a finite creature infinite; that would be to do the same, and there would be more infinites than one, which is a contradiction; he cannot raise a creature to such dignity as to have divine perfections ascribed to it, it has not, which would be a falsehood; or to have religious worship and adoration given it, which would be denying himself, detracting from his own glory, and giving it to another, when he only is to be served and worshipped: in such manner it is also said of him, that he *cannot lie*, Tit. i. 2. Heb. vi. 18. for this would be contrary to his truth and faithfulness; he can do nothing that is contrary to his attributes; he cannot commit iniquity, he neither will nor can do it; for that would be contrary to his holiness and righteousness; see Job xxxiv. 10, 12. and xxxvi. 23. he cannot do any thing that implies a contradiction; he cannot make contradictions true; a thing to be, and not to be at the same time; or make a thing not to have been that has been;[4] he can make a thing not to be, which is, or has been; he can destroy his own works; but not make that not to have existed, which has existed; nor make an human body to be everywhere; nor accidents to subsist without subjects; with many other things which imply a manifest contradiction and falsehood: but then these are no prejudices to his omnipotence, nor proofs of weakness; they arise only out of the abundance and fulness of his power; who can neither do a weak thing nor a wicked thing, nor commit any falsehood; to do, or attempt to do, any such things, would be proofs of impotence, and not of omnipotence.

The power of God may be considered as absolute, and as actual or ordinate. According to his absolute power, he can do all things which are not contrary to his nature and perfections, and which does not imply a contradiction; even though he has not done them nor never will: thus he could have raised up children to Abraham out of stones, though he would not; and have sent twelve legions of angels to deliver Christ out of the hands of his enemies; but did not, Matt. iii. 9. and xxvi. 53. He that has made one world, and how many more we know not for certainty, Heb. xi. 3. could have made ten thousand; he that has made the stars in the heaven innumerable, could have vastly increased their number; and he that has made an innumerable company of angels, and men on earth, as the sand of the sea, could have added to them infinitely more. The power of God has never been exerted to its uttermost; it is sufficient to entitle him to omnipotence, that he has done, and does, whatsoever he pleases, and that whatsoever is made, is made by him, and nothing without him; which is what may be called, his ordinate and actual power; or what he has willed and determined, is actually done; and of this there is abundant proof, as will appear by the following instances.

1. In creation; the heaven, earth, and sea, and all that in them are, were created by God, is certain; and these visible works of creation are proofs of the invisible attributes of God, and particularly, of his

---

[4] So Agathon apud Aristot. Ethic. 1. 6. c. 2.

eternal power, Acts iv. 24. Rom. i. 20. Creation is making something out of nothing; which none but omnipotence can effect; see Heb. xi. 3. no artificer, though ever so expert, can work without materials, whether he works in gold, silver, brass, iron, wood, stone, or in any thing else: the potter can cast his clay into what form and figure he pleases, according to his art, and make one vessel for one use, and another for another; but he cannot make the least portion of clay: but God created the first matter out of which all things are made; and which were made out of things not before existing by the omnipotent Being; whom the good woman animating her son to martyrdom, exhorted to acknowledge, 2 Maccab. vii. 28. Nor can any artificer work without tools; and the more curious his work, the more curious must his tools be: but God can work without instruments, as he did in creation; it was only by his all-commanding word that every thing sprung into being, Gen. i. 3. &c. Psalm xxxvi. 9. and every thing created was done at once; creation is an instantaneous act, is without succession, and requires no length of time to do it in; every thing on the several days of creation were done immediately: on the first day God said, "Let there be light;" and it immediately sprung out of darkness: on the second day he said, "Let there be a firmament," an expanse; and at once the airy heaven was stretched out like a curtain around our earth: on the third day he said, "Let the earth bring forth grass, herbs, and fruit-trees;" and they arose directly out of it, in all their verdure and fruitfulness: on the fourth day he said, "Let there be lights in the heavens; and no sooner was it said, but the sun, moon, and stars, blazed forth in all their lustre and splendour: on the fifth and sixth days orders were given for the waters to bring forth fish, and fowl, and beasts, and cattle of every kind; and they accordingly brought them forth in full perfection immediately; and last of all, man was at once made, complete and perfect, out of the dust of the earth, and the breath of life was breathed into him: and though there were six days appointed, one for each of these works, yet they were instantaneously performed on those days; and this time was allotted not on account of God, who could have done them all in a moment; but for the sake of men, who, when they read the history of the creation, there is a stop and pause at each work, that they may stand still and meditate upon it, and wonder at it. Whereas the works of men require time; and those that are most curious, longer still. Add to all this, that the works of creation were done without weariness; no labour of men is free from it: if it be the work of the brain, the fruit of close reasoning, reading, meditation, and study; *much study*, the wise man says, *is a weariness of the flesh*, Eccles. xii. 12. or if it be manual operation, it is labour and fatigue; but the everlasting God, the Creator of the ends of the earth, though he has wrought such stupendous works, *fainteth not, neither is weary*, Isa. xl. 28. and though he is said to *rest* on the seventh day, yet not on account of fatigue; but to denote he had finished his work, brought it to perfection, and ceased from it. And now, to what can all this be ascribed but to omnipotence? Which,

2. Appears in the sustentation and support of all creatures, in the provision made for them, with other wonderful works done in providence: all creatures live, move, and have their being in God; as they are made by him, they consist by him; "he upholds all things by the word of his power;" the heavens, the earth, and the pillars thereof, Acts xvii. 28. Col. i. 16, 17. Heb. i. 3. Psalm lxxv. 3. which none but an almighty arm can do: and the manner in which the world, and all things in it, are preserved, and continue, is amazing and surprising, and cannot be accounted for, no other way than by the attribute of omnipotence; for *he stretcheth out the north over the empty place, and hangeth the earth upon nothing; he bindeth up the waters in his thick clouds, and the cloud is not rent under him;* though these are no other than condensed air, which carry such burdens in them, and yet are not burst by them—he has *shut up the sea with doors;* with clifts and rocks, and even with so weak a thing as sand; *and said, hitherto shalt thou come, and no further, and here shall thy proud waves be staid*—and has *caused the dayspring to know its place*—*divided a watercourse for the overflowing of waters, and a way for the lightning of thunder, to cause it to rain on the earth;* which none of the vanities of the Gentiles can do; he gives that *and fruitful seasons, filling* men's *hearts with food and gladness*, and provides for all the fowls of the air, and "the cattle on a thousand hills; see Job. xxvi. 7, 8. and xxxviii. 10, 11, 12, 25, 26. Acts xiv. 17. But what hand can do all these but an

almighty one? To which may be added, those wonderful events in providence, which can only be accounted for by recurring to omnipotence, and to supernatural power and aid; as the drowning of the whole world; the burning of Sodom and Gomorrah, and the cities of the plain; the strange exploits of some particular persons, as Jonathan and David; the amazing victories obtained by a few over a multitude, sometimes by unarmed men, sometimes without fighting, and always by him that helps, whether with many, or with them that have no power, as the cases of Gideon, Jehoshaphat, and Asa shew; with various other things too numerous to mention, as the removing of mountains, shaking the earth, and the pillars of it, commanding the sun not to rise, and sealing up the stars, Job ix. 5, 6, 7, &c.

3. The omnipotence of God may be seen in the redemption of men by Christ, in things leading to it, and in the completion of it: in the incarnation of Christ, and his birth of a virgin, which the angel ascribes to *the power of the Highest*, the most high God, with whom *nothing is impossible*, Luke i. 35, 37. and which was an expedient found out by infinite wisdom, to remove a difficulty which none but omnipotence could surmount, namely, to bring *a clean thing out of an unclean;* for it was necessary that the Saviour of men should be man, that the salvation should be wrought out in human nature, that so men might have the benefit of it; and it was necessary that he should be free from sin, who became a sacrifice for it; yet how it could be, since all human nature was defiled with sin, was the difficulty; which was got over, through omnipotence forming the human nature of Christ in the above manner: and which was also evident in the protection of him from the womb; in his infancy, from the malice of Herod; after his baptism, from the violence of Satan's temptations, who put him upon destroying himself; and from the wild beasts of the wilderness; and from all the snares and attempts of the Scribes and Pharisees, to take away his life before his time: and in the miraculous works wrought by him, which were proofs of his Messiahship; such as causing the blind to see, the deaf to hear, the dumb to speak, the lame to walk, and cleansing lepers, and even raising the dead to life; and which were such instances of omnipotence, as caused in those that saw them amazement at the mighty power of God, Matt. xi. 5. Luke ix. 43. and more especially this might be seen in making Christ, the man of God's right-hand, strong for himself; in strengthening him in his human nature to work out salvation, which neither men nor angels could have done, by fulfilling the law, and satisfying justice; in upholding him under the weight of sins and sufferings; in enabling him to bear the wrath of God, and the curses of a righteous law, and to grapple with all the powers of darkness, and to spoil them, and make a triumph over them; and in raising him from the dead for justification, without which salvation would not have been complete; and in which *the exceeding greatness of* the divine *power* was exerted; and whereby Christ was declared to be the Son of God *with power*, Eph. i. 19. Rom. ix. 4.

4. Almighty power may be discerned in the conversion of sinners; that is a creation, which is an act of omnipotence, as has been proved. Men, in conversion, are made new creatures; "created in Christ, and after the image of God;" have new hearts and spirits, clean and upright ones, created in them; new principles of grace and holiness formed in them; "are turned from darkness to light, from the power of Satan unto God; and are made willing in the day of God's power" upon them, to be saved by Christ, and serve him; to submit to his righteousness, and to part with their sins and sinful companions: all which are effects of the exceeding greatness of the power of God towards them and upon them: they are quickened when dead in sins, and raised by Christ, the resurrection and the life, from a death of sin to a life of grace; the Spirit of life enters into them, and these dry bones live; conversion is a resurrection, and that requires almighty power. And if we consider the means of it, generally speaking, "the foolishness of preaching," the gospel put into earthen vessels, for this end, *that the excellency of the power of God may appear to be of God*, and not of men; and when these means are effectual, they are *the power of God unto salvation*, 2 Cor. iv. 7. Rom. i. 16. And also the great opposition made to this work, through the enmity and lusts of men's hearts, the malice of Satan, willing to keep possession; the snares of the world, and the influence of wicked companions; it cannot be thought to be any thing short of the omnipotent hand of God, that snatches men, as brands, out of the burning: and the same power that is put forth in the beginning of the

work of grace, is requisite to the carrying of it on; the rise, progress, and finishing of it, are not by might and power of men, but by the mighty, efficacious, and all-powerful grace of God, 2 Thess. i. 11. Zech. iv. 6.

5. That the Lord God is omnipotent, may be evinced from the rise and progress of Christianity, the success of the gospel, in the first times of it, and the continuance of it, notwithstanding the opposition of men and devils. The interest of Christ in the world rose from small beginnings; it was like the little stone cut out of the mountain without hands, which became a great mountain, and filled the whole earth; and this by means of the preaching of the gospel; and that by such, who, for the most part, were men illiterate, mean, and contemptible, the foolish things of this world; and who were opposed by Jewish *rabbins*, and heathen philosophers, by monarchs, kings, and emperors, and by the whole world; yet these went forth, and Christ with them, conquering and to conquer, and were made to triumph in him over all their enemies everywhere; so that in a short time the universal monarchy of the earth, the whole Roman empire, became nominally Christian; and the Gospel has lived through all the persecutions of Rome pagan and papal, and still continues, notwithstanding the craft of false teachers, and the force of furious persecutors; and will remain and be the everlasting Gospel; all which is owing to the mighty power of God.

6. The final perseverance of every particular believer in grace and holiness, is a proof of the divine omnipotence; it is because he is great in power that not one of them fails; otherwise their indwelling sins and corruptions would prevail over them; Satan's temptations be too powerful for them; and the snares of the world, the flatteries of it, would draw them aside; but they are *kept by the power of God*, the mighty power of God, as in a garrison, *through faith unto salvation*, 1 Pet. i. 5.

7. The almighty power of God will be displayed in the resurrection of the dead; which considered, it need not be thought incredible; though otherwise it might; for what but the all-commanding voice of the almighty God can rouse the dead, and raise them to life, and bring them out of their graves; "some to the resurrection of life, and some to the resurrection of damnation?" What else but his almighty power can gather all nations before him, and oblige them to stand at the judgment-seat of Christ, to receive their several sentences? And what but his vengeful arm of omnipotence can execute the sentence on millions and millions of devils and wicked men, in all the height of wrath, rage, fury, and rebellion? see Phil. iii. 21. John v. 28, 29. Matt. xxv. 32—46. Rev. xx. 8, 9, 10.

CHAP. IX.

OF THE OMNISCIENCE OF GOD.

HAVING considered such attributes of God, which belong to him as an active and operative Spirit; as the Life of God, and his Power, or Omnipotence; I proceed to consider such perfections, which may be ascribed to him as an intelligent Spirit; to which, rational spirits, endowed with understanding, will, and affections, bear some similarity. God is said to have a *mind* and *understanding*, Rom. xi. 34. Isa. xl. 28. to which may be referred, the attributes of *knowledge* and *wisdom*, which go together, Rom. xi. 33. I shall begin with the first of these. And,

1. Prove that knowledge belongs to God, which is objected to, and called in question, by impious and atheistical persons, Psalm lxxiii. 11. particularly with respect to human affairs; the grounds of which doubts about it, and objections to it, seem to arise, partly from the supposed distance of God in heaven, from men on earth, and partly from the thick and dark clouds which intervene between them, Job xxii. 12, 13, 14. and which are easily answered by observing the omnipresence of God, or his presence in all places; and that the darkness hides not any thing from his all-piercing, all-penetrating eye, the darkness and the light being alike to him, Psalm cxxxix. 7—12. Jer. xxiii. 23, 24. Let it be further observed, that in all rational creatures there is knowledge; there is much in angels, and so there was in man, before the fall, both of natural, divine, and civil things; and since the fall there is a remainder of it, notwithstanding the loss sustained by it; and there is more, especially divine and spiritual knowledge, in regenerate men, who are renewed in knowledge. Now if there is knowledge in any of the creatures of God, then much more in God himself. Besides, all that knowledge that is in angels or men, comes from God; he is a *God of knowledge*, or *knowledges*, of all knowledge,

1 Sam. ii. 3. the source and fountain of it, and therefore it must be in him in its perfection: knowledge of all things, natural, civil, and spiritual, is from him, is taught and given by him; wherefore strong is the reasoning of the Psalmist, *He that teacheth man knowledge, shall he not know?* Psalm xciv. 10. His knowledge may be inferred from his will, and the actings of it; that he has a will is most certain; and works all things after the counsel of his will, which cannot be resisted, Eph. i. 11. Rom. ix. 19. and this can never be supposed to be without knowledge; it is generally said and believed of the will of man, that it is determined by the last act of the understanding; and it cannot be imagined that God wills any thing ignorantly and rashly; he must know what he wills and nills, and to whom he wills any thing, or refuses, Rom. ix. 15, 18. and it appears from all his works, from the works of creation, the heavens, earth, and sea, and all in them; which are ascribed to his wisdom, understanding, and knowledge, and could never be made without them, Prov. iii. 19, 20. the government of the world, and the judgment of the last day, suppose and require the same, Rom. xi. 33. 1 Cor. iv. 5. Without knowledge God would not be perfectly happy; the blessed one, and blessed for ever, as he is. It is knowledge that gives men the preference to the brute creation, and makes them happier than they, Job xxxv. 11. and the spiritual knowledge which good men have, gives them a superior excellency and felicity to bad men; and their happiness in a future state will lie, as in perfect holiness, so in perfect knowledge, or *to know*, as they are known, 1 Cor. xiii. 12. In short, without knowledge, God would be no other than the idols of the Gentiles, who have eyes, but see not; are the work of errors, and are falsehood and vanity; but the portion of Jacob is not like them, Jer. x. 14, 15, 16. I go on,

2. To shew the extent of the knowledge of God; it reaches to all things, John xxi. 17. 1 John iii. 20. and is therefore with great propriety called *omniscience*, and which the very heathens[1] ascribe to God; and extend it to thoughts. Thales[2] being asked, Whether a man doing ill, could lie hid to, or be concealed from God? answered, No, nor thinking neither. And Pindar[3] says, If a man hopes that any thing will be concealed from God, he is deceived.

(1.) God knows himself, his nature, and perfections somewhat of this is known by creatures themselves, even by the very heathens, through the light of nature, and in the glass of the creatures, wherein God has shewed it to them; even his invisible things, his eternal power and Godhead, Rom. i. 19, 20. and which are more clearly displayed in Christ, and redemption by him; and more evidently seen by those who are favoured with a divine revelation: and if creatures know something of God, though imperfectly, then he must know himself in the most perfect manner: and rational creatures are endowed with knowledge of themselves, of their nature, and what belongs to them, as angels may reasonably be supposed to be; since even men, in their fallen and imperfect state, know something of themselves, of the constitution, temperament, and texture of their bodies, and of the powers and faculties of their souls; what is in them, in the inmost recesses of their minds, their thoughts, purposes, and intentions, 1 Cor. ii. 11. *Nosce teipsum, Know thyself*, has been reckoned a wise maxim with philosophers, and the first step to wisdom and knowledge; and good men, illuminated by the Spirit of God, attain to the highest degree of it; and if creatures know themselves in any degree, infinitely much more must the Creator of all know himself. God knows himself in all his persons, and each person fully knows one another; the Father knows the Son, begotten by him, and brought up with him; the Son knows the Father, in whose bosom he lay; and the Spirit knows the Father and Son, whose Spirit he is, and from whom he proceeds; and the Father and Son know the Spirit, who is sent by them as the Comforter; see Matt. xi. 27. 1 Cor. ii. 10, 11. God knows the mode of each person's subsistence in the Deity, the paternity of the Father, the generation of the Son, and the spiration of the Holy Ghost; that these three are one, and one in three; three persons, but one God; which is a mystery incomprehensible by us: but inasmuch as God, who knows his own nature best, has

---

[1] παντα ιδων διος οφθαλμος και παντα νοησας, Hesiod. Opera et Dies, l. 1. v. 263.

[2] Apud Laert. Vita ejus, Val. Maxim. l. 7. c. 2. extern. 8.

[3] Olymp. Ode 1. so Epicharmus apud Clement. Stromat. l. 5. p. 597.

so declared it to be, it becomes us to yield the obedience of faith unto it: he knows his own thoughts, which are the deep things of God, and as much above us as the heavens are above the earth, and as much out of our reach; but he knows them, Jer. xxix. 11. that is, his decrees, purposes, and designs, as he needs must, since they are purposed in himself; he knows the things he has purposed, and the exact time of the accomplishment of them, which he has reserved in his own power, Eph. i. 11. Eccles. iii. 1. Acts i. 6.

(2.) God knows all his creatures, there is not *any creature*, not one excepted, *that is not manifest in his sight*, Heb. iv. 13. *Known unto him are all his works*; all that his hand has wrought, Acts xv. 18. when he had finished his works of creation, *he saw every thing that he had made*, looked over it and considered it, and pronounced it good, Gen. i. 31. and his eye sees all things in their present state and condition; he knows all things *inanimate*, all that is upon the earth, herbs, grass, trees, &c. and all in the bowels of it, metals and minerals; all that are in the heavens, not only the two great luminaries, the sun and moon, their nature, motion, rising, and setting, with every thing belonging to them, but the stars innumerable; he *bringeth out their host by number*, or them as a mighty army, and numerous; and yet, as numerous as they are, *he calleth them all by names;* such a distinct and particular knowledge has he of them, and that because he *hath created* them; and he upholds them in being, *by the greatness of his might*, so that *not one faileth*, Isa. xl. 26. he knows all the *irrational* creatures, the beasts of the field, "the cattle on a thousand hills;" *I know*, says he, *all the fowls of the mountains*, Psalm l. 10, 11. as worthless a bird as the sparrow is, *not one of them falls* on the ground without the knowledge and will of God, Matt. x. 30. he knows all the fishes of the sea, and provided one to swallow Jonah, when thrown into it; and which, at his order, cast him on dry land again, Jonah i. 17. and ii. 10. And if Adam had such knowledge of all creatures, as to give them proper and suitable names, Gen. ii. 19, 20. and Solomon, a fallen son of his, could *speak of trees, from the cedar in Lebanon to the hyssop that springs out of the wall; and of beasts, fowl, creeping things, and fishes*, 1 Kings iv. 33. even of their nature, properties, use, and end; can it be thought incredible that God, the creator of them, should have a distinct and perfect knowledge of all these? he knows all *rational* beings, as angels and men; the angels, though innumerable, being his creatures, standing before him, beholding his face, and sent forth by him as ministring spirits; the elect angels, whom he must know, since he has chosen them and put them under Christ, the head of all principality and power; and confirmed them, by his grace, in their happy state; and who stand on his right-hand and left, hearkening to his voice, and ready to obey his will; and are employed by him in providential affairs, and in things respecting the heirs of salvation. Yea, the apostate angels, devils, are known by him, and are laid up in chains of darkness, reserved to the judgment of the great day, and are under the continual eye of God, and the restraints of his providence: the questions put to these by God, Job i. 7. and by Christ, Mark v. 9. do not imply any kind of ignorance of them; the one is put to lead on to a discourse concerning Job, and the other to shew the greatness of the miracle wrought in casting them out. God knows all men, good and bad, all the sons of men, the inhabitants of the earth, wherever they are, in all places and in all ages, Psalm xxxiii. 13, 14. Prov. xv. 2. he knows their hearts, for he has fashioned them alike, and is often said to be the searcher of them; he knows the thoughts of the heart: as his word, so is he a *discerner* of them, Heb. iv. 12. see Psalm cxxxix. 2. which is peculiar to God, and a strong proof of the Deity of Christ, the essential Word, Matt. ix. 4. John ii. 24, 25. Heb. iv. 12, 13. the evil thoughts of men, which are many and vain, Psalm xciv. 11. and the good thoughts of men, as he must, since they are of him, and not of themselves; and he takes such notice of them, as to write a book of remembrance of them, 2 Cor. iii. 5. Mal. iii. 16. he knows the imaginations of the thoughts of the heart, the first motions to thought, whether good or bad, Gen. vi. 5. 1 Chron. xxviii. 9. he knows all the words of men, there is not one upon their tongues, or uttered by them, but he knows it altogether, Psalm cxxxix. 4. the words of wicked men, even every idle word, which must be accounted for in the day of judgment; and much more their blasphemies, oaths, and curses; and all their hard speeches spoken against Christ and his people, Matt. xii. 36. Jude ver. 15. And the words of good men, expressed in prayer and thanksgiving, and in spiritual conversation with one another, Mal. iii. 16. And all the works and ways of men, Job xxxiv. 21. their civil ones, their down-sitting and uprising, going forth and coming in, Psalm cxxxix. 2, 3. and cxxi. 3, 8. and all their sinful ways and works, which will all be brought into judgment, and for which an account must be given at the bar of God, Eccles. xii. 14. 2 Cor. v. 10 as well as all the good works of God's people, who knows from what principles they spring, in what manner they are done, and with what views, and for what ends, Rev. ii. 2, 19.

(3.) God knows all things whatever, as well as himself and the creatures: he knows all things possible to be done, though they are not, nor never will be done; such as have been observed under the preceding attribute; and this knowledge is what is called by the schoolmen, "Knowledge of simple intelligence" of things that are not actually done. He knows what *might* be, and in course, *would* be, should he not prevent them by the interposition of his power and providence, and which he determines to do: so he knew the wickedness and treachery of the men of Keilah to David, and that if he stayed there, they would deliver him up into the hands of Saul, and therefore gave him notice of it, that he might make his escape from them, and so prevent their giving him up, according to his determinate will, 1 Sam. xxiii. 11, 12. God knows the wickedness of some men's hearts, that they would be guilty of the most shocking crimes, and that without number, if suffered to live, and therefore he takes them away by death; and that such is the temper of some, that if they had a large share of riches, they would be so haughty and overbearing, there would be no living by them: and that even some good men, if they had them, would be tempted to abuse them, to their own hurt, and therefore he gives them poverty. Moreover, God knows all things that have been, are, or shall be; and which the schools call, "knowledge of vision;" an intuitive view of all actual things; things past, present, and to come; so called, not with respect to God, with whom nothing is past nor future, but all present; but with respect to us, and our measures of time. He knows all former things, from the beginning of the world; and which is a proof of Deity, and such a proof that the idols of the Gentiles cannot give, nor any for them, Isa. xli. 22. and xliii. 9. all past transactions at the creation, the fall of Adam, and what followed on that; the original of nations, and their settlement in the world; with various other occurrences to be met with only in the Bible, inspired by God; which, as it is the most ancient, so the truest and best history in the world: nothing that has been can escape the knowledge of God, nor slip out of his mind and memory; oblivion cannot be ascribed to him; could he forget past facts, or they be lost to him, how could every thing, open or secret, be brought into account, at the day of judgment, as it will? Eccles. xii. 14. Forgetting the sins of his people, and remembering them no more, are attributed to him after the manner of men; who, when they forgive one another, do, or should, forget offences. God sees and knows all things present; all are naked and open to him, he sees all in one view; all that is done everywhere; as he must, since he is present in all places; and all live, and move, and have their being in him. He knows all things future, all that will be, because he has determined they shall be; it is his will that gives futurition to them, and therefore he must certainly know what he wills shall be: and this is another proof of Deity wanting in heathen idols, Isa. xli. 22, 23. and xliv. 7. and xlvi. 10. And this is what is called

Prescience or *Foreknowledge;* and of which Tertullian,[4] many hundreds of years ago, observed, that there were as many witnesses of it as there are prophets; and I may add, as there are prophecies; for all prophecy is founded on God's foreknowledge and predetermination of things; and of this there are numerous instances; as of the Israelites being in a strange land four hundred years, and then coming out with great substance, Gen. xv. 13, 14. of their seventy years captivity in Babylon, and deliverance from thence at the end of that time, Jer. xxix. 10. with many other things relating to that people, and other nations; the prophecies of

---

[4] Adv. Marcion. 1. 2. c. 5.

Daniel, concerning the four monarchies; the predictions of the Old Testament, concerning the incarnation of Christ, his sufferings, death, resurrection, ascension, and session at God's right-hand. And what is the book of the Revelation but a prophecy, and so a proof of God's foreknowledge of future events, which should be in the church and world, from the times of Christ to the end of the world? and this prescience, or foreknowledge of God, is not only of the effects of necessary causes, which necessarily will be, unless prevented by something extraordinary; and of which men themselves may have knowledge; as that things ponderous will fall downwards, and light things move upwards; and that fire put to combustible matter will burn; but of things contingent, which, as to their nature, may or may not be, and which even depend upon the wills of men; and which, with respect to second causes are hap and chance. Indeed, with respect to God, there is nothing casual or contingent;[5] nothing comes to pass but what is decreed by him, what he has determined either to do himself, or by others, or suffer to be done, Lam. iii. 37, 38. that which is chance to others is none to him; what more a chance matter than a lot? yet though that is cast into the lap, and it is casual to men, how it will turn up, *the whole disposing of it is of the Lord*, Prov. xvi. 33. What more contingent than the imaginations, thoughts, and designs of men, what they will be? and yet these are foreknown before conceived in the mind, Deut. xxxi. 21. Psalm cxxxix. 2. or than the voluntary actions of men, yet these are foreknown and foretold by the Lord, long before they are done; as the names of persons given them, and what should be done by them; as of Josiah, that he should offer the priests, and burn the bones of men on the altar at Bethel, see 1 Kings xiii. 2. and 2 Kings xxiii. 15, 16. and of Cyrus, that he should give orders for the building of the temple, and city of Jerusalem; and let the captive Jews go free without price, Isa. xliv. 28. and xlv. 13. Ezra i. 1, 2, 3. all which were predicted of these persons by name, some hundreds of years before they were born: how all this is reconcileable with the liberty of man's will, is a difficulty; and therefore objected to the certain foreknowledge and decree of God; but whether this difficulty can be removed, or no, the thing is not less certain: let it be observed, that God's decrees do not at all infringe the liberty of the will, nor do not put any thing in it, nor lay any force upon it; they only imply a necessity of the event, but not of coaction, or force on the will; nor do men feel any such force upon them; they act as freely, and with the full consent of their will, whether good men or bad men, in what they do, as if there were no foreknowledge and determination of them by God; good men willingly do what they do, under the influence of grace, though foreordained to it by the Lord, Eph. ii. 10. Phil. ii. 13. and so do wicked men, as Judas in betraying Christ, and the Jews in crucifying him; though both were " according to the determinate counsel and foreknowledge of God," Luke xxii. 22. Acts ii. 23.

There is another sort of *prescience*, or *foreknowledge*, the Scriptures speak of; on which the election of persons to eternal life is founded, and according to which it is, Rom. viii. 30. 1 Pet. i. 2. which is not a foreknowledge of faith, holiness, and good works, and perseverance therein, as causes of it; for these are effects and fruits of election, which flow from it; no bare foreknowledge of persons, but as joined with love and affection to the objects of it; and which is not general, but special; *The Lord knows them that are his*, 2 Tim. ii. 19. not in general, as he knows all men; but distinctly, and particularly, he loves them, approves of them, and delights in them, and takes a particular care of them; whilst of others he says, *I know you not*, Matt. vii. 23. that is, as his beloved and chosen ones. But as this belongs to the doctrine of predestination, I shall defer it to its proper place.

3. Though enough has been said to prove the omniscience of God, by the enumeration of the above things; yet this may receive further proof from the several attributes of God: as from his *infinity*; God is infinite; he is unlimited and unbounded as to space, and so omnipresent; he is unbounded as to time, and so eternal; and he is unbounded as to power,

---

[5] Mihi ne in Deum quidem cadere videatur, ut sciat quid casuc et fortuito futurum sit; si enim scit certe, illud eveniet; sin certe eveniet, nulla fortuna est, Cicero de Divinatione, l. 2.

and so omnipotent; and he is unbounded as to knowledge, and so omniscient; there is no searching, no coming to the end of his understanding. From his eternity; he is from everlasting to everlasting, and therefore must know every thing that has been, is, or shall be. Men are but of yesterday, and therefore, comparatively, know nothing; *ars longa, vita brevis;* science is of a large extent, and man's life but short, and he can gain but little of it. Likewise from the *omnipresence* of God: he is every where, in heaven, earth, and hell; and therefore must know every creature, and every thing that is done there, Psalm cxxxix. 7—12. and it may be observed, that what is said there of this attribute, follows upon an account of the omniscience of God, and serves to confirm it: it may be argued from the *perfection* of God; if any thing was wanting in his knowledge, neither that, nor he himself, would be perfect. If the circuit of the sun is from one end of the heaven to the other, and nothing is hid on earth from its light and heat; and hence the heathens[6] represent it as seeing all things; then much more may be said of God, who is a sun, that *he looketh to the ends of the earth, and seeth under the whole heaven;* see Psalm xix. 6. Job xxviii. 24. From the several works of God his omniscience may be inferred; he has made all things, and therefore must perfectly know them; every artificer knows his own work, its nature, composition, parts, use, and end. God upholds all things, and is present with them, and therefore must have knowledge of them; he governs the world, orders, directs, and disposes of all things in it; provides for all his creatures; feeds them, and gives them their portion of meat in due season; and therefore must know them all: all the deeds of men, good and evil, public and private, will be all brought into judgment by him; which to do, requires omniscience; see Eccles. xii. 14. 1 Cor. iv. 5. Rev. ii. 23.

4. The manner in which God knows all things, is incomprehensible by us; we can say but little of it, "such knowledge is too wonderful for us," Psalm cxxxix. 6. we can better say in what manner he does not know, than in what he does: he does not know things by revelation, by instruction, and communication from another; or any way by which men come at the knowledge of things from others; for *shall any teach God knowledge? or who has taught him?* Job xxi. 22. Isa. xl. 13, 14. all things were known to God from eternity, when there were none in being to inform him of any thing: besides, to suppose this, is not only contrary to his eternity but to his independency; for this would make him beholden to, and dependent on another, for his knowledge; whereas "all things are of him, for him, and through him." Nor is his knowledge attained by reasoning, discoursing, and inferring one thing from another, as man's is; who not only apprehends simple ideas, but joins and compounds them, and infers other things from them; but then this implies some degree of prior ignorance; or at best, imperfect knowledge, till the premises are clear, and the conclusion formed; which is not to be said of God: and this method of knowledge would be contrary to the simplicity of his nature, which admits of no composition, as well as to his perfection: nor does he know things by succession, one after another; for then it could not be said, that *all things are naked and open to him;* only some at one time, and some at another; which would also argue ignorance of some things, in one instant and another; and imperfection of knowledge; and would be contrary to his immutability, since every accession of knowledge would make an alteration in him; whereas with him *there is no variableness;* he sees and knows all things at once and together, in one eternal view. In a word, he knows all things in himself, in his own essence and nature; he knows all things possible in his power, and all that he wills to do in his will, and all creatures in himself, as the first cause of them; in whose vast and eternal mind are all the original ideas of them; so that the knowledge of God is essential to him, it is his nature and essence, and therefore is incommunicable to a creature, and even to the human nature of Christ; which though united to a divine person that is omniscient, yet does not thereby become omniscient; and though the human soul of Christ may know more than the soul of any man, yet not every thing; see Mark xiii. 32. The knowledge of God is also infinite, Psalm cxlvii. 5. he knows himself, that is infinite; which he could not, unless his knowledge was infinite; for it is impossible, as a

---

[6] Ηελιω, ος παντ' εφορα, Homer. Odyss. 11. v. 108. et 12. v. 323. Vid. Sophoclis Trachin. v. 102.

Jewish[7] writer observes, that he should know what is perfectly infinite, if his knowledge was not perfectly infinite; for what is finite, can never comprehend that which is infinite; and he knows all things *ad infinitum;* there is no searching of his knowledge; it is perfect, and nothing can be added to it, Job xxxvi. 4. and it is not conjectural, but certain, depending on his will; he knew from all eternity, most certainly, that all things would be, that are, because he determined they should be; and his will cannot be frustrated, nor his power resisted, Job xlii. 2.

CHAP. X.

OF THE WISDOM OF GOD.

THE next attribute of God, which requires our attention, is, the Wisdom of God, which belongs to him as an intelligent Spirit; and is a more comprehensive attribute than that of knowledge; for it not only supposes that, but directs and uses it, in the best manner, and to the best ends and purposes; as well as his power and goodness. I shall,

I. Prove that wisdom is a perfection in God, and is in him in its utmost perfection; it is consummate and infinite wisdom he is possessed of. No one that believes the being of a God, can admit the least doubt of it. An unwise being cannot be God. No man is wise, says Pythagoras,[1] but God only. That *with him is wisdom*, is frequently asserted in the sacred Scriptures, Job xii. 12, 13. Dan. ii. 20, 21. And, indeed, if this is, and is expected to be with ancient men, who have lived long, and have had a large experience of things; then much more, yea, infinitely more, may it be thought to be with him, who is *the ancient of days*, and from everlasting to everlasting, God. He is no less than three times said to be *the only wise God*, Rom. xvi. 27. 1 Tim. i. 17. Jude ver. 25. Not to the exclusion of his Son, who is called *wisdoms*, plurally, because of the infinite fulness of wisdom that dwells in him, Prov. i. 20. nor of the Spirit, who is the Spirit of wisdom and revelation, in the knowledge of him, Eph. i. 17. but with respect to creatures, who have no wisdom, in comparison of him; the angels, those knowing and wise beings, when compared with him, are chargeable with *folly*, Job. iv. 18. and as for "man, though he would be wise, he is born like a wild ass's colt;" and has very little wisdom in things civil, none in things spiritual; and though he is wise to do evil, to do good he has no knowledge, God is *all-wise;* he has all wisdom in him; there is no defect of it in him; there is nothing of it wanting in him, with respect to any thing whatever. Men may be wise in some things, and not in others; but he is wise in every thing; *nemo sapit omnibus horis;* no man is wise at all times; the wisest of men sometimes say a foolish word, and do a foolish thing: but God, neither in his word, nor in any of his works, can be charged with folly; not an unwise saying appears in all the Scriptures; nor an unwise action in any of his works; *How manifold are thy works, O Lord, in wisdom hast thou made them all!* Psal. civ. 24. God is *essentially* wise; there is the personal wisdom of God, which is Christ; who is often spoken of as wisdom, and as the wisdom of God; see Prov. viii. 12—31. 1 Cor. i. 24. and there is his essential wisdom, the attribute now under consideration; which is no other than the nature and essence of God; it is himself; as he is love itself, and goodness itself, so he is wisdom itself; his wisdom cannot be separated from his essence; this would be contrary to his simplicity, and he would not be that simple and uncompounded Spirit he has been proved to be. God is wisdom *efficiently;* he is the source and fountain of it, the God and giver of it; all that is in the angels of heaven comes from him; all that Adam had, or any of his sons; or was in Solomon, the wisest of men; or is in the politicians and philosophers of every age; or in every mechanic; or appears in every art and science; all is the gift of God; and particularly the highest and best of wisdom, spiritual wisdom, wisdom in the hidden part, the fear of God in the soul of man, is what God puts there; wherefore, as he that teacheth man knowledge, must have knowledge himself; so he that gives wisdom to the wise, must have infinite wisdom himself; for such is the wisdom of God, it is *unsearchable;* there is no tracing it; it has a βαθος, a *depth*, which is unfathomable, Rom. xi. 33. see Job xi. 6, 7, 8, 9. and xxviii. 12—23. yet, though it cannot be traced out to the full, or be found out to perfection, there are some shining appearances and striking

---

Joseph Albo in Sepher Ikkarim, fol. 68. 2.

[1] Laert. Vit. Philosoph. Prœem. p. 8.

instances of it; which clearly and plainly prove that wisdom, in its utmost extent, is with him. And which,

II. Will be next observed. And,

First, The wisdom of God appears in his purposes and decrees, and which are therefore called his *counsels*, Isa. xxv. 1. not that they are the effects of consultation with himself or others; but because such resolutions and determinations with men are generally the wisest, which are formed on close thought, on mature deliberation, and on consultation with themselves and others. Hence the decrees of God, which are at once fixed with the highest wisdom, are called counsels; though his counsels are without consultation, and his determinations without deliberation; of which he has no need. As he sees in his understanding, what is fittest to be done, his wisdom directs his will to determine, at once, what shall be done; and this is seen in appointing the end for which they are to be, in ordaining means suitable and conducive to that end; and in pitching upon the most proper time for execution; and in guarding against every thing that may hinder that. The end for which God has appointed all that has been, or shall be, is himself, his own glory, the best end that can be proposed; *the Lord hath made*, that is, appointed *all things for himself;* for the glorifying of himself, one or other of the perfections of his nature; for as all things are *of him*, as the efficient cause; and are *through him*, as the wise orderer and disposer of them; so they are *to him*, as the final cause, or last end of them, his own glory, Prov. xvi. 4. Rom. xi. 36. The means he fixes on to bring it about, are either extraordinary or ordinary; which latter are second causes depending upon him, the first Cause, and which are linked together, and under his direction and influence most certainly attain the end; see Hos. ii. 21, 22. and which is effected in the most seasonable time; for as there is a purpose for every thing done under the heavens, there is a time fixed for every purpose; and as the times and seasons are in the power of God, and at his disposal, he pitches upon that which is the most suitable; for he makes every thing beautiful in his time, Eccles. iii. 1, 11. Acts i. 7. and being the omniscient God, he foresees all future events, the end from the beginning; so that nothing unforeseen by him can occur to hinder the execution of his purposes; wherefore his *counsel shall stand*,

and he *will do all his pleasure*, Isa. xlvi. 10. and though there may be many devices formed to counter-work his designs, they are all in vain; there is no wisdom nor counsel against the Lord; he disappoints the devices of the crafty, and the counsel of the froward is carried headlong; so that his counsel always stands: and the thoughts of his heart, which are his decrees, are to all generations. All this is true of the decrees of God in general. And if the princes of this world, under a divine direction, form wise counsels, and make wise and righteous decrees; with what greater, with what consummate wisdom, must the counsels and decrees of God himself be made; concerning which the apostle breaks forth into this exclamation, *O the depth of the riches both of the wisdom and knowledge of God!* Rom. xi. 33. for he is there treating of the decrees of God, and particularly of the decree of election: and in which the wisdom of God appears, both in the end and means, and in the persons he has chosen: his end is the praise of his own grace, or the glorifying of his sovereign grace and mercy in the salvation of men, Rom. ix. 23. Eph. i. 5, 6. to shew the sovereignty of it, he passed this decree without any respect to the works of men, and before either good or evil were done; and to shew that he is no respecter of persons, he chose some out of every nation, Jews and Gentiles; and to shew the freeness of his grace, he chose the foolish and weak things of this world, and things that are not; that no flesh should glory in his presence: and as he chose those persons to be holy, and to bring them to a state of holiness and happiness, and in a way consistent with his justice; he has pitched upon means the wisest that could be devised, even " sanctification of the Spirit, and belief of the truth; the obedience and sprinkling of the blood of Jesus," the righteousness and death of Christ, 2 Thess. ii. 13. 1 Pet. i. 2. So that this decree stands firm and stable; not on the foot of men's works, but upon the will of God; the election always obtains, or its end is answered: those that are ordained to eternal life most surely believe; and they that are predestinated to it, are most certainly " called, justified and glorified," Acts xiii. 48. Rom. viii. 30. The subordinate end of election, is the salvation of the elect; that is what they are appointed to, 1 Thess. v. 9. the scheme and plan of which salvation is so wisely formed, that it is called the

F

manifold wisdom of God, in which there are various displays of it, Eph. iii. 10. and particularly, *the counsel of peace*, which was between the Father and the Son, Zech. vi. 13. for "God was in Christ reconciling the world of his elect unto himself," planning the scheme of their peace and reconciliation; *not imputing their trespasses* unto them; for then no reconciliation could have been made; but to Christ, by whom atonement is made, and so salvation effected. But of the wisdom of God, in this decree of salvation, with respect to the Author, subjects, time, and manner, more hereafter, under another head. Moreover, the decree of God, respecting the leaving, passing by, and rejection of others, and punishing them for their sins, his end in which being for the glorifying of his justice in their condemnation, is without any imputation either of unrighteousness or folly; for *what if God, willing to show his wrath*, his indignation against sin, and *to make his power known*, in taking vengeance on sinners, *endured with much long-suffering*, their sinful course of life with much patience; even *the vessels of wrath*, justly deserving of it, *fitted for destruction* by their own sins, he appointed them to it, Rom. ix. 23. What charge of injustice or folly can be brought against him? Yea, even such decrees of God as are about the sinful actions of men, are not destitute of wisdom, of the highest wisdom. The sin and fall of Adam, so momentous, and of such consequence as to affect all mankind, could never have been without the knowledge and will of God; he could have prevented it if he would; but he left, as he decreed to leave, man to the mutability of his will; the consequence of which was his fall: and, as he designed, so in his infinite wisdom, he has overruled this greatest of all evils; the source of all that has been in the world since, for the greatest good, the salvation of men by Christ; whereby all his perfections are glorified: so the sinful actions of men are, by the permissive will of God, suffered to be, and are sometimes apparently overruled for some important end: as the selling of Joseph into Egypt by his brethren: and especially the crucifixion of Christ by the wicked Jews; both decreed by God. And so wicked men are suffered to commit the grossest sins, as Pharaoh, that God may be glorified in his justice, through inflicting his judgments on them; by the execution of which he is known, and his name celebrated with praise and glory, Exod. ix. 16.

And likewise the failings and sins of God's people serve for the humbling of them, and the exercise of their graces; and so are overruled for good. But then by this we are not authorised, nor encouraged to do evil, that good may come; God only can overrule it to serve any good purpose.

The wisdom of God is displayed in his secret transactions with Christ in the covenant of grace; it appears in making such a covenant which is *ordered in all things*, for his own glory, the glory of the three divine persons, Father, Son, and Spirit; and for the good of his people in time, and for their everlasting happiness, hereafter; being stored with promises and blessings of all sorts, peculiarly suitable for them: in appointing Christ to be the Mediator and Surety of it, and putting the said promises and blessings into his hands, and also their persons, for safety and security; all which were done in Eternity. But,

Secondly, The wisdom of God is more clearly manifested in his visible works in time; *O Lord, how manifold are thy works, in wisdom hast thou made them all!* Psalm civ. 24. And,

1st. It appears in the works of creation: the making of the heavens and the earth is always ascribed to the wisdom, understanding, and discretion of God, Psalm cxxxvi. 5. Prov. iii. 19, 20. Jer. x. 12. Whole volumes have been written on this subject, the wisdom of God in creation; and more might; the subject is not exhausted. If we look up to the starry heavens, and the luminaries, the work of his fingers, curiously wrought; as what are wrought with the fingers of men usually are; we may observe a wonderful display of divine wisdom; in the sun that rules by day, and in the moon that rules by night, and in the stars also; all which shed their benign influences on the earth: particularly in the sun, the fountain of heat and light; in the situation of it, not so far from the earth as to be of no use to it, nor so near as to hurt it; in its circular motion, either about our earth, or on its own axis, whereby nothing is hid from the heat and light of it, at one time or another; and which performs its revolutions so punctually, and with so much regularity, and so exactly answers the end of its destination, that it seems as if it was wise and knowing itself; *the sun knoweth his going down*, Psalm civ. 19. If we descend into the airy region, and could but enter into the treasures of the snow and rain, which God has in reserve there, and wisely distributes on the earth at proper times; how he binds up the water in his thick cloud, and the cloud is not rent with the weight thereof; how he balances and poises these ponderous bodies, that they are not over-set, and burst, and fall with their own weight; by which they would wash away cities, towns, and villages, and the fruits of the earth; but causes them to descend in gentle showers, and in small drops; whereby the earth becomes fruitful; we cannot but observe amazing wisdom. If we come down to the earth, we may behold, besides men, the innumerable inhabitants of it, placed on it to cultivate it; "the cattle on a thousand hills;" the pastures covered with flocks; the valleys clothed with corn; grass growing for the beasts, and herb for the service of man; "wine to make his heart glad; oil to cause his face to shine; and bread that strengthens his heart:" and in the bowels of it, metals and minerals of divers sorts, gold, silver, brass, and iron, for artificers that work in each of them; and all for the use, and to increase the wealth of men: the wisdom, as well as the goodness of God, must be discerned. The structure of the bodies of creatures is very wonderfully fitted for their different actions and uses; fishes for swimming, birds for flying, beasts for walking and running; some more slowly, and some more swiftly; but especially the texture of the human body, in all its parts, is very surprising, it being *curiously wrought;* no embroidery, or work with a needle, exceeding it: the organs of the eye are admirably fitted for seeing; the parts of the ear for hearing; the instruments of speech, the tongue, mouth, and lips, for speaking; the hands and arms for working, and feet for walking; as well as all the other parts of the body, framed and disposed for various services; to which may be added, the subserviency of all creatures to one another, and especially to man, for whose sake the world was made, and all things in it; it was designed for an habitation for him, and was made and furnished with every thing for his use and service, for his convenience and pleasure, before he was created; and when he was created, in the image of God, dominion was given him over the fishes of the sea, the fowls of the air, the beasts of the field; the herbage of the earth was provided both for meat and medicine; the cattle, some for food, some for clothing, some for carriage, and some for cultivation of the earth; and all were made for the glory of God, as the ultimate end; *for* his *pleasure they are and were created,* Rev. iv. 11. and all his works, in their way, praise him, declare his glory, and shew forth his handy-work.

2dly, The wisdom of God appears in the works of providence. It may be observed in the various returning seasons; seed-time and harvest, cold and heat, summer and winter, night and day; which keep their constant revolutions and stated course; scarce any thing ever preposterous. Rain is given from heaven, and fruitful seasons. In some of the Eastern countries, as in Canaan, rain fell but twice a year, called the former and latter rain; the one when the seed was sown, to bring it up, the other just before harvest, to plump the corn; and both constantly fell at their usual and appointed times: and where rain is very scarce, as in Egypt, the river Nile overflows its banks at a certain time of the year; which leaving a slime, makes the earth fruitful, and answers all the purposes of rain. The provision made for all creatures, suitable to their natures, is an abundant proof of the wisdom of God: as it requires wisdom, as well as faithfulness, in a steward, to give to every one under his care their portion of meat in due season; so the wisdom of God is wonderfully displayed, not only in filling men's hearts with food and gladness; but in giving to the beasts their food, every one agreeable to their nature, "and to the young ravens that cry;" in opening his hand of providence and satisfying the desires of all living; in giving largely and liberally, and in a proper time, meat to all whose eyes wait on him; even his vast numerous family of creatures. He has the charge over the earth, and disposes of the whole world, and all things in it; he sits on the circle of the earth, and beholds all that are in it, and that are done in it; he places men in different stations of life, so as to have a dependance upon, and a connection with each other: he wisely governs, rules, and over-rules all things, for the mutual good of men, and his own glory: he does all things after the counsel of his will, in the wisest and best manner, and to answer the best ends and purposes; he orders the various scenes of prosperity and adversity, and sets the one against the other; so that there is no finding any thing after him, or making them otherwise and better than they are; particularly, he maketh all things work together for the good of his people;

for the trial of their grace, and to make them meet for glory; nor is there any one trial or exercise they meet with, but what there is a necessity of it, and is for the best; yea, there is infinite wisdom in the most intricate providences, and which are now difficult to account for, and to reconcile to the promises and perfections of God; but when the mystery of providence is finished, and the judgments of God are made manifest, and all are seen in one view, in an harmonious connection together; the wisdom of God, in every part, will appear striking and amazing; as when a man looks on the wrong side of a piece of tapestry, or only views it in detached pieces; he is scarcely able to make any thing of it; nor can he discern art and beauty in it; but when it is all put together, and viewed on its right side, the wisdom, the contrivance, and art of the maker are observed with admiration.

3dly, The wisdom of God is to be seen in the great work of redemption and salvation by Christ; *herein he hath abounded towards us in all wisdom and prudence*, Eph. i. 7, 8. Wisdom and prudence are displayed in other works of God; but in this *all* wisdom and prudence, and that in abundance, and which appear,

1. In pitching upon the person to be the Redeemer; not any of the sinful race of men, for they having all sinned, all need a Redeemer; nor can any one redeem himself, and much less redeem another: nor any of the angels; for whatever goodwill they might bear to such work, none were equal to it; and therefore God put no trust in them, nor committed any such trust unto them; but his own Son, him he appointed and fore-ordained to be the Redeemer of his chosen people; the middle person in the Trinity, and most proper to be the Mediator; the Word that was in the beginning with God, and was God, and by whom all things were made, and so equal to such an undertaking; the Son of God; and it was more seemly and suitable to his relation and character, as a Son, to be appointed, to be sent, and to obey, than either of the other persons, and particularly the Father; and by having two natures, divine and human, united in one person, the Immanuel, God with us, God manifest in the flesh, he was the fittest person to be employed in this service; partaking of both natures, he was the only proper person to be the Mediator between God and Man, to be the day's-man, and lay his hand on both, and reconcile those two parties at variance, and to do what respected both, even "things pertaining to God, and to make reconciliation for the sins of the people." Being man, he could have compassion, as he had, on the lost miserable race of men, and in his love and pity redeem them; he was capable of being made under the law, and yielding obedience to it; which, being broken by the sin of men, was necessary to his redemption of them, and of suffering the penalty of the law, death; both which have been done by him, and thereby the law is magnified, and made more honourable, than it could have been by the obedience of all the angels in heaven, or by the sufferings of all the damned in hell; and hereby also satisfaction was made for sin, in the same nature that sinned, which seemed necessary, or, however, it was a wise disposition, that so it should be. But what most of all displays the wisdom of God in this affair, is, that since all human nature was depraved and corrupted with sin, how a clean and sinless nature could be produced out of an unclean one, which yet was necessary to making atonement for sin in it; which difficulty infinite wisdom, and almighty power, have surmounted by Christ's birth of a virgin, under the overshadowing of the Holy Ghost; whence what was born of her was the holy Thing, and so could be, and was offered up, without spot to God. Add to this, that it was not an human person, but an human nature, Christ assumed; it was flesh he took, the seed of Abraham, and is called the holy Thing, but not a person; it never subsisted of itself, but from the moment of its production was taken into union with the person of the Son of God; which was wisely ordered for our good, and the glory of God; for had it been a distinct person of itself, the actions and sufferings of it would have been finite, and of no benefit to mankind; his righteousness would have been, though pure and spotless, but the righteousness of a creature; and could have been of no use, but to itself: whereas, through the union of the human nature to the person of the Son of God, it became the righteousness of God, and so imputable to many. Once more, through Christ's being man, he became our near kinsman, flesh of our flesh, and bone of our bone; and so the right of redemption belonged to him; hence the same word *Goel*, in the Hebrew language, signifies both a redeemer and a near kinsman.

But then the person pitched upon to be the Redeemer, is God as well as man; and so as he had pity for men as man, he had a zeal for God, and his glory, as a divine person; and would be, as he was, concerned for the glorifying all his divine perfections, one as well as another. Being God, he could put an infinite virtue into his actions and sufferings, as man, whereby the end of them would be sufficiently answered. Hence his righteousness is the righteousness of God, and is unto all, and upon all them that believe; his blood, the blood of the Son of God, which cleanses from all sin; his sacrifice, the sacrifice of his whole human nature, in union with himself, a divine person; and so sufficient to put away sin, by a full satisfaction for it; being God, he could support the human nature, under the weight of all the sins of his people, and of all the wrath and punishment due unto them; which otherwise must have been intolerable. Being the mighty God, he was mighty to save, and his own arm has wrought out salvation. The great God is our Saviour. Now the finding out such a fit person to be the Redeemer of men, is to be ascribed solely to the wisdom of God: had all men been summoned together, and this declared unto them, that God was willing they should be redeemed, could they pitch upon a proper person to redeem them; and had the angels been called in to assist with their counsel, after long consultation, they would never have been able to have proposed one fit for this work: for who could have thought of the Son of God, and proposed his becoming man, and suffering, and dying in the stead of men, to redeem them? this is *nodus deo vindice dignus;* what God only could have found out; and he claims it to himself; *I, the only wise God, have found a ransom,* Job xxxiii. 24. See Psalm lxxxix. 19, 20.

2. The wisdom of God appears in the persons fixed upon to be redeemed; not all men, but some; partly to shew the sovereignty of God, in redeeming whom he pleases; and partly, since all had sinned, and were deserving of death, to glorify his grace and mercy in the redemption of some, and his justice in the destruction of others; and in both to shew that he could, in right, have destroyed them all, if he pleased; and likewise, that it might appear he was no respecter of persons, he has not limited the grace of redemption to any particular family or nation; but has redeemed some out of every nation, tongue, kindred, and people; and whereas his view therein is to magnify the riches of his grace, in order to shew the freeness of it; he sent Christ to die for, and redeem, not the good and the righteous, who appeared so to themselves and others, but ungodly sinners, the worst and chief of sinners, Rom. v. 6, 7, 8, 10.

3. The wisdom of God may be observed in the way and manner in which redemption is obtained; which being by the price of the blood of Christ, and in a way of full satisfaction to law and justice; the different claims of mercy and justice, which seemed to clash with one another, are reconciled; mercy insisting that the sinner be pardoned and saved, that it might be glorified; and justice requiring that the law should take place, its sentence be executed, and punishment inflicted, that so the rights and honours of law and justice might be maintained; which, by this happy method wisdom has pitched upon, they both agree; "mercy and truth meet together, righteousness and peace kiss each other." Sin is condemned in the flesh of Christ, vengeance is taken on it, punishment inflicted for it, and yet the sinner saved from sin, from condemnation, wrath, and ruin. Redemption is also wrought out in a way most mortifying to Satan. Through envy he sought the ruin of men; contrived it, brought it about, and triumphed in it: but what a mortification must it be to that proud spirit, that one of the woman's seed he had ruined, should bruise his head; that the Son of God should be manifested in human nature, to destroy his works, to destroy himself, to spoil his principalities, and redeem mankind; and be exalted in the same nature, to the highest pitch of honour and glory imaginable; to sit at the right-hand of God; angels, authorities, principalities, and powers, subject to him!

4. The wisdom of God is to be discerned in the time of man's redemption; which was the most opportune and seasonable; it was in due time; in the fulness of time fixed and agreed upon between the Father and the Son, and must be the fittest; it was after the faith and patience of God's people had been sufficiently tried, even for the space of four thousand years from the first hint of a Redeemer; after the Saviour, and his sacrifice, had been prefigured, by types, shadows, and sacrifices, for so long a time, and the use, end, and efficacy of sacrifices had been sufficiently

known, and God would have them no longer; then said Christ, *Lo, I come,* &c. when the Gentile world was covered with darkness, blindness, and ignorance, and abounded with all kind of wickedness; when immorality, formality, hypocrisy, and neglect of the word and worship of God among the Jews prevailed; by all which it may be most clearly seen, there was need of a Saviour and Redeemer; for *who can declare his generation,* the wickedness of it? then, in the infinite wisdom of God, Christ was sent to redeem sinners.

4thly, The wisdom of God shines in the Gospel, the good news of salvation by Christ; in its doctrines, and in its ordinances; that itself is called, *the wisdom of God in a mystery; the hidden wisdom; the manifold wisdom of God;* 1 Cor. ii. 7. Eph. iii. 10. every doctrine is a display of it; to instance only in justification, and the pardon of sin. Justification is by the free grace of God, and yet in strict justice; grace provided Christ to work out a righteousness; grace accepts of it in the room and stead of sinners, and grace imputes it to them: the righteousness of Christ, by which men are justified, is commensurate to the law and justice of God; so that "God is just, whilst the justifier of him that believes in Jesus:" the grace of faith is wisely appointed to receive this righteousness; it is of faith, that it might appear to be of grace, and that pride and boasting might be excluded; which, had any other been appointed, would not have been so apparent; this being a soul-humbling, a soul-emptying grace, which receives all from God, and gives him all the glory. Pardon of sin is of free grace, and yet through the blood of Christ; and is both an act of grace and of justice; God is just and faithful to forgive it, as well as gracious and merciful; he forgives sin, and takes vengeance on the inventions of the sinner; pardon proceeds upon the foot of satisfaction, which grace provides; and so both grace and justice agree in it, and are glorified by it. The ordinances of the Gospel are wisely instituted to answer the end of them; baptism to represent the overwhelming sufferings of Christ, his burial, and resurrection from the dead: the ordinance of the supper, to shew forth his death; the bread broken is a proper emblem of his broken body; the wine poured out, of his blood shed, and his soul poured out unto death for sinners. Wisely has God appointed men, and not angels, to minister the word and administer ordinances; "men of the same passions with others;" who may be heard and conversed with, without dread and terror; frail, mortal men, earthen vessels, in which this treasure is put, that the excellency of the power may be of God, and not of men; and a standing ministry is wisely fixed, to be continued to the end of the world, for the use, relief, refreshment, and comfort of God's people, as well as the conversion of sinners; and all for the glory of God.

5thly, The wisdom of God may be seen in the government and preservation of the church of God, in all ages; in guiding them by immediate revelation, without the written word, when the church was in a few families, and the lives of men long; then with written laws, statutes, and ordinances, suited to the infant state of the church, among the people of Israel; and now with ordinances, more agreeable to its adult state, under the gospel dispensation, throughout the world: and as it is a church and kingdom not of this world, it is supported, not by worldly, but spiritual means; and wonderfully has it been preserved in all ages, and increased, amidst all the persecutions of men; no weapon formed against it has prospered; and God has made it, and will still more make it to appear, that he rules in Jacob unto the ends of the earth.

CHAP. XI.

OF THE WILL OF GOD, AND THE SOVEREIGNTY OF IT.

HAVING considered the attributes of God which belong to his understanding, as an intelligent Spirit, his knowledge and wisdom, I now proceed to consider his Will, and the sovereignty of it. And shall,

I. Prove that there is a Will in God; for in all intelligent beings there is a will, as well as an understanding; as in angels and men, so in God; as he has an understanding which is infinite and unsearchable; so he has a will, to do what he knows is most fitting to be done. His understanding influences and guides his will, and his will determines all his actions; and his will being thus wisely directed, is called, *the counsel of his will,* Eph. i. 11. A will is frequently ascribed to God in Scripture; *The will of the Lord be done,* Acts xxi. 14. *Who has resisted his will,* Rom. ix. 19. *Having made known unto us the mystery of his will*, Eph. i. 9. and in many other places; the will of God is no other than God himself willing; it is essential to him; it is his nature and essence; it is not to be separated, or to be considered as distinct from it, or as a part of it, of which it is composed; which would be contrary to the simplicity of God; or to his being a simple, uncompounded Spirit; which has been established. Will is ascribed to each of the divine persons; to the Father, John vi. 39, 40. to the Son, as a divine person, John v. 21. and xvii. 24. and who also, as man, has a will distinct from that, though subjected to it, John vi. 38. Luke xxii. 42. and to the Spirit, who is said to forbid, and not to suffer some things to be done; that is, to nill them; and to nill is an act of the will, as well as to will, Acts xvi. 6, 7. and he is said to divide his gifts to men severally, as he *will*, 1 Cor. xii. 11. And these three, as they are the one God, they agree in one, in one mind and will.

II. I shall next shew what the will of God is: there is but one will in God; but for our better understanding it, it may be distinguished. I shall not trouble the reader with all the distinctions of it made by men; some are false, and others vain and useless; such as into absolute and conditional, antecedent and consequent, effectual and ineffectual, &c. the distinction of the *secret* and *revealed* will of God has generally obtained among sound divines; the former is properly the will of God, the latter only a manifestation of it. Whatever God has determined within himself, whether to do himself, or to do by others, or to suffer to be done, whilst it is in his own breast, and is not made known by any event in providence, or by prophecy, that is his secret will: such are the deep things of God, the thoughts of his heart, the counsels and determinations of his mind; which are impenetrable to others; but when these open, by events in providence, or by prophecy, then they become the revealed will of God. God's secret will becomes revealed by events in providence, whether it be considered general or special; the general providence of God, with respect to the world and church, is no other than the execution, and so the manifestation of his secret will, with respect to both: to the world, its production, the origin of nations, the settlement of them in the various parts of the world; the rise of states and kingdoms, and particularly the four monarchies, and the succession of them: to the church, in the line of Seth, from Adam, and in the line of Shem, from Noah, and in the people of Israel, from Abraham, to the coming of Christ: and the book of Revelation is a discovery of the secret will of God with respect to both, from the coming of Christ, to the end of the world; the greatest part of which has been fulfilled, and the rest will be; as the destruction of antichrist, and the antichristian states; the conversion of the Jews, and the bringing in of the fulness of the Gentiles; and the spiritual and personal kingdom of Christ. These are now already revealed, though the time when they will take place is still in the secret will of God. The providence of God may be considered as special with respect to particular persons; there is a purpose or secret will of God, with respect to every man; and there is a time fixed for every purpose; a time to be born, and a time to die; and for every thing that befals men between their birth and death: all which open in time, in providence; and what was secret becomes revealed: so we know that we are born, who our parents, the time and circumstances of our birth, as related to us; we know what has befallen us, whether in an adverse or prosperous way; God has performed what is appointed for us, as Job says of himself; but then, as he observes, *many such things are with him*, in his secret will. We know not what shall befal us; and though we know that we shall die, that is revealed; but when and where, in what manner and circumstance, we know not; that remains in the secret will of God. Some things which belong to the secret will of God become revealed by prophecy; so it was made known to Abraham, that his seed, according to the secret will or purpose of God, should be in a land, not theirs, four hundred years, and be afflicted, and come out with great substance: nor did God hide from Abraham, what he secretly willed to do, in destroying Sodom and Gomorrah: and, indeed, it has been usual for the Lord to do nothing but what he reveals to his servants the prophets; particularly all things concerning Christ, his incarnation, offices, obedience, sufferings, and death, and the glory that should follow, were all signified beforehand, to the prophets, by the Spirit of Christ in them.

The will of God, which he would have done by men, is revealed in the law, that is called *his will*, Rom. ii. 18. This was made known to Adam, by inscribing it on his heart, whereby he knew his duty to God, to be performed by him; this, though sadly obliterated by sin, yet there are some remains of it in the Gentiles, who do by nature the things contained in it; which shew the work of the law written in their hearts: a new edition of this law, was delivered to the Israelites, written on tables of stone, by the finger of God; according to which they were to behave themselves, and hold the tenure of the land of Canaan, and enjoy the privileges of it: and in regeneration the law of God is put into the inward parts, and written on the hearts of God's people; who being transformed, by the renewing of their minds, come to know what is the good, perfect, and acceptable will of God, Rom. xii. 2. This respects man's duty, both to God and men.

There is the revealed will of God in the Gospel; which respects the kind intentions, and gracious regards of God to men; and discovers what before was his secret will concerning them; as, that he has chosen some to everlasting life and happiness; that he has appointed these to salvation by Christ; and appointed him to be their Saviour; that Christ undertook to do this will of God, and came from heaven to earth to do it, and has finished it; and that it is the will of God that these should be regenerated and sanctified; and "that they should never perish, but have everlasting life," Eph. i. 4, 5. John vi. 38. 1 Thess. iv. 3. John vi. 39, 40. Matt. xviii. 14. But then, though all this is the revealed will of God, in the Gospel, yet as to particular persons interested herein, it is, in a great measure, a secret; election of God, and so the rest, may be known by the Gospel coming with power into the heart, and by a work of grace upon it; and the knowledge of it should be sought after; yet it is not attained to but by such who are favoured with a full assurance of faith; and as to others, though it may, in a judgment of charity, because of their declared experiences, their savoury discourses, and holy conversation, be concluded of them, that they are the elect of God, &c. yet it cannot be certainly known, but by divine revelation, as it might be by the apostle, that Clement, and other fellow-labourers of his, had their names written in the book of life, Phil. iv. 3. It is the revealed will of God, that there shall be a resurrection of the dead, both of the just and unjust; and that all must appear before the judgment-seat of Christ; that after death there will be a judgment; and though it is revealed, that a day is fixed, as well as a person appointed to judge the world in righteousness; yet "of that day and hour knows no man;" no, not the angels; but God only. So that, upon the whole, though there is some foundation for this distinction of the secret and revealed will of God, yet it is not quite clear; there is a mixture, part of the will of God is, as yet, secret, and part of it revealed, with respect to the same subject, as what has been observed plainly shews.

The most accurate distinction of the will of God, is into that of precept and purpose; or the commanding and decreeing will of God.

God's will of precept, or his commanding will, is that which is often spoken of in Scripture; as what should be done by men, and which is desirable they might have knowledge of, and be complete in, Matt. vii. 21. and xii. 50. Col. i. 10. and iv. 12. This is the rule of men's duty; which consists of the fear of God, and keeping his commands; this is done but by a few, and by none perfectly; every sin is a transgression of it; when it is done aright it is done in faith, from love, and to the glory of God: every good man desires to do it in the best manner, and, if it could be, perfectly; even as it is done by angels in heaven. God, by the declaration of this his will, shews what he approves of, and what is acceptable to him, when done aright; and is made to render men inexcusable that do it not, and to make it appear right in justice to inflict punishment on such persons.

The decreeing will of God is only, properly speaking, his Will; the other is his Word: this is the rule of his own actions; he does all things in heaven and earth after his will, the counsel of it; and this will is always done, cannot be resisted, frustrated, and made void; he does whatever he wills; "his counsel stands, and the thoughts of his heart are to all generations;" and this is sometimes fulfilled by those who have no regard to his will of precept, and have no knowledge of this, even while they are doing it; as Herod and Pontius Pilate, the Jews and Gentiles, in doing what they did against Christ, Acts iv. 27, 28. and the ten kings, into whose hearts God put it to fulfil his will, in giving their kingdoms to the beast,

Rev. xvii. 17. and this will of God should be bore in mind in every thing we intend to do or go about; saying, if the Lord will, we will do this, and that, and the other, 1 Cor. iv. 19. James iv. 13, 14, 15. and this should be owned and acknowledged, and submitted to in every state and condition of life, whether of prosperity or adversity, or in whatsoever befals us in our own persons, or in our friends and relations, Acts xxi. 14. and this, properly speaking, is the one and only will of God. I shall next inquire,

III. What are the objects of it.

First, God himself, not his Being, perfections, and modes of subsisting; as the paternity of the Father; the generation of the Son; and the spiration of the Spirit. These naturally and necessarily exist, and do not depend upon the will of God: but it is his own glory; *The Lord hath made all things for himself;* that is, for his own glory, Prov. xvi. 4. He wills his own glory in all he does; as *all things are of him*, as the efficient Cause; and *through him*, as the wise Disposer of them; so they are *to him*, to his glory, as the final Cause, and last end of all; and this he wills necessarily; he cannot but will his own glory; as "he will not give his glory to another;" he cannot will it to another; that would be to deny himself.

Secondly, All things without himself, whether good or evil, are the objects of his will, or what his will is some way or other concerned in: there is a difference, indeed, between the objects of God's knowledge and power, and the objects of his will; for though he knows all things knowable, in his understanding, and his power reaches to all that is possible, though not made; yet he wills not all things willable, if the word may be allowed, or that might be willed; wherefore, as Amesius[1] observes, though God is said to be omniscient and omnipotent, yet not omnivolent.

1st, All good things.—1. All things in nature; all things are made by him, and all were originally good that were made by him, even *very good:* and all were made according to his will; *Thou hast created all things, and for thy pleasure;* or by thy will, *they are and were created*, Rev. iv. 11. even the heavens, earth, and sea, and all that in them are.—2. All things in providence. God's kingdom of providence rules over all, and extends to all creatures, angels and men, and every other, and to all events that befal them; not a sparrow falls to the ground without the will of God; *He doth according to his will in the army of heaven; and among the inhabitants of the earth,* Dan. iv. 35. there is nothing comes to pass but what God has willed, ordered, and appointed; *Who is he that saith, and it cometh to pass, when the Lord commandeth it not?* Lam. iii. 37.—3. All things in grace are according to the will of God, all spiritual blessings in Christ, all grace given to the elect in Christ, before the world was; the choice of them in Christ; predestination to adoption by him; redemption through his blood; regeneration, sanctification, and the eternal inheritance; all are according to the good pleasure of his will, 2 Tim. i. 9. Eph. i. 3, 4, 5, 7, 9, 11. James i. 18. 1 Thess. iv. 3.

2dly, All evil things are the objects of God's will; which are of two sorts.— 1. *Malum pœnæ*, the evil of afflictions; whether in a way of chastisement, or of punishment: if in a way of chastisement, as they are to the people of God, they are according to the will of God; they do not spring out of the dust, nor come by chance; but are by the will, order, and appointment of God; as to quality, quantity, duration, ends, and uses, Job xxiii. 14. Mic. vi. 9. 1 Thess. iii. 3. and which are consistent with the justice, holiness, wisdom, love, and goodness of God. If they are in a way of punishment, as they are to wicked and ungodly men; there is no reason to complain of them, since they are less than their sins deserve; and not at all unworthy of a righteous God to will to inflict on them, Lam. iii. 39. all judgments, calamities, and distresses, which come upon kingdoms, nations, cities, towns, and particular persons, are all of God, and according to his will, Amos iii. 6. Not that God wills these things for the sake of them; or as taking delight in the afflictions and miseries of his creatures, Lam. iii. 33. Ezek. xviii. 32. but for the sake of some good: the afflictions of his people are for their spiritual good, as well as for his own glory: and the punishment of the wicked is for the glorifying of his justice.—2. There is *malum culpæ*, or the evil of fault and blame, that is sin: about this there is some difficulty how the will of God should be concerned in it, consistent with his purity and holiness: that the will of God is some way or

---

[1] Medulla Theolog. l. 1. c. 7. s. 47.

other concerned with it is most certain; for he either wills it or not wills it: the latter cannot be said, because nothing comes to pass, God not willing it, Lam. iii. 37. or he neither wills it, nor not wills it; that is, he has no care about it, nor concern at all with it; and so it is without the verge, and not within the reach of his providence; which cannot be admitted, and which none will say, but those who are atheistically inclined, see Ezek. ix. 9. Zeph. i. 12. Besides, as Beza,[2] and other divines argue, unless God had voluntarily permitted sin to be, there could be no display, neither of his punitive justice, nor of his mercy: to which may be added, that God's foreknowledge of sin most fully proves his will in it; that God foreknew sin would be, is certain; as the fall of Adam; since he made a provision, in Christ, for the saving of men out of it, before it was; and so other sins; see 2 Sam. xii. 11. and xvi. 22. Now certain and immutable foreknowledge, such as the foreknowledge of God, is founded upon some certain and immutable cause; which can be no other than the divine will; God foreknows, certainly, that such and such things will be; because he has determined in his will they shall be. To set this affair in the best light, it will be proper to consider, what is in sin, and relative to it: there is the act of sin, and there is the guilt of sin, which is an obligation to punishment, and the punishment itself. Concerning the two last there can be no difficulty; that God should will that men that sin should become guilty; be reckoned, accounted, and treated as such; or lie under obligation to punishment; nor that he should will the punishment of them, and appoint and foreordain them to it for it, Prov. xvi. 4. Jude ver. 4. The only difficulty is, about the act of sin; and this may be considered either as natural or moral; or the act, and the ataxy, disorder, irregularity, and vitiosity of it: as an action, barely considered, it is of God, and according to his will; without which, and the concourse of his providence, none can be performed; he is the fountain and source of all action and motion; in him all live, move, and have their being, Acts xvii. 28. but then the vitiosity and irregularity of it, as it is an aberration from the law of God, and a transgression of it, is of men only; and God cannot be said to will this; he forbids it, he abhors and detests it; he takes no pleasure in it; he is of purer eyes than even to behold it with approbation and delight. God cannot will it as sin, or for the sake of itself; but for the sake of some good to be brought about through it; as the fall of Adam, for the glorifying of his justice and mercy, in punishing some of his posterity, and saving others: the sin of Joseph's brethren selling him into Egypt, for the good of Joseph and his Father's family, and others; and the sin of the Jews, in crucifying Christ, for the redemption and salvation of men. And besides, God may will one sin as a punishment for another; as it is most certain he has in the case of the Israelites, Hos. iv. 9, 10, 13. of the heathen philosophers, Rom. i. 28. and of the papists, 2 Thess. ii. 9—12. Once more, though God may be said, in such senses, to will sin, yet he wills it in a different way than he wills that which is good; he does not will to do it himself, nor to do it by others; but permits it to be done; and which is not a bare permission, but a voluntary permission; and is expressed by God's *giving* up men to their own heart's lusts, and by *suffering* them to walk in their own sinful ways, Psalm lxxxi. 12. Acts xiv. 16. he wills it not by his effective will, but by his permissive will; and therefore cannot be chargeable with being the author of sin; since there is a wide difference between doing it himself, and doing it by others, or ordering it to be done, which only can make him the author of sin; and voluntarily permitting or suffering it to be done by others. I proceed to consider,

IV. The nature and properties of the will of God. And,

First, It is natural and *essential* to him; it is his very nature and essence; his will is himself willing; and therefore there can be but one will in God; for there is but one God, whose nature and essence is one; for though there are three persons in the Godhead, there is but one undivided nature common to them all, and so but one will: they are one, and they agree in one; God is *in one mind*, or will; though there may be distinctions of his will, and different objects of it, and divers ways in which he wills, yet it is by one single eternal act of his will he wills all things. Hence also his will is incommunicable to a creature; the will of God cannot otherwise be a

---

[2] Vide Maccov. Loc. Commun. c. 24. p. 195.

creature's, but as that may approve of it, acquiesce in it, and submit unto it; even it was incommunicable to the human nature of Christ, though taken into union with the person of the Son of God; yet his divine will, and his human will, are distinct from each other, though the one is subject to the other, John vi. 38. Luke xxii. 42.

Secondly, The will of God is *eternal*, as may be concluded from the attribute of *eternity*; for if God is eternal, as he certainly is, even from everlasting to everlasting God, then his will must be eternal, since it is his nature and essence: and from his *immutability*; who changes not, and with whom there is no shadow of turning; but if any new will arises in God in time, which was not in eternity, there would be a change in him; he would not be the same in time he was in eternity; nor the same in eternity he is in time; whereas, he is the same yesterday, to-day, and for ever: and from the *foreknowledge* of God, which is eternal; *Known unto God are all his works, from the beginning of the world*, or from eternity, Acts xv. 18. and now as God's foreknowledge arises from his will, God foreknows what will be, as has been observed, because he has determined in his will, what shall be; so if his knowledge is eternal, his will must be eternal. Likewise, this may be illustrated by the decree of *election*; that was, certainly, before men had done either good or evil; was from the beginning, or from everlasting; even before the foundation of the world, Eph. i. 4. and as the decree and determination of the will of God was so early, the same may be concluded of all others: add to all which, the will of God is concerned with *all things* that have been *from the beginning* of the world, now are, or shall be to the end of it; and therefore must be prior to the existence of the world, and things in it; and if prior to them, then prior to time; and if prior to time, must be eternal; for we know of nothing before time but what is eternal.

Thirdly, The will of God is *immutable*; immutability is expressly ascribed to the counsel of God; that is, to the will and purpose of God, Heb. vi. 17. and may be established from the attribute of *immutability*; for if God is unchangeably the same, as he is, then his will must be the same, since it is his nature and essence: a change is made in the will of a creature, either by beginning to will what it did not before, or by ceasing to will what it has willed: now the cause of beginning a new will, or willing what it did not, supposes previous ignorance of the thing now begun to be willed; not knowing the fitness and propriety of it, being ignorant of its nature, excellence, and utility; for of an unknown thing there can be no desire and will: but such a change of will can never take place in God, on such a footing; since it is not only contrary to his eternity and immutability, but to his knowledge, whose understanding is infinite: or a creature changes its will, when it ceases to will what it has willed; which is either of choice, or of obligation to it; of choice, when something unforeseen occurs, which causes it to change its will, and take another course: but nothing of this kind can befal God, before whom all things are at once and together, naked and open; even from all eternity: or else of force, being obliged unto it, because it cannot accomplish its will, and therefore drops it, and takes another course: *But who hath resisted his will*, the will of God, so as to cause him to cease from it, and drop it? If God changes his will, it must be either for the better or the worse; and either way it would betray imperfection in him, and want of wisdom; God may change his outward dispensations of things, but he never changes his will: repentance attributed to him is no proof of it; *He is in one mind, and who can turn him?* his will is not to be turned nor altered, no not by the prayers of his people. But of these things, see more under the attribute of *immutability*, before treated of.

Fourthly, The will of God is always efficacious; there are no wishes, wouldbees, or feeble velleities in God; his will is always effected, never made null and void; he does whatever he pleases, or wills; his counsel always stands, and he ever does his pleasure: otherwise he would not be almighty, as he is: it must be for want of power, if his will is not fulfilled, which cannot be said; as he is omnipotent, so is his will; yea, Austin calls[3] it, his most omnipotent will: if this was not the case, there would be somewhat, or some one *superior* to him; whereas he is God over all, the most High, higher than the highest; and can never be contradicted by any: and was his will ineffectual, he would be *frustrated* and disappointed of his *end*: but as nothing comes to pass which man says,

---

[3] De Civitate Dei, 1. 13. c. 18.

and the Lord commands it not; so every thing the Lord says, wills, and orders, most certainly comes to pass; *For the Lord of hosts hath purposed, and who shall disannul* it? yea, he hath sworn, saying, *Surely, as I have thought, so shall it come to pass; and as I have purposed, so it shall stand,* Isa. xiv. 24, 27. Besides if his will was not efficacious, or it failed of accomplishment, he would not be *happy*: when a man's will is ineffectual, and he cannot accomplish it, it gives him uneasiness, it makes him unhappy; but this can never be said of God, who is the blessed, the blessed God, blessed for evermore.

Fifthly, The will of God has *no cause* out of himself; for then there would be something prior to him, and greater and more excellent than he; as every cause is before its effect, and more excellent than that; and his will would be dependent on another, and so he not be the independent Being he is: nor can there be any impulsive or moving cause of his will; because there is in him no passive power to work upon; he is purely act, *actus simplicissimus,* a pure, active Spirit: if he consisted of act and power, he would not be the simple and uncompounded Spirit he is; wherefore, to be impelled or moved by any cause, would be contrary to his simplicity, before established: he may indeed be said to will one thing for another; but then that which he wills for another, is no moving cause of his will; these may have the nature of cause and effect between themselves; but neither of them the cause of the will of God; nor is there any final cause of what he wills and does but his own glory; and it would be madness to seek for a cause of his willing that: and from this property of the will of God, it may be clearly discerned, that foreseen faith, holiness, and good works, cannot be the cause of God's will in the election of any to eternal life; and so the contrary, no cause of his will in the rejection of others.

Sixthly, The will of God, for the same reason, is not conditional; for then it would be dependent on the condition to be performed; and not the will of God, but the performance of the condition, would be the first and chief in the attainment of the end thereby. And, to say no more, if, for instance, God willed to save all men conditionally; that is, on condition of faith and repentance; and to damn them if these conditions are wanting; who does not see that this conditional will, to save and to destroy, is equally the same? destruction is equally willed as salvation; and where is the general love of God to men, so much talked of? there is none at all to any.

Seventhly, The will of God is most free and sovereign; as appears,

1. From the making of the world, and all things in it. That the world is eternal, few have asserted; that it was made, and made by God, is generally agreed; and by the will of God, as the scriptures assert, Rev. iv. 11. and the making of it, as to time and order, and things contained in it, is owing to the sovereign will of God; to what else but to his sovereignty can it be ascribed, that he has not made more worlds than he has, who could, if he would, have made ten thousand worlds? or that he should make this world when he did, and not sooner, when he could have made it millions of ages before, if he would? or that he should be six days making that, and all things in it, when he could have made them all in a moment, if he pleased? or that he made this world no larger than it is, and made no more kinds and species of creatures than he has, and those he has made no more numerous than they be? no reason can be assigned, but his sovereign will and pleasure.

2. The sovereignty of the will of God appears in providence, and in the various events of it; as in the births and deaths of men, which are neither of them of the will of men, but of the will of God; and there is a time for both fixed by his will; and in which his sovereignty may be seen; for to what else can it be ascribed, that such and such men should be born, and brought into the world, in such an age, and not before; and that they should go out of the world at the time, in the manner and circumstances they do? and that there should be such difference in men, in their states, conditions, and circumstances in life; that some should be rich, and others poor? riches and poverty are both at the disposal of God, as Agur's prayer shews; and God is the maker both of the rich and poor, not only as men, but as rich and poor men: and to what can this difference be attributed, but to the sovereign will of God? some are raised to great honour and dignity; and others live in a very low, mean, and abject state; but promotion comes neither from the East, nor from the West, nor from the South; but God puts down one, and sets up another, as he pleases; and these differences and changes may be

observed in the same persons, as in Job, who was for many years the greatest man in all the East, and, on a sudden, was stripped of all his riches, honour, and glory, and upon a dunghill; and then, after a while, restored to twice the wealth and riches he had before. So Nebuchadnezzar, the greatest monarch then on earth, and when in the most flourishing circumstances, and in the height of his grandeur, was degraded from his dignity, as a man and monarch, and driven to dwell among beasts, and to become and live like one of them; and after all, was restored to his reason, and to his throne, and former greatness; which extorted from him such an acknowledgment of the sovereign will of God as perhaps is no where more strongly expressed; *He doth according to his will in the army of heaven, and among the inhabitants of the earth; and none can stay his hand, or say unto him, what dost thou?* Dan. iv. 35. Some are free from sickness and diseases of body all their days; their strength is firm, and no bands in their death, but die in their full strength: whilst others drag on a life attended with a variety of infirmities and disorders, to their graves; and this is the case of the best of men: to what can it be imputed, but to the sovereign will of God? and how otherwise can be accounted for the many abortions, untimely births, infants that never saw light; and others, as soon as their eyes are opened in this world, are shut again; when others not only go through the stages of infancy, childhood, and manhood, but arrive to a full age, and come to their graves like a shock of corn fully ripe? And a multitude of other things might be observed, in providence; which, though God has wise reasons for them, are unaccountable to us, but are obliged to refer them to his sovereign will and pleasure; who gives no account of his matters to the children of men.

3. The will of God appears to be sovereign in things sacred, spiritual, and religious, both with respect to angels and men; as that some of the angels should be elect, and confirmed by the grace of Christ, in the estate in which they were created, and be preserved from apostasy, whilst a large number of them were suffered to rebel against God, and leave their first state; for which they were cast down from heaven, to hell, and reserved in chains of darkness, to the judgment of the great day, and no mercy shewn to any of them; as has been to many of the apostate race of Adam. What other reason can be given for all this, but the sovereign will of God? Among men, some God loves, and some he hates; and that before good or evil are done by them; some he chooses to everlasting happiness, and others he passes by and rejects; he has mercy on some, and hardens others; just as he, in his sovereignty, wills and pleases: some are redeemed from among men, by Christ, even out of every kindred, tongue, people, and nation, whom he wills, and resolves to save; when others are left to perish in their sins; for which no other cause can be assigned than the sovereign will and pleasure of God. According to which also he dispenses his gifts to men, and these of different sorts; some fitting for public service, as to ministers of the gospel; and such he makes whensoever he pleases, and gives them gifts differing from one another; to some greater to others less, to some one talent and to others five, dividing to every man severally as he wills, according to his sovereign pleasure: the means of grace, the ministry of the word and ordinances, in all ages, have been disposed of, just as seemed good in his sight; for many hundreds of years, God gave his word to Jacob, and his statutes unto Israel, and other nations knew them not; and these have been since distributed among the Gentiles, sometimes in one place, and sometimes in another; and how apparent is the sovereignty of God in favouring our British Isles, these Isles afar off, with the gospel, and gospel-ordinances, when so great a part of the world is denied them, and is covered with Pagan, Papal, and Mahometan darkness? and still more it is manifest in that these outward means are, to some, "the savour of life unto life, and to others the savour of death unto death." The special gifts of the grace of God, are bestowed upon men according to the sovereign will of God; of his own will he regenerates some, and not others; calls by his grace, whom he pleases, when and by what means, according to his purpose; reveals the gospel, and the great things of it, to whom he would make them known; and hides them from the wise and prudent; *even so Father*, says Christ, *for so it seemed good in thy sight;* nor does he give any other reason for such a conduct. The graces of the Spirit of God are given to some, and not to others; as for instance, repentance, which is a grant from God, a

gift of Christ, was bestowed on Peter, who denied his Lord; and withheld from Judas, that betrayed him. Faith, which is the gift of God, all men have it not; to some it is only given, when others have a spirit of slumber, eyes that they see not, and ears that they hear not. In short, eternal life, which is the free gift of God, through Christ, is given only by him, to as many as the Father has given him, and to these alike; the penny, which seems to mean eternal happiness, in the parable, is given to those who were called to labour in the vineyard in the eleventh hour, as to those who bore the heat and burden of the day: some do much service for Christ, and others very little, and yet all share the same glory. To what can all this be resolved, but into the sovereign will of God? who says, *Is it not lawful for me to do what I will with my own?* Matt. xx. 15. But though the will of God is sovereign, it always acts wisely: some sovereign princes will things rashly and foolishly; but God wills nothing contrary to his perfections of wisdom, justice, holiness, &c. and his will is therefore called *counsel*, and *the counsel of his will*, Isa. xxv. 1. and xlvi. 10. Eph. i. 11.

CHAP. XII.

OF THE LOVE OF GOD.

NEXT to the attributes which belong to God, as an intelligent Spirit, to his understanding and will, may be considered, those which may be called *Affections;* for though, properly speaking, there are none in God, he being a most pure and simple act, free from all commotion and perturbation; yet there being some things said and done by him, which are similar to affections in intelligent beings, they are ascribed to him; as love, pity, hatred, anger, &c. from which must be removed every thing that is carnal, sensual, or has any degree of imperfection in it; and among these, *Love* stands in the first place; and this enters so much into the nature of God, that it is said, *God is love*, 1 John iv. 8, 16. So the Shekinah, or the divine majesty and glory, is, by the Jews,[1] called אהבה *Love;* and the heathens give the same name to God; Plato expressly calls him *Love:* and Hesiod[2] speaks of love as the fairest and most beautiful among the immortal gods. In treating of this divine attribute, I shall,

I. Consider the objects of it. And,

1. The principal object of the love of God is himself. Self-love is in all intelligent beings; nor is it discommendable, when it is not carried to a criminal excess, and to the neglect of others; none are obliged to love others more than themselves, but as themselves, Matt. xxii. 39. God[3] first and chiefly loves himself; and hence he has made himself, that is, his glory, the ultimate end of all he does in nature, providence, and grace, Prov. xvi. 4. Rom. xi. 36. Rev. iv. 11. Eph. i. 6. and his happiness lies in contemplating himself, his nature and perfections; in that love, complacency and delight he has in himself; nor needs he, nor can he have any thing out of himself that can add to his essential happiness.

The three divine Persons in the Godhead mutually love each other; the Father loves the Son and the Spirit, the Son loves the Father and the Spirit, and the Spirit loves the Father and the Son. That the Father loves the Son, is more than once said, John iii. 35. and v. 20. and the Son is sometimes called the wellbeloved and dear Son of God, Matt. iii. 17. and xvii. 5. Col. i. 13. he was from all eternity as "one brought up with him;" and was loved by him before the foundation of the world; and that with a love of complacency and delight; as he must, since "he is the brightness of his glory, the express image of his person," and is of the same nature, and possessed of all the same perfections with him, Prov. viii. 30, 31. John xvii. 24. Heb. i. 3. Col. ii. 9. yea, he loved him as his Servant, as the Mediator, in his state of humiliation, and obedience, and under all his sufferings, and on account of them; and even whilst he bore his wrath as the sinner's surety, he was the object of his love, as his Son, Isa. xlii. 1. Matt. iii. 17. John x. 17. and now he is at his right-hand, in human nature, he looks upon him with delight, and is well pleased with his sacrifice, satisfaction, and righteousness. The Father

---

[1] Shirhashirim Rabba, fol. 15. 1. et Lex. Cabal. p. 43, 44.
[2] Theogonia, v. 120.
[3] Præclarum illud est et si quæris rectum quoque et verum, ut eos qui nobis carissimi esse debeant, æque ac nosmetipsos amemus; at vero plus fieri nullo facto potest, ne optandum quidem est in amicitia, ut me ille plus quam se amet, Cicero. Tusc. Quæst. 1. 3.

loves the Spirit; being the very breath of him, from whence he has his name, and proceeding from him, and possessing the same nature and essence with him, Job xxxiii. 4. Psalm xxxiii. 6. John xv. 26. 1 John v. 7. The Son loves the Father, of whom he is begotten, with whom he was brought up, in whose bosom he lay from all eternity, as his own and only begotten Son; and as man, the law of God was in his heart; the sum of which is to love the Lord God with all the heart and soul; and as Mediator he shewed his love to him by an obedience to his commandment, even though that was to suffer death for his people, Psalm xl. 8. John xiv. 31. and x. 18. Phil. ii. 8. The Son also loves the Spirit, since he proceeds from him, as from the Father, and is called the Spirit of the Son, Gal. iv. 6. and Christ often speaks of him with pleasure and delight, Isa. xlviii. 16. and lxi. 1. John xiv. 16, 17, 26. and xv. 26. and xvi. 7, 13. And the Spirit loves the Father and the Son, and sheds abroad the love of them both in the hearts of his people; he searches into the deep things of God, and reveals them to them; and takes of the things of Christ, and shews them unto them; and so is both the Comforter of them, and the Glorifier of him, 1 Cor. ii. 10, 11, 12. John xvi. 14.

2. All that God has made is the object of his love; all the works of creation, when he had made them, he looked over them, and saw that they were good, *very good*, Gen. i. 31. he was well pleased, and delighted with them; yea, he is said to *rejoice in his works*, Psal. civ. 31. he upholds all creatures in their beings, and is the Preserver of all, both men and beasts; and is good to all, and his tender mercies are over all his works, Psalm xxxvi. 6. and cxlv. 9. and particularly, rational creatures are the objects of his care, love, and delight: he loves the holy angels, and has shewn his love to them in choosing them to happiness; hence they are called *elect angels*, 1 Tim. v. 21. by making Christ the head of them, by whom they are confirmed in the estate in which they were created, Col. ii. 10. and by admitting them into his presence, allowing them to stand before him, and behold his face, Matt. xviii. 10. yea, even the devils, as they are the creatures of God, are not hated by him, but as they are apostate spirits from him: and so he bears a general love to all men, as they are his creatures, his offspring, and the work of his hands; he supports them, preserves them, and bestows the bounties of his providence, in common upon them, Acts xvii. 28. and xiv. 17. Matt. v. 45. but he bears a special love to elect men in Christ; which is called his *great love*, Eph. ii. 4. whom he has chosen and blessed with all spiritual blessings in him, Eph. i. 3, 4. and which love is distinguishing and discriminating, Mal. i. 1, 2. Rom. ix. 11, 12. I go on to,

II. Give some instances of the love of God, particularly to chosen men in Christ, and who share in the love of Father, Son, and Spirit.

The love of the Father has appeared in thinking of them, thoughts of peace; in contriving and forming the scheme of their peace and reconciliation in Christ, from eternity, 2 Cor. v. 18, 19. in choosing them in him from the beginning, even from everlasting, to salvation, by him, 2 Thess. ii. 13. in putting their persons into the hands of Christ, and securing and preserving them in him, Deut. xxxiii. 3. Jude ver. 1. in laying up all blessings in him for them, and blessing them with them so early, Eph. i. 3, 4. in appointing Christ to be the Saviour of them; in providing, promising, and sending him into the world, to work out their salvation, John iii. 16. 1 John iv. 9, 10. Tit. iii. 4, 5. in the pardon of their sins through the blood of Christ, Isa. xxxviii. 17. Eph. i. 7. in their adoption, 1 John iii. 1. in their regeneration and conversion, Jer. xxxi. 3. Eph. ii. 4, 5. and in the gift of eternal life unto them, Rom. vi. 23.

The love of the Son of God appears in espousing the persons of the elect, those sons of men, in whom his delights were before the world was, Prov. viii. 31. Hos. ii. 19. in becoming their Surety for good, undertaking their cause, engaging to do the will of God with that cheerfulness he did; which was to work out their salvation, Psalm xl. 6, 7, 8. Heb. vii. 22. in assuming their nature, in the fulness of time, to redeem them, work out a righteousness, and make reconciliation for them, Gal. iv. 4, 5. Rom. viii. 3, 4. Heb. ii. 14, 17. by giving himself a Sacrifice for them; laying down his life on their account; and shedding his blood for the cleansing of their souls, and the remission of their sins, Eph. v. 2, 25. Tit. ii. 14. 1 John iii. 16. Rev. i. 5.

The love of the Spirit, of which mention is made in Rom. xv. 30. appears in his coming into the hearts of God's elect, to convince them of sin and righteousness, and to comfort them; by shewing the grace of the covenant, and the blessings of it to them; by opening and applying the promises of it; and by shedding abroad the love of God and Christ in their hearts; by implanting every grace in them, and drawing them forth into exercise; by witnessing to their spirits their adoption; by assisting them in every duty, particularly in prayer, making intercession for them, according to the will of God; and in being the earnest, pledge, and seal of them to the day of redemption, John xvi. 7, 8. Rom. viii. 15, 16, 26, 27. Eph. i. 13, 14.

III. It may be proper next to consider the properties of the love of God towards chosen men, which will lead more into the nature of it. And,

1. There is no cause of it out of God; there is no motive or inducement to it in them, no loveliness in them to excite it; all men by nature are corrupt and abominable; rather to be loathed than loved; and those that are loved, are no better than others, all being under sin; and are, "by nature, children of wrath, as others; as deserving of that as those that are not loved, Rom. iii. 9. Eph. ii. 3. what loveliness or beauty is in saints, is owing to the righteousness of Christ, imputed to them; which is that comeliness that is put upon them, whereby they are made perfectly comely; and to the sanctifying grace of the Spirit, whereby they are all glorious within, and appear in the beauties of holiness: so that all this is the fruit of the love of God, and not the cause of it. Nor can it be any love in them to God, that is the cause of his to them; for they had no love in them when Christ died for them; nor until regenerated by the Spirit of God; and when they love him, it is because he first loved them, 1 John iv. 10, 19. and though Christ is said to love them that love him, and the Father is said to love them too; yet this must not be understood of the first love of God and Christ, unto them, nor of the first display of it; but of further and larger manifestations of it to them; and is descriptive of the persons who are most certainly and evidently the objects of their love; but not as being the cause of it, Prov. viii. 17. John xiv. 21, 23. and xvi. 27. Nor are good works the cause of this love; for this, at least, in one instance of it, was before either good or evil were done, Rom. ix. 11, 12. and in other instances it broke forth towards them, and broke in upon them while they were yet in their sins, and before they were capable of performing good works, Rom. v. 8. Tit. iii. 3, 4. Eph. ii. 2, 3, 4. and how can it be thought, that since the best works of men are so impure and imperfect as to be reckoned as filthy rags, that these should be the cause of God's love to men? no, even faith itself is not; that "is the gift of God," and flows from electing love, and is a fruit and evidence of it, Eph. ii. 8. Acts xiii. 48. Tit. i. 1. God loves men, not because they have faith; but they have faith given them, because God loves them; it is true indeed, that "without faith it is impossible to please God;" that is, to do those things which are pleasing in his sight; but then the persons of God's elect, may be, and are, well-pleasing to God, in Christ, before faith, and without it. In short, the love of God purely flows from his good will and pleasure; who "is gracious to whom he will be gracious," Exod. xxxiii. 19. it is that pure river that proceeds out of the throne of God, and of the Lamb, as an emblem of sovereignty, Rev. xxi. 1. as God loved the people of Israel because he loved them, or would love them; and for no other reason, Deut. vii. 7, 8. in like manner he loves his spiritual and mystical Israel.

2. The love of God is eternal, it does not commence in time, it is without beginning, it is from eternity: this is evident from the love of God to Christ, which was before the foundation of the world; and with the same love he loved him, he loved his people also, and as early, John xvii. 23, 24. and from various acts of love to them in eternity; as the election of them in Christ, which supposes the love of them, Eph. i. 4. the covenant of grace made with them, in which, grants of grace, and promises of glory, were made before the world began; and Christ was set up as the Mediator of it from everlasting: all which are strong pooofs of love to them, 2 Tim. i. 9. Tit. i. 2. Prov. viii. 22, 23.

3. The love of God is immutable, unalterable, and invariable; it is like himself, *the same to-day, yesterday, and for ever:* and, indeed, *God is love;* it is his nature; it is himself; and therefore must be without any variableness, or shadow of turning. It admits of no distinctions, by which it appears to alter and vary. Some talk of a love of benevolence, by which God wishes

or wills good to men; and then comes on a love of beneficence, and he does good to them, and works good in them: and then a love of complacency and delight takes place, and not till then. But this is to make God changeable, as we are: the love of God admits of no degrees, it neither increases nor decreases; it is the same from the instant in eternity it was, without any change: it is needless to ask whether it is the same before as after conversion, since there were as great, if not greater gifts of love, bestowed on the object loved, before conversion, as after; such as the gift of God himself, in the everlasting covenant; the gift of his Son to die for them when in their sins; and the gift of the Spirit to them, in order to regenerate, quicken, and convert them; heaven itself, eternal life, is not a greater gift than these; and yet they were all before conversion. There never were any stops, lets, or impediments to this love; not the fall of Adam, nor the sad effects of it; nor the actual sins and transgressions of God's people, in a state of nature; nor all their backslidings, after called by grace; for still he loves them freely, Hos. xiv. 4. for God foreknew that they would fall in Adam, with others, that they would be transgressors from the womb, and do as evil as they could; yet this hindered not his taking up thoughts of love towards them, his choice of them, and covenant with them. Conversion makes a change in them; brings them from the power of Satan to God, from darkness to light, from bondage to liberty; from fellowship with evil men to communion with God: but it makes no change in the love of God; God changes his dispensations and dealings with them, but never changes his love; he sometimes rebukes and chastises them, but still he loves them; he sometimes hides his face from them, but his love continues the same, Psalm lxxxix. 29—33. Isa. liv. 7—10. the manifestations of his love are various; to some they are greater, to others less; and so to the same persons at different times; but love in his own heart is unvariable and unchangeable.

4. The love of God endures for ever; it is an everlasting love, in that sense, Jer. xxxi. 3. it is the bond of union between God and Christ, and the elect; and it can never be dissolved; nothing can separate it, nor separate from it, Rom. viii. 35, 38, 39. The union it is the bond of, is next to that, and like it, which is between the three divine persons, John xvii. 21, 23. The union between soul and body, may be, and is dissolved, at death; but neither death nor life can separate from this; this loving-kindness of God never departs; though health, and wealth, and friends, and life itself may depart, this never will, Isa. liv. 10. whatever God takes away, as all the said things may be taken away by him, he will never take away this, Psalm lxxxix. 33. having loved his own which were in the world, he loves them to the end, to the end of their lives, to the end of time, and to all eternity, John xiii. 1.

CHAP. XIII.

OF THE GRACE OF GOD.

THIS attribute may be considered, both as it is in God himself, and as displayed in acts towards his creatures; as in himself, it is himself; it is his nature and essence; he is *Grace* itself, most amiable and lovely; hence so often called *gracious* in Scripture: it is a character expressive of the amiableness and loveliness of his nature: and thus he was before he had, and would have been for ever the same if he never had displayed his grace towards any of his creatures. And this appears from the loveliness of Christ, the image of the Father, the express image of his person; who, to them that believe, is exceeding precious, and altogether lovely; when they behold his glory, as the only begotten of the Father; the fulness of grace in him, as Mediator; the purity, perfection, and beauty of his human nature, as in union with his divine person, in which he was in high favour with God and men. Now if Christ, under these several considerations, is so graceful and amiable, he must needs be infinitely so, whose image he is, and who has all virtues, all excellencies, all perfections in him; he is said to be *glorious in holiness*, Exod. xv. 11. And if he is so glorious and graceful, viewed in one perfection of his, what must he be when all put together, and he is viewed in them all, his goodness, wisdom, power, justice, truth, &c.? and therefore is to be loved above all, and with all the heart, soul, and strength; and hence it is that good men, as Moses, David, and others, desired to see the *face* of God, so far as could be admitted, and they were capable of, Exod. xxxiii. 14, 15. Psalm xxvii. 7, 8. and cv. 4. and what a lovely sight had Moses of him in the clift of the rock, when he caused his goodness to pass, and proclaimed his name, a God gracious before him, Exod. xxxiii. 19. and xxxiv. 6. and to see the lovely face of God, so far as creatures are capable of, is the happiness of angels, and will be the happiness of saints to all eternity, Matt. xviii. 10. 1 Cor. xiii. 12. 1 John iii. 2. Rev. xxii. 4.

The grace of God may be considered as displayed in acts of goodness towards his creatures, especially men; and is no other than his free favour and good will to men; it is no other than love unmerited and undeserved, exercising and communicating itself to them in a free and generous manner; which they are altogether unworthy of. There are many things called grace, and the grace of God, because they flow from his grace, and are the effects of it; as the gospel, 2 Cor. vi. 1. Gal. v. 4. Tit. ii. 11. gifts for preaching the gospel, Rom. xii. 6. Eph. iii. 7, 8. the blessings of grace, as justification, adoption, &c. Psalm lxxxiv. 11. 2 Tim. i. 9. the several graces of the Spirit in regeneration, as faith, hope, love, &c. 2 Cor. ix. 8. Gal. ii. 9. but then these are to be distinguished from grace in God; as the Giver and the gift, the Fountain and the streams, the Cause and the effect. The grace of God arises from the *goodness* of his nature, and not from any thing in the creature; and is exercised according to his sovereign will and pleasure; *I will be gracious to whom I will be gracious,* Exod. xxxiii. 19. It is *independent* of all merit and worth in creatures, and of all works done by them, and is always opposed to them in Scripture, Rom. xi. 6. 2 Tim. i. 9. Eph. ii. 8, 9. it is quite entirely *free*, as Austin[1] said long ago, grace is not grace, unless it is altogether free. As an attribute, it wholly and only *resides* in God; and is only in men, as to the sense and perception of it, and the effects of it upon them and in them, Rom. v. 5. and viii. 38. and it is only exhibited and *displayed through* Christ, in and through whom men are elected, adopted, redeemed, justified, pardoned, regenerated, and sanctified, Eph. i. 4, 5, 6, 7. Rom. iii. 24. Tit. iii. 5, 6. And though there are various gifts and blessings, and effects of it, it is but *one* in God: there is but one Fountain, from whence they all flow. With respect to creatures, the objects of it, some distinctions are made concerning it, as of *natural* and *supernatural* grace. *Natural* grace seems to sound oddly, and unless guarded against, may tend to confound nature and grace together; but rightly applied and understood, may be admitted. What Adam enjoyed, in a state of integrity, above the rest of creatures, was all owing to the unmerited kindness and goodness of God, and so may be called grace; as the image of God, in which he was created; his holiness and righteousness; his knowledge and understanding; the communion he had with God, and his dominion over the creatures; and yet it was all natural: so many things which his posterity in their fallen state enjoy, being altogether owing to the free favour and undeserved goodness of God, may be called grace: to have a being, and life, and the preservation of it, and the mercies of life, as food and raiment, which men are altogether unworthy of, are gifts and favours; and so may bear the name of grace, though only natural blessings. *Supernatural* grace includes all the blessings of grace bestowed upon any of the sons of fallen Adam; and all the graces of the Spirit wrought in them; and which will easily be allowed to be supernatural. But that Adam had any such, in a state of innocence, for my own part, I cannot see; though some are of this opinion. Again, grace is, by some, distinguished into *common* or *general*, and *special* or *particular*. *Common* or *general* grace, if it may be so called, is what all men have; as the light of nature and reason, which every man that comes into the world is enlightened with; the temporal blessings of life, the bounties of providence, called the riches of God's goodness, or grace, Rom. ii. 4. which all partake of, more or less; and the continuance and preservation of life; for "God is the Saviour of all men," 1 Tim. iv. 10. *Special* or *particular* grace, is that which is peculiar to some persons only; such as electing, redeeming, justifying, pardoning, adopting, and sanctifying grace, Rom. viii. 30. and this special grace is, by some, distinguished into *imputed* and *inherent* grace: *imputed* grace is the holiness, obedience, and righteousness of Christ imputed to justification: *inherent* grace is what is wrought in the heart, by the Spirit of God, in regeneration. But these distinctions with others, only concern the effects of the

---

[1] Non enim Dei gratia, gratia erit ullo modo, nisi gratuita fuerit omnimodo, Aug. contra Pelag. de Peccat. Original. 1. 2. p. 338.

grace of God; that itself is but one in God; and is sure, firm, and immutable, as his nature is; and is the efficient cause, source, and spring, of all good things enjoyed by men; and should be acknowledged, as it was by the apostle, *By the grace of God I am what I am*, 1 Cor. xv. 10. whether as a man, or as a minister, or as a christian; and this is the final cause, or ultimate end of all, that God does towards, upon, or in his elect, through Christ; all is *to the glory of his grace*, Eph. i. 6. and is what appears, shines forth, and is illustrious in every part and branch of their salvation; and therefore they are said to be *saved by grace*, Eph. ii. 5, 8. as will be evident by an enumeration of them.

1. The grace of God appears in the election of men to everlasting life; and is therefore called the *election of grace*; and is denied to be of works, Rom. xi. 5, 6. and, indeed, this act of the grace of God, passed in his eternal mind, before any works were done, good or evil, and without any consideration of them, Rom. ix. 11. nor can any works truly good be done, until men become the workmanship of God in regeneration; and then they are the fruits and effects of divine preordination, Eph. ii. 10. nor were men chosen in Christ because they were holy, but that they might be holy, Eph. i. 4. And sanctification, both internal and external, is a means fixed in the decree of election; and is as absolute, unconditional, and certain, as the end, salvation, 2 Thess. ii. 13. and all the true holiness that is, has been, or will be in the world, flows from electing grace; had it not been for this, the world had been as Sodom and Gomorrah, Rom. ix. 29. Election is also irrespective of faith; that is likewise a means fixed in the decree, and most certainly follows upon it, and is therefore called the faith of God's elect, 2 Thess. ii. 13. Acts xiii. 18. Tit. i. 1. It remains, therefore, that election must be ascribed to the free favour, good will, and pleasure of God, to his unmerited grace and goodness, the true spring and cause of it; and to shew forth which is the design of it, Rom. ix. 18, 23. Eph. i. 4, 5, 6.

2. The grace of God is displayed in the covenant he has made with his elect in Christ; this, with great propriety, is commonly called by us, *the covenant of grace;* though the phrase is not in so many words to be met with in scripture; it is founded in the unmerited grace and mercy of God; and is made to establish and secure the glory of it, Psalm lxxxix. 2, 3. It was free grace that moved God to make one, to which he was not otherwise obliged: it was free grace that called, and that moved Christ to engage with his Father in it, and which *gave* him to be the covenant of the people, Psalm xl. 6, 7. Isa. xlii. 6. it was free grace that stored it with all spiritual blessings; by which it appears to be ordered in all things for the glory of God, and the good of his covenant-people; and these are grants of *grace*, made in it to them in Christ, 2 Tim. i. 9. and it was free grace that filled it with exceeding great and precious promises; promises of grace and glory, made before the world began; and which made them sure by an oath to the heirs of them; and who became heirs of them, not through any merit of theirs, but through the undeserved favour of God towards them.

3. The grace of God is very manifest in the adoption of the chosen ones; the cause of which is the good pleasure of the will of God; and the end of it, the glory of his grace, Eph. i. 5, 6. God, the adopter, stood not in any need of sons; he had a Son, an only begotten Son, a beloved Son, the dear Son of his love, who always pleased him, his Son and Heir; the adopted are altogether unworthy of such a favour, being "by nature children of wrath, as others;" and these men, and not angels, who are only servants in the family, to wait upon the children, the heirs of salvation, and minister unto them: and not all the race of men, only some, and these no better in themselves than others; and therefore their adoption cannot be ascribed to anything else but the free and distinguished grace of God; and into which relation they were taken before time, in the everlasting covenant; and Christ was sent to open the way, that they might receive this blessing of grace, and which they do by faith, the gift of God; for faith does not make them, only manifests them to be the sons of God; which relation is the ground of their having the Spirit, faith, and every other grace, Gal. iv. 4, 5, 6.

4. The grace of God shines very illustrious in redemption by Jesus Christ; free grace set infinite wisdom to work, to find out a proper person to be the redeemer and saviour; and it found out Christ to be the ransom, and provided him to be the sacrifice, Job xxxiii. 24. his incarnation was owing to God's good will to men, Luke ii. 14. and his mission to his unmerited love,

1 John iv. 10. and it was by the grace of God he tasted death for men, Heb. ii. 9. and this for sinners, the chief of sinners, ungodly men, enemies in their minds by wicked works. In short, all that are redeemed and saved, whether Old or New Testament-saints, are saved by the grace of God and Christ, Acts xv. 11.

5. The grace of God is very conspicuous in the justification of men before God, and acceptance with him; which, in the strongest terms, is said to be of grace, to be by *his grace*, the grace of God, and *freely* by his grace, and that through the redemption that is in Christ, Tit. iii. 7. Rom iii. 24. Free grace, by infinite wisdom, found out the way whereby sinful men might be just with God; which otherwise never could have been; namely, by not imputing their trespasses to them, but to Christ, the Surety free grace provided, whereby "God is just, and yet the justifier of him that believes in Jesus," 2 Cor. v. 19. Rom. iii. 25, 26. free grace appears in appointing Christ to work out, and bring in everlasting righteousness; and in sending him in the likeness of sinful flesh to do it, Dan. ix. 24. Rom. viii. 3, 4. and it was free grace moved Christ to come to do this will of God, and " become the end of the law for righteousness;" and it was free grace in God the Father to accept of this righteousness, in the room and stead of sinners, and to impute it, without works, unto them, as their justifying righteousness; and in appointing faith to be the recipient of it, that so it might clearly appear to be of grace; as the persons who are justified by it, being in themselves ungodly, more clearly shews it, Rom. iv. 5, 6, 16. Justification is always denied to be of works; and the righteousness by which men are justified, is represented as a gift, a free gift, a gift by grace, as faith that receives it also is, Rom. iii. 20, 28. and v. 15, 16, 17. Eph. ii. 8.

6. Pardon of sin is according to the riches, fulness, and freeness of the grace of God, Eph. i. 7. the promise of it in the covenant is free, absolute, and unconditional, Heb. viii. 12. the proclamation of it in the gospel, bore witness to by all the prophets, is the same, Exod. xxxiv. 6. Acts x. 43. and xiii. 38. the blood of Christ was shed freely for it; and though it cost him dear, it is all of free grace to sinners, without money and without price. Christ is exalted as a prince to *give* it; and God, for Christ's sake, frankly forgives all trespasses, Acts v. 31. Luke vii. 41, 42. Col. ii. 13. and it is vouchsafed to the worst and chief of sinners, 1 Tim. i. 13. and to great backsliders, ungrateful persons, guilty of sins of omission and commission, Hos. xiv. 4. Isa. xliii. 22, 23, 24, 25.

7. The grace of God is abundantly evident in regeneration, vocation, and sanctification; God regenerates men by his grace, and of his own good will and pleasure, James i. 18. and he calls them by his grace, and according to it, Gal. i. 15. 2 Tim. i. 9. and which always becomes effectual. There are some things which bear the name of grace, which fall short of true sanctifying grace, at least what men call so, as *restraining grace;* whereby some of God's people, before conversion, and some others, are kept from the commission of gross sins others fall into; and external *gifts* of grace, as a rational knowledge of the gospel, historical faith, and even gifts for the public ministry; which persons may have, and yet be unknown by Christ, and be cast-aways. And also what some call *sufficient grace*, though wrongly; rather it should be called, insufficient; for that can never be sufficient, which is ineffectual; as the means of grace often are. There are other distinctions of grace, which are not very material, yet, if rightly explained and understood, may be allowed, as grace *preparing, preventing, operating,* and *co-operating,* and *subsequent.* Preparing grace must be understood not of preparations, and previous dispositions in men, and of them, to the grace of God; but what is of God himself, who prepares the heart, and makes it, by his grace, good ground, fit to receive the seed of the word cast into it, where it becomes the ingrafted word, Prov. xvi. 1. Matt. xiii. 23. *Preventing* grace is that in which God goes beforehand with men, and enlightens their minds, teaches and instructs them in the knowledge of themselves, and of Christ, and guides, directs, and draws them to him, John vi. 44, 45. *Operating* grace is that by which God works in men, both to will, and to do, of his good pleasure, Phil. ii. 13. *Co-operating* grace is that by which men act, being acted or wrought upon, and by which they run, being drawn, Cant. i. 4. And *subsequent* grace is that by which the work of grace is carried on, and performed until the day of Christ, Phil. i. 6. Though there seems to be no great need of these distinctions; the most proper epithet of the grace of God, as displayed in regeneration, vocation, and conversion, is, that it is

efficacious; it never fails of its effects: and it is always *persevering* grace, and is never lost or comes to nothing; but issues in everlasting salvation; and all is owing to unmerited goodness. Every grace implanted in regeneration, flows from the free favour and good will of God. Faith is a gift, a free-grace-gift, a distinguishing gift; not given to all men, only to whom the Lord pleases, Eph. ii. 8. 2 Thess. iii. 2. Repentance is a grant of God's grace, a gift of Christ, and a blessing of the covenant, Acts v. 31. and xi. 18. Ezek. xxxvi. 26. Hope is a good hope through grace; what men, in a state of nature, are without; and which God, of his free grace, gives, 2 Thess. ii. 16. The same may be said of every other grace, love, humility, patience, &c.

8. and lastly. Eternal life is the free gift of God, through Christ, a free-grace-gift through him, Rom. vi. 23. The introduction of all the Lord's people into the enjoyment of it, will be attended with shouts and acclamations, crying *grace, grace, unto it!* Zech. iv. 7. and which will be the employment of saints to all eternity: and so the great and ultimate end of God in their salvation, will be answered, namely, *the glory of his grace*, Eph. i. 6.

CHAP. XIV.

OF THE MERCY OF GOD.

THE Mercy of God differs, in some respects, both from the love and grace of God; from the love of God in its objects, and order of operation: in its objects; which, though the same, are regarded under different considerations. Love pitched itself originally on objects, in the pure mass of creatureship, as unfallen, though it continues with them in their fallen state, and through all the imperfections of this life, to eternal happiness; mercy supposes its objects miserable, and so fallen: in order of operation.; for though they are together in God, the one as early as the other, yet love seems to work by mercy, and mercy from it; the objects being viewed as dead in sin, and for it, love stirs up mercy to quicken them with Christ, and in themselves; *God, who is rich in mercy, for the great love*, &c. Eph. ii. 4, 5.

Mercy also differs from grace; for though all mercy is grace, because it is free, unmerited, undeserved; yet all grace is not mercy:[1] much grace and favour are shewn to the elect angels; in the choice of them in Christ; in the preservation of them from the apostasy others of their species fell into; in constituting Christ the head of them, by whose grace they are confirmed in the state in which they were created; and in their being indulged with the presence of God, and communion with him; they always beholding his face in heaven; all which is abundant grace, but not mercy; since they never were miserable, and so not objects of mercy. The things to be considered respecting this attribute, are,

I. The properties of it, which will lead more clearly into its nature, and the knowledge of it.

1. Mercy is natural and essential to God; yea, it is his nature, and essence: hence he is often described as *merciful*, Exod. xxxiv. 6. Neh. ix. 17. Psalm cxvi. 5. indeed it is not to be considered as a passion, or affection in God, as it is in men; attended with grief and sorrow, with anguish and anxiety of mind for the party in misery; which become the more vehement, the nearer the relation is, and the stronger the love and affection is, bore to the object. Hence the stoic philosophers[2] denied mercy to belong to good men, and so not to God; and, indeed, it does not, in such sense, unless by an anthropopathy, or speaking after the manner of men; since he is free from all passion and perturbation of mind. The Latin word *Misericordia* signifies, as one[3] observes, having another's misery at heart; but not a miserable heart, or one made so by the misery of another, especially as applied to God; with whom it is no other than a propensity of his will to succour persons in distress, whether in a temporal or spiritual way; and this is as essential to him as is his goodness; of which it is a branch; and therefore as God is essentially, originally, independently, and underivatively good, so is he in like manner merciful. This is one of the perfections which are in some measure imitable by creatures; *Be ye merciful as your Father is merciful*, Luke vi. 36. The Socinians[4] deny that

---

[1] Vid. Maccov. Theolog. Quæst. loc. 13. p. 82.
[2] Zeno apud Cicero. Orat. 23. pro Muræna, Laert. in Vita ejus, l. 7. p. 512. Seneca de Clementia, l. 2. c. 4, 5, 6.
[3] Zanchius de Natura Dei, l. 4. c. 4. p. 372.
[4] Socinus de Servatore, l. 1. par. 1. c. 1. Prælectiones, c. 16. Racov. Catechism, c. 8. qu. 20,

mercy is essential to God, supposing that mercy and justice are opposite, whereas they are not, not even in men; a man may be just, and yet merciful, merciful and yet just: and not caring to allow justice to be essential to God, which they think they must grant, if mercy is; which would establish the doctrine of Christ's satisfaction, and make that necessary which they do not choose to embrace. But though mercy is natural and essential to God, it is not naturally and necessarily bore towards, and exercised on every object in misery; for then all would share in it, that are in misery, even all wicked men and devils; whereas it is certain they do not; but it is guided in the exercise of it by the love of God; and is governed and influenced by his sovereign will; who *hath mercy on whom he will have mercy*, Rom. ix. 15, 18. just as omnipotence is essential to God, but is not necessarily put forth to do every thing it could; but is directed and guided by the will of God; who does whatsoever he pleases.

2. Mercy being essential to God, or his nature and essence, nothing out of himself can be the cause of it; for then there would be a cause prior to him, the Cause of himself, and that would be God, and not he: the misery of a creature is not the cause of mercy in God; who is not to be moved and wrought upon as creatures are; being a most simple act, and having no passive power to work upon; besides was this the case, all must partake of mercy, since all are miserable; which they do not; see Isa. xxvii. 11. nor are the merits of the creature, or works of righteousness, the cause of mercy; these are opposed to each other in the business of salvation, Tit. iii. 5. nor are those to whom mercy is shewn, more deserving than those to whom it is not; and oftentimes less deserving, or more vile and sinful; see Rom. iii. 9. Eph. ii. 3. 1 Cor. vi. 11. 1 Tim. i. 13. Nor are even the merits of Christ, or his obedience, sufferings, and death, the cause of mercy in God; for they are the fruits and effects of it, and flow from it; it is *through the tender mercy of our God, that the day-spring from on high hath visited us*, Luke i. 78. that is, it is owing to mercy, that Christ, who is meant by *the day-spring from on high*, became incarnate, obeyed, suffered, and died, in our room and stead, and wrought out salvation for us. The mercy of God arises from the goodness of his nature, from his special love to his people, and from his sovereign will and pleasure; who, as he loves whom he pleases, and "is gracious to whom he will be gracious;" so "he has mercy on whom he will have mercy," Exod. xxxiii. 19.

3. The mercy of God is infinite; as his nature is infinite, so are each of his attributes. His *understanding is infinite*, Psalm cxlvii. 5. and so his knowledge, wisdom, justice, holiness, and goodness, and likewise his mercy; it is so in its nature, and in its effects; and this appears both by bestowing an infinite good on men, which is Christ, who is the gift of God, and owing to the love, grace, and mercy of God; and who though, as man, is finite; yet, in his divine person, infinite; and as such given, Isa. ix. 6. and by his delivering them from an infinite evil, sin: sin, as an act of the creature, is finite; but objectively, infinite, as it is committed against God, the infinite Being, Psalm li. 4. and therefore is not only infinite with respect to number, Job xxii. 5. but with respect to its object, and also with respect to punishment for it; the demerit of it is eternal death; and this cannot be endured at once, or answered for in a short time; it is carried on *ad infinitum*, without end; and therefore spoken of as everlasting and eternal. Now mercy has provided for the forgiveness of sin, and for the deliverance of men from the punishment of it, and from being liable to it, Heb. viii. 12.

4. The mercy of God is eternal; the eternity of mercy is expressed in the same language as the eternity of God himself; and, indeed, since it is his nature, it must be as eternal as he himself is; see Psalm xc. 2. and ciii. 17. it is from everlasting, as his love is; which is to be proved by the instances of it, called his *tender mercies*, which *have been ever of old*, or from everlasting, Psalm xxv. 6. the council and covenant of peace were in eternity; in which the scheme of reconciliation to God was formed, and the method of it settled, which supposed them as enemies, and so considered them as fallen creatures, and objects of mercy: and, indeed, the covenant of grace, which was from everlasting, is a superstructure of mercy, Psalm lxxxix. 1, 2, 3. and since mercy is from everlasting, not any thing in time can be the cause of it; not the misery of the creature, by the fall of Adam, nor works of righteousness done after conversion; nor the obedience and sufferings of Christ; things in time: and the mercy of God is to everlasting, in

its fruits and effects; it is kept with Christ and for him, the Mediator of the covenant; into whose hands are put all the promises and blessings of mercy; called, therefore, *the sure mercies of David*, Psalm lxxxix. 24, 28. Isa. lv. 3. even temporal blessings, which flow from the mercy of God, are new every morning, and are daily continued; and spiritual ones always remain; the mercy of God never departs from his people, notwithstanding their backslidings; and though he chides them for them, and hides his face from them, yet still he has mercy on them, Psalm lxxxix. 30—33. Isa. liv. 6—10. Jer. iii. 12, 14. Hence,

5. The mercy of God is immutable, as he himself is, and his love also; and therefore the objects of it are not consumed, Mal. iii. 6. it is invariably the same in every state and condition into which they come; it is, as the Virgin Mary expresses it, *from generation to generation*, without any variation or change, Luke i. 50.

6. It is common to all the three divine persons, Father, Son and Spirit; for as there is one common undivided essence, of which each equally partakes, the same divine perfections and attributes belong to them, and so this of mercy: mercy is ascribed to the God and Father of Christ, 1 Pet. i. 3. and to our Lord Jesus Christ, not only as Man and Mediator, but as the true God and eternal life; to whose mercy we are to look for it, Jude ver. 21. and to the blessed Spirit, who helps the infirmities of the saints, "and makes intercession for them with groanings which cannot be uttered," Rom. viii. 26.

7. Mercy is displayed only in and through Christ; God out of Christ is a consuming fire; it is only in him God proclaims his name, " a God gracious and merciful ;" he is the mercy-seat, and throne of grace, at which men obtain mercy and find grace; he is the channel through which it flows, and through whom it, in its effects, is conveyed to the sons of men: they are right who cast themselves not on the absolute mercy of God out of Christ; but upon his mercy, as displayed in him, as the Publican did, Luke xviii. 13. In a word, it is represented, as *great*, large, and ample, and very *abundant;* we read of a *multitude* of tender mercies; and God is said to be *rich* and *plenteous* in it; as will appear more fully by considering the objects and instances of it, Psalm ciii. 11. and li. 1. 1 Pet. i. 3. Eph. ii. 4. Psalm lxxxvi. 5.

II. The objects of mercy may be next observed: and that this may appear in a plain and clear light, it will be proper to remark, that the mercy of God is general and special: with respect to the general mercy of God, all creatures are the objects of it; *the Lord is good to all, and his tender mercies are over all his works*, Psalm cxlv. 9. there is not a creature in all the earth but partakes of it; hence says the Psalmist, *The earth, O Lord, is full of thy mercy!* Psalm cxix. 64. even the brute creation, the mute animals, share in it; it is owing to mercy that they are preserved in their beings, Psalm xxxvi. 5, 6. and that a provision of food is made for their sustenance; and who sometimes are in great distress, and when they cry to God he gives them their food, Joel i. 18, 19, 20. Psalm civ. 27, 28. and cxlvii. 9. Job xxxviii. 41. All men, good and bad, partake of the providential goodness and mercy of God; he is kind to the unthankful and unholy, and makes the sun to rise on the evil and on the good, and sends rain on the just and on the unjust, Luke vi. 35. Matt. v. 45. He preserves and supports all men in their beings, and so is the Saviour of all, and especially of them that believe, 1 Tim. iv. 10. and gives them the necessaries of life, food and raiment, and all things richly to enjoy, both for convenience and pleasure: yea, even the devils themselves partake of mercy, in some sense; for though God has not spared them, so as to save them, and not condemn them; yet he has given them a kind of reprieve, and reserved them to the judgment of the great day; so that they are not yet in full torments, as their sins have deserved; and as God punishes none more but less than their sins require, this may be reasonably supposed to be the case of devils, even hereafter.

As to the special mercy of God, none are the objects of that but elect men, who are called *vessels of mercy*, Rom. ix. 23. because they are filled with it, even with all spiritual blessings, which flow from it, and which are bestowed on them according as they are chosen in Christ, Eph. i. 3, 4. and so particularly regeneration, which is according to the abundant mercy of God, they are favoured with, being the elect of God, 1 Pet. i. 2, 3. and these, as they are redeemed by Christ, share in the special mercy and goodness of God; and therefore are under obligation to say, with wonder and thankfulness, "the Lord is good; his mercy endures for ever," Psalm cvii. 1, 2. and especially, being effectually called by the grace of God, they appear to be the objects of mercy; then they who *had not obtained mercy*, did not know their interest in it, nor actually enjoyed the blessings of it, *now have obtained mercy;* are blessed both with knowledge of interest in it, and with the open possession of the blessings of it, 1 Pet. ii. 10. These are described sometimes by them *that call upon* the Lord, to whom he is plenteous in mercy, Psalm lxxxvi. 5. by "them that love him, and keep his commandments; to whom he shews his mercy," Exod. xx. 6. Nehem. i. 5. Dan. ix. 4. and by them that fear him, and towards whom his mercy always is, Psalm ciii. 11, 13, 17. Not that calling upon God, love to him, and observance of his commands, and the fear of him, are the causes of his mercy to them, since that is prior to all these, and is the cause of them; but these describe the persons who openly, and manifestly, share in the mercy of God; and to whom the effects of it have been applied, and who may expect a continuance of it, and larger discoveries and displays thereof to be made unto them; as well as they shew that the mercy of God is special and distinguishing, and yet that it is not limited to any family or nation, but is enjoyed by all that love and fear the Lord in every nation, Acts x. 34, 35.

III. The instances of mercy, to the objects of it, are many and various.

1. It appears in election: it is, indeed, a controversy among divines, whether election is an act of love or of mercy; I am inclined to be of the opinion of those who take it to be an act of love, and not mercy; as God chose literal Israel, because he loved them, Deut. vii. 7, 8. so spiritual Israel are first beloved, and then chosen, 2 Thess. ii. 13. *electio præsupponit dilectionem;* but then, though the decree of election flows from love, and not mercy; yet God has in it decreed to shew mercy; he has resolved within himself, saying, *I will have mercy, and will save;* and therefore in this decree he has appointed them not unto wrath, which they deserve, but to obtain salvation by Christ; which supposes them fallen creatures, and so objects of mercy; for the decree of election may be distinguished into the decree of the end and the decree of the means; with respect to the end, the glory of God, men were considered as unfallen, in the pure mass out of which God designed to make them for himself: but with respect to the means, redemption by Christ, and faith in him, the Redeemer, and sanctification of the Spirit; here they were considered as fallen creatures; and so, with propriety, those chosen ones may be called *vessels of mercy.*

2. The covenant of grace is a display of the mercy of God, as before observed; it is built upon mercy, and built up with it; it is stored with it, and is full of it. Mercy called Christ to engage in it, and set him up as the Mediator of it, and prevented him with the blessings of goodness; the provisions of Christ, as a Redeemer and Saviour in it; of forgiveness of sins through his blood; and of reconciliation and atonement by his sacrifice; and of regeneration and sanctification by his Spirit, are so many displays of mercy.

3. Redemption itself is a glaring instance of the mercy of God. Mercy resolved upon the redemption and salvation of the elect; being viewed as fallen in Adam, and as sinners, mercy provided a Redeemer and Saviour of them, and laid their help upon him; mercy called Christ, to undertake the work of redemption, and engaged him in it; mercy sent him, in the fulness of time, to visit them, and perform it; mercy delivered him up into the hands of justice and death, in order to obtain it, and it is most illustriously glorified in it; *mercy and truth have met together,* Psalm lxxxv. 10. yea, Christ himself, in his love and pity, has redeemed his people, Isa. lxiii. 9.

4. The forgiveness of sin is another instance of the mercy of God, to which it is frequently ascribed, Psalm li. 1. Dan. ix. 9. Luke i. 77, 78. God has promised it in covenant, as the effect of his mercy; *I will be merciful to their unrighteousness,* Heb. viii. 12. He has set forth Christ, in his purposes, to be the propitiation for the remission of sins; and has sent him, in time, to shed his blood for it, Rom. iii. 25. and it is the mercy of God, which is the foundation of hope of it; and encourages sensible sinners to ask, and through which they obtain it, Psalm cxxx. 7. Luke xviii. 13. 1 Tim. i. 13.

5. The mercy of God is displayed in regeneration, to which that is ascribed in 1 Pet. i. 3. and it is wonderful and special mercy, to quicken a sinner dead in trespasses and sins; to enlighten such that sit

in darkness, and in the shadow of death; to deliver from the bondage of Satan those that are led captive by him at his will; to snatch them as brands out of the burning, and save from everlasting fire; to bring men out of a pit, wherein there was no water, no relief and comfort, and in which they must otherwise die; and to reveal Christ to them, and in them, the hope of glory; and give them a good hope, through grace, of being for ever happy. These are some of the great and good things which God does for his people in effectual vocation, having compassion on them.

6. Complete salvation, and eternal life itself, flow from the mercy of God; he saves, "not by works of righteousness, but according to his mercy," Tit. iii. 5. and when he shall put his people into the full possession of salvation, then they shall find and obtain mercy in that day, even in the day of judgment, when they shall go into life eternal; and therefore are now directed to look unto the mercy of Christ for it, 2 Tim. i. 18. Jude ver. 21.

CHAP. XV.

OF THE LONG-SUFFERING OF GOD.

THE long-suffering of God, the same with his forbearance and patience, arises from his mercy, is a display of it, or is one way in which mercy shews itself; and so, by the Cabalistic Jews, it is said to belong to the predicament of *Chesed*, or mercy, as they express themselves;[1] and it may be observed, that wherever God is said to be long-suffering, he is represented as gracious and merciful, or as of great mercy and kindness; and by this attribute, as by them and with them, he is pleased to describe and make known himself, for the encouragement of faith and hope in him, Exod. xxxiv. 6. Numb. xiv. 18. Psalm lxxxvi. 15. and therefore the consideration of it very properly follows that of mercy. The Hebrew word ארך אפים which literally signifies *long of both nostrils*, is sometimes rendered *long-suffering*, as in the places referred to; and sometimes *slow to anger*, Nehem. ix. 17. Psalm ciii. 8. and to which the Greek words μακροθυμεω, and μακροθυμια, in the New Testament, answer, Rom. ii. 4. 2 Pet. iii. 9. 15. the allusion is to the nose, the seat of anger, which restrains or shews it, as it is long or contracted.

God is sometimes called, *the God of patience*, Rom. xv. 5. not only because he is the author and object of the grace of patience, and that it is grateful to him; but because he is patient, or long-suffering in himself, and towards his creatures, and is a pattern of patience to them; for this is one of the attributes of God, in which he may in some measure be imitated; see Eph. iv. 1, 2. Col. iii. 12. This is not to be considered as a quality, accident, passion, or affection in God, as in creatures; who bear with patience things grievous, distressing, and torturing to them, Col. i. 11. but it is the very nature and essence of God, which is free from all passion and perturbation, from all suffering, grief, and pain; it springs from his goodness, and is as essential to him as that, and is joined with it, Rom. ii. 4. it is no other than a moderation of his anger, a restraint of that, a deferring the effects of it, at least for a while, according to his sovereign will; it is an extension and prolongation of mercy for a season; for mercy is always in it and with it; and in this it differs from it, that the mercy of God is from everlasting to everlasting; but the long-suffering of God, as to the exercise of it, is only for a time, until some certain end is answered, and in which it issues; either in the damnation and destruction of the wicked, when they are fitted for it, Rom. ix. 22. or in the salvation of God's elect, 2 Pet. iii. 15. for it is exercised towards both, till each take place; which will be distinctly considered.

I. The long-suffering of God is exercised towards his chosen people; they are the *us* towards whom he is said to be *long-suffering*, 2 Pet. iii. 9. even who are called *beloved*, ver. 8. not only beloved of the apostle, and by one another, but by the Lord; and the elect according to the foreknowledge of God, 1 Pet. i. 2. for to the same persons are both epistles written; and therefore being the beloved and chosen of God, it was his will that none of them should perish, but come to repentance; even all of the same character, and of the same company and society, the whole election of grace; and until every one of these are called and brought to repentance, God is, and will be, long-suffering towards them; and long-suffering to the world for their sakes; wherefore Christ's not coming

---

[1] Lexic. Cabalist. p. 155.

to judgment sooner than he will, is not owing to any negligence, dilatoriness, or slackness in God, concerning the promise of it, but to the long-suffering of God, which has been eminently displayed with respect to the people of God.

1. In the saints of the Old Testament dispensation, which time is expressly called *the forbearance of God*, Rom. iii. 25. The case stood thus; Christ became the Surety for them in eternity, engaged to assume their nature, pay their debts, and make satisfaction for their sins: this was notified immediately after the fall of Adam, Gen. iii. 15. but it was four thousand years from thence to the time fixed in Daniel's prophecy, "to finish transgression, to make an end of sin, to make reconciliation for iniquity, and bring in everlasting righteousness;" to the fulness of time when Christ should come to redeem all his people, and particularly, to obtain the redemption of transgressions that were under the first Testament, Dan. ix. 24. Gal. iv. 4. Heb. ix. 15. Now all this time, was a time of patience, forbearance, and long-suffering with God, in respect to his people under this dispensation; he did not stir up his wrath, and execute it on them; but reserved it for his Son, their Surety; he forbore to inflict the punishment on them their sins deserved; he did not impute sin to them, place it to their account, charge it on them, and demand of them satisfaction for it; but placed it to his Son's account, and expected satisfaction from him: he accepted of the sacrifices of slain beasts, as vicarious ones in their stead, though they had no true value, nor real efficacy in them, to atone for sin; only were typical of Christ's sacrifice; and were to continue, and did, until that should be offered up; God waited till he should come and make his soul an offering for sin; and, upon his credit, bore with them, and bestowed the blessings of his grace on them: they were justified by him on the foot of Christ's righteousness to be wrought out; and their sins pardoned, through his atoning sacrifice to be offered up; they were saved by the grace of the Lord Jesus, even as we are, and we as they; they were carried to heaven, and glorified, before the payment of their debts were made by their Surety, before satisfaction for their sins was given to justice, and before the actual redemption of them was obtained. All which, as it shews the trust and confidence God put in his Son, so his forbearance and long-suffering towards Old Testament-saints; which also has appeared, and does appear.

2. In and towards every one of his people in their state of unregeneracy, in every age and period of time, or of whatsoever nation, or under whatsoever dispensation they be; the Lord bears with them, whilst in a state of nature, and waits patiently all that while, to be gracious to them, Isa. xxx. 18. There was much grace in his heart, in his Son, and in his covenant, laid up for them. This is abundantly displayed in conversion, when there is an abounding and a superabounding of it. But then the vocation and conversion of them is according to purpose; and as there is a time for every purpose, for the execution of it, so for this; and till that time comes, the Lord waits, forbears, suffers much and long; he does not cut them off in their sins, as they deserve; but saves them, and sometimes from very imminent dangers, to be called, 2 Tim. i. 9. and with some he bears and waits a long time, who are called at the ninth and eleventh hours, and, as the thief on the cross, at the last day and hour of his life; and he waits, as it were, in a longing manner; speaking after the manner of men, *When will it once be?* Jer. xiii. 27.

3. The apostle Paul is a remarkable instance of God's long-suffering; which was exercised towards him throughout all his blasphemy of Christ, his persecution of his people, and the injuries he did unto them; he waited, through all, to be gracious to him; his eye was upon him, and his heart was towards him; and hence such notice is taken of him in that state, before the account is given of his vocation; see Acts vii. 58. and viii. 1, 3. and ix. 1. yea, he himself says, *For this cause I obtained mercy, that in me first Jesus Christ might shew forth all long-suffering, for a pattern to them which should hereafter believe on him to life everlasting*, 1 Tim. i. 16. meaning the people of the Jews, in the latter day: his sense seems to be this, that as Christ bore much, and exercised great long-suffering towards him, and at last shewed him mercy; so he would bear with, and shew much long-suffering to the people of the Jews, of which that towards him was a pattern, and which should issue in their salvation, as it had in his; when *all Israel shall be saved*, Rom. xi. 25. God's long-suffering towards them is very great and very remarkable; as it was towards him;

though they are under the marks of his displeasure, he has not stirred up all his wrath, so as to cut them off from being a people; but has reserved them for future times, and good things for them, and waits to be gracious to them.

II. The long-suffering of God is exercised towards the ungodly, even towards *the vessels of wrath* whom he *endures with much long-suffering, till they are fitted to destruction*, Rom. ix. 22. and this appears by his supporting them in their beings, notwithstanding their grievous provocations of him; which are such, that it is amazing he does not at once strike them dead, as he did Ananias and Sapphira; or that the earth does not open and swallow them up, as it did Dathan and Abiram. This can be attributed to nothing else but to his patience, forbearance, and long-suffering: and by the multitude of his mercies bestowed upon them, who have many of them, more than other men; and which are called *the riches of his goodness, forbearance and long-suffering;* see Job xxi. 7—13. Psalm lxxiii. 4—7. Rom. ii. 4. and by granting to many of them the outward means of grace, which are despised and rejected by them; and by deferring his judgments on them; which, because they are not speedily executed, their hearts are set in them to do evil; they are more and more hardened, and promise themselves impunity in sin. Now the ends of God's thus dealing with them, are partly for his own glory; *to shew his wrath, and make his power known;* to vindicate him from all cruelty and injustice, when he righteously executes his wrath, and exerts his power in their destruction: as in the instance of Pharaoh, Rom. ix. 17, 22. and partly for the sake of his own people who dwell among them, that they may not suffer with them; thus he would have spared Sodom, had there been ten righteous men in it, for their sakes: and he forbears to take vengeance on those that have shed the blood of his saints, until the number of his elect, in like manner, is fulfilled; and he spares a wicked world from being burnt up and destroyed, until all his chosen ones are brought to repentance, Gen. xviii. 32. Rev. vi. 11. 2 Pet. iii. 9. and another end is for their sakes, that they may be rendered inexcusable, and the execution of wrath on them at last, appear just and righteous, Rom. ii. 1, 4, 5.

There are many instances of the patience, forbearance, and long-suffering of God, with respect to the wicked; as in the men of the old world, when the long-suffering of God waited in the days of Noah, 1 Pet. iii. 20. see Gen. vi. 3. and in the inhabitants of Sodom, daring sinners, who had first hints of God's displeasure, yet had mercy shewn them, a respite for a while, and then destroyed by fire from heaven, Gen. xiii. 13. and xiv. 11, 21. and xviii. 21. and xix. 24. in Pharaoh, refusing to let Israel go, whom God had spared some time, beginning with lighter judgments, then executed heavier ones; and at last drowned him, and his host, in the Red Sea, Exod. v. 2. and chap. vii. &c. and xiv. 17, 18, 28. in the people of Israel, in the wilderness, whose manners God suffered and bore with, and was grieved with them forty years, Acts xiii. 18. in the Amorites and Canaanites, until their sin was full, and till the land itself would bear them no longer; but spewed them out of it, Gen. xv. 16. Lev. xviii. 28. in the Gentile world, during their times of ignorance, Acts xvii. 30. in fruitless professors of religion, signified by the barren fig-tree, Luke xiii. 6—9. and in antichrist, during the time of his reign, and no longer, Rev. ii. 21. and xiii. 6. and xviii. 8.

CHAP. XVI.

OF THE GOODNESS OF GOD.

HAVING treated of the love, grace, mercy, and long-suffering of God, it will be proper to take some notice of his *goodness*, from whence they all proceed; for that God loves any of his creatures, in the manner he does, bestows favours upon them, shews mercy to them, and bears much with them, is owing to the goodness of his nature. Hence one of his names and titles by which he is described and made known, is, that of *Good; thou, Lord, art good,* Psalm lxxxvi. 5. and in many other places; when God proclaimed his name before Moses, this was one part of it, *abundant in goodness,* Exod. xxxiv. 6. Philo says,[1] God is the name of goodness. And our English word *God* seems to be a contraction of the word *Good;* or however, is the same with the German *Gott* and *Godt;* which came, as it is thought,[2] from

---

[1] Leg. Alleg. 1. 2. p. 74.

[2] Vid. Hinckelman. Præfat. ad Alkoran.

the Arabic word *Gada*, which so signified; so that the German and English name of the divine Being, in common use, is taken from the attribute of his goodness. The name the heathens give to their supreme deity, is *optimus*,[3] the *best;* he being not only good, as they supposed, and better than others, but the best of beings. Our Jehovah, the true God, is superlatively good; good in the highest degree, good beyond all conception and expression. Cotta in Cicero,[4] charges Epicurus with taking away from God the property of the best and most excellent nature, by denying the grace and goodness of God; for what, says he, is better, or what is more excellent, than goodness and beneficence? It is a common notion, Sallustius says,[5] that God is good; and Simplicius[6] calls him, the Goodness of goodnesses. Concerning the goodness of God, let the following things be observed:

1. Goodness is essential to God; without which he would not be God; he is by nature good.[7] The evil god of Cerdon and Marcion is not the true God; and this being wanting in heathen deities, whatever pretensions may be made unto it, excludes them from the claim of deity; yea, goodness is itself the nature and essence of God; as he is love itself, wisdom itself, &c. so he is goodness itself, and it is himself, it includes his whole nature and essence. When God promised Moses that he would make *all* his *goodness* pass before him, it was not a single attribute only which was proclaimed and made known; but the several attributes of mercy, grace, long-suffering, truth, faithfulness, justice, and holiness, Exod. xxxiii. 19. and xxxiv. 6, 7. The goodness of God is not distinct from his essence; for then he must be compounded of that, and his essence; which is contrary to his simplicity: he is good in and of himself, and by his own essence; and not by participation of another; for if he was not good of himself, and by his own essence, but of and by another; then there would be some being, both better than him, and prior to him; and so he would not be the eternal God, nor an independant Being, since he must depend on that from whence he receives his goodness; nor would he be the most perfect being, since what communicates goodness to him must be more perfect than he: all which, to say of God, is very unbecoming. It remains, then, that he is essentially good; is so in and of himself, by his own nature and essence.

2. Goodness only belongs to God; he is solely good; *There is none good but one; that is, God;* is the assertion of Christ, Matt. xix. 17. which is to be understood not to the exclusion of the Son, and Spirit of God, who are, with the Father, the one God; and so equally good: but with respect to creatures, who are not of themselves inderivatively and independently good; this is only true of God. Whatever goodness is in creatures, it is all from him, who made them good originally; or put into them, or bestowed upon them, what goodness they have: what goodness there is in the elect angels, who never sinned; what goodness was in Adam, in a state of innocence; what goodness is in any good man, who partakes of the grace of God, or is or will be in the saints in heaven, is all from God; every good and perfect gift comes from him; nor have creatures any thing but what they receive from him; he is the source and fountain of all, and therefore all goodness, originally, ultimately, and solely, is to be referred to God.

3. God is the *summum bonum*, he is τ' αγαθον, as Plato calls him, *the Good;*[8] the chiefest good; the sum and substance of all felicity. Unwearied have been the pursuits of men to attain this; but have always failed, when they place it or expect it in anything out of God, and short of him: innumerable have been the sentiments of men about it. Solomon seems to have reduced them to these three, wisdom, riches, and pleasure; and he made an experiment of them, what happiness could be enjoyed in them, as far as a king, a wise man, and a good man, could go; and when he had finished it, pronounced all *vanity and vexation of spirit*. God only can make men happy; he is the Father of mercies, the Fountain of all goodness, the Source of all felicity. There may be a shew of happiness in such and such outward circumstances of life, some may be in, with respect to the above things; but there is no solidity in them; he is the only

---

[3] Optimus maximus quidem ante optimus, id est, beneficentissimus quam maximus, Cicero de Natura Deorum, 1. 2.
[4] Ibid. l. 1. prope finem.
[5] De Diis, c. 1.
[6] In Epictetum.
[7] αγαθος γαρ ην φυσει, Hierocles in Carmin. Pythag. p. 21.
[8] De Republica, l. 6. p. 687.

happy man *whose God is the Lord*, Psalm cxliv. 12—15. wherefore good men, who are sensible of the vanity of the creature, and all creature-enjoyments, pant after him, and are importunately desirous of the enjoyment of him, and cannot be satisfied without him, placing all their happiness in him: whilst others are saying, *Who will shew us any good?* taking up their contentment in worldly good; they say, *Lord, lift thou up the light of thy countenance upon us;* which gives the greatest pleasure, joy, and satisfaction, that can be had, Psalm iv. 6, 7. and xlii. 1. and lxxiii. 25.

4. There is nothing but goodness in God, and nothing but goodness comes from him; there is no iniquity in him, nothing evil in his nature, no unrighteousness in any of his ways and works; he is *light* itself; all purity, holiness, truth, and goodness; *and in him is no darkness at all,* of sin, error, and ignorance, 1 John i. 5. nor does any thing that is evil come from him; he is not the author of sin, nor does he impel, nor persuade to it, nor tempt with it; but strongly forbids it, under pain of his displeasure, James i. 13, 14. indeed, his decree is concerned about it; for it could not be, he not willing it by his permissive will; but then, though he suffers it to be, he overrules it for good; as in the case of the selling of Joseph, Gen. l. 20. the evil of punishment of sin, or of affliction, is from God; in this sense *there is no evil in a city, and the Lord hath not done it,* Amos iii. 6. but then punishment of sin is a good, as it is a vindication of the honour of divine justice, and of the righteous law of God; and the affliction of the people of God is for their good; and all evil things of that kind work for their good, both here and hereafter.

5. God is infinitely good; as his understanding, wisdom, knowledge, and other perfections of his, are infinite; so is his goodness; he is abundant in it: it is so great, that it cannot be said how great it is; finite minds cannot comprehend it; the height, depth, length, and breadth of it, are unmeasurable; it knows no bounds nor limits; it is so perfect that nothing can be added to it: the goodness of a creature extends not to God, nor is it capable of communicating any to him, *who hath first given to him,* &c. Rom. xi. 35, 36.

6. God is immutably and eternally good; the goodness of creatures is but as the morning cloud, and early dew, which soon passes away; of which there has been instances in angels and men : but the goodness of God is invariably the same, and endures continually; and though there has been, and are, such large communications of it to creatures, it is the same as ever, and remains an inexhaustible fountain.

7. The goodness of God is communicative and diffusive; he is good, and he does good; "the whole earth is full of his goodness," Psalm cxix. 68. and xxxiii. 5. there is not a creature but what partakes of it, more or less, in some manner or another; but then it is communicated according to his sovereign will and pleasure. A heathen writer[9] argues the goodness of God from the existence of the world; since it is by the goodness of God the world is, God must be always good.

8. This attribute of goodness belongs to each divine person, Father, Son, and Spirit; when Christ says, as quoted above, *there is none good but one, that is, God,* it is to be understood not of God personally considered, or of one person, to the exclusion of the other; but of God essentially considered: and the design of Christ was, to raise the mind of the young man to whom he spoke, to an higher opinion of himself than what he had; even of him, not as a mere man, whom, as such, he called good; but as the true God, to whom this epithet, in its highest sense, only belongs: and it is predicated of the Father, 2 Chron. xxx. 18. of Christ, John x. 11. and of the Spirit, Nehem. ix. 20. Psalm cxliii. 10. and they must, indeed, in the same sense, be good, since they partake of one common undivided nature and essence, 1 John v. 7.

The goodness of God, with respect to the several objects of it, may be considered as general and special; in like manner as his love and mercy. There is the general goodness of God, which is as extensive as his mercy; *The Lord is good to all, and his tender mercies are over all his works,* Psalm cxlv. 9. All creatures are made by God, and as they came from him, they are all *very good;* there is a goodness put into them, whereby they become good and beneficial to others, and especially to men: there is a goodness in inanimate creatures, in the metals and minerals of the earth; in the luminaries of the heavens, the sun, moon, and stars: they are pleasant, good to look at, their form, magnitude, and

---

[9] Sallust de Diis, c. 7.

splendour; they are profitably good; by their light they themselves are seen, and other objects; by this men see to walk and work, and do the several businesses of life; and through their kind and benign influences shed on the earth, many precious fruits are brought forth, and the advantages of them all men share in; God *makes his sun to rise on the evil and on the good,* Matt. v. 45. which is one great instance of his general goodness. In the vegetable creation there is a large display of the goodness of God; some herbs, plants, and trees, being good for medicine; others for food, both for the cattle of the field and for the service of men, Psalm civ. 14, 15. Among the animals, some are for one use, and some for another, and many are meat for men: and even every creature of God is good, and to be received with thanksgiving, 1 Tim. iv. 4. and all creatures, both men and beast, partake of the goodness of God in the preservation of them, Psalm xxxvi. 6. 1 Tim. iv. 10. and in the provision of food for them, Psalm civ. 27, 28. and cxlv. 15, 16. and cxlvii. 8. Acts xiv. 16, 17. and xvii. 25, 28. 1 Tim. iv. 8.

There is indeed a difference made by God in the distribution of his general goodness, in the effects of it; which are not imparted to all creatures alike. God gives more of his goodness to men than to brutes; since he gives them reason and understanding; whereby they become more knowing, and to be wiser than the beasts of the field, and the fowls of the heavens, Job xxxv. 11. and angels have a greater share of his goodness than men; who excel as in strength, so in wisdom and knowledge; hence man is said to be made a little lower than the angels, Psalm viii. 5. and some men have a greater share in the general and providential goodness of God than others; either have larger endowments of mind, are the wise and prudent of the world; or have more comeliness, strength, and health of body; or are possessed of greater wealth and riches, Eccles. ix. 11.

The special goodness of God, as to the effects of it, elect angels, and elect men, only partake of, which is sovereign and distinguishing; God is good to the elect angels, in choosing them in Christ, preserving them from apostasy, confirming them in the estate they were created in, granting them nearness to himself, and many other peculiar favours; when the angels that sinned are not spared by him, but are reserved to judgment, 1 Tim. v. 21.

2 Pet. ii. 4. Elect men, the spiritual and mystical Israel of God, have a share in his special goodness; *truly God is good to Israel,* Psalm lxxiii. 1. and that in a very distinguishing manner, as he is not to reprobates; *the election hath obtained* all the special blessings of goodness, grace here, and glory hereafter; light, life, and happiness; while *the rest* are *blinded,* Rom. xi. 7. they are made to differ from others thereby in time, and to all eternity; and yet among them there are different displays of divine goodness in the present state: some have greater spiritual gifts for usefulness than others; some have larger measures of grace; though they have all the same grace, yet not to the same degree; they have all alike precious faith, but in some it is weaker, in others stronger; and some have more spiritual light in the Gospel, and more spiritual peace and joy, and larger discoveries of the love of God, and have more communion with him. All which must be referred to his sovereign good-will and pleasure.

Many are the acts and instances of divine goodness to the people of God in common. It has been observed, that the attribute of *goodness,* and the epithet of *good,* belong to each of the three divine persons, Father, Son, and Spirit; and they have each of them manifested their goodness in acts of it.

Jehovah the Father, has displayed his goodness to his special people, in his good designs towards them, and thoughts of them; in setting them apart for himself, his own glory, and their good; in laying up all good things for them in Christ, and in the covenant of his grace; in making promises of good things to them, both for this life, and that which is to come; and in bestowing good gifts on them, the gift of himself, the gift of his Son, and the gift of his Spirit; and all the blessings of goodness, as of adoption, justification, pardon of sin, &c. and all the graces of the Spirit, as the gift of faith, of repentance, of a good hope of eternal life, and also the gift of eternal life itself. Jehovah the Son, has manifested his goodness to the same persons; in becoming a Surety, and undertaking for their good; in partaking of their nature, in which good-will to men was expressed; and in working out the great and good work of their redemption and salvation; he is the good Shepherd, and has shewn himself to be so, by laying down his life for the sheep, and by providing a good fold, and good pasture for them: he is, and has been, in all ages, the Fountain of goodness and grace to all his people, for the supply of all their wants; and he ever lives to speak a good word, and intercede for good things for them. Jehovah the Spirit, is good unto them, as a Teacher, Sanctifier, and Comforter of them, as a Spirit of adoption, grace, and supplication; as the author of the good work of grace in them; as the guide of them through this world; and as the earnest and pledge of their future glory, and a sealer of them up unto the day of redemption.

CHAP. XVII.

OF THE ANGER AND WRATH OF GOD.

BESIDES the love and kindness of God, his grace, favour, and good-will, his mercy, pity, and compassion; and his long-suffering and forbearance; which flow from the goodness of his nature; there are other things to be considered, which may come under the notion of affections; as anger, wrath, hatred, &c. The anger and wrath of God are often used promiscuously in Scripture, to signify the same thing, and yet they sometimes seem to be distinct; and according to our notion of them, as in men, they may be distinguished: anger is a lower and lesser degree of wrath, and wrath is the height of anger: and accordingly I shall distinctly consider them, as in God.

I. The Anger of God. And shall,

First, Shew that it belongs to God; and in what sense, and on what account. And,

Secondly, With whom he is angry; or on whom his anger is exercised.

First, That Anger belongs to God, or may be predicated of him. This is denied by some philosophers of the Cynic and Stoic sects, because it is a passion; they allow grace, good-will, and beneficence in God to men, but not anger; this they suppose to be a weakness, and even a sort of madness,[1] and what is unbecoming a wise and good man, and much more unbecoming Deity. The Epicureans deny that either is in God; neither favour and good-will, nor anger and wrath;[2] for they imagine he has no concern in the affairs of men, and neither regards their good actions, nor their bad ones; and so is neither pleased nor displeased with them; and is neither kind and favourable to them; nor is angry with them, nor resents what is done by them. But the Scriptures everywhere ascribe anger to God; and often speak of it, as being kindled against particular persons, and against whole bodies of men; and give many particular instances of it: to produce the whole proof of this, would be to transcribe great part of the Bible. But then anger is to be considered not as a passion, or affection in God, as it is in men; and especially as it may be defined from the etymology of the Latin word for it *ira*, as given by a learned grammarian,[3] deriving it from *ire*, to go; as if a man when in anger, goes out of himself; and when he lays it down, returns to himself again; this cannot, in any sense, be ascribed to God: rather it may be, as if it was *ura*, and so is *ab urendo*, from burning; or rather from the Hebrew word חרה which signifies to burn; and the anger of God is compared to fire in Scripture, and is often said to be kindled; but then we are not to imagine, when God is said to be angry, that there is any commotion or perturbation in God's mind; that he is ruffled and discomposed, or that there is any pain or uneasiness in him, as in human minds; so it may be in finite created spirits, but not in an infinite and uncreated one, as God is; and much less is this to be considered as a criminal passion in him, as it too often is in men; for God is a pure and holy being, without iniquity: besides, there may be anger in men without sin; we are exhorted to *be angry and sin not*, Eph. iv. 26. and it is certain there was anger in the human nature of Christ, in whom there was no sin, nor was he conscious of any, Mark iii. 5. and so there may be in the divine mind, without an imputation of weakness or sin. Anger in God is no other than a displacency with sin, and with sinners, on account of it; it is often said in Scripture, that such and such a thing displeased him, or was evil, and not right in his sight, Numb. xi. 1. 2 Sam. xi. 27. Psalm lx. 1. Isa. lix. 15. All sin is displeasing to God; he cannot take any pleasure in it, nor look upon it with delight; it is so

---

[1] Vide Senecam de Ira, 1. 1. c. 1. Sallustium de Diis, c. 14. et Demophili Sentent. p. 8. Ed. Gale.

[2] Vide Lactantium de ira Dei. c. 4 et 5.

[3] Donatus apud Zanchium de Natura Dei, 1. 4. c. 6. p. 407.

contrary to his nature, and repugnant to his will, he cannot but have an aversion to it, and an abhorrence of it; and there are some sins more especially which provoke him to anger; as the sins against the first table of the law, particularly idolatry; which, of all sins, is the most provoking to him; since it strikes at his very being, and robs him of his glory; see Deut. xxxii. 16, 21. Judg. ii. 12, 13. 1 Kings xvi. 33. Likewise distrust of the power and providence of God, murmuring at it, and complaining of it; which was often the case of the Israelites; and by which they provoked the Lord to anger; so perjury, false swearing, the taking the name of God in vain, and blasphemy of it; profanation of the Lord's day, and neglect of his word, worship, and ordinances: and not these only, but sins against the second table of the law, are highly displeasing to God, and resented by him; as disobedience to parents, murder, adultery, theft, false witness, covetousness, and every evil thing, see Isa. v. 24, 25. Now *who knoweth the power of God's anger?* Psalm xc. 11. nothing can resist it, nor stand before it; not rocks and mountains, which are overturned and cast down by it; nor the mightiest monarchs, nor the proudest mortals, nor the stoutest and adamantine hearts; none can stand before God when once he is angry, Job. ix. 5, 13. Psalm lxxvi. 7. Nahum. i. 6.

Secondly, The objects of the anger of God, or on whom it is exercised. *God is angry with the wicked every day*, Psalm vii. 11. because they are daily sinning against him; their whole lives are one continued series and course of wickedness; all they do is sin; their very actions in civil life, the *ploughing* of the wicked, is sin; and all their religious services are but *splendida peccata*, shining sins, and so are displeasing to God, and resented by him; their sacrifices, brought with a wicked mind, without a right principle, and a right end, are an abomination to him, Prov. xxi. 4, 27. being in the flesh, in an unregenerate state, they cannot please God, nor do the things which are pleasing in his sight; being destitute of the grace of God, and particularly of faith; "without which it is impossible to please him." These, though God is angry with them continually, yet they do not always appear under the visible and public tokens of his resentment; the *rod of God* is not on them; nor are they in trouble, as other men, and have more than heart can wish; oftentimes their families, flocks, and herds, increase; and they spend their days in health, wealth, and pleasure, Job xxi. 7—13. Psalm lxxiii. 3—12. and seem as if they were the favourites of heaven, and think themselves to be such. But though God is *slow to anger*, as he is often described, moves slowly to express his anger; yet he will most certainly do it in the issue of things; and though men may promise themselves impunity in sin, and fancy they shall have peace when they walk after the imagination of their evil hearts, and add sin to sin; yet at length God will not spare them; but his anger and jealousy shall smoke against them, and all the curses written in the law shall come upon them, Deut. xxix. 19, 20.

Moreover, God is angry with his own special people, holy and good men; we read of his anger being kindled against Aaron and Miriam, for speaking against Moses; and against Moses and Aaron, for not sanctifying him before the children of Israel; insomuch that neither of them were admitted to enter the land of Canaan; and against David, Solomon, and others, for sins committed by them. And this is not at all inconsistent with the love of God unto them: anger is not opposite to love; there may be anger in the nearest and dearest relatives; and where there is the most affectionate regard to each other: the anger of Jacob was kindled against his beloved Rachel; a father may be angry with his son, and chastise him for a fault, and yet dearly love him; and a son may be angry with a father, as Jonathan was with Saul, yet bear a true filial affection for him. God loves his people with an everlasting and unchangeable love, and never alters and varies in it; and yet may be angry, that is, displeased with them, and shew his resentment at sin committed by them, by his chastisement of them, and still continue his love to them; for even that is done in love. Besides, the anger of God towards them, is often only in their sense and apprehension of it; when God goes forth towards them, in some dispensations of his, which are not agreeable to them, they conclude he is angry with them; and when these dispensations are varied, then they suppose his anger is turned away from them, Isa. xii. 1. so when he hides his face from them, and unbelief prevails, they interpret it, putting them away in anger, and shutting up his tender mercies in anger, Psalm xxvii. 9. and lxxvii. 9. when he seems to turn a deaf ear to their prayers, and does not give an immediate answer to them; this they call being angry against the prayer of his people, Psalm lxxx. 4. and when he afflicts them, in one way or another, then they apprehend he comes forth in anger against them; and "they have no soundness in their flesh, because of his anger; nor rest in their bones, because of their sins," Psalm xxxviii. 3. but when he takes off his afflicting hand, grants his gracious presence, and manifests his pardoning love and grace, then they conclude he has turned himself from the fierceness of his anger, Psalm lxxxv. 2, 3. Now this apparent anger, or appearance of anger, *endures but for a moment*, Psalm xxx. 5. a very short space of time indeed; though God hides his face from his people, and chides them for their sins, yet he does not keep anger for ever: this is the criterion by which he is distinguished from other gods, in that he retains not his anger for ever, because he delighteth in mercy, Psalm ciii. 9. Mic. vii. 18. and in this the anger of God towards his people, differs from his anger to wicked men, since the one is but for a moment, and the other is continual.

II. The wrath of God is *the heat of his great anger*, Deut. xxix. 24. it is his anger not only kindled and incensed, but blown up into a flame; it is the *indignation* of his anger, the *fury* and *fierceness* of it, Isa. xxx. 30. and xlii. 25. Hos. xi. 9. and it seems to be no other than his punitive justice, and includes his will to punish sinners according to the demerit of their sins in strict justice; his threatenings to do it, and the actual execution of it; which is the vengeance that belongs to him, and he will recompence; even his vindictive wrath, or vengeful judgment; *What if God willing to shew his wrath,* &c.? Rom. ix. 22. Now the wrath of God may be considered,

1. As temporary, or what is executed in the present life; of which there have been many instances and examples, and there will be more; and a brief review of them will give a more enlarged idea of the wrath of God. Not to take notice of the apostate angels, whom God has cast down to hell; where, though they may not be in full torment, yet are dreadful instances of the wrath of God against sin; since not one of them have been spared, or have shared in pardoning grace and mercy. I shall only observe what examples of it have been, or will be, among men. The first instance of it is in the condemnation of Adam, and all his posterity, for the first sin, and for only one single sin of his. How great must that sin be! what sinfulness must there be in it! how greatly must the divine Being be incensed by it! in that, for it, he has caused death, that is, his wrath to pass sententially on him, and all his offspring; so that, in consequence of it, all the children of Adam are the children of God's wrath. The next is the drowning of the old world, when full of violence and corruption; so that God repented he had made man in it, and it grieved him to the heart; and in his wrath he determined to destroy man and beast in it; and which he did, by bringing a flood on the world of the ungodly. Then follows another, though not so general; but limited and restrained to a part of the world; the cities of Sodom and Gomorrah, and others of the plain; whose inhabitants being notorious sinners, provoked the eyes of God's glory to such a degree, that he rained fire and brimstone from heaven upon them; and set them as an example and emblem of men's suffering the vengeance of eternal fire. The plagues inflicted on the Egyptians, for not letting Israel go, when demanded of them, is another instance of the wrath of God; for by inflicting these on them, he not only made a way to his anger, to shew it forth, as the Psalmist says; but, as he also observes, "he cast upon them the fierceness of his anger, wrath, indignation, and trouble," Psalm lxxviii. 49, 50. The children of Israel themselves often provoked the Lord to wrath; and brought it down upon them, for their sins; as at Horeb, when they made the calf; at Taberah, Massah, and Kibroth-hattaavah, where they murmured against the Lord, Deut. ix. 8, 19, 22. as they did likewise at the report of the spies, concerning the land of Canaan; when "God swore in his wrath, they should not enter into his rest." And again, upon the affair of Korah, and his accomplices, when wrath went forth from the Lord, and the plague began, Numb. xiv. 23. and xvi. 46. Witness, also, their several captivities; particularly their captivity in Babylon, through their mocking at, and misuse of the prophets of the Lord; so that wrath

H

arose against them; and there was no remedy; and their last captivity, and destruction, by the Romans; when wrath came upon them to the uttermost; and under which wrath, and in which captivity they are to this day. Whenever the four sore judgments of God, the sword, famine, pestilence, and wild beasts, have been exercised in the world, as they often have been; they are always in wrath; and these with earthquakes, and such-like uncommon events, are presignifications, and foretokens of greater wrath yet to come; and in a little while, the seven vials full of the wrath of God, will be poured forth on antichrist, and on the antichristian states; and the judgment of God will come on Babylon in one day. And when the end of all things is come, the earth, and all in it will be burnt with fire, and the heavens melt away with fervent heat; the day of the Lord will burn like an oven, and the wicked, like stubble, will be burnt up by it, and will have neither root nor branch left: all which will be expressive of the great wrath of God. But there is no greater instance of it, or what more fully demonstrates it, than what our Lord Jesus Christ suffered and endured as the Surety of his people, in their room and stead; when, their sins being imputed to him, were found on him, and he was stricken for them; the sword of justice was sheathed in him; the vindictive wrath of God was poured forth upon him, to the uttermost of the demerit of sin; God spared him not: how unconceivably great must his wrath be against sin, when God spared not in the least his own dearly beloved Son, but suffered him to be put to the most exquisite pain, both in body and soul, for the sins of his people!

2. There is the wrath of God that is yet to come: the Scriptures speak of future wrath; wrath that will take place in the life which is to come; which in part, commences at the death of wicked men; and will be complete at their resurrection from the dead, Matt. iii. 7. 1 Thess. i. 10. This is expressed by fire, than which nothing is more intolerable; even devouring fire and everlasting burnings, not to be endured; this is no other than the curse of the law that is broken; which not only reaches to this life, but to that which is to come; it is the same with the second death; which lies in a separation from God, and, in a sense of his hot displeasure; it is called hell and hell-fire; the word for which, in the New Testament, is taken from Ge-hinnom, or the valley of Hinnom; where the Jews burnt their children in sacrifice to Moloch; and which place, from the beating of drums in it, that the shrieks of the children might not be heard by their parents, was called Tophet; of which the prophet says, as an emblem of hell-fire, or the fire of divine wrath; *Tophet is ordained of old—the pile thereof is fire, and much wood: the breath of the Lord, like a stream of brimstone, doth kindle it,* Isa. xxx. 33. which is an awful representation of the wrath of God. And by whatsoever term this state of wrath is expressed, it is always spoken of as what will continue for ever: it is called everlasting fire, everlasting punishment, everlasting destruction, " the smoke of torment, that ascends for ever and ever;" and for the commencement of which, in its full extent, there is a day fixed, called, " the day of wrath, and righteous judgment of God;" until which time God reserves wrath for his adversaries; it is laid up in store with him, among his treasures, and will be ever laying out, and pouring forth.

As to the objects of this wrath, seeing it is revealed against all unrighteousness and ungodliness of men; it lies against all that are unrighteous and ungodly; and as all have sinned, so all are under sin, are called *children of wrath*, Eph. ii. 3. Rom. i. 18. and iii. 9, 23. but there are some particularly described, on whom this wrath comes, and they are called *children of disobedience* Eph. v. 5, 6. Col. iii. 5, 6. such who are disobedient to the light of nature, rebel against it, and hold truth in unrighteousness, which that discovers; and so as they sin without law, they perish without law, Rom. i. 18, 19, 21, 28. and ii. 12. and who also are disobedient to the law of God, break it, and are convicted by it, as transgressors, whom it pronounces guilty, and is the ministration of condemnation and death unto them; and who are disobedient to the gospel of Christ, obey not the truth, but obey unrighteousness, and are slaves to their sinful lusts and pleasures; on these come indignation and wrath, tribulation and anguish; even on every soul of man that does evil, 2 Thess. i. 8. Rom. ii. 8, 9. they are also represented as unbelievers: *He that believeth not the Son, shall not see life; but the wrath of God abideth on him*: he that does not believe that Christ is the Son of God, that he is the Messiah and Saviour of men, the sentence of wrath, which the law has passed on him, as a transgressor of that, remains; and since he denies divine revelation, rejects the gospel-scheme, and disbelieves Christ as a Saviour, and salvation by him, there is no help for him; wrath is on him, and that without remedy, it must abide: now it is not any sort of unbelief for which this wrath is, and abides; not for that which is through the want of the means of faith, such as in heathens; for "how shall they believe on him of whom they have not heard?" Rom. x. 14, 17. nor which is through the want of the special grace of faith, which is the gift of God, and peculiar to his elect, and which he only can give, and yet denies it; and which, without his grace vouchsafed, they can never have: but it is the disbelief of the report of the gospel, by such who have the opportunity of reading and hearing it, and yet either attend not to the evidence of it; or, notwithstanding that, reject it; they receive not the record God has given of his Son, and so make him a liar, than which nothing is more provoking to wrath, 1 John v. 10. This was the case of the Jews of old, John iii. 19. and is of the deists of the present age. In short, the wrath of God comes upon men either for their sins against the light of nature, or against the law of God, or against the gospel of Christ.

There are some on whom no wrath comes here, nor hereafter; who are the vessels of mercy, afore-prepared for glory: concerning whom Jehovah says, *fury is not in me;* and to whom he is all love, *love* itself, Isa. xxvii. 4. 1 John iv. 16. being sinners indeed, and transgressors of the law of God, they are *children of wrath as others,* Eph. ii. 3. which phrase not only means that they are deserving of wrath, but that, as they are sinners, they are found guilty of it; and not only found guilty, but are condemned unto it; they are really under the sentence of wrath, condemnation, and death; they are obnoxious to the curse of the law, which is no other than the wrath of God; they are liable to it, and in danger of it; and being so near it, how is it that they escape it, and are secured from it? They are secured from it by the decree of God, who has appointed them not to wrath, but to obtain salvation, 1 Thess. v. 9. which decree is unfrustrable by the oath of God, who has sworn that he will not be wroth with them, Isa. liv. 9. which is immutable: by the suretyship-engagements of Christ for them, to bear it in their room; and till that was done, God forbore to execute the sentence; called the forbearance of God, Rom. iii. 25. by Christ's actually bearing the chastisement of their peace; by being made a curse for them, and enduring the wrath of God in their room; whereby he delivered them from wrath to come, Psalm lxxxix. 38. 1 Thess. v. 10. and by his righteousness imputed to them, through which, being justified, they are saved from wrath, Rom. v. 9. though even these persons may have, at times, some apprehensions of the wrath of God; as, particularly, under first awakenings, and convictions of sin; when the law works a sense of wrath in them, and leaves in them a fearful looking for of judgment and fiery indignation; when they flee to Christ, from wrath to come, and say, "Lord, save us, or we perish;" and afterwards, when under the hidings of God's face, or his afflicting hand is upon them, they imagine that the wrath of God lies hard upon them, and his fierce wrath goes over them, Psalm lxxxviii. 7. 16. see Lam. iii. 1. but in reality, there is no wrath comes upon them now; their afflictions and chastisements are all in love; and there will be no curse hereafter; but they shall always see the face of God, and be "in his presence, where are fulness of joy, and pleasures for evermore," Rev. iii. 19. and xxii. 3, 4.

CHAP. XVIII.

OF THE HATRED OF GOD.

THERE are some[1] that deny that hatred belongs to God; or that he hates any thing; and urge a passage in the book of Wisdom, chap. xi. 25. *Thou lovest all beings, and hatest none of these that thou hast made;* which is true of the creatures of God, as such; for as they are made by him they are all very good; and are loved, delighted in, and not hated by him. Nor is hatred to be considered as a passion in him, as it is in men; who is a pure, active Spirit, and is solely agent, and not a patient; is not capable of suffering any thing: much less as it is a criminal passion, by which men, in their worst estate, are described, *hateful,* and *hating one another,*

---

[1] Aquinas contr. Gentiles, 1. 1. c. 96. Vid. Francisc. Silvester. in ibid.

Tit. iii. 3. since he is a perfectly holy Being, and without iniquity. Yet the scriptures do, in many places, attribute to him hatred both of persons and things, Psalm v. 5. Zech. viii. 17. and most truly and rightly; and this may be concluded from love being in God, as has been shewn; though this is made use of as an argument against it, because opposite to it; but where there is love of any person or thing, there will be an hatred of that which is contrary to the object loved: thus good men, as they love those that are good, like themselves, and good things, so they hate that which is evil; they love God, the chiefest good; and they hate sin, the chiefest evil, as diametrically opposite to him, Psalm xcvii. 10. Amos v. 15. So the righteous Lord, as he loves righteousness and righteous men, his people; as they are clothed in the righteousness of Christ, and found in the ways of righteousness, so he hates unrighteousness, and unrighteous men; for to the Son of God he saith, *thou lovest righteousness, and hatest iniquity; therefore God, thy God, hath anointed thee with the oil of gladness above thy fellows,* Psalm xlv. 7. besides, it is a virtue, yea grace, in good men, to hate sin that dwells in them, and is committed by them, as the apostle did, Rom. vii. 15. for without the grace of God it is not hated; and also to hate them that hate the Lord, as David did, and for the truth of which he appeals to God, *Do not I hate them, O Lord that hate thee? I hate them with perfect hatred,* Psalm cxxxix. 21, 22. Now if it is a virtue, or owing to the grace of God in them, that they do hate sin and sinners, then this must come from God, from whom all grace, and every good gift comes; and consequently must be in him, in a higher degree, even in the most perfect manner; to all which may be added, that hatred, when ascribed to God, sometimes signifies no other than his will to punish sin and sinners, and his execution of it, Psalm v. 5, 6. and so is an act of justice, of punitive justice; *And is God unrighteous, who taketh vengeance?* No; he is righteous in that, as he is in all his works, Rom. iii. 5. For the further illustration of this point, I shall consider both what that is; and who they are God is said to hate.

1. What that is he hates, that is sin; and this is consistent with his not hating any of his creatures; for sin is no creature of his; he is not the author of sin; all the creatures he made were very good; but sin was not among them; every creature of God is good, and not to be refused, rejected, and hated by men; as none are by God, as such; but sin is not any of them. Sin must be hateful to God, since it is so contrary to his nature, to his will, and to his righteous law. All sin is an abomination to him; but there are some sins that are particularly observed as hated by him, as idolatry, Deut. xvi. 22. Jer. xliv. 3, 4, 5. perjury, Zech. viii. 17. all insincere and hypocritical acts of worship, Isa. i. 14, 15. Amos v. 21. sins against the two tables of the law; as murder, which stands among the six things which God hates, Prov. vi. 16, 17, 18. fornication, adultery, community of wives; the deeds of the Nicolaitans he is said to hate, Rev. ii. 6, 15. theft, robbery, rapine, and violence of every sort; all kind of injury to the persons and properties of men, Psalm xi. 5. Isa. lxi. 8. and every evil thing a man may imagine against his neighbour, Zech. viii. 17. And all this is true of each of the divine persons. God the Father has shewn his hatred of sin by the judgments he has executed in casting down from heaven to hell the angels that sinned, driving Adam and Eve out of Paradise, bringing a flood upon the world of the ungodly, raining fire and brimstone on Sodom and Gomorrah; with other instances in following ages, and later ones; and by the chastisements of his own people, when they sin and transgress his law; but in nothing more than by the condemnation of sin in the flesh of Christ, when he suffered in the room and stead of his people, as their Surety and Saviour; and so by the punishment of wicked men to all eternity. The Son of God has given sufficient proof of his loving righteousness, and hating iniquity, of whom these things are expressly said, Psalm xlv. 7. Heb. i. 8, 9. and are true of him as a divine person, and as Mediator, and as man; and this he has done by inveighing against the sins of the Jews in his time; by his severe usage of the buyers and sellers in the temple; and by his exhortations and threatenings to men to sin no more, lest worse things came unto them: and the Holy Ghost is not only grieved by the sinful actions and behaviour of men; but may be vexed by them, so as to turn to be their enemy, and fight against them, Isa. lxiii. 10. Which leads me to consider,

2. Who they are that God hates; and they are sinners, *workers of iniquity*, Psalm

v. 5. not men, as men, but as sinful men; and not all that sin, or have sin in them; for then all would be hated, for all have sinned in Adam, and by actual transgressions; and none, even the best of men, are without it, Rom. iii. 23. 1 John i. 8. but *workers* of it, traders in it, whose whole lives are one continued series of sinning; to those it will be said, *I never knew you; I never loved you, I always hated you; depart from me, ye that work iniquity,* Matt. vii. 23. make a trade of it; make it the business of their lives, continually and constantly commit it, John viii. 34. 1 John iii. 8, 9. and God is impartial, he hates *all the workers of iniquity;* and brings down his *indignation and wrath, tribulation and anguish, on every soul of man that does evil, of the Jew first, and also of the Gentile,* Rom. ii. 8, 9. The Scriptures speak of an hatred of some persons antecedent to sin, and without the consideration of it; which, though it may be attended with some difficulty to account for; yet may be understood in a good sense, and consistent with the perfections of God, and with what has been said of his hatred of sin and sinners; for thus it is said of Jacob and Esau, personally considered; *Jacob have I loved, but Esau have I hated,* Mal. i. 2. and which was before the one had done any good, or the other done any evil; as the apostle expressly says, Rom. ix. 11, 12, 13. *The children not being yet born, neither having done any good or evil; that the purpose of God, according to election, might stand; not of works, but of him that calleth; it was said unto her,* to Rebekah, the mother of them, whilst they were in her womb, *the elder shall serve the younger; as it is written, Jacob have I loved, but Esau have I hated.* And what is said of these, is true of all the objects of election and non-election. And now let it be observed, that this hatred is to be understood, not of any positive hatred in the heart of God towards them, but of a negative and comparative hatred of them; that whereas while some are chosen of God, and preferred by him, and are appointed to obtain grace and glory, and to be brought to great dignity and honour; others are passed by, neglected, postponed, and set less by; which is called an hatred of them; that is, a comparative one, in comparison of the love shewn, and the preference given to others; in this sense the word is used in Luke xiv. 26. *If any man hate not his father, and mother, and wife, and children, and brethren, and sisters, yea, and his own life also, he cannot be my disciple:* the meaning of which cannot be, that a man must have positive hatred of such near relations, and of his own life, but that he should be negligent of these in comparison of Christ; postpone them to him, set less by them, have a less affection for them than him, and so prefer him unto them; in like sense are we to understand the above expression concerning Esau, and all reprobates: and that this may appear yet clear, it should be observed, that in this business there are two acts of the divine will; the one is a will not to bestow benefits of special goodness; not to give grace, nor to raise to honour and glory: and this God may do antecedent to, and without any consideration of sin; but act according to his sovereign will and pleasure, since he is under no obligation to confer benefits, but may bestow them on whom he pleases; as he himself says, *Is it not lawful for me to do what I will with mine own?* Matt. xx. 15. The other act of the divine will is, to inflict evil; and that is always for sin, and in consideration of it; for though sin is not the cause of the act of the will, it is the cause of the thing willed, which is not willed without the consideration of it; they are the wicked God has made, or appointed to the day of evil, and no other; ungodly men, whom he has fore-ordained to that condemnation, vessels of wrath, fitted for destruction by sin; on whom it is the will of God to shew his wrath, and make his power known, Prov. xvi. 4. Jude ver. 4. Rom. ix. 22. In the one act, hatred, or a denial of grace, is without the consideration of sin; in the other, hatred, or a will to punish is with it; punishment being only willed for it: but then God never hates his elect in any sense; they are always loved by him; to which hatred is opposite: he may be angry with them, and chastise them for their sins; yea, he may, as he says, and as they apprehend, *in a little wrath hide* his *face* from them; but he never hates them; though he hates their sins, and shews his resentment at them, he still loves them freely; renews, and raises them up by repentance, when fallen into sin, and manifests and applies his pardoning grace to them, and never bears any hatred to their persons.

CHAP. XIX.

OF THE JOY OF GOD.

Joy, which is often attributed to God in the scriptures, bears some resemblance to the affection of joy in men; but is, by some philosophers,[1] denied of him; and, indeed, is not to be considered as a passion, in him, as in them; and particularly when in its height, or at an excess; as it is a transport of the mind, and carries it out of, and beyond itself, as it were; as in the cases of Jacob, when the news of his son Joseph's being alive were brought him; and of the disciples, when they heard of the resurrection of Christ, believed not for joy: and, indeed, all affections that are ascribed to God, are ascribed to him, not as in themselves, but as to their effects; such and such effects being done by men, when so and so affected. Hence when similar ones are done by God, the like affections are ascribed to him; and this of joy is expressed by him in very different effects; as in inflicting punishment, as well as in conferring benefits; in the one he rejoices in the glory of his justice and holiness; and in the other, in the displays of his grace and goodness; see Deut. xxviii. 63. Though joy, as ascribed to God, seems to be no other than delight and complacency in persons and things; so some philosophers and schoolmen make them to be the same; or, however, take joy to be a species of delight; only they observe a difference, with respect to brute animals, in whom there is delight, but not joy;[2] it is also made a question with them[3] whether delight is a passion? but my business with it is only as it concerns God, and is predicated of him; and who may be said,

1. To rejoice and take delight and complacency in himself, in his own nature, and the perfections of it; in which there is an all-sufficiency, and so a fulness of content and satisfaction; and he rests infinitely well-pleased in himself. Hence Aquinas,[4] who defines joy and delight a certain quietation, or rest of the will, in what is willed by it; observes, that God must greatly rest quiet and satisfied in himself, which is his principal *volitum*, or what is willed by him, as having all-sufficiency in him, and therefore by his own will greatly rejoices and delights in himself: and though he makes joy and delight in some respect to differ; delight flowing from a good really conjoined; and joy being not only of that, but of something exterior; hence, he says, it is plain God properly delights in himself; but rejoices in himself and others. So the Jews[5] interpret 1 Chron. xvi. 27. *gladness in his place*, of joy in himself.

2. He rejoices and takes delight and complacency in his works, Psalm civ. 31. In the works of creation, which, when he had finished, he not only rested from them, but rested in them, with delight and pleasure; he looked them over, and pronounced them all very good; and he still appears to have pleasure in them, by his continuance of them in being, by upholding all things by the word of his power: he rejoices and delights in the works of his providence, in which he is always concerned, John v. 17. These, so far as they are known by men, yield an unspeakable delight and pleasure in the contemplation of them; and especially when they will be manifest; and though they are now many of them, unsearchable and past finding out, yet there is a depth of riches, both of the wisdom and knowledge of God in them; but what delight must God take in them, being all according to his sovereign will and pleasure; by whom they are seen and known in their beauty, harmony, and connection; and the springs and causes of them, and the several ends answered by them? God rejoices and takes delight particularly in the great work of redemption, contrived by his infinite wisdom, and wrought out by his Son; partly because of his own glory displayed therein; as of his love, grace, and mercy, so of his truth and faithfulness, holiness and justice; and partly because of the salvation of his people, secured thereby; a thing his heart was set upon from everlasting; what he resolved should be, and what he appointed them to: he rejoices and delights in his work of grace on the hearts of his people; this is their beauty, even the beauty of holiness, which he, the king, greatly desires; by which they are all glorious within, and well-pleasing in his sight; he delights in

---

[1] Sallustius de Diis, c. 14. Plato in Philebo. p. 384.
[2] Aquin. Sum. Theolog. prima 2 par. Quæst. 31. art. 3. et Avicenna in ibid.
[3] Ibid. art. 1. et Aristot. apud ibid.
[4] Contr. Gentiles, 1. 1. c. 90.
[5] R. Joseph Albo in Sepher Ikkarim, 1. 2. c. 15.

the graces which he himself, by his Spirit, has wrought in them, and in the exercise of those graces, as drawn forth by him, their faith, hope, love, fear, &c. *The Lord taketh pleasure in them that fear him, in those that hope in his mercy,* Psalm cxlvii. 11. see Cant. iv. 9, 10. And so all his people, as they are his workmanship, his poem, curiously wrought by him; the works of his hands, in whom, and whereby he is glorified; he rejoices in them, and blesses on account of them, Isa. xix. 25. and lx. 21. Wherefore,

3. He may be truly said to rejoice, delight, and take pleasure in his people, as he often is; they are his Hephzibah, in whom he delights; his Beulah, to whom he is married; and therefore, as a bridegroom rejoices over his bride, so does the Lord rejoice over them, Psalm cxlix. 4. Isa. lxii. 4, 5. not in all men; for there are some in whom he has no joy, vessels in whom he has no delight and pleasure, Isa. ix. 17. and xxvii. 11. Mal. i. 10. but his special covenant-people, Jer. xxxii. 38—41. and these not as creatures, and still less as sinful creatures, either as considered in Adam, or in themselves, guilty and defiled; but as in Christ, in whom God is well pleased, and in all that are in him, as chosen in him, and given to him; so God the Father rejoiced in them from everlasting; for as his love to them, so his joy in them, is so early, it being a love of complacency and delight; and of which joy there are new expressions in conversion; see Luke xv. 7, 9, 22, 23, 24. And likewise the Son of God, was from all eternity rejoicing in the habitable parts of the earth; and his delights were with the sons of men, Prov. viii. 31. and which joy he felt under all his sorrows and sufferings, when working out their salvation, Heb. xii. 2. and which he expresses at their conversion; that being the time of finding his lost people; and, indeed, the day of his open espousals to them, and so of the gladness of his heart, Luke xv. 3, 4, 5. Cant. iii. 11. and they will also be his joy, and crown of rejoicing, in the last day; when they shall be introduced into his presence, not only with joy and gladness in themselves, but with it in him, who will present them before his Father and himself, with exceeding joy, Psalm xlv. 13, 14. Jude ver. 24. and this joy over them, both in him and his divine Father, is to do them good, and issues in it; to bestow benefits upon them, grace here, and glory hereafter; to beautify them with salvation; to make them prosperous, especially in spiritual things, in which prosperity he takes pleasure; and in making all things work together for their good, Jer. xxxii. 41. Psalm cxlix. 4. and xxxv. 27. which joy is full; there is a redundancy, an overflow of it; it is hearty and sincere, is the strength and security of the saints, and will remain for ever, Nehem. viii. 10. Zeph. iii. 17.

CHAP. XX.

OF THE HOLINESS OF GOD.

HAVING considered those attributes of God which bear a likeness to affections in men; I proceed to consider those which in them may be called virtues; as holiness, justice, or righteousness, truth, or faithfulness; and shall begin with the holiness of God. And,

First, Shew that it is in God, and belongs to him, and what it is. The scriptures most abundantly ascribe it to him; he is very frequently called *holy*, and *the holy One;* this title he takes to himself, Isa. xl. 25. Hos. xi. 9. and is often given him by others, angels and men; and, indeed, without holiness he would not be that *perfect* being he is; unholiness is the imperfection of every rational being in whom it is; it is what has made angels and men both impure and imperfect; and since no men, even the best, are without sin; therefore none are in themselves perfect. But as for God, his ways and works are perfect, and so is his nature; being just and true, and without iniquity, Deut. xxxii. 4. Holiness is the purity and rectitude of his nature; whose nature is so pure, as to be without spot or stain, or any thing like it: he is light and purity itself, and in him is no darkness or impurity at all; as "he is of purer eyes than to behold iniquity," so he is of a purer heart and mind than to have one sinful thought in it: his thoughts are not as ours; he is the pattern of purity and holiness, and to be copied after: men should be holy, as and because he is holy; it is one of the imitable perfections of God, in which he is to be followed; though it cannot be attained to, as it is in him, Lev. xi. 44, 45. and xix. 2. 1 Pet. i. 15, 16.

Holiness is an essential attribute of God; it is his nature and essence; it is himself; he is holiness itself; "he swears by himself, because he can swear by no greater;" and he will not swear by any less, and yet he swears by his holiness, Heb. vi. 13. Psalm lxxxix. 35. Amos iv. 2. and vi. 8. which places put and compared together shew that the holiness of God is himself; and it has been thought to be not so much a particular and distinct attribute of itself, as the lustre, glory, and harmony of all the rest; and is what is called *the beauty of the Lord*, Psalm xxvii. 4. as it is the beauty of the good angels, and of regenerate men; and, indeed, what is wisdom or knowledge, without holiness, but craft and cunning? or what is power, without it, but tyranny, oppression, and cruelty? but God is *glorious in holiness*, Exod. xv. 11. this gives a lustre to all his perfections, and is the glory of them; and therefore none of them are or can be exercised in a wrong manner, or to any bad purpose. And as it is his nature and essence, it is infinite and unbounded; it cannot be greater than it is, and can neither be increased nor diminished; when, therefore, men are exhorted to *sanctify* the Lord, and are directed to pray that his *name* may be *hallowed*, or sanctified, Isa. viii. 13. Matt. vi. 9. the meaning is not as if he was to be, or could be made more holy than he is; but that his holiness be declared, manifested, and celebrated more and more; it is so perfect that nothing can be added to it. And as it is his nature and essence, it is immutable and invariable; the holiness of a creature is changeable, as the holiness of angels and men; which has appeared by the apostasy of the one, and the fall of the other; and the holiness of saints, though its principle is the same, the acts and exercises are variable. But God is always the same holy Being, without any variableness, or shadow of turning. He is originally holy, he is so in and of himself, and of no other; there is none prior and superior to him, from whom he could derive or receive any holiness; as his Being is of himself, so is his holiness, which is himself: the holiness of angels and men is not of themselves, but of God; he is the fountain of holiness to all rational creatures that partake of it; it is peculiar to him, yea, only in him; Hannah says, in her song, *There is none holy as the Lord*, 1 Sam. ii. 2. In another song yet to be sung, the song of Moses and of the Lamb, it is said, *Who shall not fear thee, O Lord, and glorify thy name? for thou only art holy*, Rev. xv. 4. The holiness of creatures is but a shadow of holiness, in comparison of the holiness of God; the holy angels are chargeable with folly in his sight, and they cover their faces with their wings, while they celebrate the perfection of God's holiness; as conscious to themselves, that theirs will not bear to be compared with his, Job. iv. 17, 18. Isa. vi. 2, 3. God only is essentially, originally, underivatively, perfectly, and immutably holy.

This must be understood not of one person in the Deity, to the exclusion of the rest; as not of the Spirit, though he is peculiarly called the *holy Ghost*, and the holy Spirit, yet not to the exclusion of the Father and Son; so not of the Father, to the exclusion of the Son and Spirit; for as they are the one God, who is a Spirit, they partake of the same common and undivided nature, and all the perfections of it, and of this with the rest. Hence we read of the holy Elohim, or divine Persons, in the plural number; and of the holy ones, the holy Father, the holy Son, and the holy Spirit, Josh. xxiv. 19. Prov. xxx. 2. Dan. iv. 17. And no doubt respect is had to the holiness of the three divine persons, by the seraphim, when they said, *holy, holy, holy, Lord God of hosts!* Isa. vi. 3. and by the four beasts, or living creatures, continually employed in the same divine service, celebrating the perfections of God in much the same language, saying, *Holy, holy, holy, Lord God almighty!* Rev. iv. 8. As there is no doubt made of the Deity of the Father, there can be none of his holiness: our Lord addresses him under the relation of *Father*, and under the epithet of *holy Father*, John xvii. 11. and all that has been said of the holiness of God belongs to him; of which there can be no question made: and it is as true of the Son as of the Father; for as the Father is the holy Father, he must be the holy Son, since he is of the same nature, and is "the brightness of his Father's glory, and the express image of his person;" and as the Father is of purer eyes than to behold iniquity, so is the Son; as the Father loves righteousness and hates iniquity, this is expressly said of the Son, Heb. i. 8. 9. he is eminently called "the holy one of God," Psalm xvi. 10. and "the holy one of Israel," more than thirty times in the prophecy of Isaiah; and particularly is so called along with the titles of Redeemer and Husband, which are peculiar to the second Person, the Son of God, the Redeemer of his people, and the

Husband of his church, Isa. xlvii. 4. and liv. 5. yea, he is called the *most holy*, who was anointed with the Holy Ghost above his fellows, and "having the Spirit without measure," Dan. ix. 24. the title of holy he takes to himself when addressing the church, which is an emblem of the purest state of the church militant on earth, the church of Philadelphia; *These things saith he that is holy*, Rev. iii. 7. Nay, the devil himself gives it to him; *I know thee, who thou art, the holy One of God*. Luke iv. 34. Besides, Christ is not only holy in his human nature, even perfectly so, and sanctified and set apart to his office as Mediator, by his Father; for which office holiness is a necessary requisite and qualification; but he is the Fountain of holiness to his church and people; they are sanctified in him and by him; he is made sanctification to them, and all the holiness, or holy graces that are in them, are all from him, John i. 14, 16. which could not be, if he was not holy, and even holiness itself. And as for the blessed Spirit, the third Person in the Deity, the epithet of *holy* is commonly given to him, as before observed; and very truly, since he is of the same nature with the Father and the Son; and so he is holy by nature and essence, and as appears by his graces, operations, and influences; and by his being grieved, speaking after the manner of men, with the sins and impurities of men; the reason of which is, because they are so contrary to his pure and holy nature, that he cannot bear them, but expresses his dislike and displeasure at them, Eph. iv. 29, 30. And all this will be still more clear and manifest, by considering,

Secondly, The instances wherein and whereby the holiness of God is displayed, which are his works, and actions, and proceedings towards his creatures; God is *holy in all his works;* or his holiness is manifest in them, and by them, Psalm cxlv. 17.

1st, The holiness of God the Father; which is visible, 1. In the works of creation; for as he made all things by his Son, not as an instrument, but as co-efficient with him, so when he overlooked them, he pronounced them very *good;* which he would not have done, had there been any thing impure or unholy in them. Angels, not only those that stood, but those that fell, were originally holy, as made by him: the elect angels continue in the holiness in which they were created; and the angels that sinned are not in the estate in which they were at their creation; they *kept not their first estate*, which was an estate of purity and holiness; and *abode not in the truth*, in the uprightness and integrity in which they were formed, Jude ver. 6. John viii. 44. And as for man, he was made after the image, and in the likeness of God, which greatly consisted in holiness; a pure, holy, and upright creature he was; and had a law given him, holy, just, and good, as the rule of his obedience, and which was inscribed on his heart; some remains of which are to be found in his fallen posterity, and even in the Gentiles.

2. The holiness of God appears in his works of providence; which, though many of them are dark and intricate, not easily penetrated into, and to be accounted for; yet there is nothing criminal and sinful in them: the principal thing objected to the holiness of God in his providences, is his suffering sin to be in the world; but then, though it is by his voluntary permission, or permissive will, yet he is neither the author nor abettor of it: he neither commands it, nor approves of it, nor persuades to it, nor tempts nor forces to it; but all the reverse, forbids it, disapproves of it, dissuades from it, threatens to punish for it, yea, even chastises his own people for it; and, besides, over-rules it for great good, and for his own glory; as the fall of Adam, the sin of Joseph's brethren, the Jews' crucifixion of Christ; which have been instanced in, and observed under a former attribute: wherefore the dispensations of God, in his providence, are not to be charged with unholiness on this account.

3. The holiness of Jehovah the Father is to be observed in those acts of grace which are peculiar to him; as in choosing some in Christ his Son to everlasting life, before the world began. Now though not the holiness of the creature, nor even the foresight of it, is the cause of this act; yet holiness, or the sanctification of the Spirit, is fixed as a means in it; and it is the will of God, that those whom he chooses and appoints to salvation should partake of it, or come to salvation through it; nay, he has not only chosen them *through* it, as a means, but he has chosen them *to* it, as a subordinate end; he has chosen them to be holy in part, in this life, and perfectly in the life to come; and holiness of heart and life, is the evidence of interest in it, and nothing more powerfully excites and engages to it. The covenant which he has

made with his son Jesus Christ, on the behalf of the chosen ones, provides abundantly for their holiness, both internal and external; see Ezek. xxxvi. 25, 26, 27. and the promises of it serve greatly to promote it, and to influence the saints to be "perfecting holiness in the fear of God," 2 Cor. vii. 1. And in this covenant is laid up a rod of correction, in love, to chastise with it the sins of God's people, Psalm lxxxix. 29—34. Justification is an act of God's grace towards them; it is God, even God the Father, that justifies, through the imputation of his Son's righteousness to them; by which the holy law of God is so far from being made void, that it is established, magnified, and made honourable: nor are justified persons exempted from obedience to it, but are more strongly bound and constrained to serve it; and though God justifies the ungodly, yet not without a righteousness provided for them, and imputed to them: nor does he justify, vindicate, or approve of their ungodliness, nor connive at it; but turns it from them, and them from that: and faith, which receives the blessing of justification from the Lord, by which men perceive their interest in it, and enjoy the comfort of it, is an operative grace, works by love to God, to Christ, and his people; and is attended with good works, the fruits of righteousness: the like may be observed with respect to other acts of the Father's grace; as adoption, pardon, &c.

2dly, The holiness of the Son of God is to be seen in all his works; in the works of creation and providence, in common with his divine Father; and in all his works of grace; in giving himself to sanctify his church, and make it a glorious one, without spot or wrinkle, through his blood and righteousness; in redeeming his people from all iniquity, to purify them to himself a peculiar people; in bearing their sins, and making satisfaction for them, that they might live unto righteousness, and that the body of sin might be destroyed, Eph. v. 25, 27. Tit. ii. 14. 1 Pet. ii. 24. Rom. vi. 6. and so in the execution of all his offices; as a Prophet, he has appeared to be an holy one; the faith delivered by him to the saints, is a most holy faith, wholesome words, doctrines according to godliness: as a Priest, he is holy and harmless, separate from sinners, and has offered up himself without spot to God; and though he makes intercession for transgressors, it is upon the foot of his sacrifice and righteousness: as a King, all his administrations are in purity and righteousness; and his laws, commands, and ordinances, are holy ones; and when he comes as judge of the world, he will appear without sin, and "judge the world in righteousness."

3dly, The holiness of the blessed Spirit, is visible in the formation of the human nature of Christ; in separating that mass out of which it was framed in the virgin; in sanctifying it, and preserving it from the taint and contagion of original sin; in filling the human nature, when formed, with his holy gifts and graces, and that without measure; and through him it was offered up without spot; and he was declared to be the Son of God with power, by the Spirit of holiness, through the resurrection from the dead. Moreover, his holiness is manifest in the sanctification of the chosen of God, and the redeemed of the Lamb, which is therefore called, *the sanctification of the Spirit*, 2 Thess. ii. 13. 1 Pet. i. 2. in convincing them of sin, of the evil nature and just demerit of it; in converting them from it; in calling them with an holy calling, and to holiness; in implanting principles of grace and holiness in them; in purifying their hearts by faith, through the sprinkling of the blood of Jesus; in leading them in the way of holiness, in which men, though fools, shall not err; and in carrying on, and perfecting the work of sanctification in them, "without which none shall see the Lord."

CHAP. XXI.

OF THE JUSTICE OR RIGHTEOUSNESS OF GOD.

CONCERNING this attribute of God, I shall,

First, Shew that it does belong to him, and is natural and essential to him. The scriptures do abundantly ascribe it to him; all rational creatures, angels and men, good and bad, acknowledge it in him, Rev. xvi. 5. Exod. ix. 27. Jer. xii. 1. Dan. ix. 9. Psalm cxlv. 7. and remove all unrighteousness from him, and affirm there is none in him, Psalm xcii. 15. Rom. ix. 14. And, indeed, without this attribute, he would not be fit to be the Governor of the world, and the judge of the whole earth; his government would be tyranny, and not yield that pleasure and delight to the inhabitants of it, it does; the reason of which is, because *righteousness and judgment are*

Chap. XXI. OF THE JUSTICE OR RIGHTEOUSNESS OF GOD.

the habitation of his throne, Psalm xcvii. 1, 2. And from his love of righteousness, and constant performance of it, it may be concluded it is natural to him; as what is loved by men, and constantly done by them, shews it to be agreeable to the nature of them, Psalm xi. 7. and ix. 4. and indeed, it is originally and essentially in God; it is in and of himself, and not of another; it is his nature and essence, and is not derived from another. Adam was righteous, but not of himself, God made him upright, or righteous; saints are righteous, not by their own righteousness, but by the righteousness of Christ imputed to them. But God is righteous in and of himself; his righteousness is essential and inderivative, and is incommunicable to a creature; it is not that by which men are made righteous, as Osiander dreamed; for though he who is Jehovah is their righteousness, yet not as he is Jehovah; for then they would be deified by him: the righteousness of God being his nature, is infinite and immutable; the righteousness of angels and men, in which they were created, was mutable; Adam lost his, and many of the angels lost theirs; but the *righteousness* of God is *like the great mountains,* as high, firm, and stable as they, and much more so, Psalm xxxvi. 6. Righteousness in creatures, is according to some law, which is the rule of it, and to which it is conformed, and is adequate; so the law of God, which is holy, just, and true, is a rule of righteousness to men; but God has no law without himself, he is a law to himself; his nature and will the law and rule of righteousness to him. Some things are just, because he wills them, as such that are of a positive kind; and others he wills them because they are just, being agreeable to his nature and moral perfections. This is an attribute common to the three Persons in the Godhead, as it must be, since it is essential to Deity, and they partake of the same undivided nature and essence: hence the Father of Christ is called by him *righteous Father,* John xvii. 25. and Christ, his Son, is called Jesus Christ *the righteous,* 1 John ii. 1. and no doubt can be made of its being proper to the holy Spirit, who *convinces* men *of righteousness and of judgment,* John xvi. 8. But,

Secondly, I shall next consider the various sorts, or branches of righteousness, which belong to God; for though it is but one in him, being his nature and essence; yet it may be considered as diversified, and as admitting of distinctions, with respect to creatures. Some distinguish it into righteousness of words, and righteousness of deeds. Righteousness of words lies in the fulfilment of his words, sayings, prophecies, and promises; and is no other than his veracity, truth, and faithfulness; which will be considered hereafter, as a distinct attribute. Righteousness of deeds, is either the rectitude, purity, and holiness of his nature; which appears in all his works and actions, and which has been treated of in the preceding chapter; or it is a giving that which belongs to himself, and to his creatures, what is each their due. So justice is defined by Cicero,[1] an affection of the mind, *Suum cuique tribuens;* giving to every one his own. Thus God gives or takes to himself what is his due; or does himself justice, by making and doing all things for his own glory; and by not giving his glory to another, nor his praise to graven images: and he gives to his creatures what is due to them by the laws of creation, and governs them in justice and equity, and disposes of them and dispenses to them, in the same manner. Justice, among men, is sometimes distinguished into commutative and retributive. Commutative justice lies in covenants, compacts, agreements, commerce, and dealings with one another, in which one gives an equivalent in money or goods, for what he receives of another; and when integrity and uprightness are preserved, this is justice. But such sort of justice cannot have place between God and men; what he gives, and they receive from him, is of free favour and good will; and what they give to him, or he receives from them, is no equivalent for what they have from him; *What shall I render to the Lord for all his benefits towards me?* Psalm cxvi. 12. nothing that is answerable to them. Besides, God has a prior right to every thing a creature has or can give; *Who hath first given to him, and it shall be recompensed to him again?* Rom. xi. 35. Retributive justice is a distribution either of rewards or punishments; the one may be called remunerative justice, the other punitive justice; and both may be observed in God.

1. Remunerative justice, or a distribution of rewards; the rule of which is not

---

[1] De Finibus, l. 5.

the merits of men, but his own gracious promise; for he first, of his own grace and good will, makes promises, and then he is just and righteous in fulfilling them; for God, as Austin[2] expresses it, "makes himself a debtor, not by receiving anything from us, but by promising such and such things to us." And his justice lies in fulfilling his promises made to such and such persons, doing such and such things; and not in rewarding any supposed merits of theirs. Thus, for instance, *The man that endures temptation shall receive the crown of life, which the Lord has promised to them that love him*, James i. 12. but the crown of life is not given according to any merit of it arising from enduring temptation, or loving the Lord; but in consequence of the promise of God graciously made to such persons, for their encouragement thereunto. Moreover, the reward is not of debt, but of grace; or God, in the distribution of rewards to men, rewards not their works, but his own grace; he first gives grace, and then rewards that grace with glory; called, *the reward of the inheritance*, Col. iii. 24. And this seems to be no other than the inseparable connection between grace and glory, adopting grace, and the heavenly inheritance; which, he having of his own grace put, does in justice inviolably maintain. Indeed, the remunerative justice of God is sometimes represented in scripture, as rendering to every man according to his deeds, or as his work shall be, Rom. ii. 5, 6, 7, 10. Rev. xxii. 12. But still it is to be observed, that the reward given or rendered, is owing to the promise that is made to them for *godliness*, whether as a principle of grace, or as practised under the influence of grace; or godly persons have *the promise of the life that now is, and of that which is to come*, 1 Tim. iv. 8. which promise is punctually and righteously performed. Besides, God does not reward the works and godly actions of men, as meritorious in themselves; but as they are the fruits of his own grace; who works in them both *to will and to do* of his own pleasure; and therefore he is *not unrighteous to forget their work and labour of love;* which springs from love, is done in faith, and with a view to his glory, Heb. vi. 10. Moreover, the works according to which God renders eternal life, are not men's own personal works; between which, and eternal life, there is no proportion; but the works of righteousness done by Christ, of which his obedience and righteousness consist; and which being done by him, on their account, as their Head and Representative, are reckoned to them; and according to these, the crown of righteousness is given them by the Lord, as a righteous Judge, in a way of righteousness, 2 Tim. iv. 8.

2. Punitive, or vindictive justice, belongs to God; *It is a righteous thing with God to render tribulation to them that trouble* his people, 2 Thess. i. 6. and so to inflict punishment for any other sin committed by men; and this has been exercised by him in all ages from the beginning of the world; and has appeared in casting down from heaven to hell the angels that sinned; in drowning the old world; in destroying Sodom and Gomorrah; in the plagues on Egypt, on Pharaoh and his host; the righteousness of which was acknowledged, in some of the instances of it, by that wicked king, Exod. ix. 27. in the several captivities of the Jews, and in the destruction of that people; and in the judgments of God on many other nations, in several periods of time; and as will be seen in the destruction of antichrist and the antichristian states; the righteousness of which will be ascribed to God by the angel of the waters, and by all his people, Rev. xvi. 5, 6. and xix. 1, 2. and in the eternal punishment and everlasting destruction of ungodly men: and this righteousness is natural and essential to God; but this the Socinians[3] deny, because they do not choose to embrace the doctrine of the necessity of Christ's satisfaction for sin, which, if granted, they must give into. But that punitive, or vindictive justice, is essential to God, or that he not only will not let sin go unpunished, but that he cannot but punish sin, is manifest, 1. From the light of nature: hence the accusations of the natural conscience in men for sins committed; the fears of divine vengeance falling upon them for it, here or hereafter; the many ways and means devised to appease angry Deity, and to avert punishment, some absurd, and others shocking; to which may be added, the name of δικη, vengeance, or justice, punitive justice, the heathens give to deity; see Rom. ii. 14, 15. Acts xxviii. 4.——2. From the word of God, and the proclamation which God

---

[2] Enarrat. in Psalm cix. tom. 8. p. 521.
[3] Socin. de Servatore, par. 1. c. 1. Prælection. Theolog. c. 16. Crellius de Deo, ejusque attributis, c. 25. in fine.

himself has made; in which, among other essential perfections of his, this is one, that he will by no means clear the guilty, and not at all acquit the wicked, Exod. xxxiv. 6, 7. Numb. xiv. 18. Nahum. i. 3.——3. From the nature of God, "who is of purer eyes than to behold iniquity;" cannot bear it, but hates it, and the workers of it; which hatred is no other than his punishment of it, Heb. i. 13. Isa. i. 13, 14. Psalm. v. 5, 6. Now as his love of righteousness is natural and essential to him; so must hatred of sin be; to which may be added, that "he is a consuming fire," Heb. xii. 29.——4. From the nature of sin, and the demerit of it, eternal death, everlasting punishment and destruction. Now if sin of itself, in its own nature, merits such punishment at the hands of God, he is obliged to inflict it; or otherwise there can be no demerit in it.——5. From the law of God; the sanction of it, and the veracity of God in it: sin is a transgression of the law; which God, as a lawgiver, cannot but punish; otherwise his legislative power and authority is of no effect, and would be despised: he has annexed a sanction to his law, which is death; and his veracity obliges him to inflict it; nor is it any objection to all this, that then all sinners must be necessarily punished; since the perfections of God, though natural to him, the acts and exercises of them are according to his will; as has been instanced in his omnipotence and mercy. Besides, it will be readily allowed, and even affirmed, that no sin goes unpunished; but is either punished in the sinner himself, or in his Surety. The reason why some are not punished in themselves, is, because Christ has made satisfaction for their sins, by bearing the punishment due unto them. Hence, 6. From sin being punished in Christ, the Surety of his people, it may be strongly concluded, that punitive justice is essential to God; or otherwise, where is the goodness of God to his own Son, that he should not spare him, but awake the sword of justice against him, and inflict the whole of punishment on him, due to the sins of those for whom he suffered, if he could not have punished sin, or this was not necessary? and, indeed, where is his wisdom in being at such an expense as the blood and life of his Son, if sin could have been let go unpunished, and the salvation of his people obtained without it? and where is the love of God to men, in giving Christ for them, for their remission and salvation, so much magnified, when all this might have been without it? but without shedding of blood, as there is no remission, so none could be, consistent with the justice of God; no pardon nor salvation, without satisfaction to that: could it have been in another way, the prayer of Christ would have brought it out, *Father, if it be possible, let this cup pass from me,* Matt. xxvi. 39. But,

Thirdly, I shall next consider the displays of the righteousness of God in his works; and vindicate his justice in them; for *the Lord is righteous in all his ways,* Psalm cxlv. 17.

1. In his ways and works of providence: he governs the world in righteousness, orders and disposes of all things in judgment; and though he does according to his sovereign will and pleasure in heaven and in earth, yet he acts according to the strictest rules of justice and equity; *Just and true are his ways;* he is *the Judge of all the earth,* who will *do right,* Rev. xv. 3. Gen. xviii. 25. and does do it; nor is he chargeable with any unrighteousness in any of his ways and works: men may wrongly charge him, and say, as the house of Israel did; *the way of the Lord is not equal;* when it is their ways that are unequal, and not his, Ezek. xviii. 29. nor is it any sufficient objection to the righteousness of God in his providences, that good men are often afflicted, and wicked men are frequently in very prosperous circumstances: these things have been stumbling and puzzling to good men, and they have not been able to reconcile them to the justice of God; see Psalm lxxiii. 4—13. Jer. xii. 1, 2. As for the afflictions of God's people, these are not punishments for sins, but chastisements of them; were they indeed punishments for sin, it would argue injustice, for it would be unjust to punish twice for the same sins; once in their Surety, and again in themselves: but so it is not; their afflictions come not from God as a judge, but as a father; and not from his justice, but his love; and not to their detriment and injury, but for their good. In short, they are chastened by the Lord, that they might not be condemned with the world, 1 Cor. xi. 32. And as for the prosperity of the wicked, though their eyes stand out with fatness, and they have more than heart can wish, yet they are like beasts that are fattened for the slaughter; their judgment may seem to linger, and their damnation to slumber,

but they do not; sudden destruction will come upon them; the tables will, ere long, be turned, and the saints, who have now their evil things, will be comforted; and the wicked, who have now their good things, will be tormented: justice, though it may not so apparently take place now, it will hereafter; when all things will be set to rights, and the judgments of God will be manifest. There is a future state, when the justice of God will shine in all its glory.

2. God is righteous in all his ways and works and acts of grace; in the predestination of men, the choice of some, and the preterition of others. While the apostle is treating on this sublime subject, he stops and asks this question, *Is there unrighteousness with God?* and answers it with the utmost abhorrence and detestation, *God forbid!* Election is neither an act of justice nor of injustice, but of the sovereign will and pleasure of God, who does what he will with his own; gives it to one, and not to another, without any imputation of injustice: if he may give grace and glory to whom he will, without such a charge, then he may determine to give it without any. If it is no injustice in men to choose their own favourites, friends, confidents, and companions; it can be none in God to choose whom he pleases to bestow his favours on; to indulge with communion with himself now, and to dwell with him to all eternity: if it was no injustice to choose some of the angels, called elect angels, and pass by others; and even to condemn all that sinned, without shewing mercy to one individual of them; it can be no injustice in him to choose some of the race of men, and save them, and pass by others, when he could have condemned them all. Nor can the imputation of Adam's sin to all his posterity, be accounted an unrighteous action. God made man upright, he made himself a sinner: God gave him a righteous law, and abilities to keep it; he voluntarily broke it: God constituted the first man the federal head and representative of all his posterity; and who so fit for this as their natural head and common parent, with and in whom they were to stand and fall; and what injustice could be in that; since had he stood they would have partook of the benefits of it; as now he fell they share in the miseries of it? and since they sinned in him, it can be no unrighteous thing to reckon it to them; or that they should be made and constituted sinners, by his disobedience. It is not reckoned unjust, among men, for children to be punished for the sins of their parents, and particularly treason; and what else is sin against God? Exod. xx. 5. The justice of God shines brightly in redemption by Christ; "Zion, and her converts, are redeemed in righteousness;" a full price is paid for the redemption of them; and in it "mercy and truth meet together, and righteousness and peace kiss each other:" and though it is not for all men, no injustice is done to them that are not redeemed; for if God could in justice have condemned all, it can be no act of injustice to redeem and save some. Suppose one hundred slaves in Algiers, and a man out of his great generosity, lays down a ransom-price for fifty of them, does he, by this act of distinguished goodness and generosity, do any injustice to the others? or can they righteously complain of him for not ransoming them? In the justification of men, by the righteousness of Christ, the justice of God is very conspicuous; for though God justifies the ungodly, yet not without a perfect righteousness, such as is adequate to the demands of his righteous law; even the righteousness of his own Son, in the imputation of which, and justification by it, he appears to be *just, and the justifier of him which believes in Jesus,* Rom. iii. 26. Though God forgives sin, yet not without a satisfaction made to his justice; though it is according to the riches of his grace, yet through the blood of Christ shed for it; and upon the foot of the shedding of that blood, God *is faithful and just to forgive us our sins, and to cleanse us from all unrighteousness,* 1 John i. 9. and so it is both an act of grace and of justice; as is eternal glory and happiness, being the free gift of God, through Christ and his righteousness.

CHAP. XXII.

OF THE VERACITY OF GOD.

THE apostle says, *Let God be true, and every man a liar,* Rom. iii. 4. this must be affirmed of him, whatever is said of creatures, he is true and truth itself.

I. God is true in and of himself: this epithet, or attribute, is expressive, 1. Of the reality of his being; he truly and really exists: this is what every worshipper of him must believe, Heb. xi. 6.

Creatures have but a shadow of being, in comparison of his; *Every man walks in a vain shew*, or image; rather in appearance than in reality, Psalm xxxix. 6. but the existence of God is true, real, and substantial; hence he has the name Jehovah, *I AM that I AM*; which denotes the truth, eternity, and immutability of his essence. What seems to be, and is not, is not true; what seems to be, and is, is true.——2. Of the truth of his Deity; he is the true and the living God; so he is often called, 2 Chron. xv. 3. Jer. x. 10. 1 Thess. i. 9. in opposition to fictitious deities; who either have feigned themselves such, or are feigned so by others; gods only by name, not by nature; of which there have been many: but the true God is but one, and in distinction from such who are called gods in a figurative and metaphorical sense, gods by office under God; as Moses was to Pharaoh, and as kings, judges, and civil magistrates be, Exod. vii. 1 Psalm lxxxii. 1, 6, 7. But the Lord is God in a true and proper sense.——3. This title includes the truth and reality of all his perfections; he is not only omnipotent, omniscient, omnipresent, eternal, and immutable, but he is truly so: what is falsely claimed by others, or wrongly given to them, is really in him; he is not only good and gracious, holy and just, but he is truly so; what others only appear to be, he is really.——4. This may be predicated of each Person in the Godhead; the Father is the only true God, John xvii. 3. though not to the exclusion of the Son, who is also the true God and eternal life; nor of the holy Spirit, who is truth; and who, with the Father and the Son, is the one true and living God, 1 John v. 20, 6, 7. —This attribute of truth removes from the divine nature every thing imperfect and sinful: it is opposed to unrighteousness, Deut. xxxii. 4. and has the epithet of just or holy along with it, when God is spoken of in his persons, ways, and works, Rev. iii. 7. and vi. 10. and xv. 3. and xvi. 7. and xix. 2. it removes from him all imputation of lying and falsehood; he is not a man, that he should lie, as men do; the Strength of *Israel will not lie*; yea, he is God that *cannot* lie; it is even *impossible* that he should, Numb. xxiii. 19. 1 Sam. xv. 29. Tit. i. 2. Heb. vi. 18. this frees him from all deception, he can neither deceive nor be deceived; Jeremiah, indeed, says, *O Lord, thou hast deceived me, and I was deceived*, Jer. xx. 7. but this must be understood either as a misapprehension and mistake of the prophet; or the sense is, if I am deceived, God has deceived me; but as that cannot be, therefore I am not deceived: though rather the words may be rendered, *thou hast persuaded me, and I was persuaded*, to enter upon his prophetic office, and to proceed on in the execution of it. Moreover this attribute clears God of the charge of insincerity, hypocrisy, and dissimulation, which, if in him, he could not be true. Nor on the supposition of his decree to save some men, and not all, are his declarations chargeable with any thing of that kind; as that he has no pleasure in the death of him that dies, and that he will have all men to be saved, Ezek. xviii. 32. 1 Tim. ii. 4. since the former respects not eternal death, but the captivity of the Jews, their return from it, upon their obedience, to their own land, and living in it. And the latter respects the will of God to save some of all sorts, of every rank and condition in life, and particularly Gentiles as well as Jews. In short, it removes all unfaithfulness from God, or any shadow of it: it strongly expresses the faithfulness of God; hence *true* and *faithful* are joined together, when the sayings or words of God are spoken of; nor is it any objection to the veracity of God, when what he has promised or threatened is not done; since thereunto a condition is either openly annexed or secretly understood; see Jer. xviii. 7—10. but the faithfulness of God, in his promises, &c. will be distinctly considered hereafter. Concerning the veracity of God, let the following things be observed:

(1.) That it is essential to him, it is his very nature and essence; he is truth itself; he is not only called the God of truth, but *God the truth*, Deut. xxxii. 4. and so Christ asserts himself to be the *truth*, John xiv. 6. and the Spirit is likewise so called, 1 John v. 6. To be false, fallacious, and insincere, would be to act contrary to his nature, even to deny himself; which he cannot do.

(2.) It is most pure and perfect in him; as in him is light, and no darkness at all; he is righteous, and no unrighteousness is in him; is holy, and no unholiness in him; is good, and no evil in him; is wisdom, and no folly nor weakness in him; so he is truth, and no falsehood in him, not the least mixture nor appearance of it.

(3.) It is first, chief, and original in

him; it is first in him, as he is the first cause; it is chief, as it is perfect in him, and all truth is originally from him; natural and rational truth, which is clear and self-evident to the mind: as the Being of God, from the works of his hands, called the truth of God made manifest in men, and shewed unto them, Rom. i. 18, 19, 20, 25. Moral truth, by which men know, in some measure, though sadly depraved, the difference between moral good and moral evil, Rom. ii. 14, 15. Spiritual truth, truth in the inward parts, or the true grace of God; and evangelical truth, the word of truth, and the several doctrines of it; these are not of men, but of God. All untruth is from Satan, the father of lies; but all truth is from the God of truth, and from the Spirit, who leads into all truth, as it is in Jesus.

(4.) Truth, as in God, is eternal; what is truth now, was always truth with him in his eternal mind; for *known to him are all his works from the beginning*, or from eternity, Acts xv. 18. as also his *word is true from the beginning*, or from eternity, Psalm cxix. 160. What is true with us to-day, might not be true yesterday, and will not be true to-morrow, because things are in a succession with us, and are so known by us; but not so with God, in whose eternal mind all things stand in one view; and besides, as veracity is his nature, his essence, it must be eternal, since that is, which contains all truth in it; and his truth will be to all generations, even for ever, Psalm c. 5. and cxvii. 2.

(5.) It is immutable and invariable, as he himself, as his nature is; truth does not always appear in the same light to men; at first more obscurely, then more clearly; it has its gradations and increase; but in God is always the same: creatures are mutable, fallacious, and deceitful; but God is the same, true and faithful, yesterday, to-day, and for ever. An attribute on account of which he is greatly to be praised and celebrated, Psalm lxxxix. 5. Isa. xxxviii. 19.

II. God is true in his works; or all his works are true, and his veracity is displayed in them; and these are either internal or external.

1. Internal acts within himself; some relative to himself, to the divine persons, their modes of subsisting, and distinction from each other; as paternity, filiation, and spiration; which are true and real things: the Father is truly and properly the Father of Christ, and not in name only; and Christ is his own proper Son, not in a figurative sense, or by office, as magistrates are called the children of the most high; but the Son of the Father *in truth* and love, 2 John ver. 3. and the Spirit of truth is really breathed, and proceeds from the Father and the Son, John xv. 26. others are relative to creatures; the decrees of God within himself, which are the secret actings and workings of his mind, the thoughts of his heart, the deep things of God, his counsels of old, which are *faithfulness* and *truth;* truly made, and truly performed, Isa. xxv. 1.

2. External works, as the works of creation, providence, and grace, which are all true, and real things; and in which the veracity of God appears, both in making and in continuing them.

(1.) The works of creation, the heavens and the earth, which are both his handy work, and all that are in them; in which the invisible perfections of his nature are displayed and discerned, his eternal power, and Godhead, and his veracity among the rest. The heavens above us, the sun, moon, and stars we behold, and the earth on which we live, are real, and not imaginary, they truly exist. Satan pretended to shew to Christ *all the kingdoms of the world, and the glory of them,* Matt. iv. 8. but this was a false and delusive representation, a *deceptio visus,* by which he would have imposed on Christ, but could not.

(2.) The works of providence; those in an ordinary way, by which God governs the world, and disposes of all things according to truth and righteousness; and such as are of an extraordinary kind, as those done by the hands of Moses, in Egypt; and by Christ and his apostles: these were real things, to answer some wise ends and purposes in the world; when those done by the magicians were only in shew, in appearance, and by a sort of legerdemain; as those done by antichrist, in the sight of men, as they imagine, whereby he deceives them that dwell on the earth; and therefore are called *lying wonders,* feigned things, which have no truth in them, Rev. xiii. 13, 14. 2 Thess. ii. 9, 10. but the wonderful works of God are true, and without deceit, as are all his judgments he executes by the sword, famine, pestilence, &c.

(3.) The works of grace done by him, his acts of grace, both in eternity and time:

his choice of persons to eternal life, is true, firm, and real, the foundation of God, which stands sure; the covenant of grace, made in Christ, full of blessings and promises, faithfully performed; the mission of Christ into the world, and his incarnation, who was really made flesh, and dwelt among men; the truth of which the apostle confirms by the various senses of seeing, hearing, and handling, 1 John i. 1. Justification by his righteousness is really imputed to his people, and by which they truly become righteous; and not in a putative and imaginary sense; pardon by his blood, which is not merely typical, as by the blood of slain beasts, but real; atonement by the sacrifice of himself, which he really and truly offered up to God; and sanctification by the Spirit, which is the new man, created in righteousness and *true holiness;* and not outward, typical, and ceremonial, nor feigned and hypocritical: and adoption, by which the saints are now really the sons of God; though it does not yet appear what they shall be; and to which the Spirit bears a true and real witness; and which is unto an inheritance, real, solid, and substantial.

III. God is true in his words, in his essential Word, his Son, who was *in the beginning with God;* had a true and real existence with him, and *was God,* really and truly God; he is true in his person and natures, the true God and eternal life, who took unto him a true body and a reasonable soul; and whose human nature is the true tabernacle God pitched, and not man: true in his offices he bears; the true prophet raised up and sent of God, the true light, that lightens men in every sense; the true priest, not of the order of Aaron, but of the order of Melchizedek; the true and only Potentate, King of kings, and Lord of lords; the true Mediator between God and men, and not a typical one, as Moses.

God is true in his written word; the scriptures are the scriptures of truth, even the whole of them, Dan. x. 21. they are given by inspiration from God, are the breath of God, who is the God of truth, and therefore to be received, *not as the word of man, but as in truth the word of God,* 1 Thess. ii. 13. the law-part of them is truth; the apostle speaks of the *truth in the law,* known by men, Rom. ii. 20. there is not a precept in it but what is true and right; *The judgments of the Lord are true and righteous altogether,* Psalm xix. 9. And the gospel-part of them is eminently the word of truth, Eph. i. 13. and all the doctrines of it, which are *pure words, as silver tried in a furnace of earth, purified seven times,* Psalm xii. 6. And the truth and veracity of God appears in the fulfilment of the predictions, promises, and threatenings contained in his word, which is the same with his faithfulness; which we shall particularly treat of in the next chapter, being naturally led to it; the veracity of God is the foundation of his faithfulness; and his faithfulness is a branch of that; and they are often put one for the other, and signify the same thing.

CHAP. XXIII.

OF THE FAITHFULNESS OF GOD.

FAITHFULNESS is an attribute that belongs to God; from whence he is denominated the *faithful God,* Deut. vii. 9. It is essential to him, and without which he would not be God; to be unfaithful, would be to act contrary to his nature, to deny himself, 2 Tim. ii. 13. an unfaithful God would be no God at all; it is a most glorious perfection of his nature; it is *great,* like himself; yea, it is infinite; *Great is thy faithfulness,* Lam. iii. 23. it reaches to all persons and things God has any concern with; it is all *around* him; he is, as it were, clothed and covered with it; and there is none in any creature like unto it, Psalm lxxxix. 8. There is faithfulness in the holy angels, and in good men, but not like what is in God; and therefore he puts no trust in them, Job iv. 18. his faithfulness is invariably the same; it has never failed in any one instance, nor never will; it is established in the heavens, and will continue to all generations, Psalm lxxxix. 2, 24, 33. and cxix. 90. Josh. xxiii. 14. otherwise there would be no firm foundation for trust and confidence in him; but he is the *faithful Creator,* and covenant God and Father of his people; to whom they may safely commit themselves, and depend upon him for all mercies promised, both temporal and spiritual, 1 Pet. iv. 19. 1 Thess. v. 23, 24. for the faithfulness of God chiefly lies in the performance of his word, which is certain, with respect to all that is spoken by him; for *hath he said, and shall he not do it? or hath he spoken, and shall he not make it good?* Verily he will, Numb. xxiii. 19. Luke i. 45. And it appears,

First, In the performance of what he has said with respect to the world in general; as, that it shall never more be destroyed by a flood, as it once was; and for a token and confirmation of it, God has set the rainbow in the cloud; and now four thousand years are gone since the covenant was made; and God has been faithful to it, though the earth has been sometimes threatened with destruction by violent storms, and sudden inundations; see Gen. ix. 11—16. Isa. liv. 9. Also that the ordinances of heaven, the sun, moon, and stars, shall not depart, but always continue in their being, use, and influence; and now they have kept their course, or station, and have done their office, exactly and punctually, for almost six thousand years; see Jer. xxxi. 35, 36. and xxxiii. 25. Likewise that the revolutions of the time, and seasons of the year, should keep their constant course; that, *while the earth remaineth, seed-time and harvest, and cold and heat, and summer and winter, and day and night, shall not cease,* Gen. viii. 22. and so it has always been, and still is, in one part of the world, or another, according to the different climates. Remarkable was the faithfulness of God to the Jewish nation, in that their land required rain only at two seasons of the year, and God promised it to them, and which they always had; though sometimes so ungrateful as not to fear him who gave them *rain, both the former and the latter, in his season,* and *reserved* for them *the appointed weeks of the harvest,* Jer. v. 24. see Deut. xi. 14, 15. and whereas God has given reason to expect that his creatures should be preserved in their being, and provided for by him, with the necessaries of life; he has not left himself without a witness to his faithfulness, in all ages and nations, giving rain from heaven and fruitful seasons; and so filling the hearts of his creatures with food and gladness; whose eyes all of them wait upon him, and he gives them their meat in due season, Acts xiv. 17. Psalm xxxvi. 5, 6. and cxlv. 15, 16. And from all this it may be strongly concluded, that whatsoever God has said concerning the world, which is yet to be fulfilled, shall be most certainly done; as the judgment of it, the end and consummation of all things in it, the conflagration of it, and the making new heavens and a new earth, wherein will dwell righteousness, 2 Pet. iii. 7—13.

Secondly, The faithfulness of God appears in the fulfilment of what he has said with respect to Christ, and the salvation of men by him; both of what he has said of him, and of what he has said to him: and indeed, the faithfulness of God is displayed in Christ as in a mirror.

1. In the performance of what he has said of him; as that he should be born of a woman, be of the seed of Abraham, spring from the tribe of Judah, arise out of the family of David, be born of a virgin at Bethlehem, and converse much in Galilee, Gen. iii. 15. and xxii. 18. and xlix. 10. 2 Sam. vii. 12, 13. Mic. v. 2. Isa. vii. 14. and ix. 1, 2. and suffer, and die, and work out the salvation of his people, Psalm xxii. Isa. liii. and chap. xxv. 9. and xxxv. 4. and xlix. 6. all which has been fully accomplished. Matt. i. 1, 18—23. and ii. 5, 6, 8, 11, 22, 23. and iv. 13—16. Luke i. 68—72. 1 Cor. xv. 3.

2. In the performance of what he said to Christ, or promised him; as that he would help him, and strengthen him, as man and mediator, in the great work of redemption and salvation; and which help and strength Christ expected, and believed he should have, and had it, Psalm lxxxix. 21. Isa. l. 7, 9. and xlix. 8. and that though he should die, and be laid in the grave and buried; yet he would raise him from the dead, and that on the third day; and which was accordingly done, Psalm xvi. 10. Hos. vi. 2. 1 Cor. xv. 4. and that when he had done his work, being delivered unto death for the sins of his people, and raised again for their justification, he should be glorified at his right hand, in his human nature; and accordingly, Christ having done his work, pleaded this promise, and it was fulfilled, Psalm cx. 1. John xvii. 4, 5. Phil. ii. 9, 10. and that he should see his seed, have a numerous offspring, which should continue to the end of the world, Isa. liii. 10. Psalm lxxxix. 4, 29, 36. and which has been accomplished in the numerous conversions both among Jews and Gentiles, in the first ages of Christianity; and which have continued, more or less, ever since; and will still more manifestly appear when the nation of the Jews shall be born at once, and the fulness of the Gentiles be brought in.

3. The faithfulness of God is displayed in the person, office, and works of Christ. This, as all other divine perfections, is common to each person in the Godhead, and shines resplendently in the Son of God,

the brightness of his Father's glory, who has every perfection the Father has; so that he that has seen the Son has seen the Father, the same perfections being in the one as in the other, and this of faithfulness among the rest; which is to be seen in Christ as in a mirror, or glass; and an estimate may in some measure be taken, and judgment made of the faithfulness of God, by what appears in his Son; who has been *faithful to him that appointed him* to his office as Mediator. Moses was faithful in the house of God, as a servant; but Christ as a Son over his own house, Heb. iii. 2—6. and whose faithfulness may be observed,

(1.) In the performance of his engagements: he engaged to be the Surety of his people; to stand in their place and stead; to do and suffer for them what should be required, and to take care of all their affairs and concerns for time and eternity; and accordingly, he is become the Surety of the better testament, Heb. vii. 22. he engaged to be the Saviour and Redeemer of them; he is often spoken of as such in the Old Testament; that is, as one who had engaged to work out their redemption and salvation; and which he has now obtained, and become the author of, Heb. v. 9. and ix. 12. he engaged to come into the world, in order to do this work, saying, *Lo, I come;* and he is come, and has done it; and that he came into the world, and has done this for sinners, the chief of sinners, is a *faithful saying;* in which the faithfulness of God in his promises, and of Christ in his engagements, is abundantly displayed, 1 Tim. i. 15. he engaged to come and fulfil the law, both its precepts and its penalty, and to become a sacrifice for sin; ceremonial sacrifices being insufficient, Psalm xl. 6, 7, 8. and he is accordingly become the fulfilling *end of the law for righteousness to all that believe;* and has offered himself, soul and body, without spot to God; "a Sacrifice of a sweet-smelling savour;" and whereby sin has been fully expiated and put away, Rom. x. 4. Heb. ix. 14, 26. see Heb. x. 5—10. he engaged to pay off the debts of his people, and by being their Surety, become responsible for them, and to clear off all their scores; which he has done to the uttermost farthing, and blotted out the handwriting of ordinances against them. In short, he engaged to feed the flock of God, to take the whole care and oversight of it; and he does feed his flock like a shepherd, and has shewn himself to be the good and faithful one, by laying down his life for the sheep, Zech. xi. 4, 7. Isa. xl. 11. John x. 14.

(2.) The faithfulness of Christ is seen in his discharge of the trust reposed in him, which is very large and great; the Father hath *given all things into his hand,* John iii. 35. all the persons of his elect to be kept, preserved, and saved by him; and so they are and shall be, even every one of them, whom Christ will present to his Father, and say, *Behold, I, and the children which God hath given me;* not one is lost, Heb. ii. 13. Christ is entrusted with a fulness of grace, to supply the wants of his people; it has been his Father's pleasure, that it should dwell in him for their use; he has deposited it with him, to communicate it to them, as they need it; and he has been faithful to do it, in all ages and generations; he has been to all his churches, and to all his saints, in every period of time, *A fountain of gardens, a well of living waters, and streams from Lebanon,* Cant. iv. 15. saints both of the Old and New Testament, have *all received of his fulness, and grace for grace,* John i. 16. Eternal life and happiness is in his hands, and he has a power to give it to as many as the Father has given him; and he is faithful in the use of that power, and does give it to all his sheep, so that none of them shall ever perish, 1 John v. 11. John xvii. 2. and x. 28. yea, the glory of all the divine perfections, as concerned in the salvation of men, was entrusted with Christ; and he has been faithful *in things pertaining to God,* as well as in making *reconciliation for the sins of the people;* and in doing the one he has taken care of the other. The glory of God is great in the salvation of men, even of his justice and holiness; as well as of his wisdom, power, faithfulness, grace and mercy, Heb. ii. 17. Psalm xx. 5. and lxxxv. 10.

(3.) Christ has appeared to be faithful in the exercise of his offices, as Prophet, Priest, and King: in the exercise of his prophetical office; for which he was abundantly qualified, by lying in the bosom of his Father, and so privy to his whole mind and will, which he has faithfully declared; all that he heard of the Father, all the words and doctrines he gave him, as man, he made known to his disciples; in doing which, he sought not his own glory, but the glory of him that sent him; and therefore must be true and faithful, and no unrighteousness or unfaithfulness in him, John i. 18. and vii. 16, 17, 18. and xv. 15. and xvii. 8. and therefore is justly entitled to be called the Amen, and faithful Witness, Rev. iii. 14. In the exercise of his priestly office; in which he is faithful to him that appointed him; and rightly bears the character of a faithful high-priest, in that he has offered up himself to make atonement for the sins of his people; and as the advocate for them, even Jesus Christ the righteous, faithful, and true; and takes perfect care in all things, of the house of God, over which he is a priest, Heb. ii. 17. and iii. 1, 2. and x. 21. and ix. 14. 1 John ii. 1. And in the exercise of his kingly office; all whose administrations in it are *just and true;* righteousness being the girdle of his loins, and faithfulness the girdle of his reins; and with great propriety is he called *faithful and true,* since *in righteousness he doth judge and make war,* Rev. xv. 3. and xix. 11. Isa. xi. 5.

(4.) The faithfulness of Christ is manifest in the fulfilment of his promises, which he made to his disciples; as, that he would not leave them comfortless, but come and see them; as he did, after his resurrection, and comforted them with his presence, and filled them with joy at the sight of him, John xiv. 18. and xx. 20. that they should receive the gift of the Holy Spirit, and therefore were bid to wait at Jerusalem for it, and where it was bestowed upon them, on the day of Pentecost, in a very large and extraordinary manner, Acts i. 4. and ii. 4, 33. that he would be with them in the administration of his word and ordinances; and accordingly did go forth and work with them, confirming the word by signs following, Matt. xxviii. 19, 20. Mark xvi. 20. yea, he has promised his presence with his ministers and churches to the end of the world, and that even "where two or three are gathered together in his name, he will be in the midst of them," Matt. xviii. 20. and xxviii. 20. and he makes his word good, which the experience of his ministers and people in all ages confirms: he has promised also to come again, and take his disciples and faithful followers to himself, that where he is they may be also; and which was not only verified in his immediate disciples, but in his saints in all ages, whom, when they have served their generation according to the will of God, he comes and takes them to himself, by death; and "to them that look for him, will he appear a second time, without sin, unto salvation." John xiv. 2, 3. Heb. ix. 28.

(5.) The faithfulness of Christ may be observed in his concern with the covenant of grace, and the promises of it; the covenant was made with him as the Head and Representative of his people, and stands fast with him; all the blessings of it are lodged with him, and faithfully dispensed by him; the promises were made to him, who only actually existed when they were made, and to whom only they could be given; he was the Amen, and faithful Witness of them, of their being made: and they are Yea and Amen in him; by whose blood the blessings and promises of it are ratified and confirmed; and therefore called, "the blood of the everlasting covenant:" and it is in and through him that believers come to have an interest in the promises, a right unto them, and to be partakers of them, Psalm lxxxix. 3, 24. Rev. iii. 14. 2 Cor. i. 20. Heb. xiii. 20. Eph. iii. 6. And now by the faithfulness of Christ thus manifestly displayed, may be learnt somewhat more of the attribute of faithfulness, as it is in God. Which leads on to consider,

Thirdly, The faithfulness of God in the performance of what he has said in the covenant, and the promises of it, with respect to his special people. God is denominated *faithful,* from his keeping covenant and mercy with them, Deut. vii. 9. every covenant God has made with man, he has been faithful in: he made a covenant with Adam, as the head and representative of his posterity, promising a continuance of happiness to him and his, provided he remained in his state of innocence; and threatening with death in case of disobedience. Adam was unfaithful, and broke the covenant; *they, like Adam, have transgressed the covenant,* Hos. vi. 7. But God was faithful to it, and deprived him of his happiness, and pronounced the sentence of death on him and his. God made a covenant with Noah, and all the creatures, promising that he would no more destroy the world by a flood; and he has faithfully kept it, as before observed. He made a covenant with Abraham, that he would make him the father of many nations, and that kings should spring from him, and that he would give to his posterity the land of Canaan: the former part of which was verified in the Ishmaelites, Israelites, Edomites, Midianites, and others, with their kings, which were of him: and the latter part, by putting the people of Israel in possession of Canaan, by Joshua; which they held long by the tenure of their obedience, according to his promise; but when they broke the covenant, he destroyed them from it, as he threatened, Gen. xvii. 5, 6. Josh. xxi. 43. and xxiii. 16. He made a covenant at Sinai, with all the people of Israel; and, according to his engagements, continued to them their blessings, natural, civil, and religious; but they were not stedfast in his covenant, and he dispossessed them of them. But the grand and principal covenant, is the covenant of grace; which God has made in Christ with all his elect, and is ordered in all things, and sure; and which he will never break, and they cannot; and which will never be removed, but ever be inviolably kept: and there are promises of various sorts, which God has graciously made to his people, and which are faithfully performed by him.

1. Some of a temporal nature; for *godliness* and godly men have *the promise of the life that now is*, of things belonging to it, as well as *of that which is to come*, 1 Tim. iv. 8. these their heavenly Father knows they have need of, and therefore provides them for them, and promises them unto them. He has said, *that they that seek the Lord shall not want any good thing*, Psalm xxxiv. 10. they shall have that which is good, as every creature of God is good, good food and good raiment; though it may be but mean, yet it is good, and better than the best of men deserve; and they want not any, that God, in his infinite wisdom, sees is good for them; for though they and others may think it would be better for them if they had a greater affluence of the things of this life; but God thinks otherwise, and knows it would be to their hurt, as sometimes riches are; he has bid his people *trust in the Lord, and do good*, and has promised, they *shall be fed*, Psalm xxxvii. 3. not all of them with dainties and delicious food, but with food convenient for them; he has assured them their *bread shall be given them*, and their *waters shall be sure*, Isa. xxxiii. 16. and this is sufficient to support and confirm his faithfulness: nor is the poverty of some of God's people any objection to it, since he has nowhere promised them the riches of this world, and has given them no reason to expect them; but he has promised them better riches, durable riches, and righteousness, the riches of grace and glory, and these he gives to them; see a testimony from David's experience of the faithfulness of God, with respect to temporal things, Psalm xxxvii. 25. God has not promised his people security from outward afflictions; but rather has suggested to them that they may look for them; since his people are described as a poor and afflicted people; and it is their common case; many are the afflictions of the righteous; it is what they are appointed to, and what are appointed for them; but then God has promised that they shall work for their good; either for their temporal good, as Jacob's afflictions worked for his; or for their spiritual good, the exercise and increase of grace and holiness; and always for their eternal good, 2 Cor. iv. 17. and also that he will be with them in them, support them under them, and deliver out of them in due time: all which is faithfully performed by him, 1 Cor. x. 13.

2. Others are of a spiritual nature; and the principal of these is, and which is the sum of the covenant, *They shall be my people, and I will be their God*, Jer. xxxii. 38. and which appears in their election, redemption, and effectual vocation: which is saying, that he has a special love and affection for them, and will continue it, as he does: nor are his chastisements of them, his hiding his face from them for a time, his displeasure at them, and being angry with them, any objection to the perpetuity of his love; since these are not contrary to it, but rather the fruits of it, and for their good: it signifies, that they shall have his gracious presence with them, and may expect it, and which they have; nor do their doubts, and fears, and complaints disprove it, Isa. xli. 10. and xlix. 14, 15, 16. which are generally owing to their ignorance and unbelief; God is with them, and they know it; however, he is never far from them, nor long; he does not depart from them, nor withdraw his gracious presence from them totally and finally: it assures them of his protection, that he will be all-around them, guard them, and secure them, preserve and keep them by his power, through faith unto salvation, as he does; for though they may fall into sin, yet they rise again by his grace; and though they fall into temptation, and by it, yet they are delivered out of it; they are kept from a final and total falling away; they are not of them that

draw back unto perdition: in a word, this promise is expressive of their enjoyment of God here, and for evermore; and he is their shield, and exceeding great reward; their portion in life, at death, and for ever, their ALL in ALL.

There are many particular spiritual promises made to the people of God; and which are made good by him; as, that he will sprinkle clean water upon them, and cleanse them from all their sins; which is to be understood of justifying grace, through the blood of Christ; that he will forgive their iniquities, and remember their sins no more; and he is *just* in doing it, upon the account of the blood of his Son, and *faithful* to his own promise, 1 John i. 9. that he will give them new hearts and new spirits, which he does in regeneration; and take away the heart of stone, and give an heart of flesh; as he does, when he removes the hardness of the heart, and gives evangelical repentance unto life; that he will put his laws in them, and write them in their minds; not only give knowledge of them, but both a disposition and grace to observe them; working in them both to will and to do of his good pleasure: that he will put his Spirit into them, and give them spiritual strength to keep his statutes, and perform every duty; that he will carry on his good work of grace in them, and perform it, until the day of Christ; of which they may be confident, since he has promised it; that he will give them more grace, a sufficiency of it, and supply all their need out of the fulness in Christ; and that his fear shall be continually in their hearts; and they shall not depart from him, but persevere in faith and holiness to the end. All which promises, and more, are faithfully and truly performed in all his people; see Jer. xxxi. 33, 34. and xxxii. 38, 39, 40. Ezek. xxxvi. 25, 26, 27.

3. There are other promises which respect the life to come; the eternal happiness of the saints in another world: the apostle speaks of the promise of this, as *the promise*, by way of eminency, as if it was the only promise, or, however, the principal one, in which all others issue and end: *This is the promise that he has promised us*, even *eternal life*, 1 John ii. 25. and this is an ancient one, made before the world began, and by God that *cannot lie*, Tit. i. 2. who is faithful and true, and will most certainly perform it; wherefore, *Blessed is the man that endureth temptation; for when he is tried, he shall receive the crown of life*, which the Lord hath promised to them that love him, James i. 12.

Fourthly, The faithfulness of God appears in fulfilling his threatenings, as well as his promises. God threatened Adam, that in the day he eat of the forbidden fruit, he should *surely die;* and he immediately became mortal, death began at once to work in him; his soul was seized directly with a spiritual or moral death, guilt, and terror of conscience, a sense of divine wrath, and deprivation of the divine presence, and he became liable to eternal death; nor had he any reason to expect any other, until he heard that the seed of the woman should bruise the serpent's head; and the sentence of death passed on him, and all his posterity in him, as soon as he had sinned, according to the divine threatening, Rom. v. 12. God threatened the inhabitants of the old world with a flood to destroy them, for their impiety and wickedness; and though his patience and forbearance were for a long time exercised, yet he was faithful to his word, and brought it upon the world of the ungodly, and destroyed them all. God threatened the people of Israel with captivity, and other judgments, if they walked not in his ways, and broke his statutes; of which see Lev. xxvi. and Deut. xxviii. all which grievous threatenings, and sore judgments, have been exactly fulfilled in that people, and remain to this day: who are a standing proof of God's faithfulness in this respect. And as God has threatened men with the burning of the world, and the works of it, and the wicked in it; and damnation to all unbelieving and impenitent sinners, they may be assured of it, and expect it; for as it is most true, and may be depended upon, that *he that believeth, and is baptized, shall be saved;* so it is equally as true, and as surely to be depended on, that *he that believeth not, shall be damned*, Mark xvi. 16. Nor is it any objection to the faithfulness of God in fulfilling his threatenings, that Nineveh was spared, when it was threatened, that in forty days it should be overthrown; since there was a condition implied, a secret proviso made, "except they repented;" and which their hope of mercy, and the mercy shown them upon their repentance, fully confirm; and so the veracity and faithfulness of God is sufficiently secured; and, indeed, in many promises and threatenings, respecting temporal things, a condition is either openly expressed, or secretly understood; according to which God in providence proceeds, Jer. xviii. 7—10.

CHAP. XXIV.

OF THE SUFFICIENCY AND PERFECTION OF GOD.

From this attribute of God, he has one of his names, *Shaddai*, which signifies, who is sufficient, or all-sufficient; of which see Chap. III. Three things may be observed under this attribute.

I. That God is a self-sufficient Being, and needs not any thing from without himself to support himself, or to make himself happy. He is the *first* of Beings, the first and the last; before him there was no God formed, nor will be any after him; from everlasting to everlasting he is God; and therefore his existence is not owing to any; nor has he received any assistance or support from any; being self-existent, he must be self-subsistent; as he existed of himself, and subsisted in and of himself, millions and millions of ages, even an eternity, inconceivable to us, alone, before any other existed, he must be self-sufficient, and as then, so to all eternity.[1] He is an *infinite* and *all-comprehending* Being; to what is infinite nothing can be added: if anything was wanting in him he would be finite; if there was any excellency in another, which is not in him, he would not be infinite, and so not God: being infinite, he is incomprehensible by others; and comprehends in himself all excellencies, perfections, and happiness; and therefore self-sufficient; *Who hath first given to him, and it shall be recompensed to him again? for of him, and through him, and for him are all things*, Rom. xi. 35, 36. God is the *summum bonum*, the chief good, and has all that is good in him; he is good essentially, originally, and underivatively; the source and fountain of all goodness; every good and perfect gift comes from him, James i. 17. and therefore must have a fulness of goodness in him sufficient for himself, as well as for his creatures, and can receive nothing from them; otherwise he would not be the *independent* Being he is: all have their dependence on him, and owe their being, and the preservation of it, to him; but he depends on none; which he would, if he stood in need of, or received anything from them. He is possessed of *all perfections*, as has been abundantly shewed in the preceding chapters, and is sufficiently happy in them; he is perfect and entire, wanting nothing, and therefore self-sufficient:[2] he is the Fountain; creatures, and what they have, are streams; and it would be as absurd for him to need them, or anything from them, as for the fountain to need its streams. Besides, God in his *divine persons*, God Father, Son and Spirit, have enough within themselves, to give the utmost, yea, infinite complacency, delight, and satisfaction among themselves, and to one another, and had before any creatures were made, and would have had if none had been made, and so ever will; the Father delighted in the Son, "the brightness of his glory, and the express image of his person;" the Son in the Father, before whom he was always rejoicing, when as yet no creature existed; and both in the blessed Spirit, proceeding from them; and he in them, see Prov. viii. 30. for creation adds nothing at all to the perfection and happiness of God, nor makes the least alteration in him. It is indeed said, *Thou hast created all things, and for thy pleasure they are and were created*, Rev. iv. 11. but *pleasure* there does not signify delight, satisfaction, and happiness; as if they were made for the sake of that in God; to add unto it, and increase it; but the good will and pleasure of God; it is διὰ τὸ θέλημα σȣ, and should be rendered, *by thy will they are and were created:* God has made all things for himself; that is, for his glory, his manifestative glory; but then this adds nothing to his essential glory and happiness; the heavens, and so the other parts of the creation, declare his glory; but to whom? not to himself, he needs no such declaration; he knows perfectly his own glory, which is always invariably the same; but to angels and men, that they may contemplate it, and receive benefit by it. The invisible perfections of God, his eternal power and Godhead, are seen and understood by the things that are made; but not by God himself, who needs no such glass to view them in; but by men; and the design thereof is, to make

---

[1] την αριϛην εχοντα ζωην και την αυταρκεϛατην διατελει τον απαντα αιωνα, Aristot. de Cœlo, l. 1. c. 9. and this name, he says, is divinely pronounced by the ancients.

[2] το γαρ τελειον αγαθον αυταρκες ειναι δοκει, Aristot. Ethic. l. 1. c. 5.

some better and happier, and others inexcusable. All creatures stand in need of God to supply them and support them; they consist in him, are upheld by the word of his power, live, and move, and have their beings in him; but he stands in need of none of them, being self-sufficient.

And as he does not stand in need of the creation in general, so not of men and angels in particular; not of men, nor of any services of theirs, which can add nothing to his perfection and happiness; not of their worship, for he is *not worshipped with men's hands, as though he needed any thing*,[3] no not their worship, Acts xvii. 25. he is and ought to be the sole object of their worship; it is their duty to worship him, and that in a spiritual manner, suitable to his nature as a Spirit; but then not he, but they are the gainers by it; the ordinances of divine service under the former dispensation were, and those under the present are, for the instruction, edification, comfort, and peace of the worshippers, who are hereby led into communion with God, and the enjoyment of his gracious presence; and so find it is good for them to wait upon him in them. But what benefit does he receive thereby? he stands in no need of their prayers; it is both their duty and privilege to pray to him, the God of their life, for the mercies of it, temporal and spiritual; and he is pleased to express his approbation of it, and to resent a contrary behaviour: but who has the advantage of it? not he, but they; for whose sake is the throne of grace set up? not for his own sake, but for the sake of his people, that they might come to it, and find grace and mercy to help them in their time of need: nor does he want their praises, nor is he benefited by them; they are his due, and it becomes men to give them to him; and he condescends to accept of them, and express his well-pleasedness in them; but then the celebration of his praises adds nothing to his perfection, and happiness, but to the perfection and happiness of men, who are made better thereby; nor is the obedience and righteousness of men of any profit to God; obedience to his commands ought to be yielded, and works of righteousness enjoined by him ought to be performed; but then when we have done all we can, we are but *unprofitable servants* to him; *if thou be righteous what givest thou him? or what receiveth he of thine hand?* such works and such righteousness may be profitable to men, and is a reason why they are to be done; but *can a man be profitable unto God, as he that is wise may be profitable to himself*, or to others? *is it any pleasure to the almighty that thou art righteous? or is it gain to him that thou makest thy ways perfect?* Job xxii. 2, 3. and xxxv. 7, 8. Luke xvii. 10. Tit. iii. 8. Should it be said, that God is glorified by men in the worship of him, by prayer to him, and praising of him; by obedience to his will, and by living soberly, righteously, and godly, John xv. 9. Matt. v. 16. it is very true, these make for the manifestation and display of his glory among men, but make no addition to his essential glory and happiness; the same may be said of the worship and services of angels, of the imperfection and unprofitableness of which to God they are sensible themselves, and blush and cover their faces whilst performing them, Isa. vi. 2, 3. and though they are indeed made use of as instruments in providence (but not in creation) in the preservation of God's people, and in the destruction of their enemies, and in other affairs of this world, yet not of necessity, but of choice; it is not because God needs them, and cannot do without them, but because it is his will and pleasure; just as he makes use of the ministry, and ministers of the word, for the conversion of sinners and comfort of saints; not that he needs them, nor could not convert the one and comfort the other without them; for it is certain he can, and often does, but because these are the means and instruments he chooses to make use of, 1 Cor. iii. 5, 6, 7.

There is a very remarkable expression in Psalm xvi. 2, 3. *My goodness extendeth not to thee, but to the saints that are in the earth, and to the excellent, in whom is all my delight:* which if spoken by David of himself only, indeed confirms what has been before asserted, that the goodness of men, even of the best of men, is of no advantage to God himself, but to others. The goodness of David in preparing for the building of the temple, and providing for the worship of God in it, in composing

---

[3] It is a notion of the heathens themselves, that God stands in no need of anything; αυτο μεν γαρ το θειον ανενδεες, Sallust. de Diis, c. 15. θεων μεν ιδιον ειναι μηδενος δεισθαι, Diogenes apud Laert. l. 6. in Vita Menedem.

CHAP. XXIV. OF THE SUFFICIENCY AND PERFECTION OF GOD.   121

hymns and psalms to be sung by men, and in the whole of his life and conversation, was of no avail to the essential happiness of God; but was of use to the saints, both for their profit and by way of example to them: but if spoken by him in the person of Christ, as it is clear the words are, then they carry in them an higher sense still; as, that the holiness of Christ, as man, added nothing to the perfection of God and his nature; that the obedience he yielded in it was for the sake of men, who had the advantage of it, and not God; that the satisfaction he made to divine justice for his people, God stood in no need of; he could have glorified his justice in the destruction of them, as well as in the apostate angels, the old world, and Sodom and Gomorrah: though the debt of obedience paid to the law, and the debt of punishment paid to justice in their room, has magnified the law and made it honourable; the benefit of this redounds to men only; who hereby have their debts paid, their scores cleared, and they stand free and discharged in open court. Though the glory of God is greatly displayed in salvation by Christ, the good will is to men; and all the good things he is come an high priest of, and that come thereby, come not to God, but to men; as peace, pardon, righteousness and eternal life. God is then a self-sufficient being, and needs nothing from without himself; nor does he receive any thing.

II. God is an all-sufficient Being, and has enough within himself to communicate to his creatures. He is able to do whatsoever he pleases, to fulfil all his engagements and promises, and to do exceeding abundantly above all that men ask or think. And so communicative and diffusive is his goodness, that it extends to all his creatures, and every good and perfect gift comes from him; which is a full proof of his all-sufficiency: and which appears,

1. In his gifts of nature and providence; for he *gives life, and breath, and all things* to his creatures, Acts xvii. 25. A painter may paint as near to life as can be, and a sculptor may give a statue its just features, and frame its limbs in proper symmetry and proportion, but neither of them can give life and breath; but God is sufficient to do this, and has done it: he breathed into Adam the breath of life; and gives life to all his posterity; and is, with great propriety, called the God of their life,

Psalm xlii. 8. and he is sufficient to support, maintain, and preserve the life he has given, and does, as long as he pleases, Job x. 12. and xii. 10. Psalm lxvi. 9. and to provide for men all the necessaries of life, as food and raiment; which Jacob was fully satisfied of, and therefore covenanted with God for them, Gen. xxviii. 20. and to take care of all the creatures; the fowls of heaven, and of the mountains; the beasts of the field and forest; and "the cattle on a thousand hills;" which, as they are his property, they are his care; and a large family they be to provide for every day, and food suitable to them; and yet this he is sufficient to do, and does; all wait upon him, and he gives them their portion of meat in due season, Psalm l. 10, 11. and civ. 27, 28. and cxlv. 15. and cxlvii, 9. yea, he is sufficient to govern the whole world; nor does he need any wisdom, counsel, advice, and assistance in it, from any of his creatures, Isa. xl. 13, 14. he disposes and over-rules all things as he pleases; and not only influences, directs, and manages, in matters of the greatest importance, which concern kings and governors, kingdoms and states, but even those of the lowest consideration and use; and so in all things intervening, or of a class between the one and the other, Psalm xxii. 28. Prov. viii. 15, 16. Matt. x. 29, 30. in a view of which it may well be said, *O the depth of the riches both of the wisdom and knowledge of God!* &c. What an all-sufficiency must he be possessed of! Rom. xi. 33.

2. God appears to be all-sufficient in the communications of his grace; he is the God of all grace, and is able to cause all grace to abound towards his people, and to supply all their wants out of that rich and glorious plenitude, and all-sufficiency in himself, by Jesus Christ; he has stored the covenant with all the blessings of grace; he has prevented Christ, the head and mediator of it with all the blessings of goodness; he has blessed his people in him with all spiritual blessings, and given them grace in him before the world began; and caused the fulness of it to dwell in him, which is always sufficient for them, sufficient for them in all ages and periods of time; for them of all nations and kingdoms throughout the world; for them in every state and condition of life; for all believers weak or strong: and he has a sufficiency of it for all saving purposes; for their acceptance with God, and justification before

him; for the remission of their sins, and the cleansing of their souls, and for the supply of all their wants whilst they are in this state of imperfection; and he has a sufficiency of it to communicate to them at all times, when they are called to service, ordinary or extraordinary, to do or suffer for his name's sake; in times of affliction, temptation, desertion, and in the hour of death, to bear up under, and carry them through all, and bring them safe to his kingdom and glory, John i. 14, 16. 2 Cor. xii. 9. Phil. iv. 19.

III. God is a perfect Being; entirely perfect, and wanting nothing; *Be ye perfect, even as your Father which is in heaven is perfect*, Matt. v. 48. his *nature* is perfect; the more simple and uncompounded any being is, the more perfect it is. God is a Spirit, *actus simplicissimus*, the most pure, spiritual, simple, and uncompounded Being, and therefore the most perfect. No *perfection* of Deity is wanting in him; as appears from what has been under consideration. There is a fulness of the Godhead which dwells in Christ, and the same therefore must be in each divine person, and especially in God, essentially considered; and every *attribute* of his is *perfect;* he is perfectly immutable; there is no variableness in him, nor shadow of turning, James i. 17. he is perfect in knowledge, knows himself, and all creatures and things perfectly, Job xxxvii. 16. and there is a depth in his wisdom, as well as in his knowledge, which are unfathomable, Rom. xi. 33. and as for his power, nothing is too hard for him; nor is his hand shortened that it cannot save, Isa. xl. 26, 28. and lix. 1. and his holiness is without the least tarnish; in him are *light*, purity, and holiness, and *no darkness* of sin *at all*, 1 John i. 5. all the perfections and excellencies that are in creatures, angels, and men, are, in the most perfect manner, in him, agreeable to his nature; as they must, since they all come from him, James i. 17. and though there are some things which are excellencies in creatures, as the reasoning faculty in men, and faith in the christian, which, properly speaking, cannot be said to be in God; yet these are such as would be imperfections in him; since the former supposes some want of knowledge, which the reasoning power is employed to find out, and the latter is but an obscure knowledge, and proceeds upon the authority of another; neither of which can be supposed in God, whose knowledge is clear and perfect, and to whom no authority is superior; and therefore the want of them does not infer any imperfection in him, but, on the contrary, the highest perfection. Once more, he is a rock, and *his work is perfect*, Deut. xxxiii. 4. his work of creation is finished, and so is the work of redemption, and, ere long, the mystery of providence will be finished, and the work of grace on the heart of every one of his elect; and *as for God, his way is perfect*, Psalm xviii. 30. his ways of providence are without any just blame; every path of mercy and truth he pursues, he never leaves till he has finished it; and the way he prescribes to his people to walk in, is perfect; and the scriptures, which are of him, are able to make the man of God perfect, Rev. xv. 4. Psalm xxv. 10. and xix. 7. 2 Tim. i. 16, 17.

CHAP. XXV.

OF THE BLESSEDNESS OF GOD.

THAT the nature of God is most blessed, as well as eternal, Epicurus himself asserted; and Velleius, an Epicurean, in Cicero,[1] is made to say, that nothing can be thought of more blessed than the life of God, nor more abounding with all good things: he rejoices in his own wisdom and virtue, and assuredly knows that he ever shall be in the highest and eternal pleasures: this God, says he, we rightly call blessed; though he wrongly represents him as neither doing nor designing anything. Euryphamus, a Pythagorean philosopher, more clearly expresses himself; God, says he,[2] needs no external cause; for he is φυσει by nature good, and φυσει, by nature blessed, and is of himself perfect. From this attribute of blessedness the scriptures often style God the *blessed* One, and *the blessed God;* Christ is called, *the Son of the Blessed*, Mark xiv. 61, 62. the Creator of all things is said to be, *God blessed for ever*, Rom. i. 25. 2 Cor. xi. 31. 1 Tim. i. 11. and Christ, as a divine person, is so called, Rom. ix. 5. and nothing is more common with the Jews, in their writings and prayers, than to speak of God as the holy and blessed God. This attribute may be strongly concluded from

---

[1] De Natura Deorum, l. 1.

[2] Fragment. ad Calcem, Laert.

the last treated of; for if God is a sufficient, and self-sufficient, and an all-sufficient Being, he must be happy; as well as from all the perfections of God put together, before discoursed of; his simplicity, immutability, infinity, eternity, omnipresence, omnipotence, omniscience, justice, holiness, truth, and faithfulness, all-sufficiency and perfection; he that is possessed of all these, and in whom no perfection is wanting, must needs be completely blessed. It might be argued from his sovereign, extensive, and endless power and dominion; and from that light, glory, and majesty with which he is arrayed; by all which he is described, 1 Tim. vi. 15, 16. *who is the blessed and only potentate*, &c. he is a *potentate*, has power over others, but is not under the power of any; he is higher than the highest, the most high God; he is over angels and men; he rules in his own right, in right of creation; not by a delegated power; *who hath given him a charge over the earth? or who hath disposed the whole world?* Job. xxxiv. 13. he has the charge of the earth, and disposes of the whole world, and all persons and things in it; but has his authority for it of himself, and not another; he has no rival, competitor, nor partner with him in his throne; he is not accountable to any, nor to be controled by any; he is *King of kings, and Lord of lords;* and so most blessed and happy as a potentate; and as such will always continue. *Who only hath immortality* of himself, and gives it to others: and what mars the happiness of the greatest potentates on earth is, that they must and do die, like other men, Psalm lxxxii. 6, 7. and such is his light and splendour he is clothed with, so striking and dazzling, that none can bear to come unto it, and gaze upon it; *dwelling in the light* of his own essence; for he is light itself; and such is his glory and terrible majesty, as, *that no man can approach unto; whom no man hath seen, nor can see;* and which glory arises not from any single perfection of his, as his holiness, or any other, but from an assemblage of them all; see Exod. xxxiii. 18, 19. and xxxiv. 6, 7. In which glory lies his complete and perfect happiness; and which he gives not to another. The blessedness of God may be considered,

First, As it is in himself; and lies chiefly in these two things, in a freedom from all evils, and in the possession of all good things.

1. In a freedom from all evils;[3] particularly, from the evil of evils, sin; and so from all the consequences of it. Sin is an evil and bitter thing in its own nature; it is exceeding sinful, and extremely pernicious; it is the source of all disorders, disasters, distresses, and calamities that befal any of the creatures; sin has made some of the angels, and Adam and his posterity, once in a most happy state, exceeding unhappy; and it is the infelicity of good men, in the present state, that sin dwells in them, which wars against them, breaks their peace and comfort, and mars their happiness, and obliges them to say, O *wretched* men that we are! but God is just and true, there is no iniquity in him, Deut. xxxiii. 4. no darkness of this kind at all to eclipse his light, glory, and felicity: as holiness is the happiness of the elect angels, and glorified saints, who, being thoroughly holy, are completely happy; so even the most consummate and perfect holiness, is the happiness of God; yea, he is so happy as not to be tempted with the evil of sin, nor can be, James i. 13. whereas good men, in the present state, are often sadly harassed, and made unhappy, by Satan's temptations; being sifted by him as wheat is sifted; and so much trouble is given them, by being buffeted by him, and having his fiery darts thrown at them; but God is out of the reach of all; and as he is not affected with sin, nor can be tempted to it, so he is clear from all the evil consequences of it, all hurts and damages by it.

Such is his *knowledge* of all things, that he cannot make choice of any thing that will be to his detriment; men, through ignorance, mistaking one thing for another, choose what is abominable, and issues in their hurt and ruin; and such is his *wisdom*, that he cannot be imposed upon, circumvented, deceived and drawn into any thing that may make him unhappy; as Eve was, through the subtlety of the serpent; but *there is no wisdom, nor understanding, nor counsel, against the Lord*, Prov. xxi. 30. and such is his *power*, that he cannot be overcome, nor oppressed by any: with respect to men, there is, oftentimes, *power on the side of their oppressors*, to crush and distress them, and make them unhappy; but there is no power superior

---

[3] So the Stoics say of God, that he is perfect and intellectually happy; κακυ παντος ανεπιδικτον, unsusceptible of any evil, Laert. l. 7. in Vita. Zeno.

to the divine Being, to do him the least hurt, or give him the least uneasiness. It has been observed, that properly speaking, there are no affections and passions in God to be wrought upon, or worked up, so as to disturb and disquiet him, as there are in creatures; such as grief and sorrow indulged, and wrath and anger provoked, and raised to a pitch; these are only ascribed to God, speaking after the manner of men; and because some things are done by God similar to what are done by men, when they are grieved and provoked to wrath, &c. otherwise, he is invariably and unchangeably the same, and so most blessed for evermore.

2. His blessedness lies in the possession of all good. He has all good in him; he comprehends all that can be called good; he stands in no need of anything; he is perfect and entire, wanting nothing; he is the fountain of all goodness; all good things come from him; he gives all things richly to enjoy; he is good, and does good, yea, he is good to all; he gives to all, and receives from none; and therefore must be happy; for "it is more blessed to give than to receive," according to the saying of Christ, Acts xx. 35. he is the *summum bonum*, the chief, the chiefest good; in whom only happiness is to be found; when all nature is surveyed, and every place and thing searched into, it can be thought to be in God only, and he is found to be that; *Whom have I in heaven but thee? and there is none upon earth that I desire besides thee*, Psalm lxxiii. 25. Such and such persons, in such and such circumstances, may be thought to be happy; but happy, thrice happy, are the people whose God is the Lord! who, besides the good things he bestows on them here, he has laid up such goodness for them hereafter, which the heart of man cannot conceive of. How blessed and happy then must he himself be! name whatsoever it may be thought happiness consists in, and it will be found in God in its full perfection. Does it lie in grandeur and dominion? with God is terrible majesty; he is the blessed and only potentate; his kingdom rules over all, and is an everlasting one. Does it lie in wealth and riches? *The gold is mine, and the silver is mine*, saith the Lord, Hag. ii. 8. all the gold and silver in the world, that, and all the fulness of it, are his; the riches of both Indies are his property; the mines and metals of the earth, the fowls of the heaven, the beasts of the field, and "the cattle on a thousand hills," in the latter of which the substance of men formerly lay, Psalm xxiv. 1. and l. 10, 11, 12. Does it lie in wisdom and knowledge, where Solomon sought for happiness, and had of all men the greatest share of it? these are in God in the highest perfection; *O the depth of the riches both of the wisdom and knowledge of God!* Rom. xi. 33. Does it lie in might, power, and strength, as Samson's excellency did? God is *mighty in strength: if I speak of strength*, says Job, *lo, he is strong;* there is no strength nor power comparable to his; *Who is a strong Lord like unto thee?* Job ix. 4. 19. Psalm lxxxix. 8. Does it lie in pleasure; in which also Solomon sought for it, but found it not? *In the presence of God is fulness of joy, and at his right hand are pleasures for evermore*, Psalm xvi. 11. and if such as to make his creatures happy, angels and men, then certainly to make himself happy also. Does it lie in fame, in credit, and the high esteem of others? How excellent is the name of God in all the earth! his works praise him, his saints bless him, angels celebrate his glory; yea, his glory is above the heavens; his name is great from the rising of the sun to the going down of the same.

To happiness knowledge is necessary; whatever excellencies may be in creatures, if they know them not, they are not happy in them. Hence happiness is denied of brutes; for though there are many things which they excel in, as strength, swiftness, &c. as the horse and the mule, yet being without understanding, are not happy: but God knows all the excellencies and perfections in his nature; there is no searching of his understanding, and therefore most happy. That happiness is the greatest which is independent; the happiness of angels and men is dependent on God; they have nothing but what they have received, and therefore cannot glory, as though they received it not; and this is a restraint upon, and a limitation of their happiness: but the happiness of God is infinite and independent; of him, and through him, and for him, are all things, Rom. xi. 36. Add to all this, that his blessedness endures for ever; he is God blessed for ever, from everlasting to everlasting: could his happiness cease, or be known that it would, it would detract from it, even for the present; but this can no more cease than his Being.

Secondly, What may serve further to

prove and illustrate the blessedness of God is, that he is the cause of all blessedness in his creatures, angels and men. Angels have their beings from him : it is he that has made them the spirits they are, and what excellencies, as of wisdom, knowledge, strength, &c. they have, are all from him; that they are chosen in Christ, and confirmed by grace in him, see the face of God, and enjoy his favour, in which their greatest blessedness lies, all flow from his sovereign will and pleasure. The temporal happiness of men is from him ; that they have a being, are preserved in it, and have all the necessaries and comforts of life ; and that they are blessed in basket and store; that they have health and wealth, and an increase in their families, flocks, and herds ; on account of which it behoves them to say, *Blessed be the Lord, who daily loadeth us with benefits,* Psalm lxviii. 19. Their spiritual blessings come from him, who is himself their covenant-God and Father, the chief of their blessings, and therefore cannot want any good thing, nor need fear any evil : they have Christ, and all the blessings of goodness with him ; the Spirit, and all his graces, faith, hope, and love, joy, and peace ; the blessings of pardoning grace, and a justifying righteousness, and in which their blessedness greatly lies, and from whence peace and comfort flow, Rom. iv. 6, 7, 8. and v. 1. 11. They are blessed also with the word and ordinances ; which are the means of increasing grace, and spiritual peace ; and hereafter will be blessed with eternal happiness ; with the blessed hope, or the blessedness laid up in heaven, they are hoping for, which they enter upon at death, and enjoy to all eternity. Now if such blessedness comes from God, how blessed must he be in himself!

Thirdly, God is his own blessedness; it is wholly within himself and of himself; he receives none from without himself, or from his creatures ; nothing that can add to his happiness; and he himself is the blessedness of his creatures, who are made happy by him; whose blessedness lies in likeness to him ; which is begun in this life, in regeneration ; when new-born souls are made partakers of the divine nature, is increased by sights of the glory of God in Christ, and will be perfected in the future state, when they shall awake in his likeness, and bear his image in a more perfect manner ; and also it lies in communion with God ; it is the happiness of saints now, and what they exult in, when they enjoy it, that their fellowship is with the Father and his Son Jesus Christ; and it will be the blessedness of the new Jerusalem state, that the tabernacle of God will be with men, and he will dwell with them; and of the ultimate glory the saints shall then have, everlasting and uninterrupted communion with Father, Son, and Spirit, and partake of endless pleasures in the divine presence; and it will, moreover, lie in the vision of God; which, because of the happiness of it, is usually called the beatific vision ; when they shall "see God for themselves, and not another;" see him as he is in Christ, and behold the glory of Christ; see no more darkly through a glass, but face to face, and know as they are known. Wherefore,

Fourthly, God is pronounced, declared, and owned to be blessed, by all his creatures ; hence the frequent form of blessing him used, *Blessed be the Lord God,* &c. Gen. ix. 26. Psalm lxxii. 18. Luke i. 68. Eph. i. 3. Thus he is blessed by angels, who, as they are called upon to bless him, do ascribe honour, glory and blessing to him, Psalm ciii. 20. Rev. v. 11, 12. and vii. 11, 12. and by the saints, who call upon their souls, and all within them, to bless his holy name for all benefits bestowed upon them, Psalm ciii. 1, 2, 3. and cxlv. 10. Which is done, not by invoking a blessing on him ; for there is none greater than he, to invoke and ask one of, much less by conferring any upon him; for as he needs none, a creature can give him nothing but what is his own. Besides, without all contradiction, the less is blessed of the greater ; the creature of the Creator, and not the Creator of the creature: but this is done by congratulating his greatness and blessedness, and ascribing it to him, and praising him for all blessings, temporal and spiritual, bestowed on them by him; and which, as they come from him, are proofs of the blessedness that is in him. And here ends the account of the attributes of God; which all centre and terminate in his blessedness.

CHAP. XXVI.

OF THE UNITY OF GOD.

HAVING treated of the attributes of God, I shall now proceed to prove that this God, who is possessed of all these great and glorious perfections, is but *one*. This is a first principle, and not to be doubted of;

it is a most certain truth, most surely to be believed, and with the greatest confidence to be asserted; as he is a fool that says there is no God, he is equally so, who says there are more than one; and, indeed, as Tertullian [1] observes, if God is not one, he is not at all. This is the first and chief commandment which God has given, and requires an assent and obedience to; on which all religion, doctrine, and faith depend, Mark xii. 28, 29, 30. it is the voice both of reason and revelation; it is discernible by the light of nature; what teaches men there is a God, teaches them there is but one; and though when men neglected the true God, and his worship, and liked not to retain him in their knowledge, he gave them up to a reprobate mind, to judicial blindness, to believe the Father of lies, who led them on by degrees into the grossest idolatry; yet the wiser and better sort of them, though they complied with the custom of countries in which they lived, and paid a lesser sort of worship to the rabble of inferior deities, in which they are not at all to be excused from idolatry; yet they held and owned one supreme Being, whom they often call the Father of the gods and men; [2] the chief God with the Assyrians, as Macrobius relates, [3] was called Adad; which, he says, signifies *one;* and with the Phœnicians, Adodus, the King of the gods; [4] the same with אחד, *one.* That there is but one God, is an article in the Jewish Creed, and which still continues; and no wonder, since it stands in such a glaring light in the writings of the Old Testament, and is as clearly and strongly asserted in the New; so that *we* Christians *know* assuredly, *that there is none God but one,* 1 Cor. viii. 4. It is a truth agreed on by all, by Jews and Gentiles; by Jewish doctors, [5] and heathen poets and philosophers; [6] by Old and New Testament-saints; by the holy angels; and even by the devils themselves: it must be right and well to believe it. The apostle James commends the faith of it; *Thou believest that there is one God; thou doest well; the devils also believe and tremble,* chap. ii. 19. But I go on,

First, To give the proof of this doctrine; which may be taken partly from express passages of scripture, both in the Old and New Testament; see Deut. vi. 4. Psalm lxxxvi. 10. Isa. xliii. 10. and xliv. 6, 8. and xlv. 5, 6, 14, 18, 21, 22. and xlvi. 9. Mark xii. 29. John xvii. 3. Rom. iii. 30. 1 Cor. viii. 4, 5, 6. Eph. iv. 6. 1 Tim. ii. 5. The sense of these scriptures will be observed hereafter; and partly from the perfections of God, and his relations to his creatures.

The necessary existence of God is a proof of his unity. The existence of God must be either of necessity, or of will and choice; if of will and choice, then it must be either of the will and choice of another, or of his own; not of another, for then that other would be prior and superior to him, and so be God, and not he: not of his own will and choice, for then he must be before himself, and be and not be at the same instant; which is such an absurdity and contradiction as is not to be endured. It remains, therefore, that he necessarily exists; and if so, there can be but one God; for no reason can be given why there should be, or can be, more than one necessarily existent Being.

God is the first Being, the cause of all other beings; he is the first Cause, and last end of all things; the mind of man, from effects, rises to the knowledge of causes; and from one cause, to the cause of that; and so proceeds on until it arrives to the first Cause, which is without a cause, and is what is truly called God; and as therefore there is but one first Cause, there can be but one God; so, according to Phythagoras and Plato, unity is the principle of all things. [7]

God, the first Cause, who is without a cause, and is the Cause of all, is independent; all owe their existence to him, and so depend upon him for the preservation, continuance, and comfort of their being; all live, and move, and have their being in him; but he, receiving his being from none, is independent of any; which can only be said of one; there is but one independent Being, and therefore but one God.

God is an eternal Being, before all things, from everlasting to everlasting; and there can be but one Eternal, and so

---

[1] Adv. Marcion. l. 1. c. 3.
[2] Homer. Iliad. 1. Hesiod. l. 1. Opera et Dies, v. 59.
[3] Saturnal. l. 1. c. 24.
[4] Sanchoniatho apud Euseb. præpar. Evangel. l. 1. p. 38.
[5] Maimon. Yesode Hattorah, c. 1. s. 4. Joseph Albo in Sepher Ikkarim, 1, 2. c. 6, 7.
[6] Vide Mornæum de Ver. Christ. Relig. c. 3.
[7] Laert. l. 1. in Vita Pythagoræ.

but one God; *before me*, says he, *there was no God formed; neither shall there be after me*, Isa. xliii. 10. if then no other, then but one God.

God is infinite and incomprehensible; as he is not bounded by time, so not by space; he is not contained or included anywhere, nor comprehended by any. To suppose two infinites, the one must either reach unto, comprehend, and include the other, or not; if it does not, then it is not infinite, and so not God; if it does reach unto, comprehend, and include the other, then that which is comprehended, and included by it, is finite, and so not God; therefore it is clear there cannot be more infinites than one; and if but one infinite, then but one God.

Omnipotence is a perfection of God; he claims this title to himself, The Lord God Almighty: now there cannot be more than one Almighty; omnipotence admits of no degrees; it cannot be said, there is one that is almighty, and another that is more almighty, and a third that is most almighty; there is but one Almighty, and so but one God, who can do all things, whatsoever he pleases; nothing is too hard, too difficult, or impossible to him; nor can any turn back his hand, or stay and stop him from acting. To suppose two almighties, either the one can lay a restraint upon the other, and hinder him from acting, or he cannot; if he cannot, then he is not almighty, the other is mightier than he; if he can, then he on whom the restraint is laid, and is hindered from acting, is not almighty, and so not God; and therefore there can be but one God.

God is good, essentially, originally, and underivatively; the source and fountain of all goodness; *There is none good but one*, says Christ, *that is, God*, Matt. xix. 17. and therefore but one God. The heathens call their supreme God *Optimus*, the best; and there can be none better than the best. He is the *summum bonum*, the chief good; and that is but one, and therefore but one God.

God is a perfect Being; *your heavenly Father*, says Christ, *is perfect*, Matt. v. 48. he is perfect and entire, wanting nothing, completely perfect: now if there are more gods than one, there must be some essential difference by which they are distinguished from one another, and that must be either an excellency or an imperfection; if the latter, then he to whom it belongs is not God, because not perfect; if the former, he in whom it is, is distinguished from all others in whom it is not, and so is the one and only God.

The true God is *El-Shaddai*, God all-sufficient, stands in need of nothing; for of him, and by him, and for him, are all things. All-sufficiency can only be said of One, of Him who is the first Cause and last End of all things; and which, as he is but one, so but one God.

Once more, There is but one Creator; whom all receive their beings from, are supported by, and accountable to, Mal. ii. 10. but one Lawgiver, who is able to save and to destroy, James iv. 12. one King and Governor of the world; one kingdom, which belongs to him; who is the King of kings, and Lord of lords. Were there more than one, the greatest confusion would be introduced in the world; if there were more than one that had the sovereign sway, different and contrary laws, edicts, and decrees, might be published, and subjects would not know whom they were to obey, and what their duty to be performed by them; or whose laws they should pay a regard unto. I proceed,

Secondly, To explain the sense in which this article of one God is to be understood. And,

1st, It is not to be understood in the Arian sense, that there is one supreme God, and two subordinate or inferior ones. This is no other than what is the notion of the better and wiser sort of pagans, as before observed: and if revelation carries us no further than what the light of nature discovers, and that since the fall, and in its corrupt state, we gain nothing by it, with respect to the knowledge of God; nor are the expressions concerning the unity of the divine Being, which are in the Scriptures levelled so much against the notion of more supreme gods, which is a notion that could never prevail much among the heathens; and is so absurd and contradictory, that there is no danger of men's giving into it; but against petty and inferior deities men might be tempted to embrace and worship. Besides, if two subordinate and inferior deities may be admitted, consistent with one God, why not two hundred, or two thousand? no reason can be given why the one should not stand as much excluded as the other: and again, those deities are either creators or creatures; if creators, then they are the one supreme God; for to create is peculiar to him; but if creatures, for there is no medium between the Creator and the creature, then they are not gods that made the heavens and the earth; and so come under the imprecation of the prophet, *The gods that have not made the heavens and the earth, even they shall perish*, or may they perish *from the earth, and from under these heavens*, Jer. x. 11. to which may be added, that such are not entitled to religious worship, which would be worshipping the creature besides and together with the Creator, and would be a breach of the first command, *Thou shalt have no other gods before me*, Rom. i. 25. Exod. xx. 1, 2.

2. Nor is this article to be understood in the Sabellian sense, that God is but one person; for though there is but one God, there are three persons in the godhead, which the Sabellians deny; who are so called from one Sabellius who lived in the middle of the third century; though this notion was broached before him by Noetus,[8] whose followers were called Noetians and Patripassians, asserting, in consequence of their principles, that the Father became incarnate, suffered, and died: and before them Victorinus and Praxeas[9] were much of the same opinion, against whom Tertullian wrote, and who speaks [10] of one sort of the Cataphrygians, who held that Jesus Christ was both Son and Father; and even it may be traced up as high as Simon Magus, who asserted that Father, Son, and Holy Ghost, were only different names of one and the same person, according to his different way of operation:[11] and as before his pretended conversion he gave out that he was some great one, Acts viii. 9. so he did afterwards, and said he was the Father in Samaria, the Son in Judea, and the Holy Ghost in the rest of the nations.[12] Our Socinians and modern Unitarians are much of the same sentiment with the Sabellians in this respect; and some who profess evangelical doctrines have embraced it, or are nibbling at it; fancying they have got new light, when they have only imbibed an old stale error, an ancient work of darkness, which has been confuted over and over. If the Father, Son, and Spirit, were but one person, they could not be three testifiers, as they are said to be, 1 John v. 7. to testify is a personal action; and if the Father is one that bears record, the Son another, and the Holy Ghost a third, they must be three persons, and not one only; and when Christ says, *I and my Father are one*, John x. 30. he cannot mean one person, for this is to make him say what is the most absurd and contradictory; as that I and myself are one, or that I am one, and my Father who is another, are one person; but of this more hereafter.

3. Nor is this doctrine to be understood in a Tritheistic sense, that is, that there are three essences or beings numerically distinct, which may be said to be one, because of the same nature; as three men may be said to be one, because of the same human nature; but this is to assert three Gods and not one; this the Trinitarians indeed are often charged with, and they as often deny the charge; for though they affirm the Father is God, the Son is God, and the Holy Ghost is God, yet not that they are three Gods, but one God. For,

4. They assert, that there is but one divine essence, undivided, and common to Father, Son, and Spirit, and in this sense but one God; since there is but one essence, though there are different modes of subsisting in it which are called persons; and these possess the whole essence undivided; that is to say, not that the Father has one part, the Son another, and the holy Spirit a third; but as the whole fulness of the Godhead dwells in the Father, so in the Son, who has all that the Father has, John xv. 16. Col. ii. 9. and so in the Spirit, and therefore but one God. This unity of them is not an unity of testimony only; for it is not said of them as of the three that bear record on earth, that they *agree in one*, but that they *are one*, 1 John v. 7, 8. but it is an unity of nature; they have one and the same infinite and undivided nature; and this unity is not an unity of parts, which makes one compositum, as the body and soul of man do; for God is a simple and uncompounded Spirit; nor an unity of genus and species, under which may be many singulars of the same kind, but God is one in number and nature, and stands opposed to the polytheism of the heathens, who had gods many and lords many, 1 Cor. viii. 4, 5. and to all nominal and figurative deities, as angels, civil magistrates, judges, &c. even to all

---

[8] Vid. Augustin. de Hæres. c. 36.
[9] Tertullian. de Præscript, Hæret. c. 53. et Adv. Praxeam, c. 1, 2.
[10] De Præscript. c. 52.
[11] Vid. Danæum in August. de Hæres. c. 1.
[12] Irenæus Adv. Hæres. c. 23.

who are not by nature God, Gal. iv. 8. Nor is this unity of God to be objected to and set aside by the *many names* of God, as El, Elohim, Jehovah, &c. since these are names of the one God, as one and the same man may have different names, and yet but one ; nor by the *many attributes* of God, which do not differ from him, nor from one another, but are all one in God, and are himself; though distinctly considered by us, because our understandings are too weak to take them in as in the gross, but to consider them apart, as has been observed. Nor by the *persons* in the godhead being more than one ; for though three persons, they differ not from the divine essence, nor from one another, but by their distinctive modes of subsisting, and are but one God. Nor are those passages of scripture which assert the unity of God to be appropriated to one person only, to the exclusion of the others ; but to be considered as including each.

The famous passage in Deut. vi. 4. which is introduced in a solemn manner, exciting attention, *Hear, O Israel, the Lord our God is one Lord!* and which Christ refers the scribe to as the first and chief command, Mark xii. 28, 29. asserts that there is but one Jehovah ; but not that this is peculiar to the Father, and as exclusive of the Son and Spirit; for Christ the Son of God is Jehovah, and is often so called ; see Exod. xvii. 7. Num. xxi. 6. compared with 1 Cor. x. 9. Jer. xxiii. 6. Zech. xii. 10. and so the Holy Ghost, Isa. vi. 1, 5, 8, 9. compared with Acts xxviii. 25, 26. and these, with the Father, are the one Lord or Jehovah ; and are manifestly included in Elohenu, a word of the plural number, and may be rendered *our Gods*, or rather our *divine persons* are one Lord ; for Christ the Son is one of them, who is that God whose throne is for ever and ever; and the Spirit that God, or divine person, who anointed Christ as man, Psalm xlv. 6, 7. and that the three divine persons who are the one Jehovah are here meant, is not only the sense of Christian[13] writers but even of the ancient Jews ;[14] and besides, the Son and Spirit are entitled to the same sincere and fervent love of men as the Father, and which is required to be given to the one Jehovah, even Father, Son and Spirit.

The several passages in Isaiah before referred to, and which so strongly assert the unity of the Divine Being, cannot be understood to the exclusion of the Son and Spirit. In one of them, chap. xliv. 6. the only Lord God calls himself the *first and the last*, a title which also Christ the Son of God claims as his, Rev. i. 8. yea in the same passage the one God styles himself *the Redeemer*, a name very peculiar to the Son, who agreed to be the Redeemer; came in the fulness of time as such, and has obtained eternal redemption for men : and in another of those passages, chap. xlv. 21. the only Lord God is spoken of as a Saviour ; and in ver. 22. Christ is represented as a Saviour inviting and encouraging persons to look to him for salvation, enforcing it with this reason, *for I am God, and there is none else :* now as the Father cannot be supposed to be excluded hereby, so neither should the Son and Spirit be thought to be excluded by similar expressions elsewhere ; besides, the following verse (ver. 23.) is manifestly applied to Christ by the Apostle, Rom. xiv. 10, 11.

The words of our Lord Jesus Christ, John xvii. 3. which affirm the Father to be the only true God, cannot be understood to the exclusion of himself; *this is life eternal, that they might know thee the only true God, and Jesus Christ whom thou hast sent :* since Christ also is called the only Lord God, Jude ver. 4. and the true God and eternal life, 1 John v. 20. nor would he have joined himself so closely with the only true God, if he was not so ; but he thought it no robbery to be equal with him, yea one with him ; of the same nature, power, and glory ; and besides, eternal life is made as much to depend on the knowledge of Christ as of his Father ; see John vi. 47, 53, 54. the reason of this mode of expression, distinguishing the one from the other, is because Christ is described by his office as sent of God.

In Rom. iii. 30. it is said, *It is one God which shall justify the circumcision by faith, and uncircumcision through faith;* that is, there is one God of Jews and Gentiles, which this is said to prove, ver. 29. but Christ cannot stand excluded from the one God that justifies, since he is Jehovah our righteousness, and the sun of righteousness, Jer. xxiii. 6. Mal. iv. 2. and it is not only his righteousness by which men are justi-

---

[13] Vid. Fulgentii Respons. contr. Arian. Obj. 4. 10.

[14] See my Doctrine of the Trinity, p. 19. 20.

fied, Jews and Gentiles; but he himself justifies them by his knowledge, that is, by faith, Isa. liii. 11. nor the holy Spirit, who brings near Christ's righteousness, and applies it; works faith to receive it, and pronounces men justified by it, 1 Cor. vi. 11.

The text in 1 Cor. viii. 6. which expresses the faith of Christians, there is but *one God the Father, of whom are all things*, stands opposed not to any other persons in the Godhead, but to the many lords and gods among the heathens, ver. 5. nor is the Father called the Father of Christ, or opposed to him, but the Father of all; that is, the Creator; see Mal. ii. 10. in which character, the Son and Spirit are included, Eccles. xii. 1. Besides, if Christ could be thought to stand excluded from the one God, the Father, by the same rule of interpretation, God the Father must stand excluded from the one Lord, said of Christ in the same text; and these observations may be applied to Eph. iv. 5. 6. and will serve to clear and explain the words there to the same sense.

It is also said in 1 Tim. ii. 5. that *there is one God, and one Mediator between God and men, the man Christ Jesus;* now the reason why Christ is spoken of as distinct from the one God, though not different, is for the sake of the mention of him in his office as Mediator; but then if he was not the one God, with the other divine persons; or the true God, and the great God, he could not be a Mediator between God and man; he could not be a day's-man between them, and lay his hands on both; he could not draw nigh to God, and treat with him about peace and reconciliation; and much less make peace for men, and be a ransom for them; as in the following verse: but after all, though there are three persons in the Godhead, as will more clearly appear hereafter, and none of them stand excluded from Deity, yet there is but one God; this is an article that must be inviolably maintained.

The doctrine of the unity of the divine Being, is of great importance in religion; especially in the affair of worship. God, the one only God, is the object of it. This is the sense of the first and second Commands, which forbid owning any other God but one, and the worship of any creature whatever, angels or men, or any other creature, and the likeness of them; which to do is to worship the creature, besides, or along with the Creator. But this hinders not but that the Son and Spirit may have acts of worship performed to them, equally as to the Father; and for this reason, because they are, with him, the one God; hence baptism is administered equally, in the name of all Three; and prayer is jointly made unto them; both solemn acts of religious worship; see Matt. xxviii. 19. Rev. i. 4, 5. And this doctrine of the unity of the divine Being, as it fixes and settles the object of worship, so being closely attended to, it guides the mind right in the consideration of it, while worshipping, without any confusion and division in it; for let the direction, or address, be to which person it may, as each may be distinctly addressed; be it to the Father, he is considered in the act of worship, as the one God, with the Son and Spirit; if the address is to the Son, he is considered as the one God, with the Father and the Spirit; or if the address is to the Spirit, he is considered as the one God, with the Father and Son. And this doctrine also serves to fix and settle the object of our faith, hope, and love, without division and distraction of mind; which are not to be exercised on different objects, and to be divided between them; but are to centre in one object, the one only true God, Father, Son, and Spirit; whom alone we are to make our confidence, our hope, and the centre of our affections, Jer. xvii. 7. Psalm lxxiii. 25. As well as this doctrine carries a strong and powerful argument to promote unity, harmony, and concord among the saints; for which it is used in Eph. iv. 3, 4, 5, 6.

CHAP. XXVII.

OF A PLURALITY IN THE GODHEAD; OR, A TRINITY OF PERSONS IN THE UNITY OF THE DIVINE ESSENCE.

HAVING proved the unity of the divine Being, and explained the sense in which it is to be understood; my next work will be to prove that there is a plurality in the Godhead; or, that there are more persons than one, and that these are neither more, nor fewer, than three; or, that there is a Trinity of Persons in the unity of the divine essence. Some except to these terms, because not literally and syllabically expressed in scripture; as Essence, Unity,

CHAP. XXVII.   OF A PLURALITY IN THE GODHEAD, &c.

Trinity, and Person; of which see the Introduction, p. viii. I shall,

First, Prove that there is a plurality of persons in the one God; or, that there are more than one. The Hebrew word פנים which answers to the Greek word προσωπα is used of the divine persons, פני *My persons shall go with thee,* Exod. xxxiii. 14. and if פניך *thy persons go not with me,* ver. 15. and *he brought thee out* בפניו *by his persons,* Deut. iv. 37. The word is used three times in Psalm xxvii. 8, 9. and in each clause the Septuagint has the word προσωπον, and which, as Suidas[1] observes, is expressive of the sacred Trinity. That there is such a plurality of persons, will appear more clearly,

1. From the plural names and epithets of God. His great and incommunicable name Jehovah, is always in the singular number, and is never used plurally; the reason of which is, because it is expressive of his essence, which is but one; it is the same with *I AM that I AM;* but the first name of God we meet with in scripture, and that in the first verse of it, is plural; *In the beginning God* (Elohim) *created the heaven and the earth,* Gen. i. 1. and therefore must design more than one, at least two, and yet not precisely two, or two only; then it would have been dual; but it is plural; and, as the Jews themselves say, cannot design fewer than three.[2] Now Moses might have made use of other names of God, in his account of the creation; as his name Jehovah, by which he made himself known to him, and to the people of Israel; or Eloah, the singular of Elohim, which is used by him, Deut. xxxii. 15, 16. and in the book of Job frequently; so that it was not want of singular names of God, nor the barrenness of the Hebrew language, which obliged him to use a plural word; it was no doubt of choice, and with design; and which will be more evident when it is observed, that one end of the writings of Moses is to extirpate the polytheism of the heathens, and to prevent the people of Israel from going into it; and therefore it may seem strange, that he should begin his history with a plural name of God; he must have some design in it, which could not be to inculcate a plurality of gods, for that would be directly contrary to what he had in view in writing, and to what he asserts, Deut. vi. 4.

Hear, O Israel, the Lord our God is one Lord: nor a plurality of mere names and characters, to which creative powers cannot be ascribed; but a plurality of persons, for so the words may be rendered, distributively, according to the idiom of the Hebrew language; " In the beginning every one, or each of the divine persons, created the heaven and the earth." And then the historian goes on to make mention of them; who, besides the Father, included in this name, are the Spirit of God, that moved upon the face of the waters, and the word of God, ver. 2. which said, *Let there be light, and there was light;* and which spoke that, and all things, out of nothing; see John i. 1, 2, 3. And it may be further observed, that this plural word Elohim, is, in this passage, in construction with a verb singular, *bara,* rendered *created;* which some have thought is designed to point out a plurality of persons, in the unity of the divine essence; but if this is not judged sufficient to build it upon, let it be further observed, that the word Elohim is sometimes in construction with a verb plural, as in Gen. xx. 13. and xxxv. 7. 2 Sam. vii. 23. where Elohim, the gods, or divine persons, are said to cause Abraham to wander from his father's house; to appear to Jacob; and to go forth to redeem Israel; all which are personal actions: and likewise it is in construction with adjectives and participles plural, Deut. iv. 7. and v. 26. Josh. xxiv. 19. 1 Sam. vii. 26, 36. Psalm lviii. 11. Prov. xxx. 3. Jer. x. 10. in which places Elohim, gods, or the divine persons, are said to be nigh to the people of Israel; to be living, holy, and to judge in the earth; characters which belong to persons; and now, as a learned man[3] well observes, " that however the construction of a noun plural with a verb singular, may render it doubtful to some whether these words express a plurality or no, yet certainly there can be no doubt in those places, where a verb or adjective plural are joined with the word Elohim." No such stress is laid on this word, as if it was the clearest and strongest proof of a plurality in the Deity; it is only mentioned, and mentioned first, because it is the most usual name of God, being used of him many hundreds of times in scripture; and what stress is laid upon it, is not merely because it is plural, but

---

[1] In voce αγιος.
[2] Vid. Alting. Dissert. Philolog. 4. s. 6, 7.8.

[3] Allix's Judgment of the Jewish Church, p. 124.

because it appears often in an unusual form of construction; it is used of others, but not in such a form; as has been observed. It is used of angels, Psalm viii. 5. they being not only many, but are often messengers of God, of the divine persons in the Godhead, represent them, and speak in their name. And it is used of civil magistrates, Psalm lxxxii. 6. and so of Moses, as a god to Pharaoh, Exod. vii. 1. as they well may be called, since they are the vicegerents and representatives of the Elohim, the divine Persons, the Trine-une God; nor need it be wondered at, that it should be sometimes used of a single Person in the Deity, it being common to them all; and since each of them possess the whole divine nature and essence undivided, Psalm xlv. 6, 7. The ancient Jews not only concluded a plurality, but even a Trinity, from the word Elohim.[4] With respect to the passage in Numb. xv. 16. they say,[5] "There is no judgment less than three;" and that three persons sitting in judgment, the divine Majesty is with them, they conclude from Psalm lxxxii. 1. *He judgeth among the gods*, אלהים. Hence they further observe,[6] that "no sanhedrim, or court of judicature is called אלהים unless it consists of three." From whence it is manifest, that the ancient Jews believed that this name not only inferred a plurality of persons, but such a plurality which consisted of three at least.

Another plural name of God is Adonim; *If I am* (Adonim) *Lords, where is my fear?* Mal. i. 6. now, though this may be said of one in the second and third persons plural, yet never of one in the first person, as it is here said of God by himself; *I am Lords;* and we are sure there are two, *The Lord said to my Lord*, &c. Psalm cx. 1.

In Dan. iv. 17. the most high God is called the watchers and the holy ones; *This matter is by the decree of the watchers, and the demand by the word of the holy ones;* which respects the revolution and destruction of the Babylonian monarchy; an affair of such moment and importance as not to be ascribed to angels, which some understand by watchers and holy ones; but however applicable these epithets may be to them, and they may be allowed to be the executioners of the decrees of God, yet not the makers of them; nor can anything in this world, and much less an affair of such consequence as this, be said to be done in virtue of any decree of theirs: besides, this decree is expressly called, the decree of the most High, ver. 24. so that the watchers and holy ones, are no other than the divine Persons in the Godhead; who are holy in their nature, and watch over the saints to do them good; and over the wicked, to bring evil upon them: and as they are so called in the plural number, to express the plurality of them in the Deity; so to preserve the unity of the divine essence, this same decree is called, the decree of the most High, ver. 24. and they the watcher and holy one, in the singular number in ver. 13.

2. A plurality in the Deity may be proved from plural expressions used by God, when speaking of himself, respecting the works of creation, providence, and grace. At the creation of man he said, *Let us make man in our image, after our likeness*, Gen. i. 26. the pronouns *us* and *our*, manifestly express a plurality of persons; these being personal plural characters; as *image* and *likeness* being in the singular number, secure the unity of the divine essence; and that there were more than one concerned in the creation of man, is clear from the plural expressions used of the divine Being, when he is spoken of as the Creator of men, Job xxxv. 10. Psalm cxlix. 2. Eccles. xii. 1. Isa. liv. v. in all which places, in the original text, it is my Makers, his Makers, thy Creators, thy Makers; for which no other reason can be given, than that more persons than one had an hand herein; for as for the angels, they are creatures themselves, and not possessed of creative powers; nor were they concerned in the creation of man, nor was he made after their image and likeness; nor can it be reasonably thought, that God spoke to them, and held a consultation with them about it; for *with whom took he counsel?* Isa. xl. 14. Not with any of his creatures; no, not with the highest angel in heaven; they are not of his privy council. Nor is it to be thought that God, in the above passage, speaks *regio more*, after the manner of kings; who, in their edicts and proclamations, use the plural number, to express their honour and majesty; and even they are not to be considered alone, but as connotating their ministers and privy council, by whose advice they act; and,

---

[4] See my Doctrine of the Trinity, p. 30.
[5] Gloss. in T. Bab. Yebamot, fol. 46. 2.

[6] T. Bab. Beracot, fol. 6. 1. et Gloss. in ibid.

besides, this courtly way of speaking, was not so ancient as the times of Moses; none of the kings of Israel use it; nor even any of those proud and haughty monarchs, Pharaoh and Nebuchadnezzar; the first appearance of it is in the letters of Artaxerxes, king of Persia, Ezra iv. 18. and vii. 23. which might take its rise from the conjunction of Darius and Cyrus, in the Persian empire, in both whose names edicts might be made, and letters wrote; which might give rise to such a way of speaking, and be continued by their successors, to express their power and glory: but, as a learned man[7] observes, "It is a very extravagant fancy, to suppose that Moses alludes to a custom that was not (for what appears) in being at that time, nor a great while after." The Jews themselves are sensible that this passage furnishes with an argument for a plurality in the Deity.[8]

A like way of speaking is used concerning men, in Gen. iii. 22. *And the Lord God said, Behold, the man is become as one of us;* not as one of the angels, for they are not of the Deity, nor the companions of God, and equal to him; for whatever private secret meaning Satan might have in saying, *Ye shall be as gods;* he would have it understood by Eve, and so she understood it, that they should be not like the angels merely, but like God himself this was the bait he laid, and which took, and proved man's ruin; upon which the Lord God said these words either sarcastically, "Behold the man whom Satan promised, and he expected to be as one of us, as one of the persons in the Deity; see how much he looks like one of us! who but just now ran away from us in fear and trembling, and covered himself with fig-leaves, and now stands before us clothed with skins of slain beasts!" or else as comparing his former and present state together; for the words may be rendered, *he was as one of us;* made after their image and likeness: but what is he now? he has sinned, and come short of that glorious image; has lost his honour, and is become like the beasts that perish, whose skins he now wears. Philo,[9] the Jew, owns that these words are to be understood not of one, but of more; the ἓν καὶ πολλα, the *one* and *many*, so much spoken of by the Pythagoreans and Platonists; and which Plato[10] speaks of as

infinite and eternal, and of the knowledge of them as the gift of the gods; and which, he says, was delivered to us by the ancients · who were better than we, and lived nearer the gods; by whom he seems to intend the ancient Jews; this, I say, though understood by their followers of the unity of God, and the many ideas in him, the same with what we call decrees; I take to be no other than the one God, and a plurality of persons in the Deity; which was the faith of the ancient Jews; so that the πολλα, of Plato, and others, is the same with the πληθος of Philo, who was a great Platonizer; and both intend a plurality of persons.

God sometimes uses the plural number when speaking of himself, with respect to some particular affairs of providence, as the confusion of languages; *Go to, let us go down, and there confound their language;* which also cannot be said to angels; had it, it would rather have been, go ye, and do *ye* confound their language; but, alas! this work was above the power of angels to do; none but God, that gave to man the faculty of speech, and the use of language, could confound it; which was as great an instance of divine power, as to bestow the gift of tongues on the apostles, at Pentecost; and the same God that did the one, did the other; and so the *us* here, are after explained of Jehovah, in the following verse, to whom the confounding the language of men, and scattering them abroad on the face of the earth, are ascribed, ver. 8, 9. In another affair of providence, smiting the Jewish nation with judicial blindness; this plural way of speaking is used by the divine Being; says the prophet Isaiah, *I heard the voice of the Lord saying, Whom shall I send, and who will go for us?* Isa. vi. 8. not the *seraphim* say this, but Jehovah; for to them neither the name Jehovah, nor the work agree; and though there is but one Jehovah that here speaks, yet more persons than one are intended by him; of Christ, the Son of God, no question can be made, since the Evangelist applies them to him; and observes, that Isaiah said the words when he saw his glory, and spoke of him, John xii. 40, 41. nor of the Holy Ghost, to whom they are also applied,

---

[7] Kidder's Demonstration of the Messiah, part 3. p. 90. edit. fol.
[8] See my Doctrine of the Trinity, p. 35, 36.
[9] τυ ποιησωμεν πληθος εμφαινοντος, De Confus. Ling. p. 344, 345.
[10] In Philebo, p. 372, 373. Ed. Ficin. Vid. Parmenidem, p. 1111, 1112, 1117, 1120, 1122.

Acts xxviii. 25, 26. There is another passage in Isa. xli. 21, 22, 23. where Jehovah, the King of Jacob, challenges the heathens, and their gods, to bring proof of their Deity, by prediction of future events; and, in which, he all along uses the plural number; "shew *us* what shall happen, that *we* may consider them; declare unto *us* things for to come, that *we* may know that ye are gods, and that *we* may be dismayed; see also Isa. xliii. 9.

And as in the affairs of creation and providence, so in those of grace, and with respect to spiritual communion with God, plural expressions are used; as when our Lord says, *If a man love me, he will keep my words; and my Father will love him, and we will come unto him, and make our abode with him*, John xiv. 23. which personal actions of coming and making abode, expressive of communion and fellowship, are said of more than one; and we cannot be at a loss about two of them, Christ and his Father, who are expressly mentioned; and hence we read of fellowship with the Father, and his Son Jesus Christ; and also of the communion of the Holy Ghost, 1 John i. 3. 2 Cor. xiii. 14. To all these instances of plural expressions, may be added Cant. i. 11. John iii. 11.

3. A plurality in the Deity may be proved from those passages of scripture which speak of the angel of Jehovah, who also is Jehovah; now if there is a Jehovah that is sent, and therefore called an angel, and a Jehovah that sends, there must be more persons than one who are Jehovah.

The first instance of this kind is in Gen. xvi. 7. where the angel of Jehovah is said to find Hagar, Sarah's maid, in the wilderness, and bid her return to her mistress; which angel appears to be Jehovah, since he promises to do that for her, and acquaints her with future things, which no created angel, and none but Jehovah could, ver. 10, 11, 12. and what proves it beyond all dispute that he must be Jehovah, is, what is said, ver. 13. *She called the name of the Lord*, or Jehovah, *that spake unto her, thou, God, seest*.

In Gen. xviii. 2. we read of three men who stood by Abraham in the plains of Mamre, who were angels in an human form, as two of them are expressly said to be, chap. xix. 1. Dr. Lightfoot[11] is of opinion, that they were the three divine Persons; and scruples not to say, that at such a time the Trinity dined with Abraham; but the Father, and the holy Spirit, never assumed an human form; nor are they ever called angels. However, one of these was undoubtedly a divine Person, the Son of God in an human form; who is expressly called Jehovah, the Judge of all the earth, ver. 13, 20, 25, 26. and to whom omnipotence and omniscience are ascribed, ver. 14, 17, 18, 19. and to whom Abraham shewed the utmost reverence and respect, ver. 27, 30, 31. and now he is distinguished, being Jehovah in human form on earth, from Jehovah in heaven, from whom he is said to rain brimstone and fire on Sodom and Gomorrah, chap. xix. 24. which conflagration was not made by the ministry of created angels, but is always represented as the work of Elohim, of the divine Persons, Jer. l. 40. Amos. iv. 11.

An angel also appeared to Abraham at the offering up of his son Isaac, and bid him desist from it; and who appears plainly to be the same with him who ordered him to do it; expressly called God, Gen. xxii. 11, 12. compared with ver. 1, 2. and Jehovah, who swore by himself, and promised to do what none but God could do, ver. 16, 17, 18. see Heb. vi. 13, 14. where what is here said is expressly ascribed to God. Add to this, the name Abraham gave the place on this occasion, Jehovah-Jireh, because the Lord had appeared, and would hereafter appear in this place.

The angel invoked by Jacob, Gen. xlviii. 15, 16. is put upon a level with the God of his fathers Abraham and Isaac; yea, is represented as the same; and the work of redeeming him from all evil, equal to that of feeding him all his life long, is ascribed to him; as well as a blessing on the sons of Joseph, is prayed for from him; all which would never have been said of, nor done to, a created angel.

The angel which appeared to Moses in the bush, Exod. iii. 2. was not a created angel, but a divine person; as is evident from the names by which he is called, Jehovah, God, the God of Abraham, Isaac, and Jacob, *I AM that I AM*, ver. 4, 6, 14. and from the things ascribed to him; seeing the afflictions of the Israelites, coming to deliver them out of Egyptian bondage, and promising to bring them into the land of Canaan, ver. 7, 8. to which may be added, the prayer of Moses for a blessing on Joseph, because of the good-will of him that dwelt in the bush, Deut. xxiii. 16.

---

[11] Works, vol. 1. p. 13.

and the application of this passage to God, by our Lord Jesus Christ, Mark xii. 26.

Once more, the angel that was promised to go before the children of Israel, to keep and guide them in the way through the wilderness to the land of Canaan, is no other than Jehovah; since not only the obedience of the children of Israel to him is required; but it is suggested, that should they disobey him, he would not, though he could, pardon their iniquities; which none but God can do: and also it is said, the name of the Lord was in him; that is, his nature and perfections; and since it is the same the children of Israel rebelled against, he could be no other than Christ, the Son of God, whom they tempted; the angel of God's presence; who, notwithstanding, saved and carried them all the days of old, Isa. lxiii. 9. 1 Cor. x. 9.

Again, we read of the angel of the Lord, before whom Joshua the high-priest was brought and stood, being accused by Satan, Zech. iii. 1. who is not only called Jehovah, ver. 2. but takes upon him to do and order such things, which none but God could do; as causing the iniquity of Joshua to pass from him, and clothing him with change of raiment; see Isa. lxi. 10.

To these may be added, all such scriptures which speak of two, as distinct from each other, under the same name of Jehovah; as in the above-mentioned text, Gen. xix. 24. where Jehovah is said to rain fire and brimstone from Jehovah, out of heaven; and in Jer. xxiii. 5, 6. where Jehovah promises to raise up a righteous branch to David, whose name should be called *Jehovah our righteousness;* and in Hos. i. 7. where Jehovah resolves he would save his people by Jehovah their God. Other passages might be mentioned, as proving a plurality in Deity; but as some of these will also prove a Trinity in it, they will be considered under the following head; where it will be proved,

Secondly, That this plurality in the Godhead, is neither more nor fewer than three; or, that there is a Trinity of persons in the unity of the divine essence: this I have before taken for granted, and now I shall prove it. And not to take notice of the name Jehovah being used three times, and three times only, in the blessing of the priest, Numb. vi. 24, 25, 26. and in the prayer of Daniel, chap. ix. 19. and in the church's declaration of her faith in God, Isa. xxxiii. 22. and the word holy repeated three times, and three times only, in the seraphim's celebration of the glory of the divine Being, Isa. vi. 3. and in that of the living creatures, in Rev. iv. 8. which may seem to be accidental, or the effect of a fervent and devout disposition of mind; but there is not anything, no not the least thing, that is said or written in the sacred scriptures, without design.

I shall begin with the famous text in 1 John v. 7. as giving full proof and evidence of this doctrine; *For there are three that bear record in heaven, the Father, the Word, and the Holy Ghost; and these three are one:* which is not only a proof of the Deity of each of these three, inasmuch as they are not only said to be *one,* that is, one God; and their witness is called the witness of God, ver. 9. but of a Trinity of Persons, in the unity of the divine essence; unity of essence, or nature, is asserted and secured, by their being said to be *one;* which respects not a mere unity of testimony, but of nature; for it is not said of them, as of the witnesses on earth, that they *agree in one;* but that they *are one.* And they may be called a Trinity, inasmuch as they are *three,* and a Trinity of Persons, since they are not only spoken of as distinct from each other, the Father from the Word and Holy Ghost, the Word from the Father and the Holy Ghost, and the Holy Ghost from the Father and the Word; but a personal action is ascribed to each of them; for they are all three said to be testifiers, or to bear record; which cannot be said of mere names and characters; nor be understood of one person under different names; for if the one living and true God only bears record, first under the character of a Father, then under the character of a Son, or the Word, and then under the character of the Holy Ghost; testimony, indeed, would be bore three times, but there would be but one testifier, and not three, as the apostle asserts. Suppose one man should, for one man may bear the characters, and stand in the relations of father, son, and master; of a father to a child of his own; of a son, his father being living; and of a master to servants under him; suppose, I say, this man should come into a court of judicature, and be admitted to bear testimony in an affair there depending, and should give his testimony first under the character of a father, then under the character of a son, and next under the character of a master; every one will conclude, that though here was a testimony three times bore, yet there was but one, and not three, that bore record. This text is so glaring a proof of the doctrine of the Trinity, that the enemies of it have done all they can to weaken its authority, and have pushed hard to extirpate it from a place in the sacred writings. They object, that it is wanting in the Syriac version; that the old Latin interpreter has it not; that it is not to be found in many Greek manuscripts; and is not quoted by the ancient fathers who wrote against the Arians, when it might have been of great service to them. To all which it may be replied; that as to the Syriac version, though an ancient one, it is but a version, and till of late appeared a very defective one; the history of the adulterous woman in the eighth of John, the second epistle of Peter, the second and third epistles of John, the epistle of Jude, and the book of Revelation, were all wanting, till restored from a copy of archbishop Usher's, by De Dieu and Dr. Pocock; and who also, from an Eastern copy, has supplied the version with this text, so that now it stands in it. And as to the old Latin interpreter, it is certain that it is to be seen in many Latin manuscripts of an early date, and is in the vulgate Latin version of the London Polyglot Bible; and the Latin translation which bears the name of Jerom has it; and who, in an epistle to Eustochium, prefixed to his translation of those canonical epistles, complains of the omission of it, by unfaithful interpreters. As to its being wanting in some Greek manuscripts, it need only be said, it is found in many others; it is in the Complutensian edition, the compilers of which made use of various copies; out of sixteen ancient copies of Robert Stephens's, nine of them had it; and it is also said to be in an old British copy. As to its not being quoted by some of the ancient fathers, this can be no proof of its not being genuine; since it might be in the original copy, and not in that used by them, through the carelessness and unfaithfulness of transcribers; or through copies erased falling into their hands, such as had been corrupted before the times of Arius, even by Artemon, or his disciples, who lived in the second century; who held that Christ was a mere man; by whom it is said,[12] this passage was erased; and certain it is, that this epistle was very early corrupted; as the ancient writers testify:[13] or it might be in the copies used by the fathers, and yet not quoted by them, having scriptures enow without it, to prove and defend the doctrine of it; and yet, after all, it appears plainly to be quoted by many of them; by Fulgentius,[14] in the beginning of the sixth century, against the Arians, without any scruple or hesitation: and Jerom, as before observed, has it in his translation, made in the latter end of the fourth century: and it is quoted by Athanasius,[15] about the middle of it; and before him by Cyprian,[16] in the middle of the third century; and is manifestly referred to by Tertullian,[17] in the beginning of it; and by Clemens of Alexandria,[18] towards the end of the second century: so that it is to be traced up within a hundred years, or less, to the writing of the epistle; which is enough to satisfy any one of the genuineness of this text. And, besides, it should be observed, that there never was any dispute about it, until Erasmus left it out in the first edition of his translation of the New Testament; and yet he himself, upon the credit of the old British copy, before mentioned, put it into another edition of his translation. Yea, the Socinians themselves have not dared to leave it out in their German Racovian version, A. C. 1630. To which may be added, that the context requires it; the connection with the preceding verse shows it, as well as its opposition to, and distinction from, the following verse; and in ver. 9. is a plain reference to the divine witnesses in this; for the inference in it would not be clear, if there was no mention before made of a divine testimony. But I shall not rest the proof of the doctrine of the Trinity on this single passage; but on the whole current and universal consent of scripture, where it is written as with a sunbeam; according to which, a Trinity of Persons in the Godhead appears in the works of creation, providence, and grace; in all things respecting the office and work of Christ; and God's acts of grace towards and upon his people; and in their worship and duties of religion enjoined them, and practised by them.

---

[12] Vid. Wittichii Theolog. Pacific. c. 17. s. 254.
[13] Vid. Socrat. Eccl. Hist. l. 7. c. 32.
[14] Respons. contr. Arian. Obj. 10. et de Trinitate, c. 4.
[15] Contr. Arium, p. 109. de Unit. Deitat. Trin. ad Theoph. l. 1. p. 399.
[16] De Unitat. Eccles. p. 255. et in Ep. 73. ad Iubajan. p. 184.
[17] Adv. Praxeam, c. 25.
[18] Pædagog. l. 3. in fine.

CHAP. XXVII.   OF A PLURALITY IN THE GODHEAD, &c.   137

1. In the works of creation: as by these the eternal power and godhead are made manifest, so in them are plain traces of a Trinity of persons; that God the Father made the heavens, earth, and sea, and all that are in them, under which character the apostles addressed him as distinct from Christ his Son, Acts iv. 24, 27. none will doubt; and that the divine Word, or Son of God, was concerned in all this a question cannot be made of it, when it is observed that it is said, *All things were made by him, and without him was not anything made that is made*, John i. 3. And as for the Holy Spirit, he is not only said to move upon the face of the waters which covered the earth, and brought that unformed chaos of earth and water into a beautiful order, but to garnish the heavens, to bespangle the firmament with stars of light, and to form the crooked serpent, the Leviathan, which being the greatest, is put for all the fishes of the sea; as well as he is said to be sent forth yearly, and renews the face of the earth at every returning spring; which is little less than a creation, and is so called, Gen. i. 2. Job xxvi. 13. Psalm civ. 30. and all three may be seen together in one text, Psalm xxxiii. 6. *By the word of the Lord were the heavens made, and all the host of them by the breath of his mouth*; where mention is made of Jehovah, and his Word, the eternal Logos, and of his Spirit, the breath of his mouth, as all concerned in the making of the heavens, and all the host of them. And as in the creation of man, in particular, a plurality has been observed, this plurality was neither more nor fewer than three; that God the Father is the maker of men, will not be objected to; *Have we not all one father? hath not one God created us?* Mal. ii. 10. and the Son of God, who is the husband of the church, and the Redeemer of men, is expressly said to be their maker, Isa. liv. 5. and of the Holy Spirit, Elihu in so many words says, *The Spirit of God hath made me, and the breath of the almighty hath given me life*, Job xxxiii. 4.

2. A Trinity of persons appears in the works of providence. *My father*, says Christ, *worketh hitherto and I work*, John v. 17. that is, ever since the works of creation were finished, in which both had an hand, they have been jointly concerned in the works of providence, in the government of the world, and in ordering and disposing of all things in it; and not to the exclusion of the holy Spirit, for, *Who hath directed the Spirit of the Lord, or being his counsellor hath taught him?* that is, in the affair of the government of the world, as follows; *With whom took he counsel, and who instructed him and taught him in the path of judgment, and taught him knowledge, and shewed to him the way of understanding?* to manage the important concerns of the world, to do every thing wisely and justly, and to overrule all for the best ends and purposes; see Isa. xl. 13, 14. And particularly the three divine persons appear in that remarkable affair of providence, the deliverance of Israel out of Egypt, and the protection and guidance of them through the wilderness to the land of Canaan. Whoever reads attentively Isa. lxiii. 7—14. will easily observe, that mention is made of Jehovah, and of his mercy, loving-kindness, and goodness to the children of Israel; and then of the Angel of his presence, as distinct from him, shewing love and pity to them, in saving, redeeming, bearing, and carrying them all the days of old; and next of his holy Spirit, whom they rebelled against, and whom they vexed, and yet, though thus provoked, he led them on through the wilderness, and caused them to rest in the land of Canaan.

3. The three divine persons are to be discerned most clearly in all the works of grace. The inspiration of the scriptures is a wonderful instance of the grace and goodness of God to men, which is the foundation and source of spiritual knowledge, peace, and comfort; it is a divine work: *All scripture is given by inspiration of God*, 2 Tim. iii. 16. of God, Father, Son, and Spirit; and though it is particularly ascribed to the holy Spirit, *holy men of God spake as they were moved by the Holy Ghost*, 2 Pet. i. 21. yet no one surely will say, to the exclusion of the Father; nor is there any reason to shut out the Son from a concern herein; and we find all three dictating the writings David was the penman of: *The Spirit of the Lord spake by me, and his word was in my tongue; the God of Israel said, the Rock of Israel spake to me*, 2 Sam. xxiii. 2, 3. where besides the Spirit of the Lord, who spake by every inspired writer, there is the Father, the God of Israel, as he is commonly styled, and the Son, the Rock of Israel, the Messiah, often figuratively called the Rock; and in the same manner, and by the same persons David was inspired, all the other penmen of the scriptures were. Those writings acquaint us with the covenant of grace, no other

writings do, made from everlasting before the world was; this covenant was made by Jehovah the Father, and was made with his Son, who condescended and agreed to be the surety, mediator, and messenger of it; yea he is said to be the covenant itself; and in which the holy Spirit is promised, and whose part in it is, and to which he agreed, to be the applier of the blessings and promises of it to those interested therein; see Psalm lxxxix. 3. Isa. xlii. 6. Mal. iii. 1. Heb. vii. 22. and xii. 24. Ezek. xxxvi. 27. John xvi. 14, 15. and they are all three mentioned together as concerned in this covenant, in Hag. ii. 4, 5. where, for the encouragement of the people of Israel to work in rebuilding the temple, it is said, *For I am with you, saith the Lord of hosts*, according to *the word that I covenanted with you;* or rather, as Junius renders it, *with the Word* by whom I covenanted *with you, when ye came out of Egypt,* (at which time the covenant of grace was more clearly and largely revealed;) *so my spirit remaineth among you;* where may be observed, Jehovah the covenant-maker, and his Word, in, by, and with whom he covenanted; and the Spirit standing, as it may be rendered, remaining and abiding, to see there was a performance and an application of all that was promised. In the sacred writings, the economy of man's salvation is clearly exhibited to us, in which we find the three divine persons, by agreement and consent, take their distinct parts; and it may be observed that the election of men to salvation is usually ascribed to the Father; redemption, or the impetration of salvation, to the Son; and sanctification, or the application of salvation, to the Spirit; and they are all to be met with in one passage, 1 Pet. i. 2. *Elect according to the foreknowledge of God the Father, through sanctification of the Spirit, unto obedience and sprinkling of the blood of Jesus.* The same may be observed in 2 Thess. ii. 13, 14. where God the Father is said to choose men from the beginning unto salvation; and the sanctification of the Spirit, is the means through which they are chosen; and the glory of the Lord Jesus Christ, the end to which they are chosen and called: but no where are these acts of grace more distinctly ascribed to each person than in the first chapter of the epistle to the Ephesians, where God the Father of Christ, is said to bless and choose his people in him before the foundation of the world, and to predestinate them to the adoption of children by him, in whom they are accepted with him, ver. 3—6. and where Christ is spoken of as the author of redemption through his blood, which includes forgiveness of sin, and a justifying righteousness; which entitles to the heavenly inheritance, ver. 7, 11. and then the holy Spirit, in distinction from them both, is said to be the earnest of their inheritance, and by whom they are sealed until they come to the full possession of it, ver. 13, 14. The doctrine of the Trinity is often represented as a speculative point, of no great moment whether it is believed or no, too mysterious and curious to be pryed into, and that it had better be let alone than meddled with; but, alas! it enters into the whole of our salvation, and all the parts of it; into all the doctrines of the gospel, and into the experience of the saints; there is no doing without it; as soon as ever a man is convinced of his sinful and miserable estate by nature, he perceives there is a divine person that he has offended, and that there is need of another divine person to make satisfaction for his offences, and a third to sanctify him; to begin and carry on a work of grace in him, and to make him meet for eternal glory and happiness.

4. A Trinity of persons in the godhead may be plainly discovered in all things relating to the office and work of Christ, as the Redeemer and Saviour. In the mission of him into this world on that account: he, the Son of God, was sent by agreement, with his own consent, by the Father and the Spirit; this is affirmed by himself, Isa. xlviii. 16. *Now the Lord God, and his Spirit, hath sent me;* even he who says, ver. 12, 13. *I am the first and the last,* and whose hand laid the foundation of the earth, and whose right hand spanned the heaven, and who is continued speaking to ver. 16. and must be a divine person; the mighty God, who is said to be sent by Jehovah the Lord God, and by his Spirit; who therefore must be three distinct persons, and not one only; or otherwise the sense must be, "now I and myself have sent myself," which is none at all. Christ the Son of God, sent to be the Saviour, in the fulness of time was made of a woman, or became incarnate; and though he only took flesh, the three divine persons were concerned in this affair; the Father provided a body for him in his purposes and decrees, council and covenant; the Word or Son was made flesh, and dwelt among men, and that which was conceived in the

Virgin, was of the Holy Ghost, Heb. x. 5. John i. 14. Matt. i. 20. and in the message to the Virgin, and the declaration of this mysterious affair to her by the angel, mention is made distinctly of all the three Persons; there is the *highest,* Jehovah the Father; and *the Son of the highest,* who took flesh of the Virgin; and the Holy Ghost, or *the power of the highest,* to whose overshadowing influence, the mysterious incarnation is ascribed, Luke i. 32, 35. Christ, the Son of God, being incarnate, was anointed with the Holy Ghost, his gifts and graces without measure; whereby, as man, he was fitted and qualified for his office as Mediator. The anointer is said to be God, his God, the great Jehovah; the anointed, the Son of God in human nature, called therefore the Christ of God, the true Messiah; what he was anointed with was the Holy Ghost, his gifts and grace, signified by the oil of gladness; see Psalm xlv. 7. Isa. lxi. 1. Acts x. 38. when he was thirty years of age he was baptized of John in Jordan, where all the three divine persons appeared; the Son in human nature, submitting to the ordinance of baptism: the Father, by a voice from heaven, declaring him to be his beloved Son; and the holy Spirit, descending on him as a dove, Matt. iii. 16, 17. This was always reckoned so full and clear a proof of the Trinity of Persons in the Godhead, that it was a common saying with the ancients, go to Jordan, and there learn the doctrine of the Trinity. Before our Lord's sufferings and death, he gave out several promises to his disciples, that he would send the holy Spirit, the Comforter, to them; in which there are plain traces of a Trinity of Persons; as when he says, *I will pray the Father, and he shall give you another Comforter,* John xiv. 16. Here is God the Father of Christ, who is prayed unto, who is one Person; and here is the Son in human nature, praying, a second Person, the Son of God; and because he was so, his prayer was always prevalent; nor could he be a mere creature, who speaks so positively and authoritatively, he *shall* give you; and then there is another Comforter prayed for, even the Spirit of truth, distinct from the Father and the Son; the same may be observed in ver. 26. and in chap. xv. 26. and xvi. 7. Christ by his sufferings and death, obtained eternal redemption for men. The price that was paid for it, was paid to God the Father; so it is said *hath redeemed us to God by thy blood,* Rev. v. 9. What gave the price a sufficient value was, the dignity of his person, as the Son of God, 1 John i. 7. and it was *through the eternal Spirit* he offered himself to God, Heb. ix. 14. which some understand of the divine nature; but it is not usual to say, Christ did this, or the other thing, through the divine nature, but by the Spirit, as in Matt. xii. 28. Acts i. 2. besides, in some copies of Heb. ix. 14. it is read, *through the holy Spirit.* Again, Christ having suffered and died for men, he rose again for their justification; in which all the three persons were concerned; God the Father raised him from the dead, and gave him glory, 1 Pet. i. 20. and he raised himself by his own power, according to his own prediction, John ii. 19. and was *declared to be the Son of God with power, according to the Spirit of holiness* or the holy Spirit, *by the resurrection from the dead,* Rom. i. 4. see also Rom viii. 11.

5. This truth of a Trinity in the Godhead, shines in all the acts of grace towards or in men; in the act of justification; it is God the Father that justifies, by imputing the righteousness of his Son, without works, Rom. iii. 30. and iv. 6. and viii. 33. and it is not only by the righteousness of Christ that men are justified; but he himself justifies by his knowledge, or by faith in him, Isa. liii. 11. and it is the Spirit of God that pronounces the sentence of justification in the conscience of believers; hence they are *justified in the name of the Lord Jesus, and by the Spirit of our God,* 1 Cor. vi. 11. in the act of adoption; the grace of the Father in bestowing such a favour on any of the children of men, is owned, 1 John iii. 1. and through the grace of Christ, a way is opened, by redemption wrought out by him, for the reception of this blessing; and he it is that gives power to those that believe in him, to become the sons of God, Gal. iv. 4, 5. John i. 12. and the holy Spirit witnesses their adoption to them; hence he is called the Spirit of adoption, Rom. viii. 15, 16. and all three appear in one text, respecting this blessing of grace; *Because ye are sons, God hath sent forth the Spirit of his Son into your hearts, crying, Abba, Father,* Gal. iv. 6. where the Father is spoken of as distinct from the Son, and the Son from the Father, and the Spirit from them both, and all three bear their part in this wonderful favour. Regeneration is an evidence of adoption; and an instance of the great

love and abundant mercy of God; and which is sometimes ascribed to the God and Father of our Lord Jesus Christ, 1 Pet. i. 3. and sometimes to the Son of God, who regenerates and quickens whom he will, John v. 21. 1 John ii. 29. and sometimes to the Spirit of God, John iii. 3, 5. and all three are mentioned together in Tit. iii. 4, 5, 6. where God the Father called our Saviour, is said to save by the washing of regeneration, and the renewing of the Holy Ghost; which grace of his is shed abroad in men through Jesus Christ our Saviour. Once more, their unction, or anointing, which they receive from the holy One, is from God the Father, in and through Christ, and by the Spirit; *Now he which establisheth us with you in Christ, and hath anointed us, is God; who hath also sealed us, and given the earnest of the Spirit in our hearts*, 2 Cor. i. 21. 22. where God the Father is represented as the establisher and anointer, and Jesus Christ, as a distinct person, in whom the saints are established and anointed; and the Spirit, distinct from them both, as the earnest of their future glory.

6. It plainly appears that there is a Trinity of persons in the Godhead, from the worship and duties of religion enjoined good men, and performed by them. The ordinance of baptism, a very solemn part of divine worship, is ordered to be administered, and is administered, when done rightly, *in the name of the Father, and of the Son, and of the Holy Ghost*, Matt. xxviii. 19. which are to be understood, not of three names and characters, but of three persons distinctly named and described, and who are but one God, as the singular word *name*, prefixed to them, signifies; men are to be baptised in one name of three persons; but not into one of three names, as an ancient writer [19] has observed; nor into three incarnates; but into three of equal honour and glory. God alone is to be invoked in prayer, and petitions are directed sometimes to one Person, and sometimes to another; sometimes to the first Person, the God and Father of Christ, Eph. iii. 14. sometimes to Christ himself, the second Person, as by Stephen, Acts vii. 59. and sometimes to the Lord the Spirit, the third Person, 2 Thess. iii. 5. and sometimes to all three together, Rev. i. 4, 5. and whereas the saints, who are made light in the Lord, need an increase of light, prayer is made for them, that the God of our Lord Jesus Christ, the Father of glory, would give unto them the Spirit of wisdom and revelation in the knowledge of him, that is, of Christ, Eph. i. 17, 18. where the Father of Christ is prayed to; the Spirit of wisdom is prayed for; and that for an increase in the knowledge of Christ, distinct from them both: and whereas the saints need an increase of strength, as well as light, prayer is made for them, that the Father of Christ would strengthen them by his Spirit in the inward man, Eph. iii. 14, 15, 16. see Zech. x. 12. and in a forementioned text, prayer is made to the divine Spirit, to direct the hearts of good men into the love of God, and patient waiting for Christ, 2 Thess. iii. 5. where again the three divine persons are plainly distinguished; and who may easily be discerned as distinct Persons, in the benedictory prayer of the apostle, 2 Cor. xiii. 14. with which I shall conclude the proof from scripture, of a Trinity of Persons in the unity of the divine essence; *The grace of our Lord Jesus Christ, and the love of God, and the communion of the Holy Ghost, be with you all. Amen.* To which may be added; that a plurality of Persons in the Godhead, seems necessary from the nature of God himself, and his most complete happiness; for as he is the best, the greatest and most perfect of Beings, his happiness in himself must be the most perfect and complete; now happiness lies not in solitude, but in society; hence the three personal distinctions in Deity, seem necessary to perfect happiness, which lies in that most glorious, inconceivable, and inexpressible communion the three Persons have with one another; and which arises from the incomprehensible in-being and unspeakable nearness they have to each other, John x. 38. and xiv. 10, 11.

CHAP. XXVIII.

OF THE PERSONAL RELATIONS; OR, RELATIVE PROPERTIES WHICH DISTINGUISH THE THREE DIVINE PERSONS IN THE DEITY.

SINCE there are Three who are the one God; and these Three are not one and the same Person, but three different Persons, there must be something which distin-

---

[19] Ignat. Epist. ad Philip. Ascript. p. 100. Ed. Voss.

guishes them from each other; and the distinction between them is not merely *nominal*, which is no distinction at all; as when the Sabellians say, God is one Person, having three names, Father, Son, and Spirit; here is no distinction; just as when a man has three names, they no more distinguish him than one would; be he called William, Henry, Frederic, William would not distinguish him from Henry, nor Henry from William, nor Frederic from them both, he being one man, having these several names: nor is the distinction merely *modal;* rather *real modal;* for though there are three modes of subsisting in the Deity, and each Person has a distinct mode, yet the phrase seems not strong enough; for the distinction is *real* and *personal;* the Three in the Godhead are not barely three modes, but three distinct Persons in a different mode of subsisting, who are really distinct from each other; so that the Father is not the Son, nor the Son the Father, nor the holy Spirit either the Father or the Son; but the difficulty is, what that is which gives or makes the distinction between them? Now let it be observed,

1. Be it what it may, which distinguishes the divine Persons, it must be as early as the existence of God itself; God is from everlasting to everlasting; what God is now he ever was; he is the eternal and immutable *I AM;* he is what he was, and will be what he is; he is he "which is, and was, and is to come;" he is eternally and invariably the same: if the one God existed from eternity; and if the three Persons are the one God, they must exist from eternity, and exist as distinct Persons; and consequently what gives them their distinction must exist as early. Wherefore,

2. Whatever distinguishes them cannot arise from, nor depend upon any works done by them in time, since their distinction is from eternity; and besides, the works of God *ad extra*, or his external works, are common to all the three Persons; for though one may be more commonly ascribed to one Person, and another to another, yet the three Persons have a concern in each; and therefore they cannot distinguish them one from another. Creation is commonly ascribed to the Father of Christ, who is said to make the worlds, and create all things by him his Son; not as a mere instrument of action, since he is a co-efficient Cause of them; "without him is not anything made that is made;" and the holy Spirit has a concern in the same; as has been observed; see Psalm xxxiii. 6. The salvation of men is commonly attributed to the Son, and he is called Jesus Christ our Saviour; and yet, in the same place, God the Father is called God our Saviour, and is said to save " by the renewing of the Holy Ghost," Tit. iii. 4, 5, 6. Regeneration is more commonly said to be the work of the Spirit; and yet men are said to be born of God, of the Father, and of Jesus Christ, as well as of him; and God the Father is expressly said, to beget men again, according to his mercy, 1 Pet. i. 3. I have made use of the works of God, both to prove the Being of God, and to illustrate and confirm the doctrine of a Trinity of Persons in the Godhead; but these do not make God to be, but to appear to be what he is; had they never been wrought, he would have been just the same as he is in his Being, Perfections, and Persons; for,

3. His works are arbitrary, depending upon his pleasure: thus of the works of creation it is said, *For thy pleasure,* or by thy will, *they are and were created,* Rev. iv. 11. and as all things in providence, so all things in grace, are done according to the counsel of his will; it is of his will he has mercy on men, is gracious to them, regenerates and saves them; wherefore these are things that might or might not be, just as he thought fit; but not so his Being, the Persons in the Deity, and their manner of subsisting in it; for if there had never been a creature made, nor a soul saved, nor a sinner sanctified, God would have been the same he is, three Persons in one God. In the economy of man's salvation, to which some ascribe the distinction of Persons, as taking its rise from thence; the three divine Persons are manifested, but not made, nor made distinct; but were so before, and would have been so, if that had never taken place, as it might not have done, since it flows from the good-will and pleasure of God; whereas,

4. What gives the distinction, be it what it may, is by necessity of nature; God exists necessarily, and not by choice and will, as has been before argued; for if his existence is owing to will and choice, it must be either the will and choice of another, or his own; not another's, for then that other would be prior and superior to him, and so be God, and not he; not his own will, for then he must be before he

was; have will and choice before he existed, which is an absurdity not to be endured: if the one God then necessarily existed, and the three Persons are the one God, they must necessarily exist; and if they exist as three distinct Persons, that which gives them the distinction, must be necessary also, or arise from the necessity of nature; as God is, and the manner in which he is, so the distinction in him is by necessity. But,

5. When I say it is by necessity of nature, I do not mean, that the divine nature, in which the divine persons subsist, distinguishes them; for that nature is one, and common to them all; the nature of the Son is the same with that of the Father; and the nature of the Spirit the same with that of the Father and the Son; and this nature, which they in common partake of, is undivided; it is not parted between them, so that one has one part, and another a second, and another a third; nor that one has a greater, and another a lesser part, which might distinguish them; but the whole fulness of the Godhead is in each.

6. To come to the point; it is the personal relations, or distinctive relative properties, which belong to each Person, which distinguish them one from another; as paternity in the first Person, filiation in the second, and spiration in the third; or more plainly, it is *begetting*, Psalm ii. 7. which peculiarly belongs to the first, and is never ascribed to the second and third; which distinguishes him from them both; and gives him, with great propriety, the name of Father; and it is being *begotten*, that is the personal relation, or relative property of the second Person; hence called, "the only begotten of the Father," John i. 14. which distinguishes him from the first and third, and gives him the name of the Son; and the relative property, or personal relation of the third Person is, that he is *breathed* by the first and second Persons; hence called, the breath of the Almighty, the breath of the mouth of Jehovah the Father, and the breath of the mouth of Christ the Lord, and which is never said of the other two Persons; and so distinguishes him from them, and very pertinently gives him the name of the Spirit, or breath, Job xxxii. 4. Psalm xxxiii. 6. 2 Thess. ii. 8. Those men I have now respect to, hold that there are three distinct persons in the Godhead, or divine nature; and therefore it must be something in the divine nature, and not anything out of it, that distinguishes them; not any works *ad extra*, done by them; nor their concern in the economy of man's salvation; nor offices bore by them, which are arbitrary things, which might or might not, have been, had it pleased God; and what that is in the divine nature that can distinguish them, besides what has been mentioned, let it be named if it can. If one of these distinct Persons is a Father, in the divine nature, and another a Son in the divine nature, there must be something in the divine nature which is the ground of the relation, and distinguishes the one from the other; and can be nothing else than generation, and which distinguishes the third Person from them both, as neither begetting nor begotten. From generation arises the relation, and from relation distinct personality. And as an ancient writer[1] says, "unbegotten, begotten, and proceeding," are not names of essence, (and it may be added, nor of office,) but are modes of subsistence; and so distinguish persons.

Upon the whole, it is easy to observe, that the distinction of Persons in the Deity, depends on the generation of the Son; take away that, which would destroy the relation between the first and second Persons, and the distinction drops; and that this distinction is natural and necessary, or by necessity of nature, and not arbitrary, or of choice and will; which, if it was, it might not have been at all, or have been otherwise than it is: those who place it to the economy of the Persons in the redemption of men, have been urged with this, that if it was so, he that is called the Father, might have been called the Son; and he that is called the Son, might have been called the Father;[2] which has so pressed them, that they have been obliged to own, that so it might have been, if it had so seemed to God, and been agreeable to his will.[3] Moreover, those who are in this way of thinking, and explain away the generation of the Son, and make it no other than a communion of nature, and a co-existence with the first Person, though they profess there are three Persons in the Godhead, they are not able to prove it, nor to

---

[1] Justin. Expos. Fid. p. 373.
[2] Vitring. Epilog. Disput. contr. Roel. p. 3, 4.

[3] Roel. Dissert. 1. s. 39. p. 40.

point out that which distinguishes one from another; and besides, are not able to call them by any name, only say, the one is the first Person, the other the second, and the other the third; and even the reason of this order they cannot account for; for if they have their names and distinction from the economy of man's salvation, and the part they take therein, these cannot be given them antecedent to the said economy; and yet they must exist, and be considered as existing previous to it: if the first Person has the name of a Father, from his constituting and appointing Christ to be the Mediator and Saviour; and the second Person the name of a Son, from his constitution as such; though the reason of such names from hence does not appear; and the third Person has the name of Spirit, from any office or work undertook by him, to breathe into men in creation or regeneration; these names cannot be given them antecedent to such economy, constitution, and agreement, taking place; and yet they must be considered antecedent thereunto, in some view or another. To such straits are men reduced, when they leave the form of sound words, which to do is dangerous, and generally leads into one error or another. But all this will more manifestly appear, by considering each divine person particularly, his relative property, and name pertinent to it. I shall begin with,

First, The first Person; whose distinctive relative property is *begetting*, and who is very pertinently called, the Father, which distinguishes him from the second and third Persons: and here let it be observed, that it is not his being a Father with respect to the creatures, that distinguishes him; not a Father in creation, providence, and grace: not in creation; he is a Father as the Creator of all; all his creatures are his offspring; and he is particularly the Father of spirits, of angels, and the souls of men; but this does not give him the name of Father in the Trinity; so he would have been, if not one man had ever been made, or an angel formed; nor does his being a Father to creatures distinguish him from the second and third Persons, for they are equally concerned with him in creation; and being the one God that has made us, they are the one Father of us, even the second and third Persons, as well as the first: nor in providence; God is the Father that provides for all his creatures, supplies them with things necessary, and supports them in their Beings; but this is not peculiar to the first Person; in this the second Person jointly and equally operates with him, by whom all things consist, and by whose power all are upheld; and so the third Person; and therefore on this account equally entitled to the character of Father: nor in grace, in adoption, and regeneration; in which all the three persons have a concern: in adoption, as the Father bestows the wonderful grace on the sons of men, the son gives to them that believe in him power to become the sons of God; and the Spirit has so much to do with it, that he is called the Spirit of adoption: in regeneration, the Father of Christ begets men again to a lively hope of an inheritance; the Son quickens and regenerates whom he will; and those that are born again, are born of the Spirit: it is not therefore what the first Person does in either of these respects, that entitles him to the character of Father in the Godhead, and distinguishes him from the others; but it is his being the Father of the second Person, or the Father of Christ, as he is often called, and very emphatically and significantly, God the Father, Gal. i. 1. Eph. i. 3. and iii. 14. and this name he has from begetting the Son, who is therefore called his Son, his begotten, his only begotten Son, Psalm ii. 7. John. i. 14, 18. and this personal relation, or relative property, is what distinguishes the first Person in the Trinity, it being never attributed to any other.

Secondly, The second Person, whose distinctive relative property and character is, that he is *begotten*, which is never said of the other two Persons, and so distinguishes him from them, and gives him the name of *Son*; and that he is the Son of God, there is abundant proof; all the three Persons bear testimony of it; the Father at the baptism and transfiguration of Christ, Matt. iii. 17. and xvii. 5. see Psalm ii. 7. and lxxxix. 27. the Word, or Son of God himself, John xix. 7. and v. 17, 18. and x. 30. Mark xiv. 61, 62. John viii. 13—18. and the Spirit, Matt. iii. 16. 17. it is testified and acknowledged by angels, the good angels, Luke i. 31, 35. Heb. i. 6. evil angels, the devils, Matt. viii. 29. Mark iii. 11. Luke iv. 41. by men of all sorts; by good men, John i. 6, 7, 33, 34, 49. Matt. xvi. 15, 16. John vi. 67. and xi. 27. Acts viii. 37. by bad men, Matt. xxvii. 54. So that he is on all hands acknowledged and owned to be the Son of God. The Sonship of Christ is an article of the greatest importance in the christian religion; it has a very great concern in, and connection with the ordinance of christian baptism; it was declared by a voice from heaven, at the baptism of our Lord, *saying, This is my beloved Son, in whom I am well pleased,* Matt. iii. 17. That ordinance is ordered by our Lord himself to be administered *in the name of the Father, and of the Son, and of the Holy Ghost,* Matt. xxviii. 19. considered as in their natural relative characters to each other, equally divine persons, and not as sustaining any office, which no one name or term used is expressive of; and it is mentioned in the first confession of faith, and as the sum of it, in order to an admission to that ordinance the scripture gives an account of; *I believe,* says the eunuch desiring baptism of Philip; who required an express declaration of his faith; *I believe,* says he, *that Jesus Christ is the Son of God,* Acts viii. 37. and this was the sum and substance of the ministry of the apostle Paul, with which he first set out, and continued in, that Christ is the Son of God, Acts ix. 20. 2 Cor. i. 19. and, indeed, it is the distinguishing criterion of the christian religion, and what gives it the preference to all others, and upon which all the important doctrines of it depend; even upon the Sonship of Christ as a divine person; and as by generation, even eternal generation. Without this the doctrine of the Trinity can never be supported; of this the adversaries of it are so sensible, as the Socinians, that they have always set themselves against it with all their might and main; well knowing, that if they can demolish this, it is all over with the doctrine of the Trinity; for without this, the distinction of Persons in the Trinity can never be maintained; and, indeed, without this, there is none at all; take away this, and all distinction ceases. A writer of the present age, and who was the first among us who objected to the eternal generation of the Son of God, though Roell, a Dutchman, before him, attempted to explain it away; or, at least, to a different sense; indeed, pretends to hold the doctrine of three distinct Persons in the Deity, and yet explodes this: a strange paradox! He owns[4] some divines have strenuously maintained, and *judiciously defended,* the doctrine of the Trinity, who held the eternal generation of the Son, and the procession of the Holy Ghost. Why then should this judicious defence be deserted by us? he owns that these properties, begetting, begotten, and proceeding, *plainly prove* the Father, Son, and Holy Ghost, to be distinct Persons; why then should they be laid aside? and especially, since without them there is no proof to be made of their being distinct Persons *in the divine nature.* He says,[5] that his account of Christ's Sonship, that is, by office, and not by nature, does not take away any argument by which we prove his Deity. But without his eternal generation no proof can be made of his being a distinct divine Person *in the Godhead,* and so not of his Deity: he farther says, that it does not take away any argument to prove his distinct personality from the Father and the holy Ghost; whereas it takes away that which is the only proof of it, without substituting a sufficient one in its room; and, indeed, no other *in the divine nature* can be substituted in its room; not the office of Christ, as Mediator; for he must first be proved to be a distinct divine Person, before he can be considered as Mediator. The doctrines of redemption, justification, atonement, and pardon of sin, depend upon the divinity of the person of Christ, as the Son of God, Gal. iv. 4. Rom. viii. 3, 4. Heb. i. 2, 3. 1 John i. 7.

I cannot see there is any reason to object to the use of the phrase *eternal generation,* as applied to the Sonship of Christ, since one divine Person is said to *beget,* Psalm ii. 7. and therefore must be a Father; and another divine Person is said to be *begotten,* John i. 14, 18. and elsewhere, and therefore must be a Son; and if a begotten Son, as he is often said to be, then he must be a Son by generation: for he must be a very illiterate man indeed who does not know that to *beget* and *generate* are the same; and that also to be *begotten* and *generated* are the same; and therefore generation, with great propriety, may be used of the divine persons; and if used of the divine persons as in the divine nature, as if of the Father in the divine nature, then of the Son in the divine nature; and there being nothing in the divine nature but what is eternal, then this generation must be *eternal generation;* there are no persons in the divine nature but who are eternal, the eternal Father, the eternal Son, and the eternal Spirit; nor is there anything in it but what is eternal; every attribute in it is eternal, as eternal power, eternal wisdom, &c. every will, decree, and purpose in it is

---

[4] Ridgley's Body of Divinity, vol. 1. p. 121.

[5] Ibid. p. 127.

eternal, the eternal birth of the eternal mind;[6] why not then the Son of God, the Word and Wisdom of God? and indeed Wisdom, or Christ, is expressly said to be *brought forth*, חוללתי, a word expressive of generation, twice used in Prov. viii. 24, 25. and there, in some ancient versions, rendered *begotten*, as אמון *brought up*, ver. 30. is in some later versions rendered *carried in the bosom*, as a son in the bosom of the father; all which is spoken of as done in eternity: now if Christ was begotten from everlasting, or ever the earth was, before there were any fountains of water, or mountains and hills, and was as early as a son in the bosom of his father, one would think there can be no difficulty in admitting his eternal generation. To which may be added, that if no moment or instant can be given or pointed at, neither in eternity nor in time, in which Christ was not the begotten Son of the Father, then he must be eternally begotten of him, or be his Son by eternal generation; but no moment and instant can be given or pointed at, neither in eternity nor in time, in which Christ was not the begotten Son of the Father; therefore he must be eternally begotten of him; or, in other words, be the Son of the Father by eternal generation. The phrase *eternal generation* is said to be a contradiction in terms; surely, not more so, than *eternal creation*, and an *eternal creature*: it may be thought so by those who will say the same of a Trinity in Unity, or of three being one, though expressly asserted in 1 John v. 7. and so is no more a contradiction than a Trinity of persons in one God. Indeed if the phrase was used of human generation, and applied to that, it might well be thought to be a contradiction in terms; but not as used of divine generation, and as applied to that; the one being in a nature finite, the other infinite. Perhaps the distinction of a priority of order, and a priority of time, may serve to remove the seeming contradiction; the former may be in things eternal, but not the latter. Thus, for instance, God is eternal, and so are his decrees; as the decree of election, or rather God's act of choosing men before the foundation of the world; now God may be conceived of as previous to his act of choosing in priority of order, though not in priority of time, which cannot be admitted in eternity. So the Father generating the Son, may be considered in priority of order previous to the Son generated by him, though not in priority of time, of which there can be none in eternity; considering therefore the Son's generation of the Father from eternity, in a priority of order, though there can be none of time, it will not appear to be a contradiction in terms.

When the scriptures ascribe generation to the Divine Being, it must be understood in a manner suitable to it, and not of carnal and corporal generation; no man in his senses can ever think that God generates as man does; nor believe that ever any man held such a notion of generation in God; yet Sccinus[7] has the impudence to say, that some called Evangelics, hold that God generates in the divine essence one like himself, *more animantium*, as animals do. But generation must be understood of such generation as agrees with the nature of a spirit, and of an infinite uncreated spirit, as God is; that spirits generate we know from the souls or spirits we have about us and in us; our minds, which are spirits, generate thought; thought is the *conception* and *birth* of the mind; and so we speak of it in common and ordinary speech, *I conceive*, or such a man *conceives* so and so; this is my *conception* of things, such are the *conceptions* of others, &c. So with the Platonic philosophers, thought is the birth of the mind; they call it the mind begotten by the mind, as it were another like itself;[8] now as soon as the mind is, thought is, they commence together and they co-exist, and always will; and this the mind begets within itself; without any mutation or alteration in itself. Now in some respect these answer: the mind to God who is Νϖς, the eternal mind, and thought, the birth of the mind, to Christ, the eternal Λογος, word and wisdom of God; who is in some sort represented by λογος ενδιαθετος, the internal mental word. So Plato[9] says, "thought is λογος, word or speech, by which the soul declares and explains to itself what it considers;" or elsewhere,[10] "thought is a discourse within the soul to itself, without a voice." Aristotle[11]

[6] Zeph. ii. 2. בטרם לדת חק antequam nascatur decretum, Schindler. Lexic. col. 759, antequam edetur edictum, Castalio: that is, before the decree conceived or begotten in the mind of God from eternity, is born or brought forth into open execution.

[7] Quod Regn. Polon. c. 4. s. 2. p. 698. Opera, vol. 1.
[8] Vid. Zanchum de Natura Dei, c. 7. p. 145.
[9] In Theæteto, p. 138. Ed. Ficin.
[10] In Sophiste, p. 184.
[11] Apud Polan. Syntagm. Theolog. l. 3. o. 4. p. 202.

somewhere calls it the λογος, or word, τω νοι συναιδιον, co-eternal with the mind. Now if our finite created spirits, or minds, are capable of generating thought, the internal word or speech, and that without any motion, change, or alteration, without any diminution and corruption, without division of their nature or multiplication of their essence; then in an infinitely more perfect manner can God, an infinite uncreated spirit, beget his Son, the eternal Word, wisdom, reason, and understanding, in his eternal mind, which he never was without, nor was he before it: *In the beginning was the word, &c.* John i. 1. and this same Word is expressly said to be *the only begotten of the Father*, ver. 14. and this perfectly agreeable to the sense and language of the old Jewish church, as appears from the ancient paraphrases, and from Philo,[12] who says of the Λογος, or Word, that it is not unbegotten as God, nor begotten as men, and that it is the first begotten Son, with other expressions of like nature: these things considered, may serve in some measure to relieve our minds, and make it more easy to us to conceive of this wonderful and mysterious affair. " Mental or metaphysical generation, as a learned divine[13] observes, is a similitude and adumbration of divine generation; as the mind begets by nature, not by power, so likewise God; as the mind begets a birth co-essential and co-eternal, so God; as the mind simple and perfect begets a birth simple and perfect, so God; as the mind begets immutably (or without mutation) so God; as the mind begets of itself in itself, so God; as the mind does not beget out of matter without itself, so neither God; as the mind always begets and cannot but beget, so God the Father; as metaphysical generation abides, so the divine." Not but that there is in some respects a great dissimilitude between these, as the same writer observes; for the mind begets only a faculty, or an inexistent propriety, but God the Father begets a person existing by himself; the mind begins to beget in time, but God begins not to beget, but always begets from eternity, &c. To this may be added another similitude, which may help us in this matter, and serve to illustrate it; and that is the sun, to which God is sometimes compared; the sun generates its own ray of light, without any change, corruption, division, and diminution; it never was without its ray of light, as it must have been had it been prior to it; they commenced together and co-exist, and will as long as the sun endures; and to this there seems to be an allusion, when Christ is called the *brightness*, απαυγασμα, the effulgence, the beaming forth *of his Father's glory*, Heb. i. 3. *ut radius ex sole*, as the ray from the sun, as Tertullian[14] expresses it. Though such allusions are not to be stretched too far, nor admitted where they imply any imperfection.

It will be granted that the phrases *begetting* and *begotten*, as attributed to the divine persons in the godhead, are used in reference to human generation; between which and divine generation there is some resemblance; as likeness, sameness of nature, personality, &c. and as we consider divine generation, it comes nearer to generation, properly so called, than any scheme or hypothesis opposed to it; but then care must be taken to remove from our minds every thing carnal and impure; and what implies an imperfection; as division of nature, multiplication of essence, priority and posteriority, motion, mutation, alteration, corruption, diminution, cessation from operation, &c. to reason from the one to the other, as running parallel to each other, is unreasonable; to argue from human to divine generation; from that which is physical or natural, to that which is hyperphysical or supernatural; from what is in finite nature, to that which is in a nature infinite, unbounded, and eternal, is very irrational; and to reason from the one to the other, without limitation, restriction, care, and caution, is very unsafe and dangerous; since it may lead unawares into foolish and hurtful errors; and when objections of this sort are made, as they too often are, in a vain, ludicrous, and wanton manner, they are to be rejected and detested, as impious and blasphemous; and they that make them are not to be disputed with, but despised: what is objected in a modest and decent way may be attended to; and the chief that I have met with are, that the sonship of Christ by generation makes him to be later than the Father, to be dependent on him, and subordinate to him; or, in other words, that it seems to be contrary to his eternity, independence, and equality. Let us a little consider each of these objections.

---

[12] Quis Rer. Divin. Hæres. p. 509. de Agricult. p. 105. de Confus. Ling. p. 341.

[13] Polanus ut supra, p. 204.
[14] Adv. Praxeam, c. 18. 22.

CHAP. XXVIII.   RELATIVE PROPERTIES IN THE DEITY.

1. It is urged, that he that generates must be before him that is generated; a father that begets must be before the son that is begotten by him; and putting the sonship of Christ on this foot, he cannot be co-eternal with the Father, but must have a beginning. This is the old stale objection of the Arians, and of Arius[15] himself, who stumbled at this, and set out with it, reasoning thus; "If the Father begat the Son, he that is begotten must have a beginning of his existence; and from hence it must be evident that there was a time when he was not a Son; and therefore it must necessarily follow, that he has his subsistence out of nothing." And so Aetius,[16] a follower of his, could not understand how that which is begotten, could be co-eternal with him that begets. But a little attention to a plain rule will set this matter in a clear light, and remove this objection: the rule is, and I think it is a good one, and will hold good, that "correlates mutually put or suppose each other;" that is, they commence together, they exist together, they co-exist, and that one is not before the other, nor the one after the other. Now father and son are correlates, they suppose each other; a father supposes a son, and a son supposes a father; they commence and exist together, they co-exist, they are not one before nor after another: the father, as a father, is not before his son, as such; nor the son, as a son, is not later than his father, as such; let a man have a first-born son, as soon as he has one he becomes a father, and not before; and his son is as early a son as he is a father; and supposing they live together a term of years, be it an hundred years if you please, which is not an unreasonable supposition, since it has been a fact that father and son have lived together a longer term of time; now at the end of these hundred years, the father, as a father, will not be a moment older than the son as such; nor the son, as a son, one moment younger than the father, as such; their relations rise and continue together till one or other of them cease. There is no priority nor posteriority, no *before* nor *after* in these relations; and so, as an ancient writer says,[17] "with God there is no post-existence of him that is begotten, nor pre-existence of him that begets;" if there is an eternal Father, there must be an eternal Son, and therefore must be co-eternal; there cannot be a Father without a Son, that would be an absurdity, and therefore not before him.

Should it be said, that though these mutual relations exist together, and that one is not before the other; yet surely he that is a father, though not as a father, must exist before him who is his son. As plausible as this may seem to be, it may not appear so plain when examined; for this objection may arise from a false notion of animal generation. Generation is not a production of a non-entity into being, or a bringing into existence what did not exist before; for to bring that into being which was not in being before, is nothing less than a creation, and creation is too much to ascribe to the fathers of our flesh; they are not our creators, they do not give us our being; they do not bring us out of a state of non-existence into a state of existence; God only is the creator. According to the later discoveries in natural philosophy respecting generation, it appears that every man is born of an animalcule; that generation, so called, is no other than a motion of the animalcule into a more convenient place for nourishment and growth. All generation, say our modern philosophers, is with us nothing, so far as we can find, but *nutrition*, or *augmentation* of parts:[18] they conclude, that the *animalcula* of every tribe of creatures, were originally formed by the almighty Parent, to be the seed of all future generations of animals;[19] and that it seems most probable, that the *semina*, or *stamina*, as of all plants, so of animals that have been or ever shall be in the world, have been formed *ab origine mundi*, by the almighty Creator, within the first of each respective kind;[20] and that these are no other than the entire bodies themselves *in parvo;* and contain every one of the same parts and members, with the complete bodies themselves, when grown to maturity;[21] all which, they say, evidently appears, by the help of microscopes: and this is the rather to be attended to, because it

---

[15] Socrat. Hist. l. 1. c. 5.
[16] Ib. l. 2. c. 35.
[17] Justin. Qu. et Respons. qu. 16. p. 400.
[18] Whiston's New Theory of the Earth, book 4. chap. 1. p. 299, 300.

[19] Wolaston's Religion of Nature delineated, s. 5. p. 160, 164. Ed. 8.
[20] Philosophical Transact. abridged, vol. 2. p. 912. Nieuwentyt's Religious Philosopher, contempl. 23. s. 13. p. 711. Ed. 5. see vol. 3. contempl. 27. s. 9. p. 1019.
[21] Whiston ut supra.

so greatly agrees with the sacred scriptures, by which it appears, not only that Levi, the great-grandson of Abraham, was in his loins, that is, seminally in him, before his father Jacob was born; but that all mankind were in Adam, that is seminally in him, as well as representatively; the former being the foundation of the latter, Rom. v. 12. 1 Cor. xv. 22. If, therefore, the *semina* of all mankind were created together in the first man; and all men were seminally, and in *animalculo* together in Adam, then not one before another, no priority nor posteriority among them: so that these things, rightly considered, instead of weakening, serve to strengthen and illustrate the doctrine pleaded for.[22] How far this philosophy is defensible, I will not say; I only observe it to abate the force of the objection; and the confidence of those who make it, it being not easy to disprove the said hypothesis.

2. As to the objection taken from dependence, suggesting that the doctrine of Christ's Sonship by generation is contrary to the independence of Christ as a divine Person. It may be asked, what dependence has a Son upon a Father, in animal generation? Does he depend upon him as the cause of his existence? He does not. He does not bring him into being. God only is the efficient Cause and Author of his Being. He is, at most, only an instrument of removing the animalcule, created of God, into a more convenient situation for nourishment and growth; in order, at a proper time, to come forth into the world, according to the above hypothesis: a parent has no concern in the formation of his child; it is formed without his knowledge, and without asking his consent and will; he knows nothing of its shape, features, and sex, until its birth; and when it is born, its life, and the continuance of its being, do not depend upon him; a Son lives when a Father dies, and often many years after him: it is true, in some sense, he may be said to depend upon him with respect to some circumstances, especially in the former part of life; as, for the care of him, provision for him, assistance and protection given him; circumstances which argue weakness in the human nature; but not to be found in the divine nature, nor any thing analogous to them; and does not a father oftentimes depend upon his son, as in case of distress, sickness, penury, and old age? But be these things as they may, Christ, as all sound divines hold, is αυτοθεος, God of himself, and independent of any other, though he is the Son of the Father; and as the distinct personality of the Son of God arises from his relation to his Father as such, so the distinct personality of the Father arises from his relation to his Son as such; hence the distinct personality of the one, is no more dependent, than the distinct personality of the other; and both arise from their mutual relation to each other; and both arise and commence together, and not one before the other; and both are founded in eternal generation.

3. As to subordination and subjection, and inequality, which it is supposed the Sonship of Christ by generation implies; it may be answered, that Christ in his office-capacity, in which he, as Mediator, is a Servant, and as he is man, and appeared in the form of one; it will be acknowledged, that he is subordinate and subject to the Father; but not as he is the Son of God: and whatever inequality sonship may imply among men, it implies no such thing in the divine nature, among the divine persons; who in it subsist in perfect equality with one another; and in particular, the Scriptures represent the Son of God as equal to his Father, as one who thought it no robbery to be equal with God; being of the same nature, and having the same perfections with him, and that he is equal to him with respect to power and authority; for with respect to power he says, *I and my Father are one;* and they represent him as having the same claim to equal honour, homage and worship; since all men are *to honour the Son, as they honour the Father;* not as in subordination to him, but as equal with him. There is a passage which is perverted by some to the sense of subordination and subjection of the Son of God to the Father, which is in 1 Cor. xv. 24, 28. *Then cometh the end, when he shall have delivered up the kingdom to God, even the Father—and when all things shall be subdued unto him, then shall the Son also himself be subject unto him;* and *put all things under him: that God may be all in all.* It should be observed, that all this is said of something that is future; and which, as yet, is not, and so no proof of what is, or has been.

[22] See a further use made of this philosophy in the articles of Original Sin, book 3. chap. 10. and of the Incarnation of Christ, part 2. book 2. chap 1.

Besides, there is a twofold Sonship of Christ, divine and human; from the one he is denominated the Son of God, and from the other the Son of man. Now Christ in the text, is only called *the Son*, which does not determine which Sonship is meant. This is to be learnt from the context, where he is spoken of throughout as man, as man who died, and rose again from the dead; from whence, by various arguments, is proved the general resurrection; and so he is continued to be spoken of to the passage under consideration; the plain and easy sense of which is, that at the end of the world, at Christ's second coming, when all the elect of God shall be gathered in, and Christ shall have completely finished his work, as Mediator, he will deliver up the mediatorial kingdom complete and perfect, that is, the whole body of the elect, the kingdom of priests, to the Father, and say, *Lo, I, and the children whom thou hast given me;* and then the delegated power under which he acted, as the Son of man, will cease, and be no more; and that sort of rule, authority, and power, will be put down; and he, as the Son of man, be no longer vested with such authority, but shall become subject to him that put all things under him; and then God, Father, Son, and Spirit, will be all in all; and there will be no more distinction of offices among them; only the natural and essential distinctions of the divine Persons will always continue. There are various passages of scriptures in which Christ, as the Son of God, addresses his divine Father, without the least appearance of any subordination or subjection to him, but as his equal, as Jehovah's fellow, particularly John xvii. 24. But I shall proceed to examine more particularly, in what sense Christ is the Son of God, or what is the true cause and reason of this relation.

The Socinians, unwilling to own the eternal Sonship of Christ, or that he was the Son of God before he was the Son of Mary; and not caring to acknowledge the true cause and reason of it, which is but one, have devised many; which shews the puzzle and confusion they are in; Salovious[23] has collected out of their writings, no less than thirteen causes, or reasons of Christ's Sonship; some of them are so weak and trifling, as not deserving to be mentioned; and others require but little to be said to them: I shall take notice of some of the principal ones: and then proceed to place the Sonship of Christ on its true basis, and assign the proper sole cause and reason of it; his being *begotten* of the Father.

1. They say he is called the Son of God because of the great love of God to him, and make *beloved* and *begotten* to be synonymous terms; that Christ is the object of the love of God, the Son of his love, his dearly beloved Son, is most certain; but then it is not his love to him that is the foundation and cause of relation to him; he is not his Son because he loves him; but he loves him because he is his Son; it is not love among men that produces such a relation; there may be great love where there is no such relation; Jonathan loved David as his own soul; but this strong love bore to him, did not make him nor denominate him his son. On the other hand, there may be relation and not love; a father may not love his own son; neither love nor hatred effect relation; the one does not make it, nor the other destroy it.

2. Sometimes they ascribe the Sonship of Christ to his likeness to God, and make that to be the cause of it: that Christ is the image of the invisible God, the express image of his Father's Person, and so like him, that he that has seen the one, has seen the other, because the same nature and perfections are in both, is true; yet the reason why Christ is called the Son of God, is not because he is like him, but he is like him because he is his Son; of the same nature and essence with him.

3. At other times they tell us, he is the Son of God by adoption; of which the scriptures give not the least hint. To which may be objected, that Christ is God's own Son, his proper Son, the Son of himself; and therefore not adopted: who ever adopts an own son? or what reason can there be for it? adoption among men, is not of their own sons; but usually when they have none of their own; as the instances of the adoption of Moses by Pharaoh's daughter, and of Esther by Mordecai shew: besides, Christ is the *begotten* Son of God; and if begotten, then not adopted; these are inconsistent; yea, he is his *only* begotten Son; whereas, if he was his Son by adoption, he could not be said to be his only Son, since he has many adopted

---

[23] Socinism. Profligat. art. 2. controv. 6. p. 201.

ones; even as many as are predestinated to the adoption of children, by Christ; as many as the Father gave unto him; as many as he has redeemed, "that they might receive the adoption of children;" as many as receive him, that is, believe in him, "to whom he gives power to become the sons of God;" even as many sons as he brings to glory; which is a number no man can number: but the more principal causes of Christ's Sonship they insist upon, and which seem to have the most countenance from scripture, are as follow, and which I shall more particularly and largely consider.

4. The miraculous conception and birth of Christ, or his wonderful incarnation, is assigned as the reason of his Sonship; and this is founded on Luke i. 35. the words of the angel to Mary, in answer to the difficulties objected by her, to Christ being born of her; *The holy Ghost shall come upon thee, and the power of the Highest shall overshadow thee; therefore, also, that holy Thing that shall be born of thee, shall be called the Son of God.* Now let it be observed, that the angel does not say the holy Thing born of the virgin should *be*, but should be *called* the Son of God; for though sometimes the sense of such a phrase is the same as to *be*, as in Isa. ix. 6. 1 John iii. 1. yet seems not intended here; since this appellation, the Son of God, is a name which Christ has been, and is usually called by; and the angel is not giving a reason of Christ's being the Son of God; for he was so before his incarnation; but of the manifestation and declaration of him as such in the human nature; nor does the angel predict that Christ should be called the Son of God, for *this reason*, because of his miraculous birth; for either he was to call himself so, or others were to call him so, for this reason, which neither have been; or else the angel's prediction must be false, which cannot be admitted. Moreover, the particle *therefore*, is not casual but consequential; the angel is not giving a reason why Christ should be called the Son of God, but why he should be received and owned as such by his people; who would infer and conclude from his wondrous birth of a virgin, that he must be the Immanuel, the child to be born, the Son given, &c. prophesied of in Isa. vii. 14. and ix. 6. where he is called the *child born*, with respect to his human nature, and the *Son given*, with respect to his divine nature;[24] see John iii. 16. and iv. 10. Once more, the particle *also*, ought not to be neglected; *Therefore, also, that holy Thing*, &c. not only the divine person of Christ should be owned and called the Son of God; but also the human nature of Christ, thus wonderfully produced, being taken up into personal union with him, should bear the same name: so that it is not the wonderful birth of the human nature, that so much as gives the name; but the union of this nature to the person of the Son of God; whence it is called by the same name he is. The reasons why Christ cannot be the Son of God, on account of his wonderful incarnation, are the following.

(1.) If so, then the holy Spirit must be the Father of Christ, since he had such a special and peculiar concern in it; as the above passage shews; and then there must be two Fathers in the Trinity; which would introduce a wretched confusion there. But there is but one, distinct from the Word and Spirit, 1 John v. 7. Matt. xxviii. 19. Besides, the Father of Christ is, in many places, distinguished from the Spirit, and therefore cannot be the same, John xiv. 16, 17, 26. and xv. 26. Eph. i. 17. and iii. 14, 16. To which may be added, that the Spirit is called the Spirit of the Son, Gal. iv. 6. whereas, if this was the case, rather the Son should be called the Son of the Spirit; which he never is.

(2.) If the incarnation of Christ is the cause of his divine Sonship, then there was no God the Father of Christ under the Old Testament; this was what the Marcionites of old asserted; which put the ancient writers[25] on proving, as they did, that it was the Father of Christ who made the world, gave the law, spoke by the prophets, and edited the books of the Old Testament; all which appears from Heb. i. 1, 2. Besides, God existed as the Father of Christ, before the foundation of the world; for so early as such he blessed his people, and chose them in Christ, Eph. i. 3, 4.

(3.) If Christ was the Son of God, with respect to his human nature only, the distinctive phrase *according to the flesh*, when used in speaking of him, would be quite impertinent; for it is never said of any mere man, that he is the son of such an one according to the flesh, but only, that he is his son; but the phrase is very pertinently used to distinguish Christ, the

---

[24] Vitringa in loc.

[25] See Dr. Owen on the Trinity, p. 27.

Son of God, according to his divine nature, from his being the Son of David, and of the fathers, according to his human nature, Rom. i. 4. and ix. 5.

(4.) The incarnation of Christ is not the reason of his being the Son of God, but the manifestation of him as such; he was not made, but manifested thereby to be the Son of God, 1 John i. 1, 2. and iii. 8. In the fulness of time God sent forth his Son—for what? not to be made a Son; he was so before he sent him; but that this Son might be made of a woman, or be made man; that the Word might be made flesh, or become incarnate; and so God, the Son of God, be manifest in the flesh, Gal. iv. 4. For,

(5.) It is certain that Christ existed, as the Son of God, before his incarnation; and is spoken of in the Old Testament as such; even Nebuchadnezzar, an heathen prince, had a notion of the Son of God; which he might have from Daniel, and other Jews in his palace; for he had many in his dominions, from whom he might learn that there was a glorious Person, who would appear in human nature, under the name of the Son of God; and seeing four Persons in the fiery furnace, when only three were cast into it, and the form of the fourth remarkably glorious, he concluded him to be one like him, who had been described to him, Dan. iii. 25. see Ezek. xxi. 10. Agur long before knew that a divine Person existed, as the Son of God; for speaking of the Almighty, and incomprehensible Being, he asks, *What is his name, and what is his Son's name, if thou canst tell?* suggesting that as the name, that is, the nature of God is ineffable, he had a Son of the same nature with himself, equally so, Prov. xxx. 4. Earlier than he, David speaks of the Son of God, begotten by him; whom he calls all the Kings and Judges of the earth to pay divine homage and worship to; and pronounces them blessed that trust in him, Psalm ii. 7, 12. and speaks of him also as his first born, who should call him his God and Father, Psalm lxxxix. 26, 27. yea, Christ existed as a Son, not only before Solomon and David were, but before Melchisedec was, for he is said to be made like unto the Son of God, Heb. vii. 3. yea, he existed as such at the creation of the world; for God, by him his Son, made the worlds, Heb. i. 2. before any creature was in being he was the Son of God; and so the words may be rendered in Psalm lxxii. 17. *Before the sun was, his name was the Son*, the Son of God.

(6.) If Christ is only the Son of God as he was man, and so called because made man, then he would be in no other class of Sonship than creatures be. Adam being wonderfully made and created out of the dust of the earth, is called the son of God, and all his posterity are the offspring of God, Luke iii. 38. Acts xvii. 28. Angels are also the sons of God, by creation; but *to which of the angels said he* (God) *at any time, Thou art my son, this day have I begotten thee?* Heb. i. 5. and if not to them, much less to any of the sons of men; and therefore Christ's filiation must be in an higher class than theirs; and not to be ascribed to his incarnation; but must be placed to another account.

5. Another cause or reason assigned by the Socinians why Christ is called the Son of God, is his resurrection from the dead; which cannot be the true reason of it; because,

(1.) He was the Son of God before; as has been proved, and they themselves acknowledge: for if he was the Son of God, through his incarnation, as they say, though wrongly, then before his resurrection; and so not on that account: the mission of Christ into this world, as the Son of God; the testimony bore to his Sonship, at his baptism and transfiguration, by his divine Father; the confession of men and angels, good and bad, already observed; shew him to be the Son of God before his resurrection, and so not by it.

(2.) If he was the Son of God on that account, he must beget himself, and be the author of his own Sonship, which is notoriously absurd; for he raised himself from the dead, as he predicted he would; and as he had power to do, as he declared, and did it, John ii. 19. and x. 18.

(3.) If so, his Sonship must be metaphorical and figurative, and not proper; whereas, he is often called God's own Son, his proper Son, the Son of himself; and God his own proper Father, Rom. viii. 3, 32. John v. 18.

(4.) On this account, he cannot be called the only begotten Son of God; for though he may, indeed, on account of his resurrection, be called, as he is, the first-born from the dead, and the first begotten of the dead, and the first-fruits of them that sleep, Col. i. 18. Rev. i. 5. 1 Cor. xv. 20. yet cannot be called the only begotten, since many of the saints rose with him at his resurrection;

and all men will be raised at the last day.

(5.) If the resurrection of the dead entitles to Sonship, then wicked men would be the sons of God, since there will be a resurrection of the unjust, as well as of the just; of some to shame and damnation, as well as of others to everlasting life, Dan. xii. 2. John v. 28, 29. Acts xxiv. 15. yet these are never called the sons of God; as not on any other, so not on this account; indeed, the dead in Christ, who will rise first, are said to be the *children of God, being the children of the resurrection*, Luke xx. 36. not that they then become the children of God, and are so for that reason; for they are so before; but being raised, and put into the possession of the inheritance, they will be manifested, and declared the children of God, "heirs of God, and joint-heirs with Christ;" and so,

(6.) The resurrection of Christ from the dead, is only a manifestation of his Sonship; he was *declared to be the Son of God with power, by the resurrection from the dead*, Rom. i. 4. and hence it is that the words in Psalm ii. 7. *Thou art my Son, this day have I begotten thee*, are applied to the resurrection of Christ, Acts xiii. 25. not that he was then begotten as the Son of God, for he was so before, as has been proved; but he was then manifested to be the only begotten Son of God; and which words are applicable to any time when Christ was declared and manifested to be the Son of God.

6. The last reason I shall take notice of, which the Socinians give of the Sonship of Christ, is his office as Mediator; they say he is called the Son of God, because he was sanctified, or set apart to his office, as such; and was sent into the world to do it, and has executed it, and is now exalted in heaven. And it is not to be wondered at, that they should assert Christ to be the Son of God by office, when it is a notorious sentiment of theirs, that he is only God by office; for the sake of which they endeavour to support this: the text which they build this notion on is John x. 36. *Say ye of him whom the Father hath sanctified and sent into the world, thou blasphemest, because I said I am the Son of God?* That Christ is the Son of God, may be concluded from his sanctification and mission; because no other was prophesied of, or promised to be sent, and no other expected to come, but he who was the Son of God; but that his sanctification and mission are the reason of his being so called, cannot be from hence concluded; because he was the Son of God before he was sent. Christ had, in the preceding verses, asserted his equality with God, saying, that he and his Father were one; upon this the Jews charged him with blasphemy; to vindicate himself from this charge, he first argues from his inferior character, as being in office; that if magistrates, without blasphemy, might be called gods, and children of the most High, much more might he be called the Son of God, who was in such an eminent manner sanctified, and sent into the world by the Father; but then he let not the stress of the proof of his Deity and Sonship rest here; but proceeds to prove the same by his doing the same works his Father did; to which he appeals. But that Christ is not the Son of God, by his office as Mediator, the following reasons may be given.

(1.) Because if Christ is the Son of God, not by nature, but by office, then he is only the Son of God in an improper and metaphorical sense; as magistrates are called the children of the most High, or sons of God, being in an office under him: whereas, Christ, in a true and proper sense, is the Son of God; he is the *Son of the Father in truth*, 2 John ver. 3. most truly and properly his Son; his own, his only begotten Son, the Son of himself, Rom. viii. 3. his proper Son, ver. 32. therefore not so in an improper sense.

(2.) Because the mediatorial office of Christ is so far from being the ground of his Sonship, that it is his Sonship that is the ground of his mediatorship; for antecedent to his investiture with his office, he must be considered as previously existing under some character or another, and which appears to be his relation to God as his Son. Thus in his inauguration into, and investiture with his kingly office, his Father, in the performance of it, addressed him under this relative character; *unto the Son he saith, Thy throne, O God, is for ever and ever*, Heb. i. 8. and of his consecration to his priestly Office we read, *The Lord maketh men high priests which have infirmity; but the word of the oath which was since the law*, (the eternal council and covenant, made more clear and manifest since the law, Psalm cx. 4.) *maketh the Son, who is consecrated for evermore;* that is, not makes the Son a Son, but the Son a priest; Heb. vii. 28. so that he was the Son of God before he was considered as a priest: and with respect to his prophetic office, previous to his investiture with, entrance upon, and discharge of that, he was the Son of God; and, indeed, his relation to God, and nearness to him, made him the only fit and proper Person for it; *No man hath seen God at any time; the only begotten Son, which is in the bosom of the Father, he hath declared him;* his nature, will, purposes, and promises; all which he was privy to, as being the only begotten Son of the Father, and lying in his bosom, John i. 18. so that previous to his office as mediator, and the several branches of it, he was the Son of God; and therefore not so by it; when, I say, Christ, as the Son of God, must be considered previous to his being the Mediator; though he is both from eternity; it must be understood, not of priority of time, of which there is none in eternity; but of priority of order; for Christ must be considered as existing as a divine Person, under some character or relation, ere he can be considered as invested with an office; not in order of time, both being eternal; but in order of nature; even as the eternal God, must be considered as existing previous to any act of his; as of eternal election, not in priority of time, the eternal acts of God being as early as himself; but in priority of order, as one thing must be conceived of and considered by our finite minds, before another.

(3.) Because he is frequently distinguished as a Son, from the consideration of him in his mediatorial office; as in the eunuch's confession of Faith; *I believe that Jesus Christ is the Son of God,* Acts viii. 37. and in the ministry of the apostle Paul, who is said to preach *Christ in the synagogues, that he is the Son of God,* Acts ix. 20. Now the phrase Jesus Christ respects his office as the Saviour, the anointed Prophet, Priest, and King; and if the other phrase, *the Son of God,* is a term of office also, they coincide, and signify the same thing; and then the sense of them only is, that Christ is the Christ, and the Mediator; the Mediator confessed by the one, and preached by the other; which carry in them no distinct ideas; whereas the meaning is, that the one believed, and the other preached, that Jesus, the Saviour and true Messiah, who had lately appeared with all the true characters of the promised one, was no less than a divine Person, the Son of God; see also 1 John iv. 14, 15. and v. 5.

(4.) Because Christ, as Mediator, is the Servant of God; and especially so he appears in the discharge of some parts of that his office; as in his obedience and suffering death, see Isa. xlii. 1. and xlix. 3. and liii. 11. Phil. ii. 7, 8. A servant and a son are very different relations, and convey very different ideas; our Lord observes the distinction, John viii. 35. and Christ, as a Son, is distinguished from Moses, as a servant, in the house of God, Heb. iii. 5, 6. whereas, if Christ was a Son by office, or as mediator, he would be no other than a servant, as Moses was, only of an higher rank, and in a greater office; no one is ever called a son because he is a servant; one that is a son may indeed be a servant, but is never called a son on that account; so that this is to lessen the glory of Christ, as the only begotten of the Father, and reduce him to the character and state of a servant.

(5.) Because the Sonship of Christ is sometimes spoken of as adding a lustre to his office as Mediator; as when the apostle says, *Seeing then that we have a great High Priest that is passed into the heavens, Jesus the Son of God, let us hold fast our profession,* Heb. iv. 14. that which makes this High Priest so great an one, and furnishes out so strong an argument to a constant profession of him, is his being the Son of God, not by office, but by nature; for if this was only a term of office, it would not only coincide with his being an high priest, but there would be no emphasis in it, nor evidence of his greatness; nor such strength in the argument formed upon it. Likewise, the Sonship of Christ is represented as putting a virtue and efficacy into what he has done as Mediator, and therefore must be distinct from his office as such; so particularly the apostle John ascribes the efficacy of his blood, in cleansing from sin, to his being the Son of God; *And the blood of Jesus Christ his Son,* (there lies the emphasis) *cleanseth us from all sin,* 1 John i. 7. Sometimes it is observed, as wonderful, that he who is the Son of God, should perform some parts of his office as Mediator; as obedience and suffering death; *Though he were a Son, yet learned he obedience by the things which he suffered,* Heb. v. 8. but there would be nothing strange and wonderful, that he, being the Mediator, should perform the part of one; but it lies here, that he, being the Son of God, in the form of God, and equal to him, should appear in the form of a servant, and be obedient unto death, even the death of the cross.

(6.) Because the Sonship of Christ is made use of to express and enhance the love of God, in the gift of him to the sons of men, John iii. 16. 1 John iv. 9. which would not be so strongly expressed, and so greatly enhanced, and appear in such a glaring light, if Christ, in such a gift, is considered not as a Son by nature, but as a Servant, and in an office-capacity; God has given what is more than men, or than people, for the life of his chosen; to do which would be love; but he has given his own Son; which is a far greater instance of love, Isa. xliii. 4.

Lastly, If Christ is the Son of God, and may be called his begotten Son, by virtue of his constitution as Mediator, it should be shown, that there is something in that constitution which is analogous, or answers to generation and Sonship, and lays a sufficient ground and foundation for Christ being called God's own Son, his proper and only begotten Son; what is there in the first Person's appointing and constituting the second to be a Mediator, that gives him the name of a Father? and what is that in the constitution of the second Person in such an office, that gives him the name of the Son, of the only begotten Son?

Having removed the chief and principal of the false causes, and reasons of Christ's Sonship, assigned by the Socinians; I shall proceed to establish the true cause of it; and settle it on its true basis; by assigning it to its proper and sole cause, his eternal generation by the Father; which I shall attempt to do by various passages of scripture.

There are some passages of scripture, which have been made use of to prove the eternal generation of the Son of God, I shall not insist upon, particularly Isa. liii. 8. *Who shall declare his generation?* which is to be understood, neither of the human, nor of the divine generation of Christ, as it was by the ancient writers; not of his human generation; for that the prophet himself declared; as that he would be born, and be born of a virgin, chap. vii. 14. and iv. 6. nor of his divine generation, which is declared both by the Father and the Son; though, indeed, the manner of both generations is inexplicable and ineffable, and cannot be declared by men: but the words are either to be understood of Christ's spiritual generation; the seed he should see, ver. 10. his spiritual seed and offspring; a generation to be accounted of, but not to be counted by men, their number being not to be declared: or, rather, of the wickedness of that age and generation in which Christ should appear in the flesh; called by him a wicked, adulterous, and faithless generation; the wickedness then rife both in the Gentile and Jewish world, was such as not to be declared; and particularly the barbarity and cruelty of the Jews, in putting Christ to death, and persecuting his apostles, were such as no tongue and pen could fully declare.

I have not, in my Treatise on the Trinity, insisted on Mic. v. 2. as a proof of the eternal generation of the Son of God; of whom it is there said, *whose goings forth have been from of old, from everlasting;* though this has been, and still is, insisted on by great and good men as a proof of it: but when he is said to go forth from the Father, it may seem, as it does to some, rather to intend his mission in time, or as coming into the world; not by change of place, but by assumption of nature, John xvi. 28. besides, the phrase is plural, *goings forth;* which seem to denote various acts; whereas that of begetting is a single act: to which may be added, that that is an act of the Father; these seem to be acts of the Son; and therefore may seem rather to be understood of his goings forth in the covenant, in acts of grace and love towards his people, and delight in them; in approaching to God in a covenant-way, and asking them of his Father, and all blessings of grace for them; in becoming their Surety, and engaging to be their Saviour and Redeemer. However, these words are a full proof of the eternal existence of Christ; or otherwise these things could not be predicated of him and his existence so early, under the relation and character of the Son of God, and that previous to his goings forth in a mediatorial way; as before proved. Yet, after all, I see not but that the divine generation of Christ may be included in those *goings forth;* and be the first and principal, and the foundation of the rest; since the contrast in the text is between the Deity and humanity of Christ; or, between his two births and sonships, divine and human; and the phrase of going forth, suits very well with the modern notion of generation, before observed; and the word אצי is frequently used of generation, Gen. xlvi. 26. Isa. xi. i. and xlviii. 1, 19. and, indeed, in the very text itself. But,

The text in Psalm ii. 7. though some have parted with it, as a proof of this point, I choose to retain; *The Lord hath said unto me, Thou art my Son; this day have I begotten thee;* which are the words of the

Messiah, the Lord's anointed; against whom the kings of the earth set themselves, ver. 2. the King set and anointed over the holy hill of Zion, ver. 6. and who says in the beginning of this verse, *I will declare the decree;* which he speaks either as King, signifying, that he would, as such, declare and publish the laws, statutes, and judgments; so the word signifies; by which his subjects should be ruled and governed: or as a Prophet, who would declare the covenant, as the Targum, the covenant of grace, the things contained in it; and none so fit as he, who is the messenger of it: or the counsel and decree, as we render it, the scheme of man's redemption and salvation by himself; or the gospel, called the whole counsel of God, Acts xx. 27. for this respects not what follows, the sonship of Christ; though that is the ground and foundation of the whole gospel-scheme; but that depends not on any decree, counsel, or will of God, but is of nature; and the mention of it is introduced, to shew the greatness and excellency of the Person spoken of in the context; and so to aggravate the wickedness of his enemies; since the King they opposed, is no other than the natural and proper Son of God; and in like manner are these words quoted in Heb. i. 5. to shew the pre-eminence of Christ to the angels: and as for the date, *this day,* it may well enough be thought to be expressive of eternity, since one day with the Lord is as a thousand years, and as eternity itself; and which is expressed by days of eternity in Mic. v. 2. as the eternal God himself is called the Ancient of days, Dan. vii. 9. and, indeed, this passage is applicable to any day or time in which Christ is declared and manifested to be the Son of God; as at his incarnation, Heb. i. 6. John iii. 8. and at his baptism and transfiguration, Matt. iii. 17. and xvii. 5. as it is to the time of his resurrection; when he was declared to be the Son of God, Acts xiii. 25. Rom. i. 4. And agreeable to this sense of the words, as it respects his eternal generation, and his being the natural and proper Son of God, he is after treated as his heir, and bid to ask what he would for his inheritance, ver. 8, 9. and, is represented as the object of religious worship and adoration, and of trust and confidence, ver. 12. which belong to none but a divine person. So Justin Martyr[26] interprets this passage of the manifestation of Christ's generation to men.

The text in Prov. viii. 22. though a glorious proof of Christ's eternal existence, yet I formerly thought not so clear an one of his eternal generation. But, upon a more close consideration of it, it appears to me a very clear one; as the phrases in this, and some following verses, being *possessed, brought forth,* and *brought up,* clearly shew: much darkness has been spread over it, by a wrong translation in the Greek version, which renders the words, *the Lord created me,* &c. and which has led into more errors than one. Arius from hence concluded, that Christ, as a divine person, was created by his Father in some instant in eternity, and that he was made by him, not of the same nature with him, but of a like nature to him; and is his first and most excellent creature, and whom he made use of in the creation of others: but if the Wisdom of God, the person, here speaking, was created by God, then God must be without his Logos, word, and wisdom, until he was created; whereas, he was always with him; and besides, he is the Creator, and not a creature; for all things were made by him, John i. 1, 2, 3.

Some, of late, have put a new sense on these words, equally as absurd as the former, and interpret them, of the creation of the human soul of Christ, in eternity; which, they say, was then made and taken up into union with God. But to this sense it must be objected, 1. That the human soul of Christ is not a person, nor is even the whole human nature, which is called a *thing,* and not a person, Luke i. 35. it never subsisted of itself, but always in the Person of the Son of God; and there are wise reasons in the economy and scheme of man's salvation, that so it should be; whereas wisdom here speaking is all along in the context represented as a Person, *I Wisdom,* ver. 12. *the Lord possessed me,* ver. 22. *I was set up,* ver. 23, &c.—2. The human soul of Christ is only a part of the human nature; whereas Christ has assumed a whole human nature, a true body, and a reasonable soul; and both were necessary to become a sacrifice; as they have been, Isa. liii. 10. Heb. x. 10. According to this notion, Christ assumed the human nature by parts, and these as widely distant as eternity and time; one part assumed in eternity, another part in time; what a sad mangle is this of our Lord's human nature! is this to be made in all things like unto his brethren? of the

---

[26] Dialog. cum Trypho. p. 316.

two, it would be more agreeable that the whole human nature was assumed so early; but was that the case, it would not be the seed of the woman, nor the seed of Abraham, nor the son of David, nor the son of Mary; nor would Christ be a partaker of *our* flesh and blood; and it should be considered, whether this would have been of any avail to us.—3. But what of all things is most absurd, this human soul is said to be created in eternity, or before time; which is a contradiction in terms, time being nothing else but the measure of a creature's duration; as soon as a creature was, time was; time begins with that, let it be when it will; and therefore cannot be before time: suppose a creature to be made millions of ages before the common date of time, the creation of the world, time must be reckoned from the existence of that creature; but what is worst of all, is the fatal consequence of this to divine revelation; for if there was any thing created before time, or before the world was, whether an angel or a man, or a part of man, the human soul, or the whole human nature of Christ, our Bible must begin with a falsehood; and then who will believe what is said in it afterwards? which asserts, *In the beginning God created the heaven and the earth;* that is, in the beginning of time, or when time first began. And this is so agreeable to reason, that Plato[27] says, time and heaven were made together; and Timæus Locrus;[28] God made the world with time; and Plato defines time thus,[29] Time is the motion of the sun, and the measure of motion; which was as soon as a creature was made; the first things that God made were the heavens and the earth; and therefore if anything was created before them, this must be an untruth. How careful should men be of venting their own whims and fancies, to the discredit of the Bible, and to the risk of the ruin of divine Revelation. Should it be said, Were not the angels created before? I answer, No;[30] surely no man, thinking soberly, will assert it: how can it be thought, that the angels of heaven, as they are called, should be made before there was a heaven for them to be in? Should the text in Job xxxviii. 7. be produced in proof of it, let it be observed, that it is far from being clear that angels are there meant, since they are never elsewhere compared to stars, nor called the sons of God; rather good men are there meant, to whom both epithets agree; but be it understood of angels or men, it is not to be connected with ver. 6. nor respects the time of laying the foundation and corner-stone of the earth; but the phrase in ver. 4. is to be repeated at the beginning, *Where wast thou when the morning-stars sang together?* &c. and so refers to some early time after the creation of the heavens and the earth; and to a meeting, whether of angels or men, in which the praises of God, on account of his works, were celebrated, before Job had a being. No, neither angels nor men, nor any other creature, were before time; this is peculiar to Jehovah; this is a claim he makes, and none else can put in for it; *Before the day was, I am he,* Isa. xliii. 13. that is, before there was a day, before time was, I existed, when none else did; none existed in and from eternity but Jehovah, Father, Son, and Spirit; not an angel nor an human soul: it is a notion of Origen, condemned by Jerome[31] as heretical, that the soul of the Saviour was, before he was born of Mary; and that this is that which, when he was in the form of God, he thought no robbery to be equal with God.

What has led men into this notion of the human nature of Christ, either in part, or in whole, being created before time, or in eternity, is another error, or mistake, as one error generally leads to another; and that is, that Christ could not take upon him, nor execute the office of Mediator, without it; whereas, it is most certain, that a divine Person can take upon him an office, and execute it, without assuming an inferior nature; as the holy Spirit of God has; he, in the covenant of grace, took upon him the office of applying the grace and blessings of the covenant, the things of Christ in it, to the covenant-ones; in doing which he performs the part of a comforter to them, and a glorifier of Christ; and yet never assumed any inferior nature; and this without any degradation of his person: and it is easy to observe, among men, that when two powers are at variance, one, even superior to them both, will interpose as a mediator, without at all lessening his dignity and character. Christ, as a divine Person, could and did take upon him the office of Mediator, without assuming human nature;

---

[27] In Timæo, p. 1052.
[28] De Anima Mundi, p. 10. Ed. Gale.
[29] Definitiones, p. 1337.

[30] Vid. Theodoret. in Gen. Qu. 3.
[31] Apol. Adv. Ruffin. fol. 73. A. tom. 2.

it was sufficient for his constitution as such, that he agreed to assume it in time, when it was necessary; and there are several parts of his mediatorial office, which he could and did execute in eternity without it; he could and did draw nigh to his divine Father, and treat with him about terms of peace and reconciliation for men; he could and did covenant with him on the behalf of his elect; which to do, no more required an human nature in him, than in the Father; he could and did become a Surety for them in the covenant and receive promises and blessings for them; and agreed to do all for them that law and justice could require: and to make such terms, agreements, promises, &c. of what use and avail would an human soul, or the whole human nature, have been unto him? There are other parts of his office, indeed, which required the actual assumption of the human nature; and when it was proper for him to perform them, then, and not before, was it necessary for him to assume it; such as obedience to the law, shedding of blood, and suffering death to make peace, reconciliation, and atonement for his people.

Wherefore, if this translation of Prov. viii. 22. *He created me*, is to be retained, it is better to interpret it of the constitution of Christ in his office, as Mediator, as the word *create* is used in common language, of making a king, peer, judge, or one in any office: but this is rather meant in the following verse, *I was set up*, or *anointed*, invested with the office of Mediator; anointing being used at the investiture of kings, priests, and prophets, with their office, is put for the act of investiture itself; for Wisdom, or Christ, proceeds in this account of himself, in a very regular and orderly manner; he first gives an account of his eternal existence, as the Son of God, by divine generation; and then of constitution, as Mediator, in his office-capacity; this latter is expressed by his being *set up*, and the former by his being *possessed* or *begotten;* so the same Greek version renders this word in Zech. xiii. 5. and it may be rendered here, *the Lord begat me*, and so possessed him as his own Son, laid a claim to him, and enjoyed him as such; for this possession is not in right of creation, in such sense as he is the possessor of heaven and earth, Gen. xiv. 19, 22. but in right of paternity, in which sense the word is used, Deut. xxxii. 6. as a father lays claim to, possesses and enjoys his own son, being begotten by him, or signifies possession by generation, Gen. iv. 1. the following phrase, *in the beginning of his way*, should be rendered without the preposition *in*, which is not in the text; for Wisdom, or Christ, is not in this clause, expressing the date of his being begotten, but describing him himself, who is the begotten of the Father; as *the beginning of his way*, of his way of grace; with whom God first begun, taking no one step without him, nor out of him; his purposes of grace being in him, the scheme of reconciliation formed in him, the covenant of grace made with him, and all grace given to the elect in him; in whom they were chosen: and all this *before his works of old*, the works of creation; of which Christ is the beginning; the first and co-efficient cause, Rev. iii. 14. and this sense of the words, as understood of the begetting of Christ, is confirmed by some other phrases after used, as of being *brought forth*, ver. 24. as conceived, as the vulgate Latin version; or begotten, as the Targum and Syriac version; so the Greek version, of ver. 25. is, he *begat* me; and the word is used of generation in Job xv. 7. Psalm li. 5. and is repeated, ver. 25. partly to excite attention to it, as being of great moment and importance, and partly to observe the certainty of it; the eternal generation of Christ being an article of faith, most surely to be believed: Wisdom further says of himself; *Then was I by him, as one brought up with him*, ver. 30. being begotten by him, and being brought forth, he was brought up with his Father; which expresses the most tender regard to him, and the utmost delight in him. The word אמון may be rendered, *carried in his bosom*,[32] as a son by a nursing father, Numb. xi. xii. see John i. 18.

To these proofs might be added, all those scriptures which speak of Christ as the begotten, the only begotten of the Father; which have been referred to, John i. 14, 18. and iii. 16. 1 John iv. 9. which cannot be understood of him as a man, for as such he was not begotten, and so was without father, the antitype of Melchisedec; and whose generation must be understood not of his nature; for his nature is the same with the nature of the Father and Spirit, and therefore if his was begotten, theirs would be also; but of his person; as in natural, so in divine generation, person begets person, and not essence

---

[32] Noldius, N° 1884. Coccei Lexic. col 43.

begets essence; and this begetting is not *out* of, but *in* the divine essence; it being an immanent and internal act in God; and in our conception of it, as has been already observed, we are to remove every thing impure and imperfect, division and multiplication, priority and posteriority, dependence, and the like; and as for the modus, or manner of it, we must be content to be ignorant of it, as we are of our own generation, natural and spiritual; and of the incarnation of Christ, and of the union of the human nature to his divine Person. If we must believe nothing but what we can comprehend, or account for the manner, or *how* it is, we must be obliged to disbelieve some of the perfections of God; as eternity, immensity, and omniscience, &c. yea, that there is a God, or that there are three distinct Persons in the Godhead; which, however, clearly revealed in scripture *that* they are, yet the manner, or *how* they are, how they subsist distinctly as three Persons, and yet but one God, is incomprehensible and inexplicable by us: and at this rate, there are many things in nature, and in philosophy,[33] which must be given up, which yet are certain; since the manner *how* they be, cannot be explained; it is enough, that it is plain they are, though *how* cannot be said; as the union of our souls and bodies; and the influence that matter and spirit have on each other; and in the present case, it is enough that Christ is revealed as begotten of the Father; though the manner how he is begotten, cannot be explained: Athanasius[34] expresses the thing well; "*How* the Father begat the Son, I do not curiously inquire; and *how* he sent forth the Spirit, I do not likewise curiously inquire; but I believe *that* both the Son is begotten, and the holy Spirit proceeds, in a manner unspeakable and impassible." And says[35] Gregory Nazianzen, "Let the generation of God be honoured in silence; it is a great thing, (abundantly so) for thee to learn or know,

that he is begotten; but *how* he is begotten, is not granted to thee to understand, nor, indeed, to the angels." "It is enough for me, says the same ancient divine,[36] that I hear of the Son; and that he is *of* the Father; and that the one is a Father, and the other a Son: and nothing besides this do I curiously inquire after.——Do you hear of the generation of the Son? do not curiously inquire the τὸ πῶς, the *how* it is; Do you hear that the Spirit proceeds from the Father? do not curiously inquire τὸ ὅπως, the *manner* how he does;[37] for if you curiously inquire into the generation of the Son, and the procession of the Spirit; I also, in my turn, will curiously inquire of thee, the temperament of soul and body; how thou art dust, and yet the image of God; what it is that moves thee, or what is moved; how it is the same that moves, and is moved; how the sense abides in one, and attracts that which is without; how the mind abides in thee, and begets a word in another mind; and how it imparts understanding by the word: and not to speak of greater things, what the circumference of the heavens, what the motion of the stars, or their order, or measure, or conjunction, or distance; what the borders of the sea; from whence the winds blow; or the revolutions of the seasons of the year, and the effusions of showers? If thou knowest not any of these things, O man —— of which sense is a witness, how canst thou think to know God accurately, *how* and *what* he is? this is very unreasonable." Nor should the phrase, *eternal generation*, be objected to, because not syllabilically expressed in scripture; it is enough that the thing is which is meant by it: nor are the words, a *Trinity of Persons*, or three distinct Persons in one God; nor the word *satisfaction*, expressive of a doctrine on which our salvation depends. It is most certain, that Christ is the Son of God; and it is as certain, that he is the *begotten* Son of God; and if begotten, then

---

[33] A philosopher —————— must not think he has a right to deny the action of powers, because he cannot comprehend the *manner* after which things thus happen; forasmuch as according to such notions, we might reject many things likewise, which experience proves *really* to come to pass; who can conceive the *how* of what has been shewn to happen about percussion, or about the operations of light in contempl. 24.? How many effects are there in *chymistry*, as likewise in *hydrostatics*, of which we have not yet been able to comprehend the manner *how* they came to pass? no more than what has been said in contempl. 23. about the bodies and roots of plants, which perhaps would be as hardly admitted —————— if nothing must be believed to be true, but that of which we can understand the *how* and the manner. Nieuwentyt's Religious Philosopher, vol. 3. contempl. 26. s. 5. p. 897.

[34] De S. Trinitate, Dialog. 1. p. 154.
[35] Orat. 35. p. 567.
[36] Orat. 29. p. 492. 493.
[37] Like advice is given by Cyril of Jerusalem, "that God has a Son believe, τὸ δὲ πῶς, *but how*, or in what manner, do not curiously inquire, for seeking you will not find it." Cateches. xi. s. 7. p. 144.

the word generation may be used of him, for what is begotten is generated; and since he is God's own Son, or his proper Son, he must be so by proper generation, and not by improper, or figurative generation, which must be the case if a Son by office; and if he is the Son of God by proper generation, he must be so either as man, or as a divine Person; not as man, for as such he was not begotten at all; but was made of a woman, and born of a virgin: it remains, that he must be so considered, as a divine Person; and since it was from everlasting, before the earth was, or any creature had a being, that he was begotten, and brought forth, and as early brought up, as a Son with his Father; with the utmost safety and propriety may eternal generation be attributed to him; and, indeed, in no other sense can he be the Son of God.

To close all; this phrase, *the Son of God*, intends what is essential and natural to him; and suggests to us, that he is the true and natural Son of God; not a Son in an improper and figurative sense, or not by office, but by nature; that, as such, he is a divine Person, God, the true God, Heb. i. 8. 1 John v. 20. that he is equal with God, as the Jews understood him; in which they were not mistaken, since our Lord never went about to undeceive them, which he would have done had they misunderstood him, John v. 17, 18. and x. 30. and it is to be observed, that he has been concluded to be the Son of God from his divine perfections and works; from his omniscience, John i. 48, 49. from his omnipotence, Matt. xiv. 33. and from the marvellous things that happened at his crucifixion, Matt. xxvii. 54. In short, as the phrase, *the Son of man*, denotes one that is truly man; so the phrase, *the Son of God*, must intend one that is truly God, a divine Person; and as Christ is called the Son of man, from the nature in which he is man; so he is called the Son of God, from the nature in which he is God. I have been the longer upon the Sonship of Christ, because it is that upon which the distinction in the Godhead depends; take that away, and it cannot be proved there is any distinction of persons in it. I proceed,

Thirdly, To consider the third Person, and his personal relation; or distinctive relative property; which is, to be *breathed*, or to be the *breath* of God; which is never said of the Father and Son; and which, with propriety, gives him the name of *Spirit*, or *Breath*, as he is called, Ezek. xxxvii. 9. I shall treat of this very briefly, since the scriptures speak sparingly of it. It should be observed, that though he is most frequently called, the holy Spirit, yet it is not his being of an holy nature, and of a spiritual substance, which distinguishes him from the Father and the Son; for since they are of the same nature, which is perfectly pure and holy, they must be equally holy, as he is: and since God, essentially considered, is a Spirit or spiritual, such is God, personally considered; or such is each person in the Godhead. Nor does he take his name of Spirit, or Breath, from any actions of his, on, in, or with respect to creatures; as in breathing into Adam the breath of life, Gen. ii. 7. or in breathing the breath of spiritual life, in the regeneration and conversion of men, Ezek. xxxvii. 9. John iii. 8. nor from his inspiration of the scriptures, 2 Tim. iii. 16. 2 Pet. i. 21. nor from the disciples receiving the Holy Ghost through Christ's breathing upon them, John xx. 22. Though all these are symbolical of, analogous to, and serve to illustrate his original character, and personal relation and distinction, which denominates him the breath of the Almighty, Job xxxiii. 4. and distinguishes him from Jehovah the Father, the breath of whose mouth he is called, Psalm xxxiii. 6. and from Christ the Son of God, the breath of whose mouth he is also said to be, 2 Thess. ii. 8. and the Spirit, or breath, of the Son, Gal. iv. 6. and as Jehovah the Father was never without his Word, the Son, so neither the Father, nor the Word, were ever without their Breath, or Spirit: let none be offended, that the third Person is called Spirit, or Breath, since this suggests not, a mere power, or quality, but designs a Person; so an human person is called, Lam. iv. 20. and here a divine Person; to whom personal acts, and these divine, are ascribed; such as the establishing of the heavens, the making of man, the enditing of the scriptures, and filling the apostles with extraordinary gifts, Psalm xxxiii. 6. Job xxxiii. 4. 2 Pet. i. 21. John xx. 22. whose distinct personality, and proper Deity, together with the personality and Deity of the Father and Son, will be more particularly considered in the next chapters. I take no notice of the procession of the Spirit from Father and Son, which, though it illustrates his distinction from them, yet rather seems to be understood of his coming forth from them, not with respect to his Person, but his office, in a way of mission by them, to be the Convincer and Comforter of men, and the Applier of all grace unto them, see John xv. 26. and xvi. 7, 8.

CHAP. XXIX.

OF THE DISTINCT PERSONALITY, AND DEITY OF THE FATHER.

THOUGH what has been already observed, clearly shews there is a distinction of Persons in the Godhead, and wherein that distinction lies; yet other things may be added, which will serve to illustrate and confirm it; and which will be produced, not as making it, but as making it more clearly to appear. A person is by some[1] defined, "An individual that subsists, is living, intelligent, is not sustained by another, nor is a part of another;" and which is true of each of the three Persons, Father, Son, and Spirit. I shall begin with the personality of the Father; the word *Person* is expressly used of him in Heb. i. 3. where Christ his Son, by whom he made the worlds, is called, *the express image of his person*: the word ὑπόστασις, here used, is translated *substance* in chap. xi. 1. and some would have it so rendered here; and some of the Latin writers did use the word *substantia, substance*: but then they understood it, and made use of it, just in the same sense as we do the word *person;* but finding it to be an ambiguous word, and that it tended to lead men to imagine there were three distinct divine Beings, they left it off, and chose the word person, as less exceptionable; the Greek writers, and some even before the council of Nice, took the word here used, in the same sense as we do, for *subsistence*, or person;[2] and so it is here rendered by many learned men, as Valla, Vatablus, Erasmus, Calvin, Beza, Piscator, Paræus, and others; in which translation we may safely acquiesce.

The definition of a person agrees with the Father of Christ, as before observed. The Father of Christ is an individual, and so distinguishable from the divine nature he is possessed of, in common with the Son and Spirit; he subsists of himself, he does not owe his being to another, nor is he upheld in it by another; nor is he possessed only of a part, but of the whole Deity; he is the living Father, has life in himself, and not from another, John v. 26. and vi. 57. and is intelligent, knows himself, his Son and Spirit, and all things, Matt. xi. 27.

The personality of the Father may be concluded from those personal actions which are ascribed to him; for besides begetting the Son, which is what distinguishes him from the other two persons, there are other acts which illustrate and confirm the distinction made, though they do not make it; as,—1. The creation of all things is ascribed to him; he is said, as the Father of Christ, to make the worlds by him his Son, and to create all things by him; not as an instrument, but as a co-efficient cause, Heb. i. 2. Eph. iii. 9.——2. The works of providence, as upholding and sustaining all creatures in their being, supplying them with all things necessary, governing the world, ordering and disposing of all persons and things in it, are attributed to him, in distinction from his Son, though in conjunction with him, *my Father worketh hitherto, and I work*, John v. 17.——3. The mission of his Son into the world to be the Saviour of men, shews his distinct personality from him, which is often said of him; now he that sends, and he that is sent, cannot be the same person, but must be distinct; indeed the Spirit of God is said also to send Christ, as well as the Father, Isa. xlviii. 16. but then, though the Son is sent by both, and the Spirit is sent both by the Father and the Son, yet the Father is never said to be sent by either; he is always the sender, and never the sent.——4. The several distinct acts of grace towards the elect in Christ, will serve to evince the distinct personality of the Father. Men are said to be elect according to the foreknowledge of God the Father, 1 Pet. i. 2. and are said to be chosen by him in Christ unto salvation, through sanctification of the Spirit, and therefore must be distinct from Christ, in whom, and to whose salvation they are chosen; and from the Spirit, through whose sanctification they are chosen to the obtaining of the glory of Christ, Eph. i. 4. 2 Thess. ii. 13, 14. planning the scheme of man's salvation by Christ; reconciling, or forming the scheme of reconciliation in Christ; consulting in the council of peace with him about it, are personal acts, and distinguish him from Christ; making a covenant with his Son on account

---

[1] Vid. Wendelin. Christ. Theolog. l. 1. c. 2. p. 93, 94.

[2] See my Doctrine of the Trinity, p. 93.

of elect men, putting their persons into his hands, blessing them with all spiritual blessings in him, and giving grace to them in him before the world was; as they are personal acts, so they shew him to be distinct from his Son, with whom he covenanted, and whom he entrusted with the said persons and things: his drawing them by the powerful influences of his grace in time, to come to Christ and believe in him, John vi. 44. promising and giving the Spirit as a convincer, comforter, enlightener, and strengthener, with many other things, serve to illustrate and confirm his distinct personality. Now we call the Father the first person, not that he is so in order of time or causality, and as if he was the *fons Deitatis*, the fountain of Deity, as some good men have wrongly called him; for rather the Deity is the fountain of the divine persons, from whence they arise together, and in which they subsist, and in which they have no superiority and preeminence of one another; but as it is necessary to speak of them in some order, it seems most proper to place the Father first, whence we call him the first person, and then the Son, and then the Spirit; in which order they are usually put in scripture; though to shew there is a perfect equality between them, this order is sometimes inverted.

That the Father of Christ, as he is a person, so a divine person, will not be doubted; nor is his Deity called in question; and yet it may be proper to say something of it, and establish it; which may be done, not only by observing that he is expressly and distinctly called God, Rom. xv. 6. Gal. i. 1. Phil. ii. 11. but this may be proved,

1. From his divine perfections: God necessarily exists, owes his being to no other, subsists of himself, and is independent of any; such is the Father of Christ, he *has life in himself* and of himself, and does not derive it from another, John v. 26. God is from everlasting to everlasting, without beginning and end; so is the Father of Christ, he is he *which is, and which was, and which is to come*, Rev. i. 4. God is immense and omnipresent, cannot be circumscribed by space, he fills heaven and earth, and is contained in neither; such is the Father of Christ, of whom he often speaks as in heaven, and yet with him on earth, and with all his people, at all times, and in all ages, John xiv. 23. and xvi. 32. God is omniscient, knows all persons and things; and so does the Father of Christ, he knows the Son in such sense as no othe does, and knows that which neither the angels nor the Son, as man, know, even the day and hour of judgment, Matt. xi. 27. Mark xiii. 32. see Acts i. 7. 2 Cor. xi. 31. God is omnipotent, he can do all things; and so can the Father of Christ, *Abba, Father*, says Christ, *all things are possible unto thee*, Mark xiv. 36. see Matt. xvi. 53. John x. 29. Once more, God is immutable, not subject to any change and variation; God, the Father of Christ, is the *Father of lights, with whom there is no variableness nor shadow of turning*, James i. 17. he is unchangeable in his purposes and promises made in Christ, and in his love which is in Christ Jesus the Lord. In short, there is no perfection in Deity but what God, the Father of Christ, is possessed of.

2. His Deity will appear from the works which are ascribed to him, and which none but God could do; such as making the heaven, the earth and sea, and all that in them are; and who as the maker of them is addressed by the apostle, Acts iv. 24—27. and hence by Christ called *Father, Lord of heaven and earth*, Matt. xi. 25. and the works of providence, before observed, are ascribed to him, as supporting the world by his power, governing it by his wisdom, and supplying it by his goodness, which none but God could do: see Matt. vi. 26, 32. And his mighty acts of grace in quickening sinners dead in sins, in doing which the same power is put forth as in raising Christ from the dead, Eph. ii. 1. and i. 19. and in forgiving the sins of men, which none but God can do, Mark ii. 7. and for which Christ prayed to his Father on the behalf of his enemies, Luke xxiii. 34. to which may be added the resurrection of the dead, which is purely a divine work, and requires almighty power. The resurrection of Christ is most frequently ascribed to him, and he will raise the dead at the last day, 1 Cor. vi. 14. From these and from many other divine works, may the Deity of the Father be concluded, as well as,

3. From the worship due to him, and given to him. None but God is and ought to be the object of religious worship and adoration; *Thou shalt worship the Lord thy God, and him only shalt thou serve*, Matt. iv. 10. now true worshippers of God *worship the Father in spirit and in truth, for the Father seeketh such to worship him*, John iv. 23. and the Father of Christ is frequently represented as the object of faith,

hope, and love; to whom prayer is to be made, and to whom prayer was made both by Christ and his apostles; how often are grace and peace wished for from him in the several epistles? and he stands first in the form of baptism, which is a solemn act of divine and religious worship.

CHAP. XXX.

OF THE DISTINCT PERSONALITY, AND DEITY OF THE SON.

THAT the Son of God is a person, and a divine person distinct from the Father and and the Spirit, cannot be doubted; for since his Father is a person, and he is the *express image of his person*, he must be a person too; and he must be the express image of him, as he himself is a divine person, the Son of God, and truly God; and not as he is man and mediator; not as he is man, or as having an human nature, for his Father never had any, and therefore he could not be the image of him in that respect; for though man is the image of God as to some qualities in him, yet is he never called his character or express image, much less the express image of any of the persons in the Deity: nor as mediator, and in an office-capacity, for his Father was never a mediator, nor in an office: it remains therefore that it must be the express image of his person, as he himself is a divine person, abstracted from any consideration of his human nature, and of his office. For as Plato[1] says, that which is like must needs be of the same species with that to which it is like. The definition of a Person agrees with him: he is an individual, distinct, though not separate from the divine nature, he has in common with the Father and the Spirit; he subsists of himself in that nature distinctly, and independently; is not a part of another, the whole fulness of the Godhead dwells in him; nor is his human nature, which he assumed in time, a part of his person, nor adds anything to his personality; but being taken up into union with his person, subsists in it; he has life in himself, and is the living God; is intelligent, has understanding and will; knows himself, his Father and the Spirit, and all creatures and things, and does whatsoever he pleases.

Besides the distinctive, relative property, or personal relation of the Son, which is to be *begotten*, and which gives and makes the distinction of him, as a divine person, from the Father and Spirit, who are never said to be begotten; there are many other things which shew, or make him appear to be a distinct person.

1. His being with God as the Word,[2] John i. 1. and with his Father as a Son, as one brought up with him, Prov. viii. 30. clearly expresses his distinct personality; he must be a person to be *with*, and to be brought up with another; and he must be distinct from him with whom he is; he cannot with any propriety be said to be with himself, or to be brought up with himself.

2. His being set up from everlasting as mediator, and the covenant-head of the elect; the Father making a covenant with him, and putting the persons of the chosen ones, with all the blessings of grace for them, into his hands, shew him to be a person; a mere name and character could not be said to be set up, to be covenanted with, or to have persons and things committed to his care and charge; and these shew him to be a distinct person from him who set him up, and entrusted him with all these persons and things; see Prov. viii. 23. Psalm lxxxix. 3, 28. Deut. xxxiii. 3. Eph. i. 3. 2 Tim. i. 9.

3. His being sent in the fulness of time to be the Saviour of his people, and that under the character of the Son of God, shews him to be distinct from the Father, whose Son he is, and by whom he was sent; if he was not a person, but a mere name, he could not be sent; and he must be distinct from him that sent him; he that sends, and he that is sent, cannot be one and the same person; or else it must be said, that he sent himself, which is too gross and absurd to be admitted; see Rom. viii. 3. Gal. iv. 4. 1 John iv. 9, 14.

4. His becoming a sacrifice, and making satisfaction for the sins of men, and so the Redeemer and Saviour of them, plainly declare his distinct personality. Was he not a person, he could not offer himself a sacrifice, and he must be distinct from him to whom he offered himself; was he not a person, he could not make satisfaction, or reconcile men to God; or, in other words, make reconciliation and atonement for sin;

---

[1] In Parmenide, p. 1113.

[2] Of this name of the Son of God, the Word, see my Doctrine of the Trinity, ch. 5. p. 98—120.

these are personal acts, and he must be distinct from him to whom the satisfaction, reconciliation, and atonement are made; or to whom men are reconciled by him; if he has redeemed men to God by his blood, as he has, he must be a person that is the redeemer of men, and he must be distinct from him to whom he has redeemed them; for he cannot with propriety be said to reconcile and redeem them to himself; see Eph. v. 2. Heb. ix. 14. Rom. v. 10, 11. Rev. v. 9.

5. His ascension to heaven, and session at the right hand of God, shew him to be a person that ascended, and is sat down; and though it was in human nature that he ascended and sat down, yet it was God in that nature; *God is gone up with a shout,* Psalm xlvii. 5. *Thou,* the Lord God, *hast ascended on high,* Psalm lxviii. 17. 18. *The Lord said to my Lord, sit on my right hand,* Psalm cx. 1. and he must be distinct from his God and our God, from his Father and our Father, to whom he ascended, and cannot be the same person with him at whose right hand he sits, John xx. 17. Heb. i. 13.

6. His advocacy and intercession with his Father, is a plain proof of his distinct personality. He is said to be an *advocate with the Father,* 1 John ii. 1. and therefore must be a person to act the part of an advocate; and must be distinct from him with whom he advocates; unless it can be thought he is an advocate with himself; he himself says, *I will pray the Father, and he shall give you another Comforter,* meaning the Spirit of truth, as next explained, John xiv. 16, 17. Now he must be distinct from the Father to whom he prays, for surely he cannot be supposed to pray to himself; and he must be distinct from the Spirit, for whom he prays. He appears in the presence of God for his people, and ever lives to make intercession for them, and must be a person to do this; and must be distinct from him in whose presence he appears, and to whom he makes intercession; for he cannot with any propriety be said to appear in his own presence for his people, and to mediate and make intercession for them with himself; see Heb. vii. 25. and ix. 24.

7. His judging the world at the last day, with all the circumstances thereof; gathering all nations before him, dividing them, and setting them, some on his right hand and others on his left, and passing the definitive sentence on them, prove him to be a person, a divine person, and distinct from the Father and the Spirit; for as for *the Father,* he *judgeth no man, but hath committed all judgment to the Son,* John v. 22. nor is ever the final judgment of the world ascribed to the Spirit; see Matt. xxv. 31—41. Acts x. 42. and xvii. 31.

8. It is promised to the saints that they shall be with Christ, where he is; see him as he is, and behold his glory, and shall reign with him for evermore; and he is represented as the object of their praise, wonder, and worship, to all eternity; and that as distinct from the Father and the Holy Ghost; all which, and much more, shew him to be a person, and to be distinct from them both; for surely he must be a person, a divine and distinct one, whom the saints shall be, live and dwell with to all eternity; and whom they shall praise, serve, and adore, throughout endless ages.

The Deity of Christ may be next considered, and proved; or, that he is a divine Person, truly and properly God. Not a made or created God, as say the Arians. He was made flesh, and made of a woman; but not made God; for then he must make himself, which is absurd; since *without him was not any thing made that was made;* but *all things were made by him,* John i. 3. Nor God by office, as say the Socinians; for then he would be God only in an improper sense; as magistrates are called gods; and not truly and properly God: nor God by name only; as there are called lords many, and gods many; such were the gods of the heathens, inanimate, irrational, lifeless beings, and so could have no divinity in them. But he is God by nature; as these were not; having the whole essence and nature of God in him. This will appear,

First, From the names which are given to him; he has the same glorious names the most high God has; as Ejeh, I AM that I AM, Exod. iii. 14. to which our Lord refers, and takes to himself, John viii. 58. and Jehovah, which is incommunicable to a creature, and peculiar to the most High, Psalm lxxxiii. 18. it is not given to angels; for wherever an angel is so called, not a created but the uncreated angel is meant; nor to the ark, 2 Sam. vi. 2. for not the ark, but God, whose the ark was, is there called by the name of the Lord of hosts: nor to Jerusalem, Jer. xxxiii. 16. but to the Messiah, chap. xxiii. 6. for the words may be rendered, "This is the name wherewith he shall be called by her, the Lord our Righteousness:" nor to the church absolutely, Ezek. xlviii. 35. but in composition, or with addition; and is only symbolical of Jehovah's presence, being with her; and the same may be said of mount Moriah; and of some altars, called Jehovah-jireh, Jehovah-nissi, and Jehovah-shalom; which are only symbolical, and designed to call to remembrance the wonderful appearance of Jehovah; the gracious help, and divine assistance, he granted to his people in those places, Gen. xxii. 14. Exod. xvii. 15. Judg. vi. 24. nor is this name given to priests and judges, Deut. xix. 17. for Jehovah is not to be explained by them; but is distinguished from them; and though he is joined with them, this only designs his presence in judiciary affairs, agreeable to Psalm lxxxii. 1. if, therefore, it can be proved that the name Jehovah is given to Christ, it will prove him to be the most High over all the earth.

Now we are told that God spake to Moses, and said, *I am the Lord,* or Jehovah; by which name he was not known to Abraham, Isaac, and Jacob; that is, not by that only, or that was not so fully made known to them, as it had been to Moses, and to the Israelites by him, Exod. vi. 2, 3. and iii. 14. which person that appeared to Moses, and said those words, is called the Angel of the Lord, chap. iii. 2. not a created angel, ver. 6. but an uncreated one; and must be understood, not of God the Father, who is never called an angel; but of the Son of God, the Angel of his presence, who brought the children of Israel out of Egypt, went before them, and led them through the Red Sea, and wilderness, to the land of Canaan, Exod. iii. 8. and xiii. 21. and xiv. 19. and xxiii. 20. Isa. lxiii. 9. he, whom the Israelites tempted in the wilderness, is expressly called Jehovah, Exod. xvii. 7. and nothing is more evident than that this Person was Christ, 1 Cor. x. 9. he whom Isaiah saw on a throne, making a very magnificent appearance, is not only called Adonai, Isa. vi. 1. but by the seraphim, Jehovah, ver. 3. and so by Isaiah, ver. 5. who was bid to say to the Jews, ver. 8, 9. *Hear ye indeed, &c.* which words Christ applies to himself; and observes that, *those things Esaias said, when he saw his glory and spoke of him,* John xii. 39, 40, 41. There is a prophecy in Isaiah xl. 3.

The voice of him that crieth in the wilderness, Prepare ye the way of the Lord, or of Jehovah, *make straight in the desart, an highway for our God,* which, by the evangelist Matthew, is applied unto, and interpreted of John the Baptist, Matt. iii. 1, 2, 3. wherefore, the Jehovah, whose way he was to prepare, and our God, whose paths he was to make straight, could be no other than Christ; whose harbinger and forerunner John was, and whose way and paths were prepared and made straight by him, through his preaching the doctrine of repentance, administering the ordinance of baptism, and declaring the kingdom of heaven, or of the Messiah, was at hand. Moreover, the Messiah, or Christ, is expressly called, the Lord, or Jehovah, our righteousness, in Jer. xxiii. 6. it being his work, as Mediator, to bring in everlasting righteousness; and is the end of the law for it, and is made righteousness to every one that believes. Once more, Jehovah promises to pour forth the Spirit of grace and supplication on some persons described in Zech. xii. 10. and then adds, *They shall look upon me,* Jehovah, *whom they have pierced;* which was fulfilled in Christ, when one of the soldiers with a spear pierced his side, John xix. 34, 37. the same words are referred to, and applied to Christ, Rev. i. 7. Now, since in these, and in many other places, Christ is intended by Jehovah, he must be truly and properly God, since this name is incommunicable to any other.

It may be observed also, that in some places of scripture, Christ is absolutely called God; as in Psalm xlv. 6. *Thy throne, O God, is for ever and ever;* where he is distinguished from God his Father, ver. 7. and the words are expressly applied to him as the Son of God, Heb. i. 8. *But unto the Son he saith, Thy throne, O God,* &c. yea, Christ calls himself God; as he well might, since he is in the form of God, and therefore thought it no robbery to be equal to him; saying, *Look unto me, and be ye saved, all the ends of the earth; for I am God, and there is none else; I have swore by myself,* &c. Isa. xlv. 22, 23. which last words, in connection with the other, are, by the apostle Paul, applied to Christ, Rom. xiv. 10, 11, 12. The evangelist John, says of the Word, or Son of God, who was made flesh, and dwelt among men, and so cannot be understood of any but Christ, that *the Word was God,* John i. 1, 14. and the same inspired writer observes, *Hereby perceive we the love of God, because he laid down his life for us,* 1 John iii. 16. from whence it follows, that he that laid down his life for men, which can only be said of Christ, and wherein his love to them appeared, must be God.

And Christ is not only called God absolutely, but with some additional epithets, with possessive pronouns, as, *our God,* the Jews were waiting for, and John was the forerunner of, Isa. xxv. 9. and xl. 3. *your God,* who should come when miracles would be wrought as proofs of it, Isa. xxxv. 4, 5. *their God,* Luke i. 16. *my Lord,* and *my God,* by Thomas, John xx. 28. Now though angels, magistrates, and judges, are called gods in an improper and metaphorical sense; yet never called our gods, your gods, &c. Christ is said to be Immanuel, God with us, God in our nature, that is, God manifest in the flesh, Matt. i. 22. 1 Tim. iii. 16. Some additional characters are given of Christ, when he is called God; which shew him to be truly and properly God; as, *the mighty God,* in Isa. ix. 6. which is manifestly a prophecy of him; and who elsewhere is called the most Mighty, yea, the Almighty, Psalm xlv. 3. Rev. i. 8. and *over all God blessed for ever,* Rom. ix. 5. over all creatures, angels and men, who are made by him; and he is blessed for ever in himself. He is called *the great God,* whose glorious appearing, and not the Father's, saints are directed to look for; besides, this great God, is explained of Jesus Christ our Saviour in the next clause, Tit. ii. 13. compare with this Rev. xix. 17. where he who is called the great God, is the mighty warrior, whose name is the Word of God, and King of kings, and Lord of lords, ver. 11, 13, 16. Christ is also said to be the *living God,* Heb. iii. 12. for he only is spoken of in the context; and this is only said of the most high God; which distinguishes him from all other deities, Jer. x. 10. and, to add no more, he is called, *the true God,* in opposition to all false and fictitious deities, 1 John v. 20. for what is there said, is said expressly of the Son of God.

Secondly, The Deity of Christ may be proved from the divine perfections he is possessed of; *for in him dwells all the fulness of the Godhead,* Col. ii. 9. not one perfection of the divine nature excepted; or otherwise it could not be said, that all the fulness of Deity was in him. God is necessarily and self-existent, and independent on any; such is Christ, he is αυτοθεος, God of himself: as man and mediator he has a life given him for himself, and others, and lives by the Father; but, as God, he owes his life and being to none; it is not derived from another; he is over all, God blessed for ever. Eternity is a perfection of God; God is from everlasting to everlasting; Christ was not only before Abraham, but before Adam; and before any creature was in being; for he is the αρχη, the beginning, the first cause of the creation of God, Rev. iii. 14. the first-born, or rather, the first parent and producer of every creature; as the word πρωτοτοκος, by the removal of the accent, may be rendered;[3] which best agrees with the apostle's reasoning in the next verse; where all things are said to be created by him; and therefore, as the apostle argues, he must be before all things, Col i. 15, 16, 17. as Mediator, he was set up from everlasting; his goings forth in the covenant were of old; the elect were chosen in him before the foundation of the world; and had grace given them in him, before that began; all which suppose his eternal existence. Hence he is called Alpha and Omega, the first and the last, the beginning and the ending; which is, and was, and is to come; Melchisedec's antitype, having neither beginning of days nor end of life, Rev. i. 8. Heb. vii. 3. Omnipresence, or immensity, is another perfection of Deity, Jer. xxiii. 23, 24. Christ, as the Son of God, was in heaven, in the bosom of his Father; when, as the Son of man, he was here on earth, John i. 18. and iii. 13. which he could not be, if he was not omnipresent; nor could he make good his promises to his ministers, churches, and people, to be with them at all times, in all ages, and in all places, wherever they are, Matt. xviii. 20. and xxviii. 20. nor walk in the midst of his golden candlesticks, the several churches, in different places; and fill all things and persons in them, as he certainly does, Rev. i. 13. Eph. iv. 10. Omniscience is another divine perfection, and most manifestly appears in Christ; he knew what was in man, and needed not that any should testify to him what was in man; he could tell the woman of Samaria all that ever she did; he knew from the beginning who would believe in him, and who would betray him; he knew the secret thoughts of the Scribes and Pharisees; and is that

---

[3] Vid. Isidor. Pelusiot. Epist. 1. 3. ep. 31.

Word that is a discerner of the thoughts and intents of the heart; and he will hereafter let all the world and churches know, that he searches the hearts and reins. In short, he knows all things, as Peter affirmed unto him, John ii. 24, 25. and iv. 29. and vi. 64. Matt. ix. 4. Heb. iv. 12. Rev. ii. 23. John xxi. 17. and though he is said not to know the day of judgment, this is said of him as the Son of man, not as the Son of God, Mark xiii. 32. Omnipotence is a perfection that belongs to Christ, and is peculiar to God, who only can do all things; Christ is almighty, and his works declare it; the creation of all things, the sustentation of the universe, the redemption and preservation of his people, and the resurrection of them at the last day; all which are, *according to his mighty power, which is able to subdue all things to himself*, Phil. iii. 21. To observe no more, immutability belongs solely to God; who is without any variableness or shadow of turning; and such is Christ, the same to-day, yesterday, and for ever, Heb. xiii. 8. see Psalm cii. 26. compared with Heb. i. 12. and since therefore such perfections of the Godhead are in Christ, he must be truly and properly God.

Thirdly, The truth of Christ's proper divinity may be proved from the works done by him; which are the same that are done by the Father; and in which he is a co-efficient cause with him; and are done by him ὁμοίως, in like manner as by the Father, John v. 17, 19. such as the creation of all things out of nothing; of the whole world, and all things in it, visible or invisible, John i. 2, 3. Col. i. 16. the making of the worlds, the heaven and the earth, are particularly ascribed to the Word and Son of God; and he that built all things is God, Heb. xi. 3. and i. 10. and iii. 4. the work of providence, the government of the world, and the disposing of all things in it, Christ is jointly concerned in with the Father; *My Father worketh hitherto, and I work*, that is, with him, John v. 17. Christ upholds all things by his power; bears up the pillars of the earth; and by him do all things consist, Heb. i. 3. Col. i. 17. the miracles Christ wrought on earth in human nature, as they were proofs of his Messiahship, so of his Deity; such as curing the lame, the blind, and dumb, and deaf, and even raising the dead, by a word speaking; which were what none but God could do: these prove that the Father was in him, and he in the Father, Matt. xi. 4, 5. John x. 37, 38. If he was not the mighty God, he could never have been able to have wrought and obtained the redemption and salvation of his people, by his own arm: what gave virtue and efficacy to his blood, to purchase his church and people, and cleanse them from their sins, is his Deity; and so to his righteousness, to make it a justifying one before God; and to his sacrifice, to make it expiatory of sin, and acceptable to God. The acts of forgiveness of sin, and justification from it, are peculiar to God. None can forgive sin but God; yet Christ has done it, and therefore must be God, Mark ii. 7, 9, 10. it is God that justifies men from sin, and acquits them from condemnation, Rom. viii. 1, 33. and so does Christ, Isa. liii. 11. The Resurrection of the dead is a work of almighty power, and which none but God can do; and yet Christ has raised himself from the dead, and thereby is declared to be the Son of God with power; that is, truly and properly God, Rom. i. 4. see John ii. 19. and x. 18. and he will raise all the dead at the last day, by his mighty power; and at his all-commanding voice, the dead will come forth out of their graves, wherein they have lain, John v. 28, 29. 1 Thess. iv. 16, 17. The judgment of the world is committed to him; *The Father judgeth no man, but hath committed all judgment to the Son*, John v. 22. Now if he was not God omnipotent and omniscient, he would never be able to do what he will do; gather all nations before him, separate them, and place them some on his right hand, and some on his left; bring to light the counsels of the heart, and judge the secrets of it, and give to every man for the deeds done in the body, whether good or evil; pronounce the several decisive sentences, and put them in execution, Matt. xxv. 31—46. Rom. ii. 16. 1 Cor. iv. 5. 2 Cor. v. 10.

Fourthly, As a further proof of the Deity of Christ, the worship given him both by angels and men may be observed; for when he, God's first-born, was brought into the world, he said, *Let all the angels of God worship him*, Heb. i. 6. which order to the celestial inhabitants, would never have been given, if he was not God: it is also the declared will of the divine Father of Christ, *that all men should honour the Son, even as they honour the Father;* that is, worship him with the same divine worship; which he would never have declared, who will not give his glory to another besides himself, was not Christ his Son the one God with him; see Psalm ii. 12. Men are directed to exercise faith and hope on him; yea, Christ himself directs unto it, equally to be exercised on him, as on his Father; which he would never have done, but that he and his father are one, one in nature, and so in power and glory, John xiv. 1. and x. 30. yea, if he was not God, but a mere man, instead of men being blessed and happy, who make him their hope, and trust in him, they would be cursed for so doing, Jer. xvii. 5, 7. Baptism, a solemn ordinance of religious worship, is ordered to be administered in his name, equally as in the name of the Father, Matt. xxviii. 19. which, if a mere creature, would be idolatry and blasphemy; for which reason the apostle Paul was so cautious, lest any should think they were baptized by him in his own name, 1 Cor. i. 13, 14, 15. Prayer, another branch of religious worship, is often made to Christ; and that not by a single person only, as by Stephen, in his last moments, Acts vii. 58. but by whole churches and communities; who are said in every place to call upon the name of Jesus Christ our Lord; and how often are grace and peace wished for, by the apostles, as from God our Father, so from the Lord Jesus Christ? 1 Cor. i. 2, 3. all which would never be performed by saints, nor be admitted of by God, was not Christ truly and properly God; nor need we scruple to worship him, nor be fearful lest we should give him too much: and great encouragement we have to commit our souls, and the salvation of them into his hands, and trust him with our all; since he is God the only Saviour.

CHAP XXXI.

OF THE DISTINCT PERSONALITY, AND DEITY OF THE HOLY SPIRIT.

WHAT only remains now to be considered, under the article of the Trinity, are the personality and divinity of the Holy Ghost; to prove that he is a Person, a distinct Person, from the Father and Son; and a divine Person, or truly and properly God.

First, That he is a Person, and not a mere name and character, power or attribute of God; which will appear by observing,

1. That the description of a Person agrees with him; that it subsists and lives of itself, is endowed with will and understanding, or is a willing and intelligent agent. Such is the Spirit of God; as the Father has life in himself, and the Son has life in himself, so has the holy Spirit; since he is the author of natural and spiritual life in men; which he preserves unto eternal life; and therefore called, the Spirit of life; which he could not be, unless he had life in himself; and if he has life in himself, he must subsist of himself: he has a power of willing whatever he pleases: the apostle, speaking of his influences, administrations, and operations, says, *All these worketh the one and the self-same Spirit, dividing to every man severally as he will*, 1 Cor. xii. 11. and that he is an intelligent agent, is clear from his knowing the things of God; which none can know but him; and from his teaching men all things, and guiding them into all truth, and giving the spirit of wisdom and knowledge to one and another; now "he that teacheth men knowledge, shall not he know?" 1 Cor. ii. 11. and xii. 8. John xiv. 26. and xvi. 13. Psalm xciv. 10.

2. Personal actions are ascribed unto him; he is said to be a reprover and convincer of men; to reprove or convince the world of sin, righteousness and judgment, John xvi. 8. Now he that convinces another of his mistakes, brings him to a sense and acknowledgment of them, and to repentance for them, must be a Person, and not a mere name and character. He is spoken of as a teacher, that teaches all things, all doctrines necessary to salvation, and all the duties of religion: an human teacher is a person, and much more a divine one, John xiv. 26. 1 John ii. 27. he is promised as a Comforter, John xvi. 7. and which he answers to, by shedding abroad the love of God in the hearts of the Lord's people; by taking the things of Christ, and shewing them to them; by applying to them exceeding great and precious promises; by declaring to them the pardon of their sins; by pronouncing the sentence of justification in their consciences; and by being the earnest and seal of their future happiness; all which are personal actions: he is one of the three witnesses in heaven, 1 John v. 7. who particularly testifies of Christ, of his Deity, sonship, offices, and grace, John xv. 26. and bears witness to the spirits of saints, that they are the children of God, Rom. viii. 16. which a mere name and character could not do; but a person. He is represented not only as a Spirit of grace and supplication, and an helper of the infirmities of the saints in prayer, but as making intercession for them, according to the will of God, Zech. xii. 10.

Rom. viii. 26, 27. Now as the advocacy and intercession of Christ, prove him to be a Person, and a distinct one from the Father, with whom he intercedes; so the intercession of the Spirit, equally proves his personality, even his distinct personality also: to which may be added, that the Spirit is the giver of gifts to men, whereby they are qualified for the work of the ministry, 1 Cor. xii. 8—11. and he calls them to that work, and appoints and sets them as overseers of particular churches, to feed them with knowledge and understanding, Acts xiii. 2. and xx. 28. and, to observe no more, he is often described as an inhabitant in the saints, that dwells in their bodies, and in their souls, and will always abide in them, until he has wrought them up for that self-same thing, eternal glory and happiness; now to dwell with any person, or in any place, is a personal action, and describes a person, John xiv. 16, 17. 1 Cor. iii. 16. and vi. 19. Rom. viii. 9. 11.

3. Personal affections are ascribed to the Spirit; as love, grief, &c. we read of the love of the Spirit, as well as of the Father, and of the Son; and which appears in the regeneration and sanctification of men, and in the application of grace unto them, Rom. xv. 30. and of the Spirit's being grieved with the sins of God's people, and their unbecoming carriage towards God and one another, Eph. iv. 30. and of his being rebelled against, vexed, and provoked; as he was by the Israelites, Isa. lxiii. 10. All which could not be said of him, was he not a person. He is, moreover, said to be lied unto; as by Ananias and Sapphira, Acts v. 3. and to be blasphemed, and sinned against with an unpardonable sin, Matt. xii. 32, 33. which could never be, nor with propriety be said, was he not a Person, and a divine Person too.

Secondly, The holy Spirit is not only a Person, but a distinct Person from the Father and the Son; and besides his distinctive relative property, spiration, or being the breath of them both, and so distinct from each; the following things may be observed,

1. His procession from the Father and the Son: of his procession from the Father express mention is made in John xv. 26. and therefore must be distinct from the Father, from whom he proceeds; which, whether it respects his nature or his office, proves the same: it was once a warm controversy between the Greek and Latin churches, whether the Spirit proceeded from the Son or from the Father; which was denied by the former, and asserted by the latter; and which seems rightest; since he is called the Spirit of the Son, Gal. iv. 6. however, since he is the Spirit of the Son, he must be distinct from him whose Spirit he is.

2. The mission of the Holy Spirit, by the Father and the Son, clearly evinces his distinct personality from them; of his being sent by the Father, see John xiv. 16, 26. and of his being sent by the Son, see John xv. 26. and xvi. 7. Now as a mere name and character, quality, power, and attribute, could not be said to be sent, but a Person; so the Spirit that is sent, must be a distinct Person from the Father and Son, said to send him.

3. The holy Spirit is called another Comforter, John xiv. 16. the Father of Christ is one; he is the God of all comfort; that comforts his people in all their tribulations, 2 Cor. i. 3, 4. and Jesus Christ is also a Comforter; one of his names with the Jews is Menachem, a Comforter;[1] a name well known with the Jews: hence good old Simeon is said to be waiting for the *Consolation of Israel*, Luke ii. 25. that is, for the Messiah; whom the Jews expected as a Comforter: and now the Holy Ghost is another Comforter, distinct from both; from the Son, who prayed for him as such; and from the Father, prayed unto on that account.

4. The holy Spirit is represented as doing some things distinct from the Father and the Son; particularly, as directing into the love of God, that is, the Father; and into a patient waiting for Christ; and so is distinguished from them both, 2 Thess. iii. 5. and also as taking of the things of Christ, called likewise the things of the Father, and shewing them to them that are Christ's; in which also he is distinguished from the Father, and from Christ, whose things he takes and shews, John xvi. 14, 15. So regeneration, renovation, sanctification, and conversion, are distinct things, and very peculiar to the Spirit.

5. There are some distinct appearances of the Spirit, which shew his distinct personality; as at the baptism of Christ, when he descended as a dove and lighted on him; and thereby was distinguished from the

---

[1] Talmud Bab. Sanhedrin, fol. 98. 2.

Father, whose voice was heard from heaven; and from the Son, who was baptized in Jordan, and on whom the Spirit lighted, Matt. iii. 16, 17. and on the day of Pentecost the Spirit descended on the apostles, in the form of cloven tongues, as of fire; and with respect to this, the apostle Peter says, that Christ *being by the right hand of God exalted, and having received of the Father the promise of the holy Ghost, he hath shed forth this which ye now see and hear;* meaning the effusion of the Holy Ghost, and his extraordinary gifts; and who is plainly distinguished from the Father, who made promise of him, and from the Son, who received this promise, and shed his gifts in the manner he did.

6. The holy Spirit is represented as a distinct person in the ordinance of baptism; and the form of it being to be administered in his name, as distinct from the name of the Father and of the Son, in whose name also it was to be administered, Matt. xxviii. 19. and so he is mentioned as a distinct witness from the Father and the Word, in the record bore in heaven; for if he is not a distinct person from them, there could not be three testifiers, or three that bore record in heaven, 1 John v. 7.

Thirdly, The Holy Ghost is not only a person, and a distinct person from the Father and Son, but a divine person, or truly and properly God; which was denied by the Macedonians of old,[2] and by the Socinians of late;[3] and generally by all that oppose the divinity of Christ: but the Deity of the Spirit is to be proved by the same mediums and arguments which are to be fetched from the same sources as the Deity of the Son. And,

1. From the names which are given unto him; as particularly the name Jehovah, peculiar to the most High; it was Jehovah, the Lord God of Israel, that spake by the mouth of all the holy prophets from the beginning of the world; and it is certain that they spake as they were moved by the Holy Ghost, Luke i. 68, 70. 2 Pet. i. 21. it was Jehovah, the Rock and God of Israel, that spake by David; and it is clear that it was the Holy Ghost that spake by him; for so Peter says, *This scripture must needs be fulfilled, which the Holy Ghost, by the mouth of David, spoke before concerning Judas,* 2 Sam. xxiii 2, 3. Acts i. 16. it was Jehovah, the Lord God, whom the Israelites tempted, proved, and provoked in the wilderness; and this the Holy Ghost speaks of as done to himself; *Wherefore, as the Holy Ghost saith, To day if ye will hear his voice, harden not your hearts, as in the provocation, in the day of temptation in the wilderness, when your fathers tempted me, proved me;* me, the Holy Ghost, Psalm xcv. 6, 7. Heb. iii. 7—9. see Isa. lxiii. 10. it was Jehovah that said to Isaiah, *Go and tell this people, hear ye indeed, &c.* and according to the apostle Paul, the same was the Holy Ghost; for to the Jews he says, *Well spake the Holy Ghost by Esaias the prophet, saying, Go unto this people, and say, hearing ye shall hear, &c.* Isa. vi. 8, 9. Acts xxviii. 25, 26. The Greek word κυριος, used in the New Testament, answers to Jehovah and Adonai in the Old; and this is said of the holy Spirit, he is that Spirit which is the Lord, and is called the Lord the Spirit, 2 Cor. iii. 17, 18. see also 2 Thess. iii. 5. Moreover the holy Spirit is very plainly called God in scripture: when Ananias lied to the Holy Ghost, he is said to lie not unto men but unto God; wherefore if lying to the Holy Ghost is lying to God, it follows that the Holy Ghost must be God, Acts v. 3, 4. The saints of God are called the temple of God, and the reason proving it is, because the Spirit of God dwells in them, and because their bodies are the temples of the Holy Ghost, they are exhorted to glorify God in their bodies: Now if the Holy Ghost is not called God, or meant by God in these passages there is no force of reasoning in them, 1 Cor. iii. 16. and vi. 19, 20. Moreover the apostle gives to the Holy Ghost the divine names of Spirit, Lord, and God, when he is speaking of the diversities of his gifts, administrations, and operations; for of him only is he speaking by whom all these are, 1 Cor. xii. 4—6.

2. The Deity of the Spirit may be proved from the perfections of God, which are manifestly in him, as eternity; hence, as some think, he is called the eternal Spirit, Heb. ix. 14. however he was present at the creation of the heavens and the earth, and was concerned therein, Gen. i. 2. Job. xxvi. 13. and therefore must be before any creature was, before time was, and so from eternity; as God the Father never was without his Son, so never without his Spirit; when it is said in some places that the Spirit was not yet, and that

---

[2] Vid. Aug. de Hæres. c. 52. et Dænæum in ibid.

[3] Cateches. Racov. c. 1. p. 35. et c. 6. p. 214.

there were some that had not heard that there was any Holy Ghost; this is to be understood of the wonderful effusion of the gifts of the holy Spirit on the apostles at Pentecost, which was not to be until after the glorification of Christ; and of which dispensation the disciples at Ephesus had not then heard, John vii. 39. Acts xix. 2. Omnipresence, or immensity, another divine perfection, is ascribed to the Spirit; says David, *Whither shall I go from thy Spirit? and whither shall I flee from thy presence?* Psalm cxxxix. 7. he is not to be shunned and avoided; there is no going anywhere from him, for he is everywhere, otherwise he might be avoided; and if everywhere, he must be the omnipresent God: the saints are his temples in which he dwells, and he dwells in them all, at all times, in all places; which he could not do if he was not immense and omnipresent. Omniscience is another divine perfection to be observed in the Spirit of God; he knows all things, even the deep things of God, the thoughts, counsels, and purposes of his heart; which he could not know, if he was not the omniscient God, 1 Cor. ii. 10, 11. nor could he teach the saints all things, nor guide them into all truth, and much less shew things to come, John xiv. 26. and xvi. 13. as he did under the Old Testament, when he testified beforehand, by the prophets, the sufferings of Christ, and the glory that should follow, 1 Pet. i. 11. and under the New Testament, witnessing to the apostle Paul that bonds and afflictions should abide him in every city, which he found to be true; and foretelling by Agabus, that there would be a great dearth throughout the world, which came to pass in the times of Claudius Cæsar, Acts xx. 23. and xi. 28. Omnipotence is predicated of him; he is called the power of the Highest, and the finger of God; his concern in creation, and in the formation of the human nature of Christ, the miraculous signs and wonders wrought by his power, the gifts that he bestows, and the grace that he works in the hearts of men, loudly proclaim his omnipotence; and if such perfections, which are peculiar to Deity, are to be found in him, he must be truly and properly God.

3. The works which are ascribed unto him are a clear and full proof of his divinity: creation, a work of divine power, is attributed to him; he not only moved upon the face of the waters that covered the earth, at the first creation, and brought the rude and unformed chaos into a beautiful order, and garnished the heavens, and bespangled them with the luminaries and stars of light; but by him, the Breath, or Spirit of the Lord, the heavens and the host thereof were made and established, Gen. i. 2. Job xxvi. 13. Psalm xxxiii. 6. yea man, the most excellent and curious part of the creation, is made by him, as Elihu owns, *The Spirit of God hath made me, and the breath of the Almighty hath given me life,* Job xxxiii. 4. The work of providence he is jointly concerned in with the Father and the Son; *Who hath directed the Spirit of the Lord, or being his counsellor hath taught him? with whom took he counsel* (the Spirit of the Lord) *and taught him in the path of judgment? and taught him knowledge, and shewed to him the way of understanding?* Isa. xl. 13, 14. that is, how to govern the world, and manage and direct all affairs in it. The enditing of the scripture is of him; *All scripture is given by inspiration of God;* by the Breath or Spirit of God, 2 Tim. iii. 16. this is a work purely divine, and is of the Spirit; "holy men spake as they were moved by the Holy Ghost," 2 Pet. i. 21. It was the holy Spirit that formed the human nature of Christ; what was conceived in the Virgin was of the Holy Ghost; that was fearfully and wonderfully made by him, and curiously wrought by him, in the lowest parts of the earth, Matt. i. 20. Psalm cxxxix. 14, 15. and was richly anointed by him with his gifts and graces; even above his fellows, and without measure, Psalm xlv. 7. Isa. lxi. 1. John iii. 34. and the miracles of Christ were by him, the finger of God; and those which the apostles wrought for the confirmation of the gospel, were by the power of the Holy Ghost, Matt. xii. 28. Luke xi. 20. Rom. xv. 19. Heb. ii. 3, 4. the work of grace in the heart is his work; regeneration and renovation are of the Holy Ghost; sanctification is called the sanctification of the Spirit; this is not by might nor power of man, but by the Spirit of God; and in which there is such a display of the exceeding greatness of divine power, as is equal to that which was exerted in raising Christ from the dead, Tit. iii. 5. 1 Pet. i. 2. Zech. iv. 6. Eph. i. 19. yea, the resurrection of Christ himself from the dead, is attributed to the Spirit of holiness; and it is by him the Spirit which dwells in the saints, that God will quicken their mortal bodies, Rom. i. 4. and viii. 11.

4. The worship which is due to the Spirit of God, and is given unto him, proves him to be God; for were he not, such worship would never be paid him; not only temples are erected by him, but for him, in which he is worshipped and glorified, Eph. ii. 22. 1 Cor. iii. 16. and vi. 19, 20. Baptism, a solemn act of religious worship, is administered in his name, as in the name of the Father and the Son. Matt. xxviii. 19. Swearing, which is another act of worship, a solemn appeal to the omniscient God, and is mentioned as a branch of serving him, Deut. vi. 13. is made by the Spirit, and he is called upon as a witness to facts, Rom. ix. 1. And prayer, a very principal part of worship, is directed to him, sometimes singly, as in 2 Thess. iii. 5. Cant. iv. 16. and sometimes, in conjunction with the other divine Persons, Rev. i. 4, 5. All which prove him to be truly and properly God; and therefore we should be careful to give him the honour and glory due unto him, as to the Father and the Son; and as we trust the Son with the whole affair of our salvation, and trust in him for it; so we should trust the Spirit of God with the work of grace upon our souls; and be confident that he that has begun it, will perform it; since "it is God that works in us, to will and to do, of his good pleasure."

My Treatise on the Trinity, was written near forty years ago, and when I was a young man; and had I now departed from some words and phrases then used by me, it need not, at such a distance of time, be wondered at; but so far from it, that upon a late revisal of it, I see no reason to retract anything I have written, either as to sense or expression; save only, in a passage or two of scripture, before observed, which then did not stand so clear in my mind, as proofs of the eternal generation of the Son of God; but, upon a more mature consideration of them, I am inclined to think otherwise, and have accordingly altered my sense of them; which alteration, as it is no ways inconsistent with the doctrine as before held by me, so it serves but the more strongly to confirm it.

A BODY OF DOCTRINAL DIVINITY.

BOOK II.

OF THE ACTS AND WORKS OF GOD.

CHAP. I.

OF THE INTERNAL ACTS AND WORKS OF GOD; AND OF HIS DECREES IN GENERAL.

HAVING considered the nature, perfections, and persons in God, I shall now proceed to treat of his acts and operations; which are such as are worthy of a Being possessed of those perfections which have been described; and so must be worthy of our notice. God is *actus purus et simplicissimus;* he is all act; if one may so say; having nothing passive in him; and therefore must be active and operative; *My Father worketh hitherto, and I work*, John v. 17. in which words there is a term fixed, unto which God had worked, the then present time Christ spoke them; but none from whence he began to work: he had not only worked in providence till then, since the creation, and not only at the creation, but from all eternity; his active and eternal mind had always been at work; the thoughts of his heart were always employed in devising, forming, and settling things that should be done in time; and as the three divine Persons were taking infinite delight and pleasure in each other, so in the foreviews of what would be done by each of them in time, for the setting forth and manifestation of their glory.

The acts and works of God may be distinguished into internal and external. The *external* acts and works of God, are such as are done in time, visible to us, or known by us; as creation, providence, redemption, &c. His *internal* acts and works, which will be first considered, and are what were done in eternity, are commonly distinguished into personal and essential. *Personal* acts are such as are peculiar to each person, and distinguish the one from the other; and which have been taken notice of already, in treating of the doctrine of the Trinity. *Essential* acts are such as are common to them all; for as they have the same nature and essence, they have the same understanding, will, and affections; and the same acts appropriate to these belong unto them, both with respect to themselves and the creatures they meant to make; that is to say, they mutually know one another, love each other, and will each other's happiness and glory; and have the same knowledge of, will concerning, and affection for creatures to be brought into being by them; and among these internal acts of the mind of God, are his purposes and decrees; and these are *purposed in himself*, Eph. i. 9. for what is true of one of his purposes, is true of all; and that there are such in God is certain; and which respect, not only the affairs of grace, but those of providence; even the whole earth, and all things in it, Rom. ix. 11. Eph. i. 11. and iii. 11. Isa. xiv. 24, 27. and which go by various names in scripture; sometimes they are called *the thoughts of his heart;* these are the deep things of God, which lie in the inmost recesses of his mind; are only known by himself, and searched by his Spirit; as the thoughts of a man can only be known by the spirit of man within him, Psalm xxxiii. 11. Jer. xxix. 11. 1 Cor. ii. 10, 11. Sometimes they are called the *counsels* of God, said to be *of old*, ancient ones, even from eternity; and to be *faithfulness and truth;* faithfully and truly performed in time, Isa. xxv. 1. and their being so called does not suppose any degree of ignorance, or want of knowledge in God, or as if he was at a loss what to resolve upon; and therefore consulted with himself, or others, what was fittest to be determined on; but because such resolutions, that are taken after mature deliberation and consultation, are generally formed in the wisest manner; and commonly most successful in the execution of them; therefore the purposes of God, being made with the highest wisdom, from thence they have the name of *counsels*. They are sometimes called *decrees*, and so we commonly call them; being the determinations of the mind of God; what he has fixed settled, and resolved upon, Dan. iv. 17. Zeph. ii. 2. and so the *determinate counsel* of God, Acts ii. 23. sometimes they are expressed by *preordination* and *predestination;* so Christ is said to be *foreordained* before the foundation of the world, 1 Pet. i. 20. and men are said to be *predestinated* to the adoption of children, and to an inheritance, Eph. i. 5, 11. that is, afore appointed thereunto in the decrees of God; and often they are signified by his *will* and *pleasure;* by the *counsel of his will;* and by his *counsel* and *pleasure*, Rom. ix. 19. Eph. i. 11. Isa. xlvi. 10. they containing and expressing his mind and will; what it is his pleasure should be. Now concerning these may be observed,

First, The proof to be given of them, that there are decrees and purposes in God; not merely ideas of things future, but settled determinations concerning them; which may be evinced from the nature and perfections of God. God is a Spirit, uncreated, infinite, operative, and active: he is a pure act, as before observed; and must have been for ever active in himself; his eternal mind must always have been employed, and continually at work; as the mind of man is never without its thoughts, and the understanding has its acts, and the will its volitions; so God never was without the thoughts of his heart, the acts of his understanding, and the volitions of his will. The *Sovereignty* of God over all, and his *independency*, clearly shew, that whatever is done in time, is according to his decrees in eternity; for if any thing comes to pass without the will of God, or contrary to it, or what he has not commanded, that is decreed, Lam. iii. 37. how is he a sovereign Being, that does according to his will in heaven and in earth, and works *all* things

after the counsel of his will? Dan. iv. 35. Eph. i. 11. and if any thing is by chance and fortune, or the mere effect of second causes, and of the free will of men, independent of the will of God, and if he works under these, in subserviency to them, and takes his measures of operation from them, then he must be dependent on them; and how then can it be said with truth, that *of him, and through him, and to him, are all things?* Rom. xi. 36. The *immutability* of God requires eternal decrees in him, concerning every thing that is in time; for if anything is done in time, that did not fall under his notice and will in eternity, this must be new to him, and produce a change in him; or if an after-will in time arises in him, respecting anything he would have done, which he willed not before, this argues a change in him; whereas, in him there is no *variableness, nor shadow of turning*. The *knowledge* of God, supposes and clearly proves and establishes the decrees of God; he is *a God of knowledge, and by him actions are weighed,* 1 Sam. ii. 13. he has knowledge of all actions done in time; and such an exact knowledge of them, as if they were weighed by him, and before him; and this knowledge of them is not successive, as they are performed; *Known unto God are all his works from the beginning,* or from eternity, Acts xv. 18. both what he would do himself, and what he wills to be done by others: and this knowledge is founded on his decrees; he knows that such and such things will be, because he has determined they shall be. Once more, the *wisdom* of God makes it necessary that there should be eternal purposes and decrees in him, concerning things future; he is the all-wise and only wise God, and in wisdom makes all his works; which cannot be supposed to be made without previous thoughts and determinations concerning them: what wise man undertakes a building, without first determining what it shall be, of what materials it shall be made, in what form and manner, as well as for what end? And can we imagine that the all-wise God, who builds all things, should go about them without preconcerted measures, and settled determinations concerning them; *Who is wonderful in counsel, and excellent in working?* Isa. xxviii. 29.

Secondly, The extent of the decrees and purposes of God, deserve notice and consideration: and they reach to all things that come to pass in the world, from the beginning to the end of it. The world, and all things in it, were created by and according to the will and pleasure of God, Rev. iv. 11. The heavens, their creation, stability, duration, and passing away, and succeeded by new heavens, are by a decree that cannot pass, Psalm cxlviii. 6. The earth, in its different forms, before and after the flood, its continuance, and final destruction, with the day or time of it, are by the word or decree of God, 2 Pet. iii. 5, 6, 7, 10. The sea, and the place the receptacle of it, and its boundary, the sand, which its waters cannot pass, are by a perpetual decree, Job xxxviii. 10, 11. Prov. viii. 29. Jer. v. 21. The rain which is exhausted out of it, has its decree; and there is not a shower falls but by the will of God; whether it be given as a mercy, to make fruitful seasons, or whether it be withheld, or poured down in too great plenty, in a way of judgment; it is all according to the word, will, and decree of God, Job xxviii. 26. Amos iv. 7, 8. and v. 8. The peopling of the world; the distinction of nations; the rise, progress, and ruin of states, kingdoms, and empires, are all according to the decrees of God; even every petty state and kingdom, as well as the four grand monarchies; the destruction of the first of which, the Babylonian monarchy, as it was by the decree of the Watchers, and by the demand of the holy Ones; that is, by the decree of the most High; so the origin of it, and its rise to all its glory and grandeur; and the same is true of all the rest; see Deut. xxxii. 8. Dan. ii. 38—44. and iv. 17, 20. Particularly, the people of Israel, a select and distinguished people from all others; their original from Abraham, Isaac, and Jacob; their servitude in a land not theirs, for four hundred years; their settlement in the land of Canaan; their government under judges and kings; and their several captivities, were all determined; as well as their last destruction, when the desolations determined, were poured upon the desolate; and so is their future conversion and restoration, Gen. xv. 14. Exod. xv. 17. Dan. ix. 26, 27. Rom. xi. 25, 26. The church of God, in its different states, under the legal dispensation; the time appointed of the Father, when it was under tutors and governors, Gal. iv. 1, 2. and under the gospel-dispensation, the world to come, the time of reformation, when all things became new; the former covenant waxed old, and vanished away, and the ordinances of it, and new ones took place; and which continues to be the accepted time and day of salvation; all are by divine appointment. The persecutions and sufferings of the church of Christ under the ten Roman emperors, signified by ten days, Rev. ii. 10. and under Rome papal, for a time, and times, and half a time; even forty-two months, or one thousand, two hundred and sixty days or years; the time of the church's being in the wilderness, and of the witnesses prophesying in sackcloth, and of the reign of antichrist, are all fixed by the decree of God; and when the time is up, the Angel will swear by the living God, that time shall be no longer; that is, antichristian time, Rev. x. 6. and xi. 2, 3. and xii. 14. and xiii. 5. as well as the glory of the church in the latter day; for which there is a set time; and which God will hasten, in his own time; when there will be great light and prosperity, numerous conversions, a great spread of the gospel, and an enlargement of the interest of Christ, and much purity and righteousness, Psalm cii. 13. Isa. lx. 1—22. In short, every thing respecting all the individuals of the world, that have been, are, or shall be, all correspond with the decrees of God, and are according to them; men's coming into the world, the time of it, and all circumstances attending it; all events and occurrences they meet with, throughout the whole time of life; their places of habitation, their stations, calling, and employment; their circumstances of riches and poverty, of health and sickness, adversity and prosperity; their time of going out of the world, with every thing attending that; all are according to the determinate counsel and will of God, Eccles. iii. 1, 2. and vii. 14. Acts xvii. 26. Job xiv. 5. and particularly all that relate to the people of God, as well their spiritual and eternal, as temporal concerns; their election of God, their redemption by Christ, their effectual vocation, which is according to the purpose of God; the time, manner, and means of it; all their changes in life; their afflictions and distresses, deliverances, and salvations from temptation and trouble; yea, even the final state and condition of good men and bad men, is settled and determined: but this will be more particularly considered under the special decrees of God, respecting rational creatures. All that Christ was to be, do and suffer for his people, are what the hand and counsel of God before determined; his incarnation, the time of his coming into the world; all that he met with, from the hand of God, from men and devils, whilst in it; his sufferings and death, and all circumstances attending the same, Gal. iv. 4. Acts iv. 28. and ii. 23. Luke xxii. 22, 37. In a word, every thing that comes to pass in this world, from the beginning to the end of it, is pre-ordained; every thing, good and bad: good by his effective decrees; that is, such by which he determines what he will do himself, or shall be done by others; and evil things, by his permissive decrees, by which he suffers things to be done; and which he overrules for his own glory; yea, things contingent, which, with respect to second causes, may seem to be, or not be, as the free actions of men; such as the prophecies, founded on decrees, concerning the names of Josiah and Cyrus, and of actions being performed by them of their own free will, many hundreds of years before they were born; nay, even things of the least importance, as well as the greatest; the hairs of men's heads are numbered; two sparrows, not worth more than a farthing, and yet fall not to the ground, without the knowledge, will, and purpose of God, Matt. x. 29, 30.

Thirdly, The properties of the purposes and decrees of God, may next be considered.——1. As they are internal acts, they are *immanent* ones; they are in God, and remain and abide in him; and whilst they are so, they put nothing into actual being, they are concerned about, until they bring forth, or are brought forth into execution: then they pass upon their respective objects, terminate on them, and issue in actual operation; and then they are called *transient* acts; and till then they are secrets in God's breast, and are unknown to men.——2. They are eternal; as God himself is eternal, so are they; for, as some divines express it, God's decrees are himself decreeing, and therefore if he is from everlasting to everlasting, they are so likewise; if the knowledge of God, respecting all his works, is from the beginning, or from eternity, which arises from his decrees, then they themselves must be from eternity; and if the particular decree of election was before the foundation of the world, as it was, Eph. i. 4. the same must be true of all the decrees of God, which are all of a date; for no new will, nor new act of the will of God, arise in him in time.——3. The decrees of God are most free; they are the free acts of his will without any force or compulsion, and are not influenced by any motive from without himself; as "he will have mercy on whom he will have mercy," and exercises it freely, and on whom he pleases; so he freely decreed to have mercy as he pleased; as he hides the things of the gospel from the wise and prudent, and reveals them unto babes, as seems good in his sight; he freely determined so to do: indeed, having made those decrees there is a necessity of the performance of them; but the making of them was quite free.——4. They are most wise decrees; as God is a wise Being, and does all his works in wisdom, so his decrees are laid in the deepest wisdom; which, though unsearchable by us, and may be unaccountable to us; yet there is, as the apostle expresses it, speaking of them, "a depth of the riches, both of the wisdom and knowledge of God in them," Rom. xi. 33. ——5. They are immutable and unalterable; they are the mountains of brass, out of which come forth the horses and chariots, the executioners of divine providence; signified by mountains, for their immoveableness, and by mountains of brass, for their greater stability and firmness, Zech. vi. 1—8. The decrees of the Medes and Persians, when signed and sealed, were not to be changed or altered; but these are more unchangeable and unalterable than they were: we read of the immutability of the counsel of God, Heb. vi. 17. his purposes and decrees, which, like himself, are the same to-day, yesterday, and for ever; without any variableness, or shadow of turning.——6. The decrees of God are always effectual; they cannot be frustrated or disannulled, or become of no effect; *For the Lord of hosts hath purposed, and who shall disannul it? and his hand is stretched out, and who shall turn it back?* Isa. xiv. 27. The purposes of men are often frustrated, through want of foresight, not being able to foresee what may turn up, which may hinder the execution of their designs; but no unforeseen accident can arise to put any stop in the way of executing the decrees of God; since all things are at once in his eternal view, who sees the end from the beginning: men sometimes fail of bringing their resolutions into execution, for want of power; but God is omnipotent, and is able to do, and therefore does whatever he pleases; he is in one mind, and none can turn him; and what he desires, he does; his counsel stands, and he does all his pleasure; and the thoughts of his heart are to all generations. To say no more; the end of the decrees of God is his own glory; he has *made*, that is, appointed *all things for himself*, for the glorifying his perfections, Prov. xvi. 4. there may be, and are, inferior ends, as the good of his creatures, &c. but his glory is the supreme end, and all others are subordinate to it.

CHAP. II.

OF THE SPECIAL DECREES OF GOD, RELATING TO RATIONAL CREATURES, ANGELS, AND MEN; AND PARTICULARLY OF ELECTION.

THE special decrees of God respecting rational creatures, commonly go under the name of *predestination;* though this sometimes is taken in a large sense, to express every thing that God has predetermined; and so it takes in all that has been observed in the preceding chapter; which some call eternal providence, of which, temporary providence is the execution; for with God there is not only a provision of things future, but a provision for the certain bringing them to pass; and the counsel and will of God is the source and spring of all things, and the rule and measure according to which he works, Eph. i. 11. but predestination is usually considered as consisting of two parts, and including the two branches of election and reprobation, both with respect to angels and men; for each of these have place in both. Angels; some of them are called *elect* angels, 2 Tim. v. 21. others are said to be *reserved in chains*, in the chains of God's purposes and providence, *unto* the *judgment* of the great day, 2 Pet. ii. 4. Men; some of them are vessels of mercy, afore-prepared for glory; others vessels of wrath, fitted for destruction; some are the *election*, or the elect persons, that obtain righteousness, life, and salvation; and others are the *rest* that are left in, and given up to blindness, Rom. ix. 22, 23. and xi. 7. Though sometimes predestination only respects that branch of it called election, and the predestinated signify only the elect; for who else are called, justified, and glorified, enjoy adoption and the heavenly inheritance? not, surely, the non-elect, Rom. viii. 29, 30. Eph. i. 5, 11. This branch of predestination, election, must be considered first; I shall begin with,

I. The election of angels; of this the scriptures speak but sparingly, and therefore the less need to be said concerning it: that there are some angels that are elect is certain, from the proof already given; there is a similarity between their election and the election of men; though in some things there appears a little difference.—— 1. The election of angels, as well as of men, is of God; he is the efficient cause of it; it is God that has chosen them, and distinguished them from others, and therefore they are called the *angels of God*, Luke xii. 8, 9. not merely because they are his creatures, so are the evil angels; but because they are his chosen, his favourites, and appointed to be happy with him to all eternity.——2. Their election, as that of men, lies in a distinction and separation from the rest of their species; they are not only distinguished from them by their characters, the one being holy angels, the others the angels that sinned; but by their state and condition, the one being preserved from apostasy, and continued in their first estate; the other left to fall into sin, and from their former state, and reserved unto judgment. —— 3. In their election they were considered as on an equal foot with others not elected, as men are; as men are considered, when chosen, as in the pure mass, having done neither good nor evil, so were angels; this must be out of all question, with respect to them, since the elect angels never fell, never were in any corrupt state, and could not be so considered: besides, their preservation from apostasy, and their confirmation, by grace, in the state in which they were created, are in consequence of their election; and therefore must be previous to the fall of the rest, who, with them, must be considered in the pure mass of creatureship; wherefore the choice of the one, and the leaving of the other, must be entirely owing to the sovereign will of God.—— 4. Their election, though it is not said to be made in Christ, as the election of men; nor could it be made in him, considered as Mediator; since they having never sinned against God, and offended him, they needed him not to mediate between God and them, and to make peace and reconciliation; yet they might be chosen in him, as they seem to be, as an Head of conservation; as an Head both of eminence to rule over them, protect and preserve them in their state; and of influence, to communicate grace and strength to them; to confirm them in their state in which they are; for Christ is *the head of all principality and power*, Col. ii. 10.——5. Though the angels are not chosen to salvation as men are, as that signifies a deliverance from sin and misery; seeing they never sinned, and so were never in a miserable condition, and needed no Saviour and Redeemer; yet they are chosen to happiness, to communion with God now, whose face they ever behold; and to a confirmed state of holiness and impeccability, and to the enjoyment of God, and the society of elect men to all eternity.

II. The election of men to grace and glory, is next to be considered; and it may be proper in the first place to take some notice of the election of Christ, as man and mediator; who is God's first and chief elect; and is, by way of eminency, called his elect; *Behold, my servant, whom I uphold, mine elect, in whom my soul delighteth*, Isa. xlii. 1. and oftentimes the chosen of God, Psalm lxxxix. 3. Luke xxiii. 35. 1 Pet. ii. 4. Which character not only denotes his choiceness and excellency, and the high esteem he is in with God; who, though disallowed, disesteemed, and rejected by men, is chosen of God, and precious; but either, 1. It respects the choice of the human nature of Christ to the grace of union with him as the Son of God. God prepared a body, or an human nature for him, in his eternal purposes and decrees; in the book of which all the members thereof were written; which in continuance were fashioned, when, as yet, before there were none of them, Heb. x. 5. Psalm cxxxix. 16. Among all the individuals of human nature, which rose up in the divine mind, to be brought into being by him, this was singled out from among them, and appointed to union with the second Person in the Godhead; this was sanctified, and set apart, and sent into the world; in which Joseph was a type of it, who was separated from his brethren: and hence this human nature of Christ was anointed with the Holy Ghost above his fellows, and had the gifts and graces of the Spirit without measure; and was raised to such honour and dignity, as none of the angels ever were, or will be, Heb. i. 13. ——or, 2. The character of elect, as given to Christ, respects the choice of him to his office as Mediator, in which he was set up, and with which he was invested, and had the glory of it before the world began. He was first chosen and set up as an Head; and then his people were chosen, as members of him; he was chosen to be the Saviour of the body, the church; as they are appointed to salvation by him, he is appointed to be the Saviour of them; this is meant by laying help on one that is mighty; and as their salvation is through his sufferings and death, he was foreordained, before the foundation of the world, to be the slain Lamb; through whose precious blood their redemption would be obtained; he was set forth, in the eternal decree and purpose of God, to be the propitiation for sin, to make atonement and satisfaction for it, and procure the pardon of it, 1 Pet. i. 18, 19, 20. Rom. iii. 25. Christ is appointed to be the judge of quick and dead; as well as a day is appointed in which God will judge the world in righteousness, by the man Christ Jesus, whom he has ordained for that purpose, Acts x. 42. and xvii. 31. But what will now be chiefly attended to, and what the scriptures speak so largely of, is the election of men in Christ unto eternal life.

Some are of opinion that this doctrine of election, admitting it to be true, should not be published, neither preached from the pulpit, nor handled in schools and academies, nor treated of in the writings of men; the reasons they give, are because it is a secret, and secret things belong to God; and because it tends to fill men's minds with doubts about their salvation, and to bring them into distress, and even into despair; and because some may make a bad use of it, to indulge themselves in a sinful course of life, and argue, that if they are elected they shall be saved, let them live as they may, and so it opens a door to all licentiousness: but these reasons are frivolous and groundless; the doctrine of election is no secret, it is clearly and fully revealed, and written as with a sunbeam in the sacred scriptures; it is true indeed, it cannot be said of particular persons, that such a man is elected, and such a man is reprobated; and especially when both appear to be in a state of unregeneracy; yet when men, in a judgment of charity, may be hoped to be called by grace, they may be concluded to be the elect of God, though it cannot be said with precision; and on the other hand, there may be black marks of reprobation on some men, or at least things have such a very dark aspect on them, that we are apt to say, when we hear a man cursing and swearing, and see him in all excess of wickedness with boldness and impudence, what a reprobate creature is this; though indeed no man, be he ever so vile, is out of the reach of powerful and efficacious grace; and therefore it cannot be absolutely said that he is rejected of God: and whereas there may be only the appearance of grace, and not the truth of it, in such that profess to have it; it cannot be said with certainty that such an one is an elect person, yet in charity it may be so concluded; however, a truly gracious man may know for himself his *election of God*, as the apostle affirms; and that in this way, the *gospel* being *come to him, not in word only, but in power, and in the Holy Ghost,* 1 Thess. i. 4, 5. who by means of it has begun, and will carry on and perform the work of grace in him; wherefore such persons will not be filled with doubts and fears about their salvation, nor be led into distress and despair through the doctrine of election; nor need any be distressed about it that are inquiring the way of salvation, or have any knowledge of it; for the first question to be put to a man by himself, is not, am I elected; but, am I born again? am I a new creature? am I called by the grace of God, and truly converted? If a man can arrive to satisfaction in this matter, he can have no doubt about his election; that then is a clear case and out of all question. The doctrine of regeneration, which asserts that a man must be born again, or he cannot see and enter into the kingdom of heaven, may as well be objected to, as that of election; since it is as difficult to come to satisfaction about a man's regeneration, as about his election; and when once the one is a clear case, the other must be likewise; and when it is, what thankfulness and joy does it produce! And if the apostle thought himself bound to give thanks to God for his choice of the Thessalonians to salvation; how much more reason had he to bless the God and Father of Christ for his own election, as he does 2 Thess. ii. 13. Eph. i. 3, 4. With what exultation and triumph may a believer in Christ take up those words of the apostle, and use them with application to himself, *Who shall lay anything to the charge of God's elect?* Rom. viii. 33. yea our Lord Jesus Christ exhorts his disciples, rather to *rejoice* that their *names* were *written in heaven,* than that the spirits were subject to them, or that they were possessed of extraordinary gifts, as to cast out devils. With great truth and propriety it is expressed in the seventeenth article of the church of England, that the consideration of this doctrine is *full of sweet, pleasant* and *unspeakable comfort* to *godly* persons: and as for the charge of licentiousness, what is there but what a wicked man may abuse to encourage himself in sin? as even the patience and longsuffering of God; ungodly men may turn the grace of God into lasciviousness, and every doctrine of it; and so this, contrary to its nature, use, and tendency. Strange! that this doctrine should of itself lead to licentiousness, when the thing itself, contained in it, is the source of all holiness; men are chosen according to this doctrine to be holy; they are chosen through sanctification of the Spirit, which is secured by this decree as certainly as salvation itself; wherefore those reasons are not sufficient to intimidate and deter us from receiving this doctrine, professing and publishing it; and the rather, since it is the doctrine of Christ and his apostles, frequently suggested and declared by them; what means else when our Lord speaks of the elect of God, for whose sake the days of tribulation should be shortened; and that it was impossible the elect should be deceived; and that God will avenge his own elect? Matt. xxiv. 22, 24. Luke xviii. 7. how clearly and fully does the apostle Paul enlarge on this doctrine of election in Rom. ix. and xi. and in Eph. i. and 2 Thess. ii. and in other places! and since it is so plentifully declared in the Bible, and is a part of scripture given by the inspiration of God, and is profitable for doctrine, and is written for our learning, to teach us humility, to depress the pride of man, and to magnify the sovereign grace of God in his salvation; we need not be ashamed of it, nor ought we to conceal it; and the apostle exhorts to make our *election* as well as calling *sure*, 2 Pet. i. 10. but how should men do this, if they are not taught the doctrine of it; led into an acquaintance with it; instructed into the truth, nature, and use of it, and the way and means whereby it is to be made sure? I proceed then,

First, To observe the phrases by which it is expressed in scripture, whereby may be learnt what is the true meaning of the words *election* and *elect*, as used in scripture with respect to this doctrine. It is expressed by being ordained to eternal life, Acts xiii. 48. *As many as were ordained to eternal life, believed;* by which ordination is meant no other than the predestination, choice, and appointment of men to everlasting life and salvation by Jesus Christ; and from whence it appears that this is of particular persons, of some and not all, though many; that it is not to temporary privileges and enjoyments, but to grace and glory; and that faith is not the cause, but the sure and certain fruit and effect of it; and that both eternal life through Christ, and believing in him, are infallibly secured by this act of grace. Some, in order to evade the force and evidence of these words in favour of election, would have them rendered, *as many as were disposed for eternal life, believed;* but this is not agreeable to the use of the word throughout the book of the Acts by the divine historian, where it always signifies determination and appointment, and not disposition; and so by our translators it is rendered *determined* in Acts xv. 2. and *appointed* in chap. xxii. 10. and xxviii. 23. and here *preordained* in the *vulgate* Latin version, and by Arias Montanus; and besides, there are no good dispositions for eternal life in men before faith; whatsoever is not of faith, is sin; and men, in a state of unbelief and unregeneracy, are foolish and disobedient, serving divers lusts and pleasures; living in malice, hateful, and hating one another; without hope, and without God in the world; and injurious to good men, Rom. xiv. 23. Tit. iii. 3. Eph. ii. 12. 1 Tim. i. 13. and admitting there may be what may be called dispositions for eternal life; let a desire of it, and seeking for it, be accounted such; this may be where faith in Christ does not follow; as in the young man, who asked what he must do to obtain it; and yet, when instructed by Christ, was so far from receiving his instructions, and believing him, that he turned his back on him, and went away from him sorrowful, Matt. xix. 16, 22. Let an attentive hearing of the word be reckoned a good disposition for eternal life; this was found in many of Christ's hearers, and yet they believed not the report he made, of which he complains; and it is highly probable, that many of those attentive hearers of him, were, in a few days, among those that cried, Crucify him, crucify him, Luke xix. 48. and xxiii. 18, 21. Isa. liii. 1. and after all, one would think that the Jews, who were externally religious, and were expecting the Messiah; and especially the *devout* and honourable women, were more disposed for eternal life, than the ignorant and idolatrous Gentiles; and yet the latter rejoiced at hearing the word, glorified it, and believed; when the former did not, but persecuted the preachers of it: from whence it follows, that the faith of the believing Gentiles did not spring from previous dispositions to eternal life; but was the fruit and effect of divine ordination.

This act of God is also expressed by the *names* of persons being *written in heaven*, and in the *book of life*, called, *the Lamb's book of life;* because his name stands first in it, was present at the writing of it, and is concerned in that eternal life which it has respect unto, Luke x. 20. Heb. xii. 22. Phil. iv. 3. Rev. xiii. 8. All which shews that it is an act of God in heaven, and respects the happiness of men there; is of particular persons, whose names are in a special manner known of God, and as distinct from others; and is sure and certain, and will abide. But the more common phrases used concerning it, are those of being *chosen* and *elected;* hence the objects of it are called God's *elect* and the *election;* that is, persons elected, Eph. i. 4. 2 Thess. ii. 13. Rom. viii. 33. and xi. 7. which clearly imply, that only some, and not all men, are the objects of it; *I speak not of you all,* says Christ; *I know whom I have chosen,* John xiii. 18. not all, but some of you; where all are taken, whether persons or things, no choice is made; if some are chosen, others are not, but left: and in this case the number chosen is but few; *Many are called, but few chosen,* Matt. xx. 16. hence those that are chosen, are called *a remnant according to the election of grace;* and those that are not chosen, *the rest* that are left, Rom. xi. 5, 7. Wherefore the election treated of is not,

1. An election of a nation to some external privileges, as the people of Israel, who were chosen of God to be a special people, above all people on the face of the earth; not for their quantity or quality, their number or their goodness; but because such was the pleasure of God: but this choice of them as a nation, was only to some outward benefits and blessings; as, besides the good land of Canaan, the word, and worship, and ordinances of God, with others, mentioned in Rom. ix. 4, 5. but in the same context it is observed, that they were not all Israel, or God's elect, redeemed and called people, in the most special sense; nor all children of God by adopting grace; nor were all predestinated to the adoption of children by Christ: it was only a remnant of them that were of this sort, which should be eternally saved; and whom, if God had not reserved, they had been as Sodom and Gomorrah, ver. 6, 7, 8, 27, 29. And so this nation of ours is selected and distinguished from many others,

by various blessings of goodness, and particularly by having the means of grace; yet all the individuals of it cannot be thought to be the objects of election to special grace, and eternal glory.

2. Nor of an election to offices; as the sons of the house of Aaron were chosen to minister, in the office of priests, to the Lord;. and as Saul was chosen to be king over Israel; and the twelve were chosen to be the apostles of Christ; for there were many in the priestly office very bad men; and Saul behaved so ill as to be rejected of God from being king, that is, from the kingdom being continued in his family; and though Christ chose twelve to be his apostles, one of them was a devil: so that though those were chosen to offices, and even to the highest offices in the church and state, yet not to eternal life.

3. Nor of an election of whole bodies and communities of men, under the character of churches, to the enjoyment of the means of grace: Eph. i. 4. is no instance of this. It is not certain the apostle wrote that epistle to the Ephesians, as to a church, but to some there described, as saints and faithful in Christ Jesus; and it is quite certain, that those who he says were *chosen in Christ*, were not the Ephesians only, but others also; the apostle, and others, who were not members of that church, yet shared in that grace, and other blessings aftermentioned, and were they that first trusted in Christ; and though the Ephesians may be included, yet it is not said of them as a church; besides, the phrase of being *chosen in Christ*, is sometimes used of a single person, and so is not appropriate to communities and churches, Rom. xvi. 13. To all which may be added, that those said to be chosen in Christ, are not said to be chosen as a church, or to be one, or to church-privileges; but to holiness here, and to a blameless state, or a state of perfection hereafter; even to grace and glory. Nor is the character of *elect*, given to the Colossians, chap. iii. 12. given to them as a church; for the same may be observed of them as of the Ephesians, that they are not wrote to as a church; but described by the same epithets as they are; and if they were, this might be said of them in a judgment of charity, since they all of them professed faith in Christ; and the greater part of them, doubtless, in reality were possessed of it, as a fruit and effect, and so an evidence of their election; by which the apostle enforces their mutual duties to one another. And in like manner the Thessalonians are said to be chosen of God, and to know their election of God, since the gospel was come to them, attended with the power and Spirit of God, 1 Thess. i. 4, 5. 2 Thess. ii. 13. and all of them had made a profession of Christ, and therefore it might be charitably hoped they were the elect of God; not chosen merely to outward means; but, as it is said, to salvation by Christ, and to the obtaining of his glory. And when the apostle Peter speaks of some he writes to as elect, according to the foreknowledge of God, and as a chosen generation, 1 Pet. i. 2. and ii. 9. he does not write to them, and speak of them, as a church; for he writes to strangers, scattered abroad in several countries; nor as chosen barely to the means of grace and outward privileges, but to grace and glory; since they are said to be chosen *through sanctification of the Spirit, unto obedience, and sprinkling of the blood of Jesus.*

4. Nor is this act of election under consideration, to be understood of the effectual vocation of particular persons; though that is sometimes expressed by choosing men out of the world; when they are separated and distinguished from the men of it; and by choosing, that is, calling the foolish things of the world, and by choosing the poor of it, who become rich in faith, and appear to be heirs of the kingdom, John xv. 19. 1 Cor. i. 26, 27. James ii. 5. the reason of which is, because vocation is a certain fruit and effect of election, and is a sure and certain evidence of it; *For whom* God did *predestinate, them he also called*, Rom. viii. 30. But then election and vocation differ, as the cause and the effect, the tree and its fruit, a thing and the evidence of it. But,

5. This is to be understood of the choice of certain persons by God, from all eternity, to grace and glory; it is an act by which men are chosen of God's good will and pleasure, before the world was, to holiness and happiness, to salvation by Christ, to partake of his glory, and to enjoy eternal life, as the free gift of God through him, Eph. i. 4. 2 Thess. ii. 13. Acts xiii. 48. And this is the first and foundation-blessing; according to which all spiritual blessings are dispensed; and is, by the apostle, set at the front of them all; and is the first link in the golden chain of man's salvation, Eph. i. 3, 4. Rom. viii. 30.

Secondly, The next thing to be considered is, by whom election is made, and in whom it is made: it is made by God, and it is made in Christ. 1. It is made by God, as the efficient cause of it; God, who is a sovereign Being, who does and may do whatever he pleases in heaven and in earth, among angels and men; and has a right to do what he will with his own; as with his own things, temporal and spiritual blessings; so with his own creatures. Shall he be denied that which every man thinks he has a right unto and does? do not kings choose their own ministers; masters their servants; and every man his own favourites, friends, and companions? And may not God choose whom he pleases to communion with him, both here and hereafter; or to grace and glory? He does this, and therefore it is called *election of God;* of which God is the efficient cause, 1 Thess. i. 4. and the persons chosen are called *God's elect,* Rom. viii. 33. Luke xviii. 7. This act is sometimes, and for the most part, ascribed to God the Father, the God and Father of our Lord Jesus Christ; as he is said to bless men with spiritual blessings, so to choose them in Christ, before the foundation of the world, Eph. i. 3, 4. and the persons chosen are said to be *elect, according to the fore-knowledge of God the Father, through sanctification of the Spirit, unto obedience, and sprinkling of the blood of Jesus Christ,* 1 Pet. i. 2. where the Person that chooses is not only described as the Father, but is distinguished from the Spirit, through whose sanctification, and from Jesus Christ, to whose obedience, and the sprinkling of whose blood, men are chosen by him. Sometimes it is ascribed to Christ, and he takes it to himself, *I speak not of you all; I know whom I have chosen,* John xiii. 18. this cannot be understood of Christ's choosing his disciples to the office of apostleship, for all the twelve were chosen to that; but of his choosing them to eternal life; and this is what he could not say of them all, for one of them was the son of perdition; and hence the elect are called Christ's elect; not only because chosen in him, and given to him, but because chosen by him; *He* (the Son of man) *shall send his angels—and they shall gather together his elect from the four winds,* Matt. xxiv. 30, 31. Nor is the blessed Spirit to be excluded; for since he has a place in the decree of the means, in order that the end may be attained, and has so much to do in the blessings, gifts, and operations of grace, leading on to the execution of the decree; he must have a concern with the Father and the Son in the act itself, as the efficient cause of it. And this now being the act of God, it is for ever; for whatever God does in a way of special grace, it is for ever; it is unchangeable and irrevocable; men may choose some to be their favourites and friends for a while, and then alter their minds, and choose others in their room; but God never acts such a part, he is in one mind, and none can turn him; his purpose, according to election, or with respect to that, stands sure, firm, and unalterable.——2. This act is made in Christ, *according as he hath chosen us in him,* Eph. i. 4. Election does not find men in Christ, but puts them there; it gives them a being in him, and union to him; which is the foundation of their open being in Christ at conversion, which is the manifestation and evidence of this; *If any man be in Christ,* even in the secret way, by electing grace, *he is a new creature,* sooner or later; which is an evidence of it; for when he becomes a new creature, this shews him to have been in Christ before, from whence this grace proceeds; but these two, an open and secret being in Christ, differ in this, that the one is in time, and but a little while ago, the other from eternity; the one is the evidence of the other; *I knew a man in Christ above fourteen years ago,* says the apostle, 2 Cor. xii. 2. meaning himself; who was, about that time, and not before, called, converted, and become a believer in Christ, and so had open being in Christ; and, in this sense, one saint may be in Christ before another; *Salute Andronicus and Junia—who also were in Christ before me,* says the same apostle, Rom. xvi. 7. they being called and converted before he was; but with respect to electing grace, one is not before another, the whole body of the elect being chosen together in Christ; which is the sense of the text in Ephesians: and which is not to be understood of being chosen for the sake of him; for though they are predestinated to be conformed to his image, that he may be the first-born among many brethren, and in all things have the pre-eminence; and unto salvation by him, that he may have the glory of it; and to the obtaining of his glory, partake of it, and have communion with him for evermore, that he may have praise from them to all eternity: yet not his merits, his blood, righteousness, and sacrifice, not his obedience, sufferings, and death, are the cause of election; these are the meritorious cause of redemption, forgiveness of sin, and justification, and salvation; not of election: the reasons why men are elected, are not because Christ has shed his blood, died for them, redeemed and saved them; but Christ has done all this for them because they are elect; *I lay down my life for the sheep*, says Christ, John x. 15. sheep and elect are terms convertible, and signify the the same persons, even such before they are called and converted; as appears from the following verse: now it is not Christ's laying down his life for them makes them sheep, and elect; they are so previous to that; but because they are sheep, and chosen ones in Christ, and given him by his Father, therefore he laid down his life for them. Christ himself is the object of election; he is styled God's elect; and is said to be foreordained, before the foundation of the world, to be the Saviour and Redeemer of his people, Isa. xlii. 1. 1 Pet. i. 20. Now, though as a divine Person, he is, with his Father, the efficient cause of election; yet, as Mediator, he is the means, by his obedience, sufferings, and death, of executing that decree: men are chosen in him as their Head, and they as members of him; not one before another; he and they are chosen together in the same decree; they are given to him in it, and he to them; they are put into his hands, and preserved in him; and hence have a secret being in him, and union to him; hence they partake of all grace and spiritual blessings; they are first *of God in Christ* by electing grace, and then he is made every thing to them; and they receive every thing from him they want, 1 Cor. i. 30.

Thirdly, The objects of election are to be next inquired after, who are men; for with such only is now our concern; and these not as under such and such characters, as called, converted, believers in Christ, holy and good men, and persevering in faith and holiness unto the end; for they are not elected because they are called, converted, &c. but because they are elected they become all this; and if they are not elected, especially until they have persevered unto the end, I can see no need of their being elected at all; for when they have persevered unto the end, they are immediately in heaven, in the enjoyment of eternal life, and can have no need to be chose to it: and all these characters put together, only amount to such a proposition, that he that believes, and endures to the end, shall be saved. But God does not choose propositions, but persons; not characters, but men, nakedly and abstractedly considered; and these not all men, but some, as the nature of election, and the very sense of the word suggests: as in effectual vocation, the fruit and evidence of it, men are taken out of the world, and separated from the men among whom they have had their conversation in times past; so in election, they are distinguished from others; as in redemption, men are redeemed out of every kindred, tongue, people, and nation; so in election they are chosen out of the same: election and redemption are of the same persons, and are commensurate to each other; they are distinct from the rest of mankind; vessels of mercy, in distinction from vessels of wrath; a seed, a remnant, according to the election of grace; and election itself, as distinguished from the others, called the *rest*; whilst some are given up to believe a lie, that they might be damned, others being beloved of God, are chosen from the beginning to salvation by Christ; for certain it is, that all the individuals of mankind, neither partake of the means fixed in the decree of election, sanctification of the Spirit, and belief of the truth; nor attain to the end of it, which, with respect to men, is eternal life and happiness; for all men are not sanctified by the Spirit of God; nor have all men faith in Christ, the way, the truth, and the life; nor do all men enter into life, or are eternally saved; some go into everlasting punishment. But the number of the chosen ones is not confined to any particular nation: for as God is the God both of the Jews and of the Gentiles; so those whom he has in election prepared for glory; in consequence of which he calls them by his grace; these are not of the Jews only, but of the Gentiles also; and who are eventually, for the most part, the poor of this world, James ii. 5. men mean and despicable in the eyes of it; and these are but few in comparison, not only of the men of the world, but even of those that are externally called; *Many are called, but few are chosen*, Matt. xx. 16. they are but a little flock, it is the pleasure of their heavenly Father to give the kingdom to, prepared for them from the foundation of the world; though considered absolutely by themselves, they are a great multitude, which no man can number, Luke xii. 32. Rev. vii. 9.

And here is the proper place to discuss that question, Whether men were considered, in the mind of God, in the decree of election, as fallen or unfallen; as in the corrupt mass, through the fall; or in the pure mass of creatureship, previous to it; and as to be created? There are some that think that the latter, so considered, were the objects of election in the divine mind; who are called supralapsarians; though of these some are of opinion that man was considered, as to be created, or creatable; and others, as created, but not fallen. The former seems best; that of the vast number of individuals that came up in the divine mind, that his power could create, those that he meant to bring into being, he designed to glorify himself by them in some way or another; the decree of election, respecting any part of them, may be distinguished into the decree of the end, and the decree of the means. The decree of the end, respecting some, is either subordinate to their eternal happiness, or ultimate; which is more properly the end, the glory of God; and if both are put together, it is a state of everlasting communion with God, for the glorifying the riches of his sovereign grace and goodness, Eph. i. 5, 6. The decree of the means, includes the decree to create men, to permit them to fall, to recover them out of it through redemption by Christ, to sanctify them by the grace of the Spirit, and completely save them; and which are not to be reckoned as materially many decrees, but as making one formal decree; or they are not to be considered as subordinate, but co-ordinate means, and as making up one entire complete medium; for it is not to be supposed that God decreed to create man, that he might permit him to fall; nor that he decreed to permit him to fall, that he might redeem, sanctify, and save him; but he decreed all this that he might glorify his grace, mercy, and justice. And in this way of considering the decrees of God, they think they sufficiently obviate and remove the slanderous calumny cast upon them, with respect to the other branch of predestination, which leaves men in the same state when others are chosen, and that for the glory of God. Which calumny is, that according to them, God made man to damn him; whereas, according to their real sentiments, God decreed to make man, and made man, neither to damn him, nor save him, but for his own glory; which end is answered in them, some way or another. Again, they argue that the end is first in view, before the means; and the decree of the end is, in order of nature, before the decree of the means; and what is first in intention, is last in execution: now as the glory of God is the last in execution, it must be first in intention; wherefore men must be considered, in the decree of the end, as not yet created and fallen; since the creation and permission of sin, belong to the decree of the means; which, in order of nature, is after the decree of the end: and they add to this, that if God first decreed to create man, and suffer him to fall, and then, out of the fall chose some to grace and glory; he must decree to create man without an end, which is to make God to do what no wise man would; for when a man is about to do anything, he proposes an end, and then contrives and fixes on ways and means to bring about that end: and it cannot be thought that the all-wise and only-wise God should act otherwise; who does all his works in wisdom, and has wisely designed them for his own glory, Prov. xvi. 4. they think also that this way of conceiving and speaking of these things, best expresses the sovereignty of God in them; as declared in the ninth of the Romans; where he is said to will such and such things, for no other reason but because he wills them; and hence the objector to the sovereign decrees of God is brought in saying, *Why does he yet find fault? who hath resisted his will?* and the answer to it is taken from the sovereign power of the potter over his clay; to which is added, *What if God willing*, &c. to do this or that, who has anything to say against it? he is accountable to none, ver. 15, 19, 20, 22. And this way of reasoning is thought to suit better with the instance of Jacob and Esau, the *children being not yet born, and having done neither good nor evil, that the purpose of God, according to election, might stand*, ver. 10. than with supposing persons considered in predestination, as already created, and in the corrupt mass; and particularly it best suits with the unformed clay of the potter, out of which he makes one vessel to honour, and another to dishonour; on which Beza remarks, that if the apostle had considered mankind as corrupted, he would not have said, that some vessels were made to honour, and some to dishonour, but rather, that seeing all the vessels would be fit for dishonour, some were left in that dishonour, and others translated from dishonour to honour. They further observe, that elect angels could not be considered in the corrupt mass, when chosen; since they never fell, and therefore it is most reasonable, that as they, so those angels that were not chosen, were considered in the same pure mass of creatureship; and so in like manner men; to which they add the human nature of Christ, which is the object of election to a greater dignity than that of angels and men, could not be considered in the corrupt mass, since it fell not in Adam, nor never came into any corrupt state; and yet it was *chosen out of the people*, Psalm lxxxix. 19. and consequently the people out of whom it was chosen, must be considered as yet not fallen and corrupt; and who also were chosen in him, and therefore not so considered. These are hints of some of the arguments used on this side of the question.

On the other hand, those who are called sublapsarians, and are for men being considered as created and fallen, in the decree of election, urge, John xv. 19. *I have chosen you out of the world*. Now the world is full of wickedness, it lies in it, is under the power of the wicked one; the inhabitants of it live in sin, and all of them corrupt and abominable; and therefore they that are chosen out of them must be so too: but this text is not to be understood of eternal election, but of effectual vocation; by which men are called and separated from the world, among whom they have had their conversation before conversion, and according to the course of it have lived. They further observe, that the elect are called *vessels of mercy*; which supposes them to have been miserable, and so sinful, and to stand in need of mercy; and must be so considered in their election: but though through various means the elect are brought to happiness, which are owing to the mercy of God; such as the mission of Christ to save them, the forgiveness of their sins, their regeneration and salvation; and so fitly called *vessels of mercy*; yet it follows not that they were considered as in need of mercy in their choice to happiness. It is also said, that men are chosen in Christ as Mediator, Redeemer, and Saviour; which implies, that an offence is given and taken, and reconciliation is to be made, and redemption from sin, and the curse of the law broken, and complete salvation to be effected by Christ; all which supposes men to be sinful, as it does: but then men are chosen in Christ, not as the meritorious cause of election, but as the means, or medium, of bringing them to the happiness they are chosen to. It is, moreover, taken notice of, that the transitus in scripture, is not from election to creation, but to vocation, justification, adoption, sanctification, and salvation. But, for instance, can vocation be supposed without creation? It is thought that this way of considering men as fallen, in the decree of election, is more mild and gentle than the other, and best accounts for the justice of God; that since all are in the corrupt mass, it cannot be unjust in him to choose some out of it to undeserved happiness; and to leave others in it, who perish justly in it for their sins; or that since all are deserving of the wrath of God for sin, where is the injustice of appointing some not unto the wrath they deserve, but unto salvation by Christ, when others are fore-ordained to just condemnation and wrath for their sins? But on the other hand, what reason also can there be to charge God with injustice, that inasmuch as all are considered in the pure mass of creatureship, that some should be chosen in it, and others passed by in it; and both for his own glory? These are some of the principal arguments used on both sides; the difference is not so great as may be thought at first sight; for both agree in the main and material things in the doctrine of election; as,———1. That it is personal and particular, is of persons by name, whose names are written in the Lamb's book of life.———2. That it is absolute and unconditional, not depending on the will of men, nor on any thing to be done by the creature.———3. That it is wholly owing to the will and pleasure of God; and not to the faith, holiness, obedience, and good works of men; nor to a foresight of all or any of these.———4. That both elect, and non-elect, are considered alike, and are upon an equal foot in the decree of predestination; as those that are for the corrupt mass, they suppose that they are both considered in it equally alike, so that there was nothing in the one that was not in the other, which was a reason why the one should be chosen and the other left; so those that are for the pure mass, suppose both to be considered in the same, and as not yet born, and having done neither good nor evil.———5. That it is an eternal act in God, and not temporal; or which commenced not in time, but from all eternity; for it is not the opinion of the sublapsarians, that God passed the decree of election after men were actually created and fallen; only that they were considered in the divine mind, from all eternity, in the decree of election, as if they were created and fallen; wherefore, though they differ in the consideration of the object of election, as thus and thus diversified, yet they agree in the thing, and agree to differ, as they should, and not charge one another with unsoundness and heterodoxy; for which there is no reason. Calvin was for the corrupt mass; Beza, who was co-pastor with him in the church at Geneva, and his successor, was for the pure mass: and yet they lived in great peace, love, and harmony. The Contra-remonstrants in Holland, when Arminianism first appeared among them, were not agreed in this point; some took one side of the question, and some the other; but they both united against the common adversary, the Arminians. Dr. Twiss, who was as great a supralapsarian as perhaps ever was, and carried things as high as any man ever did, and as closely studied the point, and as well understood it, and perhaps better than any one did, and yet he confesses that it was only *apex logicus*, a point in logic; and that the difference only lay in the ordering and ranging the decrees of God: and, for my own part, I think both may be taken in: that in the decree of the end, the ultimate end, the glory of God, for which he does all things, men might be considered in the divine mind as creable, not yet created and fallen; and that in the decree of the means, which, among other things, takes in the mediation of Christ, redemption by him, and the sanctification of the Spirit; they might be considered as created, fallen, and sinful, which these things imply; nor does this suppose separate acts and decrees in God, or any priority and posteriority in them; which in God are but one and together; but our finite minds are obliged to consider them one after another, not being able to take them in together and at once.

Fourthly, The date of election is next to be considered. And certain it is, that it was before men were born; *The children not being yet born—that the purpose of God, according to election, might stand*, Rom. ix. 11. nor can there be any difficulty in admitting this; for if there is none in admitting that a person may be chosen and appointed to an office before he is born, as there can be none, since God has asserted it of Jeremiah; *Before I formed thee in the belly I knew thee, and before thou camest out of the womb I sanctified thee, or set thee apart, and I ordained thee a prophet unto the nations*, Jer. i. 5. then there can be none in admitting that a person so early may be chosen to grace and glory. And this also is before the new birth, or before calling; for calling is the fruit and effect of election; the apostle says of the Thessalonians, *God hath from the beginning chosen you unto salvation*, 2 Thess. ii. 13. not from the beginning of the preaching of the gospel to them, or of the coming of that unto them; for that may come to, and be preached among a people, but not to their profit; may be without success, yea, be the savour of death unto death, Heb. iv. 2. 2 Cor. ii. 16. and when the gospel first came to the Thessalonians, and was preached among them, some believed, and others did not; yea, the Beræans are preferred unto them, for their ready reception of the word; indeed, to some at Thessalonica, it came not in word only, but in power, and in the Holy Ghost; and which was an evidence of their election, and by which they might know it. But then this was only a manifestation of their election; that itself was previous to the gospel's coming to them, and its operation on them; it was displayed therein, and thereby; but it commenced before; see Acts xvii. 1, 2, 3, 4, 11. 1 Thess. i. 4, 5. nor was the choice of them from the beginning of their conversion, or when they were effectually called by the gospel; for that, as has been observed, is the effect and evidence of election; election is that according to which vocation is, and therefore must be before it; *whom he did predestinate, them he also called*, Rom. viii. 30. see 2 Tim. i. 9. Nor is this phrase, *from the beginning*, to be understood of the beginning of time, or of the creation; as in John viii. 44. 1 John iii. 8. for though election began to operate and display itself in the distinct seeds of the woman, and of the serpent, in Abel and Cain, the immediate posterity of the first man, and the distinction has continued ever since; yet the thing itself which makes this distinction, or is the ground of it, was long before; to which may be added, that this phrase is expressive of eternity; *I was set up from everlasting; from the beginning; or ever the earth was*, Prov. viii. 23. that is, before the world began, even from all eternity; as its being inclosed by such phrases as express the same shews: and in this sense is it to be taken in the text in the Thessalonians; and it is in so many words affirmed by the apostle, that this choice of men to holiness and happiness, was made *in Christ before the foundation of the world*, Eph. i. 4. and elsewhere it is said, that the book of life of the Lamb, in which the names of God's elect are set down, and the names of others left out, was written as early, Rev. xiii. 8. and xvii. 8. And that this act of election is an eternal act, or from eternity, may be concluded,——1. From the foreknowledge of God, which is eternal; God from all eternity foreknew all persons and things; there is nothing in time but what was known to him from eternity, Acts xv. 18. Now men are elected according to the foreknowledge of God; and "whom he did foreknow he did predestinate," 1 Pet. i. 2. Rom. viii. 29. wherefore, as the foreknowledge of God is eternal, the choice he makes upon it must be so too; and especially as this foreknowledge is not a bare prescience of persons and things, but what has love and affection to the objects of it joined unto it: wherefore,——2. The eternity of election may be concluded from the love of God to his people; for it is to that it is owing; *electio præsupponit dilectionem*, election presupposes love; hence the apostle sets the character of being *beloved of the Lord* first, to the Thessalonians being *chosen* by him to *salvation*, 2 Thess. ii. 13. it is the immediate effect of love, and is inseparably connected with it; yea, is expressed by it; *Jacob have I loved*, Rom. ix. 13. Now the love of God is an everlasting love; not only endures to all eternity, but was from all eternity: God loved Christ, as he affirms, before the foundation of the world; and in the same place he says, his Father loved his people as he loved him, John xvii. 23, 24.——3. It may be argued from the covenant of grace, which is an everlasting covenant, from everlasting to everlasting; in which the goings of Christ as Mediator were of old, and promises were made before the world began; and grants of grace were made, and blessings of grace provided as early; and which covenant was made with the *chosen* of God; with Christ, the chosen Head, and with his people, as chosen in him; so that if this covenant was from everlasting, and made with chosen ones in Christ, their representative, then the choice of them in him must be as early, 2 Sam. xxiii. 5. Tit. i. 2. 2 Tim. i. 9. Psalm lxxxix. 3. Mic. v. 2. and nothing is more clear than that he was set up as Mediator of this covenant from everlasting; and that his people were chosen in him, their covenant-Head, before the foundation of the world, Prov. viii. 22. Eph. i. iv.—— 5. This appears from the early preparation of grace and glory: grace was given them in Christ before the world was, and they blessed so soon with spiritual blessings in him; as they are a people afore-prepared for glory, that is, in the purpose of God; so glory is the kingdom prepared for them from the foundation of the world; which is no other than a destination, or rather a predestination of that for them, and of them to that, 2 Tim. i. 9. Eph. i. 3, 4. Rom. ix. 23. Matt. xxv. 34.——6. From the nature of the decrees of God in general, it must appear that this is eternal; for if God's decrees in general are eternal, as has been proved from his foreknowledge of whatever comes to pass; which is founded upon the certainty of his decrees, that so they shall be; and from his immutability, which could not be established if any new thoughts and resolutions arose in him, or new decrees in time were made by him; and therefore it may be reckoned a sure point, that such a special decree as this, respecting so important an affair as the salvation of all his people, as well as his own glory, must be eternal: and, indeed, the whole scheme of man's salvation by Christ, the *fellowship of the mystery* hid in him, in which there is such an amazing display of the wisdom of God, is *according to the eternal purpose, which he purposed in Christ Jesus our Lord*, Eph. iii. 9, 10, 11. and which is no other than his purpose according to election, or respecting that.

Fifthly, The impulsive, or moving cause of this act in God, or what were the motives and inducements with God to take such a step as this: and these were not—1. The good works of men; for this act passed in eternity, before any works were done; *The children not being yet born, neither having done any good or evil; that the purpose of God, according to election, might stand*, Rom. ix. 11. and since this was done before them, they could never be the moving cause of it; they are the fruits and effects of it, and so cannot be the cause of it in any sense: it is owing to electing grace that any good works have been done by men since the fall of Adam; for what the prophet says of the people of Israel, is true of the whole world; *Except the Lord of Sabaoth had left us a seed*, a remnant, according to the election of grace, a few, whom, according to this decree, he makes holy and good, and enables them to perform good works, *we had been as Sodom, and been made like unto Gomorrah*, Rom. ix. 29. should have been like to the inhabitants of those cities, both in sin and punishment; as public and abandoned sinners, given up to the vilest lusts, without any check or restraint. Good works are what God has preordained, that his chosen ones should

walk in them, Eph. ii. 10. and therefore the election of the one, and the preordination of the other, must be previous to them, and they not the cause of either; the same cannot be both cause and effect, with respect to the same things: besides, there are no good works truly such, before effectual vocation, which is the fruit of election; before that they have only the appearance of good works, but are not really such, not being done in faith; and whatsoever is not of faith is sin; nor from love to God, which is the end of the commandment; nor in the name and strength of Christ; nor with a view to the glory of God. Men must be first created in Christ, or be new creatures in him, must be believers in him, and have the Spirit of Christ, and his grace put into them, ere they can perform good works: all which are done at effectual vocation, and not before. Moreover, God does not proceed according to men's works; nor are they the moving causes to him, in other acts of his grace; as not in the mission of his Son, 1 John iv. 10. nor in vocation, 2 Tim. i. 9. nor in justification, Rom. iii. 20, 28. nor in the whole of salvation, Tit. iii. 5. Eph. ii. 8, 9. and so not in this first step to salvation, election; for then it would not be of grace, of pure free grace, unmixed and unmerited grace, as it is said to be. And in the strongest manner it is denied to be of works, and that established by an argument which is unanswerable, Rom. xi. 5, 6.——
2. Neither is the holiness of men, whether in principle or in practice, or both, the moving cause of election to eternal life; it is an end to which men are chosen; *he hath chosen us in him—that we should be holy*, Eph. i. 4. not because we were holy, but that we might be so, and so denotes something future, and which follows upon it; and it is a means fixed in the decree of election to another end, salvation; to which men are chosen, *through sanctification of the Spirit*, 2 Thess. ii. 13. yea, the sanctification of God's elect is the object of God's decree; is the thing decreed, and so cannot be the cause of the decree; *This is the will of God, even your sanctification*, 1 Thess. iv. 3. not barely the approving will of God, as being agreeable to his holy nature and holy law; nor merely the will of his precept, *Be ye holy;* but his decreeing will, or determinate counsel, that men should be holy: besides, holiness in principle and practice, does not take place until effectual vocation, and is the work of the Spirit of God in time, who calls men with an holy calling; not only to holiness, but works a principle of grace and holiness in them, whereby they are influenced and enabled, under the power of his grace, to live soberly, righteously, and godly.——
3. Nor is faith the moving cause of election; the one is in time, the other in eternity: whilst men are in a state of unregeneracy, they are in a state of unbelief; they are, as without hope in God, so without faith in Christ; and when they have it, they have it not of themselves, of their own power and free-will; but they have it as the gift of God, and the operation of his Spirit, flowing purely from his grace; and therefore cannot be the cause of electing grace: besides, it is the effect of that, it is a consequence that follows upon it, and is insured by it; *As many as were ordained to eternal life, believed*, Acts xiii. 48. it is proper and peculiar to the elect of God; the reason why some men do not believe is, because *they are not of* Christ's *sheep*, John x. 26. his elect, given him by the Father; and the reason why others do believe is, because they are of Christ's sheep, or his chosen ones, and therefore faith is given to them; which is called, *the faith of God's elect*, Tit. i. 1. Faith is not the cause of vocation, and much less of election, which precedes that: the reason why men are called, is not because they believe, but they are called that they might believe; in which effectual call, faith is given to them, as the evidence of their election. Once more, faith is fixed as a means, in the decree of election; and therefore cannot be the cause of it, 2 Thess. ii. 13. To which may be added, if faith is the moving cause of election, men might be said rather to choose God and Christ, at least first, than they to choose him; whereas our Lord says, *Ye have not chosen me, but I have chosen you*, John xv. 16. the apostles had chosen him, but not first; he first chose them; so that their choice of him had no influence on his choice of them; but if faith is the moving cause of election, then men rather choose Christ than he them; for what is faith but an high esteem of Christ, a choosing and preferring him, as a Saviour, to all others? a choosing that good part which shall never be taken away; and of the way of truth, or of Christ, who is the Way, the Truth, and the Life.
——4. Nor is perseverance in faith, holiness, and good works, the moving cause of election; but the effect of it, and what is

ensured by it: the reason why men persevere is, because they are the elect of God, who cannot be deceived totally and finally, so as to have their faith subverted, and overthrown, as that of nominal professors may be; because the foundation on which they are, stands sure; sealed with this seal, *the Lord knows them that are his*, Matt. xxiv. 24. 2 Tim. ii. 18, 19. Should it be said, that it is the foresight of these things in men, which moves God to choose them; it may be replied, that God's foresight, or foreknowledge of things future, is founded on the determinations of his will concerning them; God foresees, or foreknows, that such and such a man will believe, become holy, do good works, and persevere therein to glory; because he has determined to give faith to them, work holiness in them, enable them to perform good works, and cause them to persevere therein to the end, and so be saved; and what is this, but the doctrine contended for? it is no other than a decree to give grace and glory to some persons for his own glory, and to deny them to others.

The truth of all this might be illustrated and confirmed by the case of infants dying in infancy; who, as soon as they are in the world, almost, are taken out of it. Now such a number as they are, can never be thought to be brought into being in vain, and without some end to be answered; and which, no doubt, is the glory of God, who is and will be glorified in them, some way or another, as well as in adult persons: now though their election is a secret to us, and unrevealed; it may be reasonably supposed, yea, in a judgment of charity it may rather be concluded, that they are all chosen, than that none are; and if it is allowed that any of them may be chosen, it is enough to my present purpose; since the election of them cannot be owing to their faith, holiness, obedience, good works, and perseverance, or to the foresight of these things, which do not appear in them.

In short, these maxims are certainly true, and indisputable, that nothing in time can be the cause of what was done in eternity; to believe, to be holy, to do good works, and persevere in them, are acts in time, and so cannot be causes of election, which was done in eternity; and that nothing out of God can be the cause of any decree, or will in him; he is no passive Being, to be wrought upon by motives and inducements without him; for if his will is moved by anything without him, that must be superior to him, and his will must become dependent on that; which to say of God, is to speak very unworthily of him. God wills things because it so pleases him; predestination is according to the good pleasure of his will; election is according to his foreknowledge; which is no other than his free favour and good will to men, Eph. i. 5. 1 Pet. i. 2. no other reason can be given of God's will or decree to bestow grace and glory on men, for his own glory, and of his actual donation of them, but what our Lord gives; *Even so, Father, for so it seemed good in thy sight*, Matt. xi. 25, 26.

Sixthly, The means fixed in the decree of election, for the execution of it, or in order to bring about the end intended, are next to be inquired into; which are, the principal of them, the mediation of Christ, and redemption by him, the sanctification of the Spirit, and belief of the truth. The mediation of Christ; Christ, as God, is the efficient cause of election; in his office-capacity, as an Head, the elect are chosen in him, as members of him; and though his mediation, bloodshed, sufferings, and death, are not the meritorious cause of election, yet Christ in them is the medium of the execution of it; that is, of bringing the chosen ones, through grace, to glory, whereby God is glorified, and so the end of it is answered: men are said to be chosen *unto obedience, and sprinkling of the blood of Jesus Christ*, 1 Pet. i. 2. which words, though they seem to express the ends of election, yet are such as have the nature of means, in order to further ends, the salvation of men, and the glory of God therein. *Obedience* may intend the obedience of Christ, both active and passive, or his subjection to the law, and fulfilment of it, both with respect to its precepts and penalty, by which men are justified in the sight of God, and so are entitled to eternal life and happiness; and to the blood of Jesus Christ are owing, the redemption of men, the remission of their sins, and the atonement of them, which issue in their salvation, and make way for the glorifying of the justice of God, as well as the grace of God in it: and the *sprinkling* of this blood, denotes an application of it to the conscience, whereby it is purged from dead works, and the heart sprinkled from an evil conscience; and which speaks peace, and yields comfort, and causes the soul to rejoice in hope of the glory of God. Moreover, men are chosen to salvation, *through sanctification of the Spirit and belief of the truth*, as means to that end, 2 Thess. ii. 13. The *sanctification of the Spirit*, is the work of grace on the heart, begun in regeneration, and carried on by the Spirit, until it is perfected by him ; and this is necessary to salvation, for without holiness, even perfect holiness, no man shall see the Lord ; and therefore it is fixed as a means of it, and is made as sure and certain by the decree of election, as the end, salvation itself; and being fixed as a mean, in this decree, confirms what has been observed, that it cannot be the cause of it : and this proves that the doctrine of election can be no licentious doctrine, but a doctrine according to godliness ; since it makes such sure provision for holiness, as well as for happiness. *Belief of the truth* may signify, not a bare belief of the Gospel, and the truths of it ; for though they are to be believed by all the saved ones, yet this may be where neither election, nor vocation, nor sanctification, ever take place ; even in reprobates, and devils themselves : but faith in Christ, the Way, the Truth, and the Life ; and believing in him with the heart, unto righteousness, and with which salvation is connected, and to which it is necessary, and is a mean of it ; and which being fixed in the decree of election, as such is secured by it, and certainly follows upon it.

Seventhly, The ends settled in the decree of election are both subordinate and ultimate ; the subordinate ones have indeed the nature of means with respect to the ultimate one : there are many things to which the elect of God, predestinated or chosen, both with respect to grace and glory, which are subordinate to the grand end, the glory of God. So God is said to *predestinate* them *to be conformed to the image of his Son*, to be made like unto him, not so much in his sonship, nor in his sufferings, as in his holiness : man was made after the image of God, this by sinning, he came short of ; in regeneration the image of Christ is enstamped, the lines of his grace are drawn upon, and he himself is formed in the hearts of his people ; and into which image they are more and more changed through transforming views of his glory ; and which will be complete in the future state, when saints will see him as he is ; and to this they are predestinated, and that in order to another end, that Christ *might be the first-born among many brethren ;* the brethren are the predestinated ones, who are brethren to each other ; and these are many, the many sons Christ brings to glory ; and he is the first-born among them ; and that he may appear to be so, he is set up as the pattern of them, to whose image they are predestinated to be conformed, that in all things he might have the pre-eminence, Rom viii. 29. moreover they are said to be *predestinated to the adoption of children*, Eph. i. 5. which may be understood either of the grace of adoption, the blessing itself, which predestination to it is no other than a preparation of it in the purposes and decrees of God, in his council and covenant, 2 Cor. vi. 18. or the inheritance adopted to, which they obtain in Christ, being predestinated to it according to a divine purpose, Eph. i. 11. likewise they are chosen to be *holy and without blame*, Eph. i. 4. even to unblameable holiness, which is begun in this life, and perfected in the other ; when they will appear before the throne in the sight of God without fault, without spot or wrinkle, or any such thing : also they are said to be chosen unto faith ; *God hath chosen the poor of this world, rich in faith*, James ii. 5. not that they were, or were considered rich in faith when God chose them, but he chose them *to be* rich in faith, as the words may be supplied, as well as to be heirs of the kingdom ; and this end is always answered, such as are chosen do believe ; *as many as were ordained to eternal life believed*, Acts xiii. 48. Once more, the elect are chosen to obedience and good works ; the text in 1 Pet. i. 2. which has been already observed, will bear to be interpreted of the *obedience* of the elect, in consequence both of their election and their sanctification ; and certain it is, that *good works* are what *God has before ordained* that his elect ones *should walk in them*, Eph. ii. 10. these are subordinate ends which respect grace, and are in order to a further end, glory and happiness, which is sometimes expressed by salvation ; *God hath not appointed us to wrath, but to obtain salvation by our Lord Jesus Christ*, 1 Thess. v. 9. and again, *God hath from the beginning chosen you to salvation*, 2 Thess. ii. 13. salvation was fixed upon, and the method of it contrived in eternity ; Christ was sent into the world, and came to effect it ; he is become the author of it by his obedience and sufferings ; this is not only published in the Gospel, but it is applied to God's elect in conversion ; but the full enjoyment of it is yet to come, Rom. xiii. 11. the saints are now heirs of it, are kept unto it, and Christ will appear to put them into the possession of it, and to this they are chosen, 1 Pet. i. 2, 5. Heb. i. 14. and ix. 28. this end is also expressed by eternal life, *As many as were ordained to eternal life*, Acts xiii. 48. This is begun in grace now, which is a well of living water springing up to it; he that believes has it already in some sense; the knowledge of God and Christ is the beginning, pledge, and earnest of it; and it will lie hereafter in a life of perfect knowledge and holiness, and in uninterrupted communion with God to all eternity; and to this the elect are ordained.

Now all these ends, both respecting grace and glory, are subordinate ones to the grand and ultimate end of all, the glory of God; for as God swears by himself, because he could swear by no greater, so because a greater end could not be proposed than his own glory, he has set up that as the supreme end of all his decrees; he has *made*, that is, has appointed, *all things for himself*, for his own glory, Prov. xvi. 4. as all things are from him, as the first cause, they are all to him as the last end, Rom. xi. 36. and with respect to the decree of election, it is the glory of his grace mixed with justice, which is the end of it; the election of men to unblameable holiness, and the predestination of them to the adoption of children, are said to be *to the praise of the glory of his grace*, Eph. i. 4—6. that his free and sovereign grace might be displayed and glorified thereby; and that men who are the chosen generation and peculiar people, might shew forth the praises of it; as they do in part now, and will do it perfectly hereafter; for they are a people he has formed for himself, both in election and effectual vocation, for this end and purpose, Isa. xliii. 21. 1 Pet. ii. 9. his great end in election is *to make known the riches of his glory on the vessels of his mercy;* that is, the riches, the fulness, and plenty of his glorious and sovereign grace and mercy on the objects of it, Rom. ix. 23. and not the glory of his grace and mercy only, but of his justice also; for which provision is made in the decree of the means, by *setting forth*, or pre-ordaining, Christ *to be the propitiation*, or to make atonement, *for sin; to declare his righteousness*, the justice of God, *that he might be just, and the justifier of him that believes in Jesus*, Rom. iii. 25, 26. and so the glory of God, of his justice and holiness, as well as of his grace and mercy, appear to be great in the salvation of men; here mercy and truth meet together, and righteousness and peace kiss each other; and God is glorified in all his perfections, which is the great end in view.

Eighthly, The blessings and benefits flowing from election are many, indeed all spiritual blessings; it is as it were the rule, measure, and standard according to which they are communicated; the several chains in man's salvation are connected with it, and hang and depend upon it, Eph. i. 3, 4. Rom. viii. 30. they need only be just named in order, since they have been suggested under the former heads.——1. Vocation. *Whom he did predestinate, them he called;* all the predestinated, or chosen ones, are in time called, and are called according to the eternal purpose and grace of God in election, Rom. viii. 30. 2 Tim. i. 9.——2. Faith and holiness, and indeed every grace of the Spirit. Holiness is both an end and a mean in this decree, as before observed, and made certain by it; faith follows upon it as a free gift of grace, and so hope and love, and every other grace.——3. Communion with God. *Blessed is the man whom thou choosest, and causest to approach unto thee*, Psalm lxv. 4. to come into his presence, and enjoy it in his house, his word, and ordinances.——4. Justification; which is secretly a branch of it, and openly as to the manifestation of it, flows from it; *Who shall lay anything to the charge of God's elect? it is God that justifieth;* that is, the elect; who because they are chosen in Christ, they are justified in him, Rom. viii. 33.——5. Adoption; to which the elect are predestinated, and are denominated the children of God, being given to Christ as such when chosen in him, before the incarnation of Christ, redemption by him, or having the Spirit from him, Heb. ii. 13, 14. John xi. 52. Gal. iv. 6.——6. Glorification; *Whom he did predestinate—them he glorified*, Rom. viii. 30. the elect, the vessels of mercy, are *afore prepared for glory*, for eternal glory and happiness; and are chosen and called to the obtaining of the glory of Christ, which the Father has given to him to bestow upon them, and which they will most certainly enjoy. Rom. ix. 23. 2 Thess. ii. 13, 14.

Ninthly, The several properties of election, may be gathered from what has been said of it; as,——1. That it is eternal; it does not commence upon believing, and much less at perseverance in faith and holiness; but it was an act in God before the foundation of the world, Eph. i. 4.—— 2. It is free and sovereign; God was not obliged to choose any; and as it is, he chooses whom he will, and for no other reason excepting his own glory, but because he will; *what if God willing*, &c. and the difference in choosing one and not another, is purely owing to his will, Rom. ix. 18, 22, 23.——3. It is absolute and unconditional; clear of all motives in man, or conditions to be performed by him; for it *stands not of works, but of him that calleth*, the will of him that calls, Rom. ix. 11.—— 4. It is complete and perfect; it is not begun in eternity and completed in time, nor takes its rise from the will of God, and is finished by the will of man; nor is made perfect by faith, holiness, obedience, and persevering in well-doing, but has its complete being in the will of God at once.—— 5. It is immutable and irrevocable; God never repents of, nor revokes the choice he has made; some choose their friends and favourites, and alter their minds and choose others; but God is in one mind, and never makes any alteration in the choice he has made; and hence their state is safe and secure.——6. It is special and particular; that is, those who are chosen are chosen to be a special people above all others, and are particular persons, whose names are written in the book of life; not in general, men of such and such characters, but persons well known to God, and distinctly fixed on by him.——7. Election may be known by the persons, the objects of it; partly by the blessings flowing from it, and connected with it, before observed, bestowed upon them; for to whomsoever such blessings of grace are applied, they must be the elect of God, Rom. viii. 30. they may know it from the efficacy of the Gospel upon them, in their vocation and conversion, 1 Thess. i. 4, 5. and by the Spirit of God testifying their adoption to them, to which they are predestinated, Rom. viii. 15, 16. and they may be able to make it known to others, by their holy lives and conversations; which is meant by making their calling and election sure, even by their good works, as some copies read, 2 Pet. i. 10. since both calling and election are to be made sure, and therefore by some third thing: indeed no man can know his election of God until he is called; it would be presumption in him to claim this character, until he is born again; nor should any man conclude himself a reprobate because a sinner, since all men are sinners; even God's elect, who are by nature, and in no wise better than others, but children of wrath, even as others.

There are many things objected to this doctrine of election; but since it is so clear and plain from scripture, and is written as with a sunbeam in it, all objections to it must be mere cavil. It is urged, that God is said to be *good to all, and his tender mercies over all his works*, Psalm cxlv. 9. which seems inconsistent with his choosing some and leaving others; but this is to be understood not of his special grace, but of his providential goodness, which extends to the elect and non-elect, the evil and the good, the just and the unjust, Matt. v. 45. and in this sense he is the saviour, preserver, and bountiful benefactor of all men, but especially of them that believe, 1 Tim. iv. 10. It is observed that Christ says he was sent not to *condemn the world, but that the world through him might be saved*, and therefore not some only but all; but to understand this of all the individuals in the world is not true, because all are not saved; and so this end of Christ's mission, so understood, is not answered; but by the world is meant the world of God's elect, whom he was reconciling in Christ, and for whom Christ gave his life, and became the propitiation for their sins, even for all the chosen throughout the whole world, and particularly among the Gentiles. Nor is 1 Tim. ii. 4. any objection to this doctrine, *Who will have all men to be saved, and to come unto the knowledge of the truth;* for all men are not eventually saved, nor do all come to the knowledge of the truth of the Gospel; nor indeed have all the means of that knowledge: but the sense is, either, that all that are saved, God wills to be saved; or, that it is his will that men of all sorts and of all nations, Jews and Gentiles, should be saved; which agrees with the context, ver. 1, 2, 7. And when it is said of God, that he is *not willing that any should perish, but that all should come to repentance*, 2 Pet. iii. 9. this must be interpreted, not of all mankind, but of the elect, to whom this and the preceding epistle are inscribed, and who are in ver. 8. styled *beloved*, and in this verse, the *us* towards whom *God is long-suffering;* now it is the will and pleasure of God that none of those should perish, but all in due time be brought to faith in Christ, and to repentance towards God: but objections from hence, with others of the like kind, are not sufficient to overturn this truth, so abundantly established in the sacred scriptures.

CHAP. III.

OF THE DECREE OF REJECTION, OF SOME ANGELS, AND OF SOME MEN.

I MAKE use of the word *rejection* in this article, partly because it is a scriptural phrase and ascribed to God, and partly because it is that act of God which gives the name of reprobate to any; and is the foundation of that character, *reprobate silver shall men call them, because the Lord hath rejected them*, Jer. vi. 30. and stands opposed to election, 1 Sam. xv. 26. and x. 24. but chiefly because the other word *reprobation*, through wrong and frightful ideas being affixed to it, carries in it, with many, a sound harsh and disagreeable; or otherwise they are of the same signification, and no amendment is made in the doctrine or sense of it, by using the one instead of the other. This doctrine of rejecting some angels, and some men, from the divine favour, is spoken of but sparingly in scripture, yet clearly and plainly; though chiefly left to be concluded from that of election, and from whence it most naturally and rationally follows. I shall begin with,

I. The rejection of some of the angels, which consists of two parts:——1. A non-election, or preterition of them, a passing over them or passing by them, when others were chosen; and which may be concluded from the choice of others; for if some were elect, others must be non-elect; if some were chosen, others were not; if some were taken, others must be passed by and left: that some of them are elect is certain, they are expressly called *elect angels*, 1 Tim. v. 21. and consequently are distinguished from others who are not elected; or otherwise the title and character of *elect* must be insignificant and impertinent. Both these were considered alike, upon an equal foot, when the one were elected, and the other not; they were viewed as not yet created and fallen, but as lying in the pure mass of creatureship or creability; God saw in his power, what creatures of this kind he could produce into being, as he also saw in his will, whom he would; and of those he could and would create, he determined to choose some and leave others, and both for his own glory; for they could not be considered as fallen creatures, or in the corrupt mass, since the elect angels never fell; and the moment they were elected, the others were passed by or rejected; and so must be

under the same consideration; and consequently the election of the one, and the rejection of the other, must be wholly owing to the sovereign will of God: both these were brought into being as God determined they should, and are equally his creatures, Psalm civ. 4. and were both made pure and holy creatures, angels of light, bright morning-stars, shining in the purity and holiness of their nature; for such were Satan and his angels in their original creation; the devil, our Lord says, *abode not in the truth*, John viii. 44. which implies that he had been in the truth, though he continued not in it; in his allegiance and fidelity to God his creator; in his integrity, purity, and holiness, as a creature of veracity; but framing lies, he became the father of them. What he was in, but abode not in, is the *first estate*, of integrity, innocence, and happiness, in which he was created, but *kept* it not, Jude, ver. 6. To some angels, God decreed to give, and did give grace, to confirm them in the state in which they were created; these are the elect angels, who are said to be *mighty*, and to *excel in strength*; not only in natural, but in spiritual strength. To others he decreed not to give confirming grace, but to deny it to them; and which he was not obliged to give, it being what could not be challenged by the laws and dues of creation, and was mere favour to those on whom it was bestowed; wherefore the others were left to the mutability of their will, which is that weakness and folly, the angels were chargeable with in their creation-state, Job iv. 18. hence of their own free-will they sinned and fell, and left their habitation, 2 Pet. ii. 4. Jude, ver. 6. what their sin was by which they fell, will be considered in course, when we come to the fall of Adam, and of theirs; this leads on to observe the other part of the decree respecting them.——2. The appointment of them to wrath and damnation; in this they were viewed as sinful, fallen creatures; this decree is meant by their being *reserved in everlasting chains under darkness, unto the judgment of the great day*, Jude, ver. 6. 2 Pet. ii. 4. for by *chains* are meant the purposes and decrees of God, by which they are bound and held fast, and from which they cannot loose themselves; and as the decrees of God are called *mountains of brass*, Zech. vi. 1. so they may be called chains of iron and brass for the same reasons; namely, their firmness, immutability, and duration; they are *everlasting* chains, and in these they are reserved *under darkness;* meaning either the state of darkness in which they are, being deprived of that light and knowledge they had; and also being under horror and black despair, without the least gleam of the light of joy and comfort; or that state of darkness to which they are appointed and reserved, even that *blackness of darkness* to which the *wandering stars,* as these may be said to be, are reserved, Jude ver. 13. and moreover they are appointed and reserved *to the judgment of the great day,* to the great day of the last judgment; when they will be brought forth in chains before the judgment-seat of Christ, and will have their final sentence passed and executed on them, which as yet seems not to have been done, Matt. viii. 29. then will Christ sit on the throne of judgment, and saints will stand by, together with the good angels, as approvers of the righteous sentence: and therefore saints are said to *judge angels,* as well as the world of the ungodly, 1 Cor. vi. 2, 3. that is, the evil angels, to which judgment they are appointed by the decree of God; and to endure eternal wrath and damnation; signified by *everlasting fire, prepared,* in the decrees and purposes of God, *for the devil and his angels,* Matt. xxv. 41. I proceed to,

II. The decree concerning the rejection of some of the sons of men. It may be observed, that we can hear and read of the non-election and rejection of angels, and of their preordination to condemnation and wrath, with very little emotion of mind: the devils may be cast down to hell, to be everlastingly damned, and be appointed thereunto, and it gives no great concern; no hard thoughts against God arise, no charge of cruelty, want of kindness to his creatures and offspring, and of injustice to them; but if anything of this kind is hinted at, with respect to any of the apostate sons of Adam, presently there is an outcry against it; and all the above things are suggested. What is the reason of this difference? It can be only this, that the latter comes nearer home, and more nearly affects us; it is partiality to ourselves, our nature, and race, to which this is owing; otherwise, far greater severity, if it may be so called, is exercised on fallen angels, than on fallen man; for God has not spared one of the angels that sinned, provided no saviour for them, nor so much as given them the means of grace; but consigned them all over at once to everlasting wrath and ruin: whereas, not only a Saviour is provided for fallen men, and means of grace allowed them, but thousands, and ten thousands, millions and millions of them are saved, by the abundant mercy and grace of God, through Christ. But to go on,

First, I shall prove that there is a non-election, or rejection of some of the sons of men, when others were chosen; and, indeed, from the election of some, may fairly be inferred, the non-election of others. Common sense tells us, that of persons or things, if some are chosen, others must be left: if there is a remnant of the sons of men, according to the election of grace, then there are others not included in it, which are left unchosen, and are called the *rest. The election,* that is, elect men, *hath obtained it,* righteousness and eternal life; *and the rest were blinded,* Rom. xi. 5, 7. Our Lord says, *I speak not of you all; I know whom I have chosen,* John xiii. 18. plainly intimating, that all were not chosen, and it is certain one was not, and whom he calls *the son of perdition;* one, not only deserving of it, but appointed to it; for though chosen to an office, as an apostle, yet not to grace and glory, John xvii. 12. and how many such there be, no man can pretend to say; but it is evident there are some, and who are generally described by negative characters; as *not known* by God and Christ; the elect are God's people, whom he knows; they are elect, according to his foreknowledge; which carries in it love and affection to them; but of others Christ says, *I never knew you;* he knew them by his omniscience, but not with such knowledge as he knows the elect of God; he never knew them as the objects of his Father's love, and his own; he never knew them as the objects of his Father's choice, and his own; he never knew them in the gift of his Father to him, Matt. vii. 23. hence they are represented as *not* loved, which is meant by being hated: *Esau have I hated;* that is, had not loved him, as he had Jacob; for it cannot be understood of positive hatred, for God hates none of his creatures, as such, only as workers of iniquity; but of negative hatred, or of not loving him; which, in comparison of the love he bore to Jacob, might be called hatred: in which sense the word is used in Luke xiv. 26. Moreover, they are spoken of as *not* being given to Christ; for if there are some that are *given* to him *out of the world,* then there must be a world which are not given, and for whom he has not so much concern as even to pray for them, John xvii. 6, 9. they are frequently described, as not having their names written, and *not* to be *found written* in the Lamb's book of life, Rev. xiii. 8. and xvii. 8. and xx. 15. Now as election is signified by the writing of names in the book of life, non-election is expressed by not writing the names of some there; and if those whose names are written there, are the elect, then those whose names are not written there, but are left out, must be non-elect: to which may be added, that our Lord says of these persons, *Ye are not of my sheep*, and gives this as a reason why they believed not in him, John x. 26. But the goats he will place on his left-hand, pass sentence of condemnation on them, and send them into everlasting punishment, Matt. xxv. 33, 41, 46.

Moreover, from the effects of election not having place in some persons, it may be concluded, that there are such who are non-elect. Vocation is a certain fruit and effect of election; *Whom he did predestinate, them he also called*, Rom. viii. 30. not only externally, but internally, with an holy and heavenly calling, to grace here, and glory hereafter. But are all called in this manner? No; there are some who have not so much as the outward call by the ministry of the word, have not the external means of grace; but as they sin without law, perish without it, Rom. x. 14. and ii. 12. Those who are chosen, are predestinated to be conformed to the image of Christ; they are chosen to holiness, and through sanctification of the Spirit. But are all made like to Christ, and conformed to his image? do not many bear the image of Satan, imitate him, and do his lusts? are all men made holy, or have they the sanctification of the Spirit? Whom God predestinates he justifies, by the righteousness of his Son. But are all men justified? No; for though he justifies some of all sorts and nations; as the circumcised Jews by faith, and the uncircumcised Gentiles through faith, yet not every individual; yea, there is a world that will be condemned, and consequently not predestinated to life, 1 Cor. xi. 32. They that are chosen, are predestinated to the adoption of children, and enjoy both the grace and inheritance of children. But are all children and heirs? is there not such a distinction among men, as children of God, and children of the devil; between whom there is, and will be, an eternal difference? 1 John iii. 10. and therefore there must be an election, and a non-election among them. Moreover, whom God has predestinated, or chosen to life and happiness, these he glorifies, Rom. viii. 30. they obtain the glory of Christ, which his Father has given him for them, and to which they are chosen and called, John xvii. 22. 2 Thess. ii. 13, 14. But are all glorified? do not some go into perdition, even into everlasting punishment? and therefore must be considered as non-elect, Rev. xvii. 8. Matt. xxv. 46. To all which may be added, that those that are given to Christ, which is but another phrase for being chosen in him; these, he says, shall come to him, and he will in no wise cast them out; yea, that they are his sheep, whom he must bring to his Father, to himself, to his fold, to grace and glory, John vi. 37. and x. 16. But are there not some whom Christ will drive away from him, and to them say, *Depart from me, ye cursed, into everlasting fire*, Matt. vii. 23. and xxv. 41? All this put together most clearly and fully proves, that there are some who are not chosen of God, but rejected by him.

Secondly, The parts of this decree, concerning the rejection of men, are commonly said to be preterition and pre-damnation.

1. Preterition is God's passing by some men, when he chose others: and in this act, or part of the decree, men are considered as in the pure mass of creatureship, or creability; in which state they are found, when passed by or rejected, and in which they are left, even just as they are found, nothing put into them; but were left in the pure mass, as they lay, and so no injury done them; nor is God to be charged with any injustice towards them: in this act sin comes not into consideration, as it does in a following one; for in this men are considered as not created, and so not fallen; but as unborn, and having done neither good nor evil, Rom. ix. 11. And this is a pure act of sovereignty in God, and to his sovereign will it is to be ascribed; who has the same sovereign power, and greater, than the potter has over his clay, to make one vessel to honour, and another to dishonour, Rom. ix. 19, 20, 22. This being expressed, as before observed, by negative phrases, is, by some, called negative reprobation.

2. Pre-damnation is God's appointment, or preordination of men to condemnation for sin; and is what is spoken of in Jude, ver. 4. *There are certain men crept in unawares, who were before of old ordained to this condemnation;* and who are described by the following characters, *ungodly men, turning the grace of God into lasciviousness, and denying the only Lord God, and*, or even *our Lord Jesus Christ;* which, when observed,

is sufficient to clear this decree of God from the charge of cruelty and injustice: and this, by some, is called, positive reprobation. The word κριμα, translated *condemnation*, in the above quoted text, some render *judgment*, and interpret it of judicial blindness and hardness of heart; which appeared in the persons embracing and spreading false and pernicious doctrines spoken of; and this is, indeed, what they are foreordained, or appointed to, as a punishment of former sins; for this hardness, &c. presupposes former sins, and an obstinate continued course in them; either against the light and law of nature, which they like not to walk according to, and therefore God gives them up, pursuant to his decree, to a reprobate mind, to do things not convenient, Rom. i. 24, 28. or against divine revelation, precepts, counsels, and admonitions, like Israel of old, hearkening not to the voice of the Lord, in his word, nor paying any regard to his instructions; and therefore he gives them up, as he determined to do, to their own hearts' lusts, and to walk in their own counsels, Psalm lxxxi. 11, 12. and this is the sense of the word in John ix. 39. God hardens some men's hearts, as he did Pharaoh's, and he wills to harden them, or he hardens them according to his decreeing will; *Whom he will he hardeneth*, Rom. ix. 18. this he does not by any positive act, by infusing hardness and blindness into the hearts of men; which is contrary to his purity and holiness, and would make him the author of sin; but by leaving men to their natural blindness and hardness of heart; for the understanding is naturally darkened; and there is a natural blindness, hardness, and callousness of heart, through the corruption of nature, and which is increased by habits of sinning; men are in darkness, and choose to walk in it; and therefore God, as he decreed, gives them up to their own wills and desires, and to Satan, the god of the world, they choose to follow, and to be led captive by, who blinds their minds yet more and more, lest light should break in unto them, Eph. iv. 18. Psalm lxxxii. 5. 2 Cor. iv. 4. and also God may be said to harden and blind, by denying them that grace which can only cure them of their hardness and blindness, and which he, of his free favour, gives to his chosen ones, Ezek. xxxvi. 26, 27. but is not obliged to give it to any; and because he gives it not, he is said to hide, as he determined to hide, the things of his grace from the wise and prudent, even because it so seemed good in his sight, Matt. xi. 25, 26. Hence this blindness, hardness, insensibility, and stupidity, are represented as following upon non-election; not as the immediate effect of it, but as consequences of it; and such as neither judgments nor mercies can remove; and bring persons to a right sense of sin, and repentance for it, Rom. xi. 7—10. The sin and fall of Adam having brought him into a state of infidelity, in which God has concluded him: and he does not think fit to give to every man that grace which can only cure him of his unbelief, and without which, and unless almighty power and grace go along with the means they have, they cannot believe; whereby the decrees, predictions, and declarations of God are fulfilled in them, John xii. 37—40. yea, as Christ is said to be *set*, or appointed, *for the fall of many in Israel*, Luke ii. 34. so many are appointed to stumble at the Word, at him, the Stone of stumbling, and Rock of offence, being children of disobedience, and left as such; when, to those who are a chosen generation, he is a precious cornerstone, and they believe in him, and are saved by him, 1 Pet. ii. 7, 8, 9. hence we read of some, who, because they received not the love of the truth, that they might be saved, to them are sent by God strong delusions, and they are given up to believe a lie, that they might be damned; not that God infuses any delusion or deceit into them, but because of their disbelief of, and disrespect to him and his Word, he suffers their corruptions to break forth and prevail, not giving restraining grace to them; so that they become a prey to them that lie in wait to deceive; and being easy and credulous, they believe lies spoken in hypocrisy; which issue in their damnation; whilst others, beloved of the Lord, and chosen from the beginning to salvation, obtain the glory of Christ, 2 Thess. ii. 10—14. But though all this is a most certain truth, and is contained in the decree we are speaking of, yet condemnation, or everlasting punishment, seems to be meant in the passage quoted; or, however, this is what some men are foreordained unto.

Some will have it, that this refers to something *forewritten*, as they choose to render the word; to some prophecy concerning the condemnation of those persons, and particularly to that of Enoch, ver. 14, 15. but it is not certain that that prophecy was ever written; besides, a prophecy, or prediction, of anything future is founded upon an antecedent predetermination and appointment; God foretels by his prophets what will be, because he has determined it shall be; if, therefore, the condemnation of those persons was foretold in any written prophecy, it was because God had decreed it should come upon them, or they be brought into it. It seems to have the same sense with God's appointing men unto wrath; which, though not in so many words expressed, is manifestly implied; as when the apostle says, *God hath not appointed us to wrath*, who yet were children of wrath, and deserving of it as others; *but to obtain salvation by our Lord Jesus Christ;* it suggests, that though he had not appointed them, yet he had appointed others to wrath, and who are therefore called *vessels of wrath, fitted for destruction*, by their own sins and transgressions, 1 Thess. v. 9. Rom. ix. 22. With which agrees what is said of some wicked men, who are *reserved*, in the purposes and decrees of God, *to the day of destruction;* in consequence of which, *they shall be brought to the day of wrath*, which God has appointed for the execution of his wrath; and hence the casting of the fury of his wrath, in all the dreadful instances of it, is called *the portion of a wicked man from God, and the heritage appointed unto him of God*, Job xxi. 30. and xx. 23—29. and this is the sense of Prov. xvi. 4. for the meaning of the text is not, nor is it our sense of it, as some misrepresent it, as if God made man to damn him; we say no such thing, nor does the text; our sentiment is, that God made man neither to damn nor save him; but he made him for his own glory, and he will be glorified in him, in one way or another: nor that he made man wicked, in order to damn him; for God made man upright; men made themselves wicked by their own inventions; which are the cause of damnation: but the true sense of the passage is, that *the Lord hath made*, that is, has appointed *all things for himself*, for his own glory: and should it be objected, that the wicked could not be for his glory, it is added, *Yea, even the wicked for the day of evil;* that is, he has appointed the wicked for the day of evil, to suffer justly for their sins, to the illustration of the glory of his justice.

Thirdly, The causes of this act.——1. The efficient cause is God; it is the Lord, that makes all things for his own glory, and the wicked for the day of evil; it is God that appoints to wrath, and foreordains to condemnation; what if *God willing to shew his wrath*, &c. Prov. xvi. 4. 1 Thess. v. 9. Rom. ix. 22. And, (1.) It is an act of his sovereignty, who does what he pleases in heaven and in earth; he does according to his will in the armies of the heavens, and among the inhabitants of the earth; as he does all things, so this, according to the counsel of his will; for though it is sovereign, it is not in such sense arbitrary as to be without reason and wisdom; it is a wise counsel of his, for his own glory. The objector, introduced by the apostle, supposes this, that it is an act of his sovereign will; and therefore says, *Why does he yet find fault? for who hath resisted his will?* and which the apostle denies not, but reasons upon it, and confirms it, Rom. ix. 19—22.——(2.) It is agreeable to his justice: the same apostle treating on this subject asks, *Is there unrighteousness with God?* that is, to love one and hate another, to choose one and not another, before they were born, or had done good or evil; and he answers, *God forbid;* since in his act of passing by one, when he chose another, he left him as he found him, without putting, or supposing, any iniquity in him; without any charge of any sin or laying him under a necessity to commit any. In the act of pre-damnation, he considers him as a sinner, and foreordains him to punishment for his sins; and if it is no injustice in God to punish men for sin, it cannot be unjust in him to determine to punish for it: if the judgments of God on antichrist are true and righteous, and display his holiness and justice, it cannot be unrighteous in him to decree to inflict these judgments on him, and his followers, here and hereafter: if it is a righteous thing with God to render tribulation to them that trouble his people, and so to them that commit any other sin, it must be agreeable to his justice to appoint them to indignation and wrath, tribulation and anguish; even every soul of man that does evil, if he pleases. (3.) Nor is this act contrary to his goodness; all persons and things are his own, and he may do with them as he pleases, without an impeachment of this or any other perfection of his; *Is thine eye evil*, says he, *because I am good?* Matt. xx. 15. What distinguishing grace and goodness has been exercised towards fallen man, when no degree of sparing mercy was shewn to fallen angels! and what goodness has been laid up, and wrought out, for many of the sons of Adam, though others have been rejected! and even on them that are rejected, what riches of providential goodness have been, and are bestowed on them, in the most plentiful and liberal manner! with what lenity, patience, forbearance, and *long-suffering*, has God *endured the vessels of wrath, fitted to destruction*, fitted by themselves! Rom. ii. 4. and ix. 22. This act of God is neither contrary to the mercy, nor to the wisdom of God, nor to the truth and sincerity of God, in his promises, declarations, calls, &c. nor to the holiness and justice of God; as I have elsewhere[1] made abundantly to appear.

2. The moving, or impulsive cause of God's making such a decree, by which he has rejected some of the race of Adam from his favour, is not sin, but the good pleasure of his will: sin is the meritorious cause of eternal death, wrath, and damnation; wrath is revealed from heaven against all unrighteousness and ungodliness of men, and comes upon the children of disobedience, whom God leaves in it; the wages, or demerit of sin, is death, even death eternal; but then it is not the impulsive cause of the decree itself; not of preterition, because that, as election, was before good or evil were done, and irrespective of either; nor of pre-damnation, God, indeed, damns no man but for sin; nor did he decree to damn any but for sin; but yet, though sin is the cause of damnation and death, the thing decreed, it is not the cause of the decree itself: it is the cause of the thing willed, but not the moving cause of God's will; for nothing out of God can move his will; if it could, the will of God would be dependent on the will and actions of men; whereas, his purpose, whether with respect to election or rejection, stands not on the works and will of men, but on his own will and pleasure: besides, if sin was the cause of the decree itself, or of God's will to reject men, then all would be rejected, since all fell in Adam; all are under sin, all have sinned, and come short of the glory of God; all are, by nature, children of wrath, and deserving of it: what then could move God to choose one and reject another, but his sovereign good-will and pleasure? that then is the sole moving and impulsive cause of such a decree; when we have searched the scriptures most thoroughly, and employed our reasoning powers to the highest pitch, and racked our invention to the uttermost; no other cause of God's procedure in this affair can be assigned, but what Christ has expressed; *Even so, Father, for so it seemed good in thy sight;* as to hide the things of his grace and gospel from some, and reveal them to others; so to decree and determine within himself, to act in this manner, Matt. xi. 25, 26.

3. The final cause, or end of this decree, is his own glory; this is the ultimate end of all his decrees and appointments, and so of this, appointing the wicked for the day of evil; it was for this purpose he raised up Pharaoh, and decreed all he did concerning him, that he might shew his power in him, his sovereignty and dominion over him, and that his name and glory might be declared throughout all the earth: and the same view he has with respect to all the vessels of wrath, namely, to shew his wrath, and to make his power known, in their destruction, which is of themselves; it is not the death and damnation of the sinner, in which he delights not, that is his ultimate end; it is his own glory, the glory of his perfections, and particularly the glory of his justice and holiness, Prov. xvi. 4. Rom. ix. 17, 22.

Fourthly, The date of this decree is as ancient as eternity itself; wicked men are *before of old*, said to be *ordained to condemnation*, Jude, ver. 4. Some who would have the word rendered, *before written*, as already observed, suppose the text refers to a written prophecy, concerning the condemnation of those men, and that regard is had to a parallel place in 2 Pet. ii. 1, 2, 3. So Grotius. But if Jude had had that in his view, he would never have said that they were *of old*, a long time ago, before written, and prophesied of; since, according to the common calculation, that epistle of Peter was written in the same year that this of Jude's was: the date of election and rejection must be the same; Esau was hated, as early as Jacob was loved, or rejected when he was chosen; and both were done before they were born. If men were chosen from the beginning, that is, from eternity to salvation; then those that were not chosen, or not ordained to eternal life, were foreordained as early to condemnation; and so is the Syriac version of the text in Jude, *were from the beginning ordained;* the same date that is given of election in 2 Thess. ii. 13. And, indeed, there can be no new decree, appointment, or purpose, made by God in time; if the decree of election was from eternity, that of rejection

---

[1] See the Cause of God and Truth, part 3. chap. 1, 2.

must be so too; since there cannot be one without the other; if some were chosen before the foundation of the world, others must be left, or passed by, as early; and, indeed, those whose names are left out of the book of life, are expressly said to be *not written in the book of life, from the foundation of the world*, Rev. xvii. 8. And from the whole,

Fifthly, The properties of this decree will appear to be much the same with those of the decree of election, and need be but just mentioned: as,——1. That it is an eternal decree of God. This did not arise in the mind of God in time, as no new act does, but was made before the foundation of the world.——2. That it is free and sovereign, owing to his own will and pleasure, not moved to it by anything out of himself; *He hath mercy on whom he will have mercy, and whom he will he hardeneth*, Rom. ix. 18. and so he determined to do. ——3. It is immutable and irrevocable; is it expressed by a decree, a preordination? all the decrees of God are unalterable, there is an immutability in his counsel, let it be concerning what it may. Is it expressed by a writing, or a forewriting, as in Jude, ver. 4? It is such a writing as ever remains in full force. Did Pilate say, *what I have written, I have written*, signifying it should remain without any alteration? John xix. 22. Then it may be concluded, that what God has written shall remain, and never be revoked; for he is in one mind, and none can turn him.——4. It is of particular persons; it does not merely respect events, characters, and actions; but the persons of men; as they are persons who are chosen in Christ, and appointed, not to wrath, but to obtain salvation by him; so they are persons who are foreordained to condemnation, whose names are left out of the book of life, whilst others are written in it.——5. It is a most just and righteous decree; and no other but such can be made by God, who is righteous in all his ways, and holy in all his works.

CHAP. IV.

OF THE ETERNAL UNION OF THE ELECT OF GOD UNTO HIM.

THE union of God's elect unto him, their adoption by him, justification before him, and acceptance with him, being eternal, internal, and immanent acts in God; I know not where better to place them, and take them into consideration, than next to the decrees of God, and particularly the decree of election; since as that flows from the love of God, and is in Christ from everlasting, there must of course be an union to him so early; and since predestination to the adoption of children, and acceptance in the beloved, are parts and branches of it, Eph. i. 4, 5, 6. they must be of the same date. I shall begin with the union of God's elect in Christ.

I shall not here treat of any time-acts of union; as of our nature to the Son of God by his incarnation, when he became our brother, our near kinsman, flesh of our flesh, and bone of our bone; and we and he were of one, that is, of one nature, Heb. ii. 11, 14, 16. nor of the vital union of our persons to him in regeneration, when we are quickened by the power and grace of God, Christ is formed in our hearts, and we become new creatures in him, and are in him as living fruitful branches in him, the living vine; which is our open being in Christ, in consequence of a secret being in him from everlasting by electing grace; see Rom. xvi. 7. 2 Cor. v. 17. and xii. 2. Nor of the more open and manifest union of the saints to God hereafter; who being once in Christ, are always found in him; die in union to him, rise from the dead by virtue of that union; and who will then, in soul and body, be one in God, Father, Son, and Spirit; as the Father is in the Son, and the Son in the Father; whose union to one another is the pattern and exemplar of theirs; and for the open manifestation of which Christ prays, John xvii. 21, 23.

But I shall consider the union of the elect to God, as it is in its original, and as an eternal immanent act in God; and which is no other than the going forth of his heart in love to them, and thereby uniting them to himself; which love, as it is from everlasting, Jer. xxxi. 3. John xvii. 23, 24. so it is of a cementing and uniting nature; and, indeed, is the bond of union between God and his chosen people, or that by which he has taken them into near union with himself: love is the bond of union among men, of friendship one to another; it was this which knit the soul of Jonathan to the soul of David, so that he loved him as his own soul; it is the bond of the saints, union to each other; their hearts are *knit together in love :* hence *charity*, or love, is called, *the bond of perfectness*, or the perfect bond, which joins and keeps them together, Col. ii. 7. and

iii. 14. It was love which so closely cemented the hearts of the first christians to one another, insomuch that the multitude of them were *of one heart and of one soul*, Acts iv. 32. And now love must operate infinitely more strongly in the heart of God, attracting and uniting the objects of it to himself, giving them such a nearness and union to him which cannot be dissolved; nothing can *separate from the love of God;* not the fall of God's elect in Adam; nor their actual sins and transgressions in a state of unregeneracy; nor their revoltings and backslidings after conversion, Rom. viii. 38, 39. Eph. ii. 3, 4. Hos. xiv. 4. This bond of union is indissoluble by the joint power of men and devils. In virtue of this, the people of God become a part of himself, a near, dear, and tender part, even as the apple of his eye; have a place in his heart, are engraven on the palms of his hands, and ever on his thoughts; the desires and affections of his soul are always towards them, and he is ever devising and forming schemes for their welfare; how great is his goodness which he has laid up and wrought for them! Zech. ii. 8. Psalm cxxxix. 17. Cant. vii. 10. Isa. xlix. 16. Psalm xxxi. 19.

The love of Christ to the elect, is as early as that of his Father's love to him and them, and which, it seems, was a love of complacency and delight; for before the world was, his *delights were with the sons of men*, John xv. 9. Prov. viii. 30, 31. and this is of the same cementing and uniting nature as his Father's; it is this which causes him to stick closer than a brother to his people; and nothing can separate from his love to them, any more than from the love of the Father; having loved his own, he loves them to the end. This bond of union remains firm and sure, and gives such a nearness to him the church wished for; *Set me as a seal upon thine heart, as a seal upon thine arm*, Cant. viii. 6. see Prov. xviii. 24. Rom. viii. 35. The same may be said of the love of the Spirit; for it is the everlasting love of God, Father, Son, and Spirit, which is the bond of the union of God's elect to the sacred three; they have all three loved the elect with an everlasting love; and thereby have firmly and everlastingly united them to themselves; and hence because of the Spirit's love of them, and union to them, he, in time, becomes the Spirit of life and grace in them, Rom. xv. 30. Now of this love-union there are several branches, or which are so many illustrations and confirmations of it, and all in eternity; as,

1. An election-union in Christ: this flows from the love of God, *electio præsupponit dilectionem*, election presupposes love; see 2 Thess. ii. 13. particular persons are said to be chosen in Christ, as Rufus, Rom. xvi. 13. and the apostle says of himself and others, that God had chosen them *in Christ*, and that before the foundation of the world, Eph. i. 4. Election gives a being in Christ, a kind of subsistence in him; though not an *esse actu*, an actual being, yet at least an *esse representativum*, a representative being; even such an one as that they are capable of having grants of grace made to them in Christ, and of being blessed with all spiritual blessings in him, and that before the world began, 2 Tim. i. 9. Eph. i. 3, 4. and how they can be said to have a being in Christ, and yet have no union to him, I cannot conceive. Besides, in election there is a near relation commences between Christ and the elect; he is given to be an head to them, and they are given as members to him; and as such they are chosen together, he first in order of nature, as the head; and then they as members of him; nothing is more common with sound divines than to express themselves in this manner, when speaking of the election of Christ, and his people in him; particularly, says Dr. Goodwin,[1] "as in the womb, head and members are not conceived apart, but together, as having relation to each other; so were we and Christ (as making up one mystical body to God) formed together in the eternal womb of election." And in the same place he says, "Jesus Christ was the head of election, and of the elect of God; and so in order of nature elected first, though in order of time we were elected together; in the womb of election he, the head, came out first, and then we, the members." Now what relation can well be thought of nearer, or more expressive of a close union, than this of head and members? Christ is the chosen head of the church, the church the chosen body of Christ, the fulness of him that fills all in all, Eph. i. 22, 23. hence is the safety and security of the saints, being in Christ through electing grace, and united to him; and therefore said to be *preserved in* him; herein and hereby put into his hand,

[1] Works, vol. 1. part 1. p. 62.

made the sheep of his hand, out of whose hands none can pluck them, nor they ever fall, Jude, ver. 1.

2. There is a conjugal union between Christ and the elect, which also flows from love, and commenced in eternity. By the institution of natural marriage, the persons between whom it is contracted become one flesh, as did Adam and Eve: and a nearer union than this cannot well be conceived of; whose marriage was a shadow and representation of that between Christ and his church; whom, having espoused, he nourishes, and cherishes as his own flesh; and they become one, and have one and the same name, Christ, that is, Christ mystical, Eph. v. 29—32. 1 Cor. xii. 12. Now though the open marriage-relation between Christ and particular persons takes place at conversion, which is the day of their espousals to him, Jer. ii. 2. and the more public notification of it will be when all the elect of God are gathered in, and shall in one body be as a bride adorned for her husband, and the marriage of the Lamb shall be come; and this declared in the most open manner, and the nuptials solemnized most magnificently, Rev. xxi. 2. Yet the secret act of betrothing was in eternity, when Christ, being in love with the chosen ones, asked them of his Father to be his spouse and bride; and being given to him, he betrothed them to himself in loving-kindness, and from thenceforward looked on them as standing in such a relation to him; and which is the foundation of all other afteracts of grace unto them: hence, because of his marriage-relation to his church, he became her surety, and gave himself for her, shed his precious blood to sanctify and cleanse her from all the impurities of the fall, and other transgressions; that he might present her to himself a glorious church without spot or wrinkle or any such thing; even just such a church, and in such glory he had viewed her in, when he first betrothed her, Eph. v. 25, 26, 27. So with the Jews there was a private betrothing before open marriage, and the consummation of it; at which betrothing the relation of husband and wife commenced, Deut. xxii. 23, 24. and so Christ is said to be the husband of the Gentile church before she was in actual being, Isa. liv. 5.

3. There is a federal union between Christ and the elect, and they have a covenant-subsistence in him as their head and representative. The covenant flows from, and is the effect of the love, grace, and mercy of God; these are spoken of along with it as the foundation of it, Psalm lxxxix. 2, 3, 33, 34. Isa. liv. 10. hence it is commonly called the covenant of grace, and this was made from everlasting; Christ was set up as the mediator of it, and his goings forth in it were so early, Prov. viii. 23. Mic. v. 2. eternal life was promised before the world began, and blessings of grace so soon provided, Tit. i. 2. 2 Tim. i. 9. all which proves the antiquity of this covenant, of which more hereafter. Now this covenant was made with Christ not as a single person, but as a common head; not for himself, or on his own account only, but for and on the account of his people; as the covenant of works was made with Adam, as the federal head of all his posterity; hence he is said to be the figure or type of him that was to come, Rom. v. 14. so the covenant of grace was made with Christ as the federal head of his spiritual offspring; and for this reason a parallel is ran between them in Rom. v. and 1 Cor. xv. as if they had been the only two men in the world, the one called the first, the other the second man. Christ represented his people in this covenant, and they had a representative union to him in it; all that he promised and engaged to do, he promised and engaged in their name and on their account; and when performed it was the same with God, as if it had been done by them; and what he received, promises and blessings of grace, he received in their name, and they received them in him, being one with him as their common head and representative.

4. There is a legal union between Christ and the elect, the bond of which is his suretiship for them, flowing from his strong love and affection to them. In this respect Christ and they are one in the eye of the law, as the bondsman and debtor are one in a legal sense; so that if one of them pays the debt bound for, it is the same as if the other did. Christ is the surety of the better testament; he drew nigh to God, gave his bond, laid himself under obligation to pay the debts of his people, and satisfy for their sins; who being as such accepted of by God, he and they were considered as one; and this is the ground and foundation of his payment of their debts, of his making satisfaction for their sins, of the imputation of their sins to him, and of the imputation of his righteousness to them. In short, it is the saint's antecedent union and relation to Christ in eternity, in the several views

of it in which it has been considered, which is the ground and reason of all that Christ has done and suffered for them, and not for others; and of all the blessings of grace that are or shall be bestowed upon them, and which are denied to others: the reason why he became incarnate for them, and took upon him human nature with a peculiar regard to them, was because they were children given to him; and why he laid down his life for them, because they were his sheep; and why he gave himself for them, because they were his church; and why he saved them from their sins, because they were his people, Heb. ii. 13, 14. John x. 14, 15. Eph. v. 25. Matt. i. 21. In a word, union to Christ is the first thing, the first blessing of grace flowing from love and effected by it; and hence is the application of all others; *of him are ye in Christ Jesus*, first loved and united to Christ, and then it follows, *who of God is made unto us wisdom and righteousness, sanctification, and redemption*, 1 Cor. i. 30. So Dr. Goodwin[2] observes, that "union with Christ is the first fundamental thing of justification and sanctification and all. Christ first takes us, and then sends his Spirit; he apprehends us first; it is not my being regenerate that puts me into a right of all these privileges; but it is Christ takes me, and then gives me his Spirit, faith, holiness, &c."

CHAP. V.

OF OTHER ETERNAL AND IMMANENT ACTS IN GOD, PARTICULARLY ADOPTION AND JUSTIFICATION.

I shall not here treat of these as doctrines, in the full extent of them; or as blessings of grace actually bestowed upon, and enjoyed by believers, with all the privileges and advantages arising from thence; or as transient acts passing on them, and terminating in their consciences at believing; but as internal and immanent acts, taken up in the mind of God from eternity, and which abide in his will; in which they have their complete *esse*, or being, as eternal election has, being of the same kind and nature, and are ranked with it as of the same date, and as branches of it, Eph. i. 4—6. In the other view of them they will be considered hereafter in course, in a proper place. I shall begin with,

1. Adoption; as predestination to it stands next to election, Eph. i. 5. which is no other than his will to adopt the chosen ones, which is his adoption of them; for as the will of God to elect any is his election of them, so his will to adopt the same is his adoption of them; and the complete essence of it lies in his will, and is as such an eternal immanent act of it; in like manner as election is, and may be considered as a branch of it, at least of the same nature with it; and which agrees with the sense of the word *adopto*, from whence adoption comes, which is compounded of *ad* to, and *opto* to choose; so that adoption is God's choice or election of some to be his children; and by this option, or choice, of his they become so. The Greek word for adoption throughout the New Testament is υιοθεσια, which signifies *putting among the children*; the phrase used by God, Jer. iii. 19. *How shall I put them among the children?* or a putting one for and in the room of a son, that is a stranger and not a son by birth; a constituting and accounting such an one as a son, according to choice, will, and pleasure: and divine adoption is an act of the sovereign grace and good-will of God, Eph. i. 5. to which he is not induced by any motive out of himself; not by any excellency in the creature; nor for want of a son; one or other of which is the case in human adoptions; as of Moses, a goodly child, by Pharaoh's daughter; and of Esther, a beautiful person, and a relation by Mordecai; but divine adoption is of persons exceeding unworthy and undeserving, nothing engaging in them; not only strangers, but children of wrath even as others, and like the wretched infant in Ezek. xvi. It is an act of distinguishing grace; it is of men, and not angels; who are servants and not sons, at least not by adoption; and of some men and not of all, though all are alike in their nature-state; and it is a most amazing act of unmerited love and free-grace, 1 John iii. 1. Now this is an eternal act of grace:

First, It did not begin in time, but commenced from eternity; it is an act of God's will, and has its complete essence in it; and the will of God is eternal, no new will, nor any new act of will, arises in God in time; or otherwise he would not be the unchangeable God he is.

1. It is an act that does not first take

[2] Works, vol. 3. part 2. p. 347.

place at believing; indeed the saints are all the children of God by faith in Christ Jesus, openly and manifestatively, Gal. iii. 26. but then it is not faith that makes them children, but what makes them appear to be so; adoption is the act of God, and not of faith; it is God that says, *How shall I put them among the children?* and again, *I will be their Father, and they shall be my sons and daughters,* Jer. iii. 19. 2 Cor. vi. 18. it is the work and business of faith to receive the blessing of adoption, which it could not do, unless it had been previously provided in the mind and by the will of God, and in the covenant of his grace; for the reception of which Christ has made way by his redemption, one end of which is *that we might receive the adoption of sons,* Gal. iv. 5. that is, by faith; for God has appointed faith to be the general receiver of Christ, and of all the blessings of grace through him, and this among the rest; and to *as many as receive Christ,* he gives εξυσιαν, a power, authority, dignity, and privilege *to become the sons of God* openly; that is, to claim this as their privilege and dignity; which claim is made by faith; but not the thing itself claimed; *even to them that believe on his name,* and who are described as regenerate persons; which is an evidence of their sonship, though not the thing itself; *who are born not of blood, nor of the will of the flesh, nor of the will of man; but of God,* John i. 12, 13. But though this describes such who are the sons of God openly, and who believe; yet, 2. Adoption does not first commence at regeneration; adoption and regeneration are two distinct blessings, and the one is previous to the other; though they are commonly confounded together by divines. Regeneration is not the foundation of adoption, but adoption the foundation of regeneration; or, the reason why men are adopted, is not because they are regenerated, but they are regenerated because they are adopted. By adoption they are put into the relation of children, and by regeneration they have a nature given them suitable to that relation; and are made partakers of the divine nature, that they may be made known to be heirs apparent to, and to have a meetness for the possession, enjoyment, and use of it, the inheritance in heaven they are adopted to; for, 3. The act of adoption is previous to any work of the Spirit of God upon the hearts of his people; *Because ye are sons,* sons already, sons by adopting grace; *God hath sent forth the Spirit of his Son into your hearts,* both to convince, convert, regenerate, and effectually call by his grace, and sanctify, and also to comfort, and to enable to cry Abba Father, witnessing to their spirits, that they are the children of God; and hence he is called, *the Spirit of Adoption;* and it is his influences, teachings, and leadings, which are the evidences of adoption; *For as many as are led by the Spirit of God, they are the sons of God;* not that those influences, operations, and leadings, make them, but make them evident to be such, Gal. iv. 6. Rom. viii. 14, 15, 16.——4. Divine adoption, or sonship, took place before any work of Christ was wrought in time, for any of the sons of men; it was before his incarnation and birth; *forasmuch then,* or because *the children are partakers of flesh and blood,* the children of God, who are so by adopting grace; therefore *he also,* Christ, *himself took part of the same;* for though the nature he assumed was what was in common to all mankind, yet he assumed it with a peculiar view to the children of God, the spiritual seed of Abraham; whose nature he is said to take, and for whose sake he was the Child born, and the Son given, Isa. ix. 6. Heb. ii. 14, 16. and in consequence they must be the children of God before Christ suffered and died; and, indeed, he suffered and died for them under this character, considered as the children of God by adopting grace; for he died not only for the elect of God among the *Jews, but that also he should gather together in one the children of God that were scattered abroad;* that is, those who were already the children of God by adopting grace, who were scattered throughout the whole Gentile world. This relates to the gathering of all the elect in one, in Christ, in the dispensation of the fulness of times; when Christ suffered as their Surety, Head, and Representative; and when they were all considered as the children of God, whether in heaven or on earth, and whether among Jews or Gentiles, Eph. i. 10. John xi. 51, 52. and in order to bring these many sons to glory, it became him to be made perfect through sufferings, and that through his redemption of them thereby, they might receive, actually in their own persons, the adoption before provided for them, as before observed; see Heb. ii. 10. Gal. iv. 5.

Secondly, Adoption is an act of God's free grace from all eternity.——1. The elect of God are frequently spoken of as a distinct number of men, given to Christ, and as previous to their coming to him by faith, which is the certain fruit and consequence of that gift; see John xvii. 2, 6, 9, 24. and vi. 37. yea, they were given to Christ before the world was; for if grace was given to them in him before the world began, they themselves must be given to him, and be in him before the world began, 2 Tim. i. 9. Now these were given to Christ in the relation of children, and therefore must be children so early; *Behold I, and the children which God hath given me,* Heb. ii. 13.———2. The elect of God were espoused to Christ in eternity; as has been shewn in the preceding chapter; which serves to illustrate and prove the relation of sonship to God so early; for as in natural and civil marriage, if a man marries a king's daughter, he becomes his son in law; as David to Saul; or if a woman marries a king's son, she becomes the king's daughter; so the elect of God, his church and people, being espoused to the Son of God, they become the sons and daughters of the Lord God almighty, the King of kings: and hence the church is called the King's daughter, Psalm xlv. 13. and these persons being betrothed to Christ the Son of God, in eternity, as they were the spouse of Christ, they must be, and must be considered as being the sons of God so early.———3. The elect of God were taken by him into the covenant of his grace, as children; the sum and substance of which runs thus, *I will be a Father unto you, and ye shall be my sons and daughters,* saith the Lord almighty, 2 Cor. vi. 18. Now this covenant was from everlasting; as the setting up of Christ the Mediator of it so soon; and the promises and blessings, made and provided before the world began, do abundantly testify. Besides, in this covenant, these same persons so early were given to Christ, as his seed and offspring, his children, and he commenced the everlasting Father of them; see Isa. ix. 6. and liii. 10.———4. Predestination to the adoption of children, is mentioned along with election, as of the same date with it, and as an illustration of it, and as an addition to it, or rather, a branch of it; as men by election are not only chosen to holiness, but to adoption, and the inheritance annexed to it, Eph. i. 4, 5. Adoption is a sentence of grace conceived in the divine mind, and settled by the divine will, and pronounced in divine predestination, which is an eternal act of God; and so says Dr. Ames,[3] "Adoption is a gracious sentence of God——which sentence is pronounced in the same variety of degrees as justification; for it was first pronounced in divine predestination, Eph. i. 5. afterwards in Christ, Gal. iv. 5. then in believers themselves, ver. 6." And all these pronunciations, and so all that Christ did in redemption respecting this, or the Spirit of God does in revealing, applying, and witnessing it, yea, all that will be done in eternity to come; for though now the saints *are the sons of God, it doth not yet appear,* clearly and fully, *what they shall be,* even as sons, or what dignity and glory they shall be raised unto, in consequence of this relation; I say, all these in time, and to eternity, serve only to open and expand the original act of God's will, in appointing and constituting them his sons in an eternity past.

II. Justification is an act of God's grace, flowing from his sovereign good will and pleasure; the elect of God are said to be *justified by his grace;* and as if that expression was not strong enough to set forth the freeness of it, the word *freely* is added elsewhere; *Being justified freely by his grace,* Tit. iii. 7. Rom. iii. 24. Justification is by many divines distinguished into active and passive. Active justification is the act of God; it is God that justifies. Passive justification is the act of God, terminating on the conscience of a believer, commonly called a transient act, passing upon an external object. It is not of this I shall now treat, but of the former; which is an act internal and eternal, taken up in the divine mind from eternity, and is an immanent, abiding one in it; it is, as Dr. Ames[4] expresses it, "a sentence conceived in the divine mind, by the decree of justifying." Now, as before observed, as God's will to elect, is the election of his people, so his will to justify them, is the justification of them; as it is an immanent act in God, it is an act of his grace towards them, is wholly without them, entirely resides in the divine mind, and lies in his estimating, accounting, and constituting them righteous, through the righteousness of his Son; and, as such, did not first commence in time, but from eternity.

First, It does not begin to take place in time, or at believing, but is antecedent to any act of faith.—1. Faith is not the cause,

---

[3] Medulla Theologiæ, 1. 1. c. 28. s. 2, 3.   [4] Ibid. c. 27. s. 9.

but an effect of justification; it is not the cause of it in any sense; it is not the moving cause, that is the free grace of God; *Being justified freely by his grace*, Rom. iii. 24. nor the efficient cause of it; *It is God that justifies*, Rom. viii. 33. nor the meritorious cause, as some express it; or the matter of it, that is the obedience and blood of Christ, Rom. v. 9, 19. or the righteousness of Christ, consisting of his active and passive obedience; nor even the instrumental cause; for, as Mr. Baxter[5] himself argues, "If faith is the instrument of our justification, it is the instrument either of God or man; not of man, for justification is God's act; he is the sole Justifier, Rom. iii. 26. man doth not justify himself: nor of God, for it is not God that believes:" nor is it a *causa sine qua non*, as the case of elect infants shews; it is not in any class of causes whatever; but it is the effect of justification: all men have not faith, and the reason why some do not believe is, because they are none of Christ's sheep; they were not chosen in him, nor justified through him; but justly left in their sins, and so to condemnation; the reason why others believe is, because they are ordained to eternal life, have a justifying righteousness provided for them, and are justified by it, and shall never enter into condemnation: the reason why any are justified, is not because they have faith;. but the reason why they have faith, is because they are justified; was there no such blessing of grace as justification of life in Christ, for the sons of men, there would be no such thing as faith in Christ bestowed on them; precious faith is obtained through the righteousness of our God and Saviour Jesus Christ, 2 Pet. i. 1. nor, indeed, would there be any room for it, nor any use of it, if a justifying righteousness was not previously provided. Agreeable to this are the reasonings and assertions of Twisse,[6] Maccovius,[7] and others. Now if faith is not the cause, but the effect of justification; then as every cause is before its effect, and every effect follows its cause, justification must be before faith, and faith must follow justification.———2. Faith is the evidence and manifestation of justification, and therefore justification must be before it; *Faith is the evidence of things not seen*, Heb. xi. 1. but it is not the evidence of that which as yet is not; what it is an evidence of, must be, and it must exist before it. The *righteousness of God*, of the God-man and mediator Jesus Christ, *is revealed from faith to faith*, in the everlasting gospel, Rom. i. 17. and therefore must be before it is revealed, and before faith, to which it is revealed: faith is that grace whereby a soul, having seen its guilt, and its want of righteousness, beholds, in the light of the divine Spirit, a complete righteousness in Christ, renounces its own, lays hold on that, puts it on as a garment, rejoices in it, and glories of it; the Spirit of God witnessing to his spirit, that he is a justified person; and so he is evidently and declaratively *justified in the name of the Lord Jesus, and by the Spirit of our God*, 1 Cor. vi. 11.———3. Faith adds nothing to the *esse*, only to the *bene esse* of justification; it is no part of, nor any ingredient in it; it is a complete act in the eternal mind of God, without the being or consideration of faith, or any foresight of it; a man is as much justified before as after it, in the account of God; and after he does believe, his justification does not depend on his acts of faith; for though *we believe not, yet he abides faithful;* that is, God is faithful to his covenant-engagements with his Son, as their Surety, by whose suretiship-righteousness they are justified; but by faith, men have a comfortable sense, perception and apprehension of their justification, and enjoy that peace of soul which results from it; it is by that only, under the testimony of the divine Spirit, that they know their interest in it, and can claim it, and so have the comfort of it. But,———
4. Justification is the object, and faith the act that is conversant with it. Now every object is prior to the act that is concerned with it; unless when an act gives being to the object, which is not the case here; for faith, as has been seen, is not the cause, nor matter of justification; what the eye is to the body, that is faith to the soul: the eye, by virtue of its visive faculty, beholds sensible objects, but does not produce them; they are before they are seen, and did they not previously exist, the eye could not behold them; the sun is before it is seen; and so in innumerable other instances: faith is to the soul, as the hand is to the body, receives things for its use; but then these things must be before they are received; faith receives the blessing of

---

[5] Aphorism, 56.
[6] Vindiciæ Gratiæ, l. 1. par. 2. s. 25. p. 197.
[7] πρῶτον ψεῦδος, Arminian, c. 10.

justification from the Lord, even that righteousness by which it is justified, from the God of its salvation; but then this blessing must exist before faith can receive it, Psalm xxiv. 5. Christ's righteousness, by which men are justified, is compared to a robe or garment, which faith puts on; but then as a garment must be wrought and completely made, before it is put on, so must the justifying righteousness of Christ be, before it can be put on by faith. ——5. All the elect of God were justified in Christ, their Head and Representative, when he rose from the dead, and therefore they believe: Christ engaged as a Surety for all his people from eternity, had their sins imputed to him, and for which he made himself responsible; in the fulness of time he made satisfaction for them by his sufferings and death, and at his resurrection was acquitted and discharged: now as he suffered and died, not as a private, but as a public person, so he rose again, and was justified as such, even as the representative of his people; hence when he rose, they rose with him; and when he was justified, they were justified in him: for he was *delivered for their offences, and was raised again for their justification*, Rom. iv. 25. see 1 Tim. iii. 16. and this is the sense and judgment of many sound and learned divines; as, besides our Sandford,[8] and Dr. Goodwin,[9] the learned Amesius,[10] Hoornbeck,[11] Witsius,[12] and others. But,

Secondly, Justification, is not only before faith, but it is from eternity, being an immanent act in the divine mind, and so an internal and eternal one; as may be concluded.——1. From eternal election: the objects of justification are God's elect; *Who shall lay anything to the charge of God's elect? it is God that justifies;* that is, the elect. Now if God's elect, as such, can have nothing laid to their charge; but are by God acquitted, discharged, and justified; and if they bore this character of elect from eternity, or were chosen in Christ before the world began; then they must be acquitted, discharged and justified so early, so as nothing could be laid to their charge: besides, by electing grace men were put into Christ, and were considered as in him before the foundation of the world; and if they were considered as in him, they must be considered as righteous or unrighteous; not surely as unrighteous, unjustified, and in a state of condemnation; for *there is no condemnation to them which are in Christ*, Rom. viii. 1. and therefore must be considered as righteous, and so justified: " Justified then we were, says Dr. Goodwin,[13] when first elected, though not in our own persons, yet in our Head, as he had our persons then given him, and we came to have a being and an interest in him."——2. Justification may well be considered as a branch of election; it is no other, as one expresses it, than setting apart the elect alone to be partakers of Christ's righteousness; and a setting apart Christ's righteousness for the elect only; it is mentioned along with election, as of the same date with it; *Wherein*, that is, in the grace of God, particularly the electing grace of God, spoken of before, *he hath made us accepted in the beloved,* Eph. i. 6. What is this acceptance in Christ, but justification in him? and this is expressed as a past act, in the same language as other eternal things be in the context, he *hath* blessed us, and he *hath* chosen us, and *having* predestinated us, so he *hath* made us accepted; and, indeed, as Christ was always the beloved of God, and well pleasing to him; so all given to him, and in him, were beloved of God, well pleasing to him, and accepted with him, or justified in him from eternity. ——3. Justification is one of those spiritual blessings wherewith the elect are blessed in Christ according to election-grace, before the foundation of the world, Eph. i. 3, 4. That justification is a spiritual blessing none will deny; and if the elect were blessed with all spiritual blessings, then with this; and if thus blessed according to election, or when elected, then before the foundation of the world: and this grace of justification must be no small part of that *grace which was given in Christ Jesus before the foundation of the world was*, 2 Tim. i. 9. " We may say, says Dr. Goodwin,[14] of all spiritual blessings in Christ, what is said of Christ, that *his goings forth are from everlasting*——in Christ we were blessed with all spiritual blessings, Eph. i. 3. as we are blessed with all other, so with this also, that we were justified then in Christ! ——4. Christ became a Surety for his

---

[8] De Descensu Christi, 1. 3. s. 30. p. 59.
[9] Works, vol. 4. part 1. p. 105, 106.
[10] Medulla ut supra.
[11] Summa Controvers. 1. 10. p. 705.

[12] Animadv. Irenic c. 10. s. 2. see the words of these authors at length, and of others before referred to, in my treatise on Justification.
[13] Ut supra.
[14] Ibid.

people from everlasting; engaged to pay their debts, bear their sins, and make satisfaction for them; and was accepted of as such by God his Father, who thenceforward looked at him for payment and satisfaction, and looked at them as discharged, and so they were in his eternal mind; and it is a rule that will hold good, as Maccovius[15] observes, "that as soon as one becomes a surety for another, the other is immediately freed, if the surety be accepted;" which is the case here, and it is but a piece of common prudence, when a man has a bad debt, and has good security for it, to look not to the principal debtor, who will never be able to pay him, but to his good bondsman and surety, who is able; and so Dr. Goodwin[16] observes, that God, in the everlasting transaction with Christ, "told him, as it were, that he would look for his debt and satisfaction of him, and that he did let the sinners go free; and so they are in this respect, justified from all eternity."—— 5. The everlasting transaction, the same excellent writer thinks, is imported in 2 Cor. v. 19. *God was in Christ reconciling the world unto himself, not imputing their trespasses unto them.* And the very learned Witsius[17] is of opinion, "that this act of God may be called, the general justification of the elect." And, indeed, since it was the determination of God, and the scheme and method he proposed to take in Christ for the reconciliation of the elect, not to impute their sins to them, but to his Son, their Surety; then seeing they are not imputed to them, but to him; and if reckoned and accounted to him, then not to them; and if charged to him, then they must be discharged from them, and so justified; and a non-imputation of sin to the elect, is no other than a justification of them; and thus the apostle strongly concludes the imputation of Christ's righteousness; which is the *formalis ratio*, or the form of justification, from the non-imputation of sin, and the remission of it, Rom. iv. 6, 7, 8.——6. It was the will of God from everlasting, not to punish sin in the persons of his elect, but to punish it in the person of Christ; and that it was his will not to punish it in his people, but in his Son, is manifest from his setting him forth in his purposes and decrees, to be the propitiation for sin; and from his sending him forth in the likeness of sinful flesh, to condemn sin in the flesh; and from his being made sin and a curse, that his people might be made the righteousness of God in him. Now, as has been often observed, no new will can arise in God; God wills nothing in time, but what he willed from eternity; and if it was the eternal will of God not to punish sin in his people, but in his Son, then they were eternally discharged, acquitted from sin, and secured from everlasting wrath and destruction; and if they were eternally discharged from sin, and freed from punishment, they were eternally justified: Dr. Twisse[18] makes the very quiddity and essence of justification and remission of sin, which he takes to be the same, to lie in the will of God not to punish; and asserts, that this will not to punish, as it is an immanent act, was from eternity.——7. It deserves regard and attention, that the saints under the Old Testament, were justified by the same righteousness of Christ, as those under the New, and that before the sacrifice was offered up, the satisfaction given, and the everlasting righteousness brought in; for Christ's blood was shed for the remission of sins that were past, and his death was for the redemption of transgressions under the first Testament, Rom. iii. 25. Heb. ix. 15. Now if God could, and actually did, justify some, three or four thousand years before the righteousness of Christ was actually wrought out, taking his Son's word and bond as their Surety, and in a view of his future righteousness; why could he not, and why may it not be thought he did, justify all his elect from eternity, upon the word and bond of their Surety, and on the foot of his future righteousness, which he had engaged to work out, and which he full well knew he would most certainly work out? and if there is no difficulty in conceiving of the one, there can be none in conceiving of the other.

There are many objections made to this truth; some are so trifling as to deserve no notice; a few of the more principal ones I shall briefly answer to, and chiefly those made, for the most part, by the learned Turretine.[19]

1. It is objected, that men cannot be justified before they exist; they must *be*, before they can be justified; since *non entis*

---

[15] Theolog. Quæst. loc. 31. qu. 6.
[16] Ut supra.
[17] Ut supra.

[18] Ut supra, p. 104.
[19] Institut. Theolog. tom. 2. loc. 16. qu. 9. s. 3.

nulla sunt accidentia, &c. of a nonentity nothing can be said, nor anything ascribed to it. To which I answer, whatever is in this objection, lies as strongly against eternal election, as against eternal justification; for it may as well be said, how can a man be elected before he exists? he must be, before he can be chosen, or be the object of choice. I own, with Maccovius,[20] that this is true of non-entities, that have neither an *esse actu,* nor an *esse cognitum,* that have neither an actual being, nor is it certain, nor known that they shall have any future being: but though God's elect have not an actual being from eternity, yet it is certain, by the prescience and predetermination of God, that they shall have one; for *known unto God are all his works from the beginning,* or from eternity, Acts xv. 18. And besides this, they have an *esse representativum,* a representative being in Christ; which is more than other creatures have, whose future existencies are certain; even such a being as makes them capable of being chosen in Christ, and blessed in him before the foundation of the world, and of having grace given them in him before the world was; and why not then of being justified in him? Eph. i. 3, 4. 2 Tim. i. 9. Moreover, as the same writer[21] observes, "Justification is a moral act, which does not require the existence of the subject together with it; but it is enough that it shall exist some time or other."

2. It is farther objected, that if God's elect are justified from eternity, then they were not only justified before they themselves existed, but before any sin was committed by them; and it seems absurd that men should be justified from sins before they were committed, or any charge of them brought against them. To which may be replied, that it is no more absurd to say, that God's elect were justified from their sins before they were committed, than it is to say, that they were imputed to Christ, and he died for them, and made satisfaction for them before committed; which is most certainly true of all those that live, since the coming and death of Christ: such that believe the doctrines of the imputation of sin to Christ, and of his satisfaction for it, ought never to make this objection; and if they do, they ought to be fully content with the answer. As for the charge of sin against God's elect, that is not first made when brought to the conscience of an awakened sinner; justice brought the charge against all the elect, in the eternal transactions between the Father and the Son; or how came Christ to be bail and Surety for them? or how otherwise could there be a transfer of the charge from them to Christ? and where is the grace of a non-imputation of sin to them, and of an imputation of it to Christ, if it was not imputable to them, and chargeable on them?

3. It is urged, that strictly and accurately speaking, it cannot be said that justification is eternal, because the decree of justification is one thing, and justification itself another; even as God's will of sanctifying is one thing, and sanctification itself another; wherefore, though the decree of justification is eternal, and precedes faith, that itself is in time, and follows it. To which it may be answered, that as God's decree and will to elect men to everlasting life and salvation, is his election of them; and his will not to impute sin to them, is the non-imputation of it; and his will to impute the righteousness of Christ unto them, is the imputation of it to them; so his decree, or will to justify them, is the justification of them, as that is an immanent act in God; which has its complete essence in his will, as election has; is entirely within himself, and not transient on an external subject, producing any real, physical, inherent change in it, as sanctification is and does; and therefore the case is not alike: it is one thing for God to will to act an act of grace concerning men, another thing to will to work a work of grace in them; in the former case, the will of God is his act of justification; in the latter it is not his act of sanctification; wherefore, though the will of God to justify, is justification itself, that being a complete act in his eternal mind, without men; yet his will to sanctify, is not sanctification, because that is a work wrought in men, and not only requires the actual existence of them, but an exertion of powerful and efficacious grace upon them: was justification, as the papists say, by an infusion of inherent righteousness in men, there would be some strength in the objection; but this is not the case, and therefore there is none in it.

4. It is observed, that the apostle, reckoning up in order, the benefits which flow from the love of God to the elect, in his famous chain of salvation, sets vocation

---

[20] Loc. Commun. c. 69. p. 609.

[21] Theolog. Quæst. loc. 31.

before justification, as something antecedent to it. Rom. viii. 30. from whence it is concluded, that vocation is in order of time, before justification. To which I reply, that the order of things in scripture is frequently inverted. The Jews have a saying,[22] that there is nothing prior and posterior in the law; that is, that the order of things is not strictly observed; to put that first which is first, and that last which is last; but the order is changed, and therefore nothing strictly can be concluded from thence; even the order of persons in the Trinity is not always kept to, sometimes the Son is placed before the Father, and the holy Spirit before them both; which, though it may be improved into an argument for their equality, yet not to destroy the order among them; and so with respect to vocation, it may be observed, that it is sometimes placed before election, 2 Pet. i. 10. but none but an Arminian would argue from thence, that it is really before it in order of time, or that men are not elected until they are called: on the other hand, salvation is placed before vocation, 2 Tim. i. 9. *Who hath saved us, and called us*, &c. from whence we might, with as great propriety argue, that salvation, and so justification, precedes vocation; as to argue, from the other text in Romans, that vocation precedes justification, in order of time. Indeed, nothing is to be concluded with certainty, one way or another, from such modes and forms of expression. Justification, as a transient act, and declarative, follows vocation; but as an immanent act in God, it goes before it, of which we are only speaking, as ought always to be remembered.

5. It is affirmed, that those various passages of scripture, where we are said to be justified through faith, and by faith, have no other tendency than to shew that faith is something pre-requisite to justification, which cannot be said if justification was from eternity. To which the answer is, that those scriptures which speak of justification, through and by faith, do not militate against, nor disprove justification before faith; for though justification by and before faith differ, yet they are not opposite and contradictory. They differ, the one being an immanent act in God; all which sort of acts are eternal, and so before faith; the the other being a transient declarative act, terminating on the conscience of the believer; and so is by and through faith, and follows it. But then these do not contradict each other, the one being a declaration and manifestation of the other. What scriptures may be thought to speak of faith, as a pre-requisite to justification, cannot be understood as speaking of it as a pre-requisite to the being of justification; for faith has no casual influence upon it, it adds nothing to its being, it is no ingredient in it, it is not the cause nor matter of it; at most, they can only be understood as speaking of faith as a pre-requisite to the knowledge and comfort of it, and to a claim of interest in it; and this is readily allowed, that no man is evidentially and declaratively justified until he believes; that is, he cannot have the knowledge of it, nor any comfort from it; nor can he claim his interest in it, without faith; and this being observed, obviates another objection, that if justification is before faith, then faith is needless and useless. It is not so; it is not of use to justify men, which it is never said to do; but it is of use to receive the blessing of justification, and to enjoy the comfort of it.

6. It is asserted, that justification cannot be from eternity, but only in time, when a man actually believes and repents; otherwise it would follow, that he who is justified, and consequently has passed from death to life, and is become a child of God, and an heir of eternal life, abides still in death, and is a child of wrath, because he who is not yet converted, and lies in sin, abides in death, 1 John iii. 14. and is of the devil, ver. 8. and in a state of damnation, Gal. v. 21. but this latter especially cannot be admitted of, with respect to God's elect, even while unconverted. And now, to remove this seeming difficulty, let it be observed, that the elect of God may be considered under two different *heads*, Adam and Christ, and as related to two covenants at one and the same time; as they are the descendents of Adam, they are related to him as a covenant-head, and as such, sinned in him, and judgment came upon them all to condemnation and death, and so they are, by nature, children of wrath, even as others. But as considered in Christ, they are loved with an everlasting love, chosen in him before the world was, and always viewed and accounted righteous in him, and so secured from everlasting wrath and damnation; hence it is no

---

[22] T. Bab. Pesachim, fol. 6. 2.

contradiction to say, that the elect of God, as in Adam, and according to the covenant of works, are under the sentence of condemnation ; and that as in Christ, and according to the covenant of grace, and the secret transactions thereof, they are justified, and saved from condemnation. This is no more a contradiction, than that they were loved with an everlasting love, and yet are children of wrath, at one and the same time, as they most certainly are; nor than that Jesus Christ was the object of his Father's love and wrath at the same time, he sustaining two different capacities, and standing in two different relations, when he suffered in the room and stead of his people ; as the Son of God he was always the object of his love ; as the Surety of his people, bearing their sins, and suffering for them, he was the object of his wrath, Psalm lxxxix. 38.

7. It is urged what the apostle says, 1 Cor. vi. 11. *Now ye are justified;* as if they were not justified before; but the word *now* is not in the text; and was it, and admit that to be the sense of it, it does not follow that they were not justified before : for so they might be *in foro dei,* in the court of God, and in his account from eternity, and in Christ their Head and Surety, and especially when he rose from the dead, before now ; yet not till now be justified in *foro conscientiæ,* in their own consciences, and by the Spirit of God; which is the justification the apostle is there speaking of. In a word, the sentence of justification pronounced on Christ, the representative of his people, when he rose from the dead, and that which is pronounced by the Spirit of God in the consciences of believers, and that which will be pronounced before men and angels at the general judgment, are only so many repetitions, or renewed declarations, of that grand original sentence of it, conceived in the mind of God from all eternity; which is the eternal justification pleaded for ; and is no other than what many eminent divines of the highest character for learning and judgment, have asserted, as before observed ; and it is to such as these Dr. Owen[23] refers, when he replied to Mr. Baxter, who charged him with holding eternal justification ; " I neither am, nor ever was of that judgment; though as it may be explained, I know *better, wiser,* and *more learned* men than myself, (and he might have added, than Mr. Baxter,) that *have* been, and *are.*"

CHAP. VI.

OF THE EVERLASTING COUNCIL BETWEEN THE THREE DIVINE PERSONS, CONCERNING THE SALVATION OF MEN.

HAVING treated of the internal and immanent acts in the divine mind, and which are eternal; I shall next consider the operations and transactions among the three divine persons when alone, before the world began, or any creature was in being; and which are, chiefly the council and covenant of God, respecting the salvation of men : these are generally blended together by divines; and indeed it is difficult to consider them distinctly with exactness and precision ; but I think they are to be distinguished, and the one to be considered as leading on, and as preparatory and introductory to the other, though both of an eternal date ; and shall begin with the council of God, held between the three divine persons, Father, Son and Spirit, concerning the affair of man's salvation before the world was. And it will be proper to inquire,

First, In what sense counsel, consultation, and deliberation, can be ascribed to God, to the divine persons ; and, 1. This is not to be understood as expressive of any want of knowledge, or of the least degree of ignorance in God, or of his being at a loss in forming the scheme of salvation ; since he is a God of knowledge, of all knowledge, is perfect in knowledge, wanting nothing ; is the only wise and allwise God, whose understanding is infinite, and reaches to all things, and nothing can escape it: want of knowledge is often the case with men, and therefore they deliberate with themselves, and consult with others ; but it is not so with God ; wherefore, 2. Consultation in him is not in order to gain more knowledge, or to obtain more satisfaction, and so more pleasure in the review of things ; for since his understanding is infinite, there can be no accession to it, nor increase of knowledge in it : men consult with themselves, and reason on things in their own minds, or consult with others to gain more knowledge ; and if this is not the result of it, yet it gives them satisfaction and pleasure, when those they

---

[23] Doctrine of Justification vindicated from the animadversions of R. B. p. 9. see also p. 4.

P

have an high opinion of, agree with them, and approve of their schemes; this makes their minds more easy, and confirms and settles them; and thus in the multitude of counsellors there is safety and delight; see Prov. xi. 14. and xxvii. 9.——Nor, 3. Does a council held between the three divine persons suppose any inequality between them; usually indeed with men in matters of moment and difficulty, persons supposed to be of superior abilities are consulted, and their judgment taken; as Ahitophel by David, and the Israelites, whose counsel with them was as the oracles of God; but this is not to be supposed here, when the Father consults with the Son and Spirit, it is not because they have knowledge superior to him, or that he needs any information from them; they are one in nature, and are equal in knowledge and understanding; the Father is omniscient, the Son knows all things, and the Spirit searches the deep things of God; and yet may consult together; and three persons of equal knowledge and judgment among men may consult together about an affair of importance, without supposing any superiority and inferiority in them.—— 4. Nor is consultation in God continued, carried on and protracted to any length, as it often is with men, who when they have a matter of difficulty before them, do not suddenly and at once determine; but take time and consider it in every point of view, that they may fix on the wisest and most rational method of acting; consultations on an affair have been sometimes held many days successively; but so it is not with God, counsel with him is as quick as thought, yea, it is no other than his thought, and therefore they go together, Psalm xxxiii. 11. But, (1.) When consultation about the salvation of man is ascribed to God, it is intended to express the importance of it; not things trifling, but those of importance, are what men consult about and deliberate upon; such is the work of men's salvation of the greatest moment, not only to men, to their comfort and happiness here and hereafter, but to the glory of God; the glory of all whose perfections is greatly displayed in it, being so wisely contrived as it is for that purpose; wherefore it is not put upon any footing; nor into any hands, but into the hands of the Son of God, Psalm xxi. 5. John xvii. 4.—— (2.) This way of speaking is used to set forth the wisdom of God displayed herein; schemes, which are the fruit of consultation and deliberation, are generally the most wisely formed, and best succeed: in the scheme of salvation by Christ, God has abounded in all wisdom and prudence; it is the manifold wisdom of God, in which that is displayed in the greatest fulness and variety; insomuch that angels, those wise and knowing creatures, desire to look more and more into it, Eph. i. 7. 8. and iii. 10.——(3.) This being the effect of a council between the three divine persons, shews their unanimity in it; as they are one in nature, so they agree in one; and as in every thing, so in this, the salvation of men; the Father signified his mind that his Son should be sent to be the Saviour of men, when he may be supposed to put such a question as in Isa. vi. 8. *Whom shall I send, and who will go for us?* the Son, knowing his Father's will, and assenting to it, declared his agreement with it, *Here am I, send me;* and the Spirit approving of the Father's motion, and the Son's consent, joined with the divine Father in the mission of him; *Now the Lord God and his Spirit hath sent me,* Isa. xlviii. 16. and what inexpressible pleasure must such unanimity give to a believing soul, to declare which is the design of the divine consultation. These things being observed, I shall endeavour,

Secondly, To give some proof that there was a council between the divine persons concerning the salvation of men.——1. An argument in favour of this may be drawn from the purpose of God; all whose purposes are called his counsels, because they are founded in the highest wisdom, Isa. xxv. 1. now the purpose of God respecting the salvation of men, is the basis and foundation of the council held concerning it, in which purpose, as well as council, all the three persons are concerned; for the scheme of salvation, which is, *the manifold wisdom of God,* is *according to the eternal purpose which he* (God the Father) *purposed in Christ Jesus our Lord,* Eph. iii. 10, 11. and the Son was not only privy to this purpose or counsel, and agreed to it; but the Spirit also, who searches *the deep things of God,* and approves of them, which are no other than the purposes and counsels of his heart, 1 Cor. ii. 10.——2. It appears there was a consultation held about the salvation of men from the gospel, which is an exhibition and declaration of the scheme of salvation, being called the *counsel of God,* Acts. xx. 27. and the wisdom of God, the hidden wisdom ordained before the world, 1 Cor. ii. 6. for it is no other indeed than a transcript of the council and covenant of grace; the sum and substance of the word and ministry of reconciliation, is that eternal transaction between God and Christ concerning it, which the apostle thus expresses; *God was in Christ reconciling the world unto himself, not imputing their trespasses,* 2 Cor. v. 19.——3. It may be reasonably concluded, from the consultation had between the divine Persons, concerning the formation of man, thus expressed, *And God said, Let us make man in our image;* which was said, not to angels, but to the other two divine Persons, the Son and Spirit; and it is not necessary to understand the words as spoken the moment, or immediately before the creation of man, but as spoken in eternity, in council between the divine Persons; for it may be rendered, *God had said;* and, indeed, God had determined on this in the decree of election; for as in the decree of the end, he chose some of the creatures his power could make, to be happy with him, for his own glory; so in the decree of the means, he resolved on the creation of them; as has been before observed; however, be it, that this consultation was immediately before the creation of man, as all the three Persons were concerned in that, and in his creation; it may be reasonably argued, that if there was a consultation of the divine Persons about the making of man at first, then much more about the redemption and salvation of him. But,——4. What would put this matter out of all doubt, is the sense of a passage in Zech. vi. 13. as given by some learned men, if it can be established; *And the counsel of peace shall be between them both:* some, indeed, interpret it of the Kingly and Priestly offices meeting in Christ, and of the unanimity of them in him; since it is before said, *He shall be a priest upon the throne;* but it seems rather to respect persons and things. Others have thought of Zerubbabel the prince, and Joshua the high-priest, who were unanimously agreed in building the second temple: but an edifice of another kind, and of a spiritual nature, the church of God, seems to be intended, the building of which is ascribed to a single Person only. Rather by the *counsel of peace,* may be meant the gospel, called the counsel of God, and the gospel of peace, which was to be, and has been among Jews and Gentiles, preached to them, both as to them that are nigh, so to them afar off, as in ver. 15. and which was a means of making peace between them, and reconciling them together, Eph. ii. 17. and vi. 15. and in this sense of the words I formerly acquiesced:[1] but there is another sense of them embraced by learned men, to whose judgment I pay a great deference; such as Heidegger,[2] De Dieu,[3] Cocceius,[4] Witsius,[5] Dr. Owen,[6] and others, that this respects the council concerning the peace and reconciliation in eternity, between Jehovah and the Branch, between the Father and the Son, who in time was to become man. My objections to this sense have been, that this council in eternity was between the three Persons, and not two only; and that that is what is past; whereas this is spoken of as future: but when I consider that Jehovah and the Branch are the only Persons mentioned in the text, and so could only, with propriety, be spoken of, though the council was between the three; and that, in the Hebrew language, tenses are frequently put for one another, the past for the future, and so the future for the past; and things are said to be, when they appear to be, though they are before; the sense may be, that when the Man, the Branch, should grow out of his place, and build the temple, and bear the glory, and sit a priest on his throne, then it should clearly appear, that there had been a council of peace between them both, which was the ground and foundation of all: and in this light, this sense of the passage may be admitted, and so be a proof of the point under consideration. But if this is not the truth of this text; yet,——5. That there has been such a transaction between the Father and the Son, which, with propriety enough, may be called the *counsel of peace,* we have sufficient warrant from 2 Cor. v. 19. *God was in Christ reconciling the world unto himself, not imputing their trespasses;* by the *world* is meant the elect of God, he so loved, as to send his Son to be the Saviour of, and for the life of whom Christ gave his flesh, John iii. 16. and vi. 51. and about the peace and reconciliation of those, or in what way to make peace and atonement for them, God was in Christ, or with Christ,

---

[1] See my exposition of Zech. vi. 13.
[2] Corpus Theolog. loc. 11. s. 12. p. 376.
[3] In loc.
[4] Summa de Fœdere, c. 5. s. 88.
[5] Oeconom. Fœderum, 1. 2. c. 1. s. 7, 8.
[6] In Hebrews, vol. 2. Exercitat. 4. s. 10. p. 54.

consulting, contriving, and planning the scheme of it; which was this, not to impute their sins unto them, but to Christ, now called to be the Saviour of them; and this contains the sum of what we mean by the council of peace. I proceed,

Thirdly, To observe, that the three divine Persons, Father, Son, and Spirit, and they only, were concerned in this council.——1. Not angels, for they were not then in being, they were not made till the heavens were. But this council was before the heavens and the earth were made; and besides, the angels are the creatures of God, his ministering spirits, and therefore he would never consult with them; they knew nothing of this transaction until it was revealed unto them: and when it was, many of them, as some think, were offended at it, left their habitation, and apostatised from God; not being able to endure it, that the Son of God, in human nature, should be their Head, and so that nature be advanced above theirs, which they perceived by this step would be the case: and as for those that stood and kept their first estate, they were so far from assisting in this council, that they were entirely unacquainted with it, until it was made known unto them; and when it was, though they highly approved of it, their knowledge of it seemed to be imperfect; since they desire to look more and more into it, and *even do* learn of the church the manifold wisdom of God in it, 1 Pet. i. 12. Eph. iii. 10.—— 2. Nor were men a party in this council; *For who hath known the mind of the Lord, or who hath been his counsellor?* Rom. xi. 34. not any of the sons of men; for these also were not then in being, and when they were, were but creatures, and soon became sinful ones, and destitute of true wisdom and knowledge, and so unfit to be of such a council, had it been in time; and had God summoned all the individuals of human nature together, and proposed it to them, that if they could find out a way how they could be saved, consistent with his divine perfections, he would willingly save them; after ever so long a time allowed them for consultation about it; and even if they had had the assistance of all the angels in heaven, they must have returned an *ignoramus*, and owned they knew not any. No, none but the blessed Three in One were of this council, and fit to be of it; the thing consulted about was *nodus Deo vindice dignus*, worthy only of God.——1. Jehovah the Father, the first Person in order of nature, though not of time, may reasonably be supposed to give the lead in this affair, and proposed the thing to be debated and advised about; he who, concerning the creation of man, proposed it to the other two Persons, might, with great propriety, move for a consultation about his salvation: who is the Ancient of days, with whom is wisdom, and who hath counsel and understanding, yea, is wonderful in counsel, as well as excellent in working; and so infinitely fit to conduct an affair of this nature, Job. xii. 12, 13. Isa. xxviii. 29.——2. Jehovah the Son, has the same wisdom, counsel and understanding his Father has; for all that he hath are his; nor does Christ think it any robbery to be equal with him; he is wisdom itself, or *wisdoms*, he is possessed of the most consummate wisdom; in him, even as Mediator, are hid all the treasures of wisdom and knowledge; and he himself says, *Counsel is mine, and sound wisdom*, Prov. i. 20. and viii. 14. see Col. ii. 3. yea, he is called *the Wonderful, Counsellor*, Isa. ix. 6. which not only respects his capacity and ability to give the best counsel and advice to men, as he does, but to assist in the council of God himself; and so the *Septuagint* interpreters understood that passage, rendering it, *the Angel of the great council;* whereby it seems as if those Jews then had a notion of this great transaction, and of the concern of the Messiah in it; to whom the whole verse belongs: to which may be added, that Christ the Son of God, was as one brought up with his divine Father, lay in his bosom, was privy to his designs, and must be in his council, and was on all accounts fit for it.——3. The holy Spirit had a concern in this council, and was fit to be of it; Epiphanius says,[7] as the Son is the Angel of the great council, so is the holy Spirit; he is not only the Spirit of wisdom to men, and by whom is given to them, to one the word of wisdom, and to another the word of knowledge; and therefore must be possessed of the most perfect wisdom and knowledge himself, Eph. i. 17. 1 Cor. xii. 8. but he is the Spirit of wisdom and understanding, and of counsel and knowledge, to and resting on Christ as Mediator, Isa. xi. 2. and therefore must be a very proper Person to be concerned with

---

[7] In Ancorato, s. 70.

the Father and the Son, in this great council; for never was such a council held as this, between such Persons, and on such a momentous and interesting affair. Which,

Fourthly, Is next to be considered more particularly and distinctly. Now the affair consulted about, was not the salvation of men merely; nor who should be the persons that should be saved with it; for both that was resolved on, and the persons fixed on who were to enjoy it, in the decree of election, which stands firm and sure on the unalterable will of God; but who should be the Saviour, or be the author of this salvation; and a proper person for this work, could never have been devised, found out, and pitched upon, by men and angels; this was the business of this great council. By the decree of election the vessels of mercy were prepared for glory, or were ordained to eternal life, God resolved to have mercy on them, and save them; but who should be the Saviour, was referred to this council to agree upon; it is true, indeed, that this was, in some respect, involved and included in the Father's purpose, according to election, who appointed some, not unto wrath, but to obtain salvation by our Lord Jesus Christ, 1 Thess. v. 9. but then, though this was in the Father's purpose, it was necessary that the will of the Son should be expressed, and his approbation and consent had; for which this council was called and held.

The case stands thus: it was in Jehovah the Father's thoughts, to save men by his Son; he in his infinite wisdom saw he was the fittest person for this work, and in his own mind, chose him to it; and this is meant by laying help on One that is mighty, exalting one chosen from among the people; finding David his servant, and anointing him with his holy oil, Psal. lxxxix. 19, 20. Now in the eternal council he moved it, and proposed it to his Son as the most advisable step that could be taken, to bring about the designed salvation; who readily agreed to it, and said, *Lo, I come to do thy will, O God,* Heb. x. 7. from Psal. xl. 7, 8. and the holy Spirit expressed his approbation of him, as the fittest person to be the Saviour, by joining with the Father in the mission of him, as before observed; and by forming his human nature in time, and filling it with his gifts and graces without measure. The pleasure and satisfaction the three divine Persons had in this affair, thus advised to, consulted, and approved of, is most clearly to be seen and observed at our Lord's baptism, Matt. iii. 16, 17.

But not only it was in this council consulted, who should be the Author of salvation; but also in what way and manner it should be effected, both for the security of men, and for the display of the glory of the divine perfections. Now it should be observed, that the elect of God, the persons to be saved, were considered in this transaction as fallen creatures, which salvation by Christ supposes; as sinners in Adam, on whom judgment came unto condemnation, as obnoxious to the curses of the righteous law, and to the resentments of divine justice; and therefore satisfaction must be made to the law and justice of God, the law must be fulfilled, and justice satisfied, by an atonement made; this was signified to the Saviour found, who approved of it, as a most fit thing to be done; hence God is gracious, and saith, *Deliver him from going down to the pit; I have found a ransom,* Job xxxiii. 24. this was found by infinite wisdom in this council; and whereas this ransom, satisfaction, and atonement, must be made by obeying the precepts of the law, and by the suffering of death, the penalty of it; this the law required of the transgressor of it; *Thou shalt surely die;* and so of the Surety for him; wherefore, since it was necessary that the Captain and Author of salvation, in bringing many sons to glory should be made perfect through sufferings; it was proper that he should assume a nature in which he would be capable of obeying and suffering, even a nature of the same kind with that which sinned; this was notified in council to the Son of God, and he approved of it as right and fit, and said, *A body hast thou prepared me,* a whole human nature, in purpose; and now in council, signified he was ready to assume it in time. Moreover, it was seen proper and advisable, that the human nature assumed, should be holy and pure from sin, that it might be offered up without spot to God; and be a sacrifice to take away sin, which it could not be, if sinful; now here a difficulty arises, how such a nature could be come at, since human nature would be defiled by the sin of Adam; and who would be able to bring a clean thing out of an unclean? This difficulty infinite wisdom surmounts, by proposing that the Saviour should be born of a virgin; that this individual nature to be assumed, should not descend from Adam by ordinary generation, but be formed in an extraordinary manner by the power of the Holy Ghost; and this was approved in council, by both the Son and Spirit, since the one readily assumed this nature in this way, and the other formed it. Once more, it appeared necessary that this nature should be taken up into personal union with the Son of God; or, that the Saviour should be God and man in one person; that he should be man, that he might have somewhat to offer, and thereby make reconciliation for the sins of the people; and that he should be God, to give virtue to his deeds and sufferings, to make them effectual to the purposes of them, and he be a fit Mediator, a day's-man between God and men, and take care of the things belonging to both. In short, the affair debated and consulted between the three divine persons, was the peace and reconciliation of God's elect by Christ, and the way and manner of doing it; and therefore, as before observed, this transaction may, with great propriety, be called, *the council of peace;* and which issued in a covenant of peace, next to be considered; in this council every thing relative to it was advised, consulted, and contrived; and in the covenant the whole was adjusted and settled; and therefore I have considered the council as the preparation and introduction to the covenant.

CHAP. VII.

OF THE EVERLASTING COVENANT OF GRACE, BETWEEN THE FATHER, AND THE SON, AND THE HOLY SPIRIT.

The council before treated of, is the basis and foundation of the covenant of grace, and both relate to the same thing, and in which the same persons are concerned. In the former, things were contrived, planned, and advised; in the latter, fixed and settled. The covenant of grace is a compact or agreement made from all eternity among the divine Persons, more especially between the Father and the Son, concerning the salvation of the elect. For the better understanding these federal transactions between them, before the world was, when there were no creatures, neither angels nor men in being; and which lay the foundation of all the grace and glory, comfort and happiness, of the saints in time and to eternity; it may be proper to consider,

I. The etymology and signification of the words used for *covenant,* in the writings of the Old and New Testament, by which it will appear with what propriety these transactions may be called a *covenant.* The books of the Old Testament were written in Hebrew, and the Hebrew word for *covenant,* throughout those writings is ברית *Berith;* which, by different persons, is derived from different roots. There are a set of men[1] lately risen up, who derive the word from ברר *Barar,* which signifies, to *purify;* and because the word we translate *make,* which usually goes along with *covenant,* signifies, to *cut off,* they warmly contend, that wherever we meet with this phrase, it should be rendered, *cut off the Purifier,* by whom they understand the Lord Jesus Christ. Now, though it will be allowed, that Christ is sometimes called a Refiner and Purifier, Mal. iii. 3. yet not by any word or name derived from this root; nor is it likely, that a *Purifier,* or *he that purifies,* should be expressed by a noun feminine, as *Berith* is; and not by a noun masculine, or a participle belonging to this root; and though such a version of the phrase may happen to suit tolerably well with a passage or two; yet there are many places in which, were it so rendered, no sense could be made of them. If the word has the signification of purity, as a word of the same letters, though differently pointed has, being twice translated *sope,* Jer. ii. 22. Mal. iii. 2. which is of a detersive, cleansing, and purifying nature. Rather as this is used for covenant, it may denote the purity of intention, and sincerity of heart, that ought to be in all persons that enter into covenant with each other; and which is most eminently true of the pure and holy divine persons, in their covenant-engagements. But the word *Berith, covenant,* may rather be derived, as it more commonly is, either from ברא *Bara;* which, in the first sense of the word, signifies to *create;* a covenant being made with man, as soon almost as he was created, which covenant he transgressed, Hos. vi. 7. but the covenant of grace was made before the creation of man; though it was first made manifest quickly after his fall, which was not long after his creation; the sum and substance of which lies in those words *The seed of the woman shall bruise the serpent's head,* Gen. iii. 15. The word, in a secondary sense, may signify, to *order* or

---

[1] Called Hutchinsonians.

dispose of things; as in creation, things were disposed and put in an orderly manner, and with this may agree, the words διατιθεμαι, and διαθηκη, used of a covenant in the New Testament, which signify, a disposing of things in a covenant or testamentary way. It is further observed by some, that the same Hebrew word, in another conjugation, signifies to *cut* in pieces and divide, and think that a covenant has its name from hence, because it was usual at making covenants, to slay creatures for sacrifice, and cut them in pieces, and lay them by each other, and the covenanters to pass between them; of which rite see Gen. xv. 9, 10, 17. Jer. xxxiv. 18. to which way of making a covenant by sacrifice, the allusion may be in Psalm l. 5. Or else the word may be derived from ברה *Barah;* which, among other things, signifies to *eat* food; it being usual, when covenants were made and confirmed, for the parties covenanting, to eat and feast together; as did Abimelech and Isaac, Laban and Jacob, Gen. xxvi. 30. and xxxi. 46. and it may be observed, that the Lord's Supper, which is a feast, is a commemoration of the ratification of the covenant of grace, by the blood of Christ, and wherein and whereby the faith of God's people is strengthened and confirmed, as to their interest in it. But after all, it may be best to derive the word from this root, as it signifies to *select* and *choose*, and the rather, since all those roots, ברה ברא ברר, have this signification; and which well agrees with a covenant, into which persons of their own will and choice, enter; choose the persons to be concerned with them, the terms and conditions on which they covenant with each other, and the things and persons they covenant about; all which entirely agrees with this federal transaction, or covenant of grace we are about to treat of.

The word used in the new Testament for *covenant* is διαθηκη, by which word the *Septuagint* interpreters almost always translate the Hebrew word *berith* in the Old, and comes from a word which signifies to *dispose*, and that in a covenant-way, as in Luke xxii. 29. where the Father is said to appoint, or dispose of his Son, as he also is said to appoint, or dispose by covenant, a kingdom to his people; and the word from it, is used for a covenant in Acts iii. 25. and in other places; and sometimes for a testament, or a man's last will, Heb. ix. 16, 17. and we shall see the use of the word in this sense hereafter, as it may be applicable to the covenant of grace; the word signifies both covenant and testament, and some have called it a covenant-testament, or a testamentary covenant; hence the different administrations of the covenant of grace in time, are called the first and second, the old and new testament; and even the books of scripture, written under those different dispensations, are so distinguished; see Heb. viii. and ix. 2 Cor. iii. 6, 14. In the next place it may not be improper to observe,

II. In what sense the word *covenant* is used in scripture, which may serve to lead into the nature of it. And, 1. It is sometimes used for an ordinance, precept, and command; so the order for giving the heave-offerings to the sons of Aaron, is called a covenant of salt, a perpetual ordinance, Numb. xviii. 19. the law for releasing servants after six years service, has the name of a covenant, Jer. xxxiv. 13, 14. and this may account for the Decalogue, or Ten Commands, being called a covenant, Deut. iv. 13. for whatsoever God enjoins men, they are under an obligation to observe, nor have they a right to refuse obedience to it; and, indeed, the covenant of works made with Adam, was much of the same nature, only he had a will, consenting to obey, the bias of it being to the will of God, as well as power to perform. ———2. A covenant, when ascribed to God, is often nothing more than a mere promise; *This is my covenant with them, saith the Lord, my Spirit that is upon thee,* &c. Isa. lix. 21. hence we read of *covenants of promise,* or promissory covenants, Eph. ii. 12. and, indeed, the covenant of grace, with respect to the elect, is nothing else but a free promise of eternal life and salvation by Jesus Christ, which includes all other promises of blessings of grace in it; *This is the promise that he hath promised us,* the grand comprehensive promise, *even eternal life,* 1 John ii. 25. and which is absolute and unconditional, with respect to them; whatever condition is in that covenant, lay only on Christ to perform; he and his work are the only condition of it. And so.———3. We often read of covenants of God only on one side; of this kind is his covenant of the day and of the night, Jer. xxxiii. 20. which is no other than a promise that these should always continue, without requiring any condition on the part of the creature, Gen. viii. 22. and the covenant he made with Noah and his posterity, and with every living creature, with which latter especially, there could be no restipulation, Gen. ix. 9—17. and so the covenant he promised to make for his people, with the beasts of the field, could be no other than a mere promise of security from hurt by them, Hos. ii. 18. But,——4. A covenant properly made between man and man, is by stipulation and restipulation, in which they make mutual promises, or conditions, to be performed by them; whether to maintain friendship among themselves, and to strengthen themselves against their common enemies, or to do mutual service to each other, and to their respective posterities; such was the confederacy between Abraham, Aner, Eshcol, and Mamre; and the covenant between Abimelech and Isaac, and between David and Jonathan, Gen. xiv. 13. and xxvi. 28. 1 Sam. xx. 15, 16, 42. and xxiii. 18. Now,——5. Such a covenant, properly speaking, cannot be made between God and man; for what can man restipulate with God, which is in his power to do or give to him, and which God has not a prior right unto? God may, indeed, condescend to promise that to man, which otherwise he is not bound to give; and he may require of man, that which he has no right to refuse, and God has a right unto, without making any such promise; and therefore, properly speaking, all this cannot formally constitute a covenant, which is to be entered into of free choice on both sides; and especially such a covenant cannot take place in fallen man, who has neither inclination of will to yield the obedience required, nor power to perform it. But,——6. The covenant of grace made between God and Christ, and with the elect in him, as their Head and Representative, is a proper covenant, consisting of stipulation and restipulation; God the Father in it stipulates with his Son, that he shall do such and such work and service, on condition of which he promises to confer such and such honours and benefits on him, and on the elect in him; and Christ the Son of God, restipulates and agrees to do all that is proposed and prescribed, and, upon performance, expects and claims the fulfilment of the promises: in this compact there are mutual engagements each party enters into, stipulate and restipulate about, which make a proper formal covenant; see Isa. xlix. 1—6. and liii. 10, 11, 12. Psalm xl. 6, 7, 8. John xvii. 4, 5. Which passages of scripture will be produced, and more fully opened hereafter.

III. The names and epithets given to this federal transaction, or covenant of grace, between the Father and Son, both in the scriptures and among men, may deserve some notice, since they may help to give a better and clearer idea of this transaction.——1. It is called, *a covenant of life*, Mal. ii. 5. for though it is said of Levi, yet of him as a type of Christ; and if the covenant with Levi might be so called, much more that with Christ. Some divines call the covenant of works, made with Adam, a covenant of life, and so it may be; but then only as it respected that natural happy life Adam then lived, and as it contained a promise of continuance of it, and confirmation in it, should he stand the trial of his obedience; but not a promise of eternal life and happiness, such as the saints enjoy in heaven; for such a life was never designed to be given by, nor could come through a covenant of works; see Gal. iii. 21. But the covenant of grace contains such a promise, a promise that was made by God, that cannot lie, before the world was; that is, a promise made to Christ, in the covenant of grace, from eternity, who then existed as the federal Head of his people, to whom it was made, and in whose hands it is put for them; he asked life of his father for them in this covenant, and he gave it to him, even length of days for ever and ever; and therefore with great propriety may this covenant be called, a covenant of life; see Tit. i. 2. 2 Tim. i. 1. Psalm xxi. 4.——2. It is called *a covenant of peace*, Mal. ii. 5. Isa. liv. 10. As the transaction between the eternal Three, in which the plan and method of the peace and reconciliation of God's elect was consulted, may be called *the council of peace;* because that was a principal article considered in it; so, for the same reason, the covenant may be called the covenant of peace; for what was concerted in the council of peace concerning it, was fixed and settled in the covenant: as, that the Son of God, in human nature, should be the Peace-Maker, and should make peace by the shedding of his blood; and hence, in the fulness of time, he was sent to be the Man, the Peace, according to promise and prophecy, founded upon this covenant, Mic. v. 2, 5. and had the *chastisement of peace* laid upon him; that is, the punishment for the sins of the elect inflicted on him, whereby their peace and reconciliation was made, Isa. liii. 6. all which was by his own consent, and in consequence of the covenant made between him and his Father, and which, therefore, is rightly called *the covenant of peace*.—— 3. It is commonly called by men, *the covenant of grace;* and properly enough, since it entirely flows from, and has its foundation in the grace of God: it is owing to the everlasting love and free favour of God the Father, that he proposed a covenant of this kind to his Son; and it is owing to the grace of the Son, that he so freely and voluntarily entered into engagements with his Father; the matter, sum, and substance of it is grace; it consists of grants and blessings of grace to the elect in Christ; and the ultimate end and design of it is the glory of the grace of God.—— 4. It is by some divines called, *the covenant of redemption;* and very truly, because the redemption of God's elect is a principal article in it: the Father proposed to the Son, that he should raise up, restore, redeem Israel, his chosen ones; the Son agreed to it, and hence he was declared and promised, and expected as the Redeemer, long before he came into this world to do this service; Job knew him as his living Redeemer, and all the old-testament saints waited for him as such, having had a promise of it, which was founded on this covenant-agreement; for as it was proposed to him, and he agreed to it, to be the Redeemer, so it was promised him, that upon the condition of giving himself, the redemption and ransom-price for the elect, they should be delivered from all their sins, and the effects of them, and out of the hands of all their enemies; see Isa. xlix. 5. and lix. 20. Job xxxiii. 24. But then,—— 5. This covenant is the same with the covenant of grace; some divines, indeed, make them distinct covenants; the covenant of redemption, they say, was made with Christ in eternity; the covenant of grace with the elect, or with believers, in time: but this is very wrongly said; there is but one covenant of grace, and not two, in which the Head and Members, the Redeemer and the persons to be redeemed, Christ and the elect, are concerned; in which he is the Head and Representative of them, acts for them, and on their behalf. What is called a covenant of redemption, is a covenant of grace, arising from the grace of the Father, who proposed to his Son to be the Redeemer, and from the grace of the Son, who agreed to be so; and even the honours proposed to the Son in this covenant, redounded to the advantage of the elect; and the sum and substance of the everlasting covenant made with Christ, is the salvation and eternal happiness of the chosen ones; all the blessings and grants of grace to them, are secured in that eternal compact; for they were blessed with all spiritual blessings in him, and had grace given them in him before the world was; wherefore there can be no foundation for such a distinction between a covenant of redemption in eternity, and a covenant of grace in time.

IV. The contracting parties concerned in this covenant, are next to be considered more particularly and distinctly. This covenant is commonly represented as if it was only between the Father and the Son; but I see not why the holy Spirit should be excluded, since he is certainly promised in it both to Head and members; and in consequence of it, is sent down into the hearts of God's covenant-ones, to make application of the blessings, promises, and grace of the covenant to them, and to work a work of grace in them; all which must be by agreement, and with his consent; and I think there are some traces, and some footsteps of all the three Persons, as concerned in it, in the dispensation and manifestation of this covenant to the people of Israel, Hag. ii. 4, 5. However, as in all covenants the contracting parties are,——
1. Distinct from each other, so in this; a covenant is not of one, but of more than one; no man covenants with himself; at least such a covenant is not properly one; Job is, indeed, said to make a covenant with his eyes, chap. xxxi. 1. but that was no other than a resolution within himself to lay a restraint upon his eyes, not to make use of them in such a manner as might tend to sin. The divine Persons of the sacred Trinity are distinct Persons, as has been proved in the article on that subject. And so they appear to be in their federal transactions with each other. He that called his son to service, and directed him, or proposed the work he should do, *to raise up the tribes of Jacob, and restore the preserved of Israel, &c.* Isa. xlix. 3, 5, 6. must be distinct from him to whom he proposed all this; and he who in compliance with it said, *Lo, I come to do thy will, O my God!* Psalm xl. 7, 8. Heb. x. 7. must be distinct from him whose will he was so ready to do, and whom he calls his Lord and God, as he was, by virtue of his covenant-relation to him: and the Spirit, who was sent by them both, in consequence of a covenant-

agreement, to be the Comforter of the covenant-ones, must be distinct from either.

——2. As they are distinct Persons, so they have distinct acts of will; for though their nature and essence is but one, which is common to them all, and so their will but one; yet there are distinct acts of this will, put forth by and peculiar to each distinct Person: thus their nature being the same, their understanding must be the same; and yet there are distinct acts of the divine understanding, peculiar to each Person; the Father knows the Son, and the Son knows the Father, and they have a distinct knowledge and understanding of one another, and the Spirit knows them both, and they know him. And as their nature and essence, so their affections are the same; and yet there are distinct acts of them, peculiar to each Person; the Father loves the Son, and has put all things into his hands; the Son loves the Father, and is in all things obedient to him; the Spirit loves the Father and the Son, and they both love him: so their will, though the same, there are distinct acts of it, peculiar to each Person; and which appear in their covenanting with each other, and are necessary to it: there is the Father's distinct act of will notified in the covenant, that it is his will and pleasure his Son should be the Saviour of the chosen ones; and there is the Son's distinct act of will notified in the same covenant, he presenting himself, and declaring himself willing, and engaging himself to be the Saviour of them; which distinct acts of the divine will thus notified, formally constituted a covenant between them; and as the holy Spirit dispenses his gifts and grace, the blessings of this covenant, *severally as he will*, 1 Cor. xii. 11. this is pursuant to an agreement, to a notification of his will in covenant also.——

3. These contracting Parties entered into covenant freely and voluntarily, of their own choice, as all covenanters do, or should; hence the Hebrew word for covenant, as has been observed, comes from a root, which signifies to *choose;* because men choose their own terms and conditions, on which they agree to enter into covenant with each other, not being compelled and forced thereunto. So it is in this everlasting covenant, the parties were at entire liberty to enter or not into it: the Father was under no necessity, nor under any obligation to save men; he could, in consistence with his justice, and the other perfections of his nature, have destroyed the whole world of men, as he destroyed all the angels that sinned; he was not obliged to make a covenant with his Son to save them; it was of his own choice he did it; who will have mercy on whom he will have mercy: nor was the Son compelled to enter into this covenant; but knowing his Father's will, and agreeing to it, voluntarily engaged in it, and said, *Lo, I come to do thy will:* and as the Spirit freely bestows his grace, and the gifts of it in time, so he freely engaged to do it in the covenant in eternity.——4. What they agreed in covenant, was what was in their power to perform; if one man enters into a covenant with another, and agrees to do what is not in his power, and which he knows it is not, when he enters into covenant, this is a fraud and an imposition on him, with whom he covenants; and in course the covenant is null and void. But the contracting parties in the covenant of grace, are able to perform whatever they covenanted about: the Father is able to make good all that he has promised in it, either to his Son or to the elect in him; and the Son is able to do the work he engaged to do; he had power to assume human nature into union with his divine Person, and to lay down his life in that nature, having such a power over his own life, and to dispose of it at pleasure, as no mere man ever had; and so being God, as well as man, was able to work out the salvation of his people, which he undertook; the Father knew he was able to save them, and therefore laid help on him, and called him to this work; and he knew himself to be equal to it, and therefore engaged in it: and the holy Spirit is a Spirit of power and might, and so able to perform the part he took in this covenant.——5. As in all covenants, however, the persons covenanting may be equal in other respects, yet in covenanting there is an inequality and subordination; especially in covenants, in which there is service and work to be done on one side, and a reward to be given in consideration of it on the other; of which nature is the covenant of grace and redemption; and though the contracting parties in it are equal in nature, perfections, and glory, yet in this covenant-relation they voluntarily entered into, there is by agreement and consent a subordination; hence the Father, the first Person and Party contracting, is called by his Son, his Lord and his God, a phrase always expressive of covenant-relation; see Psalm xvi. 2. and xxii. 1. and xl. 8. and

xlv. 7. John xx. 17. and the Son, the second Person and party contracting, is called by the Father his Servant; *Thou art my servant, &c.* Isa. xlix. 3. hence the Father is said to be *greater than he*, John xiv. 28. not merely on account of his human nature, about which there could be no difficulty in admitting it; but with respect to his covenant-relation to him, and the office-capacity he has taken and sustains in it: and the Spirit, the third Person and contracting Party, he is said to be sent both by the Father and the Son, to perform that part which he undertook in it: and this economy and dispensation of the covenant, thus settled in subordination among themselves by agreement and consent, is done with great propriety, beauty, and decency, suitable to their natural relations they bear to each other, as equal divine Persons; for who so proper to be the proposer of terms in the covenant, to direct and prescribe them, and to exercise a kind of authority, as he who is the first Person in order of nature, and that stands in the relation of a Father to the second Person; and since here was work and service to be done, the salvation of the elect, and that in an inferior nature, in human nature, who so proper to engage in this service, and to assume this nature, and in it yield obedience to the will of God, than the second Person, who stood in the relation of a Son to the First? and with what congruity is the third Person, the holy Spirit, sent by both, to make application of the grace of both; who is said to be their Breath, and to proceed from both.——6. As in all covenants some advantages are proposed unto, and expected by all parties concerned, so in this; as God's end in all things, in nature, providence, and grace, is his own glory, so it is in this covenant, even the glory of Father, Son, and Spirit; which must be understood, not of any addition unto, or increase of their essential glory, but of the manifestation of it; otherwise, as Christ is represented saying to his Father, *My goodness extendeth not to thee;* thou art not the better for my suretiship-engagements in covenant, and the performance of them; thou hast no real profit and advantage thereby; no new accession of glory and happiness accrues to thee by it; *but* the real profit and advantage resulting from hence is, *to the saints that are in the earth,* and *to the excellent, in whom is all my delight,* Psalm xvi. 2, 3. As for the glory promised to Christ, and which he expected and pleased on his finishing his work, John xvii. 4, 5. this was either the manifestation of the glory of his divine Person, hid in his state of humiliation; or his glory as Mediator, his kingdom and glory, as such appointed to him, and promised him, upon the performance of his engagements, Luke xxii. 29. 1 Pet. i. 21. Heb. ii. 9. of which more hereafter; and yet, even the benefit of this redounds to the advantage of God's elect, John xvii. 22, 24. it is their salvation and happiness that is the grand thing in view in these covenant-transactions; this is *all my salvation,* 2 Sam. xxiii. 5. As the sum of the gospel, which is no other than a transcript of the covenant of grace, is the salvation of lost sinners by Christ; so the covenant, of which that is a copy, chiefly respects that, and that is the result of it: hence Christ, the Covenantee, has the name of Jesus, because he undertook to save, and came to save, and has saved his people from their sins, in consequence of his covenant-engagements.

CHAP VIII.

OF THE PART WHICH THE FATHER TAKES IN THE COVENANT.

THE several parts which each contracting Party take in this covenant, are next to be considered.

The Father, the first person in the Trinity, takes the first place, and gives the lead in this covenant. *All things are of God,* that is, of God the Father; they are of him originally, they begin with him; all things in creation; he has made the world, and created all things by his Son; and so all things in the salvation of men, *who hath reconciled us to himself by Jesus Christ;* he set on foot the council of peace, and so the covenant of peace, *God was in Christ reconciling the world to himself;* that is, God the Father; he planned the reconciliation of men in council, and proposed it in covenant, and settled it with the other two persons; and he is not only the proposer, but the prescriber and enjoiner of things in the covenant; he both proposed the work to be done, and took upon him the authority, by agreement, to prescribe and enjoin it: hence we read of the injunctions and commands laid on Christ with respect to his discharge of his office, as the mediator of this covenant, John x. 18. and xii. 49. and xiv. 31. it was the Father that called Christ from the womb of eternity to be his servant, and directed and enjoined his work and service, as appears from Isa. xlix. 1—6. and promised a reward to him on condition of his performing the service, and to bestow benefits on the elect in him, and for his sake. And let us,

1st, Consider the work he proposed to Christ, which is the great and only condition of the covenant, and which he prescribed and enjoined him to do; which was, 1. To take the care and charge of the chosen ones; these, as he chose them in him, he put them into his hands, not only as his property, but for their safety; and here they are safe, for none can pluck them out of his hands; hence they are called *the sheep of his hand*, not only because they are guided by his hand as a flock, but because they are under his care and custody; they were not only given him as his portion and inheritance, but to be kept and saved by him; when they were committed to him, he had this charge given to him by his Father, that *of all* that he had *given* him he *should lose nothing*, not any one of them; they were told into his hands, and the full tale of them was expected to be returned: and which respects the whole of them, as their souls which he has redeemed, and does preserve, so their bodies likewise; for the injunction was that he *should lose nothing*, no part of them, not even their dust in their graves, *but should raise it up again at the last day*, John vi. 39. as he will. God not only made a reserve of them in Christ for himself, but they were *preserved in* him, and therefore are called the *preserved of Israel*, Jude, ver. 1. Isa. xlix. 6. and that Christ, in a covenant-way, by his own consent, was laid under such an obligation to keep and preserve his elect safe to glory, appears from his own account, both from what he says in his intercessory prayer; *those that thou gavest me, I have kept, and none of them is lost*, John xvii. 12. and from what he will say at the last day, when they are all brought in; *Behold, I, and the children which God hath given me*, Heb. ii. 13. all kept safe, and presented faultless; the kingdom of priests, the whole number of the chosen vessels of salvation, will be delivered up complete and perfect, agreeable to the charge committed to him, and his own voluntary undertakings.——2. Whereas these same Persons made his care and charge, would fall in Adam, with the rest of mankind, and that into a state of sin and misery, and under the curse and condemnation of the law, he proposed it to him, and enjoined it as his will, that he should redeem them from all this; and hence agreeing to it, he was sent to do it, and has done it; this work, as proposed and prescribed in the covenant of grace, is expressed by various phrases, in Isa. xlix. 5, 6. as by *bringing Jacob again to him*; by Jacob is meant the elect of God, especially among the Jews, the remnant according to the election of grace: and *bringing* them *again*, supposes they were gone aside, apostatized from God, and turned their backs on him, and were gone out of the right way, gone astray, and become lost sheep: and the work of Christ, as enjoined him in covenant, and he undertook, was to bring them unto God, and set them before him, to use Judah's words, when he offered to be surety for Benjamin, Gen. xliii. 9. to bring them nigh to God; which he has done, by his obedience, sufferings, and death, Eph. ii. 13. 1 Pet. iii. 18. and also this work of Christ is expressed by *raising up the tribes of Jacob*; meaning the same persons, sunk into a low estate through the fall, into an horrible pit, into the mire and clay, into a pit wherein is no water: out of this low estate Christ was to raise them, as he did by the blood of the covenant, and made them kings and priests unto God; and likewise by *restoring the preserved of Israel*, even the same chosen ones, among the people of Israel; who, by the fall, lost their righteousness, and forfeited their happy life in innocence; these Christ was to recover from their fallen and sinful estate, and restore them, as he has done, to a better righteousness, and to a life more abundant than what they lost, to an higher state of grace, glory, and happiness: and if this should be thought by Christ to be too *light* and too *low* a thing for him to be the Saviour of the elect among the Jews; it is farther proposed, that he should be *the light of the Gentiles*, and *the salvation* of God *unto the end of the earth*, be the Saviour of all God's elect, both among Jews and Gentiles; not only to die for his people among the Jews, but to bring again, raise up, restore, and gather together the children of God, scattered abroad throughout the whole world; and be the propitiation, not for the sins of the chosen among the Jews only, but of those in the whole world of the Gentiles; so that this takes in the whole work of redemption and salvation, the work which Christ's Father gave him to do, and which he undertook, and has finished, John xvii. 4. and with respect

to the Gentiles, as well as Jews, our Lord says, *Other sheep I have* to take care of, to lay down his life for, besides those among the Jews, *which are not of this fold*, of the Jewish church-state, but out of it; the Gentiles, *them also I must bring*, bring them again, raise up, and restore, and set before his Father; bring them into his church, and among his people, into an open state of grace, and to eternal glory; and this he says he *must* do, because his Father enjoined it, and he agreed to do it.——3. In order to this, the Father proposed to the Son to assume human nature in the fulness of time, which was necessary to the work of redeeming the chosen people; as this was advised to in council, it was fixed in the covenant; *A body hast thou prepared me*, Heb. x. 5. not only in the purposes and decrees of God, in the book of which *all* the *members* of it *were written, which, in continuance, were fashioned, when, as yet, there was none of them*, before they were in actual being, Psalm cxxxix. 16. nor only in the prophesies of the Old Testament, in which it was foretold and promised, that the Messiah should become man, be the child born, and born of a virgin, and that the Man, the Branch, should grow up out of his place; but this was provided in covenant, not an human body only, nor an human soul only, but the whole human nature; which, though it had not a real and actual, yet had a covenant-subsistence, as it may be called; that is to say, the Father proposing it, and the Son assenting as he did, by the above words; there was an agreement, a compact between them, that he should take into union with himself, a true body, and a reasonable soul; both which were necessary, to suffer the whole curse of the law; a true body, in which he might get his bread by the sweat of his brow, and suffer pains, sorrows, and death; bear the sins of many in it, and be offered up for them; and a reasonable soul, that he might endure the punishment of loss and sense; of loss, in being deprived for a while of the gracious presence of God, as when on the cross; of sense, in feeling the wrath poured into his soul, which made it exceeding sorrowful, as in the garden. And this nature proposed to be assumed, and was assumed, is of the same kind with that which sinned, and to which death was threatened, as it seems proper it should; the same flesh and blood with the children, and in which he was made like unto his brethren, excepting sin; and to assume such a nature was necessary, that Christ might have somewhat to offer, that would be acceptable to God, and satisfactory to his justice; this was part of the will of God enjoined in covenant, and which Christ agreed to do; that whereas ceremonial sacrifices would be disapproved of by him, as insufficient to take away sin, he would assume the body, or human nature, prepared and provided in covenant for him, and offer it up, that sin might be condemned, and the righteousness of the law be fulfilled; for it is *by* this *will*, or the doing of it, that *we are sanctified through the offering of the body of Jesus Christ once for all*, Heb. x. 5—10. and this being the will of the Father, what he proposed and prescribed to be done; hence he is always represented as concerned in this affair: he promised to bring forth his Servant the Branch, the Man the Branch, that should grow out of its place; and he sent his Son, in the fulness of time, made of a woman, and in the likeness of sinful flesh, to put away sin by the sacrifice of himself, Zech. iii. 8. and vi. 12. Rom. viii. 3. Gal. iv. 4.——
4. Another branch of the work assigned to Christ, in the covenant, by his Father, and to which he agreed, was to obey the law in the room and stead of his people, to which Christ has respect when he says, *thy law is within my heart*, or I am heartily willing and ready to obey and fulfil it; and which designs not only the law of mediation, or the command enjoined Christ as Mediator, with respect to the performance of his several offices as such: so with respect to his prophetic office Christ says, *The Father which sent me, he gave me a commandment what I should say, and what I should speak——whatsoever I speak, therefore, even as the Father said unto me, so I speak*, John xii. 49, 50. And with respect to his priestly office, his laying down his life for his people; *I have power to lay it down, and I have power to take it up again; this commandment have I received of my Father*, John x. 18. see chap. xiv. 31. And with respect to his kingly office; *I will declare the decree;* that is, of his Father, the ordinance, statute, law, and rule of governing his people; for this refers not to what follows concerning the generation of Christ, but to what goes before, concerning his kingly office: but also the moral law, which he agreed to be made under, and was willing to fulfil, and for which he came into the world, and did become the fulfilling end of it, whereby he magnified it, and made it

honourable; as it became him to do, as the Surety of his people, and which was necessary to their justification; for *by the obedience of One, many are made righteous*, Rom. v. 19.——5. Another part of the work proposed to him, and enjoined him by his Father, was to suffer the penalty of the law, death; which must be endured, either by the sinner himself, the transgressor of the law, or by his Surety, Gen. ii. 17. wherefore it *became* the wise, holy, and righteous Being, *for whom, and by whom, are all things—to make the Captain of salvation*, his Son, whom he appointed to be the Saviour of men, *perfect through sufferings*, for the satisfaction of law and justice; and therefore he enjoined him to bear them, Heb. ii. 10. hence Christ says, speaking of laying down his life for the sheep, *This commandment have I received of my Father*, John x. 18. and hence his sufferings are called, *the cup* which his Father had *given* him; not just then put into his hands, for he spake of it long before, as what he was to drink of; but was what was ordered him in the everlasting covenant, John xviii. 11. Matt. xx. 22. and hence also they are spoken of by all the prophets from the beginning of the world: and this being the Father's will in covenant, hence likewise it is that the Father had so great an hand in them, as to bruise him, and put him to grief, to awake the sword of justice against him, and smite him; not to spare him, but deliver him up by his determinate counsel, into the hands of wicked men, and to death itself; and the covenant having somewhat of the nature of a testament, or of a man's last will, there was a necessity of the death of the testator to ratify and confirm it; which was to be done by the blood of Christ, called therefore, the blood of the everlasting covenant, Heb. ix. 15, 16, 17. and xiii. 20.——6. When the Father signified in covenant, his dislike of the continuance of legal sacrifices, as insufficient to take away sin; he strongly suggested it was his will that his Son should become a sacrifice for it, and therefore prepared him a body, or human nature, in the covenant, capable of being offered up; and it was by his will expressed therein, that his covenant-people are sanctified through the offering up of the body of Christ, Heb. x. 5—10. This is the great condition of the covenant, and on which all the blessings of it depend: *When thou shalt make his soul an offering for sin*, or rather, *When his soul shall make an offering for sin;* that is, when he shall heartily and willingly offer up himself, soul and body, a sacrifice for sin, then the benefits following should be conferred both on Christ, and on his spiritual seed, Isa. liii. 10, 11, 12. And,—— 7. Farther, it was the will of the Father, in the covenant, that Christ should hereby make atonement for the sins of the chosen ones; this was the work which was assigned him in covenant, and is marked out in prophecy for him to do; namely, *To finish the transgression, to make an end of sin, and to make reconciliation for iniquity*, Dan. ix. 24. and as he agreed to do it, for this purpose he became man, and by his bloodshed, sufferings, and death, has made it; which lays a foundation of solid joy in his people, Heb. ii. 17. and ix. 26. and x. 14. Rom. v. 10, 11.——8. In close connection with the former, his work assigned him in covenant was, *to bring in everlasting righteousness*, for the justification of the elect. God the Father in covenant, *called him in righteousness*, or *to righteousness*, to work out a righteousness for his people, commensurate to the demands of law and justice; and this call and proposal he answered and agreed to; hence the church of old could say, *Surely in the Lord have I righteousness and strength;* and by virtue of the suretiship-righteousness of Christ, and his engagements in covenant, all the old-testament saints were justified, Isa. xlii. 6. and xlv. 24, 25.——*Lastly*, The work which the Father proposed to, and prescribed to the Son was, *to feed the flock of slaughter;* to which he replied, *I will feed the flock of slaughter;* even all the elect of God, Zech. xi. 4, 7. and this feeding the flock committed to his charge, takes in his whole work as a shepherd; taking care of his sheep, laying down his life for them, gathering the lambs in his arms, carrying them in his bosom, gently leading those with young, protecting them from all harms and enemies, bringing them into his fold here and above, setting them at his right hand, and introducing them into his kingdom and glory. This is the work that was before him; and his reward was with him, next to be observed, Isa. xl. 10, 11.

2dly, On condition of Christ's engaging to do the above work proposed and prescribed to him, the Father promised in the covenant many things; some to him personally, and others to the elect, whom he personated and represented in it.——1. Some things to himself, respecting his work, assistance in it, &c. a glory on the nature in which he should do it, the honourable offices he should be invested with in it, and the numerous offspring he should have. ——(1.) As the work assigned him was to be done in human nature, which needed qualifications for it, strength to do it, help and assistance in it, support under it, preservation from enemies, and encouragement of success: all this was promised him, that as his human nature should be formed by the Holy Ghost without sin, so it should be filled with his gifts and graces; that the Spirit should be put upon him, and rest on him, as a Spirit of wisdom, counsel, might, knowledge, and of the fear of God, whereby he would be qualified to execute his offices of Prophet, Priest, and King, Isa. xi. 1, 2. and xlii. 1. and lxi. 1. and which was bestowed upon him without measure, Psalm xlv. 7. John iii. 34. and that whereas the human nature, in which this work was to be done, would be attended with weakness, with all the sinless infirmities of human nature, as it was at last crucified through weakness; God promised to strengthen him, and he believed he would be his strength, and, accordingly, he was the Man of his right hand, whom he made strong for himself, Psalm lxxxix. 21. Isa. xlix. 5. Psalm lxxx. 17. and that, as he would need help and assistance in that nature, it was promised him, and he expected it, asked for it, and had it, Psalm xxii. 1, 19. Isa. l. 7, 8. and xlix. 8. and as it would want support, under the mighty load of sin, and sense of wrath, that it might not sink under it, this was promised and granted; so that he failed not, nor was he discouraged or broken, Isa. xlii. 1, 4. and as it would have many enemies, who would seek to take its life away before its time; God promised that he would keep and preserve him, and hide him in the shadow of his hand, and in his quiver, and so secure him, as he did from Herod, and the wicked Jews, Isa. xlii. 6. and xlix. 2, 6. and since he would be treated with great contempt in that nature, be despised by men, abhorred by the nation of the Jews, and be a servant of rulers; he was told, for his encouragement, that the Lord would choose him, and express delight and pleasure in him as his elect; and though disallowed of men, would be chosen of God, and precious, Isa. xlii. 1. and xlix. 7. and accordingly, delight and well-pleasedness in him were expressed by his Father, when both obeying and suffering, Mat. iii. 17. John x. 17.

yea, success in his work was promised him, that *the pleasure of the Lord* should *prosper in his hand;* that is, the work of the Lord be succeeded, which it was his will and pleasure to put into his hand. Now all this was promised him in covenant, as an encouragement to engage in this work. ——(2.) As he was to do and suffer much in his human nature, so it was promised him, that he should have a very great glory conferred on him in that nature; not only that the glory of his Deity should be manifested and displayed, which was hid, especially from many, during his state of humiliation; for which, when he had done his work, he may be thought to pray, pleading a promise made to him, John xvii. 4, 5. But there was a glory to be put on his human nature, which was promised in the everlasting covenant, and which he had with his Father, in promise, before the world was; hence the prophecies of the Old Testament, which are founded on covenant-engagements, speak, as of the sufferings of Christ, so of the glory that should follow, and of Christ's entering through sorrows and sufferings, into his kingdom and glory; and Christ believed and expected that he should be *glorious*, notwithstanding all his meanness in a state of humiliation, Isa. xlix. 5. Luke xxiv. 26. particularly it was promised him, that though he should die and be laid in the grave, yet that he should not lie so long as to see corruption, but be raised again the third day, as he was, and so had the glory given him, and which he had faith and hope of, Psalm xvi. 9, 10, 11. 1 Pet. i. 21. as also, that he should ascend to heaven, and receive gifts for men, or in man, in human nature; and accordingly he did ascend above all heavens, to fill all things, and gave the gifts to men he received, and that in a very extraordinary manner; whereby it appeared he was glorified, as was promised him, because the Spirit was not given in such a plentiful manner till Jesus was glorified, exalted at the right hand of God, and made and declared Lord and Christ, Psalm lxviii. 18. Eph. iv. 8, 9, 10. John vii. 39. Acts ii. 33, 36. Moreover, it was promised him, that in human nature he should sit at the right hand of God; a glory and honour which none of the angels was ever admitted to; but, in consideration of his obedience, sufferings, and death, he was highly exalted, as it was promised he should, and a name given him above every name; being placed on the right hand of

God, angels, authorities, and powers being made subject unto him! Psalm cx. 1. Heb. i. 13. Phil. ii. 7, 8, 9. 1 Pet. iii. 23. and now he is seen crowned with glory and honour, and will come a second time in his own glory, and in his Father's glory, and in the glory of the holy angels, all according to the covenant-agreement. In a word, it was promised him in covenant; on condition of making his soul an offering for sin, among other things, that God would *divide him a portion with the great;* give him as large and ample a portion, yea, a larger one, than any of the great men of the earth; that he would make him his first-born, higher than the kings of the earth: and that he should *divide the spoil with the strong*, or take the prey out of the hands of the mighty, and deliver the lawful captive; which spoil and prey being taken out of the hands of the strong, should be his portion and inheritance; and that because he poured out his soul unto death, was numbered with the transgressors, and bore the sins of many, Isa. liii. 12.——
(3.) As an encouragement to Christ to engage in the above work proposed to him in covenant, it was promised him, that he should be invested with, and sustain several honourable offices, which he should execute in human nature; as, that he should be the great Prophet of the church; not only *the minister of the circumcision for the truth of God* to the Jews, but be *for a light of the Gentiles;* which is twice promised, where plain traces of this everlasting covenant are to be seen, Isa. xlii. 6. and xlix. 6. and he accordingly was expected to be a light to lighten the Gentiles, as well as to be the glory of the people of Israel, Luke ii. 32. and he was so, by the ministry of his apostles, in the Gentile-world, and still is, by the preaching of his ministers in it; whereby men are turned from darkness to light, and to shew forth the praises of him who has called them out of the one to the other, 1 Pet. ii. 9. Eph. ii. 17. Acts xxvi. 18.——It was also promised, and swore to by an oath in covenant, that he should be a Priest; an honour which no man takes to himself, but he that is called to it, as was Aaron; even Christ glorified not himself, to be called an High-Priest; but his Father, who invested him with this office, by an oath, to shew the immutability of it; and that he should continue in it, and be a priest on his throne, Psalm cx. 4. Heb. v. 4, 5. and vii. 21. Zech. vi. 13. Likewise, that he should be King of Zion, of saints, over his church and people, and have a kingdom very large, from sea to sea, from the river to the ends of the earth; of which government, and the increase of it, there should be no end; a dispensatory kingdom, besides that of nature and providence, which he had a right to, as a divine Person; but this is a kingdom disposed of to him in covenant and by promise; *I appoint unto you a kingdom*, says Christ, *as my Father hath appointed me*, διέθετο, has disposed of or appointed in covenant to me, Luke xxii. 29. Once more, God has appointed him in covenant to be the judge of quick and dead; and has appointed a day in which he will judge the world in righteousness, by that man whom he has ordained; and accordingly he has committed all judgment to him, that all men should honour him as they honour the Father, Acts x. 42. and xvii. 31. John v. 22, 23.
——(4.) In consequence of fulfilling the condition of the covenant, engaging to do, and doing the above work proposed in it; it was promised to Christ, that he should *see his seed, and prolong his days*, Isa. liii. 10. that is, that he should have a spiritual offspring, a seed that should serve him, and be accounted to him for a generation; that he should be an everlasting Father to them, and they be his everlasting children; that as the first Adam was the common parent, and federal head of all his posterity, who sinning, conveyed sin and death to them; so the second Adam becomes the Father and federal Head of a spiritual offspring, and conveys grace, righteousness, and life unto them; it was promised him, that this seed of his should be numerous, and continue long; yea, that these children should endure for ever, and his throne be as the days of heaven; and that these should be his portion, and his inheritance; not only the elect among the Jews, but those among the Gentiles also; and therefore he was bid to *ask* of his Father in covenant, and he would *give* him *the heathen for his inheritance*, and the uttermost parts of the earth for his possession; which accordingly he asked, and has, and is well pleased with his portion, and says, the lines are fallen to him in pleasant places, and he has a goodly heritage, Isa. ix. 6. Psalm xxii. 30. and lxxxix. 29, 36. and ii. 8. and xvi. 6. yea, it was promised him, that all persons and things should be put into his hands, to subserve his mediatorial interest, and the good of his spiritual seed, his covenant-people; even all the wicked

CHAP. VIII. FATHER TAKES IN THE COVENANT.

of the earth, whom he disposes of as he pleases, and rules with a rod of iron : he is given to be an Head over all things to the church ; for its preservation and security ; and has power over all flesh, that he may give eternal life to as many as the Father hath given him ; and accordingly all things are put into his hand, and all creatures are at his dispose ; all power in heaven and in earth is given unto him, so that he can order and appoint whatsoever he pleases for the good of his people, Psalm ii. 9. Eph. i. 22. John xvii. 2. and iii. 35. Matt. xxviii. 18.——2. There are other things which God the Father promised in covenant, respecting the elect, the persons for whom Christ was a covenantee, and whom he represented in the covenant, and for whose sake he was to do all the work proposed to him, and which he undertook. And,——(1.) It was promised, that upon Christ's engaging in, and performing the work of redemption, they should be delivered out of that state of misery sin brought them into, even out of the pit wherein is no water, through the blood of the everlasting covenant, Zech. ix. 11. that they should be redeemed from all their iniquities, original and actual, which should be cast behind God's back, and into the depths of the sea, never to be seen and remembered more to their condemnation, Psalm cxxx. 8. that they should be ransomed from the hand of Satan, stronger than they, and the prey be taken from the mighty, and the lawful captive delivered, Jer. xxxi. 11. Isa. xlix. 24, 25. that they should be freed from the law, its curse, and condemnation, Christ being made a curse for them, and sin condemned in his flesh, Rom. viii. 1, 3, 33. Gal. iii. 13. and that they should be secured from hell, wrath, ruin, and everlasting destruction their sins deserved, Job xxxiii. 24.——(2.) That upon the faithful discharge of his office, as a Servant, particularly in bearing the sins of his people, they should be openly justified and acquitted ; that his righteousness he would bring in, should be made known unto them, and received by faith ; and so they should be manifestatively, and in their own consciences, justified in the name of the Lord Jesus, and by the Spirit of our God, Isa. liii. 11. 1 Cor. vi. 11. Ezek. xxxvi. 25.——(3.) That all their iniquities should be forgiven them, for Christ's sake, and their sins and transgressions be remembered no more. This is a special and particular article in the covenant, to which all the prophets bear witness. Jer. xxxi. 34. Acts x. 43.——(4.) That they should be openly adopted, and declared the children of God, and be dealt with as such ; that God should be their God, their Father, their Portion, and Inheritance ; and they should be his people, his children, and heirs of him, and be treated as such by him ; as they would be when chastised for their sins, the rod being provided for them in covenant, as well as their inheritance, Jer. xxxii. 38. 2 Cor. vi. 18. Psalm lxxxix. 30, 34. Heb. xii. 7.——(5.) That they should be regenerated, their hearts spiritually circumcised to love the Lord, and his fear put into them, and be made willing in the day of his power upon them, to be saved by him, and to serve him, Deut. xxx. 6. Jer. xxxii. 39. Psalm cx. 3. that they should be made new creatures, have new hearts and new spirits put within them, in which are new principles of light, life, and love, grace and holiness, joy, peace, and comfort ; that the stony heart should be taken out of them, the hardness and impenitence of it removed, and an heart of flesh given them, soft, penitent, and contrite ; or, in other words, that true, spiritual, evangelical repentance for sin should be granted to them, Ezek. xxxvi. 26.——(6.) That they should have knowledge of God, as their covenant-God and Father ; even the least, as well as the greatest, be all taught of God, as his children, and so believe in Christ ; for those that hear and learn of the Father, come to Christ ; that is, believe in him, Jer. xxxi. 34. Isa. liv. 13. John vi. 45. So that repentance and faith are not terms and conditions of the covenant, but are free grace-gifts granted, and blessings of grace promised in the covenant, and are as sure to the covenant-people, as any other blessings whatever, Acts xi. 18. and v. 31. Eph. ii. 8.——(7.) It is another promise in this covenant, that the law of God should be put into their inward parts, and written on their hearts ; that they should have a spiritual knowledge of it, and a cordial respect unto it, a real delight in it, and serve it with their minds and spirits, and yield a constant, ready, and cheerful obedience to it, Jer. xxxi. 33. Rom. vii. 22, 25. as well as be the epistles of Christ, and have the law of faith, or doctrine of the gospel, take place in their hearts, and dwell richly in them, and they yield a professed subjection to it.——(8.) It is further promised by the Lord, in this covenant, that whereas

Q

they are weak and strengthless, and unable to do anything spiritually good of themselves, that he will put his Spirit within them, who should work in them both to will and to do; and strengthen them with strength in the inward man, and enable them to walk in his statutes, and to keep his judgments, and do them, Ezek. xxxvi. 27. so that likewise new spiritual and evangelical obedience, both to law and gospel, is no term and condition of the covenant, but a blessing secured in it, which absolutely provides with grace and strength to perform it.——(9.) Another article in this covenant, respecting the chosen and covenant-people, is, that they shall persevere in grace, in faith, and holiness, to the end; this is absolutely promised in it, and the faithfulness of God is engaged to perform it; *I will put my fear in their hearts, that they shall not depart from me*, Jer. xxxi. 40. see 1 Thess. v. 23, 24.——(10.) Glory, as well as grace, is promised in this covenant; and to whom God gives the one, he gives the other; eternal life was promised before the world began; and the promise of it was made unto Christ in the everlasting covenant, and put into his hands for his people; and it is represented as if it was the only promise in it, being the grand, principal, and comprehensive one; *This is the promise that he has promised us*, even *eternal life*, Tit. i. 2. 2 Tim. i. 1. 1 John ii. 25. hence our Lord, in an authoritative way, as it were, demands the glorification of ALL the Father has given him, and he undertook for in covenant, John xvii. 24.

CHAP IX.

OF THE PART THE SON OF GOD, THE SECOND PERSON, HAS TAKEN IN THE COVENANT.

THE part which the Son of God takes, and the place and office he has in the covenant of grace, are next to be considered. Christ has so great a concern in the covenant, that he is said to be the Covenant itself; *I will give thee for a Covenant of the people*, Isa. xlii. 6. and xlix. 8. his work, that which was proposed to him, and he agreed to do, is, as has been observed, the grand condition of the covenant, and he himself is the great blessing of it; he is the Alpha and the Omega, as of the scriptures, so of the covenant of grace; he is the first and the last in it, the sum and substance of it; he is every thing, ALL in ALL in it; all the blessings of it are the sure mercies of him, who is David, and David's Son; he is prevented with all the blessings of goodness, and the covenant-people are blessed with all spiritual blessings in him, as their covenant-head; all the promises are made to him, and are all yea and amen in him; he sustains various characters and offices in the covenant. He is the representative-Head of his people in it; he is the Mediator, Surety, Testator, and Messenger of it; of all which, more particularly and distinctly hereafter. At present I shall only observe Christ's assent to his Father's proposals, his acceptance of them, and open declaration of his readiness and willingness to act according to them, which formally constitute the covenant and compact between them; his consent thereunto is fully expressed in Psalm xl. 6, 7, 8. *Sacrifice and offering thou didst not desire; mine ears hast thou opened: burnt-offering, and sin-offering, hast thou not required. Then said I, Lo, I come; in the volume of the book it is written of me: I delight to do thy will, O my God! yea, thy law is within my heart.* Which words, though spoken and written by David, yet as personating the Messiah, as is certain from the application of them to him by the apostle, in Heb. x. 5—10. according to whom, the time when these words were spoken, was when *he cometh into the world*, that is, at his incarnation, when he came from heaven to earth, by the assumption of human nature, to do the will and work of his Father, which he proposed unto him; then he said all the above in fact, what he had before said in word, in promise; *Lo, I come to do thy will;* for that this was said before is plain, since it was known to David, in his time, and written by him, as the pen-man of the Holy Ghost, and as personating Christ, and was repeated and confirmed by Christ at his coming into the world: and when could it be said before, but in the covenant of grace? Likewise it appears, that this was said on the account of the insufficiency of legal sacrifices to atone for sin; in proof of which the apostle quotes the words, *It is not possible that the blood of bulls and goats should take away sin;* wherefore——he saith, *Sacrifice and offering thou wouldst not, &c.* that is, though they were the institutions and appointment of God, yet he would not have them continued any longer than the coming of Christ, because of the weakness and unprofitableness of them to take away sin, and because they were to have, and had, their accomplishment in him; in the fore-views of which this was said in David's time, and earlier by Christ, in the covenant of grace; in which, knowing his Father's will concerning sacrifices, and their continuance, as well as the insufficiency of them, freely declared that he was ready to come, in the fulness of time, and give himself an offering for sin; as his Father had proposed to him he should, Isa. liii. 10. This assent and consent of his is first more obscurely and figuratively expressed; *Mine ears hast thou opened*, digged or bored; expressive of his great attention, hearkening and listening with great diligence, to what his Father proposed to him; see Isa. l. 4, 5. and of his ready and cheerful obedience to his Father's will, signified thereby: the phrase seems to be used in allusion to the boring the servant's ear, who cared not to quit his master's house, but was willing to serve him for ever, Exod. xxi. 5, 6. the Septuagint, and so the apostle renders the words, *A body hast thou prepared me;* a part being put for the whole; and which is supposed; for the ear could not be opened, unless a body was prepared; by which is meant, not a part, but the whole of the human nature, soul and body; prepared not only in the purposes and decrees of God, but in the covenant of grace, where it had a covenant-subsistence, by the joint-agreement of the divine Persons; for as the Father proposed it to the Son, that he should have such a nature, he agreed to assume it, and therefore takes up these words, to shew his ready assent to it; *A body hast thou prepared me;* as it is thy pleasure I should have one, I am ready to take it, at a proper time; that I might have something to offer, an offering of more avail, and more acceptable, than the legal ones. This acceptance of his Father's proposals is more clearly and fully expressed; *Lo, I come to do thy will;* that is, to assume human nature, to lay down his life in it, to suffer death, make atonement for the sins of his people, and obtain their redemption and salvation: his willingness to do all this freely, and without compulsion; he himself, and not another, and immediately, as soon as ever it should be necessary; he declares, with a note of admiration, attention, and asseveration; and his heartiness in it is still more fully signified, by saying, *I delight to do thy will;* it was with the utmost pleasure and complacency that he complied with it, and it would be his meat and drink, as it was, to do it: and it is added; *Yea,*

thy law is within my heart; it is in my heart to fulfil it; I am ready to yield a cordial and cheerful obedience to it. Now all this was *written* concerning him *in the volume of the book;* not of the scriptures in general only, nor of the Pentateuch in particular, the only volume extant in David's time, εν κεφαλιδι, at the head and beginning of which is a declaration of the grace, will, and work of Christ, Gen. iii. 15. nor only of the book of God's purposes, Psalm cxxxix. 16. but of the covenant; alluding to the writing, signing, and sealing of covenants; the covenant at Sinai is called, the book of the covenant, Exod. xxiv. 8. Now in this volume, or book, as the Father's proposal is there written and contained, so is the Son's assent unto it, and acceptance of it. Add to all this, that the character in which Christ here addresses his divine Father, *My God*, is a phrase expressive of covenant-relation, and is frequently so used both with regard to Christ and his people. But, to observe no more, nothing more fully proves Christ's free and full assent and consent to do the will of his Father, proposed in covenant, than his actual performance of it. Was it his will that he should take the care and charge of all his elect, and lose none? he has done it, John xvii. 12. Was it his will that he should assume human nature? the Word has been made flesh, and dwelt among men, John i. 14. Was it his will that he should obey the law? he is become the end of the law for righteousness, Rom. x. 4. Was it his will that he should suffer death, the penalty of it? he has suffered, the just for the unjust, to bring them to God, 1 Pet. iii. 18. Was it his will that he should make himself an offering for sin? he has given himself to God, an Offering and a Sacrifice, of a sweet-smelling savour, Eph. v. 2. In a word, Was it his will that he should redeem his people from all their iniquities? he has obtained an eternal redemption of them, Heb. ix. 12.

CHAP. X.

OF CHRIST, AS THE COVENANT-HEAD OF THE ELECT.

THERE are various characters, relations, and offices, which Christ sustains in the covenant of grace; among which, that of a federal Head is one: Christ is often said to be the *Head of the Church;* not of any particular congregation of saints, in this or the other part of the world; but of the church of the first-born, whose names are written in heaven, even of all the elect of God, that ever have been, are, or will be in the world, Eph. i. 22, 23. and v. 23. Col. i. 18. and he is a Head to them in different senses; he is that to them as a natural head is to a natural body, and the members of it; which is of the same nature with it, superior to it, communicates life, sense, and motion to it, as well as overlooks and protects it; such an Head of influence is Christ to the church, the source of life to it, from whom nourishment is derived, and all the supplies of grace, Eph. iv. 15, 16. Col. ii. 19. He is an Head in a political sense, as a captain-general is head of his army, and a king is head of his subjects, Judg. x. 18. and xi. 11. Hos. i. 11. and in an economical sense, as the husband is the head of the wife, and a father the head of his children, and a master the head of his servants and of his whole family, Numb. i. 4. Eph. v. 23, 24. Isa. ix. 6. Matt. xxiii. 10. The headship of Christ in these several senses, chiefly belongs to his Kingly office; but besides these, he is the representative-head of his church, or of all the elect of God; they were all considered in him, and represented by him, when he covenanted with his Father for them; all that he engaged to do and suffer, was not only on their account, but in their name and stead; and all that he received, promises and blessings, were not only for them, but he received them as personating them. As Christ was given to be the covenant of the people, so to be an Head of them in it, Eph. i. 22. And thus,

1. Christ was considered in election; he was chosen as Head, and his people as members in him, and so they had union to him, and a representative-being in him before the world began: they did not then personally exist, but Christ did, who represented them, and therefore were capable of being chosen in him, as they were, Eph. i. 4.

―――2. Such a relation Christ stood in to them in the covenant, that was made, not with him alone, but with all the elect of God, considered in him as their head and representative; hence we read of *the covenant that was confirmed before of God in Christ;* which was of God made sure and firm with his covenant-people, in Christ, as their Head, before the foundation of the world; when as yet they had not an actual being, only a representative one in Christ, Gal. iii. 17. and hence the covenant was made sure to them in him, before the manifestation and application of it to Abraham, and his spiritual seed spoken of in the preceding verse; so that *the law, which was four hundred and thirty years after* that revelation and manifestation of the covenant to Abraham, *cannot disannul, that it should make the promise of none effect;* for what commences in time, can never make void what was confirmed in eternity.―――

3. The promises of grace and glory, made to the elect of God in covenant, were made to them, as considered in Christ, their head and representative; for whereas these promises were made before the world began, Tit. i. 2. they could not be made to them in their own persons, but as personated by Christ, and therefore were made to him their Head, and to them in him; and hence the promise of life is said to be *in* him, 2 Tim. i. 1. and indeed, all the promises are Yea and Amen *in him*, 2 Cor. i. 20. The apostle having said, that *to Abraham and his seed were the promises made,* observes, *he saith not* and *to seeds, as of many, but as of one, and to thy seed, which is Christ;* who is the head and representative of all his spiritual offspring, and in whom they are all collected and considered; all the promises made, manifested and applied to Abraham, and his spiritual seed, were originally made to Christ, the everlasting Father of his spiritual offspring, the common Head and Parent of them, Gal. iii. 16.

―――4. All the blessings of grace, and grants of them in the covenant of grace, given and made to the elect in it, were given and made to Christ first in their name, and as personating them, and to them in him, as considered in him, their head and representative; for when these grants were made, and blessings bestowed, they were not in actual being, only had a representative one in Christ their head; hence grace is said to be given them *in Christ Jesus,* before the world began; and they to be blessed with all spiritual blessings in heavenly places *in Christ,* as they were chosen in him before the foundation of the world, 2 Tim. i. 9. Eph. i. 3, 4.―――5. Christ, in the everlasting covenant, engaged in the name of his people, to obey and suffer in their stead; and accordingly he did both in time, as their Head and Representative. He obeyed the law, and fulfilled all righteousness, not as a single individual of human nature, and for himself, but as the federal Head of his people, as representing them; *That so the righteousness of the law might be fulfilled in us*, says the apostle, Rom. viii. 4. that is, in the elect of God, they being considered in Christ their Head, when he became the fulfilling End of the law for righteousness unto them; and so they were made, or accounted, the righteousness of God *in him* their Head, Rom. x. 4. 2 Cor. v. 21. in like manner as he in their name engaged to suffer for them; so in time he suffered in their room and stead, as their head and representative; insomuch that they may be truly said to suffer with him; they were all gathered together, recollected in one Head, *in Christ*, and sustained and represented by him when he hung upon the cross, and are said to be *crucified with* him, Eph. i. 10. Col. ii. 12.

———6. In consequence of Christ's covenant-engagements and performances, when he rose from the dead, he rose not as a private Person, but as a public Person, as the head and representative of all those for whom he obeyed and suffered; and therefore they are said to be quickened and raised together with him, as they were then also justified in him, when he himself, as their Head and Surety was, Eph. ii. 5, 6. Col. iii. 1. 1 Tim. iii. 16. Yea, Christ is also gone to heaven, not only as the Forerunner of his people, but as their Head and Representative; he has taken possession of heaven in their name, appears in the presence of God for them, and personates them, as the high-priest did the children of Israel, in the holy of holies; and hence they are said to be made to sit together in heavenly places *in Christ Jesus*, Eph. ii. 6.

———7. The federal headship of Christ, may be argued and concluded from Adam being a federal head and representative of all his natural offspring; in which he was *the figure of him that was to come*, that is, Christ; for it was in that chiefly, if not solely, that he was a figure of Christ; at least, that is the chief, if not the only thing the apostle has in view, Rom. v. 14. as appears by his running the parallel between them, as heads and representatives of their respective offspring: Adam, through his fall, conveying sin and death to all his natural descendents; and Christ, through the free gift of himself, communicating grace, righteousness, and life to all his spiritual seed, the elect, the children his Father gave him: and hence these two are spoken of as the first and last Adam, and the first and second man; as if they were the only two men in the world, being the representatives of their several seeds, which are included in them, 1 Cor. xv. 45, 47.

Now, as Christ stands in the relation of an Head to the elect, he has all things delivered into his hands: in honour to him, and in love both to him and them, and for their good; God has given him to be *Head over all things* to the church, Matt. xi. 27. John iii. 35. Eph. i. 22. all persons and things are under his command, and at his dispose, to subserve his interest as Head of the church; even angels and men, good and bad, and all things in heaven and in earth; all power therein to protect and defend his people, and to provide for them; all fulness of grace, and the blessings of it to supply them; the government of the church, and of the world, is on his shoulders, who represents them; and therefore their persons, grace, and glory, must be safe in him; the covenant, and all its blessings and promises, are sure in him, the Head and Representative of his people in it.

CHAP. XI.

OF CHRIST, THE MEDIATOR OF THE COVENANT.

ANOTHER relation, or office, which Christ bears in the covenant, is that of *Mediator;* three times in the epistle to the Hebrews is he called the Mediator of the new, or better covenant or testament, chap. viii. 6. and ix. 15. and xii. 24. the same with the everlasting covenant, only so called in reference to a former administration of it. The apostle Paul asserts, that there is *one Mediator between God and men, the man Christ Jesus,* 1 Tim. ii. 5. Both Jews and Gentiles have a notion of a Mediator; the Jews[1] call the Messiah אמצעי, the Mediator, or middle one; and so Philo the Jew,[2] speaks of the most ancient Word of God, as μεσος, a middle Person between God and men, not unbegotten as God, nor begotten as man, but the middle of the extremes, one between both. The Persians[3] call their God Mithras, μεσιτης, a Mediator; and the Demons, with the heathens, seem to be, according to them, mediators between the superior gods and men; but we have a more sure word of prophecy to direct us

---

[1] R. Joseph Albo, Ikkarim, Orat. 2. c. 28.
[2] Quis Rer. Divin. Hæres. p. 509. Vid. ibid. de Cherubim, p. 112.

[3] Plutarch. de Isid. et Osir.

in this matter; Christ is the one and only Mediator. It will be proper to enquire,

First, In what sense Christ is the mediator of the covenant; not as Moses, who stood between God and the people of Israel, *to shew* them *the word of the Lord*, Deut. v. 5. to receive the law, the lively oracles, and deliver them to them, said to be ordained, or disposed by angels, in the hand of a mediator, supposed to be Moses, Gal. iii. 19. Christ indeed is the revealer and declarer of his Father's mind and will, and the dispenser of the covenant of grace in the different administrations of it, in the several periods of time; but this more properly belongs to him as the *angel* or *messenger of the covenant*, as he is called, Mal. iii. 1. than the mediator of it. Christ is a mediator of reconciliation; such an one as interposes between two parties at variance, in order to bring them together, and in some way or other reconcile them to each other. *A mediator is not of one*, of one party; for where there is but one party there can be no difference, and so no need of a mediator; but *God is one*, he is one party, the offended party, and man is the other, the offending party; and Christ is the mediator between them both to bring them together, who are through sin at as great distance as earth and heaven; and he is the antitype of Jacob's ladder, that reaches both and joins them together; the days-man between them, who lays his hand on them both, and makes peace between them; and so a learned Grecian[4] interprets the word for *mediator* ειρηνο ποιος, *a peace-maker;* and this work he performs not merely by way of intreaty, as one man may intreat another to lay aside his resentment against an offender, and not pursue him to his destruction, which lies in his power; or as Moses intreated God with great vehemence and importunity to forgive the Israelites, or blot him out of his book; for however commendable this may be for one man to intercede with another, or with God for an offender, in such a manner; yet it seems too low and mean an office for Christ the Son of God, barely to intreat his Father to lay aside the marks of his displeasure against a sinner, and not so honourable for God to grant it, without satisfaction; wherefore Christ acts the part of a mediator, by proposing to his Father to make satisfaction for the offence committed, and so appease injured justice. Christ is a mediator of reconciliation in a way of satisfaction; reconciliation in this way is Christ's great work as mediator; this is what was proposed in covenant, and what he therein agreed to do, and therefore is called the mediator of the covenant.

Reconciliation supposes a former state of friendship, a breach of that friendship, and a renewal of it; or a bringing into open friendship again. Man in a state of innocence was in a state of friendship with God, had many high honours and special favours conferred upon him; being made after the image and likeness of God, had all the creatures put in subjection to him, was placed in a delightful garden, had a right to eat of the fruit of all the trees in it but one; to him the creatures were brought to give them names, and an help meet was provided for him; but man being in this honour abode not long, sin soon separated chief friends, and he was drove out of his paradisaical Eden; and appeared to be, as all his posterity are, not only at a distance from God, and alienation to him, but enmity against him, as the carnal mind of man is; and in this state the elect of God were considered, when Christ undertook in covenant to be the mediator of reconciliation for them; and in this condition he found them, when he came to make actual reconciliation for them; *you that were sometimes alienated and enemies in your minds by wicked works, yet now hath he reconciled*, Col. i. 21. and hereby has brought them into an open state of grace and favour with God; into greater nearness to him, and into a more exalted state of friendship with him than was lost by the fall.

It should be observed, that the elect of God are considered in the covenant of grace as fallen creatures; and that Christ being a mediator of reconciliation and satisfaction for them, supposes them such. In the covenant of works there was no mediator; whilst that covenant remained unbroken, and man continued in a state of integrity, he needed none; he could correspond and converse with God without one; though he might have knowledge of Christ as the Son of God, and second person in the Trinity, which was necessary to his worship of him, yet he knew nothing of him as mediator, nor needed him as such; he could hear the voice of God, and abide in his presence without fear or shame; it was after he had sinned, and not before,

---

[4] Suidas in voce μισιτης.

that he hid himself among the trees, on hearing the voice of God: nor is there any mediator for angels, none was provided, nor admitted, for the fallen angels, they were not spared; and the good angels needed not any, having never sinned; they are admitted into the divine presence without a mediator to introduce them; they stand before God, and behold his face continually. Some have thought that Christ is the medium of union of angels with God, and of elect men, chosen in Christ, and considered as unfallen, which I will not object to; but a mediator of reconciliation and satisfaction, Christ is only to fallen men, and they needed one; a reconciliation was necessary, and without such a mediator the purposes of God concerning elect men, the covenant of grace made on their account, the prophecies of the Old Testament, and the salvation of men could not have been accomplished; nor the perfections of God, particularly his justice and holiness, glorified in it.

Sin has been committed, which is offensive to God, provoking to the eyes of his glory, and deserving of his wrath, even of eternal death; the law broken, which reflects dishonour on the lawgiver, who is able to save and to destroy; justice injured and affronted, and which insisted on making a satisfaction, and that nothing less than perfect obedience to the law, and a bearing the penalty of it; fallen man could not make his peace with God, nor reconcile himself to him on such terms; Christ, as mediator of the covenant, undertook to make reconciliation for elect men; and God set him and sent him forth to be, and he is become the propitiation for their sins; and God is pacified towards them for all that they have done, and has taken away all his wrath, and turned himself from the fierceness of his anger, and removed all the visible marks and effects of his displeasure.

Nor is this reconciliation Christ is the mediator of, as thus stated, any contradiction to the everlasting love of God to his elect in Christ; where there is the strongest love amongst men, when an offence is committed, there is need of reconciliation to be made. David had the strongest affection for his son Absalom as can well be imagined; Absalom committed a very heinous offence, murdered his brother Amnon, David's first-born, and heir to his crown; he fled from justice, and from his father's wrath and vengeance he might justly fear; Joab became a mediator between them, first more secretly, by means of the woman of Tekoah, and then more openly in his own person, and succeeded so far as to obtain leave that the young man be called from his exile; nevertheless, when returned, David would not admit him into his presence until two years after, when, and not before, a full and open reconciliation was made and declared; and yet all this while the heart of David was towards his son, and continued, even notwithstanding his unnatural rebellion against him. And so the love of God to his people is from everlasting to everlasting, invariably the same: with him there is no shadow of turning; there is no change in God, as not from love to hatred, so not from hatred to love; he is in one mind, and none can turn him, no, not Christ himself; nor was it the work of Christ's mediation, nor the design of it, to turn the heart of God; for that proceeded according to the unalterable and unchangeable will of God; nor did the mediation of Christ procure, nor was it intended to procure the love and favour of God to his elect; so far from it, that itself is the fruit and effect of that love, John iii. 16. Rom. v. 8. 1 John iv. 10. It was love that set forth and sent forth Christ to be the propitiation for sin; it was owing to the good-will and free favour of God, that a Mediator was admitted for sinful men; and it appeared still greater, in providing one to be a Mediator of reconciliation for them; and the reconciliation the scriptures speak of, as made by the blood, sufferings and death of Christ, is not a reconciliation of God to them, as to his love, but justice; but a reconciliation of them to God; and that not so much of their persons, which are always acceptable and well-pleasing to God, as considered in Christ, in whom they were chosen, as for their sins, Rom. v. 10. 2 Cor. v. 19. Col. i. 20, 21. Heb. ii. 17. and which is no other than a satisfaction for them to divine justice; for the reconciliation of their persons in that way, is not to the love and affections of God, from which they were never separated, but to the justice of God, offended by their sins; and the whole is a reconciliation of the divine perfections to each other in the business of salvation; for though these agree among themselves, yet with respect to that, had different claims to make; the love and grace of God pleaded for mercy, and mercy pleaded for itself, that it might be shewn to the objects of love; but justice insisted on it, that satisfaction be made for the offences committed; the difficulty was how to answer these several pleas; Christ interposed, and offered himself in the covenant, to be a Mediator of reconciliation, or to make satisfaction for sin; and so mercy and truth have met together, and righteousness and peace have kissed each other. Reconciliation then is the principal branch of Christ's office in the covenant as Mediator. Another follows, namely,

His intercession, or advocacy, which proceeds upon reconciliation or satisfaction made; *If any man sin, we have an Advocate with the Father, Jesus Christ the righteous; and he is the Propitiation for our sins,* 1 John ii. 1, 2. and it is his being the Propitiation for sin, that is the foundation of his advocacy, or on which is grounded his plea for the remission of it; he is the Angel of God's presence, who always appears there for his people, and ever lives to make intercession for them; he is first the Mediator of reconciliation, and then of intercession; as they are reconciled to God by his sufferings and death, they are saved through his interceding life. He is called the Angel of God's presence, not only because he enjoys it himself; but because he introduces his people into it, and presents their petitions to God, offers up the prayers of all saints, perfumed with the much incense of his mediation; through which they become acceptable to God. Christ is the medium of access to God, to the throne of his grace; there is no drawing nigh of sinful men to God without a Mediator, without him he is a consuming fire; no man can come to the Father but by Christ; he is the only Way, the new and the living Way; and through him, his blood, righteousness, and sacrifice, there is access with boldness and confidence. And he is the medium of acceptance, both of persons and services, which are only accepted in the Beloved, and become acceptable through his prevalent mediation and intercession; and he is the medium of conveyance of all the blessings of the covenant of grace to his people, which are all communicated in virtue of his advocacy for them; and he is the medium of the saints' communion and fellowship with God now, as he will be the medium of their glory and happiness to all eternity. The next thing to be considered is,

Secondly, The fitness of Christ for his work and office, as the Mediator of the covenant; since a mediator was necessary, and he must be one of the divine Persons in the Trinity; the Son of God being the middle Person in it, seems most proper and suitable to preserve the order, name, and place of the Persons in it: it does not seem so decent, that the first Person should be a Mediator to the second; but rather, since, as Dr. Goodwin expresses it, the suit of trespass was commenced, and ran in the name of the Father, of the first Person for the rest; it seems most agreeable that the reconciliation be made to him by one of the other Persons; and since the second Person bears the name of a Son, as the first of a Father, it seems most in character, that the Son should mediate with the Father, than the Father with the Son; and since it was proper that the Mediator should become the son of man, as will be seen hereafter, it seems most agreeable, that he who is the Son of God should become the Son of man; otherwise there would be two Sons in the Trinity, or two Persons so called: and for the first or third Person to become a Mediator between God and man, does not seem so becoming, as he who is the second or middle Person among them. But the principal fitness of Christ for his office, as Mediator, at least for the execution of it, lies in the union of the two natures, human and divine, in his one Person; whereby he is the Immanuel, God with us, God manifest in the flesh; and as he partakes of both natures, he has an interest in, and a concern for both; he is fit to be a Mediator between God and man; both to take care of things pertaining to God and his glory, and to make reconciliation for the sins of the people.—1. It was requisite that he should be man, assume human nature into union with his divine Person, even a true body, and a reasonable soul.——(1.) That he might be related to those he was a Mediator, Redeemer, and Saviour of; that he might be their brother, their near kinsman, their Goel, and so have an apparent right to redeem them, as the near kinsman, according to the law, had, Lev. xxv. 48, 49.——(2.) That sin might be satisfied for, and reconciliation be made for it, in the same nature which sinned; and whereas, according to the scheme of mediation and salvation by Christ, the same individuals that sinned were not to suffer; it seems requisite and reasonable that an individual of that nature should, in their room and stead, that so it might come as near to what the law required as could be, Gen. ii. 17.——(3.) It was proper that the Mediator should be capable of obeying the law, broken by the sin of man: as a divine Person could not be subject to the law, and yield obedience to it; and had he assumed the angelic nature, that would not have been capable of obeying all the precepts of the law, which are required of men; and universal perfect obedience was necessary for the justification of a sinner before God; hence Christ was made of a woman, that he might be made under the law, and yield obedience to it; by which obedience men are made righteous in the sight of God, Gal. iv. 4. Rom. v. 19.—— (4.) It was meet the Mediator should be man, that he might be capable of suffering death; as God he could not die, and had he assumed the nature of an angel, that is uncapable of dying; and yet suffering the penalty of the law, death, was necessary to make reconciliation; a sacrifice for sin was to be offered, and therefore it was proper Christ should have somewhat to offer; even a true body, and a reasonable soul, which he did offer; peace was to be made by blood, and reconciliation by the sufferings of death, and therefore a nature must be assumed capable of shedding blood, and of suffering death; and without which he could not be made sin, and a curse for men, as the law required he should. In a word, it was highly becoming, that the Captain of our salvation should be made perfect through suffering, that he might be a perfect Saviour, which could not be, without the assumption of human nature; see Heb. ii. 10, 14, 15. and v. 9. and viii. 3.——(5.) It was fit the Mediator should be man, that he might be a merciful, as well as a faithful High Priest, have a fellow-feeling with his people, and sympathize with them under all their temptations, afflictions, and distresses, and succour and relieve them, from love and affection to them, as their friend and brother, Heb. ii. 17, 18. and iv. 15. ——(6.) It was necessary that he should be holy and righteous, free from all sin, original and actual, that he might offer himself without spot to God, take away the sins of men, and be an advocate for them, Heb. vii. 26. and ix. 14. 1 John iii. 5. and ii. 1. but it was not enough to be truly man, and an innocent person; he must be more than a man, to be a mediator between God and man; it was requisite, therefore, 2. That he should be God as well as man.——(1.) That he might be able to draw nigh to God, and treat with him about terms of peace, and covenant with him; all which a mere man could not do; and therefore it is with wonder said, and as expressive of the arduousness of the task, of the difficulty of the work, and of the necessity of a divine Person to do it; *Who is this that engaged his heart to approach unto me, saith the Lord?* Jer. xxx. 21. to mediate between him and sinful men, to lay his hands on both, and reconcile them together; none but Jehovah's fellow could or dared to do this.——(2.) That he might give virtue and value to his obedience and sufferings; for if he had been a mere man, his obedience and righteousness would not have been sufficient to justify men, nor his sufferings and death a proper sacrifice and atonement for sin. But being God as well as man, his righteousness is the righteousness of God; and so sufficient to justify all that believe in him, and them from all their sins; and his blood is the blood of the Son of God, and so cleanses from all sin, and is a proper atonement for it.——(3.) Being Mediator, Redeemer and Saviour, it naturally and necessarily leads men to put their trust and confidence in him, and rely upon him, for peace, pardon, and salvation; whereas, if he was a mere man, and not God, this would entail a curse upon them; *for cursed is the man that trusteth in man, and maketh flesh his arm,* Jer. xvii. 5. and even to worship and adore him, and ascribe divine honour and glory to him; which to do would be idolatry, was he not God; for though he that is Mediator is to be worshipped by angels and men, yet not as mediator, but as God; for it is his Deity that is the foundation of worship, and renders him the proper object of it; God will *not give* his *glory to another,* Isa. xlii. 8. not even the glory of being a Mediator to any other but a divine Person; for of Christ, in his mediatorial capacity, are the words spoken, as appears from the whole preceding context: it is necessary that the Mediator should be God, that he might be the proper object of trust, worship, honour, and glory divine.

Nor is it any objection to his being a Mediator, as to his divine nature, that then the Father and the Spirit would be Mediators too, the divine nature being common to them all; since it is not in the divine nature, essentially considered, but as it subsists in the second Person, the Son of God, that Christ is Mediator, and performs his office; and to exercise this office in it, is no lessening and degrading of his Person, since it is a glory that none but a divine Person is fit to bear: and it may be observed, that among men this office is sometimes assumed and exercised by one superior to either of the parties between whom he mediates; and though the Father may be said to be greater than Christ, considered in his office-capacity, yet this does not suppose any subjection or inferiority of his divine Person: nor is it any objection to Christ being Mediator, as to his divine nature, that then he must be a Mediator to himself, or reconcile men to himself; for not to observe, that Christ in his office may be distinguished from himself, as a divine Person; as one may be distinguished from himself as to different circumstances of age, office, &c. there is no impropriety that Christ is a Mediator for himself, or has made reconciliation and satisfaction to himself; for if the Father may be said to reconcile men to himself by his Son, as in 2 Cor. v. 18, 19. Col. i. 20. why may not the Son be said to reconcile men to himself, as God, by his sufferings and death as man? There is no impropriety, that if a man has offended a society of men, one of that society should take upon him to be a mediator for him, and reconcile him to that society, though he himself is a part of it, and as such, equally offended as they: or, still nearer to the case in hand, supposing a rebellion in a nation, against the king of it, and this king should have a son, who is heir to his throne, and so must be equally offended with the rebels as his father, and yet should take upon him to be a mediator between his father and the rebels, and make peace between them; where would be the impropriety of it, though he himself, with his father, is the party offended?

The mediation of Christ thus stated, meets with and militates against two errors; one of those, who say he is only a Mediator as to his human nature; and that of others, who assert him to be only a Mediator as to his divine nature. But most certain it is, that there are several acts and works of Christ, as Mediator, in which both natures manifestly appear, and are concerned; not to make mention of the incarnation itself, or Christ's assumption of human nature, which manifestly implies both; for it was a divine Person that partook of flesh and blood, or assumed, not an angelic, but an human nature: it was the Word, which was in the beginning with God, and was God, that was made flesh, and dwelt among men; it was he that was in the form of God, and thought it no robbery to be equal with him, that was found in fashion as a man, and took on him the form of a servant; it was God manifest in the flesh. In the obedience of Christ both natures are to be perceived; not only the human nature, in his being obedient unto death, even the death of the cross; but the divine nature also; or otherwise, where is the wonder, that *though he was a Son, yet learned he obedience by the things that he suffered,* Heb. v. 8. and it was that which gave virtue to his obedience, and made it satisfactory to the justice of God, and made the law more honourable than the perfect and perpetual obedience of angels and men could do. In the act of laying down his life for men, both natures appear; the human nature, which is passive in it, and is the life laid down; the divine nature, or the divine Person of Christ, who is active in it, and laid down his life of himself, he having such a power over his life as man, and that at his dispose, as no mere creature ever had; and both are to be observed in his taking of it up again; his human nature, in his body being raised from the dead; his divine nature or person, in raising it up of himself, whereby he was declared to be the Son of God with power: he was put to death in the flesh, in human nature, and quickened in the Spirit, or by his divine nature; the sacrifice of himself, was his own act, as Mediator; what was offered up were his soul and body, his whole human nature; this was offered by his eternal Spirit, or divine nature, which gave virtue to it, and made it a proper atoning sacrifice for sin. To observe no more, the redemption and purchase of his people, is a plain proof of both natures being concerned in his work as Mediator; the purchase-price, or the price of redemption, is his precious blood, his blood as man; but what gave virtue to that blood, and made it a sufficient ransom-price, is, that it was the blood of him that is God as well as man; and therefore God is said to purchase the church with his own blood, Acts xx. 28.

3. It was not only requisite and necessary, that the Mediator should be God and man, but that he should be both in one Person, or that the two natures should be united in one Person; or, rather, that the

CHAP. XI. OF CHRIST, THE MEDIATOR OF THE COVENANT. 235

human nature should be taken up, and united to, and subsist in the Person of the Son of God; for the human nature, as it has no personality of itself, it adds none to the Son of God; it is no constituent part of his Person; he was a divine Person, before his assumption of human nature; and what he assumed was not a person, but a nature, and is called a *thing, nature, seed*, Luke i. 35. Heb. ii. 16. had it been a person, there would be two persons in Christ, and so two mediators, contrary to the express words of scripture, 1 Tim. ii. 5. and if the human nature was a person, as it must be a finite one, what was done and suffered by it, must be finite also, and of no use but to that person, and could have no sufficient virtue and value in them to justify men, and atone for sin; but these two natures being in personal union, the works and actions of either, though distinct and peculiar to each, yet belong to the whole Person, and are predicated of it; and so those of the human nature have virtue and efficacy in them, from the personal union, to make them effectual to the purposes for which they were designed, without which they would be ineffectual. Hence it may be observed, that Christ is described in one nature, by qualities, works, and actions, which belong to him in the other, and is what divines call a communication of idioms or properties; thus the Lord of glory is said to be crucified; God is said to purchase the church with his blood; and the Son of man is said to be in heaven, while he was here on earth, 1 Cor. ii. 8. Acts xx. 28. John iii. 13. the advantage of this personal union is, that the divine nature has an influence upon, and gives virtue and dignity to whatsoever is done or suffered in the human nature; which is of the utmost concern in the mediation of Christ: nor is it any objection that two natures should influence one and the same action, or be concerned in the production or perfection of it; when it is observed, that the soul and body of man, united together, concur in the performance of the same action, whether good or bad. I shall next enquire,

Thirdly, How Christ came to be the Mediator of the covenant, even the Mediator of reconciliation in it: it was owing originally to a thought in the heart of God, the offended Party; whose thoughts were *thoughts of peace, and not of evil*, towards offending man; this affair began with God the Father; *All things are of God*, that is, the Father, as appears by what follows; *Who hath reconciled us to himself by Jesus Christ, and hath given to us the ministry of reconciliation;* the doctrine of it, to publish and declare to the world; the sum and substance of which is, *to wit, that God was in Christ reconciling the world unto himself,* 2 Cor. v. 18, 19. that is, consulting with Christ his Son, and with him contriving the scheme and method of reconciling to himself the world of his elect, considered as sinful fallen creatures in Adam: upon the first thought of peace and reconciliation, a council of peace was held between the divine Persons, which issued in a covenant of peace, in which it was proposed to Christ, and he agreed to it, to be the Peace-maker, upon which he was constituted the Mediator of it; *I was set up from everlasting,* Prov. viii. 23. says Christ; that is, by his divine Father; though not without his own consent: or, *I was anointed*, which does not design a collation of any gifts, qualifying him for the office of Mediator; as when he is said to be anointed with the Holy Ghost; only his investiture with that office, so expressed, because the rite of anointing was used in the consecration of kings, priests, and prophets to their office. And God not only set him up, but *set* him *forth*, in his eternal purposes and decrees, to be the *propitiation for sin*, to make reconciliation and satisfaction for it, Rom. v. 25. and declared him in prophecy to be the Prince of peace, and the Man that should appear in human nature, and make peace and reconciliation between him and men; he sanctified him, or set him apart to this office before the world began; and in the fulness of time, sent him to be the propitiation, or propitiatory-sacrifice, for the sins of men; and even before his incarnation, being constituted in covenant the Mediator of it, he acted as such, throughout the whole old testament-dispensation: he exercised his several offices then; his prophetic office, by making known to Adam the covenant of grace immediately after his fall; by preaching by his Spirit to the disobedient in the times of Noah, the spirits that were in prison, in the times of the apostle Peter; and by his Spirit, in the prophets testifying beforehand his own sufferings, and the glory that should follow. His kingly office, in gathering, governing, and protecting his church and people, who acknowledged him as their King, Judge, and Lawgiver: and his priestly office, through the virtue of his blood reaching backward to the foundation of the world, and therefore said to be the Lamb slain so early, Rev. xiii. 8. and instances there are of his intercession under the former dispensation, Zech. i. 12, 13. and iii. 1, 2, 3, 4. the actual existence of Christ's human nature from eternity, was not necessary to his being a Mediator of the covenant; it was enough that he agreed in covenant, to be man in time; that this was known he would be, and was certain he should be; and accordingly he was, from the instant of the covenant-making, reckoned and accounted, and bore the name of the God-man and Mediator, and acted as such. Some parts of his work did not require the actual existence of the human nature; he could draw nigh to God, as Jehovah's fellow, without it; he could treat with God about terms of peace, and promise to fulfil them, and covenant with God without it: it no more required the actual existence of his human nature, to covenant with his Father, about the reconciliation and redemption of man, than it required that the Father should assume such a nature to covenant with his Son about the same: there were other parts of Christ's work as Mediator, which required its actual existence; as obedience to the law, and suffering death, the penalty of it; but then, and not before, was it necessary for him to assume it, when the fulness of time was come agreed on, to obey and suffer. It only remains now,

Fourthly, To shew what a Mediator Christ is, the excellency of him, and the epithets which belong to him as such. And, 1. He is the one and only Mediator; *There is one Mediator between God and man, the Man Christ Jesus;* and there is no other: the papists plead for other mediators, angels and saints departed; and distinguish between a Mediator of redemption, and a mediator of intercession; the former, they own, is peculiar to Christ, the latter common to angels and saints; but there is no Mediator of intercession, but who is a Mediator of redemption and reconciliation; the instances produced are insufficient, and respect either the uncreated angel, Jesus Christ himself, Zech. i. 12. Rev. viii. 3. or saints, ministers, and members of churches in the present state, and not as departed, Rev. v. 8. and if Rev. vi. 9. is to be understood of departed spirits, it is only an instance of prayer for themselves, and not for others: the passages in Exod. xxxii. 13. Job. v. 1. with others, are quite impertinent.———2. Christ is a Mediator of men only, not of angels; good angels need not any, and as for evil angels, none is provided nor admitted, as before observed. Yet not of all men; for the world, said to be reconciled to God by Christ, is not all the individuals in it; but the world Christ gave his flesh, or human nature for the life of, since there is a world for which he is not so much as a Mediator of intercession, and much less a Mediator of reconciliation; see 2 Cor. v. 19. John vi. 51. and xvii. 9. The persons for whom Christ acted as a Mediator, by means of death, for the redemption of their transgressions, were such as were called, and received the promise of the eternal inheritance, Heb. ix. 15.———3. Yet he is the Mediator both for Jews and Gentiles; for some of both these are chosen vessels of mercy; and God is a covenant-God, not to the Jews only, but to the Gentiles also; and Christ is a Propitiation, not for the sins of the Jews only, but for the sins of the whole world, or of God's elect throughout the whole world: and therefore both have access to God through the one Mediator, Christ, Rom. ix. 23, 24. and iii. 29, 30. 1 John ii. 2. Eph. ii. 18.———4. Christ is Mediator both for old and new testament-saints; there is but one Mediator for both, but one Way to the Father, which is Christ the Way, the Truth, and the Life; but one Way of life, peace, reconciliation, and salvation; but one Redeemer and Saviour; but one name given under heaven among men, whereby they can be saved; old and new testament-saints are saved by the grace of our Lord Jesus; he is the Foundation of the apostles and prophets.———5. Christ is a prevalent Mediator, his mediation is always effectual, ever succeeds, and is infallible; as his work was to make peace and reconciliation, and he agreed and engaged to make it; he has made it, the thing is done, and done effectually; and as for his prayers, they are always heard, his intercession ever prevails, and is never in vain; *I knew that thou hearest me always*, John xi. 42.———6. Christ is an everlasting Mediator; he was Mediator from everlasting, and acted as such throughout the whole old testament-dispensation, and still continues; he has an unchangeable priesthood; his blood always speaks peace and pardon, and he ever lives to make intercession; and when his mediatorial kingdom will be completed, and there will be no need of him, either as a Mediator of reconciliation or intercession, at least in the manner he has been, and now is; for sin being wholly removed from the saints, even as to the being of it, they may have access to God, and he may communicate unto them, without the intervention of a Mediator; as is the case of the holy angels; though Christ may be the medium of the glory and happiness of his people to all eternity; and since the happiness of the saints will greatly lie in beholding the glory of Christ as God-man, and the glory of God will be most illustriously displayed in him, it may be admitted: I shall observe no more, only that this office of Christ, as Mediator, includes his kingly, priestly, and prophetic offices; all which will be considered in their proper place.

CHAP. XII.

OF CHRIST, THE SURETY OF THE COVENANT.

THE suretiship of Christ is a branch of his mediatorial office; one way in which Christ has acted the part of a Mediator between God and men, is by engaging on their behalf, to do and suffer whatever the law and justice of God required, to make satisfaction for their sins. The Greek word for *surety* εγγυος, is used but once throughout the whole New Testament, Heb. vii. 22. and there of Christ; where he is said to be made, or become, *the Surety of a better testament*, or covenant. And the word is derived either from εγγυς, *near*, because a surety draws nigh to one on the behalf of another, and lays himself under obligation to him for that other; thus Christ drew nigh to his Father, and became a Surety to him for them; hence those words, *I will cause him to draw near, and he shall approach unto me; for who is this that engaged his heart to approach unto me, saith the Lord?* Jer. xxx. 21. or rather, it is derived from γυιον, which signifies the *hand*;[1] because when one becomes a Surety, he either puts something into the hand of another for security, or rather puts his hand into the hand of another, or strikes hands with him; a rite much used in suretiship, and is often put for it, and used as synonymous; see Prov. vi. 1. and xvii. 18. and xxii. 26. Suidas[2] derives it from γη, για, the *earth*, because it is that is the firmest of the elements, and remains immoveable, and may denote the firmness and security of the promise, or bond, which a surety gives to one for another. The Hebrew word for a *surety*, in the Old Testament, ערב, Gen. xliii. 9. and elsewhere, has the signification of *mixing*, because, as Stockius[3] observes, in suretiship persons are so mixed among themselves, and joined together, that the one is thereby bound to the other: and, upon the whole, Christ, as a Surety, drew nigh to his Father on the behalf of the elect, struck hands with him, and gave him firm security for them, and put himself in their place and stead, and engaged to perform every thing for them that should be required of him; for the better understanding this branch of Christ's office in the covenant, it may be proper to consider,

First, In what sense Christ is the Surety of the covenant. And, 1st, He is not the Surety for his Father, to his people, engaging that the promises made by him in covenant shall be fulfilled; which is the Socinian sense of Christ's suretiship;[4] for though the promises were made to Christ, and are Yea and Amen in him; and many of them, such as respect him, were fulfilled in him, and by him, as the minister of the circumcision, Gal. iii. 16. 2 Cor. i. 20. Rom. xv. 8. Yet, such is the faithfulness of God that has promised, that there needs no surety for him; his faithfulness is sufficient, which he will not suffer to fail; he is God, that cannot lie, nor deny himself; there is no danger of his breaking his word, and not fulfilling his promise, which may be depended on, and strongly confided in; and if his word was not enough, he has joined his oath to it; so that by two immutable things, in which it was impossible for God to lie, the heirs of promise might have strong consolation, in believing the fulfilment of every promise made, Heb. vi. 18. Besides, though Christ is equal with his Father, is Jehovah's fellow, and has all the perfections of Deity in him, yet he is not greater than he; and, with reverence to him be it said, he cannot give a greater security, than the word and oath of God, or that will lay a firmer foundation for confidence in the promises of God; and it is with an ill grace these men advance such a notion; since they make Christ to be but a mere man; and what dependence can

---

[1] So Hesychius and others.
[2] In voce εγγυη.
[3] Clavis Ling. Sanct. p. 810.
[4] Crellius et Schlichtingius in Heb. vii. 22.

there be upon him, when cursed is the man that trusts in man, and makes flesh his arm? Jer. xvii. 5. and what greater security is it possible that a mere man should give, than what the promise of God itself gives? or what additional strength can a creature give to that, to induce a stronger belief of it? Nor,

2dly, Is Christ in such sense a Surety, as civilians call a *fidejussor*, or such a surety that is jointly engaged with a debtor, for the payment of a debt; or is so bound for another, as that that other remains under obligation, and the obligation of the surety is only an accession to to the principal obligation, which is made stronger thereby, and the creditor has the greater security; yet still the principal debtor is left under his debt, that is not removed from him, and he is under obligation to pay it, if able; and it is first to be demanded of him, or should his surety desert his suretiship, and not make satisfaction. But now none of these things are to be supposed in Christ's suretiship.——1. He is not a mere accessory to the obligation of his people for payment of their debts; he and they are not engaged in one joint-bond for payment; he has taken their whole debt upon himself, as the apostle Paul did in the case of Onesimus; and he has paid it off, and entirely discharged it alone.——2. Nor was any such condition made in his suretiship-engagements for his people, that they should pay if they were able; for God the Father, to whom Christ became a Surety, knew, and he himself, the Surety, knew full well, when this suretiship was entered into, that they were not able to pay, and never would be; yea, that it was impossible for them, in their circumstances, ever to pay; for having failed in their obedience to God, all after acts of obedience, though ever so perfect, could not make amends, or satisfy for that disobedience, since to those God has a prior right; and their failure in obedience, brings upon them a debt of punishment, which is everlasting, and *ad infinitum*; and, if left on them, would be ever paying, and never paid; see Luke vii. 41, 42. Matt. xviii. 24, 25. and v. 26. and xxv. 46.——3. Nor is such a supposition to be made, that Christ might desert his suretiship, withdraw himself from it; this indeed has been supposed by some: but though Christ was not obliged to become a Surety, he voluntarily engaged in this work, and cheerfully took it on him; yet when he had undertaken it he could not relinquish it, without being guilty of disobedience to his Father, and of unfaithfulness to his own engagements; for from the instant he became a Surety for his people, he became a Servant to his Father, and he called and reckoned him as such; *Thou art my servant, O Israel; behold my servant whom I uphold*, Isa. xlix. 3. and xlii. 1. and laid his commands upon him, both to obey his law, and lay down his life for his people, both which he undertook to do, and did perform; or otherwise he could not have had the character of God's *righteous Servant*, nor would have been faithful to him that appointed him, nor to himself, Isa. liii. 10. Heb. iii. 2. and consequently could not be without sin, which God forbid should ever be said or supposed of the holy Jesus, who did no sin, nor was guile found in his mouth; yet this has been supposed of him by some, and the dreadful consequences of it, which have been blasphemously uttered by some schoolmen and popish-writers, not fit to be mentioned.
——4. Nor is it to be supposed, that Christ might not fulfil his suretiship-engagements, or not make satisfaction, as might be expected; since if he did not, it must be either for want of will, or want of power; not of will, since the persons he became a surety for, he bore the strongest affection to; these were the sons of men, in whom was all his delight from everlasting; and such his love to them, that nothing whatever could separate from it: nor could it be for want of power, since, as a divine Person, he is the mighty God; as Mediator, has all power in heaven and in earth; as man, was made strong by the Lord for this work, and had a power, as such, to lay down his life, and take it up again: and should he have deserted his suretiship, and not have made the promised and expected satisfaction, the purposes of God, respecting the salvation of the elect by Christ, must have been frustrated, and made null and void; the council of peace held concerning it would have been without effect; the covenant of grace abolished; the salvation of God's people not obtained, and the glory of God, of his grace, mercy, truth, and faithfulness lost; yea, Christ himself must have been deprived of his mediatorial glory; all too shocking to be admitted. But,

3dly, Christ is in such sense a Surety, as civilians call an *expromissor*, one that promises out and out, absolutely engages

CHAP. XII.   OF CHRIST, THE SURETY OF THE COVENANT.   239

to pay another's debt; takes another's obligation, and transfers it to himself, and by this act dissolves the former obligation, and enters into a new one, which civilians call *novation*; so that the obligation no longer lies on the principal debtor, but he is set free, and the Surety is under the obligation, as if he was the principal debtor, or the guilty person. Now this sort of suretiship being most similar, and coming nearest to Christ's suretiship, is made use of to express and explain it; though they do not in every thing tally; for the civil law neither describes nor admits such a Surety among men as Christ is; who so substituted himself in the room and stead of sinners, as to suffer punishment in soul and body for them; but in some things there is an agreement.——1. Christ, by his suretiship, has took the whole debt of his people upon himself, and made himself solely responsible for it; he has dissolved thereby their obligation to payment or punishment, having taken it on himself; so that they were by it entirely set free from the very instant he became their Surety; it is a rule that will hold good, as Maccovius[5] observes, that as soon as any one becomes a surety for another, the other is immediately freed, if the surety be accepted: which is the case here; for from henceforward, God the Father looked for his debt, and expected satisfaction of Christ, and let the sinners go free, for whom he engaged; he was gracious, and said, *deliver them from going down to the pit; I have found a Ransom*, Job xxxiii. 24. just as when the apostle Paul became a surety for Onesimus; supposing him accepted as such by Philemon, Onesimus was set free; the apostle taking the whole debt and wrong upon himself, and promising to repay and make satisfaction, and which he wrote and signed with his own hand.——2. When Christ became a Surety for his people, their sins were no longer imputed to them, but were imputed to Christ, were placed to his account, and he became responsible for them; it was not at the time of his sufferings and death, that God laid on him first the iniquities of his people, and they were imputed and reckoned to him, and he accounted them as his own, 2 Cor. v. 19. Isa. liii. 6. Psalm xl. 12. and lxix. 5. by which it appears, that obligation to payment of debts, or punishment, did not lie upon the principal debtor, or guilty person, but upon Christ, who became their Surety; for,——3. The old testament-saints were really freed from guilt, condemnation, and death, before the actual payment was made by Christ their Surety; some had as full an application of the pardon of their sins, and as clear a view of their interest in Christ's righteousness, as their justifying righteousness before God, as any of the new testament-saints ever had; the one were saved by the grace of Christ as the other; yea, they were received into heaven, and actually glorified, before the suretiship-engagements of Christ were fulfilled, Isa. xliii. 25. and xlv. 24, 25. Acts xv. 11. Heb. xi. 13—16. So that it is a plain case, that the obligation to payment and punishment lay not on those for whom Christ became a Surety, but was transferred from them to him; unless this absurdity can be admitted, that such an obligation lay on glorified saints, till the actual payment was made by Christ; or that there was a *limbus patrum*, as the papists say, where the saints, before Christ's coming, were detained; but were set free by him when he came.——4. It is certain that the old testament-saints had knowledge of the suretiship-engagements of Christ, and prayed and pleaded for the application of the benefits of them to them, Job xix. 25. Psalm cxix. 122. Isa. xxxviii. 14. and which they enjoyed: and such was the dignity of Christ's person, and his known faithfulness to his engagements, and the eternity of them, which with God has no succession, they were always present with him, and in full view, as if actually performed; before and after made no difference in the sight of God, with whom a thousand years are as one day, and eternity itself as but a moment. And now, from this suretiship of Christ arise both the imputation of sin to Christ, and the imputation of his righteousness to his people; this is the ground and foundation of both, and on which the priestly office of Christ stands, and in virtue of which it is exercised, 2 Cor. v. 21. Heb. vii. 20, 21, 22. I proceed,

Secondly, To consider what Christ as a Surety, engaged to do. And, 1st, He engaged to pay the debts of his people, and satisfy for the wrong and injury done by them; this may be illustrated by the instance of the apostle Paul engaging for Onesimus; which is thus expressed, *If he*

---

[5] Theolog. Quæst. loc. 31. qu. 6.

hath wronged thee, or oweth thee ought, put that on my account; I, Paul, have written it with mine own hand, I will repay it, Philem. ver. 18, 19. Sin is a wrong and injury done to divine justice, and to the holy law of God, broken by it; which Christ undertook to satisfy for; and sins are debts; see Matt. vi. 12. compared with Luke xi. 4. not proper ones, for then they might be committed with impunity, since it is right and commendable to pay debts: but in an improper sense, as debts oblige to payment, so sins to punishment; even to endure the curse of the law, and death eternal, the sanction of it: these debts, or sins, are infinite objectively, as they are contracted and committed against an infinite being, and require punishment of a creature *ad infinitum;* and therefore not to be paid off, or answered, by a finite creature; but Christ being an infinite Person, as God, was able to pay off those debts, and answer for those sins, and engaged to do it, and has done it.

There is a twofold debt paid by Christ, as the Surety of his people; the one is a debt of obedience to the law of God; this he engaged to do, when he said, *Lo, I come to do thy will; thy law is within my heart:* and accordingly he was made under the law, and yielded perfect obedience to it, by which his people are made righteous; and the other is a debt of punishment, incurred through failure of obedience in them; the curse of the law he has endured, the penalty of it, death; and by paying both these debts, the whole righteousness of the law is fulfilled in his people, considered in him their Head and Surety. Now let it be observed, that these debts are not pecuniary ones, though there is an allusion to such, and the language is borrowed from them; but criminal ones, a wrong and injury done, as supposed in the case of Onesimus; and are of such a nature as deserve and require punishment in body and soul, being transgressions of the righteous law of God; and God is to be considered, not merely as a creditor, but as the Judge of the whole earth, who will do right, and who will by no means clear the guilty, without a satisfaction to his justice; and yet there is a mixture of grace, mercy, and goodness in God, with his justice in this affair, by admitting a Surety to obey, suffer, and die, in the room and stead of his people, which he was not obliged unto; nor does the law give the least hint of an allowance of it; nor do the civil laws of men admit of any such thing, that an innocent person should suffer death in the room of one that is guilty, even though he consents to it, and desires it; because no man has a power over his own life, to dispose of it at pleasure; but God, who can dispense with his own law, if he pleases, has thought fit to explain it, and put a construction on it in favour of his people, where it is not express; and allow of a commutation of persons, that his Son should stand in their law-place and stead, obey, suffer, and die for them, that they might be made the righteousness of God in him. This is owing to his sovereign grace and mercy; nor is at all inconsistent with his justice, since Christ fully consented to all this, who is the Prince of life, and had power over his own life, as man, to lay it down, and take it up again; and since justice is fully satisfied, by the obedience and death of Christ, and the law magnified and made honourable, and more so than it could have been by all the obedience and sufferings of angels and men put together.

2dly, Another thing which Christ as a Surety engaged to do, was to bring all the elect safe to glory; this may be illustrated by Judah's suretiship for Benjamin; thus expressed to his father, *I will be surety for him; of my hand shalt thou require him; if I bring him not unto thee, and set him before thee, then let me bear the blame for ever,* Gen. xliii. 9. And thus Christ became a Surety to his divine Father, for his beloved Benjamins, the chosen of God, and precious; as he asked them of his Father, and they were given into his hands, to be preserved by him, that none of them might be lost; he agreed that they should be required of his hand, every one of them, and pass under the hand of him that telleth them, and their whole number appear complete, and none missing; as will be the case, when he shall say, *Lo, I, and the children which God hath given me,* Heb. ii. 13. Christ engaged to *bring* his people to his Father; this was the work proposed to him, and which he agreed to do; *to bring Jacob again to him, and to restore the preserved of Israel,* Isa. xlix. 5, 6. to recover the lost sheep, to ransom them out of the hands of him that was stronger than they; to redeem them from all iniquity, and from the law, its curse and condemnation, and save them with an everlasting salvation, and bring them safe to his Father in heaven; and because he laid himself under obligation to do all this; hence he says, *them also I must bring*, into his fold here, and into heaven and glory hereafter, John x. 16. and *set* them *before* his Father; as he did at his death, when all the elect were gathered together in one Head, even in him, to present them in the body of his flesh, through death, holy, unblameable, and unreproveable in the sight of God; and as he now does in heaven, where he appears in the presence of God for them, and they are set down in heavenly places in him, as their Head and Surety; and as he will at the last day, when he will deliver up the kingdom to the Father, the mediatorial kingdom, the kingdom of priests, complete and perfect, as he received them; and having first presented them to himself, as a glorious church, without spot or wrinkle, he will present them faultless before the presence of his Father's glory, with exceeding joy; and will be so far from bearing any blame, having so fully discharged his suretiship-engagements, that he will appear without sin unto salvation; even without sin imputed, without the wrong done by his people put on his account; all being fully answered for according to agreement.

CHAP. XIII.

OF CHRIST, THE TESTATOR OF THE COVENANT.

FIRST, The covenant of grace bears the name, and has the nature of a testament: it is often called the new and better testament, as administered under the gospel-dispensation, Matt. xxvi. 28. Heb. vii. 22. and ix. 15. in distinction from the former; it is called a testament, in allusion to the last will and testament of men. And, 1. Because it is the will of God himself, and not another; the will of him that is sovereign and absolute, who does according to his will in heaven and in earth, in nature, providence, and grace. The covenant is founded on the will of God, and is the pure effect of it; he was not obliged to make it; he freely and of his own accord came into it; so all the contracting parties in it, as has been before observed. A man's will or testament ought to be voluntary; he is not to be forced nor drawn, nor pressed to make it, contrary to his inclination; or otherwise it is not his own will. The covenant, or testament of God, is of his own making, without any influence from another; all the articles in it are of his free good will and pleasure; as, that he will be the covenant-God of his people; that they shall be his sons and daughters; that they shall be his heirs, and joint-heirs with Christ; that they shall enjoy all the blessings of grace, redemption, pardon, justification, regeneration, perseverance in grace and glory; for he hath bequeathed, in this will, both grace and glory to his people, Psalm lxxxiv. 11. Luke xii. 32.

——2. As a will consists of various legacies to various persons, so does the covenant of grace; some to Christ, for he under different considerations, is a legatee in it, and a testator of it: all the elect, his spiritual seed and offspring, are bequeathed unto him, as his portion and inheritance, and with which he is greatly delighted, Deut. xxxii. 9. Psalm ii. 8. and xvi. 6. *As my Father hath appointed unto me a kingdom*, says he, Luke xxii. 29. his mediatorial kingdom, a kingdom of priests, and which he disposed of to him in a testamentary-way, as the word there used signifies. There are other legacies, such as before suggested, respecting grace and glory, left in this will for the brethren of Christ, among whom he is the first-born, and so appointed principal heir, yea, heir of all things, and they joint-heirs with him; and what is given to them, is in trust with him for them, particularly the inheritance bequeathed, which they obtain in him, and is reserved with him in heaven for them.

——3. In wills, what a man disposes of, is, or should be, his own; no man has a power to dispose, nor ought to dispose of, what is another's, or not his own; or otherwise, his will is a void will, and such bequests void bequests. All the blessings of goodness, whether of nature, providence, or grace, are all the Lord's own, and he has a sovereign right to dispose of them as he pleases, and to give them to whomsoever he will; and against which no one has any just cause or reason to object; and if he does, it is to no purpose; *Is it not lawful for me*, says the Testator of the covenant, *to do what I will with mine own? Is thine eye evil, because I am good?* Matt. xx. 15.——4. This will, or testament, of Jehovah, is an ancient one, it was made in eternity; it is called an everlasting covenant or testament; not only because it always continues, and will never become null and void, but because it is from everlasting; the bequests and donations made in it were made before the world began,

2 Tim. i. 9. It is, indeed, sometimes called a new testament, not because newly made, but because newly published and declared, at least in a more clear and express manner; a new and fresh copy of it has been delivered out to the heirs of promise.——5. It is a will or testament that is unalterable; *Though it be but a man's covenant*, or testament, *yet if it be confirmed* by his own hand-writing and seal, and especially by his death, *no man disannulleth or addeth thereunto*, Gal. iii. 15. The covenant of grace is ordered in all things, and sure; this testament, or will, is founded upon the immutability of the divine counsel; so that the heirs of promise, the legatees in it, may have strong consolation, and be fully assured of enjoying their legacies in it; which are the sure mercies of David, of David's Son and Antitype, as all the promises of it are Yea and Amen in him.—— 6. Testaments, or wills, are generally sealed as well as signed: the seals of God's will or testament are not the ordinances; circumcision was no seal of the covenant of grace; it was a seal to Abraham, and to him only, that he should be the father of believing Gentiles; and that the same righteousness of faith should come upon them, which came upon him, when in uncircumcision: nor is baptism, which is falsely said to come in the room of it, and much less is it a seal of the covenant; nor the ordinance of the Lord's Supper; for though the blood of Christ, one of the symbols in it, is yet not that itself: but the seals are the holy Spirit of God, and the blood of Christ; and yet the holy Spirit is not such a seal that makes the covenant, or testament, surer in itself, only assures the Lord's people of their interest in it, by witnessing it to their spirits, by being in them the earnest of the inheritance bequeathed them, and by sealing them up unto the day of redemption; properly speaking, the blood of Christ is the only seal of this testament, by which it is ratified and confirmed; and therefore called the blood of the covenant, and the blood of the new testament, Zech. ix. 11. Matt. xxvi. 28. Heb. xiii. 20.——7. To all wills there are commonly witnesses, and often three, and in some cases three are required. Now as God sware by himself, because he could swear by no greater; so because no other and more proper witnesses could be had, to witness this will made in eternity, God himself, or the three divine Persons, became witnesses to it, the Three that bare record in heaven, the Father, the Word, and the holy Ghost, 1 John v. 7. Unless we choose to conceive of things in this manner; that as the Father, the first Person, gives the lead in all things in nature and in grace, and as he did in the council of peace, so in the covenant of grace, or in this testament, he may be considered as the maker of the will, or testament, and the Son and Spirit as witnesses to it.—— 8. This will, or testament, is registered in the sacred writings, from thence the probate of it is to be taken; the public notaries, or amanuenses, that have copied it under a divine direction, are the prophets and apostles; hence the writings of the one are called the Old Testament, and the writings of the other the New Testament, the latter being the more clear, full, and correct copy.

The covenant of grace having the nature of a testament, shews that there is no restipulation in it on the part of men; no more than there is a restipulation of legatees in a will; what is bequeathed to them being without their knowledge and consent, and without anything being required of them, to which they give their assent. The covenant of grace is properly a covenant to Christ, in which he restipulates; but a testament to his people, or a pure covenant of promise. Also it may be observed, that the legacies in this testament are owing to the good-will of the testator, and not to any merit in the legatees; *For if they which are of the law be heirs*, if they that seek eternal life by the works of the law be heirs of grace and glory, then, says the apostle, *faith is made void, and the promise made of none effect*, which declare it to be a free donation: and so again, *If the inheritance be of the law*, or to be obtained by the works of it, *it is no more of promise;* these will not consist with, but contradict one another; *but God gave it to Abraham by promise;* as he has done to all the legatees in his covenant or will; see Rom. iv. 14. Gal. iii. 18.

Secondly, The Son of God, the Lord Jesus Christ, may be considered as testator of the covenant of grace, as it is a will or testament, and which is plainly suggested in Heb. ix. 15—17. for,——1. Christ as God has an equal right to dispose of things as his divine Father, seeing all that the Father has are his; as all the perfections of deity, so all persons, and all things in nature, providence, and grace; particularly all the blessings of grace and of glory. He is over all God blessed for ever, and all things are of him and owe their being to him, and are at his dispose; yea, all things are delivered by the Father to him as mediator: and if the Spirit disposes of his gifts and graces, dividing them to every man severally as he will; the Son of God may be reasonably thought to have a power and right to dispose of the blessings of his goodness to whomsoever he pleases.——2. Nothing is disposed of in the covenant, or testament, without his counsel and consent; for though with respect to creatures, angels and men, it may be said of God, *with whom took he counsel?* yet with his Son, the Wonderful Counsellor, the Angel of the great council, he did; for the council of peace was between them both, the Father and the Son, which respected the salvation of men, and the donation of grace and glory to them.——3. Nor was anything given in covenant, or disposed of in the will and testament of God, but with respect to the death of Christ; all promised in covenant was on condition of Christ's making his soul an offering for sin, and of pouring out his soul unto death, Isa. liii. 10—12. all the blessings of grace bestowed on Old Testament-saints, as they were legacies in this testament, so they were given forth in virtue of the blood of the covenant, which had a virtue that reached backward; Christ being the lamb slain from the foundation of the world; and there is no blessing of grace in the covenant, but what is on account of the death of Christ the testator; redemption of transgressions, that were under both the first and second testaments, was by means of death; and without shedding of blood there was no remission under either dispensation; and it is the death of Christ that secures from condemnation, as well as by it reconciliation is made.——4. Whatever is given in this will, is given to Christ first to be disposed of by him, so that he is the executor as well as the testator of it; he was set up as mediator from everlasting; was prevented with the blessings of goodness, or had them first given to him; he was possessed of a fulness of grace, and grace was given to the elect in him before the world began; not only the blessings of grace were put into his hands to dispose of, but eternal life, for he has power to give eternal life to as many as the Father hath given him; whether this be considered as an inheritance which He, the Word of God's grace, the essential Word, is able to give among them that are sanctified by faith in him; or as a kingdom prepared for them in the purposes of God, and which Christ gives a right unto, and a meetness for; yea, he himself disposes of it in a testamentary way, *and I appoint unto you a kingdom,* dispose of it to you by will and testament, Luke xxii. 29. Wherefore,

Thirdly, The death of Christ is necessary to put this will in force, to give strength unto it, that it may be executed according to the design of the maker of it; *for where a testament is, there must also of necessity be the death of the testator; for a testament is of force after men are dead, otherwise it is of no strength at all, whilst the testator liveth,* Heb. ix. 16, 17. It is not the death of any only of the testator himself, that gives validity to his will, or renders it executable; and it is only the death of Christ that gives force and strength unto, or ratifies and confirms the covenant of grace; not the death of slain sacrifices, for though by the blood and death of these the first testament was dedicated, ratified, and confirmed in a typical way, as these were types of Christ in his bloodshed and death, Heb. ix. 19—22. yet the new testament is only, really, truly, and properly ratified and confirmed by the death of Christ itself; and whereas the Father and the Spirit were jointly concerned with Christ in making this will or testament, it was not necessary that they should die, nor could they, since they never assumed a nature capable of dying; only it was necessary that one of the testators should assume a nature capable of death, and in it die to give force to this will; and infinite wisdom judged it most proper and fitting that the Son of God should do it, who took upon him, not the nature of angels, who are incorporeal, immaterial and immortal spirits, and die not; but he became a partaker of flesh and blood, of human nature, that he might die and ratify the testament and will he was concerned in the making of; and this was necessary to give it strength and force: not as if it was alterable until the death of Christ, as the wills of men are until their death, which while they live are liable to be altered again and again; for the first thoughts of God always remain, and that to all generations; his mind is never turned, his counsel is immutable, and so his covenant and testament founded thereon is unalterable; nor that the inheritance bequeathed in this will could not be enjoyed before the death of Christ; this indeed is the case with respect to the wills of men, the legacies are not payable, nor estates bequeathed enjoyed, until the testator dies; but such is not only the certainty of Christ's death, and which with God was as if it was, before it really was; but such is the virtue and efficacy of it, that it reaches backward to the beginning of the world, as before observed; wherefore the Old Testament-saints not only received the promise of eternal inheritance, but enjoyed it before the death of Christ, though in virtue of it, for they are said to *inherit the promises,* that is, the things promised, Heb. ix. 15. and vi. 11. but the death of Christ was necessary to confirm the covenant or testament, that the legatees might appear to have a legal right to what was bequeathed to them, law and justice being satisfied thereby; so that no caveat could be put in against them, and no obstruction made to their claim of legacies, and their enjoyment of them; and no danger of this will being ever set aside. There is another concern and part which Christ has in the covenant, and that is the *messenger* of it, Mal. iii. 1. but as that respects the administration of it, it will be considered in its proper place, after the fall of man.

CHAP. XIV.

OF THE CONCERN THE SPIRIT OF GOD HAS IN THE COVENANT OF GRACE.

HAVING considered the parts which the Father and the Son have taken in the covenant, the part which the holy Spirit has in it is next to be treated of; who was not a mere bystander, spectator, and witness of this solemn transaction, compact, and agreement, between the Father and the Son, but was a party concerned in it. And,

First, The third person, the Spirit, gave his approbation of, and assent unto every article in the covenant.——1. In general, what respected the salvation of the chosen ones; for that is the grand and principal article of the covenant; *this,* says David, speaking of the covenant, *is all my salvation,* 2 Sam. xxiii. 5. that is, the whole of his salvation; all things relative to it were provided for in it, and secured by it; in the economy of which each Person took his part; and that of the Spirit is sanctification; which makes meet for the enjoyment of complete and eternal salvation; hence called *the sanctification of the Spirit,* 2 Thess. ii. 13. 1 Pet. i. 2. And this clearly shews, that the Spirit approved of, and assented to the whole scheme of salvation, or of the thing itself in general; or otherwise he would never have taken a part in it; and as it was the purpose and will of God the Father to save men by his Son, and he appointed them to obtain salvation by him; so the Son of God came to seek and save men, being sent of God for that purpose; in which mission of him the Spirit joined; *Now the Lord God, and his Spirit, hath sent me,* Isa. xlviii. 16. which is a plain proof that he approved of and assented to it, that the Son of God should be the Saviour of men; and whereas it was proper that the Son of God should assume human nature, and in it work out the salvation of men; and which was agreed upon between the Father and the Son; so it was approved of and assented to by the Spirit; as appears from his concern in the incarnation of Christ; for what was *conceived in the Virgin was of the Holy Ghost,* Matt. i. 18, 20. and, seeing it was necessary that the Saviour of men should suffer and die for them, to satisfy law and justice; and the divine Father enjoined his Son to lay down his life for them; to which command he became obedient; so the Spirit declared his approbation of it, by testifying beforehand, in the prophets, *the sufferings of Christ, and the glory that should follow;* as well as was assisting to the human nature of Christ, in the sacrifice of himself; since it was *through the eternal Spirit,* he offered up himself without spot to God, 1 Pet. i. 11. Heb. ix. 14. Once more, as it was highly proper, that as Christ should be delivered to death for the offences of men, so that he should rise again for their justification; or otherwise, the whole affair of salvation would have miscarried; hence the Father in covenant enjoined his Son, as to lay down his life, so to take it up again; and which he did, and in which the Spirit was concerned; and which shewed his approbation of this closing part of the scheme of salvation by Christ; see Rom. i. 4.——2. The Spirit of God approved of and assented to all the promises in the covenant: there are many exceeding great and precious promises in the Scriptures, which are transcribed from the covenant, and are all Yea and Amen in Christ, and in which the Spirit has a concern; hence he is called *the holy Spirit of promise,* Eph. i. 13. indeed, he himself is the great promise of the covenant; promised both to Christ the Head, and to his members, Matt. xii. 18. Isa. xlii. 1. and xliv. 3. Gal. iii. 14. and he is concerned in the application of every promise to the elect;

it is he that remembers to them the word of promise, on which the Lord has sometimes caused them to hope; and it is he that opens the promise to them, instructs them in it, and shews them what is contained in it, the nature, use, and suitableness of it; it is he that applies the promises to them at a proper season, when they are like apples of gold in pictures of silver; and he it is that keeps up their faith and hope, as to the grand promise of eternal life; so that they, *through the Spirit, wait for the hope of righteousness by faith,* John xiv. 26. Prov, xxv. 11. Gal. v. 5. by which it appears, that he approved of every promise of the covenant made in eternity, or he would never act the part he does, in the application of them in time.
———3. The blessed Spirit approved of and gave his assent to all the grants made to Christ, and to his people in the covenant, to the sure mercies of David, to the spiritual blessings wherewith the elect are blessed in heavenly places in Christ; for he takes of these in time, and shews them to the persons interested in them, and their interest therein, John xvi. 14. which he would not do, if he had not approved of the grants of these blessings to them, in the everlasting covenant; as for instance, the blessing of a justifying righteousness, to be wrought out by Christ, was provided in the covenant; and which being brought in, is revealed in the gospel from faith to faith: and besides the external revelation of it in the gospel, the Spirit of God brings near this righteousness, and sets it in the view of an awakened sinner, and shews him its suitableness, fulness, and excellency, works faith in him to receive it, and pronounces in his conscience his justification by it; hence it is said of such, that they are *justified in the name of the Lord Jesus, and by the Spirit of our God,* 1 Cor. vi. 11. Pardon of sin is another blessing of the covenant through Christ, and the Spirit takes the blood of Christ, the blood of the covenant, shed for the remission of sin, and sprinkles it on the conscience, and thereby speaks peace and pardon to it; saying, *Son,* or *daughter, be of good cheer, thy sins are forgiven thee,* Heb. viii. 12. and x. 22. and xii. 24. Adoption also, a blessing of grace, provided in the covenant, and which the Spirit bears witness to and makes application of, and is sent down into the hearts of the covenant and adopted ones for that purpose, and is hence called *the Spirit of adoption,* 2 Cor. vi. 18. Gal. iv. 6.

Rom. viii. 15, 16. In short, all the grace given to the elect in Christ, before the world began, all the things that are freely given them of God in the covenant, the Spirit in time makes known unto them, and declares and testifies their interests in them, 1 Cor. i. 12. and ii. 9, 10, 11. All which abundantly prove his approbation of and assent unto every thing contained in the covenant of grace.

Secondly, There are many things which the holy Spirit himself undertook and engaged in covenant to do; and nothing more strongly proves this than his doing them; for had he not agreed to do them, they would not have been done by him. And,

1st, Some things he has done, as he agreed to do, with respect to Christ; he formed the human nature of Christ, in which he obeyed and suffered for the salvation of the elect: every individual of human nature is, indeed, made by him; *The Spirit of God hath made me,* says Elihu, Job xxxiii. 4. but the individual of Christ's human nature, was *fearfully and wonderfully made* by him, as David, personating him, says he was *in secret, and curiously wrought in the lowest parts of the earth,* in the womb of the Virgin, according to the model of it, in the book of God's purposes and decrees; it was produced by the power of the Highest, the overshadowing of the Holy Ghost, without the instrumentality of man; and so was free from the pollution of sin, propagated by ordinary and natural generation, and therefore called the *holy thing,* born of the Virgin, Psalm cxxxix. 14, 15, 16. Luke i. 35. The Spirit of God filled the same human nature with his gifts and graces without measure, which are the oil of gladness he anointed him with above his fellows, and thereby fitted and qualified him as man, for the discharge of his office as Mediator, Isa. xi. 1, 2, 3. and xlii. 1. and lxi. 1. he descended upon him as a dove at his baptism; which was the signal by which John the Baptist knew he was the Messiah, and pointed him out as such to others; he assisted him as man, in the ministry of the gospel, whereby he spake as never man did, and with an authority the Scribes and Pharisees did not; and in the performance of miracles; for he cast out devils, as he himself says, by *the Spirit of God,* Matt. xii. 28. He also was concerned in Christ's offering up himself a Sacrifice; and in his resurrection from the dead, as before observed; whereby he glorified him, as well as by other things, Christ said he would, John xvi. 14. All which he did according to covenant-agreements and settlements.

2dly, There are other things he has done, as he agreed to do, with respect to men; either,

1. To such as are in a public office and capacity, as the prophets of the Old Testament; whom he inspired to speak and write as they did, 2 Pet i. 21. and the apostles of the New, who were endowed with power from on high, with his extraordinary gifts to preach the gospel, in all languages, to all people, and to confirm it with miracles, Acts i. 4, 5. and ii. 4. Heb. ii. 3, 4. and ordinary ministers of the word, in all succeeding generations, with gifts and grace suitable to their office; whom he calls and separates to it, directs where they should go, he has work for them to do, and makes them overseers of flocks or churches committed to their care, Acts xiii. 2. and xvi. 6, 7. and xx. 28. and it is he that makes the word preached by them effectual to the conviction and conversion of sinners, and to the comfort and edification of saints; and whereby he conveys himself into the hearts of men, 1 Thess. i. 5, 6. 2 Cor. iii. 6, 8. Gal. iii. 2. All which he undertook to do, and has done. Or,

2. To such as are in a private capacity, to whom he is, (1.) A Spirit *of conviction;* he convinces them of sin, original, actual, of all their sins of thought, word, and deed; of the demerit of sin, and of the inability of men to make atonement for it; and brings them to such a sense of it, as to loath it, and themselves for it; to blush and be ashamed of it, and to have such a godly sorrow for it, which works repentance unto salvation. And *of righteousness;* of the insufficiency of their own righteousness to justify them before God; and of the excellency and suitableness of the righteousness of Christ. And *of judgment;* that there is one not to be escaped, and at which all must appear, and in which there will be no standing, but in the righteousness of Christ, John xvi. 8.——(2.) A Spirit *of regeneration* and *renovation;* men must be born again, and they that are born of God, even of the Spirit of God, are renewed by him in the Spirit of their minds; all things are made new; a new man is created in them, a new heart and a new spirit are given unto them, according to the covenant of grace; hence we read of *regeneration,* and *the renewing of the Holy Ghost,* Tit. iii. 5.——(3.) A Spirit *of faith;* all men have not faith, only God's elect; and therefore true faith is called the faith of God's elect; and those that have it, have it not of themselves, it is the gift of God; it is of the operation of God, a work of his almighty power, begun, carried on, and performed with power, and that by the Holy Ghost: and therefore he is called *the Spirit of faith,* 2 Cor. iv. 13.——(4.) A *Comforter,* under which character he is often spoken of, and promised by Christ, that he should be sent by him, and from his Father, according to covenant-agreements; and which office, as he freely undertook in covenant, he performs, by shedding abroad the love of God and Christ in the hearts of his people; by leading into the comfortable doctrines of the gospel; by opening and applying the precious promises of it; by taking of the things of Christ, and shewing them to them; and by witnessing to them their adoption; and by being the earnest of their inheritance, and the sealer of them up unto the day of redemption.——(5.) A *Sanctifier;* if any are sanctified, it is by the Spirit of God; sanctification is his work, and therefore called *the sanctification of the Spirit,* as before observed: it is the Spirit that begins, and carries on, and finishes the work of grace and holiness upon the hearts of God's elect, without which no man shall see the Lord. He is the Spirit of strength to the saints, to enable them to exercise grace, and to perform duties; he is put into them according to the covenant of grace, to cause them to walk in the statutes and judgments of the Lord to do them; to strengthen them to walk on in the ways of the Lord, and to persevere in faith and holiness to the end. And all this the Spirit of God does, as he engaged and undertook to do, in the everlasting covenant; and therefore he is said to *come,* being sent, to do these things; not without his will and consent, but according to his voluntary engagements in covenant, without which he could not be sent by the Father and the Son, being equal to them; and this will account for the several passages where he is said to be sent by the Father, in the name of Christ, and by Christ, from the Father, John xiv. 16, 26. and xv. 26. and xvi. 7. Gal. iv. 6. This being all agreed on, and settled in the covenant between them.

CHAP. XV.

OF THE PROPERTIES OF THE COVENANT OF GRACE.

I SHALL close the account of the covenant of Grace with the epithets or properties of it; which may serve to lead more fully and clearly into the nature, use, and excellency of it; and which may in some measure be collected from what has been already observed. And,

1. It is an *eternal* covenant; not merely as to duration, being what will continue to eternity, and so is called an everlasting covenant, but as to the original of it; it was made in eternity, and commenced and bears date from eternity. The spring of it is the mercy, grace, and love of God; *I said,* says God, *mercy shall be built up for ever;* there shall be such a display of it, as shall always abide; and in order to this it follows; *I have made a covenant with my chosen,* with Christ, and the elect in him; which is a standing everlasting monument of mercy; and now *the mercy of the Lord is from everlasting;* not only as an attribute of God, but in the display of it to sinful miserable creatures; and where is there a display of it so early but in the covenant? Psalm lxxxix. 2, 3, 28. and ciii. 17. and which mercy is no other than the love and free favour of God exercising itself in such a manner towards sinful men; and which love, as it was bore to Christ, so to his people in him, before the foundation of the world, John xvii. 23, 24. The basis of the covenant, is God's election of men to eternal life; the foundation of God, which stands sure, and which laid a foundation for the covenant of grace; it is built upon it; the covenant is made with Christ, God's elect, and with men chosen in him, and who were chosen in him to be holy and happy, before the foundation of the world, Eph. i. 4. The council of peace, which was introductory to the covenant of grace, was of old, from everlasting; as all the counsels of God are; in this Christ was the everlasting Counsellor; as well as in the covenant the everlasting Father: God was in Christ from eternity, forming the scheme of man's peace, reconciliation, and salvation; which prepared and furnished sufficient matter for the everlasting covenant: Christ was set up as the Mediator of it *from everlasting;* from the beginning, or ever the earth was; his goings forth in it, in acts of love and grace towards his people, *were of old, from everlasting;* drawing nigh to his divine Father, and becoming their Surety, interposing between him and them as Mediator, engaging to do every thing for them law and justice could require; and receiving on their account, all grants and promises made unto them, Prov. viii. 23. Mic. v. 2. The blessings of the covenant were put into the hands of Christ so early, and the elect were blessed with them in him, as they were chosen in him before the foundation of the world, and are the *grace* given to them in him, *before the world began,* Eph. i. 3, 4. 2 Tim. i. 9. There were also promises made, particularly the grand promise of eternal life, which God, that cannot lie, promised before the world was; and which promise of life is in Christ, as all the promises of the covenant are, being put into his hands so early; the heirs of them not having an actual being, yet a representative one in him their Head, Tit. i. 2. 2 Tim. i. 1.

Now all this proves the antiquity of the covenant of grace; nor is it any objection to it, that it is sometimes called the *second* and *new* covenant, Heb. viii. 7, 8, 13. and ix. 15. and xii. 24. for it is so called, not with respect to the covenant of works made with Adam, as if it was the second to that, and newer and later than that; for it was made long before that, even in eternity, as has been shewn; but the distinctions of *first* and *second*, *old* and *new*, respect the different administrations of the same covenant of grace in time: the first administration of it began immediately after the fall of Adam, and continued under the patriarchs, and under the Mosaical dispensation, unto the coming of Christ; and then a new administration of it took place, which made the first old, and is called the second, with respect to that; and yet both, for substance, are the same covenant, made in eternity, but variously administered in time.

There are several time-covenants made with men; as with Adam, Noah, Abraham, the children of Israel, Phinehas, David, &c. But the covenant made with Christ, and the elect in him, was not made in time, but in eternity. It is a notion that commonly obtains, that God makes a covenant of grace with men when they believe, repent, &c. but it is no such thing; the covenant of grace does not then begin to be made, only to be made manifest; it then openly takes place, its blessings are bestowed, its promises applied, its grace is wrought in the hearts of men, when God puts his fear there, gives a new heart, and a new spirit, and puts his own Spirit there, to work faith, repentance, and every other grace; but then the covenant is not new made, but all this is done in virtue and in consequence of the covenant of grace made in eternity, and according to the tenor of that.

2. The covenant of grace is entirely *free*, it is altogether of free grace; grace is the moving cause of it; God was not induced to make it from any motive and condition in men. The several parties entered freely into it; the Father, of his own grace and good will to men, proposed the terms of the covenant to his Son; and the Son of God, from his great love he bore to the same persons, voluntarily agreed unto them; and the same love in the blessed Spirit, engaged him to undertake what he did in it; hence we read, as of the love of the Father, and of the love of the Son, so of the love of the Spirit, Rom. xv. 30. which love of the three divine Persons, no where more clearly and fully appears, than in the covenant of grace, and the performance of it. The act of election, which is the basis of the covenant, on which it proceeds, and to which it is commensurate, is entirely of grace, and not of works, and therefore called *the election of grace*, Rom. xi. 5, 6. the matter, sum and substance of the covenant is of grace; the blessings of it are all of grace, they all go by the name of *grace*, given in Christ before the world began, 2 Tim. i. 9. Adoption is owing to the free favour of God; a justifying righteousness is the gift of his grace; pardon of sin is according to the riches of his grace; and so every other blessing. The promises of it, which are exceeding great and precious, flow from the grace of God: when promises are made, the faithfulness of God is engaged to fulfil them; but it is of his grace and good will that he makes them; he is not obliged to make promise of any thing to his creatures. The grace of God greatly appears in making faith the recipient of all blessings and promises; which itself is not of men, but is the gift of God; and by divine wisdom is put in the place it is, to receive all the blessings and promises of the covenant; *That it might be by grace;* that it might appear that all is of grace; *to the end the promise,* and so every blessing, *might be sure to all the seed,* Rom. iv. 16. The end of making the covenant is, the glory of the grace of God; as God has made all things for himself, for his own glory, in nature and providence; so all things in grace, and particularly the covenant of grace, is made and stored with all the blessings of it, to the glory of his grace, Eph. i. 3—6. and therefore with great propriety, may, on all accounts, be called the covenant of grace.

3. This covenant is absolute and *unconditional*: the covenant of works is conditional; Adam, according to it, was to continue in that happy state in which he was created and put, whilst he obeyed the voice of God, and abstained from the forbidden fruit; but if he eat of that, he was to be stripped of his happiness, and die; the language of that covenant is, do this and live; if obedient to it, then blessing and life; but if disobedient, then cursing and death. The covenant God made with Abraham and his seed, concerning their having the land of Canaan for an everlasting possession, was conditional; if willing and obedient, and so long as they behaved themselves well, according to the laws of God given them, they were to possess it, and enjoy the good things of it, Isa. i. 19. but if otherwise, to be dispossessed of it; and accordingly, when they broke the laws of God, their neighbouring nations were let in upon them, and harassed and distressed them, or they were carried captive by them out of it; as, first by the Assyrians, then by the Chaldeans, and at last by the Romans; in which state they now are. But not such is the covenant of grace, that is without any conditions on the part of men. Some, indeed, make it to be a conditional covenant, and faith and repentance to be the conditions of it. But these are not conditions, but blessings of the covenant, and are as absolutely promised in it, as any thing else; the promise of a *new heart*, and of a *new spirit*, includes the gift of faith, and every other grace; and that of taking away the *stony heart*, and giving an *heart of flesh*, is fully expressive of the gift of the grace of repentance, Ezek. xxxvi. 26. Besides, if these were conditions of the covenant, to be performed by men in their own strength, in order to be admitted into it, and receive the benefits of it; they would be as hard, and as difficult to be performed, as the condition of the covenant of works, perfect obedience; since faith requires, to the production of it, almighty power, even such as was put forth in raising Christ from the dead,

Eph. i. 19, 20. and though God may give men means, and time, and space of repentance, yet if he does not give them grace to repent, they never will. Christ's work, and the Spirit's grace, supersede all conditions in the covenant, respecting men; since they provide for every thing that can be thought of, that is required or is wanting: Christ's work of redemption, atonement, and satisfaction for sin, as has been observed, is the only condition of the covenant; and that lies on the Mediator and Surety of the covenant, and not on the persons for whose sake it is made. *When thou shalt make his soul,* or, *if his soul shall make an offering for sin,* Isa. liii. 10. then such and such things are promised in the covenant, both to him and to his seed. Otherwise, the promises to them are absolute and unconditional, and run in this strain, I *will,* and they *shall,* without any *ifs* or conditions; as, I *will* be their God, and they *shall* be my people; I *will* put my law in their hearts; I *will* forgive their iniquities; they *shall* all know me, from the least to the greatest; I *will* put my fear in their hearts, that they *shall* not depart from me; I *will* sprinkle clean water upon you, and ye *shall* be clean; I *will* give you a new heart, and a new spirit, and an heart of flesh; and I *will* take away the stony heart, and I *will* put my Spirit within you, and *cause* you to walk in my statutes, and ye *shall* keep my judgments, and do them, Jer. xxxi. 33, 34. and xxxii. 38, 40. Ezek. xxxvi. 25, 26, 27. The blessings of the covenant are not suspended on any conditions to be performed; they do not wait for any, but take place without them. Redemption by Christ, the great article of the covenant, was not deferred on account of any condition to be performed by men; but Christ, in the fulness of time agreed on in covenant, when men were without strength to do anything, died for the ungodly; while they were yet sinners Christ died for them; and when enemies, they were reconciled to God by the death of his Son; and herein appeared the love of God; not that we loved God, but that he loved us, and sent his Son to be the propitiation for our sins, Rom. v. 6, 8, 10. 1 John iv. 10. Adoption takes place among men, who were not the people of God; and justification has for its objects the ungodly; and God forgives the iniquities of men, and remembers them no more, though they have done nothing to deserve it, but are guilty of the greatest ingratitude and unkindness; and regeneration finds men dead in trespasses and sins, foolish, disobedient, serving divers lusts and pleasures, without any previous dispositions or preparations in them for it, Hos. i. 10. Rom. iv. 5. Isa. xliii. 25. Eph. ii. 4, 5.

4. The covenant of grace is *perfect* and complete, wanting nothing; it is *ordered in all things;* and if in all things, nothing can be wanting in it, 2 Sam. xxiii. 5. It is full of precious promises; promises of all sorts, promises of things temporal, spiritual, and eternal; so that there is nothing that a believer stands in need of, nor any state nor condition he can come into, but there is a promise of what he wants, and which is suitable to him, 1 Tim. iv. 8. Heb. xiii. 5, 6. it is full of rich blessings of grace; of all spiritual blessings, of blessings of goodness, which Christ, as Mediator, is made most blessed with; of goodness inconceivable and inexpressible, laid up in the covenant, and in the hands of Christ, for the covenant-ones: it provides all things pertaining to life and godliness; for the implantation of life itself, and of every grace; for the beginning, carrying on, and finishing the work of grace on the heart; for the food, nourishment, support, and maintenance of the spiritual life in it; for the peace, joy, and comfort of believers; for grace, and spiritual strength to exercise grace, perform duties, bear and suffer all that they are called unto; for their perseverance in faith and holiness to the end; and for their eternal life and happiness; grace and glory are secured in this covenant; even *all salvation,* the whole of it, and all the parts of it, 2 Sam. xxiii. 5. And it is so ordered, as to secure the spiritual and eternal welfare of God's elect, so to advance the glory of God, Father, Son, and Spirit; the Father is glorified in and by Christ the Mediator of it; and Christ is glorified by the Spirit, who takes of the things of Christ, and shews them to his people; and the Spirit is glorified by being the earnest, pledge, and seal of the heavenly inheritance, Isa. xlix. 3. John xvi. 14. Eph. i. 14.

5. It is an *holy* covenant; so it is called, Luke i. 72. where God, by visiting and redeeming his people, and raising up an horn of salvation for them, or by sending Christ to be the Redeemer and Saviour of them, and to be his salvation to them, which is the grand article of the covenant of grace, is said by all this, *to remember his*

holy covenant. The contracting parties in this covenant are, the holy Father, and the holy Son, and the holy Spirit, with respect to whom this epithet is thrice expressed in Isa. vi. 3. see Psalm cxi. 9. the matter of it is holy; the promises of it are holy, Psalm cv. 42. the blessings of it are holy; what are called the mercies of David, Isa. lv. 3. are called οσια, the *holy* things of David, in Acts xiii. 34. and nothing can more strongly engage to a concern for holiness of heart and life, than the promises of the covenant; see 2 Cor. vi. 18. and vii. 1. yea, the covenant provides fully for the sanctification of all the covenant-ones; expressed by writing the laws of God in the hearts of them, putting his fear into them, giving them new hearts and new spirits, taking away the stony heart from them, and putting his own Spirit within them, to enable them to walk in his statutes, keep his judgments, and do them, Jer. xxxi. 33. and xxxii. 39, 40. Ezek. xxxvi. 26, 27.

6. It is a *sure* covenant, firm and immoveable, more immoveable than rocks and mountains; they may depart, but this covenant shall never depart, 2 Sam. xxiii. 5. Isa. liv. 10. it is *kept*, or *observed*,[1] as the word rendered *sure*, in the first of those places, signifies; it is kept inviolably by God that made it; hence he is sometimes described as a God *keeping covenant*, Nehem. ix. 32. his faithfulness, which he will never suffer to fail, is engaged to keep it, and therefore it is he will not break it, and men cannot, Psalm lxxxix. 33, 34. it is secured by the oath of God, and the immutability of that; for as the counsel of God is confirmed by his oath, so is the covenant of God; for it follows in the place now referred to, ver. 35. *Once have I sworn by my holiness, that I will not lie unto David*. And that is another reason why the covenant will not be broken; and why the word or promise that is gone out of his mouth shall not be altered. The covenant is also ratified and confirmed by the death of Christ, the Testator, as has been shewn in a former chapter; whence the blood of Christ is called the blood of the covenant, which has sealed and confirmed it. The promises of the covenant are Yea and Amen in Christ; that is, sure and firm; and the blessings of it are the sure mercies of David, and the whole of it is confirmed in Christ, 2 Cor. i. 20. Isa. liv. 3. Gal. iii. 17.

7. It is frequently called an *everlasting* covenant, 2 Sam. xxiii. 5. Isa. liv. 3. Heb. xiii. 20. It is a covenant that will stand fast with Christ for ever, with whom it is made, and is what God has commanded for ever, and will be always fulfilling; the effects of it will be always seen and enjoyed, in time and to all eternity, Psalm lxxxix. 28. and cxi. 9. It is a covenant that will never be antiquated, nor give way to, nor be succeeded by another; the covenant of works is broken, and has been succeeded by an administration of the covenant of grace; and that first administration being not faultless, but deficient with respect to clearness and extensiveness, is waxen old, and vanished away, and has given place to a new administration of it; which will continue unto the end of the world, until all the covenant-ones are gathered in: but though these two administrations differ in some things, as to some external circumstances and ordinances; yet the matter, sum, and substance of them is the same, even Christ, who is the same yesterday, to-day, and for ever: he is the foundation of the apostles and prophets, of old and new testament-saints, who all partake of the same spiritual benefits and blessings, and of the same promises; and both are saved in the same way, by the grace of our Lord Jesus Christ; even by the grace of the covenant, which is invariable and perpetual.

CHAP. XVI.

OF THE COMPLACENCY AND DELIGHT GOD HAD IN HIMSELF, AND THE DIVINE PERSONS IN EACH OTHER, BEFORE ANY CREATURE WAS BROUGHT INTO BEING.

HAVING finished what I had to say concerning the internal acts of God, and the eternal transactions between the three divine Persons, before any creature, angel or man, was made; I should now have entered upon the external acts and works of God in time, but that I thought it might be proper, first, to observe the complacency, delight, and satisfaction God had in himself, in his own nature and perfections, before any creature existed; and would have had, if none had ever been brought into being: as also the pleasure he took in the foreviews of his eternal purposes and decrees being executed in time; and of the

---

[1] שמרה servatum, Tigurine Version.

success of those transactions, which were between the divine Persons in God, in the council of peace, and covenant of grace; and especially the mutual delight and complacency each divine Person had in one another, when alone, in a boundless eternity, and all of them had in the chosen vessels of salvation.

First, The complacency, delight, and satisfaction, which the divine Being had in himself, in his own nature and perfections, before the existence of any creature; and would have had the same if no creature had ever existed; in his nature, in the contemplation of the unspeakable glories of Deity, and in the special properties and mutual relations of the three persons to each other, and in the perfections of his nature. God is a most perfect being, entire and wanting nothing; he is El-shaddai, God all-sufficient, who has a sufficiency in and of himself, and needs nothing from creatures; he is the blessed one, God blessed for evermore; completely happy in himself, as has been proved, when his perfections were considered; whatever perfection or excellency is in creatures, angels or men, it is all from him, and is in him to the highest degree, and therefore as in them can add nothing to his pleasure and happiness: the perfections of God are indeed displayed in the creatures in a glorious manner; the heavens declare his glory, and the earth is full of it; but then these displays are made not for his own sake, but for the sake of others, that they may understand his eternal power and godhead, or be left without excuse; and though his perfections are very brightly displayed herein, yet they are clearer in himself, and so can give him no new pleasure and satisfaction, nor add anything to his felicity and blessedness; for though it is said, *For thy pleasure they are and were created*, Rev. iv. 11. *pleasure* here does not signify delight, but *will;* and so it should be rendered *by thy will,* or according to it, *they are and were created;* and though when they were made, and he had reviewed them, they appeared to him all very good, and he expressed his well-pleasedness in them; yet this raised no new joy in him, nor added anything to his happiness, complete in himself; which would have been the same if a creature, or any of the works of creation had never been made, nor if any of the sons of men had ever been redeemed; for the benefit arising from the redemption of men by Christ, and the satisfaction made for them by him, redounds not to God, but to the redeemed, and for whom the satisfaction is made; *My goodness extendeth not to thee,* says Christ, *but to the saints that are in the earth, and to the excellent in whom is all my delight,* Psalm xvi. 2, 3. nor does he need the worship and obedience of angels or men; nor does he receive any additional pleasure and happiness from them; what are the highest and loudest praises of angels, to him who is exalted above all blessing and praise? or the prayers and petitions of indigent creatures? the benefit from them is to them, and not to him; what is all the righteousness, and what are the best works done by men to him? *Is it any pleasure to the Almighty that thou art righteous? or is it gain to him that thou makest thy ways perfect? If thou be righteous, what givest thou him? or what receiveth he of thine hand? Can a man* by all this *be profitable to God?* No, he cannot; when the best of men have done all they can, they must own they are but *unprofitable servants,* with respect to him. *Who hath first given to him, and it shall be recompensed to him again; for of him, and through him, and to him are all things,* Job xxii. 2, 3. and xxxv. 7. Luke xvii. 10. Rom. xi. 35, 36. Since then nothing in time, in and from creatures, add anything to the essential glory, bliss, and happiness of the divine Being; it clearly appears, that his going forth in the works of creation, did not arise from necessity of nature, but was according to his sovereign will; and that he had infinite delight, pleasure, and complacency in himself, before any creature was made, and would have had the same, if they had never been.

Secondly, As Jehovah took delight and pleasure in himself, in his own nature, and the perfections of it, so in the internal and eternal acts of his mind; his purposes and decrees, formed in his eternal mind, according to the good pleasure of his will; these concern all things done in time, from the beginning to the end of the world; the formation of the heaven, earth, and sea, and all that are in them; every thing that has been, is, or shall be, since the world began to the consummation of all things; for there is a purpose for every thing under heaven, and a time for every purpose, Eccles. iii. 1. And these all lay before God, at once and together, in his all-comprehending mind; he saw the end from the beginning, and every intervening thing;

Known unto God are all his works from eternity, Acts xv. 18. and he delighted in them, as he saw them in himself, in his mind and will, and in the foreviews of the accomplishment of them in time; who calls things that are not, as though they were; they stood all before him in his view, as if really in execution; nor does the execution of them add any new joy and pleasure to him: particularly all those purposes and resolutions of his mind, concerning the redemption, conversion, and salvation of his chosen ones, and the state and condition of his church, in all the periods of time, were viewed within himself, with the utmost delight and pleasure; the plan of their peace and reconciliation, drawn in the council of peace, and every thing respecting their salvation, settled in the covenant of grace. These transactions gave him infinite pleasure and satisfaction; and on these his thoughts have ran ever since, with the utmost delight, in the foreviews of all things, taking place in time and to eternity, according to these ancient settlements. But what I would chiefly attend unto is,

Thirdly, The delight and complacency which each divine Person had in one another, before any creature was in being; with respect to two of the divine Persons, this is strongly expressed in Prov. viii. 30. *Then I was by him*, as *one brought up* with him, *and I was daily* his *delight, rejoicing always before him;* when all this was, may be learned from the preceding verses; when there were no depths, no fountains abounding with water; before the mountains were settled, while as yet he had not made the earth, &c. ver. 24—29. and the third Person is not to be excluded.

1*st*, The delight and complacency of the Father in the Son, is declared in the following expressions; which are borrowed from the delight and pleasure parents take in their children; being *by* them, *brought up* with them, *nursed* up by them, *playing* before them; which must be understood with a decency becoming the divine Persons, and not be strained beyond their general design, which is to express the mutual delight of the Father and the Son in each other: *Then I was by him*, from eternity, or before the world was; *I*, a person, as the pronoun is expressive of; not a nature, not the human nature of Christ, which is no person; and still less a part of it, the soul of Christ, which then had no existence; but I, a divine Person, the eternal *Logos*, the Word and Wisdom of God, who is all along speaking from ver. 12. *I Wisdom, &c.* to this very passage, the same with the Word John speaks of, and much in the same language, chap. i. 1. *In the beginning was the Word, and the Word was with God, and the Word was God;* to which Word he ascribes the creation of all things, and therefore must be before them, as well as be a divine Person; and he is in both places represented as a distinct Person, as he must be, from him, by whom, and with whom, he was a Person eternally existing; being not only before Abraham, but before Adam, or any creature was in being; a Person co-existing, as a Son with the Father, being co-essential and co-eternal with his Father; and was by him, and at his side, on a level with him; Jehovah's fellow, equal to him, possessed of the same perfections; and being by him, and in his presence, was infinitely delighted in by him; and was *as one brought up with him*, as a Son with a Father, and so denotes his relation to him, being begotten of him, his own Son, the Son of the Father, in truth and love; and the Father's tender regard of him, and delight in him; being, as some render the word, *nursed up* by him, and carried in his bosom, as a nursing Father bears the sucking child; so to express the exceeding great tenderness of the Father to the Son, and his delight in him, the only begotten Son, he is said to be *in the bosom of the Father*, John i. 18. Though the phrase may also have respect to Christ, in his mediatorial capacity, who was foreordained and constituted as Mediator by his Father, and trained up in his office, and to whom he pointed out the work he was to do as such; to bring Jacob again, to raise up the tribes of Jacob, and restore the preserved of Israel; and be his salvation unto the ends of the earth, Isa. xlix. 5, 6. *And I was daily his delight;* day by day, or every day; not that there are, properly speaking, days in eternity; but the phrase is expressive of the constant and invariable delight the Father had in his Son; as well as the greatness of it is signified by the word in the plural number, *delights;* he was his exceeding great delight, superlatively delightful to him; and so he was, as he was his Son, a Son of delights, the dear Son of his love; whom he loved before the foundation of the world, with a love of complacency and delight; he was always his beloved Son, in whom he was well pleased; partly because of his likeness to him, being the image of the invisible God, the express image of his Person ; as every like loves its like ; and partly because of the same nature with him, having the same perfections, even the whole fulness of the Godhead in him : he was also his delight, considered in his office as Mediator ; *Behold my Servant, whom I uphold ; mine elect, in whom my soul delighteth,* Isa. xliii. 1. He delighted in him, as engaging in covenant to be the Mediator and Surety of it ; as with admiration, so with the utmost pleasure and delight, he said, *Who is this that engaged his heart to approach unto me, saith the Lord?* Jer. xxx. 21. to strike hands with me, and become a Surety for my people. And with equal pleasure did he behold him acceding and assenting to his proposals in covenant, saying, *Lo, I come to do thy will, O my God!* Psalm xl. 7, 8. He delighted in him as the God-man ; being fit, as such, for the work he assigned unto him ; and whereas he proposed to him in covenant, to assume human nature in time, for that purpose, and he agreed unto it, he viewed him henceforward as the God-man ; and he bore the repute of it with him, and considered him under this character ; he delighted in the foreviews of his future assumption of human nature ; and a little before the time, by Zechariah, one of the last of the prophets, expressed his joy at the near approach of it ; *Behold, I will bring forth my Servant, the Branch:* that is, speedily, in a very short time and again, *Behold the Man, whose name is the Branch, he shall grow up out of his place,* Zech. iii. 8. and vi. 12. which is signified to be future, yet near. And he delighted in the foreviews of that obedience to his will his Son should yield in that nature, by which the law would be magnified and made honourable ; and of his sufferings and death in it, whereby full satisfaction would be given for the sins of his people ; and of his glorification at his right hand in that nature he had promised him ; and of his own glory displayed in the salvation of men by him, and a full accomplishment of that ; an affair his heart was so much set upon from everlasting. In the foreviews of all this was Christ as Mediator, Redeemer, and Saviour, as well as God's own Son, the object of his infinite delight and pleasure from everlasting.

2dly, The Son of God also had the same delight and pleasure in his divine Father, before the world was ; and when there was no creature in being, he was then *rejoicing always before him ;* rejoicing in being possessed of the same nature and perfections his Father was, being like and equal to him in all things ; and rejoicing that he stood in such a relation to him as a Son to a Father ; with what exultation does he repeat the words of his Father to him, declaring this relation ; *The Lord hath said unto me,* and that was in eternity, *Thou art my Son, this day have I begotten thee,* Psalm ii. 7. He delighted in the foreviews of his future incarnation, as being agreeable to his Father's will ; *A body hast thou prepared me,* Heb. x. 5. which he spoke with pleasure, and as being willing and desirous to assume it ; in which he should do his Father's will and work, and which would be his meat and drink, and accomplish the salvation of his people, which was the *joy set before him ;* and he rejoiced in the foreviews of his Father being glorified by it, and of his own glory upon it, John xiii. 31, 32. and xvii. 1, 4, 5.

3dly, Though the third Person, the holy Spirit, is not mentioned in the passage in Proverbs ; yet as the Father delights in the Son, and the Son in the Father, so both of them delight in the Spirit, as proceeding from them, and he in them ; for these Three are One, of the same nature and perfections, and have a mutual in-being in each other, and so a complacency in one another ; for as the Father is in the Son, and the Son in the Father, John x. 38. and xiv. 10. so the Spirit is in them, and they in him ; and in consequence must have a mutual delight in each other : the Spirit, as he is of the same nature with the Father and the Son, always took infinite delight in his own nature and perfections ; and as he was privy to all the thoughts, purposes, and counsels of God, which are the deep things he searches and reveals ; he must have taken pleasure in them, and in the foreviews of the execution of them ; and as he approved and assented to all the articles in the council and covenant of peace, he must have had infinite delight in the view of the accomplishment of them, as well as of those things which he himself in covenant undertook to perform.

4thly, This mutual delight and complacency which each Person had in one another, lay in and arose from the perfect knowledge they had of each other ; *As the Father knoweth me,* says Christ, *so know I the Father,* John x. 15. and the Spirit knows them both, and the things that are in them, 1 Cor. ii. 10, 11. and hence arises mutual love to each other; the Father loves the Son, and the Son loves the Father, John iii. 35. and v. 20. and xiv. 31. and the Spirit proceeding from them both, loves them both; and it cannot be otherwise, since there is such a nearness to, and mutual in-being in each other. Moreover,

Fourthly, The three divine Persons had from eternity, and before any creature was in actual being, the utmost delight and complacency[2] in the elect of God, and in the foreviews of their salvation and happiness. The joy and delight of the Son in them are strongly expressed in Prov. viii. 31. *Rejoicing in the habitable part of his earth, and my delights were with the sons of men;* that is, from everlasting; before ever the earth was made, or any creature in it; then was the Son of God *rejoicing in the habitable part of the earth;* in the foreviews of those spots of ground, houses, and cottages, where it was known the chosen vessels of mercy would dwell: for God has *determined the times before appointed, and the bounds of their habitation;* and Christ knew beforehand in what places he should have a people, and in which this and that man should be born again, Acts xvii. 26. and xviii. 10. Psalm lxxxvii. 4, 5, 6. and as lovers express their love to the objects of their love, by saying they love the ground on which they tread; so Christ having loved his people with a love of complacency and delight, rejoiced in the foresight of those parts of the habitable world, where he saw their habitations would be: the church of God on earth may be called the habitable part of his earth, being the dwelling-place which he has chosen for himself as such, and where he delights to dwell, and they were from everlasting his Hephzibah and Beulah. Some respect may be had to the new earth, or the second Adam's earth; in which only righteous persons will dwell; and where the tabernacle of God will be with men, his chosen ones; and where he will dwell with them a thousand years; and in this also the Son of God was rejoicing in the foreviews of: nor am I averse to take in the human nature of Christ, into the sense of the words; who, though with respect to his divine Person, and mediatorial office, is the Lord from heaven; yet, as to his human nature, he was *curiously wrought,* by the power and skill of the Holy Ghost, *in the lowest parts of the earth,* in the womb of the Virgin, and therefore called *the fruit of the earth,* being born of an earthly woman, Psalm cxxxix. 15. Isa. iv. 2. and which human nature is a tabernacle God pitched and not men; a tabernacle for the eternal Word to dwell in, and where the fulness of the Godhead dwells bodily; and in the views of this the Son of God was rejoicing before the world was; and in time expressed his desire of it, and delight in it, before it became his habitation; as may be concluded from his frequent appearances in an human form, before his incarnation, as preludiums of it; as to Adam, Abraham, Jacob, and other patriarchs; he rejoiced in the foreviews of it, as it would be of the same kind with that of the children given him, and he had undertook to redeem and save; and as it would be the produce of the holy Spirit, and so free from sin; and as it would be filled and adorned with his gifts and graces; and as after he had done the will of God in it, it would be crowned with glory and honour, and set down at the right hand of God: and all this joy and delight were with a peculiar respect unto the elect of God, as follows; *And my delights were with the sons of men,* the posterity of Adam, fallen creatures, the chosen of God among them, who sinned in him, and on whom judgment came unto condemnation, and who are conceived and born in sin, and are by nature children of wrath as others; and yet the delights of Christ, his exceeding great delight, expressed by the plural number, were with them as they were loved by his Father, chosen in him, and given to him; and as he viewed them redeemed by him, washed in his blood, and clothed with his righteousness; and as he saw them in the glass of his Father's purposes and decrees, in all the glory he designed to bring them to, even to be a glorious church without spot or wrinkle, or any such thing.

Now not only the Son of God took delight and complacency in the elect of God, before the world was; but the Father and Spirit also; for God the Father of Christ loved them, and chose them in him, before the foundation of the world, 2 Thess. ii. 13. Eph. i. 4. And this love was a love of complacency and delight; because he delighted in them, therefore he chose them to be his peculiar people, as he did Israel

---

[2] Of the love of delight and complacency of God towards the elect, see a Treatise of mine, called the Doctrines of God's Everlasting Love to his Elect, &c. p. 52. &c.

of old, in a national sense, Deut. x. 15. And from the same delight in them arose the council held by him with the other two Persons concerning them; and the covenant of grace he entered into with them. And so the holy Spirit, his delights were with the same Persons, as they were chosen in Christ, through sanctification by him; and in the foreviews of their being temples for him to dwell in; and in whom he should abide as the earnest and pledge of their future glory; and as the sealer of them to the day of redemption; and as they should be sanctified and made meet by him for eternal glory and happiness.

Thus we see what delight and complacency, satisfaction and happiness, God had in himself before any creature existed; and would have continued the same, if none had ever been created: so that he needed not for his own sake, to go forth in acts of power, to bring creatures into being, since he would have been as happy without them as with them; wherefore the production of them into being, is purely the effect of his sovereign will and pleasure; and we see what the thoughts of God were employed about, and chiefly concerned in, in eternity; and the whole furnishes an answer to those curious questions, if it is proper to make them; What was God doing in eternity? what did his thoughts chiefly run upon then? and wherein lay his satisfaction, delight, and happiness?

A BODY OF
DOCTRINAL DIVINITY.

BOOK III.

OF THE EXTERNAL WORKS OF GOD.

CHAP. I.

OF CREATION IN GENERAL.

HAVING considered the internal and eternal acts of the divine mind, and the transactions of the divine Persons with each other in eternity; I proceed to consider the external acts and works of God, or his goings forth out of himself, in the exercise of his power and goodness in the works of creation, providence, redemption, and grace; which works of God, without himself, in time, are agreeable to the acts of his mind within himself, in eternity. These are no other than his eternal purposes and decrees carried into execution; for *he worketh all things after the counsel of his own will*, Eph. i. 11. I shall begin with the work of creation, which is what God himself began with; and shall consider the following things concerning it.

1. What creation is. Sometimes it only signifies the natural production of creatures into being, in the ordinary way, by generation and propagation; so the birth of persons, or the bringing them into being, in the common course of nature, is called the creation of them, and God is represented as their Creator, Ezek. xxi. 30. and xxviii. 14. Eccles. xii. 1. Sometimes it designs acts of providence, in bringing about affairs of moment and importance in the world; as when it is said, *I form the light, and create darkness;* which is explained by what follows, *I make peace and create evil:* it is to be understood of prosperous and adverse dispensations of providence; which are the Lord's doings, and are according to his sovereign will and pleasure, Isa. lv. 7. So the renewing of the face of the earth, and the reproduction of herbs, plants, &c. in the returning spring of the year, is called a creation of them, Psalm civ. 30. And the renewing of the world, in the end of time, though the substance of it will remain, is called a creating new heavens and a new earth, Isa. lxv. 17. Sometimes it intends the doing something unusual, extraordinary, and wonderful; such as the earth's opening its mouth, and swallowing up the rebellious Israelites in the wilderness, Numb. xvi. 30. and the wonderful protection of the church of God, Isa. iv. 5. and particularly the amazing incarnation of the Son of God, Jer. xxxi. 22. But, to observe no more, creation may be distinguished into mediate and immediate; mediate creation is the production of beings, by the power of God, out of pre-existent matter, which of itself was not disposed to produce them; so God is said to create great whales and other fishes, which, at his command, the waters brought forth abundantly; and he created man, male and female; and yet man, as to his body, was made of the dust of the earth, and the woman out of the rib of man, Gen. i. 21, 27. and, indeed, all that was created on the five last days of the creation, was made by the all-commanding power and will of God, out of matter which before existed, though indisposed of itself for such a production. Immediate creation, and which is properly creation, is the production of things out of nothing, or the bringing of a nonentity into being, as was the work of the first

day, the creating the heavens and the earth, the unformed chaos, and the light commanded to arise upon it, Gen. i. 1, 2, 3. And these are the original of all things; so that all things ultimately are made out of nothing, which is the voice of divine revelation, and our faith is directed to assent unto and receive. *Through faith we understand that the worlds were framed by the word of God; so that things which are seen were not made of things which do appear*, Heb. xi. 3. but of things unseen, and indeed, which had no existence; for God, by his all-commanding word and power, *called things that are not as though they were*, Rom. iv. 17. that is, called and commanded by his mighty power, non-entities into being; and this is what is meant by a creation of things out of nothing; and so the word ברא, used for the making of the heavens and the earth in the beginning, signifies, as Aben Ezra and Kimchi observe; and indeed it cannot be conceived of otherwise, but that the world was made out of nothing; for,

If nothing existed from eternity but God, or if nothing existed before the world was but himself, by which his eternity is described, and which he claims as peculiar to himself, Psalm xc. 2. Isa. xliii. 10. and if the world was made by him, as it most certainly was, it must be made by him out of nothing, since besides himself, there was nothing existing, out of which it could be made; to say it was made out of pre-existent matter, is to beg the question; besides, that pre-existent matter must be made by him; for he has *created all things*, Rev. iv. 11. and if all things, nothing can be excepted; and certainly not matter; for be that visible or invisible, one of them it must be; and both the one and the other are created of God, Col. i. 16. and this matter must be made out of nothing, so that it comes to the same thing, that all things are originally made out of nothing. Besides, there are some creatures, and those the most noble, as angels and the souls of men, which are immaterial, and therefore are not made out of matter, and consequently are made out of nothing; and are brought from nonentity into being, by the almighty power of God; and if these, why not others? and if these and others, why not all things, even matter itself? As for that old and trite maxim, so much in the mouths of the ancient philosophers,[1] as well as modern reasoners, *Ex nihilo nihil fit*, out of nothing, nothing is made; this only holds true of finite nature, finite beings, second causes; by them out of nothing, nothing can be made; but not of infinite nature, of the infinite Being, the first Cause, who is a God of infinite perfection and power; and what is it that omnipotence cannot do? Plato[2] owns that God is the Cause, or Author of those things, which before were not in being, or created all things out of nothing.

II. The object of creation, all things, nothing excepted in the whole compass of finite nature; *Thou hast created all things, and for thy pleasure, or by thy will, they are and were created*, Rev. iv. 11. these all things are comprehended by Moses under the name of the heavens and the earth, Gen. i. 1. and more fully expressed by the apostles in their address to God, who is described by them as having *made heaven, and earth, and the sea, and all that in them is*, Acts iv. 24. and still more explicitly by the angel, who swore by the living God *who created heaven, and the things that therein are; and the earth, and the things that therein are; and the sea, and the things which are therein*, Rev. x. 6.

1*st*, The heavens and all in them; these are often represented as made and created by God, and are said to be the work of his fingers and of his hands; being curiously as well as powerfully wrought by him, Psalm viii. 3. and xix. 1. and cii. 25. They are spoken of in the plural number, for there are more heavens than one; there are certainly three, for we read of a *third* heaven, which is explained of *paradise*, 2 Cor. xii. 2, 4. this is, 1. The heaven of heavens, the superior heaven, and the most excellent, the habitation of God, where his glorious presence is, where he has his palace, keeps his court, and is indeed his throne, Isa. lxv. 15. and lxvi. 1. and where angels dwell, and therefore they are called the angels of heaven, are in the presence of God there, and behold the face of our heavenly Father, Matt. xxiv. 36. and xviii. 10. and where glorified saints will be in soul and body to all eternity. Now

---

[1] So Democritus, Diogenes, Epicurus, vid. Laert. 1. 9, 10. in Vita eorum.——nullam rem è nihilo gigni; nil posse creari, de nihilo——Lucretius, l. 1. so Persii Satyr. 3. v. 84. erit aliquid quod aut ex nihilo oriatur, aut in nihilum subito occidat, quis hoc physicus dixit unquam? Cicero de Divinatione, 1. 3. c. 37.

[2] Sophista, p. 185.

this is a place made and created by God, and as such cannot contain him, though his glory is greatly manifested in it, 1 Kings viii. 27. it is where the angels are, who must have an *ubi* somewhere to be in, being finite creatures, and who are said to ascend unto, and descend from thence, John i. 51. and here bodies are, which require space and place, as those of *Enoch* and *Elijah*, translated thither, and the human nature of Christ, which has ascended to it, and will be retained in it, until his second coming; and where the bodies of those are, who rose at the time of his resurrection; as well as all the bodies of the saints will be to all eternity: and this is expressly called a *place* by Christ, and is distinguished as the place of the blessed, from that of the damned, John xiv. 2, 3. Luke xvi. 26. and is sometimes described by an house, a city, a country, kingdom, and an inheritance; and particularly it is called a *city whose builder and maker is God*, Heb. xi. 10. for he that built all things built this; it is a part of his creation; and all things in it are created by him; he the uncreated Being excepted; even God, Father, Son, and Spirit; but the angels of it are his creatures; *He makes his angels spirits*, Psalm civ. 5. of their creation, and the time of it, of their nature, number, excellency, and usefulness, I shall treat in a particular chapter hereafter.—— 2. There is another heaven, lower than the former, and may be called the *second*, and bears the name of the starry heaven, because the sun, and moon, and stars are placed in it; *Look towards heaven, and tell the stars*, Gen. xv. 5. see Isa. xl. 26. Job xxii. 12. this reaches from the region of the moon to the place of the fixed stars, and to that immense space which our eyes cannot reach. Now this, and all that in it are, were created by God; he made the sun to rule by day, and the moon to rule by night; and he made the stars also, Gen. i. 16.——3. There is another heaven lower than both the former, and may be called the aërial heaven; for the air and heaven are sometimes synonymous; hence the fowls are sometimes called the fowls of the heaven, and sometimes the fowls of the air, they being the same, Gen. vii. 3, 23. Now this wide expanse, or firmament of heaven, is the handy-work of God, and all things in it; not only the fowls that fly in it, but all the meteors gendered there; as rain, hail, snow, thunder, and lightning. *Hath the rain a father?* None but God; and the same may be said of all the rest: Job xxxvii. 6. and xxxviii. 28, 29.

2dly, The earth, and all that is therein. This was first made without form; not without any, but without the beautiful one in which it quickly appeared; and when the waters were drained off from it, and became dry land, it was called earth, Gen. i. 2, 9, 10. and as this was made by God, so all things in it; the grass, the herbs, the plants, and trees upon it; the metals and minerals in the bowels of it, gold, silver, brass, and iron; all the beasts of the field, and "the cattle on a thousand hills;" as well as the principal inhabitants of it, men, called eminently the inhabitants of the earth, Dan. iv. 35. Of the creation of man I shall treat in a distinct chapter by itself.

3dly, The sea, and all that is in that; when God cleaved an hollow in the earth, the waters he drained off of it, he gathered into it; and gave those waters, thus gathered into one place, the name of seas, Gen. i. 10. and which were of his creating; *The sea is his, and he made it*, Psalm xcv. 5. and all in it: likewise the marine plants and trees, with other things therein; and all the fishes which swim in it, great and small, innumerable, Psalm civ. 25, 26. Now these, the heavens, earth, and sea, and all that are in them, make up the world which God has created, and which is but one; for though we read of worlds, God has made by his Son, and which are framed by the word of God, Heb. i. 2. and xi. 3. yet these may have respect only to the distinction of the upper, middle, and lower world; for the numerous worlds some Jewish writers speak of, they are mere fables; and that the planets are so many worlds as our earth is, and that the fixed stars are so many suns to worlds unknown by us, are the conjectures of modern astronomers, and in which there is no certainty; revelation gives no account of them, and we have no concern with them; and were there as many as are imagined, and can be conceived of, this we may be assured of, they were all created by God.

III. The next thing to be inquired into is, When creation began? or God began to create and bring things into being? and this was not in eternity, but in time; an *eternal creature*, or a creature in eternity, is the greatest absurdity imaginable; to assert it is an insult on the common sense and understanding of men: it was in the beginning of time, or when time first began, as it did, when a creature was first made, that God made all things; *In the beginning God created the heaven and the earth*, Gen. i. 1. *And thou, Lord, in the beginning hast laid the foundation of the earth*, &c. Heb. i. 10. these were the first that were created, and with these time begun; and every creature has a beginning, creation supposes it; for that is no other than bringing a nonentity into being; and therefore since what is created, once was not, it must have a beginning. Some philosophers, and Aristotle at the head of them, have asserted the eternity of the world; but without any reason; and is abundantly refuted by scripture; and therefore cannot be received by those that believe its divine authority; for that not only assures us that it was created in the beginning, and so had a beginning; but gives us an account of what was before it; as, that before the mountains were brought forth, or ever the earth and world were formed, God was, even from everlasting; so that an eternity anteceded the making of the world. Christ also, the Wisdom and Word of God, was before the earth was; even when there were no depths, nor fountains abounding with water; before the mountains and hills were settled, and the highest part of the world made, Psalm xc. 2. Prov. viii. 24—30. A choice of men was made in Christ unto eternal life, before the foundation of the world; and grace was given to them in him, as their head and representative, before the world began, Eph. i. 4. 2 Tim. i. 9. A full proof that the world had a beginning; and that there were things done in eternity, before the world was in being. To say the world, or matter, was coeternal with God, is to make that itself God; for eternity is a perfection peculiar to God; and where one perfection is, all are: what is eternal, is infinite and unbounded; and if the world is eternal, it is infinite; and then there must be two infinites, which is an absurdity not to be received. Besides, if eternal, it must necessarily exist; or exist by necessity of nature; and so be self-existent, and consequently God; yea, must be independent of him, and to which he can have no claim, nor any power and authority over it; whereas, according to divine revelation, and even the reason of things, all things were according to the pleasure of God, or by his will, Rev. iv. 11. and therefore must be later than his will, being the effect of it.

And as the world had a beginning, and all things in it, it does not appear to be of any great antiquity; it has not, as yet, run out six thousand years, according to the scriptural account, and which may be depended on. Indeed, according to the Greek version, the age of the world is carried fourteen or fifteen hundred years higher; but the Hebrew text is the surest rule to go by: as for the accounts of the Egyptians, Chaldeans, and Chinese, which make the original of their kingdoms and states many thousands of years higher still; these are only vain boasts, and fabulous relations, which have no foundation in true history. The origin of nations, according to the Scriptures, which appears to be the truest; and the invention of arts and sciences, and of various things necessary to human life; as of agriculture, the bringing up of cattle; making of various utensils of brass and iron, for the various businesses of life; and the finding out of letters; with many other things, which appear to be within the time the Scripture assigns for the creation; plainly shew it could not be earlier, since without these men could not be long: nor does any genuine history give an account of anything more early, nor so early, as the Scriptures do; and therefore we may safely conclude, that the origin of the world, as given by that, is true; for if the world had been eternal, or of so early a date as some kingdoms pretend unto, something or other done in those ancient times, would have been, some way or another, transmitted to posterity.

Under this head might be considered, the time and season of the year when the world was created. Some think it was in the vernal equinox, or spring of the year, when plants and trees are blooming, look beautiful, and all nature is gay and pleasant; and at which season in every year, there is a renewing of the face of the earth: and some have observed, in favour of this notion, that the redemption of man was wrought out at this time of the year, which is a restoration of the world; but these seem not sufficient to ascertain it. Others think the world was created in the autumnal equinox, when the fruits of the earth are ripe, and in their full perfection; which seems more probable: and certain it is, that some nations of old, as the Egyptians and others, began their year at this time; as did the Israelites, before their coming out of Egypt, when they were ordered by the Lord to make a change; and from thenceforward to reckon the month

Abib, or Nisan, in which they came out of Egypt, the first month of the year, and which answers to part of March and part of April; and which they always observed for the regulation of their ecclesiastical affairs, though with respect to civil matters, they still continued to reckon the year from Tisri, which answers to some part of our September; and it may be observed, that the feast of ingathering the fruits of the earth, is said to be *in the end of the year;* and when a new year begun; see Exod. xii. 2. and xxiii. 16. But this is a matter of no great moment, which way soever it is determined; what follows is of more importance.

IV. The author of creation is God, and he only; hence he is called the creator of the ends of the earth, of the whole world, to the utmost bounds of it; and claims the making the heavens and the earth to himself alone; and a curse is pronounced on those deities that made not the heavens and the earth; and it is declared, that they should perish from the earth, and from under those heavens, Isa. xl. 28. and xlii. 5. and xliv. 24. Jer. x. 11. and more divine persons than one were concerned in this work, for we read of creators and makers in the plural number, Eccl. xii. 1. Job xxxv. 10. Psalm cxlix. 2. Isa. liv. 5. and a plural word for God is made use of at the first mention of the creation, Gen. i. 1. and these divine Persons are Father, Son, and Spirit, the one only living and true God; of the Father of Christ there can be no doubt; our Lord addresses his Father as Lord of heaven and earth, the possessor and governor of both, being the creator of them, Matt. xi. 25. and the apostles expressly ascribe to him the making of the heavens, earth, and sea, and all that is in them, Acts iv. 24, 27. and he is said to make the worlds by his Son, and to create all things by Jesus Christ, Heb. i. 2. Eph. iii. 9. not by him as an instrument, but as a co-efficient cause; for the particle *by* does not always signify an instrument; see Rom. xi. 36. besides it is expressly said of the Word and Son of God, who is God, that *all things were made by him, and without him was not anything made that is made;* and of him, the image of the invisible God and first-born, or first parent and producer of every creature, that *all things were created by him, and for him;* by him as the first cause, and for him as the chief end, John i. 1—3. Col. i. 15, 16. and the Son is addressed by his divine Father after this manner, *And thou, Lord, in the beginning hast laid the foundation of the earth, and the heavens are the works of thine hands;* and by him, the eternal Logos, the essential Word of God,[3] the worlds are said to be framed, Heb. i. 8—10. and xi. 3. nor is the holy Spirit to be excluded from having a concern in the works of creation; since he not only moved upon the face of the waters at the first creation, and brought the unformed earth into a beautiful order, and by him the heavens were garnished, and bespangled with luminaries, Gen. i. 2. Job xxvi. 13. but the formation of men is ascribed to him, *The Spirit of God hath made me,* saith *Elihu, and the breath of the Almighty hath given me life,* Job xxxiii. 4. and since the Spirit of God is the author of regeneration, which is a re-creation, or a new creation, and which requires the same almighty power to effect it, as the old creation did; and since he is the giver of all grace, and of every spiritual gift, which he dispenses to every one severally as he will; no doubt ought to be made of it, that he had an hand in the creation of all things.

And this work of creation was wrought by God, Father, Son, and Spirit, without any other cause, principal or instrumental; not principal, for then that would be equal with God; nor instrumental, since creation is a production of things out of nothing, there was nothing for an instrument to operate upon; and since it was an instantaneous action, done in a moment, there could be no opportunity of using and employing one: besides, this instrument must be either God or a creature; not God, because it is supposed to be distinct from him, and to be made use of by him; and if a creature, it must be used in the creation of itself, which is an absurdity; for then it must be and not be at the same moment: nor could nor can creative power be communicated to a creature; this would be to make finite infinite, and so another God, which cannot be; this would be to make God to act contrary to his nature, to deny himself, which he cannot do; and to destroy all distinction between the crea-

---

[3] Pretty remarkable is the account given by Laertius in vita Zeno, of the notion of the Stoics concerning creation, "with them," he says, "there are two principles of all things, an agent and a patient; the patient is substance, matter without quality; the agent on it is τον εν αυτη λογον τον Θεον, God the Word; for he being eternal, effects or creates every thing by or through the whole of it.

ture and the Creator, and to introduce and justify the idolatry of the heathens, who worshipped the creature besides the Creator.

V. The manner and order of the creation; it was done at once by the mighty power of God, by his all-commanding will and word, *He spake and it was done, he commanded and it stood fast*, Psalm xxxiii. 9. he gave the word, and every creature started into being in a moment; for though God took six days for the creation of the world and all things in it, to make his works the more observable, and that they might be distinctly considered, and gradually become the object of contemplation and wonder; yet the work of every day, and every particular work in each day, were done in a moment, without any motion and change, without any labour and fatigue, only by a word speaking, by an almighty *fiat*, let it be done, and it immediately was done; thus on the *first* day, by the word of the Lord the heavens and the earth were at once made, and light was called into being, *Let there be light, and there was light*. On the *second* day the firmament of heaven, the great expanse, was formed in the same manner, to divide the waters above it, gathered up and formed into clouds, from those that were under it upon the surface of the earth; and on the *third* day, in one moment of that day, God ordered the waters under the heavens to be gathered into one place called the sea, and leave the land dry, which he called earth; and in another moment of that day, he commanded the earth to bring forth grass, herbs, and trees, and they sprung up at once. On the *fourth* day he made the sun, moon, and stars in an instant, and directed their several uses; on the *fifth* day, in one moment of it, he bid the water bring forth fowls, and in another moment of it created great whales, and the numerous fishes of the sea; and on the *sixth* day, in one moment of it, he ordered the earth to bring forth living creatures, beasts, and cattle, wild and tame; and in another moment on the same day he created man after his image, his soul immaterial out of nothing, his body out of the dust of the earth; and in another moment on the same day created the woman out of the rib of man, immediately infusing into her a rational soul as into man, since both were made after the image of God; and thus God proceeded in the creation of things in the visible world, from things less perfect to those more perfect, and from inanimate creatures to animate ones, and from irrational creatures to rational ones; and in his great wisdom provided food and habitations for living creatures before he made them; and when he had finished his works he overlooked them and pronounced them all *very good*. Nor is it any objection to the goodness of them that some creatures are noxious and hurtful to men, since they become so through the sin of men; and others are of a poisonous nature, since even these may be good and useful to others; and God has given man capacity and sagacity to distinguish between what may be hurtful to him, and what is salutary. There remains nothing more to be observed but,

VI. The end of the creation of all things: and, 1. The ultimate end is the glory of God: *The Lord hath made*, in every sense, *all things for himself;* that is, for his glory, Prov. xvi. 4. and his glory is displayed in all, the heavens declare it, and the earth is full of it, even the glory of all the divine perfections; *for the invisible things of him*, his nature, perfections, and attributes, *from the creation of the world*, or by the works of creation, *are clearly seen, being understood by the things that are made*, which could never be made without them, *even his eternal power and godhead;* all the perfections of deity, particularly his infinite and almighty power, Rom. i. 20. for as the prophet Jeremy says, *Lord God, thou hast made the heaven and the earth by thy great power and stretched-out arm*, Jer. xxxii. 17. moreover the goodness of God is remarkably displayed in the creation; God appears therein to be communicative of his goodness, since he has not only made all things very good, but all conducive to the good of his creatures; the whole earth is full of his goodness; and men are called upon by the Psalmist to give thanks to God because he is good; and the principal things instanced in, in which his goodness appears, are the works of creation; see Psalm xxxiii. 5. and cxxxvi. 1, 4, &c. to all which may be added, the rich display that is made of the wisdom of God in the several parts of the creation; *The Lord by wisdom hath founded the earth, by understanding hath he established the heavens, by his knowledge the depths are broken up*, Prov. iii. 19, 20. The wisdom of God appears in every creature he has made, in their form, shape, texture, and nature, suitable for what they are designed, and in their subserviency to each other, so that the Psalmist well might say, *O Lord, how* manifold are thy works, in wisdom hast thou made them all! Psalm civ. 24.——2. The subordinate end is the good of man, of men in general; the earth is made to be inhabited by man, and all the creatures on it are put in subjection to him, and are for his use and service, as well as all that grows upon it, or are in the bowels of it, Isa. xlv. 12, 18. Psalm viii. 6—8. the celestial bodies, the sun, moon, and stars, and all the influences of the heavens, are for his benefit, Gen. i. 14—18. Hos. ii. 21, 22. particularly the world, and all things were made for the sake of God's chosen people, who in the several ages of time were to be brought forth and appear on it; and in which, as on a stage and theatre, the great work of their redemption and salvation was to be performed in the most public manner; and they have the best title to *the world*, even the present world, Christ being theirs, whose is the world and the fulness of it, 1 Cor. iii. 22, 23. Psalm xxiv. 1. as well as the new heavens and the new earth, as they will be when refined and purified, the second Adam's world, are for their sakes; and in which none but righteous persons will dwell, even the whole church of God, when prepared as a bride for her husband, and where the tabernacle of God will be with men, 2 Pet. iii. 13. Rev. xxi. 1—4. yea the angels of heaven are created for their use and service; they are all *ministering spirits, sent forth to minister for them who are heirs of salvation*, Heb. i. 14. wherefore upon the whole it becomes us to glorify and worship God our creator, to fear him and stand in awe of him, and to put our trust and confidence in him, both for things temporal and spiritual.

CHAP. II.

OF THE CREATION OF ANGELS.

From considering the creation in general, I descend to particulars; not to all the creatures that are made; to treat of the nature, form, figure, and qualities of every creature in heaven, earth, and sea, would be a work too large and tedious, and what belongs to naturalists and philosophers, and not divines: I shall only consider angels, the chief of God's works in the heavens; and man, the principal of his creatures on earth. And begin with the angels.

Though the creation of angels is not expressly mentioned in the account of the creation by Moses, yet it is implied in it; for the heavens include all that are in them; which are said to be created by God; and among these must be the angels: besides, Moses, in closing the account of the creation, observes, *Thus the heavens and the earth were finished, and all the host of them*, Gen. ii. 1. Now of the hosts of heaven, the angels are the principal part; they are expressly called, the heavenly host, and the armies of heaven, Dan. iv. 35. Luke ii. 13. and therefore must have been created within the six days of the creation; though on what particular day is not certain, whether on the first, second, third, or fourth; all have been pitched upon by one or another; most probably the first, on which day the heavens were created; and that first, and then the earth; so that the angels might be created with the heavens, whose nature is most similar to the heavens, and the heavens the habitation of them; and accordingly might be present at the forming and founding of the earth, on the same day, and sing on that occasion, Job xxxviii. 7. which if the sense of that text, the time of their creation is plainly pointed out by it; for though they were created very early, some time within the creation of the six days, since some of them fell before man did; and one of the apostate angels was concerned in the seduction of our first parents, and was the instrument of their fall and ruin, quickly after their creation; yet they were not created before the world was, as some have fancied, and which is a mere fancy; for there was nothing before the world was, but the supreme Being, the Creator of all things; *Before the world was*, is a phrase expressive of eternity, and that is peculiar to God, and whose eternity is expressed by the same phrase; *Before the mountains were brought forth, or ever thou hadst formed the earth and the world; even from everlasting to everlasting thou art God*, Psalm xc. 2. Besides, though angels have not bodies, and so are not in place circumscriptively; yet, as they are creatures, they must have an *ubi*, a somewhere, in which they are definitively; so that they are here, and not there, and much less every where: now where was there an *ubi*, a somewhere, for them to exist in, before the heavens and the earth were made? it is most reasonable therefore to conclude, that as God prepared an habitation for all the living creatures before he made them; as the sea for the fishes; the expanse, or air, for the fowls; and the earth for men and beasts; so he made the heavens first, and then the angels to dwell in them; and these were made all at once and together; not like their kindred, the souls or spirits of men, which are made one by one, as their bodies are; for they are created, not without them, but in them, by God, *who formeth the spirit of man within him*, Zech. xii. 1. But the angelic spirits were made altogether; for *all* those morning-stars, the sons of God, were present, and shouted at the foundation of the earth; and all the host of heaven, which must be understood chiefly of angels, were made by the breath of God, when the heavens were created by his word, Job xxxviii. 7. Psalm xxxiii. 6. and their numbers are many; there was a multitude of them at the birth of Christ, Luke ii. 13. and our Lord speaks of twelve legions of them and more, that he could have had at asking them of his Father, Matt. xxvi. 53. According to the vision in Dan. vii. 10. thousand thousands of these ministering spirits, ministered to the Ancient of days, and which number is greatly exceeded in the vision John saw, Rev. v. 11. where those in worship with the living creatures and elders are said to be ten thousand times ten thousand, and thousands of thousands, and may well be called an innumerable company, Heb. xii. 22. and yet the passages referred to only speak of good angels; the evil angels are many also; we read of a legion of them in one man, Mark v. 9. perhaps those that fell, may be as many as those that stood; and if so, how great must be the number of them all together, at their creation? Now these are all the creatures of God; *who maketh his angels spirits*, Psalm civ. 5. they are made by Jehovah the Father, who is called from hence, as well as from his making the souls of men, *the Father of spirits*, Heb. xii. 9. and by Jehovah the Son, *for by him were all things created that are in heaven, and that are in earth, visible and invisible;* and among the latter, angels must be reckoned; and who are further described by *thrones, dominions, principalities, and powers; these all were created by him and for him*, Col. i. 16. Nor is Jehovah the Spirit to be excluded from a concern in the creation of them, since, as *by the word of the Lord were the heavens made, so all the host of them*, the angels, *by the breath*, or Spirit, *of his mouth*, Psalm xxxiii. 6. Concerning these excellent creatures of God, the following things may be observed:

First, Their names: as for proper names, though there are many of them in the Apocryphal and Jewish writings, yet in the sacred scriptures but few, perhaps no more than one, and that is Gabriel, the name of an angel sent with dispatches to Daniel, Zacharias, and to the Virgin Mary, Dan. viii. 16. and ix. 21. Luke i. 19, 26. for as for Michael, the Archangel, he seems to be no other than Christ, the Prince of angels, and Head of all principality and power; who is as God, like unto him, as his name signifies; yea, equal with him. The names, titles, and epithets of angels, are chiefly taken from their nature, qualities, appearances, and offices; some that are ascribed to them, do not seem to belong to them, as *cherubim*, and *seraphim*, which are names and characters of ministers of the word, as I have shewn in a sermon of mine published;[1] and the *Watchers*, in Nebuchadnezzar's dream, thought to be angels by many, more probably are the divine Persons in the Godhead, the same with the holy Ones, and the most High, Dan. iv. 17, 24. The name of Elohim is their principal one, translated *gods*, Psalm xcvii. 7. and interpreted of angels, Heb. i. 6. the same word is translated angels, Psalm viii. 5. and which is justified by the apostle, Heb. ii. 9. Now angels have this name because they have been sent with messages from God, in his name, to men; and they have spoken in his name, and been his representatives; and may be called so, as magistrates sometimes are, because God's vicegerents, and act under him, and for a like reason have the names of *thrones, dominions, principalities, and powers*, Col. i. 16. Not because of hierarchy, or order of government, established among themselves, which does not appear; but rather because of the dignity they are advanced unto, being princes in the court of heaven; and because of that power and authority which, under God, and by his direction, they exercise over kingdoms, provinces, and particular persons on earth: and if the text in Job xxxviii. 7. is to be understood of angels, it furnishes us with other names and titles of them; as *morning-stars*, and *sons of God;* and they may be called *morning-stars*, because of the brightness, splendour, and glory of their nature; and because of the clearness of

---

Called the Doctrine of the Cherubim opened and explained from Ezek. x. 20. printed in 1764.

their light, knowledge, and understanding; in which sense they are *angels of light;* and into one of which Satan sometimes transforms himself, who was once a bright morning-star: and these may be said to be *sons of God;* not by grace and adoption, as saints are; much less by divine generation, as Christ is; *For unto which of the angels said he at any time, Thou art my son, this day have I begotten thee?* Heb. i. 5. but by creation, being made in the image of God, which consists in wisdom and knowledge, in righteousness and holiness; and being his favourites, and beloved of him. They sometimes have the name of *men* given them; because they have appeared in an human form; such were two of those who appeared like men to Abraham, and afterwards to Lot; and two others seen by the women at Christ's sepulchre, Gen. xviii. 2. and xix. 1, 5, 8. Luke xxiv. 4. The more common name given to these celestial spirits, is that of *angels;* the word for which in the Hebrew language, and which is used of them in the Old Testament, signifies *messengers;* and so the uncreated Angel, Christ, is called the Angel, or Messenger of the covenant, Mal. iii. 1. and it comes from a root, preserved in the Ethiopic dialect, which signifies to send,[2] because these spirits have been often sent with messages and dispatches to the children of men: the word *angels* we use, comes from a Greek word,[3] which signifies the same; and are so called, from their being sent on, and bringing messages, which they declare, publish, and proclaim.

Secondly, The nature of angels, which is expressed by the word *spirits;* so good angels are called spirits, and ministering spirits, Heb. i. 7, 14. and evil angels, unclean spirits, Christ gave his apostles power to cast out of the bodies of men, Mat. x. 1. Luke x. 17, 20. that is, spiritual subsistences, they are real personal beings, that subsist of themselves. There was a sect among the Jews, the Sadducees, who said there was *neither angel nor spirit,* Acts xxiii. 8. and our modern Sadducees are not less absurd, who assert that good and evil angels are no other than good and evil thoughts; but this is to be confuted, from the nature and names of angels; from the offices they bear, and are employed in; from the works and actions ascribed unto them; from the powers and faculties of will, understanding, and affections they are possessed of; and from the happiness and misery assigned to them that do well or ill. From all which it appears, that they are not imaginary, or *entia rationis;* nor mere qualities, but personal beings; and they are of a *spiritual* nature; not compounded of parts, as bodies are; and yet they are not so simple and uncompounded as God is, who is a Spirit; in comparison to him, they approach nearer to bodies; wherefore Tertullian, and some other of the fathers, asserted them to be corporeal, though with respect to bodies they are incorporeal. It is difficult with us to form any idea of a spirit; we rather know what it is not, than what it is; *A spirit hath not flesh and bones as ye see me have,* says Christ, Luke xxiv. 39. was it corporeal, a legion of spirits could never have a place in one man; nor penetrate and pass through bodies, through doors bolted and barred, as these angelic beings have: nor is it any objection to their being *incorporeal,* that they have sometimes appeared as men, since they have only seemed so; or they have assumed bodies only for a time, and then laid them aside: nor that they ascend and descend, and move from place to place; for this is said of the souls of men, which are incorporeal; and being spirits, or of a spiritual nature, they are possessed of great agility, and with great swiftness and speed descend from heaven, on occasion; as Gabriel did, who flew swiftly, having his order to carry a message to Daniel, at the beginning of his prayer, and was with him before it was ended; who must move as swift as light from the sun, or lightning from the heavens: and being without bodies, they are *invisible,* and are among the invisible things created by the Son of God, as before observed; and though it was a notion that obtained among the Jews in Christ's time, and does among the common people with us, that a spirit may be seen; it is a vulgar error, Luke xxiv. 37. Indeed, when angels have assumed an human form they may be seen, as they were by Abraham and Lot; and so when they appeared in the forms of chariots and horses of fire, around Elisha, they were seen by his servant, when his eyes were opened; but then these bodies seen were not their own; and these appearances were different from what they really were in themselves.

---

[2] לאך legavit, misit nuncium, Ludolf. Lexic. Ethiop. p. 19. vid. Hottinger. Smegma Oriental. l. 1. c. 5. p. 88.

[3] αγγελλω nuntio, nuntium affero, Scapula.

Once more, being incorporeal and immaterial, they are *immortal;* they do not consist of parts, of matter capable of being disunited or dissolved; and hence the saints in the resurrection will be like them in this respect, that *neither can they die any more,* Luke xx. 36. God, who only has immortality originally and of himself, has conferred immortality on the angelic spirits; and though he can annihilate them, he will not; for even the evil spirits that have rebelled against him, though they die a moral and an eternal death, yet their beings, their substances, continue and perish not; everlasting fire, eternal punishment, is prepared for the devil and his angels.

Thirdly, The qualities and excellencies of angels may be next considered; and they are more especially *three,* holiness, wisdom, or knowledge, and power.——
1. Holiness; they are holy creatures, called *holy angels,* Mark viii. 38. and so they were created, even all of them: not indeed so holy as God is; for *there is none holy as the Lord,* 1 Sam. ii. 2. in comparison of him all creatures are unholy; *the heavens are not clean in his sight.* Job. xv. 15. that is, the inhabitants of them, the angels; nor were they created immutably holy, but so as that they were capable of sinning, as some of them did; who, being left to the mutability of their own free will, departed from their *first estate,* which was a state of holiness, as well as happiness; and *abode not in the truth,* in the truth of holiness, in that uprightness and righteousness in which they were created; and they are called the *angels that sinned,* 2 Pet. ii. 4. Jude ver. 6. John viii. 44. But others of them stood in their integrity, and are become impeccable; not owing to the power of their free-will, and their better use of it than the rest; but to the electing grace of God, and the confirming grace of Christ, who is the Head of all principality and power, 1 Tim. v. 21. Col. ii. 10. These now, as they persist in their obedience, they are perfect in it; hence the petition Christ directed his disciples to; *Thy will be done in earth as it is in heaven,* Matt. vi. 10. they are subject to the same laws and rules of morality and righteousness that men are, excepting such as are not suitable to their nature; as some duties belonging to the fourth, fifth, seventh, eighth, and tenth commands of the Decalogue; but to the rest in such manner as their nature will admit of; with all other orders, prescriptions, and directions of the divine will, they cheerfully and constantly yield an obedience to; for they *do his commandments, hearkening to the voice of his word,* Psalm ciii. 20.——2. Wisdom and knowledge; angels are very wise and knowing creatures; it is an high strain of compliment in the woman of Tekoah to David; *My Lord is wise, according to the wisdom of an angel of God; to know all things that are in the earth,* 2 Sam. xiv. 20. yet it shews the general opinion entertained of the wisdom of angels; though in comparison of the all-wise and only-wise God, they are by him chargeable *with folly,* Job. iv. 18. Very wise and knowing creatures no doubt they are; but they are not omniscient; they know much, but not every thing; they know much of themselves, through the strength and excellency of their nature, being rational and intelligent creatures, of the highest form and class; and by observation and experience, for which they have had a long time, and great opportunity; and also by divine revelation, through which they are acquainted with many things they otherwise would not know: they know much of God, being always in his presence, and beholding his face, and whose perfections displayed in his works, they have the clearest knowledge of; and much of their fellow-creatures, of the same species with them, the holy angels; who having a language peculiar to themselves, can converse with, and communicate to each other; and much of the apostate angels, who they are set to oppose, conflict with, and counterwork; and much of men, of wicked men, on whom, by divine direction, they inflict the judgments of God; and of good men, the heirs of salvation, to whom they are sent, as ministering spirits: they know much of the mysteries of providence, in the execution of which they are often employed; and of the mysteries of divine grace, not only by divine revelation, but by the church, and by the ministry of the word, they attending the congregations of the saints; though it seems that this their knowledge is imperfect, since they bow their heads, and desire to pry more into these things: and there are many things which they know not, unless by marks and signs, in a conjectural way, or by a particular revelation; as the thoughts of men's hearts, which of others, men themselves know not, only the spirits of men within them; and which to know, peculiarly belongs to God, the searcher of the

hearts, and trier of the reins of the children of men: nor do they know future contingencies, or what shall be hereafter, unless such as necessarily and ordinarily follow from natural causes, or may be guessed at, or are revealed unto them of God, in order to impart them to others; of the day and hour of the end of the world, and the last judgment, as no man knoweth, so neither the angels of heaven, Matt. xxiv. 36. Rev. i. 1.——3. Power is another excellency of the angels; they are called *mighty* angels, and are said to *excel in strength;* that is, other creatures, 2 Thess. i. 7. Psalm ciii. 20. their strength is great, and their power and authority under God very large, yet finite and limited; they are not omnipotent; nor sovereign; they do not preside over the celestial bodies, move the planets, dispose of the ordinances of heaven, bind or loose their influences, and set their dominion in the earth; they have not the power of the air, nor the command of the earth; the world is not in subjection to them: they are capable indeed, under a divine influence, and by divine direction, help, and assistance, of doing great and marvellous things; of holding the four winds of heaven; of quenching the violence of fire; and of stopping the mouths of lions; and of re-restraining other hurtful things: they have great power over the bodies of men, of moving them from place to place; as an evil spirit, by permission, carried Christ, and set him upon the pinnacle of the temple; and a good spirit caught away Philip, and carried him to Azotus: they have power, when they have leave, or are ordered, to smite the bodies of men with diseases; as the men of Sodom with blindness, yea, with death itself, as seventy thousand Israelites, on account of David's numbering the people; and a hundred and forty-five thousand Assyrians in one night, as they lay encamped against Jerusalem; and Herod the king, who, being smitten by an angel, was eaten of worms, and died. But the power of angels will still more appear under the following head, concerning,

Fourthly, Their office and employment.
——1*st,* With respect to God; their work is to praise him, to celebrate the glory of his perfections; *Praise ye him, all his angels,* Psalm cxlviii. 2. and to worship him with his saints; we find them sometimes joining with men, with the living creatures and elders, in John's visions, in ascribing blessing, glory, wisdom, thanksgiving, honour, power, and might unto God; and the same, in the same company, to the Lamb that was slain, Rev. v. 11, 12. and vii. 11, 12. and their work also lies in keeping the commandments of God, and doing his will in heaven and in earth; these are the four spirits of the heavens, which go forth from standing before the Lord of all the earth, to do his will and work in it; they wait his orders, and immediately go forth and execute them, Zech. vi. 4, 5.

2*dly,* With respect to Christ, on whom they are said to ascend and descend, as they did on Jacob's ladder, a type of him, Gen. xxviii. 12. John i. 51. these attended at the incarnation of Christ; one informed the Virgin of her conception of him, removed her doubts about it, and explained to her the mystery of it; another encouraged Joseph to take her to wife, who thought to put her away, because of her pregnancy; and a third published the news of his birth to the shepherds; and who was presently joined with a multitude of them, who in chorus celebrated the glory of God, displayed therein. Yea, when God brought him, his first-begotten, into the world, and manifested him to it in human nature, he gave orders to all the angelic host, to do him homage and worship, saying, *Let all the angels of God worship him,* Luke i. 30—35. Matt. i. 19, 20. Luke ii. 10—14. Heb. i. 6. these had the care and charge of him in his state of humiliation; they were solicitous for the preservation of his life in his infancy; when Herod sought to take it away, an angel gave notice of it to Joseph, in a dream, and directed him to take the child and his mother, and flee into Egypt: and I see no reason why those wonderful escapes of Christ out of the hands of his enemies, in riper years, when just going to destroy him, may not be ascribed to the ministration of angels; since it is most certain, that God gave his angels charge over him, to keep him in all his ways; see Matt. ii. 13. Luke iv. 29, 30. John viii. 59. Psalm xci. 11. When he had fasted forty days and nights in the wilderness, these same excellent creatures came and ministered food unto him, Matt. iv. 11. and one of them attended him in his agony in the garden, and strengthened and comforted him, Luke xxii. 43. they were present at his resurrection, and rolled away the stone from the sepulchre; and declared to the women at it, that he was risen from the dead, Matt. xxviii. 2. Luke xxiv. 4, 6, 23.

they accompanied him at his ascension to heaven, even thousands of them; though only in the Acts of the Apostles two are mentioned; by whom he was seen, and escorted through the region of the air, the territory of Satan, in triumph; and was received and welcomed to heaven, Psalm lxviii. 17, 18. Acts i. 10, 11. 1 Tim. iii. 16. and by whom he will be attended at his second coming; for they will make a part of his glorious appearing, which will be in his own glory, and in the glory of his Father, and in the glory of his holy angels, 2 Thess. i. 7. Luke ix. 26.

3dly, With respect to the saints, to whom they are sent as ministering spirits; for though in some instances they may have a concern with others, yet that is chiefly in the behalf of the church and people of God, who are more especially their charge and care, both in respect to things temporal and spiritual.———1. With respect to things temporal, instances of which are, (1.) Preserving them in their infant state; there is a special providence concerned with the elect; as soon as they are born they are under the particular watch and care of it, and are distinguished by it; which is what the apostle means when he says, that *God separated him from his mother's womb*, Gal. i. 15. and which providence may be thought to be chiefly executed by the ministry of angels; for though it is not certain, which yet some scriptures countenance, Matt. xviii. 10. Acts xii. 15. that every one has his guardian angel, since sometimes more angels are deputed to one, and sometimes but one to many; yet doubtless saints from their birth are under the care of angels, and are preserved by them to be called; it is not known how many difficulties and dangers they are preserved from in infancy, in childhood, and in youth, as well as in riper years, by means of angels. ———(2.) Providing food for them when in want of it, or that they might not want it; as they ministered food to Christ in the wilderness; and prepared manna, called angels' food, because prepared by them in the air, and let down by them from thence, for the Israelites during their forty years' travels; and as an angel dressed food for the prophet Elijah, and called upon him to arise and eat, Matt. iv. 11. Psalm lxxviii. 25. 1 Kings xix. 5—8.———(3.) Keeping off diseases from them, and healing of them according to the promise, *He shall deliver thee from the noisome pestilence—neither shall any plague come nigh thy dwelling;* *for he shall give his angels charge over thee*, &c. Psalm xci. 3, 7, 10, 11. and if evil angels can, by divine permission, inflict diseases, as appears from the case of Job, and doubtless they would oftener do it, was it not for the interposition of good angels, why may not good angels be thought capable of healing diseases? and those many strange and wonderful cures wrought when all means have been ineffectual, may be ascribed, at least many of them, to the good offices of angels in directing to simple things, whose nature and virtue they are well acquainted with; and even they have cured diseases in a miraculous way, witness the pool of Bethesda, whose healing virtue for all diseases was owing to the agitation of its waters by an angel, John v. 4.———(4.) Directing and protecting in journies, and at other times; thus Abraham, when he sent his servant to Mesopotamia to take a wife for his son Isaac, assured him that God would send an angel before him to direct and prosper him, which the servant found to be true, and blessed God for it, Gen. xxiv. 7, 27, 48. so Jacob, as he was travelling, was met by the angels of God, who divided themselves into two hosts for his guard, and one went on one side of him and the other on the other; or one went before him, and the other behind him; wherefore he called the name of the place where they met him Mahanaim, which signifies two camps or armies, Gen. xxxii. 1, 2. and even all that fear the Lord have such a guard about them, for *the angel of the Lord encampeth round about them that fear him*, Psalm xxxiv. 7.———(5.) Keeping from dangers, and helping out of them : when Lot and his family were in danger of being destroyed in Sodom, the angels laid hold on their hands and brought them forth, and set them without the city, and directed them to escape for their lives to an adjacent mountain, Gen. xix. 15—17. the preservation of Shadrach, Meshech, and Abednego, in the furnace of fire, and of Daniel in the lions' den, is ascribed to angels, Dan. iii. 28. and vi. 22. the opening of the doors of the prison where the apostles were, and setting them free; and the deliverance of Peter from prison, whose chains fell from him, and the gate opened before him, were done by angels, Acts v. 19, 20. and xii. 7, 10. ———2. With respect to things spiritual. ———(1.) Angels have been employed in revealing the mind and will of God to men. They attended at mount Sinai, when the law was given; yea, it is said to be ordained by angels, and to be given by the disposition of angels, and even to be the word spoken by angels, Deut. xxxii. 2. Acts vii. 59. Gal. iii. 19. Heb. ii. 2. And an angel published the gospel, and brought the good news of the incarnation of Christ, and salvation by him, Luke ii. 10, 11. An angel made known to Daniel the time of the Messiah's coming; as well as many other things relating to the state of the church and people of God, Dan. viii. 16—19. and ix. 21—27. and xii. 5—13. And an angel was sent to signify to the apostle John the things that should come to pass in his time, and in all ages to the end of the world, Rev. i. 1.——(2.) Though the work of conversion is the sole work of God, yet as he makes use of instruments in it, as ministers of the word, why may he not be thought to make use of angels? they may suggest that to the minds of men which may be awakening to them, and may improve a conviction by a providence, which may issue in conversion. However, this is certain, they are acquainted with the conversions of sinners; and there is joy in heaven, and in the presence of the angels of God, over one sinner that repenteth, more than over ninety and nine just persons that need no repentance, Luke xv. 7, 10.——(3.) They are useful in comforting the saints when in distress; as they strengthened and comforted Christ in his human nature, when in an agony, so they comfort his members, as Daniel, when in great terror, and the apostle Paul, in a tempest, Dan. ix. 23. and x. 11, 12. Acts xxvii. 23, 24. and as when in temporal, so when in spiritual distresses; for if evil angels are capable of suggesting terrible and uncomfortable things, and of filling the mind with blasphemous thoughts, and frightful apprehensions; good angels are surely capable of suggesting comfortable things, and what may relieve souls distressed with unbelief, doubts and fears, and the temptations of Satan; for—— (4.) They are greatly assisting in repelling the temptations of Satan; for if they oppose themselves to, and have conflicts with evil angels, with respect to things political and civil, the affairs of kingdoms and states, in which the interests and church of Christ are concerned; see Dan. x. 13, 20. Rev. xii. 7. they, no doubt, bestir themselves in opposition to evil spirits, when they tempt believers to sin, or to despair; so that they are better able to wrestle against principalities and powers, against the rulers of the darkness of this world, and against spiritual wickednesses in high places, Eph. vi. 12. see Zech. iii. 1, 2, 3, 4. ——(5.) They are exceeding useful to saints in their dying moments; they attend the saints on their dying beds, and whisper comfortable things to them against the fears of death; and keep off the fiends of hell from disturbing and distressing them; and they watch the moment when soul and body are parted, and carry their souls to heaven; as they carried the soul of Lazarus into Abraham's bosom, Luke xvi. 22. and thus Elijah was carried to heaven, soul and body, in a chariot of fire, and horses of fire, which were no other than angels, which appeared in such a form, for the conveyance of him, 2 Kings ii. 11.—— (6.) Angels, as they will attend Christ at his second coming, when the dead in Christ shall rise first; so they will be made use of by him, to gather the risen saints from the four quarters of the world, and bring them to him; to gather the wheat into his garner, and to take the tares, and even all things out of his kingdom that offend, and burn them, Matt. xiii. 40, 41. and xxiv. 31. From the whole it appears, that angels are creatures, and so not to be worshipped; which kind of idolatry was introduced in the apostles' time, but condemned, Col. ii. 18. the angels themselves refuse and forbid it, Rev. xix. 10. and xxii. 8, 9. yet notwithstanding, they are to be loved, valued, and esteemed by the saints, partly on account of the excellency of their nature, and partly because of their kind and friendly offices; and care should be taken to give them no offence, in public or private; see 1 Cor. xi. 10. for the saints are highly honoured, by having such excellent spirits to wait upon them, and minister unto them, and be guards about them; and it is no small part of their gospel privileges, for which they should be thankful, that they are come to an innumerable company of angels, Heb. i. 14. and xii. 22.

CHAP. III.

OF THE CREATION OF MAN.

MAN was made last of all the creatures, being the chief and master-piece of the whole creation on earth, whom God had principally and first in view in making the world, and all things in it; according to that known rule, that what is first in intention, is last in execution; God proceeding in his works as artificers in theirs, from a less perfect to a more perfect work, till they come to what they have chiefly in view, a finished piece of work, in which they employ all their skill; and which, coming after the rest, appears to greater advantage. Man is a compendium of the creation, and therefore is sometimes called a microcosm, a little world, the world in miniature; something of the vegetable, animal, and rational world meet in him; spiritual and corporal substance, or spirit and matter, are joined together in him; yea, heaven and earth centre in him, he is the bond that connects them both together; all creatures were made for his sake, to possess, enjoy, and have the dominion over, and therefore he was made last of all: and herein appear the wisdom and goodness of God to him, that all accommodations were ready provided for him when made; the earth for his habitation, all creatures for his use; the fruits of the earth for his profit and pleasure; light, heat, and air for his delight, comfort, and refreshment; with every thing that could be wished for and desired to make his life happy.

Man was made on the *sixth* and last day of the creation, and not before; nor were there any of the same species made before Adam, who is therefore called *the first man Adam*: there have been some who have gone by the name of Præadamites, because they held there were men before Adam. So the Zabians held; and speak of one that was his master;[1] and in the last century one Peirerius wrote a book in Latin, in favour of the same notion; which has been refuted by learned men over and over. It is certain, that sin entered into the world, and death by sin, by one man, even the first man Adam; from whom death first commenced, and from whom it has reigned ever since, Rom. v. 13, 14. Now if there were men before Adam, they must have been all alive at his formation; there had been no death among them; and if they had been of any long standing before him, as the notion supposes, the world, in all probability, was as much peopled as it may be now; and if so, why should God say, *Let us make man*, when there must be a great number of men in being already? And what occasion was there for such an extraordinary production of men? Why was Adam formed out of the dust of the earth? and Eve out of one of his ribs? and these two coupled together, that a race of men might spring from them, if there were men before? But it is certain that Adam was the first man, as he is called; not only with respect to Christ, the second Adam; but because he was the first of the human race, and the common parent of mankind; and Eve, the mother of all living; that is, of all men living. The apostle Paul says, that God *has made of one blood*, that is, of the blood of one man, *all nations of men to dwell on all the face of the earth*, Acts xvii. 26. and this he said in the presence of the wise philosophers at Athens, who, though they objected to the new and strange deities, they supposed he introduced, yet said not one word against that account he gave of the original of mankind. But what puts this out of all question, with those that believe the divine revelation, is, that it is expressly said, that before Adam was formed, *there was not a man to till the ground*, Gen. ii. 5.

Man was made after, and upon a consultation held concerning his creation; *Let us make man*, Gen. i. 26. which is an address, not to second causes, not to the elements, nor to the earth; for God could, if he would, have commanded the earth to have brought man forth at once, as he commanded it to bring forth grass, herbs, trees, and living creatures of all sorts, and not have consulted with it: nor is it an address to angels, who were never of God's privy council; nor was man made after their image, he being corporeal, they incorporeal. But the address was made by Jehovah the Father to, and the consultation was held by him, with the other two divine Persons in the Deity, the Son and Spirit; a like phrase see in chap. iii. 22. and xi. 7. Isa. vi. 8. and such a consultation being held about the making of man, as was not at the making of any of the rest of the creatures, shews what an excellent and finished piece of work God meant to make. Concerning the creation of man, the following things may be observed.

I. The author of his creation, God; *So God created man*, Gen. i. 27. Not man himself; a creature cannot create, and much less itself; nor angels, for then they would be entitled to worship from men, which they have refused, because their fellow-servants, and it might be added, their fellow-creatures. But God, who is

---

[1] Sepher Cosri, par. 1. s. 61. p. 27.

the Creator of the ends of the earth, was the Creator of the first man, and of all since; for we are all his offspring, and therefore are exhorted to *remember* our *Creator*, Eccles. xii. 1. or *Creators;* for so it is in the original text; for as there were more concerned in the consultation about man's creation, so in the creation of him; and the same that were in the one, were in the other, even Father, Son, and Spirit; hence we read of God our *Makers* in various passages of scripture, Job xxxv. 10. Psalm cxlix. 2. Isa. liv. 5. that God the Father, who made the heavens, earth, and sea, and all that in them are, made man among the rest, and particularly made him, will not be questioned; nor need there be any doubt about the Son of God; since *without him,* the eternal Word, *was not anything made that was made;* then not man; and if all things were made and created by him, whether visible and invisible, then man was made by him, who must be reckoned among these all things, John i. 1, 2, 3. Col. i. 16. The character and relation of an husband to the church, more particularly belongs to Christ; and her husband is expressly said to be her maker, Isa. liv. 5. compare also Psalm xcv. 6, 7, 8. with Heb. iii. 6, 7. Nor is the holy Spirit to be excluded from the formation of man, who had a concern in the whole creation, Gen. i. 3. Job xxvi. 13. Psalm xxxiii. 6. and to whom Elihu particularly ascribes his formation, Job xxxiii. 4. and why not the first man made by him also? yea, the act of breathing into man the breath of life, when he became a living soul, seems most agreeable to him, the Spirit and Breath of God; and who has so great a concern in the re-creation, or renovation of man, even in his regeneration. Wherefore the three divine Persons should be remembered as Creators, and be feared, worshipped, and adored as such; and thanks be given them for creation, preservation, and for all the mercies of life, bountifully provided by them. It is pretty remarkable that the word *created* should be used three times in one verse, where the creation of man is only spoken of; as it should seem to point out the three divine Persons concerned therein, Gen. i. 27.

II. The constituent and essential parts of man, created by God, which are two, body and soul; these appear at his first formation; the one was made out of the dust, the other was breathed into him; and so at his dissolution, the one returns to the dust from whence it was; and the other to God that gave it; and, indeed, death is no other than the dissolution, or dis-union of these two parts; *the body without the Spirit is dead;* the one dies, the other does not.

First, The body, which is a most *wonderful* structure, and must appear so when it is considered, with what precision and exactness every part is formed for its proper use, even every muscle, vein, and artery, yea, the least fibre; and that every limb is set in its proper place, to answer its designed end; and all in just symmetry and proportion, and in a subserviency to the use of each other, and for the good of the whole: to enter into a detail of particulars, more properly belongs to anatomy; and that art is now brought to such a degree of perfection, that by it most amazing discoveries are made in the structure of the human body,[2] as the circulation of the blood, &c. so that it may well be said of our bodies, as David said of his, *I am fearfully and wonderfully made,* Psalm cxxxix. 14. The erect posture of the body is not to be omitted, which so remarkably distinguishes man from the four-footed animals, who look downward to the earth; and by which man is fitted and directed to look upward to the heavens, to contemplate them, and the glory of God displayed in them; and even to look up to God above them, to worship and adore him, to praise him for mercies received, and to pray to him for what are wanted; as well as instructs men to set their affections not on things on earth, but on things in heaven; and, indeed, it is natural for every man, whether in any great distress, or when favoured with an unexpected blessing, and when he receives things that surprise him, whether of good or of bad things, to turn his face upwards. In the Greek language man has his name $\alpha\nu\vartheta\rho\omega\pi\sigma\varsigma$,[3] from turning and looking upwards.

The body of man is very *fair* and beautiful; for if the children of man, or of Adam, are fair, as is suggested, Psalm xlv. 2. then most certainly Adam himself was created fair and beautiful; and some think he had the name of Adam given him from his beauty; the root of the word, in the Ethiopic[4] language, signifies to be fair

---

[2] See Nieuwentyt's Religious Philosopher, vol. 1.
[3] Vide Platonem in Cratylo.

[4] Vide Ludolph. Hist. Ethiop. 1. 1. c. 15.

and beautiful; and though external beauty is a vain thing to gaze at, and for men to pride themselves with, in this their fallen state, when God can easily by a disease cause their beauty to consume away as a moth; yet it is a property and quality in the composition of man at first not to be overlooked, since it greatly exceeds what may be observed of this kind in the rest of the creatures.

The body of man was also originally made *immortal;* not that it was so of itself, and in its own nature, being made of the elements of the earth, and so reducible to the same again; and was supported, even in the state of innocence, with corruptible food; but God, who only has immortality, conferred it on the body of man; so that if he had never sinned, his body would not have been mortal, or have died: nor is it any objection to it, that it was supported with food; for God could have supported it with or without food, as long as he pleased, or for ever: he could have supported it with food, not to take notice of the tree of life, which some think was designed as the means of continuing man's life perpetually, if he had not sinned; but without that, as God could and did support the body of Adam with food, even when it was become mortal, through sin, for the space of nine hundred years and more; he could have supported it for the space of nine thousand, and so onward, had it been his pleasure; and therefore there can be no difficulty in conceiving that he could have supported it in an unfallen state, when it had the gift of immortality, in the same way for ever. Besides, God could, by a new act of his special grace and goodness, have translated Adam to heaven, or to an higher state of life, to greater nearness and communion with him, and supported his body without food for ever; as the bodies of Enoch and Elijah, translated, that they should not see death; and have been some thousands of years supported without food; and as the body of Christ is, and the bodies of the saints that rose at his resurrection are; and all the bodies of men, after the resurrection, will be; and it is most clear from the word of God, that death did not arise from a necessity of nature; but from sin: *Sin entered into the world, and death by sin*——and, *through the offence of one, many be dead*——*the wages of sin is death* ——yea, it is expressly said, *the body is dead because of sin*, Rom. v. 12, 15. and vi. 23. and viii. 10. and, indeed, to what purpose was that threatening given out, *In the day thou eatest thereof thou shalt surely die*, Gen. ii. 17. if man of necessity must have died, whether he had sinned or no? as say the Pelagians and Socinians;[5] and which, if they could, they would maintain, in order to avoid the force of the argument, in favour of original sin, they deny, from death being the fruit, effect, and punishment of the sin of Adam. But now, though this body was so wonderfully and beautifully formed and gifted with immortality, yet it was made out of the dust of the earth, Gen. ii. 7. that is, macerated with water, and so properly clay; hence man is said to be made out of the clay, and the bodies of men to be like bodies of clay; and to have their foundation in the dust, Job iv. 18. and xiii. 12. and xxxiii. 6. Isa. lxiv. 8. Hence some think that Adam had his name from *adamah*, earth, out of which he was formed, red earth, as Josephus[6] calls it; as in Latin he is called *homo*, from *humus*, the ground. And this is an humbling consideration to proud man, and especially in the sight of God, when compared with him; and still more, as this clay of his is now, through sin, become frail, brittle, and mortal; and his dust, sinful dust, and ashes, Gen. xviii. 27. and it may serve to take down the haughtiness and pride of some men, who vaunt over their fellow-creatures, and boast of their blood, and of their families, when all are made out of one mass and lump of clay, and of one blood all the nations of men are formed.

Secondly, The soul is the other part of man created by God; which is a *substance* or subsistence; it is not an accident, or quality, inherent in a subject; but is capable of subsisting of itself; it is not a good temperament of the body, as some have fancied; nor is it mere thought; it is indeed a thinking substance, in which thought is, and is exercised by it, but is distinct from it; it cannot be a mere quality, or accident, because that is not properly created, at least by itself, but is concreated, or created with the subjects in which it is; whereas the Spirit of man is formed or created of God within him, Zech. xii. 1. it is itself the subject of qualities, of all arts and sciences, and in its depraved state, the subject of *vices*, and of virtues

---

[5] Socinus de Statu primi hominis ante lapsum, s. 8, 9, 10. et de Servatore, par. 3. c. 8. et par. 4. c. 6.

[6] Antiq. l. 1. c. 1. s. 2.

and graces; it is an inhabitant of the body, dwells in it, as in a tabernacle, and removes from it at death, and exists in a separate state after it; all which shew it is a substance, or subsistence of itself. It is not a corporal[7] but a *spiritual* substance; not a body, as Tertullian,[8] and others, have thought; but a spirit, as it is often called in scripture, Eccles. xii. 7. Matt. xxvi. 41. Acts vii. 59. And the souls of men are called the spirits of all flesh, to distinguish them from angelic spirits, which are not surrounded with flesh, as the spirits of men are, Numb. xvi. 22. The soul is immediately breathed from God, as Adam's soul was; and in it chiefly consists the image of God in man, and therefore must be a spirit, as he is, though in a finite proportion, a created spirit; it is also *immaterial*; it does not consist of flesh, and blood, and bones, as the body does, and so is *immortal*, and dies not when that does; when that goes to the dust, the soul returns to God; the body may be killed by men, but not the soul; when they have killed the one, they can proceed no farther; the soul survives the body, and lives for ever,[9] it consists of various powers and faculties, the understanding, will, &c. and performs various operations of life, either immediately by itself, or mediately by the organs of the body, in the vegetable, animal, and rational way; and therefore is called the *spirit*, or *breath of lives*, Gen. ii. 7. and yet is but one; for though sometimes mention is made of soul and spirit, as if they were distinct, 1 Thess. v. 23. Heb. iv. 12. yet this only respects the superior and inferior powers and faculties of one and the same soul; for otherwise the scriptures always represent man as having but one soul; and this is *created* by God; it is not uncreated, as he is; nor is it created by angels, as some have fancied; nor of itself; nor is it generated by and derived from immediate parents. The soul of Adam was most certainly created of God, and immediately, and breathed into him; and the same may be believed of the soul of Eve; for it cannot be thought that that was contained in, and educed out of the rib, from which her body was made; but that when that was made, God breathed into her the breath of life, as he did into Adam; and there is no reason why the souls of all men should not be made, or created, in like manner.

Some have been, and are of opinion, that the souls of men are *ex traduce*, as Tertullian; or generated by and derived from their parents, with their bodies. But against this it may be observed, that Christ was made in all things like unto us, having a true body and a reasonable soul; which soul of his could not be generated by and derived from his parents, not from a father, because he had none, as man; nor from his mother, for then she, being a sinful woman, it must have been infected and defiled with the contagion of sin, the corruption of nature; whereas he was holy and harmless, without spot and blemish. Moreover, if souls are by natural generation from their immediate parents, they must be derived either from their bodies, or from their bodies and souls, or from their souls only; not from their bodies, for then they would be corporeal, whereas they are not; not from both bodies and souls; for then they would be partly corporeal, and partly incorporeal, which they are not; not from their souls only, for as an angel is not generated by an angel, so not a soul by a soul. Besides, if the souls of men are derived from the souls of parents, it is either from a part of them, or from the whole; not from a part, for then the soul would be partible and divisible, as matter is, and so not immaterial; and as not a part, so neither can their whole souls be thought to be communicated to them, for then they would have none, and perish; to such absurdities is this notion reducible. Besides, what is immaterial, as the soul is, can never be educed out of matter; if the soul is generated out of the matter of parents, then it is and must be material; and if material, then corruptible; and if corruptible, then mortal; and it is a maxim, that what is generated may be corrupted; and if the soul may be corrupted, then it is not immortal; the doctrine of the soul's immortality, becomes indefensible by this notion; for if this be admitted, the other must be relinquished.[10] But what puts this matter out of all doubt is, the distinction the apostle makes between the *fathers of our*

---

[7] Aristotle says, that την ψυχην ασωματον, Laert. 1. 5. in Vita ejus.
[8] De Resurrectione Carnis, c. 17.
[9] The arguments proving the immortality of the soul are reserved to the doctrine of a future state, and the resurrection of the body to be considered with them.
[10] Nam de mortalibus non potest quicquam nisi mortale generari, Lactant. de Opificio Dei. c. 19.

CHAP. III. OF THE CREATION OF MAN.

flesh, and the *Father of spirits*, Heb. xii. 9. Man consists of two parts, of *flesh* and *spirit*, body and soul; the former the apostle ascribes to immediate parents, as instruments thereof; and the latter to God, as the Father, Author, and Creator of it. Nor is it an objection of any moment, to the soul being of the immediate creation of God, that then a man does not generate a man: to which it may be replied, that he may be said to generate a man, though strictly speaking he only generates a part of him; as when one man kills another, he is truly said to kill a man, though he only kills his body; so a man may be said to generate a man, though he only generates the body; from whence in this case man is denominated. Moreover, as in death, the whole man may be said to die, because death is a dissolution of the whole, though each part remains; so the whole man may be said to be generated, because in generation there is an union and conjunction of the parts of man; though one part is not generated, yet because of the union of the parts, the whole is said to be so. Nor is it an objection of greater weight, that man does not do what other creatures do, generate the whole of their species; as a horse a horse, not only the flesh, but the spirit of it; since it is not at all derogatory to man, but it is his superior excellency, that his soul is not generated as the spirit of a beast is, but comes immediately from the hand of God. Such who are otherwise right in their notion of things, give into this, in order to get clear of a difficulty attending the doctrine of original sin, and the manner of its propagation, which they think is more easily accounted for, by supposing the soul derived from parents by natural generation, and so corrupted; but though this is a difficulty not easily to be resolved, how the soul coming immediately from God, is corrupted with original sin; it is better to let this difficulty lie unresolved, than to give up so certain a truth, and of so much importance, as the doctrine of the immortality of the soul is; which, as has been seen, must be given up, if this notion is received; but there are ways and methods for the clearing of this difficulty, without being at the expense of the loss of such an important truth; as will be shewn when we come to treat of the doctrine of original sin. In the meanwhile, let us take it for granted, that souls are of God's immediate creation; the making of them he claims to himself; *The souls that I have made*, Isa. lvii. 16. see Jer. xxxviii. 16.

The souls of men were not made in eternity, but in time. The pre-existence of all human souls before the world was, is a notion held by Plato among the heathens, and espoused by Origen, among christians; but is exploded by all wise, thoughtful, and judicious men; for whatsoever was before the world was, is eternal; if souls were created before the world, then they are eternal; whereas there was nothing before the world but God, to whom eternity only belongs, Psalm xc. 2. nor were souls created together, as angels were; but they are created one by one, when their bodies are prepared to receive them; they are not created without the body, and then put into it; but they are formed in it; *Who formeth the spirit of man within him*, Zech. xii. 1. not brought Συραθιν, from without, as Aristotle,[11] expresses it; but when the *embryo* is fit to receive it, it is created by God, and united to it; but how it is united, and what is the bond of that union, we must be content to be ignorant of; as well as of the particular place of its abode, whether diffused through the whole body, as some think, or has an apartment in the brain, or has its seat in the heart, which is most likely, and most agreeable to scripture, and to that known maxim, that the heart is the first that lives, and the last that dies.

III. The difference of sex in which man was created, is male and female, Gen. i. 27. that is, man and woman; not that they were created together; though on the same day, and perhaps not long one after the other: the male was created first, and out of him the female, as the apostle says, *Adam was first formed, then Eve*, 1 Tim. ii. 13. which he observes, to shew that the woman should not usurp authority over the man, since he was before her; and by which it appears, that *the man was not created for the woman, but the woman for the man*, as he elsewhere asserts, 1 Cor. xi. 9. and therefore ought to be in subjection to him: nor were they made out of the same matter, at least not as in the same form; their souls, indeed, were equally made out of nothing, out of no pre-existent matter, but their bodies differently: the body of

---

[11] De Generat. Animal. l. 2. c. 3.

Adam was formed out of the dust of the earth, and the body of Eve out of a rib of Adam, though both originally dust and clay, to which they both returned: the woman was very significantly made out of man's rib; not out of the upper part of man, lest she should be thought to have a superiority over him; nor out of the lower part of man, lest she should be despised and trampled upon; but from a rib of him, to signify that she should be by his side, a companion of him, and from a part near his heart, and under his arm, to show that she should be the object of his love and affection, and be always under his care and protection: and thus being *flesh of his flesh*, as he himself owned, it became him to nourish and cherish her as his own flesh. Man is a social creature, and therefore God in his wisdom thought it not proper that he should be alone, but provided an helpmeet for him, to be a partner and companion with him, in civil and religious life; and in this difference of sex were they created for the sake of procreation of children, and of the propagation of their species, in their successive offspring, to the end of the world; and there were but one male and one female, at first created, and which were joined together in marriage by the Lord himself, to teach, that but one man and one woman only are to be joined together at one time in lawful wedlock; and these two, male and female, first created, were made after the same image; for the word *man* includes both man and woman; and Adam was a name common to them both in their creation, and when said to be made after the image of God, Gen. i. 26, 27. and v. 1, 2. which image, as will hereafter be seen, lies much in righteousness and holiness. Now God *made man*, that is, both man and woman, *upright; but they*, Adam and Eve, *sought out many inventions*, sinful ones, and so lost their righteousness: nor is it any objection to the woman being made after the image of God, part of which lies in dominion over the creatures, as will hereafter be observed, that she is in subjection to the man; for though her husband ruled over her, yet she had equal dominion with him over the creatures. Which leads on to consider,

IV. The image of God, in which man was created; *God said, Let us make man in our image, and after our likeness——so God created man in his own image*, Gen. i. 26, 27. Whether image, and likeness are to be distinguished, as by Maimonides,[12] the one respecting the substantial form of man, his soul; the other certain accidents and qualities belonging to him; or whether they signify the same, is not very material; the latter seems probable; since in Gen. i. 27. where *image* is mentioned, *likeness* is omitted; and, on the contrary, in Gen. v. 1. the word *likeness* is used, and *image* omitted. Now though this is only said of man, that he is made after the image and likeness of God,[13] yet he is not the only creature so made; angels are like to God, and bear a resemblance to him, being spirits, immaterial, immortal, and invisible, and are also righteous and holy in their nature, and are sometimes called Elohim; yet the image of God in man, differs in some things from theirs: as that part of it especially, which lies in his body, and in his connection with and dominion over the creatures; and yet he is not in such sense the image of God, as Jesus Christ the Son of God is, who is the image of the invisible God, yea, the express image of his Father's Person, having the same divine nature and perfections he has; but man, though there was in him some likeness and resemblance of some of the perfections of God; which are called his imitable ones, and by some communicable; as holiness, righteousness, wisdom, &c. yet these perfections are not really in him, only some faint shadows of them, at least not in the manner and proportion they are in God, in whom they are infinite, in man finite; and though the renewed and spiritual image of God in regenerate persons, which is of an higher and more excellent kind than the natural image of God in Adam, is called a partaking of the *divine nature*, 2 Pet. i. 4. yet not to be understood as if any partook of the nature and essence of God, and the perfections of it; only that that is wrought in them, and impressed on them, which bears some resemblance to the divine nature.

The seat of the image of God in man, is

---

[12] Moreh Nevochim, par. 1. c. 1.
[13] So Plato de Republ. l. 6. p. 682, from Homer, represents the human form as Θεοειδης, for Homer often speaks of one man and another as Θεοεικελος and Θεοειδης, Iliad. 1. v. 131. and 2. 623. and 3. 16.

and 6. 290. Eurysus the Pythagorean says, that the Maker in making man used himself as an exemplar, Apud Clement. Alex. Stromat. l. 5. p. 558.

the whole man, both body and soul; wherefore God is said to create *man* in his image; not the soul only, nor the body only; but the whole man, Gen. i. 27. and v. 1. Even as the whole man, soul and body, are the seat of the new and spiritual image of God in regeneration and sanctification; *The very God of peace sanctify you wholly;* which the apostle immediately explains of their *whole spirit, and soul and body*, being *preserved blameless unto the coming of our Lord Jesus Christ;* when and at the resurrection of the dead, the saints will most fully appear to *bear the image of the heavenly One*, 1 Thess. v. 23. 1 Cor. xv. 49.

First, The first man was made in the image of God in his *body* in some respect; hence this is given as a reason why the blood of a man's body is not to be shed, because, *In the image of God made he man*, Gen. ix. 6. though this image must not be thought to consist in the lineaments and figure of a man's body; this would be to conceive of him as altogether such an one as ourselves, and as the Anthropomorphites do; who, because they find bodily members ascribed to God in scripture, as eyes, hands, &c. fancy that he has a body like ours, and that our bodies are like his; but, as Job says, *Hast thou eyes of flesh?* Job x. 4. No; he has not; and the same may be observed of other members ascribed unto him; for we are not to entertain such gross notions of God as if he was corporeal, or that man was like unto him in the structure of his body; not but that there is something divine and majestic in the countenance of man, in comparison of brute creatures; and what is superexcellent to them, is the erectness of his posture, as has been before observed; which fits and directs him to look up to God, whereby he has a nearness to him, and communion with him, through which he becomes more like unto him. And it may be observed, that the perfections of God, many of them, are represented by the members of the human body; as his omniscience and all-seeing providence by *eyes*, which go to and fro throughout the whole earth. His omnipresence and close attention to the petitions of his people, and readiness to help and assist them, by *ears* open to their cries; and his might and power to deliver, protect, and defend them, by an *arm* and *hand;* and his pleasure and displeasure, by his *face* being towards good men, and against bad men; with others that might be added. Some qualities in the body of the first man, he had from God, which made him in some sense like unto him : such as *immortality;* for not only the soul of man breathed into him, was immortal, but his body also, as has been before observed; and in this there was in him some likeness to God, who only hath immortality, in the highest sense of it. Likewise *righteousness* and holiness, another branch of the divine image, as will be hereafter taken notice of; of which the body, as well as the soul, is the seat; for as that is defiled, since the fall, with the corruption of nature; so before, it was pure and holy; as when sanctified by the Spirit of God, it becomes a temple, in which he dwells; and particularly at the resurrection, when it is raised a powerful, incorruptible, spiritual, and glorious body, saints will then awake in the likeness of God, and appear to bear the image of the heavenly One, as in soul so in body; and whereas another branch of this image lies in dominion over the creatures, that is chiefly exercised by the organs of the body. To say no more, I see no difficulty in admitting it; that whereas all the members of Christ's human body were written and delineated in the book of God's eternal purposes and decrees, before they were fashioned, or were in actual being; and God prepared a body for him in covenant, agreeable thereunto; or it was concluded in it, he should assume such a body in the fulness of time, Psalm cxxxix. 16. Heb. x. 5. I say, I see no difficulty in admitting that the body of Adam was formed according to the idea of the body of Christ in the divine mind; and which may be the reason, at least in part, of that expression; *Behold, the man is*, or rather *was, as one of us;* and so as Eve was flesh of Adam's flesh, and bone of his bone, the members of Christ are also flesh of his flesh, and bone of his bone, Gen. iii. 22. and ii. 23. Eph. v. 30. But,

Secondly, The principal seat of the image of God in man, is the soul, which was immediately breathed of God into man, and so bears the greatest resemblance of him; and thus the spiritual image of God, enstamped in regeneration and renovation, is chiefly seated in the soul; *Be renewed in the spirit of your mind*, Eph. iv. 23. And this appears,

1. In the nature of the soul, which is spiritual, immaterial, immortal, and invisible, as God is; God is a Spirit, most simple and uncompounded; more so than any created spirit can be supposed to be;

yet the soul, which is often called a spirit, bears some likeness to him: he is expert of all matter, and only hath immortality; and so the soul is not a material being, but a spirit, it has not flesh and bones, as a body has; and is not capable of being brought to the dust of death, or to be killed; and as no man has seen God at any time, he is the King eternal, immortal, and invisible; so the soul is not to be seen; who ever saw his own soul, or the soul of another? Moreover, the soul carries some shadow of likeness to God in its powers and faculties, being endowed with understanding, will, and affections; which are, in some respects, similar to what is in God; or there is that in God which these are a faint resemblance of; and though it consists of various faculties, there is but one soul; as God, though his perfections are many, and his Persons three, yet there is but one God.

2. The image of God in the soul of man, of the first man particularly, appeared in the qualities of it; especially in its wisdom, knowledge, and understanding, and in its righteousness and holiness; for if the spiritual image in regeneration consists in these things, though in a higher and more excellent manner, and of a superior nature; it may be reasonably thought, the natural image of God in man consisted of these things in a natural way; see Col. iii. 10. Eph. iv. 24.

(1.) It lay in knowledge and understanding. Adam, in his state of innocence, had a large share of natural knowledge; he knew much of himself, both of the constitution of his body, and the powers of his mind; he knew much of the creatures made and given for his use, and over which he had the dominion, and to whom he gave names suitable to their nature; he had a large knowledge of God, as his Creator and Benefactor in a natural way, through the creatures; for if God, and the perfections of his nature, are in some measure to be known from his works by the light of nature, now man is fallen, and so as to be left without excuse; a much greater degree of knowledge of him, must man unfallen be supposed to have: and who, doubtless, had knowledge of a Trinity of Persons in the Godhead, since they were so manifestly concerned in the creation of all things, and particularly in his own; and this seems necessary, that he might yield that worship and adoration which was due from him to each of them; but then he knew nothing of Christ, as Mediator, Redeemer, and Saviour; this was not revealed to him until after his fall, nor did he need it before; on which it was made known to him, that the seed of the woman should bruise the serpent's head, and be the Saviour of him and his posterity: nor did he know any thing of pure, spiritual, and evangelic truths, and which were not suitable to the state in which he was; such as justification by the righteousness of Christ; pardon of sin through his blood; atonement by his sacrifice; and eternal life, as the free gift of God through him: these were things his eye had not seen, nor his ear heard of, nor did it enter into his heart to conceive of before his fall, and the revelation of them to him, which was made upon that; but then he knew all things necessary to be known by him; all things natural, moral, and civil; yea, he had some things revealed to him, and which he knew under a prophetic spirit; some things past, as the formation of Eve out of his rib; and, no doubt, his own formation, and the manner of it; and the whole creation, and the order of it, in six days; and other things to come, as that Eve should be the mother of all living; and that marriage, as it was appointed, would be continued in the world for the propagation of his species.

(2.) The image of God in Adam, further appeared in that rectitude, righteousness, and holiness, in which he was made; for *God made man upright;* a holy and righteous creature, Eccles. vii. 29. which holiness and righteousness were, in their kind, perfect; his understanding was free from all error and mistakes; his will biassed to that which is good; his affections flowed in a right channel, towards their proper objects; and there were no sinful motions and evil thoughts in his heart; nor any propensity and inclination to that which is evil; and the whole of his conduct and behaviour was according to the will of God. And this righteousness of his was *natural*, and not personal and acquired; it was not obtained by the exercise of his free will; it was lost, but not got that way; had it been personal, and acquired by his own power, and made up of acts of his own, when lost, it would only have been lost for himself; and his posterity would have had no concern in it; but it was the righteousness of his nature, it was concreated, or created with it, and so common to it; and had he stood in it, would have been propagated to his posterity; but, on the contrary, he sinning, whereby his nature was defiled, a corrupt nature is propagated instead of it. The *papists*, and those of the same complexion with them, say that Adam was created in his pure naturals; their meaning is, that he was created neither holy nor unholy; neither righteous nor unrighteous; but capable of being either the one or the other, as he made use of the power of his free-will. This notion is advanced in favour of man's free-will, and to weaken the doctrine of original sin.

(3.) This image also lies in the freedom of the will, and the power of it. As God is a free agent, so is man; and as the freedom of the divine will does not lie in an indifference and indetermination to good and evil, but is only to that which is good; so was the will of man in his state of integrity: as likewise the will of the good angels and glorified saints. And man had a power to obey the will of God, and do his commands; and as he had not only a positive law given him to abstain from the forbidden fruit, as a trial of his obedience; so he had the moral law written on his heart, as the rule of his obedience, and had power and ability to keep it; for as it was required of him to love the Lord his God with all his heart, and soul, and strength; so he could, if he would, have performed the same; and such strength and ability were due unto him, from the laws of creation; for if God required of him obedience to his holy law, it was but fit and right that he should give him a conformity of nature and will to it, and power to obey it; though he was not obliged to give him grace and strength to persevere, nor to render him impeccable and immutable; wherefore, leaving him to the mutability of his will, he sinned, and fell from his former estate, which on that account is called *vanity*, Psalm xxxix. 5.

3. The image of God in the whole man, soul and body, or in his person, lay in his immortality, natural to his soul, and conferred on his body; and also in his dominion over the creatures; for this was the end God proposed in the creation of him, that he might have dominion over the beasts of the field, the fowls of the air, and the fishes of the sea; and accordingly all were put in subjection to him; see Gen. i. 26, 28. Psalm viii. 6, 7, 8. in which he resembled God, the Governor of the universe; and hence kings, governors, and civil magistrates are called gods, because they bear such a likeness to him, Psalm lxxxii. 6.

4. And lastly: this image lay in the blessedness of man, in his original state; for as God is God over all and blessed, and is the blessed and only Potentate; so man, in a lower sense, was blessed above all the creatures; having an healthful constitution, an immortal body, and every thing grateful and suitable to it; and a soul knowing, wise, holy, just, and good; and be placed in the most delightful spot in the whole globe, with all the profusion of nature about him, and all creatures subject to him, enjoying communion with God, through the creatures, though but in a natural way; and God was pleased sometimes to appear to him, and talk with him; and yet man, being thus in honour, abode not long, but became like the beasts that perish; so that we may look back and see from what an high estate man is fallen, and to what a low estate sin has brought him, by means of which he is come short of the image and glory of God, in which he was created; and yet may adore the grace and wisdom of God, which has brought us into a more excellent state by Christ; a state more spiritual, firm, and secure. Adam's knowledge was natural knowledge; his holiness and righteousness natural holiness and righteousness; the covenant made with him a natural covenant; the communion he had with God was in a natural way; and all his benefits and blessings natural ones: but believers in Christ are blessed with all spiritual blessings in him; and have a spiritual image enstamped upon them, which can never be lost; and into which they are changed from glory to glory, till it becomes perfect.

CHAP. IV.

OF THE PROVIDENCE OF GOD.

THE next eternal work of God is *Providence;* by which all the creatures God has made are preserved, governed, guided, and directed. The word itself is never used of the divine Being syllabically, or in so many syllables in scripture; yet the thing itself, or what is meant by it, is fully declared and clearly expressed; as, that God upholds all things by his power; governs the world by his wisdom; looks down upon the earth, takes notice and care of all his creatures in it, and makes provision for them, and guides and directs them to answer the ends for which they were made; which is the sum and substance of Providence: nor need we abstain from the use of the word on that account, since there are many other words used to express Christian doctrines, not to be found in the Bible, though the things expressed by them are, as trinity, satisfaction, &c. nor because it is taken from the school of Plato, who is said [1] to be the first that made mention of the providence of God in so many words, as he often [2] does: nor because used by the Stoic philosophers, and other heathens, who have wrote and spoken well of divine providence. It is once used in scripture, of the civil administration of a Roman governor, Felix, by Tertullus the orator, when he pleaded before him against the apostle Paul, whom he compliments on the *great quietness* the Jews enjoyed under his government, and *the very worthy deeds done unto* their *nation by* his *providence*, Acts xxiv. 3. that is, by his wise and prudent administration of government, and the provident care he took of the peace and welfare of the Jewish nation; as he would be understood. And if the word may be used of such an administration of government; or of that of a civil magistrate; then much more of the great Governor of the world, whose is the kingdom of the whole world, and he is the Governor among the nations; whose kingdom rules over all, and who does according to his will and pleasure in heaven and in earth; and does all things well and wisely.

Providence, of which we are now about to treat, must be considered as distinct from prævidence, prævision, prescience, foresight, foreknowledge, and predestination; which all respect some act in the divine mind in eternity; and are no other than the eternal purposes and decrees of God, who foresaw and foreknew all persons and things that would be; he determining within himself that they should be; for *known unto him* were *all his works from the beginning*, or from eternity; even all that would be done in time, from the beginning to the end of the world; he knew they would be, because he decreed they should be; this may be called eternal providence, virtual providence, providence in purpose; but providence in time, which is what is now under consideration and may be called actual providence, is the execution of whatsoever God has foreknown and determined; *Who worketh all things after the counsel of his will*, Eph. i. 11. the eternal will of God is the rule of his conduct in providence according to which he proceeds in it; and his wisdom, which fixed his will, and therefore said to be the counsel of his will, presides, guides, and directs in the execution of it; which execution of it is called his working; wherefore providence is to be reckoned as his work. The wise man says, *There is a time to every purpose under the heaven;* whatever is done under the heavens in time, there was a purpose for it in eternity; and for the execution of that purpose a time was fixed; and at that time it is brought about by the providence of God; who *makes every thing beautiful in his time;* in the time and season in which he appointed it to be done, Eccles. iii. 1, 11. Purpose and providence exactly tally and answer to each other; the one is the fulfilment of the other; *Surely, as I have thought,* saith the Lord, *so shall it come to pass; and as I have purposed, so shall it stand,* Isa. xiv. 24.

The providence of God is not only expressed in scripture, by his sustaining, upholding, and preserving all things; and by his government of the world, and the execution of his purposes; but by his looking down upon the earth, and the inhabitants of it; taking a prospect of them, and notice of their ways, and works, and actions, and dealing with them according to them; *The Lord looked down from heaven upon the children of men,* &c. Psalm xiv. 2. and xxxiii. 13, 14. The providence of God may be argued from, and illustrated by the senses which he imparts to men, for their good, preservation, and safety; particularly those of hearing and seeing. He has placed the eyes and the ears in the head of the human body, to look out after and listen to what may turn to the advantage or disadvantage of the members of the body; hence the Psalmist reasons, *He that planted the ear, shall he not hear? he that formed the eye, shall he not see?* He must needs hear all that is said, and see all that is done in the world, and must know and take notice of all persons in it, their works, their words, and even their very thoughts; as it follows; *The Lord knoweth the thoughts of men, that they are vanity,* Psalm xciv. 9, 10, 11. All which is observed, to convince such brutish and ignorant people, who act as if they disbelieved the providence of God, ver. 3—8.

The words *provide* and *providing,* are

---

[1] Vid. Laert. 1. 3. in Vita Platonis.

[2] In Timæo et Phædro, et alibi.

sometimes used of men in general, and of masters of families in particular, who are to *provide things honest in the sight of all men*, both for themselves and for all under their care; and, *If any provide not for his own, he is worse than an infidel*, Rom. xii. 17. 1 Tim. v. 8. and which provision, incumbent on such persons, may give us an idea of the providence of God; in that branch of it particularly, which concerns the provision which he, as the great Master of his family, throughout the whole universe, makes for it, even from the greatest to the least; *The eyes of all wait upon thee, and thou givest them their meat in due season; thou openest thine hand, and satisfiest the desire of every living thing*, Psalm cxlv. 15, 16. see Psalm civ. 27, 28. even the very ravens and their young, such mean and worthless creatures, are provided for by him; *Who provideth for the raven his food, when his young ones cry unto God?* Job xxxviii. 41. see Luke xii. 24. and how much more does he not, and will he not provide for rational creatures? It was an instance of great ingratitude and unbelief in the Israelites, that after many tokens of divine goodness to them, they questioned the power of God to take care of them; saying, *Can God furnish a table in the wilderness?——Can he give bread also?——Can he provide flesh for his people?* Yes, he could and did for six hundred thousand Israelites, besides women and children; and he can and does provide food for all creatures, rational and irrational; and he can and does provide for men, what is necessary for them, when in the greatest extremity. From God's providing a sacrifice in the room of Isaac, when just going to be slain on mount Moriah, it became a proverbial expression in after times, *In the mount of the Lord it shall be seen;* or, *the Lord will appear;* or, *will provide*, and grant supplies, and deliver out of difficulties, Gen. xxii. 8, 14. and from the provision which God makes for all his creatures, as the great Master of the family, Providence, which with the heathens was reckoned as a deity, is represented like a good housewife, or mistress of a family, administering to the whole universe, and was pictured like a grave elderly matron,[3] and this is one of the titles of the goddess Minerva.[4]

Once more: the providence of God is expressed by his *care* of his creatures; *Doth God take care of oxen?* 1 Cor. ix. 9. He does, and even of creatures inferior to them; and much more then of those who are superior to them; even of all rational creatures; and especially of them that believe; who therefore are encouraged to be *casting all* their *care upon him, for he careth for them*, 1 Pet. v. 7. It is particularly said of the land of Canaan, that it was *a land which the Lord careth for;* from one end of the year to the other, Deut. xi. 12. and it is true of the whole world in general, that God cares for it, and all creatures in it; not only from year to year, and from age to age, but from the beginning of the world to the end of it. Now God's sustentation of the world, his government of it, the view and notice he takes of it, the provision he makes for all creatures in it, and his care of and concern for them; this is providence. And now, having considered the name and thing, and what is meant by it, I shall proceed,

I. To prove a divine providence, by which all things are upheld, governed, guided, and directed. And,

1. This appears from the light of nature; for as by that it may be known that there is a God who has created all things; so by the same that there is a providence that superintends, orders, and disposes all things. Hence the heathens held a providence; all nations, even the most barbarous;[5] all the sects of the philosophers owned it, but one, the Epicureans, and that from a foolish notion that it was unworthy of God, affected his happiness, and interrupted his peace and quiet. Pythagoras[6] asserted, there is a kindred between God and men; and that God exercises a providence over us. Plato[7] gives this reason for his being the soul of the universe, or why he thought that was a living creature, because it was under the providence of God; and it is affirmed by the Stoics,[8] that the world is inhabited by the mind and providence of God; the mind dispensing and administering through every part of it, as the soul in us; and that God governs the world by his providence, and all things in it. Seneca wrote a book on providence, in which he says,[9] providence presides over all, and God is in the midst of us. Menedemus,

---

[3] Vid. Chartarium de Imag. Deorum, p. 8, 9.
[4] Pausan. Phocica, sive l. 10. p. 623.
[5] Ællan. Var. Hist. l. 2. c. 81.
[6] Laert. in Vita Pythagor.
[7] In Timæo. fol. 30.
[8] Laert. l. 7. in Vita Zenonis. Arrian. Epictet. l. 2. c. 14.
[9] De Providentia, c. 1.

the philosopher, was an advocate for the doctrine of providence.[10] Chrysippus wrote on the same subject also.[11] They are the words of Cicero,[12] that by the providence of God, the world and all the parts of it, were both constituted at the beginning, and administered by it at all times: and the apostle Paul, in a discourse of his before the philosophers at Athens, concerning God and his providence, produces a passage from Aratus, one of their own poets, in proof of the same; *We are also his offspring*, Acts xvii. 28. his creatures, his children, and his care; in whom we live, move, and have our being. Even God's sustentation of irrational creatures, his preservation of them, and the provision he makes for them, prove a providence; wherefore Job, chap. xii. 7—10. sends his friends to them to learn this; *Ask now the beasts, and they shall teach thee*, &c.

2. Divine providence may be concluded from the Being of God; the same arguments that prove the one prove the other; if there is a God, there is a providence; and if there is a providence, there is a God; these mutually prove each other; as he is a fool that says there is no God, he is equally a fool that says there is no providence: these are closely connected together and cannot be the one without the other; wherefore, when the Psalmist had observed, that *the fool said in his heart, there is no God*, he immediately observes the providence of God; *The Lord looked down from the heaven upon the children of men*, Psalm xiv. 1. 2. And such in all ages who have denied a providence, have been looked upon as atheists. Hence Cicero[13] observes of Epicurus, that though he made use of the word God in his philosophy, that he might not offend the Athenians; yet in reality removed him from it. And the same writer[14] thus reasons, If it is granted there is a God, it must be owned, that the administration of the world is by his counsel; and again, those who allow there is a God, must confess that he does something, and something famous and excellent; and nothing is more excellent than the administration of the world; and therefore it must be by his counsel. And to me, says Lucilius,[15] he that does nothing, (as such Epicurus makes God to do) seems entirely not to be, to have no being; so closely connected are God and his providence, according to the reasoning of this wise heathen: the oracle of Apollo, at Miletus, calls providence the first-born of God:[16] and it is easy to observe, that the Lord puts the idolatrous heathens upon proving the truth of the deities they worshipped, by acts of providence; by declaring things past; foretelling things to come; and by doing good or evil; bestowing good things on their votaries, and avenging their enemies; all which he claims to himself, and which could not be proved to belong to them; and therefore no deities; for a deity without foresight, and without forecast, unactive and impotent to do good or evil, to reward or chastise men, could be no deity; see Isa. xli. 22, 23. and xlii. 8, 9. and xliii. 9. and xlvi. 9, 10.

3. The providence of God may be argued from the creation of the world; as the Being of God may be proved from thence, so the providence of God; for if the world was created by him, it must be upheld by him; for as it could not make itself, so neither could it sustain itself; the same power that was requisite to create it, is necessary to uphold it; and therefore it may be observed, that creation and conservation, which is one branch of providence, are closely joined together, Col. i. 16, 17. see also Nehem. ix. 6. Heb. i. 2, 3. God, the great builder of all things, does not act by them as an architect, that builds an house and has no further concern with it, but leaves it to stand or fall of itself; or that builds a ship, and has nothing more to do with it; he takes the government of it, and steers and directs it; he that is the Creator of the world, is the Governor of it; the Creator is not one, and the governor another, but the same; and is as equal to the government of it, as to the creation of it; and creation gives him a right to govern; and without his support and government of it, it could not long subsist: besides, there must be some ends for which it is created; which ends it cannot attain and answer of itself; but must be directed and influenced by the Creator of it. Wherefore,

4. The perfections of God, and the display of them, make a providence necessary,

---

[10] Tertullian. Apolog. c. 18.
[11] A. Gell. Noct. Attic. 1. 6. c. 1. Laert. 1. 7. in Vita Zeno.
[12] De Natura Deorum, 1. 2.
[13] Epicurus re tollit, oratione relinquit Deos, ibid. 1. 1. in fine.
[14] De Natura Deorum, 1. 2.
[15] In Cicero. ibid.
[16] Apud Lactant. 1. 7. c. 13.

particularly his power, wisdom, and goodness: since God has created the world, had he not supported it, but left it to chance and fortune, it would have seemed as if he could not have supported it; then where had been the greatness of his power, and the glory of it, who is said to be the Almighty? and since he made it with some views, and to answer some ends, had it not been influenced, guided, and directed by him, to answer these ends; where had been the wisdom of him, who is called the all-wise and the only-wise God? and to make a world of creatures, and then neglect them, and take no care of them, where would have been his goodness? Whereas, the whole earth is full of it; and he is good to all his creatures; and his tender mercies are over all his works; so that from these perfections of God, we may be assured of his providence.

5. It may be concluded from the worship of God; which this is a powerful inducement to, and the ground of. The Being of God is the object of worship; and his providence is the basis of it: without this there would be no fear of God, no reverence for him, no adoration of him: the two main branches of worship are prayer and praise; but if God has no regard to his creatures, and they receive nothing from him, nor have an expectation of any from him, what have they to pray to him for? or what to praise him for? Nor what have they to fear from him, if they have no connection with him, and are not accountable to him? Hence Cicero,[17] an heathen, could say, "There are some philosophers, (meaning the Epicureans) who suppose that God takes no care at all of human affairs; but, says he, if this is true, what piety can there be? what sanctity? what religion?" Wherefore they are the libertines of the age, who in any period, as the followers of Epicurus, deny the providence of God; and this they do, that they may have the reins loose on their own necks, and be under no restraint, but at liberty to indulge to the gratification of every sensual lust; such were those of that cast among the Jews, who said, *The Lord hath forsaken the earth; and the Lord seeth not;* and therefore we may do as we please; there is none to observe what we do, nor to call us to an account for it; *The Lord will not do good, nor will he do evil;* neither bestow favours on good men, nor correct and punish evil men, Ezek. ix. 9. Zeph. i. 12. And hence, because it has been observed, that good men are afflicted, and wicked men prosper, which some have improved into an argument against divine providence, which will be considered hereafter; this has been inferred from it, that it is in vain to serve God, and no profit to keep his ordinances, Mal. iii. 14, 15.

6. The settled and constant order of things, from the beginning of the world to this time, clearly evince a divine Providence; the ordinances of the heavens, of the sun, moon, and stars,[18] have never departed from their stated and fixed order and appointment; nor the covenant of the day and of the night ever been broken, Jer. xxxi. 35. and xxxiii. 20. the sun goes forth every morning, like a giant to run his race; takes his circuit from one end of the heavens to the other, and with great exactness observes his rising and setting, and makes every day in the year; and who also performs his annual course with great precision, and who also finishes every returning year; and this course he has constantly ran almost six thousand years: can this be thought to be the effect of chance, and not of an all-wise, all-powerful, and all-disposing Providence, which has so long supported it in its being, supplied it with light and heat, given and continued its motion unto this day? the constant revolution of night and day; and of the seasons of the year; of seed-time and harvest; of cold and heat; and of summer and winter, are standing and perpetual proofs of a divine providence; since these take place every year in their order, throughout the whole world, according to the different climates of it. Were there only now and then an instance of such an order of things, it might not deserve so much notice; but that it should be constant and continued, can never surely be thought to be the sports of chance and fortune; and especially when it is observed, that so much, and things of the greatest importance, depend upon such a constant revolution of them, with respect to the welfare of mankind. Every year, in the winter-season, grass, herbs, and plants, wither and seem to die; trees are stripped of all

---

[17] De Natura Deorum, 1. 1.
[18] Supervacuum est in præsentia ostendere, non sine aliquo custode tantum opus stare, nec nunc fiderum certum discursum fortuiti impetus esse, Seneca de Providentia, c. I.

their fruit and verdure, and look as if they were dead; when, in the returning spring, which never fails to come, there is a reproduction of all these, a sort of a new creation of them; *Thou sendest forth thy Spirit; they are created, and thou renewest the face of the earth*, Psalm civ. 30. Can this be observed, as it may with amazement, and a Providence denied! To all which may be added, the constant succession of men in all ages; *One generation passeth away, and another generation cometh*, Eccles. i. 4. so that the earth is continually replenished with inhabitants, notwithstanding so many are daily taken off by death, in various shapes. All which can never be without an all-wise disposing Providence.

7. Were there not a supporting and superintending providence concerned in the world, and the things of it, all would soon fall into confusion and destruction. If God, that has hung the earth upon nothing, without any support than his own power, was to withdraw his hand and let go his hold, it would drop into its original chaos, into Tohu and Bohu;[19] the earth, and the inhabitants of it, would soon and easily be dissolved, did not the Lord bear up the pillars of it, Psalm lxxv. 3. and where anarchy takes place, and no government is, there is confusion and every evil work. In families, in bodies of men gathered tumultuously together, and in towns, cities, kingdoms, and states, where there is no head, no governor, none to preside, guide, and direct, dissipation and ruin quickly ensue; and so it would be with the world in general, if not governed and superintended by a divine providence. The founding of kingdoms and states, and the setting up of political government in the world, are a proof of divine providence; and one way and means by which it is exercised, as will be seen hereafter; and even the erection of the great monarchies of the earth, Babylonian, Persian, Grecian, and Roman, and the dissolution of them, shew a divine providence: those monarchies could never have risen to the height they did, nor come to the destruction they have, but by that providence *that removeth kings and setteth up kings* at pleasure, Dan. ii. 21.

8. The many blessings of goodness, the daily benefits and favours, which are continually bestowed by God on his creatures, manifestly declare his providence; all creatures partake of his goodness, he is kind to the unthankful and to the evil, he makes his sun to rise on the evil and on the good, and sends rain on the just and on the unjust; he has not left himself without a witness of his providential goodness in any age to any people, Jews or Gentiles, in that he has done good unto them, given them rain and fruitful seasons, filling their hearts with food and gladness, Luke vi. 35. Matt. v. 45. Acts xiv. 17.

9. The judgments of God in the earth, at different periods of time, are a demonstration of the providence of God. Who can believe that the universal deluge, the sweeping away of a world of ungodly men by a flood, and saving eight persons only in an ark, were the effects of chance, and not of providence? and that the burning of Sodom and Gomorrah, with the cities of the plain, by fire and brimstone from heaven, was by accident, as a common fire is sometimes said to be? the same may be observed of the plagues of Egypt, the drowning of Pharaoh and his host in the Red Sea, the captivities of the Israelites, the destruction of their neighbours, the Moabites, Edomites, &c. so that the name of one of them is not to be found in the world, as was foretold; when they, though scattered up and down in it, are yet preserved. The earthquakes, famine, pestilence, fire and sword, which are frequently in the world, shew a divine providence; for God is *known by the judgments which he executeth*, Psalm ix. 16.

10. The fears of punishment and hopes of reward in men, shew the consciousness they have of the notice God takes of them and their actions, which is one branch of providence. Their fears, either of judgments coming upon them now, or of a future judgment, at which Felix trembled when he heard of it, plainly declare their sense of a divine Being, and of his knowledge of their conduct and behaviour, and resentment of it; who they justly fear will punish them for it, here or hereafter; why else were some of the Roman Cæsars, as Augustus, Tiberius, and Caligula, so terribly frighted at thunder and lightning; but because they were convinced there was a God in the heavens, from whence they came, who saw and knew all their wicked actions, and to whom they were accountable? and this is to be observed, more or less, in all man-

---

[19] Vis illum (custodem rectoremque universi) providentiam dicere? recte dices; est enim cujus consilio huic mundo providetur ut inconcussus eat, et actus suos explicet. Seneca, Nat. Quæst. l. 2. c. 45.

kind; whose consciences accuse or excuse, according to their actions; if evil, their minds are filled with dread, and a fearful expectation of wrath and vengeance; if good, they entertain hopes of receiving good things here, and better hereafter; which is a clear proof from men themselves, and they are obliged to own it, and say, *Verily, there is a reward for the righteous; verily, he is a God that judgeth in the earth,* Psalm lviii. 11. I proceed,

II. To observe some distinctions which have been used by some, and may be useful to explain and confirm the doctrine of providence.

1st, Providence may be considered as *immediate* and *mediate.* 1. Immediate providence, is what is exercised by God of himself, without the use of any mean, instrument, or second cause: thus the world is upheld by himself, by his own power, without the intervention of any other; and every creature, as to its being and subsistence, is immediately dependent upon him; in whom all live, move, and have their being, Heb. i. 3. Acts xvii. 24. God sometimes works without means, as when he made the earth fruitful before any rain, or dew, or mist, fell upon it, or before there was any man to till it, Gen. ii. 5, 6. and as he supported the body of Moses in the mount, and of Christ in the wilderness, without food, for the space of forty days and forty nights; and as he sometimes has wrought salvation in the midst of the earth; which is one branch of providence; and has given victory over enemies without fighting, as to the Israelites at the Red Sea; to the same, in the times of Joshua, before the walls of Jericho; and in the times of Gideon over the Midianites; and in the days of Jehosaphat over the Ammonites, and others. Sometimes he works over and above means, and what means cannot reach unto, which exceeds the power of nature; of this kind are all miraculous operations; such as those wrought in Egypt; and by Christ and his apostles; as turning water into wine; and multiplying a little food for the supply of multitudes. Yea, God works sometimes contrary to the nature of things, of means, and second causes; as when he caused waters, which naturally flow or stand, to rise up and become heaps, and divide, and be as a wall, to the right and left, as the waters of the Red Sea and Jordan were to the Israelites, and through which they passed as on dry land; and as when he caused the sun, which naturally goes forth and forward as a giant to run his race, to stand still, as in the days of Joshua; and to go back ten degrees on the dial of Ahaz, in the times of Hezekiah; and he suffered not fire to burn, which it naturally does, combustible things; even not so much as to singe the garments of Daniel's three companions, when cast into a furnace of fire; and to cause lions, naturally voracious, to shut their mouths and not touch Daniel, when cast into their den. All which God sometimes does; that is, acts immediately, and without the use of means, and even above them, and contrary to them; to shew that he is not tied to means and second causes; and that his people, those that trust in him, may not despair when things are at the worst, and there appears no way of deliverance; but to exercise faith in the God of providence, who is all-wise and all-powerful, and can and will appear for them, and be seen in the mount of difficulties; see Dan. iii. 16, 17.——2. Mediate providence is what is exercised in the use of means, or by them; and which God does, not from any defect of power in him; but, as Dr. Ames[20] observes, because of the abundance of his goodness, that he might communicate, as it were, some dignity of efficiency to the creatures; and in them make his own efficiency the more discernible: hence it may be observed, that he sometimes makes use of means to produce great and noble effects, which are unlikely, and for which they do not seem to have any aptitude; as when, with a small army, an handful of men, comparatively speaking, he gives victory over a large one; for there is no restraint or hinderance to him; and it is nothing with him to save by many or by few; and whether with many, or with them that have no power, 1 Sam. xiv. 6. 2 Chron. xiv. 11. and xxiv. 24. see 1 Cor. i. 27, 28. And sometimes he makes proper means ineffectual to answer the end of them, and for which they seem to be well adapted; for what seems more for the safety of a king and his country than a well-mounted cavalry, and a well-disciplined and numerous army? and yet these are sometimes of no service, and are vain things for safety, Psalm xxxiii. 16, 17. And what more fit to support the lives of men, and to refresh and nourish when hungry, than wholesome food? yet

---

[20] Medulla Theolog. l. i. c. 9. s. 6.

men may eat, and not have enough, or be nourished by it, Hos. iv. 10. Indeed, ordinarily God does work by means; he makes the earth fruitful by snow and rain descending upon it; whereby it gives seed to the sower, and bread to the eater; produces grass for cattle, and herb for the service of men; with other necessaries of life. There is a chain of second causes that depend upon the first, and are influenced by it, and act in subordination to one another; the Lord hears the heavens, and the heavens hear the earth, and the earth hears the corn, and the wine, and the oil, and they hear Jezreel, Hos. ii. 21, 22. And usually God supplies and supports the bodies of men by mean sof food, the whole stay of bread, and the whole stay of water, by giving a blessing thereunto. And he exercises his providence, commonly by the use of means, to shew men that they are to make use of means, and not slight them; no, not even when events are certain to them; as the cases of Hezekiah and Paul's mariners shew, Isaiah xxxviii. 21. Acts xxvii. 31. Yet means, or second causes, are never to be depended on; but the first Cause is to be looked unto for success, and to him the glory is to be given, Psalm cxv. 1, 2, 3. and cxxvii. 1, 2.

2*dly*, Providence may be considered both as *ordinary* and *extraordinary.*——1. Ordinary providence is what is exercised in the common course of means, and by the chain of second causes; and according to the original law of nature impressed on beings from the beginning. From this law, the ordinances of heaven, the sun, moon, and stars, have not departed, except in extraordinary cases; and the revolutions of day and night, and of the seasons of the year, are constantly and regularly observed; and all things act and move by an inclination of nature settled in them; fire burns, and sparks fly upwards; heavy bodies descend, and light ones ascend; in animate and irrational creatures there is an instinct of nature suitable to their natures, by which they are guided and directed, and do not ordinarily swerve from it; and even in inanimate creatures, as the meteors of the air, snow, rain, hail, &c. there is an obediential power and influence, by which they perform the will of their Creator, and answer the ends for which they were made, Psalm cxlviii. 8.——2. Extraordinary providence is that in which God goes out of his common way; and which consists of miraculous operations, as before observed, such as exceed the power of nature; as when he ordered rocks to be smitten, and waters gushed out to supply the Israelites, their flocks and their herds; and rained manna about their tents every morning in the week, excepting one, by which he supported them near forty years in a wilderness; and so the prophet Elijah, though the food he was fed with was ordinary and common, yet it was in an extraordinary manner that he was furnished with it; ravens brought him bread and flesh morning and evening, whilst he was by the brook Cherith; and he was supplied with food at Zarephath, in a widow's house, through the very extraordinary multiplication of an handful of meal in a barrel, and a little oil in a cruse; and when in a wilderness, had a cake baked for him by an angel, and a cruse of water set at his head, of which he eat and drank; and in the strength of which he travelled forty days and forty nights, 1 Kings xvii. 6, 12—16. and xix. 5—8.

3*dly*, Providence may be considered as *universal* and *singular;* or, as general and particular.——1. Universal or general providence, is what is concerned with the whole world, and all things in it; and is expressed by upholding and preserving all things that are created; it is God's sustentation, preservation, and continuance of creatures in their being; this is acknowledged by some, who yet do not agree to ——2. A singular or particular providence, as concerned with every individual, and especially with rational creatures and their actions. But most certain it is, that God not only in his providence is concerned for the world in general, but for all individuals in it; every star in the heavens is known by him, taken notice of, and preserved; *He bringeth out their host by number; he calleth them all by names——for that he is strong in power; not one faileth,* Isa. xl. 26. the cattle on a thousand hills, and the thousands of cattle on those hills, are known and provided for by him; and so are all the fowls of the air, and of the mountains; and even a sparrow does not fall to the ground without his notice and will, Psalm l. 10. 11. Matt. x. 29. And he looks down upon all the inhabitants of the earth, and considers their ways, and works, and actions, Psalm xxxiii. 13, 14, 15. The sentiments of the Stoic philosophers come the nearest to those of divine revelation, concerning this matter; which,

CHAP. IV. OF THE PROVIDENCE OF GOD.

according to Cicero,[21] are, that not only mankind in general, but that singulars, or individuals, are cared and provided for by the immortal gods: and yet Seneca,[22] one of that sect, says, that the gods take a greater care of universals than of singulars; and elsewhere, that they take care of mankind in general, and *sometimes* are careful of singulars,[23] as if they were not always careful of them; and Cicero,[24] though he represents Balbus the Stoic, as saying that the gods take care of singulars; yet with this exception, that with respect to some externals, they take care of great things, but neglect small ones. Sallustius,[25] the Cynic philosopher, is very express; he says, Providence and fate, as they are concerned about nations and cities, so about every man; and so Plato[26] strongly argues, that the providence of God is concerned about less as well as greater matters; and according to the christian doctrine, as will be seen hereafter; not only men, but the most minute things, are under the notice of providence.

4thly, Providence may be considered as both *common* and *special*. Common providence is that which belongs to the whole world, and all the creatures in it, and to all mankind, and is exercised in the common and ordinary way; for God is *good to all, and his tender mercies are over all his works*, Psalm cxlv. 9. *Special* providence is what concerns the church of God in all ages. The Jewish church, under the former dispensation, was distinguished from all the people of the earth, and chosen to be a special and peculiar people, and had special favours bestowed upon them; and the Christian church, under the gospel dispensation, was particularly cared for at the beginning of it, and remarkably increased and preserved under the persecution of the heathen emperors; and which has been, and will be, nourished for a time, and times, and half a time, in the wilderness, during the reign of antichrist, and then will become great and glorious. Moreover God, as the God of providence, is the Saviour and Preserver of all men; but especially of *them that believe*, 1 Tim. iv. 10. And the providence respecting God's elect will be particularly considered hereafter.

5thly, Providence may be considered as real and moral: real, is what concerns things, and the essence of them, by which they are sustained and preserved. Moral providence, or what is commonly called God's moral government of the world, respects rational creatures, angels, and men, to whom God has given a law, as the rule of their actions, which consists of precepts and prohibitions, the sanctions of which are promises and threatenings; and it is explained and enforced by instructions, persuasions, admonitions, &c. and according to which reasonable law, a reasonable service is required of reasonable creatures. God deals with them as their works and actions appear to be. Of this providence of God, respecting angels and men, especially in their first estates, and change of them, a particular notice will be taken of in some following chapters. I shall next observe,

III. The Author of providence, the efficient Cause of it, and the instruments made use of by him in the administration of it. God, that is in the heavens, and looks down upon the earth, does in it whatever he pleases; he sitteth King for ever, and his kingdom rules over all. Elihu puts such a question as this, *Who hath disposed the whole world?* Job xxxiv. 13. the answer to it must be, He that made it has a right to dispose it, and of all things in it; and he does dispose thereof according to his pleasure; *All things are of him*, in creation; and all things are *through him*, in providence; and all things are *to him*, directed and ordered to his glory, Rom. xi. 36. God, Father, Son, and Spirit, are the one efficient Cause and Author of providence. God, the Father of Christ; *My Father worketh hitherto;* not in creation, for the works of creation were finished in six days; and then God ceased from his work; but in providence, in which he worked from the beginning of the world to the time of Christ on earth; and continued to work; for he says not, my Father hath worked, but *worketh*, continues to work in a providential way; for the work of providence is his work; *Who worketh all things after the counsel of his will*, Eph. i. 11. which is said of the God and Father of our Lord Jesus; who has blessed his people in Christ, chosen them in him, and predestinated them by him to the adoption of children; and who is spoken of all along in the

---

[21] De Natura Deorum, 1. 2. prope finem.
[22] De Providentia, c. 3.
[23] Epist. 95.
[24] Ut supra.

[25] De Diis, c. 9.
[26] De Legibus, 1. 10. p. 95, &c. in Epinomide, p. 1008.

context to the passage cited. Our Lord addresses his Father as *the Lord of heaven and earth*, the Maker and Possessor of both and Governor of them, when he is speaking of a sovereign act of his in providence; hiding some things from the wise and prudent, and revealing them to babes; and adds, *All things are delivered unto me of my Father*, to subserve the ends of his mediatorial kingdom in a providential way, Matt. xi. 25, 26, 27.

Christ, the Son of God, is equally concerned with his divine Father in the work of providence; *My Father worketh hitherto*, as before observed; *and I work*, the same work jointly along with him; for *whatsoever things he* (the Father) *doth, those also doth the Son likewise*, John v. 17, 19. *By him all things consist;* are sustained, upheld, preserved, and supplied, and guided, to answer the ends for which they are created by him, Col. i. 16, 17. see Heb. i. 2, 3. Nor is the holy Spirit to be excluded from the work of providence, who had so great a concern in that of creation; the heavens were garnished by him; yea, the host of them were made by him; he moved upon the waters that covered the chaos, and brought it into a beautiful form and order; and several of the works of providence are particularly ascribed to him; the renovation and reproduction of things every returning spring are ascribed to him; *Thou sendest forth thy Spirit, and they are created; thou renewest the face of the earth*, Psalm civ. 30. The government of the world, and the ordering and disposing of all things in it, are attributed to him, without the counsel and direction of others; *Who hath directed the Spirit of the Lord*, &c. or, *being his counsellor, hath taught him?* &c. Isa. xl. 13, 14. And he that is so much concerned in the regeneration, conversion, and sanctification of men, and has been in all ages of the world, with which the affairs of providence are so closely connected in numberless instances, can never be shut out of the administration of them. Father, Son, and Spirit, are the efficient cause of providence; and to whom, and not to fate, fortune, and chance, are all things in it to be ascribed. The instruments God makes use of in the administration of providence are many; some of the principal of which are as follow:

1. Angels, good and bad. Good angels are the ministers of God that do his pleasure; these stand continually before him, wait his orders, hearken to the voice of his commandments, and are ready to perform any service he shall enjoin them, or send them to do; *These are the four spirits of the heavens, which go forth from standing before the Lord of all the earth*, into the several parts of the world, when sent by him, to execute his will and pleasure; they are *ministering spirits, sent forth to minister for them who are heirs of salvation;* to guard and protect them, and do many good offices for them, as has been observed in a preceding chapter; see Psalm ciii. 19, 20. Zech. vi. 5. Heb. i. 14. Evil angels are also sometimes employed in the affairs of providence; either for the inflicting of punishment on wicked men, or for the correction and chastisement of the people of God. They were made use of in the plagues of Egypt; for the Psalmist says, God *cast* upon the *Egyptians the fierceness of his anger, wrath, and indignation, by sending evil angels among them*, Psalm lxxviii. 49. In the execution of what particular plagues they were concerned it is not easy to say; probably they were sent at the time of the plague of darkness, to terrify and affright, and add to the horror of that dreadful scene. An evil spirit offered himself to be a lying spirit, in the mouths of Ahab's prophets, which he had leave to be, and thereby brought about, in providence, the death of that prince, in a battle at Ramoth-Gilead, as was foretold, 1 Kings xxii. 21—34. Satan, the adversary of good men, obtained leave from the Lord, to destroy the substance, family, and health of Job; which was granted for the chastisement of him, and for the trial of his faith and patience. The same malicious spirit put it into the heart of Judas Iscariot to betray his Lord, as was foretold; whereby the crucifixion of Christ, according to the determinate counsel and foreknowledge of God, was effected; and by that the redemption and salvation of men. The coming of antichrist, was after the working, and through the efficacy of Satan, by divine permission, with all power, and signs, and lying wonders; with which so many things in providence have been so closely connected for more than a thousand years past, and will be to the end of his reign.

2. Kings, princes, and civil magistrates, good and bad, have been, and are, instruments in the hands of God, for the executing of his providences in the world; the powers that be, are ordained of God, and are ministers of his, to some for good, who

do good and behave well; to others for evil, for vengeance, to execute wrath upon them, Rom. xiii. 1, 4. and because they have their power and authority, their commission and capacity from God, and are his vicegerents, and act under him, and personate him, and are representatives of him; hence they are called gods, Psalm lxxxii. 6. *By* him good *kings reign, and princes decree justice;* from him they have wisdom and capacity to make good laws, and power to put them in execution, for the good of men; such an one was David, raised up by God to fulfil his will; there have been but few of this sort; but some there have been, and more there will be in the latter day, when kings shall be nursing fathers to Zion, and queens nursing mothers; the seven angels that shall have the vials of God's wrath to pour forth on the antichristian states to their destruction, are seven christian kings, or protestant princes, who will have a commission from God to do that work. Evil kings, however, such who have had no true knowledge of God, have been raised up, and made use of in providence, to do great things in it; either for the good of the church and people of God, as Cyrus king of Persia, whom the Lord girded, though he knew him not, and held his right hand to subdue nations, 'and particularly Babylon; that he might be in a capacity, and have an opportunity of letting go the captive Jews in it, and of delivering them from their bondage, and of giving them liberty to rebuild Jerusalem, and the temple in it, as was foretold of him two hundred years before he was born, Isa. xliv. 28. and xlv. 1—13. And sometimes wicked princes have been used as scourges of God's people, and for the correction of them; as Sennacherib king of Assyria; of whom it is said; *O Assyria, the rod of mine anger, and the staff in their hand is mine indignation!* that is, the indignation of God, the execution of it, was put into his hands, as a rod and staff, to chastise the people of the Jews for their hypocrisy and other sins, which were provoking to God; *Howbeit he,* the Assyrian monarch, *meaneth not so; neither doth his heart think so,* that he is an instrument, in the hand of God, to correct his people; *but it is in his heart to destroy and cut off, nations not a few,* to gratify his ambition, pride, and cruelty, Isa. x. 5, 6, 7. So the ten kings who have given their kingdoms to the antichristian beast, and become vassals to him, God put it into their hearts to do it, to fulfil his will in providence, which they knew nothing of, Rev. xvii. 17. And Psammon,[26] an Egyptian philosopher, made use of this as an argument of divine providence, shewing that all men were governed by God, since in every thing that ruled and governed, there was something divine.

3. Ministers of the word, and masters of families, are, in their respective stations, instruments in the execution of the affairs of providence. The work of ministers lies much in convincing men of sin, and in turning them from it, and directing them in the way of their duty, as well as in the way of salvation; and it has a very close connection with the providence of God, which is exercised therein and thereby. Masters of families, both by their instructions and examples, are very serviceable in providence, to those that are under them; and, indeed, every man, in whatsoever station he is, has a work to do, which, in providence, is ordered and disposed to answer some end or another.

4. Even irrational creatures are employed in providence to execute some parts of it; the beasts of the field, the fowls of the air, and the fishes of the sea, being at the beck and command of the great Creator of them. The noisome beast is one of God's four judgments which God has sometimes inflicted on wicked men; this he threatened the Jews with in case of disobedience to him, Ezek. xiv. 21. Lev. xxvi. 22. two she-bears, by divine direction, came out of a wood, and tore in pieces two and forty children, for mocking a prophet of the Lord; and lions were sent among the idolatrous Samaritans, to punish them for their idolatry, 2 Kings ii. 24. and xvii. 25. nay, not only creatures of such bulk and strength have been made use of in providence, but even the meanest and most minute, as flies, frogs, lice, and locusts, which were four of the plagues of Egypt; and the latter is called the Lord's army, and his great camp, which sometimes have a commission to destroy a whole country, and strip it of herbs and plants, and every green thing, Joel ii. 11. the fowls of the air, the ravens, those voracious creatures, were employed in providence, to carry bread and flesh, morning and evening, to the prophet Elijah; and the fishes of the sea also have been made use of; God

---

[26] Plutarch. Alexander, p. 680.

prepared a fish to swallow up Jonah when he was cast into the sea, and he spake unto it, commanded and gave it orders, to throw him upon the shore again; and a fish furnished Peter with a piece of money to pay the tribute for himself and his Master.

5. Inanimate creatures, the several meteors in the air, are under the direction of providence, and subservient to it. God has his treasures of snow and hail, which he reserves against the day of trouble, against the day of battle and war, Job xxxviii. 22, 23. and which artillery of heaven he sometimes plays upon the inhabitants of the earth; hail was one of the plagues of Egypt, by which, not only grass, herbs, plants, and trees were battered down, but both cattle and men destroyed; and in a battle with the Canaanites, in Joshua's time, more of them were killed by hail-stones from heaven, than by the Israelites; and sometimes others of the meteors are made use of in a way of mercy, as those mentioned in a way of judgment; so snow and rain, by commission, descend on the earth to refresh it, and make it fruitful, whereby it brings forth what is beneficial to man and beast: in short, every meteor in the heavens is at the command of God, and does his will; *Fire and hail, snow and vapour, stormy wind fulfilling his word,* Psalm cxlviii. 8.

Now, whatever good or evil come to the children of men, by any and all of these instruments, are not to be attributed to them, but to the God of providence, who makes use of them to bring about his designs. All the good things of life, the wealth and riches men are possessed of, let them come by them in what way they may, by inheritance, by bequest, or by their own industry, yet all must be ascribed to God; *Riches and honour come of thee,* says David, 1 Chron. xxix. 12. he had amassed together a vast quantity of riches, great part of which, at least, he got by his victories over the Moabites, Syrians, &c. but who gave him the victory? God; and therefore, as he ascribes his military honour and glory, so his riches to him; in like manner as Job, through the providence of God, became the greatest man in the East for worldly substance, as well as other things; so by the same providence he lost all; and though the Sabeans and Chaldeans were the instruments of it, he does not impute it to them, nor to Satan, who instigated them to it; but to the Lord: saying, *The Lord gave, and the Lord hath taken away; blessed be the name of the Lord!* Job. i. 21.

IV. The several parts and branches, or acts of providence, of which it consists, are next to be considered; and they are chiefly these two, conservation, or preservation of all things created, and the government of them; or the wise and orderly disposal of them, to answer the ends for which they are made and preserved.

First, Conservation, or preservation of creatures, and the sustentation of them in their being; which is expressed by these several phrases, *Thou preservest them all;* that is, the heaven, and the heaven of heavens, with all their host, the earth and seas, and all therein, Nehem. ix. 6. *Upholding all things by the word of his power;* that is, the worlds made by him, Heb. i. 2, 3. *By him all things consist,* even all things created by him in heaven and in earth, visible and invisible, Col. i. 16, 17. It may be proper to consider the necessity of God's sustaining and preserving the creatures made by him; and then shew to what and to whom this preservation extends and reaches.

1. That the sustentation and preservation of the creatures in their being, is of God, and must be so, and which may be proved,

(1.) From the nature and perfections of God, particularly his independence. God is an independent Being; all creatures depend on him, but he on none; *Of him, through him, and to him are all things,* Rom. xi. 36.

If creatures could or do support and preserve themselves in their being, they would be independent, and then there would be more independents than one, and so more gods than one; which cannot be admitted; there is but one potentate, God over all, on whom all depend.

(2.) From the nature of creatures, which is to be dependent on the Creator; he that gives them life and breath, gives them all things for the support and preservation thereof; yea, in himself they live and move and have their being; he not only grants them life and favour, but his visitation preserves their spirits; and this is true of all the creatures that have life and breath and motion; all depend upon God for the continuance of them; and even of rational creatures, *he holdeth our soul in life,* in union with the body, in which it lives, Acts xvii. 25, 28. Job x. 12. Psalm lxvi. 9.

(3.) From the weakness of creatures to support and preserve themselves. If any creature could preserve itself, it might be thought that man could; but he cannot; he cannot preserve himself from disorders and diseases of body; if he could, he would not be attended with them: he cannot preserve himself from death; could he, none would ever die; but *there is no man that hath power over the Spirit, to retain the Spirit; neither hath he power in the day of death,* to keep it off from him; *there is no discharge in that war,* Eccles. viii. 8. nor can any man preserve his brother, friend, or near relation, so as that they *should live for ever, and see no corruption;* for then none, for whom an affectionate regard is had, would ever die; nay, men cannot preserve their cattle, in which the chief substance of some men lies; could they, these would always be in good plight and case, and stand, and never fail; their sheep would continue to bring forth thousands, and their oxen would be always strong to labour, Psalm xlix. 7, 9. and cxliv. 13, 14.

(4.) The same power that was put forth in creation, is required and is necessary, for the preservation of the creatures made; eternal power was exerted, and is to be seen in the things that are made, and by the same almighty power all things are upheld, Rom. i. 20. Heb. i. 3. hence creation and preservation are so closely connected, Nehem. ix. 6. and, indeed, preservation is no other than a continued creation.

(5.) Was God to withdraw his supporting hand and preserving power and influence, creatures would soon come to destruction and perish; the whole fabric of the world would at once fall to pieces; *The earth, and all the inhabitants of it, are dissolved,* that is, they would be, were it not for what follows, *I bear up the pillars of it,* Psalm lxxv. 3. Creatures, whilst God supports and supplies them with his hand of providence, they live; but when he hides his face, or withdraws his hand, they are troubled, die, and return to their dust, Psalm civ. 27, 28, 29. Job was sensible of this, that he was held in life by the hand of God; he therefore desires he would *let loose his hand,* let go his hold of him, and then he knew he should drop and die, for which he was solicitous, Job vi. 9.

(6.) The whole world is a building, and God is the architect of it; *He that built all things is God;* but this building differs from any building of man. A man may erect an edifice, and when he has done, leave it to itself, to stand or fall; and it does stand without him, and oftentimes subsists many years after the architect is dead; the reason of which is, that such an edifice is only the effect of art; the builder does not make the materials of it, the stone and the timber; he finds them made to his hand; he only figures them for his purpose, and puts them together; and this is all that is necessary for him to do. But God, the great architect, has not only put together the world, and all things in it, in the beautiful order he has; but he has made the very matter of which it consists, and for the support of that his almighty power that created it, is requisite and necessary.

(7.) Every creature is made for some end, and therefore it is necessary it should be preserved and continued until that end is answered; *The Lord hath made all things for himself;* for his own glory, Prov. xvi. 4. wherefore it may be strongly concluded, that as God has made all things to answer some subordinate ends to one another, and ultimately for his own glory; he will, as it is necessary he should, preserve them, that such an end may be answered, as it is, in fact; *All thy works shall praise thee, O Lord!* Psalm cxlv. 10.

2. To what and to whom this preservation extends and reaches. It includes all the creatures God has made; the phrases by which it is expressed, as before observed, shew this; which declare that God preserves them *all;* that he upholds *all* things, and that by him *all* things consist; the world in general, and every individual in it; *O Lord, thou preservest man and beast,* Psalm xxxvi. 6. yea, every other creature.

(1.) Some of the individuals of the creation are sustained and preserved, as they were from the beginning; the *prima materia,* the first matter, of which all things were made, still continues; for matter is never annihilated, though it passes into different forms and figures. The whole world, which was made of it, is so established as that it cannot be moved, Psalm xciii. 1. and xcvi. 10. the form, figure, and fashion of it pass away, but the matter and substance of it remain. The ordinances of the heavens, and the heavens themselves, are as they were when first created; the sun is supported in its being, continued in its motion, and constantly supplied with light and heat, which it continually emits; for nothing is hid, as from the light, so neither from the heat of it;

the stars, every one of them, keep their place, their station, or course; because that God is *strong in power,* who sustains and preserves them, *not one faileth,* Isa. xl. 26. for what are called falling stars, are not stars, but meteors kindled in the air, which burn and blaze awhile, and then run and fall. A new star, so called, because not seen before, sometimes appears, but no one is lost. The heavens God has established by his understanding and power, ιϲ that they remain as they were; and though it is said they *shall perish, wax old as a garment, and as a vesture be changed and folded,* Prov. iii. 19. Psalm cii. 25, 26. Heb. i. 11, 12. yet as a garment folded up still remains, though in a different form; so the heavens will not perish, as to matter and substance, but be changed, as to form, quality, and use, in which respect they will be new and continue; and the same may be said of the earth; for God *has laid the foundations of it, that it should not be removed for ever,* Psalm civ. 5. and though it underwent some change at the universal deluge, so that the apostle distinguishes the earth that then was, from that which now is, yet as to substance it is the same; and though at the general conflagration, the earth, and the works that are therein, shall be burnt up, and a new earth will rise up out of it; yet the same as to matter and substance, only different as to form, an earth without a sea; and as to quality, being purified and refined; and as to use, only to be inhabited by righteous persons, 2 Pet. iii. 5, 6, 7, 10, 11, 12, 13. Rev. xxi. 1. Angels and the souls of men, are preserved in being, as they were first created; angels die not, nor do the souls of men, when their bodies do, but survive them, and live in a separate state till the resurrection.

(2.) Some of the individuals of creatures, which are subject to corruption and death, are yet preserved, as long as it is the pleasure of God; as the beasts of the field and the bodies of men; for *he preserveth man and beast,* Psalm xxxvi. 6. the brute creatures wait upon him, and he gives them food for their sustenance, by which they are supported; and then when he pleases he takes away their breath and they perish. Man springs up like a flower, and flourishes for a while, and then is cut down; God sends him into the world to do his will, or to do some work by him, and when that is done, he changes his countenance, and sends him away, Psalm civ. 28, 29. Job xiv. 20. but though the individuals of various sorts of creatures die, yet they are preserved and continued in their species; thus, though herbs, and plants, and trees, wither and seem to be dead, or are dead in the winter-season; yet in the spring those that were withered revive; or, if dead, others spring up in their room, or are raised up by seed; so that there is a constant succession of vegetables. Cattle, and fowls, and fishes, though consumed in great numbers for the use of man, or on other accounts; yet their species is propagated by them, so that there is the same sort of creatures of all kinds, as were at the first creation; and though thousands of men die every day, in one place or another, all put together, yet still a race of men is continued; *One generation passeth away, and another generation cometh, but the earth abideth for ever,* and is full of inhabitants, Eccles. i. 4.

Secondly, The other branch of providence is government, or the wise and orderly disposal of all creatures, to answer the ends for which they are made and preserved. God is the Governor of the whole universe; and he has a right to govern it, who is the Creator of it; the kingdom of nature is his, and so is the kingdom of providence; and he is the Governor among the nations; his government is very extensive, all creatures are subject to him; his kingdom rules over all, and it is an everlasting one; and his dominion endures throughout all generations, Psalm xxii. 28, and ciii. 19. and cxlv. 13. And as the government of the world is a branch of providence; so from the wise and orderly disposition of things in it, it may be strongly concluded there is a Providence; or that there is a God, who by his providence governs, guides, orders, and directs all things in the world. For, as Cicero[27] observes, if a man comes into an house, or a school, or a court of judicature, and takes notice of the order, manner, and discipline of things observed therein, he must conclude within himself, there is some one who presides there, and who is obeyed; and much more in such motions, in such vicissitudes and orders, and of so many and such great things, in which there is never any failure, one must needs conclude, that such motions of nature are governed by an intelligent Being.

---

[27] De Natura Deorum, 1. 2,

1. Inanimate creatures are governed, and guided, and directed by the providence of God, to do those things for which they were created, and so answer the ends of their creation; there is a law of nature, as has been before observed, impressed upon such creatures, which they constantly obey; there is an inclination of nature in them to such and such actions, which they perpetually follow; so the sun naturally pursues his course, and takes both his daily and yearly circuit from one end of the heavens to the other, and exactly knows and observes his rising and setting; there is an obediential power and influence, by which creatures without life and sense are actuated, and to which they attend with as much precision, as if they heard the order, and understood the will of their Creator; thus the rain and the snow come down from heaven, and fall upon the earth, by direction; that drinks in the rain that comes upon it, receives the seed cast into it, cherishes and fructifies it, and throws it up again; whereby it brings forth seed to the sower, and bread to the eater; and so in numerous other instances.

2. Animate creatures, but irrational, are governed, guided, and directed in providence, by an instinct of nature, placed in them by their Creator, to such actions as are agreeable to their nature, and from which they scarce ever swerve; thus with what art and skill do birds build their nests? with what tenderness do they cherish and provide food for their young? that little creature the ant, though it has no *guide, overseer, or ruler*, no visible and external one, yet *provides its meat in the summer, and gathers its food in harvest;* an example this of industry and diligence, care and foresight, to human creatures; this is one of the *four little* things on earth Solomon speaks of, which, though little, are *exceeding wise*, through an instinct in nature, put into them by the God of nature and providence. The *ants*, he says, *are a people not strong*, far from it, very weak, *yet prepare their meat in the summer* against winter; *the conies are but a feeble folk*, yet are so wise under the direction of providence, and by an instinct in nature, as to *make their houses in the rocks*, to shelter them from danger and hurt; *the locusts have no king*, to command and direct them, *yet they go forth all of them by bands*, march in rank and order, like a well-disciplined army; *the spider taketh hold with her hands*, on the thread of her webs, she spins, and is in kings' *palaces*, where, though her webs are often destroyed, she weaves them again, Prov. vi. 7, 8. and xxx. 25, 26, 27. Birds of passage, as the stork, the turtle, the crane, and the swallow, know the appointed times of their going and coming, and exactly observe them, Jer. viii. 7. Multitudes of instances of this kind might be given.

3. Rational creatures, as angels and men, are governed in a moral way, by a law, which for substance is the same to both, according to their different nature and circumstances; particularly men have either the law and light of nature to guide them, or a written law to direct them; and according as they behave towards it, they are dealt with; to those that are good, and do good, it is well with them, now and hereafter; and for the present, God makes all things work together for their good; to the evil, and them that do evil, it goes ill with them, and they shall eat the fruit of their doings, now, or in the world to come.

And there is a concourse of providence which attends all men, all their actions, yea, even their words and thoughts, Prov. xvi. 1, 9. and xxix. 21. all which are overruled by providence, to answer some end or another; yea, even evil actions themselves, as in the case of Joseph's brethren selling him into Egypt; they, in so doing, thought evil against him, and did evil in it; but God meant it for good, and overruled it for that purpose, to save many people alive, Gen. l. 20. but of this more hereafter. Moreover, men are governed as rational creatures, in a political way; kings and princes, as has been before observed, are instruments by whom God governs and administers this part of the affairs of providence; he sets up kings and judges at his pleasure, and enjoins men obedience to them; who are ministers of his, and through the power and authority they are entrusted with, are terrors to evil doers, and a praise to them that do well. I proceed to consider,

V. The object of providence; which is the whole universe, all the creatures of it, and whatever is done in it.

First, The whole inanimate creation, or creatures without life, whether in the heavens or in the earth,[28] are subject to divine providence, and under the direction of it, and act according to ancient and original laws,

---

[28] Aristotle owned, that the providence of God reached to heavenly things, and to earthly ones according to their sympathy or congruence with the heavenly. Diog. Laert. l. 5. in Vita ejus.

which the Author of them has imposed upon them, and from which they do not swerve.

1. The luminaries of the heavens, the sun, moon, and stars, these were made at first for various uses, for signs and seasons, and for days and years, and to give light to the earth by day and by night; and they are continued and employed by divine providence, for the said purposes and uses for which they were created. The sun is not only supported in its being, directed in its course, and continued to perform its office, as has been observed, but it daily sheds its benign influences upon the earth, to make it fruitful; hence we read of *precious fruits brought forth by the sun*, Deut. xxxiii. 14. and by the order of God in providence, all men partake of the benefits of it; for *he maketh his sun to rise on the evil and on the good*, Matt. v. 45. it is at his command and beck, he can stop it at his pleasure, and hide it from men; *He commandeth the sun, and it riseth not;* or, is not seen for days together; he causes it *to go down at noon*, as it seems to do in an eclipse, *and darkens the earth in a clear day*, Job ix. 7. Amos viii. 9. the same may be said of the moon, that is supported, continued, and directed in providence to answer the ends of its creation; it was *appointed for seasons*, to distinguish times, as it does; to give light by night, of which use it is, and to influence the earth and seas; hence we read of precious things brought forth by the moon; and that it is at the command of the God of providence, appears by its being stopped and stayed, when the sun was, in the days of Joshua; the stars are the hosts of heaven, God's militia, which he sometimes employs in providence, in favour of his people, and against their enemies; *The stars in their courses fought against Sisera*, Judg. v. 20. they are of use, in providence, to mariners on the mighty waters; the loss of which was sensibly felt by the apostle Paul, and those with him, when for many days neither sun nor stars appeared, Acts xxvii. 20. and when such is the case, then it is that God *sealeth up the stars*, Job ix. 7.

2. The meteors in the heavens are under the direction of providence; the clouds and winds, hail, rain, snow, and dew, thunder and lightning: the providence of God is greatly concerned in the ordering, directing, and managing of the clouds; *He bindeth up the waters in his thick clouds, and the cloud is not rent under them*, Job xxvi. 8. amazing it is, that such a body of waters should be wrapped up in so thin a garment as a cloud is, which is only thickened air; and that the cloud should not be rent and burst with the weight of the waters in it; and that these should not fall at once, in the vast quantity of which they are, which should they, would wash away the increase of the earth, and destroy men and cattle on it. But God, in his infinite wisdom and providence, causes them to fall in gentle showers, and in small drops, as if they passed through a sieve or colander, and so refresh and make the earth fruitful, Job xxxvi. 27, 28. and in ver. 29. Elihu asks, *Can any understand the spreadings of the clouds?* how from a small appearance, like that of a man's hand, on a sudden they spread themselves all over the heavens; as in the times of Ahab, 1 Kings xviii. 44, 45. and elsewhere he asks, *Dost thou know the balancings of the clouds, the wondrous works of him which is perfect in knowledge?* Job xxxvii. 16. how such vast bodies, holding such large quantities of water, are poised in the air, without turning aside, or falling at once; but move on evenly from place to place, and fall on those parts where in providence they are directed.

3. The winds are also at the dispose of providence: God has his treasures of them, and he brings them out from thence when he pleases, and holds them in his fists, restrains them, or lets them loose at his pleasure; he commands and raises the stormy wind, and bids it blow, and it obeys his orders, and fulfils his word; and he makes a weight for it, and causes it to subside, Psalm cxxxv. 7. and cvii. 25, 29. and cxlviii. 8. Prov. xxx. 4. Job xxviii. 25. And as all this is the work of providence, and which God only can do, so it is a clear proof of the Deity of our Lord; who, when he rebuked the winds and sea, and there was a calm, when before a violent tempest, the men in the ship with him said, *What manner of man is this, that the winds and the sea obey him?* Matt. viii. 26, 27. Hail is at the command of God, and which he sometimes in providence makes use of to the hurt and destruction of wicked men, as the Egyptians and Canaanites, as before observed, and will be one of the plagues on the antichristian states, Rev. xvi. 21. and we frequently hear of damages by it. On the other hand, in a way of mercy, God sends dew, and rain, and snow upon the earth, to water it, and make it fruitful; and which are what none of the vanities of the Gentiles can give; rain is a wonderful

blessing of providence, and falls by divine direction, sometimes on one part of the earth, and sometimes on another, as God pleases to dispose of it to the benefit of it, Amos iv. 7, 8. Thunder and lightning are of God; lightning is directed by him, and it runs from one end of the heavens to the other, and very many and wonderful are the effects of it; thunder is the voice of God; *Canst thou thunder with a voice like him?* Job. xl. 9. *The voice of the Lord is upon the waters; the God of glory thundereth;* and strange effects are produced by it, Psalm xxix. 3—9. God sometimes causes this his voice to be heard, to awaken and terrify secure sinners and atheistical persons, and let them know there is a God in the heavens that takes notice of them, and to whom they are accountable; and sometimes God in his providence does execution upon them this way; thus with a great thunder the Lord discomfited the army of the Philistines, in the days of Samuel, 1 Sam. vii. 10.

4. The providence of God is not only concerned with things inanimate in the heavens, but also in the earth, the several metals and minerals there; such as gold, silver, brass, iron, &c. *There is a vein for silver, and a place for gold——iron is taken out of the earth, and brass is molten out of the stones,* Job xxviii. 1, 2. God has made a provision of these metals for the use of men, and betows them on them in providence; *The silver is mine, and the gold is mine, saith the Lord,* Hag. ii. 8. and he gives them to whom he pleases, and as much of them as seems meet to him; and directs men how to employ them and improve them in trade and commerce, and in several arts and manufactories.

5. The sea, as well as all that are therein, is at his command; this unruly and unwieldy creature is managed by him at his pleasure, as easily as an infant by its nurse; he puts on its garment, wraps it in a swaddling band; he has broke up its decreed place for it, and has set bars, and doors, and bounds unto it, to stop and stay its proud waves from proceeding any further; he has placed that small creature the sand for a boundary of it; and though the waves thereof toss themselves, as it were in scorn and contempt of this their boundary; yet notwithstanding their haughty airs, they cannot prevail and pass over, Job xxxviii. 8—11. Jer. v. 22. see also Psalm lxv. 7.

Secondly, Animate creatures, or creatures with life; though they have only either a vegetative life, or a sensitive animal life, are under the care of divine providence; vegetables, herbs, plants, and trees, grass for the cattle, and herb for the service of man; and of great use, profit, and advantage, are they to both; when they are withered, or they do not spring up, not only the *beasts groan, the herds of cattle are perplexed, and the flocks of sheep are made desolate, because they have no pasture,* Joel i. 18. but men sensibly feel the loss of them; for God sometimes in providence turns a *fruitful land into barrenness, for the wickedness of them that dwell therein,* Psalm cvii. 34. As every spire of grass proclaims a God, so it also declares a providence, and instructs men to trust therein; *Consider the lilies of the field, how they grow, they toil not, neither do they spin;* but being raised by providence, they thrive, and are clothed with a beauty and glory, which Solomon, in all his glory, was not arrayed with: *Wherefore, if God so clothe the grass of the field,* with such verdure and gaiety, *which to-day is, and to-morrow is cast into the oven; shall he not much more clothe you, O ye of little faith?* Matt. vi. 28, 29, 30. Other creatures that live a sensitive, animal life, yet irrational, are cared for in providence; *He giveth to the beast his food, and to the young ravens that cry,* Psalm cxlvii. 9. All the creatures look up unto him, wait upon him, and he gives them their meat in due season; the beasts of the field, and the fowls of the air, God knows them all, and provides for them, and takes care of them, and preserves them; not a sparrow falls to the ground without him, without his knowledge, will, and providence; and the doctrine of providence, and trust in it, are to be learned from these creatures; *Behold the fowls of the air, for they sow not, neither do they reap, nor gather into barns; yet your heavenly Father feedeth them; are ye not much better than they?* Matt. vi. 26. The heathens acknowledge the providence of God, as regarding the most mean and minute. Plato says,[29] that things small and great are not neglected by God, neither through ignorance nor sloth; and that such an imagination is false and wicked; so Chrysippus.[30] Indeed, some are for exempting creatures mean and small, as well as trivial things, from the providence of God, being

---

[29] De Legibus, 1. 10, p. 956.

[30] Apud Plutarch. de Stoic. repugn. p. 1056.

of the Stoic's mind, who said,[31] *Dii magna curant, parva negligunt;* the gods take care of great things, but neglect small ones: but what is more mean and worthless than a sparrow? and yet under the care of the providence of God; and what smaller than some insects, as flies, &c. and yet as the wisdom and power of God are seen in creating them, they are no less displayed in the use he makes of them, in doing great things by them; as in the plagues of Egypt; and if they are not unworthy of his creation, they cannot be unworthy of his providence.

Thirdly, Rational creatures, angels and men, are more especially the objects of divine providence. Angels good and bad. Good angels are not only upheld in their beings by God, but are directed by his providence, and ordered by his will, here and there; and he does according to his will among them, even in the armies of the heavens, which they are, Dan. iv. 35. He orders them to do his pleasure in the several parts of the world, gives them a charge over his people, to keep and guard them in all their ways. Christ says, he could have asked twelve legions of them from his Father, and have had them, Psalm xci. 11. Matt. xxvi. 53. But of the offices and employment of good angels we have treated elsewhere. Evil angels are under the restraints and checks of providence; they are held in the chains of it, nor can they go any where, nor any further, nor do anything but what they have leave for; as the cases of Job, and of the man possessed of a legion, and of Peter, shew, Job i. 11, 12. and ii. 5, 6. Mark v. 10—13. Luke xxii. 31. but of the providence of God, respecting angels in their first estate, and at their fall, I shall treat more particularly hereafter; and proceed to consider the providence of God concerning men, men in general, and the people of God in particular.

1*st*, Men in general. As all men have their life and breath, and all things, from God; they live, and move, and have their being in him; he looks down from heaven, and beholds them all, takes care of them, and provides for them, and preserves them; *Thou preservest man and beast;* as all sorts of beasts, so the whole of mankind, Acts xvii. 25, 28. Psalm xxxiii. 13, 14. and xxxvi. 6. the providence of God is concerned in the production of every man into being, and attends him in every stage and step of life, even unto death.

1. It is concerned in the production of them into being; it was the will of God, declared from the beginning, that there should be a propagation of the human species; God made man, male and female, for that purpose, joined them together in marriage, and enjoined them the first law of nature; *Increase and multiply;* and blessed this ordinance and institution of his to the peopling of the old world; and when that was overrun with wickedness, and destroyed by him for it with a flood, he by his providence preserved eight persons in an ark; and renewed the original law, *increase and multiply;* and by them repeopled the whole earth; and though ever since one generation of men has been going off by death, yet another generation comes and succeeds by birth; so it has been, is, and will be to the end of the world. To be a little more particular; the providence of God is concerned in the birth of every man, with respect to time when, place where, and persons of whom he is born; for as each of these are fixed in the purposes of God, the providence of God exactly executes those purposes, Eccles. iii. 1, 2. Acts xvii. 26. Gen. xxxiii. 5. and xlviii. 9. the conception of man in the womb, the formation of every member of the body, in the curious and wonderful manner in which they are wrought, and the whole progress thereof, are under the direction of providence, and owing to it, Job x. 8, 9. Psalm xciv. 9. and cxxxix. 14, 15, 16. the production of the soul in, and the union of it to the embryo, when in a fit and proper state to receive it, whereby it is quickened, are performed by the same hand, Psalm xxxiii. 15. Zech. xii. 1. Acts. xvii. 25. and when all things are ripe for the birth, God, by his power and providence, takes it out of the womb, and brings it forth into the world; for to him is this act ascribed, rather than to the midwife. Job, in his distress, complains of it, and wishes it had not been; but the Psalmist blesses and adores the providence of God for it, Job x. 18. Psalm xxii. 8, 9. and lxxi. 6. and how wonderful does the providence of God appear in the case of a new-born infant, that when it cannot help itself, nor tell its wants, care is taken that such things should be done for it in that instant which are necessary, Ezek. xvi. 4. and that as it has been marvellously fed and nourished, in the dark cell of nature,

---

[31] Balbus apud Ciceron. de Natura Deorum, l. 2. in fine.

as soon as it is brought to the light, the mother's breasts are filled with milk, to which it has a natural desire; and her heart is filled with tenderness to it, to do all that is in her power for it, and rather suffer herself than that should want; this is all owing to divine providence, Psalm xxii. 8. Isa. xlix. 15.

2. The providence of God attends men in every stage of life into which they come, and in every step in it, as in the first moment of their birth, so throughout their infancy; providing things necessary for them, and preserving them from many dangers the infant-state is exposed unto: it appears in their education, the foundation of which is laid in childhood; some have a better education than others, by which their tender minds are opened and improved; and some have greater capacities to receive and take in the instructions given them; but all have either more or less to fit them for the stations in life which are designed for them; all that come into the world are enlightened with the light of nature and reason; there is a rational spirit in every man; and the inspiration of the Almighty gives him understanding in natural things, and teaches him, and makes him wiser than the beasts of the earth, and the fowls of the heaven; whereby he is qualified, in a course of time, for such employments in life he is designed unto, Job xxxii. 8. and xxxv. 11. and when fit for business, the providence of God is greatly seen in directing to such callings, occupations, and stations in life they are fittest for; and it is easily discerned in giving to each an inclination to such and such services, some to one, and some to another; some choose an employment on the sea, others on land; some take to agriculture or husbandry, in one branch of it or another; some to mechanic trades and manufactories, of different sorts: in all which the providence of God greatly appears; for as it is in the natural body, *If the whole body were an eye, where were the hearing? if the whole were hearing, where were the smelling?* So it is in the body politic, if all chose and were concerned in one sort of business and employment, that would soon be overdone, and the rest neglected; the consequence of which would be distress and confusion. But God, in his providence, has ordered every man's calling for his own particular good, and the good of the public; therefore, *let every man abide in the same calling wherein he is called,* 1 Cor. vii. 20, 24. and xii. 17. the places of abode where every man is settled, to do the business of his calling, are under the direction of the providence of God, who has *determined the times before appointed, and the bounds of men's habitation.* God not only at the first peopling of the world, divided to the nations their inheritance, and set the bounds of the people; particularly after the flood, disposed of the sons of Noah, and their posterity, some in one part of the world, and some in another; but he has appointed to every man the place of his settlement, and in his providence directs unto it, Deut. xxxii. 8. Acts xvii. 26. The marriage-state of life, into which most men enter, is too important an affair to escape the providence of God; there is more truth in that common saying, than many are aware of, that *marriages are made in heaven;* that is, they are appointed of God, and brought about in providence; and very often in a most remarkable manner; instances of this may be observed in the direction of Abraham's servant, sent to take a wife for Isaac; and in the case of Boaz and Ruth, Gen. xxiv. 14, 15, 21, 27. Ruth iv. 13, 14. When persons are got into the world, and set up in business in it, their success therein depends on the providence of God, which is different, to some greater, to others less; some rise early, and sit up late, and it is as much as they can do to live; others, through the blessing of God on their diligence and industry, become rich; which is not to be ascribed to chance and fortune, but to divine providence, Psalm cxxvii. 2. Prov. x. 4, 22. for poverty and riches are both in the hand of God, and he disposes of them at his pleasure; *The rich and the poor meet together; the Lord is the maker of them all,* both rich and poor; not the maker of them as men, though he is, which is an observation any one could make, as well as the wise man; but the maker of them both as rich and poor; this is an observation worthy of the wisest of men; for *the Lord maketh poor and maketh rich.* Agur was sensible of this, and therefore desires that God would give him neither poverty nor riches, for reasons he mentions; see Prov. xxii. 2. and xxx. 8. 1 Sam. ii. 7. All afflictions, of whatsoever sort, are under the direction of providence; they do not spring out of the ground, or come by chance, but by the appointment of God; and are overruled, in providence, to answer some

ends or other; be they personal or family, or crosses, losses, and disappointments in trade and business, they are all sent, and set and bounded by the providence of God; prosperity and adversity are set by him, the one against the other; so that men can find nothing after him, Job v. 6. and xxiii. 14. Eccles. vii. 14. All diseases of bodies are the servants of God, are at his beck and command, and sent here and there to do his pleasure; he says to one, go, and it goes, and to another, come, and it comes; he sends them on, and calls them off, as he pleases; he chastens with sore pain, consumes their flesh, weakens their strength in the way, and brings near to the grave; *These things worketh God* in his providence, *oftentimes with men*, Job xxxiii. 29. And as the providence of God attends men in their infancy, childhood, youth, and manhood, and in all circumstances relative to them, in the course of these, so in old age; he that has been the guide of their youth, and conducted them in every part of life, is the staff of old age, and will not then cast off, leave, nor forsake; he carries from the womb even to old age and hoary hairs, Psalm lxxi. 9, 18. Isa. xlvi. 3, 4. The term of life, as it is fixed by God, it is finished by providence, exactly in the manner, and at the time appointed; some die a violent, and others for the most part, a natural death; some in the prime of life, others in old age; some suddenly, and in their full strength, whilst others drag on a tedious life, and consume and pine away gradually; but all come by the appointed means, and in the appointed manner, and at the appointed time, under the direction of providence, 1 Sam. xxvi. 10. Job. xxi. 23, 24, 25. Eccles. iii. 2. Nor can the term of life be protracted beyond the bounds of days, months, and years which God has fixed;[32] nor be shortened, as not to be reached unto, Job xiv. 5. Nor are the fifteen years added to Hezekiah's days, an objection to this; since that addition was not to the days which God had appointed he should live, but to his own, which he thought were at an end; when he had the sentence that he should die, being stricken with a mortal disease, which none but God could cure him of: nor what is said of some, that they die before their time, Eccles. vii. 17. since that does not respect God's time, but their own time; what, according to the course of nature, humanely speaking, they might have lived to; and which both they and their friends might expect they would; the passage respects such who by capital crimes fall under the notice and vengeance of the civil magistrate, and so come to what is usually styled an untimely end. And when some are said not to live out half their days; these live out all the days they are designed in providence to live, and yet live but half of those which, according to their own, and the expectation of their friends, and according to the common term of life, threescore years and ten, it might be supposed they would have lived; so that if a person dies under five-and-thirty years of age, he may be said to live not half the days of man, though he has lived all the days that were allotted to him in providence; see Psalm lv. 23. and xc. 10.

2*dly*, There is a special providence, which is concerned with the people of God in particular; God is *the Saviour of all men*, in a providential way, but *especially of those that believe*, 1 Tim. iv. 10. not only is the eye of love, grace, and mercy, on those that fear the Lord, but his eye of providence. The providence of God is signified by seven eyes, that run to and fro through the earth, to denote the perfection and extensiveness of it; and it takes this course, particularly that God may *shew himself strong on the behalf of them whose heart is perfect towards him*, Psalm xxxiii. 18. Zech. iv. 10. 2 Chron. xvi. 9. Many are the instances on divine record, of the special providence of God respecting the saints; as Abraham and Sarah, who being called from their native country to a strange land, through which they travelled with safety, though the Canaanite was in it; and were eminently preserved both in Egypt and Gerar; Abraham, when his life, as he supposed, was in danger, and Sarah, when her chastity was ready to be violated, Gen. xii. 1, 6, 10, 12, 13, 20. and xx. 6, 15, 16. Isaac, in obedience to the divine command, Abraham took, and was about to sacrifice, all things being ready for that purpose, and his hand stretched out to give the fatal blow; when he was restrained from it by a voice from heaven, and was directed to a ram caught in a thicket, to offer in his room; and this providence being at mount

---

[32] Fixus est cuique terminus; manebit semper ubi positus est; nec illum ulterius diligentia aut gratia promovebit, Senecæ Consolatio ad Marc. c. 20.

Moriah, occasioned a proverb in future ages, for the encouragement of faith in times of distress; *In the mount of the Lord it shall be seen*, Gen. xxii. 2, 10, 11, 14. Jacob is another instance of the special care of divine providence, in directing him to flee from the wrath of his brother, who intended to kill him; and in preserving him in his journey, and bringing him safe to Laban's family; in prospering him in it, and in securing him from his fury, when he departed from him; in guarding him with an host of angels when his brother Esau came out to meet him; all which, and other providences, were remarked by him; which occurred in the way in which he was led by his God, who fed him, and protected him all his days, Gen. xxvii. 42, 43. and xxix. 1. and xxx. 43. and xxxi. 29, 42. and xxxii. 1, 2. and xxxv. 3. and xlviii. 15. Joseph, whose party-coloured coat was an emblem of the various providences of his life, is a remarkable instance of this kind; in being preserved from the designs of his brethren upon his life; in his being sold and carried into Egypt; in the disposal of him there, and the favour he had both in Potiphar's family, and in the prison into which he was cast by him; in interpreting the dreams of two of Pharaoh's servants, which was the means of his being brought from thence into Pharaoh's presence and court; where he was advanced to the highest honour and office, next the king, and was of eminent use to the whole nation, and to his father's family, Gen. xxxvii. 3, 18, 21, 26, 27. and xxxix. 4, 21, 23. and xli. 14, 41. and l. 20. To observe no more, David was also remarkably the care of providence. Samuel was directed by the providence of God to anoint him king, when all his brethren, elder than he, were passed by; and by the same providence he was brought to Saul's court, and more than once was he eminently preserved from his fury; as when he threw a javelin at him, and sent messengers to beset his house, and take him; and when he pursued him in various places, and particularly when he lay with his army on one side of the mountain where David and his men were, and was just about to surround him, but was called off by a messenger that acquainted him the Philistines had invaded the land: with many other signal appearances of divine providence in his favour, both in his exile and in his wars, 1 Sam. xvi. 13, 18—23. and xix. 10, 12. and xxiii. 26, 27. But besides those instances, and many others, there is a special providence that attends all the people of God.

1. Before conversion, even as soon as they are born; this is what the apostle seems to intend in Gal. i. 15. With respect to himself; *When it pleased God, who separated me from my mother's womb;* which cannot be understood of the separation of him in election, which was done earlier than this, even in eternity; nor of his separation from others in effectual vocation, for that was not done so early; but of his being taken under the care of divine providence in a distinguished manner, as soon as he was taken out of his mother's womb; God's eye was upon him all along, from thence to the time of his conversion, waiting to be gracious to him; see Acts vii. 58. and viii. 1, 3. and ix. 1—5. Though it is not the only, nor the principal thing, that may be intended in 2 Tim. i. 9. yet it seems to be part of the sense of it, and not to be excluded from it; *Who hath saved us, and called us;* since the people of God are often saved from many imminent dangers, to which their lives are exposed before conversion; and so are saved before called, and saved to be called. Many of them are greatly preserved from the grosser sins of life before conversion, though this is not the case of all; and many are blessed with a religious education, which is a means of their preservation from scandalous sins; though this also every one has not; yet where it is, it is a providential favour.

2. At conversion; as effectual calling itself is according to the purpose of God, as to time, place, and means; so the providence of God is concerned in the bringing of it about agreeable thereunto; there is a time fixed for it, called the time of life, and the time of love; because there is then the first appearance of both; this is sometimes in the earlier, and sometimes in the latter part of life, and is not restrained to any, but is always at the time appointed by God, and then it is providentially brought about; the time being come for the conversion of the woman of Samaria, and for the call of Zaccheus, Christ must needs go through Samaria and Jericho, when it does not appear that he had any reason to go through either, but on those accounts. The place where conversion shall be made is also fixed, Psalm lxxxvii. 4, 5, 6. Acts xviii. 10. wherefore the providence of God is often remarkably concerned either in

bringing the gospel to such places, as it was brought to Philippi, for the sake of the conversion of Lydia and her household, and of the gaoler and his, Acts xvi. 6—12, 14, 15, 33, 34. or in bringing persons to the places where the gospel is, and casting them under the sound of it. Very remarkable and uncommon was the conversion of Onesimus, a fugitive servant, who ran away from his master, was taken up and cast into the same prison where the apostle Paul was, by whom he was begotten in his bonds, through the ministry of the gospel to him, Philem. ver. 10. And as the gospel is the ordinary means of conversion, how providentially are some persons brought under it, and converted by it, led by curiosity to hear it, or with a malignant spirit to scoff at it, oppose and persecute it; and ministers, how providentially are they directed to insist on such a subject, to say such things, and drop such expressions, and which, perhaps, they thought not of before, which, accompanied with a divine power, issue in conversion. Thus Austin, losing his subject, and digressing from it, fell upon the error of the Manichees, which proved the conversion of a great man of that heresy; and at most, ministers draw the bow at a venture; it is divine providence, in a gracious manner, directs the arrow of the word to the sinner's heart, where, through the power of divine grace, it does execution.

3. After conversion the providence of God appears, as well as before, in preserving his people from many evils and dangers; angels are ministering spirits to them, have the charge of them, encompass about them, and protect them, Psalm xci. 11. and xxxiv. 7. in providing for their temporal good, so that they shall want no good thing fitting and convenient for them; rather than they shall suffer want, God will open rivers in high places, and fountains in the midst of the vallies, Psalm xxxiv. 9, 10. and lxxxiv. 11. Isa. xli. 17, 18. And in directing them in all their ways, to take such steps as will be most for their good and the glory of God, Psalm xxxvii. 23. and in delivering them out of their afflictions, and causing all things to work together for their good; and in being their God and guide even unto death, Rom. viii. 28. Psalm xxxiv. 19. and xlviii. 14.

Fourthly, The providence of God is concerned in all actions; in every thing that is done in the world, from the beginning to the end of it. God is a *God of knowledge, and by him actions are weighed,* 1 Sam. ii. 3. not only are they known, considered, and examined by him, but he has some way or other, or in some sense or another, a concern in them; all action is from motion, and all motion comes originally from the first Mover, who is God, *in whom we live, and move, and have our being,* Acts xvii. 28.

1st, All natural actions, which are common or peculiar to every creature, as flying to the fowls of the air, swimming to fishes, walking to men and beasts; all muscular motion is of God; and is continued by his providence; by which we can move from place to place, rise, walk, run, &c. eat and drink, and do every action, and the several businesses of life.

2dly, All necessary actions; such as either arise from the necessity of nature, or are so by the ordination and appointment of God. Some are so by the necessity of nature; as waters naturally and necessarily descend and flow; and fire naturally and necessarily burns what is combustible, when put to it; and heavy things descend, and light things ascend; they necessarily move and act according to their nature, which is preserved in them by the providence of God; and that they are under the direction of providence is clear, because they are sometimes controlled by it: so the waters rose up and stood on an heap in the Red Sea, and the river of Jordan, and made dry land for the Israelites to pass through. The nature of fire was so restrained in Nebuchadnezzar's furnace, that it did not so much as singe nor scent the clothes of the three companions of Daniel, cast into it. There are other things that are necessary by the appointment of God, or must be, because he has appointed them; and, indeed, every thing is necessary in this sense, because he has foreordained whatsoever comes to pass; so for instance, the sufferings of Christ being by the determinate counsel of God, were necessary; hence those phrases, *ought* not Christ to suffer; the Son of man *must* suffer many things; so likewise offences *must* come, and heresies *must* be; they were necessary, by a necessity of immutability; that is, they must and do unchangeably come to pass in providence; but not by a necessity of coaction, or force, on those that are the authors of them, who do what they do most freely: as the crucifiers of Christ; men could not act more freely than they did; and as those by whom offences come, they give them freely, and are pleased when they are taken. Heretics form their corrupt schemes of doctrine with their whole hearts and will, and freely spread them; so that the divine determination, and providential bringing about of necessary actions, are consistent with the liberty of man's will. Hence,

3*dly*, All free and voluntary actions, which depend upon the free-will of man, are under the direction of the providence of God. The thoughts, purposes, schemes, and determinations of the will of men, than which nothing is more free; yet these are under the influence of divine providence; *A man's heart deviseth his way;* forms schemes, which he purposes to execute; settles the method of the execution of them, according to his will; and chooses the way he proposes to walk in; *But the Lord directeth his steps*, and guides him in providence to take a quite different course; *The preparations of the heart in man, and the answer of the tongue, are from the Lord;* the thoughts of the heart, by which a man is prepared to speak his mind, are under a divine influence; as free as thought is, it is not exempt from the providence of God, which both directs and overrules it; and the answer the tongue is thereby prepared to give, is under the same influence and restraint; Balaam would willingly have given an answer to the wishes of Balak, in order to have got his money, but could not; when he had devised what to say, and was just ready to open his mouth to curse Israel, God put another word into his mouth; and instead of cursing, he blessed Israel. What more free and arbitrary than the heart, mind, and will of a sovereign despotic prince? yet *the king's heart is in the hand of the Lord, as the rivers of water, he turneth it whithersoever he will;* as resolute and determined as it may be, it is in the hands of God; and it is in his power to turn it as easily as canals of water may be cut by a gardener to water his garden; or as the river Euphrates was cut by Cyrus, and its course diverted, and its waters drained; so that he could march his army into the midst of Babylon, through which it ran. So the cabinet councils of princes, in which they consult, debate, and speak their minds freely, are all overruled by the providence of God, to answer his own purposes; see Prov. xvi. 1. 9. and xxi. 1.

4*thly*, All contingent actions, or such as are called chance matters, these fall under the divine providence. What may seem more a contingency, or matter of chance, than the shooting of a bird flying, and fetching it to the ground? When the bow is drawn, or the piece presented and levelled, how uncertain is it whether it hits the bird or no? And yet, *One sparrow shall not fall on the ground,* that is, be shot and drop on the ground, *without your Father;* without his knowledge, will, and providence, Matt. x. 29. and what is more contingent than the killing of a man unawares, as it is described, Deut. xix. 4, 5.? and yet the providence of God is so far concerned in such an affair, that God is said to *deliver* such a man *into the hand* of his neighbour, Exod. xxi. 13. What we call accidental death is providential: what can be thought more a chance matter than the casting of a lot, how it will issue? and yet the issue, which is of God, is certain; *The lot is cast into the lap, but the whole disposing thereof is of the Lord,* Prov. xvi. 33. The first lot mentioned in scripture is that which was cast on the account of Achan, who had stolen a Babylonish garment, and a wedge of gold; to find out which, Joshua had recourse to a lot; this was cast first for the tribe the guilty person belonged to, and it fell on the tribe of Judah; then for the family of it, and it fell on the family of the Zarhites; and next for the household, and it fell upon the household of Zabdi; and then for the person, and it fell upon Achan: and in the whole process, how remarkable is the providence of God, which directed to the tribe, to the family, to the household, and to the guilty person; for that he was so, is certain from his own confession, Josh. vii. 16—20. The next lot was that which was cast for the division of the land of Canaan to the tribes of Israel; and which fell exactly agreeable to the prophecies of Jacob and Moses: thus for instance, it is suggested in both of them, that the tribe of Zebulon should have its situation by the sea, Gen. xlix. 13. Deut. xxxiii. 19. and by lot this situation was assigned unto it, Josh. xix. 11. The third lot we read of was that cast by Saul, to find out the person that had sinned, on whose account no answer was returned by the Lord to an inquiry made; and Saul desired a perfect lot might be given between the people, and him and Jonathan; it was cast, and the people escaped; it was cast again, and it fell on Jonathan, who had tasted honey that day, contrary to the charge and oath of Saul, 1 Sam. xiv. 40—43

Once more, Jonah fleeing from the presence of the Lord, took shipping at Joppa, for Tarshish, when a tempest arose and endangered the ship, and frightened the mariners; who supposed it was for some evil done by some among them, and therefore cast lots to find out the person, and the lot fell on Jonah. Now how careful and just was this disposition made in providence, that it might not fall upon any of the innocent mariners, but upon the guilty person; and for whom God in his providence had provided a fish to swallow him, when cast into the sea! Jonah i. 7, 17.

Fifthly, All actions and things done in the world and among men, whether good or evil, are under the direction of providence; or that is some way or other concerned in them.

1st, Good actions. Those are of God, the fountain of all goodness; there is no good thing in fallen man naturally, and therefore no good thing comes out of him, nor is any good thing done by him; and without the grace of God, he can do nothing of that kind; neither think a good thought, nor do a good action, an action that is spiritually good; in this God is concerned; this is one branch of his gracious dealings in providence with men: and he does not only uphold them in their beings, whilst they are doing good; for this he does to wicked men, whilst they are doing evil things; nor does he only give them a law, which shews them that which is good, what is to be done, and what to be avoided, and what is the perfect and acceptable will of God; to love God and their neighbour; to do nothing injurious to the glory of the one, and the good of the other: nor does he barely make use of moral suasion by his ministers, to persuade with arguments taken from fear or love, from loss or profit, to avoid evil and do good, Deut. xxx. 19. 2 Cor. v. 11. But God works efficaciously in the hearts of his people, both to will and to do, of his good pleasure; he opens their hearts to attend to the word spoken to them; he bends their wills, and inclines their hearts to that which is good, and gives them power and grace to effect it; he circumcises their hearts to love him, the Lord their God; he creates them anew in Christ, that they may be capable of performing good works; for though without him they can do nothing, yet through him strengthening them, they can do all things; he puts his Spirit within them, to enable them to walk in his statutes, and to keep his judgments and do them. But of this more, when we come to treat of the doctrine of efficacious Grace.

2dly, There are many evil things done in the world, in which the providence of God is concerned; and these are of two sorts, the evil of calamities, distress, and afflictions, and the evil of sin.

1. The evils of calamities, &c. and these are either more public or more private. (1.) More public; such are the calamities and distresses on nations and kingdoms, and bodies of men, and which are never without the providence of God; *I make peace and create evil; I the Lord do all these things*, in a providential way, Isa. xlv. 7. When peace obtains and continues in states and kingdoms, it is God that makes peace in their borders; this is a blessing of his providence; and the evil which is set in contrast with it, said to be of his creating, is war; and this, and all the calamities and distress that attend and follow it, are by the providence of God. In this sense are we to understand the prophet when he says, *Shall there be evil in the city, and the Lord hath not done it?* Amos iii. 6. he means any public calamity, affliction, and distress; even cities themselves come to destruction, and their memorial perishes with them: where is now Thebes with its hundred gates, and Babylon, with its broad walls, and the famous Persepolis, and Jerusalem the joy of the whole earth? it cannot be thought that these cities came to destruction without the concern of providence therein: yea, where are the famous monarchies which made such a figure in the world, the Babylonian, Persian, Grecian, and Roman, of which the latter only has a name, and that is all? the fall of these, according to divine prediction, has been accomplished by divine providence. Under this head may be observed the judgments of God in the world, as the sword, famine, pestilence, earthquakes, &c. When the sword is drawn, it is God that gives it a charge, and appoints it against such a state and kingdom; and it cannot be sheathed again, and be at rest and quiet, until he gives a counter-order in providence, Jer. xlvii. 6, 7. Famine is one of God's arrows shot out of the bow of providence; wherever it is, it is of his calling for and sending, Amos iv. 6. Hag. i. 11. and pestilence is another of his arrows, an arrow which flies by day and walks in darkness, and wastes at noon-day by his order; concerning which he says, *I will send*, or

I have sent the pestilence among them, Jer. xxix. 17. Amos iv. 10. and who has foretold there shall be earthquakes in divers places, as have been in our times as well as others, and cannot be thought to be without the providence of God, Matt. xxiv. 7. (2.) There are other calamities and afflictions which are of a more private nature, and are either inflicted on wicked men by way of punishment for sin, nor can they justly complain of the providence of God as acting unrighteously by them, *Wherefore should a living man complain, a man for the punishment of his sins?* Lam. iii. 39. or they are inflicted on good men in love, and as fatherly corrections and chastisements; *for whom the Lord loveth he chasteneth, and scourgeth every son that he receiveth*, Heb. xii. 6. and this now (the afflictions of good men) is made an objection, though not justly, against the providence of God: this was the grand objection of Epicurus [33] and his followers, to divine providence, the only persons among the heathens that objected to it: because they observed that wicked men for the most part prospered, and good men, or virtuous men, as they called them, were generally afflicted and distressed; and therefore they could not believe that God concerned himself with human affairs; [34] and this has been a stumbling to good men, which they know not how well to reconcile to the justice of God, as it was to Asaph and Jeremiah, Psalm lxxiii. 2, 3, 12, 13, 14, Jer. xii. 1, 2. But it should be observed, (1.) That wicked men, though they prosper and abound in riches, and are not seemingly in trouble as other men, yet they are not so happy as they may be thought to be; for as our Lord says, *A man's life*, that is, the happiness of it, *consisteth not in the abundance of the things which he possesseth*, Luke xii. 15. Some have much, and have not a power to make use of it, either for their own comfort or the good of others; and where is the difference then between having and not having it? Others, on the contrary, are profuse and extravagant, and live very luxurious and debauched lives, and bring upon themselves painful or nauseous diseases, and distress of mind; so that they have neither ease of body nor peace of conscience, but racking pain and dreadful remorses; some, their abundance will not suffer them to sleep, either through fear of losing what they have by thieves, &c. or through care contriving schemes to increase it; and some, envy seizes them and gnaws upon them, and they cannot enjoy themselves because a neighbour exceeds them in grandeur and wealth.——(2.) It should be also observed that a good man, though afflicted, is not so unhappy as is imagined; he has more peace, satisfaction, and contentment in what he has, though mean and little, than the wicked rich man in all his abundance; see Psalm xxxvii. 16. Prov. xv. 16, 17. besides, the good man, though poor in one sense, he is rich in a better; and is not only heir of a kingdom, but is possessed of one which cannot be moved, the kingdom of grace; he is possessed of the riches of grace, and is entitled to the riches of glory; and in the meanwhile has the love of God shed abroad in his heart, communion with God, and joy and peace unspeakable, which none can take away; and even his very afflictions work together for his good, temporal, spiritual, and eternal; and he has the presence of God, and a rich experience of his grace in them; so that he has reason to count it all joy when he falls into temptations, that is, into afflictions; for though they are not in themselves joyous, but grievous, yet they yield to them to whom they are sanctified, the peaceable fruits of righteousness; so that the balance is now on the afflicted good man's side.—— (3.) Hereafter, in a future state, this difficulty will be quite removed, and entirely vanish, when the wicked rich man, that was clothed in purple, and fared sumptuously every day, and had his good things here, will have his evil things; and Lazarus, the afflicted man, that was clothed with rags, and covered with ulcers, and had his evil things, will now have his good things; the one will be tormented, and the other comforted; the wicked will go into everlasting punishment, and the righteous into life eternal; and then justice will shine in its true lustre and glory.

2. There are the evils of fault, or sinful actions, from which the providence of God is not to be excluded. This is the greatest difficulty to be met with in the article of providence, how it should have a concern with sinful actions, or with actions to which sin is annexed, as some choose to express themselves. There are two things to be set down for certain and eternal truths,

---

[33] Vid. Lactant. Institut. l. 5. c. 10.
[34] ——Hominum nimium securus ades, non solicitus prodesse bonis, nocuisse malis? Senecæ Hippol. v. 971.

whether we are capable of reconciling them to our own satisfaction and that of others, or no; the one is, that God is not and cannot be the author of sin; the other is, that the providence of God has a concern with and in all sinful actions in some sense or another: that God is not the author of sin is most certain, there is nothing sinful in his nature;[35] Plato[36] says of good things there is no other cause, but of evil things we must seek for any other cause but God: he is without iniquity, is of unspotted purity and holiness; there is nothing but good in him, and therefore nothing sinful can come from him, nor be done by him; he takes no pleasure in sin, nor in those that do it, which the authors of sin do; he cannot look upon it with approbation and delight, it is abominable and hateful to him; for he has not only forbidden it by his law, but is the avenger of it; indignation and wrath, tribulation and anguish, come from him on every soul that does evil; wherefore *let no man say when he is tempted, I am tempted of God*, James i. 13. and on the other hand, to exclude the providence of God from all concern in the sinful actions of men, is contrary to the independency of God, in whom all live and move and have their being, and of whom, through whom, and to whom all things are: creatures depend upon God, as in their being so in their operation, or they would be in action independent of him, and so there would be other independents besides him; moreover to exempt the providence of God from all concern in sinful actions, or in actions to which sin is annexed, would be to banish providence, in a good measure, out of the world; for, comparatively speaking, what is done in the world but what is sinful? for these are the all, or the chief things in the world; *The lust of the flesh, the lust of the eye, and the pride of life*, 1 John ii. 16. Let the following things be observed for the settling of this point, and the removing of the above difficulty,——(1.) That God supports men in their being, whilst they are sinning. This is certain; he upholds them in life, his visitation preserves their spirits; was he to withdraw his power and providence from them, they would cease to be, and become incapable of action; but this he does not; he could have struck Ananias and Sapphira dead, before they committed the sin they did, and so have prevented it; but he did not; but when they had committed it, then he did it. ——(2.) God, in innumerable instances, does not hinder the commission of sin, when he could do it, if he would: that he can do it is certain, because he has done it; he withheld Abimelech from sinning against him, as he told him, Gen. xx. 6. and he that withheld Abimelech, could have withheld Adam, and any of his sons, from sinning, whom he has not. He restrained Laban from hurting Jacob, as Laban himself owned; and hindered Balaam from cursing Israel, which he would gladly have done. And so God could prevent the innumerable sins of men, which yet he does not. We, as creatures, are bound to hinder all the evil we can; but God is under no such obligation.——(3.) God permits sin to be done, or suffers it to be, in his providence. This is the language of scripture; *Who in time past suffered all nations to walk in their own ways;* and these ways were sinful ones, Acts xiv. 16. And this permission is not a connivance at sin; nor a concession or grant of it; much less does it express any approbation of it; nor is it barely a leaving men to the liberty of their wills, to do as they please; as Moses suffered the Jews to put away their wives when they pleased; as though he was careless and indifferent about it: nor is it a mere naked permission, but a voluntary one, yea, an efficacious one; God's will is in it, and efficacy attends it. Hence, ——(4.) God is represented as active in things relative to it; he not only suffers men to walk in their sinful ways, but *he gives them up to their own hearts' lusts; he gives them over to a reprobate mind, to do those things which are not convenient; he sends them strong delusion, that they may believe a lie*, Psalm lxxxi. 12. Rom. i. 28. 2 Thess. ii. 11. Joseph's brethren sold him into Egypt, but God sent him thither; he bid Shimei curse David; he gave the evil spirit a commission to go forth and do what he proposed, to be a lying spirit in the mouths of Ahab's prophets, Gen. xlv. 5. 2 Sam. xvi. 10. 1 Kings xxii. 21, 22. ——(5.) It will be proper to distinguish between an act, and the obliquity of it; every action, as an action, a natural one, is of God, the first Mover, in whom all move; the creature is dependent on God,

---

[35] εν μεν θεοις (κακον) ουκ εςιν, επειδε πας θεος αγαθος, Sallust. de Diis, c. 12.

[36] De Republica, l. 2. p. 605.

as the Creator, in every action, as well as in his being; but the obliquity and irregularity of the action, as it swerves from the rule of God's law, is from man: this is sometimes illustrated by divines in such an instance as this; a man that rides on a lame horse, he by whipping and spurring is the cause and occasion of his motion of going forward; but he is not the cause of his going lamely; that arises from a disorder in the creature itself: also the sun in the firmament, when it exhales a nauseous scent from a dunghill, it is the cause of the exhalation; but it is not the cause of the ill scent of it, that arises from the dunghill; the heat and force of the sun may be the occasion of the ill scent being drawn forth, but not of that itself. So, ——(6.) God in his providence, may put in the way of persons, things that are good in themselves; which may give an opportunity, and be the occasion of drawing out the corruptions of men's hearts; thus God in his providence, directed Joseph to dream, and to tell his dreams; which drew upon him the envy of his brethren; and God put it into the heart of Jacob to send him to visit them in the fields, where they were feeding their flocks, which gave them an opportunity to form and execute evil against him. David was brought by providence into afflicted circumstances, which obliged him to flee, and pass by the way where Shimei lived; and which gave him an opportunity of doing that with his mouth, which very probably he had done in his heart before; and, now it was, as it were, saying, Go curse David; the object was presented, and a fit opportunity in providence offered. There is sometimes a concurrence of things in providence, which in themselves are not sinful, yet are the occasion of sin; as in the affair of David and Bathsheba. Various things met together, which gave an opportunity, and were the occasion of committing sin, which David fell into, not being restrained by the grace of God; and to be preserved from opportunities, the occasion of sinning, is owing to the kind providence of God. Of this an heathen [37] was sensible, and therefore gave thanks to God, that when he had a disposition to sin, and should have committed it, had an occasion offered; yet $\Theta\iota\omega\nu\ \iota\upsilon\pi o\iota\iota\alpha$, by the good providence of God, no such occasion, from the concourse of things, did offer for his commission of it. God gives to some men wealth and riches, and these are the occasions of much sin to them. He gives a law, which forbids men to sin; but as the poet says, *Nitimur in vetitum;* or rather as the apostle says, *Sin taking occasion by the commandment, wrought in me all manner of concupiscence,* Rom. vii. 8. the gospel also sent to men, is the occasion of the stirring up the corruption of their nature, their pride, and passion, to an opposition to it, and it becomes *the savour of death unto death* unto them, 2 Cor. ii. 16.——(7.) The concern of providence about sinful actions, further appears in limiting and setting bounds; as to the waves of the sea, saying, *hitherto shalt thou come, and no further,* Job. xxxviii. 11. Thus Joseph's brethren would have run greater lengths in sin, had they not been restrained by the overruling providence of God; their first scheme was to put him to death; this was disconcerted by Reuben, who proposed putting him into a pit, and let him starve there; from this also they were diverted by a motion of Judah's to take him from thence, and sell him to the Ishmaelites, who were coming that way. And though it is amazing to observe how much sin is committed in the world; yet considering the wretched depravity of human nature, the temptations of Satan, and the snares of the world, it is most amazing that no more is committed; which can only be ascribed to the restraining providence of God.——(8.) God in the affairs of providence, is to be considered as the Rector and Governor of the world, and the Judge of the whole earth; and in this branch of it, respecting sin, which he overrules either for the punishment of those who commit it, or of others, or else for good; he sometimes punishes one sin with another. Plato [38] says, a licence to sin, is the greatest punishment of sin. So disobedient Israel, because they would not hearken to the voice of God, and would have nothing to do with him, therefore he gave them up to their own hearts' lust: and the heathens, because they liked not to retain God in their knowledge, therefore he gave them up to a reprobate mind, to commit things sinful; and because the followers of antichrist believed not the truth, but had pleasure in unrighteousness; therefore he sent them strong delusions to believe a lie; and when he is said to harden the hearts, and blind the minds of

---

[37] Antoninus de Seipso, l. 1. s. 17.

[38] In Theæteto.

men, it is done in a judicial way, by giving them up to greater hardness and blindness, for their wilful obstinacy, and affected ignorance, Psalm lxxxi. 11. Rom. i. 28. 2 Thess. ii. 11, 12. Rom. ix. 18. and xi. 8, 10. Thus God corrected David's sin with Bathsheba, by the incest of his son with his wives and concubines; and punished the hypocrisy and idolatry of Israel, through the pride, ambition, and cruelty of the Assyrian monarch, who was in his hand the rod of his anger, and the staff of his indignation, 2 Sam. xii. 11. Isa. x. 6, 7. Sometimes God overrules the sins of men for good;[39] as the sin of Adam, for the glorifying of his perfections; the crucifixion of Christ, for the salvation of men; and Joseph's being sold into Egypt, for the saving many persons alive, Gen. 1. 20.[40]

To conclude this article of providence; let it be observed,——1. That all the providences of God are executed in the wisest manner; though they may not sometimes appear clear to us, and are inscrutable by us, and the causes and reasons of them not to be accounted for; yet even in such a view of them it should be said with the apostle, *O the depth of the riches, &c.* Rom. xi. 33.——2. They are all done in the most holy and righteous manner; even such as are concerned about sin, are clear from any imputation of it; *The Lord is righteous in all his ways, and holy in all his works*, Psalm cxlv. 17.——3. They are executed with power irresistible; they are immutably performed, according to the unchangeable will of God, who works all things in providence after the counsel of his will; he does what he pleases; his counsel always stands; and he does all his pleasure. Wherefore,——4. We should give to him the glory of all; observe with wonder and gratitude, the several steps of it respecting ourselves and others; and put our trust in him for things temporal and spiritual; and at all times cast our care upon him, who cares for us; seeing it is, and always will be, well with the righteous, in time and to all eternity.

CHAP. V.

OF THE CONFIRMATION OF THE ELECT ANGELS, AND THE FALL OF THE NON-ELECT.

HAVING considered at large the doctrines of creation and providence; I proceed to observe the first and principal events of providence relating to angels and men; and shall begin with the angels, the first of rational creatures that were created, and in whom the providence of God first took place; and whereas there was a distinction made between them, of elect and non-elect, as has been shewn in a preceding chapter. I shall take notice,

I. Of the confirmation of the elect angels; for as God chose them to a state of holiness and happiness; as soon as he created them, he confirmed them in that state; the providence of God was not only concerned in the preservation and sustentation of them in their being when created, Col. i. 16, 17. but in the government of them, which are the two parts and branches of providence. Now the government of rational creatures is in a moral way, by giving a law to them as the rule of their obedience; and such a law was given to angels, not of a positive nature, similar to what was given to Adam, forbidding him on pain of death, to eat of the fruit of a certain tree, as a trial of his obedience to the whole will of God; since we read of no such law, or like it, given to angels; nor a law in the form of a covenant, as to men, since the angels do not appear to have had any federal head, they standing singly and alone, and each for themselves; nor do we ever read of good angels keeping covenant; nor of the evil angels being charged with the breach of covenant; but it was a law implanted in their nature, concreated with them in like manner, as the law of nature was inscribed on Adam's heart, some remains of which are to be observed in his fallen posterity, and even among the Gentiles, Rom. ii. 14, 15. which is the same in substance with the moral law written; and with which angels are concerned, so far as the precepts of it are suitable to spiritual substances; for such of them, and so much of them, as relate to the body, and to corporeal actions, cannot agree with angels, who are incorporeal; as the fifth, sixth, seventh, and eighth commands: but such as relate to the fear and worship of God in a spiritual manner; to love to God, and love to fellow-creatures; these are binding on angels, and are perfectly obeyed by the good angels; and in this their

---

[39] δι αγαθοτητα γινεται τα κακα, Sallust, ut supra.
[40] Clemens of Alexandria says, Stromat. l. 1. p. 312. "it is the greatest argument of divine providence that he does not suffer evil, which arises from a voluntary defection, to remain useless and unprofitable, nor to be altogether hurtful; but, as he after expresses it, that which is devised by evil persons, God brings on to a good and useful end."

perfect obedience and holiness, are they immutably confirmed, from the moment of their creation; for this their confirmation is not owing to any merits of theirs, through the good use of the freedom of their wills: some have fancied that they were first in a state of probation, and having stood some time in their obedience, through the power of their free will, merited confirmation in that state from God; but a creature, even of the highest rank, can merit nothing at the hand of God; for *Who hath first given to him, and it shall be recompensed to him again?* Rom. xi. 35. The obedience of angels was due to God, and could merit nothing of him; nor was their confirmation owing to the merits of Christ. Christ is a Mediator between God and men; but not between God and angels; for though he may be allowed to be a medium of conservation of angels; yet not a Mediator of peace and reconciliation, which they needed not; he is not a Saviour and Redeemer of them; he merited nothing for them by his incarnation, sufferings, and death; these were not on their account; hence the angels say, *Unto you is born this day* (not unto *us*) *a Saviour, which is Christ the Lord*, Luke ii. 11. see Heb. ii. 14, 16, 17. But their confirmation is owing to the free favour and good will of God, choosing them to a state of holiness and happiness; and to his putting them under the care and charge of Christ, as the Head of all principality and power, 1 Tim. v. 21. Col. ii. 10.

Now in this state of constant obedience and perfect holiness, they are immutably fixed by the will of God, and have from their creation continued in it, and ever will; as appears by their enjoyment of the presence of God perpetually; they always behold the face of God in heaven; they never left their habitation, but have always resided in heaven, where they were first placed; hence called the *angels of heaven*, Matt. xviii. 10. and xxiv. 36. and by their constant and perfect obedience to the will of God, and which is made the pattern of obedience to it in men; or we are directed to pray that it might be like it; *Thy will be done in earth, as it is in heaven;* that is, by the angels there, Matt. vi. 10. and by the consummate happiness of the saints at the resurrection being like to theirs; which supposes them to have continued in their original state, and that the saints will be like unto them, not only in the immortality of their bodies, but in perfect holiness and impeccability, as perfectly holy as they, and no more subject to sin than they are, Luke xx. 36. and by what is said of them with relation to the second coming of Christ, and their estate to all eternity; as that he shall descend from heaven with his mighty angels; shall come, not only in his own, and in his Father's glory, but in the glory of the holy angels; that he will employ them in gathering in the elect from the four parts of the world; that he will then confess the names of his faithful followers before them; and that the wicked will be tormented with fire and brimstone in their presence; the smoke of whose torment shall ascend for ever and ever; and consequently the holy angels will be free from that torment, and be happy for ever and ever; see 2 Thess. i. 7. Luke ix. 26. Matt. xxiv. 31. Rev. iii. 5. and xiv. 10, 11.

II. The next remarkable event respecting angels, is the sin and fall of the non-elect angels. The heathens seem to have had some notion of the fall of the evil angels; for Plutarch speaks[1] of demons or devils as θηλατοι and ὐρανοπιται, expelled by the gods, and fallen from heaven. The providence of God was equally concerned in the sustentation and conservation of them in their beings, as of the elect angels; and in which they are and will be everlastingly preserved. The same law also for the government of them, and as a rule of obedience, was given to them; or otherwise they could not be chargeable with sin, as they are; they are called the angels that sinned. Now sin is a transgression of the law; where there is no law there is no transgression, 2 Pet. ii. 4. 1 John iii. 4. Rom. iv. 15. These angels, in their original estate of creation, were in a capacity of obeying the law that was given them; their will was inclined to it; and the bias of their mind was towards it; for they were created holy, just, and good; the estate they are now in, is not that in which they were made; it is expressly said of them, that they *kept not their first estate,* and *abode not in the truth*, Jude ver. 6. John viii. 44. which supposes a better estate than what they are now in, and that they were originally in an estate of *truth;* that is of integrity, righteousness, and holiness, though

---

[1] De Vitando ære Al. p. 830.

they did not abide in it, but fell from it; for being left to the freedom of their will, which was mutable, and is that folly and weakness which angels in their original state were chargeable with by God, and in comparison of him; they sinned and fell, to which fall of theirs our Lord has respect, when he says, *I beheld Satan, as lightning fall from heaven,* Luke x. 18. that is, suddenly, swiftly, and irresistibly, and which proves the existence of Christ before his incarnation; as that not only he was before Abraham, but before Adam; however, before the fall of Adam, for he was before the fall of the angels, he was present at it, and a witness of it. Now concerning this, the following things may be inquired into.

First, What was the sin of the angels, by which they fell? this cannot be said with precision, the scriptures being silent about it; yet it is generally supposed, and it is probable from the scriptures, that their sin was,

1. Pride; and which seems probable from 1 Tim. iii. 6. *Not a novice, lest being lifted up with pride, he fall into the condemnation of the devil;* being guilty of the same sin, he is in danger of the same condemnation; and usually so it is, as the wise man observes, *that pride goes before destruction; and an haughty spirit before a fall,* Prov. xvi. 18. And so it might, before the fall of the angels, and be the cause of it. They might first begin with contemplating their own perfections and excellencies, which were very great; as their wisdom, knowledge, strength, &c. which might lead on to self-admiration, and issue in an over-weening opinion of themselves, so as to think more highly of themselves than they ought to have done; and to conclude, that creatures of such an high rank and class, as they were, ought not to be subject to a law, and therefore cast off the yoke of the law, and departed from their allegiance, and obedience to God; hence one of the names of Satan is Belial, without a yoke; and the children of the devil are called sons of Belial; not being subject to the law of God, 2 Cor. vi. 15. 2 Sam. xxiii. 6. upon which they seem to have affected deity; and having revolted from God, set up for gods themselves; and this may be thought to be confirmed from the manner in which they tempted our first parents to rebel against God; to do which they might hope to prevail with them, as it was the snare in which they themselves were taken; *Ye shall be as Gods, knowing good and evil,* Gen. iii. 5. as also by all the methods they have since taken to get themselves worshipped as gods. Satan has usurped to himself the title of the god of this world; and very early did he introduce into the world the worship of idols, and the offering of sacrifice to them; which to do is no other than to sacrifice to devils, 2 Cor. iv. 4. 1 Cor. x. 20. yea, he has prevailed upon the poor Indians, both Eastern and Western, to worship him openly as a devil; and nothing can be a greater instance of his pride, arrogance, and impudence, than the proposal he made to Christ, to give him all the kingdoms of this world, if he would but fall down and worship him, Matt. iv. 9.

2. Some have thought that envy was the sin of the devils, by which they fell; led thereunto by a saying in the Apocryphal book of Wisdom, chap. ii. 24. *By the envy of the devil, death entered into the world:* and, indeed, envy and pride are inseparable; a proud man is always envious at others; he cannot bear that any should be above him, or even equal to him: the apostle joins these sins together, James iv. 5, 6. the angels might envy the superior power and excellencies of God himself, and therefore withdrew from him, as not bearing his superiority over them, envying that he should be above them, and higher than they; if there was any superior rank and class of angels above these, since some are called dominions, thrones, principalities, and powers, they might be the object of their envy, and be displeased that they were not of the same, or of a superior class; however, it seems highly probable, that they envied the state and happiness of man,[2] and, therefore contrived his fall and ruin; as that he should be made after the image and likeness of God, which is never said of them, however like to God angels may be; and that man should be the Lord of the whole world, and all the creatures put in subjection to him; which they might think more properly belonged to them. And especially they might be envious at the Son of God, who they might understand, would in time assume human nature; though the end and design of it they might not know; and that in that nature

---

[2] It is an ancient tradition of the heathens, that the evil demons envied good men, Plutarch, in Dio, p. 958.

he should sit at the right hand of God, which they were not admitted to; and that he should in that nature be the Head of all principality and power; and that angels, authorities, and powers, should be subject to him in it. Now this they could not brook and bear, that the human nature should be advanced above that of theirs; and therefore broke away from God in envy, wrath, and malice; and hence there has been from the beginning, a continued enmity and opposition by the devil, to Christ, the seed of the woman, that should bruise the head of the serpent; hence Satan always sought to oppose Christ in his person and offices, and to lead men into errors and mistakes about them; denying him in one or other of his natures, and depreciating him in his offices; and hence he set up antichrist, whose coming was after the working of Satan; and whose doctrines are doctrines of devils, and diametrically opposite to the glory of Christ.

3. Unbelief may also be taken into the account of the sin of the angels; they must disbelieve the eternal power of God, and his truth and faithfulness to his word, or they would not have dared to have sinned against him; and as the apostasy of our first parents began with that, and disregard unto, and a disbelief of the threatening word of God; it may be reasonably thought that something of the same kind led on to the rebellion and fall of the angels; indeed, their sin seems to be a complication of iniquity, of pride, envy, and unbelief.

Secondly, There are several questions commonly asked, relative to the fall of angels; to which a short answer may be returned; as,

1. How and by what means they came to fall? they had no tempter; there were no creatures in being capable of tempting them to sin; not irrational creatures, who could have no influence on them; and if man was then created, as it is a question whether he was or no; and if he was, he had no disposition to anything of this kind; but, on the other hand, his fall was through the temptation of an evil angel; there was none but God to tempt them, and he *tempts none*, neither angel nor man, James i. 13, 14. and this indeed was the case, as before observed; the angels were left to their own free will, which was mutable, and so of themselves, and not through any temptation without them, sinned and fell, this is always spoken of as their own voluntary act and deed, without any force or persuasion used with them; they kept not their first estate, left their habitation, and abode not in the truth. It is very probable, that one of them, famous above the rest for his wisdom and strength, might begin the apostasy; and being in high esteem for his excellent qualifications, he gave the lead, and others followed his example; hence we read of the prince of devils, and of the prince of the power of the air, or of the posse of devils in it, and of the devil and his angels, Matt. xii. 24. and xxv. 41. Eph. ii. 2.

2. It is sometimes asked, When the angels fell? to which it may be answered, Not before the sixth day of the creation: as it is probable they might be created on the first day, when the heavens, their habitation, was made, and light was formed; so they continued in their first estate, during the six days of the creation; for on the sixth day, when all the creatures were made, *God saw every thing that he had made, and behold it was very good;* not only when made, but to this time had continued so. Now if the angels had sinned before, this could not have been said; and yet they must have fallen before Adam fell, because it was the serpent, or the devil in the serpent, either in a real one, or in the form of one, that beguiled Eve, and so was the cause and means of the fall of man. But however, certain it is, that the fall of the angels was very early; since the devil is called, *a murderer from the beginning,* John viii. 44. a destroyer of mankind, either from the beginning of the world, that is, quickly after it was made; or from the beginning of his creation, not long after he began to be; or from the beginning of man's creation, who abode not long in his happy state, but soon fell from it, through the temptation of the devil.

3. This question is sometimes put, What number of the angels fell? This cannot be said with any precision; some have thought that as many fell as stood; grounding it on a passage in Ezek. xli. 18. where it is said, that on the wall of the temple were carved, with cherubim and palm-trees, a palm-tree between a cherub and a cherub; by cherubim they understand angels, and by palm-trees good men, said to flourish like the palm-tree; and who are supposed to fill up the places of fallen angels; and so conclude the same number fell as stood; but as such a sense of the text cannot easily be established, it is insufficient to build such a

notion upon. Others have thought, that not so many fell as stood; since evil angels are never said to be innumerable, as the good angels are, Heb. xii. 22. And which they also gather from the words of Elisha to his servant; *Fear not; for they that be with us, are more than they that be with them;* and the servant's eyes were presently opened, and he saw the *mountain full of horses and chariots of fire round about;* that is, angels in such forms, 2 Kings vi. 16, 17. but then the comparison is not between good and bad angels; but between the good angels and the Syrian host. Others fancy that a third part of the angels fell; this they take from Rev. xii. 4. where the *dragon* is said to *draw* with *his tail the third part of the stars of heaven*, but by the stars are not meant angels, but such who bore the character of the ministers of the word, who in that book are called stars, chap. i. 20. whom Satan, through his influence, prevailed upon to drop their character, and desert their office. However, it is certain, that not a few of the angels, but many of them, fell; even as many as to form a kingdom, with a prince at the head of it; and there were so many that possessed one man, as to be called a legion, which consisted of some hundreds; for when the devil in him was asked his name, he answered, *My name is legion, for we are many,* yea, it seems there are various kinds and sorts of them; for when the disciples asked Christ the reason why they could not cast out a certain devil, our Lord, among other things, says, *this kind goeth not out but by prayer and fasting*, Matt. xii. 24, 26. and xvii. 19, 20, 21. Mark v. 9.

Thirdly, The state and condition into which the angels were brought by sin, may next be considered. They were originally angels of light; full of light, knowledge, and understanding; but by sinning are become angels of darkness; and are called the power of darkness, and the rulers of the darkness of this world, blind, and blinding others, Col. i. 13. Eph. vi. 12. 2 Cor. iv. 4. for whatever light and knowledge of natural things they retain, and which may be increased by long observation and experience; or whatever notional knowledge they have of evangelic truth, they have no spiritual and experimental knowledge; not the light of faith; nor rejoicing of hope;

nor heat of love; no light of spiritual joy and gladness; but all black despair. They were once pure and holy creatures; but through their sin and fall, became impure and unholy; and therefore called *unclean spirits;* who delight in the impurities of sin; and take pleasure in drawing men into them, to the commission of them; the devil is called emphatically and eminently, *the wicked one*, being notoriously and superlatively wicked; even wickedness itself, Matt. x. 1. and xiii. 38. 1 John iii. 12. and v. 18. Once they were lovers of God, and of their fellow-creatures; but now at enmity to God, and all that is good; and spiteful and malicious to mankind. Satan is called emphatically the *enemy*, the enemy of God and of Christ, and of all good men; desirous of doing all the hurt and mischief to them he can, or gets leave to do; the case of Job abundantly proves this; whose substance, family, and health, by permission, he destroyed; and would have taken away his life, could he have obtained leave: and as also the possessions of men by him, in the times of Christ shew; to the torment of their bodies, and the distraction of their minds; and, indeed, he is always going about seeking whom he may devour, 1 Pet. v. 8. These fallen angels, who were once in a guiltless state, are now in the most desperate circumstances; are in chains of darkness and black despair, under irremissible guilt; no pardon for them, nor hope of it for evermore; which leads on to observe,

Fourthly, Their punishment; and which is both of loss and sense; they have lost the favour and presence of God, and they sensibly feel his wrath and indignation on them. Sinning, they were hurled out of heaven, and deprived of their blissful state they left; being forced to leave their habitation there; nor will their place be any more found there; the apostle Peter says, they were *cast down to hell*, 2 Pet. ii. 4. but where that is, it is not easy to say; very probably upon their ejection out of heaven, they fell down into the air, since Satan is said to be the *prince of the power of the air*, Eph. ii. 2. Not that he has a power of moving the air, and of raising storms and tempests; but he is the ruler of the posse of devils that dwell in the air;[3] from whence, by divine permission, they

---

[3] It was a notion of the Chaldeans, that the air is full of dæmons, Laert. Proem. ad Vit. Philos. p. 5. and of Pythagoras, ibid. Vit. Philosoph. l. 8. in Vita ejus; and of Plato, Apuleius de Deo Socratis; and of the Jews, so R. Joseph Ben Gekatilia in Shaare ora, fol. 4. 1.

descend and patrol; and rove about the earth, in chains, limited and restrained for the punishment of wicked men, and for the trial of the graces of good men; but as yet they do not seem to have their full punishment inflicted on them; or are not yet in full torment; as may be learnt from their words to Christ; *Art thou come hither to torment us before our time?* and are said to be *reserved unto judgment, and unto the judgment of the great day;* when their full sentence will be pronounced upon them, and be carried into execution, Matt. viii. 29. 2 Pet. ii. 4. Jude, ver. 6. which they *believe and tremble* at, James ii. 19. and which punishment will be everlasting; there will be no end of it, no deliverance from it; it is called *everlasting fire, prepared for the devil and his angels;* the fire of divine wrath, which will never be quenched, but always burn without intermission, to all eternity; and a *lake of fire and brimstone,* where the devil, with the beast and false prophet, will be *tormented day and night for ever and ever,* Matt. xxv. 41. Rev. xx. 10.

CHAP. VI.

OF THE HONOUR AND HAPPINESS OF MAN IN A STATE OF INNOCENCE.

HAVING considered the first and principal events of providence respecting angels, I shall proceed to consider such as respect man, as soon as created, and when in his first estate, and the honour and happiness of that estate; not what regard his internal honour and excellency, being created in the image and likeness of God, which lay in his wisdom and knowledge; in his holiness and righteousness; in the right use of his rational powers, his understanding, will, and affections; in communion with God, and in his frequent appearances to him, which have been treated of; but what regard his external honour and happiness; as,

First, His being placed in the garden of Eden; for an habitation to dwell in; for the support of his animal life; and for his exercise in the culture and dressing of it.

1st, For his habitation; *And the Lord God planted a garden eastward in Eden;* and there he put the man whom he had formed. Gen. ii. 8. Indeed, the whole earth was made to be inhabited by man, as it has been ever since the creation of it; *the heaven,* even *the heavens are the Lord's;* he has reserved that part of his creation for himself, for the habitation of his holiness; and for his attendants, the holy angels; *But the earth hath he given to the children of men,* for them to dwell in; see Isa. xlv. 18. Psalm cxv. 16. And though Adam was heir and lord of the whole world, yet there was one particular spot more excellent than all the rest, assigned him for his residence; even as a king of a large country, has his royal seat, palace, and court, in some particular part of it: and it appears that this garden of Eden was not the whole world, as some have thought, which, for its delightfulness and fertility, might be called a garden; but though it was exceeding delightful and fruitful, in comparison of what it is now; yet it is certain, that the garden of Eden was a distinct spot from the rest of the world; this is clear from the man being said to be put into it when created, which shews that he was formed without it, and when made, was removed into it; as also from his being driven out of it when he had sinned. To which may be added, that we read of a land that was at the East of it; see Gen. ii. 8. and iii. 24. and iv. 16. It is called the garden of God, because of his planting; and of Eden, because of the pleasantness and delightfulness of it, as the word signifies; hence any spot that was uncommonly fruitful and delightful, is compared unto it, Gen. xiii. 10. Where this garden was, cannot be said with any certainty; whether in Armenia, Assyria, or in Judea; most probably it was in Mesopotamia, since we read of an Eden along with some places in that country, Isa. xxxvii. 12. However, it is not to be known at this day; and there are many things that contribute to the obscurity of it; as its being left without any to cultivate it, upon Adam's being ejected from it, and so, in course of time, must become ruinous and desolate; and from the curse taking place upon it, as no doubt it did, and upon it chiefly and in the first place, as being man's peculiar habitation; *Thorns and thistles shall it bring forth:* besides, fire might spring up out of the earth, and destroy the trees and ornaments of it; or they might be washed away afterwards by the waters of the flood; and what through the change it might then undergo, as the whole earth did; and through the alteration of the course of the rivers of it, it is no wonder it should not be known at this day where it was. However, it was so delightful a spot, at its first plantation, that the church of Christ is compared unto it, and is called, in allusion to it, *a garden inclosed*——*and her plants, an orchard*, or *paradise of pomegranates*, Cant. iv. 12, 13. Moreover, it was an emblem of the heavenly state, which is therefore called paradise, Luke xxiii. 43. 2 Cor. xii. 3, 4. Rev. ii. 7.

2*dly*, Adam was put into the garden of Eden for the support of his animal life; where grew trees, not only pleasant to the sight, but good for food; and Adam was allowed to eat of them all excepting one, Gen. ii. 9, 16, 17. there are two trees particularly taken notice of; *the tree of life, in the midst of the garden, and the tree of knowledge of good and evil:* the former is so called, because with the other trees of the garden, it was a means of maintaining Adam's animal life, and perhaps the chief means of it; and so of the continuance of his life, so long as he stood in his integrity; for notwithstanding his body was gifted with immortality, this it had not from the constitution of it, but from the gift of God; and was to be continued in the use of means, and by eating of the fruit of this tree in particular; though what it was, and its fruit, are not now to be known by us; not that it had such a virtue in it as to prevent diseases; to which Adam's body was not, as yet, subject; nor such as to give and preserve immortality, and continue it, as Adam vainly thought it would, after he had sinned; which seems to be supposed in Gen. iii. 22, spoken according to his sense of things; but this tree was planted and pointed at, and called by this name, because it was a token that Adam had his natural life from God, the God of his life; and that it depended upon him, and that he might expect the continuance of it so long as he kept his state of integrity: it was also an emblem of Christ, who is therefore called the tree of life, Prov. iii. 18. Rev. ii. 7. and xxii. 2. But not then to Adam, unless of him as his Creator, from whom, as such, he had his life and being; but not of him as Mediator, who, as such, is the author and giver of life, spiritual and eternal; but of him, as such, Adam had no knowledge; and so could not be a symbol of spiritual and eternal life to him, in that his then present state, though it might be after his fall. There was another tree, called *the tree of knowledge of good and evil:* what that tree was, cannot be said; it is generally thought to be the apple tree; founded upon a passage in Cant. viii. 5. Others have thought of the fig-tree, because that Adam and Eve immediately plucked the leaves of that tree, to cover their naked bodies with; but after they had suffered so much by eating the fruit of it, it can hardly be supposed, if this was the tree, that they would have so much as touched its leaves, and much less have wrapped their bodies with them; and there is no sufficient foundation for either of them; nor for any other suggested; as the vine-tree, stalks of wheat, &c. and though this tree might be as good for food as any other of the trees, yet it was forbid to be used for that purpose, as a trial of man's obedience. It had its name, not from any virtue that it had of ripening the rational powers of man, and of increasing and improving his knowledge, as say the Jews and Socinians, who take Adam to be but a great baby, an infant in knowledge;[1] whereas his knowledge of God, and of things natural and moral, was very great: and besides, had he wanted knowledge, this tree could not be the means of accelerating and increasing it, since he was forbid to eat of it; nor was it so called from the lie of the serpent; *God doth know that in the day ye eat thereof, ye shall be as gods, knowing good and evil.* But this tree had its name before that lie was told, or any temptation was offered to Eve, Gen. ii. 9, 17. and iii. 5. but it was so called, either because God hereby tried and made known, whether Adam would obey his will or no; or eventually, since hereby Adam knew by sad experience, what the good was he had lost, and might have enjoyed; and what a bitter and evil thing sin was, and what evil it had brought on him and his posterity; otherwise Adam full well knew before, in the theory, the difference between good and evil; but by his fall, or eating of the fruit of this tree, he knew these things practically; to his great grief and distress.

3*rdly*, Adam was put into the garden of *Eden to dress it and to keep it*, Gen. ii. 15. for the culture of it; not to worship and serve God in it, as some give the sense of the word; indeed as Adam had a right knowledge of God, and knew it was his

---

[1] Vid. Joseph. Antiq. l. i. c. 1. s. 4. Socinum de Stat. prim. hom. c. 4. et Smalcium apud Peltii Harmon. Remonstr. et Socin. art. 6. p. 39.

duty to worship, serve, and glorify God, he took every opportunity of doing it in the garden; and the various trees and plants, and beauties of it, must needs lead him into adoring views of the great Creator; and he might often take his walks in the garden to contemplate the perfections of God displayed in it; even as Isaac went into the field to meditate on divine things. But the sense of the passage is, that he was put into the garden to cultivate it and keep it in good order, and keep out of it every thing that might be injurious to it; and this was a proper exercise for man in his state of innocence; for it was never the will of God that men should in any state live an idle and lazy life; nor indeed any of his creatures, the most exalted; the angels are *ministering spirits*, employed in the service of God, and in ministrations to their fellow-creatures. Yet the work of man in the garden was without toil and fatigue, he did not eat his bread with the sweat of his brow, as after the fall; but his service in it was attended with the utmost delight and pleasure; nor was it at all dishonourable to him, nor inconsistent with the high, honourable, and happy estate in which he was.

4*thly*, What added to the delight and fruitfulness of the garden of Eden, was a river that went out of it to water it; which was parted into four heads or branches, the names of which were Pison, Gihon, and Hiddekel or Tigris, and Euphrates; which may be symbols of the gospel and its doctrines, which, like a fountain or river, went forth out of Zion the church, and makes it cheerful and fruitful; and of the ordinances of it, those still waters of the sanctuary; or of the Spirit and his grace, which are rivers of living waters which flow from them that believe; or rather of the everlasting love of God, that pure river of water of life, a river of Eden, or of pleasure; the four heads and branches of which are election, redemption, effectual vocation, and eternal life, Rom. viii. 30.

Secondly, Another remarkable event in providence, relating to the honour of man in his estate of innocence, is the bringing of all the creatures to him to give names unto them, and whatsoever names he gave them they were called by, Gen. ii. 19. which was a proof and instance of his great wisdom and knowledge, part of the image of God he was created in; for to give names to creatures suitable to their nature, required a large share of knowledge of them; insomuch that Plato[2] said, that it seemed to him that that nature was more than human that gave names to things; and besides, by the creatures being brought unto him for such a purpose, whether by the ministry of angels, or by an instinct in them, it was putting him into the possession of them, as being their lord and proprietor; whose dominion over them was declared when created, and now confirmed by this act.

Thirdly, Another providential event, and which shews the care of God over Adam, and his concern for him, is providing an help-meet for him, and a partner with him in civil and religious things, man being a sociable creature; and whereas no suitable one could be found among the creatures, he cast man into a deep sleep, and took out a rib from him, and of that made a woman, brought her to him and joined them together in marriage, by whom he could propagate his species and live a social life; which shews that marriage is honourable, being instituted in paradise, and not at all inconsistent with the pure state of man in innocence; and it was also typical of the marriage of Christ, the second Adam, and his church; and of their mutual union and communion; see Eph. v. 31, 32.

CHAP. VII.

OF THE LAW GIVEN TO ADAM, AND THE COVENANT MADE WITH HIM IN HIS STATE OF INNOCENCE; IN WHICH HE WAS THE FEDERAL HEAD AND REPRESENTATIVE OF HIS POSTERITY.

THE manner in which God governs rational creatures is by a law, as the rule of their obedience to him, and which is what we call God's moral government of the world; and as he gave a law to angels, which some of them kept, and have been confirmed in a state of obedience to it; and others broke it, and plunged themselves into destruction and misery: so God gave a law to Adam, and which was in the form of a covenant, and in which Adam stood as a covenant head to all his posterity. And I shall endeavour to shew what that law was, that it was in the form of a covenant, and that Adam was a federal head in it.

---

[2] In Cratylo, p. 268—270.

First, The law given him was both of a natural and positive kind. God, who is the Creator of all, Judge of all the earth, and King of the whole world, has a right to give what laws he pleases to his creatures, and they are bound as creatures, and by the ties of gratitude, to observe them. The natural law, or law of nature, given to Adam, was concreated with him, written on his heart, and engraved and imprinted in his nature from the beginning of his existence; by which he was acquainted with the will of his Maker, and directed to observe it; which appears from the remains of it in the hearts of all men, and even of the Gentiles; and from that natural conscience in every man, which, if not by some means lulled asleep, that it does not perform its office, excuses men from blame when they do well, and accuses them, and charges them with guilt when they do ill, Rom. ii. 14, 15. and likewise from the inscription of this law, in a spiritual and evangelic manner, on regenerate persons, according to the tenor of the covenant of grace; *I will put my law in their inward parts, and write it in their hearts,* Jer. xxxi. 33. so that they become the epistle of Christ, having the law as from him, and by his Spirit written in them, and the Spirit put into them, to enable them to walk in his statutes, and keep his judgments, and do them; and this law that was written on Adam's heart, and is reinscribed in regeneration, is the same with the Decalogue, as to the substance of it; and excepting such things in it as were peculiar to the Jews, all of a moral nature; and which is comprised in these two precepts, to which it is reduced by Christ; *Thou shalt love the Lord thy God with all thy heart; and thou shalt love thy neighbour as thyself;* this was binding on Adam, and on all his posterity.

Besides, this natural law, or law of nature, given to Adam, there were others of a positive kind, which were positive institutions of God, such as man could never have known by the light of nature; but were made known by the revelation of God; such as relate to divine worship, and the manner of it; that there was a God, and that he was to be worshipped, Adam knew by the light of nature; but how, or in what manner, and with what rites and formalities he would be worshipped, this he could not know, but by divine revelation. In all dispensations there have been ordinances of divine service; there now are; and there were under the former dispensation; and so in a state of integrity; which were appointed of God, and revealed to man; for the law that forbid the eating of the fruit of a certain tree, is not the only positive law of God; however, it is certain that was one; *Of the tree of the knowledge of good and evil thou shalt not eat,* Gen. ii. 17. which was given as a trial of man's obedience to the will of God, whether he would observe it or no; for the evil of the act of eating did not arise from the nature of the tree, and its fruit, which was as good for food as perhaps any tree in the garden; but from its being disobedience to the will of God. And be it what it may, in which God is disobeyed, it matters not; and by so much the lesser is that which is forbidden, by so much the greater is the sin of disobedience, the more aggravated, and the more inexcusable.

Secondly, This law given to Adam, taken in its complex view, as both natural and positive, was in the form of a covenant; the same to be both a law and a covenant, is not at all inconsistent; so the law given to the people of Israel from mount Sinai, is also called a covenant, Exod. xxiv. 7. and Deut. v. 1, 2, 3. yea, the covenant of grace is called a *law*, the law of Christ's mediatorship, which was in his heart to fulfil; even the covenant he made with his Father, and his Father with him, Psalm xl. 8. The law given to Adam, as it was a law, sprung from the sovereignty of God, who had a right to impose a law upon him, whatsoever he thought fit; as it was a covenant, it was an act of condescension and goodness in God, to enter into it with man, his creature; he could have required obedience to his law, without promising anything on account of it; for it is what God has a prior right unto, and therefore a recompense for it cannot be claimed; if, therefore, God thinks fit, for the encouragement of obedience, to promise in covenant any good, it is all condescension, it is all kindness.

Moreover, It may be observed, that the law given to Adam is expressly called a covenant, as it should seem in Hos. vi. 7. *but they, like men,* (or like Adam) *have transgressed the covenant:* the sense of which seems to be, that as Adam transgressed the covenant God made with him; so the Israelites had transgressed the covenant God made with them; for as well may Adam's transgression of the law or covenant be referred to here, as his palliating his sin, after the commission of it, is referred to in Job xxxi. 33. Besides, the terms by which the positive law given to Adam is expressed, manifestly imply a covenant; as that if he eat of the forbidden fruit, he should surely die; which implies, that if he abstained from it, he should surely live; which formally constitute a covenant; even a promise and a threatening. To which may be added, the distinction of two covenants of grace and works, called the law of faith, and the law of works; and a twofold righteousness and obedience yielded to the one, and to the other, the righteousness which is of faith, and the righteousness which is of the law. Gal. iv. 24. Rom. iii. 27. and x. 5, 6. for without the law of Adam, as a covenant, two covenants cannot be fairly made out; for though in Heb. viii. 7, 13. we read of a first and second, an old and a new covenant; yet these respect one and the same covenant, under different dispensations; and though in the passage referred to, the covenant at Sinai may be intended as one, yet as a repetition, and a new edition of the covenant made with Adam.

This covenant is by divines called by various names; sometimes a covenant of *friendship*, man being in friendship with God when it was made with him; of which there are many instances; as the placing him in the garden of Eden, putting all the creatures in subjection to him, and providing an help-meet for him; appearing often to him, and talking friendly with him, and granting him communion with him; and it was an act of friendship to him to enter into covenant with him; and whilst Adam observed this, he remained in friendship with God; and it was the breach of this covenant that separated chief friends. Sometimes they call it a covenant of *nature*, it being made with Adam as a natural man, and a natural head of his posterity; and promised natural blessings to him and his; was coeval with his nature; and was made with all human nature, or with all mankind, in Adam. It is also called a covenant of *innocence;* because made with man in his innocent state; and who, as long as he kept this covenant, continued innocent; but when he brake it, he was no more so. And it is frequently called the *legal* covenant, the covenant of *works*, as the Scripture calls it, *the law of works,* as before observed; it promised life on the performance of good works; its language was, Do this and live. And it sometimes has the name of the covenant of *life* from the promise of life in it; though not in such sense as the covenant with Levi, as a type of Christ, is called, *the covenant of life;* for it is life of a lower kind that was promised to Adam, than what was promised to Christ, for his people, as will be seen hereafter.

Thirdly, As in all covenants there are contracting parties, so in this. 1. God is one of the parties, in this covenant; nor was it unworthy of God to enter into a covenant with Adam; for if it was not unworthy of God to make a covenant of conservation with Noah; a covenant of circumcision with Abraham; and a covenant of royalty with David; a covenant respecting the kingdom, and the continuance of it in his family; men in a fallen state; then it could not be unworthy of God to make one with Adam in his perfect state; yea, even since, on the behalf of his people, he makes a covenant with the beasts of the field, the fowls of heaven, and the creeping things of the ground, Hos. ii. 18. Besides, to make a covenant with Adam, was a display of his goodness to him. As he was the work of his hands, he must have a regard to him; as every artificer has for his work; and would not despise him, but be concerned for his good; and therefore in covenant promised good things to him, in case of obedience to his will: this his covenant also flowed from his sovereignty; since all his good things are his own, and he can do with them as he pleases; make promises of them in a covenant-way; in like manner he disposed of some of them in such a way to Adam.

2. The other contracting party was Adam; who gave a full and hearty assent to what was proposed to him. The stipulation, on the part of God, was proposing and promising good, on condition of obedience. The stipulation, or restipulation on the part of man, was his free and full consent to yield the obedience proposed, in expectation of the promise fulfilled; and this may be concluded from the law he was to obey being written on his heart; which he had full knowledge of, approved of, and assented to; for which he had the most sincere affection; and the inclination and bias of his will were strongly towards it: and as for the positive law, which forbid him to eat of a certain tree; his will was to observe it; his resolution to keep it; as appears from what Eve said to the serpent, tempting her; *God hath said, Ye shall not eat of it, neither shall ye touch it, lest ye die,* Gen. iii. 3. which shews,

that she and her husband believed what God had said; judged it to be reasonable to hearken to it; and were determined to observe it: and man had also power to keep this covenant; being made after the image, and in the likeness of God; pure and upright, possessed of a clear understanding of it, a strong affection for it, and a full resolution to keep it; for it was not till sin took place, that the nature of man was weakened, and, he unable to keep the law; *For what the law could not do, in that it was weak through the flesh, &c.* or what man could not do in fulfilling the law, his nature being weakened by sin; for then, and not before, was it in such an incapacity. Though it should be observed, that man was not left to his liberty; it was not at his option, whether he would assent to the proposal in the covenant, and the condition of it; he had not an alternative given him, to agree or not agree, since obedience was due to God, whether he promised him any thing or no. Wherefore this covenant differs from any covenants among men; in which the parties not only freely agree to make a covenant, but it is at the option of the one, whether he will accept of and agree to the proposal of the other. So that this covenant made with Adam, is not strictly and properly a covenant, such as is among men; but is rather a covenant on one side, as a covenant of promise is; and a covenant of God with man, rather than a covenant of man with God.

The obedience required of man in this covenant, was personal, perfect, and perpetual. It was *personal;* it was to be performed in his own person, and not by another for him; as is the obedience of Christ, which is not personal to them, who are made righteous by it; or as would have been the obedience of Adam, had he stood, as reckoned to his posterity; which, though personal to him, would not have been so to them; as his disobedience, by which they are made sinners, is not personal to them, Rom. v. 19. It was *perfect* obedience that was required of him, both as to parts and as to degrees; it was to be yielded to all the commandments of God, without exception, and to be performed in the most perfect manner; as to matter, all the commands of God, natural and positive, were to be observed; and as to manner, just as the Lord commanded them. And then this obedience was to be *perpetual;* it was not to be done for a time only, but always; life and the continuance of it, depended on it; otherwise, if a stop was made in it, the law condemned, and the man became accursed; *Cursed is every one that continueth not in all things written in the book of the law to do them,* Gal. iii. 10. So that man was bound by it for ever, as a law; but as considered as the condition of a covenant, it was to be yielded to as such, until man was confirmed in his estate, as the angels are; and, as some divines think, until he had children arrived to an age capable of obeying or sinning.

Fourthly, The law given to Adam, as it had the nature of a covenant, it contained a promise in it, and had a sanction annexed to it.

1. It contained a promise; which was a promise of life, of natural life to Adam, and of a continuation of it so long as he should observe the condition of it; just as life was promised to the Israelites, and a continuance in it, in the land of Canaan, so long as they should observe the law of God; for neither the law of Moses, nor the law of nature, made promise of any other than of a natural life. Some divines, and these of great name and figure in the churches of Christ, think, and indeed it is most generally received, that Adam continuing in his obedience, had a promise of eternal life. I cannot be of that mind. There is, indeed, an ambiguity in the phrase *eternal life;* if no more is meant by it than living for ever in his present life, it will not be denied; but if by it is designed such a state of glory and happiness, which saints shall enjoy in heaven to all eternity; that must be denied for the following reasons:

(1.) Adam's covenant was but a natural covenant; and which was made with a natural man, as Adam is called by the apostle 1 Cor. xv. 46, 47. and which covenant promised no supernatural blessing, neither grace nor glory; for as for spiritual blessings, these the elect are blessed with only in heavenly places in Christ, Eph i. 3. ———(2.) It was in another covenant more early than that of Adam's, in which eternal life was promised and secured; God, that cannot lie, promised it before the world began; and this promise was put into Christ's hands, even from all eternity; and the blessing itself was secured in him for all for whom it was designed, Tit. i. 2. 2 Tim. i. 1. 1 John v. 10.———(3.) Eternal life is only through Christ as the Mediator of the covenant of grace; it comes by no other hands but his; it is *through Christ Jesus our Lord;* he came to open the way of it, that *we might have life, and that more abundantly;* a more abundant, durable, and excellent life, than Adam had in innocence: Christ, as Mediator, had a *power to give eternal life* to as many as the Father has given him; and he does give it to all his sheep, that know his voice, hearken to him, and follow him, Rom. vi. 23. John x. 10. and xvii. 3. and x. 28.——(4.) If eternal life could have been by Adam's covenant, it would have been by works; for that covenant was a covenant of works; and if by works, then not of grace; it would not have been the gift of God, as it is said to be; *The Gift of God is eternal life,* χαρισμα, a free grace gift. Eternal life is no other than consummate salvation in the future state; and that is said to be of grace, and denied to be of works; see Rom. vi. 23. Eph. ii. 8, 9. Should the question of the young man in the gospel, and Christ's answer to it, be objected, Matt. xix. 16—22. *Good Master, what good thing shall I do that I may inherit eternal life?—If thou wilt enter into life, keep the commandments;* it may be observed, Christ answers him, and deals with him on his own principles; the man was upon the bottom of his own good works, and seeking for eternal life by them; and since he sought for life that way, Christ directs him to keep the commands. there being no good thing better than keeping them; the young man asked him what they were; he tells him; upon which he was very alert, and thought himself in a very good way for heaven: but Christ, further to try him, and to convince him that eternal life was not to be enjoyed by any good thing done by him, bids him, if he would be perfect, sell all that he had, and give to the poor; on which he went away sorrowful, unwilling to part with his possessions; and so found that eternal life was not to be had by doing.——(5.) Life and immortality, or an immortal, eternal life, and the way to it, are only brought to light by the Gospel, 2 Tim. i. 10. not by the light of nature, nor by the law of Moses; only by the Gospel of Christ.——(6.) There is no proportion between the best works of man, even sinless obedience and eternal life; wherefore, though the threatening of death to Adam contains in it eternal death, it does not follow that the promise of life includes eternal life; since, though eternal death is the just wages and demerit of sin; yet eternal life is not the wages and merit of the works of men; it is the free gift of God, Rom. vi. 23.

2. The sanction of the law and covenant made with Adam, was death; *In the day thou eatest thereof thou shalt surely die,* Gen. ii. 17. which includes death corporal, spiritual, or moral, and eternal.——1. A *corporal* death; which lies in a separation of soul and body; as this was threatened, so the sentence of it was pronounced on the day the man ate of the tree; *Dust thou art, and to dust thou shalt return,* Gen. iii. 19. Adam was at once stripped of the immortality of his body, that gift was at once withdrawn from him, and he became a mortal man; the seeds of death took place in him; and he was immediately subject to diseases, disorders, and miseries, which issue in death.——2. A spiritual, or rather moral death seized upon him; which lies in a separation of the soul from God, and communion with him; in an alienation from the life of God; in a deformation of the image of God; in a corruption and defilement of the several powers and faculties of the soul; in an impotency and disinclination to that which is good; he became dead in trespasses and sins, as all his posterity are.——3. An *eternal* death, which lies in a separation of soul and body from God; in a loss of the divine presence, and in a sense of divine wrath; both which are contained in these words, *Depart from me ye cursed into everlasting fire;* a symbol of which was the ejection of Adam out of paradise; as eternal life is the gift of God, so eternal death is the wages of sin, Matt. xxv. 41. Rom. vi. 23.

Fifthly, In this covenant Adam acted not as a private person for himself only, but as a federal head[1] and representative of his whole posterity; and in this he was alone; Eve was not a federal head with him, he was alone, before an help-meet was found for him; yet she was included in it, being formed out of him; and all his posterity, who spring from him; but the man Christ Jesus is to be excepted, since he descended not from him by ordinary generation, and was a Mediator, the Head of another and better covenant. But as to

---

[1] The Jews had a notion of Adam being a head to all mankind; see my Exposition of Rom. v. 12. and some think Plato, who borrowed many of his notions from the Jews, gives an hint of it, when he speaks of a corruption εν κιφαλη, in an head, derived from the first birth, in Timæo, p. 1087. ed. Ficin.

his natural posterity, it may be observed, there were many things which were common to him and them; and in which they had an equal concern; as in dominion over the creatures, the increase and propagation of their species, the food granted them, and the law of marriage, Gen. i. 28, 29. and ii. 24. However, that in the covenant with him he was the federal head of them, appears,

1. From Adam being a figure or type of him that was to come; that is, of Christ, Rom. v. 14. Now in what was Adam a type of Christ, but in his being the federal head of his posterity? Not as a man; so all his sons might be: nor on account of his extraordinary production; for though that of both was in an uncommon way, yet in a different way; the one was created out of the earth; the other, though not begotten of man, was born of a woman, as other men be; but they were both covenant-heads to their respective offspring; and the parallel between them as such, is formed by the apostle in the context of the place referred to; that as the one, Adam, as an head, conveyed sin and death to all his natural seed; so the other, Christ, as an head, conveyed grace, righteousness, and life to all his spiritual offspring.——2. From Adam being called the first man, and the first Adam, and described as natural and earthly, in distinction from whom, Christ is called the second man, and the last Adam, and described as spiritual, and the Lord from heaven; and these are represented as if the only two men in the world, because the two heads of their respective offspring.——3. From the threatening taking place upon the sin of Adam, not on himself only, but on all his succeeding offspring; as they were in him, they sinned in him; and death, the sentence of death, passed on them in him. In him they all died; through his offence death reigned over them, and judgment came upon them all to condemnation, and by his disobedience they were made, accounted, and charged as sinners, Rom. v. 12, 15—19. 1 Cor. xv. 22.——4. It was no unusual thing with God to make covenants with men, and their posterity, unborn; thus God made a covenant with Noah, and all that should descend from him, that he would no more destroy the earth with a flood; and with Abraham, and his natural seed, a covenant of circumcision, which should continue till the Messiah came; and the covenant at Horeb, with the children of Israel, was not only with them that were then present, and on the spot, but with those that should be hereafter descendents of them, Gen. ix. 9. and xvii. 4. Deut. xxix. 14, 15. And so the covenant of grace was made with Christ, as the Head of his chosen ones, who were considered in him, and had grace and all spiritual blessings given them in him before the world was.——5. Nor have any of Adam's posterity reason to complain of such a procedure; since if Adam had stood in his integrity, they would have partook of all the blessed consequences of his standing, and enjoyed all the happiness that he did; and therefore should not murmur, nor esteem it any injustice in God, in putting their affairs in his hand, that they share in the miseries of his fall; for if they would have received good things through him, had he stood, why should they complain of receiving evil things through his fall? And if this does not satisfy,——6. Let it be considered, that since God in his infinite wisdom, thought proper that men should have an head and representative of them, in whose hands their good and happiness should be placed; who so fit for it as the first man, the common parent of mankind, made after the image of God, so wise, so holy, just, and good? and could it have been possible for all men to have been upon the spot at once, and it had been proposed to them to choose an head and representative for themselves; who would they, who could they have chose, but the first man, that was their natural parent, of whose blood they were made; and who, they might reasonably think, had the most tender affection for them, and would take the greatest care of them, and of their good, put into his hands? so that it is reasonable to conclude, they would all to a man have united in the choice of him. But,——7. To silence all complaints and murmurings, let it be observed, that what God gave to Adam, as a federal head, relating to himself and his posterity, he gave it in a way of sovereignty; that is, he might, and might not have given it; he was not obliged to it; it was his own that he gave, and therefore might choose whom he pleased in whose hands to deposit it; and who can say to him, What dost thou?

CHAP. VIII.

OF THE SIN AND FALL OF OUR FIRST PARENTS.

THE law that was given to our first parents, and the covenant that was made with them, were soon broken by them; *They like men* (or like Adam) *have transgressed the covenant*, Hos. vi. 7. They continued not long in their obedience to it, and in that state of integrity in which they were created; but sinning, fell from it, into an estate of sin and misery.

First, I shall consider the persons sinning, the same to whom the law was given, and with whom the covenant was made; the common parents of mankind, Adam and Eve; first Eve and then Adam: for Eve was first in the transgression, and then Adam; though Adam was formed first, Eve sinned first, 1 Tim. ii. 13, 14.

1*st*, Eve, she was beguiled and deceived by the old serpent the devil, to eat of the forbidden fruit, by which she sinned and fell from her original state; her sin may be thought to begin in holding a parley with the serpent; especially on such a subject as the forbidden fruit; she might have suspected that there was some design upon her, by introducing such a subject of conversation, by so extraordinary a creature; and therefore should have broke off at once, and have abstained from all appearance of evil, from every thing that tended, or might be a leading step unto it; though there is what may be said in excuse of her, that she took the question put to her, to be a very harmless and innocent one; and to which, in the innocence and integrity of her heart, she gave a plain and honest answer: some have thought she failed in the account she gave of the law concerning the tree forbid to be eaten of; both by adding to it, saying, *neither shall ye touch it;* and by diminishing the sense of it, *lest ye die*, or, *lest perhaps ye die;* as if it was a question or a doubt with her, whether they should die or no, if they eat of it; whereas God had said, *Thou shalt surely die*, chap. ii. 17. But she is to be defended in all this; for though *touching* is not expressed in the prohibition, it is implied; since the fruit could not be plucked from the tree, nor taken in the hand, nor put to the mouth, without touching: besides, this may be considered as an argument of Eve's from the lesser to the greater, that if they might not so much as touch the fruit, then most certainly not eat of it. And as for the other phrase, *least*, or *lest perhaps ye die*, this does not always express a doubt, but the certainty of the event that would follow; see Psalm ii. 12. But her sin lay in giving credit to what the serpent said, *Ye shall not surely die;* in direct opposition to the word of God, *Thou shalt surely die;* which she now began to doubt of, and disbelieve; and for the strengthening of which doubt and disbelief, the serpent might take of the fruit, eat of it himself, and not only commend it as a most delicious fruit, but observe to her, that she saw with her eyes that no such effect as death, or any symptom of it, followed upon his eating it; and he might further suggest, that that superior knowledge and wisdom to the rest of the creatures he had, was owing to his eating this fruit; and that if she and her husband did but eat of it, they would increase and improve their knowledge as to be equal to angels; and which, he observed, was known to God. Now upon all this there arose a lustful inordinate desire of eating the fruit, it being of so lovely an aspect, so good for food, and having such a virtue in it as to make wiser and more knowing; so that at once there sprung up in her, *the lust of the flesh, the lust of the eye, and the pride of life:* hence she inwardly sinned, before she eat of the forbidden fruit. Much the same progress may be observed in her sinning, which the apostle James observes of sin in common; *When lust hath conceived, it bringeth forth sin*, James i. 15. for lust being conceived, she could no longer abstain, but took of the fruit, either from the serpent or from the tree, and eat of it, and so finished her transgression; and not content with eating it herself, but she gave to her husband to eat of it also; who either was with her, or at some distance, to whom she went directly, with some of the fruit in her hand, as may be supposed, eating it all the way she went; and when she came to Adam, held it up to him to look at, as most lovely to behold, and commended the deliciousness of it; and no doubt used the same arguments with him to eat, the serpent had made use of with her; and he hearkening to her, eat of it, and sinned also. For,

2*dly*, That Adam sinned as well as Eve, is most certain; for though it is said, *Adam was not deceived;* the meaning is, that he was not first deceived, that he was not deceived by the serpent, but by his wife; and when she is said to be *in the transgression*, the sense is, that she was in the transgression first; but not only in it; for Adam was also; hence we read of Adam's *transgression*, Rom. v. 14. And if he was with his wife when she eat of the fruit, as seems from the letter of the text, Gen. iii. 6. he sinned in not attempting to detect the sophistry of the serpent; in not defending his wife from his assaults; in not persuading her not to eat of the fruit; in not warning her of her danger; yea, in not using his conjugal authority, and laying his commands upon her not to eat; for if he was present and silent, he must be criminal and accessary to her sin; but perhaps he was not with her. But his sin lay in *hearkening* to his wife, to her solicitations and requests, upon which it is put, Gen. iii. 17. And she might urge, that they must be mistaken about the sense of the law; that God never meant by it that they should certainly die for eating the fruit, since she had eat of it, and was alive and well; by such insinuations Adam was prevailed upon to eat also. Though some think that he was not deceived by her; that he knew what he did, and what would be the consequence of it; he sinned with his eyes open; knew full well the sense of the law, and what would be the effect of it; but what he did was in complaisance to his wife, and from a vehement passionate love and affection for her; because he would not grieve her; and that she might not die alone, he chose to eat and sin and die with her: but then this was all very criminal; it was his duty to love his wife, as his own flesh; but then he was not to love her more than God: and to hearken to her voice more than to the voice of God. However Adam sinned, and his sin is more taken notice of than the sin of Eve; and it is to his sin that all the sad effects of the fall are imputed; sin entered into the world by him, and death; in Adam all died; for he being the federal head of all his posterity, he sinned not as a single private person, but as the common head of all mankind, Rom. v. 12—19. 1 Cor. xv. 21, 22. Some have thought, that if Eve only had sinned, and not Adam, her sin would have been personal, and only affected herself, she not being a federal head with Adam; but she could not have been the mother of a sinless posterity; for *Who can bring a clean thing out of an unclean?* and she must have died for her offence; indeed God could have created another woman for Adam; from whom an holy seed might have sprung, had he stood. But this is all conjecture; nor is it so clear a point that Eve had no concern in federal headship; since though the law was given to Adam, and the covenant was made with him before she was formed; yet it was made known unto her, and she assented to it, and looked upon herself as equally bound by it, and shared in the same privileges Adam did; particularly in having dominion over the creatures; and she was, as he, the common parent of their posterity, the mother of all living; was one flesh with him, and both the one Adam, Gen. v. 2. the head of all mankind.

Secondly, How creatures, so wise and knowing, so holy, just, and good; made after the image and likeness of God, came to sin as they did, deserves an enquiry: To what could their sin and fall be owing? Not unto God; he is not the author of sin, nor tempts unto it; nor is he tempted by it: nor to Satan, only as an instrument, enticing and deceiving; but to themselves, to their own will, it was their own act and deed.

1st, Not to God; he forbad it; was displeased with it; and resented it to the highest degree. Those who are differently minded from us, represent our sentiments about Adam's sin, as chargeable with making God the author of sin; which we abhor and detest. Let us therefore a little consider what concern God had in this affair; by which it will appear that the charge is false and groundless. And,

1. What he did not do.——(1.) He did not restrain the serpent from tempting; nor withhold man from sinning. He could have kept the serpent out of the garden, and laid his commands on Satan, not to tempt our first parents; and he could have hindered the temptation from having any influence upon them; but this he did not; nor did he withhold Adam from sinning, which he could have done; as well as he withheld Abimelech from sinning against him, as he told him he had; and Laban and Esau from hurting Jacob; and Balaam from cursing the people of Israel; he could have done the one as well as the other; but he did not; nor was he obliged to it. And on the other hand, he did not force nor impel either Satan to tempt, or man to sin; they both acted their part freely, without any force or compulsion. Satan, full of spite and malice, and moved with

CHAP. VIII.   OF THE SIN AND FALL OF OUR FIRST PARENTS.   319

envy at the happiness of man, most freely and voluntarily entered into a scheme to destroy him, and with all his heart pursued it, and carried it into execution; and our first parents, with the full consent of their wills, and without any force upon them, took and eat the forbidden fruit; none of Adam's sons and daughters ever eat a heartier meal, and with more good will, or with greater gust, than our first parents eat the forbidden fruit; stolen waters are sweet, and bread eaten in secret pleasant.

(2.) God did not withdraw any favour from man he had bestowed upon him, nor any power and strength to stand which he had given him; for when God does anything of this kind, it is by way of punishment for a preceding sin or sins; but no such punishment could be inflicted on Adam, because as yet he had not sinned; but God left him in the full possession of all the powers and abilities he had conferred upon him; so that he could have stood if he would; he did not indeed grant him new favours, nor give him additional power and strength, which he was not obliged unto; he gave him enough, had he made right use of it, to have continued in his integrity; and to have resisted every temptation. Now these negative acts of God could never make him chargeable with being the author of Adam's sin and fall.

2. There are other things which God did do, or acts which are ascribed unto him, relative to this affair.——(1.) He foreknew the sin and fall of Adam; as he foreknows all things that come to pass in this world, which none will deny that own the omniscience and prescience of God; and if God foreknew the most trivial and contingent events that befal any of his creatures; then surely such an event as the fall of Adam, so important in its consequences, could never escape his foreknowledge; now God's foreknowledge of things future flows from the determinations of his will; he foreknows that things will be, because he has determined they shall be. Wherefore, (2.) God predetermined the fall of Adam; this fell under his decree, as all things do that come to pass in the world; there is nothing comes to pass without his determining will, *Who is he that saith and it cometh to pass,* when *the Lord commandeth it not?* Lam. iii. 37. nothing is done, or can be done, God not willing it should be done: that the fall of Adam was by the determinate counsel and foreknowledge of God is certain; because the sufferings and death of Christ, by which is the redemption of men from that sin, and all others, were ordained before the foundation of the world; and which must have been precarious and uncertain, if Adam's fall was not by a like decree, Acts ii. 23. and iv. 28. 1 Pet. i. 20. but then neither the foreknowledge of God, nor any decree of God, laid Adam under a necessity of sinning; it is true there arises from hence a necessity of immutability, that is, that the things God has decreed should unchangeably come to pass, but not a necessity of co-action or force; as Judas and the Jews sinned freely, the one in betraying, the other in putting Christ to death; so Adam sinned freely without force or compulsion, notwithstanding any decree of God concerning him; so that these do not make God at all chargeable with being the author of his sin; he and he alone was the author of it.——(3.) God permitted or suffered Adam to sin and fall, which permission was not a bare permission or sufferance; God was not an idle spectator of this affair; the permission was voluntary, wise, holy, powerful, and efficacious, according to the unchangeable counsel of his will; he willed, and he did not will the sin of Adam, in different respects; he did not will it as an evil, but as what he would overrule for good, a great good; he willed it not as sin, but as a mean of glorifying his grace and mercy, justice and holiness: and that this was not a bare and inefficacious permission, but attended with influence, is clear; because, (4.) There was a concourse of divine providence attending this action, and influencing it as an action, without which it could never have been performed; as divine providence supports every wicked man in his being throughout the whole course of his vicious life, and so while he is sinning; the same providence upheld Adam in his being, whilst he was eating the forbidden fruit; otherwise, as Eve could not have stretched out her hand and taken of the fruit of the tree and eaten it, so neither could Adam have put forth his hand and taken it of her. The influences of divine providence concur with every action, be it what it may, as an action, since all live, and move, and have their being in God; every action, as an action, is from God; but the obliquity, irregularity, and sinfulness of the action, is from the creature: wherefore God is not the author of any sin; as he is not the author of sin in any man, notwithstanding the concourse of his providence with every

action of his, as an action, so neither of the sin of Adam.——(5.) God may be said, by planting a garden, and that particular tree of the knowledge of good and evil in it, and by forbidding him to eat of that fruit, to afford an occasion of sinning to Adam; but had he not a right, as the Lord of the world, to plant a garden; and as a sovereign Lord to plant what tree he pleased in it, and to forbid the eating of it, without being blamed for it? especially when he gave to Adam a power to abstain from it, had he made use of it; and God can no more on this account be chargeable with being the author of Adam's sin, than by giving wealth and riches to a wicked man, which are occasions of his sinning, by consuming them on his lusts.

2*dly*, The concern that Satan had in this affair may next be considered; and what he did was not by force or compulsion, but by persuasion; he acted the part of a tempter, and from thence he has that appellation, Matt. iv. 3. 1 Thess. iii. 5. he enticed and seduced by lies and false reasonings, and so prevailed; he is said to beguile Eve, and to deceive the whole world, the representatives of it, 2 Cor. xi. 3. Rev. xii. 9. in order to which he made use of a serpent, and not a mere form and appearance of one that he assumed; as is clear from its being reckoned one of the beasts of the field, and said to be more subtil than the rest, for which this creature is notorious; and from the curse denounced on it to go on its belly; and eat dust all its days: and yet it was not merely a serpent, or a serpent only, but Satan in it; as appears not only from its having the faculty of speech, which such creatures have not; but from its being possessed of reasoning powers, capable of forming an artful scheme, and of conducting it and carrying it into execution, so as to gain his point; and from the seduction and ruin of men being ascribed to the old serpent the devil, John viii. 44. 2 Cor. xi. 3. Rev. xii. 9.

Satan shewed great craftiness and cunning throughout this whole affair; in making use of the serpent, the most subtil of all creatures, which could easily creep into the garden unobserved, which some other creatures could not; and it might be a very lovely creature to look at, adorned with beautiful spots, and of a bright shining golden colour, which when the rays of the sun struck on it, made it look very lovely, as such creatures in those parts are said to be; all which might recommend it to Eve: she might take particular notice of it, and have a particular fondness for it; it might be very familiar to her, she might wrap it or suffer it to wrap itself about her arms; and what might make her still more fond of it, was its faculty of speaking; whereby she could converse with it about indifferent things; and this familiarity might continue some time before Satan in it made his attack upon her; so that she was used to it, and it was no surprise to her to hear it speak. Satan's cunning also appeared in going to work with our first parents so early, as soon as they were well settled in their state of happiness, and when they had but just tasted of the pleasures of it, and before the habits of virtue and goodness were more strengthened, when it might have been more difficult for him to have worked upon them, and gained his point; as also in making his attack on Eve first, and when she was alone, and her husband not with her, to aid and assist, counsel and protect her. Nor did he discover himself to be what he really was; had he declared himself to be an apostate spirit, that had left his first estate, not bearing to be under the government of God, he was so cruel and tyrannical; had he set out with such outrageous blasphemy against God as this, the woman would have fled from him at once, with the utmost abhorrence and detestation of him, which would have marred his scheme at once; but he begun, seemingly with owning the authority of God; and that he had power to forbid the use of any of the trees of the garden; and only questioned whether he had done so or no; he could scarcely believe that a God so good as he was, and particularly to Adam and Eve, had planted a garden for them, and stored it with all manner of fruit, that he would ever restrain them from eating the fruit of any of the trees, and especially would never inflict death upon them for so slight a matter as that; they must surely misunderstand him, and mistake his meaning: and after this, and more conversation, the woman began to doubt whether God had said so or no; or, however, that her husband had mistook his meaning, and had made a wrong report of it to her, who was not present when the law was given. Satan perceiving that he had gained ground, boldly affirmed, that though they eat, they should not die; and that God knew that such was the virtue of the fruit of that tree, that it would make them wiser and more knowing, even as knowing as God, at least as the angels of God : the woman by this finding that there were an order of creatures superior to them in knowledge, what with the lovely sight of the fruit, and the usefulness of it, especially to make wiser, took of it and eat, and prevailed upon her husband to do so likewise. And thus they sinned and fell, not through any force and compulsion, but through the temptation of Satan, and his seduction. Wherefore,

3dly, The sin, fall, and ruin of man were of himself. It was not through ignorance and want of knowledge that Adam fell; he was created after the image of God, one part of which lay in wisdom and knowledge; he had no darkness, blindness, nor hardness of heart; he knew God, his Creator and Benefactor; he knew his will, he knew his law, and what would be the consequence of disobedience to it; indeed, he was not so perfect but that he might be imposed upon by the appearance of a false good, presented to his understanding, which his will made choice of, under a shew of good : nor was it through a defect of holiness and righteousness in him; for *God made man upright,* endued him with rectitude and holiness of nature, with a bias to that which is good, and with an aversion to that which is evil ; but as he was made mutable, which he could not otherwise be, he was left to the mutability of his will, and so sinned and fell ; which is that folly, or rather weakness, which the highest rank of creatures, in their original estate, are chargeable with in comparison of God, the Creator : should it be said, Why did God make man mutable? it might as well be asked, Why did not he make him God ? for immutability, in the strict sense of it, is peculiar to God. Should the question be altered, Why did not he confirm him in the state in which he was created, as he confirmed the elect angels ? to which it may be replied, That it is not improbable but that he would have confirmed him, had he continued a little longer in his state of probation. But the truest answer is, that it did not so seem good in his sight; and to shew his sovereignty, he confirmed the elect angels; but did not confirm, as not the rest of the angels, so neither man. And this should satisfy.

CHAP. IX.

OF THE NATURE, AGGRAVATIONS, AND SAD EFFECTS OF THE SIN OF MAN.

First, The nature of this sin : It seems to have been brought on through inadvertency, thoughtlessness, and being off of guard ; it began with doubting and disbelief of what God had said ; appeared in an inordinate desire after the forbidden fruit ; and in an unlawful curiosity of knowing more than he did ; and in pride, affecting to be as God ; at least to be upon an equality with angels.

The nature of it may be learnt in some measure from the names it goes by ; it is called *sin*, and the *sin*, the grand *sin*, the first and fountain of all sin among men, Rom. v. 12. It is called a *transgression*, ver. 14. a transgression of the law, as every sin is defined, 1 John iii. 4. a transgression of the covenant, a breach of that; and what is more heinous than covenant-breaking ? to break covenant with men is a great evil; but to break the covenant with God is a greater still. It is called *disobedience*, Rom. v. 19. disobedience to the will of God, and to his law; and as obedience to God is well pleasing to him; so disobedience, in any case, is highly resented by him. It is often called the *offence*, ver. 15. 17, 18, 20. it being in its nature, and in all its circumstances, very offensive to God, and abominable in his sight, as all sin is ; and in the last-mentioned places the word used signifies a *fall;* and hence it is common with us to call this sin the *fall of Adam;* it being that by which he fell from a state of integrity, honour, and happiness, into an estate of sin and misery.

Secondly, The aggravations of this sin were, the place where it was committed, and the time when, with other things.

1. With respect to place; it was committed in the garden of Eden. Here man was put when he was formed ; nor was he cast out of it till after he had sinned, and for that reason : here were all manner of trees for his use ; and he was allowed to eat of them all excepting one, which was forbidden him ; and not to attend to that prohibition was great ingratitude to his Creator and Benefactor, who had so richly provided for him ; and in the midst of all which plenty he sinned. Had it been in a remote part of the world, or in a desert, where this tree grew, and where scarce any

thing else was to be had, it would in some measure have extenuated the crime; but in a garden, where he had enough of every thing, it was a very aggravated crime; and by how much the less that was which was forbidden him, by so much the greater was his crime in not abstaining from it.

2. With respect to the time when it was committed; that is, how long after the creation of our first parents. This cannot be precisely determined: some make the time after it too long, and others too short. Some think that the first Adam kept his state of integrity as long as the second Adam lived here on earth; but this is a mere fancy, without any foundation. Some have fancied that he fell on the tenth day of September, and they suppose the creation of the world began with that month; so that as Adam was created on the sixth day, his standing could be no longer than three or four days; and this is supposed for no other reason, but because the Jews in aftertimes had their grand fast on that day; but that was not for Adam's sin, but their own; and had it been for that, it should have been general, and kept by all mankind, if at all. And others are of opinion that he fell the same day he was created; but the text on which it is founded will not support it, Psalm xlix. 12. since it speaks not of the first man, but of his sons, and those in honour, whose continuance in it is not long; and the word for *abideth* or *lodgeth*, as some choose to render it, signifies often a longer duration than a night's lodging. However, it must be very early that man fell, since the account of his fall is very closely connected with what was done on the first day of his creation; and Satan is said to be a *murderer*, that is a destroyer of mankind *from the beginning.* John viii. 44. Now this was an aggravation of Adam's sin, that he should be guilty of it so soon, having just received his being from God; placed in so happy a situation; and blessed with so much honour, power, and authority, and with so many indulgent favours; he and his consort taking their walks in the garden, no doubt, often *sung the praises* of their great Creator and kind Benefactor, in tuneful lays, in melodious strains; but, like some of their sons afterwards, *soon forgat his works.*

3. The sin of Adam was a complicated one; he sinned against light and knowledge, and when he was in full power to have resisted the temptation; he could neither plead ignorance nor weakness in excuse of his sin; it was the height of ingratitude to his Maker; it was affronting him in the highest degree, by disbelieving his word, and thereby making him a liar; it was intolerable pride, an affectation of deity or of equality to God; a want of thought, of care, concern, and affection for his posterity, with whose all he was intrusted. In short, it included all sin in it. For the laws of God are so connected together, that he that *offends in one point is guilty of all,* James ii. 10.

Some have laboured to make it appear, that Adam by his sin transgressed the whole Decalogue, or the law of the ten commandments, and no doubt but many, the most, if not all, were broken. Dr. Lightfoot[1] expresses it thus, "Adam, at one clap, breaks both the tables, and all the commandments.——1. He chose him another God, when he followed the devil. ——2. He idolized and deified his own belly, as the apostle's phrase is; his belly he made his God.——3. He took the name of God in vain, when he believed him not. ——4. He kept not the rest and estate wherein God had set him.——5. He dishonoured his Father which was in heaven; wherefore his days were not long in that land which the Lord his God had given him.——6. He massacred himself and all his posterity.——7. In eyes and mind he committed spiritual fornication.——8. He stole that (like Achan) which God had set aside not to be meddled with; and this his stealth is that which troubles all Israel, the whole world.——9. He bore witness against God when he believed the witness of the devil above him.——10. He coveted an evil covetousness, which cost him his life, and all his progeny."

Thirdly, The sad effects and consequences of this sin. The account of what befel Adam after his fall, is so short, that much is not to be expected from it; and besides, he was so quickly recovered by the grace of God, and brought to repentance for his sin, and had a better image restored to him than what he had lost; and had so early the revelation of the seed of the woman, as a Saviour from this and all other sins; so that the mischiefs that personally accrued to him, are not so manifest; but appear more clearly in his posterity. However, there are so many things said, and hints

---

[1] Works, vol. i. p. 1027, 1028.

given, as may lead us plainly to observe some of the sad effects of this sin.

1. A loss of original righteousness followed upon it. God made man upright; but sinning, he lost the uprightness and rectitude of his nature; or the righteousness in which he was created; so that he became unrighteous, nay, full of all unrighteousness; hence it is that there is none of his posterity righteous, no not one. Now this was signified by the nakedness of our first parents, which was immediately perceived by them after their fall; for though it primarily respects the nakedness of their bodies, which was the same before the fall, but then was no occasion of shame to them; but afterwards it was; the reason of which was, because of the loss of their inward clothing, the righteousness and holiness of their nature; the want of which the nakedness of their bodies was now an emblem to them of: and as Adam immediately betook himself to get something to cover himself with, so natural it is for men to seek to obtain a righteousness of their own, to cover their naked souls with; for to be self-righteous is as natural to man as to be sinful; and what men do attain to as a righteousness by their own works, is of no more avail than Adam's fig-leaves were to him; cannot cover a man from the sight of divine Justice, nor shelter him from the stormy winds of divine wrath and vengeance; nor justify him in the sight of God; nor entitle him to heaven and happiness, nor introduce him into it.

2. Guilt on the consciences of our first parents presently appeared, and that in an endeavour to hide themselves from the presence of God among the trees of the garden. Guilt is the consequence of sin in all men; the whole world of Adam's posterity is guilty before God; and this is sometimes intolerable, and nothing can remove it but the blood of Christ. And from this consciousness of guilt, flow shame, fear, and hiding themselves from God; they were ashamed to appear before him; and sin causes shame in every one, more or less, unless hardened, stupified, and past all sense, and are like those that declare their sin, as Sodom: hence men choose to commit sin in secret, in the dark, that their sins may not be seen; nor do they care to come to the light, lest their deeds should be reproved. Fear followed upon a consciousness of guilt in Adam; *I was afraid because I was naked;* as there is in every man, more or less, a fearful looking for of judgment and indignation, even in the more audacious; yea, those daring creatures the devils themselves, believe and tremble; and through guilt, shame and fear, Adam hid himself, but to no purpose; there is no fleeing from the presence of God, to whom the darkness and the light are both alike; of what avail could the shade cast by the trees in the garden be to Adam, to hide him from the all-seeing eye of God? and yet such a notion possesses his posterity; see Amos ix. 2, 3. Rev. vi. 15, 16, 17.

3. Loss and want of knowledge and understanding, were soon perceived in him. The last instance, of hiding himself, betrays his ignorance and folly; as if the trees in the garden could secure him from the sight and vengeance of the Almighty; instead of gaining the knowledge he unlawfully sought after, he lost much of what he had; hence he is ironically and sarcastically upbraided with it; *Behold, the man is become as one of us, to know good and evil!* and his posterity are represented as foolish, ignorant, and devoid of understanding; *There is none that understandeth,* Rom. iii. 11. Though they may understand natural things, and civil things, and somewhat of moral things, though not clearly and distinctly, at least so as to do them; to do good they have no knowledge: but they understand not spiritual things, the things of the Spirit of God, which they neither receive nor know, because they are spiritually discerned. They know not God, so as to glorify him; and much less as in Christ; they know not Christ, nor the way of peace, life, and salvation by him; they know not the Spirit of God, his person, office, and operations: yea, men are as stupid as the beasts of the field, and in some things more so; man is born like a wild ass's colt, and is more ignorant, and less knowing than the ox and ass, which know their owner; and than birds of passage, which know the time of their coming and going, when men know not the Lord and his judgments, Job xi. 12. Isa. i. 3. Jer. viii. 6, 7.

4. Our first parents, upon their sinning, were immediately obnoxious to the curse of the law, and it was pronounced on them along with the serpent; though it is expressed as if it only concerned the body, and temporal things; in which strain run the several curses of the law afterwards; *Cursed shalt thou be in the city,* &c. Gen. iii. 16—19. Deut. xxviii. 15, 18. yet they

extend further, even to the wrath of God on the soul, both here and hereafter; for the curse of the law is no other than the sanction of it, *death;* and which, as has been seen, is death corporal, spiritual or moral, and eternal; Adam, upon sinning, was at once stripped of the immortality of his body, which God had bestowed on it, and became mortal, subject to diseases, and a corporal death, and so all his posterity; *In Adam all die;* and a spiritual or moral death seized on all the powers and faculties of his soul; his understanding darkened; his mind and conscience defiled; his affections inordinate; his will biassed to that which is evil, and to every good work lifeless and reprobate, until restored by the grace of God; as every man is dead in trespasses and sins, until quickened. And eternal death is the just wages of sin, which is no other than the wrath of God revealed against all unrighteousness, and which comes upon the children of disobedience: and there are none of the sons of Adam but as such, and in themselves, are obnoxious to it; even God's elect are *by nature children of wrath as others,* Eph. ii. 3. This is the grand curse, the flying roll in Zechariah's vision, that goes over the face of the whole earth, and cuts off the sinner on this and the other side; and which the wicked will hear at last denounced on them, *Go ye cursed!* But the righteous will be saved from it, because Christ has redeemed them from the curse of the law, and delivered them from wrath to come,

5. Ejection out of paradise is another thing which followed on the sin of Adam; *So he drove out the man,* Gen. iii. 24. An emblem of that alienation from God, from the life of God, and communion with him, which sin has produced, and which has set man at a distance from God; hence Christ suffered, to bring his people near unto him; and by his blood, they that were afar off were made nigh unto God. And besides these,

There are many others, which are the effects of the sin and fall of Adam; as a general corruption and depravity of all the powers and faculties of the soul, which are all immersed in sin, and full of it; and all the members of the body yielded as instruments of unrighteousness; a propensity and proneness to all that is sinful; an inordinate desire after the lusts of the flesh, and of fulfilling them; a serving of divers lusts and pleasures; a serving lusts as pleasures, being lovers of sinful pleasures more than lovers of God. There is, moreover, a disinclination to all that is good, yea, an aversion to it; an hating the good, and loving the evil; yea, the carnal mind is enmity itself to God, and all that is good; and there is also an impotency, an inability to do that which is good; hence man is represented as without strength, having lost it, and become unable to do anything that is spiritually good; to which may be added, that sin has brought man into a state of slavery to sin, Satan, and the world; this is what we commonly call the corruption and depravity of nature, the effect of the first sin of Adam. This is the *pandora* from whence have sprung all spiritual maladies and bodily diseases; all the disasters, distresses, mischiefs and calamities, that are, or have been in the world.

CHAP. X.

OF THE IMPUTATION OF ADAM'S SIN TO ALL HIS POSTERITY.

HAVING considered the disobedience of our first parents, and the sad effects of it to themselves, I shall next consider the concern their posterity have in it, and how much they are affected by it. There are two things follow on it with respect to them; the imputation of the guilt of it to them, and the corruption of nature derived to them from it.

I shall begin with the first, as being previous to the other, and the foundation of it, and which is expressed in very strong terms, Rom. v. 19. *For as by one man's disobedience many were made sinners, so by the obedience of one shall many be made righteous.* The apostle is upon the doctrine of justification by the righteousness of Christ; and whereas it might be a difficulty in the minds of some, how any could be justified by the righteousness of another; and he had to do greatly with Jews as well as Gentiles; the former of which might better understand the doctrine of the imputation of Adam's sin to his posterity; or how all men are made sinners by his sin, than the doctrine of justification by Christ's righteousness; he observes, it is as easy to conceive how men may be made righteous by the obedience of another, namely, through the imputation of that obedience to them, as it is to conceive how all men are made sinners by the disobedience of one man, even through the imputation of that disobedience to them. To set this doctrine in the best light I can, I shall, 1. Observe the act of disobedience, by which men are made sinners.——2. Who they are that are made sinners by it.——3. In what sense they are *made* so through it.

First, The act of disobedience; whose it is, and what.——1. Whose it is: it is sometimes expressed by *one that sinned;* and more than once called, the *offence of one,* Rom. v. 15, 16, 18. and yet more clearly; *By one man sin entered;* and is called, *one man's offence,* and *one man's disobedience,* ver. 12, 17, 19. for it is not the sin of one of the apostate spirits, by which men are made sinners; but the sin of one of their own species, one of the same nature, even the common parent of all mankind, and who is expressed by name, ver. 14. where this offence and disobedience is called *the transgression of Adam;* and so in 1 Cor. xv. 22. *In Adam all die,* being all in him, and having sinned in him, death comes upon them for it; but then this is to be understood of Adam not to the exclusion of Eve, who was also in the transgression, and first in it, and was the mother of all living. They both have the same name, the same appellative name, *man;* the same proper name, Adam, Gen. v. 1, 2. were of the same nature; nay, Eve was formed out of a rib of Adam; was flesh of his flesh, and bone of his bone; a part of himself; and by their marriage-relation became one flesh, Gen. ii. 21—24. they had the same law given them, which forbid the eating of the fruit of a certain tree; the same covenant was made with them, and they were both guilty of the same act of disobedience; and had a sentence of punishment pronounced on them both; and which did not rest on their own persons only, but is common to all their posterity, and still continues; which shews that their posterity had a concern in their act of disobedience, in the guilt of it, since they share in their punishment, as all the sons and daughters of Adam and Eve do; as in the toil and labour of the one, and his return to the dust; so in the pains of child-bearing in the other, and subjection to the man.——2. What this disobedience was; which appears from what has been already said, it was disobedience to the law and will of God, in eating the fruit which he had forbid; so disbelieving the word of God, and giving credit to the serpent. Now it was this one act of disobedience, by which Adam's posterity were made sinners; and therefore is sometimes called the *one* sin, and the *one* offence; so in Rom. v. 16. some copies read ενος αμαρτηματος, *by one sin;* and so in ver. 17. ιν τω ενι παραπτωματι, *by one offence;* and so ver. 18. may be translated as it is in the margin of our bibles; it was a single sin, and the first sin committed in our world; I say in our world, because sin was committed before, in the world above, in heaven, by the apostate spirits, the angels that sinned; but with their sin men have no concern; or they are not made sinners by it; but by that sin which first entered into our world, by the one man, Adam; and this the only one of his sins, and that which was first committed by him, and not any after-sins of his; it is what, and it is the only one that was committed by him, whilst he stood the federal-head of his posterity: that he was a covenant-head to us has been proved already; and that he was such when this was committed by him is plain, because his posterity were then considered in him, as a federal-head, and sinned in him, which brought death upon them all, Rom. v. 12. But no sooner had Adam committed this first sin, by which the covenant with him was broke, but he ceased to be a covenant-head; the law given him, as a covenant of works, was no more so; the promise of life by it ceased; the sanction of it, death, took place; and he was no more in a capacity of yielding sinless obedience; and so could not procure life for himself and his; wherefore he no longer standing as a federal-head to his posterity, they had no more concern with his after-sins, than with his repentance and good works, both of which, no doubt, were performed by him; yet by his repentance they are not reckoned repenting sinners; nor are his good works accounted to them.

Secondly, Who they are that are made sinners by the disobedience of Adam. They are said to be *many;* not only Adam and Eve, who were transgressors, and so became guilty and polluted sinners, through their disobedience, as they most certainly did; as appears from their consciousness of nakedness; from the shame and confusion of face that covered them; from the fear and dreadful apprehensions of the wrath and vengeance of God; and from their fleeing from his presence, and hiding themselves; but even all their posterity, descending from them by ordinary generation, were made sinners hereby; for though they are only said to be *many*, these many signify *all*; the reason of the use of this word, is to answer to the next clause, to the *many* that are *made righteous by the obedience of one Man;* and yet the *many* there, signify all that are in Christ, as their covenant-head; even all his spiritual seed and offspring, given to him and chosen in him: and so all the natural seed and offspring of Adam, to whom he stood as a federal-head, are all made sinners by his disobedience; which is thus strongly expressed, *As by one man sin entered into the world, and death by sin; and so death passed upon all men, for that* or *in whom all have sinned*, Rom. v. 12. And again, *By the offence of one, judgment came upon all men to condemnation*, ver. 18. I say, all descending from him by ordinary generation, are made sinners by his sin, and none else. Had God made more worlds than one, as he could if he would, and worlds of men too; yet as these would not have descended from Adam, they would have had no concern in his sin: had God raised up, children to Abraham out of stones, which he could have done; yet such so raised up, in such a miraculous manner, and not descending from Adam, could not be affected with his sin; and for a like reason the human nature of Christ must be excepted from any concern in it, and from any effect of it, guilt, or pollution; for though he was a partaker of the same human nature, of the same flesh and blood with other men, and made in all things like unto them, yet not by ordinary generation; he was made of a woman, but not begotten by man; God, his Father, prepared a body for him in covenant; and in the fulness of time his human nature was formed by the holy Spirit, in a wonderful manner; it was an extraordinary production; it was a new thing, which God created in the earth, and so an holy thing; was holy, harmless, and separate from sinners, without spot and blemish, and any consciousness of sin; and thus as it was clear of the taint and corruption of nature from Adam's sin, so it was exempt from the guilt of it; see Luke i. 34, 35. And besides that, Christ not descending from Adam by ordinary generation, could not be a federal-head to him on that account;[1] so neither because of the dignity of his person; the human nature being personally united to the Son of God, could never be under a creature as its federal-head, or be represented by one. Moreover, Christ was the head of another and better covenant than Adam's, and was previous to it, even before Adam and his covenant were in being. Christ was an head to Adam, as he was chosen in him, given to him in covenant to be redeemed and saved by him; but Adam was no head to him; *The Head of Christ is God*, and he only, 1 Cor. xi. 3.

Thirdly, In what sense all Adam's posterity are *made* sinners by his disobedience.
———1. Not by imitation, as say the Pelagians; men may become more sinful by imitation, but they do not first become sinful by it: men may, by example, be drawn in to commit sin more frequently, and to commit greater ones; and therefore the company of wicked men is to be shunned, since *Evil communications corrupt good manners;* especially persons of power and authority, their examples have great weight and influence; as civil magistrates, ministers, parents, and masters. So Jeroboam caused Israel to sin, was the occasion of it, and drew them into it by his authority and example. But this cannot be the case here; for,———(1.) Death, the effect of Adam's sin, and the punishment inflicted for it, takes place on such who never *sinned after the similitude of Adam's transgression*, Rom. v. 14. namely, infants dying in their infancy; who, though not without the corruption of nature in them, yet without any actual sin committed by them, like to that of Adam's transgression; dying so soon, they have neither capacity nor opportunity of committing any sin similar to his; that is, any actual transgression; and therefore said, in that respect, to be innocent, Jer. xix. 4. not free from the taint, but from the act of sin. Now since death, which is the punishment of sin, takes place on them, that supposes guilt, or otherwise punishment could not in justice be inflicted on them; and as they are not made sinners by Adam's sin, through imitation of it, they must become guilty, or be made sinners in some other way.———(2.) Death, the effect of Adam's sin, and the punishment of it, takes place on such who never heard of it, and consequently cannot be made sinners by it, through imitation of it; for *death passes upon all men*, all nations of the world, and all individuals in it, through the sin of one man, Adam; even on such who never heard of the law which forbid the eating of

---

[1] See more of this in Book V. of this Work, Chap. I.

the fruit of the tree of knowledge; nor, indeed, ever heard of the law of Moses, and the sins forbidden by that; are acquainted only with the law and light of nature; the law written in their hearts, according to which their minds, consciences, and thoughts, accuse or excuse one another; and yet they that are without law, perish without law, being sinners; and therefore as they cannot be made sinners by Adam's sin, through imitation of it, they must be made so another way; see Rom. ii. 12—15. ——(3.) This sense makes a man no more a sinner by Adam's disobedience than he is by the disobedience of his immediate parents, or any other whose ill examples he follows. Adam seems to be too remote an ancestor to imitate; more likely immediate parents; and yet this is not always the case; children do not always follow the examples of parents, bad or good. Some may have evil parents, and, like the Jews, fill up the measure of their father's sins, and do as they did, and appear to be a generation of vipers; and others have good parents, who give them a religious education, and set them good examples, and yet they take very bad courses; and so not by imitation, at least of their parents. And indeed, sin in general does not come by imitation; but it is from a corrupt nature; and there are many sins which are never seen committed, yet are committed by those who never saw them; as murder, acts of uncleanness, &c. Did Cain sin by imitation when he murdered his brother? Did Lot's daughters sin by imitation when they contrived to commit incest with their father, and did? It is possible that all these defects in nature may meet in one man, as to be born blind, deaf, and dumb; and so not capable of seeing and hearing, and knowing what sins are committed, and yet be as vicious as any of the sons of Adam.

2. Nor is the sense of the phrase, "made sinners by one man's disobedience," what the more modern Pelagians and Arminians give into; that by a metonymy of the effect, sin being put for the punishment of it, men become sufferers, or are obnoxious to death, and suffer death on the account of Adam's disobedience; but this is to depart from the common and constant sense of this word, *sinners*. Nor can any instance be given of the apostle's use of the word in this sense, either in the context or elsewhere; it always signifying a sinful, guilty, and defiled creature; one that is guilty of a crime, and obnoxious to death for it; it is contrary to the apostle's scope and design in the context, which was to shew how death came into the world, namely, by sin; and to the distinction he all along makes between sin and death; the one he represents as the cause, the other as the effect; whereas this sense confounds cause and effect, sin and death, together; and makes the apostle guilty of such bad reasoning as can never be charged upon him, and which a man of such large reasoning powers, abstracted from his being an inspired writer, could never be capable of; for then the sense of these words, ver. 12. *Death passed upon all men, for that all have sinned*, must be, death passed upon all men, because it has passed upon all men; or all men are obnoxious to death, and suffer it, because they are obnoxious to it, and suffer it. Besides, it is granting us too much for themselves; it makes their cause indefensible, and even destroys it, and cuts the throat of it; for if men are obnoxious to death, even though but a corporal death, which is what they mean, and suffer such a death on the account of Adam's sin, they must have a concern in it, and be, in some way or other, guilty of it; or such a punishment, in justice, could not be inflicted on them. What greater punishment is there among men, for the most enormous crime, than death? And why should men suffer death for Adam's sin, of which they are in no sense guilty? Let this be reconciled, if it can be, to the justice of God.

3. Nor is the sense of the phrase, "made sinners by one man's disobedience," that Adam's posterity derive a corrupt nature from him, through his sin; this is indeed a truth, but not the truth of this passage; it is true that all men are made of one man's blood, and that blood tainted with sin; and so a clean thing cannot be brought out of an unclean; what is born of the flesh is flesh, carnal and corrupt; every man is conceived in sin, and shapen in iniquity, as David was; but then there is a difference between being *made* sinners, and *becoming* sinful, the one respects the guilt, the other the pollution of nature; the one is previous to the other, and the foundation of it; men receive a corrupt nature from their immediate parents; but they are not made sinners by any act or acts of their disobedience. Wherefore,

4. It remains that the posterity of Adam are only *made* sinners through the imputa-

tion of his disobedience to them. And this imputation is not to be considered in a *moral* sense, as the action of a man committed by himself, whether good or bad, is adjudged and reckoned unto him as his own, whether in a way of praise or dispraise; as the zealous good work of Phinehas in slaying two persons in the very act of sin, was *counted unto him for righteousness;* that is, was judged, reckoned, and esteemed a righteous, worthy, and commendable action; but in a *forensic,* judicial, and law-sense; as when one man's debts are in a legal way, placed to the account of another, as if they were his, though not personally contracted by him. An instance of this we have in the apostle Paul, who said to Philemon, concerning Onesimus; *If he hath wronged thee, or oweth thee anything,* ελλογει, *let it be imputed to me,* or placed to and put on my account. And thus the posterity of Adam are made sinners by Adam's disobedience, that being imputed to them, and put to their account, as if it had been committed by them personally, though it was not. And this sense is to be confirmed and illustrated,——1. From the signification of the word here used, κατεςαθησαν, *constituted* in a judicial way, ordered and appointed in the dispensation of things, that so it should be; just as Christ was made sin, or a sinner by imputation, by the constitution of God, laying upon him, reckoning, placing to his account the sins of all his people, and dealing with him as though he was the guilty person, and as if he had committed the sins, though he had not; and not imputing trespasses to them, though they were the actual transgressors; see Isa. liii. 6. 2 Cor. v. 19, 21. ——2. From its being the disobedience of another, by which men are made sinners; and therefore they can in no other way be made sinners by it, than by the imputation of it to them; just as the righteousness of Christ being not our own, but his, another's; we cannot be made righteous by it, but by the imputation of it to us.——3. From the punishment inflicted on persons for it. The punishment threatened to Adam in case of disobedience to the law and will of God, was death, Gen. ii. 17. which includes death, corporal, moral, and eternal; a corporal death has been taken notice of already, and which is allowed to be suffered on account of the sin of Adam; and if so there must be guilt; and that guilt must be made over to the sufferer; and which can be done in no other way than by the imputation of it. A moral death is no other than the loss of the image of God in man, which consisted in righteousness and holiness; and particularly it is a loss of original righteousness: in the room of which succeeded unrighteousness and unholiness; and is both a sin, and a punishment for sin; it is a sin as it has malignity in it, and a punishment for sin; and so it was threatened to Adam, and came upon him as such; and so to all his posterity, by the ordination and appointment of God; for which there can be no other foundation but the imputation of Adam's disobedience to them; nor can anything else vindicate the righteousness of God; for if the law of nature was sufficient, why should this original taint infect men, rather than the sins of immediate parents? Now if this comes upon men as a punishment, it supposes preceding sin; and what can that be but Adam's disobedience, the guilt of which must be made over to Adam's posterity, or it could not in justice take place; and that could no other way be made over to them but by imputation. And if eternal death is taken into the punishment, as it must be; for the wages of sin is death, even death eternal; and this can never be inflicted on guiltless persons; if men are thus punished for Adam's sin, the guilt of that sin must be imputed to them: in Rom. v. 18. it is said, *By the offence of one, judgment came upon all men to condemnation;* that is, the righteous sentence of God passed upon the whole posterity of Adam, to the condemnation of them for his offence; be that condemnation to a corporal, or to a moral, or to an eternal death, to any or all of them, it supposes them guilty of that offence, and that the guilt of that offence is made over to them, and reckoned as theirs; which can only be done by imputation; or they cannot be righteously condemned and punished for it in either sense.——4. That this is the sense of the clause, *made sinners by the disobedience of one,* appears from the opposite clause; *So by the obedience of one shall many be made righteous:* now the many ordained to eternal life, for whom Christ died, and whom he justified, are made righteous, or are justified only through the imputation of his righteousness to them; and he is made sin by the imputation of their sins to him, 2 Cor. v. 21. In like manner are Adam's posterity, or all men, made sinners through the imputation of his disobedience to them. And this is the sense of this clause, notwithstanding what may be objected to it.

It is no objection, that Adam's disobedience or sin is not now in act; as soon as it was committed as an act, it ceased; and therefore not to be imputed. The same may be objected to the obedience of Christ; or rather a course of obedience, a series of actions, which when performed, ceased to be in act; but then the righteousness arising from them continues; and is in Christ, The Lord our Righteousness; and is unto all and upon all that believe. And so Adam's sin, though it ceased to be in act, the guilt of it continues, and is imputed to all his posterity. In like manner the sins of the saints, before the coming of Christ, ceased to be in act as soon as committed; and yet Christ died for the redemption of transgressions that were under the first Testament, and the sins of all the people of God were laid upon him by imputation. Nor is it any objection to this truth, that Adam's posterity were not in being when his disobedience was committed, and so could have no concern in it; but though they had not an actual being, yet they had a virtual and representative one; they were in him both seminally and federally; and *sinned in him* too, Rom. v. 12. as Levi was in the loins of Abraham, and paid tithes to Melchizedek, Heb. vii. 9, 10. I say, both seminally and federally; and it is their being in him seminally that is the foundation of their being in him federally, and makes it reasonable that so they should be; and this may be greatly illustrated and confirmed by modern philosophy, according to which all kinds of plants of the same sort to be produced in all following ages, were actually formed in the first seed that was created; and that all the *stamina* and *semina*, not only of plants but of animals, and so of men, were originally formed of the almighty Parent, within the first of each respective kind, and to be the seed of all future generation:[2] thus all mankind being formed in the first man, in this manner, it easily accounts for it, how they came to have a share in the guilt of his sin, and that to be imputed to them; as also to have the corruption and pollution of it derived to them. Nor does this act of imputation of Adam's sin to his posterity, make God the author of sin; since this act makes men sinners not inherently, but imputatively; it puts no sin in them, though it reckons sin to them; and though this imputation is God's act, it makes him no more the author of sin, than the imputation of Christ's obedience, makes God the author of that obedience; as not God, but Christ, is the author of the obedience imputed; so not God, but Adam, is the author of that disobedience imputed to his posterity: nor is this doctrine chargeable with cruelty and injustice; it has never been reckoned either, that children should suffer for the sins of their parents; or rather, that parents should be punished in their children; God describes himself as a God visiting the iniquity of the fathers upon the children unto the third and fourth generation of them that hate him; and yet it is impossible that he should be guilty either of a cruel or unjust action: when Achan sinned, his sons and his daughters, and all that he had, were ordered to be brought forth, and they were all burnt with him. The Amalekites, for the injury they did to Israel, when they first came out of Egypt, Saul had orders, some hundreds of years after, to go and smite them, and utterly destroy all they had, men and women, infants and sucklings, and all their cattle: the blood of all the righteous persons that had been shed from the beginning of the world to the times of Christ, was then avenged on the wicked Jews. And such a procedure in subjecting children to penalties for the sins of their parents, is justified by the laws, customs, and usages of all nations, who make treason punishable in the posterity of men. A nobleman when he commits treason against his sovereign, he is not only stripped of his titles, honour, and estates himself, but his children are also, and reduced to poverty and misery, until the attainder is taken off. And if treason against an earthly king is punishable in this manner, then much more treason against the King of kings, and Lord of lords, as Adam's sin was.

The text in Ezek. xviii. 2, 3, 4. is not to the purpose; that the proverb, *The fathers have eaten sour grapes, and the childrens' teeth are set on edge*, should be no more used in Israel, but the soul that sins should die; since this speaks not a word of Adam, and his sin, nor of his posterity suffering for it; nor even of such men that commit the same sins their fathers have;

---

[2] See the Philosophical Transactions abridged, vol. ii. p. 912. Nieuwentyt's Religious Philosopher, vol. ii. contempl. 23. s. 13. p. 711. ed 5. Wolaston's Religion of Nature, s. 5. p. 160, 164. ed. 8.

but of good men and just men, that do not follow their fathers' evil ways, and so shall not be punished for any sins of theirs, and is restrained to a certain case and time. The case of the man born blind, is also quite impertinent; since that also respects not Adam's sin, but the sin of the man and his parents, and a particular disaster, blindness. The disciples put this question to Christ upon it; *Who did sin, this man or his parents, that he was born blind?* Christ's answer is, *Neither hath this man sinned, nor his parents*: not but that they had both sinned, but their sin was not the cause and reason of his blindness; but the sovereign will and pleasure of God, *That the works of God should be made manifest in him;* that there might be an opportunity for Christ to give proof of his Deity and Messiahship, by performing such a cure as was never heard of before, John ix. 2, 3.

To close this point; let it be observed, that the ground of the imputation of Adam's sin to his posterity, is not his being the natural head, and common parent of them; for so are immediate parents to their respective offspring; but their particular sins are not imputed to them; Adam, being the common parent of mankind, may be considered as the ground of the derivation of a corrupt nature to them, and yet the justice of that will not clearly appear without their being considered as made sinners by the imputation of Adam's sin to them: but the ground of this imputation is the federal headship of Adam or his standing as a covenant-head to all his posterity; so that what he did as such, is reckoned as if done by them; which is not the case of immediate parents; and therefore their sins are not imputed: that Adam stood in the relation of a federal-head to his posterity, has been proved in a former chapter, and vindicated from exceptions to it.

CHAP. XI.

OF THE CORRUPTION OF HUMAN NATURE.

HAVING proved the imputation of the guilt of Adam's sin to his posterity, what follows upon this is, the corruption of nature derived unto them from him; by which is meant, the general depravity of mankind, of all the individuals of human nature, and of all the powers and faculties of the soul, and members of the body.

First, I shall prove that there is such a depravity and corruption of mankind.

1. The heathens themselves have acknowledged and lamented it; they assert, that no man is born without sin;[1] that every man is naturally vicious;[2] that there is an evil disposition, or vicious affection, that is implanted and grows up in men;[3] and that there is a fatal portion of evil in all when born, from whence are the depravity of the soul, diseases, &c.[4] and that the cause of viciosity is rather from our parents, and from first principles, than from ourselves:[5] and Cicero[6] particularly laments that men should be brought into life by nature as a step-mother, with a naked, frail, and infirm body, and with a mind or soul prone to lusts.——2. Revelation asserts it; the scriptures abound with testimonies of it, affirming that no man can be born pure and clean; that whatever is born of the flesh, or comes into the world by ordinary generation, is flesh, carnal and corrupt; that all men, Jews and Gentiles, are under sin, under the guilt, pollution and dominion of sin; that the imagination of the thoughts of man's heart is only evil, and that continually; that the heart is deceitful and desperately wicked; and that out of it proceeds all that is vile and sinful, Job xiv. 4. John iii. 6. Rom. iii. 9. Gen. vi. 5. Jer. xvii. 9. Matt. xv. 19.——3. Reason confirms it, that so it must be; that if a tree is corrupt, it can bring forth no other than corrupt fruit; that if the root of mankind is unholy, the branches must be so too; if the fountain is impure, the streams must be so likewise; if immediate parents are unclean, their posterity must be unclean, since a clean thing cannot be brought out of an unclean; and if God has made of one man's blood all nations that are upon the face of the earth, and that blood is tainted with sin, all that proceed from him by ordinary generation must have the same taint.——4. All experience testifies the truth of this; no man was ever born into the world without sin;

---

[1] Which Plato calls κακοφυια, and defines it κακια εν φυσει, an evil in nature, Plato. Definitiones. Nam vitiis nemo sine nascitur——Horat. Satyr, 1. 1. satyr 3. v. 68.

[2] Unicuique dedit vitium natura creatâ, Propert. 1. 2. eleg. 22. ver. 17.

[3] Laertius, 1. 2. in vita Aristippi.

[4] Plutarch, de Consol. ad Apoll. vol. 2. p. 104.

[5] Timæus Locrus de Natura Mundi, p. 21.

[6] De Republica, 1. 3. apud August. contr. Julian 1. 4. c. 12.

CHAP. XI. OF THE CORRUPTION OF HUMAN NATURE. 331

no one has ever been exempt from this contagion and defilement of nature, *there is none that doeth good, no not one,* Rom. iii. 10. that does good naturally and of himself; the reason is, because there is none by nature good; of all the millions of men that have proceeded from Adam by ordinary generation, not one has been found without sin; there is but one individual of human nature that can be mentioned as an exception to this, and that is the human nature of Christ; and that is excepted because of its wonderful production, and did not descend from Adam by ordinary generation.——5. The necessity of redemption by Christ, and of regeneration by the Spirit of Christ, shews that men must be in a corrupt state, or there would have been no need of these. The redemption of men from sin, and from a vain conversation, supposes them to be under the power of sin, and the influence of it, to lead a vain sinful life; and if men were free from the pollution of sin, the blood of Christ to cleanse from all sin would have been unnecessary; his being made wisdom, righteousness, and sanctification, and redemption to them, implies that they were foolish and unwise, that they were unrighteous and unholy, and slaves to sin and Satan: regeneration and sanctification are absolutely necessary to a man's enjoyment of eternal happiness; *except a man is born again, he cannot see the kingdom of God;* and *without holiness no man shall see the Lord,* John iii. 3. Heb. xii. 14. but what occasion would there have been for man's being born again, or having a new or supernatural birth, if he was not defiled by his first and natural birth; or of being sanctified, if he was not unholy and unclean? see 1 Cor. vi. 9—11.

Secondly, The names by which this corruption of nature is expressed in scripture deserve notice, since they not only serve to give more light into the nature of it, but also to confirm it; it is often called *sin* itself, being a want of conformity to to the law of God, and contrary to it; it is represented as very active, working all manner of concupiscence, and death itself; deceiving, slaying, killing, and as exceeding sinful, even to an hyperbole, being big with all sin, and the source of all, Rom. vii. 8, 11, 13. It has the name of *indwelling sin;* the apostle speaks of it as such with respect to himself, *it is no more I that do it, but sin that dwelleth in me,* Rom. vii. 17, 20. it is not what comes and goes, or is only a visitor now and then, but an inhabitant, and a very troublesome one; it hinders all the good, and does all the evil it can; and it abides, and will abide, as long as men are in this tabernacle, the body, and even in the saints, until the earthly house of this tabernacle is dissolved; it is like the spreading leprosy in the house, which was not to be cured until the house was pulled down, and the stones and timber carried into an unclean place: so the tabernacle of the body will not be rid of the corruption of nature, until it is unpinned and taken down, and carried to the grave. It is said to be the *law of sin,* and a *law in the members;* which has force, power, and authority with it; it reigns like a king; yea, rather as a tyrant; for it reigns unto death unless grace prevents it; it enacts laws, and requires obedience to them; and obedience is yielded to the lusts of it; men serve divers lusts and pleasures, Rom. vii. 23. and viii. 2. and vi. 12. and v. 21. Tit. iii. 3. Sometimes it is called the *body of sin,* because it consists of various parts and members as a body does; it is an aggregate, or an assemblage of sins, and includes all in it, Rom. vi. 6. Col. iii. 5. Sometimes it goes by the name of the *old man,* because it is the effect of the poison of the old serpent; it is near as old as the first man; and is as old as every man in whom it is: it exists as early as man himself does, Rom. vi. 6. Eph. iv. 22. Very often it is called *flesh,* because it is propagated by the flesh, and is carnal and corrupt, and is opposed to the spirit or principle of grace, which is from the Spirit of God; and in which no good thing, nothing that is spiritual, dwells, John iii. 6. Gal. v. 17. Rom. vii. 18, 25. Once more, it is named, *lust* or *concupiscence;* which is sin itself, and the mother of all sin; it consists of various branches, called fleshly lusts, and worldly lusts, the lust of the flesh, the lust of the eyes, and the pride of life, Rom. vii. 7. James i. 15. 1 John ii. 15. The Jews commonly call it, the evil figment, or imagination.

Thirdly, This corruption of nature is universal,——1. With respect to the individuals of mankind. Our first parents were, and all descending from them by ordinary generation are tainted with it. This corruption, immediately upon the sin of our first parents, took place in them; as appears from the shame, confusion, and fear, they were at once filled with; from their gross stupidity and folly, in thinking to hide themselves from God among the trees of the garden; from their attempts to conceal, palliate, and excuse their sin, the woman by laying the blame on the serpent, the man on the woman, and ultimately on God himself. Their immediate offspring took the contagion from them; the first man born into the world, Cain, the corruption of nature soon appeared in him, in his wrathful and envious countenance, when his brother's sacrifice was preferred to his; nor could he be easy until he had shed his brother's blood, which he did: and though Abel is called righteous Abel, as he was, through the righteousness of Christ imputed to him, and on account of the new man created in him unto righteousness and true holiness; in consequence of which he lived soberly and righteously; yet he was not without sin, or otherwise, why did he offer sacrifice, and by faith looked to the sacrifice of Christ, which was to be offered up to make atonement for his sins, and those of others? In the room of Abel, whom Cain slew, God raised up another seed to Adam, whom he begot in his own likeness, after his image; not in the likeness and image of God, in which Adam was created; but in that which he had brought upon himself, through his sin and fall: the posterity of this man, and of Cain, peopled and filled the whole world before the flood. And what is the account that is given of them? It is this, that the earth was corrupt through them; that all flesh had corrupted his way on the earth; and that only one man found grace in the sight of God; and that the imagination of the thoughts of man's heart was only evil continually, Gen. iv. 25. and v. 3. and vi. 5, 8, 11, 12. And as for the inhabitants of the new world, who sprung from Noah and his three sons, who descended in a right line from Seth, much the same is said of them, Gen. viii. 21. In short, all nations of the earth, which may be divided into Jews and Gentiles, and which include the whole, are all under sin, under the guilt and pollution of it; not the Gentiles only, whose times of ignorance God winked at, and whom he suffered to walk in their own ways, which were sinful ones; but even the people of Israel, whom God chose to be a special and peculiar people, these were always rebellious, from the time they were a people; all the while Moses was with them; in the times of the Judges; and when under the government of Kings; as their several captivities testify; they were a seed of evil doers, a people laden with iniquity; in every age or period of time, whenever God took a survey of the state and condition of mankind, this was the sum of the account, *They are corrupt, &c.* Psalm xiv. 1, 2, 3. See Rom. iii. 9, 10, 11, 12. The contentions, quarrels, and wars, which have been in the world, in all ages, are a strong, constant, and continued proof of the depravity of human nature; *for these come of lusts that war in the members,* James iv. 1. which, as it is true of the war between flesh and spirit in the soul; and of the animosities and contentions among professors of religion; so of wars among nations, in a civil sense; and which have been from the beginning, and still continue: a quarrel there was between the first two men that were born into the world, which issued in bloodshed; and as soon as kingdoms and states were formed, and kings over them, we hear of wars between them. Look over the histories of all ages, and of all nations in them, and you will find them full of accounts of these things; all which have risen from the pride, ambition, and lusts of men. Yea, this depravity and corruption of nature has appeared, not only among the men of the world in all ages, but even among the people of God, and after they have been called by grace; there never was a just man that did good, and sinned not; in many things, in all things, they sin and offend; in them, that is, in their flesh, their corrupt part, no good thing dwells: such that say they have no sin, deceive themselves, and the truth is not in them.

2. This corruption of nature is general, with respect to the parts of man, to all the powers and faculties of his soul, and to the members of his body.———(1.) To the powers and faculties of the soul of man, to all that is within him; his heart is deceitful and desperately wicked; his inward part is wickedness itself; the thoughts of his heart are evil, vain, and sinful; yea, the imagination of the thoughts of his heart, the very substratum of thought, the first notions that are in man that way; the mind and conscience, are defiled, and nothing can remove the pollution but the blood of Jesus: the understanding is darkened through the blindness and ignorance that is in it; so that a mere natural man cannot discern the things of the Spirit of God; whatever knowledge men

have of things natural and civil, they have none of things spiritual; wise they are to do evil, but to do good they have no knowledge; they know not, nor will they understand; the will is averse to that which is good; the carnal mind is enmity to God, and not subject to the law of God; nor can it be, without his grace; it is hard, stiff, obstinate, and perverse, until the stony heart is taken away, and a heart of flesh is given. The affections are inordinate, run in a wrong channel, are fixed on wrong objects; men hate what they should love, and love what they should hate; they hate the good, and love the evil; they are lovers of pleasures, of sinful lusts and pleasures, rather than lovers of God, good men, and good things. In short, there is no place clean, no part free from the pollution and influence of sin.——(2.) All the members of the body are defiled with it; the tongue is a little member, and is a world of iniquity itself, and defiles the whole body; the several members of it are used as instruments of unrighteousness; several of them are particularly mentioned in the general account of man's depravity, Rom. iii. as the throat, lips, mouth, and feet, all employed in the service of sin.

Fourthly, The time when the corruption of nature takes place in man; the lowest date of it is his youth; *The imagination of man's heart is evil from his youth*, Gen. viii. 21. that is, as soon as he is capable of exercising his reason, and of committing actual sin; and which, at this age, chiefly appears in lying and disobedience to parents; and this is said, not of some particular men, or of some individuals, but of men in general; and not only as in the times of Noah, but in all succeeding generations to the end of the world. This depravity of nature is in some passages carried up higher, even to a man's birth; *The wicked are estranged from the womb;* that is, from God, alienated from the life of God; being under the power of a moral death, or being dead in trespasses and sins; *They go astray as soon as they be born, speaking lies*, Psalm lviii. 3. that is, as soon as they are capable of speaking; and the sin of lying, children are very early addicted to; and this is said, not only of such who in the event turn out very wicked, profligate and abandoned sinners, but even such as are born of religious parents, have a religious education, and become religious themselves, are *called transgressors from the womb*, Isa. xlviii. 8. that is, as soon as capable of committing actual transgression. David carries the pollution of his nature still higher, when he says; *Behold, I was shapen in iniquity; and in sin did my mother conceive me*, Psalm li. 5. which he observes, not to extenuate, but rather to aggravate, his actual transgression he was confessing, in that he had been so early and so long sinful; and that whereas he was not ignorant of the corruption of his nature, and how prone he was to sin, that he should be no more upon his guard against it. He does not say, *my sin, and my iniquity*, though it was his, being in his nature; but *sin* and *iniquity*, being what was common to him with the rest of mankind; and what had attended him at the formation of him in the womb, and so before he could commit any actual sin; and therefore must design the original corruption of his nature; and that as soon as soul and body were united together he was a sinful creature. To this sense of the words it is objected, that David speaks only of his mother's sin; and broad hints are given that her sin was the sin of adultery. This shews how much the advocates for the purity of human nature are pinched with this passage, to betake themselves to such an interpretation of it, at the expense of the character of an innocent person, of whom nothing of this kind is suggested in the sacred writings; but, on the contrary, that she was a pious and religious person; David valued himself upon his relation to her, and pleads to be regarded for her sake, Psalm lxxxvi. 16. and cxvi. 16. Besides, if this had been the case, David would have been illegitimate; and, by a law in Israel, would have been forbid entering into the congregation of the Lord, and could not have bore any office in church and state; nor did it answer the scope and design of David, to expose the sins of others, especially his own parents, whilst he is confessing and lamenting his own; nor does the particle *in* belong to his mother, but to himself; the sense is not, that his mother being in sin or that she *in* and *through sin* conceived him; but that he was conceived being in sin, or that as soon as the mass of human nature was shaped and formed in him, and soul and body were united together, he was in sin, and sin in him; or he became a sinful creature. Some who do not go the above lengths, yet suppose that the sin of his immediate parents, in begetting and conceiving him, though in lawful wedlock, is meant; but this cannot be; since the propagation of the human species by generation, is a principle implanted in nature by God himself, and so not sinful. It was the first law of nature, *Increase and multiply;* given in the state of innocence. Marriage was instituted in Paradise, and has been always esteemed honourable when the bed is undefiled. Besides, one of the words used, translated *shapen*, is in the passive form, and respects what neither David nor his parents could be active in; and the whole refers to the amazing work of his formation, which he so much admires, Psalm cxxxix. 14, 15, 16. It is objected by others, that he goes no higher than his mother; and takes no notice of Adam. Nor was there any need of it; for since the corruption of nature goes in the channel of generation, he had no occasion, in speaking of that, to take notice of any other but his immediate parents, through whom it was conveyed to him: it is further urged, that David speaks not of other men, only of himself. But that all mankind are corrupted in the same manner, other passages are full and express for it, Job xiv. 4. John iii. 6. Psalm lviii. 3. Eph. ii. 3. And if David, a man so famous for early piety and religion, one after God's own heart, whom he raised up to fulfil his will, was tainted with sin in his original formation, then surely the same must be true of all others; who, after him, can rise up and say, it was not so with him? Lastly, some will have these words to be figurative and hyperbolical, and only mean, that he had often sinned from his youth: but men, in confessing sin, do not usually exaggerate it, but declare it plainly, ingenuously, just as it is; and, indeed, the sinfulness of nature, cannot well be hyperbolized; and, if such a figure was attempted, it might be allowed of, without lowering it; see Rom. vii. 13.

Fifthly, The way and manner in which the corruption of nature is conveyed to men, as to become sinful by it.———1. It cannot be of God, or by infusion from him; he is of purer eyes than to behold it; he has no pleasure in it; it is abominable to him, and therefore would never infuse and implant it in the nature of men. Some of the ancient heretics fancied, there were two first principles, or beings; the one good, and the other evil; and that all that is good comes from the one, and all that is evil from the other: but this is to make two first causes, and so two gods; and those diametrically opposite to each other. ———2. Nor can it be by imitation of parents, either first or immediate; there are some who never sinned after the similitude of Adam's transgression, and yet die; which they would not, were they not guilty and polluted; there are many born into the world who never knew their immediate parents, and therefore could not imitate them. Some their fathers die before they are born; and some lose both parents before capable of imitation; and if the taint is at their formation, and before their birth, it is impossible to be by imitation.——— 3. Nor does this come to pass through souls being in a pre-existent state. Some of the heathen philosophers, as Pythagoras and Plato, held a pre-existence of souls before the world was; and which notion was adopted by Origen, who held, that souls in this pre-existent state sinned each separately for themselves; and for their sins were thrust in time into human bodies, or into others, in which they suffer. Some think this notion was embraced by some of the Jews in Christ's time, and even by some of his followers; as is urged from John ix. 1, 2, 3. but then it is not allowed of by him. And some modern Christians have imbibed the same heathenish and Jewish notion; who, observing that some passages of scripture speak of the pre-existence of Christ, in his divine nature, or as a divine Person, have interpreted them of the pre-existence of his human soul; and have proceeded to assert the pre-existence of all souls, but without any colour of reason or scripture authority. ———4. Nor is this to be accounted for by the traduction of the soul from immediate parents; or by the generation of it, together with the body, from them. Could this indeed be established, it would greatly remove the difficulty which attends the doctrine of the propagation of the corruption of nature by natural generation; hence Austin was once inclined to it on this account; but it is so big with absurdities, as has been seen in a preceding chapter, that it cannot be admitted; as, that spirit is educed out of matter, and generated from it, and therefore must be material, corruptible, and mortal; for whatever is generated is corruptible, and consequently the soul is not immortal; a doctrine never to be given up: and, besides, according to the Scriptures, the soul is immediately created by God, Zech. xii. 1. Heb. xii. 9. That this corruption of

CHAP. XI.   OF THE CORRUPTION OF HUMAN NATURE.   335

nature is conveyed by generation, seems certain; see Job. xiv. 4. John iii. 6. Eph. ii. 3. for since nature is conveyed in that way, the sin of nature also must come in like manner. But how to account for this, consistent with the justice, holiness, and goodness of God, is a difficulty, and is one of the greatest difficulties in the whole scheme of divine truths; wherefore some have thought it more advisable to sit down and lament this corruption, and consider how we must be delivered from it, than to inquire curiously in what way and manner it comes into us; as a man that is fallen into a pit, does not so much concern himself how he came into it, as how to get out of it, and to be cleansed from the filth he has contracted in it. But a sober inquiry into this matter, with a due regard to the perfections of God, the sacred Scriptures, and the analogy of faith, may be both lawful and laudable. The difficulty is chiefly occasioned by the manner in which the the case is put; as, that a soul that comes pure and holy out of the hand of God, should be united to a sinful body, and be defiled by it; but if it can be made out, that neither of these is the fact, that the body is not properly and formally sinful, when the soul is first united to it, nor the soul pure and holy when created by God; that is, not in such sense as the soul of Adam was when created; the difficulty will be greatly lessened, if not entirely removed.

1. Let it be observed, then, that the contagion of sin does not take place on the body apart, nor on the soul apart; but upon both when united together, and not before: it was not the body apart in the substance of Adam's flesh that sinned; nor was the soul apart represented by him; but both as in union, and as one man, one person; for not bodies and souls separately, but men, were considered in Adam, and sinned in him; and so as the imputation of the guilt of his sin is not made to the body apart, nor to the soul apart, but to both as united; when, and not before, it becomes a son of Adam, a member of him; so the corruption of nature, derived from him, takes place on neither apart, but upon them as united together, and constituted man. The body, antecedent to its union to a rational soul, is no other than a brute, an animal, like other animals; and is not a subject either of moral good or moral evil; as it comes from a corrupt body, and is of a corruptible seed, it has in it the seeds of many evils, as other animals have, according to their nature; but then these are natural evils, not moral ones; as the savageness, fierceness, and cruelty of lions, bears, wolves, &c. But when this body comes to be united to a rational soul, it becomes then a part of a rational creature, it comes under a law, and its nature not being conformable to that law, its nature and the evils and viciosities of it, are formally sinful. It has before a disposition, an aptitude to what is sinful; and contains fit fuel for sin, which its vicious lusts and appetites kindle, when these become formally sinful, through its becoming a part of a rational creature; and these increasing, operate upon and gradually defile the soul. Should it be said, that matter cannot operate on spirit; this may be sooner said than proved. How easy is it to observe, that when our bodies are indisposed through diseases and pain, what an effect this has upon our minds; from the temperament and constitution of the body many incommodities and disadvantages arise unto the soul: persons that have much of the *atra bilis*, or black choler in them, a melancholy and bodily disorder, what a gloominess does it throw upon the mind! and to what passion, anger, and wrath, are men of a sanguine complexion subject? and to what is insanity owing, but to a disorder in the brain? and to a defect there must it be attributed, that some are idiots, and others of very mean capacities, and very short memories; and where the bodily organs are not well attempered and accommodated, the soul is cramped, and cannot duly perform its functions and offices; and a man must be inattentive to himself, if he does not observe, that as by thoughts in the mind, motions are excited in the body, whether sinful, civil, or religious; so motions of the body are often the means and occasion of exciting thoughts in the mind.

2. It is not fact that souls are now created by God pure and holy; that is, as Adam's soul was created, with original righteousness and purity; with a propensity to that which is good, and with power to do it. But they are created with a want of original righteousness and holiness; without a propensity to good, and without power to perform; and a reason will be given presently, why it is so; and why it should be so. And such a creation may be conceived of without any imputation of unrighteousness to God, and without making

him the author of sin. It may be conceived of without any injury to the perfections of God; as, that he may create a soul in its pure essence, with all its natural powers and properties, without any qualities of moral purity or impurity, holiness or unholiness; or that he may create one with a want of righteousness, and with an impotence to good, and without any propensity to it; since by so doing he does not put any sinfulness into the soul, nor any inclination to sin. And that the souls of men should be now so created, it is but just and equitable, as will appear by the following considerations: Adam's original righteousness was not personal, but the righteousness of his nature; he had it not as a private single person, but as a public head, as the root, origin, and parent of mankind; so that had he stood in his integrity, it would have been conveyed to his posterity by natural generation; just as he having sinned, the corruption of nature is derived to them in the same way; what he had, he had not for himself only, but for his posterity; and what he lost, he lost not for himself only, but for his posterity; and he sinned not as a single private person, but as the head, root, origin, and parent of all his offspring; they were all in him, and sinned in him as one man; so that it was but just that they should be deprived, as he, of the glory of God, that is, of the image of God, which chiefly lay in original righteousness, in an inclination to good, and a power to perform it; and, being stripped of this, or being devoid of it, an inclination to sin follows upon it, as soon as it offers; and in the room of it unrighteousness and unholiness take place; for as Austin says, the loss of good takes the name of evil; and this being the case, how easily may it be accounted for, that a soul without any fence or guard, wanting original righteousness, be gradually mastered and overcome by the corrupt and sensual appetites of the body. And to all this agrees what a learned author[7] well observes, "God is to be considered by us, not as a Creator only, but also as a Judge; he is the Creator of the soul, as to its substance; in respect to which it is pure when created. Moreover, God is a Judge, when he creates a soul, as to this circumstance; namely, that not a soul simply is to be created by him; but a soul of one of the sons of Adam: in this respect it is just with him to desert the soul, as to his own image lost in Adam; from which desertion follows a want of original righteousness; from which want original sin itself is propagated,"

Should it be said, that though the justice and holiness of God are cleared from all imputation, in this way of considering things; yet it does not seem so agreeable to the goodness and kindness of God to create such a soul, and unite it to a body, in the plight and condition before described; since the natural consequence of it seems to be unavoidably the moral pollution of them both. To which may be replied, that God in this proceeds according to the original law of nature, fixed by himself; and which according to the invariable course of things, appears to be this, with respect to the propagation of mankind: that when matter generated is prepared for the reception of the soul, as soon as that preparation is finished, that very instant a soul is created, and ready at hand to be united to it, and it is. Now the law for the propagation of mankind by natural generation, was given to Adam in a state of innocence, and as soon as created, *Increase and multiply*; he after this corrupted and defiled the whole frame of his nature, and that of all his posterity. Is it reasonable now, that because man has departed from his obedience to the law of God, that God should depart from his original law, respecting man's generation? It is not reasonable he should, nor does he, nor will he depart from it: this appears from cases, in which, if in any, he could be thought to do so; as in the case of insanity, which infects a man's blood and family, and becomes a family disorder; and yet to put a stop to this God does not depart from the order of things fixed by him; and so in the case of such who are unlawfully begotten in adultery or fornication; when what is generated is fit to receive the soul, there is one prepared and united to it. And sometimes in this way God brings into the world some that belong to the election of grace; one of our Lord's ancestors came into the world in this way, Gen. xxxviii. 29. Matt. i. 3. What if Adam eats the forbidden fruit, and men drink water out of another's cistern, stolen waters, which are sweet unto them, and thereby transgress the law of God; must he forsake his own stated law and order of things? No; nature itself does not do so: a man

---

[7] Sandford or Parker de Descensu Christi ad inferos, 1. 3. s. 65. p. 121, 122.

steals a quantity of wheat, and sows it in his field; nature proceeds according to its own laws, fixed by the God of nature; the earth receives the seed, though stolen, into its bosom, cherishes it, and throws it out again, and a plentiful crop is produced. And shall nature act its part, and not the God of nature? He will; and the rather he will go on in his constant course, that the sin of men might be manifest, and that sin be his punishment. And in this light, indeed, we are to consider the corruption of nature; a moral death, which is no other than a deprivation of the image of God, a loss of original righteousness, and an incapacity to attain to it, was threatened to Adam, and inflicted on him as a punishment. And since all his posterity sinned in him, why should not the same pass upon them? and, indeed, it is by the just ordination of God that things are as they be, in consequence of Adam's sin, who cannot do an unjust thing; there is no unrighteousness in him; he is righteous in all his ways, and holy in all his works; and so in this. And here we should rest the matter; in this we should acquiesce; and humble ourselves under the mighty hand of God.

CHAP. XII.

OF ACTUAL SINS AND TRANSGRESSIONS.

FROM the sin of Adam arises the corruption of nature, with which all mankind, descending from him by ordinary generation, are infected; and from the corruption of nature, or indwelling sin, arise many actual sins and iniquities; which are called in scripture, *The works of the flesh*, Gal. v. 19. or corrupt nature, in distinction from the fruits of the Spirit, or inward principles of grace and holiness; see ver. 17, 22. These are the same with the *lusts of the flesh*, and *the desires* or *wills of the flesh*, Eph. ii. 3. The internal sinful actings of the mind and will; even all manner of concupiscence, which lust or corrupt nature works in men, and which war against the soul: they are called sometimes, *the deeds of the body*, of the body of sin; which, through the Spirit, are mortified, weakened, kept under, so as not to be frequently committed, and be a course of sinning, Rom. viii. 13. and vi. 6. And sometimes, *the deeds of the old man*, the old principle of corrupt nature, to be put off, with respect to the outward conversation, and not be governed by the dictates of it, Col. iii. 9. Eph. iv. 21. Sometimes they are represented by *corrupt fruit*, brought forth by a corrupt tree; such is man's sinful heart and nature, and such the acts that spring from it: if the tree is not good, good fruit will not grow upon it; the heart must be made good, ere good works can be done by men, Matt. vii. 16—20. and xii. 33. Those actual sins are the *birth* of corrupt nature, which is like a woman that conceives, bears, and brings forth; *When lust hath conceived, it bringeth forth sin,* James i. 15. see Rom. vii. 5. Corrupt nature is the fountain, and actual sins, whether internal or external, are the streams that flow from it; *Out of the heart,* as from a fountain, *proceed evil thoughts,* &c. Matt. xv. 19. as is the spring, so are the streams; if water at the fountain-head is bitter, so are the streams; *Doth a fountain send forth at the same place, sweet water and bitter?* No.

Actual sins are deviations from the law of God; for *sin is the transgression of the law,* 1 John iii. 4. Actions, as natural actions, are not sinful; for all actions, or motions, are from God, the first Cause; from whom nothing sinful comes; creatures depend on him in acting, as well as in subsisting; *In him we move;* or otherwise they would be independent of him; whereas, *all things are of him.* But an action is denominated good or bad, from its agreement or disagreement with the law of God, its conformity or disconformity to it; it is the irregularity, obliquity, and aberration of the action from the rule of the divine law, that is sin; and this whether in thought, word, or deed; for actual sins are not to be restrained to outward actions, performed by the members of the body, as instruments of unrighteousness; but include the sinful actings of the mind, evil thoughts, carnal desires, the lusts of the heart, *heresies,* errors in the mind, false opinions of things, and *envyings,* are reckoned among the *works of the flesh,* Gal. v. 20, 21. And when we distinguish actual sins from original sin, we do not mean thereby that original sin is not actual. The first sins of Adam and Eve were actual sins, transgressions of the law of God; *Eve was in the transgression;* that is, guilty of an act of transgression; and we read of *Adam's transgression,* which designs the first sin he committed, 1 Tim. ii. 14. Rom. v. 14. And original sin, as derived from the sin of our first parents, is also actual; it is a want of conformity to the law of God, and is very active and operative as it dwells in men, it works in them all manner of concupiscence; it hinders all the good, and puts upon doing all the evil it can; and is itself exceeding sinful. But actual sins are second acts, that flow from the corruption of nature. My business is not now to enlarge on particular sins, by explaining the nature, and shewing the evil of them; which more properly belongs to another part of my scheme that is to follow, even *Practical Divinity*. I shall therefore only treat of actual sins very briefly, in a doctrinal way, by giving the distribution of sins into their various sorts and kinds, reducing them to proper classes, and ranging them under their respective heads.

First, With respect to the object of sin, it may be distinguished into sins against God; sins against others, our neighbours, friends, and those in connection with us; and against ourselves; for which distinction there seems to be some foundation in 1 Sam. ii. 25. *If one man sin against another, the Judge shall judge him; but if a man sin against the Lord, who shall entreat for him?*——1. There are some sins that are more immediately and directly against God; all sin, indeed, is ultimately against him, being contrary to his nature and will; a transgression of his law; a contempt and neglect, and indeed a tacit denial of his legislative power and authority; who is that *Lawgiver that is able to save and to destroy*. The sins of David against Uriah are confessed by him to be against the Lord; *Against Thee, Thee only have I sinned*, Psalm li. 4. But there are some sins more particularly pointed at him, committed against him, in an open, bold, and audacious manner; *Their tongues and their doings are against the Lord*, Isa. iii. 8. Such are they as Eliphaz describes, who *stretch out their hands against God*, Job xv. 25, 26. their carnal minds being enmity against God. Particularly sins against the first table of the law, are sins against God; such as *atheism* in theory and in practice; which is, a denying that there is a God, and strikes at the very Being of him: blasphemy of his name, his perfections, and providences; which is one of the things that proceed from the evil heart of man: idolatry, having other gods before him, and serving the creature besides the Creator; bowing down to, and worshipping idols of gold, silver, brass, wood, and stone: to which may be added, sensuality, voluptuousness, making the belly a god, and covetousness, which is idolatry: taking the name of God in vain, using it on trifling occasions, and in a light and irreverent manner: cursing fellow-creatures in the name of God, and swearing falsely by it, which is perjury: want of love to God, and of fear of him; having no regard to his worship, private and public; a profanation of the day of worship, and a neglect of the ordinances of divine service.——
2. Sins against others, are the violations of the second table of the law; as disobedience to parents; not giving that honour, shewing that reverence and respect, and paying that regard to their commands that ought to be: to which head may be reduced, disobedience to all superiors; the king as supreme, the father of his country; subordinate magistrates; ministers of the word, masters, &c. Murder, or the taking away of the life of another, is a sin against the sixth command, as the former are against the fifth; of this there are divers sorts; as parricide, fratricide, &c. which last is the first actual sin we read of after the sin of our first parents: it seems as if the sin of murder greatly abounded in the old world, since at the beginning of the new, a special law respecting it was made; *Whoso sheddeth man's blood, by man shall his blood be shed*, Gen. ix. 6. All sins of unchastity, in thoughts, and by obscene words and filthy actions, are violations of the seventh command, which forbids adultery, fornication, incest, and all unnatural lusts: taking away a man's property, privately or publicly, by force or fraud, by false accusations, and by circumventing and overreaching in trade and business, are breaches of the eighth command; and not only doing injury to the persons and properties of others, but to their good name, credit, and reputation, comes under the name of actual sins against others; for taking away a man's good name is as bad as taking away his money, and is next to taking away his life.——3. There are sins against a man's self; the apostle reckons fornication as sinning *against* a man's *own body*, 1 Cor. vi. 18. what is a pollution of it brings dishonour upon it, fills it with nauseous diseases, and weakens the strength of it. Drunkenness is another sin against a man's self; it is what deprives him of the exercise of his reason, impairs his health, wastes his time, his substance, and at last his body. Suicide is a sin against a first principle of nature, self-preservation. The Stoics applaud it as an *heroic* action; but it is a base, mean, and cowardly one; and betrays

CHAP. XII. OF ACTUAL SINS AND TRANSGRESSIONS.

want of fortitude of mind to bear up under present adversity, and to meet what is thought to be coming on. However, no man has a right to dispose of his own life; God is the giver, or rather lender, of it, and he only has a right to take it away.

Secondly, With respect to the subject of sin, it may be distinguished into internal and external; sins of heart, lip, and life; or of thought, word and action.——1. Internal sins, sins of the heart; the plague of sin begins there, that is the seat of it; it is desperately wicked, it is wickedness itself; and out of it all manner of sin flows; the thoughts of it are evil, they are abominable to God, and very distressing to good men, who hate vain thoughts; the very thought of foolishness or wickedness is sin.[1] The imagination of the thoughts of the heart is evil continually; the very substratum of thought, the motions of sin in the mind, work to bring forth fruit unto death; the desires and lusts of the mind are carnal and sinful, which are various; the lust of uncleanness in the heart; the lust of passion, wrath, and revenge; the lust of envy, which the object of it cannot stand before, and which slays the subject of it; the lusts of ambition and pride; and which are thus summed up by the apostle, *the lust of the flesh, the lust of the eye, and the pride of life*, 1 John ii. 15.

Errors in the mind, false opinions of things contrary to the word of God; all unreasonable doubts, even in saints themselves; and all the actings of unbelief, which proceed from an evil heart, come under this sort of sins, internal ones, or sins of the heart.——2. Sins of the lip, or of words, which are external, openly pronounced, whether respecting God or man, and one another; as all blasphemy of God, evil speaking of men, cursing and swearing, lying one to another; all obscene and unchaste words, every sort of corrupt communication; all bitterness, wrath, anger, clamour, and evil speaking; all foolish talking and jesting, which are not convenient; yea, every idle word, comes into the account of sin, and will be brought to judgment; see Eph. iv. 25, 29, 31. and v. 4. Matt. xii. 36, 37.——3. Outward actions of the life and conversation; a vain conversation, a course of sin, the garment spotted with the flesh, right eye and right hand sins, and all that the members of the body are used as instruments in the commission of.

Thirdly, With respect to the parts of sin: they may be divided into sins of omission and sins of commission; when some things are left undone which should be done, and which are done when they ought not to be; such a distinction may be observed in the words of Christ, or however a foundation for it there is in them, Matt. xxiii. 23. and xxv. 42—44. and both these sorts of sins are very strongly expressed in Isa. xliv. 22—24. Sins of omission are against affirmative precepts, not doing what is commanded to be done; sins of commission are against negative precepts, doing what is forbidden to be done; see James iv. 17.

Fourthly, Sin may be distinguished by the principle from whence it arises. Some sins arise from ignorance, as in the princes of the world, that crucified the Lord of life and glory; in the apostle Paul when unregenerate, in persecuting the saints, and doing many things contrary to the name of Jesus; and which he did ignorantly, and in unbelief; and in others who know not their master's will, and so do it not, and yet pass not uncorrected; especially whose ignorance is wilful and affected, who know not, nor will understand, but reject and despise the means of knowledge, and say to God, depart from us, we desire not the knowledge of thy ways; the sins of others are presumptuous ones, and are done wilfully, knowingly, and of choice, and who are worthy of many stripes; see Luke xii. 47, 48. Some sins are through infirmity of the flesh, the power of Satan's temptations, and the snares of the world, which men are betrayed into through the deceitfulness of sin, and are overtaken and overpowered at an unawares, and surprised into the commission of them; and which is the case oftentimes of the people of God.

Fifthly, Sins may be distinguished by the degrees of them into lesser and greater; for all sins are not equal, as the Stoics say;[2] and some are more aggravated than others, with respect to the objects of them; as sins against God are greater than those against men; violating of the first table of the law, greater than that of the second: and with respect to persons that commit

---

[1] Prov. xxiv. 9. This is a Christian doctrine; apud nos et cogitare, peccare est, Minutius Felix in Octavio, p. 39. and yet an heathen poet asserts it, from whom one would not have expected it: nam scelus intra se tacitum qui cogitat ullum, facti crimen habet——Juvenal, Satire 13. v. 209. Vid. Alex. ab Alex. Genial. Dier. 1.2. c. 16.

[2] Laert. 1. 7. Vita Zeno, p. 510.

them, and with respect to time and place when and where they are committed, with other circumstances; some are like motes in the eye, others as beams. Our Lord has taught us this distinction, not only in Matt. vii. 3, 4, 5. but when he says, *He that delivered me unto thee, hath the greater sin,* John xix. 11. And this appears from the different degrees of punishment of sin, which are allotted in proportion to it; so as our Lord speaks of some cities, where his doctrines were taught, and his miracles wrought, and repented not, that it would be *more tolerable for Tyre, Sidon, and Sodom, than for* them, Matt. xi. 20—24. According to the laws of Draco, all sins were equal, and all were punished with the same capital punishment; the stealing of an apple, as the murder of a man. Hence it was said, that Draco wrote his laws, not in ink, but in blood.[3] Not such are the laws of God; nor such the nature of sin according to them.

Sixthly, Sins may be distinguished by their adjuncts. As, 1. Into secret and open sins. Secret sins are such as are secretly committed, or sins of the heart; which none but God, and a man's own soul, are privy to; and some pass through it unnoticed and unobserved by the good man himself; and are opposed to presumptuous sins; which distinction may be observed in Psalm xix. 12, 13. Others are done openly, publicly, before the sun, and in sight of all, without fear or shame. Some men's sins go beforehand to judgment; they are notorious ones; condemned by all, before the judgment comes; and others more secretly committed, they follow after; for all will be brought into judgment, 1 Tim. v. 24. Eccles. xii. 14. —— 2. The papists distinguish sin into venial and mortal: which cannot be admitted without a limitation or restriction; for though all sin is venial or pardonable, through the grace of God and blood of Christ, and is pardoned thereby, excepting one, that will be hereafter mentioned; yet none are pardonable in their own nature; or are so small and trifling as to be undeserving of death, only of some lesser chastisement; for all sin is mortal, and deserving of death; *The wages of sin,* of any and every sin, without distinction of greater and lesser, *is death,* eternal death, as it must be; for *Cursed is every one that continueth not in all things,* be they greater or lesser, *written in the book of the law to do them*: if, therefore, every breach of the law subjects to the curse of it, which is death, then every sin is mortal. Yet,——3. Sin may be distinguished into remissible and irremissible. All the sins of God's people are remissible, and are actually remitted. God forgives them all their iniquities, and heals all their diseases, their spiritual maladies; and on the other hand, all the sins of reprobates, of abandoned sinners, that live and die in final impenitence and unbelief, are irremissible; *He that made them will not have mercy on them,* to forgive their sins; *And he that formed them will shew them no favour* that way, Isa. xxvii. 11. There is one sin which is commonly called the *unpardonable sin,* which is the sin, or blasphemy, against the Holy Ghost; and of which it is expressly said, that *it shall not be forgiven, neither in this world, nor in the world to come,* Matt. xii. 31, 32. But not every sin against the Holy Ghost is here meant; every sin committed against God is committed against the Holy Ghost, as well as against the Father and the Son; he, with them, being the one God, against whom all sin is committed: nor is it a denial of his deity, and of his personality, though sins against him, yet they arise from ignorance of him, and are errors in judgment; and from which persons may be recovered, and repent of, and renounce: nor is a denial of the necessity of the operations of his grace on the souls of men, in order to their regeneration, conversion, and sanctification, this sin, for the same reasons: men may, and good men too, grieve the Holy Spirit by their sins; yea, vex him, as the Israelites; and yet not sin the unpardonable sin; yea, a man may break all the Ten Commandments, and not sin the sin against the Holy Ghost; it is a sin not against the law, but against the gospel; it lies in the denial of the great and fundamental truth of the gospel, salvation by Jesus Christ, in all its branches; peace and pardon by his blood, atonement by his sacrifice, and justification by his righteousness; and this, after he has received the knowledge of this truth, under the illuminations, convictions, and demonstrations of the Spirit of God; and yet, through the instigation of Satan, and the wickedness of his own heart, knowingly, and wilfully, and maliciously denies this truth, and obstinately persists therein. So that as he

---

[3] Plutarch in Solon. p. 87.

never comes to repentance, he has no forgiveness, here nor hereafter. Not because the Holy Spirit is superior to the other divine Persons; for they are equal: nor through any deficiency in the grace of God, or blood of Christ; but through the nature of the sin, which is diametrically opposite to the way of salvation, pardon, atonement, and justification; for these being denied to be by Christ, there can be no pardon; for another Jesus will never be sent, another Saviour will never be given; there will be no more shedding of blood, no more sacrifice, nor another sacrifice for sin; nor another righteousness wrought out and brought in. And, therefore, there remains nothing but a fearful looking for of judgment and indignation, to come on such persons.

Upon all which it may be observed, from what a small beginning, as the sin of our first parents might seem to be, what great things have arisen; what a root of bitterness that was which has brought forth so much unwholesome and pernicious fruit; such a vast number of sins, and of such an enormous size: what a virtue must there be in the blood of Christ, to cleanse from such sins as these, and all of them; and in his sacrifice to make atonement for them; and in his righteousness to justify from them! And how great is the superabounding grace of God, that where sin has thus abounded, grace should superabound!

CHAP. XIII.

OF THE PUNISHMENT OF SIN.

As to the punishment of original sin on those who, it may be thought, not to have added to it any actual sin and transgression, as infants, dying in infancy, I shall be silent; at least, say little. Not that I doubt of the right of justice to punish that sin on Adam's descendants, who have not actually sinned after the similitude of his transgression; since corporal death, a part of the punishment threatened, does pass upon them, and they are born with a want of original righteousness, a considerable branch of moral death; but if divine justice proceeds further, and inflicts eternal death, or everlasting punishment on them, I think it must be in a more mild and gentle manner than what is inflicted on those who have also been guilty of actual sins and transgressions; seeing, as

there are degrees of punishment respecting them, as they are greater or lesser, Matt. xi. 20—24. so there must be a difference of the punishment of original sin, separately considered; and of that attended with numerous actual transgressions. Many unguarded expressions have been dropped, concerning the punishment of such infants, as before mentioned, which are not at all to the credit of truth. Many conjectures have been made, and schemes formed, that are scarcely worth mentioning. Some have fancied that all such infants are lost; which seems to have something in it shocking, especially to parents. And others think they are all saved, through the electing grace of God, the redeeming blood of Christ, and the regeneration of the blessed Spirit; to which I am much rather inclined, than to the former: but think it best to leave it among the secret things that belong to God; who, we may be assured, cannot do an unjust thing, nor do any injury to any of his creatures: and who, as he is just in his nature, he is merciful in Christ.

In this article I have nothing to do with men as elect or non-elect; but as they are all the fallen race of Adam. The elect, as considered in Christ, the Head of the covenant of grace, are not subject, or liable to any punishment, here or hereafter; *There is no condemnation to them that are in Christ Jesus:* their afflictions are not punishments for sin; nor is corporal death inflicted on them as a penal evil; nor will any curse befal them in a future state. But my concern is with men considered in Adam, as the head of the covenant of works, and the representative of all mankind; as they sinned and fell in him, and were involved in the guilt of his sin; and as they are actual transgressors in themselves; and as they are chargeable with sin, according to the declaration, sanction, and tenor of the law; and considered as such, all mankind descending from Adam by ordinary generation, without any exception and distinction, are subject, obnoxious, and liable to punishment.

Punishment of sin, original and actual, may be considered as temporal and eternal; both in this life, and that which is to come. There is an everlasting punishment into which the wicked go after death; and there is a punishment in this life; *Wherefore should a living man complain, a man for the punishment of his sin?* Lam. iii. 37. that is, for punishment in the present state.

First, Temporal punishment, or punishment in this life, is due to sin; and is inflicted on account of it; and this is both inward and outward, or of soul and body.

1. Punishment inward, or of the soul, lies, (1.) In a loss of the image of God upon it; all have sinned and *come short*, or *are deprived of the glory of God;* that is, of the image of God, in which his glory on man lay; one principal part of which image was righteousness and holiness. This man is stripped of, and is become unrighteous; *There is none righteous, no not one*, Rom. iii. 10, 23.

(2.) In a loss of the freedom of will, and of power to do good. Man has not lost the natural liberty of his will to things natural; but the moral liberty of his will to things moral; his will is not free to that which is good, only to that which is evil; and that liberty is no other than bondage. Man's free-will is a slave to his lusts; he is a home-born slave, Jer. ii. 14. Man has lost his power to do good; how to perform that he knows not; through the weakness of the flesh, or corrupt nature, he cannot do what the law requires; he cannot of himself think anything; and, without the grace of God, cannot do anything as it ought to be done; for he has no principle of life and motion in him to it; he is dead in trespasses and sins.

(3.) In a loss of knowledge of divine things; his understanding is darkened with respect to them; he is darkness itself; he has lost his knowledge by sinning, instead of gaining more; *There is none that understandeth*, and seeks after God, and the knowledge of him. Spiritual things men cannot discern; to do good they have no knowledge; they know not, nor will they understand. And many, through an habitual course of sinning, become hardened; and God gives them up to a judicial blindness and hardness of heart; to vile affections, and a reprobate mind, to do things not convenient; to strong delusions, to believe a lie; and to their own hearts' lusts; and nothing worse can well befal men than that.

(4.) In a loss of communion with God. Adam sinned, and was drove out of paradise, and was deprived of communion with God through the creatures; and all his sons are alienated from a life of fellowship with him: their sins separate between God and them; and, indeed, what communion can there be between light and darkness, righteousness and unrighteousness? the throne of iniquity, or where iniquity reigns, can have no fellowship with God, who commit sin as though they had a law to do it.

(5.) In being destitute of hope, and subject to horror and black despair. The sinful soul of man is hopeless and helpless: men live without real hope of future happiness, and without God in the world; if their consciences are not lulled asleep, they are continually accusing of sin; the arrows of the Almighty stick in them; the poison of his wrath drinks up their spirits; and his terrors set themselves in array against them: having no view of pardon, peace, and righteousness by another, there is nothing but a fearful looking for of judgment; indignation and wrath, tribulation and anguish, are due to every soul of man that does evil, and to which he is liable; unless the grace of God prevents.

2. Outward punishments or of the body, or what relate to the outward things of life, are as follow:

(1.) Loss of immortality of the body. Adam's body was gifted with immortality; but sinning, he was stripped of it, and became mortal, and so all his posterity are; which arises not from the constitution of their nature, and the appointment of God, barely, but from sin; *The body is dead*, or is become mortal, *because of sin*, Rom. viii. 10. and it is liable, on the same account, to various diseases; they all have their foundation in and their original from sin; God threatens men for it with a consumption, and with a fever, and with an inflammation, and with extreme burning, Deut. xxviii. 22. and these, with many others, are inflicted on account of it. To one cured of a disease, Christ said; *Go home, sin no more, lest a worse thing come upon thee*, John v. 14. signifying, that his former disease came upon him for sin, and a worse would, should he continue in it.

(2.) Labour of body, with toil, fatigue, and weariness, is another penal effect of sin. Though Adam dressed the garden of Eden, in his state of innocence, it was done without toil and fatigue; but when he had sinned, the earth was cursed for his sake, and brought forth thorns and thistles; and he was doomed to labour in it, to dig in it, to weed and purge it, to cultivate and manure it; and thereby to get and eat his bread in sorrow, and in the sweat of his brow. And this doom continues still in his posterity; man is born *to labour* as the sparks fly upward; so the word may be rendered, Job v. 7. The earth remains in such a state as requires cultivation, ploughing, sowing, weeding, &c. in which men must work with their own hands, in a toilsome and laborious manner, or in other arts, to get bread for themselves and families, and have wherewith to give to others. And it may be observed, that the punishment pronounced on Eve, that her conception and sorrow should be multiplied; and that in sorrow she should bring forth children, is continued in her daughters; and it is remarked, that of all the creatures, none bring forth their young in so much pain as women; and hence some of the greatest calamities and distresses in life, are described and expressed by the pains of a woman in travail; see Gen. iii. 16—19.

(3.) Loss of dominion over the creatures is another sort of punishment of sin. Adam had a grant of dominion over all the creatures, and these were in subjection to him. But by sin man has lost his power over them; and many of them, instead of fearing and serving him, rebel against him, and are hurtful to him; he is afraid of coming near them, unless God makes peace with them for him, and preserves him from them; yea, the noisome beast is one of God's sore judgments with which he threatens to punish sinful men, Hos. ii. 18. Ezek. xiv. 21.

(4.) The many distresses in person, in family, and in estate, are the penal effects of sin; the curses of the law, for the transgressions of it, come upon men, and on what they have; in the city, and in the field; in basket, and in store; in the fruit of their body, and of their land; in the increase of their kine and flocks of sheep; when these are affected, and there is a failure in them, it is for sin, Deut. xxviii. 16, 20.

(5.) Public calamities are to be considered in this light, as punishments of sin, as the drowning of the old world; the burning of Sodom and Gomorrah; the captivities of the Jews; the destruction of other nations and cities; the devastations made by wars, famines, pestilences, earthquakes, &c.

(6.) Last of all, as to outward temporal punishment, corporal death, which is the disunion of soul and body, is the just *wages* and demerit of sin; it was threatened in case of it, and it is inflicted for it; it came upon Adam, and it comes upon all his posterity; and sin is the cause of it; *The sting of death is sin;* sin gives it its destructive power and force, and makes it a penal evil.

Secondly, There is an eternal punishment of sin, or the punishment of it in the world to come for ever. This takes place in part on wicked men as soon as soul and body are separated; their souls, during their separate state, until the resurrection, are in a state of punishment; the wicked rich man when he died, *in hell he lift up his eyes, being in torment,* Luke xvi. 22, 23. At the resurrection the bodies of wicked men will come forth from their graves, to the resurrection of damnation; when soul and body will be destroyed in hell, and punished with an everlasting destruction from the presence of God, John v. 29, Matt. x. 28. 2 Thess. i. 9. This punishment will be both of loss and sense; it will lie in an eternal separation from God, from any enjoyment of his favour, and fellowship with him; but such will have their eternal abode with devils and damned spirits; and in an everlasting sense of the wrath of God, which will be poured forth like fire; and both are expressed in that sentence, *Depart from me, ye cursed, into everlasting fire,* Matt. xxv. 41. Now this punishment is eternal; it is called everlasting punishment, everlasting destruction; everlasting fire; fire that is not quenched; the smoke of it ascends for ever and ever, Matt. xxv. 41, 46. 2 Thess. i. 9. Mark ix. 42. Rev. xiv. 11. The reasons of the eternal duration of punishment for sin, are, because it is committed against an infinite and eternal Being, and is objectively infinite, and requires infinite satisfaction, which a finite creature cannot give; and this not being given, punishment must proceed on *ad infinitum,* and so be eternal. Could satisfaction be made, punishment would cease; but no satisfaction can be made in hell by the sufferings of finite creatures; which, therefore, must be continued until the uttermost farthing is paid, or full satisfaction made, which can never be done. Besides, the wicked in the future state, will always continue sinning, and be more and more outrageous and desperate in their blasphemy and hatred of God; and, therefore, as they will sin continually, it will be just that they be punished continually; to which may be added, that there will be no repentance for sin there, no pardon of it, no change of state; *He that is unjust, let him be unjust still; and he that is filthy, let him be filthy still,* Rev. xxii. 11. But of this more hereafter, towards the close of this work.

Now this punishment of sin, both temporal and eternal, is due to all the fallen ace of Adam; to all descending from him by ordinary generation, without any distinction or exception, as they are considered in him, and transgressors of the righteous law of God. All equally sinned in him, and died in him; all are made sinners by the imputation of his disobedience to them; the guilt of which sin, and of their own actual transgressions, they are chargeable with: the whole world is become guilty before God; and which guilt in his sight, and as pronounced by him according to his law, is an obligation to punishment: all the transgressors of the law, as all men are, stand cursed and condemned by it; nay, *by the offence of one*, of the one man Adam, *judgment came upon all men to condemnation;* so that all Adam's posterity are under a sentence of condemnation; and as considered in him, and in themselves, are subject, exposed, and liable to the above punishment; being all *by nature children of wrath*, one as well as another, deserving of it, and so liable to it; that is, to punishment. The reason why this punishment, to which all are subject, is not inflicted on some, is because of the suretiship engagements of Christ for them, and his performance of those engagements; whereby he endured all that wrath and punishment due to their sins in their room and stead; and so delivered them from it, which otherwise they were exposed unto; the dawn of which distinguishing grace the next part of this work will open and display.

A BODY OF DOCTRINAL DIVINITY.

BOOK IV.

OF THE ACTS OF THE GRACE OF GOD TOWARDS AND UPON HIS ELECT IN TIME.

CHAP. I.

OF THE MANIFESTATION AND ADMINISTRATION OF THE COVENANT OF GRACE.

HAVING treated of the sin and fall of our first parents, and of the breach of the covenant of works by them, and of the sad effects thereof to themselves, and of the woeful consequences of the same to their posterity; of the imputation of their sin, and the derivation of a corrupt nature unto them; and of actual sins and transgressions flowing from thence, and of the punishment due unto them: I am now come to the dawn of grace to fallen man, to the breakings forth and application of the covenant of grace, and the blessings of it to the spiritual seed of Christ among the posterity of Adam.

I have considered the covenant of grace in a former part of this work, as it was a compact in eternity, between the three divine persons, Father, Son, and Spirit; in which each person agreed to take his part in the economy of man's salvation: and now I shall consider the administration of that covenant in the several periods of time, from the beginning of the world to the end of it. The covenant of grace is but one and the same in all ages, of which Christ is the substance; being given for *a covenant of the people*, of all the people of God, both Jews and Gentiles, who is *the same* in the *yesterday* of the Old Testament, and in the *to-day* of the New Testament, and *for ever*; he is *the way, the truth, and the life*, the only true way to eternal life; and there never was any other way made known to men since the fall of Adam; no other name under heaven has been given, or will be given, by which men can be saved. The patriarchs before the flood and after, before the law of Moses and under it, before the coming of Christ, and all the saints since, are saved in one and the same way, even *by the grace of our Lord Jesus Christ*; and that is the grace of the covenant, exhibited at different times, and in divers manners. For though the covenant is but one, there are different administrations of it; particularly two, one before the coming of Christ, and the other after it; which lay the foundation for the distinction of the *first* and *second*, the *old* and the *new* covenant, observed by the author of the epistle to the Hebrews, chap. viii. 7, 8, 13. and ix. 1, 15. and xii. 24. for by the *first* and *old* covenant, is not meant the covenant of works made with Adam, which had been broke and abrogated long ago; since the apostle is speaking of a covenant waxen old, and ready to vanish away in his time: nor was the covenant of works the first and most ancient covenant; the covenant of grace, as an eternal compact, was before that; but by it is meant the first and most ancient administration of the covenant of grace which reached from the fall of Adam, when the covenant of works was broke, unto the coming of Christ, when it was superseded and vacated by another administration of the same covenant, called therefore the *second* and *new* covenant. The one we commonly call the Old Testament-dispensation, and the other the New Testament-dispensation; for which there seems to be some foundation in 2 Cor. iii. 6, 14. Heb. ix. 15. these two covenants, or rather the two administrations of the same covenant, are allegorically represented by two women, Hagar and Sarah, the bond-woman and the free, Gal. iv. 22—26. which fitly describe the nature and difference of them. And before I proceed any farther, I shall just point out the agreement and disagreement of those two administrations of the covenant of grace.

First, The agreement there is between them.——1. They agree in the efficient cause, God: the covenant of grace in its original constitution in eternity, is of God, and therefore it is called his covenant, being made by him; *I have made a covenant—my covenant I will not break*, Psalm lxxxix. 3, 34. and whenever any exhibition or manifestation of this covenant was made to any of the patriarchs, as to Abraham, David, &c. it is ascribed to God, *I will make my covenant—he hath made with me an everlasting covenant*, Gen. xvii. 2. 2 Sam. xxiii. 5. so the new covenant, or new administration of it, runs in this form, *I will make a new covenant, &c.* Heb. viii. 8. ——2. In the moving cause, the sovereign mercy, and free-grace of God, which moved God to make the covenant of grace at first, Psalm lxxxix. 2, 3. And every exhibition of it under the former dispensation, is a rich display of it, and therefore it is called, the *mercy promised to the fathers* in his *holy covenant*, Luke i. 72. and which has so largely appeared in the coming of Christ, which is ascribed to *the tender mercy of our God*, that *grace* and *truth*, in the great abundance of them, are said to come by him; by which names the covenant of grace, under the gospel-dispensation, is called, in distinction from that under the Mosaic one, Luke i. 78. John i. 17.——3. In the Mediator, who is Christ; there is but one Mediator of the covenant of grace, let it be considered under what dispensation it will; even Christ, who under the former dispensation was revealed as the seed of the woman that should bruise the serpent's head, and make atonement by his sufferings and death, signified by the expiatory sacrifices, under the law; the Shiloh, the peaceable One, and the Peace-Maker, the living Redeemer of Job, and of all believers under the Old Testament. Moses, indeed, was a Mediator, but he was only a typical one. There is but *one Mediator between God and man, the Man Christ Jesus;* there never was any other, and he is the *Mediator of the new covenant,* 1 Tim. ii. 5. Heb. xii. 24.——4. In the subjects of these covenants, or administrations of the covenants of grace, the elect of God, to whom the blessings of it are applied. It was with the chosen people of God in Christ, the covenant of grace was originally made; and according to election-grace are the spiritual blessings of it dispensed to the children of men, Psalm lxxxix. 3. Eph. i. 3, 4. so they were under the former dispensation, from the beginning of the world, to the seed of the woman, in distinction from the seed of the serpent; to the remnant according to the election of grace among the Jews, the children of promise that were counted for the seed; and election, or elect men, obtain the blessings of the covenant in all ages, and under the present dispensation more abundantly, and in greater numbers.——5. In the blessings of it; they are the same under both administrations. Salvation and redemption by Christ is the great blessing held forth and enjoyed under the one as under the other, 2 Sam. xxiii. 5. Heb. ix. 15. Justification by the righteousness of Christ, which the old testament-church had knowledge of, and faith in, as well as the new, Isaiah xlv. 24, 25. Rom. iii. 21, 22, 23. Forgiveness of sin through faith in Christ, all the prophets bore witness to; and the saints of old, as now, had as comfortable an application of it, Psalm xxxii. 1, 5. Isa. xliii. 25. Mic. vii. 18. Acts x. 43. Regeneration, spiritual circumcision, and sanctification, were what men were made partakers of under the first, as under the second administration of the covenant, Deut. xxx. 6. Phil. iii. 3. Eternal life was made known in the writings of the Old Testament, as well as in those of the New; and was believed, looked for, and expected by the saints of the former, as of the latter dispensation, John v. 39. Heb. xi. 10, 16. Job xix. 26, 27. In a word, they and we eat the same spiritual meat, and drink the same spiritual drink, for they drank of that Rock that followed them, and that Rock was Christ, 1 Cor. x. 3, 4.

Secondly, In some things there is a disagreement between these two administrations of the covenant of Grace.——

1. Under the first administration, saints looked forward to Christ that was to come, and to the good things that were to come by him, and so were waiting, expecting, and longing for the enjoyment of them; but under the second and new administration, believers look backwards to Christ as being come, before whose eyes he is evidently set forth in the word and ordinances, as crucified and slain; and they look to the blessings of the covenant through him as brought in; to peace, pardon, atonement, righteousness, redemption, and salvation, as wrought out and finished.——2. There is a greater clearness and evidence of things under the one than under the other; the law was only a shadow of good things to come; did not so much as exhibit the image of them, at least but very faintly. The obscurity of the former dispensation, was signified by the veil over the face of Moses, when he spoke to the children of Israel; so that they could not see to the end of what was to be abolished; whereas, believers under the present dispensation, with open face, with faces unveiled, behold, as in a glass, the glory of the Lord clearly and plainly, Heb. x. 1. 2 Cor. iii. 13, 18. then, comparatively, it was night, now broad day; the day has broke, and the shadows are fled and gone.——3. There is more of a spirit of liberty, and less of bondage, under the one, than under the other; saints under the one differed little from servants, being in bondage under the elements of the world; but under the other are Christ's freemen, and receive not the spirit of bondage again, to fear; but the spirit of adoption, crying, Abba, Father; which is a free spirit, and brings liberty with it; and for this reason the two different administrations of the covenant, are signified, the one by Hagar, the bond-woman, because it gendered to bondage, and those under it were in such a state; and the other by Sarah, the free-woman, an emblem of Jerusalem, which is free, and the mother of us all, Gal. iv. 1, 2, 3, 24, 25, 26. Rom. viii. 15.——4. There is a larger and more plentiful effusion of the Spirit, and of his gifts and graces, under the one, than under the other; greater measures of grace, and of spiritual light and knowledge were promised, as what would be communicated under the new and second administration of the covenant and accordingly *grace* in all its fulness, and *truth* in all its clearness and evidence, are *come by* *Jesus Christ*, John i. 17. see Jer. xxxi. 31—34.——5. The latter administration of the covenant extends to more persons than the former. The Gentiles were strangers to the covenants of promise, had no knowledge nor application of the promises and blessings of the covenant of grace, except now and then, and here and there one; but now the blessing of Abraham is come upon the Gentiles, and they are fellow-heirs of the same grace and privileges, and partakers of the promises in Christ by the gospel, Eph. ii. 12. and iii. 6. Gal. iii. 14.——6. The present administration of the covenant of grace, will continue to the end of the world; it will never give way to, nor be succeeded by another; it is that which remains, in distinction from that which is done away, and so exceeds in glory: the ceremonial law, under which the former covenant was administered, was *until the time of reformation*, until Christ came and his forerunner; *The law and the prophets were until John*, the harbinger of Christ, the fulfilling end of them; see 2 Cor. iii. 11. Heb. ix. 10. Luke xvi. 16.——7. The ordinances of them are different. The first covenant had ordinances of divine service; but those, comparatively, were carnal and worldly, at best but typical and shadowy, and faint representations of divine and spiritual things; and were to continue but for a while, and then to be shaken and removed, and other ordinances take place, which shall not be shaken, but remain to the second coming of Christ; and in which he is more clearly and evidently set forth, and the blessings of his grace, Heb. ix. 1, 10. and xii. 27.——8. Though the promises and blessings of grace under both administrations are the same, yet differently exhibited; under the former dispensation, not only more darkly and obscurely, but by earthly things, as by the land of Canaan, and the outward mercies of it; but under the latter, as more clearly and plainly, so more spiritually and nakedly, as they are in themselves spiritual, heavenly, and divine; and delivered out more free, and unclogged of all conditions, and so called *better promises*, and the administration of the covenant, in which they are, *a better testament;* God having *provided* for new testament-saints some *better thing*, at least held forth in a better manner; that old testament-saints might not be *made perfect* without them, Heb. viii. 6. and vii. 22. and xi. 40.

CHAP. II.

OF THE EXHIBITIONS OF THE COVENANT OF GRACE IN THE PATRIARCHAL STATE.

Though the administration of the covenant of grace may be considered in a threefold state; as in the patriarchal state, before the giving of the law; and then under the Mosaic dispensation; and last of all under the gospel-dispensation; yet more agreeable to the apostle's distinction of the first and second, the old and the new covenant, observed in the preceding chapter, I shall choose to consider it in the distinct periods under these two: and I shall begin with the administration of it under the first testament, as reaching from the fall of Adam to the coming of Christ, and consider it as held forth in the several periods in that long interval of time.

The *first* period shall be from Adam to Noah. And those in this period to whom the covenant of grace, and the blessings of it it were manifested and applied, were, 1. Our first parents themselves, Adam and Eve, and that both by words and actions. By words, and these spoken not directly to them, nor by way of promise to them; but to the serpent, and threatening-wise to him; and yet were the first dawn of grace to fallen man, Gen. iii. 15. from whence it might be at once concluded by Adam and Eve, that they should not immediately die, but that a seed should be of the woman, who would be the ruin of Satan, and the Saviour of them; which must spring light, life, and joy, in their trembling hearts: and though these words are short and obscure, yet contain some of the principal articles of faith and doctrines of the gospel; as the incarnation of the Son of God, signified by the *seed of the woman*, who should be made of a woman, born of a virgin, unbegotten by man, and without father as man; the sufferings and death of Christ for the sins of men, signified by the serpent's *bruising his heel*, bringing him to the dust of death in his inferior nature, sometimes expressed by his being bruised for the sins of his people; and may hint at the manner of his death, and crucifixion, since his feet could not well be pierced with nails without bruising his heel; also the victory he should obtain over Satan, signified by *bruising his head*, destroying his power and policy, his schemes and works, his authority, dominion, and empire; yea, him, himself, with his principalities and powers; and may express the bruising him under the feet of his people, the deliverance of them from him; the taking the captives out of the hand of the mighty, and the saving them with an everlasting salvation. Which is the sum and substance of the gospel, and matter of joy to lost sinners.

The grace of the covenant, and the blessings of it, were manifested and applied to our first parents, by certain actions and things done; as by the Lord God making *coats of skin*, and *clothing them with them*, which were emblems of the robe of righteousness, and garments of salvation, Christ has wrought out; that righteousness which God imputes without works; and is unto all, and upon all them that believe, as their clothing and covering: and those coats being made of the skins of slain beasts, very probably slain for sacrifice, which man was soon taught the use of; may have respect to the sacrifice of Christ, the woman's seed, which should be offered up, as was agreed on in the covenant of grace, and by which atonement would be made for sin, and upon which justification from it proceeds; all which are momentous articles of faith. The *cherubim* and *flaming sword*, placed at the East end of the garden of Eden, to keep the way of the tree of life, were not for terror, but for comfort; and were an hieroglyphic, shewing that God in succeeding ages would raise up a set of prophets, under the old-testament, and apostles and ministers of the gospel, under the new testament, who should hold forth the word of light and life; that word which is quick and powerful, sharper than any two-edged sword; that has both light and heat in it; and who should shew to men the way of salvation, and observe unto them the true tree of life, and the way to it; even Christ, the way, the truth, and the life; see Gen. iii. 21, 24.

2. Abel, the Son of Adam, is the next person to whom an exhibition of the covenant, and of the grace of it, was made; he was an instance of electing grace, according to which the blessings of the covenant are dispensed: a hint was given in the serpent's curse, that there would be two seeds in the world, the seed of the serpent, and the seed of the woman; this distinction took place in the first two men that were born into the world. Cain was of the wicked one, the seed of the serpent; Abel was one of the spiritual seed, of Christ, a

chosen vessel of salvation; and, in virtue of electing grace, was a partaker of the blessings of grace in the covenant; particularly of justifying grace: he is called *righteous* Abel, not by his own righteousness, but by the righteousness of faith, by the righteousness of Christ received by faith; for he had the grace of faith, which is a covenant-grace, bestowed on him; by which he looked to Christ for righteousness and eternal life; *By faith Abel offered unto God a more excellent sacrifice than Cain; by which he obtained witness that he was righteous*, Heb. xi. 4. His sacrifice was a more excellent one; not only as to its kind, being a lamb, and so typical of the Lamb of God; but as to the manner in which it was offered, by faith, in the view of a better sacrifice than that; even the sacrifice of Christ, by which transgression is finished, sin made an end of, reconciliation for it made, and an everlasting righteousness brought in; all which Abel, by faith, looked unto, and God had respect to him, and to his offering; which he testified in some visible way; perhaps by sending down fire upon it; which drew the envy of his brother upon him, who could not rest until he had slain him: in this Abel was a type of Christ, as well as in his being a keeper of sheep; who, through the envy of the Jews, who were in some sense his brethren, was delivered to the Roman governor, to be put to death; so that they are justly said to be the betrayers and murderers of him; and a like punishment of their sin came on them as on Cain; as he was drove from the presence of God, was an exile from his native place, and wandered about in another land; so they were carried captive by the Romans, and dispersed throughout the nations of the world, among whom they wander about to this day. Abel was a type of Christ also in his intercession; for as he *being dead, yet speaketh;* so Christ, though he was dead, yet is alive, and ever lives to make intercession, to speak on the behalf of his people, and be an Advocate for them; and his blood has a speaking voice in it, and speaks better things than that of Abel; it calls for peace and pardon.

3. Seth, the other seed appointed in the room of Abel, whom Cain slew, is not to be overlooked; since the appointment of him was of grace, and to fill up the place of righteous Abel, and be the father of a race of men that should serve the Lord; and was put, set, and laid as the foundation, as it were, of the patriarchal church-state, as his name signifies; and was a type of Christ, the foundation God has laid in Zion: and in the days of his son Enos, as an effect of divine grace, and the displays of it, *Men began to call upon the name of the Lord*, Gen. iv. 25, 26. not but that they called upon the Lord personally, and in their families, before; but now being more numerous, families joined together, and set up public worship; where they met, and socially served the Lord, and called upon him in the name of the Lord, in the name of Christ, who, as Mediator, might be more clearly manifested; or they called themselves by the name of the Lord, of the Lord's people, and the sons of God, in distinction from the sons of men, the men of the world, irreligious persons, profane and idolatrous; which distinction took place before the flood, and perhaps as early as the times of Enos; see Gen. vi. 2.

4. Enoch is the only person in this period besides, who is taken notice of for the grace of God bestowed on him; though, no doubt, there were thousands who also were made partakers of it. He was *trained* up in a religious way, as his name signifies; he was eminent for his faith, and was high in the favour of God: he had a testimony that he pleased God, which could not be without faith, by which he drew nigh, had much nearness to, fellowship and familiarity with him; he *walked with God*, enjoyed much communion with him, and had large communications of grace, light, and knowledge from him; was even favoured with a spirit of prophecy, and foretold a future judgment, and the coming of Christ to it; and as he was made acquainted with the second coming of Christ, so, no doubt, with his first coming to save lost sinful men: and as Abel was a type of Christ in his low estate, in his sufferings and death, Enoch was a type of him in his ascension to heaven; for he *was not* on earth any longer than the time of his life mentioned; *for God took him*, translated him from earth to heaven, took him to himself; so Christ, when he had finished his work on earth, was taken to heaven, a cloud received him out of the sight of his apostles, and he ascended to his God and their God, to his Father and their Father.

Secondly, The next period of time in which an exhibition of the covenant of grace was made, is that from Noah to Abraham. And Noah is the principal person taken notice of in it. His father, at his birth, thought there was something remarkable in him, and designed to be done by him, and thus expressed himself; *This same shall comfort us concerning our work, &c.* Gen. v. 29. and therefore called his name Noah, which signifies *comfort* and is derived from נחם, to *comfort*, the last letter being cut off. And in this Lamech has respect, not so much to things temporal, and to that benefit that should be received through Noah's invention of instruments for the more easy cultivating of the earth, and by bringing agriculture to a greater perfection, as he did; whereby the curse of the earth was, in a great measure, removed, which made it very difficult, through great toil and labour, to get a livelihood; but not so much to these as to things spiritual, respect is had by Lamech; and if he did not think him to be the promised Seed, the Messiah, the Consolation of Israel; yet he might conclude, that he would be an eminent type of Christ, from whom all comfort flows, the Saviour of men from their sins, their evil works, and from the curses of the law, on account of them; and who has eased them from the toil and labour of their hands, to get a righteousness of their own for their justification, having wrought out one for them. However, in this person, Noah, there was a rich display of the grace of the covenant.

1. In his person, both in his private and public capacity. *He found grace in the eyes of the Lord;* that is, favour and good will, which is the source of all the blessings of grace, of electing, redeeming, justifying, pardoning, adopting, and sanctifying grace; of all the graces of the Spirit, as faith, hope, love, &c. all which Noah was a partaker of, and this in the midst of a world of ungodly men; which shewed it to be free and distinguishing: he was a *just*, or righteous man; not by his own works, by which no man can be justified, but by the *righteousness of faith*, of which he was an *heir*, Heb. xi. 7. even the righteousness which is by the faith of Christ: and he was *perfect in his generations;* not in himself, but in the righteousness of Christ, by which he was justified, and was a truly sincere and upright man, and *walked with God*, as Enoch did, and was favoured with much communion with him: and in his public capacity he was a *preacher of righteousness;* of righteousness to be done between man and man; of the righteousness of God in bringing a flood upon the world to destroy it; and also of the righteousness of Christ; for no doubt he was a preacher of that of which he was an heir, and so had knowledge of and faith in it: the persons to whom he preached, or Christ in him by his Spirit, were the spirits that are now in prison; but then in the days of Noah, while he was preparing the ark, were on earth; to whose ministry they were disobedient, and so it was without success; see 2 Pet. ii. 5. 1 Pet. iii. 19, 20.

2. There was a display of the grace of God in the ark which Noah was directed to make for the saving of his family, Heb. xi. 7. which may be considered either as an emblem of the church of God, which is to be formed in all things according to the pattern given by God himself, as that was; and which weathers the storms and tempests, and beatings of the waters of affliction and persecution, as that did in a literal sense; and in which are carnal professors, hypocrites, and heretics, as well as God's chosen people, and truly gracious souls; as there were all sorts of creatures in the ark: or else the ark may be considered as a type of Christ, the cover and shelter from the storm and tempest of divine wrath and vindictive justice, and in whom spiritual rest is to be had for weary souls; just as the dove let out of the ark found no rest until it returned to it again; and as in the ark few souls were saved, only Noah and his family, and none but those that were in the ark; so there are but few that seek and find the way of salvation, and eternal life by Christ; and there is salvation in no other, but in him; nor are there any saved, but who are saved in and by him.

3. This sacrifice of Noah, after he came out of the ark, was typical of the sacrifice of Christ, both with respect to the matter of it, clean creatures; expressive of the purity of Christ's sacrifice, who is the Lamb of God without spot or blemish; and who offered himself without spot to God; and who, having no sin himself, was fit to be a sacrifice for the sins of others: and also with respect to the acceptance of it; *God smelled a sweet savour;* that is, he was well-pleased with, and graciously accepted of Noah's sacrifice; and the same phrase is used of the acceptance of Christ's sacrifice, Eph. v. 2. see Gen. viii. 20, 21.

4. The covenant made with Noah, though it was not the special covenant of grace, being made with him and all his

posterity, and even with all creatures; yet, as it was a covenant of preservation, it was a covenant of kindness and goodness in a temporal way; and it bore a resemblance to the covenant of grace; inasmuch as there were no conditions in it, no sign or token to be observed on man's part; only what God himself gave as a token of his good-will, the rainbow in the cloud; and seeing that it is a covenant durable, lasting, and inviolable; see Isaiah liv. 9, 10. The rainbow, the token of it, shewed it to be a covenant of peace, which is one of the titles of the covenant of grace in the text referred to. So Christ, the Mediator of it, is said to have a rainbow upon his head; and a rainbow is said to be round about the throne, signifying, that access to the throne of grace is only through the peace-maker, Jesus Christ, Rev. x. 1. and iv. 3. To which may be added, that if this covenant of preservation had not taken place; but mankind had been now destroyed; the covenant of grace would have been made void, and of no effect; since the promised Seed, the great blessing of that covenant, was not yet come, and if so, never could, in the way promised.

5. Noah's blessing of Shem is not to be omitted; *Blessed be the Lord God of Shem!* in which is a display of covenant-grace; for to be the Lord God of any person, is the sum and substance of the covenant of grace, which always runs in this style, *I will be their God*. Moreover, Noah foretold spiritual blessings of grace, which should be enjoyed by his posterity in future time; *God shall enlarge Japhet, and he shall dwell in the tents of Shem*, Gen. ix. 26, 27. The tents of Shem signify the church of God in its tabernacle-state; and which continued among the Jews who were of the race of Shem, until the coming of Christ; and then God sent the gospel into the Gentile world, among the posterity of Japhet, and enlarged, or *persuaded* them, as some choose to render the word, to come and join with the believing Jews in the same gospel-church-state; whereby they became of the same body, and partakers of the same promises and blessings of the covenant; by which the above prophecy was in part fulfilled, and will be more completely in the latter day; see Isa. lx. 1—8.

Thirdly, The next period of time in which an exhibition was made of the covenant and of the grace of it, is that from Abraham to Moses. And, 1. Abraham himself stands foremost in it; he was an eminent instance of the grace of God, of the electing and calling grace of God. He was born in an idolatrous family, and lived in an idolatrous land; and he was called from his own country, and his father's house, to forsake it, and go elsewhere and serve the Lord; and to be separate from them, and the rest of the world; as the people of God are, when effectually called: he was an eminent instance of justifying grace; he was justified, but not by works, and so had not whereof to glory before God; but he was justified by faith in the righteousness of Christ; *He believed in the Lord, and he counted it to him for righteousness*, Gen. xv. 6. Not the act of faith, but the object of it, what he believed in, the Lord and his righteousness; for what was imputed to him, is imputed to all that believe in Christ, Jews or Gentiles, in all ages; now whatsoever may be said for Abraham's faith, being imputed to himself for righteousness; it can never be thought, surely, that it is imputed to others also for the same. Besides, it is the *righteousness of faith*, the righteousness of Christ received by faith, which Abraham, when uncircumcised, had; and which is imputed to them also that believe, whether circumcised or uncircumcised, Rom. iv. 2, 3, 11, 13, 22, 23, 24. To which may be added, that the gospel was preached to Abraham; the good news of his spiritual seed, those that walk in the steps of his faith, whether Jews or Gentiles, being blessed with all spiritual blessings in the Messiah, who should spring from him, Gal. iii. 8.

But what more especially deserve attention, are the several appearances of God unto Abraham, and the manifestations of the covenant of grace then made unto him. The first appearance was at the time of his call from his idolatrous country and kindred, when the covenant of grace was broke up to him, and he was assured of the blessings of it, Gen. xii. 1, 2, 3. as it is to the chosen ones in effectual calling; and that it was this covenant that was then made known to Abraham, is clear from Gal. iii. 17. where it is said to be *confirmed before of God in Christ;* which certainly designs the covenant of grace; for what else could be said to be thus *confirmed?* and which indeed was made with him, and confirmed in him in eternity, and was now made manifest to Abraham; and from the time of the manifestation of it to him at his call from Chaldea, to the giving of the law on mount Sinai, were four hundred and thirty years there mentioned. The next appearance of God to him I shall take notice of, (for I propose not to consider every one) is that which is recorded in Gen. xv. 1. where in a vision God said unto him, *I am thy shield, and thy exceeding great reward;* his shield, to protect him from all enemies, temporal and spiritual; his reward, portion, and inheritance in this life and that to come; and which is an exceeding great one, and is the sum and substance of the covenant of grace. Another appearance of God to Abraham was, when he was ninety-nine years of age; when, besides the covenant of circumcision, God gave to him, and his natural seed of the male kind, and a promise of the land of Canaan to his posterity, as he had done before, he made himself known to him as the *Almighty God*, or God all-sufficient; whose power and grace were sufficient to support him in his walk before him, and bring him to a state of perfection, Gen. xvii. 1. and particularly in ver. 4. he said to him, *As for me, behold my covenant is with thee, and thou shalt be a father of many nations;* which the apostle explains of his being the father of all that believe, whether circumcised or uncircumcised; even of all that walk in the steps of his faith, and believe unto righteousness, as he did; these are blessed, with faithful Abraham, with all the blessings of the covenant of grace, as he was, Rom. iv. 9—17. Gal. iii. 9, 29. Once more, the Lord appeared to him in the plains of Mamre. Three appeared to him in an human form, two of them were angels, and one was Jehovah, the Son of God; who not only foretold the birth of a Son to Abraham, but made known to him the design to destroy Sodom; and gave an high encomium of his piety and justice; and allowed him to expostulate with him about the destruction of Sodom; admitted him to stand before him, and he communed with him. All which shewed him to be a friend of God, and interested in the covenant of his grace, Gen. xviii. 3, 10, 17, 22, 33. At the time of the offering up of his son Isaac, by the command of the Lord, he appeared to him, and restrained him from the actual performance of it; upon which he called the name of the place Jehovah Jireh, the Lord will see, or will appear in the mount of difficulties, as he had to him; and when he made a further manifestation of the covenant of grace in that important article; *In thy seed shall all the nations of the earth be blessed*, Gen. xxii. 14—18. meaning the promised Seed, the Messiah, that should spring from him, as he did, and is called the Son of Abraham, Matt. i. 1. in whom all the elect are blessed with all spiritual blessings, the blessings of the everlasting covenant. Not to omit the interview Abraham had with Melchizedek, who met him upon his return from the slaughter of the kings, and blessed him in the name of the most high God; this man was an eminent type of Christ; his name and title agree with his, king of righteousness, and king of peace; the righteous and peaceable king; a priest continually, and of whose order Christ was; and whose eternity is shadowed forth in his genealogy being unknown, in which he was made like unto the Son of God, the eternal Son of the eternal Father: it may be our Lord has respect to this interview, when he says, *Abraham saw my day, and was glad;* saw him in the promise, and saw him in this type, John viii. 56. see Heb. vii. 1, 2, 3. Gen. xiv. 18, 19.

2. Isaac, the son of Abraham, is the next instance of covenant-grace in this period of time; in his line from Abraham it was promised the Messiah should come, and did: the same covenant of grace that was exhibited to Abraham, was manifested to Isaac in the same words, Gen. xxvi. 3, 4. And he was himself an eminent type of Christ, the promised Seed, and the great blessing of the covenant, both in his sacrifice and in his resurrection. Isaac was Abraham's own son, his only son, his beloved son, whom he took to offer on mount Moriah; Isaac went with him without reluctance, carrying the wood on which he was to be laid, and was laid; by which it appeared that Abraham withheld him not. So Christ, who has been offered a sacrifice by the will of God, is his own Son, his begotten Son, his only begotten Son, and his beloved Son, when it was his pleasure to make his soul an offering for sin, he willingly went, as a lamb to the slaughter, bearing on his shoulders the cross on which he was crucified; and was not spared by his divine Father, but delivered up for us all. And though Isaac died not, yet he was reckoned by Abraham as dead; who accounted that God was able to raise him from the dead; from *whence also he received him in a figure*, Heb. xi. 19. a ram caught in a thicket being shewn him, and

which he offered in his room; and so Isaac was delivered, and went home alive to his father's house; and this was on the third day from the time Abraham reckoned him as a dead man. So Christ was *put to death in the flesh*, signified by the ram in the thicket; and *quickened in the Spirit*, typified by Isaac saved alive; who, after his resurrection, went to his God and our God, to his Father and our Father; and his resurrection was on the third day, according to this scripture-type of him.

3. Jacob, the son of Isaac, is another instance in whom there was a display of covenant-grace, in the period of time between Abraham and Moses. He was an eminent and illustrious instance of electing grace, according to which the blessings of the covenant are dispensed. He and Esau were brothers, twins, and if any, Esau had the precedence; yet before their birth it was notified to Rebekah, that *the elder should serve the younger*, Gen. xxv. 23. which the apostle makes use of to illustrate and exemplify the grace of God in election, Rom. ix. 11, 12, 13. The same covenant of grace that was manifested to Abraham and Isaac, was repeated and made known to Jacob, Gen. xxviii. 13, 14, 15. Christ also was represented to him by a ladder, whose top reached to heaven, and on which he saw the angels of God ascending and descending, Gen. xxviii. 12. The same is said of Christ, John i. 51. who in his divine nature reached to heaven, and was in heaven when in his human nature he was here on earth; and to whom angels ministered, and who is the only Mediator between God and man, and the way of access to God, and communion with him. Christ in an human form appeared to Jacob, and wrestled with him, with whom Jacob had so much power as to prevail, and obtain the blessing from him, and got the name of Israel, Gen. xxxii. 24—28. The Messiah was prophesied of by him, under the name of Shiloh, the prosperous and the peaceable; in whose hands the pleasure of the Lord prospered, and who made peace for men by the blood of his cross; and that he should spring from his son Judah, and out of his tribe, as he did; and that he should come while civil government, in some form or another, was in Judah; and that when he came, there should be a great gathering of the Gentiles to him; all which have been exactly fulfilled: and for Christ, as the author of salvation, provided and promised in the covenant of grace, did the patriarch Jacob wait. Gen. xlix. 10, 18.

4. Within this period of time, about the time the children of Israel were in Egypt, and before the times of Moses, lived Job, and his three friends: who, though they were not of Israel, but of the race of Esau, yet the covenant of grace, and the blessings of it, were made known to them, as a pledge and earnest of what would be done in after-times. Job was an eminent instance of the grace of God; his character, as given by God himself, is, that he was *a perfect and upright man;* perfect, as justified by the righteousness of Christ; upright and sincere, as sanctified by the Spirit; and who, in his walk and conversation, appeared to be *one that feared God and eschewed evil,* Job i. 8. and as he was a man of great knowledge of natural and civil things, so of things divine, spiritual, and evangelical; of the impurity of nature; of the insufficiency of man's righteousness to justify him before God; and of the doctrine of redemption and salvation by Christ. How many articles of faith, and doctrines of grace, are contained in those words of his; *I know that my Redeemer liveth? &c.* from whence it appears, that he knew Christ as the Redeemer and as his Redeemer, provided and promised in the covenant of grace; that he then existed; that he would be incarnate, and dwell among men on earth; and come a second time to judge the world; and that there would be a resurrection of the same body, and a beatific vision of God in a future state; see Job ix. 2, 20, 30, 31. and xiv. 4. and xix. 25, 26, 27. Job's three friends, though they mistook his case, and misapplied things to him, yet were men that knew much of divine things; of the corruption of nature; of the vanity of self-righteousness; this, indeed, was their quarrel with Job, imagining, though wrongly, that he was righteous in his own eyes: and how gloriously does Elihu speak of the great Redeemer as the *Messenger* of the covenant, the uncreated Angel, Christ; as *an Interpreter* of his Father's mind and will; *One among a thousand,* the Chiefest of ten thousand, whose office it is *to shew unto men his uprightness,* his own righteousness, to declare and preach it, Psalm xl. 9. And as a Ransom found in council and covenant; a proper Person to give his life a ransom for men: see Job iv. 17, 18. and xv. 14, 15, 16. and xxv. 4, 5, 6. and xxxiii. 23, 24.

Thus the covenant of grace was exhibited, held forth, displayed, and manifested in the grace and blessings of it in the times of the patriarchs.

CHAP. III.

OF THE EXHIBITION OF THE COVENANT OF GRACE UNDER THE MOSAIC DISPENSATION.

HAVING traced the manifestation and application of the Covenant of Grace from the times of our first parents, through the patriarchal state, to the times of Moses; I shall now consider it as exhibited in his time, and unto the times of David and the prophets; and shall begin,

1. With Moses himself, who was a great man of God; and though the law was by him, he had large knowledge of Christ; of his person, offices, and grace; of the covenant of grace, and the blessings of it. *Had ye believed Moses,* says Christ to the Jews, *ye would have believed me, for he wrote of me,* John v. 46.

Moses was an eminent type of Christ, in whom the grace of Christ, and of the covenant, was eminently displayed. The apostle in Heb. iii. runs the parallel between Moses and Christ, though he gives the preference to Christ, as it was just he should; they were both, he observes, concerned in the house of God; both faithful therein; with this difference, Moses as a servant, and Christ as a Son in his own house. Moses was a mediator when the covenant on Sinai was given, at the request of the people of Israel, and by the permission of God; and stood between God and them, to deliver his word to them, Gal. iii. 19. Deut. v. 5. in which he was a type of Christ, the Mediator of the new and better covenant, and the Mediator between God and man. He was a prophet, and spoke of Christ as who should be raised up a prophet like unto him, and was to be hearkened to; and who has been raised up; and God has spoken by him all his mind and will to the sons of men. When Moses and Elias were with Christ on the mount, which shewed harmony and agreement between them; a voice was heard, saying, *This is my beloved Son, in whom I am well pleased, hear ye him,* as the great Prophet of the church; see Deut. xviii. 15. Heb. i. 1, 2. Matt. xvii. 5. Moses was a priest, and officiated as such before Aaron was appointed to that office; and he, indeed, invested him with it by the offering of sacrifices, Exod. xxix. 1. see Psalm xcix. 6. in which he prefigured Christ in his priestly office, who became man, that he might be a merciful and sympathizing one; and being holy, harmless, and separate from sinners, was fit to be one, and to offer a pure sacrifice for sin. Moses was also a king and a lawgiver under God; a ruler and governor of the people of Israel, Deut. xxxiii. 4, 5. Christ is King of Zion and King of saints; by the designation of his Father, and with the acknowledgment of his people, who own him, and submit to him as such; and of whose government there will be no end, Psalm ii. 6. Isa. xxxiii. 22. and ix. 7. Once more, Moses was a deliverer or redeemer of the people of Israel, out of that state of bondage in which they were in Egypt, Acts vii. 35. and in this bore a figure of Christ the Redeemer of his people, from a worse than Egyptian bondage, the bondage of sin, Satan, and the law; and herein and hereby through him were held forth the grace of the covenant, and the blessings of it in Christ to the faith of God's people.

There were many things done by him, and under him, and in his time, which exhibited and shewed forth the covenant of grace, and the things contained in it. The whole ceremonial law was nothing else than a shadowy exhibition of it; it was a shadow of good things to come by Christ, the great high Priest, which are come by him; as peace, pardon, righteousness, and salvation. The priests, their garments, and their sacrifices, with other numerous rites, all prefigured Christ, and the grace of the covenant, which is by him: the ceremonial law was the gospel of the Israelites, it was their pedagogue, their schoolmaster, that taught them the A B C of the gospel in their infant state. Christ was the mark and scope it aimed at, the end of it, and in whom it had its full accomplishment; the Israelites, by reason of darkness, could not see to the end of those things, which are now abolished, and which we with open face behold. It would be too tedious to go over the several particulars in the former dispensation, which held forth the grace of Christ, and of the covenant to the faith of men. It may be sufficient to instance in three or four of them, which were protempore, or of longer continuance; and were either stated ordinances, or extraordinary works of providence, which typified spiritual things.

The passover, which was instituted at the time of Israel's going out of Egypt, was kept by faith; not only of deliverance from Egyptian bondage, but in the faith of a future redemption and salvation by Christ; hence he is called *Christ our passover*, 1 Cor. v. 7. see Heb. xi. 23. The passover was a lamb without blemish, slain by the congregation of Israel, between the two evenings; it was then roasted with fire, and eaten whole with bitter herbs, and its blood was sprinkled upon the doorposts of the houses of the Israelites; that when the destroying angel passed through Egypt, to destroy their first-born, seeing the blood where it was sprinkled, passed by the houses in which the Israelites were, and left them unhurt; and hence the institution had the name of the passover; see Exod. xii. All which was typical of Christ, who is the Lamb of God, without spot or blemish; who was taken by the Jews and crucified and slain; who endured the fire of divine wrath, whereby his strength was dried up like a potsherd; is to be, and is fed upon by faith; even a whole Christ, in his person, and offices, and grace, attended with repentance and humiliation for sin; believers in him, when they look to him by faith, mourn; and a profession of him is, more or less, accompanied with bitter afflictions, reproaches, and persecutions; and his blood, which from hence is called the blood of sprinkling, that being shed and sprinkled on the hearts of men, not only purges their consciences from dead works, but secures them from the wrath and justice of God; who, looking upon this blood, which is ever in sight, is pacified towards them, and passes by them, when he takes vengeance on others.

The manna was another type of Christ; that was typical bread, Christ is the true bread; hence Christ, speaking of the manna, and of himself, says, *My Father giveth you the true bread from heaven,* John vi. 32. meaning himself, the truth of the type; the manna was only a shadow, Christ is the substance, the solid and substantial food, signified by it, and therefore is called *the hidden manna*, Rev. ii. 17. which every believer in Christ has a right to eat of, and does; so the old and new testament-saints *all eat of the same spiritual meat,* 1 Cor. x. 3. The Israelites being in the wilderness, and hungry, complained for want of food, and murmured; God promised to give them bread from heaven, which he did: this when they first saw, they knew not what it was; and asked one another, What is it? it was small in bulk, white in colour, and sweet in taste; this they gathered every day for their daily food, as they were directed; and ground it in mills, or beat it in a mortar, and baked it in pans: and on this they lived whilst in the wilderness, until they came to the land of Canaan; see Exod. xvi. and Numb. xi. and Josh. v. 12. All which pointed to Christ and his grace, the food of faith; who, when he came into the world, the world knew him not; nor is he known to the Israel of God before conversion; they are without Christ, without the knowledge of him whilst unregenerate; until it pleases God to call them by his grace, and reveal his Son in them. And he is entirely hidden from the men of the world; in whose eyes, and in the eyes of carnal professors, he is little, mean, and contemptible; yet white and ruddy, comely and beautiful, pure and holy, and desirable, to truly gracious souls; to whose taste his fruits, the blessings of his grace, his doctrines, his word, and ordinances, are sweet and pleasant; and a crucified Christ, whose sufferings are signified by the manna being ground, beaten, and baked, is the food of believers in this present state; what is their daily food, and which they live upon whilst they are in the wilderness, till they come to Canaan's land, and eat of the *old corn,* the things which God from all eternity has prepared for them that love him.

The water out of the rock the Israelites drank of in the wilderness, was another emblem and representative of Christ and his grace; hence called *spiritual drink,* and the rock a *spiritual rock; and that Rock was Christ,* 1 Cor. x. 4.

The Israelites wanting water in the wilderness, murmured, when Moses was ordered by the Lord to smite a rock at two different times and places, from whence water gushed out for the supply of them, their flocks and herds. Christ was signified by the rock, who may be compared to one for height, shelter, strength, and duration; and with which they are followed and supplied whilst they are in this world: and as it was by the rod of Moses the rock was smitten; so Christ was stricken and smitten in a legal and judicial way, being the surety and representative of his people, by which means the blessings of grace flow unto them; as justification, pardon, &c. just as the blood and water sprung from his side when pierced with the spear; and this rock being thus smitten for believers, they have a never-failing supply of grace through the wilderness.

The brazen serpent was another figure of Christ and his grace. The Israelites being bitten with fiery serpents, of which many died; Moses was ordered by the Lord to make a fiery serpent of brass, and set it on a pole, that whoever was bitten might look unto it and live; which was done accordingly, and the promised effect followed, Numb. xxi. 6, 7, 8, 9. Our Lord takes notice of this very significant type himself, and applies it to himself, John iii. 14, 15. The serpent Moses made had the form of a serpent, but not the nature of one: Christ was in the likeness of sinful flesh, but his flesh was not sinful; he was without the poison of the serpent, sin, original or actual: it was a fiery one, denoting either the wrath of God sustained by Christ, or the vengeance he took on his and our enemies when on the cross; or rather, it may denote his flaming love to his people, expressed in his sufferings and death. It being of brass, denoted not only his lustre and glory, but his strength; who, being the mighty God, is able to save to the uttermost all that come and look unto him for salvation. The situation of the serpent of Moses on a pole, may signify the crucifixion of Christ, which he himself expressed by being lifted up from the earth, John xii. 32. or his exaltation at the right hand of God; or rather, the setting of him up in the ministry of the gospel, where he is erected as an ensign and standard to gather souls to him; and where he is held forth evidently as crucified and slain, as the object and ground of hope. And as the end of the erection of the serpent was, that such who were bitten by the fiery serpents might look to it and live; so the end of Christ's crucifixion, and of the ministration of him in the gospel is, that such who are envenomed with the poison of the old serpent, the devil, and whose wound is otherwise incurable, might, through looking to Christ by faith, live spiritually, comfortably, and eternally; as all such do who are favoured with a spiritual sight of him, John vi. 40.

2. Besides Moses, there were others in his time, in whom the grace of the covenant was remarkably displayed and manifested; particularly Aaron, his brother, called *the saint of the Lord*, Psalm cvi. 16. the holy one, with whom were the Urim and Thummim, Deut. xxxiii. 8. a type of Christ, in whom all lights and perfections are; and though Christ, as a priest, was not of the order of Aaron, but of another; yet Aaron in his priestly office, prefigured him; he was taken from among men, from among his brethren, to offer gifts and sacrifices for sin, and did not take this honour to himself, but was called of God to it; *so Christ glorified not himself to be made an high-priest;* but was made so by his divine Father, Heb. v. 4, 5. and has offered up a sacrifice for the sins of his people, of a sweet smelling savour to God; which the sacrifices of Aaron and his sons were typical of, by which the faith of believers in those times was led to the great and better sacrifice of Christ. Aaron was also a type of Christ in his intercession, as well as in his sacrifice; he could speak well, and therefore was appointed the spokesman of Moses unto the people, Exod. iv. 14, 15, 16. Christ is an advocate for his people; he can speak well to their case for them, and ever lives to appear in the presence of God, and to make intercession for them, and is always heard.

3. Joshua, the successor of Moses, was also a type of Christ, and in him the grace of Christ, and of the covenant, was evidently displayed. Their names agree, both signify a Saviour; Joshua is called Jesus, Heb. iv. 8. Moses conducted the people of Israel through the wilderness, to the borders of the land of Canaan, but was not allowed to lead them into it; intimating, that it is not by the works of the law, or by the works of righteousness, done by men, that they are or can be saved; that a man must have a better righteousness than his own, or he will never enter into the kingdom of heaven; there is no salvation but in and by the name of Jesus, the antitype of Joshua: as Joshua led the people of Israel into the land of Canaan, and settled them there; so Christ, by his blood and righteousness, has opened a way for his people into the heavenly state, and gives them an abundant entrance into his kingdom and glory. Joshua did not give the true rest in Canaan; for then another would not have been spoken of; it was only a typical one he gave; but Christ, our spiritual Joshua, gives spiritual rest here, and eternal rest hereafter.

The scarlet thread which Rahab the harlot was ordered by the spies in the times of Joshua, to bind at her window, that her house might be known by them, in order to save her, and all in it, when Jericho was destroyed, was an emblem of the blood of Christ, by which are peace, pardon, righteousness, and salvation for the chief of sinners; for Gentile sinners, as well as Jews; and through which is security from wrath, ruin, and destruction. Joshua was favoured with an appearance of Christ unto him, with a sword drawn in his hand, who declared unto him, that he came as the Captain of the host of the Lord, to animate, encourage and assist him. Christ is the Captain of salvation, who has fought the battles of his people for them; conquered all their enemies, and made them more than conquerors through himself. There were after appearances of Christ to others in this period of time, as to Manoah and his wife, who declared to them his name was Pele, a Wonder, or Wonderful, which is one of the names of Christ, Isa. ix. 6. and to Gideon, Samuel, and others, I shall take no further notice of.

CHAP. IV.

OF THE COVENANT OF GRACE, AS EXHIBITED IN THE TIMES OF DAVID, AND THE SUCCEEDING PROPHETS, TO THE COMING OF CHRIST.

CHRIST, the great blessing of the covenant, was spoken of by all *the holy prophets which have been since the world began;* by the patriarch prophets; by Moses and others; but more abundantly by the prophets of a later date; *God, who at sundry times,* in different ages of the world; *and in divers manners,* as by angels, by vision, by dreams and impulses on the mind; *spake in times past to the fathers by the prophets,* concerning his mind and will, the covenant of his grace, and the blessings of it; to which dispensation of things is opposed that which is by Christ; *hath in these last days spoken unto us by his Son,* Luke i. 70. Heb. i. 1, 2. From whence it appears, that the first administration of the covenant of grace, as has been observed, reached from the beginning of the world, or near it, to the coming of Christ; and now having traced it from Adam to Noah, from Noah to Abraham, from Abraham to Moses, and from Moses to David; I shall next consider it as more clearly manifested in the times of David, and by succeeding prophets, to the coming of Christ. And begin,

First, with David, who was a prophet, and by whom the Spirit of God spake concerning Christ, and the covenant of grace made with him, Acts ii. 30. and i. 16. 2 Sam. xxiii. 2, 3, 4, 5. The grace of the covenant was displayed in him, the blessings of it were bestowed on him, the covenant itself was made with him; not only the covenant of royalty, concerning the succession of the kingdom of Israel in his family; but the special covenant of grace, in which his own salvation lay; a covenant ordered in all things and sure, and an everlasting one, 2 Sam. xxiii. 5. This was made with him, as he declares, that is, made manifest and applied unto him, and he was assured of his interest in it. He was an eminent type of Christ, who is therefore often called by his name, Psalm lxxxix. 3, 20. Ezek. xxxiv. 23, 24. and xxxvii. 24. Hos. iii. 5. In his person, in the comeliness of it; in his character and employment, as a shepherd; in his offices, of prophet and king; in his afflictions and persecutions; and in his wars and victories. And great light and knowledge he had of things respecting Christ and his grace, as the book of Psalms, written by him, under divine inspiration, abundantly shews; as, of the person of Christ; of his divine and eternal sonship; of his being the eternal begotten Son of God, to whom this was first, at least, so clearly made known, Psalm ii. 7. From whence are taken all those expressions in the New Testament, of Christ's being the only begotten Son, the only begotten of the Father, his own and proper Son: phrases expressive of Christ's co-essentiality, co-eternity, and co-equality with his Father. David speaks of the humanity of Christ, of a body being prepared for him in covenant, of the formation of it in the womb of the virgin; of his being of his seed, and springing from him as man, as he did, Psalm xl. 6. compared with Heb. x. v. Psalm cxxxix. 15, 16. and cxxxii. 11, 17. Acts xiii. 23. He speaks very expressly of his sufferings and death, in Psalm xxii. uses the very words Christ uttered on the cross; exactly describes the persons that surrounded him, and mocked at him when on it, as well as the manner of his death, by crucifixion, signified by his hands and feet being pierced; and also the dreadful pains and agonies he was then in, by which he was brought to the dust of death; yea, some minute circumstances of his sufferings are observed, as casting lots on his vesture, and parting his garments; and elsewhere, the giving him gall and vinegar to drink, Psalm lxix. 21. He foretels his burial in the grave, which should not be so long as to see corruption, and his resurrection to an immortal life, Psalm xvi. 10, 11. see Acts ii. 25—31. His ascension to heaven, Psalm lxviii. 18. compared with Eph. iv. 8, 9, 10. His session at the right hand of God, Psalm cx. 1. see Heb. i. 13. He treats of his suretiship-engagements, and of his offices, as Prophet, Priest, and King, Psalm xl. 6—9. and cx. 4. and ii. 6. and lxxxix. 27. and lxxii. 8.

Secondly, Solomon, the Son of David, and his successor in the kingdom, had not only the covenant of royalty established with him, but the special covenant of grace was made with him, or made known unto him; *I will be his Father and he shall be my Son*, 2 Sam. vii. 14. He was both a preacher and king of Israel; and, no doubt, a good man, notwithstanding his fall; his prayer at the dedication of the temple shews it; as well as his being the amanuensis of the holy Spirit, in various writings: an eminent type he was of Christ, who is therefore called Solomon, Cant. iii. 7, 9, 11. and viii. 11. 12. in his name, which signifies peaceable, and agrees with Christ, the Prince of peace; in his descent, the Son of David; in his wisdom, in which Christ is greater than Solomon; in his wealth and riches; and in the peaceableness and extent of his kingdom. Much of Christ, and the blessings of grace through him, were made known unto him. He writes of him under the name of Wisdom, as a divine Person, the same with the Logos, the Word, and Son of God; of his eternal existence; of the eternal generation of him; of his being brought forth, and brought up as a Son with his Father from everlasting, as is declared in the eighth of Proverbs; which when one reads, might be tempted to think he was reading the first chapter of John, there being such a similarity, yea, sameness of diction, sentiment, and doctrine. Solomon or Agur speaks of Christ under the names of Ithiel and Ucal; the one signifies, *God is with me*; as he always was with Christ, and Christ with him: the other, *the mighty One*, or, *I am able*, I can do all things; as he could, being the Almighty. He speaks in the same place of the infinite, omnipresent, and omnipotent Being, whose name, that is, his nature is incomprehensible and ineffable; and to whom he ascribes a Son as a divine, distinct Person from his Father; as of the same incomprehensible and ineffable nature with him, and so co-essential, co-eternal, and co-equal with him, Prov. xxx. 1, 4. The book of Canticles, written by Solomon, is a rich display of the glories and excellencies of Christ, of his great love to his church, and of the covenant-blessings of grace bestowed upon her. Pass we on now,

Thirdly, To the prophets who lived in the succeeding reigns of the kings of Israel and Judah; as Isaiah, Jeremiah, &c. who were holy men of God, and spake and wrote as they were moved by the holy Spirit; the Spirit of God, was in them, and spoke by them; and the sure word of prophecy they delivered, was as a light or lamp in a dark place; the gospel-day not as yet being broke, nor the shadows of the ceremonial law fled, nor Christ, the Sun of Righteousness, yet up and risen. These,

1. Speak much of the covenant of grace. Of it as a covenant of life and peace, in which provision is made for the spiritual and eternal life of the covenant-ones; and in which the plan and model of their peace and reconciliation by Christ was formed, Mal. ii. 5. Isa. liv. 10. Of it as an everlasting one, which should continue for ever, and never be altered, nor removed, Isa. lv. 3. and liv. 10. Of the persons who engaged and entered into it, Jehovah and the branch, that should build the temple of the Lord, between whom the council of peace was; yea, Jehovah the Father, the Word of God, and his Spirit, who were each of them concerned in the covenant of grace, Zech. vi. 12, 13. Hag. ii. 4, 5. Of Christ, as the sum and substance of it, said to be the covenant of the people, in whom are all the blessings and promises of it, called the sure mercies of David; and whose blood is said to be the blood of the covenant, by which it is ratified and confirmed; and he is spoken of as the messenger of it, Isa. xlii. 6. and xlix. 8. and lv. 3. Zech. ix. 11. Mal. iii. 1. Mention is made by them of the persons on whose account the covenant of grace was made, the elect of God, both Jews and Gentiles, Isa. xlix. 5, 6, 8. yea, they speak of the new covenant, or of the administration of it under the new-testament dispensation, and give the several articles of it; which would be more clearly known, and more powerfully have their effect, Jer. xxxi. 31—34. Which may lead on to observe,

2. That the prophets in this period of time speak very plainly of the blessings of the covenant of grace, even more plainly and fully than heretofore. As of,

(1.) The blessing of pardon of sin through Christ, which is a blessing of the covenant, Heb. viii. 10, 12. Not only Moses relates, that God appeared to him, and caused his goodness to pass before him, and proclaimed his name, a God gracious and merciful, pardoning iniquity, transgression, and sin; and David describes the blessedness of the man whose iniquities are forgiven, and instances in himself, Exod. xxxiv. 6, 7. Psalm xxxii. 1, 2, 5. But the apostle Peter observes, that to Christ *give all the prophets witness, that through his name whosoever believeth in him shall receive remission of sins*, Acts x. 43. They speak of it as belonging to God, and him only, even every act of it, and as flowing from his mercy; on which account there is none like unto him, Dan. ix. 9. Mic. vii. 18. and of his being abundant in it, or abundantly pardoning, even all that apply to him for it; and all their sins and transgressions, though ever so many and great, Isa. lv. 7. and i. 18. and of the freeness of pardon, as the effect of the free favour, love, grace, and mercy of God, which is very strongly expressed in Isa. xliii. 25. after so many aggravated sins of omission and commission are observed; and yet they speak of it as founded upon the sufferings of Christ, and redemption, reconciliation, atonement, and satisfaction procured thereby, Zech. iii. 9. Isa. xliv. 22. Dan. ix. 24. They also describe the persons that share in this blessing, even such whom God has reserved for himself in election, and in the covenant of grace, and who are the remnant of his heritage, his portion, and the lot of his inheritance, Jer. l. 20. Mic. vii. 18.

(2.) The blessing of justification by the righteousness of Christ; which though a doctrine more clearly revealed under the gospel-dispensation, yet is *witnessed by the law and prophets*, Rom. iii. 21, 22. The prophets speak of the righteousness by which men are justified as an everlasting righteousness, that was then to be brought in by Christ, the Surety and Saviour of his people, Dan. ix. 24. and as *well-pleasing to God*, because by it the *law is magnified*, all its demands answered, and it made *honourable*, and more so than it could have been by the most perfect obedience of angels and men, Isa. xlii. 21. They speak of Christ as the author of it; and hence he is called by them, *The Lord our Righteousness;* and *the Sun of Righteousness;* because righteousness is wrought out by him, and springs from him, as light from the sun, Jer. xxiii. 6. Mal. iv. 2. They speak of Christ as the justifier of them that know him, and believe in him, Isa. liii. 11. And of the seed of Israel being justified in him, and glorying of him, as the Lord their Righteousness, even all the elect of God, both Jews and Gentiles; and the church is represented by them as expressing her strong faith of interest in the righteousness of Christ, as her justifying one; *Surely shall one say, in the Lord have I righteousness and strength,* Isa. xlv. 24, 25. Under the emblem of Joshua, the high-priest, accused of, and charged with sin and guilt, yet acquitted by Christ the Angel of the Lord, is represented an elect sinner, charged with sin by law and justice, by Satan and his own conscience; but cleared from all by the application and imputation of the righteousness of Christ, to him expressed by those strong terms, *causing his iniquity to pass from him,* and *clothing him with change of raiment,* Zech. iii. 1, 2, 3, 4. The same with *the garments of salvation,* and *robe of righteousness,* the church declares she was clothed and covered with, and in which she rejoiced, Isa. lxi. 10.

(3.) The blessing of adoption is another covenant-blessing, spoken of by the prophets; not national adoption, included in the national covenant made with the people of Israel; but adoption by special grace. The prophets speak of God's putting some among the children that were unlovely, unworthy, and deserving of his displeasure, and yet were the objects of his love and delight; his dear sons and pleasant children, and whom he owned in such a relation, Jer. iii. 19. and xxxi. 20. of some that were given to Christ as his children, and to whom he stood in the relation of an everlasting Father, Isa. viii. 18. and ix. 6. see Heb. ii. 13. And though the saints under the former dispensation, for the most part had not such a measure of the Spirit of adoption, as under the New Testament, yet they were then heirs, and so children; and some of them had a strong assurance of their interest in God, as their Father; *Doubtless, thou art our Father,* Isa. lxiii. 16. And the prophets also speak of a large number of adopted sons and daughters of God, as in the latter-day, in the several parts of the world, both among the Gentiles and among the Jews, Isa. xliii. 6. and xlv. 11. Hos. i. 10.

(4.) Salvation, spiritual and eternal, in general, is the great blessing of the covenant of grace, 2 Sam. xxiii. 5. and this the prophets enquired after, and diligently searched into and spoke of; of the author of it, declaring it was not in hills and mountains, nor to be expected from thence, but in the Lord God only; they affirm that Christ was appointed as God's salvation to the ends of the earth; that he would come and save, and as having salvation; they represent him as mighty to save, yea as if salvation was then already wrought out by him, Jer. iii. 23. Isa. xlix. 6. and xxxv. 4. and lxiii. 1, 5. Zech. ix. 9. They speak of the nature of it as an everlasting salvation, and describe the persons interested in it as the Israel of God, both Jews and Gentiles; even such who are at the ends of the earth, and who are encouraged to look to Christ for salvation, Isa. xlv. 17, 22. and they speak of the time when it should be wrought out, Dan. ix. 24. see 1 Pet. i. 10, 11.

3. There are various things relating to Christ, his person, office, and grace, which are copiously and frequently spoken of by the prophets in this period of time; as his incarnation, which though not till many hundred years after, is spoken of as if then done, because of the certainty of it in the purpose and promise of God, *to us a child is born*, Isa. ix. 6. his birth of a virgin, with the name given him, Immanuel, God with us; and which is represented as wonderful, new and unheard of, as it justly might, Isa. vii. 14. with Matt. i. 23. Jer. xxxi. 22. Dan. ii. 45. The place of his birth, Bethlehem Ephratah, Mic. v. 2. see Matt. ii. 4, 5, 6. John vii. 41, 42. Some things following his birth, as the murder of the infants about Bethlehem; his being carried to Egypt, and called again from thence, and residing in Nazareth, Jer. xxxi. 15. Hos. xi. 1. see Matt. ii. 13—23. The parts where he should chiefly live, converse, and minister, Isa. ix. 1. see Matt. iv. 13, 14. His state of humiliation, sufferings, and death, which are particularly described in Isa. liii. The circumstances of his being sold for thirty pieces of silver by one of his disciples, forsaken by them all, and his side pierced with a spear, Zech. xi. 12, 13. and xiii. 7. and xii. 10. see Matt. xxvii. 3—10. and xxvi. 31. John xix. 34—37. The prophets also speak of the time of his coming and of his sufferings: Daniel fixes the exact time of them, from a date given; and Haggai and Malachi declare he should come into the second temple, and give it a greater glory than the former; so that he must come and suffer as he did, before the destruction of that, Dan. ix. 24, 26. Hag. ii. 7, 9. Mal. iii. 1. And the same prophets, with Zechariah, who were the last of the prophets, speak of his near approach, that he was just at hand, and would soon, suddenly, and at unawares, come into his temple; and of his forerunner, Zech. iii. 8. and vi. 12. and ix. 9. Hag. ii. 6. Mal. iii. 1. and iv. 5. but though the prophets mentioned were the last of the inspired writers, prophecy did not wholly cease with them; as appears by the instances of Zechariah the father of John the Baptist, who prophesied of him, and of the Messiah; and good old Simeon, to whom it was revealed by the holy Spirit that he should not see death before he had seen the Lord's Christ; and Anna the prophetess, who spoke of him to those that looked for redemption in Jerusalem, Luke i. 67. and ii. 25, 26, 36, 38. So true is what our Lord says, that *the law and the prophets were until John;* which finishes the old-testament dispensation, and the first and old administration of the covenant of grace; after which the kingdom of God, or gospel of Christ, was preached more clearly and fully, and God spake no more by the prophets, but by his Son, Luke xvi. 16. Heb. i. 1, 2. when the second and new covenant, or administration of it, took place; of which we shall treat in the next chapter. And from what has been observed it appears, that the former administration of the covenant of grace, reaching from the fall of Adam to the coming of Christ, was by types and figures, by shadows and sacrifices, and by promises and prophecies of future things, which are now fulfilled; Christ, the sum and substance of all, being come, the great blessing of the covenant of grace, and in whom all are included.

CHAP. V.

OF THE ABROGATION OF THE OLD COVENANT, OR FIRST ADMINISTRATION OF IT, AND THE INTRODUCTION OF THE NEW, OR SECOND ADMINISTRATION OF IT.

WHEN we speak of the Abrogation of the Covenant this is to be understood, not of the covenant of grace, as to the matter and substance of it, which remains invariably the same in all periods of time; it is an everlasting covenant; it is ordered in all things and sure; it can never be broken and made void; every promise of it is unalterable, and every blessing irreversible; the covenant of peace can never be removed; it will stand firm to all generations; but with respect to the form of the administration of it only, even the form of it, under the former, or old-testament dispensation, before described; and in order to set this in its true and proper light,

First, Let it be observed, that it was never designed that the first administration of the covenant of grace should continue always in that form; it was foretold that there should be a cessation of it, and therefore it might be expected.

1. It was only intended to continue for a certain time, called, *The time of reformation,* Heb. ix. 10. when there would be a reform from burdensome rites and ceremonies; or *of correction,* when what was faulty and deficient would be corrected, amended, and become perfect; or *of direction,* when the saints would be directed to look to Christ, the substance of types and figures, and for perfection in him; the same with *the time appointed of the Father,* until which time, children, though heirs, are under tutors and governors; so the Israelites were under the elements of the world, the ceremonies of the former dispensation, under the tutorage and pædagogy of the law: for the *law,* the ceremonial law, was their *schoolmaster unto Christ,* that led them to him, and instructed them in him; but when he came, they were no longer under a schoolmaster; and this was when *the fulness of time was come,* agreed on between the Father and the Son; at which time the Son was sent, *that they might receive the adoption of children,* and be no more considered as in their nonage, and as needing the instructions of a schoolmaster, Gal. iii. 1, 2, 3, 4. and iii. 24, 25.

2. The ancient form of the administration of the covenant of grace, in a course of time, was limited to a certain people in a certain country, worshipping at a certain place, and sacrificing on the same altar. The word, worship, and service of God, peculiarly belonged to the Jews, which was their distinguishing privilege above all the nations of the world, Psalm cxlvii. 19, 20. Rom. iii. 1, 2. and ix. 4. All their males were obliged three times in the year to appear at Jerusalem and worship together; and all their offerings and sacrifices were to be brought and offered on the altar there, and no where else, Deut. xii. 11, 14. and xvi. 16. Now such a state of things was never designed to continue always; since when Shiloh, the Messiah, should come, there would be a gathering of the people to him, of people out of all nations of the world, who were to be blessed in him; he was to be set up as an ensign to them, to whom they would seek; from the rising of the sun to the going down of the same, his name was to be great among the Gentiles, and incense to be offered to it in every place, Gen. xlix. 10. Isa. xi. 10. Mal. i. 11. Now to such a dispensation the former state of things could never suit, and therefore could not be intended to be continued; the people of all nations could never be convened into one country, and worship at one place, and sacrifice on one altar.

3. It is expressly foretold, that there would be *a new covenant,* or a new administration of it; and that the former, in course, would cease, Jer. xxxi. 31, 32. and it is upon this the apostle reasons, and proves the abrogation of the former covenant, *in that he saith a new covenant, he hath made the first old,* Heb. viii. 8, 13. Particularly it was foretold, that sacrifices should cease, and be no longer acceptable to God; which were a considerable branch of the administration of the old covenant. These were from the beginning, as early as the first manifestation of the covenant of grace to fallen man: indeed, while they were in use by divine appointment, they were not in such high esteem with God as moral obedience and spiritual services, 1 Sam. xv. 22. Psalm lxix. 30, 31. Hos. vi. 6. And plain hints were given, that the time would come when they should be no more practised and regarded. David had knowledge, by the inspiration of the Spirit of God, of what Christ, the surety of his people, said to his divine Father in the council and covenant of peace, and what he would say again when he came into the world to be their Saviour; *Sacrifice and offering thou didst not desire, &c. Then said I, Lo, I come, &c.* Psalm xl. 6, 7. see Heb. x. 5, 6, 7. Christ's coming into the world to offer up himself a sacrifice for the sins of his people, was virtually saying, that God would have legal sacrifices no longer offered up, and would no more accept of them. And Daniel expressly says, that the Messiah would *cause the sacrifice and the oblation to cease;* the daily sacrifice, and every other offering according to the law, Dan. ix. 27. And the Jews them-

selves say,[1] "that all sacrifices will cease in time to come (in the time of their vainly expected Messiah) but the sacrifice of praise."

According to prophecy, the Levitical priesthood, with which so many rites and ceremonies were connected, and upon which sacrifices were established, and in the exercise of which they were performed, was to be changed; the Messiah was to come, an High-Priest of another order of priesthood than that of Aaron; *Thou art a priest for ever after the order of Melchizedek*, Psalm cx. 4. which are the words of God the Father to Christ, and from whence the apostle argues the imperfection of the Levitical priesthood, and the change of it; and also of necessity the change of the whole law, on which it was founded, Heb. vii. 11, 12, 15, 16, 17.

The ark was something very remarkable in the former dispensation; in it was the Decalogue, and on the side of it the whole body of the Jewish laws; it was a token, and indeed the place of the divine presence, and a type of Christ, a symbol of the covenant; and therefore called the ark of the covenant, and included the whole of the ceremonial law; and is put for the whole service and worship of that dispensation. Now of this it is foretold, that there would be a time when it should be no more, and should not be so much as thought of any more, Jer. iii. 16.

The ecclesiastical, as well as civil state of the Jews, was to be shaken and removed; the one is signified by the shaking of the heaven, as the other by the shaking of the earth, in Hag. ii. 6. which the apostle explains of *the removing of things shaken, that those things which cannot be shaken may remain*, Heb. xii. 26, 27. even of the immoveable kingdom after spoken of; the second administration of the covenant of grace, which is to remain, and the ordinances of it, until the second coming of Christ; whereas the ordinances of divine service under the first covenant were so shaken as to be removed; and which were made to be removed, as they have been, according to the above prediction.

Prophecy was another considerable way and means by which the covenant of grace was administered, throughout the whole old testament-dispensation; and it was foretold that this should be sealed up, finished, and cease; for one part of the Messiah's work, when come, was to seal up the *vision and prophecy*, Dan. ix. 24. all the visions and prophecies of the Old Testament were to have, and had their accomplishment in Christ; were to be sealed up and fulfilled in him, the sum and substance of them; or to *seal up the vision and prophet*; the prophets were to be till John, the forerunner of Christ, and no longer: after Christ, the great Prophet to be raised up, like unto Moses, there was to be no other, he only is to be heard; whatever scheme of things, either as to doctrine or worship, is set up, through pretended vision and prophecy, is to be disregarded; nor has any prophet risen up since prophecy, as foretold, was at an end. From all this now it might be expected, that the first and old administration of the covenant would in time cease.

Secondly, There are reasons to be given why the first covenant should and must cease. 1. It was a typical covenant; the people on whose account it was made, was a typical people, typical of the whole Israel of God, consisting of Jews and Gentiles; of the spiritual Israel, chosen of God, redeemed by Christ, and who shall be saved with an everlasting salvation; the works, duties, and services, enjoined them, and required of them with so much strictness, rigour, and severity, were typical of the obedience of Christ, the surety of the spiritual Israel; of that righteousness he was to fulfil and bring in, by which they are made righteous in the sight of God. The blessings promised unto them were typical ones; they were only shadows of good things, of spiritual blessings that were to come by Christ, Heb. x. 1. and ix. 11. As the earthly Canaan was a type of the heavenly inheritance, obtained in him; the sacrifices offered under that covenant were typical ones; the priests that offered them, the garments they offered them in, and the gifts and sacrifices offered by them, *served to the example and shadow of heavenly things*, Heb. viii. 4, 5. and ix. 23. The mediator of it, Moses, was a typical mediator, typical of Christ, the Mediator of the new covenant; the blood with which the first testament, or covenant, was dedicated and confirmed, was typical blood, typical of the blood of Christ, called, *The blood of the everlasting covenant*, Heb. ix. 18.

---

[1] Vajikra Rabba, s. 9. fol. 153, 1. and s. 27. fol. 168, 4.

CHAP. V.   OF THE ABROGATION OF THE OLD COVENANT.   363

and xiii. 20. Now when the Antitype of all this came, the types must cease; when Christ, the body, the sum and substance, appeared, these shadows must flee away, and disappear, in course, Col. ii. 17.

2. It was a faulty covenant, and therefore it was proper it should give way to a new and better covenant; so the apostle reasons; *for if that first covenant had been faultless, then should no place have been sought for the second*, Heb. viii. 7, 8. Not that there was anything sinful or criminal in the first covenant, but it was defective; there were some deficiencies in it, which made the abrogation of it necessary.——(1.) It did not exhibit Christ present, only in figure, in promise, and in prophecy; it only signified, that he would come and save his people; but it did not hold forth salvation as wrought out by him; it gave an intimation of the righteousness of Christ, that he was to bring in, but not as brought in; under it the propitiation, reconciliation, and satisfaction for sin, were not made, nor redemption from it obtained; wherefore Christ became the propitiation *for the remission of sins that are past;* and he suffered death *for the redemption of the transgressions that were under the first testament*, Rom. iii. 25. Heb. ix. 15.——(2.) The sacrifices then offered were imperfect; for some sins there were no sacrifices appointed, as for sabbath-breaking, murder, adultery, &c. and those that were appointed, could not really take away sin; at most they only made a typical expiation, not a real one; they sanctified only *to the purifying of the flesh;* but could not remove sin from the conscience, and *purge* that *from dead works;* that only the blood of Christ could do, Heb. ix. 13, 14.——(3.) There was but a small measure of the gifts and graces of the Spirit bestowed on men under the first covenant; for though there were here and there one on whom great gifts, and much grace were bestowed, as Abraham and David, &c. yet in common, it was but a scanty measure of grace, light, knowledge, and holiness, that was given to ordinary saints; and the communication was made, for the most part, only to Israelites, and but to a few among them, a remnant, according to the election of grace.—— (4.) It was a state of darkness and obscurity under that covenant; it was like a night season, in which lamps are lighted, and torches used; such was the sure word of prophecy; it was like a light or lamp in a dark place; there was light in some particular persons, as in the prophets, and it was held forth by them; but in general there was but little among the people, who *could not stedfastly look to the end of that which is abolished*, the ceremonial law; under which the mysteries of grace were couched, were clouded, and lay hid; they could not clearly see the end, design, and scope of them; though there were glorious promises of grace, these were covered with the veil of ceremonies, of which the veil, on the glory of the face of Moses, was a type, 2 Cor. iii. 7, 13.——(5.) It was a state of bondage; this covenant was signified by Hagar the bond-woman, and by mount Sinai, which gendered to bondage, and answered to Jerusalem, as it was in the apostle's time; to the state of the Jews then, who were in bondage with their children: and the Israelites, whilst in their nonage, whilst children, were in bondage, under the elements of the world, which brought upon them a spirit of bondage to fear; for such a number of laws and ordinances being given them, to the breach of which death was annexed without mercy; and they so liable to break them, they, through fear of death, were all their life-time subject to bondage, Gal. iv. 3, 24, 25. Rom. viii. 15. Heb. ii. 15.

3. The rites and ceremonies by which this covenant was greatly administered, are by the apostle called, *weak and beggarly elements;* and being *weak* and *unprofitable*, there was, therefore, a *disannulling* of them, Gal. iv. 9. Heb. vii. 18, 19. The sacrifices, which were a principal part of them, could not make, neither them that did them, nor the comers unto them, perfect, as to the conscience; they could not purge the worshippers, or those that attended ceremonial services, so as that they should have no more conscience of sin; they could not take away sin, neither from the sight of God, nor from the conscience of the sinner; nor so as that there should be no remembrance of them; for notwithstanding the daily sacrifices, morning and evening, and others on particular accounts, there was an annual remembrance made of them all, on the day of atonement, Heb. ix. 9. and x. 1, 2, 3, 4. And especially when the great high-priest was come, and his sacrifice was offered, they were quite impotent and useless, to answer any end at all: and therefore of right ought to cease, and be no more used; which leads,

Thirdly, To the abrogation of the first covenant, or of the administration of it; which was signified by the rending of the veil between the holy place and the holy of holies, at the death of Christ; whereby the way into the holiest of all was made manifest, and all within exposed to open view; as are the mysteries of grace, the veil of ceremonies being removed; and now, with boldness and freedom, entrance is had into the holiest of all by the blood of Jesus, by a new and living way, consecrated through the veil of his flesh, which the former veil was a type of. The abrogation of the old covenant is expressed by *breaking down the middle wall of partition*, which stood between Jews and Gentiles; such the ceremonial law was, and is so called in allusion to the inclosure of the court of the Israelites, in the temple, over which the Gentiles might not pass; and by *abolishing* and *slaying* the *enmity*, even *the law of commandments contained in ordinances;* the same ceremonial law, which had this name; because it indicated the hatred of God against sin, and irritated the hatred of natural men to it, by its numerous and wearisome rites; and because it was the occasion of enmity between Jew and Gentile, Eph. ii. 14, 15, 16. It is moreover expressed by a *disannulling of the commandment*, the commandment of the priesthood, and of sacrifices and rites belonging to it; and even the whole ceremonial law, as to be of no more force, nor any longer binding; so that no man, henceforward, ought to *judge* another, with respect to them, nor take upon him to command an observance of them, and require obedience to them, Heb. vii. 19. Col. ii. 16, 17. It is likewise expressed by *a blotting out the hand-writing of ordinances that was against us;* being an accusation for sin, containing a charge of sin, and implying an acknowledgment of it; as if they had given it under their hands, and showing and owning that satisfaction for sin, and that expiation were not yet made; wherefore when Christ came and paid the debt, he took up his bond, and cancelled it, and blotted out this hand-writing against his people, that it might not be read any more, and nailed it to his cross; where law and justice are directed to go for satisfaction, Col. ii. 14. Once more, the abolition of the first covenant, and its form of administration, is signified by the fleeing away and disappearance of *shadows*. The law and its ceremonies were only shadows of good things to come by Christ; when he, the Sun of Righteousness, arose, these shadows fled; when he, the body, sum, and substance appeared, these disappeared: to this the church has respect, Cant. ii. 17. and iv. 6.

Now the abrogation of the first and old covenant, or of that form of administration of the covenant of grace, was made, not at once, but gradually; and which the apostle suggests, when he says; *In that he saith a new covenant, he hath made the first old; now that which decayeth and waxeth old is ready to vanish away*, Heb. viii. 13. It began to decay, and there were some symptoms of a decay of it at the Babylonish captivity, and under the second temple; when the land of Canaan, a type of the heavenly inheritance, was seized upon by the Chaldeans, the inhabitants carried captive, a governor appointed over it by the king of Babylon, and people left in it to till it for his use; the temple was burnt, and temple worship and service ceased for many years, and the vessels of it were carried to Babylon; and though after a term of years there was a return of the people to their own land, and the temple was rebuilt, and worship restored; yet, as the Jews themselves own,[2] the ark and many other things were wanting in that temple; great declensions there were, both in doctrine and worship; the sect of the Pharisees arose, and set up their own traditions upon a level with the written word, if not above it; and great confusion there was in the priesthood, that and the civil government being blended together; and men were put into it, especially towards the close of this period, that were very unfit for it; and oftentimes obtained it by corruption and bribery; all which shewed a decay, and foreboded a change of things as near.

John the Baptist, the forerunner of Christ, came and proclaimed the near approach of the Messiah; he declared, that *the kingdom of heaven was at hand*, Matt. iii. 2. The gospel dispensation, the new administration of the covenant of grace, and the blessings of it: his father, at his birth, called him *the prophet of the Highest* who was to *prepare* his way, and *give knowledge of salvation* to his people; and when he entered upon his office, he directed the people to believe on Christ, who was to come; and quickly pointed him to them, saying, *Behold the Lamb of God, which*

---

[2] T. Bab. Yoma. fol. 21. 2.

taketh away the sin of the world, John i. 29. which the lambs of the daily sacrifice, and all other sacrifices, could not do. Christ himself appeared, and preached the same as John had done, and began his ministry with the same words; but during his life the ceremonies of the law continued in use: he himself was circumcised the eighth day; his mother purified herself according to law, at the proper time, and presented him in the temple, according to the usual manner; at twelve years of age he went up with his parents to Jerusalem, to keep the passover; and when he had entered on his public ministry, he attended synagogue and temple worship; when he healed the leper, he sent him to the priest to offer his gift; and one of the last actions of his life, was keeping the passover with his disciples; but at his death, of right, though not in fact, all ceremonies ceased, and even the whole dispensation or administration of the covenant, as it had been before in use; all *things now concerning him had an end,* Luke xxii. 37. all types and figures, shadows, sacrifices, promises, and prophecies; he by his sacrifice, by his sufferings and death, caused *the sacrifice and oblation to cease,* of right; nor should any afterwards have been offered up, Dan. ix. 27. nor any other rite and ceremony observed: yet, through the influence of Judaizing teachers over weak minds, it was thought advisable to continue the use of some of the ceremonies, at least for a time; after it was known by Peter and others, that they were no longer in force, yet because of the many thousands of Jews, who were all zealous of the law, it was judged proper that compliances should be made, and charity and prudence to be exercised, that weak minds might not be offended, until they were better instructed in the doctrine of Christian liberty; which when that was done, the use of them was strongly opposed against the obstinate and self-willed, who were resolved to retain them at any rate; and the saints were exhorted to stand fast in the liberty wherewith Christ had made them free, and not to be entangled with the yoke of bondage; by which means the Christian churches were freed from those burdensome rites and ceremonies. But still the carnal Jews continued them, and even sacrifices, until the destruction of Jerusalem, which put an end to them; for according to the law of God, no sacrifice might be offered but at Jerusalem, and upon the altar there; so that when the city, temple, and altar were destroyed, they ceased to offer any sacrifice, and never have offered any since; whereby that prophecy is remarkably fulfilled; *the children of Israel shall abide many days without a sacrifice,* Hos. iii. 4. as they have for seventeen hundred years, and still do; not even a passover lamb is slain by them, as well as no other sacrifice offered; which yet they would gladly offer in defiance of Christ, the great Sacrifice, were it not for the above law, which stands in their way, and by which they are awed; and which is no small instance of the wisdom and goodness of God in providence. Now it was a little before the destruction of Jerusalem the apostle wrote the epistle to the Hebrews, and therefore, with great propriety, he says of the old covenant, that it was not only decayed, and waxen old, but was *ready to vanish away,* Heb. viii. 13. This being the case,

Fourthly, The new covenant, or the new administration of the covenant of grace, took place; and as the one was gradually removed, the other was gradually introduced; and this observation will serve to reconcile the different æras fixed by different persons, for the beginning of the new dispensation; some placing it at the birth of Christ; others at the ministry of John the Baptist; others at the death of Christ, and his resurrection from the dead; and others at his ascension, and the effusion of the Holy Spirit on the day of Pentecost; whereas these were so many gradual manifestations of it: at the birth of Christ, undoubtedly, *the fulness of time* was come for the redemption of his people from the law who were under it; and on which very day the gospel was first preached by the angels to the shepherds, and afterwards more clearly and fully by John, by Christ and his apostles: Mark the evangelist, seems to make the beginning of the gospel of Jesus Christ the Son of God, to be with the ministry of John the Baptist, Mark i. 1, 2, 3. and which agrees with what Christ says; *the law and the prophets were until John;* they terminated in him, his ministry put a period to them; *since that time the kingdom of God is preached* in a clearer manner, and attended to by more than it was before, Luke xvi. 16. Christ appeared and preached the gospel as never man did; grace and truth came by him in a clearer and fuller manner than it ever had: he not only preached that the kingdom of heaven was at hand, as John did, but that it was already come; though not with pomp, with outward show and observation, and was actually among the people, Luke xvii. 20, 21. At his death, and by the shedding of his blood, the New Testament was sealed, ratified, and confirmed by him, as the Testator of it; and therefore called, *the blood of the New Testament*, and *the blood of the everlasting Covenant*, Matt. xxvi. 28. Heb. xiii. 20. of that new administration of the covenant which should always continue; but this new dispensation more clearly appeared at his ascension, and by the effusion of the holy Spirit on the apostles at the day of Pentecost; at his resurrection he gave them a commission to go into all the world and preach the gospel to every creature; and ordered them to wait at Jerusalem until they were endued with the holy Spirit, as they were on the above day; whereby they were furnished and qualified to carry the gospel, and preach it among all nations, as they did. And now it may be observed, that the new administration of the covenant, under the gospel dispensation, lies in the following things:

1. In an exhibition of Christ as come, and as become the author of eternal salvation; in it he is set and held forth as incarnate; as having obeyed, suffered, and died, and has made peace and reconciliation, and full satisfaction for sin; and has obtained eternal redemption; has risen from the dead, and ascended to heaven, and has received for and given gifts to men to preach his gospel; these several articles of grace are comprised in the *great mystery of godliness*, 1 Tim. iii. 16. and in those words, which are the sum of the gospel declaration, *this is a faithful saying*, &c. 1 Tim. i. 15.

2. In a more clear and extensive ministration of the gospel: it first began to be spoken by Christ in the clearest and fullest manner it possibly could be; and then by his apostles, who received it from him, and gifts to minister it; and who by his orders carried it throughout the world, and preached it to every creature under heaven, first to the Jews, and then to the Gentiles; and is, *according to the commandment of the everlasting God made known to all nations, for the obedience of faith*, Rom. xvi. 25, 26. so that the administration of the covenant is no longer restrained to a certain people, but men of all nations have the benefit of it.

3. In a freedom from all bondage and servitude: not from the bondage of sin and Satan, common to all believers under every dispensation; but from the rigorous exaction of the law, as a covenant of works; from the yoke of the ceremonial law, and from the judicial laws, as peculiar to the Jews; and which further lies in the free use of things indifferent, and in the enjoyment of the privileges and immunities of the gospel church state: this is the glorious liberty of the children of God, the liberty with which Christ has made them free; and who receive the Spirit of adoption, by whom they cry, Abba, Father; and who is a free Spirit, and where he is, there is liberty.

4. In a large communication of the gifts and graces of the Spirit: of extraordinary gifts which in the first part of this administration were bestowed, not only upon the apostles, but upon common Christians, men and women, sons and daughters, servants and handmaids, according to the prophecy of Joel, chap. ii. 28, 29. of common and ordinary gifts to fit men for the ordinary ministry of the word; and of the special graces of the Spirit, in a greater degree to saints in common; as a larger measure of faith, peace, joy, and comfort, and of light and knowledge; for according to this covenant, and the administration of it, all know the Lord from the least to the greatest; and though John was greater than the prophets, the least in this kingdom of heaven, or gospel dispensation, is greater than he, Jer. xxxi. 34. Matt. xi. 11.

5. In ordinances more spiritual than the ordinance of divine service under the first covenant were, which are called *carnal* ones; but these, which are Baptism and the Lord's Supper, do in a very lively and spiritual manner represent the sufferings, death, burial, and resurrection of Christ; and hold forth the blessings of the covenant of grace in a comfortable way, and are the means of applying them to believers, to the increase of their joy and peace; and these will continue throughout the present administration of the covenant, even to the end of the world, Matt. xxviii. 19, 20. 1 Cor. xi. 26. Of these ordinances I shall particularly treat elsewhere.

Now as the former administration of the covenant was carried through the various periods of time from the first exhibition, after the fall of Adam, to the first coming of Christ; so this second and new administration of the covenant is carried through various successive periods, unto his second coming. The book of the Revelation exhibits the state of the church from the resurrection of Christ to his personal coming; and particularly the seven churches of Asia are emblematical of it in the several successive periods of time within that interval; and represent it in its various changes and vicissitudes, as sometimes in prosperity and sometimes in adversity; sometimes in the freer use and enjoyment of the ministry of the word and ordinances, and sometimes as under clouds, darkness, and discouragements, through persecutors and false teachers, until the spiritual reign of Christ takes place; when the whole earth will be full of the knowledge of the Lord, and be enlightened with his glory; when the gospel will be in its purity everywhere, and the ordinances kept as they were first delivered, and gospel churches set up, and gospel discipline maintained everywhere; which will be followed with the personal reign of Christ, the resurrection of the dead, the last judgment, and the ultimate glory: of each of which in their proper place.

CHAP. VI.

OF THE LAW OF GOD.

It appears by what has been observed, that there was an intermixture of law and gospel under the former dispensation, as there also is in the present one; they are interspersed in both testaments; though the law was more largely held forth than the gospel, under the former dispensation; and therefore we commonly call it the legal dispensation; and there is more of the gospel than of the law under the present dispensation; for which reason we call it the gospel dispensation; yet there are of each in both; and here will be a proper place to treat of law and gospel distinctly, which will connect what has been already said to what is yet to be said; and by the latter I shall be naturally led to the great and glorious truths of the gospel, I intend to treat distinctly of. And shall begin with the law.

The word *law* is variously used, sometimes for a part of the Scriptures only, the Pentateuch, or five books of Moses; as when it is mentioned in the division of the Scriptures by Christ, Luke xxiv. 44. and along with the prophets, and as distinct from them, John i. 45. see also chap. viii. 5. Sometimes for all the books of the Old Testament, which in general go by the name of the Law, as does the book of Psalms on that account, as the places quoted out of it, or referred to in it, show, John x. 34. and xii. 34. and xv. 25. Sometimes it signifies the doctrine of the Scriptures in general, both legal and evangelical, Psalm xix. 7. and the doctrine of the gospel in particular, even the doctrine of the Messiah, Isa. ii. 3. and xlii. 4. called in the New Testament *the law*, or doctrine *of faith*, Rom. iii. 27. and sometimes it signifies the whole body of laws given from God by Moses to the children of Israel, as distinct from the gospel of the grace of God, John i. 17. and which may be distinguished into the laws ceremonial, judicial, and moral.

1. The ceremonial law, of which little need be said, since much has been observed concerning it already; this concerns the ecclesiastical state of the Jews, their priests, sacrifices, feasts, fasts, washings, &c. and though some of these rites were before the times of Moses, as sacrifices, the distinction of clean and unclean creatures, circumcision, &c. yet these were renewed and confirmed, and others added to them; and the whole digested into a body of laws by Moses, and given by him under a divine direction to the people of Israel. This law was a shadow of good things to come by Christ, of evangelical things, and indeed was no other than the gospel veiled in types and figures; the priests served to the example and shadow of heavenly things; the sacrifices were typical of the sacrifice of Christ; the festivals were shadows, of which Christ was the body and substance; the ablutions typified cleansing by the blood of Christ; and the whole was a schoolmaster to the Jews, until he came; but when faith came, that is, Christ, the object of faith, they were no longer under a schoolmaster, nor had they need of the law as such; there was a disannulling of it, because of its weakness and unprofitableness; for it became useless and unnecessary, having its accomplishment in Christ.

2. The judicial law, which respects the political state or civil government of the Jews, and consists of statutes and judgments, according to which the judges in Israel determined all causes brought before them, and passed sentence; in which sentence the people were to acquiesce, Deut. xvii. 8—11. Such as related to any injuries done to their persons or property, and to the punishment of offences, both of a greater and of a lesser kind; these were given by Moses, but not made by him; they were made by God himself. The government

of the Jews was a very particular form of government; it was a theocracy, a government immediately under God; though he is King of the whole world, and Governor among and over the nations of it, yet he was in a special and peculiar manner King over Israel; and he made laws for them, by which they were to be ruled and governed: nor had the commonwealth of Israel a power to make any new laws; nor any of their judges and rulers, not even Moses, their lawgiver under God; and therefore when any matter came before him, not clearly determined by any law given by God, he suspended the determination of it until he knew the mind of God about it; see Lev. xxiv. 12. Numb. xv. 34. And when the people of Israel were desirous of a king, after the manner of neighbouring nations, it was resented by the Lord, and reckoned by him as a rejection of him from being their King; and though he gave them a king, or suffered them to have one, it was in anger; and so far he still kept the peculiar government of them in his hands, that their kings never had any power to make new laws; nor did their best and wisest of kings make any, as David and Solomon; and when a reformation was made among them, as by Hezekiah and Josiah, it was not by making any new regulations, but by putting the old laws into execution; and by directing and requiring of the judges, and other officers, to act according to them.

It may be inquired, whether the judicial laws, or the laws respecting the Jewish polity, are now in force or not, and to be observed or not; which may be resolved by distinguishing between them; there were some that were peculiar to the state of the Jews, their continuance in the land of Canaan, and whilst their polity lasted, and until the coming of the Messiah, when they were to cease, as is clear from Gen. xlix. 10. such as related to inheritances, and the alienation of them by marriage or otherwise; the restoration of them when sold at the year of jubilee; the marrying of a brother's wife when he died without issue, &c. the design of which was, to keep the tribes distinct until the Messiah came, that it might be clearly known from what tribe he sprung. And there were others that were peculiarly suited to the natural temper and disposition of that people, who were covetous, cruel, and oppressive of the poor, froward and perverse, jealous and revengeful; hence the laws concerning the manumission of servants sold, at the end of the sixth year; the release of debts, and letting the land rest from tillage every seventh year; concerning lending on usury; leaving a corner in the field for the poor, and the forgotten sheaf;—and others concerning divorces, and the trial of a suspected wife, and the cities of refuge to flee to from the avenger of blood: these, with others, ceased when the Jewish polity did, and are not binding on other nations. But then there were other judicial laws, which were founded on the light of nature, on reason, and on justice and equity, and these remain in full force; and they must be wise as well as righteous laws, which were made by God himself, their King and Legislator, as they are said to be, Deut. iv. 6, 8. And they are, certainly, the best constituted and regulated governments that come nearest to the commonwealth of Israel, and the civil laws of it, which are of the kind last described; and where they are acted up unto, there what is said by Wisdom is most truly verified, *By me kings reign, and princes decree judgment;* and if these laws were more strictly attended to, which respect the punishment of offences, especially capital ones, things would be put upon a better footing than they are in some governments; and judges, in passing sentences, would be able to do that part of their office with more certainty and safety, and with a better conscience. And whereas the commonwealth of Israel was governed by these laws for many hundreds of years, and needed no other in their civil polity, when, in such a course of time, every case that ordinarily happens, must arise, and be brought into a court of judicature; I cannot but be of opinion, that a digest of civil laws might be made out of the Bible, the law of the Lord that is perfect, either as lying in express words in it, or to be deduced by the analogy of things and cases, and by just consequence, as would be sufficient for the government of any nation: and then there would be no need of so many law books, nor of so many lawyers; and perhaps there would be fewer law-suits. However, we Christians, under whatsoever government we are, are directed to submit to every ordinance of man for the Lord's sake, and for conscience sake; even to every one that is not contrary to common sense and reason, and to religion and conscience; see Rom. xiii. 1—7. Titus iii. 1. 1 Peter ii. 13, 14.

3. The moral law, which lies chiefly in the Decalogue, or Ten Commandments, Exod. xx. 3—17. and which our Lord has reduced, even both tables of the law, to two capital ones, love to God, and love to our neighbour, Matt. xxii. 36—40. as the apostle has reduced the commands of the second table to one, that is, love—which he calls the fulfilling of the law, Rom. xiii. 9, 10. And this law, to love God and our neighbour, is binding on every man, and is eternal, and remains invariable and unalterable; and concerning which I shall treat more largely. And shall consider,

First, The author and giver of this law; God was the author and maker of it; Moses the giver and minister of it from God; it was God that first spoke the ten words, or commands, to the children of Israel; and it was he that wrote and engraved them on tables of stone; the writing was the writing of God, and the engraving was by the finger of God; it was from his right hand this fiery law went: the ministry of angels was made use of in it; it is called, the word spoken by angels; it was given by the disposition of them; it was ordained by them in the hands of a mediator, who was Moses, who stood between God and the people, received the lively oracles from him, and delivered them to them. There was a law in being before the times of Moses; or otherwise there would have been no transgression, no imputation of sin, no charge of guilt, nor any punishment inflicted; whereas death, the just demerit of sin, reigned from Adam to Moses; and besides the positive law, which forbade the eating of the fruit of the tree of knowledge of good and evil; and was given as a trial of man's obedience to the whole moral law, and in the form of a covenant, in which Adam stood as a federal head to all his posterity; and which covenant he broke, and involved himself and his in misery and ruin. Besides this, there was the law of nature, inscribed on his heart by his Maker, as the rule of his obedience to him; and by which he knew much of God, and of the nature of moral good and evil; and which, though much obliterated by the fall, some remains of it are to be discerned in Adam's posterity, and even in the Gentiles, Rom. i. 19, 20. and ii. 14, 15. and which is re-inscribed in the hearts of God's people in regeneration, according to the tenor of the covenant of grace, Jer. xxxi. 33. Now, the law of Moses, for matter and substance, is the same with the law of nature, though differing in the form of administration; and this was renewed in the times of Moses, that it might be confirmed, and that it might not be forgotten, and be wholly lost out of the minds of men; of which there was great danger, through the great prevalence of corruption in the world: and it was written, that it might remain, *litera scripta manet;* and it was written on tables of stone, that it might be the more durable; the apostle says, *it was added because of transgressions,* to forbid them, restrain them, and punish for them; and it *entered that the offence might abound,* the sin of Adam; that the heinousness of it might appear, and the justness of its imputation to all his posterity might be manifest; as well as all other offences might be seen by it to be exceeding sinful, and righteously punishable: see Gal. iii. 19. Rom. v. 20. and vii. 13. It was not delivered as a pure covenant of works, though the self-righteous Jews turned it into one, and sought for life and righteousness by it; and so it gendered to bondage, and became a killing letter; nor a pure covenant of grace, though it was given as a distinguishing favour to the people of Israel, Deut. iv. 6, 8. Psalm cxlvii. 19, 20. Romans ix. 4. and much mercy and kindness are expressed in it; and it is prefaced with a declaration of the Lord being the God of Israel, who had, of his great goodness, brought them out of the land of Egypt, Exod. xx. 2, 6, 12. But it was a part and branch of the typical covenant, under which the covenant of grace was administered under the former dispensation; and of what it was typical, has been observed before; and a principal end of its being renewed was, that Christ, who was to come of the Jews, might appear to be made under the law, as the surety of his people, the righteousness of which he was to fulfil, and, indeed, all righteousness; being the end of the law, the scope at which it aimed, as well as the fulfiller of it.

Secondly, The epithets of this law, or the properties of it, may be next considered; such as the scriptures expressly give to it; and which will lead into the nature and quality of it. As,——1. That it is perfect. *The law of the Lord is perfect*, Psalm xix. 7. which is true of the moral law, by which men come to know *what is that good, and acceptable, and perfect will of God*, Rom. xii. 2. what it is

his will should be done, and what not be done; it takes in the whole duty of men, both to God and man; for to fear God, and keep his commandments, is the whole duty of man; it includes love to God, and love to our neighbour; and which are comprehensive of every duty to both; it is very large and capacious; it is the commandment which is exceeding broad; it is so complete and perfect, that as nothing is to be subtracted from it, so nothing is to be added to it, nor can be added to it, to make it more perfect: the papists talk of counsels, exhortations, &c. as additions; but these belong either to law or gospel. And the Socinians say, that Christ came to make the law more perfect; which they infer from some passages in Matt. v. where Christ observes, that it had been said by some of the ancients of old, thus and thus; but he said, so and so; which is not to be understood of any new laws made by him, but as giving the true sense of the old laws, and vindicating them from the false glosses and interpretations of the Scribes and Pharisees: and when the apostle John speaks of a new commandment, he means the old commandment to love one another, as he himself explains it, 1 John ii. 7, 8. and which he calls new, because enforced by a new instance and example of Christ's love in dying for his people, and by new motives and arguments taken from the same.——
2. It is spiritual; *We know that the law is spiritual*, says the apostle, Rom. vii. 14. which is to be understood of the moral law; for as for the ceremonial law, that is called, *The law of a carnal commandment;* and is said to stand in *carnal ordinances,* Heb. vii. 16. and ix. 10. which only reached the flesh, and the sanctifying of that: but the moral law is so spiritual in its nature and requirements, that so holy and spiritual a man as the apostle Paul, when he compared himself with it, and viewed himself in the glass of it, thought himself *carnal, and sold under sin*. The law reaches to the thoughts and intents of the heart, and the affections of the mind, and forbids and checks all irregular and inordinate motions in it, and the lusts of it. Thus, for instance, the sixth command not only forbids actual murder, but all undue heat, passion, anger, wrath, malice, resentment, and revenge, conceived in the mind, and expressed by words. So the seventh command not only prohibits the outward acts of uncleanness, as fornication, adultery, &c. but all unclean thoughts, impure desires, and unchaste affections, as well as looks and words. The law directs, not only to an external worship of God, but to an internal, spiritual one; as to love the Lord, to fear him, and put trust and confidence in him, suitable to his nature as a Spirit; it requires of a man to serve it with his own mind and spirit, with his whole heart, as the apostle did, Rom. vii. 25. and the assistance of the Spirit of God is necessary to the observance of it; and God in covenant has promised his people, that he *will put his spirit within them*, and *cause them to walk in his statutes*, and *keep his judgments, and do them*, Ezek. xxxvi. 27.——
3. The law is *holy;* so it is said to be, Rom. vii. 12. and the commandment holy; it comes from an holy God, from whom nothing unholy can proceed; for holiness is his nature, and he is holy in all his works; and the law is a transcript of his holy will; the matter of it, or what it requires, is holy; even sanctification of heart and life; and it directs to live holily, soberly, righteously, and godly in this evil world.——4. It is also *just*, as well as holy and good, Rom. vii. 12. There are no laws so righteous as the laws of God; the judgments of the Lord are true and righteous altogether, Deut. iv. 8. Psalm xix. 9. It is impartial unto all, and requires the same of one as of another, and renders to every man according to his works; it is just in condemning wicked men for sin, and in justifying those that have a righteousness answerable to its demands; for God is just, according to his law, whilst he is the justifier of those that believe in Jesus.——5. The law is *good;* the author of it is good only, essentially, originally good; from whom every good and perfect gift comes, and nothing that is evil and bad. The law is materially good, it is morally good; as God by the light of nature, so much more by the law of Moses, does he shew to men that which is good; in it he sets before them the good they are to do; and the evil they are to avoid: it is pleasantly good; not to an unregenerate man, whose carnal mind is enmity to all that is good, and so to the law of God; but to a regenerate man, who, as the apostle, delights in the law of God after the inner man, and loves it, as David did, and meditates on it, as every good man does, Rom. vii. 22. Psalm cxix. 97. and i. 2. And it is also profitably good; not to God, for when men have done all they can, they are,

with respect to God, unprofitable servants, Luke xvii. 10. but to men, their fellow-creatures, and fellow-christians, to whom they are serviceable, by their good works, Tit. iii. 8. and also to themselves; for though not *for*, yet *in* keeping the commands there is great reward, as peace of conscience, Psalm xix. 11. and cxix. 165. The law is good, *if a man use it lawfully*, 1 Tim. i. 8. There is a lawful and unlawful use of the law; it is used unlawfully when men seek to obtain life and righteousness by it; for the law cannot give life, nor is righteousness by it; nor can men be justified by the works of it, in the sight of God; for no man can perfectly keep it; there is not a just man that does good and sins not: but it is lawfully used when obeyed in faith, from a principle of love, with a view to the glory of God, without any selfish and sinister ends. Which leads me to consider more particularly,

Thirdly, The uses of the law both to sinners and saints.——1. To sinners.—— (1.) To convince of sin. Sin is a transgression of the law, by which it is known that it is sin, being forbidden by the law; *By the law is the knowledge of sin;* not only of gross actual sins; but of the inward lusts of the mind; *I had not known lust,* says the apostle, *except the law had said, Thou shalt not covet*, Rom. iii. 20. and vii. 7. Yet only as it is used by the Spirit of God, who holds it up to a mind enlightened by him, whereby it sees the sinfulness of it; for it is the Spirit's work savingly to convince of sin; which he does by means of the law.——(2.) To restrain from sin; of this use are the laws of men; hence civil magistrates are terrors to evil doers: so the law, by its menaces, deters men from sin, when they are not truly convinced of the evil of it, nor humbled for it; though by such restraints, it does but rise and swell, and rage the more within, like a flood of water stopped in its course.—— (3.) To condemn and punish for sin; for sinners it is made, and against them it lies, to their condemnation, unless justified in Christ, 1 Tim. i. 9, 10. It accuses of sin, charges with it; brings evidence of it; stops the sinner's mouth from pleading in his own cause; pronounces guilty before God; and curses and condemns: it is the ministration of condemnation and death; and its sentence takes place where the righteousness of Christ is not imputed.

2. It is of use to saints and true believers in Christ.——(1.) To point out the will of God unto them; what is to be done by them, and what to be avoided; to inform them of, and urge them to their duty, both towards God and man; for in that the whole of it lies.——(2.) To be a rule of life and conversation to them; not a rule to obtain life by; but to live according to; to guide their feet, to direct their steps, and preserve them from going into bye and crooked paths. The wise man says, *The commandment is a lamp, and the law is light,* Prov. vi. 23. And the wise man's father says, *Thy word is a lamp unto my feet, and a light unto my path,* Psalm cxix. 105.—— (3.) It is as a glass, in which a believer, by the light of the Spirit of God, may see his own face, what manner of man he is; how deformed, how carnal and corrupt, when compared with this law; and how far short of perfection he is in himself; *I have seen an end of all perfection,* says David; *Thy commandment is exceeding broad;* to which the imperfect works of men are not commensurate; hence good men are sensible that their own righteousness is insufficient to justify them before God, it being but as rags, and those filthy ones. Hence,——(4.) They are led to prize and value the righteousness of Christ, since that is perfectly agreeable to the holy and righteous law of God; yea, by it the law is magnified and made honourable; wherefore they desire to be found in Christ, not having on their own righteousness, but his; who is the end of the law for righteousness, to every one that believes. Now,

Fourthly, The law of God continues under the present dispensation for the said uses; Christ came not to destroy it, and loosen men's obligations to it; but to fulfil it: nor is the law made null and void by faith; by the doctrine of justification by faith in the righteousness of Christ; so far from it, that it is established by it:[1] there is a sense in which the law is *done away,* and saints are *delivered* from it; *that being dead wherein* they *were held,* as in a prison; and they *become dead to it by the body of Christ,* by his obedience and sufferings in it, 2 Cor. iii. 11. Rom. vii. 4, 6.

1. It does not continue as a covenant of works; and, indeed, it was not delivered to the children of Israel as such, strictly and properly speaking, only in a typical sense; though the Jews turned it to such

---

[1] See a Sermon of mine called, "The Law established by the Gospel."

a purpose, and sought righteousness and life by it; but God never made a covenant of works with men since the fall, in order to their obtaining life and salvation by it; for it never was in the power of man since, to perform the conditions of such a covenant; however, it is certain, believers are not under the law as a covenant of works; but under grace as a covenant of grace.

2. Nor does it continue as to the form of administration of it by Moses; it is now no longer in his hands, nor is to be considered as such; the whole Mosaic economy is broke to pieces, and at an end, which was prefigured by Moses casting the two tables of stone out of his hands, and breaking them, when he came down from the mount: the law, especially as it lies in the Decalogue; and as to the form of the administration of that by Moses, was peculiar to the Jews; as appears by the preface to it, which can agree with none but them; by the time of worship prescribed them in the fourth command, which was temporary and typical; and by the promise of long life in the land of Canaan, annexed to the fifth command.

3. It continues not as a terrifying law to believers, who are not come to mount Sinai, and are not under that stormy and terrible dispensation; but they are come to mount Sion, and to all the privileges of a gospel-church-state: nor are they brought into bondage by its rigorous exactions; on a strict compliance to which, or perfect obedience thereunto, their peace and comfort do not depend: nor are they awed and urged by its menaces and curses, to an observance of it; but are constrained, by the love of God and Christ, to run with cheerfulness the way of its commandments: they are made willing to serve it with their mind and spirit, through the power and efficacy of divine grace upon them; and they do serve it, not in the oldness of the letter but in the newness of the spirit; or, as they are renewed by the free Spirit of God.

4. Nor is it a cursing and condemning law to the saints. As sinners and transgressors of it, they are subject to its curses; but Christ has redeemed them from the curse of the law, being made a curse for them; and so there is no more curse to them here or hereafter; they are out of the reach of its curses, and of condemnation by it; there is none to them that are in Christ: Who shall condemn? it is Christ that died; and who by dying has bore their sentence of condemnation, and freed them from it; and having passed from death to life, they shall never enter into condemnation, Gal. iii. 10, 13. Rom. viii. 1, 33. John v. 24.

5. Yet it continues as a rule of walk and conversation to them, as before observed; and is to be regarded by them as in the hands of Christ;[2] by whom it is held forth as King and Lawgiver, in his church; and who, not Moses, is to be heard, and his voice hearkened to, as the Son and Master, in his own house. Believers though freed from the law, in the sense before declared, yet are *not without law to God, but under the law to Christ,* and obliged to regard it; and the rather, as it was in his heart, and he was made under it, and has fulfilled it; and therefore may be viewed and served with pleasure, 1 Cor. ix. 21.

CHAP. VII.

OF THE GOSPEL.

THERE was Gospel in the former dispensation, though called the legal dispensation; it was preached to Adam, to Abraham, and by Isaiah, and other prophets as has been observed. Yet there is a clearer revelation and ministration of it under the present dispensation; as the law was by the ministration of Moses; *Grace and truth,* the word of grace and truth, the gospel, *came by Jesus Christ,* in a clearer and fuller manner than it had been made known before, John i. 17. Concerning which the following things may be noted.

First, The name and signification of it. The Greek word ευαγγελιον, used for it throughout the New Testament, signifies, a good message, good news, glad tidings; such the gospel is; a message of good news from God, from heaven, the far country, to sinners here on earth: such was the gospel Christ was anointed to preach, and did preach, even good tidings, Luke iv. 18. compared with Isa. lxi. 1. and which his ministers bring, whose feet are beautiful upon the mountains, Isa. lii. 7. Acts xiii. 32, 33. The Hebrew word בשרה used for the gospel, and the preaching of it, signifies good tidings also; and it is observed by some, to have the signification of *flesh* in it, which has led them to think of the

---

[2] See another Sermon of mine, called, "The Law in the hand of Christ."

incarnation of Christ; which is, undoubtedly, good news to the children of men; and a considerable branch of the gospel of Christ; what has given Isaiah the character of an evangelic prophet is, because he so clearly spoke of the incarnation of Christ, as well as of his sufferings and death, as if then present in his time: *To us a child is born, to us a Son is given,* Isa. ix. 6. see chap. vii. 14. And when the angel proclaimed the birth of Christ to the Shepherds, he is said, *to bring good tidings of great joy to all people,* Luke ii. 10, 11. And this is one principal part of the gospel, the great mystery of godliness; *God manifest in the flesh,* 1 Tim. iii. 16. Our English word *gospel,* is of Saxon derivation; in which language *spel* signifies speech; and so gospel is either *good speech,* which carries in it the same idea with the Greek and Hebrew words; or God's speech, which he has spoken by his Son, by his prophets, and by his ministers; and is the voice of God the Son, the voice of Christ speaking in his ministers, and the voice of the Holy Ghost also.

Now this word is variously used; sometimes it is put for the history of Christ's birth, life, and actions; such are the Gospels according to Matthew, Mark, Luke, and John. Mark begins his history thus; *The beginning of the Gospel of Jesus Christ the Son of God,* Mark i. 1. And Luke calls his Gospel; *The former treatise* he had made, *of all that Jesus began, both to do and teach,* Acts i. 1. And hence these four writers are commonly called *evangelists;* though this title is sometimes given to others, as distinct from apostles, Eph. iv. 11. and even to ordinary ministers of the word, when they do the work of an evangelist, or preach the gospel faithfully, and make full proof of their ministry, 2 Tim. iv. 5. Sometimes the gospel is to be taken in a large sense, as including the word and ordinances, Matt. xxviii. 19, 20. Mark xvi. 15, 16. And sometimes strictly, for the doctrine of peace, pardon, righteousness, and salvation by Christ; hence gospel-ministers, who bring good tidings of good, are said to publish peace, and to publish salvation, Isa. lii. 7. the sum of which is expressed by the apostle, when he says, *This is a faithful saying, &c.* 1 Tim. i. 15. Hence,

1. The gospel is called, the gospel of salvation, the word of salvation, and salvation itself, Eph. i. 13. Acts xiii. 26. and xxviii. 28. because it gives an account of Christ, the author of salvation; of his appointment to it; of his mission, and coming into the world, to effect it; and of his actual performance of it; of his being the able, willing, and only Saviour; and of the salvation itself, as great and glorious, perfect and complete, spiritual and everlasting; and because it describes also the persons that share in it, sinners, sensible sinners, and who believe in Christ; and who, according to the declaration of it, shall certainly be saved, Mark xvi. 16. Acts xvi. 30, 31. and because it is, not only the means of revealing, but of applying salvation; for it is to them that believe *the power of God unto salvation,* Rom. i. 16.

2. It is called, *The gospel of the grace of God,* Acts xx. 24. because the several doctrines of it are doctrines of grace, or which exhibit blessings as flowing from the grace of God; as election, redemption, pardon, justification, adoption, and eternal life; and particularly, that salvation, from first to last, is all of grace, and not of works, Eph. ii. 8.

3. It is called, *The gospel of peace,* the word of reconciliation, the word preaching peace by Christ, Eph. vi. 15. 2 Cor. v. 19. Acts x. 36. because it relates the steps taken in council and covenant; to form the scheme of man's peace with God; to lay the foundation of it; and to bring it about; hence called the council of peace, and the covenant of peace, Zech. vi. 13. Isa. liv. 10. And also relates the actual making of it; by whom, and by what means; by Christ, who is our peace; by the chastisement of our peace being laid on him; by the shedding of his blood on the cross; and by his suffering of death, Eph. ii. 14. Isa. liii. 5. Col. i. 20. Rom. v. 10.

4. It is called, *The gospel of the kingdom,* Matt. iv. 23. because it treats both of the kingdom of grace here, shewing wherein it lies; and of the kingdom of glory hereafter, pointing out the proper meetness for it, regeneration by the Spirit of God; and the right and title to it, the righteousness of the Son of God; and that itself, as the Father's free gift to his people, flowing from his good will and pleasure, John iii. 5. Matt. v. 20. Luke xii. 32.

Secondly, The author and origin of the gospel.——1. It is not of man, a device and invention of men; a system of things schemed and formed by the art and wit of men; says the apostle, *I neither received it of men, nor was I taught it;* that is, by men, as human arts and sciences are,

Gal. i. 11, 12. It is not discoverable by the light of nature and reason; the law, and the things of it, may be known thereby, as what is morally good and evil, as were by the Gentiles, Rom. ii. 14, 15. but not the things of the gospel; they are what eye has not seen, nor ear heard, nor has it entered into the heart of man to conceive of; as for instance, that fundamental doctrine of the gospel, that Jesus Christ is the Son of the living God, believed and confessed by Peter, was declared by our Lord to be what *flesh and blood* had *not revealed* to him, but his *Father in heaven*, Matt. xvi. 16, 17. Hence the gospel is frequently called, a mystery; the wisdom of God in a mystery; the hidden wisdom; and the doctrines of it, the mysteries of the kingdom; which are only known by those to whom it is given by the Spirit and grace of God to know them, Matt. xiii. 11. and when they are externally revealed, and men have got some little notion and idea of them, they are disapproved of by them; for natural men receive not with approbation, and a good liking, the things of the Spirit of God, the doctrines of the gospel, which he searches and reveals; for they are foolishness, insipid things to them; for which they have no taste; as the doctrine of a crucified Christ, and salvation alone by him, 1 Cor. ii. 14. and i. 18, 23.——2. The gospel is from heaven; it is good news from a far country, which far country is heaven; the gospel is, with the Holy Ghost, sent down from heaven; and Christ that spoke it, is He that speaketh from heaven: the question put concerning the baptism of John; *Whence was it? from heaven, or of men?* may be put concerning the gospel, and answered as that; that it is from heaven, and not of men, 1 Pet. i. 12. Heb. xii. 25. Matt. xxi. 25. It comes from God, Father, Son, and Spirit; from God the Father, and is therefore called the gospel of God; that is, the Father, concerning his Son Jesus Christ, Rom. i. 1, 3. which he ordained before the world was; and in time committed into the hands of men to preach, whom he made, and makes, able ministers of it, and which he blesses and succeeds. It comes also from Christ, the Son of God; and is called, the gospel of his Son, the gospel of Christ, the word of Christ, and the testimony of our Lord, Rom. i. 9. 16. Col. iii. 16. 2 Tim. i. 8. of which Christ is the subject, sum, and substance, as well as the author; even his person, offices, and grace; and of which he was the preacher when here on earth; for which he was qualified by the Spirit without measure, and spake and preached it as never man did; and by whom it was revealed and brought to light in the clearest manner; hence the apostle says, he received it *by the revelation of Jesus Christ*, Gal. i. 12. It may be said likewise, to come from the holy Spirit of God, the inditer of the scriptures, wherein it lies; who searches the deep things of it, and reveals them to men; who leads the ministers of it into all the truths thereof; and makes their ministrations of it powerful and successful; and whereby he and his grace, comparable to the golden oil, are conveyed and received into the hearts of men. The instruments of declaring, publishing, and proclaiming the gospel, and its truths, to the children of men, are the prophets of the Old Testament, who made a report of it, though believed but by few; the angels, who descended at the birth of Christ, and brought the good news of it; John the Baptist, the forerunner of Christ, who pointed him out as the Son of God, and as the Lamb of God that took away the sin of the world; the apostles of Christ, who had a commission from him to preach the gospel to every creature; and all ordinary ministers of the word, whose business it is to publish good tidings of good things.

Thirdly, The effects of the gospel when attended with the power and Spirit of God. ——1. The regeneration of men, who are said to be born again by the word of God, and to be begotten again with the word of truth, 1 Pet. i. 23. James i. 18. hence ministers of the gospel are represented as spiritual fathers, 1 Cor. iv. 15. ——2. As in regeneration, souls are quickened by the Spirit and grace of God, this is ascribed to the gospel as an instrument, hence it is called the Spirit which giveth life, and said to be the savour of life unto life, 2 Cor. ii. 16. and iii. 6.——3. The gospel is frequently spoken of as a light, a great light, a glorious light; and so is in the hands of the Spirit a means of enlightening the dark minds of men into the mysteries of grace, and the method of salvation; *the entrance of thy word giveth light, it giveth understanding unto the simple*, Psalm cxix. 130. The Spirit of God gives the gospel an entrance into the heart, being opened by him to attend unto it; and when it has an entrance, it gives light into a man's self, his state and condition, and into the way of life by Christ; it is a glass in which the glory of Christ, and of the riches of his grace, may be seen.——4. By it faith in Christ comes, and is ingenerated in the heart by the Spirit of God attending it; hence, among other reasons, it is called *the word of faith*; and ministers, by preaching it, are instruments of confirming and increasing faith, and of perfecting what is lacking in it, Rom. x. 8, 17. 1 Thess. iii. 10.——5. When faith is wrought in the soul, the righteousness of Christ is revealed unto it in the gospel; and not at first believing only, but at after times; for it is revealed therein *from faith to faith*, from one degree of it to another, giving thereby clearer views of it, and of interest in it, Rom. i. 17. hence it is called the word of righteousness, and the ministration of righteousness, Heb. v. 13. 2 Cor. iii. 9.——6. It affords spiritual food, and is the means of feeding and nourishing souls unto everlasting life; it contains words of faith and good doctrine, even the wholesome words of our Lord Jesus; it has in it milk for babes, and meat for strong men; and when it is found by faith, it is eaten by it with pleasure, and fills with spiritual joy, 1 Tim. iv. 6. and vi. 3. Heb. v. 13, 14. Jer. xv. 16. which—— 7. Is another effect of it in gracious souls, it yields much spiritual peace, joy, and comfort; the doctrines of it are calculated for such a purpose; it is good news and glad tidings of good things; as of peace, pardon, righteousness, and salvation by Christ, which, when applied, cannot fail of producing spiritual joy in sensible sinners; when Philip preached Christ and his gospel in Samaria, there was great joy in that city, Acts viii. 5, 8. all this must be understood of the gospel, not as producing these effects of itself, but as it comes, not in word only, but with the power and in the demonstration of the Spirit; when it is sent forth out of Zion as the rod of God's strength, and it becomes the power of God unto salvation, 1 Thess. i. 5, 8. Psalm cx. 2. Rom. i. 16.

Fourthly, The properties of the gospel. ——1. It is but one, there is not another, as the apostle says, Gal. i. 6, 7. the same gospel which was in the beginning, and will be to the end of the world, the same under the Old Testament as under the New; the subject of it, Christ and salvation by him; the doctrines of it, of justification, remission of sins, &c. the same, only now more clearly revealed; then it was in types and figures, now more plainly set forth, and more clearly and fully expressed; the same was preached by Christ and his apostles, and by all faithful ministers since, and will be to the end of time; for it is true of the gospel what is said of Christ, it is *the same yesterday, to-day, and for ever*, Heb. xiii. 8.——2. It is called, from the objects of it, the gospel of the circumcision, and the gospel of the uncircumcision, Gal. ii. 7. not that the gospel of the one is different from that of the other; it is the same gospel, only dispensed to different persons; the circumcised Jews and the uncircumcised Gentiles; it was first ordered to be preached to the Jews, and to them only, in Christ's life-time; after his death and resurrection he enlarged the commission of his disciples, and sent them forth to preach the gospel to every creature, both Jews and Gentiles; yet the special revelation and application of it are made only to some; to some it is the savour of life unto life, to others the savour of death unto death; there are some to whom God would make it known; it was his determinate pleasure to make known the riches of the glory of the mystery of it; to others it is hid, even to the wise and prudent, whilst it is revealed unto babes; of which no other reason can be given, but the sovereign will and pleasure of God, 2 Cor. ii. 16. and iv. 3. Col. i. 27. Matt. xi. 25, 26. ——3. It is a glorious gospel: so it is called, 2 Cor. iv. 4. 1 Tim. i. 11. it has a glory in it exceeding that of the law, and the dispensation of it, 2 Cor. iii. 11. for the clearness, fulness, and suitableness of its doctrines to the state and condition of men; and in which the glory of the person of Christ as the Son of God, and of his offices as mediator, and of the blessings of grace that come by him, is held forth in great splendour and brightness.——4. It is an everlasting gospel, which is the epithet given it, Rev. xiv. 6. it was ordained in the council and covenant of God before the world was, of which it is a transcript, and so was from everlasting, 1 Cor. ii. 7. and *the word of the Lord endureth for ever, and this is the word which by the gospel is preached*, 1 Pet. i. 25. and which will continue until all the elect of God are gathered in, maugre all the craft and cunning, force and power of earth and hell.

Fifthly, I shall close this chapter with a brief answer to some queries relating to faith, repentance, and good works; as, to what they belong, whether to law or gospel.

1. Whether faith is a duty of the moral law, or is to be referred to the gospel? to which it may be answered, that as the law is not of faith, so faith is not of the law. There is a faith indeed which the law requires and obliges to, namely, faith and trust in God, as the God of nature, and providence; for as both the law of nature, and the law of Moses, shew there is a God, and who is to be worshipped; they both require a belief of him, and trust and confidence in him; which is one part of the worship of him enjoined therein: moreover the law obliges men to give credit to any revelation of the mind and will of God he has made, or should think fit to make unto them at any time; but as for special faith in Christ as a Saviour, or a believing in him to the saving of the soul; this the law knows nothing of, nor does it make it known; this kind of faith neither comes by the ministration of it, nor does it direct to Christ the object of it, nor give any encouragement to believe in him on the above account; but it is a blessing of the covenant of grace, which flows from electing love, is a gift of God's free grace, the operation of the Spirit of God, comes by the hearing of faith, or the word of faith as a means, that is, the gospel; for which reason, among others, the gospel is so called; and it is that which points out Christ, the object of faith; and directs and encourages sensible sinners under a divine influence to exercise it on him; its language is, *believe on the Lord Jesus Christ, and thou shalt be saved*, Acts xvi. 31.

2. Whether repentance is a doctrine of the law or of the gospel? the answer to which is, that such who sin ought to repent of sin; this God has commanded, the law of nature teaches; and so far as this is to be considered as a duty incumbent on men, it belongs to the law, as all duty does; but then the law makes no account of repentance for sin; nor does it admit of it as a satisfaction for it; nor gives any encouragement to expect that God will receive repenting sinners into his grace and favour upon it; this is what the gospel does, and not the law; the law says not, repent and live, but do and live. Moreover, there is what may be called a legal repentance and contrition; for by the law is the knowledge of sin, without which there can be no repentance; and it works a sense of wrath in the sinner's conscience, and a fearful looking for of judgment and fiery indignation from an incensed God; but if it stop here, it will prove no other than a worldly sorrow, which worketh death. The Spirit of God may make use of this, and go on and produce spiritual repentance, such a repentance as is unto life, even life eternal; and unto salvation, which needeth not to be repented of: but such a repentance is not the work of the law; for life and salvation come not by any work of the law; but true repentance, which has salvation annexed to it, is, as faith, a blessing of the covenant of grace; a grant from God, a gift of Christ as a Saviour, and with it remission of sins; a grace produced in the soul by the Spirit of Christ, by means of the gospel, which only encourages to the exercise of it; see Acts v. 31. and xi. 18. 2 Cor. vii. 10. Gal. iii. 2. And so is a doctrine of the gospel, and not of the law, as appears from the ministry of John the Baptist, the forerunner of Christ, who exhorted and encouraged to repentance from gospel-motives; and preached the baptism of repentance for the remission of sins, Matt. iii. 2. Mark i. 4. But what has the law to do either with baptism or the remission of sins? His ministry was evangelical, and ran in the same strain with the apostles, as appears from their answer to a question put to them; *Men and brethren what shall we do?* A serious question, put upon thought and reflection by persons upon the bottom of a covenant of works,[2] as the Jews generally were; and especially under a sense of guilt, as those were, desirous to know what *must be done* by them, that they *might be saved;* as it may be supplied from the jailor's words, when in the same case; or whereby they might make atonement for, and obtain the pardon of so great a sin, of which they were guilty:[3] to which a proper answer is returned, putting them off of legal works for such purposes, and directing them to evangelical ones; *Repent and be baptized, every one of you, for the remission of sins,* Acts ii. 37, 38. And this is also clear from the ministry of Christ himself; who came, not to call the righteous, but sinners, to repentance; which was not a legal, but evangelical repentance. He began his

---

[1] Surely no man can take this to be the same as an Anglicism, or as an unmeaning phrase used among us sometimes by persons in distress, "What shall we do? what shall we do? what shall we do? &c."

[3] So Piscator, Pricæus, et alii in loc.

ministry thus; *Repent, and believe the gospel*, see Matt. ix. 13. Mark i. 15. With which agrees the ministry of the apostles in general; who, by the direction of Christ, preached repentance and remission of sins in his name; which most certainly was the gospel; the one, as well as the other, a doctrine of the gospel, Luke xxiv. 47. And the apostle Paul, who was a most evangelical preacher, divides his whole ministry into these two parts; *Repentance towards God, and faith towards our Lord Jesus Christ*, Acts xx. 21.

3. Whether good works belong to the gospel, or to the law? or rather, whether there are any works that belong to the gospel distinct from the law? to which it may be replied, That the gospel, taken in a large sense, as has been observed in the beginning of this chapter, includes both the doctrines and ordinances of the gospel; and the one, as well as the other, are taught, and directed to be observed; yea, all good works, which the law requires, are moved and urged unto in the ministry of the gospel, upon gospel-principles and motives: the gospel of the grace of God, which brings the good tidings of salvation, instructs and urges men to do good works, and to avoid sin, Tit. ii. 11, 12. and iii. 8. But the gospel, strictly taken, is a pure declaration of grace, a mere promise of salvation by Christ. All duty and good works belong to the law; promise and grace belong to the gospel; the works of the law, and the grace of the gospel, are always opposed to each other, Rom. iii. 20, 24, 28. Eph. ii. 8. And if there were any works distinct from the law, and not required by it, which, if not performed, would be sin; then the apostle's definition of sin, as a transgression of the law, would not be a full and proper one, 1 John iii. 4. since then there would be sins which were not transgressions of the law; wherefore, as all evil works are transgressions of the law, all good works are required and enjoined by it.

A BODY OF
DOCTRINAL DIVINITY.

BOOK V.

OF THE GRACE OF CHRIST, AS EXPRESSED IN HIS STATES OF HUMILIATION AND EXALTATION, AND IN THE OFFICES EXERCISED BY HIM IN THEM.

CHAP. I.

OF THE INCARNATION OF CHRIST.

HAVING treated in the preceding Book, of the exhibition of the covenant of grace, both under the Old and New Testament dispensations, and of the law and gospel, as held forth in both; and of the latter only in a general way; I shall now proceed to consider, the particular, special, and important doctrines of the gospel, which express the grace of Christ, and the blessings of grace by him; and shall begin with the Incarnation of the Son of God. This is a very considerable part of the glad tidings of the gospel, and which give it that name; when the angel related to the shepherds the birth of Christ, he said unto them; *Behold I bring you good tidings of great joy, &c.* Luke ii. 10, 11. The whole gospel is a mystery; the several doctrines of it are the mysteries of the kingdom; the knowledge of which is given to some, and not to others; it is the mystery of godliness, and, without controversy, great; and this stands the first and principal article of it; *God manifest in the flesh,* 1 Tim. iii. 16. This is the basis of the christian religion; a fundamental article of it; and without the belief of it no man can be a christian; *Every spirit that confesseth that Jesus Christ is come in the flesh, is of God;* born of God, and belongs to him, and is on the side of God and truth; *And every spirit that confesseth not that Jesus Christ is come in the flesh, is not of God,* 1 John iv. 2, 3.

The incarnation of Christ is a most extraordinary and amazing affair; it is wonderful indeed, that the eternal Son of God should become man; that he should be born of a pure virgin, without any concern of man in it; that this should be brought about by the power of the Holy Ghost, in a way unseen, imperceptible, and unknown, signified by his overshadowing; and all this in order to effect the most wonderful work that ever was done in the world, the redemption and salvation of men: it is a most mysterious thing, incomprehensible by men, and not to be accounted for upon the principles of natural reason; and is only to be believed and embraced upon the credit of divine revelation, to which it solely belongs. The heathens had some faint notions of it; at least say some things similar to it. The Brachmanes among the Indians, asserted, that Wistnavius, the second person of the trine-une god with them, had nine times assumed a body, and sometimes an human one; and would once more do the same again; and that he was once born of a virgin.[1] Confucius, the famous Chinese philosopher, who lived almost five hundred years before Christ, it is said,[2] foresaw that the Word would be

---

[1] Huet. Quæst. Alnetan. 1. 2. c. 13. p. 234. et c. 15. p. 241. See Philosoph. Transact. abridged, vol. v. part 2. p. 168.

[2] Martin. Sinic. Hist. 1. 4. p. 131, 132. Vid. Huet. ut supra, p. 235.

made flesh; and foretold the year in which it would be; and which was the very year in which Christ was born: but this seems to savour too much of the tale of a christian in later times. However, several of the deities and heroes of the heathens, Greeks and Romans, are represented as having no father.[3] Now whatever notion the heathens had of an incarnate God, or of a divine person born of a virgin, in whatsoever manner expressed; this was not owing to any discoveries made by the light of nature, but what was traditionally handed down to them, and was the broken remains of a revelation their ancestors were acquainted with. Otherwise the incarnation of the Son of God, is a doctrine of pure revelation; in treating of which I shall consider,

First, The subject of the incarnation, or the divine Person that became incarnate. The evangelist John says it was the Word, the essential Word of God; *The word was made flesh, and dwelt among us*, John i. 14. And therefore not *the Father;* for he is distinguished from the *Word*, in the order of the Trinity, 1 John v. 7. And he is said to be the *Word with God;* that is, with God the Father; and therefore must be distinct from him, Rev. xix. 13. Acts xx. 32. John i. 1. Besides, the Father never so much as appeared in an human form; and much less took real flesh; nay, never was seen in any shape by the Jews, John v. 37. And though their ancestors heard a voice, and a terrible one at Sinai, they saw no similitude, Deut. iv. 12. And wherever we read of any visible appearance of a divine Person in the Old Testament, it is always to be understood, not of the first, but of the second Person. And it may be further observed, that the Father prepared a body, an human nature in his purpose, council and covenant, for another, and not for himself, even for his Son, as he acknowledges; *A body hast thou prepared me;* Heb. x. 5. To which may be added, that that divine Person who came in the flesh, or became incarnate, is always distinguished from the Father, as being sent by him; *God sending his own Son in the likeness of sinful flesh*, Rom. viii. 3. And again; *God sent forth his Son made of a woman*, Gal. iv. 4. that is, God the Father, in both passages; as appears from the relation of the Person to him, sent in the flesh, his Son. Once more, if the Father had been incarnate, he must have suffered and died; for that is the end of the incarnation, that the Person incarnate, might obey, suffer, and die, in the room of sinners; so Christ suffered in the flesh, and was put to death in the flesh. There were a set of men in ancient times, who embraced the Sabellian folly, and were called Patripassians, because they held that the Father suffered; and, indeed, if there is but one Person in the Deity, and Father, Son, and Spirit are only so many names and manifestations of that one Person; then it must be equally true of the Father as of the Son, that he became incarnate, obeyed, suffered, and died. But this notion continued not long, but was soon rejected, as it must be by all that read their Bible with any care. Nor is it the holy Spirit that became incarnate, for the same reasons that the Father cannot be thought to be so: and besides, he had a peculiar hand, and a special agency, in the formation of the human nature, and in its conception and birth: when the Virgin hesitated about what was told her by the angel, she was assured by him, that the Holy Ghost should come upon her, and the power of the Highest should overshadow her; and accordingly the birth of Christ was on this wise, when Joseph and Mary were espoused, before they came together, *she was found with child of the Holy Ghost;* and Joseph was told, in order to encourage him to take her to wife, that what was *conceived in her*, was *of the Holy Ghost;* and therefore he himself was not incarnate; see Luke i. 35. Matt. i. 18, 20. It remains, that it is the second Person, the Son of God, who is meant by *the Word that was made flesh*, or became incarnate; and, indeed, it is explained of him in the same passage; for it follows, *And we beheld his glory, the glory as of the only-begotten of the Father*. And it is easy to observe, that the same divine Person that bears the name of the Word, in the order of the Trinity, in one place, has that of the Son in another; by which it appears they are the same; compare 1 John v. 7. with Matt. xxviii. 19. When this mystery of the incarnation is expressed by the phrase, *God manifest in the flesh;* not God the Father, nor the holy Spirit, but God the Son is meant, as it is explained, 1 John iii. 8. for *this purpose the Son of God was manifested;* that is, in the flesh; and as before observed, it was the Son of God that was sent in the likeness of sinful flesh, and in the fulness of time was

---

[3] Hesiod. Theogon. v. 927. Apollodor. de Deor. Orig. l. 1. p. 8. Vid. Huet. ut supra, c. 15. p. 237, 238.

sent forth, made of a woman, Rom. viii. 3. Gal. iv. 4. He, therefore, is the subject of the incarnation, or the divine Person that became incarnate.

Now the Logos, the Word and Son of God, who is made flesh or become incarnate, is not to be understood of the human soul of Christ; for this word was *in the beginning with God;* that is, was with him from all eternity; see Prov. viii. 22—30. whereas the human soul of Christ is one of the souls that God has made; a creature, a creature of time, as all creatures are; time is an inseparable adjunct and concomitant of a creature; a creature before time, is a contradiction: besides, this Word *was* God, a divine Person, distinct from the Father, though with him, the one God; which cannot be said of the human soul. Likewise, to it is ascribed the creation of all things; *All things were made by him;* not as an instrument, but as the efficient cause; *And without him was not any thing made that was made;* and since the human soul is what is made, being a creature; if that is the Word and Son of God, it must be the maker of itself, seeing nothing that is made is made without it; which is too great an absurdity to be admitted. So the creation of all things is elsewhere ascribed to the Son of God, who therefore cannot be a creature; see Heb. i. 1, 2, 10. Col. i. 16, 17. To which may be added, that the human soul of Christ is a part of the human nature assumed by him; it is included in the word *flesh*, the Word, or Son of God, is said to be made, as will be shewn presently; it is a part of that nature of the seed of Abraham, in distinction from the nature of angels, which the Word, or Son of God, a divine Person took upon him, and into union with him, and therefore cannot be the assumer; the assumer and the assumed cannot be the same, but must be distinct from each other; see Heb. ii. 14, 16.

Nor by the Logos, or Word, made flesh, are we to understand the divine nature, essentially considered, or the essence of God, as common to the three divine Persons, Father, Son, and Spirit; for then it would be equally true of the Father and the Spirit, that they are made flesh, or become incarnate, as of the Son; as it must needs be, if the divine nature, so considered, was incarnated; or the human nature was united to it as such: such phrases are therefore unsound, unsafe, and dangerous; as that the man Christ stands in the divine nature; and that the human nature is united to Deity: this is not the truth of things; the human nature is not united to Deity absolutely considered; but as that in a distinct mode of subsisting, is in the second Person, the Son of God; it was the Son of God, by whom God made the world, and by him speaks to men, in these last days, who is the brightness of his Father's glory, and the express image of his person; the Creator of angels, and the object of their worship and adoration; and who upholds all things by the word of his power, who partook of the same flesh and blood with the children, and has taken upon him, and assumed to him, not the nature of angels, but the seed of Abraham; he who was in the form of God, of the same nature with him, and thought it no robbery to be equal with God, is he that took upon him the form of a servant, the nature of man in a servile state, was made in the likeness of man, and found in fashion as a man, or really became man. I proceed,

Secondly, To observe, in what sense the Word, or Son of God, was *made flesh*, became a partaker *of flesh and blood, came in the flesh*, and was *manifest in the flesh:* all which phrases are made use of to express his incarnation, John i. 14. Heb. ii. 14. 1 John iv. 2, 3. 1 Tim. iii. 16. and signify, that he who is truly God really became man, or assumed the whole human nature, as will be seen presently, into union with his divine person. Socinus is so bold as to say,[4] that if any passages of scripture could be found, in which it is expressly said that God was made man, or put on and assumed human flesh, the words must be taken otherwise than as they sound, this being repugnant to the majesty of God. The contrary to this will soon appear; and though this is not to be found in scripture just syllabically, the sense clearly is, as in the scriptures referred to. But there is no dealing with such a man who will talk at this rate; and who elsewhere[5] says, on another account, that the greatest force must be used with the words of the apostle Paul, rather than such a sense be admitted, which yet is obvious. It will be proper to inquire, both what is meant by *flesh*, and what by being *made* flesh.

1st, What is meant by *flesh*, in the

---

[4] Opera, tom. 1. De Christi Natura Disput. p. 784.

[5] Ibid. Ep. 2. ad Balcerovicium. p. 425.

phrases and passages referred to. And by it is meant, not a part of the human body, as that may be distinguished from other parts, as the bones, &c. nor the whole human body, as that may be distinguished from the soul or spirit of a man; as in Matt. xxvi. 41. but a whole individual of human nature, consisting of soul and body; as when it is said, *There shall no flesh be justified in his sight:* and again, *That no flesh should glory in his presence*, Rom. iii. 20. 1 Cor. i. 29. with many other passages; see Gen. vi. 12. Luke iii. 6. for such acts as being justified and glorying, can never be said of the flesh or body, abstractly considered; but of the whole man, or of individuals of human nature, consisting of soul and body; and in this sense are we to understand it, when it is used of the incarnation of the Son of God, who took upon him the whole nature of man, assumed a true body and a reasonable soul, being in all things made like unto his brethren; so his flesh signifies his human nature, as distinct from the Spirit, his divine nature, Rom. i. 3, 4. 1 Pet. iii. 18.

1. He took a true body, not a mere phantom, spectre, or apparition, the appearance of a body, and not a real one; as some fancied, and that very early, even in the times of the apostle John, and afterward; and who imagined, that what Christ was, and did, and suffered, were only seeming, and in appearance, and not in reality; and hence they were called *Docetæ:* and this they argued from his being sent in the *likeness* of sinful flesh; and being found in fashion *as* a man; and from the appearances of Christ before his coming; of which same kind they supposed his appearance was when he came. As for the text in Rom. viii. 3. *likeness* there, is not to be connected with the word *flesh*, but with the word *sinful;* he was sent in real flesh, but that flesh looked as if it was sinful: it might seem so to some, because he took flesh of a sinful woman, was attended with griefs and sorrows, the effects of sin; had the sins of his people imputed to him, and which he bore in his own body on the tree; all which made his flesh appear as if it was sinful, though it was not; and hindered not its being real flesh. As to Phil. ii. 7. 8. the *as* there, is not a note of similitude, but of certainty; as in Matt. xiv. 5. and signifies, that Christ was really a man, as John was accounted a real prophet, and not merely like one; and which is evident by his being obedient unto death, as follows: and as for the appearances of Christ in an human form, before his coming in the flesh, the Scriptures speak of; admitting they were only appearances, and not real, it does not follow, that therefore his coming in the flesh, in the fulness of time, was of the same kind; but rather the contrary follows; and since these were preludes of his incarnation, that must be real; though some of these previous appearances were not merely appearances, but realities: real bodies were formed and animated, and made use of for a time, and then laid aside; as seems to be the case of the three men that appeared to Abraham, two of which were angels, and the other the Lord, Jehovah, the Son of God; who were clothed with bodies, capable of walking and travelling, of talking and conversing, of eating, and drinking in; so the man that wrestled with Jacob, who was no other than the Angel of the covenant, the promised Messiah; the body he appeared in was not a mere phantom, spectre, and apparition, but palpable flesh, that was felt and handled, and grasped, and held fast, by Jacob; and which he would not let go till he had received the blessing. However, it is certain that Christ partook of the same flesh and blood as his children and people do; and therefore, if theirs is real, his must be so. Likewise, his body is called the body of his flesh, his fleshly body, Col. i. 22. to distinguish it from the token of his body in the supper; and from his mystical and spiritual body, the church: all his actions, and what is said of him from his birth to his death, and in and after it, show it was a true body that he assumed; he was born and brought into the world as other men are; and when born, his body grew and increased in stature, as other human bodies do: the Son of man came eating and drinking; he travelled through Judea and Galilee; he slept in the ship with his disciples; he was seen, and heard, and handled by them; he was buffeted, scourged, bruised, wounded, and crucified by men; his body, when dead, was asked of the governor by Joseph, was taken down from the cross by him, and laid in his tomb; and the same identical body, with the prints of the nails and spear in it, was raised from the dead, and seen and handled by his disciples; to whom it was demonstrated, that he had flesh and bones, a spirit has not: yea, the very infirmities that attended him, though sinless, were proofs of his body being a true and real one; such as his fatigue and weariness in travelling, John iv. 6.

his tears at the grave of Lazarus, and over Jerusalem; and his sweat in the garden, John xi. 35. Luke xix. 41. and xxii. 44. In short, it was through weakness of the flesh that he was crucified; which was not in appearance, but in reality. The body he assumed was mortal, as it was proper it should be, since the end of his assumption of it was to suffer death in it; but being raised from the dead, it is become immortal, and will never die more, but will remain, as the pledge and pattern of the resurrection of the bodies of the saints, which will be fashioned like to his glorious body; and which will be the object of the corporal vision of the saints after their resurrection, with joy and pleasure, to all eternity.

2. Christ assumed a reasonable soul, with his true body, which make up the nature he took upon him, and are included in the flesh he was made, as has been seen; and is the flesh and blood he partook of; which is sometimes understood of an individual of human nature, as flesh is; see Matt. xvi. 17. Gal. i. 16. The Arians deny that Christ has an human soul; they say, that the Logos, or the divine nature in him, such a one as it is, supplied the place of an human soul. This nature, they say, is not the same, but like to the nature of God; that it was created by him; which they ground on Prov. viii. 22. and read, *He created me;* and they make this the first and principal creature God made, and by which he created others; that it is a superangelic spirit, and is in the room of an human soul to Christ. But Christ asserts, that he had a soul; and which, he says, was exceeding sorrowful; and which was an immaterial and immortal Spirit; and which, when his body died, and was separated from it, he commended into the hands of his divine Father, Matt. xxvi. 38. Luke xxiii. 46. Had he not an human soul, he would not be a perfect man; and could not be called, as he is, the man Christ Jesus: the integral parts of man, and which constitute one, are soul and body; and without which he cannot be called a man; these distinguish him from other creatures: on the one hand he is distinguished from angels, immaterial and immortal spirits, with which his soul has a cognation, by having a body, or by being an embodied spirit; whereas they are incoporeal; so, on the other hand, he is distinguished from mere animals, who have bodies as well as he, by his having a rational and immortal soul: and if Christ was without one, he could not be in all things like unto us; being deficient in that which is the most excellent and most noble part of man. But that he is possessed of an human soul, is evident from his having an human understanding, will, and affections; he had an human understanding, knowledge, and wisdom, in which he is said to grow, and which in some things were deficient and imperfect, Luke ii. 52. Mark xiii. 32. He had an human will, distinct from the divine will, though not opposite, but in subjection to it, John vi. 38. Luke xxii. 42. And he had human affections, as love, Mark x. 21. John xiii. 23. And joy, Luke x. 21. Yea, even those infirmities, though sinless passions, prove the truth of his human soul; as sorrow, grief, anger, amazement, and consternation, Matt. xxvi. 38. Mark iii. 5. and xiv. 33. Besides, if he had not had an human soul, he could not have been tempted in all points like as we are, Heb. iv. 15. since the temptations of Satan chiefly respect the soul, the mind, and the thoughts of it, and affect and distress that: nor could he have bore the wrath of God, nor have had a sensation of that; which it is certain he had, when the weight of the sins of his people lay on him, and pressed him sore; see Psalm lxxxix. 38. Matt. xxvi. 38. Nor could he have been a perfect sacrifice for their sins; which required his soul as well as his body, Isa. liii. 10. Heb. x. 10. nor have been the Saviour of their souls; as he is both of body and soul, giving life for life, body for body, soul for soul, 1 Peter i. 9.

2ndly, In what sense the Word, or Son of God, was *made* flesh, and so became incarnate; the Word could not be made at all, that is, created, since he is the Maker and Creator of all things; and therefore he himself could not be made or created; nor was he, nor could be, made, converted, and changed into flesh; the divine nature in Christ could not be changed into human nature; for he is the Lord, that changes not; he is the same in the *yesterday* of eternity, in the *day* of time, and *for ever* to all eternity. By the incarnation nothing is added to, nor altered in the divine nature and personality of Christ. The human nature adds nothing to either of them; they remain the same they ever were; Christ was as much a divine Person before his incarnation as he is since; the union of the human nature to the divine nature, is to it as subsisting in the Person of the Son of God; so it is always to be understood, whenever we speak of the union of the human nature to the divine nature; for it is not united to the divine nature, simply considered; or as that is common to the three Persons; for then each would be incarnate; but as it has a peculiar subsistence in the Person of the Son of God: and so the human nature has its subsistence in his Person, and has a glory and excellency given it; but that gives nothing at all to the nature and person of the divine Word and Son of God. But, as other scriptures explain it, God the Word, or Son, was made and became *manifest in the flesh*; the Son that was in the bosom of the Father, the Word of life, that was with him from all eternity, was manifested in the flesh in time, to the sons of men; and that in order to take away sin, and destroy the works of the devil, 1 Tim. iii. 16. 1 John i. 1, 2. and iii. 5, 8. And the incarnation of the Word or Son of God, is expressed and explained by his partaking of flesh and blood; and by a taking on him the nature of man; or by an assumption of the human nature into union with his divine Person; so that both natures, divine and human, are united in one Person; and there is but one Lord, and one Mediator between God and man. The Nestorians so divided and separated these natures, as to make them distinct and separate Persons; which they are not, but one. And the Eutychians, running into the other extreme, mixed and confounded the natures together; interpreting the phrase, *the Word was made flesh*, of the divine nature being changed into the human nature; and the human nature into the divine nature; and so blended together as to make a third; just as two sort of liquors, mixed together, make a third different from both. But this is to make Christ neither truly God, nor truly man; the one nature being confounded with and swallowed up in the other. But this union of natures is such, that though they are closely united, and not divided, yet they retain their distinct properties and operations; as the divine nature to be uncreated, infinite, omnipresent, impassible, &c. the human nature to be created, finite, in some certain place, passible, &c. at least the latter, before the resurrection of Christ. But of this union, and the nature of it, more hereafter.

Thirdly, The causes of the incarnation, efficient and moving, or to whom and what it is to be ascribed; and the final cause, for the sake of whom, and what.——1. The efficient cause of it, God, Father, Son, and Spirit; all the three Persons have a concern in it, it being a work *ad extra*. The Father prepared a body for the Son in his purpose, and proposed it to him in council and covenant to assume it; and he sent him forth in the fulness of time, made of a woman, in the likeness of sinful flesh, Heb. x. 5. Gal. iv. 4. Rom. viii. 3. The Son having agreed to it, being sent, came in the flesh, by the assumption of it; he took upon him the nature of the children, and partook of the same flesh and blood with them; he took upon him the form of a servant, and was found in fashion as a man, Heb. ii. 14, 16. Phil. ii. 7, 8. The Holy Ghost had a very great concern in this affair; for that which was conceived in the Virgin was of *the Holy Ghost*, Matt. i. 20. not of his substance, nature, and essence; for then he would have been the Father of it, which he is never said to be; Christ, as man, was *without Father*, and so a proper antitype of Melchizedec, Heb. vii. 3. Besides, the body of Christ would have been not human, but spiritual: but it was of him as the efficient cause of it; it was through his over-shadowing power and influence that it was conceived and formed, Luke i. 35. Now, though all the three Persons in the Deity had an hand in the wondrous incarnation, yet only one of them became incarnate; only the Son assumed the human nature, and took it into union with his divine Person; it is the Word only that was made flesh. Some have illustrated this, by three virgins concerned in working a garment; when only one of them puts it on and wears it.——2. The moving cause of the incarnation of Christ, is the love of the Father, and of the Son, to mankind. God so loved the world, that he gave his only begotten Son to become man, obey, suffer, and die for sinners; herein is love, and this love manifested, that God sent his Son in human nature to be the propitiation for the sins of his people, and save them from death, John iii. 16. 1 John iv. 9, 10. And such was the love and condescending grace of the Son, that though he was in the form of God, of the same nature with him, and equal to him; yet he took upon him the form and nature of man in a servile condition, humbled himself, and died in it. The grace of our Lord Jesus Christ is well known; who, though rich in his divine Person, became poor in human nature, to make his people rich, Phil. ii. 6, 7, 8. 2 Cor. viii. 9.——3. The final cause, or for whose sake, and for what the Son of God became incarnate. It was for the sake of the elect of God; *To us*, or *for us*, for our sakes, *a Child is born; a Son is given*: it was *unto all people;* or rather, *unto all the people;* for the sake of the whole people of God among Jews and Gentiles, that Christ was born a Saviour, or to be a Saviour of them; for which reason, as soon as he was born, his name was called Jesus, because he was to save his people from their sins; for which end he was born and came into the world. But of this more hereafter; see Isa. ix. 6. Luke ii. 10, 11. Matt. i. 21.

Fourthly, The parts of the incarnation are next to be considered, conception and nativity.

1*st*, Conception; this is a most wonderful, abstruse, and mysterious affair; and which to speak of is very difficult.—— 1. This conception was by a virgin; it was a virgin that conceived the human body of Christ, as it was foretold it should; which was very wonderful, and and therefore introduced with a note of admiration; *Behold a virgin shall conceive and bear a Son!* This was a *new thing;* unheard of and astonishing; which God *created in the earth*, in the lower parts of the earth, in the virgin's womb; *A woman compassed*, or conceived, *a man*, without the knowledge of man, Isa. vii. 14. Jer. xxxi. 22. This was not natural, but supernatural; though Mela,[6] the geographer, speaks of some women in a certain island who conceived without copulation with men; but that is all romance; Plutarch[7] asserts, such a thing was never known. This conception was made *in* the virgin, and not without her; for so says the text; *That which is conceived in her, is of the Holy Ghost;* this I observe to meet with, and confute the heretical illapse, as it is sometimes called; it was a notion of some of the ancient heretics, the Valentinians,[8] and of late, the Mennonites,[9] that the human nature of Christ was formed in heaven, and came down from thence into the virgin, and passed through her as water through a pipe, as their expression was; so that according to them, he was not conceived in her, nor took flesh of her: to countenance this, it is observed, that the *second man* is said to be *the Lord from heaven*, 1 Cor. xv. 47. But the words are not to be understood of the descent of the human nature of Christ from heaven; but of his divine Person from thence; not by change of place, but by assumption of the human nature into union with him; by virtue of which union the man Christ has the name of the *Lord from heaven;* and not because of the original and descent of the human nature from thence; and in this sense, and in this sense only, are we to understand the words of Christ, when he says, *I came down from heaven*, John vi. 38. namely, that he descended in and by the human nature; not by bringing it down from thence, but by taking it into union with his divine Person.——2. This conception was through the power and influence of the Holy Ghost, overshadowing the virgin. His operations in this affair may be considered in this manner, and after this order; He first took a part and portion of the virgin, of her *semen*, or blood, and conveyed it to a proper place; and purified and sanctified it or separated it, not from any moral impurity, which it was not capable of, being an unformed mass; but from a natural indisposition in it, which, had it not been removed, might hereafter have occasioned sin; to prevent which this was done; and then he impregnated it with a fructifying virtue, and formed the members of the human body, in order, at once, and in a fitness (being properly organized) to receive the human soul; for to consider its immediate formation in such a state, is much more agreeable to the formation of the first man, more becoming the workmanship of the Holy Ghost, and more suitable to the dignity of the Son of God to assume it into union with himself, than to suppose it an unformed and unshapen embryo. Yet this is to be understood, not as if it was in such a state as not to admit of a future increase, both before and after birth; nor to contradict its continuance in the womb of the virgin the usual time of every man. Now though this affair has been spoken of as in several processes, yet must be understood as all instantaneously done by the almighty power of the holy Spirit: in the same instant the human body was thus conceived, formed, and organized, the human soul of Christ was created and united to it, by Him who *forms the spirit of man within him;*

---

[6] De Situ Orbis, 1. 3. c. 9.
[7] Conjugial Præcept. p. 145.
[8] Irenæus Adv. Hæres. l. 1. c. 1. p. 29.

[9] Socini Disput. Adv. Mennonitas in Oper. tom. 2. p. 461,

and in that very instant the body was conceived and formed, and the soul united to it, did the Son of God assume the whole human nature at once, and take it into union with his divine Person, and gave it a subsistence in it; so that the human nature of Christ never had a subsistence of itself; but from the moment of its conception, formation, and creation, it subsisted in the Person of the Son of God: and hence the human nature of Christ is not a person; a person is that which subsists of itself; but that the human nature of Christ never did; wherefore,——3. It was a nature, and not a person, that Christ assumed so early as at its conception; it is called *the holy Thing*, and not a person; *The seed of Abraham*, or the nature of the seed of Abraham; the *form* and *fashion* of a man, that is, the nature of man; as *the form of God*, in the same passage, signifies the nature of God; see Luke i. 35. Heb. ii. 16. Phil. ii. 6, 7, 8. The Nestorians asserted the human nature of Christ to be a person; and so made two persons in Christ, one human and one divine; and of course four persons in the Deity, contrary to 1 John v. 7. but there is but one Person of the Son, one Son of God, one Lord of all, one Mediator between God and man: if the two natures in Christ were two distinct separate persons, the works and actions done in each nature could not be said of the same Person; the righteousness wrought out by Christ in the human nature, could not be called the righteousness of God: nor the blood shed in the human nature the blood of the Son of God; nor God be said to purchase the church with his blood; nor the Lord of life and glory to be crucified; nor the Son of man to be in heaven, when he was here on earth: all which phrases can only be accounted for, upon the footing of the personal union of the human nature to the Son of God, and his having but one Person; of which these several things are predicated. Besides, if the human nature of Christ was a person of itself, what it did and suffered could have been of no avail, nor of any benefit to any other but itself; the salvation wrought out in it, and by it, would not have been *the common salvation*, or common to elect men; but peculiar to that individual human person; and the righteousness he is the author of, he would only have had the benefit of, being justified by it, and accepted with God in it; whereas, it being wrought out in the human nature, as in personal union with the Son of God, this gives it an enlarged virtue, and spread; and so it comes to be *unto all, and upon all them that believe*.

I treat of the union of the two natures, divine and human, in the person of the Son of God, under the article of conception, and before the birth of Christ, as it certainly was; hence when Mary paid a visit to her cousin Elizabeth, before the birth of Christ, and just upon the conception of him, she was saluted by her thus; *Whence is this to me, that the mother of my Lord should come unto me?* Luke i. 43. Wherefore, before I proceed to consider the second part of the incarnation, the nativity of Christ, I shall farther observe some things concerning the union, which took place at the conception; and of the effects of it.

1. Of the union itself; concerning which let it be observed,——(1.) That though Christ, by assuming the human nature, united it to his divine Person; yet there is a difference between assumption and union; assumption is only of one nature; union is of both: Christ only assumed the human nature to his divine Person; but both natures, human and divine, are united in his Person: that he has two distinct natures is evident; in that, according to the flesh, or human nature, he is the Son of David; and according to the Spirit of holiness, or the divine nature, he is the Son of God; he was of the father's, according to the flesh or human nature; but, according to the divine nature, God over all, blessed for ever: he was put to death in the flesh, in the human nature; but quickened in or by the Spirit, the divine nature, Rom. i. 3, 4. and ix. 5. 1 Pet. i. 18. yet but one Person.——(2.) This union is hypostatical, or personal; but not an union of persons: the union of Father, Son, and Spirit in the Deity, is an union of three Persons in one God; but this is not an union of two persons; but of two natures in one person.——(3.) This an union of natures; but not a communication of one nature to another; not of the divine nature, and the essential properties of it, to the human nature; for though *the fulness of the Godhead dwells bodily* in Christ, Col. ii. 9. that is, substantially and really, not in shadow and type; yet the perfections of the Godhead are not communicated to the manhood, as to make that uncreated, infinite, immense, and to be every where, &c. the properties of each nature remain distinct, notwithstanding this union.——

(4.) This union lies in a communication of, or rather in making the personality of the Word, common to the human nature; or giving it a subsistence in the Person of the Word or Son of God; hence because of this union and community of person, it has the same name with the Word; and is called, *the Son of God*, Luke i. 35. And hence it appears, that the human nature of Christ is no loser, but a gainer, and is not inferior, but superior to other individuals of human nature, by its not being a person, subsisting of itself; because it has a better subsistence in the Person of the Son of God, than it could have had of itself; or than any creature has, angel or man.——
(5.) This union is indissoluble: though death dissolved the union between the body and soul of Christ, it did not, and could not, dissolve the union between the human nature and person of Christ; wherefore, in consequence of this union, he raised up the temple of his body, when destroyed, the third day, and thereby declared himself to be the Son of God with power, John ii. 19. Rom. i. 4.

2. The effects of this union, both with respect to the human nature, and to the Person of Christ. With respect to the human nature;——(1.) Pre-eminence to all other individuals of human nature; it is chosen and preferred to the grace of union with the Son of God, above them all; it has a better subsistence than they have, and has obtained a more excellent name than they, and even than the angels; and is possessed of glory, blessings, and privileges above all creatures; as will appear from what will be further observed. All which is not of any merit in it, but of the free grace of God.——
(2.) Perfect holiness and impeccability: it is called, *the holy Thing;* it is eminently and perfectly so; without original sin, or any actual transgression; it is not conscious of any sin, never committed any, nor is it possible it should.——(3.) A communication of habitual grace to it in the greatest degree; it is, in this respect, fairer and more beautiful than any of the sons of men; grace being poured into it in great plenty; it is anointed with the oil of gladness above its fellows; that is, with the gifts and graces of the holy Spirit; it has the Spirit given unto it, but not by measure; the Spirit of God rests upon it, in his several gifts, and graces, in a most glorious and perfect manner, Psalm xlv. 2, 7. John iii. 34. Isa. xi. 2. And should it be asked, if the same graces were in it, and exercised by it, as love, faith, and hope, in the saints? it may be answered, they were, and were exercised by it in its state of humiliation, as its circumstances required: Christ trusted and hoped in God, when upon his mother's breasts, Psalm xxii. 9, 10. When in suffering circumstances, he exercised faith on him, that he would justify, help, and deliver him, Isa. l. 7, 8, 9. When the time of his death drew nigh, he expressed his love to God by a readiness to submit to his will, and obey his command, John xiv. 31. And when his body lay in the grave, he rested in hope of the resurrection of it, Psalm xvi. 10.——
(4.) A very high and glorious exaltation of it, after his death and resurrection from the dead: it was highly exalted by being united to the Person of the Son of God; and though it came into a state of humiliation in it, yet being raised from the dead, is highly exalted, far above all principality and power, and might and dominion, and above every name that is named in this world or in that to come; it is set down at the right hand of God, where angels are never bid to come; and where angels, authorities, and powers, are made subject to it, Eph. i. 20, 21. Phil. ii. 9, 10. Heb. i. 13. 1 Pet. iii. 22.

With respect to the Person of Christ, the effects of this union are,——(1.) A communication of idioms, or properties, as the ancients express it; that is, of the properties of each nature; which are, in common, predicated of the Person of Christ, by virtue of the union of natures in it; for though each nature retains its peculiar properties, and does not communicate them to each other; yet they may be predicated of the person of Christ: yea, he may be denominated in one nature, from a property which belongs to another; thus in his divine nature he is God, the Son of God, the Lord of glory; and yet in this nature is described by a property which belongs to the human nature, which is to be passible, and suffer; hence we read of God purchasing the church with his blood; and of the blood of the Son of God cleansing from all sin; and of the Lord of glory being crucified, Acts xx. 28. 1 John i. 7. 1 Cor. ii. 8. And on the other hand, in his human nature he is called the Son of man; and yet as such, is described by a property which belongs to the divine nature, which is to be omnipresent, to be every where. So it is said; *No man hath ascended to* heaven, but he that came down from heaven, even the Son of man, which is in heaven, John iii. 13. who was in heaven at the same time he was here on earth; which was true of his Person, though denominated from his human nature; and thus what cannot be said of Christ in the abstract, is true of him in the concrete, by virtue of this union; it cannot be said, that the Deity of Christ suffered; or that the humanity of Christ is every where: but it may be said, that God, the Son of God suffered; and that the Son of man was in heaven when on earth, or every where. It cannot be said, that the Deity is humanity; nor the humanity Deity, nor equal to God: but it may be said, that God the Word is man, and the man Christ is God, Jehovah's Fellow; because these names respect the Person of Christ, which includes both natures.——(2.) A communion of office, and of power and authority to exercise it in both natures: thus by virtue of this union Christ bears the office of a Mediator, and exercises it in both natures; there is *one Mediator between God and man, the Man Christ Jesus*, 1 Tim. ii. 5. but he is not Mediator only in his human nature, and only exercises it in that; he took upon him, and was invested with this office before his assumption of human nature; and could and did exercise some parts of it without it, as has been shewn in its proper place; but there were others that required his human nature; and when, and not before it was requisite, he assumed it; and in it, as united to his divine Person, he is God-man, is Prophet, Priest, and King, Judge, Lawgiver, and Saviour; and has power over all flesh, to give eternal life to as many as the Father has given him; and upon his resurrection, had all power in heaven and earth given him, to appoint ordinances, and commission men to administer them; and had authority also to execute judgment, both in the world and in the church; because he is the Son of man, Matt. xxviii. 18. John xvii. 2. and v. 27.——(3.) A communion of operations in both natures, to the perfecting of the same work; which, therefore, may be called *theandric*, or the work of the God-man; there being a concurrence of both natures in the performance of it; which, when done, is ascribed to his Person: thus, for instance, the sacrifice of himself, as the propitiation for the sins of men; as God-man and Mediator, he is the Priest that offers; his human nature, consisting of soul and body, is the Sacrifice; and his divine nature is the altar which sanctifies it, and gives it its atoning virtue, his blood was shed in the human nature, to cleanse from sin; but it is owing to its union with the Son of God that such an effect is produced by it. The redemption of men is by the ransom-price of the life and blood of Christ; but it is the divine nature, to which the human is united, in the person of the Son of God, that makes it a sufficient one. The mission of the Spirit, by Christ, is owing both to his intercession in the human nature, and to his power and authority in the divine nature, according to the economy of things settled between the divine Persons.——(4.) The adoration of the Person of Christ, having both natures united in him, is another effect of this union. The human nature of Christ is not the formal object of worship; it is a creature, and not to be worshipped as such; nor is worship given for the sake of it, or as singly considered; but then the divine Person of Christ having that nature in union with him, is the object of worship; the flesh of Christ is not worshipped, but the incarnate God is; a whole Christ is worshipped, but not the whole of Christ. *When he bringeth in the first-begotten into the world*, which was at the time of the incarnation, *he saith, let all the angels of God worship him*, Heb. i. 6. And upon his resurrection from the dead, God has *given him a name which is above every name; that at the name of Jesus every knee should bow;* that is, in a way of religious adoration, Phil. ii. 9, 10. and though Christ, as man, is not the object of such adoration; yet what he has done in the human nature, is a motive and argument why blessing and honour should be given to his Person, having both natures united in him; *Worthy is the Lamb that was slain, to receive power, &c.* Rev. v. 12, 13.

2*dly*, The birth, or nativity of Christ, the other part of the incarnation, is next to be considered.

1. Of whom born; of a virgin, of the house of David, and of the tribe of Judah. ——(1.) Of a virgin: this was hinted at in the first promise of *the seed of the woman;* and is fully expressed by Isaiah; *A virgin shall conceive and bear a Son;* to fulfil which prophecy, before Joseph and Mary cohabited as man and wife, and so, whilst she was a virgin, *she was found with child of the Holy Ghost,* Matt. i. 18—23. And it was brought about in this manner,

that the human nature of Christ might be clear of original sin, which it otherwise must have been infected with, had it been conceived and born in the ordinary and natural way of generation; for *whatsoever is born of the flesh, is flesh*, carnal and corrupt; but being produced in this extraordinary and supernatural way, by the power of the Holy Ghost, that which was born of the virgin is *the holy Thing;* free from all spot and blemish of sin. This is most surprisingly accounted for, by the more modern philosophy respecting generation, that every man is born of an animalcule; which agrees with the sacred philosophy[10] in Job xxv. 6. and that all the animalcula from which millions of men spring in all ages, were originally formed by the great Creator in the first man; which, as it accounts for the guilt and pollution of all men in him; so for the purity of Christ's human nature, since that was not born of an animalcule, as other men are; nor was it of man, nor of the seed of man;[11] but was according to the first promise, the pure seed of the woman; nor was it ever in Adam, in the first man; no, not in *animalculo*, as the rest of the individuals of human nature, according to this hypothesis, and so was not represented by him; nor did he stand related to it, as a covenant-head; nor did it descend from him by ordinary generation; but was conceived in the virgin through the power of the Holy Ghost; and did not exist in any respect before; no, not in *animalculo;* which lies strongly against the pre-existence of Christ's human nature in any sense whatever; and so, being free from sin, was fit to be a sacrifice for sin, since it could be offered up to God without spot, by the eternal Spirit. Moreover, so it was, that as the ruin of men came by means of a virgin; for the fall of Adam was before he knew his wife; so the Saviour of men from that ruin, came into the world by a virgin: and so it was ordered by the wisdom of God, that Christ should appear to have but one Father, having none as man, and so be but one Person; whereas, had he had two fathers, there must have been two persons.—— (2.) Christ was born of a virgin of the house of David; as in Luke i. 27. for the phrase of the house of David, is equally true of the virgin, as of Joseph, and may be connected with her. God promised to David, that the Messiah should be of his seed; and accordingly, of his seed he raised up unto Israel, a Saviour Jesus, who is therefore called the Son of David; and is both *the root and offspring of David;* the root of David, as God, and David's Lord; and the offspring of David, as man, descending from him, Acts xiii. 23. Rev. xxii. 16.——(3.) He was born of a virgin of the tribe of Judah; as she must be, since she was of the house of David, which was of that tribe; and it is manifest, as the apostle says, that our Lord sprung out of the tribe of Judah, as it was foretold he should, Gen. xlix. 10. see Heb. vii. 14.

2. The birth of Christ, or his coming into the world, was after the manner of other men; his generation and conception were extraordinary; but his birth was in the usual manner; he came into the world after he had lain the common time in his mother's womb; for it is said, *the days were accomplished that she should be delivered;* she went her full time with him, and brought forth him, her first-born Son, as other women do; and no doubt with pains and sorrow, as every daughter of Eve does: and presented him to the Lord when the days of her purification were ended, according to the law, as it is written, *Every male that openeth the womb, shall be called holy to the Lord,* Luke ii. 6, 22, 23. So that in these respects Christ was made in all things like unto his brethren.

3. The place of his birth was Bethlehem, according to the prophecy in Mic. v. 2. here it was expected he would be born; and this was so well known to the Jews, that when Herod enquired of the chief priests and Scribes where Christ should be born; they, without any hesitation, immediately reply, in *Bethlehem of Judea,* and quote the above prophecy in proof of it, Matt. ii. 4, 5, 6. yea, this was known by the common people, John vii. 42. and so it was wonderfully brought about in providence; that though Joseph and Mary lived in Galilee, yet through a decree of Cæsar Augustus to tax the whole empire, they were both obliged to come to the city of Bethlehem, the city of David, to be taxed, being of the lineage and house of David; and whilst they were on that business there, the virgin was delivered of her

---

[10] Omnia nimirum animalia, etiam, perfecta similiter ex vermiculo gigni, Harveus de Generat. Animal. Exercit. 18. p. 144.

[11] The animalcula are only "in semine masculo;" see the Philosophical Transactions abridged, vol. 2. p. 912, 913.

Son, Luke ii. 1—7. Bethlehem signifies the house of bread; a fit place for the Messiah to be born in, who is the bread that came down from heaven, and gives life unto the world.

4. The time of his birth was as it was fixed in prophecy; before the sceptre, or civil government, departed from Judah: Herod was king in Judea when he was born; before the second temple was destroyed; for he often went into it, and taught in it: and it was at the time pointed at in Daniel's weeks; see Gen. xlix. 10. Mal. iii. 1. Hag. ii. 6, 7, 9. Dan. ix. 24. &c. The exact year of the world in which he was born, is not agreed on by chronologers; but it was about, or a little before or after the four thousandth year of the world; nor can the season of the year, the month and day in which he was born, be ascertained. However, the vulgar account seems not probable; the circumstance of the shepherds watching their flocks by night, agrees not with the winter-season. It is more likely it was in autumn, sometime in the month of September, at the feast of tabernacles, which was typical of Christ's incarnation; and there seems to be some reference to it in John i. 14. *The Word was made flesh, and dwelt*, or *tabernacled*, among us; the temple of Solomon, a type of Christ's human nature, was dedicated at the feast of tabernacles: and as Christ, the passover, was sacrificed at the very time of the passover; and the Holy Ghost was given on the very day of Pentecost, typified by the first-fruits offered on that day; so it is most reasonable to suppose, that Christ was born at the very feast of tabernacles, a type of his incarnation; and which feast is put for the whole ministry of the word and ordinances, to be observed in gospel-times. Zechariah xiv. 16. However, it was in the fulness of time, or when the time was fully up he was to come, that God sent him, and he came; and in due time, in the fittest and most proper time, infinite Wisdom saw meet he should come: God could have sent him sooner; but he did not think fit to do it; but he sent him at the most seasonable time; when the wickedness of men was at its height, both in Judea and the Gentile world; and there appeared a necessity of a Saviour of men from it; and when the insufficiency of the light of nature, of the power of man's free-will, which had been sufficiently tried among the philosophers; and of the law of Moses, and of the works and sacrifices of it, to take away sin, and save men from it, had been clearly evinced. To conclude, it was in time, and not before time, that Christ became man. To talk of the human nature of Christ, either in whole or in part, as from eternity, is contrary both to scripture and reason; nor can that man, or human nature, be of any avail or benefit to us; but he that is the Seed of the woman, the Son of Abraham, the Son of David, and the Son of Mary.

Fifthly, The ends of Christ's incarnation are many; there is a cluster of them in the song of the angels at his birth; *Glory to God in the highest; and on earth peace, good-will towards men*, Luke ii. 14.
——1. One end of Christ's incarnation was, to shew forth the glory of God in it; the glory of his grace, kindness, and goodness to men, in the mission of his Son in this way; the glory of his faithfulness in fulfilling his promise of it; the glory of his power in the miraculous production of Christ's human nature; and the glory of his wisdom in bringing it into the world in such a manner as to be free from sin, and so fit for the purpose for which it was designed: and all this that God might be glorified in these his perfections; as he was by the angels, by Mary, by the father of John the Baptist, and by Simeon, at, or about, the time of Christ's birth; and as he has been by saints in all ages since.
——2. Another end of Christ's incarnation was, to make peace with God for men on earth; to make reconciliation for sin, was the work appointed him in covenant; and to do this, was the reason of his being made in all things like unto his brethren; and this end is answered; he has reconciled sinners to God by his death, and made peace for them by the blood of his cross.——3. Another end of Christ's incarnation was, not only to shew the good will of God to men, but that they might receive the fruits of his good will and favour towards them; even all the blessings of grace, those spiritual blessings provided in covenant, and laid up in Christ; and which came by him our High-priest, and through his blood, called therefore, the blood of the everlasting covenant.——
4. Particularly, Christ became man that he might be our Goel, our near kinsman, and might appear to have a right to redeem us; and he was, in the fulness of time, made of a woman, to redeem men from the law, its curse and condemnation; and

that they might receive the adoption of children, and every other blessing included in or connected with redemption; as peace, pardon, and justification; for he was sent in the likeness of sinful flesh, that by the sacrifice of himself for sin, he might condemn it in the flesh; and that the righteousness of the law might be fulfilled in us, as represented by him, and so be completely justified in him; see Gal. iv. 4, 5. Rom. viii. 3, 4.——5. Christ became man, that he might be a Mediator between God and men; and the better to perform several parts of his office as such, he took upon him the nature of man; that he might have something to offer as a Priest to be a Sacrifice for sin, and that he might make satisfaction for it in that nature that sinned; and that he might be a prophet like unto Moses, raised up, as he was, among his brethren; and having the Spirit of the Lord God upon him, might preach glad tidings to the meek; and that he might appear to be a King taken from among his brethren, as the kings of Israel were; and to be the Ruler, Noble, and Governor, that proceeded from the midst of them, as was predicted he should, Jer. xxx. 21. and so sit and reign upon the throne of his Father David.

CHAP. II.

OF CHRIST'S STATE OF HUMILIATION.

CHRIST's state of humiliation began at his incarnation, and was continued through the whole of his life unto death, which is fully and clearly expressed in a few words in Phil. ii. 7, 8. *but made himself of no reputation, &c.* and which the apostle illustrates and confirms by placing it in a contrast with his glorious estate previous to it; for by how much the higher he was in that state, the lower and meaner he appears in this; and higher it was not possible for him to be, than as described by the apostle, as *in the form of God*, in his nature and essence; and as *equal with* God his Father; having the same perfections, names, works, and worship, ascribed to him. Now in this state of humiliation he appeared the reverse of this; he who was in the form of God, was not only made in the likeness of man, and in fashion as a man, but took on him the form of a servant, of one of the meanest of men; and he, who was equal to his divine Father, made himself of no account among men, and became obedient in all things to his Father, and that even to death itself, the accursed death of the cross.

1. The humiliation of Christ took place at his incarnation, and therefore in the above account of it, the phrases of being *made in the likeness of men*, and of *being found in fashion as a man*, are used as expressive of it; and which are to be understood of his being really and truly man, as has been observed in the preceding chapter; for though the assumption of the human nature into union with the person of the Son of God was an exaltation of it, and gave it a pre-eminence to all the other individuals of human nature, and even to angels themselves, as has been shewn; see Psalm lxxxix. 19. yet it was an humbling of the person of Christ to take a nature so inferior to his into union with him; for I see not why the phrase of *humbling* may not be used with respect to this matter of the person of the Son of God, since it is used of the divine Being, Psalm cxiii. 6. and if it is an humbling of God, a stoop of Deity, to look upon things in heaven and earth; a condescension in him to dwell on earth, whom the heaven of heavens cannot contain, 1 Kings viii. 27. it must be much more so for the Word and Son of God, who was in the beginning with God, and was God, and to whom the creation of all things is ascribed, to be made flesh and dwell among men, John i. 1, 2, 3, 14.

First, The humiliation of Christ appeared both in his conception and birth; though there were some things relating to his conception which were very illustrious and glorious; as a remarkable prophecy concerning it some hundreds of years before it was, Isa. vii. 14. the dispatch of an angel to the virgin to acquaint her with it, when near or at the instant of it, and that it itself was of the mighty power of the holy Spirit, Luke i. 26, 31, 35. yet it was amazing humility that he who was the Son of God, lay in the bosom of his Father, should by assumption of human nature into union with his divine person, lie nine months in the womb of a virgin; and he that ascended on high, should first descend into these lower parts of the earth. And though there were many great and glorious things that attended his birth, which made it very illustrious; as an unusual star, which guided the wise men from the east to the place of his nativity, who worshipped him, and presented gifts unto him; and an angel appeared in a glorious form to the shepherds, who acquainted them with his birth; and a multitude of the heavenly host descended and joined with him, singing *Glory to God in the highest* on account of it; yet, besides many things that followed it, very inglorious; as Herod's search after him to take away his life; the flight of his parents with him into Egypt, where they continued a while in fear and obscurity; and the massacre of a great number of infants in and about Bethlehem: it may be observed, ——1. That he was *born of a woman*, which very phrase is expressive of meanness, Job xiv. 1. born of a sinful woman, though he himself without sin; *made of a woman*, as the expression is in Gal. iv. 4. made of one that was made by him, and to whom he stood in the character of Creator, Lord and Saviour, as she herself owned, Luke i. 46, 47.——2. Born of a poor woman; for though his mother, the virgin, was of the house of David, of that illustrious family, yet when that family was become very low, like a tree cut down to its roots; for when in such a state was the Messiah to spring from it, as he did, according to the prophecy, Isa. xi. 1. that his mother was a poor woman, appears from the usage she met with at the time of her delivery in the inn, where there was no room for her to be received in, because of her poverty; and therefore was obliged to lay her new-born infant in a manger. Into what a low estate was our Lord brought! As also from her bringing the offering of the poorer sort at her purification. Persons of ability were obliged to offer a lamb on such an occasion, but if poor, a pair of turtle doves or two young pigeons, which she did, Luke ii. 7, 24. hence the Jews upbraided Christ with the meanness of his parentage, saying, *Is not this the carpenter's son? is not his mother called Mary?* plain *Mary; and his brethren James and Joses, and Simon and Judas? and his sisters, are they not all with us?* do not we know them, what a low-life family they are?——3. He was born in a poor country village; for though it was the birth-place of David, and called his city, and so famous on that account; yet in Christ's time was mean and obscure, and said to be *little among the thousands of Judah;* and he afterwards lived in a very despicable place, where he was brought up; despicable to a proverb; *Can any good thing come out of Nazareth?* John i. 46.——4. The nature he was conceived and born in, and which he assumed, though without sin, yet had all the sinless infirmities of human nature: his soul was subject to sorrow, grief, anger, &c. and his body to hunger, thirst, weariness, &c. it was a nature inferior to angels; at least, he was for a while, through the sufferings of death, made a little lower than they, Heb. ii. 9. and who at certain times, when in distress, ministered to him and relieved him, Matt. iv. 11. Luke xxii. 43. into such a low estate and condition did Christ come in our nature.

Secondly, The humiliation of Christ appeared in all the stages of life into which he came; for he passed through the states of infancy, childhood, and youth, as other men do; he was wrapped in swaddling bands, as new-born infants are; hung upon his mother's breasts as soon as born, and received his nourishment from thence, as infants do; he endured the painful rite of circumcision when eight days old, and was presented in the temple according to usual custom; he continued in the infant-state, both with respect to body and mind, the usual time, for ought appears: his case was not like the first Adam's; he was created as one in the prime of life, a grown man, and in the full exercise of his rational powers at once: but so it was not with the second Adam; he was an infant of days, he grew in body as children do; and his reasoning faculties were not opened at once, but gradually, for it is said, he *increased in wisdom* as well as *in stature*, Luke ii. 40, 52. as he grew up in his childhood and youthful state, though we have but little account of it, it appears to be attended with much meanness and obscurity, even to his manhood; we have but one circumstance related of him in this time, which is that of his coming up to Jerusalem with his parents at the passover, when twelve years of age; and though there were some things then appeared in him very remarkable and uncommon, in taking his place among the doctors, hearing and asking them questions; yet he returned with his parents, and lived in subjection to them, Luke ii. 42—51. and it seems as if he was brought up to a mechanic business; it was a commonly received tradition of the ancients, that he was brought up to the trade of a carpenter; and there are some things which make it probable; it is a question put by the Jews, *Is not this the carpenter?* Mark vi. 3. nor was it ever denied that he was; they suggest, that he had no liberal education, was not brought up in any of their public schools or academies: *How knoweth this man letters, having never learned?* John vii. 15. and it cannot be supposed that he should live an inactive life the greater part of his days; but besides the poverty of his parents, which would not admit of the maintenance of him without business, what greatly prevails upon me to give into this sentiment is, that the second Adam must bear the first Adam's curse, even that part of it which lay in getting his bread by the sweat of his brow, Gen. iii. 19. O what a low estate was our Lord brought into on our account! Add to all this, that his whole life, until he was thirty years of age, was a life of obscurity; for from the time of his coming out of Egypt and being had to Nazareth in his infancy, we hear nothing of him, excepting that single instance of being at Jerusalem when twelve years of age, until he came from Galilee to Jordan unto John to be baptized of him; and then he was about thirty years of age, Luke iii. 23. Now what astonishing condescension and humility is this, and how great was the humiliation of Christ in this state! that the greatest personage that ever was in the world, the Son of God in human nature, and who came to do the greatest work that ever was done in the world, should be in the world thirty years running, and scarce be known at all by the inhabitants of it; at least not known who and what he was, John i. 10. at most but by very few.

Thirdly, The public life of Christ began at his baptism, for by that he was made manifest in Israel; and for that purpose John came baptizing with water; and who had this signal given him, that on whomsoever he should see the Spirit of God descending, the same was He; which when he saw he bore testimony of him that he was the Son of God, and pointed him out as the Lamb of God, that takes away the sin of the world; and though there were some things attending the baptism of Christ which made it illustrious, as not only John's testimony of him, but the descent of the Spirit on him as a dove, and a voice from his Father heard, saying, *This is my beloved Son, in whom I am well-pleased*, John i. 29—36. Matt. iii. 16, 17. yet his submission to the ordinance itself was an instance of his humiliation; his coming many miles on foot, from Galilee to Jordan, to John to be baptized of him, is a proof of it; he that had the power of baptizing with the holy Ghost and with fire, was baptized in water; he that knew no sin, nor did any, was baptized with the baptism of repentance, as though he had been a sinner; and he that was John's Lord and Master, was before him, and preferred to him, and whose shoe-latchet John was not worthy to unloose; and who could have ordered him to attend him, at any place convenient for baptism, which for some reasons he thought fit to submit unto; yet took the pains and fatigue of a journey to go to him for that purpose; and though John modestly declined it at first, having some hint of him who he was, yet being pressed by him, he agreed to administer the ordinance to him, and did; and which was done to fulfil all righteousness, and in obedience to the will of God, and to set an example to us, that we should tread in his steps; and in all which appear wonderful humility and condescension; see Matt. iii. 13—15.

Fourthly, Immediately after his baptism Christ was harassed with the temptations of Satan, which was another branch of his humiliation and low estate he came into; for *he suffered being tempted;* and he *was tempted in all points like as we are, yet without sin*, Heb. ii. 18. and iv. 15. that is with all sorts of temptations, though not altogether in the same manner, nor had they the same effect on him as on us. Satan tempted him, not by stirring up any corruption, or provoking any lust in him, as he provoked David, stirred up the lust of pride and vanity in him to number the people; for in Christ was no sin, lust, or corruption to stir up; Satan could find nothing of this kind in him to work upon: nor did he tempt him by putting any evil into him, as he put it into the heart of Judas Iscariot to betray his Lord, and into the hearts of Ananias and Sapphira to lie unto the holy Ghost: nor could he get any advantage over Christ by any of his temptations; he was forced after all his temptations in the wilderness to leave him, and in the garden and on the cross, he was foiled by him; yea he, and his principalities and powers, were spoiled and triumphed over; but inasmuch as by these temptations Christ in his human nature was harassed and distressed, they are a part of his humiliation, and require a particular consideration; and those we have the clearest account of are they which began in the wilderness; for he was *led up of the Spirit into the wilderness to be tempted of the devil*, Matt. iv. 1. that is, he was influenced and directed by the Spirit of God, who had lighted on him at his baptism, under an impulse of his, both inward and outward, to go up from the habitable parts of the wilderness, where John was preaching and baptizing, and where he himself had been baptized, to the mountainous and uninhabitable parts of it, which were quite desolate and uncultivated; where were no provisions, nor any man to converse with, none but wild beasts, to whom he was exposed, and with whom he was, Mark i. 13. another instance of his low estate. The time when he was here tempted was quickly after his baptism; Matthew says *then* he was led to be tempted, that is, when he had been baptized; and Mark says it was *immediately;* and thus as it was with Christ the head, so it often is with his members; that as he was tempted, after his baptism, after the Spirit of God had descended upon him, and filled him with his gifts and graces without measure; and after he had had such a testimony from heaven of his divine Sonship: so his people, after they have had communion with God in ordinances, and have had some sealing testimonies of his love, fall into temptations, and fall by them; as the disciples of Christ after the supper, who, when tempted, all forsook him and fled, and one denied him. Moreover, it was after Christ had fasted forty days, and when he was hungry, that the tempter came to him and attacked him; two of the evangelists say he tempted him forty days; so he might tempt him, more or less, all the forty days, at times; but when they were ended, and Christ was an hungry, then he set upon him with greater violence, as judging it a proper opportunity to try the utmost of his power and skill with him: so Satan suits his temptations to the constitutions, circumstances, and situation men are in.

The first temptation was by putting an *if* upon the Sonship of Christ; *If thou be the Son of God;* though there could be no doubt made of this, since a testimony of it from heaven had just been given; and the devils themselves have acknowledged, that Christ is the Son of God, Luke iv. 41. And thus the children of God are sometimes tempted to call in question their sonship, because of inward corruptions and outward afflictions; or it may be, Satan argued from hence, *if,* or *seeing*, thou art the Son of God, as has been testified by a voice from heaven, and thou thyself affirmest; as a proof of it, *command that these stones be made bread,* or *this stone,* as Luke expresses it; that is, one of the stones which lay hard by, and were in sight: and Satan might hope to succeed in this temptation, since Christ was now hungry, and he might insinuate a concern for his welfare; and the rather as he succeeded with the first Adam, in tempting him to eat of the forbidden fruit; and as he might suggest, he would, by such an act of omnipotence, give proof of his divine Sonship: but though Christ could have done this, as well as God could raise up out of stones children unto Abraham; yet as it was needless to do it in proof of his Sonship, since that had been so well attested already, by a voice from heaven; nor for his sustenance, since he had been sustained by the power and providence of God forty days without food, he might be longer. Besides, he never wrought a miracle for his own support; nor would he do it now, at the instance of the devil, which was what he wanted him to do, in obedience to him, and at his motion; wherefore Christ's answer is; *It is written, Man shall not live by bread alone, but by every word that proceedeth out of the mouth of God,* Deut. viii. 3. which signifies, that men may live by that which is not properly bread, as by manna, on which the Israelites lived in the wilderness to which the passage quoted refers: nor does man live by bread, when he has it, abstracted from the blessing of the mouth of God with it, which gives it nourishment; and besides, without bread, in any sense, a man may be supported by the power and providence of God, as Moses and Elijah were, and as Christ now had been; and therefore, to take such a method as he was tempted to, would have seemed to have been a distrust of that power and providence by which he had been sustained; and thus, by quoting scripture, to repel Satan's temptations, Christ has taught us to make use of the sword of the Spirit, which is the word of God, to withstand the temptations of Satan also.

The second temptation was, after Satan had prevailed on Christ, or he condescended to go along with him, or he suffered him to take him to the city of Jerusalem, and place him on the pinnacle of the temple, or on the battlements of it, *to cast* himself *down* from thence; in order to give proof of his divine Sonship, in a public manner, before the inhabitants of Jerusalem, Priests, Scribes, and common people;

by which he might suggest it would gain him great credit and esteem; and as for his preservation in it, he quotes, in imitation of him, a passage of scripture, where it is written, *He shall give his angels charge concerning thee, &c.* which, however applicable to Christ, as well as to his members, is perverted, since a material clause is omitted, *to keep thee in all thy ways;* whereas Satan was endeavouring to lead him out of the right way, tempting him to the sin of self-murder; which he did, either out of envy and malice, and the malignity of his nature; or to prevent, if he had any notion of it, Christ's dying in the room and stead of his people, in a judicial way, for their salvation: however, Christ resisted the temptation, by saying, *It is written again, Thou shalt not tempt the Lord thy God,* Deut. vi. 16. as Christ was; which was testified by a voice from heaven, declaring him to be the Son of God, and so Lord and heir of all things. In like manner the children of God are often tempted by Satan to destroy themselves; which shews the similarity between Christ's temptations and theirs.

The third temptation was, after the devil had taken Christ, by his permission, to an exceeding high mountain, one of those about Jerusalem, or not far from it, and had shewed him, by a diabolical and false representation of things to the sight, *all the kingdoms of the world, and the glory of them;* alluring him with a promise of these to *fall down and worship him.* To promise Christ these was impertinent; since the earth is his, and the fulness thereof, the world, and they that dwell therein, as the maker of them; and all power in heaven and earth is given him as Mediator; to pretend that these were in his power to dispose of to whomsoever he pleased, as it is in Luke, was intolerable arrogance; when he had not the least thing in the world at his dispose; could not touch any of Job's substance without permission, and a grant from God; nor go into a herd of swine without leave: but to propose to Christ, that he should fall down and worship him, was the height of insolence and impudence! This shews what the original sin of the devil was, affectation of Deity, and to be worshipped as God; hence he has usurped the title of the God of this world; and has prevailed upon the ignorant part of it, in some places, to give him worship; and, indeed, to sacrifice to idols, is to sacrifice to devils: but, not content with this, he sought to be worshipped by the Son of God himself; than which nothing could be more audacious and impious; wherefore Christ rejected his temptation with indignation and abhorrence; saying, *Get thee hence, Satan;* or, as Luke has it, *Get thee behind me, Satan; for it is written, Thou shalt worship the Lord thy God, and him only shalt thou serve,* Deut. vi. 13. upon which the devil left him, finding he could do nothing with him; and angels came and ministered to him. After which we hear no more of him, till the time of Christ's death drew nigh, when Christ observed to his disciples, that *the prince of this world cometh,* to meet him in the garden, where he was in an agony, and had a combat with him; and his sweat was as drops of blood falling to the ground; and when were the hour and power of darkness, when all the posse of devils were let loose upon him, and cast their fiery darts at him; but he got the victory over them all; yet, notwithstanding that, these several assaults and temptations of Satan, to which he was subject, and by which he was harassed, must be considered as a part of his humiliation, and of that low estate he was brought into.

Fifthly, Christ's humiliation appeared in the reproaches, indignities, and persecutions he endured from men, even contradiction of sinners against himself; the reproaches with which God and his people were reproached, fell on him; and these so thick and fast, and so heavily, that, in prophetic language, reproach is said to have broken his heart, Psalm lxix. 9, 20. Sometimes his enemies the Jews upbraided him with the meanness of his descent and pedigree, the low estate of his family, as has been observed; with his illiberal education, and the illiterateness of his followers: sometimes they attacked his moral character, affirmed they knew him to be a sinner; charged him with sabbath-breaking, with being a glutton and a wine-bibber, and an encourager of men in sinful practices; they traduced his miracles, which they could not deny as facts, as if done by the help of the devil; and said he had a devil, and was familiar with one, by whom he did his works; they called him a deceiver of the people, and charged him with preaching false doctrines, and delivering out hard sayings not to be borne with; nay, they endeavoured to fix the imputation of blasphemy on him, because, being a man, he made himself God, and equal to him; they represented him as a seditious person, that went about teaching men not to give tribute to Cæsar; as well as having an intention to destroy their law; and as setting men to pull down their temple. In short, they not only rejected him as the Messiah, with the greatest contempt and abhorrence of him; but sought to take away his life in a violent manner; sometimes by having him to the brow of an hill to cast him down headlong; and at other times they took up stones to stone him; nor were they satisfied until they had brought him to the dust of death.

Sixthly, There was a very great degree of meanness and poverty which appeared throughout the whole life of Christ, private and public; to which the apostle has respect when he says; *Ye know the grace of our Lord Jesus,* &c. 2 Cor. viii. 9. where he puts Christ's riches and poverty in contrast, that by so much the greater his riches were in his former state, by so much the more does his poverty seem to be in his low estate; he was rich in the perfections of his nature, in the possession of heaven and earth, and all therein; and in the revenues of glory arising from the kingdom of nature and providence; and yet he who was Lord of all became poor to make us beggars rich. And this is to be understood of poverty in a literal sense; for Christ was not spiritually poor. Some instances of his meanness and poverty in private life have been observed before; as, that he was born of poor parents, had not a liberal education, and was brought up to a mechanic business. When he came into public life, it does not appear that he had any certain dwelling-house to live in; so that *the foxes, and the birds of the air,* enjoyed more than he did, Matt. viii. 20. To what a low estate was our Lord brought! though he could have supported himself, and his twelve apostles, by working miracles for his and their sustenance; yet he never did, but lived upon the contributions and ministrations of some good women, and others, mentioned in Luke viii. 2, 3. When the collectors of tribute came to him for the tribute-money, he had none to pay them, but ordered Peter to cast his hook into the sea, and take up a fish, and out of that a piece of money, and pay the tribute for him and for himself, Matt. xvii. 24—27. At his death he had nothing to leave his mother for her support; but seeing her, and his disciple John, when on the cross, said to her, *Behold thy son;* and to him, *Behold thy mother;* signifying, that he should take care of her; and from that time that disciple took her to his own house, John xix. 26, 27. Nor had he any tomb of his own, or family vault to be interred in; but was laid in one belonging to another, even Joseph of Arimathea. And this poverty of his was signified by hints, types, and prophecies, that he should be thus poor and needy; and which were hereby fulfilled, Psalm xl. 17. Eccles. ix. 14. Zech. ix. 9.

Seventhly, Upon the whole, it clearly appears, that Christ indeed *humbled himself, and made himself of no reputation,* as in Phil. ii. 7, 8. or *emptied himself;* not of the fulness of grace it pleased the Father should dwell in him; this was with him, and seen in him, when he became incarnate; and still continues with him; out of which saints receive grace for grace, John i. 14, 16. much less of the perfections of his divine nature, the whole fulness of which dwells in him bodily, Col. ii. 9. Every perfection in Deity was asserted by him in his state of humiliation, as omniscience, omnipresence, omnipotence, &c. John ii. 24, 25. and iii. 13. Rev. i. 8. Christ did not lay aside the form of God, in which he was; or lay down his divine nature, which was impossible; nor deny his equality with God, which would be to deny himself; but he consented to have his divine glory covered and veiled, as to the ordinary manifestation of it, and in common; I say as to the ordinary manifestation of it; for it sometimes did break forth in an extraordinary way by miracles, John ii. 11. and there were some, though but few, which saw his glory as the glory of the only begotten of the Father; the greater part saw no form nor comeliness in him, wherefore he should be desired by them, John i. 14. Isa. liii. 3. He did not give up his equality with God the Father; but he was content that that for a time should be out of sight; and so behave, and be so treated, as if he was not his fellow; he was willing, in the human nature, and in his office capacity, to act in subordination to his Father; to say what he bid him say, and do what he bid him do; even to the laying down of his life; for which he had a commandment from his Father; yea, he owned that in that his present state and circumstances, his Father was greater than he, John xii. 49, 50. and x. 18. and xiv. 28. He was content to be had in the utmost disesteem by men, to be emptied of his good name, character, and reputation, to be reckoned a worm, and no man; to be a Samaritan, and have a devil; and to be called and abused as if he was the worst of men; and to be made sin, and a curse for his people, to repair the loss of honour sustained by the sins of men; so that Christ's humiliation was his own voluntary act and deed.

CHAP. III.

OF THE ACTIVE OBEDIENCE OF CHRIST IN HIS STATE OF HUMILIATION.

II. The humiliation of Christ may be seen in his obedience to God, through the whole course of his life, even unto death; in order to which,

First, He took upon him *the form of a servant*, Phil. ii. 7. and really became one; even the Servant of God: and this is an instance of his amazing humility and condescension; that he, who was the Son of God, of the same nature with God, and equal to him, the brightness of his Father's glory, and the express image of his person, should voluntarily become the Servant of Him; which the apostle observes with astonishment; *though he were a Son, yet learned he obedience by the things which he suffered!* Heb. v. 8. He was chosen of God, in his eternal purposes, to be his Servant; and therefore is called, his Servant elect, Isa. xlii. 1. He called him to the work and office of a servant; and said unto him, in the everlasting council and covenant of grace and peace, *Thou art my Servant, O Israel, in whom I will be glorified*, Isa. xlix. 3. And Christ, the Son of God, accepted of this office; agreed to be the Servant of God, to come into the world, and do his will and work, Psalm xl. 7, 8. And accordingly, he was prophesied of as the Servant of the Lord, that should come, Zech. iii. 8. Isaiah xlii. 1. In the fulness of time he was sent, and came not to be ministered unto, as a monarch, but to minister as a servant; and he quickly appeared to be under a law, and was subject to the law of circumcision; and being had in his infancy to Egypt, the house of servants; to his ancestors, according to the flesh, was an emblem of that servile state he was come into; and very early did he declare, that he must be about his Father's business: as a servant, he had work to do, and much to work, and that very laborious; which lay, not only in working miracles, which were works his Father gave him to finish, as demonstrations of his Deity, and proofs of his Messiahship; nor only in going about from place to place, healing all manner of diseases, and so doing good to the bodies of men; nor only in preaching the gospel, for which he was qualified and sent, and thereby did good to the souls of men; but chiefly in fulfilling the law of God, both in the preceptive and penal part of it, in the room and stead of his people; and thereby wrought out the great work of all he came to do, the redemption and salvation of men; for this was the work assigned him by God his Father, as his Servant; *to raise up the tribes of Jacob, and to restore the preserved of Israel;* that is, to redeem and save the chosen people: this was the work his Father gave him to do; this was the work which was before him when he came; and this is the work which he has finished; for he has obtained eternal redemption; and is become the author of eternal salvation. Now throughout the whole of his work, as a servant, he appeared very diligent and constant; very early he discovered an inclination to be about it; very eager was he at it; when in it, it was his meat and drink; and he was continually, constantly employed in it, John iv. 34. and ix. 4. Nor did he leave working till he had completed the whole. In all which he was faithful to him that appointed him; and very justly did he obtain the character of God's *righteous Servant*, Isaiah xi. 5. and liii. 11.

Secondly, When Christ became incarnate, and took upon him the form of a servant, and really was one; he, as such, was subject to the law of God: hence these two things are joined together, as having a close connection with each other; *Made of a woman; made under the law*, Gal. iv. 4.

1st, Christ was made under the judicial, or civil law of the Jews; he was by birth a Jew, and is called one, Zech. viii. 23. It is manifest that he sprung from the tribe of Judah; which tribe, in process of time, gave the name of Jews to the whole people of Israel; and because our Lord was of that tribe, he is called the Lion of the tribe of Judah, Heb. vii. 14. Rev. v. 5. He was born at Bethlehem, in the tribe of Judah, and was of the seed of David, who was of that tribe; and is therefore said to be the root and offspring of David, Rev.

xxii. 16. Wherefore, since he, the salvation of God, and Saviour of men, as to his human nature, was of the Jews; it was fit and proper he should be subject to their civil government, and to the laws of it, as he was: for though he was charged with sedition, yet falsely, for he was subject to their government, though it was then in the hands of the Romans; and not only paid tribute himself, but directed others to do the same, saying, *Render unto Cæsar the things that are Cæsar's*, Matt. xvii. 24—27. and xxii. 17—21. And to this law he submitted,——1. That it might appear he was of the nation of the Jews, as it was prophesied of, and promised he should; as that he should be of the seed of Abraham, of the tribe of Judah, and of the Jewish fathers, according to the flesh; all which he was, Gen. xxii. 18. and xlix. 10. Matt. i. 1. Rom. ix. 5.——2. That it might be manifest that he came before the Jewish polity was at an end; as it was foretold he should, Gen. xlix. 10. And Christ being under and subject to the civil law, shewed that the sceptre and lawgiver had not departed, but civil government yet continued; though now, for many hundreds of years it has wholly departed, and is not, in any form or shape, among that people; which has fulfilled the prophecy in Hos. iii. 4. *The children of Israel shall be many days without a king;* and therefore the Messiah must be come long ago, before they were without one, as he did; for Herod was king when he was born.——3. Christ became subject to the civil law, to teach his followers subjection to civil magistrates; and this is the doctrine of his apostles, frequently inculcated by them, to be subject to the higher powers, to obey magistrates, and submit to every ordinance of men, Rom. xiii. 1. Tit. iii. 1. 1 Pet. ii. 13.

2dly, Christ was made under the ceremonial law, and became subject to that; he was circumcised when eight days old, according to that law; and was presented in the temple at the time of his mother's purification, as the law required: at twelve years of age he came with his parents to Jerusalem, to keep the passover; and when he had entered on his public office, it was his custom constantly to attend synagogue-worship; and it was one of the last actions of his life, to keep the passover with his disciples. Now he became subject to this law,——1. Because it looked to him, and centered in him; it was a shadow of good things to come by him: the feasts of tabernacles, passover, and pentecost; the sabbaths of the seventh day of the week, and of the seventh year, and of the seven times seventh year, were shadows, of which he is the substance: all the ablutions, washings, and purifications enjoined by it, were typical of cleansing by his blood; and all the sacrifices of it, daily, weekly, monthly, and yearly, all pointed to his sacrifice.——2. He was made under this law, in order to fulfil it; for it became him to fulfil all righteousness, ceremonial as well as moral righteousness; and all things in it were to have an end, and had an end, even a fulfilling end in him.——3. He was made under it, that by fulfilling it he might abolish it, and put an end to it; for when it was fulfilled, it was no longer useful; and there was a necessity of the disannulling of it, because of its weakness and unprofitableness; and accordingly this law of commandments was abolished; this handwriting of ordinances was blotted out; this middle wall of partition between Jews and Gentiles was broken down; and the rituals of it pronounced weak and beggarly elements; and believers in Christ were directed to take care they were not entangled with this yoke of bondage; nor should they judge and condemn one another for any neglect of it; Christ has answered to the whole, by being made under it.

3dly, Christ was made under the moral law; under this he was as a man; being *made of a woman*, in course he was made under the law; for every man, as a creature of God, is subject to him, its Creator and Lawgiver, and to his law: to fear God, and keep his commandments, is the whole duty of man; and is the duty of every man; and was the duty of Christ, as man. But besides this, Christ was made under it, as the surety and substitute of his people; as he became their surety, he engaged to fulfil the law in their room and stead; this is a very principal part of that will of God, which he declared his readiness to come and do; saying, *Lo, I come to do thy will, O God! thy law is within my heart*, Psalm xl. 7, 8.——1. He was made under it, in order to fulfil the precepts of it; which to do is righteousness, Deut. vi. 25. and is that righteousness which he undertook to work out in perfect agreement with the commands of the law; and which he perfectly obeyed; for he always did the things which pleased the Father, and all that was pleasing to him; even every command of his righteous law; nor did he fail in any one instance; he never committed one sin; and so did not transgress the law in any one particular; but was holy and harmless throughout the whole of his life and conversation.——2. He submitted to the penal part of the law; the law pronounces a curse on all those that do not perfectly observe its precepts; Christ being the Surety of his people, was made a curse for them; or endured the curse of the law in their stead, that he might redeem them from it, Gal. iii. 10, 13. The penal sanction of the law was death; it threatened with it, in case of sin or disobedience to it; the wages of sin is death; Christ therefore, as the substitute of his people, became obedient to death, even the death of the cross, for them.——3. All this he became and did, to fulfil the law in their room; and that the righteousness of it might be fulfilled in them, and so deliver them from the bondage, curse, and condemnation of it; that being, through Christ, dead to them, and they to that, that they might live unto God in a spiritual and evangelic manner.

Thirdly, Christ taking upon him the form of a servant, in human nature, and being made under the law, he was obedient to it, throughout the whole course of his life, to the time of his death; which is meant by that phrase, *Became obedient unto death;* that is, until death, as well as in it, and by submission to it. And,

1. There is the obedience of Christ to men; he was obedient to his earthly parents; he not only lived in a state of subjection to them in his childhood and youth, but continued his filial affection for them, and regard to them, particularly to his mother, when a grown man: his words to her in John ii. 4. do not express irreverence towards her; nor did she so understand them, shewing no resentment at them; but on the contrary: nor do those in Matt. xii. 48, 49. signify any disrespect to her, nor want of affection to her; but his great affection for his spiritual relations; and that he retained his filial duty and regard to her to the last, appears by his bequeathing her to the care of one of his disciples, John xix. 27. Christ also yielded obedience to civil magistrates, as before observed, by paying the tribute-money; hence in prophecy he is called, *the Servant of rulers*, Isa. xlix. 7. But,

2. There is the obedience of Christ to God; for his Servant he was; and it was his law he was made under; and to which he yielded obedience; and is that obedience by which his people are made righteous; though there are many things in which Christ was obedient to God, which do not come into the account of his obedience for the justification of men. As,——(1) The miraculous actions which were performed by him: these were necessary to be done, for they were predicted of him, and were expected from him; hence the Jews said, *When Christ cometh, will he do more miracles than these which this man hath done?* John vii. 31. see Isa. xxxv. 5, 6. And these were done to prove his proper Deity, that he was truly God; that he was in the Father, and the Father in him; that is, that he was of the same nature with him, and equal to him; for the truth of which he appeals to those works of his, John x. 38. and xiv. 11. These were also proofs of his being the true Messiah; and were given by him as evidences of it to the two disciples John sent to him, to know whether he was the Messiah expected or not, Matt. xi. 3, 4, 5. Now these were done in obedience to his Father; he gave him those works to finish, and because they were done by his direction, and in his name, and by his authority, they are called the works of his Father, John v. 36. and x. 25, 37. And yet these are no part of that obedience by which men are made righteous; these were done to answer the above ends; and they are recorded, that we might believe in the Son of God, and in his righteousness; but, as Dr. Goodwin observes,[1] they are not ingredients in that righteousness in which we believe. Nor,——(2.) His obedience in the ministration of the gospel: he had from God his mission and commission to preach the gospel; he was qualified for it as man, through the unction of the holy Spirit; he was sent of God to preach to this and the other city; to these and the other people: he became the minister of the circumcision, or a minister to the circumcised Jews; both for the truth and faithfulness of God, to confirm the promises made to the fathers; and in obedience to the will of God, who gave him a commandment what he should say, and what he should speak; and accordingly he said and spoke what was delivered to him; not his own doctrine, but his Father's, in which he sought, not his own, but his glory; and so

---

[1] Works, vol. 3. part 3. p. 336.

shewed himself to be true, and no unrighteousness in him, Rom. xv. 8. John viii. 28. and xii. 49, 50. and vii. 16, 17, 18. But now it was not his faithful execution of this his prophetic office, nor of the whole of his office as Mediator, which is the obedience or righteousness by which a sinner is justified; for though it is the righteousness of the Mediator; yet not the fidelity and righteousness he exercised in the execution of his office, is that by which men are justified. Nor,——(3.) His obedience to the ceremonial law, which he was under, as has been shewn; and to which he yielded obedience; of which many instances have been given; but this is no part of our justifying righteousness; for the greater number of those that are made righteous by Christ's obedience, were never under this law; and so under no obligation to yield obedience to it; nor their surety for them. But,——(4.) It is Christ's obedience to the moral law, which he was under, and to which he was obedient throughout his life, unto death; and is what all men are subject, and ought to be obedient to; and for lack of which obedience, Christ has yielded a perfect one, in the room and stead of his people; concerning which may be observed, his qualifications and capacity for it, his actual performance of it, and the excellency of his obedience, whereby it appears to have answered the end and design of it.

1*st*, The qualifications and capacity of Christ to yield perfect obedience to the law. ——1. His assumption of human nature, which was necessary to his obedience: as God he could not obey; he therefore took upon him a nature in which he could be subject to God, and yield obedience to him; and which was fit and proper to be done in that nature in which disobedience had been committed.——2. He was made under the law, for this purpose; which has been particularly explained and enlarged on.——3. He had a pure and holy nature, quite conformable to the pure, holy, and righteous law of God; clear of all irregular affections, desires, motions, or lusts; is called, *the holy Thing*, said to be *without spot or blemish*, harmless and undefiled; entirely free from both original and actual transgression, and so fit for pure and perfect obedience to be performed in it.—— 4. Was possessed of a power of free-will to that which is holy, just, and good, agreeable to the law of God. In the state of innocence the will of man was free to that which is good only: in man fallen, his will is only free to that which is evil; in a man regenerate, there being two principles in him, there is a will to that which is good, and a will to that which is evil; so that he cannot do oftentimes what he would: but the human will of Christ was entirely free to that which is good; and as he had a will and power to do, so he always did the things which pleased his Father.——5. He had a natural love to righteousness, and an hatred of sin, Psalm xlv. 7. and from this principle flowed an entire conformity to the law, throughout the whole of his life, and all the actions of it.

2*dly*, His actual performance of it; for as he came to fulfil it, he has fulfilled it; and is become the end of it, for righteousness, to every one that believes. The moral law consists of two tables; and is reduced, by Christ, to two heads, love to God, and love to our neighbour; and both have been exactly observed and obeyed by Christ.

1. The first table of the law; which includes,——(1.) Love to God; *Thou shalt love the Lord thy God with all thy heart, &c.* Matt. xxii. 37, 38. and which was never obeyed and fulfilled to such perfection and purity as by Christ; and which he has fully shewn by his regard to the whole will of his Father, to all his commands, even to the laying down of his life for men; and therefore voluntarily went forth to meet the prince of this world in the garden, and deliver up himself into the hands of his emissaries, in order to suffer and die, according to his Father's will; hence he said, *That the world may know that I love the Father——Arise, let us go hence,* John xiv. 31.——(2.) Faith and trust in God; for to believe God, and to believe in him, is to have him before us, as the law requires: Christ very early exercised faith and hope on him as his God; even when he was upon his mother's breasts; and when in the midst of his enemies, and in suffering circumstances, he expressed the strongest degree of confidence in him; *The Lord God will help me, therefore I shall not be ashamed,* Psalm xxii. 9, 10. Isa. l. 7, 8, 9.——(3.) The whole worship of God; not only internal, which lies in the exercise of faith, hope, love, &c. just observed; but external, as prayer and praise; both which Christ was often in the exercise of, Luke vi. 12. and x. 21. and who not only directed to the worship and service of God, and of him only; but set an

example by his constant attendance on public worship on sabbath-days; and he shewed his regard to it, by inveighing against all innovations in it, the doctrines, traditions, and commandments of men, as vain and superstitious; and by resenting every degree of profanation, even of the place of public worship, Matt. iv. 10. and xiii. 54. and xv. 3, 6, 9. and xxi. 12, 13.——(4.) Honour and reverence of the name of God; and though Christ himself was dishonoured by men, he was careful to honour his God and Father, and not take his name in vain; *I honour my Father*, says he, *and ye dishonour me*. With what reverence does he address him in his prayer; saying, *Holy Father, and righteous Father?* see John viii. 49. and xvii. 11, 25.——(5.) Sanctification of the sabbath; for though Christ was charged with breaking it, by doing acts of mercy on it; which he vindicated, and so cleared himself from the aspersion of his enemies; yet he was constant in the observation of it for religious service; it was his constant custom to go to the synagogue on sabbath-days, and there either hear or read the scriptures, and expound them. Luke iv. 16, 31.

2. The second table of the law; which includes,——(1.) Honouring of parents, and obedience to them; the first commandment with promise, and the first in this table; and which, how it was observed by Christ, both in youth and manhood, has been remarked already; see Luke ii. 51. and in which he was a pattern to others of filial obedience.——(2.) Love to our neighbour as one's self, and which is the second commandment, and like to the first, Matt. xxii. 39. And this was never fulfilled by any as by Christ; who has shewn the greatest love, pity, and compassion, both to the bodies and souls of men: greater love hath no man, than what he has expressed to men, by suffering and dying for them, and working out their salvation, John xv. 13.——(3.) Doing all good to men the law requires; and no injury to the persons and properties of men, which that forbids; and which Christ punctually observed: he went about continually from place to place, doing good to the bodies of men, by healing all manner of diseases; and to the souls of men, by preaching wholesome doctrine to them; nor did he ever, in one single instance, do any injury to the person of any man, by striking, smiting, or killing; nor to the property of any one; he did *no violence*, committed no act of rapine or robbery, or took away any man's substance by fraud or force, Acts x. 38. Isa. liii. 9.——(4.) As all malice, impurity, and evil concupiscence, are forbid in this table of the law; none of these appeared in Christ; no, not the least shadow of them; no malice prepense, nor hatred of any man's person; no unchaste desires, looks, words, and actions; no evil covetousness, or lust after what is another's; nor after any worldly riches and grandeur: so that the law in both its tables, was precisely obeyed by him.

3*dly*, The obedience which Christ yielded to the law, has these peculiar excellencies in it.——1. It was voluntary; he freely offered himself to become man, to be made under the law, and yield obedience to it; or, in other words, to do the will of God; saying, *Lo, I come to do thy will, O God!* and when he was come, it was meat and drink; or, he took as much delight and pleasure in doing the will and work of God, and went about it as willingly and as cheerfully, as a man does in eating and drinking, Heb. x. 7. John iv. 34.——2. It is perfect and complete; there is no command but what Christ inviolably kept; no one, in any one instance, was broken by him; *He did no sin;* whatever was commanded, he did; and whatever was forbidden, he avoided: hence those that are justified by his obedience and righteousness, are all fair, without spot, perfectly comely through his comeliness put upon them.——3. It excels the obedience of men and angels; not only the obedience and righteousness of the Scribes and Pharisees, who pretended to a strict observance of the law, but of the most truly righteous persons; for *there is not a just man upon earth, that does good and sinneth not*, Eccles. vii. 20. But Christ did all that was good, without sin: the obedience and holiness of angels is chargeable with folly, in comparison of the purity and holiness of God; but the obedience and righteousness of Christ is without any blemish, weakness, or imperfection.—— 4. It was wrought out in the room and stead of his people; he obeyed the law, and satisfied it in all its demands, that the righteousness of it might be fulfilled in them, or for them, in him, as their head and representative; hence he, being the end of the law for righteousness unto them, it is unto them, and comes upon them.—— 5. It is the measure and matter of the justification of them that believe in him; *By the obedience of one shall many be made* *righteous*, Rom. v. 19. that is, by the imputation of this obedience, or righteousness, unto them; see 1 Cor. i. 30. 2 Cor. v. 21.——6. It is an obedience well-pleasing in the sight of God; because voluntary, perfect, super-excellent, performed in the room and stead of his people, and by which they are justified. God is well-pleased with his Son, and with his people, considered in him; and with his righteousness and obedience imputed to them; because by it the law is magnified and made honourable; Christ always did the things which pleased his Father; his obedience, in all the parts of it, is acceptable to him; and so are his people on account of it, in whose room and stead it was performed; this is what is commonly called the active obedience of Christ, which he performed in life, agreeable to the precepts of the law.

CHAP. IV.

OF THE PASSIVE OBEDIENCE OF CHRIST, OR OF HIS SUFFERINGS AND DEATH.

III. ANOTHER part of Christ's humiliation, lies in his sufferings and death; to which he readily submitted; he was *obedient unto death*, and in it. He cheerfully endured all sufferings for the sake of his people, it was his Father's will and pleasure he should; he *was not rebellious, neither turned away his back from the smiters, nor his face from shame and spitting*: and when the time was come to suffer death; in the room and stead of his people, according to the counsel of God, and his own agreement; he was like the innocent dumb sheep, *So he opened not his mouth;* said not one word against the sentence of death being executed on him; was not reluctant to become a sacrifice for the sins of men; but as he had *received a commandment* from his Father to lay down his life, as well as to take it up again, he readily and voluntarily obeyed that commandment; and this is what is sometimes called his passive obedience, Isa. l. 5, 6. and liii. 7. John x. 18.

First, I shall observe what the sufferings of Christ were which he endured. They were foretold by the prophets, *who testified beforehand* of them; and the apostles said no other things than what *Moses and the prophets did say should come, that Christ should suffer, &c.* 1 Pet. i. 11. Acts xxvi. 22, 23. This was intimated in the first revelation made of the Messiah; *Thou shalt bruise his heel*, Gen. iii. 15. The twenty-second Psalm, and fifty-third of Isaiah, and ninth of Daniel, are illustrious prophecies of his sufferings; and which have had their exact accomplishment in him. Christ's whole life was a life of sufferings, from the cradle to the cross; he suffered very early from Herod, who sought to destroy him; and which obliged his parents to flee with him into Egypt; he suffered much from Satan's temptations; for his temptations were sufferings, *He suffered, being tempted;* and from the reproaches and persecutions of men; his life, throughout, was a life of meanness and poverty, which must be reckoned a branch of his sufferings: but what may more eminently and particularly be called his sufferings, are those which he endured as preparatory to his death, which led on to it, and issued in it; and death itself, and what attended it.

1st, The things preparatory to his death, and which led on to it, and issued in it.——1. The conspiracy of the chief priests and elders to take away his life; this they had often meditated, and had made some fruitless attempts upon him: but a few days before his death it became a more serious affair; and they met together in a body, in the palace of the high-priest, to consult the most crafty methods to take him and kill him, Matt. xxvi. 3, 4. whereby was fulfilled what was foretold, *the rulers take counsel together;* the ecclesiastic rulers, as well as the civil ones, Psalm ii. 2.——2. The offer of Judas Iscariot to them, to betray him into their hands. A little before the passover, Christ and his disciples supped at Bethany, when Satan put it into the heart of Judas to betray him; which Christ, being God omniscient, knew, and gave an hint of it at supper; and said to Judas, *That thou doest, do quickly:* upon which, he set out for Jerusalem that night, and went to the chief priests, where they were assembled, and covenanted with them to betray his Master into their hands for thirty pieces of silver. This was one part of Christ's sufferings, to be betrayed by one of his own disciples; and which in prophecy, is observed as such; and the sum of money is foretold for which he agreed with them; and which also is observed as an instance of great disesteem of him, Psalm xli. 9. Zech. xi. 12, 13.——3. After Christ had eat his last passover with his disciples, and had instituted and celebrated the ordinance of the Supper; he went into a garden, where he used sometimes to go: here more manifestly his sufferings began; he saw what was coming upon him; the sins of his people he stood charged with as their surety, and the wrath of God for them; this caused him to be exceeding sorrowful, even unto death; at this his human nature shrunk; and he prayed, that, if possible, the cup might pass from him; and the agony he was in was so great, and the pressure on his mind so heavy, and so much affected his body, that his sweat was, as it were, great drops of blood falling to the ground; this was a foretaste of what he was after more fully to endure, Matt. xxvi. 38, 39. Luke xxii. 44.

―――4. Judas knowing the place Christ resorted to, and where he now was, came with a band of soldiers he had from the chief-priests, and with a multitude of others, armed with swords and clubs, as if they came out against a thief, to take him, as our Lord observed to them; when with a kiss he betrayed him to them; and, after he had given them proof of his almighty power, and how easily he could have made his escape from them, voluntarily surrendered himself unto them; who laid hold on him, and bound him as a malefactor, and had him to Caiaphas the high-priest.―――
5. In whose palace he endured much from men, rude, and inhuman; some *spat in his face, and buffetted him; and others smote him with the palms of their hands;* one particularly struck him with the palm of his hand, as with a rod, saying, *Answerest thou the high-priest so?* all which Christ took patiently, whereby the prophecies concerning him were fulfilled, Isa. l. 6. Micah v. 1.
―――6. Still more he endured in the hall of Pilate the Roman governor, to whom the Jews delivered him bound. Here he was accused of sedition, and of stirring up the people against the Roman government; as he had been before in the high-priest's palace of an evil design to destroy the temple; which were all forged and false; as is said in prophetic language, Psalm xxxv. 11. and though he appeared to be innocent, and that to the judge himself, who would willingly have let him go; yet such were the enmity and malice of the chief-priests and elders, and of the multitude of the people, that they were the more vehement and incessant in their cries, to have Barabbas, a robber, released, and Jesus crucified; which verified what David in the person of the Messiah, said, Psalm lxix. 4. Upon which he was scourged by Pilate, or by his orders; to which he willingly submitted, according to Isa. l. 6. and then was delivered to the Roman soldiers, who used him extremely ill; who platted a crown of thorns, and put it upon his head, which gave him pain, as well as disgrace, which is now crowned with glory and honour; and put a reed in his right hand, for a sceptre, whose proper sceptre is a sceptre of righteousness; and, in a mock-way, bowed to him, to whom every knee shall bow in the most solemn manner; having before stripped him of his garments, and put on him a soldier's coat, as fit apparel for a king; and then having put on his clothes again, when they had sated themselves with sport, led him forth to be crucified, according to the sentence the governor had passed upon him, at the instance of the Jews; bearing his own cross they laid upon him, as was the custom with the Romans. Plutarch[1] says, when malefactors were brought out to be punished, every one carried his own cross: only Christ meeting with Simon, a Cyrenean, by the way, they obliged him to bear the cross after him, that is, one end of it; and so crucified him: which leads on to consider,

2*dly*, The death itself he died. He was obedient to *the death of the cross,* the death he died on the cross; hence his blood shed on it is called, *the blood of the cross;* and the cross is put for the whole of his sufferings and death, Col. i. 20. Eph. ii. 16. This was plainly foretold and pointed out in prophecy, particularly in the twenty-second Psalm, described by the dislocation and starting out of his bones; by the fever upon him, which usually attended crucifixion; and especially by the piercing of his hands and feet; and was typified by the lifting up of the brazen serpent by Moses in the wilderness; and the phrase of lifting up from the earth, is used by Christ himself, to signify what death he should die, John iii. 14. and xii. 32, 33. This kind of death was a shameful one; hence Christ is said to endure the cross, and despise the shame; that is, the shame that attended it, Heb. xii. 2. which lay not so much in his being crucified naked, and so exposed, was that truly the case, as in its being the punishment of strangers, of servants, and slaves,

---

[1] De sera Num. Vindict. p. 554.

and such like mean persons; but not of freemen and citizens of Rome; hence it was called *servile supplicium*,[2] a servile punishment; and it was also a painful and cruel one, as the thing itself speaks; to have the whole body stretched to the uttermost; the hands and feet, those sensible parts of it, pierced; and to have the weight of the body depending on them! it was so cruel, that the most humane[3] among the Romans, wished to have it disused, even to servants; and the more mild and gentle of the emperors[4] would order persons to be strangled before they were nailed to the cross: and it was reckoned an accursed death.[5] And though Christ was not accursed of God, but was his beloved Son, while he was suffering this death; yet it was a symbol of the curse; and he was hereby treated as if he was one accursed; and it became a clear case hereby, that he bore the curse of the law in the room and stead of sinners; yea, that he was *made a curse* for them; *for it is written, Cursed is every one that hangeth on a tree*, Gal. iii. 18.

There were several circumstances which attended the death of Christ, which made it the more ignominious and distressing; as the place where he suffered, Golgotha, so called from the skulls of malefactors executed there; and was as infamous as our Tyburn; and it was as scandalous to be crucified in the one place, as to be hanged in the other. Here he was crucified between two thieves; as if he had been guilty of the same, or a like transgression, as theirs; and so fulfilled the prophecy in Isa. liii. 12. *He was numbered among the transgressors;* and, instead of giving him a cup of wine with frankincense, which they used to give in kindness to a person about to be executed, to intoxicate him, that he might not be sensible of his misery; they gave to Christ vinegar mixed with gall, or sour wine with myrrh, and such like bitter ingredients, the more to distress him; of which he, in prophecy, complains, Psalm lxix. 21. Then they parted his garments, and cast lots upon his vesture; by which it seems that he was crucified naked, the more to expose him to shame and contempt; and which was predicted in Psalm xxii. 18. and while he was suffering, he endured the trial of cruel mockings, from all sorts of people; not only from travellers that passed by, and from the multitude of common people, assembled on the occasion; but from the chief-priests, scribes, and elders; and even from the thieves, with whom he was crucified: to all which respect is had in prophecy, Psalm xxii. 7, 8, 12, 13, 16. And for three hours together, whilst he was on the cross, there was darkness over all the land; the sun, as it were, blushing and hiding its face at the heinousness of the sin now committed by the Jews; or as refusing to yield any relief and comfort to Christ, now sustaining as a surety the wrath of God, for the sins of his people; and might be an emblem of that greater darkness upon his soul, being now forsaken by his Father; see Amos viii. 9. And when this was over, he quickly gave up the ghost.

Let it be observed, that Christ was *put to death in the flesh;* as the apostle expresses it, 1 Peter iii. 18, that is, *in the body;* that only suffered death; not his soul, that died not; but was commended into the hands of his divine Father; nor his Deity, or divine nature, which was impassible, and not capable of suffering death; and yet the body of Christ suffered death, in union with his divine person: hence the Lord of glory is said to be crucified; and God is said to purchase the church with his blood, 1 Cor. ii. 8. Acts xx. 28. And the death of Christ, as the death of other men, lay in the disunion of, or in a dissolution of the union between soul and body; these two were parted for a while; the one was commended to God in heaven; the other was laid in the grave: but hereby he was not reduced to a state of non-existence, as say the Socinians; his soul was with God in paradise; and his body, when taken from the cross, was laid in a sepulchre, and where it saw no corruption. The death of Christ was *real*, not in appearance only, as some of the ancient heretics affirmed; nor was he taken down from the cross alive; but was really dead, as appears by the testimony of the centurion that guarded the cross, to Pilate; by the soldiers not breaking his legs, with the others crucified with him, perceiving he was dead; and by one of them piercing his side, the

---

[2] Valer. Maxim. 1. 2, s. 7. s. 12 it is called the grave of servants, Plaut. Miles, 2, 4, 19. Pone crucem servo, Juvenal. Satyr. 6. v. 248.
[3] As Cicero in Orat. pro. Rabirio.
[4] Sueton. Vit. Jul. Cæsar. c. 74.
[5] It is called "arbor infelix," in Cicero ibid. abire in malam crucem, is often used as a curse by Plautus, vide Parei Lexic. Plaut. in voce crux.

pericardium, from whence flowed blood and water; after which, had he not been dead before, he must have died then. And lastly, his death was *voluntary;* for though his life was taken from the earth, seemingly in a violent manner, with respect to men, being cut off in a judicial way; yet not without his full will and consent; he laid it down of himself, and gave himself freely and voluntarily to be a sacrifice, through his death, for the sins of his people.

Now, besides this corporal death which Christ endured, there was a death in his soul, though not of it, which answered to a spiritual and an eternal death; for as the transgression of the first Adam, involved him and all his posterity in, and exposed them to, not only a corporal death, but to a moral or spiritual, and an eternal one; so the second Adam, as the surety of his people, in order to make satisfaction for that transgression, and all others of theirs, must undergo death, in every sense of the threatening, Gen. ii. 17. And though a moral or spiritual death, as it lies in a loss of the image of God; in a privation of original righteousness; in impotence to that which is good, and in an inclination, bias, and servitude of the mind to that which is evil; could not fall upon the pure and holy soul of Christ; which must have made him unfit for his mediatorial work; yet there was something similar to it, so as to be without sin and pollution; as darkness of soul, disquietude, distress, want of spiritual joy and comfort, amazement, agony, his soul being sorrowful even unto death, pressed with the weight of the sins of his people on him, and a sense of divine wrath on account of them; and what he endured both in the garden and on the cross, especially when he was made sin and a curse, and his soul was made an offering for sin, was tantamount to an eternal death, or the suffering of the wicked in hell;[6] for though they differ as to circumstance of time and place; the persons being different, the one finite, the other infinite; yet, as to the essence of them, the same: eternal death consists in these two things, punishment of loss, and punishment of sense; the former lies in an eternal separation from God, or a deprivation of his presence for ever; *Depart from me, ye cursed;* the latter is an everlasting sense of the wrath of God, expressed by *everlasting fire.* Now Christ endured what was answerable to these; for a while he suffered the loss of his Father's gracious presence, when he said, *My God, my God, why hast thou forsaken me!* And he endured the punishment of sense, when God was wroth with him, his anointed; when his wrath was poured out like fire upon him; and his heart melted like wax within him, under it; and *the sorrows of hell* compassed him about, Psalm lxxxix. 38. and xxii. 14. and xviii. 5. Eternity is not of the essence of punishment; and only takes place when the person punished cannot bear the whole at once; and being finite, as sinful man is, cannot make satisfaction to the infinite Majesty of God, injured by sin, the demerit of which is infinite punishment: and as that cannot be borne at once by a finite creature, it is continued *ad infinitum;* but Christ being an infinite Person, was able to bear the whole at once; and the infinity of his Person, abundantly compensates for the eternity of the punishment.[7]

Secondly, Let us next enquire into the cause, reason, and occasion of the sufferings and death of Christ; and how he came to undergo them.

1. With respect to God, and his concern in them. To trace this, we must go back as far as the eternal decrees and purposes of God; which are the foundation, source, and spring of them; for it was by the determinate counsel and foreknowledge of God, that Christ was delivered into the hands of the Jews, and was taken, and by wicked hands was crucified and slain; Herod and Pontius Pilate, the Gentiles, and the people of the Jews, did no other things against him than what the hand and counsel of God determined before should be done; and therefore it was necessary they should be done, Acts ii. 23. and iv. 27, 28. Hence all things were overruled by the providence of God in time, to bring about what he had decreed should be; and without it nothing could have been done; Pilate had no power over him but what was given him from above: so great an hand had God in the sufferings of his Son, that he is said to bruise and put him to grief; to awake the sword of justice against him, to

---

[6] Ita quidem ut brevis passio Christi æternæ damnandorum æquipolleat, Witsius in Symbol. Exercit. 15. s. 16.

[7] Of Christ's enduring the same sufferings his people should, and undergoing the same punishment threatened in the law, see Dr. Owen, Exercit. 5. on Heb. vol. 2. p. 80, &c. and his Vindiciæ Evangel. c. 26. s. 28. p. 564, &c.

OF THE PASSIVE OBEDIENCE OF CHRIST.

spare him not; but deliver him up for us all, into the hands of men, to justice and to death: and the moving cause of all this was, the great love he bore to his chosen ones in Christ; *God so loved the world, &c. In this was manifested the love of God towards us, &c.* John iii. 16. 1 John iv. 9, 10. see Rom. v. 8.

2. With respect to Christ, and his will, as to his sufferings and death; we must have recourse to the council and covenant of grace and peace; in which the plan of salvation was formed upon the obedience, and sufferings, and death of Christ; these were proposed to him, and he readily assented to them; and said, *Lo, I come to do thy will, O God!* which was, to become incarnate; to obey, suffer, and die, in the room and stead of his people; and what moved him thereunto was, his free and unmerited love to them; and which is so fully and strongly expressed therein, John xv. 13. 1 John iii. 16. Eph. v. 2, 25.

3. With respect to Satan; the concern he had therein, in putting it into the heart of Judas, to betray his Lord and Master; and in stirring up the chief priests and elders of the Jews to conspire to take away his life; and so strongly to move for it, and insist upon it with the Roman Governor: this arose from that old enmity that was between him and the woman's seed; in which he betrayed great ignorance of the way of man's salvation, or else acted in great contradiction to himself, and to his own scheme.

4. With respect to men; these acted from different motives, and with different views: Judas from a spirit of covetousness, to gain a small sum of money from the Jews; they, from envy and malice to the Person of Christ, delivered him to Pilate, and moved to have him crucified; and he, against his own conscience, and the remonstrance of his wife, passed sentence of death on him, and delivered him to be crucified, to get and continue an interest in the affections of the Jews, and retain the good-will and favour of his prince, the Roman emperor.

5. But the true causes and reasons why it was the pleasure of God, and the will of Christ, from their great love to men, that he should suffer for them, were their sins and transgressions; to make satisfaction for them, and save them from them; it was not for any sin of his own, for he never committed any, but for the sins of others; he was wounded for our transgressions; he was bruised for our sins; he was stricken for the transgression of his people; he died for their sins, according to the scriptures, Isa. liii. 5, 8. 1 Cor. xv. 3.

Thirdly, The effects of the sufferings and death of Christ, or the things procured thereby, are many. As,

1. The redemption of his people from sin, from Satan, from the curse and condemnation of the law, and from wrath to come; which is through his blood, his sufferings, and death: he gave his flesh for the life of the world of his elect; and gave his life a ransom for them; and being made perfect through sufferings, became the author of salvation to them, Eph. i. 7. John vi. 51. Matt. xx. 28. Heb. ii. 10. and v. 9.

2. Reconciliation, which is by the death of Christ; and peace, which is made by his blood; even a complete atonement for sin; which is obtained through Christ's being a propitiation for it, which he is, through his blood; that is, his sufferings and death, Rom. iii. 25. and v. 10. Col. i. 20.

3. Pardon of sin; which is a branch of redemption, through the blood of Christ, which was shed for the remission of sin; and without shedding of blood there is no remission, Eph. i. 7. Matt. xxvi. 28. Heb. ix. 22.

4. Justification, which is sometimes ascribed to the blood of Christ; that is, to his sufferings and death; the consequence of which is, deliverance, and security from wrath to come, Rom. v. 9.

5. In short, the complete salvation of all God's elect: Christ came to gather together the children of God that were scattered abroad, by dying for them; to seek and to save that which was lost; even to save all his people from their sins, by finishing transgression, making an end of sin, making reconciliation for iniquity, and bringing in everlasting righteousness; and by obtaining an entire conquest over all enemies, sin, Satan, and death, and hell, John xi. 51, 52. Matt. i. 21. Dan. ix. 24.

6. In all which the glory of God is great; the glory of his mercy, grace, and goodness; the glory of his wisdom, truth, and faithfulness; the glory of his power, and the glory of his justice and holiness.

Fourthly, The properties of Christ's death and sufferings.——1. They were real; and not imaginary, or in appearance only: as he really became incarnate, so he really suffered and died; which was confirmed by the testimony of the centurion, and the soldiers that guarded him; by his hands, feet, and side being pierced, and the prints of these being seen after his resurrection.

2. They were voluntary; he willingly agreed in council and covenant to undergo them; he came readily into the world, in the time appointed for that purpose; and was earnestly desirous of, and even straitened until they were accomplished; he freely surrendered himself into the hands of his enemies; and cheerfully laid down his life, and resigned his breath.

3. They were necessary; he ought to suffer; he could not be excused from suffering, because of the decrees of God; the covenant and agreement he entered into with his Father; the prophecies concerning them; and the types and figures on them. Besides, the redemption and salvation of his people could not be procured in any other way.

4. They were efficacious, or effectual to the purposes for which they were endured; as redemption, reconciliation, &c. which efficacy they had from the dignity of his Person, as the Son of God; hence his blood cleansed from all sin; and his righteousness justified from all; and it is unto all, and upon all them that believe, to the justification of them; and his sacrifice is of a sweet-smelling savour with God; and a full and proper atonement for the sins of men. For,

5. They are expiatory and satisfactory. The sufferings of saints are by way of fatherly chastisement; but they have no efficacy to expiate sin, or make atonement for it. But Christ's sufferings, through the infiniteness of his Person, are a complete atonement for all the sins of his people; by his sacrifice and death he has put away sin for ever, and perfected for ever them that are sanctified.

CHAP. V.

OF THE BURIAL OF CHRIST.

IV. THE last degree of Christ's humiliation, and which it ended in, is his burial, or his being laid in the grave; where he continued under the dominion of death for a time. This is one of the articles of the christian faith, *that he was buried—according to the scriptures*, 1 Cor. xv. 4. Wherefore it will be proper to observe,

First, That Christ was to be buried, according to scripture-prophecies and types of it; and what they were.

1*st*, Scripture-prophecies; which are the following.——1. Psalm xvi. 10. *For thou wilt not leave my soul in hell*, or body in the grave. The whole Psalm is concerning Christ, and this verse particularly is applied to him, and strongly argued to belong to him, and not to David, by two apostles, Peter and Paul, Acts ii. 25—31. and xiii. 34—37. Indeed, they produce it in proof of Christ's resurrection; but it is, at the same time, a proof of his burial in the grave, from whence he was raised. Some understand it, of his *descent into hell;* as it is expressed in some creeds, that of the Apostles, the Nicene, and the Athanasian creeds, though foisted into them in later times; and which the papists interpret of the local descent of the soul of Christ into hell, as it signifies the place of the damned, at least into an apartment of it, they call, *limbus patrum;* whither they say he went, to complete his sufferings; to preach the gospel to the old testament saints; to fetch their souls from thence, and to triumph over Satan. But it is certain, that the soul of Christ upon its separation from his body, went not to hell, but to heaven, being committed by him into the hands of his Father: nor needed he to go thither to complete his sufferings, which ended on the cross, when he said, *It is finished ;* nor to preach the gospel, which belongs to the present life, and not to the state of the dead; and which had been preached to the old testament saints in their life time; nor to fetch their souls from thence, which were in heaven; as not only Enoch and Elijah, both in soul and body; but the souls of Abraham, Isaac, and Jacob; and all the rest of the saints; nor to triumph over the devil and his angels, that he did when on the cross, Col. ii. 15. The passages of scripture which all this is chiefly grounded upon, and brought for the confirmation of, are in 1 Pet. iii. 19, 20. and iv. 6. which are misunderstood, and wrongly applied; for the words are to be understood, not of Christ's going down into the prison of hell, after his death, and preaching to the spirits there; but of his preaching by his Spirit, to the disobedient ones, who lived in the times of Noah; whose spirits, for their disobedience to it, were, in the apostle's time, in the prison of hell. In like manner the dead, to whom the gospel is said to be preached, in chap. iv. 6. are those that were then dead when the apostle wrote, but were alive when the gospel was preached unto them. Nor are the words in the sixteenth Psalm, and with which the article in the creed is allowed by some to agree, to be understood of the soul-sufferings of Christ; the anguish and distress of his mind, under a sense of wrath, and under divine desertion; which have been spoken of in the preceding chapter; though Calvin, and many that follow him, so interpret the phrases, both in the Psalm and in the Creed: but these were what he endured in the garden and on the cross, before his death, and not after it. By *hell*, is meant the grave; and so the word is used in many places, Genesis xlii. 38. 1 Samuel ii. 6. Isaiah xxxviii. 18. And by *soul*, is meant the dead body of Christ; as the word *nephesh* sometimes signifies; see Lev. xxi. 1. and then the sense is, that God would not leave his dead body in the grave, at least not so long as to see corruption, to putrify and corrupt, as bodies begin to do, usually, on the fourth day of their being laid in the grave, John xi. 39. but Christ was to be, and was raised, on the third day, which prevented that. Now this prophecy manifestly implies that Christ's dead body should be laid in the grave, though it should not be left there; and though it should not lie there so long as to be corrupted, or that any worm or maggot should have power over him, as the Jews[1] express it.

2. Another passage is in Psalm xxii. 15. *Thou hast brought me into the dust of death;* not only to death, but to dust after death; to lie in the dusty grave, according to the threatening; *To dust thou shalt return*, Gen. iii. 19. and to which the body does return when laid in the grave; and the soul to God that gave it, Eccles. xii. 7. So Kimchi interprets the passage; " I am ready to be put into the grave, which is the dust of death."

3. Some take the words in Isa. xi. 10. to be a prophecy of Christ's burial; *And his rest shall be glorious;* that the passage belongs to the Messiah, is clear from ver. 1, 2, and following; and from the quotation and application of it to the times of Christ, Rom. xv. 12. And the *vulgate* Latin version of the words is, *His grave shall be glorious:* and the grave, as it is a resting-place to the saints, so it was to Christ; where his *flesh rested in hope* of the resurrection from the dead, Psa. xvi. 9. And though his being buried was an instance of his humiliation, and a proof of the low estate into which he was brought; yet it was, in some sense, glorious, inasmuch as he was honourably interred in the grave of a rich man; as the next prophecy suggests.

4. In the passage in Isa. liii. 9. *and he made his grave with the wicked, and with the rich in his death;* in which words there is some difficulty: could they be transposed thus, *he made his grave with the rich, and he was with the wicked in his death,* facts would exactly answer to it; for he died between two thieves, and so was with the wicked in his death; and he was buried in the sepulchre of Joseph of Arimathea, a rich man, and so had his grave with the rich; but it might be using too much freedom with the text to transpose it at pleasure. The general sense of the words may be this, that after his death both rich men and wicked men were concerned in his burial, and were about his grave; Joseph and Nicodemus, two rich men, in taking down from the cross his body, and laying it in the tomb, enwrapped by them in linen with spices; and wicked soldiers were employed in guarding the sepulchre: or the first clause may respect the intention of the Jews, *he* or *it*, the Jewish people and nation, *gave*, appointed, and intended that *his grave* should be *with the wicked*, that he should be interred in the common burying-place for malefactors; and the latter clause may respect the will of God, but *he made it*, that is, God in his providence ordered it, that it should be *with the rich in his death;* that he should be buried in a rich man's grave when dead. Aben Ezra says the word במתו translated *in his death*, signifies a structure over a grave, a sepulchral monument; and so the sense may be, that though his grave was put under the care and watch of the wicked soldiers, yet he had a famous monument erected at the charge of a rich man, where he was laid.[2]

2*dly*, There was a scripture-type of his burial, and which our Lord himself takes notice of; for *as Jonas was three days and*

---

[1] Midrash apud Kimchium, in v. 9.

[2] See my Book of the Prophecies of the Old Testament fulfilled in Jesus, p. 166.

three nights in the whale's belly, so shall the son of man be three days and three nights in the heart of the earth, Matt. xii. 40. that is, as Jonas was as it were buried so long in the belly of the whale, so Christ should lie a like time under the earth, called *the heart of it*, as elsewhere *the lower parts* of it, into which Christ *descended*, that is, the grave, Eph. iv. 9.

Secondly, As Christ should be buried according to prophecy and type, so in fact he was buried, as all the evangelists relate, Matt. xxvii. 59, 60. Mark xv. 46, 47. Luke xxiii. 53, 55. John xix. 39—42. though with different circumstances, yet not contradictory; what is omitted by one is supplied by another; and from the whole we learn,——1. That the body being begged of Pilate by Joseph of Arimathea, a rich man, it was taken down from the cross, and was wrapped or wound about in fine clean linen, as was the manner of the Jews; see John xi. 44. when he was bound hand and foot like a prisoner; and which may denote the dominion death had over him; for when the apostle says, *death hath no more dominion over him*, Rom. vi. 9. it supposes that it once had; as it had when he was bound with grave-clothes and was laid in the grave, until he was loosed from the pains or cords of death, and declared to be the Son of God with power by his resurrection from the dead: the fine clean linen, in which he was wrapped, may be an emblem of his innocence, purity, and holiness; who notwithstanding all appearances and charges, was holy, harmless, and as a lamb without spot and blemish; and likewise of his pure and spotless righteousness, now wrought out, and brought in by his active and passive obedience completely finished, called fine linen, clean and white, which is the righteousness of the saints, Rev. xix. 8. and in which his dead members, his people, who are in themselves dead in law, and dead in sin, being enwrapped, or having his righteousness imputed to them, it is unto justification to life.——2. Nicodemus, another rich man, brought a mixture of myrrh and aloes, about an hundred pound weight; which spices, along with the linen clothes, were wound about the body of Christ; which may denote the savouriness and acceptableness of the righteousness of Christ to God, and to sensible sinners; all whose garments smell of myrrh, aloes, and cassia, as those his sepulchral garments did, Psalm xlv. 8. so the smell of the church's garment's which she has from Christ, is like the smell of Lebanon, or like the smell of a field which the Lord has blessed; as the smell of Jacob in his brother's garments was to Isaac, Cant. iv. 11. Gen. xxvii. 27. also the savouriness of Christ's death and sacrifice, how agreeable to God, being satisfactory to his justice, and so of a sweet smelling savour to him, Eph. v. 2. and the savour of a crucified Christ diffused through the preaching of the gospel, which is like a box of ointment poured forth, and emits such a sweet savour as attracts the love and affections of souls unto him; and whereby the ministers of it become a sweet savour to God and men, 2 Cor. ii. 14, 15. Cant. i. 3.——3. The body being thus enwrapped was laid in Joseph's own tomb, a new one, in which no man had been laid; and this was cut out of a rock. As Jacob, the patriarch and type of Christ, was honourably buried by his son Joseph, so Christ, the antitype of him, and who is sometimes called Israel, was honourably buried by another Joseph, and he a *rich* man, which fulfilled the prophecy in Isa. liii. 9. Christ was laid, not in his own, but in *another's* tomb; which, as it is expressive of his meanness and low estate, who in his lifetime had not where to lay down his head to sleep in, and at his death had no tomb of his own to lay his dead body in; so it denotes, that what he did and suffered, and was done to him, were not for himself but for others; he died not for his own sins, but for the sins of others; and he was buried, not so much for his own sake, but for others, that they and their sins might be buried with him; and so he rose again for their justification: it was a *new* tomb in which Christ was laid, who wherever he comes makes all things new; he made the grave for his people quite a new and another thing to what it was; as, when he is formed, and lies, and dwells in the hearts of men, old things pass away, and all become new: and in this tomb *was never man yet laid;* and which, as the former circumstance, was so ordered in providence, that it might not be said that not he but another man rose from the dead; or that he rose not by his own power, but by the touch of another body, as a man once rose by the touch of the body of Elisha, 2 Kings xiii. 20. moreover this tomb was *hewn out in the rock*, as was sometimes the manner of rich men to do, to prepare such sepulchres whilst living for the greater security of their bodies when dead, Isa. xxii. 16.

and this prevented any such objection to be made to the resurrection of Christ, that the apostles through some subterraneous passages got to the body of Christ and took it away; and to all this may be added, that at the door of this new tomb hewn out of a rock a great stone was rolled, and this stone sealed by the Jews themselves; so that no pretence could be made for a fraud or imposture in this affair.

4. The tomb in which Christ's body was laid was *in a garden;* nor was it unusual for great personages to have their sepulchres in a garden, and there to be buried. Manasseh and Amon his son, kings of Judah were buried in a garden, 2 Kings xxi. 18, 26. Christ's sufferings began in a garden, and the last act of his humiliation was in one; this may put us in mind of the garden of Eden, into which the first Adam was put, and out of which he was cast for his sin; and may lead us to observe, that as sin was first committed in a garden, whereby Adam and his posterity came short of the glory of God, so sin was finished in a garden; there it was buried, there the last act of Christ's humiliation for it was performed; and hereby way was made for our entrance into the garden of God, the heavenly paradise above. A garden is a place where fruit-trees grow, and fruit is in plenty; and may direct us to think of the fruits of Christ's death, burial, and resurrection; who compares himself to a grain of wheat, which unless it falls into the ground and die, it abides alone; but if it dies, it brings forth much fruit, John xii. 24. such as redemption, reconciliation, pardon of sin, &c. as also that as Christ's remove from the cross was to a garden, so the remove of saints at death will be from the cross of afflictions and tribulations, to the garden of Eden, the paradise of God where there are pleasures for evermore.——5. The persons concerned in the burial of Christ, and attended his grave, were many and of divers kinds, and on different accounts: the persons principally concerned in the interment of him were Joseph of Arimathea and Nicodemus, both rich men; and though before they did not openly profess Christ, yet now being wonderfully animated, influenced, and strengthened by the power and grace of God, boldly appear in his cause, and are not ashamed to own him, and act on his behalf, though crucified and slain, and lay under so much ignominy and contempt. And this was so ordered by the wise providence of God, that it might appear, that though Christ was loaded with the reproaches of the multitude of the people of all sorts, yet he had some friends among the rich and honourable, who had courage enough to espouse his cause; and such faith in him, and love to him, as publicly to do the kind offices they did to him, in his greatest debasement and lowest state of humiliation. There were some women also who attended his cross, and followed him to his grave; and continued sitting over against the sepulchre, saw where he was laid, and how his body was laid there; and who went and prepared spices to anoint it, and with which they came early on the first day of the week; but were prevented doing it by his resurrection from the dead; here the power and grace of God were seen in spiriting and strengthening the weaker vessels to act for Christ, and shew their respect to him, when all his disciples forsook him and fled; and this conduct of the women was a rebuke of theirs. Besides these, there were the Roman soldiers, who were placed as a guard about the sepulchre; and which, not only gave proof of the truth of his death, and of the reality of his burial; but also of his resurrection; though they were tampered with to be an evidence against it.

The continuance of Christ in the grave, was three days and three nights; that is, three natural days, or parts of them; which answered the type of Christ's burial, Jonas; who lay so long in the belly of the whale, Matt. xii. 40. Christ was buried on the sixth day, and so lay in the grave part of that natural day, and the whole seventh day, another natural day, and rose again on the first day, and so must lie a part of that day in it; and in like manner, and no longer, it may reasonably be supposed, Jonas lay in the whale's belly.

Thirdly, The ends, uses, and effects of Christ's burial, require some notice.—— 1. To fulfil the prophecies and type before mentioned; for as this was predicted of him, it was necessary it should be fulfilled in him.——2. To shew the truth and reality of his death; for though there were other proofs and evidences of it; yet this must be a very convincing one, since he was taken down from the cross, and buried, not by his enemies, but by his friends, who would never bury him alive; nor, indeed, did Pilate, nor would he deliver the body to them until he was certified by the centurion that he was really dead; and if any doubt could remain after that, it must be removed by the burial of him.——3. That it might appear, that by his death and sacrifice, he had made full satisfaction for sin, and a complete atonement for it; that as by his hanging on the tree, it was manifest that he bore the curse, and was made a curse for his people; so by his body being taken down from the cross, and laid in the grave, it was a token that the curse was at an end, and entirely abolished, agreeable to the law in Deut. xxi. 23.—— 4. To sanctify the grave, and make that easy and familiar to saints, and take off the dread and reproach of it: Christ pursued death, the last enemy, to his last quarters and strong hold, the grave; drove him out from thence, and snatched the victory out of the hand of the grave; so that believers may, with pleasure, go and see the *place where their Lord lay;* which is now sanctified, and become a sleeping and resting place for them until the resurrection-morn; and may say and sing, in the view of death and the grave; *O death, where is thy sting? O grave, where is thy victory?* For,—— 5. In Christ's burial, all the sins of his people, are buried with him; as the *old man was crucified with him; that the body of sin might be destroyed,* Rom. vi. 6. So being dead, that, and its deeds, are buried with him; these may be signified by the grave-clothes with which he was bound, and from which being loosed, he left them in the grave; signifying that the sins of his people, with which he was held, but now freed from, having atoned for them, would never rise up against them; being left in his grave, and cast into the depths of the sea, and, by the Lord, behind his back, so as never to be seen and remembered more; and which is emblematically represented in the ordinance of baptism, designed to exhibit to view the death, burial, and resurrection of Christ, and of believers in him, Rom. vi. 4, 5, 6. Col. ii. 12.——6. This is an instance of the great humiliation of Christ; not only to be brought to death, but to the dust of death. The body of man, when laid in the grave, is a *vile* body, mean, abject and contemptible; it is sown in dishonour and weakness; and so was the body of Christ; he descended into, and lay in the lower parts of the earth, where death and the grave had dominion, and triumphed over him for a while; and so did the enemies of Christ, as the enemies of the two witnesses will, over their dead bodies, saying, as in prophetic language, *And now that he lieth,* that is, in the grave, *he shall rise up no more,* Psalm xli. 8. But they were mistaken; though he died once, he will die no more; death shall have no more dominion over him; though whilst he was in the grave it had dominion over him; but now he is loosed from the cords and pains of death, and lives for evermore, having the keys of hell and death; and he is quickened and justified in the Spirit; and is risen again for the justification of his people; which is the next thing to be considered.

CHAP. VI.

OF THE RESURRECTION OF CHRIST FROM THE DEAD.

HAVING gone through Christ's state of humiliation, I pass on to his state of exaltation; which immediately took place on the ending of the former: these two are closely connected by the apostle, Phil. ii. 6—10. for having fully described the humiliation of Christ; he adds, *Wherefore God also hath highly exalted him,* &c. see Acts ii. 33. and v. 31. The several steps and instances of his exaltation are, his resurrection from the dead, ascension to heaven, session at the right-hand of God, and his second coming to judge the world at the last day. I shall begin with the first of these; for the first step of Christ's exaltation is, his resurrection from the dead; *God raised him from the dead and gave him glory,* 1 Pet. i. 21. This is one of the principal articles of the Christian faith; a very important one, and on which the truth of the whole gospel depends, 1 Cor. xv. 4, 14.

First, I shall consider the prophecies and types of Christ's resurrection from the dead, and how they have been fulfilled.

1*st,* Scripture-prophecies; and the apostle Paul takes notice of several of them in one discourse of his, in Acts xiii. 33, 34, 35. ——1. A passage in Psalm ii. 7. *Thou art my Son, this day have I begotten thee;* which was not said to David; nor could it be said to any other man, since it never was said to any of the angels, Heb. i. 5. yet not so to be understood of Christ, as if his resurrection was the cause of his being, or of his being called the son of God; since, before that, his divine Sonship was witnessed to by his Father, by angels, by men, good and bad, yea, owned by devils; and

was the charge brought against him, for which the Jews said he ought to die, John xix. 7. But the sense is, that by his resurrection from the dead, he would be declared, as he was, to be the Son of God with power; and the truth of his divine Sonship confirmed thereby; and so this prophecy fulfilled; see Rom. i. 4.——
2. Another prophecy of Christ's resurrection is in Psalm xvi. 10. which is produced both by the apostle Peter, and by the apostle Paul, as foretelling the resurrection of Christ, Acts ii. 31. and xiii. 35, 36, 37. for as it is a proof that his dead body would be laid in a grave, and lie buried there for a time, as has been observed in the preceding chapter, so that it would not be left there, not so long as to be corrupted, but would be raised from thence.——3. Another scripture quoted by the apostle Paul, Acts xiii. 34. as referring to the resurrection of Christ, and as a proof of it, is in Isa. lv. 3. *I will give you the sure mercies of David;* by David is meant Christ, as he often is in prophecy, Jer. xxx. 9. Ezek. xxxiv. 23, 24. and xxxvii. 24, 25. Hos. iii. 5. and by his *mercies,* the blessings of the covenant of grace, which are with him; so called, because they flow from the grace and mercy of God; and which being put into his hands, are sure to all the elect through him; and particularly through his resurrection from the dead; for had he died, and not rose again from the dead, the blessings of the covenant would not have been ratified and confirmed; the impetration of them is owing to his death; but the application of them to his resurrection from the dead; which, therefore, was necessary to make them sure. Besides these,——
4. There is another passage, foretelling the resurrection of Christ, in Isa. xxvi. 19. *Thy dead men shall live, together with my dead body shall they arise;* which is an answer to the complaint of the prophet, concerning the sad estate of his people, ver. 14, &c. and are not spoken by him, but by the Messiah to him, the Lord Jehovah, in whom is everlasting strength, the desire of his people, the ordainer of peace for them, and the worker of their works in them; and who is acknowledged by them as being Lord of them, ver. 4, 8, 9, 12, 13. and who assures the prophet, that whereas he should arise from the dead, others should rise with him, as a pledge of the resurrection of his people at the last day; and which was fulfilled at the resurrection of Christ, when the graves were opened, and many of the saints arose from the dead, Matt. xxvii. 52, 53. or if the words are to be rendered, *As my dead body;* or, *as sure as my dead body shall they arise;* either way they predict the resurrection of Christ, of Christ's dead body; which is both the exemplar, earnest, and pledge of the resurrection of the saints. Once more.——
5. Another prophecy of the resurrection of Christ, and of its being on the third day, is, as is generally understood, in Hos. vi. 2. *after two days will he revive us,* &c. which words are thought to be spoken of the Messiah, whose coming is prophesied of in the following verse; and though they are expressed in the plural number, this may be no objection to the application of them to Christ, and his resurrection; since he rose again, not as a single Person, but as a public Head, representing all his people, who are therefore said to be raised up together with him, Eph. ii. 6. Col. iii. 1.

2*dly,* Scripture-types; some of which are,——1. Types of the thing itself in general; or at least thought to be so; as the first Adam's awaking out of a deep sleep, when the woman was presented to him, formed of one of his ribs; the deliverance of Isaac, when his father received him in a figure as from the dead; the bush Moses saw burning with fire, and not consumed; the budding and blossoming of Aaron's dry rod; the living bird let fly, after it had been dipped in the blood of the slain bird, used in the purification of the leper; and the scape-goat, let go into the wilderness, when the other taken with it was slain.——2. Others are types of the time of it in particular; as well as of the thing itself; as the rescue of Isaac from the jaws of death, on the third day, from the time Abraham had the order to sacrifice him, and from which time he was looked upon by him as a dead man; to which others add the preferment of Joseph in Pharaoh's court, on the third year from his being cast into prison by Potiphar; putting a year for a day, as sometimes a day is for a year; but the principal type of all, respecting this matter, is that of the deliverance of Jonas from the whale's belly, when he had been three days in it, at least part of three natural days, and which our Lord himself makes mention of as such, Matt. xii. 40.

Secondly, As it was foretold that Christ should rise from it, and that on the third day; accordingly he did; of which there were many witnesses and full evidence.

As,———1. The testimony of angels. Matthew speaks of but one angel, that descended and rolled away the stone from the sepulchre; but Luke makes mention of two men in shining garments, that is, angels, who appeared in such a form; and John calls them angels, and represents them as sitting, the one at the head and the other at the feet, where the body of Jesus had lain; and who told the women that came to the sepulchre, that Christ was not there, but risen; and so as angels were the first that brought the tidings of Christ's incarnation and birth to the shepherds, they were the first that made the report of his resurrection to the women, Matt. xxviii. 2, 5, 6. Luke xxiv. 5, 6. John xx. 12. Who,———2. Were good and sufficient witnesses of what they saw and heard; they were present when the body of Christ was laid in the sepulchre; they saw where it was laid, and how it was laid; they went home to prepare spices, and when the sabbath was over, came with them to the sepulchre, to anoint the body with them; where, to their great surprise, they saw the stone was rolled away from it; they entered into it, and found the body was gone; they saw the angels, who assured them that Christ was risen; and as they were returning to the disciples with the news, Christ himself met them, whom they knew and worshipped, and held by the feet: so that they had all the evidence of his being risen they could well have, and of his being risen in a real body; which was not only visible to them, but palpable by them, Mark xvi. 4. Luke xxiv. 2, 3. Matt. xxviii. 9.———3. Even the soldiers that guarded the sepulchre were witnesses of Christ's resurrection; they saw the angel roll away the stone, they were terrified with the sight, and with the earthquake they felt; they left their station, and went to the chief priests, and reported what was done, that Christ was risen from the dead; as appears by the method the priests took to stifle the matter, by bribing them with money, to contradict what they had said, and give out that the disciples came by night, and took the body away, whilst they slept; which is so far from invalidating their first report, that it serves but to corroborate it, that they spoke the truth at first, but a lie at last; since, if asleep, how could they know and attest the coming of the disciples to the grave, and taking the body from thence? Matt. xxviii. 4, 11—15.———4. After this, Christ was seen of many men, even of many hundreds; first he was seen of Cephas, or Peter; then of the twelve disciples; after that of above five hundred brethren at once; next of James, then again of all the apostles; and, last of all, he was seen of the apostle Paul, both at his conversion, and afterwards in in the temple; see 1 Cor. xv. 5—8. Acts xxvi. 16, 19. and xxii. 17, 18. Now the apostles were witnesses chosen before of God for this purpose, Acts x. 41. and are to be credited; for———(1.) They were such who knew Christ full well, who had been some years his disciples and followers, had attended his ministry, had seen his miracles, and had been his constant companions in his life-time; and after he was risen from the dead, had ate and drank with him; and had not only a glance or two of him, but he was seen by them at certain times for the space of forty days; and shewed himself alive to them by infallible proofs, Acts i. 3. and x. 41.———(2.) They were men not over credulous, nay, slow of heart to believe, as our Lord upbraids them; and even with respect to this matter; though the women that had been at the sepulchre gave such a plain account of things, with such striking circumstances; yet *their words seemed to them as idle tales, and they believed them not;* nay, when Christ had appeared to all the disciples but one; and they were fully convinced of the truth and reality of his resurrection, and reported this to Thomas, who was not with them; yet so incredulous was he, and would not receive their united report, that he declared he would not believe that Christ was risen, unless he saw the print of the nails in his hands, and put his finger into it, and thrust his hand into his side; all which he was indulged with by Christ; and then, and not before, declared his faith in it. Now had they been a credulous sort of men, easy of belief, ready to receive anything that was told, their testimony might have been objected to; but they were all the reverse; see Luke xxiv. 11. John xx. 25, 27.———(3.) The disciples were men of holy lives and conversation, of strict probity, honesty, and integrity; never charged with any vice or immorality: it may be said of them what the apostle Paul said of himself, that *in simplicity and godly sincerity they had their conversation in the world:* and the testimony of such persons merits regard in any affair.———(4.) They could have no sinister end, or any worldly advantage in view, in contriving and telling such a story; they could expect no other but to be mocked and hated, reproached and persecuted, by all sorts of men, by Jews and Gentiles; as in fact they were, Acts iv. 1, 2, 3. and xvii. 18. nay, not only they risked their credit and reputation, but life itself; and exposed themselves to the severest sufferings, and most cruel death; see 1 Cor. xv. 29, 30, 32. nay, even risked the salvation of their immortal souls; for how could such men but expect the wrath of God, eternal damnation, that could frame and propagate such a falsehood, if it was one?

5. The resurrection of Christ is not only confirmed by the above witnesses, but the Holy Ghost himself is a witness of it, by the miracles which were wrought under his influence, in confirmation of it; the apostles, *with great power*, that is, with miracles, signs, and wonders, and mighty deeds, *gave witness of the resurrection of the Lord Jesus Christ;* see Acts iv. 32. and v. 30, 31, 32.

6. It is as certain, and of it there is full evidence, that Christ rose again from the dead on the third day, according to scripture prophecies and types. It was on the first day of the week Christ rose from the dead. All the evangelists agree that it was on that day the women came to the sepulchre with their spices, and found things as they were; which showed that Christ was risen, Matt. xxviii. 1. Mark xvi. 1, 2. Luke xxiv. 1. John xx. 1. which laid the foundation for the observation of that day to be kept by Christians in a religious manner, Acts xx. 7. 1 Cor. xvi. 1, 2. and it was early in the morning on that day, about the break of it, towards sun-rising; a fit time, very suitable to the Sun of righteousness, who arises on his people with healing in his wings; and this day was the third day from his death. On the evening of the sixth day, on which he died, he was buried, and he rested in the grave on the seventh day, the Jewish sabbath; and fulfilled thereby that type of him, and put an end to it; which made way for the first day, as a day of religious worship, which immediately succeeded it, as none so proper as the next day: so that a time, or day of worship, was not in the least intermitted, nor ever since was one wanted; and on the first day, which was the third from his death, he rose from the dead, and so fulfilled the type of Jonah; who, it is reasonable to suppose, lay no longer in the belly of the whale than our Lord did in the earth; namely, one whole natural day, and parts of others; the Jews having no other name for a natural day than a night and a day; which the Greeks call a night-day; and a part being put for the whole, both might be said to lie three days and three nights; that is, three natural days; the one in the whale's belly; the other in the heart of the earth: they lying there some part of two natural days, whether the night or day part of them, and one whole natural day, Matt. xii. 40.

Thirdly, The manner of Christ's rising from the dead comes next to be considered.
———1. It was in his body; not in his divine nature; which, as it was not capable of suffering and dying, so not the subject of the resurrection; nor his human soul; for that died not with the body, but went to heaven, to paradise, on its separation from it; but in his body: as he was put to death in the flesh, so he was raised from the dead in it; it was the body only that died, and that only was raised again; when Christ said, *Destroy this temple, and in three days I will raise it up;* the evangelist observes, that *he spoke of the temple of his body,* John ii. 19, 21.

2. It was the same body that was raised that died, and was laid in the grave; it was a real body, consisting of flesh, blood, and bones; and was not only to be seen, but to be handled; and it was the same identical body, as appears from the print of the nails in his hands, and the mark in his side made by the spear, Luke xxiv. 39, 40. John xx. 25, 27.

3. It was raised immortal, clear of all former infirmities, as weariness, hunger, thirst, &c. it was, before, mortal, as the event showed; Christ was crucified through weakness; but was raised powerful, immortal, and incorruptible, never to die more; nor shall death have any more dominion over him; he lives for evermore, and has the keys of hell and death, the government of the grave, and can open it at his pleasure, and let out the inhabitants of it free, Rom. vi. 9. Rev. i. 18.

4. It was raised very glorious; of which his transfiguration upon the mountain, before his decease, was an emblem and pledge: and though he might not appear in so much glory immediately after his resurrection, and during his stay with his disciples, before his ascension, they not being able to bear the lustre of his countenance, it really had; yet now, being crowned with glory and honour, his body is a *glorious* one, according to which the bodies of the saints will be fashioned,

at the resurrection of the just, Phil. iii. 21.

5. Yet it has the same essential parts and properties of a body it ever had, not only being flesh and blood, which a spirit has not, but circumscribed by space; not every where, but limited to some certain place; it is received up into heaven, and there it is retained, and will be retained, until the restitution of all things.

6. And lastly, The resurrection of Christ was attended with wonderful events; as with an earthquake, which made it grand and solemn, and alarmed the watch to be attentive to it, and be witnesses of it; and was expressive of the mighty power of God, by which it was performed; and it was followed with a resurrection of many of the saints, shewing the efficacy of it; and as a pledge, earnest, and confirmation of the future resurrection of all the righteous at the last day, Matt. xxviii. 2. and xxvii. 52, 53.

Fourthly, The causes of the resurrection of Christ from the dead deserve notice; it is frequently ascribed to God, without any distinction of persons; it being a divine work, which none but God could do, and is a work of the exceeding greatness of his power, Eph. i. 19. see Acts ii. 24, 32. and iii. 13, 15. and iv. 10. and v. 30. yet being a work *ad extra*, all the three divine persons were concerned in it. It is sometimes ascribed to God the Father, as in Eph. i. 17—20. again in Acts xiii. 30, 33. which words are said to the Son by God the Father, who raised him from the dead; see also 1 Pet. i. 3. At other times it is ascribed to the Son himself: he declared beforehand, that when the temple of his body was destroyed, he would raise it up again; and that, as he had power to lay down his life, he had power to take it up again, which he did; and was thereby declared to be the Son of God with power, John ii. 19, 21, and x. 18. Rom. i. 4. see also 1 Pet. iii. 18. The Spirit, the third Person, had also a concern in it; for the declaration of Christ's Sonship with power was *according to the Spirit of holiness*, or the holy Spirit, *by the resurrection from the dead;* that is, by raising Christ from the dead; and as God, by his Spirit, will raise the members of Christ at the last day, so by the same Spirit, he raised Christ, their Head, on whose resurrection theirs depends, which is intimated by the apostle, Rom. viii. 11.

Fifthly, The effects of Christ's resurrection from the dead, or the ends which were to be, and have been, or will be, answered by it.

1st, With respect to God, the chief end of all, was his glory; for *Christ was raised from the dead by*, some read it, to *the glory of the Father*, Rom. vi. 4. that is, *to the glory of God the Father*, as in Phil. ii. 11. to the glory of his perfections; as particularly, his *truth* and *faithfulness*, in fulfilling types, promises, and prophecies concerning this matter; for what the apostles and ministers of the New Testament say of it, is no other than what Moses and the prophets did say should come to pass; namely, *that Christ should suffer, and that he should be the first that should rise from the dead*, Acts xxvi. 22, 23. and since God spoke of it by them, the veracity of God required it should be done, and that is glorified by it. Also the *power* of God; to raise one from the dead, is the work of almighty power; as is both the resurrection of Christ, and of the saints; *God hath both raised up the Lord, and will also raise up us by his own power:* and the exceeding greatness of his power was exerted in a most glorious manner in the resurrection of Christ, 1 Cor. vi. 14. Eph. i. 19, 20. Moreover, the *justice* of God is glorified in it; when Christ had done his work as a Surety, it was but just and equitable that he should be discharged, be loosed from the cords of death, and be detained no longer a prisoner in the grave; and that he should be honourably and legally acquitted; as he was when a messenger was dispatched from heaven to roll away the stone of the sepulchre, and set him free; and being thus raised from the dead, he was justified in the Spirit; and hereby the justice of God was glorified, as also his *wisdom, grace,* and *goodness;* which appeared in forming the scheme of salvation, and in the kind designs of God to his people; all which would have been defeated, if Christ had not been raised from the dead.

2dly, With respect to Christ.——1. Hereby is given further proof of his proper Deity, and divine Sonship; by this it appears, that he is the Lord God Almighty, who could and did raise himself from the dead! this declares him to be the Son of God with power; shews that he is the Lord of all, both of the dead and of the living; that he has the keys of hell and death, and can and will unlock the graves of his people, and set them free, as he has himself, Rom. i. 4. and xiv. 9. Rev. i. 18.——2. By this it is a clear case, that Christ has done his work as the Surety of his people; that he has paid all their debts, finished transgression, made an end of sin, made reconciliation for iniquity, and brought in everlasting righteousness; that he has fulfilled the law, satisfied justice, and obtained eternal redemption, having given a sufficient price for it; and, in short, has done every thing he agreed to do, to the full satisfaction of his divine Father; and therefore he is raised from the dead, received into glory, and set down at the right-hand of God, having answered all his suretiship-engagements.——3. This shews that he has got the victory over death and the grave; that he has not only destroyed him that had the power of death, the devil, but has abolished death itself, the last enemy, and has brought life and immortality to light; that he has done what he resolved to do; *O death, I will be thy plague! O grave, I will be thy destruction!* so that the believer, in a view of interest in a risen Saviour, who has conquered death and the grave, may triumph and say, *O death, where is thy sting? O grave, where is thy victory?* 2 Tim. i. 10. Hos. xiii. 14. 1 Cor. xv. 55.——4. It was necessary that Christ should rise from the dead, in order to enter into the glory promised him, and he prayed for: the prophets not only spoke of the sufferings of Christ, but of the glory that should follow; which could not be enjoyed by him, unless after he had suffered death, he was raised again; wherefore God raised him from the dead, and gave him the promised glory, 1 Pet. i. 11, 21.

3*dly* With respect to his people; *the power of Christ's resurrection is great;* the effects of it are many, Phil. iii. 10.
——1. The blessings of the covenant of grace in general are enjoyed by the saints in virtue of it; for though reconciliation, and other blessings of grace, are by the death of Christ; yet the application and enjoyment of them are through his interceding life, in consequence of his resurrection from the dead; to which life the whole of salvation is ascribed, Rom. v. 10. Heb. vii. 25.——2. Justification, in particular, is observed as one special end and effect of Christ's resurrection; *he was delivered for our offences, and was raised again for our justification;* and the triumph of faith, in the view of that blessing of grace, is rather, and more principally founded on Christ's resurrection, than on his sufferings and death, Rom. iv. 25. and viii. 33, 34.——3. Regeneration is another effect of Christ's resurrection; as the elect of God were *quickened with him,* and in him, as their head and representative, when he was quickened and raised from the dead; hence, said to be *raised up together,* Eph. ii. 5, 6. so they are quickened in regeneration, in consequence and virtue of his resurrection, to which it is ascribed, 1 Pet. i. 3.——4. The resurrection of the saints at the last day is the fruit and effect of Christ's resurrection, and which is ensured by it. Christ's glorious body is the exemplar, according to which the bodies of the saints will then be formed; and his resurrection is the earnest and pledge of theirs; he is *the first-fruits of them that slept,* that is, of the dead; the first-fruits are the sample, and what ensure a following harvest; so the resurrection of Christ is the sample, and gives assurance of the resurrection of the saints in time to come: so that Christ's resurrection being certain, the resurrection of the saints is also, 1 Cor. xv. 20, 23. 1 Thess. iv. 14.

CHAP. VII.

OF THE ASCENSION OF CHRIST TO HEAVEN.

THE ascension of Christ to heaven was, as his death, burial and resurrection, according to the scriptures; he himself gave hints of it to his disciples, even before his death, as well as after his resurrection: *What and if ye shall see the Son of man ascend up where he was before?* John vi. 62. see also John xvi. 28. and xx. 17. It was pre-signified both by scripture-prophecies, and by scripture-types.

First by scripture-prophecies; of which there are many; some more obscurely, others more clearly point unto it. As,

1*st*, A passage in Psalm xlvii. 5. *God is gone up with a shout; the Lord with the sound of a trumpet.* The whole Psalm is applied, by some Jewish writers, to the times of the Messiah, and this verse particularly, who is the great King over all the earth, ver. 2, 7. and more manifestly appeared so at his ascension, when he was made and declared Lord and Christ; and who subdued the Gentile world, ver. 3, through the ministration of his gospel; by which, after his ascension, he went into it, conquering and to conquer; and caused his ministers to triumph in it. And though it was in his human nature that he went up from earth to heaven; yet it was in that, as in union with his divine Person; so that it may be truly said, that God went up to heaven; in like sense as God is said to purchase the church with his blood; even God in our nature; God manifest in the flesh; Immanuel, God with us: and though the circumstance of his ascension, being attended with a shout, and with the sound of a trumpet, is not mentioned in the New Testament, in the account of it; yet there is no doubt to be made of it, since the angels present at it, told the disciples on the spot, that this same Jesus should so come, in like manner as they saw him go into heaven: now it is certain that Christ will descend from heaven with the voice of an archangel, and with the trump of God; and also, since he was attended in his ascension with the angels of God, and with some men who rose after his resurrection; there is scarce any question to be made of it, that he ascended amidst their shouts and acclamations; and the rather, since he went up as a triumphant conqueror, over all his and our enemies, leading captivity captive.

2*dly*, The words of the Psalmist, in Psalm cx. 1. *The Lord said unto my Lord, Sit thou at my right hand;* though they do not express, yet they plainly imply, the ascension of Christ to heaven; for unless he ascended to heaven, how could he sit down at the right hand of God there? and hence the apostle Peter thus argues and reasons upon them; *For David is not ascended into the heavens;* not in his body, and therefore the words are not spoken of him, but of one that is ascended; *But he himself saith,* not of himself, but another, even of his Lord the Messiah; *The Lord said unto my Lord, &c.* Acts ii. 34, 35.

3*dly*, The vision Daniel had of the Son of man, in chap. vii. 13, 14. is thought by some to have respect to the ascension of Christ to heaven; he is undoubtedly meant by *one like unto the Son of man;* that is, really and truly man; as he is said to be *in the likeness of men,* and to be *found in fashion as a man;* the same *came in the clouds of heaven;* so a cloud received Christ, and conveyed him to heaven, at his ascension, and he was *brought near to the Ancient of days,* to God, who is from everlasting to everlasting; and was received with a welcome by him; and there were given him *dominion, glory, and a kingdom;* as Christ, at his ascension, was made, or made manifest, openly declared Lord and Christ, Head and King of his church. Though this vision will have a farther accomplishment at the second coming of Christ, when his glorious kingdom will commence in the personal reign; who will not deliver up the kingdom until that reign is ended. Once more,

4*thly*, The prophecy in Mic. ii. 13. may be understood as referring to this matter; *The breaker-up is come up before them;* which, in the latter part of the verse, is thus explained; *And their King shall pass before them, and the Lord on the head of them;* so that a divine Person is meant, who is head and king of the church, and plainly points to Christ, who may be called Phorez, the breaker; as Pharez had his name from the same word, because he broke forth before his brother; as Christ, at his birth, broke forth into the world in an uncommon way, being born of a virgin; and at his death, broke through the troops of hell, and spoiled principalities and powers; broke down the middle wall of partition, that stood between Jews and Gentiles; and at his resurrection, broke the cords of death, as Sampson did his withs, with which he could be no more nor longer held by them, than he with them; and at his ascension he broke up, and broke his way through the region of the air, and through legions of devils; at the head of those that were raised with him when he rose, angels and men shouting as he passed along. But,

5*thly*, What most clearly foretold the ascension of Christ to heaven, is in Psalm lxviii. 18. which is, by the apostle Paul, quoted and applied to the ascension of Christ, Eph. iv. 8, 9, 10. and all the parts of it agree with him: he is spoken of in the context, in the words both before and after. He is the Lord that was among the angels in Sinai, who spoke to Moses there; and from whom he received the oracles of God, to give to Israel; and he is the God of salvation, the author of it to his people. And of him it may be truly said, that he *ascended on high,* far above all heavens, the visible heavens, the airy and starry heavens, and into the third heaven, the more glorious seat of the divine Majesty: he has led *captivity captive;* either such as had been prisoners in the grave, but freed by him, and who went with him to heaven;

or the enemies of his people, who have led them captive, as Satan and his principalities; the allusion is to leading captives in triumph for victories obtained. Christ *received*, upon his ascension, *gifts for men;* and, as the apostle expresses it, *gave* them to men; he received them in order to give them; and he gave them, in consequence of his receiving them: and even he received them for, and gave them to, *rebellious* men, as all by nature are *foolish and disobedient;* and even those be to whom he gives gifts fitting for public usefulness; and such an one was the apostle Paul, as the account of him and his own confessions show, who received a large measure of those gifts of grace; the end of bestowing which gifts was, *That the Lord God might dwell among men*, gathered out of the world, through the ministry of the word, into gospel-churches, which are built up for an habitation for God, through the Spirit.

Secondly, The ascension of Christ was presignified by scripture-types; personal ones, as those of Enoch and Elijah. The one in the times of the patriarchs, before the flood, and before the law; the other in the times of the prophets, after the flood, and after the law was given. Enoch, a man that walked with God, and had communion with him, *was not;* he was not on earth, after he had been some time on it; *God took him* from thence up to heaven, soul and body, Gen. v. 24. Elijah went up to heaven in a whirlwind, in a chariot, and horses of fire; was carried up by angels, who appeared in such a form; when he and Elisha had been conversing together, 2 Kings ii. 11. So Christ was carried up to heaven, received by a cloud, attended by angels, while he was blessing his disciples: more especially, the high-priest was a type of Christ in this respect, when he entered into the holiest of all once a year, with blood and incense; which were figures of Christ's entering into heaven with his blood, and to make intercession for men, Heb. ix. 23, 24. The ark in which the two tables were, was a type of Christ, who is the fulfilling end of the law for righteousness; and the bringing up of the ark from the place where it was to mount Zion, which some think was the occasion of penning the twenty-fourth Psalm, in which are these words, *Be ye lift up, ye everlasting doors, and the King of Glory shall come in;* and of the forty-seventh Psalm, where are the above words, *God is gone up with a shout, &c.* the bringing up of which ark to Zion, may be considered as an emblem of Christ's ascension to heaven, sometimes signified by mount Zion.

Now as it was foretold by prophecies and types, that Christ should ascend to heaven, so it is matter of fact, that he has ascended thither; concerning which may be observed,

First, The evidence of it; as the angels of God, who were witnesses of it; for as Christ went up to heaven in the sight of his apostles, *two men stood by them in white apparel*, who were angels, that appeared in an human form, and thus arrayed, to denote their innocence and purity; and other angels attended him in his ascent, when it was that he was seen *of angels*, who were eye-witnesses of his ascension; see Acts i. 10. 1 Tim. iii. 16. The eleven apostles were together, and others with them, when this great event was; and while he was pronouncing a blessing on them, he was parted from them, and carried up to heaven; they beheld him, and looked stedfastly towards heaven, as he went up, until a cloud received him, out of their sight, Luke xxiv. 33, 50, 51. Acts i. 9, 10. Yea, after this, when he had ascended to heaven, and had entered into it, and was set down on the right-hand of God, he was seen by Stephen the proto-martyr, and by the apostle Paul: whilst Stephen was suffering, looking stedfastly to heaven, he saw the glory of God, and Jesus standing at the right-hand of God; and at the same time declared it to the Jews, that he saw the heavens opened, and the Son of man standing on the right-hand of God, Acts vii. 55, 56. Christ *appeared* to the apostle Paul at his conversion, when he was caught up into the third heaven, and heard and saw things not to be uttered; and afterwards, when in a trance in the temple, he says, *I saw him*, Acts xxvi. 16. and xxii. 18. see also 1 Cor. xv. 8. Moreover, the extraordinary effusion of the Spirit, on the day of Pentecost, is a proof of Christ's ascension to heaven, Acts ii. 33. for before this time, the Spirit was not given in an extraordinary manner; *Because Jesus was not yet glorified;* but when he was glorified, and having ascended to heaven, and being at the right-hand of God, then the Spirit was given; and the gift of him was a proof of his ascension and glorification, John vii. 39.

Secondly, The time of Christ's ascension, which was forty days from his resurrection;

which time he continued on earth that his disciples might have full proof, and be at a certainty of the truth of his resurrection; *to whom he shewed himself alive after his passion, by many infallible proofs, being seen of them forty days;* not that he was with them all that forty days, but at several times in that interval: on the first day he appeared to many, and on that day sennight again to his disciples; at another time at the sea of Tiberias; and again on a mountain in Galilee. Now by these several interviews the apostles had opportunities of making strict and close observation, of looking wistly at him, of handling him, of conversing with him, of eating and drinking with him, of reasoning upon things in their own minds, and of having their doubts resolved, if they entertained any; and had upon the whole infallible proofs of the truth of his resurrection: in this space of time also he renewed their commission and enlarged it, and sent them into the whole world to preach and baptize, and farther to instruct those that were taught and baptized by them; now it was he opened the understandings of his apostles, that they might more clearly understand the scriptures concerning himself, which he explained unto them, that so they might be the more fitted for their ministerial work; he also spoke to them *of the things pertaining to the kingdom of God*, the gospel-church-state; of the nature of a gospel-church, of the officers of it, of ordinances in it, and discipline to be observed therein; wherefore all that they afterwards delivered out and practised, were according to the directions and prescriptions given by him: and as all this required time, such a length of time was taken as that of forty days; yet longer it was not proper he should continue with them in this state, lest his apostles should think he was about to set up a temporal kingdom on earth, which their minds were running upon, and inquiring after and expecting, Acts i. 5, 6. and besides, it was proper that they should be endued with the Holy Ghost in an extraordinary manner, to qualify them for the important work Christ gave them a commission to do; and which they could not receive until Christ was ascended and glorified.

Thirdly, The place from whence, and the place whither Christ ascended, may next be considered.——1. The earth on which he was when he became incarnate, the world into which he came to save men, out of which he went when he had done his work, John xvi. 28. the particular spot of ground from whence he ascended was mount Olivet, as appears from Acts i. 12. a place he frequented much in the latter part of his life; and it was in a garden at the bottom of the mount where his sufferings began, where his soul was exceeding sorrowful, even unto death; and where he put up that prayer, *Father, if it be possible, let this cup pass from me;* and where he was in such an agony, that his sweat was as drops of blood falling to the ground; and from this very spot he ascended to his God and Father, to enjoy his presence, and all the pleasures of it, and partake of the glory promised him, Luke xxi. 37. and xxii. 39, 44. One of the evangelists tells us, that he led his disciples as far as Bethany, and there blessed them, and was parted from them; which must not be understood of the town of Bethany, but of a part of mount Olivet near to Bethany, and which bore that name, and which signifies the house of affliction, from whence Christ went to heaven; and as it was necessary he should suffer the things he did, and enter into his glory, so his people must through many tribulations enter the kingdom, Luke xxiv. 50, 51. and xxv. 26. Acts xiv. 22.

2. The place whither he ascended, heaven, even the third heaven; hence Christ is often said to be carried up into heaven, taken up into heaven, towards which the disciples were gazing as he went up; passed into heaven, and was received into heaven, where he remains; and which is to be understood, not merely of a glorious state, into which he passed, exchanging a mean, uncomfortable, and suffering one, for a glorious, happy, and comfortable one; which is meant by the two witnesses ascending to heaven, even a more glorious state of the church, Rev. xi. 12. but a place in which he is circumscribed in his human nature, where he is, and not elsewhere, nor every where; which has received him, and where he is, and will be retained until the times of the restitution of all things; from whence he is expected, and from whence he will descend at the last day; he is gone to his Father there, and has taken his place at his right hand; who, though every where, being omnipresent, yet heaven is more especially the place where he displays his glory; and who is called *Our Father*, and Christ's Father, who is *in heaven;* and of going to

CHAP. VII. OF THE ASCENSION OF CHRIST TO HEAVEN. 419

him at his ascension he often spoke, John xvi. 10, 16, 17, 28. and xx. 17.

Fourthly, The manner of Christ's ascension, or in what sense he might be said to ascend; not *figuratively*, as God is sometimes said to go down and to go up, Gen. xi. 6. and xvii. 22. which must be understood consistent with the omnipresence of God; not of any motion from place to place, but of some exertion of his power, or display of himself; nor in *appearance* only, as it might seem to beholders, but in reality and truth; nor was it a *disappearance* of him merely, as in Luke xxiv. 31. for he was seen going up, and was gazed at till a cloud received him out of sight; nor was it in a *visionary* way, as the apostle Paul was caught up into the third heaven, not knowing whether in the body or out of the body; nor in a *spiritual* manner, in mind and affections, in which sense saints ascend to heaven, when in spiritual frames of soul; but really, *visibly* and locally: this ascension of Christ was a real motion of his human nature, which was visible to the apostles, and was by change of place, even from earth to heaven; and was sudden, swift, and glorious, in a triumphant manner: and he went up as he will come again, in a cloud, in a bright cloud, a symbol of his divine majesty, either literally taken; or if understood of the appearance of angels in the form of a bright cloud, as by Dr. Hammond, it is expressive of the same; nor does it at all affect the reality, locality, and visibility of Christ's ascension, so to understand it: nor can Luke, as an historian, be chargeable with an impropriety in his relation of it in such sense, any more than in the same account by representing angels as appearing in an human form, and in white apparel; nor than that the author of the book of Kings is, in relating the ascent of Elijah to heaven in a chariot and horses of fire, generally understood of angels in such a form, 2 Kings ii. 11. as the horses and chariots of fire also are in chap. vi. 17. which yet were really and visibly seen; and the rather it may be thought that the angels are intended in the account of Christ's ascension, since as the Lord makes *the clouds his chariots*, Psalm civ. 3. so certain it is, the angels are the twenty thousand chariots of God among whom Christ was, and inclosed, as in a bright cloud when he ascended on high, Psalm lxviii. 17, 18. all which serve to set forth the grandeur and majesty in which Christ ascended.

Fifthly, The cause or causes of Christ's ascension; it was a work of almighty power to cause a body to move upwards with such swiftness, and to such a distance; it is ascribed to the right hand of God, that is, of God the Father; to the power of God, by which he is said to be lifted up and exalted, Acts ii. 33. and v. 31. and therefore it is sometimes passively expressed, that he was *carried up*, *taken up*, and *received up* into heaven; and sometimes actively, as done by himself, by his own power; so it is said, *he went up*, he lifted up his own body through the union of it to his divine person, and carried it up to heaven; so *God went up with a shout*; see Acts i. 10. and often he speaks of it as his own act, *What if the son of man ascend, &c. I ascend to my God, &c.* the *efficient* cause of it is God; and being a work *ad extra*, Father, Son, and Spirit were concerned in it. The *procuring* or *meritorious* cause of it was the *blood* of Christ; by which he made full satisfaction to divine justice, and obtained eternal redemption for his people: and therefore having done the work he engaged to do, it was but fit and just that he should be, not only raised from the dead, but ascend to heaven, and be received there; hence it is said, *by his own blood*, through the virtue of it, and in consequence of what he had done by it, *he entered in once into the holy place, having obtained eternal redemption for us*, Heb. ix. 12. The *instrumental* or ministering causes, were the *cloud* and the attending angels.

Sixthly, The effects of Christ's Ascension, or the ends to be answered, and which have been answered, are,——1. To fulfil the prophecies and types concerning it, and particularly that of the high-priest's entering into the holiest of all once a year, to officiate for the people; and so Christ has entered into heaven itself, figured by the most holy place, there to make, and where he ever lives to make, intercession for the saints.——2. To take upon him more openly the exercise of his kingly office; to this purpose is the parable of the nobleman, Luke xix. 12. by the *nobleman* is meant Christ himself; see Jer. xxx. 31. by the *far country* he went into, heaven, even the third heaven, which is far above the visible ones; his end in going there, was *to receive a kingdom for himself*, to take possession of it, and exercise kingly power; to be made and declared Lord and Christ, as he was upon his ascension, Acts ii. 36. which kingdom will be delivered up at the close of his personal reign, and not before.———3. To receive gifts for men, both extraordinary and ordinary; and this end has been answered, he has received them, and he has given them; extraordinary gifts he received for, and bestowed upon the apostles on the day of Pentecost; and ordinary ones, which he has given since, and still continues to give, to fit men for the work of the ministry, and for the good of his churches and interests in all succeeding ages, Eph. iv. 8—13.———4. To open the way into heaven for his people, and to prepare a place for them there; he has by his blood entered into heaven himself, and made the way into the holiest of all manifest; and given boldness and liberty to his people through it to enter thither also, even by a new and living way, consecrated through the vail of his flesh, Heb. ix. 8, 12. and x. 19, 20. he is the forerunner for them entered, and is gone before-hand to prepare by his presence and intercession mansions of glory for them in his Father's house, Heb. vi. 20. John xiv. 2, 3.———5. To assure the saints of their ascension also; for it is to his God and their God, to his Father and their Father, that he is ascended; and therefore they shall ascend also, and be where he is, and be glorified together with him; and all this is to draw up their minds to heaven, to seek things above, where Jesus is; and to set their affections, not on things on earth, but on things in heaven; and to have their conversation there; and to expect and believe that they shall be with Christ for evermore.

CHAP. VIII.

OF THE SESSION OF CHRIST AT THE RIGHT-HAND OF GOD.

This follows upon the Resurrection and Ascension of Christ to heaven; it is in this order things stand according to the scriptures; Christ was first raised from the dead; then he went to heaven, and was received up into it; and then sat down at the right-hand of God, Eph. i. 20. 1 Pet. iii. 22. Mark xvi. 19. I shall treat this article much in the same manner as the former.

First, Shew that it was foretold in prophecy that Christ should sit at the right-hand of God; hence it may be thought, that in prophetic language, and by anticipation, he is called *the man of God's right-hand*, Psalm lxxx. 17. not only because beloved of God, and dear to him as a man's right-hand is to him; so Jacob called his youngest son Benjamin, the son of the right-hand, because of his great affection to him; nor because Christ would be held and sustained by the right-hand of God in the discharge of his mediatorial office, Isa. xlii. 1. but because when he had done his work on earth, he should be received to heaven, and placed at the right-hand of God; of which there is a plain promise and prophecy in Psalm cx. 1. *The Lord said unto my Lord, Sit thou at my right-hand;* which words are spoken, not of Abraham by Melchizedek, nor by Eliezer the servant of Abraham; not by Melchizedek, for he was greater than Abraham, Heb. vii. 6, 7. and therefore would not call him his Lord; and though he might be so called by Eliezer, yet he could not say of him, that he was a priest after Melchizedek's order, ver. 4. nor are they said of David; for as the apostle Peter argues, *David is not ascended into the heavens; but he saith himself, The Lord said unto my Lord, Sit thou at my right-hand,* &c. nor indeed could they be said to, or of any man; not of the saints, for though they sit down together with Christ, their head and representative; and will sit on the same throne with him, and be glorified with him; yet are never said to sit at the right-hand of God; nor indeed are they spoken to or of angels, for *to which of the angels said he at any time, Sit on my right-hand?* &c. Heb. i. 13. but on the contrary, angels, authorities, and powers, are subject to him who sits at the right-hand of God, 1 Pet. iii. 22. and who is the Messiah, Christ, the Son of God, of whom the text in the Psalms is spoken, and was so understood by the ancient Jews, and even by the Jews in Christ's time, as is clear from Matt. xxii. 42—45. where Christ puts a question to which they could give no answer, but were nonplussed and confounded; but could they have given, or had they known any other sense of the words, they could easily have made answer by denying they belonged to the Messiah, but to some other person, and so have freed themselves from the embarrassment they were in; but they knew that this was the universal and acknowledged sense of their nation. The words were spoken by Jehovah the Father, to his Son, in the everlasting council and covenant of grace; even to him who was David's Adon, or Lord: Christ himself also foretold that he should sit down at the right-hand of God; *Hereafter shall ye see the Son of man sitting on the right-hand of Power*, Matt. xxvi. 64.

Secondly, It is fact; Christ is set down at the right-hand of God, and the above prophecies are fulfilled; the evidences of this fact are,——1. The effusion of the Spirit on the day of Pentecost, after Christ had ascended and took his place at the right-hand of God. The Spirit was not given until he was glorified in heaven, by his session there at God's right-hand; upon which, *having received of the Father, the promise of the Holy Ghost, he hath shed forth this which ye now see and hear*, says the apostle, Acts ii. 33. And again, *And we are his witnesses of these things; and so is also the Holy Ghost, whom God hath given to them that obey him*, on his exaltation at the right-hand of God, Acts v 31, 32.—— 2. Stephen, the proto-martyr, while he was suffering, was an eye-witness of this; he saw Christ at the right-hand of God; and declared to the Jews that stoned him, that he did see him; only with this difference, in all other places Christ is spoken of as sitting; but Stephen saw him standing, at the right-hand of God; having risen up, as it were, from his seat, to shew his resentment at the usage of his servant; but this circumstance makes no difference, nor creates any objection to the thing itself, which is, Christ's being exalted in human nature, at the right-hand of God, Acts. vii. 55, 56. I shall next,

Thirdly, Endeavour to explain this article, and shew what is meant by it; what by the right-hand of God; and what by sitting at it; how long Christ will sit there; and what the use and benefits of his session there, are to his people.

1st, What is meant by the right-hand of God, at which Christ is said to sit. This is variously expressed; sometimes by the right-hand of the throne of God; sometimes by the right-hand of the throne of the Majesty in the heavens; and elsewhere, by the right-hand of the Majesty on high, Heb. xii. 2. and viii. 1. and i. 3. By *Majesty*, as it is in some of these places, is meant God himself; as is clear from others, to whom majesty, grandeur, and glory belong; with whom is terrible majesty; it is not only before him, but he is clothed with it. By his *throne*, heaven is sometimes meant, where he more especially displays his majesty and glory; and may be put for him that sits upon it; and he, and that, are said to be on high, in the heavens, in heavenly places; for though God is every where, yet, as now observed, his majesty and glory are most conspicuous in heaven; and here the human nature of Christ is; who in it, is at God's right-hand, being in a certain place, where he is, and will continue till his second coming, and from whence he is expected: and the right-hand of God is not to be taken in a literal sense, but figuratively, and signifies the power of God, and the exertion of that, Psalm lxxxix. 13. and cxviii. 16, and is such a glorious perfection of God, that it is sometimes put for God himself; and even when this article of Christ's session at his right-hand is expressed, Matt. xxvi. 64.

2dly, What is meant by Christ's *sitting* at God's right-hand.——1. It is expressive of great honour and dignity; the allusion is to kings and great personages, who, to their favourites, and to whom they would do an honour, when they come into their presence, place them at their right-hand; so Bathsheba, the mother of Solomon, when she came with a petition to him, he caused her to sit on a seat on his right-hand, 1 Kings ii. 19. in allusion to which, the queen, the church, is said to stand on the right-hand of Christ, Psalm xlv. 9. see also Matt. xx. 21. This supposes such a person, next in honour and dignity to the king; as Christ, under this consideration, is to the Majesty on high, on whose right-hand he sits; and therefore is not to be understood with respect to his divine nature, abstractly considered, or as a divine Person; for as such he is Jehovah's fellow, who thought it no robbery to be equal with God: nor with respect to his human nature merely, and of any communication of the divine perfections to it; for though the fulness of the Godhead dwells bodily in him, yet this is not communicated to, or transfused into his human nature, as to make that omnipotent, omniscient, and omnipresent, or equal to God, or give it a right to sit on his right-hand; but this is to be understood of him as Mediator, with respect to both natures; who, in that office-capacity, is inferior to his Father, and his Father greater than he; since the power in heaven and in earth he has, is given to him by him, and received from him; and he is made subject to him, that put all things under him, by placing him at his right-hand; where he is next unto him, in his office as Mediator.

2. It is expressive of his government and dominion over all; for this phrase of sitting at the right-hand of God is explained by reigning or ruling; for it follows, in the original text, as explanative of it; *Rule thou in the midst of thine enemies*, Psalm cx. 2. and so the apostle interprets it, in 1 Cor. xv. 25. Now this government and dominion is not to be understood of what is natural to Christ, and common to him, with the other two divine Persons; the kingdom of nature and providence equally belongs to him, as to his divine Father, of whom he says, *My Father worketh hitherto, and I work*; jointly with him, having the same power, operation, and influence in all things, he has, John v. 17. Psalm xxii. 28. but of his mediatorial kingdom and government; which dominion, glory, and kingdom, were given to him, and received from the Ancient of days; a delegated kingdom, for the administration of which he is accountable to his Father, and will deliver it up to him, when completed; in respect of which he may be said to sit at the right-hand of God, and to be next unto him in power and authority, Dan. vii. 14. Luke xix. 12. 1 Cor. xv. 28. and yet superior to all created beings, of the highest form, and of the greatest name, which are all subject to him, Eph. i. 20, 21. Phil. ii. 9, 10. 1 Pet. iii. 22.

3. Sitting at the right-hand of God, supposes Christ has done his work, and that to satisfaction, and with acceptance: as the work of redemption, which was given him, and he undertook, and came to work out, and has finished; upon which he *entered in once into the holy place*; that is, into heaven, Heb. ix. 12. and the work of making atonement for sin, reconciliation for iniquity, and full satisfaction for it; which was cut out in council and covenant for him, and he agreed to do; and having done it, *sat down on the right-hand of God*, Heb. i. 3. and x. 12. And also the work of bringing in an everlasting righteousness, for the justification of his people; this he engaged to do, and for this end came into the world, and is become the end of the law for righteousness, to every one that believes; and being raised from the dead for our justification, and gone to heaven, *is at the right-hand of God;* which the apostle observes for the strengthening of his own faith, and the faith of others, with respect to their full acquittance, and complete justification before God, Rom. iv. 25. and viii. 33, 34. All which, and more, he has done with acceptance: God is well-pleased with his righteousness, because the law is by it magnified, and made honourable; his sacrifice is of a sweet-smelling savour to God; and all being done he agreed to do, to entire satisfaction, he was received up into heaven with a welcome; and, as a token of it, placed at God's right-hand.

4. Sitting at God's right-hand, supposes ease and rest from labour; for Christ, upon his resurrection, and ascension to heaven, came into the presence of God; in whose presence is fulness of joy, and at whose right-hand are pleasures for evermore; and when he was made glad with the light of his countenance; and when having entered into his rest, he ceased from his own works, as God did from his at creation, Psalm xvi. 11. Heb. iv. 10. Not that Christ ceased to act for his people in heaven, when set down at the right-hand of God; for he passed into the heavens for them, for their service and good; he entered as the forerunner for them, and appears in the presence of God for them; and, as their high-priest, transacts all affairs for them, and ever lives to make intercession for them; but he ceases now from his toilsome and laborious work: for though it was his Father's business, and which he voluntarily engaged in, and it was his meat and drink to do; yet it was very fatiguing, not merely in going about continually to do good to the bodies and souls of men; but in the labour and travail of his soul, when he bore the wrath of God, and endured the curse of the law, in his sufferings and death: and now, being freed and eased from all this, he sits down, and looks with pleasure on all that he has done; as God, when he had finished the works of creation, took a survey of them, and saw they were all very good, and then rested from his works; so Christ, with pleasure, sits and sees the travail of his soul, the blessings of grace, through his blood, applied to his people; and a continued succession of his seed to serve him, who, ere long, will be all with him where he is, and behold his glory; which is the joy that was set before him when he suffered for them.

5. Sitting denotes continuance; Christ sits as a priest upon his throne, and abides continually: the priests under the law did not abide continually, by reason of death; but Christ lives for ever, and has an

unchangeable priesthood; they stood daily offering the same sacrifices, because sin was not effectually put away by them; but Christ, by one offering, has made full and perfect expiation for sin; and therefore is set down, and continues to do the other part of his priestly office as an intercessor; and to see the efficacy of his sacrifice take place: he also sits King for ever; his throne is for ever and ever; and his kingdom an everlasting kingdom, of which, and the peace thereof, there shall be no end. Which leads,

3*dly*, To observe how long Christ will sit at the right-hand of God; namely, *until all enemies are put under his feet, and made his footstool.* It began at his ascension to heaven, and not before; the Word and Son of God was with God in the beginning from all eternity; and was co-eternal with him, and had a glory with him before the world was; but he is never said to sit at the right-hand of God till after his incarnation, death, resurrection from the dead, and ascension to heaven; then, and not before, he took his place at the right-hand of God, where he will continue till his second coming, when all enemies shall be subdued under him. Some are subdued already; as sin, which is made an end of; the devil, who is destroyed; and the world, which is overcome by him: others remain to be destroyed; all, as yet, are not put under him, as the man of sin, and son of perdition, who will be destroyed with the breath of his mouth; the anti-christian kings, who will be gathered to the battle at Armageddon and slain; the beast, and the false prophet, who will be cast into the burning lake: now Christ sits and reigns till all these are vanquished, and the last enemy destroyed, which is death.

4*thly*, The use of Christ's session at the right-hand of God to his people, and the benefits and blessings arising from thence to them, are,——1. Protection from all their enemies. Being raised, and set down at the right-hand of God, he has a name, power, and authority, over all principalities and powers, might and dominion in this world and that to come; all things are put under his feet, and he is given to be an head over all things to the church; all are put into his hands, to subserve his own interest, and the interest of his people; he has all power in heaven and in earth given him, and which he uses for their good, and for the protection of them from all evil, Eph. i. 20, 21, 22. Matt. xxviii. 18.

2. In consequence of this is, freedom from fear of all enemies; some are destroyed already; those that remain will be; so that there is nothing to be feared from them by those that believe in Jesus, 1 Cor. xv. 25, 26, 27.

3. The perpetual and prevalent intercession of Christ, on the behalf of his chosen ones, is another benefit arising from his session at the right-hand of God; there he sits as their high-priest; and being made higher than the heavens, ever lives to make intercession for them, by representing their persons, presenting their petitions, and pleading their cause; though Satan sometimes stands at their right-hand to resist and accuse them; Christ sits at the right-hand of God as their advocate with the Father, to rebuke him, and answer to, and remove his charges; in a view of which every saint may say with the apostle; *Who shall lay any thing to the charge of God's elect?* Romans viii. 33, 34.

4. Hence great encouragement to come with boldness and freedom to the throne of grace; since we have such an high-priest who is passed into the heavens for us, is our forerunner for us entered, appears in the presence of God for us, is on the throne of glory, and at the right-hand of God, to speak a good word for us; and this serves to draw up our hearts heavenwards, to seek things above, where Christ sitteth at the right-hand of God; and to set our affections on things in heaven, and not on things on earth, Heb. iv. 14, 16. Col. iii. 1, 2.

5. This raises the expectation of the saints, with respect to Christ's second coming, and gives them assurance of it; Christ sits at the right-hand of God, expecting till his enemies be made his footstool; and they look for, and expect him from heaven, who is gone thither to prepare a place for them; and has assured them, that he will come again, and take them to himself, that where he is they may be also, and sit upon the same throne, and be for ever with him, Heb. x. 12, 13. Phil. iii. 20. John xiv. 2, 3. Rev. iii. 21. 1 Thess. iv. 16, 18. Another branch of Christ's exaltation lies in his second coming to judgment, when he will come in great glory. But that I shall reserve to treat of in a more proper place.

CHAP. IX.

OF THE PROPHETIC OFFICE OF CHRIST.

Having gone through Christ's estates of humiliation and exaltation, I shall next consider the offices sustained and executed by him in those estates. His office in general is that of Mediator, which is but one; the branches of it are threefold, his prophetic, priestly, and kingly offices; all which are included in his name, Messiah, or Christ, the anointed; prophets, priests, and kings, being anointed, when invested with their several offices; as Elisha the prophet, by Elijah; Aaron the priest, and his sons, by Moses; Saul, David, and Solomon, kings of Israel: these offices seldom, if ever, met in one person; Melchizedek was king and priest, but not a prophet; Aaron was prophet and priest, but not a king; David and Solomon were kings and prophets, but not priests: the greatest appearance of them was in Moses, but whether all together is not so clear; he was a prophet, none like him arose in Israel till the Messiah came; he was king in Jeshurun; and officiated as a priest, before his brother Aaron was invested with that office, but not afterwards: but in Christ they all meet; he is a Prophet mighty in deed and word, a Priest after the order of Melchizedek, and is King of kings and Lord of lords. The case and condition of his people required him to take upon him and execute these offices. They are dark, blind, and ignorant, and need a prophet to enlighten, teach, and instruct them, and make known the mind and will of God unto them; they are sinful, guilty creatures, as all the world are before God, and need a Priest to make atonement for them; in their unconverted state they are enemies to God, and disobedient to him, and need a powerful Prince to subdue them; to cause his arrows to be sharp in their hearts, whereby they fall under him, and become willing to serve him, in the day of his power: and in their converted state are weak and helpless, and need a King to rule over them, protect and defend them. And though there are many other names and titles of Christ, yet they are all reducible to these offices of Prophet, Priest, and King; and it may be observed, that these are executed by Christ in the order in which they are here put: he first exercised the prophetic office, which he entered into upon his baptism, and continued it throughout his life; at his death, as a Priest, he offered himself as a sacrifice to God for the sins of his people, and now ever lives to make intercession for them; and upon his ascension to heaven, was made and declared Lord and Christ, and sits as a King on his throne, and has been ever since exercising his kingly office; and will do so more apparently hereafter. I shall begin

With his prophetic office; which was foretold in the writings of Moses and the prophets; the proof and evidence of which as belonging to Jesus, lies in his miracles; the several parts of his office will be inquired into; and the time of his execution of it.

First, It was foretold that Christ should appear in the character of a Prophet, and therefore was expected by the Jews as such; hence when they saw the miracles he wrought, they said; *This is of a truth that Prophet that should come into the world*, John vi. 14. meaning, that was prophesied of by Moses, to whom the Lord said, *I will raise them up a Prophet from among their brethren like unto thee*, Deut. xviii. 15, 18. which cannot be understood of a succession of prophets, as say the Jews;[1] for a single Person is only spoken of; and this not Joshua, nor David, nor Jeremiah; only Jesus of Nazareth, to whom they are applied, Acts iii. 22. and vii. 37. and with whom all the characters agree: he was *raised* up of God as a Prophet; this the people of the Jews were sensible of; and therefore glorified God on that account, and considered it as a kind and gracious visitation of his, Luke vii. 16. He was raised up *from among his brethren*, being the Son of Abraham, the Son of David; of the tribe of Judah; born in Bethlehem; and so was of the Israelites, according to the flesh: he was *like unto Moses*; a prophet, like unto him, and greater than he; as the Law came by Moses, grace and truth came by Christ: as Moses was raised up, and sent to be a redeemer of Israel out of Egypt; Christ was raised up, and sent to be a Saviour and Redeemer of his people, from a worse than Egyptian bondage: as Moses was faithful in the house of God, so Jesus; they are compared together, but the preference is given to Christ,

---

[1] See my Book of Prophecies literally fulfilled in Jesus, p. 134, &c.

CHAP. IX.   OF THE PROPHETIC OFFICE OF CHRIST.

Heb. iii. 2—6. The words of God were *put into the mouth* of Christ; the doctrine he preached was not his own, but his Father's; he spoke not of himself; what he spoke, as the Father said unto him, so he spoke; and he spoke *all* that he received from him, and that he commanded him; and so was faithful to him that appointed him, John vii. 16. and viii. 29. and xii. 49, 50. and xv. 15. and xvii. 6, 8. and therefore to be hearkened to; as his Father directed his apostles to do; saying, *This is my beloved Son; hear ye him:* plainly referring to the above prophecy, Matt. xvii. 5.

The qualifications of Christ for this prophetic office were also foretold; which lie in the gifts and graces of the Spirit, which he received without measure: *The Spirit of the Lord God is upon me, because the Lord hath anointed me to preach good tidings unto the meek,* Isa. lxi. 1. from which passage of scripture Christ preached his first sermon, at Nazareth; and having read the text, said, *This day is this scripture fulfilled in your ears,* Luke iv. 16—21. see also Isa. xi. 1, 2. There are also several names of Christ, by which he is called in the Old Testament, which refer to his prophetic office; as a *Messenger*, the messenger of the covenant, whose work it was to explain it, and declare the sense of it; the same with the apostle of our profession, *an interpreter, one among a thousand, to shew unto man his uprightness;* an interpreter of the mind and will of God, who lay in his bosom, and has revealed it, and whose business it was to preach righteousness, even his own, in the great congregation, and has done it, Job. xxxiii. 23. Psalm xl. 9. He goes by the name of *Wisdom*, who cries and calls to the sons of men, and gives instructions to them, Prov. i. 20. and viii. 1, 2. He is called a *Counsellor;* not only because he was concerned in the council of peace; but because he gives counsel and advice in the Gospel, and by ministering of it, both to saints and sinners, Isa. ix. 6. see Rev. iii. 18. He is represented as a *Teacher* of the ways of God, and of the truths of the Gospel, called his law, or doctrine, Isa. ii. 2, 3. and xlii. 4. see Joel ii. 23. Likewise, as a *Speaker*, who has the tongue of the learned, to speak a word in season, Isa. l. 4. and lii. 6. Heb. ii. 3. Moreover, he is called a *Light* to lighten the Gentiles, as well as the Jews; and to give a clear knowledge of the truth as it is in himself, Isa. ix. 2. and xlii. 6. And likewise, *a Witness of the people,* Isa. lv. 4. and to bear witness to the truth he came into the world; and a faithful witness he is, John xviii. 37. Rev. iii. 14. All which belonged to, and pointed at the prophetic office of Christ, and have all appeared and met in our Jesus; yea, the very place, and more particular parts of Judea, where he was chiefly to exercise as a prophet were foretold; see Isa. ix. 1. compared with Matt. iv. 12—15.

Secondly, The evidence and proof of Jesus being that prophet that was to come, are the miracles which were wrought by him: upon Christ's working the miracle of feeding five thousand persons with five loaves and two small fishes; some of the Jews, that saw the miracle, were convinced, and said, *This is of a truth that Prophet that should come into the world,* John vi. 14. And upon his raising from the dead the widow's son of Nain, as he was carrying to the grave, they said, *A great Prophet is risen up among us,* Luke vii. 16. So Nicodemus was convinced that Christ was *a Teacher come from God,* from his miracles, John iii. 2. The Jews expected, that when the Messiah came he would do many and great miracles; as they had just reason for it; for it was foretold he should, Isa. xxxv. 4, 5, 6. wherefore, when they saw what kind of miracles, and what numerous ones were wrought by Christ, some of the Jews were convinced by them that he was the Christ, John vii. 31. When John sent two of his disciples to Christ, to inquire of him, whether he was *he that should come,* the prophet that was to come; or whether they were to *look for another;* he bids them go and tell John what they had seen and heard, meaning the miracles wrought by him, which he particularly mentions, and closes the account with saying, *the poor have the gospel preached to them;* plainly intimating, that he was that prophet that should preach glad tidings to the poor; and his miracles were a confirmation of it, Matt. xi. 2—5. And he frequently appeals to his miracles, not only as proofs of his Deity, but of his Messiahship, John v. 36. and x. 37, 38. which miracles were true and undoubted ones; they were such as exceed the laws and power of nature; what a mere creature could never perform; nor could they be attributed to diabolical influence; for Satan, had he a power to work miracles, would never assist in them, to confirm doctrines subversive of his kingdom and interest, as our Lord argues, Matt. xii. 24, 25, 26. Nor did Christ ever work any miracles to serve any temporal interest of his own, but purely for the good of men, and the glory of God; and these were openly and publicly done, and liable to the strictest examination; so that there could be no fraud nor deceit in them. The next thing to be considered is,

Thirdly, The parts of the prophetic office executed by Christ; and which lay,

1*st*, In foretelling future events; as he is God omniscient, he knew all things future, even the more contingent, and did foretel them; as of a colt tied at a certain place, which he bid his disciples go and loose; and intimated to them what would be said by the owners of it, and what they should say to them; and of a man's carrying of a pitcher of water, whom his disciples were to follow, which would lead them to the master of a house, where the passover was to be provided for him and them, Mark xi. 2—6. and xiv. 13, 16. But more particularly and especially, Christ foretold his sufferings and death; and the kind and manner of it, crucifixion, Matt. xvi. 21. and xx. 18, 19. John xii. 31, 32. the means by which his death should be brought about, by one of his disciples betraying him into the hands of his enemies: he knew from the beginning who would betray him; and declared to his disciples in general, that one of them would do it; and to Judas in particular he directed his discourse, and bid him do what he did quickly: and when the time drew nigh for the execution of the scheme Judas had formed, Christ said to his disciples with him, *He is at hand that doth betray me;* and immediately Judas appeared with a great multitude, and a band of soldiers, to seize on Jesus, upon a signal given them, John vi. 64. and xiii. 18, 21. Matt. xxvi. 46, 47. Christ foretold the behaviour of his disciples towards him, upon his being apprehended, that they would all be offended with him and forsake him; and that, particularly, Peter would deny him thrice before the cock crew: all which exactly came to pass, Matt. xxvi. 31, 34, 56, 74, 75. Likewise, his resurrection from the dead, on the third day; which he gave out, both in more obscure and figurative expressions, and in more plain and easy ones, and directed to the sign of the prophet Jonah, as a token of it; and notwithstanding all the precautions of the Jews, so it came about, who owned, that in his lifetime he predicted it, John ii. 19. Matt. xvi. 21. and xii. 39, 40. and xxvii. 63—66. He spoke beforehand of the treatment and usage his disciples should meet with from men after he was gone; that they should be delivered up to councils, and scourged in synagogues, and be brought before kings and governors for his sake; and that they should be put to death, and those that killed them think they did God good service: all which came to pass, and was fulfilled in all his disciples, Matt. x. 17, 18. John xvi. 2. He predicted the destruction of Jerusalem; the signs going before of it, its distresses, and what followed upon it, Matt. xxiv. which, in every particular, was accomplished, as the History of Josephus abundantly shews. To observe no more, the Book of the Revelation is a prophecy delivered by Christ to John, concerning all that were to befal the church and world, so far as the church was concerned with it, from the resurrection of Christ to his second coming; the greater part of which has been most amazingly fulfilled; and there is the utmost reason to believe the rest will be fulfilled in due time.

2*dly*, Another part of the prophetic office of Christ lay in the ministration of the word; which is sometimes in scripture called prophecy, 1 Cor. xiv. 3. and this was not only exercised by Christ, in interpreting the law, giving the true sense of it, and pointing out its spirituality and extensiveness, and vindicating it from the false glosses of the Pharisees, Matt. v. but chiefly in preaching the gospel; for which he was in the highest degree qualified; and was most assiduous in it, preaching it in one city, and then in another, whereunto he was sent, and that throughout all Galilee, and other parts, Luke iv. 43. Matt. iv. 23. and which he delivered with such authority as the Scribes and Pharisees did not, Matt. vii. 29. even the whole of it; declaring all that he had heard of the Father, and who spoke his whole mind and will by him; and so sealed up prophecy: hence no regard is now to be had to the pretended prophecy and revelations of men, inconsistent with the word of God, John i. 17. and xv. 15. Heb. i. 1, 2. Dan. ix. 24. and which he taught freely, boldly, and without fear or respect of persons, as the Jews themselves acknowledged, Matt. xxii. 16. and with such wisdom, prudence, and eloquence, as never man spake, John vii. 46. and with such gracefulness, and such gracious words, grace being poured into his lips, as was astonishing to those that heard him, Psalm xlv. 2. Luke iv. 22.

and this part of his prophetic office lay not only in the external ministry of the word, but in a powerful and internal illumination of the mind, in opening the heart, as Lydia's was, to attend to the things spoken; and in opening the understanding to understand the Scriptures, and to receive and embrace the truths thereof; the word coming not in word only, but with power, and in the Holy Ghost, and much assurance.

Fourthly, The time when this office was executed by Christ; and it may be observed, that this office may be considered as executed either *immediately* or *mediately*.——1. Immediately, by Christ, in his own Person, by himself; and this was here on earth, in his state of humiliation; for he came *a Teacher from God;* being sent and anointed by him to preach the gospel; and on which office he entered quickly after his baptism, and continued in the exercise of it until his death; but only to the lost sheep of Israel, to whom he was sent, and to them only did he give his apostles a commission to preach the gospel during that time; for he was *a Minister of the circumcision;* that is, a Minister to the circumcised Jews, and to them only, Rom. xv. 8.——2. Mediately, by his Spirit, and by the prophets of the Old Testament, and by the apostles and ministers of the New; and in this sense he exercised the office of a Prophet both before and after his state of humiliation.——(1.) Before his incarnation: he did indeed sometimes personally appear in an human form, and preached the gospel to men, as to our first parents in the garden of Eden, immediately after their fall; declaring, that *the Seed of the woman,* meaning himself, would *bruise the serpent's head:* and thus the gospel, strictly speaking, *began to be first spoken by the Lord,* Gen. iii. 15. Heb. ii. 3. And so, under the name of the Angel of the Lord, and very probably in an human form, he appeared to Abraham, and preached the gospel to him; saying, *In thy seed shall all the nations of the earth be blessed,* Gen. xxii. 15—18. Gal. iii. 8. He was with the thousands of angels at mount Sinai, even he who ascended on high, and led captivity captive: he was with Moses in the wilderness, to whom he spoke at Sinai; and gave unto him the lively oracles of God, Psalm lxviii. 17, 18. Acts vii. 38. But at other times we read of his preaching by his Spirit unto men; Noah was a preacher of righteousness, even of the righteousness of faith; and Christ preached in him, and by him: he, by his Spirit, went and preached to the ungodly world, to those who were disobedient in the times of Noah; the same who in the times of the apostle were spirits in prison: and as Christ was spoken of by all the holy prophets that were from the beginning of the world; so he, by his Spirit, spoke in them, and testified of his own sufferings, and the glory that should follow, 1 Pet. iii. 18, 19, 20. and i. 11.——(2.) Christ continued to exercise his prophetic office, after his state of humiliation was over, and he was raised from the dead, and had glory given him; for he appeared to his disciples after that, and expounded to them the scriptures concerning himself, and opened their understanding, that they might understand them; and spoke unto them of the things concerning the kingdom of God, and instructed them in them, and renewed their commission to preach and baptize, and enlarged it; promised his presence with them, and with their successors to the end of the world; and by them, and not in his own person, after his ascension to heaven, he went and preached peace to them that were nigh, and to them that were afar off, both Jews and Gentiles, Christ speaking in and by his ministers; so that they that hear them, hear him; and they that despise them, despises him: and so he continues, and will continue to exercise his prophetic office in and by his ministers, and by his Spirit attending their ministrations, throughout all ages, to the end of time, until he has gathered in all his chosen ones.

CHAP. X.

OF THE PRIESTLY OFFICE OF CHRIST.

I. CHRIST was to be a Priest; this was determined on in the purposes and decrees of God: God set him *forth* προεθετο, foreordained him, *to be a propitiation,* Rom. iii. 25. that is, to be a propitiatory sacrifice, to make atonement and satisfaction for sin; which is one part of Christ's priestly office; on which, redemption by his blood is founded; to which he was *verily foreordained before the foundation of the world,* 1 Pet. i. 18, 19, 20. The sufferings and death of Christ, whatever he endured from Jews and Gentiles, were all according to the *determinate counsel and foreknowledge of God;* and were no other than what his hand and counsel determined before to be *done*, Acts ii. 23. and iv. 27, 28. and which he endured in the execution of his priestly office; of which, the decrees of God are the spring and rise. To this office Christ was called of God; he did not glorify himself to be called an High Priest, but his divine Father, whose only-begotten Son he is, called him to take upon him this office, invested him with it, and swore him into it, in the council and covenant of peace; for he was made a Priest with an oath, Psalm cx. 4. to shew the importance, dignity, validity, and perpetuity of his priesthood: to all which Christ agreed; saying, *Sacrifice and offering thou wouldst not;* "I foresee that sacrifices of slain beasts, offered by sinful men, will not be, in the issue, acceptable to thee; nor be sufficient to atone for sin; *But a body hast thou prepared me,* in purpose, council, and covenant; which I am ready, in proper time, to assume, and offer up a sacrifice to divine justice," Heb. x. 5. And these eternal decrees, and mutual transactions, are the basis and foundation of Christ's priesthood; and made it sure and certain.

In the prophecies of the Old Testament Christ is spoken of as a Priest. Some think he is meant in 1 Sam. ii. 35. the characters agree with him; however, it is certain, David, under divine inspiration, had knowledge of the above divine transactions, in which the Son of God was constituted a priest, and spoke of him as such, Psalm xl. 6, 7. and cx. 4. he is the priest, the Tirshatha, as Nehemiah the governor said should arise with Urim and Thummim, or what were signified thereby, even all light and perfection, Neh. vii. 65. but still more plainly in Zech. vi. 12, 13. where the Messiah, called the Man the Branch, who was to spring up and build the temple, and bear the glory, is said to be *a priest upon his throne*. Moreover, the several parts of Christ's priestly office are particularly prophesied of, as that he should *make his soul an offering for sin*, and should make *intercession for the transgressors*, Isa. liii. 10, 12. to which may be added, that he sometimes appeared in the habit of a priest, clothed in linen; see Ezek. ix. 2. Dan. x. 5.

There were several types of Christ as a priest; among these the first and principal was *Melchizedek, king of Salem, and priest of the most high God*, Gen. xiv. 18. according to whose order Christ was to be, and is a priest, Heb. v. 10. and vii. 17. who this illustrious person was, is not easy to say, and it looks as if it was the will of God that he should not be known with certainty and precision; the Jews generally suppose that he was Shem, the son of Noah; and it is certain that Shem was living at the time that Abraham was met by this person; and he was also a very pious person, and in whose posterity the church of God continued till the Messiah came, and who sprung from them; but this is to be objected to him, that it was well known who was his father, when born, how long he lived, and when he died: it is not worth while to take notice of the various opinions of those that have borne the christian name; they are so fanciful, and without any foundation, as that he was an angel, or a man created at once perfect and sinless, or the Holy Ghost; that which may seem at first sight more probable is, that he was the Son of God himself; and to this interview with him it is thought Christ had respect in John viii. 56. *Abraham saw my day and was glad;* and since of Melchizedek it is said, *That he liveth and abideth a priest continually*, Heb. vii. 3, 8. but then this may be understood of him in his antitype; besides, he is said to be *made like unto the Son of God*, and therefore not he himself; and this would destroy his being a type of Christ, and Christ's being after his order. It seems best to suppose that he was some Canaanitish king, famous for his extraordinary piety, princely dignity, and divine priesthood; whose genealogy and descent were purposely concealed that he might be a fit type of Christ, who was to be of his order; that is, after the similitude of him, as it is explained, Heb. vii. 15. and a very great similarity and likeness there is between them: Melchizedek was a type of Christ in his person, and the eternity of it, he being *without father* as man, and *without mother* as God; who as such had no genealogy or descent, but is from everlasting to everlasting; and in his offices, kingly and priestly; his name was Melchizedek, king of righteousness; as Christ, the church's king, is said to be, just and having salvation, to reign in righteousness, and to be the Lord our righteousness; and his title, king of Salem, that is, peace, agrees with Christ, who is the prince of peace, and who is both king and priest on his throne, as this person was; and Christ's perpetual never-changing priesthood is shadowed out by his being a priest, *not after the law of a carnal commandment, but after the power of an endless life*, Heb. vii. 16.

Aaron the high-priest was an eminent

type of Christ, though Christ was not of the same tribe with him, nor made a priest after the same law, nor of the same order, but of one more ancient than his, and which continued in Christ when his was abolished. Yet there are many things in which Aaron typified Christ; in his priesthood, as in the separation of him from his brethren; in the unction of him when installed into his office; in his habit and several vestments with which he was clothed, his mitre, robe and broidered coat, ephod and the girdle of it, with the breast-plate of judgment; but especially in the sacrifices which he offered, which were all typical of the sacrifice of Christ; and in his entrance into the most holy place, bearing the names of the children of Israel in the breast-plate of judgment on his heart; in carrying in the burning coals and incense, with the blood of slain beasts, all typical of the intercession of Christ, as founded on his sacrifice; as well as he was a good spokesman, one that could speak well; as Christ has the tongue of the learned to speak on the behalf of his people: and even all the common priests were types of Christ, in their ordination from among men, and for men, and to offer gifts and sacrifices for them, though they were many, and he but one; and their sacrifices many, and were daily offering, and his but one, and once offered, and which was sufficient. Indeed all the sacrifices offered up from the beginning of the world, were all typical of the sacrifice of Christ our great high-priest. The sacrifice of Abel, which was offered up in the faith of the sacrifice of Christ; and those of Noah, which for the same reason were of a sweet-smelling savour to God; the passover lamb was a type of Christ, our passover, sacrificed for us; and so were the lambs of the daily sacrifice morning and evening, and all other sacrifices offered up to the times of Christ's coming, sufferings, and death, which put an end to them all.

II. Christ is come in the flesh, and is come as an high-priest; he came to give his life a ransom for many, and he has given himself a ransom-price for all his people, which has been testified in due time; and which is a considerable branch of his priestly office; for the whole of which he was abundantly qualified, being both God and man.

1. As man; he is mediator according to both natures, but the mediator is particularly said to be *the man Christ Jesus*, 1 Tim. ii. 5. he became man, and was made in all things like unto his brethren, persons of that nature elect; that he might be fit to be a priest, and officiate in that office, and *that he might be a merciful and faithful high-priest in things pertaining to God*, the glory of the divine perfections, and particularly his justice; to *make reconciliation for the sins of the people*, atonement for them, whereby the justice of God and all his perfections would be glorified, Heb. ii. 17. Christ being man, is taken from among men, and ordained for men, for their use and service, as the priests of old were: not for angels; the good angels needed none, and those that sinned were not spared; no priest, no saviour, nor salvation were provided for them, and therefore Christ took not on him their nature; but that of men, that they and they only might reap the benefit of his priestly office; and being man he had something to offer for them, an human body and an human soul, which as God he had not; as such he was impassible, not capable of sufferings and death; and had he assumed an angelic nature, that is not capable of dying, for angels die not; which it was necessary our high-priest should, that by means of death he might obtain redemption from transgressions, both under the Old and under the New Testament; and it was proper that satisfaction should be made in that nature that sinned, and that those of that nature, and not others, should enjoy the advantages of it: also by being man he has another qualification of a priest, which is to be compassionate to persons in ignorance, difficulties, and distress; and hereby Christ becomes a merciful high-priest, one that has a fellow-feeling with his people in all their infirmities, afflictions, and temptations; to which may be added, that Christ's human nature is holy, harmless, and undefiled; clear of original and actual transgression; and such an high-priest became us, is suitable for us, since he could, as he did, offer himself without spot to God; and being Jesus Christ the righteous, he is a very proper person to be an advocate or intercessor for transgressors.

2. As God, or a divine person; being the great God, he was able to be a Saviour, and to work out a great salvation; being the mighty God, he was mighty to save to the uttermost; and being an infinite person, could make infinite satisfaction for the sins of men, and render his sacrifice acceptable to God, and sufficient to put away, and to put an end unto the sins of

his people; and could put a virtue and efficacy into his blood, to cleanse from all sin, and bring in a righteousness that could justify from all, and could make his intercession and mediation for his people always prevalent with God.

III. Christ has executed, and is executing, and will continue to execute, his priestly office; the parts of which are more principally these two, offering sacrifice, and making intercession; to which may be added, a third, blessing his people; for it was the work of the highpriest, as to do the two former, so the latter.

First, Offering a sacrifice. The work of the priests was to offer sacrifice for sin; Christ was once offered up to bear the sins of many, and the punishment of them, and to make atonement for them; he has offered himself a sacrifice to God, of a sweet-smelling savour, Heb. v. 3. and ix. 28. Eph. v. 2.—It may be inquired, 1. Who is the sacrificer? Christ is altar, sacrifice, and priest: as he had something to offer as man, he has offered it; and as it became him as a priest to do it, he has done it; it is his own act and deed, and is frequently ascribed unto him; *He offered up himself unto God, &c.—He gave himself an offering and sacrifice, &c.* Heb. ix. 14. Eph. v. 2.

2. What it was he offered; or what was the sacrifice? Not slain beasts; their blood could not take away sin; it was not their blood he shed; but it was his own, with which he entered into the holy place; it was his flesh he gave for the life of the world, of his chosen ones; it was his body which was offered up once for all; and it was his soul that was made an offering for sin; and all as in union with his divine Person; and therefore said to be himself which was the sacrifice: strictly speaking, it was his human nature which was the sacrifice; the divine nature was the altar on which it was offered, which sanctified the gift or offering, and gave it a virtue and efficacy to atone for sin; it was through the *eternal Spirit* he offered up himself, Heb. ix. 14.

3. To whom was the sacrifice offered? It was offered to God; as it is often said to be, Eph. v. 2. Heb. ix. 14. to God, against whom sin is committed; and therefore to him was the sacrifice for it offered; whose justice must be satisfied; without which, God will by no means clear the guilty: and therefore Christ was set forth and appointed to be the propitiation for sin, to declare the righteousness of God, to shew forth his justice, the strictness of it, and give it satisfaction, Rom. iii. 25, 26. and being satisfied, the sacrifice of Christ became acceptable, and of a sweet-smelling savour to God, Eph. v. 2.

4. For whom was the sacrifice offered? Not for himself; he needed none, as did the priests under the law; he was cut off, but not for himself, being without sin: nor for angels; the elect angels needing no sacrifice, having not sinned; and evil angels were not spared, and so their nature was not taken by him, nor a sacrifice offered for them: but for elect men, called his church, his sheep, his children; for whom he laid down his life, and gave himself an offering to God. His sacrifice was a vicarious one; as were those under the law, which were typical of his; Christ our passover was sacrificed for us, in our room and stead; Christ suffered, the just for the unjust, in the room and stead of them; he died for the ungodly, or they must have died; and became the ransom-price for them.

5. What the nature, excellency, and properties of this sacrifice of Christ? It is a full and sufficient sacrifice, *adequate* to the purposes for which it was offered: such were not the legal sacrifices; they could not make those perfect for whom they were offered; nor purge their consciences from sin; nor take it away from them: but Christ has, by his sacrifice, perfected for ever all those for whom it is offered, Heb. x. 1, 2, 3, 4, 14. It is an *unblemished* sacrifice, as all under the law were to be, which was typical of this; as the passover-lamb, the lambs for the daily sacrifice; Christ the sacrifice is a Lamb without spot and blemish, free from original and actual sin; in him was no sin, and so fit to be a sin-offering for the sins of others; and was offered up, *without spot*, to God. This sacrifice was free and *voluntary;* Christ gave himself an offering; he laid down his life *freely;* he showed no reluctance, but was *brought as a lamb to the slaughter*, &c. Isa. liii. 7. It was but *one* offering, and but *once* offered up. The priests under the law stood daily offering the same sacrifices, because insufficient; but Christ having offered one sacrifice for sin, offered no more, that being sufficient and effectual to answer the designs of it; wherefore in the Lord's Supper, which is only a commemoration of

this sacrifice, there is no reiteration of it; it is not an offering up again the body and blood of Christ, as the papists in their mass pretend; that has been done once, and it is needed no more.

6. What are the ends and uses of this sacrifice, and the blessings which come by it? Christ *is come an High-priest of good things to come,* Heb. ix. 11. or there are many good things which come through Christ's priesthood; particularly through his sacrifice is a full *expiation* of sin, and *atonement* for it; Christ has, by the sacrifice of himself, put away sin for ever; finished it, made an end of it, and reconciliation for it. And the *perfection* of his sanctified ones, that were set apart for himself in eternal election; those he has *perfected for ever,* by his one sacrifice, Heb. x. 14. they are perfectly redeemed, justified, pardoned, and saved by it: by giving himself for them a sacrifice, in their room and stead, he has obtained *eternal redemption* for them; through it he has redeemed them from all iniquity, Tit. ii. 14. *peace* is made for them by the blood of his cross; and through his sufferings and death they are reconciled unto God, Rom. v. 10. full *pardon* of sin is procured, which was not to be had without shedding of blood; and a full satisfaction is made for sin; which is made through the sacrifice of Christ; and so there is redemption through his blood, even the forgiveness of sins, free and full forgiveness of them, Eph. i. 7. In a word *eternal salvation* is the fruit and effect of this sacrifice; Christ being *made perfect* through sufferings; and thereby made perfect satisfaction for sin, he is *become the author of eternal salvation* to his people; and which is owing to his being *called,* and officiating, as *an High-priest after the order of Melchizedek,* Heb. v. 9, 10.

CHAP. XI.

OF THE INTERCESSION OF CHRIST.

SECONDLY, another branch of Christ's priestly office is his intercession; and this may be considered much in the same method as the former, by showing,

I. That Christ was to be an Intercessor, or was to make intercession for his people: when Christ was called to the office of a priest, and invested with it, which was done in the council and covenant of grace; he was put upon making request on their behalf; he is bid to ask them of his Father, as his portion and inheritance, to be possessed and enjoyed by him; which is promised him on making such a request as he did, and they were given him, Psalm ii. 8. John xvii. 6. and he not only asked them, but life for them, spiritual and eternal life, with all the blessings and comforts of life; which, upon asking, were given; God gave him the desires of his heart, and did not withhold the request of his lips: all blessings were bestowed upon his chosen in him; and grace, which is comprehensive of all blessings, was given them in him before the world began, Psalm xxi. 2, 4. Eph. i. 3. 2 Tim. i. 9. and this asking, or requesting, is a species of Christ's intercession, and an early instance of it, and of his success in it; and a specimen of what was to be done by him hereafter.

The intercession of Christ was spoken of in prophecy in the books of the Old Testament; Elihu, in Job xxxiii. 23. not only speaks of him in his prophetic office, as an *interpreter* of his Father's mind and will; but as an advocate, pleading on the behalf of the man to whom he shows and applies his righteousness; that he be delivered from the evil of destruction, from wrath and ruin; since he had found a ransom, a ransom-price, and redemption by it; as in Heb. ix. and xii. and therefore insists, in point of right and justice, that he be secure from condemnation and death: again, in Psalm xvi. 4. which is a Psalm concerning Christ, whose dead body would not be left in the grave so long as to see corruption; but be raised and shown the path of life, ver. 10, 11. now two sorts of persons are spoken of in it; one who are called saints, excellent ones, in whom was all Christ's delight, ver. 3. and another sort, that *hastened after another god,* another saviour, and not Christ; concerning whom he says, *I will not take up their names into my lips;* that is, he would not pray or make intercession for them; and has the same sense as the words in John xvii. 9. *I pray for them; I pray not for the world:* and saying that he would not take the names of some into his lips, supposes that he would take the names of others; that is, pray and intercede for them: but what most clearly foretels the intercession of Christ, and is a prophecy of it, is a passage in Isa. liii. 12. *and made intercession for the transgressors;* that is, would make intercession for them, according to the prophetic style used in that chapter; and which was particularly fulfilled, when Christ upon the cross prayed for his enemies, Luke xxiii. 34.

The types of Christ's intercession are many. As Abel's sacrifice was a type of Christ's, so his speaking after his death was a type of Christ's speaking since his death; it is said of Abel, that he, *being dead, yet speaketh*, Heb. xi. 4. so Christ, though dead, is alive, and lives for ever, and makes intercession, and speaks for his people; as Abel's blood had a voice in it, so has the blood of Christ; but with this difference, the blood of Abel cried against his brother; Christ's blood cries for his brethren, on their behalf: Abel's blood cried for vengeance on the murderer; Christ's blood calls for, and speaks peace and pardon to guilty men, Heb. xii. 24. Melchizedek, as he was a type of Christ, in his kingly and priestly offices, so in that part of the latter which respects intercession; he prayed for Abraham, that he might be blessed both with temporal and spiritual blessings, with blessings both in heaven and on earth, Gen. xiv. 19. so Christ prays and intercedes for his people, that they may have all the blessings of goodness here and hereafter bestowed upon them. Abraham likewise was a type of Christ in his intercession, when he so warmly interceded for Sodom and Gomorrah, at least for the righteous in those cities; in which he so far succeeded, that righteous Lot and his, were delivered from destruction in them. Aaron being a good spokesman, one that could speak well, was a type of Christ, who has the tongue of the learned, and can speak well on the behalf of his distressed ones; and who can plead their cause thoroughly, effectually, and infallibly: so was Moses, when the children of Israel had sinned in making the golden calf, and were threatened with destruction, he interposed in their behalf, and pleaded they might be spared; or otherwise, that he might be blotted out of the book of life, or die: and such is the love of Christ to the spiritual Israel of God, that he has died for them; and pleads his death that they might live. Particularly the entrance of the high-priest once a year, with the blood of beasts, with a censer of burning coals, and an handful of incense, was an eminent type of Christ's entrance into heaven, and his intercession there; who went in thither, not with the blood of beasts, but with his own blood; and so to a better purpose: the burning coals were emblems of his painful sufferings; and the incense put upon them represented his powerful mediation and intercession, founded upon his sufferings and death, and satisfaction for sin made thereby. Likewise the high-priest going into the most holy place, with the names of the children of Israel on his breast-plate, and bearing their judgment before the Lord, and taking away the sin of their holy things, typified Christ as the representative of his people in heaven; appearing in the presence of God for them, presenting his sacrifice for the taking away of their sins, even those of their most solemn services; see Lev. xvi. 2, 12, 13, 14. Exod. xxviii. 29, 30.

II. Christ is an intercessor; he has executed, he is executing, and will continue to execute this office; and the inquiries to be made concerning it are, where, when, and in what manner, he has made, or does make intercession? for what he intercedes, and for whom; and the excellency and usefulness of his intercession?

First, Where, when, and in what manner his intercession has been and is performed? And it may be considered as,

1. Before his incarnation: that he then interceded, and was a Mediator between God and man, is evident from that access to God which was then had: upon the sin and fall of our first parents they were driven from the presence of God, and no access could be had unto him, nor communion with him, on the foot of works; none, but through Christ, the Mediator, who is the only Mediator between God and men; there never was, nor never will be any other; through him both Jews and Gentiles, old and new testament saints, have access to God; those under the former dispensation put up their prayers to God through Christ, and for his sake and through his mediation and intercession they were heard and accepted. So Daniel prayed to be *heard for the Lord's sake;* that is for Christ's sake, Dan. ix. 17. Christ was then *the Angel of God's presence;* who was not only in the presence of God, but appeared there for his people, and by whom they were introduced and admitted into the presence of God, had audience of him, and acceptance with him, Isa. lxiii. 9. We have an instance of Christ's intercession for the people of the Jews, when in distress, who is represented as an angel among the myrtle-trees in the bottom; signifying the low estate the Jews

CHAP. XI. OF THE INTERCESSION OF CHRIST.

were in; and as interceding and pleading with God for them; *and the Lord answered the angel that talked with me, with good and comfortable words:* his intercession was acceptable, prevalent, and succeeded, Zech. i. 11, 12, 13. But a more clear and full instance of Christ's intercession for his people in distress, through sin, is in chap. iii. 1—4. where Joshua, a fallen saint, is represented as greatly defiled with sin; and Satan standing at his right-hand, to accuse and charge him, and get judgment to pass against him; when Christ, the angel of the covenant, appears on his behalf, rebukes Satan, and pleads electing and calling grace in favour of the criminal; and, on the foot of his own sacrifice to be offered, satisfaction to be made, orders his filthy garments to be taken away, and him to be clothed with change of raiment, his own righteousness, and dismissed.

2. Christ acted as an intercessor in his state of humiliation. We often read of his praying to God, and sometimes a whole night together, and of his offering up prayers and supplications, with strong crying and tears, especially in the garden and on the cross; which might be chiefly on his own account, though not without regard to his people: at other times we find him praying for particular persons; as at the grave of Lazarus, where he wept and groaned in Spirit, and inwardly put up supplications, which were heard; for he thanks his Father for hearing him; and declared he always heard him, John xi. 41, 42. And he prayed for Peter particularly, when tempted, that his *faith* might *not fail*, and was heard; for though he fell by the temptation, he was at once recovered, Luke xxii. 32. He prayed for all his disciples, in John xvii. which is a specimen of his intercession in heaven for all his elect: yea, he prayed for his enemies, and such of his elect who were then in a state of enmity; and who, in consequence of his intercession, were converted and comforted; though they had been concerned in taking away his life, Luke xxiii. 34. Acts ii. 36—41. Such virtue is there in his blood, and in his intercession founded upon it!

3. Christ is now interceding in heaven for his people; he is gone to heaven, entered there, and is set down at the right-hand of God; where he ever lives to make intercession, Rom. viii. 34. Heb. vii. 25. for so his intercession is sometimes represented, as after his death and resurrection from the dead, and session at God's right-hand; and which is performed, perhaps not vocally, as on earth; for as he could request and intercede before he assumed an human nature, even in the council and covenant of peace, without a voice, so he can now in heaven; though it is not improbable but that he may make use of his human voice at his pleasure; though it cannot with certainty be affirmed, yet it is not to be denied: however it is certain that he does not intercede in like manner as when on earth, with prostration of body, cries, and tears; which would be quite inconsistent with his state of exaltation and glory, being set down at the right-hand of God, and crowned with glory and honour; nor as supplicating an angry Judge, and entreating him to be pacified, and show favour; for peace is made by the blood of Christ's cross; and God is pacified towards his people for all that they have done: nor as litigating a point in a court of judicature; for though Christ has names and titles taken from such like procedures, as counsellor, pleader, and advocate; yet not as engaged in a cause dependant and precarious: but the intercession of Christ is carried on in heaven, by appearing in the presence of God there for his people; it is enough that he shows himself, as having done, as their Surety, all that law and justice could require; by presenting his blood, his sacrifice, and righteousness: Christ is gone with his blood into the holiest of all, and sprinkled it on the throne of mercy, before God; and where he is in the midst of the throne, as a Lamb that had been slain; his sacrifice being always in view of his divine Father, and his righteousness always in sight; with which God is well pleased, because by it his law is magnified and made honourable, and his justice satisfied: all which, of themselves, speak on the behalf of his people. Moreover, Christ intercedes, not as asking a favour, but as an advocate in open court, who pleads, demands, and requires, according to law, in point of right and justice, such and such blessings to be bestowed upon, and applied unto such persons he has shed his blood for; he speaks, not in a charitative, but in an authoritative way, declaring it as his will, on the foot of what he has done and suffered, that so it should be; a specimen of this we have in the finishing blessing of all, glorification, John xvii. 24. Christ performs this his office also by offering up the prayers and praises of his people; which become acceptable to God through

the sweet incense of his mediation and intercession, Rev. viii. 3, 4. Heb. xiii. 15. 1 Pet. ii. 5. Once more, Christ executes this office by seeing to it, that all the blessings of grace promised in covenant, and ratified by his blood, are applied by his Spirit to the covenant ones; and so he sits as a Priest on his throne, and sees the travail of his soul with satisfaction; when, as those he engaged for are reconciled by his death, so they are saved by his interceding life; are effectually called by grace, and put into the possession of what was stipulated and procured for them.

Secondly, The next thing to be considered is, what Christ makes intercession for more particularly? For the *conversion* of his unconverted ones: *Neither pray I for those alone*, says he, meaning his disciples that were called; *but for them also which shall believe on me through their word*, John xvii. 20. And for the *comfort* of those that are convinced of sin, distressed with a sense of it, and need comfort; in consequence of his intercession, he sends the Comforter to them, to take of his things, and show them to them, and shed abroad his love in them, and so fill them with joy and peace in believing; insomuch that they have peace in him while they have tribulation in the world. And particularly for discoveries and applications of pardoning grace and mercy; *If any man sin, we have an Advocate with the Father;* not that he pleads for sinning, nor that any may be connived at in it; but that he may have a manifestation and application of the pardon of it, in consequence of his blood shed for it. And as Christ has a fellow-feeling with his people under temptations, and succours them that are tempted; this is one way of doing it, interceding for *strength* for them to bear up under temptations, to be carried through them, and delivered out of them; and so that they might have *persevering grace* to hold on, and out, unto the end; he prays not that they be taken out of the world, but that they may be kept from the evil of it, John xvii. 11, 15. Lastly, he intercedes for their *glorification;* one principal branch of which will lie in beholding his glory, John xvii. 24. This was the joy set before him, and which he kept in view in all his sufferings; and for the sake of which he endured them so cheerfully; and it is that which is uppermost in his heart, in his intercession for them; nor will he cease pleading till he has all his people in heaven with him.

Thirdly, The persons Christ makes intercession for are not the *world*, the men of it, and all that are in it; for Christ himself says, *I pray not for the world;* but for those that were chosen and given him out of the world; and who, in due time, are effectually called out of it by his grace: the objects of Christ's intercession are the same with those of election, redemption, and effectual calling; to whom Christ is a propitiation, for them he is an advocate, John xvii. 9. 1 John ii. 1, 2. The high-priest bore upon his heart, in the breast-plate of judgment, only the names of the children of Israel, and they are only the spiritual Israel of God whom Christ bears upon his heart, whom he represents and intercedes for in the holiest of all; and not for those only who actually believe, but for those who shall hereafter; even who are, for the present, enemies to him, and averse to his rule over them; as his prayers in the garden, and on the cross, show, John xvii. 20. Luke xxiii. 34. It is for all the elect Christ intercedes, that have been, are, or shall be, scattered up and down in the several parts of the world, and in all ages and periods of time, that they be partakers of his grace here, and be glorified with him hereafter; hence says the apostle, *Who shall lay any thing to the charge of God's elect?* since not only God justifies them, Christ died for them, is risen again, and is at the right-hand of God; but makes intercession for them, and answers to, and removes all charges brought against them, Rom. viii. 33, 34. and for those even though and while they are sinners and transgressors; for so it is said of him in prophecy; *and hath made intercession for the transgressors*, Isa. liii. 12. and as he died for such, yea, the chief of sinners, and calls them by his grace, and receives them into fellowship with himself, it is no wonder that he should pray and intercede for them.

Fourthly, The excellent properties and use of Christ's intercession. Christ is an only intercessor; *there is but one Mediator between God and men, the man Christ Jesus*, 1 Tim. ii. 5. though the Spirit of God makes intercession for the saints, it is within them, not without them, at the right-hand of God; and it is with groans unutterable; not so Christ in heaven; saints in heaven are no intercessors for saints on earth; they are ignorant of their persons and cases, and therefore cannot intercede for them; nor angels, as say the papists, who distinguish between mediators of redemption and mediators of intercession; the latter they say angels are, and Christ the former: but the Scripture knows no such distinction; he that is the Redeemer is the only Intercessor; he that is the Propitiation is the sole Advocate; and he is every way fit for it: being the Son of God, he has interest in his Father's heart; being the mighty God, he is mighty to plead, thoroughly to plead the cause of his people; and having offered up himself as man, to be a sacrifice for them, he has a sufficient plea to make on their behalf; and having the tongue of the learned, can speak well for them; and being Jesus Christ the righteous, the holy and harmless High-Priest, is a proper person to be the *advocate* for those that sin; as such he is with the Father, at hand, and to be called unto; is ready to defend[1] the cause of his people, and deliver them from their adversary; and he is a *prevalent advocate* and intercessor; he is always heard; he was when on earth, and now in heaven; his mediation is always acceptable, and ever succeeds, John xi. 41, 42. And he performs this his office *freely*, willingly, and cheerfully; he never rejects any case put into his hands, nor refuses to present the petitions of his people to his divine Father; but is always ready to offer up the prayers of all saints with the much incense of his mediation, Rev. viii. 3, 4. And his intercession is *perpetual*; though he was dead he is alive, and lives for evermore; and *he ever lives to make intercession for them* that come unto God by him, Heb. vii. 25. Many are the benefits and blessings of grace derived to saints from Christ's intercession for them; such as access to God through him, acceptance with God in him, both of persons and services, communications of grace from him, the application of every blessing of the covenant to them; for though the impetration of them is by the death of Christ, the application of them is owing to his life, Rom. v. 10.

CHAP. XII.

OF CHRIST'S BLESSING HIS PEOPLE AS A PRIEST.

THIRDLY, I proceed in this chapter to consider another part of Christ's priestly office; which lies in blessing his people; for this was what belonged to the priests. Aaron and his sons were appointed to bless the people of Israel in the name of the Lord; and had a form of blessing prescribed them; which they were to use, and did use on that occasion, Deut. xxi. 5. Numb. vi. 23—26. Indeed, the blessing of the priests was only prayerwise; they could not confer a blessing, only prayed for one; yet when they did, the Lord promised to give one, ver. 27. and some think Christ's blessing his people is only a species or branch of his intercession; though Christ does not only intercede for blessings for his people, but he actually confers them; and whether this is to be considered as a branch of Christ's intercession; which is made, not in a supplicant, but in an authoritative manner, as has been shown; or whether as a distinct part of Christ's priestly office; I shall treat of it particularly and separately, and much in the same method as the other parts have been treated of; by showing,

I. That Christ was to bless his people; this was promised and prophesied concerning him, and was prefigured in types of him.

First, It was promised to Abraham, that in his *seed all the nations of the earth should be blessed,* Gen. xxii. and xviii. and which was renewed to Isaac, Gen. xxvi. 4. and also again to Jacob, Gen. xxviii. 14. and which contains the sum of the gospel preached unto Abraham; for by *seed* is meant, not his numerous natural seed, descending from him by ordinary generation, in successive periods of time; but his single, special, and principal seed, the Messiah, who was to spring from him, Gal. iii. 8, 16. and by *all nations* are meant some of all nations, the chosen vessels, who consist both of Jews and Gentiles, the redeemed of the Lamb, who are by him redeemed out of every kindred, tongue, people, and nation; and are effectually called, by the Spirit and grace of God, out of the world, and the nations of it, in the several periods of time, and so are all blessed, both in time and to eternity; and on this account Christ is truly called, *the desire of all nations,* Haggai. ii. 7. whose coming as an Highpriest with good things being promised, might be expected and desired by them; and those may be said not only to be

---

[1] Advocatus appellatur, etiamsi nihil dicat, neque agat, sed qui tantum paratus sit defendere, Vallæ Elegantiar. 1. 4. c. 12.

blessed in him as their representative, as they are, both in eternity and in time, Eph. i. 3, 4. and ii. 5, 6. and not only *through him*, all the blessings of goodness being put into his hands for them; and so they come to them, through his hands, and through the efficacy of his blood, as redemption, pardon, grace, and eternal life, Eph. i. 7. Acts xiii. 38. Tit. iii. 6. Rom. vi. 23. but they are blessed by him as it is his own act and deed; and so the apostle interprets and explains the phrase; *In thy seed shall all the kindreds of the earth be blessed; unto you first, God having raised up his Son Jesus, sent him to bless you, in turning away every one of you, from his iniquities*, Acts iii. 25, 26.

Secondly, Christ's blessing his people was prefigured in Melchizedek, the type of him, and of whose order he was. This illustrious person met Abraham returning from the slaughter of the kings, *and blessed him, and said, Blessed be Abraham of the most high God, possessor of heaven and earth*, Gen. xiv. 19. that is, may Abraham be blessed of God with both temporal and spiritual blessings, which he who is Lord of both worlds is able to bestow upon him: and on this benediction the apostle observes that Melchizedek, who *received tithes from Abraham, blessed him who had the promises;* not only of a Son to be his heir, and of the land of Canaan for his seed, but of the Messiah, and of the heavenly inheritance; from whence he infers the greatness, the excellency, and the superiority of Melchizedek, as a type of Christ, Heb. vii. 6, 7. The priests under the law, one part of whose work and office it was to bless the people, and who did bless them, were types and figures of Christ in that action, and foreshowed what he was to do when he came, Lev. ix. 22. Psalm cxviii. 26.

II. Christ has blessed his people, does bless them, and will continue to bless them: he blessed them under the Old Testament; he appeared in an human form to Jacob, and wrestled with him; nor would Jacob let him go except he blessed him; and he had power with him, and prevailed, and got the blessing; as appears by the name of Israel he gave him; and having such an experience of his ability to bless, he addressed him for a blessing on his grandchildren, saying, *The angel which redeemed me from all evil, bless the lads;* meaning Christ the uncreated Angel, the Angel of God's presence, the Angel of the covenant, who had protected him from all evil throughout his life, and particularly from the evil he feared from his brother Esau; when he appeared to him, and for him, and blessed him, as before observed, Gen. xxxii. 24—29. and xlviii. 16. and as Christ came in the fulness of time, an Highpriest of good things; he blesses his people with them, of which his blessing his disciples is a specimen; and which was done by him after he had offered himself a sacrifice, and was risen from the dead, and before his ascension to heaven; *he lift up his hands and blessed them: and it came to pass while he blessed them he was parted from them*, Luke xxiv. 50, 51.

First, Observe the qualifications of Christ to bless his people, his fitness, ability, and sufficiency for such a work.

1. As he is God, or a divine person, he must be able to bless; God is blessed; this is an epithet of his; blessedness is a perfection of Deity; it is a principal one; yea, all his perfections are comprehended in it, and serve to complete it; and hence he is the fountain of all blessedness to his creatures. Now Christ is *over all, God blessed for ever*, Rom. ix. 5. all the fulness of the Godhead is in him; all that the Father hath are his, he is the Lord God omnipotent, *and able to do exceeding abundantly above all that we ask or think*, Eph. iii. 20. he is El-Shaddai, God all-sufficient; as such he is the Creator of all things; nothing is made without him, but all by him and for him; and he has all the blessings of nature in his hands to dispose of; the earth is his, and the fulness thereof, and he can give it to whom and when he pleases: as such he is the God of providence; and as such jointly works in providence with his divine Father; and has all providential goodness to bless men with; as such he is the God of all grace, the God of his people, their sun and shield, who gives grace and glory; and his grace is sufficient for them; every good and perfect gift of grace comes from him; and grace and peace are equally prayed and wished for from him as from the Father; as in all the epistles.

2. Christ, as Mediator, has a fitness, ability, and sufficiency to bless his people; as such, God has *made him most blessed for evermore*, and *prevented him with the blessings of goodness*, Psalm xxi. 3, 6. by laying up in him the blessings of the covenant of grace, to communicate to his people; by first giving all the blessings of grace to him, and then to them in him.

As God, he has a natural claim and right to all blessedness; he has it to the full, infinitely, in right of nature; it is independent of, and underived from another: but as Mediator, he is *made* blessed by the will and pleasure of his Father; the blessings of grace and goodness are given unto him; it is his Father's good pleasure, that all the fulness of grace should dwell in him; out of which, his people, in all ages, receive grace for grace; and all their spiritual wants are supplied from thence; nor can they want any good thing; his grace is sufficient for them, and he has enough to dispense unto them. Besides, as Mediator, he has obtained all blessings for them, in a way consistent with all the perfections of God, to bestow them on them. Who can doubt of his abilities to bless his people with deliverance from sin, Satan, the law, its curses and condemnation, and from ruin and destruction; since he has obtained *eternal redemption* for them? or with a justifying righteousness; since, as he came to bring in everlasting righteousness, he is become the end of the law for righteousness to every one that believes? or with spiritual peace, he has promised to give, since he has made peace by the blood of his cross? or with salvation, and all things appertaining to it; since he is become the author of eternal salvation, and is able to save to the uttermost all that come unto God by him?

Secondly, The persons who are blessed by Christ; though *all nations* of the earth are said to be blessed in him, and by him; yet not every individual of all nations; for at the same time that this was promised to Abraham, God declared that he would curse them that cursed him; and so all such that curse his people, and blaspheme his name; yea, there are some whose very blessings are cursed, as well as their persons; and, indeed, all that are of the works of the law, or seek for justification by them, are cursed, *that continue not in all things written in the book of the law to do them*, Gal. iii. 10. which no man does; and therefore is cursed by that very law by which he seeks for justification. To which may be added, that all graceless and Christless sinners, instead of being blessed by Christ, will, at the last day, be bid to depart from him, saying, *Depart from me, ye cursed*, Matt. xxv. 41. But,

1. All that are blessed of the Father are blessed by Christ; God, as the God and Father of Christ, blessed his people with all spiritual blessings in him; and those that are blessed in him are blessed by him; the same the Father blesses, the Son does also; to whom he will say at the great day, *Come, ye blessed of my Father*, Eph. i. 3. Matt. xxv. 34.——2. All that are chosen of God in Christ are blessed by him; for they are blessed with all spiritual blessings according as they are chosen in him; their election of God is the standard, rule, and measure, of all after blessings; that stands at the front of them and secures all the rest; *whom he did predestinate, them he also called, &c.* Rom. viii. 30. The elect of God are the objects of all the blessings of grace which arise from Christ's death, resurrection, session at the right-hand of God, and his intercession there; or otherwise there would be no strength nor force in the triumphant challenge of the apostle, ver. 33, 34.——3. All that are given to Christ by the Father are blessed by him; for these he prays for blessings, on these he bestows them; he manifests the name of God unto them, his favour and grace, and the blessings of it; his gospel, and the privileges belonging to it; he confers grace on them, keeps them by his power, and gives unto them eternal life, John xvii. 2, 6, 8, 9, 11, 12, 24.—— 4. All the covenant-ones are blessed by Christ; all that are in covenant have a right to the blessings of it, and they are blessed with it; God is their covenant-God, and happy are they whose God he is; God, even their own God, will bless them. The covenant of grace is ordered in all things and sure; and Christ, the mediator of it, in whose hands they are, gives them the sure mercies of David.——5. All the spiritual Israel of God, the whole Israel of God, consisting both of Jews and Gentiles, are blessed by Christ; what is said of literal Israel, *Happy art thou, O Israel, ——O people saved by the Lord*, Deut. xxxiii. 29. is true of mystic Israel, or the elect of God among all nations; that Israel whom God has chosen, and Christ has redeemed and called by name; these are the seed of Israel that are justified in Christ, and saved in the Lord with an everlasting salvation, Psalm cxxxv. 4. Isa. xliii. 1. and xlv. 17, 25.

Thirdly, The blessings Christ blesses his people with, some of which are as follow.——1. With a justifying righteousness; this is a great blessing: David describes *The blessedness of the man to whom God imputeth righteousness without* works, Rom. iv. 6. and that is the righteousness of Christ; and this Christ has not only wrought out, and brought in, but he brings it near to his people; he puts it upon them, he clothes and covers them with it; so that they are justified from all their sins, and secured from condemnation and death, and are saved from wrath to come; their persons and services are acceptable unto God; and it is well with them at all times, in life, in death, and at the last judgment.——2. With the pardon of their sins, which is another great blessing: *Blessed is the man whose transgression is forgiven,* Psalm xxxii. 1. and Christ has not only shed his blood to obtain remission of sins for his people, but through the ministry of his gospel, and by his Spirit and grace he applies it to them, Matt. ix. 2. and which fills their hearts with joy and gladness.——3. Christ blesses his people with the adoption of children; they are not only predestinated of God unto it by him, and he has redeemed them that they might receive it, but he himself bestows it on them; John i. 12.——4. Those are blessed by Christ with regeneration and conversion by his Spirit and grace through the ministration of his gospel; this is the instance mentioned by the apostle, of Christ's blessing his people, for whose sake he was raised up, and to whom sent, Acts iii. 26. His blessing then lay in this, in turning them from sin and self; and in turning them to himself, to his blood, righteousness, and sacrifice, for peace, pardon, justification, and eternal salvation.——5. The same persons are blessed by Christ with the Spirit, which he has received without measure; and with the graces thereof in an abundant manner, at first conversion, which are richly shed on them, through Christ, their Saviour; and by whom they are blessed with all after supplies of grace, till he brings them to glory.——6. The Lord blesses his people with peace, Psalm xxix. 11. which flows from his peace-speaking blood, his perfect righteousness, and atoning sacrifice; with peace which passeth all understanding; and in what the world can neither give nor take away.——7. He blesses them with the gospel, the ordinances of it, and the privileges of his house. He favours them with the joyful sound, with the good-news and glad-tidings of his gospel: he satisfies them with the goodness and fatness of his house; he gives them a place, and a name in it, better than that of sons and daughters; he makes them fellow-citizens with the saints, and takes them into the household of God, and causes them to partake of every blessing and privilege of the children of God.——8. And lastly, Christ blesses his people with eternal life and happiness; he not only intercedes for them that they may be with him where he is, and behold his glory; and not only is gone beforehand, to prepare mansions of glory for them; but, according to his promise, will come and take them to himself, and introduce them into his kingdom and glory, where they shall be for ever with him.

Fourthly, The nature and excellencies of these blessings.——1. They are covenant-blessings; which are laid up and secured in the covenant of grace, ordered in all things and sure; and which are very comprehensive, and include both grace and glory.——2. They are spiritual blessings, Eph. i. 2. such as are of a spiritual nature, relating to the spiritual welfare of men, and suited to spiritual men; and for the good of their souls or spirits; and are what the Spirit of God takes, shews, and applies unto them.——3. They are solid and substantial ones; blessings indeed, such as Jabez prayed for; saying, *O that thou wouldst bless me indeed!* 1 Chron. iv. 10. Earthly and temporal blessings, as riches and honours, are things that are not, nonentities, comparatively speaking, have no solidity and substance in them; but the blessings of Christ, both of grace and glory, have substance in them; faith is the *substance* of things hoped for; and heaven is a more *enduring substance;* which wisdom, or Christ, causes his people to inherit, Heb. xi. 1. and x. 34. Prov. viii. 21. and xxiii. 5.——4. They are irreversible blessings; the blessing with which Isaac blessed Jacob was confirmed by him with a resolution not to alter it: and the blessing Balaam was commanded to bless Israel with, was what he could not reverse, whatever good-will he had to it: but the blessings of grace by Christ, are such as God never repents of, revokes, or reverses; these are *the gifts and calling of God* to grace and glory, which *are without repentance,* Rom. xi. 29.——5. These blessings are eternal; whatever is done in this way of Christ's blessing his people *is for ever,* Eccles. iii. 14. Christ's righteousness is an everlasting righteousness; pardon of sin ever remains; once a child of God, always so; no more a servant, but a son, an heir of God, and a joint-heir of Christ; so every blessing of grace, with glory and happiness, in the world to come.

CHAP. XIII.

OF THE KINGLY OFFICE OF CHRIST.

THE prophetic and priestly offices of Christ having been considered; the kingly office of Christ is next to be treated of. Christ is king in a twofold sense: he is a king by nature; as he is God, he is God over all; as the Son of God, he is heir of all things; as he is God the Creator, he has a right of dominion over all his creatures: and he is king by office, as he is mediator; and accordingly he has a twofold kingdom, the one natural, essential, universal, and common to him with the other divine persons; the kingdom of nature and providence is his, what he has a natural right unto, and claim upon; it is essential to him as God; dominion and fear are with him; it is universal, it reaches to all creatures visible or invisible, to all in heaven, earth, and hell; it is common to the three divine persons, Father, Son, and Spirit, who are joint-creators of all the creatures, and have a joint rule, government, and dominion over them; and as Christ is the creator of all, nothing that is made being made without him, but all things by him, he has a right to rule over them. This kingdom of his extends to angels, good and bad; he is the head of all principality and power; of the good angels, he is their creator, lord and king, from whom all worship, homage, and obedience are due unto him; and who are at his command to do his will and pleasure; and whom he employs as ministering spirits in nature, providence, and grace, as he pleases: and the evil angels, though they have left their first estate, cast off their allegiance to him, and rebelled against him, yet whether they will or no they are obliged to be subject to him; and even when he was manifest in the flesh, they trembled at him, and were obliged to quit the possession of the bodies of men at his command, and could do nothing without his leave. Men also, good and bad, are under the government of Christ as God, who is Lord of all; he not only is king of saints, who willingly become subject to him; but even those who are sons of Belial, without a yoke, who have cast off the yoke, and will not have him to reign over them; whether they will or no, they are obliged to yield unto him; over whom he rules with a rod of iron, and will break them in pieces as a potter's vessel; so easy, so inevitable, and so irreparable is their ruin and everlasting destruction by him. This his kingdom rules over all men, of all ranks and degrees, the highest and the greatest; he is King of kings, and Lord of lords; he sets them up and puts them down at his pleasure; by him they reign, and to him they are accountable. But besides this, there is another kingdom that belongs to Christ as God-man and Mediator; this is a special, limited kingdom; this concerns only the elect of God, and others only as they may have to do with them, even their enemies; the subjects of this kingdom are those who are chosen, redeemed, and called from among men by the grace of God, and bear the name of saints; hence the title and character of Christ with respect to them is *king of saints;* this kingdom and government of his is what is put into his hands to dispense and administer, and may be called a dispensatory, delegated government; what is given him by his Father, and he has received authority from him to exercise, and for which he is accountable to him; and when the number of his elect are completed in effectual vocation, he will deliver up the kingdom to the Father, perfect and entire, that God may be all in all. And this is the kingly office of Christ, now to be treated of; and which will be done much in the same manner the other offices have been treated of.

I. I shall shew that Christ was to be a king; as appears by the designation of his Father, in his purposes, council, and covenant; by the types and figures of him; and by the prophecies concerning him.

1. That he was to be a king, appears by the designation and appointment of him by his Father to this office; *I have set my king upon my holy hill of Zion*, says Jehovah, Psalm ii. 6. that is, he had set up Christ his Son, in his eternal purposes, to be king over his church and people; and therefore calls him his king, because of his choosing, appointing, and setting up. And as he appointed him to be a king, he appointed a kingdom to him; which is observed by Christ; *I appoint unto you a kingdom, as my Father hath appointed unto me,* Luke xxii. 29. In the council and covenant of grace, Christ was called to take upon him this office, *feed the flock of slaughter,* the church, subject to the persecutions of men; and the act of feeding

them, designs the rule and government, care and protection of the people of God; in allusion to shepherds, by which name kings and rulers are sometimes called: to which Christ assented and agreed; saying, *I will feed the flock of slaughter*, take the care and government of them, Zech. xi. 4, 7. upon which he was invested with the office of a king, and was considered as such; *Unto the Son he saith, Thy throne, O God, is for ever and ever*, Heb. i. 8.

2. It appears from the types and figures of Christ, in his kingly office. Melchizedek was a type of him; not only in his priestly office, of whose order Christ was; but in his kingly office; both offices meeting in him, as they do in Christ, who is a priest upon his throne; from his quality as a king he had his name Melchizedek, king of righteousness, or righteous king; and such an one is Christ, a king that reigns in righteousness; and from the place and seat of his government, king of Salem; that is, king of peace; agreeable to which, one of Christ's titles belonging to him, in his kingly office, is, prince of peace; see Heb. vii. 1. Isa. ix. 6. David was an eminent type of Christ in his kingly office; for his wisdom and military skill, his courage and valour, his wars and victories, and the equity and justice of his government; hence Christ, his antitype, is often, with respect to the Jews, in the latter days, called David their king, whom they shall seek and serve; and who shall be king over them, Jer. xxx. 9. Ezek. xxxiii. 23. and xxxvii. 24. Hos. iii. 5. Solomon also was a type of Christ as king; hence Christ, in *the Song of Songs*, is frequently called Solomon, and king Solomon, Cant. iii. 7, 9, 11. and viii. 11, 12. because of his great wisdom, his immense riches, the largeness of his kingdom, and the peaceableness of it; in all which he is exceeded by Christ; and who, speaking of himself, says, *a Greater than Solomon is here*, Matt. xii. 42.

3. This still more fully appears, that Christ was to be a King, by the prophecies concerning him, in this respect; as in the very first promise or prophecy of him, Gen. iii. 15. that *the Seed of the woman*, meaning Christ, should bruise the *serpent's head;* that is, destroy the devil, and all his works; which is an act of Christ's kingly power, and is expressive of him as a victorious prince, and triumphant conqueror over all his and his people's enemies. Balaam foretold, that *there should come a Star out of Jacob, and a Sceptre*, that is, a Sceptrebearer, a King, should *rise out of Israel,* Numb. xxiv. 17. which prophecy, some way or other, coming to the knowledge of the magi, or wise-men in the East, upon the appearance of a new star, led them to take a journey into Judea, to inquire after the birth of the King of the Jews, where he was born. In the famous prophecy of Isaiah, concerning Christ, chap. ix. 6, 7. it is said, that *the government should be upon his shoulders;* one of his titles be, *the Prince of peace;* and that of his government, and the peace of it, there should be no end; as well as it should be ordered and established with justice and judgment: and to the same purpose is another prophecy in Jeremiah, chap. xxiii. 5, 6. of the Messiah, the Man the Branch, it is said, *And a King shall reign and prosper, and shall execute judgment and justice in the earth; and this is his name whereby he shall be called,* The Lord our righteousness: and there can be no doubt but Christ is here meant; as well as in that known prophecy of the place of his birth, Bethlehem Ephratah; of which it is said, *Out of thee shall he come forth unto me, that is to be Ruler in Israel*, the King of Israel, as Christ is sometimes called, Mic. v. 2. To which may be added, another prophecy of Christ, as King, and which was fulfilled in him; *Rejoice greatly, O daughter of Zion ——behold thy King cometh unto thee,* Zech. ix. 9. see Matt. xxi. 4, 5. yea, the angel that brought the news to the Virgin Mary, of Christ's conception and incarnation, foretold unto her, that this her Son should be *great, and be called the Son of the Highest;* and that *the Lord God would give unto him the throne of his father David;* and that he should *reign over the house of Jacob for ever; and of his kingdom there should be no end,* Luke i. 32, 33.

II. I proceed to shew, that Christ is a King; as it was decreed and determined he should be, and according to the types of him, and prophecies concerning him. And,

1. Christ was a King before his incarnation, during the old testament dispensation. He was King over the people of Israel; not as a body politic; though their civil government was a theocracy; but as a church, a kingdom of priests, or a royal priesthood; and he is the Angel that was with them, the church in the wilderness, which spoke to Moses on mount Sinai; from whose right-hand went the fiery law, the oracles of God; for the rule,

government, and instruction of that people: he is the Angel that went before them, to guide and direct them, and to rule and govern them, whose voice they were to obey: he appeared to Joshua, with a drawn sword in his hand, and declared himself to be the Captain of the Lord's hosts, to fight their battles for them, and settle them in the land of Canaan. David speaks of him as a King in the forty-fifth Psalm, and represents him as a very amiable Person, grace being poured into his lips, and he fairer than the children of men; as a majestic and victorious Prince, whose queen stands at his right-hand, in gold of Ophir, his church, who is called upon to worship him, to yield homage and subjection to him; because he is her Lord and King; and as such he is acknowledged by the church in the times of Isaiah; *The Lord is our Judge; the Lord is our Lawgiver; the Lord is our King*, Isa. xxxiii. 22. and xxvi. 13.

2. Christ was King in his state of incarnation; he was born a King, as the wise-men understood it he was, by the prophecy of him, and by the star that appeared, that guided them to come and worship him as such. The angel that brought the news of his birth to the shepherds, declared, that that day was born a Saviour, Christ the Lord, Head and King of his church; agreeable to the prophecy of him by Isaiah, that the Child born, and Son given, would have the government on his shoulders, and be the Prince of peace; and Christ himself acknowledges as much, when he was asked by Pilate, whether he was a King? he answered in a manner which implied it, and gave assent unto it; though at the same time, he declared his kingdom was not of this world, but of a spiritual nature, John xviii. 36, 37. He began his ministry with giving notice, that the *kingdom of heaven was at hand;* that is, his own kingdom, which was going to take place, with some evidence of it; and he assures the Jews, that the kingdom of God was then within them, or among them; though it came not with the observation of the vulgar; nor with outward shew, pomp, and splendour, like that of an earthly king, Matt. iv. 17. Luke xvii. 20, 21. and Christ was known, and owned by some, as a King, though not by many: Nathanael made the following noble confession of faith in him, respecting his person and office, upon a conviction of his being the omniscient God; *Rabbi, thou art the Son of God! thou art the King of Israel!* John i. 49. When Christ entered into Jerusalem, in a very public manner, whereby was fulfilled the prophecy of him as a King, Zech. ix. 9. not only the children cried, Hosanna to the Son of David! expressive of his royal character and dignity; but the disciples, in so many words, said, *Blessed be the King, that cometh in the name of the Lord!* Matt. xxi. 4, 5, 9. Luke xix. 38. Moreover, Christ, in the days of his flesh on earth, received authority from his divine Father, to execute judgment; that is, to exercise his kingly office in equity and justice; and this before his sufferings and death; and had all things requisite to it, delivered unto him by his Father, John v. 22, 27. Matt. xi. 27. and after his resurrection from the dead, and before his ascension to heaven, he declared, that *all power was given him in heaven and in earth;* in virtue of which, he appointed ordinances, renewed the commission of his disciples to administer them, promising his presence with them, and their successors, to the end of the world, Matt. xxviii. 18, 19, 20. All which shews how false the notion of the Socinians is, that Christ was no King, nor did he exercise his kingly office before his ascension to heaven. It is true, indeed,

3. That upon his ascension to heaven, he *was made both Lord and Christ,* Acts ii. 36. not but that he was both Lord and Christ before, of which there was evidence; but then he was declared to be so, and made more manifest as such; then he was exalted as a Prince, as well as a Saviour, and highly exalted, and had a name given him above every name; and angels, authorities, and powers, were made subject to him. He then received the promise of the Spirit, and his gifts from the Father, which he plentifully bestowed upon his apostles; whom he sent forth into all the world, preaching his gospel with great success, and causing them to triumph in him in every place where they came; and so increased and enlarged his kingdom: he went forth by them with his bow and arrows, conquering and to conquer, making the arrows of his word sharp in the hearts of his enemies, whereby they were made to submit unto him; sending forth the rod of his strength out of Zion, the gospel, the power of God unto salvation; he made multitudes willing in the day of his power on them, to be subject to him; whereby his kingdom and interest were

greatly strengthened in the world; and from small beginnings, his kingdom being at first but like a grain of mustard-seed, became very flourishing and populous: and in this way more or less, Christ has been exercising his kingly office in the world; which, though sometimes it has been in great obscurity, yet will more gloriously appear in the latter day, in that remarkable period of time which may be properly called, *the spiritual reign of Christ;* when he shall take to himself his great power and reign; not begin to take it, nor begin to reign; but shall take it and exert it in a more conspicuous manner; and will reign before his ancients gloriously; when the kingdoms of this world shall become his, and he shall be King over all the earth; and there shall be one Lord, and his name one; and more especially when the kingly office of Christ shall appear in its full glory, in his *personal reign* on earth a thousand years; of which two species of his kingly office, I shall treat separately and distinctly, in their proper place; and at present shall only observe,

4. That all the rites and ceremonies used at the inauguration of kings, and their *regalia,* are to be found with Christ. Were kings anointed? as Saul, David, and Solomon were, so was Christ, from whence he has his name, Messiah; he whose throne is for ever and ever, is anointed with the oil of gladness above his fellows; that is, with the gifts and graces of the holy Spirit without measure; as he more eminently was, upon his ascension to heaven, when he was made or declared, Lord and Christ; and, indeed, because of this ceremony used at the instalment of kings into their office, the original investiture of Christ with the kingly office is expressed by it; *I have set,* or as in the Hebrew text, *I have anointed my King upon my holy hill of Zion,* Psalm ii. 6. see Psalm xlv. 6, 7. Were kings crowned at the time of their inauguration? so was Christ at his ascension to heaven; he was then *crowned with glory and honour;* his Father set *a crown of pure gold on his head;* not a material one; the phrase is only expressive of the royal grandeur and dignity conferred upon him: his mother, the church, is also said to crown him; and so does every believer set the crown on his head, when, rejecting all self-confidence, and subjection to others, they ascribe their whole salvation to him,

and submit to him, as King of saints; and he, as a mighty Warrior, and triumphant Conqueror, is represented as having many crowns on his head, as emblematical of the many great and glorious victories he has obtained over all his, and the enemies of his people, Heb. ii. 9. Psalm xxi. 3. Cant. iii. 11. Rev. xix. 12. Do kings sometimes sit on thrones when in state? Isaiah, in vision, saw the Lord sitting on a throne, high and lifted up, when he saw the glory of Christ, and spake of him: and when our Lord had overcome all his enemies, he sat down with his Father on his throne, as he makes every overcomer sit down with him on his throne; and this throne of his is for ever and ever: and when he comes to judge the world, he will sit on a great white throne; an emblem of his greatness, purity, and justice, in discharging this part of his kingly office, judging quick and dead, Isa. vi. 1. Psalm xlv. 6. Rev. iii. 21. and xx. 11. Do kings sometimes hold sceptres in their hands, as an ensign of their royalty? so does Christ; his sceptre is a *sceptre of righteousness;* he reigns in righteousness; he has a golden sceptre of clemency, grace, and mercy, which he holds forth towards his own people, his faithful subjects; and he has an iron one, with which he rules his enemies; see Psalm xlv. 6. and ii. 9. Do kings sometimes appear in robes of majesty and state? Christ is arrayed with majesty itself; *The Lord reigneth, he is clothed with majesty,* Psalm xciii. 1. and so he is apparelled, as now set down on the right-hand of the throne of the Majesty in the heavens; of which his transfiguration on the mountain was an emblem, when his face did shine as the sun, and his raiment was white as the light, Heb. viii. 1. Matt. xvii. 2.

III. Having shewn that Christ was to be a King, and is one; I shall next consider the exercise and administration of the kingly office by him; and observe,

First, His qualifications for it. David, who well knew what was requisite to a civil ruler, or governor, says, *He that ruleth over men, must be just, ruling in the fear of God;* and this he said with a view to the Messiah, as appears by what follows, 2 Sam. xxiii. 3, 4. and with whom these characters fully agree; he is the righteous Branch, raised up to David; and sits upon his throne, and establishes it with judgment and justice; a king that

CHAP. XIII. OF THE KINGLY OFFICE OF CHRIST.

reigns in righteousness, and governs according to the rules of justice and equity; who with righteousness judges, and reproves with equity; the girdle of whose loins is righteousness, and faithfulness the girdle of his reins, all the while he is executing his kingly office; his sceptre is a sceptre of righteousness; and his throne is established by it; and one of the characters of Zion's King, by which he is described, is just, as well as lowly; see Jer. xxiii. 5, 6. Isa. ix. 7. and xi. 4, 5. Psalm xlv. 6. Zech. ix. 9. And the other character, *ruling in the fear of God*, is found in him; on whom the Spirit of the fear of the Lord rests, and makes him of quick understanding in the fear of the Lord, so that he judges impartially; not through favour and affection to any, nor according to the outward appearance; but with true judgment, Isa. xi. 2, 3. and a king should be as wise as an angel of God, to know all things appertaining to civil government, as the woman of Tekoah said David was; even to know and to be able to penetrate into the designs of his enemies, to guard against them, to provide for the safety and welfare of his subjects: and such is David's Son and Antitype, the Messiah; on whom rests *the Spirit of wisdom and understanding, of counsel and of knowledge;* and who has all the treasures of wisdom and knowledge, and all that wisdom by which kings reign, and princes decree judgment, is from him; to which may be added, *the Spirit of might* rests upon him, Isa. xi. 2. he has power and authority to execute judgment, to enforce his laws, and command obedience from his subjects; all power in heaven and on earth is given to him, and which he exercises; yea, he is the Lord God omnipotent; and as such reigns, Matt. xxviii. 18. Rev. xix. 6. and how capable therefore, on all accounts, must he be to exercise his kingly office? The next enquiry is,

Secondly, Who are his subjects? a king is a relative term, and connects subjects: a king without subjects, is no king. The natural and essential kingdom of Christ, as God, reaches to all creatures; as has been observed; *His kingdom ruleth over all*, Psalm ciii. 19. but his kingdom, as Mediator, is special and limited, and is over a certain number of men; who go under the names of Israel, the house of Jacob, the holy hill of Zion, and are called saints; hence Christ is said to be *King of Israel;* to reign over *the house of Jacob;* to be set King upon *the holy hill of Zion;* and to be *King of saints*, John i. 49. Luke i. 33. Psalm ii. 6. Rev. xv. 3. and by Israel, and the house of Jacob, are not meant the people of the Jews, as a body politic, of whom Christ was never king in such a sense; nor carnal Israel, or Israel according to the flesh, especially the unbelieving part of them, who would not have him to reign over them, in a spiritual sense; nor only that part of them called the election of grace among them; the lost sheep of the house of Israel Christ came to seek and save, and so to rule over, protect, and keep; but the whole spiritual Israel of God, consisting both of Jews and Gentiles; even that Israel God has chose for his special and peculiar people, among all nations; whom Christ has redeemed by his blood, out of every kindred, tongue, and people; and whom, by his Spirit, he effectually calls, through grace; and who are saved in him, with an everlasting salvation: and these are meant by the holy hill of Zion, over which he is set, appointed, and anointed King; even all those whom God has loved with an everlasting love, and chosen in Christ his Son, and who are sanctified and made holy by his Spirit and grace; and are brought to make an open profession of his name, and become members of his visible church, and are immoveable in grace and holiness; for all which they are compared to mount Zion, the object of God's love and choice, a hill visible, holy, and immoveable: and to these Christ stands in the relation, and bears the office of a King; and they are his voluntary subjects; and who say of him and to him, *Just and true are thy ways, thou King of saints!* Rev. xv. 3. the church of God is Christ's kingdom, and the members of it his subjects.

Thirdly, The form and manner of Christ's executing his kingly office; which is done,——1*st*, Externally, by the ministry of the word, and administration of ordinances; and in the exercise of discipline in his church, which is his kingdom. And,——2*dly*, Internally, by his Spirit and grace, in the hearts of his people; and by his power with respect to their enemies.

1*st*, Externally, by the word and ordinances, and church-discipline.——1. By the ministry of the word; which is his sceptre he holds forth, and by which he invites his people to come and submit to him; and by which he rules and governs them when come; it is the rod of his strength he sends out of Zion, and which is the power of God unto salvation to them that believe: it is signified by the weapons of warfare, the sword of the Spirit, the bow and arrows with which Christ rides forth, conquering and to conquer; with which he smites the hearts of his people, while enemies to him, and causes them to fall under him, and be subject to him; it is the rule and standard of their faith and practice, he sets before them, shewing them what they are to believe concerning him, and what is their duty in obedience to him; it is the *magna charta* which contains all their privileges and immunities he grants them; and which he, as their King, inviolably maintains; and it is according to this his word, that he will execute that branch of his kingly office, judging the world in righteousness at the last day.

2. By the administration of ordinances; as baptism: Christ, in virtue of that power in heaven and earth, which he received as King of saints, issued out a command, and gave a commission to his apostles, as to preach the gospel, so to baptize, such as are taught by it, in the name of the three divine Persons; and directed that all such who become members of his visible church, the subjects of his kingdom, should first submit to this ordinance of his; as the instance of the first converts after the commission given shews; who were first baptized, and then added to the church: this is part of that yoke of Christ's kingdom, which is easy; and one of those commandments of his, which are not grievous. The Lord's Supper is another of the ordinances kept by the church at Corinth, as delivered to them; for which the apostle commends them; the account of which he had from Christ himself, and delivered to them; and which he suggests was to be observed in his churches, and throughout his kingdom, to the end of the world. Public prayer in the house of God, is another appointment in Christ's kingdom, the church; which is distinct from the duty of private prayer, in private meetings, and in the family, and closet; and is what goes along with the public ministry of the word; and is meant by what the apostles proposed to give themselves continually to; and which was attended to by the first christians, and continued in, and by which they are described, and for it commended; see Acts ii. 42. and iv. 31. and vi. 4. Singing of psalms, hymns, and spiritual songs, in a public manner, in the churches, is another ordinance of Christ, enjoined them, Eph. v. 19. Col. iii. 16. and in doing which, they express their joy and gladness, in Zion's King, Psalm cxlix. 2.

3. In the exercise of church-discipline; about which Christ, as King in his church, has given orders and directions; in case of private offences, the rules how to proceed, are in Matt. xviii. 15—18. In case of public, scandalous sins, which bring a public disgrace on religion, and the church; the delinquents are to be rebuked before all in a public manner, and rejected from the communion of the church, 1 Tim. v. 20. In case of immoralities and disorderly walking, such are to be withdrawn from, till repentance is given to satisfaction; and in case of false doctrines, and heretical opinions, such that hold them, are not only to be rebuked sharply, in a ministerial way, that they may be sound in the faith; but being incorrigible, are to be cut off from the communion of the church, Tit. i. 13. and iii. 10.

4. For the execution and due performance of all this, the ministry of the word, administration of ordinances, and exercise of church-discipline, Christ has appointed officers in his church and kingdom; whom he qualifies and empowers for such purposes; who have a rule and government under Christ, and over the churches, to see his laws and rules carried into execution; and who are to be known, owned, and acknowledged, as having rule over the churches; and to be submitted to, and obeyed by them, so far as they act according to the laws of Christ, Eph. iv. 10, 11, 12. 1 Thess. v. 12. Heb. xiii. 7, 17.

2dly, The kingly office of Christ is exercised internally, by his Spirit and grace in the hearts of his people, and by his power, with respect to their enemies; and which chiefly lies in the conversion of his people; in the protection of them from their enemies; and in the utter abolition and destruction of them.

1. In the conversion of his people; which is no other than a rescue of them out of the hands of those who have usurped a dominion over them. Whilst unregenerate, they are in a state of enmity to Christ, and in open rebellion against him; they who are reconciled by him, are not only enemies in their minds, by wicked works, but enmity itself, whilst their

minds remain carnal; and such they were when reconciled to God, by the death of Christ; and so they continue until the enmity is slain, by his powerful grace in them; by which the arrows of his word are made sharp in them; and thereby they are conquered, and fall under him. Whilst in a state of nature, other lords have dominion over them, sin, Satan, and the world; sin reigns in their mortal bodies, and they yield their members instruments of unrighteousness! and are servants and slaves to sin, even unto death; for it reigns in them to death; and though its reign is so severe and rigorous, yet they yield a ready obedience to it; *We ourselves,* says the apostle, *were foolish and disobedient,* disobedient to God, and disobedient to Christ, *serving divers lusts and pleasures.* Satan, the prince of the power of the air, works in them, whilst they are the children of disobedience; and they have their conversation according to him, and according to the course of the world, whilst in such a state; and live according to the will of men, and not according to the will of God, Isa. xxvi. 13. Tit. iii. 3. Eph. ii. 2, 3. Satan particularly, the god of this world, has power over them, and leads them captive at his will, until the prey is taken from the mighty, and the lawful captive is delivered; he is the strong man armed, that keeps the palace and goods in peace, till a stronger than he comes; who is Christ, the King of glory, who causes the everlasting doors of men's hearts to lift up, and let him in, when he enters, binds the strong man armed, dispossesses him, and spoils his armour, wherein he trusted; sets up a throne of grace in the heart, where he himself sits and reigns, having destroyed sin, and caused grace to reign, through righteousness; and will not suffer sin to have any more dominion there. By the power of his grace he makes those his people willing to submit to him, and serve him, and him only, disclaiming all other lords, Isa. xxvi. 13. and xxxiii. 22. Christ, as King in Zion, enacts laws, appoints ordinances, and gives out commands, which he enjoins his subjects to observe and obey; and those he writes, not on paper, nor on tables of stone, nor on monuments of brass, but upon the tables of the heart; and puts his Spirit within his people, to enable them to walk in his statutes, and to keep his judgments, and do them. Moreover, Christ being set up as an ensign to the people, they flock unto him, and enlist themselves under his banner, and become volunteers, in the day of his power, or when he musters his armies; and declare themselves willing to endure hardness, as good soldiers of Christ; to fight the Lord's battles, the good fight of faith, and against every enemy; when they are clad by him with the whole armour of God, and become more than conquerors, through their victorious Lord and King; by, and under whom, they abide as his faithful subjects and soldiers unto death.

2. Christ's kingly office is further exercised, in the protection and preservation of his people from their enemies; out of whose hands they are taken, and who attempt to reduce them to their former captivity and slavery; they are protected and preserved from sin: not from the indwelling and actings of it in them; but from its dominion and damning power; and the grace that is wrought in them is preserved, and its reigning power is continued and confirmed. Christ, as a Prince, as well as a Saviour, gives repentance to his people, attended with the manifestation and application of pardon of sin; and he not only gives this grace; but every other, faith, hope, and love: these are his royal bounties, and are principles of grace, wrought in the souls of his people; according to which, and by the influence of which, he rules and governs them; and these he preserves, that they are not lost; that their faith fail not; their hope remain, as an anchor, sure and stedfast; and their love continue; and the fear of God, put into them, abide; so that they shall never depart from him: he is able to keep them from falling, finally and totally, and he does keep them; they are in his hand, out of which none can pluck them; they are protected by him from Satan; not from his assaults and temptations, to which the most eminent saints are exposed; but from being destroyed by him, who goes about like a roaring lion, seeking whom he may devour, and would gladly devour them: but Christ is able to succour them, and does; and knows how to deliver them out of temptation, and does, in his time and way, and bruises Satan under their feet; so that, instead of being destroyed by him, he himself is destroyed by Christ: and they are protected from the world, its force and fury; he makes their wrath to praise him, and restrains the remainder of it. In short, he protects them from every enemy; and from the last enemy, death;

not from dying a corporal death, but from the sting of it; and from it as a penal evil; and from a spiritual death ever more taking place in them; and from an eternal death, by which they shall not be hurt, and which shall have no power over them.

3. Christ's kingly office appears to be exercised in the utter destruction of the said enemies of his people. He came to finish transgression, and make an end of sin; and he did it meritoriously, on the cross; where the old man was crucified, that the body of sin might be destroyed; and by his Spirit and grace he weakens the power of sin in conversion; and will never leave, till he has rooted out the very being of it in his people: he came to destroy Satan, and his works; and he has destroyed him; and spoiled his principalities and powers, on the cross; and rescued his people out of his hands, at conversion; and will not only bruise him under their feet shortly, but will bind him, and cast him into the bottomless pit for a thousand years; and after loosed from thence, will cast him into the lake which burns with fire and brimstone, where he will continue for ever. Christ has also overcome the world; so that it could not hinder him from doing the work he came about: and he gives his people that faith by which they overcome it also; and nothing they meet with in it, even tribulation, persecution, and every thing of that kind, shall not be able to separate them from Christ, from a profession of him, and love unto him; but they become more than conquerors over the world, through Christ that loved them; and who must reign till all enemies are put under his feet; and the last enemy that shall be destroyed is death: which will be destroyed at the resurrection; when mortal shall put on immortality, and corruption incorruption; and then that saying will be brought to pass, that *death is swallowed up in victory;* in a victory obtained by Christ over that and every other enemy, 1 Cor. xv. 25, 26, 54.

Fourthly, The properties of Christ's kingdom and government; shewing the nature and excellency of it.

1. It is spiritual; not carnal, earthly, and worldly: *My kingdom,* says Christ, *is not of this world,* John xviii. 36. Though it is in the world, it is not of it; its original is not from it; it is not founded on maxims of worldly policy; it is not established by worldly power, nor promoted and increased by worldly means, nor attended with worldly pomp and grandeur; *The kingdom of God,* that is, of Christ, *cometh not with observation,* with outward glory and splendour, Luke xvii. 20. The Jews, at the coming of Christ, having lost the notion of the spirituality of his kingdom, thought of nothing but an earthly and worldly one; and expected the Messiah as a temporal king, who would deliver them from the Roman yoke; and make them a free and flourishing people, as in the days of David and Solomon: and this was the general and national belief; the disciples and followers of Christ were possessed of it; as appears from the request of the mother of Zebedee's children, Matt. xx. 20, 21. and from the question of the apostles to Christ, even after his resurrection, Acts i. 6. But this notion was contrary to the prophecies of the Messiah; which represent him as poor, mean, and abject; a man of sorrows and griefs, despised of men; and should be treated ill, and be put to death, Isa. liii. 2, 3, 4, 8, 12. Zech. ix. 9. and not being able to reconcile these prophecies, with those which speak of him as exalted and glorious, they have feigned and expect two messiahs; the one they call the son of Ephraim, who shall make a poor figure, be unsuccessful, and shall be slain in the war of Gog and Magog; the other they call the son of David, who shall be prosperous, gain many victories, and shall live long; restore the Jews to their own land, and make them an happy people. But the true Messiah was neither to destroy his enemies with carnal weapons; but smite them with the rod of his mouth, and consume them with the breath of his lips, his gospel; nor to save his people by bow, by sword, by horses and horsemen; but by himself, his righteousness and sacrifice. His kingdom was not to be, and has not been, set up and spread by the sword, by dint of arms; as the kingdom of Mahomet has been; but by his Spirit and grace attending the ministration of his gospel. Christ never had, nor never will have, an earthly, worldly kingdom; such will not be his personal reign on earth a thousand years, as some have fancied, imagining it will be a state of worldly grandeur, riches, and civil power; which has brought the doctrine of the millennium into disgrace and contempt; whereas they that are worthy to obtain that world and kingdom, which will take place at the first resurrection, will neither eat nor drink, nor marry, nor be given in marriage; but will be like the angels of

God: there will be nothing carnal nor worldly in it; it will be a spiritual state, suited to bodies raised spiritual; and to the spirits of just men made perfect: what will have the greatest appearance of a worldly kingdom, will be in what we call the spiritual reign of Christ, when multitudes of all ranks and degrees shall be converted; and great personages, as kings and queens, shall be nursing fathers and nursing mothers to the churches; shall join them, and submit to the ordinances in them; and when they shall bring their riches and wealth into them; and all civil power and authority shall be in the hands of true christians; and the kingdom under the whole heaven, shall be given to the saints of the most High; but then there will be such a pouring down of the Spirit, which will be an over-balance to this worldly grandeur, and shall check it, that it shall not hurt, or do prejudice to the spirituality of God's people. But of this, more hereafter, in its proper place. The kingdom of Christ is spiritual; he is a spiritual King, the Lord from heaven, the second Adam, that is spiritual, the Lord and Head of his church; his throne is spiritual, he reigns in the hearts of his people by faith; his sceptre is a spiritual sceptre, a sceptre of righteousness; his subjects are spiritual men, born of the Spirit, and savour the things of the Spirit of God; they are subdued, and brought to submit to Christ by spiritual means; not by carnal weapons of warfare, but by the sword of the Spirit, which is the word of God; the kingdom of God is within them, set up in their hearts, where grace reigns; and it lies not in outward things; it is *not meat and drink*, and such like carnal things; *but righteousness, and peace, and joy in the Holy Ghost;* they are spiritual promises Christ makes to them, to encourage them in their obedience to him; and spiritual blessings and favours are bestowed upon them by him; and even their enemies, with whom their conflict is, are spiritual wickednesses in high-places; and are not to be fought with carnal weapons; nor to be subdued and conquered by means of them; but by the shield of faith and sword of the Spirit; even by the rod of Christ's mouth, and the breath of his lips.

2. Christ's kingdom is a righteous one; this has been suggested already; the whole administration of it is righteous; he is a King that reigns in righteousness, his throne is established by it; his sceptre is a right sceptre; justice and judgment are executed in his kingdom, and nothing else, by Christ the King; no injustice, violence or oppression; just and true are his ways, who is King of saints.

3. Christ's kingdom is a peaceable kingdom: he is the prince of peace; his gospel, which is his sceptre, is the gospel of peace; his subjects are sons of peace; the kingdom of grace in them, lies in peace and joy in the Holy Ghost; and in the latter day, there will be abundance of peace in Christ's kingdom, the church; and of it, and its increase, there will be no end.

4. Christ's kingdom is gradually carried on; so it has been from the first; it arose from a small beginning, in the external administration of it; it was like a little stone cut out of the mountain, without hands, which will, in due time, fill the face of the whole earth; it was like a grain of mustard-seed, the least of all seeds, in the times of Christ, which grows up to a large tree; as Christ's kingdom afterwards greatly increased, first in Judea, and then in the Gentile world; notwithstanding all the opposition made unto it; until the whole Roman empire became christian, and paganism abolished in it; and though it has met with some stops, in some periods, yet it has revived again; as at the reformation; and will hereafter be extended from sea to sea; and from the river to the ends of the earth: and the internal kingdom of Christ in the hearts of his people is gradually carried on; it is like seed sown in the earth, which springs up, and whose appearance is but small, and by degrees grows up to maturity; as grace in the heart does, until it arrives to the fulness of the stature of Christ.

5. Christ's kingdom is durable; of his government there will be no end; his throne is for ever and ever; he will reign over the house of Jacob evermore; his kingdom is an everlasting kingdom. Christ will never have any successor in his kingdom; for he lives for evermore, and has the keys of hell and death in his hands: as his Priesthood is an unchangeable priesthood, which passes not from one to another, as the Aaronical priesthood did, by reason of the death of priests; so his kingdom is an unchangeable kingdom, which passes not from one to another; he being an everliving and everlasting King; his kingdom will never give way to another; nor be subverted by another; as earthly kingdoms are, and the greatest monarchies have been:

the Babylonian monarchy gave way to the Persian and Median, and was succeeded by that; the Persian to the Grecian; and the Grecian to the Roman: but Christ's kingdom will stand for ever; his church, which is his kingdom, is built on a rock; and the gates of hell shall not prevail against it. The word and ordinances of the gospel, by which the government of Christ is externally administered, will always continue; the gospel is an everlasting gospel, the word of God, which abides for ever; and the ordinances of baptism, and the Lord's Supper, are to be administered until the second coming of Christ; and the internal kingdom of grace, set up in the hearts of Christ's subjects, is a kingdom that cannot be moved; grace can never be lost; it is a governing principle, and reigns unto eternal life by Christ: and even when Christ shall have finished his mediatorial kingdom, and delivered it up to his Father, complete and perfect; all the elect of God being gathered in; he will not cease to reign, though in another and different manner: he will reign after the spiritual kingdom is ended, a thousand years with his saints, in a glorious manner on earth; and when that is ended, he will reign with them, and they with him, in heaven, for ever and ever.

CHAP. XIV.

OF THE SPIRITUAL REIGN OF CHRIST.

It has been observed in the preceding chapter, that Christ has been exercising his kingly office in all ages of time, both before and since his incarnation; and there are two remarkable periods of time yet to come, in which Christ will exercise his kingly office in a more visible and glorious manner; the one may be called the *spiritual reign of Christ;* and the other, his *personal reign;* it is the former of these that will now be attended to; and which is no other than the present reign continued; and which will be administered in the same manner: only,

First, With greater purity, and to a greater degree of perfection; both as to doctrine and practice.

1. The kingdom of Christ will be carried on by the ministry of the word, as now; the gospel will then be preached; and in this the spiritual reign will differ from the personal one, in which there will be no ministry of the word, all God's elect being gathered in, and the saints in a perfect state; but in this there will be multitudes to be converted, and will be converted by the word, and saints be in an imperfect state, and to be edified and comforted. The gospel is to be preached unto the end of the world, and Christ has promised his presence with his ministers so long; and hence the gospel is called the *everlasting gospel,* Matt. xxviii. 19, 20. Rev. xiv. 6. but in the spiritual reign it will be preached, ——(1.) With more light and clearness than now. The light of the present time is fitly described as being neither *clear nor dark;* not so clear as in the first times of the gospel, nor so dark as in the darkest times of popery, or as it may be before a brighter day appears. It is *one day,* a remarkable uncommon day; *known to the Lord,* how long it will last, and to him only; *not day nor night,* not clear day nor dark night, but a sort of an evening twilight; and at *evening time,* when a greater darkness may be expected to be coming on, *it shall be light,* Zech. xiv. 6, 7. a blaze of light shall break out, and that to such a degree, that *the light of the moon,* which at most is the light we now have, *shall be as the light of the sun* in its meridian splendour; and *the light of the sun shall be sevenfold, as the light of seven days;* as great as the light of seven days could it be collected together; so great will be the difference between the gospel-light as now, and as it will be then, Isa. xxx. 26. *The angel having the everlasting gospel to preach;* by whom is meant a set of gospel-ministers in the spiritual reign; is said to *fly in the midst of heaven* with it, which not only denotes the public but the clear ministration of it, Rev. xiv. 6.——(2.) The gospel will be preached with greater consistence; a principal fault in the present ministry of the word is inconsistence; not only in different ministers, but in the same ministers at different times, and even in the same discourse; *the trumpet gives an uncertain sound;* but *in that day,* in the spiritual reign, *the great trumpet* of the gospel will be *blown* with great strength and fervour, and with a more even and unwavering note, and so be understood by saints and sinners, and be a better direction to them; there will not be that yea and nay as now, but the ministry of the word will be uniform and all of a piece.——(3.) There will be an agreement in the ministers of it; now they clash with one another, scarce two persons think and speak the same thing;

and some so widely different, that it seems to be another gospel preached by some than what is by others; though indeed there is not another gospel: but in the spiritual reign the *watchmen*, Christ's ministers, who watch for the good of the souls of men, *shall see eye to eye, when the Lord shall bring again Zion*, or restore his church to its former state and glory, Isa. lii. 8. their light will be the same, their ministry will be alike, they will see things in the same light, and speak the same things, and in the same manner.——(4.) There will be one faith, one doctrine of faith or system of truths, which will be preached and professed by all; there will be no more an Arian, a Socinian, a Pelagian and Arminian, or any other heterodox person; as there will be but one Lord, *his name* will be *one*, one religion professed by all that name the name of Christ; they will be all of one accord, of one mind, Zech. xiv. 9.——(5.) The gospel will have a greater spread than now; at present it lies in a narrow compass, chiefly in the isles, very little on the continent; and in the countries where it is, it is but in few places there; but hereafter many will run to and fro, and knowledge, evangelical knowledge, will be increased; the earth shall be full of it, as the waters cover the sea; the angel, or a set of gospel-ministers, shall have it to preach to every nation, kindred, tongue, and people. Those *living waters*, the doctrines of grace, which are the means of quickening sinners and enlivening saints, *shall go out from Jerusalem*, the church of God; *half of them towards the former*, or eastern *sea*, and *half of them towards the hinder*, or western *sea;* that is, they shall go east and west, even into all parts; *in summer and in winter shall it be;* these waters shall be always flowing, or these doctrines constantly and continually preached, Dan. xii. 4. Isa. xi. 9. Rev. xiv. 6. Zech. xiv. 8.——(6.) The gospel will be preached with greater success; there will be no more such complaints, as *Who hath believed our report?* the report of the gospel will be generally believed; and *to whom is the arm of the Lord revealed?* the power of God will go along with the word, to the conversion of multitudes; who, to the great surprise of the church, will *fly as a cloud* for number; so that there shall scarce be room enough in the church for them; and it will be said, *The place is too strait for me, give place to me that I may dwell;* the place of her tent must be enlarged, the curtains of her habitation stretched forth, and her cords lengthened, since she shall break forth on the right-hand and on the left, and her seed shall inherit the Gentiles, Isa. xlix. 18—20. and liv. 2, 3. and lx. 4—8.

2. The same ordinances will be administered in the spiritual reign as now; in this it will differ also from the personal reign; for then the *city*, the church, will have no *need of the sun nor moon* of gospel-ordinances, the Lord himself personally will be the light of his people; but in this state the ordinances of baptism and the Lord's Supper will be celebrated; for they are to continue till Christ's second coming and personal appearance. Matt. xxviii. 19, 20. 1 Cor. xi. 26. but not as they are commonly administered now, but as they were first delivered; through a course of time and prevailing corruption, men *have transgressed the laws, changed the ordinances, and broken the everlasting covenant*, Isa. xxiv. 5. so that were the apostles to rise from the dead, they would not know the ordinances as in general use, to be the same that were given to them; but in the spiritual reign of Christ they will be restored to their primitive purity, and be observed clear of all innovation and corruption; we shall no more hear of that absurd notion of transubstantiation, or of the bread and wine in the ordinance of the supper being transubstantiated into the very body and blood of Christ; nor of withholding the cup from the laity; nor of kneeling at the reception of the elements, as if adored; nor of the prostitution of this sacred ordinance to secular purposes, to qualify for places of honour or trust, or profit in civil things; nor shall we hear any more of the childish practice of infant-sprinkling; the ordinance of baptism will be administered only to its proper subjects, believers in Christ, and in its proper manner by immersion.

3. The same discipline will be observed in the churches of Christ as now; only with greater strictness, and more agreeable to the laws and rules of Christ: in this also the spiritual reign will differ from the personal; there will be no temple seen in that, but the Lord God Almighty, and the Lamb will be the temple of it, Rev. xxiii. 22. The worship and discipline of Christ's house will not be carried on in the manner as in the present state: but in the

spiritual reign, *the temple of God will be opened in heaven, and the ark of his testament will be seen* in it: the affairs of the church will be restored as at first; and all things will be done according to the pattern Christ has given; the form and fashion of the house, the church, its comings in, and goings out, admission and exclusion of members, the laws and ordinances of it, respecting discipline, will be shewn most clearly to it; and which will be strictly and punctually observed: there will be no more controversies about the nature of a church, and the government of it, and of officers in it; and in whom the exercise of power lies; and who to be admitted into it, and rejected from it, and by whom; see Rev. xi. 19. Isa. i. 26. Jer. xxx. 18. Ezek. xliii. 10, 11,—Churches will be formed and governed upon the plan they were in the times of the apostles.

Secondly, The spiritual reign of Christ will be more large and ample than now it is; it will reach all over the world.

1. The first step towards the increase and enlargement of Christ's kingdom, will be the destruction of antichrist; who, in the prophecy of Daniel, is spoken of as a *little horn;* an *horn*, which is an emblem of strength, power, and dominion: a *little* one, as at his first rise, and in comparison of other powers; having eyes like *the eyes of man;* denoting his sagacity, penetration, and looking out sharp on all sides, to enlarge his power and dominion; and a *mouth speaking great things* in favour of himself, and against the most High, and his people; and a *look more stout than his fellows,* than his fellow-bishops, more bold, arrogant, and impudent; making *war with the saints,* the Waldenses and Albigenses; and thinking to *change times and laws;* to change times and seasons, for different purposes than for what they were designed; and to dispense with the laws of God and man, and make new ones: but though he should continue thus great and mighty for a time, it is said, his *dominion shall be taken away, consumed and destroyed;* and that he should *come to his end, and none shall help him,* Dan. vii. 20—26. and xi. 45. In the New Testament he is called, *the man of sin,* because extremely wicked; and *the son of perdition,* because not only deserving of it, but shall certainly come into it; who *opposeth* Christ in his offices; *exalteth himself above all that is called god;* above heathen deities, above angels, and above civil magistrates; *sits in the temple of God,* the church, over which he sets himself as head; *shewing himself that he is God;* taking the name of God to himself; and assuming the prerogative of God, to forgive sin: he is called, *that wicked* and lawless one, and *mystery of iniquity,* that began doctrinally and practically to work in the times of the apostles; though this evil one lay greatly hid for a while, and was let and hindered from a more open appearance by the Roman emperor; yet, upon his removal from Rome to Constantinople, way was made for him to take his seat, and shew his power: but notwithstanding his long and tyrannical reign, Christ will consume him *with the Spirit of his mouth,* and destroy him *with the brightness of his coming,* 2 Thess. ii. 3—8. In the book of Revelation, he is described by two beasts, one rising out of the sea, the other out of the earth; signifying his twofold capacity, civil and ecclesiastical; and his twofold power, temporal and spiritual: great things are ascribed to him, and said to be done by him; who shall continue long, but at last go into perdition: this mother of harlots, with whom the kings of the earth have committed fornication, shall be hated by them, and she be burnt with fire; see Rev. xiii. and xvii. 8, 16. then they that destroyed the earth with false doctrines and worship shall be destroyed, Rev. xi. 18. the man of the earth shall no more oppress and tyrannize over the consciences of men; the Heathen, or Gentiles, by which name the papists are sometimes called, shall perish out of the land; and those sinners shall be consumed out of it, and those wicked ones be no more; see Psalm x. 16, 18. and civ. 35. so the judgment and burning of the beast, antichrist, is related as previous to the kingdom of Christ, the Son of man, Dan. vii. 12, 13, 14.

The reign of antichrist is fixed in prophecy, for a certain time; in Daniel vii. 25. for a time, and times, and the dividing of time; that is, for three years and a half; the same with forty-two months, and one thousand two hundred and sixty days; which are so many years: but when these will end, cannot be said with any precision, because it is difficult to settle the beginning of his reign; could that be done, it would easily be known when it would end: there have been many conjectures made, and times fixed, but without effect; even this very year, one

CHAP. XIV.   OF THE SPIRITUAL REIGN OF CHRIST.   451

thousand, seven hundred, and sixty-six,[1] has been pitched upon as the time of antichrist's destruction, and the beginning of the millennium; but nothing of this kind appears; or as being very near at hand: however, what is said of the ruin of antichrist, and of the antichristian states, will be fulfilled by the Lord in his own time. And this will be done, partly by the preaching of the gospel, which is the spirit and breath of Christ's mouth; with which antichrist will be consumed and destroyed, upon the angel flying in the midst of heaven, with the everlasting gospel to preach to all nations; and upon another angel appearing with such splendour, power, and glory, as to lighten the whole earth, the fall of Babylon will immediately follow, and be proclaimed; the gospel then preached, will give such a light as to open the eyes of men, to behold the abominable doctrines and practices of the church of Rome, so as to hate it, depart from it, and leave it desolate; see Rev. xiv. 6, 7, 8. and xviii. 1, 2. and xvii. 16. and partly the ruin of antichrist, and the antichristian states, will be effected by the pouring out of the seven vials of God's wrath upon them; which will be put into the hands of seven angels, or protestant princes, by one of the four beasts, or living creatures, the emblems of gospel-ministers; who having some knowledge of the time of antichrist's destruction being near, will stir up the protestant princes to take this work in hand; who will carry their victorious arms into popish countries, and make a conquest of them; first into Germany, then into France, Spain, Portugal, and Italy; and into the very kingdom and seat of the beast; for the first five vials will be poured out on the Western antichrist, and his dominions; which will cause revolutions in them from popery, and where the gospel will take place; and all those countries now under the power of papacy, will become the kingdom of Christ, and will make a large addition to his interest in the world; see Rev. xv. and xvi.

2. The next step to the increase and enlargement of Christ's kingdom and government in the world, will be the conversion of the Jews, which will follow upon the destruction of antichrist; for the Popish religion is the great stumbling-block which lies in the way of the Jews; and therefore must be first removed. There are many prophecies that speak of their conversion; as that they shall be *born* at once; not in a civil sense, set up and established as a nation; but in a spiritual sense, born again of water and of the spirit; they shall be brought into a thorough conviction of sin, and a true sense of it, and shall mourn for it; particularly the sin of their obstinate rejection of the true Messiah, and their continued unbelief in him; when they shall be led and go forth with weeping and with supplication, and shall seek the Lord their God, and David their king, the Messiah, and receive him and submit unto him; and join themselves to christian churches, and be subject to the ordinances of Christ: and this will be universal; all Israel shall be saved, the whole nation shall be born at once, suddenly; for which for many hundreds of years they have been kept a distinct people, and have not been reckoned and mixed among the nations, though scattered in the midst of them; which is a most marvellous thing in providence, and plainly shews that God has some great things to do for them and by them. In the reign of the late king, and within our knowledge and memory, was a very surprising event respecting this people, yet little taken notice of; a bill was brought into our British Parliament to naturalize them; I then thought in my own mind it would never pass; God would not suffer it in providence, being so contrary to scripture-revelation and prophecy, and the state of that people, in which they are to continue until their conversion; but the bill did pass to my great astonishment, not knowing what to think of prophecy, and of what God was about to do in the world, and with what people. But lo! the bill was repealed, and that before one Jew was naturalized upon it; and then all difficulties were removed, and it appeared to be the will of God, that an attempt should be made, and that carried into execution as near as possible, without crossing purposes, and contradicting prophecy; and to let us see what a watchful eye the Lord keeps upon the counsels of men, and that there is no counsel against the Lord; and that the Jews must remain a distinct people until the time of their conversion. How otherwise at that time would it appear that a nation is born at once, if not then a people that dwell alone, and not reckoned

---

[1] The substance of this Chapter was preached in that year.

among the nations? These two sticks, Jews and Gentiles, will become one; but it will be in and by the hand of the Lord; it will not be effected by Acts of Parliament, but by works of grace upon the souls of men; the Jews will never be naturalized until they are spiritualized; and when they are, they will return to their own land and possess it, being assisted, as they will be, by Protestant princes, who will drive out the Turk and establish them in it; this will be another addition to the kingdom of Christ.

3. By this means, the conversion of the Jews, and the settlement of them in their own land, a way will be opened for the great spread of the gospel in the Eastern nations, and for the enlargement of Christ's kingdom there; for the Protestant princes, who will be assisting to the Jews in replacing them in their own land, will carry their victorious arms into other parts of the Turkish dominions, and dispossess the Turk of his empire; which will be effected by the pouring out of the sixth vial upon the river Euphrates, which will be dried up; an emblem of the utter destruction of the Ottoman empire; whereby way will be made for the kings of the East; or for the gospel being carried into the kingdoms of the East; not only into Turkey, but Tartary, Persia, China, and the countries of the Great Mogul; which, upon the passing away of the second, or Turkish woe, the kingdoms of this world, those vast kingdoms just mentioned, will become the kingdoms of our Lord, and of his Christ, Rev. xvi. 12. and xi. 14, 15. And now will the fulness of the Gentiles be brought in; and those vast conversions made among them, prophesied of in Isa. lx. And now will the interest and church of Christ, make the greatest figure it ever did in the world; now kings shall come to the brightness and glory of Zion; her gates shall stand open continually for the kings of the Gentiles to enter in; who will become church-members, and submit to all the ordinances of Christ's house; their kings shall be nursing fathers, and their queens nursing mothers: and this will be the case, not only of one or two, or a few of them; but even of all of them; for all kings shall fall down before Christ, and all nations shall serve him: churches shall be raised and formed every where; and those be filled with great personages: now will be the time when the kingdom, and dominion, and greatness of the kingdom under the whole heaven, shall be given to the people of the saints of the most High, Isa. lx. 3, 10, 11. and xlix. 23. Psalm lxxii. 10, 11. Dan. ix. 27. Yet such will be the spirituality of this state, that it will be a counterbalance to the grandeur and riches of it; so that the saints shall not be hurt thereby; as in former times, particularly in the times of Constantine; which leads me further to observe,

Thirdly, That the reign of Christ in this state, will be more spiritual than now; from whence it has its name.

1. There will be a more plentiful effusion of the Spirit of God upon ministers and churches, in this state: the prophecy of Joel, concerning the pouring forth of the Spirit, had a very great accomplishment on the day of Pentecost, upon the apostles; but not its whole accomplishment; for the Spirit was not then poured forth upon *all* flesh, as promised; nor upon the Gentiles: but now it will be poured out on them in general from on high; so that the wilderness of the Gentiles shall become a fruitful field, Isa. xxxii. 15, 16. and to this will be owing the above things; as the destruction of antichrist, which will be by the Spirit of Christ accompanying his word; and the conversion of the Jews will follow, upon the spirit of grace and supplication being poured forth on the house of David, and the inhabitants of Jerusalem; and the many and great conversions in the Gentile world, will be, not by might or power of men, but by the Spirit of the Lord of hosts.

2. The saints in general will be more spiritualized than now: they will have more spiritual frames of soul; and will more mind, savour, and relish the things of the Spirit of God; and with their whole hearts and spirits, seek more after God, and communion with him; they will have more spiritual light and knowledge in the doctrines of the gospel; and the light of Zion will rise, and be very bright and glorious, conspicuous to others, and be very inviting; it will be like the shining light, that shines more and more unto the perfect day. The saints will be more spiritual in their conversation; there will be less of that frothiness, vanity, and emptiness, which now too often appear in them; they will frequently meet together, and speak often one to another, about divine, spiritual and experimental things. They will be more spiritual in their worship; they will worship God in the Spirit, with their spirits,

and under the influence and conduct of the divine Spirit; and will enjoy more of the spiritual presence of God and Christ; who will come down upon them like rain upon the mown grass, and as showers of rain upon the earth, very refreshing and delightful.

3. The graces of the Spirit of God will be more in exercise. Faith, which a little before this time will be scarce found in the earth, will now be in high exercise; and especially the grace of love, which will be the distinguishing character of this state; and which will answer to its name, Philadelphia, which signifies brotherly love; for in that church-state, the spiritual reign will be: then the saints will be of one heart, and of one soul; as the primitive christians were; they will be kindly affectioned one to another; no animosities and contentions among them, on any account, civil or religious; Ephraim shall not envy Judah. nor Judah vex Ephraim; but all being of one mind, having one Lord, one faith, one baptism, they will keep the unity of the spirit in the bond of peace; see Isa. xi. 13. Eph. iv. 2, 3, 4.

4. There will be abundance of peace in this reign, even of outward peace; no more wars, nor rumours of wars; swords and spears will be beaten into plow-shares and pruning hooks; and war shall be learnt no more; no more persecution, nor persecutors; there will be none to hurt and destroy in all God's holy mountain; and such as were like wolves, and leopards, and bears, shall be as tame as lambs, kids, and calves; and shall feed and lie down together: there shall be an abundance of peace of every kind, and of it no end; and particularly internal and spiritual peace; for as grace will be high in exercise, joy and peace will increase and abound; see Psalm lxxii. 7, 8. Isa. ix. 7. and xi. 6—9.

5. There will be a great degree of holiness in all saints, of every class and rank; all the Lord's people will be righteous; *Every pot in Jerusalem, and in Judea;* that is, every member of the church, *shall be holiness unto the Lord;* in his sight and to his glory; yea, *holiness to the Lord shall be upon the bells of the horses;* signifying how common it should be, and appear in every civil action of life, as well as in religious ones; and that holiness shall then be as common as unholiness is now; and that it shall be visible in the lives and conversations of saints; and be seen of all; see Isa. lx. 21. Zech. xiv. 20, 21.

The other period of time in which Christ will, in a most glorious manner, reign with his people on earth, and which may be called, his *personal reign;* being what will take place at his second coming to judgment, and personal appearance then, and upon the first resurrection; it will be most proper to defer it, until those articles come under consideration.

A BODY OF DOCTRINAL DIVINITY.

BOOK VI.

OF THE BLESSINGS OF GRACE, WHICH COME BY CHRIST; AND OF THE DOCTRINES IN WHICH THEY ARE HELD FORTH.

CHAP. I.

OF REDEMPTION BY CHRIST.

HAVING, in the preceding book, gone through the twofold state of Christ, his humiliation and exaltation; and considered the several offices of Prophet, Priest, and King, sustained and exercised by him therein; I shall now proceed to consider the blessings of grace, which come by him, through the exercise of them; and especially his priestly office; for he is *come an High-priest of good things to come,* Heb. ix. 11. which were future, under the former dispensation, were promised, prophesied of, and prefigured in it; but not accomplished; for *the law* had only a shadow of these good things to come, Heb. x. 1. but now they are come, and are actually obtained, through Christ's coming in the flesh; and through what he has done and suffered in it; as redemption, satisfaction, and reconciliation for sin, remission of sin, justification, adoption, &c. and as redemption stands in the first place, and is a principal and most important blessing and doctrine of grace, I shall begin with that. And,

First, I shall settle the meaning of the word; and shew what it supposes, includes, and is designed by it. Our English word Redemption, is from the Latin tongue, and signifies, buying again; and several words in the Greek language, of the New Testament, are used in the affair of our Redemption, which signify the obtaining of something by paying a proper price for it; sometimes the simple verb αγοραζω, to *buy,* is used: so the redeemed are said to be *bought unto God* by the blood of Christ; and to be *bought* from the earth; and to be *bought* from among men; and to be *bought* with a price; that is, with the price of Christ's blood, Rev. v. 9. and xiv. 3, 4. 1 Cor. vi. 20. hence the church of God is said to be purchased with it, Acts xx. 28. Sometimes the compound word εξαγοραζω, is used; which signifies, to *buy again,* or *out* of the hands of another; as the redeemed are bought out of the hands of justice; as in Gal. iii. 13. and iv. 5. In other places λυτροω, is used, or others derived from it; which signifies, the deliverance of a slave, or captive, from his thraldom, by paying a ransom-price for him: so the saints are said to be redeemed, not with silver or gold, the usual price paid for a ransom; but with a far greater one, the blood and life of Christ, which he came into this world to give, as a ransom-price for many; and even himself, which is αντιλυτρον, an answerable, adequate, and full price for them, 1 Pet. i. 18. Matt. xx. 28. 1 Tim. ii. 6. There are various typical redemptions, and that are of a civil nature, which may serve to illustrate our spiritual and eternal redemption by Christ. As,

1. The deliverances of the people of Israel out of their captivities, Egyptian and Babylonian; the latter I shall not much insist upon; since, though the Jews were exiles in Babylon, they did not appear to

be in much slavery and thraldom; but built houses, planted gardens, and had many privileges; insomuch that some of them, when they might have had their liberty, chose rather to continue where they were; and though their deliverance is sometimes called a redemption, yet sparingly, and in an improper sense, Jer. xv. 21. for they were redeemed without money; and Cyrus, their deliverer, neither gave nor took a price for them; and is never called a redeemer; see Isa. xlv. 13. and lii. 3. But the deliverance of the people of Israel out of Egypt, was a very special and remarkable type of redemption by Christ, out of a worse state of bondage than that of Egypt. The Israelites were made to serve with rigour, and their lives were made bitter with hard bondage, in brick and mortar, and service in the field; and they cried to God, by reason of their bondage, it was so intolerable; and it was aggravated by the taskmasters set over them; who, by the order of Pharaoh, obliged them to provide themselves with straw, and yet bring in the full tale of brick as before: which fitly expresses the state and condition that men are in; who through sin, are weak and unable to fulfil the law; yet is it as regardless of want of strength, as the Egyptian taskmasters were of want of straw: it requires sinless and perfect obedience to it; and curses and condemns such as continue not in all things to do it. The deliverance of the people of Israel, is called a redemption; God promised to rid them out of their bondage, and to *redeem* them with a stretched-out arm; and when they were delivered, he is said to have led forth the people he had *redeemed;* and the bringing them out of the house of bondage, or redeeming them out of the house of bondmen, is used as an argument to engage them to regard the commandments of God, Exod. vi. 6. and xv. 13. and xx. 2. Deut. vii. 8. And which redemption by Christ, from sin, the law, and death, lay the redeemed under a still greater obligation to do; Moses, who was the instrument God raised up, and whom he called and sent to redeem Israel, is said to be a *deliverer,* or as it should be rendered, a *redeemer,* Acts vii. 35. in which he was a type of Christ, whom God raised up, called, and sent to be a Redeemer of his spiritual Israel: and there was, in some sense, a price paid for the redemption of literal Israel; since they are expressly said to be a purchased people, bought by the Lord, Exod. xv. 16. Deut. xxxii. 6. and their deliverance was owing to blood, the blood of the passover-lamb, sprinkled on their door-posts; typical of the blood of Christ, the price of our redemption. Besides, as it has been observed by some, the redemption of the people of Israel, being the Lord's people, was by virtue of their future redemption by Christ; whose sufferings and death were for the *redemption of transgressions,* or of transgressors, who were *under the first testament;* and that the temporal deliverance of none but the Lord's people, is called a redemption, not that of his and their enemies.

2. The ransom of the people of Israel, when numbered, was typical of the ransom by Christ; which was made by paying half a shekel, called the atonement-money for their souls, and which was paid alike for a rich man, as a poor man; whereby they were preserved from any plague among them, Exod. xxx. 12—16. None but Israelites were ransomed; and none are ransomed by Christ, but the spiritual Israel of God whom he has chosen, Christ has redeemed, and who shall be saved with an everlasting salvation; even the whole Israel of God, Jews and Gentiles: they were a numbered people for whom the ransom was paid; and so are they that are redeemed and ransomed by Christ; whose names are written in the Lamb's book of life; who have passed under the hands of him that telleth them, and have been told into the hands of Christ; and are particularly and distinctly known by him, even by name; the sheep for whom he has laid down his life; and are a special and peculiar people. The half-shekel was paid alike for rich and poor, for one neither more nor less. Christ's people, though some may be redeemed from more and greater sins than others; yet they are all redeemed from all their sins, and with the same price, the price of his blood; and which is, as the half-shekel was, an atonement for their souls; by which peace and reconciliation, and full satisfaction are made for sin, so that no plague shall come nigh them; they are delivered from going down to the pit of destruction; and are saved from the second death; see Job xxxiii. 24.

3. The buying again of an Israelite, waxen poor, and sold to another, by any near akin to him; is a lively representation of the purchase and redemption of the Lord's poor people, Lev. xxv. 47, 48, 49. who, in a state of nature, are poor, and wretched, and miserable; even so as to be like beggars on the dunghill; when such

was the grace of Christ, who, though rich, for their sakes became poor, that they, through his poverty might be made rich; and to such a degree, as to be raised from the dunghill and sit among princes, and inherit the throne of glory. Though some may not sell themselves to work wickedness, as Ahab did, yet all are sold under sin; for if this was the case of the apostle Paul, though regenerate, much more must it be the case of an unregenerate man; who through sin, is brought into subjection to it, a servant of it, and a slave to it; as the poor Israelite, sold to a stranger, was a bond-man to him; and such an one cannot redeem himself, being without strength, unable to fulfil the law, and to make atonement for sin; nor can any of his friends, though ever so rich, redeem him, or give to God a ransom for him; such may redeem a poor relation, or friend from a prison, by paying his pecuniary debts for him; but cannot redeem his soul from hell and destruction; may give a ransom-price to man for one in slavery and bondage; but cannot give to God a ransom to deliver from wrath to come: only Christ, the near kinsman of his people, can do this, and has done it; he that is their *Goel*, their near *Kinsman*, partaker of the same flesh and blood with them, is their Redeemer, who has given himself a ransom for them.

4. The delivery of a debtor from prison, by paying his debts for him, is an emblem of deliverance and redemption by Christ; a man that is in debt, is liable to be arrested, and cast into prison, as is often the case; where he must lie till the debt is discharged, by himself or another: sins are debts; and a sinner owes more than ten thousand talents, and has nothing to pay; he cannot answer to the justice of God for one debt of a thousand; nor can he, by paying a debt of obedience he owes to God, pay off one debt of sin, or obligation to punishment; and so is liable to a prison, and is in one; is concluded under sin, under the guilt of it, which exposes him to punishment; and he is held with the cords and fetters of it; which he cannot loose himself from; and he is shut up under the law, in which he is held, until delivered and released by Christ; who, as he has engaged to pay the debts of his people, has paid them, cleared the whole score, and blotted out the hand-writing that was against them; in consequence of which is proclaimed, in the gospel, liberty to the captives, and the opening of the prison to them that are bound; and in effectual vocation Christ says *to the prisoners, Go forth*, opening the prison-doors for them; and to them that sit in darkness, in the gloomy cells of the prison, *shew yourselves;* all which is done in virtue of the redemption price paid by Christ for his people.

5. The ransoming of persons out of slavery, by paying a ransom-price for them, serves to give an idea of the redemption of the Lord's people by Christ. They are in a state of slavery, out of which they cannot deliver themselves; Christ is the ransomer of them out of the hands of such that are stronger than they; his life and blood are the ransom-price he has paid for them; and they are called, the ransomed of the Lord; their deliverance from present bondage, and future ruin and destruction, is in consequence of a ransom found and given; *Deliver him from going down to the pit; I have found a ransom*, Job. xxxiii. 24. see Zech. ix. 11. In which there is an allusion to a custom in the eastern countries, to put their slaves in an evening into a pit, where they are close shut up till the morning, and then taken out, to be put to their slavish employments; but not delivered, unless a sufficient ransom is given for them; and such is the blood of the covenant. Now all these views of redemption plainly point out to us the following things with respect to the redemption of the Lord's people.

1. That they are previous to their redemption, and which that supposes, in a state of captivity and bondage; they are sinners in Adam, and by actual transgressions; and so come into the hands of vindictive justice, offended by sin; and which will not clear the guilty without satisfaction given to it; which is made by paying a price: redemption by Christ is nothing more nor less than buying his people out of the hands of justice, in which they are held for sin; and that is with the price of his blood; which is therefore paid into the hands of justice for them; hence they are said to be redeemed, or bought unto God by his blood, Rev. v. 9. Being sinners, and offenders of the justice of God, that holds under sin; under the guilt of it, which binds over to punishment, unless delivered from it; it holds them under the sentence of the law, transgressed by them; which not only accuses of and charges with sin, but pronounces guilty, and condemns and curses: it holds them in subjection to death, even eternal death; which is the

wages and just demerit of sin; the law threatened with it in case of sin; sin being committed, the sentence of death passed upon all men; all having sinned, judgment, or the judicial sentence, came upon all men to condemnation in a legal way; and sin reigned unto death in a tyrannical manner; or, in other words, man became not only deserving of wrath, but obnoxious to it; the wrath of God was revealed from heaven against all unrighteousness and ungodliness of men; and indignation and wrath, tribulation and anguish, come upon every soul of man, as upon the children of disobedience, unless delivered from it, through the redemption that is by Christ. In such an enthralled state are men to sin, to the justice of God, to death, and wrath to come.

2. That redemption by Christ is a deliverance from all this. It is a redemption from sin; from all iniquities whatever, original and actual, Psalm cxxx. 8. Tit. ii. 14. from avenging justice, on account of sin; from the guilt of sin; for there is no condemnation by it to them that are interested in redemption by Christ; *Who shall condemn? it is Christ that died!* and by dying, has redeemed his people from sin, and secured them from condemnation, Rom. viii. 1, 33. and in virtue of this they are delivered from the dominion of sin; for though this is done in effectual vocation, by the power of divine grace, it is in virtue of redemption by Christ, by whom sin is crucified, and the body of it destroyed; so that it shall not reign in them, or have dominion over them: one branch of redemption lies in being delivered from a vain conversation; and, ere long, the redeemed shall be delivered from the very being of sin; when their redemption, as to the application of it, will be complete; as it will be in the resurrection; when the soul will not only be among the spirits of just men made perfect; but the body will be clear of sin, mortality, and death; which is called redemption that draws near, the redemption of the body waited for, and the day of redemption, Luke xxi. 28. Rom viii. 23. Eph. i. 14. and iv. 30. Redemption is a deliverance from the law, from the bondage of it, and from the curse and condemnation by it; so that there shall be no more curse; and from eternal death and wrath to come: life is forfeited into the hands of justice by sin; which life is redeemed from destruction, by Christ giving his life a ransom for it; he, by redeeming his people, has delivered them from wrath to come; being justified through the redemption that is in Christ, by his blood, they are, and shall be saved, from everlasting wrath, ruin, and destruction.

3. That redemption by Christ is such a deliverance, as that it is setting persons quite free and at entire liberty; such who are dead to sin by Christ are freed from it, from the damning power of it, and from its dominion and tyranny; and though, not as yet, from the being of it; yet, ere long, they will be; when, with the rest of the members of the church, they will be presented glorious, without spot or wrinkle, or any such thing: and such are free from the law; though not from obedience to it, yet from the bondage of it; they are delivered from it, and are no longer held in it, as in a prison; but are directed and exhorted to stand fast in the liberty from it, with which Christ has made them free; and this will have its full completion on all accounts, when the saints shall be delivered from every degree of bondage, into the glorious liberty of the children of God.

CHAP. II.

OF THE CAUSES OF REDEMPTION BY CHRIST.

SECONDLY, The next thing to be considered are the causes of redemption; what it springs from, by whom, and by what means it is obtained; and for what ends and purposes it is wrought out.

1st, The moving cause of it, or from whence it springs and flows; and that is, the everlasting love of God; which, as jt is the source and spring of every blessing of grace; as of election, regeneration, and effectual vocation; so of redemption. The gift of Christ to be the Redeemer of his people flows from this love. Christ was given to be a Redeemer before he was sent; when he was given for a covenant to the people he was given in covenant to be the Redeemer of them; and this gift was the effect of love; to this Christ himself ascribes it; *God so loved the world, that he gave his only begotten Son;* that is, to be their Redeemer; hence, before he came, Job had knowledge of him as his living Redeemer; and all the old testament saints waited for him as such. The mission of Christ in the fulness of time, to be the propitiation for the sins of men, and to redeem them from them, is given as a manifest, clear, and undoubted instance of his love; *In this was manifested the love of God*, &c. *Herein is love*, &c. 1 John iv. 9, 10. and God's not sparing his Son, but delivering him into the hands of justice and death, to die in the room and stead of sinners, while they were such, is a full demonstration and high commendation of his great love unto them, Rom. v. 8. The free grace of God, for grace, if it is not altogether free, is not grace; and which is no other than unmerited love, clear of all conditions, merit and motives in the creature; it is at the bottom of our redemption by Christ; for as we are *justified freely by his grace, through the redemption that is in Jesus Christ;* so that redemption that is in and by Christ is of free grace; the gift of Christ is a free grace gift; his being sent and delivered up to death are owing to the grace of God; it is *by the grace of God he tasted death for every one;* for every one of the sons of God: and this cannot be attributed to any merit or desert in those for whom Christ died; since they were without strength, ungodly wicked sinners, the chief of sinners, and enemies in their minds, by wicked works, Rom. v. 6, 7, 8, 10. Mercy, which is no other than the love and grace of God, exercised towards miserable creatures, gives rise to this blessing of redemption: God first resolved to have mercy on sinful men; and then determined to redeem and save them by his Son; and it is through the tender mercy of our God, that Christ, the day-spring from on high, visited and redeemed his people; and so performed the mercy promised to men, Luke i. 68, 69, 72, 78. hence God is said to save men according to his mercy; and mercy is glorified in their salvation and redemption by Christ; and they are under obligation to sing of mercy, to praise the Lord, and give thanks unto him, on account of it, Tit. iii. 5. Psalm cvii. 1, 2. and cxxxvi. 23, 24. it is now, by the love, grace, and mercy of God to sinful men, that his will is determined, and his resolution fixed, to redeem them; for redemption is according to an eternal purpose he has purposed in Christ; who was fore-ordained before the foundation of the world, to redeem men from a vain conversation, with his precious blood: he was set forth, in the decrees and purposes of God, to be the propitiation for sin; God appointed him to be the Redeemer and Saviour; and appointed men, not unto wrath, which they deserved, but to obtain salvation by him; even the vessels of mercy afore prepared for glory; and being moved, from his love, grace, and mercy, within himself, to determine upon the redemption of them, his wisdom was set to work to find out the best way and method of doing it: upon this a council was held; God was, in Christ, forming a scheme of peace, reconciliation, and redemption; in which he has *abounded towards us in all wisdom and prudence*, in 'fixing upon the most proper person, and the most proper means, whereby to effect it: and hence the scheme of redemption, as formed in the eternal mind and council of God, is called *the manifold wisdom of God*, Eph. i. 7, 8. and iii. 10. But of the wisdom of God, as it appears in redemption by Christ, I have more largely treated when on the attribute of Wisdom. All these workings in the heart and will of God, issued in a covenant between him and his Son; in which he proposed to his Son, that he should be the Raiser-up, Restorer, and Redeemer of his people, both among Jews and Gentiles; and to which he agreed; and said, *Lo, I come to do thy will!* which was no other, than to work out the redemption of his people, Isa. xlix. 5, 6. Psalm xl. 7, 8. Hence this covenant is by some called, the covenant of redemption, in which this great affair was settled and secured. Now upon all this, the love, grace, and mercy of God, the good-will and purpose of his heart, his council and covenant, the plot of man's redemption is formed; this is the source and spring of it.

2dly, The procuring cause, or author of redemption, is Christ, the Son of God; he was appointed to it, and assented to it; was prophesied of as the Redeemer that should come to Zion; he was sent to redeem them that were under the law; and he has obtained eternal redemption; and in him believers have it, through his blood, and he is of God made redemption to them.

1. If it be asked, how Christ came to be the Redeemer? it may be answered, as the love, grace, and mercy of God the Father moved him to resolve upon redemption, and appoint his Son, and call him to this work; so like love, grace, and mercy, wrought in the heart of the Son of God to accept of this call, and engage in this work; the love of Christ, which was in his heart from everlasting, and was a love of complacency and delight; this

showed itself in various acts, and especially in giving himself for his people to redeem them; in giving himself an offering and a sacrifice for their sins; in laying down his life for them; all which is frequently ascribed to his love, Tit. ii. 14. Eph. v. 2, 25. 1 John iii. 16. and this love is unmerited, as appears from the characters of the persons for whom he died, observed before; and so is called the grace of Christ, free grace, unmoved and unmerited by any thing in the creature; and to this is attributed the whole affair of our redemption and salvation by Christ, 2 Cor. viii. 5. pity and compassion in his heart towards his people in their miserable and enthralled state, moved him to undertake and perform the work of their redemption: *in his love and in his pity he redeemed them*, as he did Israel of old, Isa. lxiii. 9. This love, grace, and mercy, influenced and engaged him to resolve upon the redemption of them; hence he said, *I will ransom them, I will redeem them;* as from the grave and death, so from every other enemy, Hos. xiii. 14. and as he entered into covenant engagements with his Father from everlasting, he considered himself as under obligation to perform this work, and therefore spoke in language which imports the same; as that he *must* work the works of him that sent him, of which this is the principal; that he *ought* to suffer and die as he did; and that he *must* bring in those the Father gave him, and he undertook for, and bring them safe to glory.

2. The fitness of Christ to be a Redeemer of his people is worthy of notice. As he engaged in it, he was every way fit for it; none so fit as he, none fit for it but himself; no creature, man or angel: no man, for all have sinned, and so every one needs a redeemer from sin, and can neither redeem himself nor any other; nor could an angel redeem any of the sons of men; God has put no trust of this kind in those his servants the angels, knowing that they were unequal to it: the angel Jacob speaks of, that redeemed him from all evil, was not a created but the uncreated angel; the angel and messenger of the covenant, the Messiah. Now Christ's fitness for the work of redemption lies in his being God and man in one person. It was the Son of God that was sent to redeem men, who is of the same nature, and possessed of the same perfections his divine Father is; the brightness of his glory, and the express image of his person; who was in the form of God, and thought it no robbery to be equal to him: this Son of God is the true God, the great God, and so fit to be the Redeemer and Saviour of men; and a mighty redeemer he must be, since he is Jehovah, the Lord of hosts, and therefore equal to such a work as this, Gal. iv. 4. 1 John v. 20. Tit. ii. 13. Jer. l. 34. and he is both God and man; he is the child born, as man, and the son given, as a divine person; he is Immanuel, God with us, God in our nature, God manifest in the flesh, and so fit to be a mediator between God and man; and to be an umpire, a days-man to lay hands on both; and to do the work required of a redeemer of men, to make reconciliation for their sins, and to take care of things pertaining to the glory of God, his justice and holiness. As man he could be made, as he was made, under the law, and so capable of yielding obedience to it, and of bearing the penalty of it; which it was necessary he should, as the surety and redeemer of men; as man he had blood to shed, with which most precious blood he could redeem them unto God; had a life to lay down, a sufficient ransom-price for his people, and was capable of suffering and dying in their room and stead, and so of making full satisfaction for them. As God, he would be zealously concerned for the glory of the divine perfections, and secure the honour of them in the redemption wrought out by him; as such, he could put an infinite virtue into his blood, and make it a full and adequate price for the purchase of his church, and the redemption of it; as such, he could support the human nature under the load of sin and of sufferings for it, and of carrying it through the work, otherwise insupportable; and as both God and man he had a right to redeem; as Lord of all, he had a right as well as power to redeem them that were his; and being, as man, their near kinsman, the right of redemption belonged to him, and therefore bears the name of Goel, which signifies a redeemer, and a near kinsman; see the law in Lev. xxv. 47—49. and who so fit to be the redeemer of the church as he who is her head and her husband?

3. The means by which redemption is wrought out by Christ; and that is by his blood, his life, to which it is often ascribed, Eph. i. 7. 1 Pet. i. 18, 19. Rev. v. 9. this was shed, and shed freely, for the remission of sins, and for the redemption of men; had it been shed involuntarily, by accident, or by force, against his will, it would not

have been a proper redemption price, or have answered such an end; but it was purposely and voluntarily shed, and with full consent; Christ, as he had the full disposal of his own life, freely *gave* his life a ransom-price for many; *I lay down my life for the sheep*, says he, as a ransom-price for them; *I lay it down of myself*, Matt. xx. 28. John x. 15, 18. and the blood that was thus freely shed was the same with that of those for whom it was shed, which was necessary; not the blood of bulls and goats, which could not be an adequate price of redemption, but human blood; Christ partook of the same flesh and blood with the children for whom he died; only with this difference, it was not tainted with sin as theirs is; which is another requisite of the ransom-price; it must be the blood of an innocent person, as Christ was: much notice is taken in scripture of the innocence, holiness, and righteousness of the Redeemer; that he was holy in his nature, harmless in life, knew no sin, nor ever committed any; that he, the just and holy one, suffered for the unjust; a great emphasis is put upon this, that the price with which men are redeemed is *the precious blood of Christ, as of a Lamb without blemish and without spot*, 1 Pet. i. 18, 19. for if he had had any sin in him, he could not have been a redeemer from sin, nor his blood the price of redemption: and yet more than all this, it is necessary to make this price a full and adequate one, it must not be the blood of a mere creature, but of one that is God as well as man, and such is Christ; hence *God*, who is Christ, is said to *purchase the church with his own blood;* being God and man in one person, this gave his blood a sufficient virtue to make such a purchase; and a peculiar emphasis is put upon his blood, being the *blood of* Jesus Christ *the Son of God*, which cleanses from all sin, Acts xx. 28. 1 John i. 7. Now this price is paid into the hands of God, whose justice is offended, whose law is broken, and who is the lawgiver, that is able to save and to destroy; and against whom all sin is committed: and who will not clear the guilty unless his justice is satisfied; for he is the judge of all the earth, who will do right; wherefore Christ is said *to redeem* men *unto God by his blood*, Rev. v. 9. The price of redemption, which is the blood of Christ, was paid unto God, whereby redemption from vindictive justice was obtained; it was not paid into the hands of Satan, or any other enemy that had power over the redeemed; for the power of Satan was only an usurpation; he had no legal right to hold them captives; and therefore the delivery of them out of his hand is by power and not by price: but the justice of God had a legal right to shut them up, and detain them as prisoners, till satisfaction was given; and therefore redemption from avenging justice, which is properly the redemption that is by Christ, is by a price paid to justice for the ransom of them.

3*dly*, The final cause, or causes, or ends, for which redemption was wrought out and obtained by Christ in this way; and they are these.———1. That the justice of God might be satisfied in the salvation of a sinner; that God might appear to be just, whilst he is the justifier of him that believes in Jesus; and be just and faithful in forgiving sins, and cleansing from all unrighteousness; that the attributes of his justice, holiness, truth, and faithfulness, might be glorified in the redemption of men, as well as the other perfections of his, Rom. iii. 25, 26. 1 John i. 9. Psalm lxxxv. 10.———2. That the people of God might be reconciled unto him, and have peace with him, and joy through believing in Christ; for the price of redemption being paid for them and satisfaction given, they are reconciled to God by the death of his Son; even to his justice, as they always stood in his love and favour; and peace being made by the blood of Christ on such a footing, they may joy in God through Christ, by whom they have received the atonement, Rom. v. 10, 11.———3. Another end of redemption by Christ is, that the redeemed might enjoy the blessing of adoption; for so it is said, that God sent his Son *to redeem them that were under the law, that we might receive the adoption of sons*, Gal. iv. 4, 5. for though the saints are predestinated to the adoption of children in the purpose of God from everlasting; and this blessing is provided and secured in the covenant of grace; yet sin having thrown a remora in the way of the enjoyment of it in their own persons, consistent with the holiness and justice of God, this is removed by the redemption which is through Christ; so that they come to receive and enjoy this blessing of grace in themselves in virtue of their redemption by Christ, and through believing in him.———4. The sanctification of God's elect is another end of redemption by Christ; *who gave himself for them, that he might redeem them from all iniquity, and purify unto himself a peculiar people zealous of good works*,

Tit. ii. 14. and again, Christ is said to love the church, *and give himself for it*, a ransom-price for it, *that he might sanctify and cleanse it*, Eph. v. 25, 26. and the redeemed are said to be redeemed by his blood *from a vain conversation*, 1 Pet. i. 18. for in consequence of redemption by Christ, the Spirit of Christ comes as a Spirit of sanctification, and begins and carries on that work in the souls of God's people; and by applying the grace and benefit of redemption, lays them under the highest obligation to holiness of life and conversation; see Gal. iii. 14.———5. In a word, the end of Christ's redeeming his people is, that they might be freed from all evil, from every enemy, and all that is hurtful, sin, Satan, the world, law, hell, and death; and that they might be put into the possession of every good thing. *Christ has redeemed them from the curse of the law, being made a curse for them, that the blessing of Abraham*, even all the blessings of the covenant of grace, in which Abraham was interested, *might come on them through Jesus Christ*, Gal. iii. 13, 14.———6. and lastly, The subordinate end of redemption is the everlasting salvation of God's elect, and their eternal life and happiness; and the ultimate end is the glory of God, of his grace and justice, and of all the perfections of his nature.

CHAP. III.

OF THE OBJECTS OF REDEMPTION BY CHRIST.

Thirdly, The objects of redemption come next under consideration. These are a special and distinct people; they are said to be *redeemed from the earth;* that is, from among the inhabitants of the earth, as after explained, *redeemed from among men;* and one end of Christ's redemption of them is, *to purify to himself a peculiar people*, Rev. xiv. 3, 4. Tit. ii. 14. The inspired writers seem to delight in using the pronoun *us*, when speaking of the death of Christ, and redemption by it; thereby pointing at a particular people, as the context shows: *Christ died for us;* God *delivered him up for us all; who gave himself for us, that he might redeem us; hath redeemed us unto God by thy blood*, Rom. v. 8. and viii. 32. Tit. ii. 14. Rev. v. 9. They are many indeed for whom Christ has *given his life a ransom*, a ransom-price, the price of their redemption, Matt. xx. 28. But then these are so described as show they are a peculiar people; they are the *many* who are ordained unto eternal life; the *many* the Father has given to Christ; the *many* whose sins he bore on the cross; the *many* for whom his blood was shed for the remission of their sins; the *many* who are made righteous by his obedience; the *many* sons, he, the Captain of their salvation, brings to glory. That the objects of redemption are a special people, will appear by the following observations.

1. The objects of redemption are such who are the objects of God's love; for redemption, as has been observed, flows from the love of God and Christ; and which love is not that general kindness shown in providence to all men, as the creatures of God; but is special and discriminating; the favour which he bears to his *own* people, as distinct from others; *Jacob have I loved, but Esau have I hated:* and the love which Christ has expressed in redemption is towards his *own* that were in the world, whom he has a special right and property in, *his* people, *his* sheep, *his* church; as will be seen hereafter.

2. The objects of election and redemption are the same; *Who shall lay any thing to the charge of God's elect?—It is Christ that died!* died for the elect: so the same, *us all*, for whom God delivered up his Son, are those whom he foreknew, and whom he predestinated; and whose calling, justification, and glorification are secured thereby, Rom. viii. 30—33. and the same *us*, who are said to be chosen in Christ, before the foundation of the world, have redemption in him through his blood, Eph. i. 4, 7. Election and redemption are of equal extent; no more are redeemed by Christ than are chosen in him; and these are a special people: what is said of the objects of the one is true of the objects of the other. Are the elect the beloved of the Lord? and does the act of election spring from love? Election presupposes love; so the redeemed are the beloved of God and Christ; and their redemption flows from love. Are the elect a people whom God has chosen for his peculiar treasure? the redeemed are purified by Christ, to be a peculiar people to himself. Do the vessels of mercy, afore prepared for glory, consist of Jews and Gentiles; even of them who are called of both? so Christ is the propitiation, not for the sins of the Jews only, or the Redeemer of them only; but for the sins of the Gentile world also, or the Redeemer of his

people among them. Are the elect of God a great number, of all nations, kindreds, people, and tongues? Christ has redeemed those he has redeemed unto God, out of every kindred, tongue, people, and nation. Is it true of the elect, that they cannot be totally and finally deceived and perish? it is true of the ransomed of the Lord, that they shall come to Zion with everlasting joy; Christ will never lose any part of the purchase of his blood.

3. Those for whom Christ has died, and has redeemed by his blood, are no other than those for whom he became a Surety. Now Christ was the Surety of the better testament, or covenant of grace; and of course became a Surety for those, and for no other, than who were interested in that covenant, in which he engaged to be the Redeemer: Christ's suretiship is the ground and foundation of redemption; the true reason of the sin of his people, and the punishment of it, being laid upon him, and of his bearing it; of the payment of the debts of his people, and of redeeming them out of the hands of justice; was because he engaged as a Surety, and laid himself under obligation to do all this. But for those for whom he did not become a Surety, he was not obliged to pay their debts, nor to suffer and die in their room and stead. Christ's suretiship and redemption are of equal extent, and reach to the same objects, they are the Lord's Benjamins, the sons of his right-hand, his beloved sons, that Christ, the antitype of Judah, became a Surety for, and laid himself under obligation to bring them safe to glory, and present them to his divine Father.

4. The objects of redemption are described by such characters as show them to be a special and distinct people; particularly they are called, the people of God and Christ; *for the transgressions of my people*, saith the Lord, *was he stricken;* that is, Christ was, or would be, stricken by the rod of justice, to make satisfaction for their sins, and thereby redeem them from them, Isa. liii. 8. and when he was about to come and redeem them, Zechariah, the father of John the Baptist, at his birth said, *Blessed be the Lord God of Israel! for he hath visited and redeemed his people;* by sending Christ, the day-spring from on high, as he afterwards calls him, to visit them, and redeem them by his blood, Luke i. 68, 78. Hence, also, the angel that appeared to Joseph, and instructed him to call the Son that should be born of his wife by the name of Jesus, gives this reason, *for he shall save his people from their sins*, Matt. i. 21. Now though all men are, in a sense, the people of God, as they are his creatures, and the care of his providence; yet they are not all redeemed by Christ; because those that are redeemed by Christ, are redeemed *out of every people;* and therefore cannot be every or all people, Rev. v. 9. the redeemed are God's covenant-people; of whom he says, *They shall be my people, and I will be their God:* they are his portion and his inheritance; a people *near* unto him, both with respect to union and communion; a people given to Christ, to be redeemed and saved by him; of whom it is said, *Thy people shall be willing*, &c.

5. The objects of redemption; or those for whom Christ laid down his life a ransom-price, are described as *sheep;* as the sheep of Christ, in whom he has a special property, being given him of his Father; and who are represented as distinct from others, who are not his sheep, John x. 15, 26, 29. and such things are said of them as can only agree with some particular persons; as, that they are known by Christ; *I know my sheep*, not merely by his omniscience, so he knows all men; but he knows them distinctly as his own; *the Lord knows them that are his*, from others; he has knowledge of them, joined with special love and affection for them; as he has not of others, to whom he will say, *Depart from me; I know you not.* Likewise Christ is *known* by those sheep of his he has laid down his life for; they know him in his person, offices, and grace; whereas there are some that neither know the Father nor the Son; but those know the voice of Christ; that is, the gospel of Christ, the joyful sound; whereas the gospel is hid to them that are lost: and the sheep Christ has died for, *follow* him, imitate him in the exercise of grace, of love, patience, humility, &c. and in the performance of duty; and this is said of the redeemed from among men; that they *follow the Lamb whithersoever he goes*, Rev. xiv. 4. It is also affirmed of those sheep, that they shall *never perish;* whereas the goats, set on Christ's left-hand, shall he bid to go, as *cursed*, into everlasting fire, Matt. xxv. 33, 34.

6. The objects of redemption are the sons of God; redemption and adoption belong to the same persons; according to the prophecy of Caiaphas, Christ was to die, not for the nation of the Jews only, but to *gather together in one the children of*

CHAP. III.   OF THE OBJECTS OF REDEMPTION BY CHRIST.   463

God that were scattered abroad throughout the Gentile world, John xi. 52. and those who are predestinated to adoption by Christ, are said to have redemption in him, through his blood, Eph. i. 5, 7. and the blessing of adoption, in the full enjoyment of it, in the resurrection, is called *the redemption of the body;* when redemption, as to the application of it, will be complete also, Rom. viii. 23. Now these sons, or children of God, are a peculiar number of men, who are given of God to Christ, to redeem; the seed promised to him in covenant, that he should see and enjoy; and to whom he stands in the relation of the everlasting Father; these are they on whose account he became incarnate, *took part of the same flesh and blood;* and these are the many sons he brings to glory, Heb. ii. 10, 13, 14. Now these are not all men; *the children of the flesh,* or such as are never born again, they are *not the children of God;* only such are openly and manifestatively the children of God who believe in Christ; and this is owing to special grace, to distinguishing love; and is a favour that is only conferred on some, Rom. ix. 8. Gal. iii. 26. John i. 12. 1 John iii. 1.

7. The objects of redemption are the church and spouse of Christ; it is the church he has loved, and given himself as a sacrifice and ransom-price for; it is the church he has purchased with his blood; even the general assembly, the church of the first-born, whose names are written in heaven; that is, the elect of God, whose names are written in the Lamb's book of life, Eph. v. 25. Acts xx. 28. of that church of which Christ is the head and husband, he is the Redeemer; *thy Maker is thine husband; and thy Redeemer the Holy One of Israel!* Isa. liv. 5. This cannot be said of all communities and bodies of men: the whore of Babylon is not the spouse of Christ; nor sects under the influence of false teachers, though there may be *threescore queens, and fourscore concubines,* of this sort; yet, says Christ, *my dove, my undefiled, is but one;* and who only is redeemed by Christ, and espoused to him, Cant. vi. 9.

Now from all this it appears, that redemption is not universal, is not of all men; for though they are many for whom the ransom-price is paid; yet though all are many, many are not all; and if the redeemed are such who are the objects of God's special love and favour, then not all men; for there are some of whom it is said, *He that made them, will not have mercy on them; and he that formed them, will shew them no favour,* Isa. xxvii. 11. If they are the elect of God who are redeemed by Christ, and them only, then not all men; for all are not chosen; *The election hath obtained it;* and *the rest are blinded,* Rom. xi. 7. if only those are redeemed for whom Christ became a surety, then not all men; since Christ did not engage to pay the debts of all men; and if they are the people of God and Christ, then not all; since there are some on whom God writes a *lo-ammi,* saying, *Ye are not my people; and I will not be your God,* Hos. i. 9. And if they are the sheep of Christ, to whom he gives eternal life; then not the goats, who will go into everlasting punishment; and if they are the children of God, and the church and spouse of Christ; then not all men; for all do not bear these characters, nor stand in these relations. What may be farther necessary, will be to produce some reasons, or arguments, against universal redemption; and to give answer to such scriptures as are brought in favour of it. It should be observed, that it is agreed on both sides, that all are not eventually saved: could universal salvation be established, there would be no objection to universal redemption; the former not being the case, the latter cannot be true; Christ certainly saves all whom he redeems.

First, I shall give some reasons, or produce some arguments against the universal scheme of redemption. And,

1*st,* The first set of arguments shall be taken from hence, that universal redemption reflects highly on the perfections of God; and what is contrary to the divine perfections, cannot be true; for God cannot deny himself, nor say, nor do anything contrary to his nature and attributes.

1. The universal scheme greatly reflects on the love of God to men: it may, at first sight, seem to magnify it, since it extends it to all; but it will not appear so; it lessens it, and reduces it to nothing. The scriptures highly commend the love of God, as displayed in the death of his Son, and in redemption by him; but what kind of love must that be, which does not secure the salvation of any by it? it is not that love which God bears to his own people, which is special and distinguishing; when, according to the universal scheme, God loved Peter no more than he did Judas; nor the saints now in heaven, any more

than those that are damned in hell; since they were both loved alike, and equally redeemed by Christ; nor is it that love of God, which is immutable, invariable, and unalterable; since, according to this scheme, God loves men with so intense a love, at one time, as to give his Son to die for them, and wills that they all should be saved; and afterwards this love is turned into wrath and fury; and he is determined to punish them with everlasting destruction. What sort of love must this be in God, not to spare his Son, but deliver him up to death for all the individuals of mankind, for their redemption; and yet, to multitudes of them, does not send them so much as the gospel, to acquaint them with the blessing of redemption by Christ; and much less his Spirit, to apply the benefit of redemption to them; nor give them faith to lay hold upon it for themselves? Such love as this is unworthy of God, and of no service to the creature.

2. The universal scheme, highly reflects on the wisdom of God: it is certain, God is *wonderful in counsel*, in contriving the scheme of redemption; and is *excellent in working*, in the execution of it; he is the wise God, and our Saviour; and is wise as such. But where is his wisdom in forming a scheme, in which he fails of his end? there must be some deficiency in it; a want of wisdom, to concert a scheme, which is not, or cannot be carried into execution, at least as to some considerable part of it. Should it be said, that the failure is owing to some men's not performing the conditions of their redemption required of them; it may be observed, either God did know, or did not know, that these men would not perform the conditions required; if he did not know, this ascribes want of knowledge to him; which surely ought not to be ascribed to him that knows all things: if he did know they would not perform them, where is his wisdom, to provide the blessing of redemption, which he knew beforehand, would be of no service to them? Let not such a charge of folly, be brought against infinite Wisdom.

3. The universal scheme, highly reflects on the justice of God: God is righteous in all his ways and works; and so in this of redemption by Christ; and, indeed, one principal end of it is, *To declare the righteousness of God, that he might be just*, or appear to be just, *and the justifier of him which believeth in Jesus*. But if Christ died for the sins of all men, and the punishment of their sins is inflicted on him, and bore by him, and yet multitudes of them are everlastingly punished for them, where is the justice of God? It is reckoned unjust with men, to punish twice for the same act of offence: if one man pays another man's debts, would it be just with the creditor to exact, require, and receive payment again at the hands of the debtor? If Christ has paid the debts of all men, can it be just with God to arrest such persons, and cast them into the prison of hell, till they have paid the uttermost farthing? Far be it from the Judge of all the earth to do so, who will do right.

4. The universal scheme, reflects on the power of God; as if he was not able to carry his designs into execution; whereas, *The Lord's hand is not shortened, that it cannot save;* but, according to this scheme, it seems as if it was; for if Christ has redeemed all men, and all men are not saved, it must be either from want of will in God to save them, or from want of power: not from want of will; for, according to this scheme, it is the will of God that every individual man should be saved; it must be therefore for want of power; and so he is not omnipotent. Should it be said, that some men not being saved, is owing to evil dispositions in them, obstructing the kind influences and intentions of God towards them; to the perverseness of their wills, and the strength of their unbelief. But, what is man mightier than his Maker? Are the kind influences of God, and his gracious intentions, to be obstructed by the corrupt dispositions of men? Is not he able to work in them, both to will and to do, of his good pleasure? Cannot he remove the perverseness of their wills, and the hardness of their hearts? Cannot he, by his power, take away their unbelief, and work faith in them, to believe in a living Redeemer? Far be it to think otherwise of him, with whom nothing is too hard, nor any thing impossible.

5. The universal scheme reflects on the immutability of God, of his love, and of his counsel: God, in the scripture, says, *I am the Lord, I change not; therefore ye sons of Jacob are not consumed*, Mal. iii. 6. But, according to this scheme, it should be, rather, I am the Lord, I change; and therefore the sons of men, or at least some of them, are consumed, are lost and perish, though redeemed by Christ; for the love of God, as has been observed, is changeable with respect unto them: one while he

loves them, so that he wills their salvation; at another time his love is changed into hatred, and he is resolved to stir up his wrath to the uttermost against them. He is said to be *in one mind, and who can turn him?* and yet, according to this scheme, he is sometimes in one mind, and sometimes in another; sometimes his mind is to save them; and at another time his mind is to damn them. But let not this be said of him, *with whom there is no variableness, nor shadow of turning.*

6. The universal scheme disappoints God of his chief end, and robs him of his glory. The ultimate end of God, in the redemption of men, as has been observed, is his own glory; the glory of his rich grace and mercy; and of his righteousness, truth, and faithfulness: but if men, any of them who are redeemed, are not saved, so far God loses his end, and is deprived of his glory; for should this be the case, where would be the glory of God the Father, in forming a scheme which does not succeed, at least with respect to multitudes? and where would be the glory of the Son of God, the Redeemer, in working out the redemption of men, and yet they not saved by him? And where would be the glory of the Spirit of God, if the redemption wrought out, is not effectually applied by him? But, on the contrary, the *glory of God*, Father, Son, and Spirit, *is great in the salvation* of all the redeemed ones, Psalm xxi. 5.

2*dly*, Another set of arguments against universal redemption, might be taken from its reflecting on the grace and work of Christ: whatever obscures, or lessens, the grace of Christ in redemption, or depreciates his work as a Redeemer, can never be true. Whereas,

1. The universal scheme reflects on the love and grace of Christ. The scripture speaks highly of the love of Christ, as displayed in redemption; and Christ himself intimates, that he was about to give the greatest instance of his love to his people, by dying for them, that could be given; even though and while they were enemies to him, John xv. 13. But what sort of love is that, to love men to such a degree as to die for them, and yet withhold the means of grace from multitudes of them, bestow no grace upon them, and at last say to them, *Depart from me, ye cursed, into everlasting fire!*

2. The universal scheme reflects upon the work of Christ; particularly his work of satisfaction, which was to finish transgression, to make an end of sin, by satisfying divine justice for it; by putting away sin by the sacrifice of himself. Now, either he has made satisfaction for every man, or he has not: if he has, then they ought to be set free, and fully discharged, and not punishment inflicted on them, or their debts exacted of them; if he has not made satisfaction by redeeming them, this lessens the value of Christ's work, and makes it of no use, and ineffectual; and indeed, generally, if not always, the advocates for general redemption deny the proper satisfaction, and real atonement by Christ; plainly discerning, that if he has made full satisfaction for the sins of all men, they must all be saved; and so the work of reconciliation, which is closely connected with, and involved in satisfaction, is not perfect according to the scriptures. Christ, by redeeming men with the price of his blood, has made satisfaction to justice for them, and thereby has procured their reconciliation; for they are said to be reconciled unto God by the death of his Son; and peace is said to be made by the blood of his cross, which is the redemption-price for them; and he is pacified towards them for all that they have done; which is meant by Christ being a propitiation for sin, whereby justice is appeased. But, according to the universal scheme, God is only made reconcileable, not reconciled, nor men reconciled to him, notwithstanding what Christ has done, there may be no peace to them, not any being actually made for them; and, indeed, the work of redemption must be very incomplete; though Christ is a *Rock*, as a Saviour and Redeemer, and his *work is perfect*, his work of redemption; and hence called a *plenteous* one; and Christ is said to have obtained *eternal redemption* for us; and yet if all are not saved through it, it must be imperfect; it cannot be a full redemption, nor of eternal efficacy; the benefit of it, can at most, be only for a time to some, if any at all, and not be for ever; which is greatly to depreciate the efficacy of this work of Christ.

3. According to the universal scheme, the death of Christ, with respect to multitudes, for whom he is said to die, must be in vain; for if Christ died to redeem all men, and all men are not saved by his death, so far his death must be in vain: if he paid a ransom for all, and all are not

ransomed; or if he has paid the debts of all, and they are not discharged, the price is given, and the payment made, in vain. According to this scheme, the death of Christ is no security against condemnation; though the apostle says, *Who shall condemn? It is Christ that died!* so that there is no condemnation to them whose sins are condemned in Christ; and he has condemned them in the flesh, Rom. viii. 1, 33. and yet there is a world of men that will be condemned, 1 Cor. xi. 32. and therefore it may be concluded, that Christ did not die for them, or otherwise they would not come into condemnation; or else Christ's death has no efficacy against condemnation.

4. The universal scheme separates the works of Christ, the work of redemption, and the work of intercession; and makes them to belong to different persons; whereas they are of equal extent, and belong to the same; for whom Christ died, for them he rose again from the dead; and that was for their justification; which is not true of all men: for those he ascended to heaven, to God, as their God and Father, for the same he entered into heaven, as their forerunner, and appears in the presence of God for them, and ever lives to make intercession for them; and for the same for whom he is an advocate, he is the propitiation; for his advocacy is founded upon his propitiatory sacrifice: now those for whom he prays and intercedes, are not all men, himself being witness; *I pray for them; I pray not for the world*, John xvii. 9. Yet, according to the universal scheme, he died for them for whom he would not pray; which is absurd and incredible.

5. If Christ died for all men, and all men are not saved, Christ will not see of the travail of his soul and be satisfied; as was promised him, Isa. liii. 11. for what satisfaction can he have to see his labour, with respect to multitudes, all lost labour, or labour in vain? it was the joy that was set before him, of having those for whom he suffered and died, with him in heaven: but what joy can he have, and what a disappointment must it be to him, to see thousands and millions whom he so loved as to give himself for, howling in hell, under the everlasting displeasure and wrath of God?

3dly, Other arguments against universal redemption, may be taken from the uselessness of it to great numbers of men. As

1. To those whose sins are irremissible; whose sins will never be forgiven, neither in this world, nor in that which is to come: that there are such sinners, and such sins committed by them, is certain, from what Christ himself says, Matt. xii. 31, 32. and the apostle speaks of a sin which is *unto death*, unto eternal death; which he does not advise to pray for, 1 John v. 16. and surely Christ cannot be thought to die for such sins, for which there is no forgiveness with God, and no prayer to be made by men for the remission of them; to say that Christ died for those, is to say that he died in vain: besides, there were multitudes in hell at the time when Christ died; and it cannot be thought that he died for those, as he must, if he died for all the individuals of mankind; as the men of Sodom, who were then, as Jude says, *suffering the vengeance of eternal fire;* and the inhabitants of the whole world, the world of the ungodly, destroyed by the flood; those that were disobedient in the times of Noah; whose spirits, as the apostle Peter says, were, in his time, in the prison of hell, Jude ver. 7. 1 Pet. iii. 20. if he died for these, his death must be fruitless and useless; unless it can be thought, that a jail delivery was made at his death, and the dominions and regions of hell were cleared of their subjects.

2. Redemption, if for all, must be useless to those who never were favoured with the means of grace; as all the nations of the world, excepting Israel, for many hundred of years were; whose times of ignorance God winked at and overlooked, and sent no messengers, nor messages of grace unto them; see Psalm cxlvii. 19, 20. Acts xvii. 30. and since the coming of Christ, though the gospel has, in some ages, had a greater spread, yet not preached to all; nor is it now, to many nations, who have never heard of Christ, and of redemption by him, Rom. x. 14.

3. The universal scheme affords no encouragement to faith and hope in Christ: redemption, as it ascertains salvation to some, it encourages sensible sinners to hope in Christ for it; *Let Israel hope in the Lord, for with him is plenteous redemption*, Psalm cxxx. 7. a redemption full of salvation; and which secures that blessing to all that believe. But, according to the universal scheme, men may be redeemed by Christ, and yet not saved, but eternally perish: what hope of salvation can a man have upon such a scheme? it

requires no great discernment, nor judgment of things, to determine, which is most eligible of the two schemes, that which makes the salvation of some certain; or that which leaves the salvation of all precarious and uncertain; which, though it asserts a redemption of all; yet it is possible none may be saved.

4. Hence, even to those who are redeemed and saved, it lays no foundation for, nor does it furnish with any argument to engage to love Christ, to be thankful to him, and to praise him for the redemption of them; since the difference between them and others, is not owing to the efficacy of Christ's death, but to their own wills and works; they are not beholden to Christ, who has done no more for them than for those that perish; they are not, from any such consideration, obliged to walk in love, as Christ has loved them, and given himself for them; since he has loved them no more, and given himself for them no otherwise, than for them that are lost; nor are they under obligation to be thankful to him, and bless his name, that he has redeemed their lives from destruction; since, notwithstanding his redemption of them, they might have been destroyed with an everlasting destruction; it is not owing to what Christ has done, but to what they have done themselves, performing the conditions of salvation required, that they are saved from destruction, if ever they are, according to this scheme: nor can they indeed sing the song of praise to the Lamb, for their redemption; saying, *Thou art worthy—for thou wast slain, and hast redeemed us to God by thy blood, out of every kindred, and tongue, and people, and nation!* since, according to this scheme, Christ has redeemed every kindred, every tongue, every people, and every nation.

CHAP. IV.

OF THOSE TEXTS OF SCRIPTURE WHICH SEEM TO FAVOUR UNIVERSAL REDEMPTION.

THERE are several passages of scripture, which at first sight, may seem to countenance the universal scheme; and which are usually brought in support of it; and which it will be necessary to take under consideration: and these may be divided into *three* classes,——1. Such in which the words *all*, and *every* one, are used, when the death of Christ, and the benefits of it are spoken of.——2. Those in which the words *world*, and the *whole world*, occur, where the same subjects are treated of. And,——3. Those that seem to intimate, as if Christ died for some that may be destroyed and perish.

I. Such in which the words *all*, and *every* one, are used; when the death of Christ, and the benefits of it, particularly redemption and salvation by him, are spoken of. As,

1. The declaration of the angel, in Luke ii. 10, 11. *Behold, I bring good tidings of great joy, which shall be to all people; for unto you is born this day, in the city of David, a Saviour, which is Christ the Lord.* Let it be observed, that Christ is not here said to be the Saviour of all men; but to be born for the sake of some, that he might be the Saviour of them; *Unto* YOU *is born a Saviour;* to you the shepherds, who appear to be good men, waiting for the salvation of God, and the coming of their Saviour, and therefore praised and glorified God for what they heard and saw; the words fully agree with the prophetic language, in which the birth of Christ is signified, in Isa. ix. 6. *To us a Child is born:* indeed, it is said, that the news of the birth of a Saviour, would be great joy *to all people*, or *to all the people;* not to all the people of the world, many of whom never heard of it; nor to all the people of the Jews, who did hear of it; nor to Herod the king, and to the Scribes and Pharisees, and to many, at least, of the inhabitants of Jerusalem; for when he and they heard the report the wisemen from the East made, of the birth of the king of the Jews, *Herod was troubled, and all Jerusalem with him,* Matt. ii. 3. but to all the people of God and Christ; to the people Christ came to save, and does save; on whose account his name was called *Jesus, for he shall save* HIS *people from their sins;* the people given him in covenant, and for whose transgressions he was stricken, and for whose sins he made reconciliation, Matt. i. 21. Isa. liii. 8. Heb. ii. 17. at most, the birth of Christ, as a Saviour, can only be matter of great joy to whom the tidings of it come; whereas there are multitudes that come into the world, and go out of it, who never hear of the birth of Christ, and of salvation by him; and where the gospel, the good tidings of salvation by Christ, does come, it is only matter of great joy to them to whom it comes in power, and who are, by it, made sensible of their lost, perishing estate, of their want of a Saviour, and of the suitableness of salvation; such as the

three thousand convinced and converted under Peter's sermon; and the jailor and his household, who cried out, sirs, what must I do to be saved? To such, and to such only, the news of Christ as a Saviour, is matter of great joy.

2. The account given of John's ministry and the end of it; *That all men, through him, might believe,* John i. 7. from whence it is concluded, that all men are bound to believe that Christ came to save them, and that he died for them; and if he did not die for them, then they are bound to believe a lie, and if condemned for not believing, they are condemned for not believing an untruth. But John's ministry only reached to the Jews, among whom he came preaching; and the report he made of Christ they were bound to believe, was, not that he died for them; as yet he had not died; but that he was the Messiah: and their disbelief of this was their sin and condemnation; as it is the sin of the deists, and of all unbelievers, to whom the gospel-revelation comes; and they give not credit to it; for such are bound to believe the report it makes, and give an assent to the truth of it; and which is no other than an historical faith, and which men may have and not be saved; and which the devils themselves have: so that men may be bound to believe, and yet not to the saving of their souls; or that Christ died for them. As is the revelation that is made to men, so they are under obligation to believe; if no revelation is made, no faith is required; *How shall they believe in him, of whom they have not heard?* The Indians who have never heard of Christ, are not bound to believe in him; nor will they be condemned for their unbelief; but for their sins against the light of nature, they have been guilty of; see Rom. x. 14. and ii. 12. Where a revelation is made, and that is only external, and lies in the outward ministry of the word, declaring in general such and such things, concerning the person and office of Christ, men are obliged to give credit to them, upon the evidence they bring with them, and for their unbelief will be condemned; not because they did not believe that Christ died for them, to which they were not obliged; but because they did not believe him to be God, the Son of God, the Messiah, and the Saviour of men. Where the revelation is internal, *By the Spirit of wisdom, and revelation in the knowledge of Christ;* shewing to men their lost estate, and need of a Saviour; acquainting them with Christ, as an able and willing Saviour; setting before them the fulness and suitableness of his salvation; such are, by the Spirit and grace of God, influenced and engaged to venture their souls on Christ, and to believe in him, to the saving of them; but then the first act of faith, even in such, is not to believe that Christ died for them; for it is the plerophory, the full assurance of faith to say, *He hath loved me, and given himself for me!* Gal. ii. 20.

3. The words of Christ in John xii. 32. *And I, if I be lifted up from the earth will draw all men to me;* are expressive of the death of Christ, and of the manner of it, crucifixion; which would be the occasion of drawing a great number of persons together, as is usual at executions; and more especially would be and was at Christ's, he being a remarkable and extraordinary person; some to deplore his case and bewail him, and others to mock at him and reproach him. Though rather this is to be understood of the great multitude of souls who should be gathered to Christ through the ministry of the word after his death, as the fruit and consequence of it; who should be *drawn* and influenced by the powerful and efficacious grace of God to come to Christ, and believe in him; in which sense the word *draw* is used by Christ in John vi. 44. but this is not true of all and every individual person; for there were multitudes then, as now, who will have no will to come to Christ, and are never wrought upon by the grace of God, or drawn by it to come unto him and believe in him; and will be so far from being gathered to him, and into fellowship with him, that they will be bid to depart from him another day, with a *Go, ye cursed;* and in the words before the text, mention is made of the *judgment,* or condemnation of the world, as being then come; as well as of the prince of it being cast out. But by all men, are meant some of all sorts, Jews and Gentiles, more especially the latter, that should be gathered to Christ after his death, through the gospel preached unto them; as was foretold, that when Shiloh, the Messiah, came, who now was come, *to him should the gathering of the people be;* that is, the Gentiles: and it may be observed, that at this time, when Christ spoke these words, there were certain Greeks that were come to the feast to worship, who were desirous of seeing Jesus; with which he was made acquainted by his disciples, and occasioned the discourse of which these

words are a part; and in which our Lord suggests, that at present these Greeks could not be admitted to him, but the time was at hand when he should be *lifted up from the earth*, or die; by which, like a corn of wheat falling into the ground and dying, he should bring forth much fruit; and should be lifted up also as an ensign in the ministry of the word, when the Gentiles in great numbers should flock and seek unto him.

4. The passage of the apostle in Rom. v. 18. *By the righteousness of one, the free gift came upon all men unto justification of life;* is undoubtedly meant of the righteousness of Christ, called the *free gift*, because it was freely wrought out by Christ, and is freely imputed without works; and faith, which receives it, is the gift of God; but then this does not come upon, or is imputed to, every individual son and daughter of Adam; for then they would be all justified by it, and entitled to eternal life through it, and would be glorified; for *whom he justified, them also he glorified:* and being justified by the blood and righteousness of Christ, they would be secure from condemnation, and saved from wrath to come; but this is not true of every one; there are some who are righteously *foreordained to condemnation;* yea, there is a *world* of ungodly men, a multitude of them, that will be *condemned*, Jude ver. 4. 1 Cor. xi. 32. The design of the apostle in the text and context is to shew, that as all men are sinners, and are originally so through the sin and offence of the first man Adam; so all that are righteous become righteous, or are justified, only through the righteousness of Christ imputed to them to their justification; and those who are justified by it, are described by the apostle in this epistle as the elect of God; *Who shall lay any thing to the charge of God's elect? it is God that justifies;* as believers in Christ, on whom his righteousness comes, or is imputed to their justification; that is, *unto all, and upon all them that believe;* and such who receive that, receive also *abundance of grace,* chap. viii. 33. and iii. 22. and v. 17. all which cannot be said of every individual of mankind. But what will set this matter in a clear light is, that Adam and Christ, throughout the whole context, are to be considered as two covenant-heads, having their respective seed and offspring under them; the one as conveying sin and death to all his natural seed, and the other as conveying grace, righteousness, and life to all his spiritual seed; now as through the offence of the first Adam judgment came upon all to condemnation, who descended from him by natural generation, and upon none else; as not upon the human nature of Christ, which did not so descend from him; nor upon the angels that sinned, who were condemned and punished for their own offences, and not his, being none of his offspring; so the free gift of Christ's righteousness comes upon all to justification, and to none else, but those who are the spiritual seed of Christ; given to him as such in the covenant of grace in which he stands an head to them; and *in whom all the seed of Israel,* the spiritual Israel of God, *are justified,* and shall glory, Isa. xlv. 24, 25.

5. The parallel place in 1 Cor. xv. 22. *As in Adam all die, so in Christ shall all be made alive;* which is similar to the preceding in some respect, though not in every thing; it is similar to it in that Adam and Christ are to be considered as representative heads of their respective offspring. Though these words have no respect at all to justification of life, nor to men being quickened together with Christ, nor to the quickening of them by the Spirit and grace of God; but of the resurrection of the dead, when men that have been dead will be made alive, or quickened; see ver. 36. and the design of them is to shew, as in the preceding verse, that *as by man came death, by man came also the resurrection of the dead;* as death came by the first Adam, the resurrection of the dead comes by the second Adam; as the first Adam was a federal head and representative of all that naturally descended from him, and they were considered in him, and sinned in him, and death passed upon all in him, and actually reigns over all his posterity in all generations; so Christ is a federal head and representative of all his spiritual seed, given to him in covenant, and who, though they die a corporal death, shall be made alive, or raised from the dead, by virtue of union to him; for of those only is the apostle speaking in the context, even of such of whom Christ is the first fruits, and who belong to him, ver. 23. for though all shall be made alive, or raised from the dead, by Christ, through his mighty power; yet only those that belong to him, as his seed and offspring, or the members of his body, shall be raised through union to him, and in the first place, and to everlasting life; others will be raised to shame and everlast-

ing contempt, and to the resurrection of damnation.

6. The text in 2 Cor. v. 14, 15. is sometimes brought as a proof of Christ's dying for all men in an unlimited sense; *if one died for all, then were all dead:* now let it be observed, that in the supposition *if one died for all,* the word *men* is not used; it is not *all men,* but all, and may be supplied from other scriptures, *all* his *people,* whom Christ came to save; and *all the sheep,* he laid down his life for; all the members of the *church* for whom he gave himself; *all the sons* whom he brings to glory: and the conclusion, *then were all dead,* is not to be understood of their being dead *in* sin, which is no consequence of the death of Christ; but of their being dead *to* sin in virtue of it; and could it be understood in the first sense, it would only prove that all for whom Christ died are dead in sin, which is true of the elect of God as of others, Eph. ii. 1. but it would not prove that Christ died for all those that are dead in sin, which is the case of every man; but the latter sense is best, for to be dead to sin is the fruit and effect of Christ's death; Christ bore the sins of his people on the cross, that they being *dead to sin, should live unto righteousness;* through the death of Christ they become dead to the damning power of sin; and to the law, as a cursing law; that they might serve the Lord in newness of spirit: this puts them into a capacity of living to him, and affords the strongest argument, drawn from his love in dying for them, to such purposes; to influence and engage them to live to his glory; see Rom. vi. 2, 6. and vii. 4, 6. And let it be further observed, that the same persons Christ died for, for them he rose again; now as Christ was delivered for the offences of men unto death, he was raised again for their justification; and if he rose for the justification of all men, then all would be justified; whereas they are not, as before observed.

7. The words in 1 Tim. ii. 4. *Who will have all men to be saved, and to come unto the knowledge of the truth.* It is certain that all that are saved, it is the will of God they should be saved, and that by Christ, and by him only; *I will save them by the Lord their God;* salvation of whomsoever, is not of the will of men, but flows from the sovereign will and pleasure of God; and if it was the will of God that every individual of mankind should be saved, they would be saved; for *who hath resisted his will?* he works all things after the counsel of it; he does according to it in heaven and in earth; but as it is certain in fact that all are not saved, it is as certain that it is not the will of God that every man and woman should be saved; since there are some who are *fore-ordained to condemnation;* and if there are any he appoints to condemnation, it cannot be his will that the self-same individuals should be saved; besides, there are some of whom it is clearly signified that it is his will they should be damned; as the man of sin, and the son of perdition, Antichrist and his followers; to whom *God sends strong delusions; that they should believe a lie, that they might be damned,* 2 Thess. ii. 11, 12. Besides, those it is the will of God that they should be saved, it is his will that they should *come unto the knowledge of the truth;* both of Christ, who is the way, the truth, and the life, the true way to eternal life; through the faith of whom, as well as through sanctification of the Spirit, men are chosen unto salvation; and of the truth of the gospel; not a notional and superficial, but an experimental knowledge of it; now to all men it is not the will of God to give the means of knowledge, of Christ, and the truths of the gospel: for hundreds of years together, God gave his word to Jacob, and his statutes unto Israel, a small people in one part of the world; and as for other nations, they knew them not; God winked at and overlooked the times of their ignorance, and sent not the gospel, the means of knowledge, unto them; and this is the case of many nations at this day; yea, where the gospel is sent and preached, it is the will of God to hide the truths of it from many, and even from those who have the most penetrating abilities; *even so, Father,* says Christ, *for so it seemeth good in thy sight,* Matt. xi. 25, 26. it was his will it should be so, and therefore it could not be his will they should be saved, and come to the knowledge of the truth. It is best therefore to understand by *all,* some of all sorts, as the word *all* must be understood in many places, particularly in Gen. vii. 14. and this sense agrees with the context, in which the apostle exhorts that prayers and thanksgivings be made for all men, for kings, and for all in authority; not only for men of low degree, but for men of high degree also; for all sorts of men; this being agreeable to God, and acceptable in his sight; whose will it is that men of all sorts should be saved, and know the truth.

Though it is best of all to understand this of the Gentiles, some of whom God would have saved, as well as of the Jews; and therefore had chosen some of both unto salvation; and had appointed his Son to be his salvation to the ends of the earth; and therefore had sent his gospel among them, declaring that whoever believed in Christ should be saved, whether Jew or Gentile; and had made it the power of God unto salvation to the Jew first, and also to the Gentile; and therefore it was proper that prayers and thanksgivings should be made for Gentiles in every class of life.

8. Another passage in the same context, in which Christ is said to *give himself a ransom for all*, ver. 6. or a *ransom-price*, αντιλυτρον, in the room and stead of all; but this cannot be understood of all and every individual man; for then all would be ransomed, or else the ransom-price must be paid in vain; but of many, as it is expressed by Christ, Matt. xx. 28. and particularly of the Gentiles, as before; the truth contained herein being what has been testified in the gospel, of which the apostle was ordained a preacher, a teacher of the Gentiles in faith and verity, when the Jews forbade him and other apostles to preach unto them; but as he opposed this prohibition of theirs, so another notion of theirs in the next verse, which confined public prayer to a certain place; all which shew whom the apostle had in view throughout the whole context, and intended by the word *all*.

9. Another passage in the same epistle is sometimes brought in favour of the general scheme, 1 Tim. iv. 10. where God is said to be *the Saviour of all men;* but the passage is not to be understood of Christ, and of spiritual and eternal salvation by him; which it is certain all men do not share in; but of God the Father, and of temporal salvation by him; and of his preservation of all his creatures; who is the *preserver of men*, supports and upholds them in being, and supplies them with the necessaries of life; and in a providential way is *good to all;* but his providence is extended in a special manner towards those that trust and believe in him; he takes a particular care of them, and makes particular provisions for them; these being his people, his portion, and the lot of his inheritance, like Israel of old, he surrounds them by his power, leads them about by his wisdom, and keeps them as tenderly as the apple of his eye.

10. So the words of the apostle, in Tit. ii. 11, 12. *For the grace of God, that bringeth salvation, hath appeared to all men:* but it is not said, that this grace brings salvation to all men, but has appeared to all men; nor that it teaches all men to deny ungodliness, &c. but only *us*, to whom the gospel of the grace of God comes with power; for that is to be understood by it; not the grace and love of God, in his own heart, towards men; for this is not manifested to all men; but is a favour he bears to his own people: nor grace, as wrought in the heart by the Spirit of God; for this is not vouchsafed unto all men; all men have not faith; and some are without hope and God in the world, and have no love to God and Christ, and to his people; but the gospel, which often goes by this name, because of the doctrines of grace contained in it; this had been like a candle lighted up in a small part of the world, in Judea; but now it was like the sun in its meridian glory, and appeared to Gentiles as well as Jews, being no longer confined to the latter; and where it came with power, as it did not to every individual, it produced the effects herein mentioned; from whence it appears, the apostle is speaking only of the external ministration of the gospel, and of the extent of that; and not of redemption and salvation by Christ; of which, when he speaks, in a following verse, it is in a very different form; *Who gave himself for us*, not for all, *that he might redeem us*, not every man, *from all iniquity, and purify unto himself a peculiar people*, a special and distinct people, *zealous of good works*.

11. Likewise what the author of the epistle to the Hebrews says, chap. ii. 9. *That he* (Christ) *by the grace of God, should taste death for every man:* but the word *man* is not in the text; it is only for *every one;* and is to be interpreted, and supplied, by the context, for every one of the sons Christ brings to glory, ver. 10. for every one of the brethren whom he sanctifies, and is not ashamed to own in that relation, ver. 11. and for every one of the members of the church, in the midst of which he sung praise, and for the whole of it, ver. 12. for every one of the children given him by his Father, and for whose sake he became incarnate, ver. 13, 14. Besides, the words may be rendered, *that he should taste of every death*, of every kind of death, which it was proper he should, in bringing many sons to glory, ver. 10. and as he did; of the death of afflictions, of which he had

waters of a full cup wrung out to him; of corporal death, being put to death in the flesh; and of spiritual and eternal death, or what had a semblance thereof, and was tantamount thereunto, when he was deprived of the divine presence, and had a sense of divine wrath; as both in the garden, when his soul was *exceeding sorrowful, even unto death;* and on the cross, when he said, *My God, my God, why hast thou forsaken me!*

12. One passage more, is in 2 Pet. iii. 9. *God is long-suffering to us-ward, not willing that any should perish; but that all should come to repentance.* This cannot be understood of every individual of mankind; for certain it is, that God is willing that some should perish; *What if God willing, &c.* Rom. ix. 22. Nor is it true, that it is the will of God that all men should have repentance unto life; for then he would give it to them; for it is solely in his own gift; at least, he could give them the means of it, which he does not: the key to this text lies in the phrase, *to us-ward,* to whom God is long-suffering; these design a society to which the apostle belonged, and not all mankind; and who are distinguished, in the context, from scoffers and mockers, that would be in the last days, ver. 3, 4. and are described by the character of beloved, ver. 8. beloved of God and Christ, and of his people; for whose sake he waited, and did not bring on the destruction of the world so soon as, according to his promise, it might be expected; but this was not owing to any dilatoriness in him; but to his long-suffering towards his beloved and chosen ones, being unwilling that any of them should perish; but that they should all come to, and partake of, repentance towards God, and faith in Christ; and when every one of them are brought thereunto, he would delay the coming of Christ, and the destruction of the world, no longer; when the last man was called by grace, and converted, and became a true believer, and a real penitent; when the head, or last, stone was laid upon the top of the building, the church, and that edifice completed thereby, he would stay no longer, but come suddenly, as a thief in the night, and burn the world about the ears of the ungodly: this world is but like scaffolding to a building, which, when finished, the scaffolding is taken down and destroyed, and not before; the building is the church, for the sake of which this world was made; and when this edifice is finished, which will be when all the elect of God are called, and brought to repentance, then it will be destroyed; the earth, and all therein, will be burnt with fire; as in ver. 10.

II. A second class of scriptures, which may seem to favour, and are sometimes brought in support of the universal scheme, are such in which the words *world,* and the *whole world,* are used; when the death of Christ, and the benefits of it, are spoken of. As,

1. The words of John the Baptist to his hearers, in John i. 29. *Behold the Lamb of God, which taketh away the sin of the world!* which are to be understood, neither of original sin, which is common to the whole world; but is not taken away, with respect to all: nor of the actual transgressions of every person; which is not true in fact; and is only true of such whose sins are laid on Christ, and imputed to him; and which he bore, and the whole punishment of them; and so has taken them away, as to be seen no more; which cannot be said of the sins of all men, 1 Tim. v. 24. they are the sins of *many,* and not all, which have been made to meet on Christ, and he has borne them, and took them away, Isa. liii. 6, 12.

2. The words of Christ himself, in John iii. 16. *God so loved the world, that he gave his only begotten Son, &c.* But all the individuals in the world are not loved by God in such a manner; nor is Christ the special gift of God to them all; nor have all faith in him; nor can it be said of all, that they shall never perish, but have everlasting life; since many will go into everlasting punishment: but by the world, is meant the Gentiles; and Christ opposes a notion of the Jews, that they themselves only were the objects of God's love, and that the Gentiles had no share in it, and would not enjoy any benefit by the Messiah when he came; but, says Christ, I tell you, God has so loved the world of the Gentiles, as to give his Son, that whosoever believes in him, be he of what nation soever, shall be saved with an everlasting salvation.

3. The words of the Samaritans to the woman of Samaria, in John iv. 42. *We know that this is indeed the Christ, the Saviour of the world,* of Gentiles as well as Jews; this they learnt from what Christ had made known of himself, and of his grace to them; for they were originally Gentiles, and were now reckoned by the Jews as heathens; see also 1 John iv. 14.

4. The words of our Lord in his discourse about himself, as the bread which *giveth life unto the world; and which is his flesh he gave for the life of the world:* now no more can be designed by the *world,* than those who are quickened by this bread applied unto them, and received by them, and for the obtaining of eternal life; for whom the flesh, or human nature of Christ, was given, as a sacrifice for sin, whereby that is secured unto them; but this is not true of all men; since even the gospel, which exhibits the heavenly manna, and holds forth Christ, the bread of life, is to some *the savour of death unto death,* whilst to others it is, *the savour of life unto life,* 2 Cor. ii. 16.

5. The words of the apostle, in 2 Cor. v. 19. *God was in Christ, reconciling the world unto himself:* these are the same with the *us,* in the preceding verse, which were a special and distinct people; for it cannot be said of every man what follows, *not imputing their trespasses unto them;* which is a special blessing, that belongs to some; for though it comes upon both Jews and Gentiles, that believe, yet not upon all and every man, Rom. iv. 6, 7, 8. for some men's sins will be charged upon them; and they will be punished for them, with an everlasting destruction; by various circumstances in the context it seems, that by the *world* the Gentiles are meant.

6. The famous, and well-known text, in this controversy, is 1 John ii. 2. where Christ is said to be, *the propitiation for the sins of the whole world.* Now let it be observed, that these phrases, *all the world,* and *the whole world,* are often in scripture to be taken in a limited sense; as in Luke ii. 1. *that all the world should be taxed;* it can mean no more than that part of the world the Roman empire, which was under the dominion of Cæsar Augustus: and in Rom. i. 8. it can only design the christians throughout the world, not the heathens; and when the gospel is said to be *in all the world, and bring forth fruit,* Col. i. 6. it can only intend true believers in Christ, in all places, in whom only it brings forth fruit; and when it is said, *all the world wondered after the beast,* Rev. xiii. 3. at that same time, there were saints he made war with, because they would not worship him: and so in other places; and in this epistle of John, the phrase is used in a restrained sense, 1 John v. 19. where those that belong to God, are distinguished from the whole world, described by lying in wickedness, which they do not. And as John was a Jew, he spake in the language of the Jews, who frequently in their writings, use the phrase כולי עלמא *the whole world,* in a limited sense: sometimes it only signifies a large number of people;[1] sometimes a majority of their doctors;[2] sometimes a congregation;[3] or a whole synagogue;[4] and sometimes very few:[5] and so here in the text under consideration, it cannot be understood of all men; only of those for whom Christ is an advocate, ver. 1. whose advocacy is founded on his propitiatory sacrifice; now Christ is not an advocate, or does not make intercession for all men; for he himself says, *I pray not for the world:* and Christ can be a propitiation for no more than he is an advocate; if he was a propitiation for all, he would surely be an advocate for all; and plead on their behalf his propitiatory sacrifice; but Christ was *set forth,* or preordained, to be *a propitiation,* not for all men; but for such only, who, *through faith in his blood,* receive the benefit of it, and rejoice in it, Rom. iii. 25. and v. 11. moreover, in this epistle, the persons for whom Christ is a propitiation, are represented as a peculiar people, and the objects of God's special love, 1 John iv. 10. but what may be observed, and will lead more clearly into the sense of the passage before us, is, that the apostle John was a Jew, and wrote to Jews; and in the text speaks of them, and of the Gentiles, as to be distinguished; and therefore says of Christ, *he is* the propitiation *for our sins; and not for ours only,* for the sins of us Jews only; *but for the sins of the whole world;* of the Gentiles also, of all the elect of God throughout the Gentile world: in which a notion of the Jews is opposed, that the Gentiles would receive no benefit by the Messiah, as has been observed, on John iii. 16. and here the apostle takes up the sentiment of his Lord and Master, in whose bosom he lay, and expresses it. Nothing is more common in Jewish writings, than to call the Gentiles the world, the whole world, and the nations of the world; as they are by

---

[1] T Bab. Yoma, fol. 71. 2.
[2] Ibid. Bava Metzia, fol. 33. 2.
[3] Ibid. Megillah, fol. 22. 2.
[4] Ibid. Horaoit, fol. 33. 2.
[5] Vid. Mill. Form. Talmud. p. 41, 42.

the apostle Paul, in distinction from the Jews, Rom. xi. 12, 15.

III. Another class of scriptures, which may seem to favour the universal scheme, and are usually brought in support of it, are such which it is thought, intimate that Christ died for some that may be destroyed and perish.

1. The first passage is in Rom. xiv. 15. *Destroy not him with thy meat for whom Christ died:* which can never design eternal destruction; for that cannot be thought to be neither in the will nor power of men; could it be supposed, that it was in the will of any, or that any were of such a malicious disposition, as to wish for, and seek the eternal damnation of another; which surely cannot be imagined among men professing religion; yet it could never be in their power; for none but God can destroy soul and body in hell, Matt. x. 28. nor can one instance be produced, of any that were eventually destroyed for whom Christ died; nor can such destruction be brought about by eating meat, of indifferent use, that might, or might not be eaten, of which the apostle is speaking, neither through themselves nor others eating it: for that can never affect the eternal state of men, which makes a man neither better nor worse, 1 Cor. viii. 8. But the passage is to be understood of the destruction of a weak brother's peace and comfort, through the imprudent use of things indifferent, by a stronger brother; who thereby may be the occasion of offending and grieving his brother, and of his stumbling and falling, so as to wound and distress him, though not as to perish eternally; thus it is explained, ver. 13, 21. and is to be taken in the same sense as the phrase in ver. 20. *for meat destroy not the work of God;* not saints, as the workmanship of God; for as that is not of man's making, it is not of man's marring; nor the work of grace, which being begun, will be perfected; nor the work of faith, which will be performed with power; but the work of peace in individual persons, and in the church of God.

2. A similar passage, and to be understood in much the same manner, is in 1 Cor. viii. 12. *And through thy knowledge shall thy weak brother perish, for whom Christ died?* which intends, not the perishing of his immortal soul; or of his perishing eternally in hell; which can never be the case of any for whom Christ died; for then the death of Christ would be so far in vain; and not be a security from condemnation; contrary to Rom. viii. 33. nor be a full satisfaction to justice; or God must be unjust, to punish twice for the same offence: but it intends, the perishing of his peace and comfort for a time; and is explained by *defiling* and *wounding* his conscience, and making him to *offend*, through the imprudent use of christian liberty, in those who had stronger faith and greater knowledge, ver. 7, 12, 13. of which they should be careful, from this consideration; that a weak brother is as near and dear to Christ, since he died for him, as a stronger brother is.

3. Another passage urged for the same purpose, is in 2 Pet. ii. 1. which speaks of false teachers that should be among the saints, who would bring in *damnable heresies, denying the Lord that bought them; and bring upon themselves swift destruction:* from whence it is concluded, that such as are bought by Christ, may be destroyed; but Christ is not here spoken of, but God the Father; and of him the word δισποτης is always used, when applied to a divine Person, and not of Christ; nor is there any thing in this text that obliges us to understand it of him; nor is there here any thing said of Christ dying for any persons, in any sense whatever; nor of the redemption of any by his blood; and which is not intended by the word *bought:* where Christ's redemption is spoken of, the price is usually mentioned; or some circumstance or another, which plainly determines the sense; see Acts xx. 28. 1 Cor. vi. 20. Eph. i. 7. 1 Pet. i. 18, 19. Rev. v. 9. and xiv. 3, 4. Besides, if such as Christ has bought with his blood, should be left so to deny him, as to bring upon themselves eternal destruction, Christ's purchase would be in vain, and the ransom-price be paid for nought; which can never be true. The *buying*, spoken of in the text, respects temporal deliverance, particularly the redemption of Israel out of Egypt; who are therefore called, a *purchased* people, Exod. xv. 16. the phrase is borrowed from Deut. xxxii. 6. where, to aggravate the ingratitude of the people of Israel, it is said, *Is not he thy Father that hath bought thee?* And this is not the only place Peter refers to in this chapter; see ver. 12, and 13. compared with Deut. xxxii. 5. Now the persons the apostle writes unto were Jews, scattered about in divers places; a people that in all ages valued themselves upon, and boasted of their being the Lord's peculiar people, bought and purchased by him:

wherefore the phrase is used here as by Moses, to aggravate the ingratitude and impiety of the false teachers among the Jews; that they should deny, in works at least, if not in words, that mighty Jehovah who had of old redeemed their fathers out of Egypt, and had distinguished them with peculiar favours.

Of these various passages of scripture, see more at large, in my *Cause of God and Truth*, Part. I. and of the objections and answers to them, taken from reason, and the absurd consequences following the denial of universal redemption, as supposed; see the same Treatise, Part III.

From what has been observed concerning redemption, the nature and properties of it may be learnt. As,

1. That it is agreeable to all the perfections of God: it springs from his love, grace, and mercy, and glorifies them; it is planned and conducted by his infinite wisdom, which is illustriously displayed in it; and it is wrought out to declare his justice and honour; that all the perfections of God meet in it, mercy and truth, peace and righteousness: the glory of all his attributes is great, in the redemption and salvation of his people.

2. It is what a creature could never obtain; none but the Son of God: no man could have redeemed himself, or any other, nor given to God a ransom for either; a creature could never have redeemed himself, neither by power nor by price; not by power, he could not have loosed the fetters of sin, with which he was held; nor delivered himself out of the hands of Satan, the gaoler, stronger than he: nor by price, for the infinite justice of God being offended by sin, required an infinite satisfaction, an infinite price to be paid into its hands, for redemption and deliverance; and to which no price was adequate, but the precious blood of Christ.

3. The redemption obtained by Christ resides in him, as the subject of it, who is the author of it; *In him we have redemption, through his blood*, Eph. i. 7. and the benefits of it are communicated from him by the Father, through his gracious imputation and application of it, and of them to his people, 1 Cor. i. 30.

4. It is special and particular; they are many, and not all that are ransomed and redeemed; they that are redeemed, are redeemed out of every kindred, tongue, people, and nation; they are the elect of God, and sheep of Christ; a peculiar people, Rev. v. 9.

5. It is a plenteous one, full and complete, Psalm cxxx. 7. by it men are brought, not into a mere salvable state; but are actually, and to all intents and purposes, saved by it; God, through it, is not made merely reconcileable to them; but the redeemed are actually reconciled to God, through the death of his Son. Salvation is obtained for them, not conditionally, but absolutely; Christ came to seek and save what was lost; even the lost sheep of the house of Israel; and he has found them in redemption, and saved them. Redemption includes the several blessings of grace; as justification, pardon of sin, adoption, and eternal life; and secures all to the redeemed ones.

6. It is eternal, Heb. ix. 12. so called, in distinction from the typical and temporary expiations, by the blood of slain beasts, which could not take away sin; but there was an annual remembrance of them; but by the blood of Christ men are eternally redeemed from all iniquity: and in distinction from temporary redemption and salvation; as of the people of Israel out of Egypt and Babylon; which were types of this; and because it extends, as to ages past, and was a redemption of transgressions and of transgressors, that were under the first testament; so to ages to come; the benefits and blessings of which reach to the saints in all generations: the blessings of it are eternal; an everlasting righteousness for justification; pardon of sin is once and for ever; and once a child of God, always so, and the inheritance secured by it; redemption is eternal; and the redeemed ones shall be saved in the Lord, with an everlasting salvation; none of them shall ever perish, but have everlasting life.

CHAP. V.

OF THE SATISFACTION OF CHRIST.

Though the doctrine of satisfaction is not only closely connected with, but even included in, the doctrine of redemption, made by paying a satisfactory price into the hands of justice, and is a part of it; yet, it is of such importance, that it requires it should be distinctly and separately treated of: it is the glory of the christian religion, which distinguishes it from others; what gives it the preference to all others, and without which it would be of no value itself: and though the word *satisfaction* is not syllabically expressed in scripture, as used in the doctrine under consideration, the thing is abundantly declared in it; which yet Socinus[1] denies; though he himself owns,[2] that a thing is not to be rejected, because not expressly found in scripture; for he says, it is enough with all lovers of truth, that the thing in question is confirmed by reason and testimony; though the words which are used in explaining the question are not found expressly written. What Christ has done and suffered, in the room and stead of sinners, with content, well-pleasedness, and acceptance in the sight of God, is what may, with propriety, be called, *satisfaction;* and this is plentifully spoken of in the word of God; as when God is said to be *well-pleased for Christ's righteousness sake*, and with it, it being answerable to the demands of law and justice; and is an honouring and magnifying of it; and when the sacrifice of Christ, and such his sufferings are, is said to be of a *sweet-smelling savour to God;* because it has expiated sin, atoned for it; that is, made satisfaction for it, and taken it away; which the sacrifices under the law could not do; hence there was a remembrance of it every year, Isa. xlii. 21. Eph. v. 2. and there are terms and phrases which are used of Christ, and of his work; as *propitiation, reconciliation, atonement*, &c. which are equivalent and synonymous to *satisfaction* for sin, and expressive of it; concerning which may be observed the following things:

I. The necessity of satisfaction to be made for sin, in order to the salvation of sinners; for without satisfaction for sin, there can be no salvation from it; *for it became him for whom are all things, and by whom are all things, in bringing many sons unto glory, to make the Captain of their salvation perfect through sufferings;* that is, it became the all-wise and all-powerful Former and Maker of all things for himself; it was agreeable to his nature and perfections; it was fitting, and so necessary, that it should be done; that whereas it was his pleasure to bring many of the sons of men, even as many as are made the sons of God, to eternal glory and happiness by Christ; that the author of their salvation should perfectly and completely suffer, in their room and stead, all that the law and justice of God could require; without which not a sinner could be saved, nor a son brought to glory. If two things are granted, which surely must be easily granted, satisfaction for sin will appear necessary: 1. That men are sinners; and this must be owned, unless any can work themselves up into such a fancy, that they are an innocent sort of beings, whose natures are not depraved, nor their actions wrong; neither offensive to God, nor injurious to their fellow-creatures; and if so, indeed then a satisfaction for sin would be unnecessary: and one would think the opposers of Christ's satisfaction must have entertained such a conceit of themselves; but if they have, scripture, all experience, the consciences of men, and facts, are against them; all which declare men are sinners, are transgressors of the law, and pronounced guilty by it before God; and are subject to its curse, condemnation, and death, the sanction of it; and *every transgression* of it, and *disobedience* to it, has *received*, does receive, or will receive, *a just recompense of reward;* that is, righteous judgment and punishment, either in the sinner himself, or in a surety for him, Heb. ii. 2. God never relaxes the sanction of the law; that is, the punishment for sin it threatens; though he favourably admits one to suffer it for the delinquent. By sin men are alienated from God, set at a distance from him, with respect to communion; and without reconciliation or satisfaction for sin, they never can be admitted to it; a sinner, not reconciled to God, can never enjoy nearness to him, and fellowship with him; and this, when ever had, is the fruit of Christ's sufferings and death; he suffered, in the room and stead of the unjust, to bring them to God; and it is by his blood making peace for them, that they that were afar off, with respect to communion, are made nigh and favoured with it, 1 Pet. iii. 18. Eph. ii. 13, 14. the satisfaction of Christ does not procure the love of God, being the effect of it; yet it opens the way to the embraces of his arms, stopped by sin. Moreover, men by sin, are declared rebels against God, and enemies to him; hence reconciliation,

---

[1] Prælection. Theolog. c. 15. T. 1. Oper. p. 565.

[2] De Adorat. Christ. Disp. inter. Opera ejus, tom. ii. p. 978.

atonement, or satisfaction, became necessary; as they are enemies in their minds, by wicked works; yea, their carnal mind is enmity itself against God. And, on the other hand, on the part of God, there is a law-enmity, which must be slain, and was slain, through the sufferings of Christ on the cross; *Having slain the enmity thereby*, Eph. ii. 16. and so made peace and reconciliation; for this designs not any internal disposition in the mind of God's people, before conversion, which is overcome in it, by the love of God implanted in them; but the declared enmity of the moral law against them, broken by them; of which the ceremonial law was a symbol, in the slain sacrifices of it, and stood as an hand-writing against them; all which were necessary to be removed.——2. The other thing to be taken for granted is, that it is the will of God to save sinners, at least some of them; for if it was not his will to save any from sin, there would be no need of a satisfaction for it. Now it is certain, that it is the will and resolution of God to save some; whom he appointed not to the wrath they deserve, but to salvation by Christ; whom he has ordained to eternal life, and are vessels of mercy, afore prepared for glory; and for whose salvation a provision is made in the council and covenant of grace, in which it was consulted, contrived, and settled, and Christ appointed to be the author of it; and who, in the fulness of time, was sent and came about it, and has obtained it; and which is ascribed to his blood, his sufferings, and death, which were necessary for the accomplishment of it.

Some have affirmed, that God could forgive sin, and save sinners, without a satisfaction; and this is said, not only by Socinians,[3] but by some, as Twisse, Dr. Goodwin, Rutherford, &c. who own that a satisfaction is made, and the fitness and expedience of it: but then this is giving up the point; for if it is fitting and expedient to be done, it is necessary; for whatever is fitting to be done in the affair of salvation, God cannot but do it, or will it to be done. Besides, such a way of talking, as it tends to undermine and weaken the doctrine of satisfaction; so to encourage and strengthen the hands of the Socinians, the opposers of it; much the same arguments being used by the one as by the other. It is not indeed proper to limit the holy One of Israel, or lay a restraint on his power, which is unlimited, boundless, and infinite; with whom nothing is impossible, and who is able to do more than we can conceive of; yet it is no ways derogatory to the glory of his power, nor is it any impeachment of it, nor argues any imperfection or weakness in him, to say there are some things he cannot do; for not to be able to do them is his glory; as that he cannot commit iniquity, which is contrary to the purity and holiness of his nature; he cannot do an act of injustice to any of his creatures, that is contrary to his justice and righteousness; he cannot lie, that is contrary to his veracity and truth; he cannot deny himself, for that is against his nature and perfections; and for the same reason he cannot forgive sin without a satisfaction, because so to do, does not agree with the perfections of his nature. It is a vain thing to dispute about the power of God; what he can do, or what he cannot do, in any case where it is plain, what it is his will to do, as it is in the case before us; at the same time he declared himself a God gracious and merciful, forgiving iniquity, transgression, and sin; he has, in the strongest terms, affirmed, that he *will by no means clear the guilty;* see Exod. xxxiv. 6, 7. Jer. xxx. 11. Nahum. i. 3. Numb. xiv. 18. or let him go unpunished; that is, without a satisfaction. Besides, if any other method could have been taken, consistent with the will of God, the prayer of Christ would have brought it out; *Father, if it be possible, let this cup* of suffering death *pass from me :* and then adds, *not my will, but thine be done!* what that will was, is notorious; see Heb. x. 5—10. It may be said, this is to make God weaker than man, and to represent him as not able to do what man can do;[4] one man can forgive another the debts that are owing to him; and in some cases he should, and is to be commended for it; and one may forgive another an offence committed against himself, and ought to do it; especially when the offender expresses repentance. But it should be observed that sins are not pecuniary debts, and to be remitted as they are; they are not properly debts, only so called allusively: if they

---

[3] Socinus de Jesu Christo Servatore, par. 1. c. 1 et par. 3. c. 1. Prælection. Theolog. c. 16, 17, 18. p. 566, 567, 570. Racov. Catechés. c. 8. qu. 12:

[4] Prælection. ut supra, c. 16.

were proper debts, they might be paid in their kind, one sin by committing another, which is absurd; but they are called debts, because as debts oblige to payment, these oblige to punishment; which debt of punishment must be paid, either by the debtor, the sinner, or by a surety for him; sins are criminal debts, and can be remitted no other way. God, therefore, in this affair, is to be considered not merely as a creditor, but as the Judge of all the earth, who will do right; and as the Rector and Governor of the world; that great Lawgiver, who is able to save and to destroy; who will secure his own authority as such, do justice to himself, and honour to his law, and shew a proper concern for the good of the community, or universe, of which he is the moral Governor. So though one man may forgive another a private offence, committed against himself, as it is an injury to him, yet he cannot forgive one, as it is an injury to the commonwealth, of which he is a part; a private person, as he cannot execute vengeance and wrath, or inflict punishment on an offender; so neither can he, of right, let go unpunished one that has offended against the peace and good of the commonwealth; these are things that belong to the civil magistrate, to one in power and authority: and a judge that acts under another, and according to a law which he is obliged to regard, can neither inflict punishment, nor remit it, especially the latter, without the order of his superior. God indeed is not under another; he is of himself, and can do what he pleases; he is the Maker and Judge of the law, but then he is a law to himself; his nature is his law, and he cannot act contrary to that; wherefore, as Joshua says, *he is an holy God; he is a jealous God; he will not forgive your transgressions, nor your sins;* that is, without a satisfaction; and which comports with his own honour and glory; of which he is a jealous God. Sin is *crimen læsæ Majestatis;* a crime committed against the majesty of God; it disturbs the universe, of which he is Governor, and tends to shake and overthrow his moral government of the world; to introduce atheism into it, and bring it into disorder and confusion, and to withdraw creatures from their dependence on God, and obedience to him, as the moral Governor of it; and therefore requires satisfaction, and an infinite one, as the object of it is; and cannot be made, but by an infinite Person, as Christ is; such a satisfaction the honour of the divine Being, and of his righteous law, transgressed by sin, requires. Which leads to observe,

That to forgive sin, without a satisfaction, does not accord with the perfections of God.

1. Not with his justice and holiness: God is naturally and essentially just and holy; all his ways and works proclaim him to be so; and his creatures own it, angels and men, good and bad; as he is righteous, he naturally loves righteousness; and naturally hates evil, and cannot but shew his hatred of it; and which is shewn by punishing it. God is a consuming fire; and as fire naturally burns combustible matter, so it is natural to God to punish sin. Wherefore, punitive justice, though denied by Socinians,[5] in order to subvert the satisfaction of Christ, is natural and essential to him; he cannot but punish sin; it is a righteous thing with him to do it; the justice of God requires it; and there is no salvation without bearing it;[6] and he is praised and applauded for it, by saints and holy angels; and to do otherwise, or not to punish sin, would be acting against himself and his own glory.

2. To forgive sin, without satisfaction for it, does not agree with his veracity, truth, and faithfulness, with respect to his holy and righteous law; it became him, as the Governor of the universe, to give a law to his creatures; for where there is no law, there is no transgression; men may sin with impunity, no charge can be brought against them; sin is not imputed, where there is no law; but God has given a law, which is holy, just, and good; and which shews what is his good and perfect will; and this law has a sanction annexed to it, as every law should have, or it will be of no force to oblige to an observance of it, and deter from disobedience to it; and the sanction of the law of God is nothing less than death, than death eternal; which is the just wages, and proper demerit of sin, and which God has declared he will inflict upon the transgressor; *In the day thou eatest thereof thou shalt surely die:* now the veracity, truth, and faithfulness of God, are engaged to see this sanction

---

[5] Socin. Prælection, ut supra, c. 16. Racov. Catechcs, c. 8. qu. 20.

[6] See Dr. Owen's Preface to Vindiciæ Evangel. p. 26. Sandford De Descensu Christi. 1. 3. p. 106.

established, and threatening executed; either upon the transgressor himself, or upon a surety for him; for the judgment of God is, that such a person is worthy of death; and his judgment is according to truth; and will and does most certainly take place.

3. The wisdom of God makes it necessary that sin should not be forgiven, without a satisfaction; for it is not the wisdom of any legislature, to suffer the law not to take place in a delinquent; it is always through weakness that it is admitted, either through fear, or through favour and affection; and this may be called tenderness, lenity, and clemency; but it is not justice: and it tends to weaken the authority of the legislator, to bring government under contempt, and to embolden transgressors of the law, in hope of impunity. The all-wise Lawgiver can never be thought to act such a part: besides, the scheme of men's peace and reconciliation by Christ, is represented as the highest act of wisdom, known to be wrought by God; for *herein he has abounded towards us in all wisdom and prudence:* but where is the consummate wisdom of it, if it could have been in an easier way, at less expense, without the sufferings and death of his Son? had there been another and a better way, infinite wisdom would have found it out, and divine grace and mercy would have pursued it.

4. Nor does it seem so well to comport with the great love and affection of God, to his Son Jesus Christ, said to be his beloved Son, the dear Son of his love; to send him into this world in the likeness of sinful flesh—to be vilified and abused by the worst of men—to be buffeted, lashed, and tortured, by a set of miscreants—and to put him to the most cruel and shameful death, to make reconciliation for sin, if sin could have been forgiven, and the sinner saved, without all this, by a hint, a nod, a word speaking; *Thy sins are forgiven thee,* and thou shalt be saved! Nor does it so fully express the love of God to his saved ones; but tends to lessen and lower that love. God giving his Son to suffer and die, in the room and stead of sinners, and to be the propitiation for their sins, is always ascribed to the love of God, and represented as the strongest expression of it! But where is the greatness of this love, if salvation could have been done at an easier rate? and, indeed, if it could have been done in another way? the greatness of it appears, in that either the sinner must die, or Christ die for him; such was the love of God, that he chose the latter! To all this may be added, as evincing the necessity of a satisfaction for sin, that there is something of it appears by the very light of nature, in the heathens, who have nothing else to direct them; they are sensible by it, when sin is committed, deity is offended; else what mean those accusations of conscience upon sinning, and dreadful horrors and terrors of mind? witness also, the various, though foolish and fruitless methods they have taken, to appease the anger of God; as even to give their first-born for their transgression, and the fruit of their body for the sin of their souls; which shews their sense of a necessity of making some sort of satisfaction for offences committed; and of appeasing justice, or vengeance, as they call their deity, Acts xxviii. 4. The several sacrifices of the Jews, they were directed to under the former dispensation, plainly shew the necessity of a satisfaction for sin; and plainly point out forgiveness of sin, as proceeding upon it; though they themselves could not really, only typically, expiate sin, make atonement and satisfaction for it. But if God could forgive sin without any satisfaction at all, why not forgive it upon the foot of those sacrifices? The reason is plain, because he could not, consistent with himself, do it without the sacrifice of his Son, typified by them. Wherefore it may be strongly concluded, that a plenary satisfaction for sin, by what Christ has done and suffered, was absolutely necessary to the forgiveness of sin; *Without shedding of blood is no remission,* neither typical nor real; without it there never was, never will be, nor never could be, any forgiveness of sin, Heb. ix. 22.

II. The ground and foundation of satisfaction for sin by Christ, and the cause and spring of it.

First, The ground and foundation on which it is laid, and upon which it proceeds, are the council and covenant of grace, and the suretiship-engagements of Christ therein.

1. The scheme of making peace with God, or of appeasing divine justice, and of making reconciliation for sin, that is, satisfaction for it, was planned in the everlasting council; which, from thence is called, *the council of peace,* Zech. vi. 13. *God was* then *in Christ,* or with Christ, *reconciling the world,* the whole number of the elect, *to himself;* that is, they were

consulting together to form the plan of their reconciliation and salvation; and the method they pitched upon was, *not imputing their trespasses to them;* not to reckon and place to their account, their sins and iniquities, and insist upon a satisfaction for them from themselves; for God knew, that if he made a demand of satisfaction for them on them, they could not answer him, one man of a thousand, no, not one at all; nor for one sin of a thousand, no, not for a single one; and that if he brought a charge of sin against them, they must be condemned; for they would not be able to give one reason, or say any thing on their own behalf, why judgment should not proceed against them; wherefore, *Who shall lay any thing to the charge of God's elect?* since God will not, whoever does, it will be of no avail against them; for *it is God that justifies* them: and happy are the persons interested in this glorious scheme, to whom the Lord *imputeth not iniquity;* and it was also further devised in this council, to impute the transgressions of the said persons to Christ, the Son of God; which, though not expressed in the text referred to, 2 Cor. v. 19. yet it is implied and understood, and in clear and full terms signified, in the verse following but one, in which the account of the scheme of reconciliation is continued; *For he hath made him to be sin for us, who knew no sin;* that is, the sinless Jesus, who was made sin, not inherently, by a transfusion of sin into him, which his holy nature would not admit of; but imputatively, by a transfer of the guilt of sin unto him, by placing it to his account, and making him answerable for it; which was done, not merely at the time of his sufferings and death, though then God openly and manifestly *laid upon him,* or made to meet on him, *the iniquity of us all,* of all the Lord's people, when *the chastisement of their peace was on him;* or the punishment of their sin was inflicted on him, to make peace for them; but as early as the council of peace was held, and the above method was concerted and agreed to, or Christ became a Surety for his people, so early were their sins imputed to him, and he became responsible for them; and this laid the foundation of his making satisfaction for sin. For,

2. The scheme drawn in council, was settled in covenant; which, on that account, is called *the covenant of peace,* Isa. liv. 10. Mal. ii. 5. in which covenant Christ was called to be a Priest; for Christ glorified not himself to be called one; but his father bestowed his honour on him, and consecrated, constituted, and ordained him a Priest with an oath, Psalm cx. 4. Now the principal business of a priest, was to make reconciliation and atonement for sin; for the sake of this, Christ was called to this office; and it was signified to him in covenant, that he should not offer such sacrifices and offerings as were offered up under the law, which could not take away sin, or atone for it; and though God would have these offered, as typical of Christ's atoning sacrifice, from the beginning, throughout the former dispensation, to the coming of Christ; yet it was not his will that any of this sort should be offered by him; *Sacrifice and offering thou wouldst not:* and therefore, though Christ was a Priest, he never offered any legal sacrifice; but when any thing of this kind was necessary to be done for persons he was concerned with, he always sent them to carry their offerings to a priest; as in the case of cleansing lepers, Matt. viii. 4. Luke xvii. 14. a sacrifice of another kind, and to answer a greater purpose, was to be offered by him, and which in covenant was provided; *A body hast thou prepared me,* which is put for the whole human nature; for not the body of Christ only, but his soul also, were made an offering for sin, Heb. x. 5, 10. Isa. liii. 10. and this offering for sin was made by Christ's suffering and dying in the room and stead of sinners, when he was wounded for their transgressions, and bruised for their sins, and stricken for their iniquities; that is, to make satisfaction for them; this was what was enjoined in covenant; this commandment he received from his Father, and he was obedient to it, even to die the death of the cross; and this work was proposed and appointed to him in covenant, and declared in prophecy, in order to finish transgression, make an end of sin, and make reconciliation for iniquity; and this he did by the sacrifice of himself. Now as this whole scheme was drawn in council, and settled in covenant, it was proposed to Christ, and he readily agreed to it, and became the surety of the covenant, the better testament; and engaged to sssume human nature, to do and suffer in it, all that the law and justice of God could require, and should demand of him, in the room and stead of sinners, in order to make full satisfaction for their sins, of which the above things are the ground and foundation. Now,

3. There is nothing in this whole transaction that is injurious to any person or thing, or that is chargeable with any unrighteousness; but all is agreeable to the rules of justice and judgment.

(1.) No injury is done to Christ by his voluntary substitution in the room and stead of sinners, to make satisfaction for their sins; for as he was able, so he was willing to make it; he assuming human nature, was qualified to obey and suffer, he had somewhat to offer as a sacrifice; as man, he had blood to shed for the remission of sin, and a life to lay down for the ransom of sinners; and as God, he could support the human nature in union with him, under the weight of sin laid on it; and bear the whole of the punishment due unto it with cheerfulness, courage, and strength: and as he was able, so he was willing; he said in covenant, when it was proposed to him, *Lo, I come to do thy will;* and at the fulness of time he readily came to do it, went about it as soon as possible, counted it his meat and drink to perform it, and was constant at it; and what was most distressing and disagreeable to flesh and blood, he most earnestly wished for, even his bloody baptism, sufferings, and death; and *volenti non fit injuria.* Besides, he had a right to dispose of his own life; and therefore in laying it down, did no injustice to any: the civil law will not admit that one man should die for another; the reason is, because no man has a right to dispose of his own life; but Christ had, *I have power,* says he, *to lay it down;* that is, his life, John x. 18. hence he is called, *The prince of life,* both with respect to his own life, and the life of others, Acts iii. 15. and accordingly it was in his power to give it as a redemption-price for his people; wherefore he says, he came *to give his life a ransom for many,* Matt. xx. 28. and which he did give; and he also had a power to take it up again: was a good man admitted by the civil law to die for a bad man, it would be a loss to the commonwealth, and is another reason why it is not allowed of; but Christ, as he laid down his life for sinners, so he could and did take it up again, and that quickly; he was delivered to death for the offences of men, to satisfy justice for them; and then he rose again for the justification of them; he died once, and continued a little while under the power of death, but it was not possible for him to be held long by it; when through it he had made satisfaction for sin, he rose from the dead, and will die no more, but will live for ever for the good of his people. Nor is the human nature of Christ a loser but a gainer by his sufferings and death; for having finished his work, he is glorified with the glory promised him in covenant before the world was; is crowned with glory and honour, highly exalted above every creature, has a place at the right-hand of God, where angels have not; angels, authorities, and powers, being subject to him; nor has the human nature any reason to complain, nor did it ever complain of any loss sustained by suffering in the room and stead of sinners, and by working out their salvation.

(2.) Nor is there any unjust thing done by God throughout this whole transaction; there is no unrighteousness in him, in his nature, nor in any of his ways and works; nor in this affair which was done *to declare his righteousness, that he might be just,* appear to be just, *and be the justifier of him that believes in Jesus;* upon the foot of a perfect righteousness, and full satisfaction made for sin. The person sent to do this work, and who was given up into the hands of justice, and not spared, was one God had a property in, he was his own Son, his only begotten Son; and it was with his own consent he delivered him up for all his people; and who being their surety, and having engaged to pay their debts, and to answer for any hurt, damage, or wrong done by them; and having voluntarily taken their sins upon him, and these being found on him by the justice of God; it could be no unrighteous thing to make a demand of satisfaction for them; and accordingly *it was exacted, and he answered,* as the former part of Isa. liii. 7. may be rendered; that is, satisfaction was required of him, and he answered to the demand made upon him; and where is the unrighteousness of this? Christ's name was in the obligation, and that only; and therefore he was the only person that justice could lay hold upon, and get satisfaction from: besides, there was a conjunction, an union, a relation between Christ and his people, previous to his making satisfaction for them; which lay at the bottom of it, and shewed a reason for it: as in all such cases where the sins of one have been punished on another; as when God has visited the iniquities of fathers upon the children, there is the relation of fathers and children; and the fathers are punished in the children, as being parts of them; thus Ham, the son of Noah, was the transgressor, but the curse was denounced and fell on Canaan his son, and Ham was punished in him; when David numbered the people, and so many thousands suffered for it, here was a relation of king and subjects, who were one in a civil sense, and the one were punished for the other. Thus Christ and his people are one, both in a natural sense, being of the same nature, and partakers of the same flesh and blood; and so satisfaction for sin was made in the same nature that sinned, as it was fit it should; and in a law-sense, as a surety and debtor are one, so that if one pay the debt it is the same as if the other did it; and in a mystical sense, as head and members are one, as Christ and his people are head and members of the same body, so that if one suffer, the rest suffer with it; nor is it any unjust thing, if one part of the body sins, another suffers for it; as, if the head commits the offence, and the back is punished: Christ and his people are one, as husband and wife are, who are one flesh; and therefore there can be no impropriety, much less injustice, in Christ's giving himself a ransom-price for his church, to redeem her from slavery; or an offering and sacrifice for her, to make atonement for her transgressions: and as there appears to be no unrighteousness in God through this whole affair, so far as he was concerned in it, so there is no injury done him through a satisfaction being made by another; for hereby all the divine perfections are glorified, Psalm lxxxv. 10.

(3.) Nor is there any injury done to the law of God; it has the whole of its demands, no part remaining unsatisfied; for it is neither abrogated nor relaxed; there is a change of the person making satisfaction to it, which is favourably allowed by the lawgiver; but there is no change of the sanction of the law, of the punishment it requires; that is not abated. The law is so far from being a loser by the change of persons in giving it satisfaction, that it is a great gainer; *the law is magnified and made honourable;* more honourable by Christ's obedience to it, than by the obedience of the saints and angels in heaven; and is made more honourable by the sufferings of Christ, in bearing the penal sanction of it, than by all the sufferings of the damned in hell to all eternity, Isa. xlii. 21.

Secondly, The causes, spring, and source of satisfaction.——1. So far as God the Father was concerned in it, he may be said to be an efficient cause of it, and his love the moving cause; he was at the first of it, he began it, made the first motion, set it awork; *All things are of God, who hath reconciled us to himself by Jesus Christ,* 2 Cor. v. 18. he called a council upon it, he contrived the scheme of it, he *set forth* Christ in his eternal purposes and decrees *to be the propitiation* for sin, to make satisfaction for it; and he sent him in the fulness of time for that purpose; he laid on him the iniquities of his people, and made him to be sin for them by imputation; he bruised him, and put him to grief, and made his soul an offering for sin; he spared him not, but delivered him into the hands of justice and death; and what moved him to this, was his great love to his people, John iii. 16. 1 John iv. 10.

2. In like manner Christ may be considered as an efficient cause, and his love as a moving cause in this affair; he came into the world to die for sinners, and redeem them to God by his blood; he laid down his life for them; he gave himself for them an offering and a sacrifice unto God, a propitiatory, expiatory one; and what moved him to it, was his great love to them, and kindness for them; *Hereby perceive we the love of God,* that is, of God the Son, *because he laid down his life for us,* 1 John iii. 16. and the love of Christ is frequently premised to his giving himself to die in the room of his people, Gal. ii. 20. Eph. v. 2, 25.

III. The matter of satisfaction, or what that is which gives satisfaction to the justice of God; so that a sinner upon it, or in consideration of it, is acquitted and discharged; and this is no other than Christ's fulfilling the whole law, in the room and stead of sinners; this was what he undertook in covenant; hence he said, *Thy law is within my heart;* he was willing and ready to fulfil it; and when he came into the world by his incarnation, he was *made under* it voluntarily, and became subject to it, for he came not to *destroy* it, but to fulfil it; and he is become *the end of the law,* the fulfilling end of it, to every one that believes: he has fulfilled it,

1. By obeying the precepts of it, and answering all that it requires. Does it require an holy nature? it has it in him, who is *holy, harmless,* and *undefiled;* does it require perfect and sinless obedience?

it is found in him, who did no sin, never transgressed the law in one instance, but always did the things which pleased his Father; and who has declared himself *well pleased for his righteousness sake*, and with it; and that as wrought out for his people by his active obedience to the law, which is so approved of by God, that he imputes it without works for the justification of them, Rom. iv. 6. and v. 19. Nor is it any objection to this doctrine that Christ, as man, was obliged to yield obedience to the law for himself, which is true; but then it should be observed, that as he assumed human nature, or became man, for the sake of his people, *to us*, or for us, *a child is born ;* so it was for their sake he yielded obedience to the law. Besides, though he was obliged to it as man, yet he was not obliged to yield it in such a state and condition as he did; in a state of humiliation, in a course of sorrow and affliction, in a suffering state throughout the whole of his life, even unto death; for the human nature of Christ, from the moment of its union to the Son of God, was entitled to glory and happiness; so that its obedience to the law in such a low estate was quite voluntary, and what he was not obliged unto: nor is it to be argued from Christ's yielding obedience for his people, that then they are exempted from it; they are not; they are *under the law to Christ*, and under greater obligation to obey it; they are not obliged to obey it in like manner, or for such purposes that Christ obeyed it, even to justify them before God, and entitle them to eternal life.

2. Christ has fulfilled the law and satisfied it, by bearing the penalty of it in the room and stead of his people, which is death of every kind, Gen. ii. 19. Rom. vi. 23. corporal death, which includes all afflictions, griefs, sorrows, poverty, and disgrace, which Christ endured throughout his state of humiliation; for he took our infirmities, and bare our sicknesses; and was a man of sorrows, and acquainted with griefs all his days; and all that he suffered in his body, when he gave his back to the smiters, and his cheeks to them that plucked off the hair; when he was buffeted and smitten with the palms of the hand in the palace of the high-priest; and was whipped and scourged by the order of Pilate; his head crowned with thorns, and his hands and feet pierced with nails on the cross, where he hung for the space of three hours in great agonies and distress; and some have confined his satisfactory sufferings to what he underwent during that time, which though very great indeed, and none can tell what he endured in soul and body, in that space of time; yet these, exclusive of what he endured before and after, must not be considered as the only punishment he endured by way of satisfaction for the sins of men; the finishing and closing part of which was death, and what the law required; and hence making peace and reconciliation are ascribed to the bloodshed and death of Christ on the cross, Col. i. 20. Rom. v. 10. which death was a bloody, cruel, and painful one, as the thing itself speaks, and the description of it shews, Psalm xxii. 15, 16. and was also a very shameful and ignominious one, the death of slaves, and of the worst of malefactors; and was likewise an accursed one, and shewed, that as Christ was made sin for his people, and had their sins charged upon him, so he was made a curse for them, and bore the whole curse of the law that was due unto them, Gal. iii. 13. Moreover, Christ not only endured a corporal death, and all that was contained in it, and connected with it, or suffered in his body; but in his soul also, through the violent temptations of Satan, *he suffered, being tempted ;* and through the reproaches that were cast upon him, which entered into his soul, and broke his heart; and through his agonies in the garden, when his soul was exceeding sorrowful, even unto death; and especially through his sufferings on the cross, when his soul, as well as his body, was made an offering for sin; and when he sustained what was tantamount to an eternal death, which lies in a separation from God, and a sense of divine wrath; both which Christ then endured, when God deserted him, and hid his face from him; which made him say, *My God, my God, why hast thou forsaken me !* and he had a dreadful sense of divine wrath,[7] on the account of the sins of his people laid upon him, the punishment of

---

[7] Some say Christ did not suffer the wrath of God against sin, Lightfoot, Works, v. 2. p. 1255, 1347, &c. But, to the contrary, vid. Witsii Oeconom. Foederum, l. 2. c. 4. s. 21. and c. 6. s. 12, 38, 45. in Symbolum Exercitat. 15. s. 9. and 18. s. 19, 20, 35, 39. and Irenic. c. 3. s. 6, 10. and many others; see this body of Divinity, book 5. chap. 4. of the sufferings of Christ.

which he bore; when he said, *Thou hast cast off and abhorred, thou hast been wroth with thine anointed,* thy Messiah, Psalm lxxxix. 38. and thus by doing and suffering all that the law and justice of God could require, he made full and complete satisfaction thereunto for his people; it was not barely a something, some little matter, which Christ gave, and with which God was content, and what is called *acceptilation;* but a proper, full, and adequate satisfaction, which he gave, so that nothing more in point of justice could be required of him.

IV. The form or manner in which satisfaction was made by Christ; which was by *bearing* the sins of his people, under an imputation of them to him, and by dying for their sins, and for sinners; that is, in their room and stead, as their substitute; these are the phrases by which it is expressed in scripture.

First, By bearing the sins of his people, which we first read of in Isa. liii. 11, 12. where two words are made use of, both alike translated; *And he bare the sin of many,* נשׂא he took, he lifted them up, he took them off of his people, and took them upon himself; and again, *He shall bear their iniquities,* יסבל as a man bears and carries a burden upon his shoulders; and from hence is the use of the phrase in the New Testament: the author of the epistle to the Hebrews, chap. ix. 28. observes, that *Christ was once offered to bear the sins of many;* pointing at the time when he bore the sins of many; it was when he was offered up a sacrifice to make atonement for them; and the apostle Peter observes where he bore them; *Who his own self bare our sins in his own body on the tree!* 1 Pet. ii. 24. *He bore them in his own body,* in the body of his flesh; when that was offered once for all; and *on the tree,* upon the cross, when he was crucified on it. Now his bearing sin, supposes it was upon him; there was no sin *in* him, inherently, in his nature and life; had there been any, he would not have been a fit person to take away sin, to expiate it, and make satisfaction for it; he was *manifested to take away our sins;* that is, by the sacrifice of himself; and *in him is no sin,* 1 John iii. 5. and so a fit sacrifice for it: but sin was upon him, it was *put* upon him, as the sins of Israel were *put upon* the scape-goat, by Aaron. Sin was put upon Christ by his divine Father; no creature could have done it, neither angels nor men; but *the Lord hath laid on him,* or made to meet on him, *the iniquity of us all,* Isa. liii. 6. not a single iniquity, but a whole mass and lump of sins collected together, and laid, as a common burden, upon him; even *of us all,* of all the elect of God, both Jews and Gentiles; for Christ became the propitiation, or made satisfaction, for the sins of both, 1 John ii. 2. This phrase, of laying sin on Christ, is expressive of the imputation of it to him; for as it was the will of God, not to impute the trespasses of his elect to themselves; it was his pleasure they should be imputed to Christ, which was done by an act of his own; *For he hath made him to be sin for us;* that is, by imputation, in which way we are *made the righteousness of God in him;* that being imputed to us by him, as our sins were to Christ: the sense is, a charge of sin was brought against him, as the surety of his people; *he was numbered with the transgressors;* bearing the sins of many, he was reckoned as if he had been one, sin being imputed to him; and was dealt with, by the justice of God, as such; sin being found on him, through imputation, a demand of satisfaction for sin was made; and he answered it to the full. All this was with his own consent; he agreed to have sin laid on him, and imputed to him, and a charge of it brought against him, to which he engaged to be responsible; yea, he himself took the sins of his people on him; so the evangelist Matthew has it; *Himself took our infirmities, and bare our sicknesses,* chap viii. 17. as he took their nature, so he took their sins, which made his flesh to have *the likeness of sinful flesh,* though it really was not sinful.

What Christ bore, being laid on him, and imputed to him, were *sins,* all sorts of sin, original and actual; sins of every kind, open and secret, of heart, lip, and life; all acts of sin committed by his people; for he has redeemed them from all their iniquities; and God, for Christ's sake, forgives all trespasses; his blood cleanses from all sin, and his righteousness justifies from all; all being imputed to him, as that is to them: all that is in sin, and belongs to sin, were bore by him; the turpitude and filth of sin, without being defiled by it, which cannot be separated from it; and the guilt of sin, which was transferred to him, and obliged to punishment; and particularly the punishment itself, sin is often put for the punishment of sin, Gen. iv. 13. Lam. v. 7. and is greatly meant, and always included, when Christ is said to bear it; even all the punishment due to the sins of his people; and which is called, *the chastisement of our peace*, said to be *upon him*, Isa. liii. 5. that is, the punishment inflicted on him, in order to make peace, reconciliation, and atonement for sin. Bearing sin, supposes it to be a burden; and, indeed, it is a burden too heavy to bear by a sensible sinner, when sin is charged home upon the conscience, and a saint groans, being burdened with it; what must that burden be, and how heavy the load Christ bore, consisting of all the sins of all the elect, from the beginning of the world to the end of it? and yet he sunk not, but stood up under it, failed not, nor was he discouraged, being the mighty God, and the Man of God's right-hand, made strong for himself; and he himself bore it; not any with him, to take any part with him, to help and assist him; his shoulders alone bore it, on which it was laid; and his own arm alone brought salvation to him. And he bore it, and bore it away; he removed the iniquity of his people in one day; and that as far as the East is from the West: and in this he was typified by the scape-goat, on whom were put all the iniquities, transgressions, and sins, of all the children of Israel, on the day of atonement, and which were all borne by the scape-goat to a land not inhabited, Lev. xvi. 21, 22. Aaron was also a type of Christ, in bearing the sins of the holy things of the people of Israel, when he went into the holy place, Exod. xxviii. 38. And the sin-offering was typical of the sacrifice of Christ, which is said to bear the iniquities of the congregation, and to make atonement for them, Lev. x. 17.

Secondly, The form and manner in which Christ made satisfaction for sin, is expressed by *dying for sin*, that is, to make atonement for it; and *for sinners*, that is, in their room and stead, as their substitute.

1. By dying *for the sins* of his people; this the apostle represents as the first and principal article of the christian faith, *that Christ died for our sins, according to the scriptures*, 1 Cor. xv. 3. according to the scriptures of the Old Testament, which speak of Christ being *cut off*, in a judicial way, by death, but not for himself, for any sin of his own; and of his being wounded, bruised, and stricken, but not for his own transgressions and iniquities; but as *wounded for our transgressions, bruised for our iniquities, and stricken for the transgressions of his people*, Dan. ix. 26. Isa. liii. 5, 8. that is, wounded and bruised unto death, and stricken with death; which death was inflicted on him as a punishment for the sins of his people, to expiate them, and make atonement for them, being laid on him, and bore by him: the meaning of the phrases is, that the sins of his people were the procuring and meritorious causes of his death; just as when the apostle says, *for which things sake*; that is, for sins before mentioned; *the wrath of God cometh on the children of disobedience*, Col. iii. 6. the sense is, that sins are the procuring, meritorious causes of the wrath of God, being stirred up, and poured down upon disobedient sinners; so, in like manner, when Christ is said to be delivered into the hands of justice and death, *for our offences*; the sense is, that our offences were the meritorious cause why he was put to death, he bearing them and standing in our room and stead; as his resurrection from the dead, having made satisfaction for sins, was the meritorious and procuring cause of our justification from them; as follows, *and was raised again for our justification*, Rom. iv. 25. The Socinians urge, and insist upon it, that the particle *for*, used in the above phrases, signifies not the procuring, meritorious cause, but the final cause of Christ's death; which they say was this, to confirm the doctrines and practices he taught, that men, by obedience to them, might have the forgiveness of their sins; which is a doctrine very false; for though Christ did, both by the example of his life, and by his sufferings and death, confirm the truths he taught, which is but what a martyr does; and that though through the grace of God, his people do obey from the heart the doctrines and ordinances delivered to them; yet it is not by their obedience of faith and duty, that they obtain the forgiveness of their sins; but through the blood of Christ, shed for many, for the remission of sins.

2. By dying for sinners, as their substitute, in their room; so the several Greek particles, αντι, υπερ, περι, used in this phrase, and others equivalent to it, signify a surrogation, a substitute of one for another; as in divers passages in the New Testament; see Matt. ii. 21. and v. 38. and in various writers, as has been observed by many, with full proof and evidence, and most clearly in the scriptures, where Christ's sufferings and death are spoken of as for others; thus Christ gave his life *a ransom for many*, in the room and stead of many,

Matt. xx. 28. so he himself is said to be αντιλυτρον, *a ransom for all*, in the room and stead of *all* his people, Jews and Gentiles. The prophecy of Caiaphas was, *That one Man should die for the people*, in the room and stead of them, John xi. 50. *Christ died for the ungodly*, in the room and stead of the ungodly; *While we were yet sinners Christ died for us*, in our room and stead, Rom. v. 6, 7, 8. Again, *Christ also hath once suffered for sins, the just for the unjust*, in the room and stead of the unjust, 1 Pet. iii. 18. The Socinians say, that these phrases only mean, Christ died for the good of men: that Christ became a Surety for good to his people, and has obtained good for them, by performing his suretiship-engagements, is certain; yet this good he has obtained by obeying, suffering, and dying, in their room and stead; thus that the blessing of Abraham, even all the spiritual blessings of the everlasting covenant, might come upon the Gentiles, through Christ, he was *made a curse for them*, in their room; he bore the whole curse of the law for them, as their substitute, and so opened a way for their enjoyment of the blessings, or good things, in the covenant of grace; and that sinners might be made the righteousness of God in him, or have his righteousness imputed to them for their justification; he was *made sin for them*, had their sins laid on him, and imputed to him, as their substitute; and was made a sacrifice for sin in their room and stead, to make atonement for it; see Gal. iii. 13, 14. 2 Cor. v. 21. This is the greatest instance of love among men, *that a man lay down his live* υπερ, *for*, in the room and stead of, *his friend*, John xv. 13. and such was the love of Christ to his church, *that he gave*, delivered *himself* to death υπερ αυτης *for her*, in her room and stead,[8] Eph. v. 25.

V. The effects of satisfaction made by Christ, or the ends that were to be, and have been answered by it.

1. The finishing and making an entire end of sin; this was Christ's work assigned him in covenant, and asserted in prophecy; and which was done when he made reconciliation or atonement for sin, Dan. ix. 24. not that the being of sin was removed thereby; for that remains in all the justified and sanctified ones, in this life, but the damning power of it; such for whom Christ has made satisfaction, shall never come into condemnation, nor be hurt of the second death, that shall have no power over them; sin is so done, and put away, and abolished, by the sacrifice of Christ for it, that no charge can ever be brought against his people for it; the curse of the law cannot reach them, nor light upon them; nor any sentence of condemnation and death can be executed on them; nor any punishment inflicted on them; they are secure from wrath to come. Sin is so finished and made an end of, by Christ's satisfaction for it, that it will be seen no more by the eye of avenging Justice; it is so put away, and out of sight, that when it is sought for, it shall not be found; God, for Christ's sake, has cast it behind his back, and into the depths of the sea.

2. In virtue of Christ's satisfaction for sin, his people are brought into an open state of reconciliation with God; atonement being made for their sins, their persons are reconciled to God, and they are admitted into open favour with him; and he declares himself *pacified towards them, for all that they have done*, Ezek. xvi. 63.

3. Sin being atoned for, and made an end of, an everlasting righteousness is brought in, with which God is well-pleased; because by it his law is magnified and made honourable; all its demands being fully answered, by Christ's obeying its precepts, and bearing its penalty; which righteousness God so approves of, that he imputes it to his people, without works; and so it is unto all, and upon all, them that believe, as their justifying righteousness; which acquits them from sin, and entitles them to eternal life.

4. Immunity from all evil; that is, from all penal evil, both in this life, and in that to come, is an effect of Christ's satisfaction for sin; since sin being removed by it, no evil can come nigh them; no curse attends their blessings; no wrath is in their afflictions; all things work together for their good; it is always well with them in life, in all the circumstances of it; at death, they die in the Lord, in union to him, in faith, and hope of being for ever with him; and at judgment, the Judge will

---

[8] So Plato observes in his Convivium, p. 1178, that only lovers are willing υπεραποθνησκειν, to die for another, that is, in the room and stead of another; of which, he says, there is a sufficient testimony in Alcestis, who only was willing to die υπερ του αυτης ανδρος, "for her husband," in his room and stead, when he had both a father and a mother.

be their Friend and Saviour, and it will be well with them to all eternity; they will be eternally delivered from wrath to come.

5. With respect to God, the effect of Christ's satisfaction is the glorifying of his justice; for, for that end was Christ *set forth to be the propitiation,* or to make atonement for sin; *to declare the righteousness* of God, to shew it in all its strictness, *that he might be just, and the justifier of him that believes in Jesus;* appear to be just in so doing; yea, all the divine perfections are glorified hereby; see Rom. iii. 25, 26. Psalm xxi. 5.

There are many objections made by the Socinians, to this important doctrine, and article of faith; some of the principal of which are as follow:

1. It is suggested, as if the doctrine of satisfaction for sin to the justice of God, is inconsistent with the mercy of God, and leaves no room for that.[9] But the attributes of mercy and justice, are not contrary to each other. They subsist and accord together, in the same divine nature; *Gracious is the Lord, and righteous; yea, our God is merciful,* Psalm cxvi. 5. merciful, though righteous; and righteous, though gracious and merciful; see Exod. xxxiv. 6, 7. and as they agree as perfections in the divine Being; so in the exercise of them, they do not clash with one another, no, not in this affair of satisfaction; justice being satisfied, a way is opened for mercy to display her stores, Psalm lxxxv. 10.

2. It is objected, that pardon of sin, upon the foot of a full satisfaction for it, cannot be said to be free,[10] but eclipses the glory of God's free grace in it: it is certain, that remission of sin is through the tender mercy of God, and is owing to the multitude of it; it is according to the riches of free grace, and yet through the blood of Christ; and both are expressed in one verse, as entirely agreeing together; *In whom* (Christ) *we have redemption through his blood, the forgiveness of sins, according to the riches of his grace,* Eph. i. 7. the free grace of God is so far from being eclipsed, in the forgiveness of sin, through the satisfaction of Christ, that it shines the brighter for it; for consider, that it was the free grace of God which provided Christ to be a sacrifice for sin, to atone for it; as Abraham said to Isaac, when he asked, *Where is the lamb for a burnt-offering?*

My son, says he, *God will provide himself a lamb for a burnt-offering,* Gen. xxii. 7, 8. so God, of his rich grace and mercy, has provided Christ to be an offering for sin; and his grace appears more, in that it is his own Son, his only begotten Son, he provided to be the atoning sacrifice; it was grace that set forth Christ in purpose, proposed him in council and covenant, and sent him forth in time to be the propitiation for sin; it was grace to us that he spared him not, but delivered him up for us all; and it was grace in God to accept of the satisfaction made by Christ; for though it was so full and complete, as nothing could be more so; yet it would have been a refusable one, had he not allowed Christ's name to be put in the obligation; had it not been for the compact and covenant agreed to between them, God might have marked, in strict justice, our iniquities, and insisted on a satisfaction at our own hands; he might have declared, and stood by it, that the soul that sinned, that should die: it was therefore owing to the free grace and favour of God, to admit of a Surety in our room, to make satisfaction for us, and to accept of that satisfaction, as if made by ourselves. Moreover, though it cost Christ much, his blood, his life, and the sufferings of death, to make the satisfaction for sin, and to procure forgiveness by it; it cost us nothing; it is all of free grace to us. Besides, grace in scripture is only opposed to the works of men, and satisfaction by them, and not to the works of Christ, and to his satisfaction.

3. It is pretended, that this scheme of pardon, upon the foot of satisfaction, makes the love of Christ to men, to be greater than the love of the Father; it represents the one as tenderly affectionate, compassionate, and kind to sinners; and the other as inexorable, not to be appeased, nor his wrath turned away without satisfaction to his justice; and so men are more beholden to the one than to the other:[11] but the love of both is most strongly expressed in this business of Christ's satisfaction; and he must be a daring man that will take upon him to say, who of them shewed the greatest love, the Father in giving his Son, or the Son in giving himself, to be the propitiatory sacrifice for sin; for as it is said of Christ, that he loved the people, and gave himself for them, an offering and a

---

[9] Socin. de Servatore, p. 1. c. 1. et Prælect. Theolog. c. 18. p. 571.

[10] Racov. Cateches. c. 8. qu. 15.

[11] Racov. Cateches. c. 8. qu. 15.

sacrifice of a sweet-smelling savour to God, Eph. v. 2, 25. Gal. ii. 20. so it is said of the Father, that he *so loved the world*, that he gave his only begotten Son to suffer and die for men; and that herein his love was manifested; and that he commended it towards us, in sending Christ to be the propitiation for sin, John iii. 16. 1 John iv. 9, 10. Rom. v. 8. Can there be greater love than this expressed by both? and which is greatest is not for us to say.

4. It is said, that if Christ is a divine Person, he must be a party offended by sin; and if he has made satisfaction for it, he must have made satisfaction to himself; which is represented as an absurdity.[12] All this will be allowed, that Christ is God, and, as such, equally offended as his Father; and that he made satisfaction to the offended, and that, in some sense, to himself too; and yet no absurdity in it. Indeed, in case of private satisfaction, for a private loss, it would be quite absurd for one to make satisfaction to himself; but in case of public satisfaction, for a public offence to a community, of which he is a part, he may be said, by making satisfaction to the whole body, to make satisfaction to himself, without any absurdity. A member of parliament, having violated the rules and laws of the house, when he makes satisfaction for the same to it, may be said to make satisfaction to himself, being a member of it. It is possible for a lawgiver to make satisfaction to his own law broken, and so to himself, as the lawgiver: thus Zaleucus, a famous legislator, made a law which punished adultery with the loss of both eyes; his own son first broke this law, and in order that the law might have full satisfaction, and yet mercy shewn to his son, he ordered one of his son's eyes, and one of his own, to be put out; and so he might be said to satisfy his own law, and to make satisfaction to himself, the lawgiver. But in the case before us, the satisfaction made by Christ, is made to the justice of God, subsisting in the divine nature, common to all the three Persons; this perfection subsisting in the divine nature, as possessed by the first Person, is offended with sin, resents it, requires satisfaction for it; and it is given it by the second Person, in human nature, as Godman: the same divine perfection subsisting in the divine nature, as possessed by the second Person, shews itself in like manner, loving righteousness, and hating iniquity; affronted by sin, and demanding satisfaction for it, it is given to it by him, as the God-man and Mediator; who, though a Person offended, can mediate for the offender, and make satisfaction for him. And the same may be observed concerning the justice of God, as a perfection of the divine nature, possessed by the third Person, the Spirit of God; the satisfaction is made to the justice of God, as subsisting in the divine nature, common to the three Persons; and is not made to one Person only, singly, and separately, and personally; but to God, essentially considered, in all his Persons; and to his justice, as equally possessed by them; and that as the Lord, Judge, and Governor of the whole world; who ought to maintain, and must and does maintain, the honour of his Majesty, and of his law.

5. Once more, it is said that this doctrine of Christ's satisfaction for sin, weakens men's obligation to duty, and opens a door to licentiousness.[13] But this is so far from being true, that, on the contrary, it strengthens the obligation, and excites a greater regard to duty, in those who have reason to believe that Christ has made satisfaction for their sins; for the love of Christ in dying for them—in being made sin and a curse for them, to satisfy for their sins, constrains them, in the most pressing manner, to live to him, according to his will, and to his glory; being bought with the price of Christ's blood, and redeemed from a vain conversation by it; they are moved the more strongly to glorify God with their bodies and spirits, which are his, and to pass the time of their sojourning here in fear; the grace of God, which has appeared in God's gift of his Son, and in Christ's gift of himself to be their Redeemer and Saviour, to be their atoning sacrifice; teaches them most effectually to deny ungodliness and worldly lusts, and to live soberly, righteously, and godly in this evil world, 2 Cor. v. 14. 1 Cor. vi. 20. 1 Pet. i. 17, 18. Tit. ii. 11, 12.

CHAP. VI.

OF PROPITIATION, ATONEMENT, AND RECONCILIATION, AS ASCRIBED TO CHRIST.

HAVING observed, that though the word *satisfaction* is not syllabically used in

---

[12] Socin. de Servatore, par. 3. c. 4. p. 102.

[13] Racov. Cateches. c. 8. q. 17.

scripture, when the doctrine of Christ's satisfaction is spoken of; yet that there are words and terms equivalent to it, and synonymous with it; as *propitiation, atonement*, and *reconciliation ;* it may be proper to explain these terms, and give the sense of them; which may serve the more to clear and confirm the doctrine of satisfaction; and to begin,

First, With *Propitiation :* the first time we meet with this word, and as applied to Christ, is in Rom. iii. 25. *Whom God hath set forth to be a propitiation ;* either to be the author of propitiation; for whose sake, and on account of what he was to do and suffer, God would be propitious to men—his justice be appeased—and he be at peace with them; laying aside all marks of displeasure, anger, and resentment against them: for this was Christ's work as Mediator; he drew nigh to God, and treated with him about terms of peace, and entered into measures of peace with him; interposed between justice and them, became a Mediator between God and man, to bring them together; hence he has the names of Shiloh, the Prince of peace, the Man the Peace, and Jesus our peace, who has made both one: or else to be the propitiatory sacrifice for sin; such hilastic, propitiatory, and expiatory sacrifices there were under the law; typical of the expiatory and propitiatory sacrifice of Christ; and as God in them smelled a sweet savour of rest, as types of Christ; so his sacrifice was an offering of a sweet-smelling savour to him; he was well-pleased with it, it gave him content and satisfaction, because his justice was appeased by it, and the demands of his law were answered, yea, it was magnified and made honourable; the word used in the above text ιλαςηριον, is the same which the Greek version of Exod. xxv. 21. and which the apostle, in Heb. ix. 5. use of the *mercy-seat ;* which, with the cherubim upon it, and the ark, with the law therein under it, to which it was a lid or cover, formed a seat for the divine Majesty; and which was an emblem of his mercy and justice shining in the atonement made by Christ, which this exhibited to view; and gave encouragement to draw nigh to this mercy-seat, or throne of grace in hope of finding grace and mercy, and enjoying communion with God: a glimpse of this the poor publican had, when he said, *God be merciful,* ιλασθητι, *propitious, to me a sinner !* or be merciful to me, through the propitiation of the Messiah. Now Christ was *set forth* to be the propitiation in the purposes and decrees of God, προοθιτο, God *fore-ordained* him, as he was fore-ordained to be the Lamb slain, as the ransom-price and propitiatory sacrifice; whose sufferings and death, which were the sacrifice, were according to the determinate counsel and fore-knowledge of God, 1 Pet. i. 19. Acts ii. 23. and iv. 28. and he was set forth in the promises and prophecies spoken of by all the holy prophets that were from the beginning of the world; as the seed of the woman that should bruise the serpent's head, destroy him and his works, among which this is a principal one, making an end of sin, by a complete atonement for it; and he was set forth as such in the types and shadows of the law, the trespass-offerings, and sin-offerings, which are said to bear the sins of the congregation, and to make atonement for them; which were typical of Christ, who was made an offering for sin, bore the sins of many, and made atonement for them, Lev. x. 17. and he has been set forth, in the fulness of time, in the exhibition of him, in human nature, in which he was manifested to take away sin; and he has put it away, and even abolished it, by the propitiatory sacrifice of himself; and he is still set forth in the gospel, as the sin-bearing and sin-atoning Saviour, who has satisfied law and justice, and made peace by the blood of his cross; and therefore it is called the word of reconciliation, the gospel of peace and the word preaching peace by Jesus Christ, who is Lord of all.

There are two other places where Christ is spoken of as ιλασμος, the *propitiation ;* and these are in the first epistle of the apostle John; in one of them, chap. iv. 10. it is said, *God sent his Son to be the propitiation for our sins ;* that is, sent him in human nature, to offer up soul and body as a sacrifice, and thereby make expiation of sin, and full atonement for it; and in the other it is said, chap. ii. 2. *And he is the propitiation for our sins,* both of Jews and Gentiles ; for which he is become a propitiatory sacrifice; upon which God is *merciful,* ιλως, *propitious* to his people, notwithstanding all their *unrighteousness, sins, and transgressions,* or is *pacified towards them for all that they have done,* Heb. viii. 12. Ezek. xvi. 63.

Secondly, The word *atonement,* though often used in the 'Old Testament, of typical sacrifices, making expiation of sin; as in Lev. i. 4. and iv. 20, 26, 31, 35. and v. 6, 10, 13, 16, 18. and xvi. 6, 10, 11, 16, 17, 18, 27, 30, 32, 33, 34. and xvii. 11. where the word כפר is used, which signifies to *cover;* and Christ, by his sacrifice, the antitype of these, is a covering to his people, from the curses of the law they have broken—from the wrath of God they have deserved—and from avenging justice their sins exposed them to. Yet it is but once used in the New Testament, Rom. v. 11. *By whom we have received the atonement* made for them by Christ their surety, head, and representative; that is, the benefit of it, the application of it by the Spirit of God, who takes the blood, righteousness, and sacrifice of Christ, and applies it to his people, and shews them their interest therein; the effect of which is joy, peace, and comfort. The word used properly signifies *reconciliation;* and so it is elsewhere translated; and the Hebrew word כפר is sometimes rendered to *reconcile,* Lev. vi. 30. atonement and reconciliation for sin, design the same thing, and both satisfaction for it. Which leads to observe,

Thirdly, That the word *reconciliation* is frequently used with respect to this doctrine. Reconciliation began with God himself; *All things are of God,* originally in nature, providence, and grace; particularly this, *Who hath reconciled us to himself by Jesus Christ,* 2 Cor. v. 18. It began in the thoughts of his heart, which were thoughts of peace; it was brought into council and settled in covenant, called the council and covenant of peace. It was carried into execution by Christ, who is frequently represented as the author of it, by his death, and the blood of his cross, Rom. v. 10. Eph. ii. 16. Col. i. 20, 21, 22. and it was made unto God, against whom sin is committed, whose law is broken, and his justice offended; and who is the Lawgiver, who is able to save and to destroy, Rom. v. 10. Eph. ii. 16. and it is a reconciliation for sin, to make atonement for it, Dan. ix. 24. Heb. ii. 17. and of sinners and enemies in their minds to God, Rom. v. 10. Col. i. 21. which may be further illustrated,

1st, By observing the character of the persons reconciled; which will shew the cause, reason, and necessity of a reconciliation to be made; they are *enemies;* and in one of the texts referred to, they are said to be *enemies in their minds by wicked works;* which is expressive, 1. Of the internal enmity there is in their minds and hearts; *the carnal mind,* as every man's mind is naturally carnal, is not only an enemy, but *enmity* itself, *against God,* Rom. viii. 7. to the Being of God—wishing there was no God—to the nature and perfections of God, denying some of them, misrepresenting others, and framing him in their minds, as altogether such an one as themselves—to the purposes and decrees of God, which they cannot bear, and to which they insolently reply; and to the providences of God, they charge with inequality and unrighteousness: and they are inwardly and secretly enemies to Christ, to his person and offices; particularly his kingly office, being unwilling that he should reign over them; and to his gospel, and the special doctrines of it; and to his ordinances, they care not to be subject unto: and so they are to the Spirit, to his Person, whom they know not, nor can receive; to his operations, which they deride and ridicule; the things of the Spirit of God are foolishness to them: and they are enemies to the people of God, there is an old and implacable enmity between the seed of the woman and the seed of the serpent; the saints are hated by the world, because chosen and called out of the world; God's elect themselves, whilst in a state of nature, are hateful, and hating one another; Paul, a chosen vessel of salvation, was, whilst unregenerate, exceeding mad against the saints. But,

2. There is an external enmity, which appears by wicked works and sinful actions openly committed; which are acts of hostility against God, are contrary to his nature and will, are abominable in his sight; provoke the eyes of his glory, excite his wrath, and cause it to be revealed from heaven, and for which it comes on the children of disobedience; and all are deserving of it: sins are breaches of the law of God, render men liable to the curses of it, and to death itself, the sanction of it; they not only fill with enmity to God, and shew it to him, but set men at a distance from him; so that they have no communion with him, are afar off, are without him, and separate from him. But,

3. Men are not only enemies internally, and externally to God, but there is an enmity on the part of God to them; there is a law-enmity, or an enmity declared in the law against them; they are declared by the law of God as enemies, traitors, and rebels to him; and as such

God's elect were considered, when Christ died to make reconciliation for them; for it is said, *while they were sinners Christ died for them, and when they were enemies they were reconciled to God, by the death of his Son*, Rom. v. 8, 10. Now the far greater part of those for whom Christ died, were not then in an actual sinful state, nor in actual rebellion and enmity against God; for then they were not in actual being; but they were considered as in their apostate head, as sinners in him, and so as rebels and traitors; as such they were deemed by the law, and proceeded against, proclaimed guilty, judgment came upon them to condemnation; they were, in the eye of the law, and in the sight of justice, viewed as enemies, and declared such: and this law-enmity is what was slain by Christ, and removed at his death; and not that enmity that was in their minds; that was not removed by and at the death of Christ; that is removed at conversion, when the arrows of the word become sharp in these enemies, which bring them to fall under, and be subject to Christ; when they are made willing in the day of his power, to be saved by him, to submit to his righteousness, and to have him to reign over them; this is the work of the Spirit of Christ: there is a two-fold reconciliation, one of which is the work of Christ, and was made at his death; the other the work of his Spirit, at conversion; when by his grace, men are reconciled to the way of salvation by Christ; and both may be seen in one text, Rom. v. 10. If there had been no other enmity than what is in the hearts of men against God, there would have been no need of the sufferings and death of Christ to make reconciliation; but there was a law-enmity on the part of God, and his justice, which required the death of Christ to take it away. Not that there was any enmity in the heart of God to his elect; that would be inconsistent with his everlasting and unchangeable love, which appeared strongly towards them at the time Christ died for them, reconciled them, and became the propitiation for their sins, Rom. v. 8, 10. Tit. iii. 3, 4. 1 John iv. 10. But they were, according to the law, and in the view of justice, deemed and declared as the enemies of God. So when the subjects of a king rise up in rebellion against him, there may be no enmity in his heart to them; yet they are, according to law, proclaimed rebels, and enemies to him, and may be treated as such, and proceeded against in due form of law; and yet, after all, be pardoned by him. There was, in some sense, a reciprocal enmity between God and men, which made a reconciliation necessary; and which was brought about by the bloodshed, sufferings, and death of Christ, when he slew the enmity of the law, and blotted out the handwriting of ordinances that were against sinners, so making peace, Eph. ii. 14, 15, 16. Col. ii. 14. Which will further appear,

2*dly*, By observing what reconciliation signifies and imports: there is something similar and analogous in a case when it is made between man and man, though not altogether the same; and some caution must be taken, lest we go into mistakes: reconciliation between man and man, supposes a former state of friendship subsisting between them, a breach of that friendship, and a renewing and restoration of it; and there is something like it in reconciliation between God and man; man, in his primeval state, was in strict friendship with God, not only Adam personally, being made after the image, and in the likeness of God, having dominion over all the creatures, made for his use, and which were brought to him, to be named by him; and having an habitation in a most delightful garden, where he was allowed to eat of all kind of fruit in it, but one; and where he enjoyed communion with God: in all this honour he was; and not he only, but all his posterity, considered in him, as their head and representative, were in a state of friendship with God; hence the covenant made with him, in which he was their federal-head, is rightly called by divines, *foedus amicitiæ*, a covenant of friendship: but man abode not long in this state; sin, that whisperer and make-bate, soon separated chief friends; alienated man from the life of God, caused him to apostatize from him, and to become a traitor to him; filled him with enmity to him, and set him at a distance from him; and in this state of alienation and enmity, all his posterity naturally are; with respect to the elect of God among them, Christ has interposed, appeased justice, satisfied the law, and made reconciliation for them, and brought them into an open state of friendship with God; so that they are considered, in consequence of this, as Abraham was, the friends of God, and are treated as such, James ii. 23. Cant. v. 1. John xv. 15. have the blessings of divine favour bestowed upon them, and rich communications of grace made unto them.

But here we must proceed warily, and observe some things to prevent mistakes and misrepresentations; for perhaps there is not one thing in the whole scheme of evangelical truths more difficult rightly to fix than this. It should be considered, that properly speaking, there are no passions nor perturbations of mind in God, who is a spirit, simple and uncompounded, and not capable of such things; when therefore displeasure, anger, provocation, resentment, &c. are ascribed to him, it must be understood after the manner of men; that he says something in his word, and does something in his providence, and the outward dispensations of it, which is somewhat similar to what men say and do, when the above is the case with them; otherwise we are not to conceive that God is in a passion, and is ruffled, and his mind disturbed, as they are. Nor are we to imagine there is any change in God, as in men, who are sometimes friends, then enemies, and then friends again; he changes not, there is no variableness nor shadow of turning in him; he may change his voice to his people, and speak comfortably to them in his gospel, who before spake terribly to them in his law; he may change his outward conduct and behaviour towards them, and carry it friendly to them, when before as at a distance: but he never changes his mind, counsel and affections to them; his love is everlasting and invariable; he ever rested in it, and nothing can separate from it; his love is never changed to enmity, and from enmity to love again; his special secret favour, as it is never lost, needed no recovery; nor did Christ, by making satisfaction and reconciliation for sin, procure the love and favour of God to his people; for Christ's being sent to be the propitiation, his sufferings and death, sacrifice and satisfaction, were the fruit and effect of the love of God, and not the cause of it, John iii. 16. Rom. v. 8. 1 John iv. 10 The reconciliation made by Christ was not to the love of God, which was never lost, but to the justice of God, offended by sin; the flaming sword, which turned every way and threatened vengeance, was plunged into the heart of Christ, the surety of his people, which was done to declare the righteousness and satisfy the justice of God; and to open a way for mercy to display itself, and turn its hand upon the little ones; and thus justice and mercy happily met together, and were reconciled to one another in their different pleas and demands, Zech. xiii. 7. Rom. iii. 25, 26. Psalm lxxxv. 10. The reconciliation made by Christ is for sin, to make satisfaction for it, Dan. ix. 24. Heb. ii. 17. and on that account it is a reconciliation of sinners to God, he being thereby pacified towards them for all that they have done; being well pleased with what Christ has done and suffered for them; he is well pleased with him, and with all that are considered in him, who are accepted in him the beloved, and are admitted into an open state of favour; which is meant by their having access through Christ into the grace wherein they stand, Matt. iii. 17. Eph. i. 6. Rom. v. 2. for though the love of God to his elect is invariable and unchangeable in itself, yet the manifestation of it is different; and it may be distinguished into secret and open love; there are obstructions by sin thrown in the way of love, which must be removed, in order to enjoy open favour and the blessings of it, and which are removed by Christ; thus Christ was made under the law, to redeem his people, that they might receive the adoption of children; and was made a curse for them, that the blessings of grace, love had provided in covenant for them, might come upon them; and he was made sin, and a sin-offering for them, that they might be made the righteousness of God in him; and be brought into a state of open fellowship and communion with him, who before were kept at a distance. Thus David, though he most affectionately loved his son Absalom, and longed for him, when for an offence he fled; and though through the mediation of Joab he was allowed to return to Jerusalem, yet the king would not suffer him to see his face for the space of full two years; when by the mediation of the same person, he was admitted into the king's presence, taken into open favour, and kissed by him, 2 Sam. xiii. 39. and xiv. 1, 21, 24, 33.

3*dly*, The means by which this reconciliation is made, are the blood-shed and death of Christ; he only is the reconciler and peace-maker; a sinner cannot make peace with God or reconciliation, that is, satisfaction for his sins; not by his works of righteousness, which are impure and imperfect; nor by repentance, which the law does not admit of, nor is it any satisfaction to it; nor by faith, for that does not make, only receives the atonement made by Christ; there is nothing a sinner can do, will make peace and reconciliation for him; and what will, he cannot do; which is no less than fulfilling the whole law, and answering all the demands of law and justice, Rom viii. 3, 4. death being the sanction of the law, and the wages of sin, there is no reconciliation to be made but by death; not by the death of slain beasts, which could not take away sin; nor by the death of the sinner himself: the Jews having lost the true notion of the atonement by the Messiah, fancy that a man's death atones for his sins; but it is a false notion, there is no other way of peace, reconciliation, and atonement being made, but by the death of the Son of God; who being God as well as man, could and did give virtue and efficacy to his blood, sufferings and death, in human nature united to his person, as to make them adequate to the said purposes.

CHAP. VII.

OF THE PARDON OF SIN.

THE doctrine of pardon properly follows the doctrine of satisfaction; for pardon of sin proceeds upon satisfaction made for it. Forgiveness of sin, under the law, followed upon typical atonement for it; four times, in one chapter, it is said, the priest shall make atonement for sin, and it shall be forgiven, Lev. iv. 20, 26, 31, 35. and as often in the next chapter, v. 10, 13, 16, 18. and in other places. This doctrine is of pure revelation; it is not to be known by the light of nature; *as many as have sinned without law shall also perish without law*, Rom. ii. 12. for any thing the light of nature suggests, concerning the pardon of it; men may fancy, from the goodness and mercy of God, that he will forgive their sins; but they cannot be certain of it that he will, since he is just as well as merciful; and how to reconcile justice and mercy in the pardon of sin, the light of nature leaves men in the dark; they may conjecture, that because one man forgives another, upon repentance, God will do the same; but they cannot be sure of it: besides, grace must be given to a man to repent, as well as remission of sins, or else he never will repent. Nor is this a doctrine of the law, which gives not the least hint of pardon, nor any encouragement to expect it; *as many as have sinned in the law shall be judged by the law*, condemned without any hope of pardon, Rom. ii. 12. *Every transgression and disobedience* of the law, or word spoken by angels, *received a just recompence of reward;* that is, proper and righteous punishment, Heb. ii. 2. Nor does the law regard a man's repentance, nor admit of any; *he that despised Moses's law died without mercy!* Heb. x. 28. But the doctrine of pardon is a pure doctrine of the gospel, which Christ gave in commission to his disciples to preach, and which they preached in his name, and to which all the evangelic prophets bore witness, Luke xxiv. 47. Acts xiii. 38. and x. 43. Concerning which may be observed,

First, The proof that may be given of it, that there is such a thing as pardon of sin: this is asserted in express words by David; *There is forgiveness with thee*, Psalm cxxx. 4. and by Daniel, *To the Lord our God belong mercies and forgiveness*, full and free pardon of sin, Dan. ix. 9. It is a blessing provided and promised in the covenant of grace, ordered in all things, which, without this, it would not be; this is a principal blessing in it; the promise of which runs thus; *I will be merciful to their unrighteousness, and their sins and their iniquities will I remember no more*, Heb. viii. 12. It is in the gracious proclamation the Lord has made of his name, and makes a considerable part of it; as *the Lord, the Lord God, merciful and gracious, forgiving iniquity, transgression, and sin!* Exod. xxxiv. 7. Christ was *set forth*, in the purposes of God, to be *a propitiation, through faith in his blood, for the remission of sins;* and he was sent forth, in the fulness of time, to shed his blood for it; and his blood has been *shed for many for the remission of sins!* and it is procured by it; or otherwise his bloodshed and death would be in vain, Rom. iii. 25. Matt. xxvi. 28. Eph. i. 7. and it is in his hands to bestow it; having ascended on high, he has received gifts for men, *even for the rebellious;* and among the gifts for them, pardon of sin is one; Christ is *exalted to be a Prince and a Saviour, to give repentance unto Israel and forgiveness of sins*, Acts v. 31. and it is by his orders, published in the gospel, as before observed; to which may be added, the numerous instances of it, both under the Old and under the New Testament; as of the Israelites, who, as they often sinned, God had compassion on them, and forgave their iniquities; even though he took vengeance on their inventions, Psalm lxxviii. 38. and xcix. 8. and of David, Manasseh, and others, and of Saul the blasphemer, the persecutor, and injurious person; and of other notorious sinners, Psalm xxxii. 5. 1 Tim. i. 13. Luke vii. 37, 47. It is in this way God would have his people comforted, when burdened and distressed with the guilt of sin, Isa. xl. 1, 2. Matt. ix. 2. and they are, at times, favoured with a comfortable experience of it, and peace of soul from it, Psalm lxxxv. 1, 2, 3, Rom. v. 11. they are directed to pray for it, and do pray for it; to which there would be no encouragement if there was no such thing, Psalm xxxii. 5. and li. 1, 2, 7, 8, 9. Dan. ix. 19. Matt. vi. 12. To add no more, forgiveness of sin is included in complete salvation, and is a part of it, and without which it would not be complete; nay, without it there could be no salvation; forgiveness of sin is a branch of redemption by the blood of Christ, which is explained by it, Eph. i. 7.

Secondly, The phrases by which the pardon of sin is expressed, and which will serve to lead into the nature of it.

1. By lifting it up, and taking it away; *Blessed is he whose transgression is forgiven,* נשׂא is *lifted up,* taken off from him, and carried away, Psalm xxxii. 1. Sin lies upon the sinner, and lays him under obligation to punishment, unless it is taken off; and the sins of God's elect are taken off of them, and laid on Christ, and bore by him, and removed from them, as far as the East is from the West; so that when sought for they shall not be found, God having pardoned those he has reserved for himself: and sin lies upon the conscience of an awakened sinner, as a burden too heavy for him to bear; which is taken away by the application of the blood of Christ; and who gives orders to take away the filthy garments of his people, and clothe them with change of raiment, and puts away their sins, that they shall not die.

2. By the covering of it; *Blessed is he whose sin is covered,* Psalm xxxii. 1. *Thou hast forgiven the iniquity of thy people; thou hast covered all their sin,* Psalm lxxxv. 2. Sin is something impure, nauseous, and abominable, in the sight of God, and provoking to the eyes of his glory, and must he covered out of sight; and this cannot be done by any thing of man's; not by his righteousness, which is but rags, a covering too narrow to be wrapped in, and can no more hide his nakedness than Adam's fig-leaves could hide his; nay, it is no better than a spider's web; and of which it may be said, *Their webs shall not become garments, neither shall they cover themselves with their works,* Isa. lix. 6. sin is only covered by Christ, who is the antitype of the mercy-seat, which was a lid or cover to the ark of the same dimensions with it, in which was the law, and prefigured Christ, as the covering of the transgressions of it by his people, from the sight of avenging Justice; and whose blood is the purple covering in the chariot of the covenant of grace, under which his people ride safe to glory; all their iniquities being out of sight; and whose righteousness is unto and upon all that believe; a garment that reaches to the feet, that white raiment with which being clothed, the shame of their nakedness does not appear; yea, being clothed with this robe of righteousness and garments of salvation, are as ornamented as the bridegroom and bride on the wedding-day; hereby their sins are covered, so as not to be seen any more, and they appear unblameable and irreproveable in the sight of God.

3. By a non-imputation of it; *Blessed is the man to whom the Lord imputeth not iniquity,* Psalm xxxii. 2. does not reckon it, or place it to his account, or bring any charge against him for it, or punishes for it; but acquits him from it, having imputed it to Christ, placed it to his account, charged him with it, laid the chastisement of it on him, or the punishment of it on him, and received satisfaction from him for it.

4. By a blotting of it out: in such language David prays for the forgiveness of sin; *Blot out my transgressions, and blot out all mine iniquities,* Psalm li. 1, 9. and in the same way God declares his will to forgive the sins of his people; *I, even I, am he that blotteth out thy transgressions,* Isa. xliii. 25. which language is used, either in allusion to the crossing of debt-books, drawing a line over them; or to the blotting out a man's hand-writing to a bond or note, obliging to payment of money; hence the phrase of *blotting out the hand-writing of ordinances that was against us,* Col. ii. 14. Sins are debts, and these are numerous, and sinners poor, and unable to pay them; wherefore God, for Christ's sake, freely forgives, and draws the line of Christ's blood over them, and cancels the obligation to payment: or else to the dissipation of a cloud, by the sun rising or breaking forth through it; *I have blotted out, as a thick cloud, thy transgressions; and as a cloud thy sins,* Isa. xliv. 22. Sins may be

compared to clouds for their quantity, their number being many; for their quality, being exhaled out of the earth and sea, and mount up to heaven, cause darkness, and intercept light; sin rises out of the earthly minds of men, who mind earthly things, and who are like the troubled sea which cannot rest; and the sins of some, like those of Babylon, reach up to heaven, and call for wrath and vengeance to come down from thence; sin causes the darkness of unregeneracy, and is often the reason of darkness to such who have been made light in the Lord; it intercepts the light of his countenance, and of Christ, the Sun of righteousness: now as a cloud is dispersed and dissipated by the breaking forth of the sun, which, overcoming the cloud, scatters it, so as it is seen no more; in like manner, through the rising of the Sun of righteousness, with healing in his wings, an application of pardoning grace is made for his sake; upon which darkness is dispersed, light and joy introduced, a serene heaven of peace and comfort follow: and as a cloud is so dispersed that it is seen no more, so sin is pardoned, in such sort as not to be seen any more, or to be set in the light of God's countenance unto condemnation; and though as fresh clouds may arise, so new sins may be committed, which yet are removed and cleansed from, by the blood of Christ, and the efficacy of it, for the continual pardon of it, through the repeated application of that blood.

5. By a non-remembrance of it; *And their iniquities will I remember no more,* Heb. viii. 12. Isa. xliii. 25. God forgives and forgets; having once forgiven them, he thinks of them no more; they are out of sight and out of mind; his thoughts are thoughts of peace, and not of evil; he remembers not former iniquities, but his tender mercies, which have been ever of old.

6. By making sin, or rather sinners, white as snow: so David prays, *Wash me, and I shall be whiter than snow,* Psalm li. 7. So the Lord promises; *Thy sins shall be as white as snow,* Isa. i. 18. *Her Nazarites were purer than snow,* Lam. iv. 7. Being justified by the righteousness of Christ, clothed with that fine linen, clean and white, washed in his blood, and their garments made white therein, and all their sins forgiven for his sake, and so all fair without spot or blemish.

Thirdly, What sins are pardoned; sins both with respect to quality and quantity.

1*st,* For quality; they are called *trespasses.* Sin is a walking on forbidden ground, for which a man must suffer, unless forgiven; and *transgressions* of the law of God, a passing over and going beyond the bounds and limits prescribed by it; and *iniquities,* which are contrary to the rules of justice and equity; and *sins,* errors, aberrations, straying from the rule of God's word: when God is said to forgive *iniquity, transgression,* and *sin,* it takes in every kind and sort of sin; every sin is against God, though some are more immediately against him than others; they are contrary to his nature, which is pure and holy; whereas, nothing is more impure, and unholy than sin is; and therefore it is abominable to him, and hated by him; and hence sins are called abominations; not that they are so to sinners, for they delight in them; but to God, to whom they are so very disagreeable: there is an enmity in sin, and in every sinner's heart, to God; every sin is an act of hostility against him, it is a stretching out the hand against God, and a strengthening a man's self against the Almighty; it strikes at his Deity, and is a contempt of his authority; and yet he forgives it: it being committed against him, an infinite Being, it is objectively *infinite,* and requires an infinite satisfaction; and without it is punished *ad infinitum.* Sin is defined, *a transgression of the law,* 1 John iii. 4. a breach, a violation of it; which accuses of it, pronounces guilty for it, and curses and condemns; and is only forgiven by the Lawgiver, who is able to save and to destroy. Sins are sometimes represented as *debts;* because being committed, they oblige to the debt of punishment, which God remits; the sinner owing more than ten thousand talents, and not able to pay, he frankly forgives all for Christ's sake; of which the year of release from debts under the law, was typical: sins, with respect to men, are called diseases, and they are incurable, but by the grace of God and blood of Christ; and pardon of sin is expressed by healing them; *who forgiveth all thine iniquities, who healeth all thy diseases,* Psalm ciii. 3. see Isa. xxxiii. 24. Mal. iv. 2.

2*dly,* For quantity; all trespasses, sins, and transgressions are forgiven, Col. ii. 13. Psalm ciii. 3. Original sin, the sin of the first man, and the sin of all men in him, by which all are made, constituted, and accounted sinners; which is the source and fountain of all sin, and is the iniquity of us all, which was laid on Christ, and he satisfied for, and is forgiven for his sake; of all sin, it cannot be thought this should be left unforgiven: all actual sins which spring from thence; the works of the flesh, which are many and manifest; some are more secret, some more open, some lesser, others greater, more daring and presumptuous; some sins of commission, others sins of omission; but all are forgiven; see Isa. xliii. 22, 23, 24, 25. and not only daily failings and infirmities, but all backslidings, revoltings, and partial apostacies, Jer. iii. 12, 13, 14, 22. Hos. xiv. 4. and, indeed, every sin, excepting the sin against the Holy Ghost, Matt. xii. 31, 32. and why that is unpardonable has been observed, book iii. chap. 12.

Fourthly, The causes of the pardon of sin.

1*st*, The efficient cause is God, and not any creature, angels or men.——1. It is not in the power of men to forgive sin; one man may forgive another an offence, as committed against himself, but not as committed against God; saints ought to forgive one another's offences that arise among them; as God, for Christ's sake, has forgiven them, Eph. iv. 32. Col. ii. 13. Ministers can remit sin ministerially and declaratively, but not authoritatively; no man that goes under the name of a priest, or a minister of the word, has a power of absolution, or has authority to absolve men from their sins: all that a true and faithful preacher of the gospel can do, is to preach remission of sins in the name of Christ; and to declare, that whoever repent of their sins, and believe in Christ, shall receive the forgiveness of them; and which declaration of theirs, God abides by, and confirms; and whose sins, in this sense, they remit, they are remitted, John xx. 23. To assume a power to forgive sin, and absolve from it, is the height of antichristianism; it is with respect to this that antichrist is said to sit in the temple of God, *shewing himself that he is God,* by taking that to himself which belongs to God only; namely, to forgive sin; this is one of the blasphemies, and a principal one, which his mouth is opened to utter, to dispense with sin, grant indulgencies of it, and pardons for it, 2 Thess. ii. 4. Rev. xiii. 5, 6. the highest angel in heaven cannot forgive nor procure the forgiveness, of one sin; they could not for those of their own kind that sinned; nor can they for any of the sons of men.

2. There is nothing a man has, or can do, by which he can procure the pardon of sin, either for himself, or for others: no man, by his riches, and the multitude of his wealth, can give to God a ransom for himself, or his brother, make atonement and satisfaction for sin, and obtain the pardon of it; *riches profit not in the day of wrath:* when God comes to deal with men for their sins, and pour out his wrath upon them for them, bags of gold and silver will be of no avail. Nor is pardon of sin to be obtained by works of righteousness; could it, it would not be of grace; for grace and works are opposed to each other; men would be saved by works, contrary to the scriptures, since pardon is included in salvation, and that is by grace, and not works: besides, the blood of Christ would be shed in vain; for as if righteousness, or justification, came by the law, then Christ died in vain; so if pardon of sin came by the works of the law, and obedience to it, in like manner Christ must have died in vain. Once more, the best works of men are due to God; he has a prior right unto them, and therefore cannot be meritorious of pardon; nor is there any just proportion between them and pardon, and eternal life; one debt cannot be paid by another, or the debt of punishment be remitted by the debt of obedience. Nor is pardon procured by repentance; they are both gifts of grace; and though given to the same persons, the one is not the cause of the other; at least, repentance is not the cause of remission; for true, evangelical repentance, flows from, and in the exercise of it is influenced by the discovery and application of pardoning grace; see Ezek. xvi. 63. Brinish tears will not wash away sin; notwithstanding these, it will remain marked before God; the tears the woman, a sinner, shed, and with which she washed Christ's feet, were not shed to procure the pardon of her sins; but flowed from a sense of pardoning love manifested to her, Luke vii. 37, 47. Nor is pardon procured by faith, as the cause of it; faith does not obtain it by any virtue of its own, but receives it as obtained by the blood of Christ, Acts x. 43. and xxvi. 18. Nor is it procured by a submission to the ordinance of water-baptism; baptism neither takes away original sin, nor actual sin; not as to the guilt thereof, as the case of Simon Magus shews; for though the three thousand are directed to be *baptized in the name of Christ for the remission of sins;* and Saul was

advised by Ananias, to *arise, and be baptized, and wash away his sins*, Acts ii. 38. and xxii. 16. yet the meaning is not, as if remission of sins was to be obtained by baptism, or sinners to be cleansed from them by it; but that by means of this ordinance, they might be led to the sufferings, death, and bloodshed of Christ, represented in it; for whose name's-sake remission of sins is granted, and whose blood was shed for it, and cleanses from it.

3. God only can forgive sin; it is his sole prerogative; it belongs to him, and to no other, Mark ii. 7. Isa. xliii. 25. Dan. ix. 9. And this appears from the nature of sin itself; it is committed against God; and none but he against whom it is committed can forgive it; it is a breach of his righteous law; and none but the Lawgiver, who is able to save and to destroy, can remit it, or free from obligation to punishment for it. Besides, if there was any other that could forgive sin, then there would be one equal to God; whereas, *Who is a God like unto him that pardoneth iniquity?* Mic. vii. 18. and it may be observed, that saints in all ages, under the Old and under the New Testament, never made their application to any other but to God for the forgiveness of sin; nor are they ever directed to any other for it, Psalm li. 1. Dan. ix. 19. Matt. vi. 9, 12. Acts viii. 22.

4. Yet all the three Persons, Father, Son, and Spirit, have a concern in it. God the Father made an early provision of this blessing of pardon in his heart, in his purposes, in his council and covenant; and sent his Son to be the propitiation for it, and for the remission of it, through faith in his blood; and does bestow it for his sake; in which he shows, not only his grace, but his justice and faithfulness; for upon the bloodshed of his Son for it, he is *just and faithful to forgive sin;* just, in that the blood of Christ is a sufficient atonement for it; and faithful to his counsels, covenant, and promises, concerning it. Christ, as God, and the Son of God, has power to forgive sin, even as Immanuel, God with us. God in our nature, and when he was here on earth; of which he gave proof, by another act of his divine power, bidding a lame man take up his bed and walk, Matt. ix. 2, 6. As Godman and Mediator, his blood was shed for the remission of sin; and by it it was obtained; as the Advocate of his people he calls for it, and demands and requires the application of it when it is wanted;

and as the exalted Saviour he gives it, and in his name it is preached, according to his orders, by the ministers of the gospel. The holy Spirit of God has also a concern in it: he convinces men of sin, and of their need of the pardon of it; he makes it manifest; he takes the blood of Christ, and applies it to the conscience, which speaks peace and pardon; he pronounces the sentence of it in the conscience of a sinner; he is the holy Spirit of promise, and he seals up the pardon of sin in a promise; and witnesses to the spirits of God's people that they are pardoned ones.

2dly, The impulsive moving cause of pardon, is neither man's misery nor his merits; not any works of righteousness done by him; nor even any of the graces of the Spirit in him; but the sovereign grace and mercy of God, through Christ, Eph. i. 7. Psalm li. 1. Luke i. 77, 78.

3dly, The procuring meritorious cause of it, is the blood of Christ, which was shed for it, has obtained it, and for the sake of which God forgives sin; which virtue it has from the human nature being in union with the divine Person of the Son of God; see Heb. ix. 14. 1 John i. 7.

Fifthly, The effects of pardon, that is, when applied; for the effects of it are not sensibly perceived unless applied; which are, 1. Peace of conscience: when sin is charged upon the conscience, and there is no sight and sense of pardon, there is no peace; but no sooner is there a view of interest in justification, by the righteousness of Christ, and pardon by his blood, but there is peace, which that blood speaks and gives; and which the world cannot take away; a peace that passeth all understanding, and it is better experienced than expressed.

2. Cheerfulness of spirit: when sin lies as an heavy burden, without a view of pardon, the mind is depressed; it is filled with gloominess, and melancholy apprehensions of things, if not with despair, as in the case of Cain: a spirit, wounded with a sense of sin, and without a view of pardon, who can bear? But when the Lord says, *Son,* or *daughter, be of good cheer, thy sins are forgiven thee!* cheerfulness takes place; the spirits, that were sunk, are raised; the head that was bowed down, is lifted up; that countenance, that looked dejected, smiles; the soul is caused to hear joy and gladness; and the bones that were broken are made to rejoice.

3. Comfort of soul: whilst a gracious

soul, under a sense of sin, apprehends that God is angry with him, he has no comfort; but when he manifests his pardoning grace then he concludes his anger is turned away and he is comforted: and this is one of the ways and means in which God would have his people comforted by his ministers; *Speak ye comfortably to Jerusalem; cry unto her, that her iniquity is pardoned*, Isa. xl. 1, 2. and when their ministry is accompanied by the Spirit of God, comfort is enjoyed.

4. Access to God with boldness and confidence: a soul, under the weight and pressure of the guilt of sin, moves heavily to the throne of grace; and when it comes there, cannot lift up his eyes, but looking downward, and smiting on his breast, says, *God be merciful*, or propitious, *to me, a sinner!* but when it has a view of the blood, righteousness, and sacrifice of Christ, it comes with liberty, boldness, and confidence; particularly when it has a clear and comfortable sight of the pardon of sin, through the blood of Jesus, it has boldness to enter into the holiest of all, and come up to the seat of God, and claims interest in him.

5. Attendance on divine worship with pleasure and delight: this flows from a sense of forgiveness of sin, and is one end of it; *there is forgiveness with thee, that thou mayest be feared*, that is, worshipped; for fear is put for worship, both inward and outward; and especially denotes, serving the Lord with reverence and godly fear. And to have the conscience purged from dead works by the blood of Christ, both puts a soul into the best capacity, and into the most suitable frame to serve the living God, Psalm cxxx. 4. Heb. xii. 28. and ix. 14.

6. Love to God and Christ is raised, promoted, and increased, by an application of pardon; which, as it is an evidence of the love of God to a sinner, it produces love again; the poor woman in the gospel, the notorious sinner as she had been, loved much, many sins having been forgiven her, Luke vii. 47.

7. Evangelical repentance, and the exercise of it, are much influenced by pardon of sin being applied: the tears of repentance, shed by the poor woman before mentioned, flowed from a sense of pardoning grace and mercy; sin never appears more odious than in the glass of forgiving love; shame, confusion of face, and silence, are never more manifest, than when a soul knows that God is pacified towards it for all that it has done; this produces a godly sorrow, a sorrow after a godly sort, for sin committed against a God of love, grace, and mercy; faith first looks to Christ, and beholds pardon through him; and then evangelical mourning and repentance follow upon it, Ezek. xvi. 63. Zech. xii. 10.

8. Thankfulness of soul for such a mercy; than which there cannot be a greater: if a man is truly impressed with a sense of it, he will call upon his soul, and all within him, to bless and praise the Lord for all his benefits; and particularly for this, *who forgiveth all thine iniquities*, Psalm ciii. 2, 3. Think with what gratitude and thankfulness a condemned malefactor, and just ready to be executed, receives his pardon from the king! with that, and much more, souls sensible of sin, the demerit of it, and danger by it, receive pardon of all their sins, through the blood of Christ, from the King of kings.

Sixthly, The properties of pardon. 1. It is an act of God's free grace; it is according to the *riches* of it; that is, the plenty of it, which is abundantly displayed in it; and according to the *multitude of his tender mercies*, mercy being richly shown forth in it, Eph. i. 7. Psalm li. 1. It is an act of the Father's grace, who has found the ransom; and, upon it, delivered men from going down to the pit of corruption; has set forth Christ to be the propitiation, through faith in his blood, for the remission of sins, and does, for his sake, freely forgive them: and it is an act of the Son's grace, in shedding his blood for the remission of it: and it is an act of the Spirit's grace, to lead to the blood of Jesus, which speaks peace and pardon; to that fountain opened to wash in for sin and uncleanness; to take of the things of Christ, his blood, righteousness, and sacrifice, and shew interest in them, and make application of them. Pardon of sin is one of the things freely given of God, which the Spirit gives knowledge of; and it is an act of sovereign, unmerited, and distinguishing grace. God bestows it on whom he pleases, according to his sovereign will, and on persons altogether undeserving of it, who have been guilty of all manner of sin, of sins of omission and commission; and yet to such he says, *I, even I, am he that blotteth out thy transgressions for mine own sake*, Isa. xliii. 25. and it is bestowed on some, and not on others, who are equally as bad as the others; and on men, and not angels; for to the angels that sinned, no sparing pardoning mercy is extended; only to rebellious, sinful men.

2. It is a point of justice; God is just, whilst he pardons those that repent of their sins, confess them, and believe in Christ; *If we confess our sins, he is faithful and just to forgive us our sins,* 1 John i. 9. just, on account of the blood of his Son being shed for the remission of sin; and faithful, to his counsel, covenant, and promises, to grant it upon that footing; and hence also Christ, as an advocate, calls for it, and demands it in right of justice; that it be applied to his people, for whom he shed his blood; and became the propitiatory sacrifice for their sins; which he powerfully and effectually pleads on their behalf, 1 John ii. 1, 2.

3. It is a complete act; it is a forgiveness of all the sins and trespasses of God's people, not one is left unforgiven; and it is done *simul* and *semel,* together and at once; though the manifestation and application may be made at different times, as wanted by believers; yet in the mind of God it passed at once; even a full as well as free forgiveness of all sins, past, present, and to come. Nor is it any objection to this, that then sins must be forgiven before they are committed; so they are, in virtue of Christ's suretiship engagements, and the performance of them.[1]

4. It is an act that will never be repealed; it is one of those gifts of grace which are without repentance, and will never be revoked; it is a blessing God has given in covenant, and in and with his Son Jesus Christ, and it is irreversible; it is one of those things which God does, which are for ever; sins once pardoned are always so; when sought for they shall not be found; they are removed from the pardoned sinner as far as the east is from the west; God has cast them behind his back, and will never set them more in the light of his countenance; he has cast them into the depths of the sea, and will never fetch them up again.

5. It is one of the chief articles of faith, and blessings of grace; it stands the first of those benefits, on account of which the Psalmist called upon his soul to bless God for, Psalm ciii. 2, 3. next to eternal election, it is reckoned among the spiritual blessings saints are blessed with in Christ; being a branch of redemption through his blood, Eph. i. 3, 4, 7. and happy is the man that has an interest in it; he has peace and comfort now, and may rejoice in hope of the glory of God hereafter!

Seventhly, Answer some questions relating to pardon of sin; which do not so naturally fall under the above heads.

Qu. 1. Whether any sin is venial or pardonable in its own nature, and does not deserve eternal death? The reason of this question is the distinction the Papists make between venial and mortal sins; some sins, they say, are in their own nature venial, pardonable, or not deserving of eternal death, only some lesser chastisement, whilst others are mortal, and deserving of death: but there is no room nor reason for such a distinction; no sin is venial or pardonable in itself, but mortal, and deserving of death; though every kind of sin is venial or pardonable, or rather is pardoned through the grace of God and blood of Christ, excepting one. There is a difference in sins, some are greater, others lesser; see John xix. 11. some are breaches of the more weightier matters, or precepts of the law, as those against the first table of it; others of the lesser matters, or precepts of it, as those against the second table; some are attended with more aggravated circumstances than others, being committed against light and knowledge, and under the enjoyment of great blessings and privileges, Luke xii. 47, 48. Matt. xi. 22, 24. whilst others are done ignorantly without knowledge of the Lord's will, and not favoured with means that others have; yet every sin is mortal, or deserving of death: death was threatened to sin before it was committed, in case it should; and the first sin brought death into the world with it, and the end of all other sins is death; death is the wages and just demerit of sin; every sin is committed against God, and is objectively infinite, and deserving of infinite and everlasting punishment; it is a breach of his law, and every disobedience to that, has a just recompence of reward annexed to it; righteous punishment, or the wrath of God it reveals and works; the breach of the least of the commands of it is liable to divine resentment; and he that offends in one point is guilty of all; the least sin leaves a stain which what is done or used by the sinner cannot remove; and such pollution excludes from

---

[1] Justificatio virtualiter peracta est——cum filius statim post lapsum datus est mediator et sponsor electorum ex decreto, Gen. iii. 15. itaque hoc sensu quadam ratione peccata possunt dici fidelibus remissa, antequam sunt commissa Leydecker. Synops. Theolog. Christian. 1. 5. c. 5. s. 33.

the kingdom of God; the least sin, even every sin of thought, word, and deed, will be brought into judgment, and must be accounted for: though all manner of sin is venial, or pardonable, or is pardoned through the grace of God and blood of Christ; God forgives iniquity, transgression, and sin, which include all sorts of sins; sins of the greatest magnitude, and of the deepest die, are blotted out for Christ's sake; such as are like crimson and scarlet, become through him as white as wool, as white as snow; his blood cleanses from sin; every sin is forgiven, but the sin against the Holy Ghost, Matt. xii. 31, 32.

Qu. 2. Whether any sin will be forgiven in the world to come? The reason of this question is, because it is said of the sin against the Holy Ghost, that it shall *not be forgiven, neither in this world, nor in the world to come;* which seems to imply, that though *that* sin shall not then be forgiven, others may: but the meaning of the expression is, that it shall never be forgiven; it is a phrase expressive of endless duration, that that sin shall always remain unpardonable, and does not suppose any thing concerning other sins; and therefore the answer to be returned to the question is, that there will be no forgiveness of any sin at all in the other world. As for the sins of God's people, the remission of them is perfect; all of them have been laid on Christ, and bore by him; and he has finished and made an end of them all; and has made perfect reconciliation and satisfaction for them; and God, for Christ's sake, has forgiven all trespasses, and no new sins will be committed by them; the will of God will be done by them with the same perfection as by the angels; there will be no sin in them, and done by them, to be pardoned; there will be indeed a general declaration of pardon, and of their being blessed with that, and all other blessings comprehended in Christ's address to them, *Come, ye blessed of my Father;* and they will live under a continual sense of pardoning grace, and in admiration of it, and thankfulness for it; but no particular act of pardon will be passed by God, nor applied to them for any particular sin: and as for others, the door will be shut upon them at the day of judgment; the door of the ministry of the word; repentance and remission of sins will be no more preached in the name of Christ; after this there will be no repentance of sin in sinners, nor faith to believe in Christ for the remission of sins; these graces will not be bestowed on any in the other world, the door of mercy will be shut, and never opened to men any more.

Qu. 3. Whether the sins of pardoned ones will be made known and exposed to others in the day of judgment? I think not; my reasons are, because none but their good works are taken notice of in Matt. xxv. because it does not seem consistent with the nature of pardon: pardon of sin is expressed by a covering of it; when God forgives sins he covers them, and he will never uncover them, or take off the blood and righteousness of his Son; and if he does not uncover them, who can? neither angels, nor men, nor devils: it is a blotting them as a cloud; and when a cloud is broke to pieces and scattered, it can never be collected together any more; sins are cast behind the back of God, and into the depths of the sea; and are removed as far as the east is from the west, and can never, though sought for, be found more. Nor does it consist with the state and condition of the pardoned ones that their sins should be exposed; Christ, who has taken so much pains to sanctify and cleanse his church, that he might present her to himself a glorious church, without spot or wrinkle or any such thing, will never suffer their sins ever more to appear; the church will now descend from heaven as a bride adorned and prepared for her husband, having the glory of God upon her, and clothed with the shining robes of immortality and glory, as well as with the fine linen, clean and white, the righteousness of her Lord; it will now be her open and consummate marriage with the Lamb; and it seems quite out of all character, that he should suffer her faults, failings, sins, and transgressions, to be exposed on her wedding day; and which would, one would think, cause shame and blushing, which seems not consistent with that state of happiness.

Qu. 4. Whether it is now the duty of saints to pray for the pardon of sin? Prayer itself is a moral duty, and incumbent on all; and the light of nature will direct persons in distress to pray to God for relief; and when they suppose they have offended Deity by sin, and he is angry with them, and his judgments are, or they fear will come upon them; it is natural to them to pray unto him to forgive them, and deliver them out of present troubles, or what they fear are coming upon them;

as may be observed in Jonah's mariners, who were heathens; and the apostle directed Simon Magus, an unregenerate man, and known by him to be so, to *pray* to God, if perhaps *the thought of his heart might be forgiven him*, Acts viii. 22. But this comes not up to the question, which is, Whether pardoned sinners should pray for the pardon of sin? to which it may be answered, That either these pardoned ones have a comfortable sense and perception of the pardon of their sins, or they have not; if they have, they have no need, at present at least, to pray even for the manifestation of it to them, since they have it already; if they have not a comfortable view of it, which is sometimes the case of pardoned ones, as it was of the church, when she said, *We have transgressed and rebelled, thou hast not pardoned*, Lam. iii. 42. they will then see it both their duty, and privilege, and interest, to pray for a comfortable view and fresh manifestation of it: and whereas saints are daily sinning in thought, word, or deed, Christ has directed to make a daily petition of it, that when we pray that God would give us *day by day our daily bread*, that he would also *forgive us our sins*, Luke xi. 3, 4. and it appears to have been the practice of saints in all ages to pray for the pardon of sin in some sense, and as it seems in the sense suggested; so Moses prayed when the people of Israel had sinned at Sinai, *Pardon our iniquity and our sin*, Exod. xxxiv. 9. so David prayed, *For thy name's-sake, O Lord, pardon mine iniquity, for it is great*, Psalm xxv. 11. A strange plea this! a reason, one would think, why it should not be pardoned, than why it should be pardoned; and it was so great in his apprehension, that if he had not a discovery and application of pardon made to him, he could not bear up under it; and as he prayed thus, and with success, he observes it for the encouragement of other saints to do so likewise; *I said, I will confess my transgressions unto the Lord*, and so he did; *and thou forgavest the iniquity of my sin; for this shall every one that is godly pray unto thee in a time when thou mayest be found*, Psalm xxxii. 5, 6. that is, for the pardon of their sins, and the evidence of it, when they stood in need thereof; so Daniel prayed for himself and others, *O Lord hear, O Lord forgive*, Dan. ix. 19.

and so New Testament saints are directed by Christ to pray, as has been observed: but then it must be understood in an explained sense, consistent with the nature of pardon, as procured by Christ, and passed by God; it cannot be supposed that saints should pray that Christ's blood may be shed again to procure fresh pardon for them; nor that any fresh act of pardon should be passed in the divine mind, since God has forgiven all trespasses through the blood of his Son, shed once for all; but that they might have fresh manifestations, discoveries, and application of pardon, as they stand in need of them, being continually sinning against God: in no other sense can I understand that pardon of sin can be prayed for by the saints.[2]

There are several other questions that might be put, but they are superseded by what has been already said concerning them; as, Why the sin against the Holy Ghost is said to be unpardonable? the reason of which is given, in book iii. chap. 12. And whether one man can forgive another? and in what sense? to which the answer is, He may, and in some cases, ought; as it is an injury and offence to himself: and whether sins against God can be forgiven by himself, without a satisfaction to his justice? and whether if, upon a satisfaction, how can pardon be free, or of free grace? The answer to these questions may be found in a preceding chapter.

CHAP. VIII.

OF JUSTIFICATION.

PARDON of sin, and justification from it, are very closely connected; the one follows upon the other; according to the position of them in some passages of scripture, pardon is first, and justification next; as in Acts xiii. 38, 39. and xxvi. 18. though they are not, the one, in reality, prior to the other; they are both together in the divine mind, and in the application of them to the conscience of a sinner; indeed, according to the order of causes, justification by the righteousness of Christ, imputed, may be considered as before pardon; since God forgives sin for Christ's sake; that is, for the sake of his righteousness imputed. Now that for the sake of which a thing is, must be before that for which it is, as the

---

[2] Petitur quotidie remissio peccatorum a justificatis, ut sensus et manifestatio ejus magis magisque percipiatur, prout singularia peccata postulant, Amesii Medulla Theolog. l. 1. c. 27. s. 25.

cause is before the effect. Some take them to be the same, and that justification lies solely in the remission of sins; and others more rightly make the imputation of Christ's righteousness, and forgiveness of sins, the two parts of justification, distinct ones; whilst others think they are not two integral parts, really distinct, but only one act, respecting two terms, *a quo et ad quem*; just as by one and the same act, darkness is expelled from the air, and light is introduced; so by one and the same act of jusfication, the sinner is absolved from guilt, and pronounced righteous; hence they suppose such express the whole of justification, who say, it consists in the remission of sins, and those that say it consists in the imputation of righteousness; because when God forgives men their sins, he pronounces them righteous, through the imputation of Christ's righteousness to them; and when he pronounces them righteous, by that he forgives them their sins; remission of sin supposes the imputation of Christ's righteousness; and the imputation of Christ's righteousness infers the remission of sin. But though these are not to be separated, yet they are to be distinguished; and I should choose to consider them, not as distinct parts of the same thing, but as distinct blessings of grace; for though pardon and justification agree in some things, in others they differ. In some things they agree.

1. In their efficient cause, God: as God only can and does forgive sin, it is his prerogative, it is peculiar to him; so it is God that justifies the sinner, and he only; *there is one God, who justifies the circumcision by faith, and the uncircumcision through faith;* that is, that justifies both Jews and Gentiles, who believe in Christ, Mark ii. 7. Rom. iii. 30.

2. In their moving cause, the free grace of God: pardon of sin is owing to the riches of God's grace, and the multitude of his tender mercy; and justification is ascribed to the grace of God, and is said to be freely by his grace, Eph. i. 7. Psalm li. 1. Tit. iii. 7. Rom. iii. 24.

3. In their procuring cause, the blood of Christ: the blood of Christ was shed to procure the remission of sins, and it is by it; and so likewise justification is by the same blood, Matt. xxvi. 28. Rom. v. 9.

4. In the objects of it: the same persons that are pardoned are justified, and the same that are justified are pardoned; to whom God imputes the righteousness of Christ, to their justification, to them he gives the remission of sin; and to whom he does not impute sin, but forgives it, he imputes righteousness without works, Rom. iv. 6, 7, 8.

5. In their commencement and completion: pardon and justification commence together, and both are finished at once, *simul* and *semel;* and are not carried on in a gradual and progressive way, as sanctification is, Col. ii. 13. Acts xiii. 39.

6. In the manner of actual enjoying them, which is in a way of receiving, and that by faith; it is by faith men receive the forgiveness of sins; and by it they receive abundance of grace, and the gift of righteousness to justification of life; and this is what the Scriptures call justification by faith, Acts xxvi. 18. Rom. v. 1, 17, 18. But though they agree in these things, in others they differ.

1. Pardon is of men that are sinners, and who remain such, and may be called so, though pardoned sinners; but justification is a pronouncing persons righteous, as if they had never sinned; it is one thing for a man to be arraigned at the bar as a criminal, and be tried, cast, and condemned, and after that be pardoned; and another thing for a man to be tried by law, and to be found and declared righteous by it, as though he had not transgressed it.

2. Pardon takes away sin from the sinner, but does not give him a righteousness, as justification does; pardon takes away the filthy garments; but it is justification that clothes with change of raiment, with the robe of Christ's righteousness; these are two distinct things, Zech. iii. 4.

3. Pardon frees from punishment, and an obligation to it, as it takes away guilt; *the Lord hath put away thy sin; thou shalt not die,* 2 Sam. xii. 18. but does not entitle to everlasting life, happiness, and glory: that justification does, and therefore is called *justification of life;* and in consequence of which men are made heirs, according to the hope of eternal life, Rom. v. 18. Tit. iii. 7. When a king pardons a criminal, he does not by that act entitle him to an estate, much less to his crown and kingdom; but if he will, when he has pardoned him, take him to court, and make him his son and heir, it must be by another distinct act of royal favour.

4. More is required for justification than for pardon; the blood of Christ was sufficient to procure pardon, and did procure it; but to the justification of a sinner, the holiness of the human nature of Christ, the

perfect obedience of his life, and his bloodshed, and sufferings of death, are and must be imputed.

5. The righteousness of Christ, by which men are justified, is the fulfilling of the law; Christ came to fulfil it in the room of his people; and he is the fulfilling end of it to them, for righteousness; which is inherent in him, the author of it: not so pardon; that does not fulfil the law, gives no righteousness; nor does it reside in Christ, as righteousness does, Rom. x. 4. Isa. xlv. 24.

6. Pardon lies in the non-imputation of sin; justification in the imputation of righteousness: righteousness is imputed, but pardon is not, Rom. iv. 6, 7.

7. Justification passed on Christ, as the head and representative of his people; but not pardon: Christ having had the sins of his people imputed to him, and having made satisfaction to the justice of God for them, he was acquitted, discharged, and justified; but not pardoned: we may truly say, Christ was justified, and that God justified him, because the Scriptures say so; but not that he was pardoned; such an expression would sound harsh, and be very unwarrantable; see Isa. l. 8, 9. 1 Tim. iii. 16.

8. An innocent person, falsely charged, may be acquitted and justified, when he cannot be said to be pardoned; yea, such who need no pardon, as Adam did not in his state of innocence, and the elect angels in heaven; yet may be said to be justified, that is declared to be just and righteous: so men, in the present state, could they perfectly fulfil the law, as they cannot, would be justified by it; for *the doers of the law are justified; he that does these things shall live by them*, Rom. ii. 13. and x. 5. Moreover, if justification and pardon are to be considered as cause and effect, as before observed, they must be distinct, and are not to be confounded.

The doctrine of justification by the righteousness of Christ, is a doctrine of great importance; the apostle speaks of it as if the essence of the gospel lay in it; and calls the opposite to it, justification by the works of the law, another gospel; see Gal. i. 6, 7. and iii. 8. it is a fundamental article of the gospel; some have called it, the *basis* of christianity; it was the great doctrine of the reformation; what our first reformers made their chief study; and by it cut the sinews of *popery*, the antichristian doctrines of penance and purgatory, of pardons and indulgencies, of the merit of good works, works of supererogation, &c. Luther used to call it, *articulus stantis vel cedentis ecclesiæ*, the article of the church, by which it stands or falls; as this is, the church is; if this obtains, the church is in a well-settled and prosperous state; but if this loses ground, and is rejected, it is in a ruinous one: if this is a rule to judge by, it may be easily discerned, in what case the church, and interest of religion, now are. This doctrine is the ground and foundation of all solid joy, peace, and comfort, in this life, and hope of eternal glory hereafter.

I have, in a former part of this work, book ii. chap. 5. treated of justification, as an immanent and eternal act in God; and so it may be said to be from eternity, and before faith; and in what sense it is so, with a removal of objections, has been shewn in the place referred to; and therefore shall only now discourse concerning justification, as it terminates in the conscience of a believer; and which the scriptures style justification by faith. I shall,

I. Consider the act of justification, and in what sense the word is to be taken. And,

1. It is not to be understood of instructing men in the scheme and method of justification, whether in a legal or evangelical way, Acts xv. 1. 1 Tim. i. 7. Dan. xii. 3.

------ 2. Nor is it to be understood of making men righteous, by infusing righteousness into them; for this is to confound justification and sanctification together, which are two distinct things, 1 Cor. i. 30. and vi. 11. this is sanctification: the righteousness by which men are justified, is *imputed* to them; but the righteousness of sanctification is *inherent* in them; that by which men are justified, are the obedience and blood of Christ; but infused holiness is neither of these.

The word *justify* is never used in a physical sense, for producing any real internal change in men; but in a forensic sense, and stands opposed, not to a state of impurity and unholiness, but to a state of condemnation; it is a law-term, and used of judicial affairs, transacted in a court of judicature see Deut. xxv. 1. Prov. xvii. 15. Isa. v. 22. Matt. xii. 37. where justification stands opposed to condemnation; and this is the sense of the word whenever it is used in the doctrine under consideration; so in Job ix. 2, 3. and xxv. 4. so by David, Psalm cxliii. 2. and in all Paul's epistles, where the doctrine of justification is treated of, respect is had to courts of judicature, and to a judicial process in them; men are represented as sinners, charged with sin, and pronounced guilty before God, and subject to condemnation and death; when, according to this evangelic doctrine, they are justified by the obedience and blood of Christ, cleared of all charges, acquitted and absolved, and freed from condemnation and death, and adjudged to eternal life; see Rom. iii. 9, 19. and v. 9, 16, 18, 19. and viii. 1, 33, 34. Gal. ii. 16, 17. Tit. iii. 7.

3. Justification is to be understood in this doctrine, not of justification before men, before whom men may appear righteous, Matt. xxiii. 28. but in the sight of God, in whose sight they cannot be justified by the works of the law, Rom. iii. 20. Nor of the justification of a man's cause; or of his vindication from the calumnies of men, 1 Sam. xii. 5, 6. Psalm vii. 8. Job xiii. 18. Nor of the justification of a man's faith by his works, thereby proving the genuineness and sincerity of it: so the faith of Abraham, and of Rahab, was justified by their works; or their faith in the promises made unto them, was proved to be genuine and sincere; the one by offering up his son; and the other by hiding the spies, James ii. 21—25. But of the justification of the persons of men before God; and this is either legal or evangelical: legal, on condition of a person's fulfilling the whole law, or yielding perfect obedience to it; which, in man's present state and circumstances, is impossible, Rom. ii. 13. and x. 5. and viii. 3, 4. evangelical, which is an act of God's grace, accounting and pronouncing a person righteous, through the righteousness of Christ imputed to him, and received by faith; so *by the obedience of one many are made righteous;* and, Christ is of God, *made righteousness to them;* and they are *made the righteousness of God in him;* are reckoned perfectly righteous through him, and so stand justified and accepted in the sight of God, Rom. v. 19. 1 Cor. i. 30. 2 Cor. v. 22. and this is the justification we are treating of; concerning which farther observe,

II. The causes of it. The *moving cause* is the grace of God; it was the sovereign grace, favour, and good-will of God, which put him upon forming the scheme and method of justification; which moved him to appoint and send his Son, to work out, and bring in a righteousness for the justification of his people; and then to accept of it as their justifying righteousness, and to impute it freely to them without works: the procuring, meritorious, or material cause of justification, is the righteousness of Christ imputed, which will be treated of more largely, when we come to consider the matter of justification; or what that is, for the sake of which, any of the sons of men are justified before God. At present, I shall only attend to the *efficient* cause of justification, who is God; *It is God that justifies*, Rom. viii. 33. see also chap. iii. 26, 30. Gal. iii. 8. which is marvellous; since,

1. He is the Judge of all the earth, who will do right, and will by no means clear the guilty. Judges among men, by his orders and instructions, and as they would forfeit his displeasure, were not to justify the wicked; and yet he, who is Judge himself in the earth, *justifies the ungodly:* but then it should be observed, that he does not justify them without a righteousness, but upon the foot of Christ's righteousness; so that though he justifies the ungodly, yet not as ungodly, but as righteous, through the righteousness of his Son; hence it is, that it is one of the privileges of such persons, that they can *come to God, the Judge of all*, without fear and dread, appearing before him perfectly righteous in Christ the Mediator, Heb. xii. 23, 24.

2. Whose law is the rule by which he judges, and that law broken by men, and yet he justifies them. The law is holy, just, and good, and requires perfect, sinless obedience of men, but is broken by them in ten thousand instances; and he that offends in one point, is guilty of all, and the law pronounces him guilty, and curses and condemns him; and yet God, who judges according to this law, justifies them, Rom. ii. 12. but then it should be observed, that Christ has fulfilled the law, in the room and stead of these persons; so that the *righteousness of the law* is said to be *fulfilled in them;* and it is considered as if it was fulfilled by them; and on this account they are legally acquitted, discharged, and justified, according to this law; its demands being fully satisfied by Christ.

3. Sin, the breach of the law of God, is committed against him, and is hateful to him, and yet he justifies from it; every sin, being a transgression of the law, is against God, the Lawgiver, and cannot but be resented by him, and be an abomination to him; he hates it, and the workers of it; well then might Bildad say, *How then can*

man be justified with God? Job. xxv. 4. and yet he is.

4. It is that God that justifies, who will not admit of an imperfect righteousness, in the room of a perfect one: man's righteousness is imperfect, and cannot be reckoned as a perfect one by him, whose judgment is according to truth; nor will it stand in judgment, nor answer for the sinner at the bar of God, and justify in his sight; and yet God justifies; but then it is through the perfect righteousness of Christ, who is *the end of the law for righteousness to every one that believes*, Rom. x. 4.

5. That God, who is the Lawgiver, and is able to save and to destroy, who has the power to destroy both body and soul in hell, and would be just in so doing, and into whose hands it is a fearful thing to fall, yet he justifies. Now this act of justification, as ascribed to God, belongs to all the three Persons in the Godhead; they are all concerned in it, Father, Son, and Spirit.

First, God the Father; who, in many places where he is spoken of as a justifier, is distinguished from Christ; as where it is said, *It is God that justifieth—who shall condemn? It is Christ that died!* Again, God is said to *be just, and the justifier of him that believeth in Jesus*, Rom. viii. 34. and iii. 25, 26. the same that justifies the head, justifies the members; now it is the Father that justified Christ, the head of his elect, of whom Christ says, *He is near that justifieth me*, Isa. l. 8.

1. God the Father contrived the scheme and method of justification; it would have been a puzzling question to angels and men, had not he resolved it; *How should man*, sinful man, *be just with God?* But God, in his infinite wisdom, *found a ransom*, a Ransomer, a Redeemer of his people, to bring in everlasting righteousness for them, and thereby acquit and discharge them, and *deliver them from going down to the pit* of ruin and destruction; *God was in Christ reconciling the world to himself;* was, with him, forming the scheme of their peace and reconciliation, of their redemption, justification, and salvation; *not imputing their trespasses*, but the righteousness of his Son unto them, Job xxxiii. 24. 2 Cor. v. 19.

2. He sent his Son, in the fulness of time, to execute this scheme; he sent him in human nature, *made under the law*, subject to it, in the room and stead of his people, and to yield a perfect obedience to it; and he sent him *in the likeness of sinful flesh*, with their sins imputed to him; and by making him a sacrifice for sin, through his sufferings and death, he bore the penalty of the law, that so the whole *righteousness of the law*, or all it could demand, both with respect to precept and penalty, *might he fulfilled in* them; they being represented by him, Gal. iv. 4. Rom. viii. 3, 4.

3. A perfect righteousness being wrought out by Christ, agreeable to the requirements of law and justice, by which the law is magnified and made honourable, and justice satisfied; God the Father approves of it, is well-pleased with it, and accepts of it as the justifying righteousness of them that believe in Christ.

4. He imputes this righteousness to believers as their own: this is the Father's act of grace, Rom. iv. 6. *Of Him*, that is, of God the Father, *are ye in Christ Jesus*, chosen in him, and united to him; *who, of God* (the Father) *is made unto us righteousness;* which is done by his act of imputation, Rom. iv. 6. 1 Cor. i. 30.

Secondly, God the Son, the second Person, is concerned in the justification of men; *By his knowledge*, says Jehovah the Father, *shall my righteous Servant justify many*, Isa. liii. 11.

1. Christ, as a divine Person, as he has power to forgive sin, so to absolve and justify from it; of which we have some instances, even when he was here on earth, in human nature, as to the man sick of the palsy he said, *Thy sins are forgiven thee!* and to the woman taken in adultery, *Neither do I condemn thee!* which was a full acquittance and discharge; and to his apostles he said, *Ye are clean*, every whit clean, free from sin, and fully absolved from it, *Through the word I have spoken to you;* the sentence of justification by his blood and righteousness he had pronounced upon them, Matt. ix. 2. John viii. 11. and xv. 3. and xiii. 10.

2. As Mediator, Christ is the author of that righteousness by which sinners are justified; as he was to bring in an everlasting righteousness, he has brought in one; hence he is called, The Lord our Righteousness, the Sun of righteousness, and the end of the law for righteousness; and men are made righteous by his obedience, and justified by his blood, Jer. xxiii. 6. Mal. iv. 2. Rom. x. 4. and v. 9, 19.

3. As the head and representative of his people, they are justified in him; as Adam's natural posterity, sinning in him, were

condemned in him, judgment came upon them all unto condemnation; so all Christ's spiritual seed and offspring are justified in him; for *in the Lord shall all the seed of Israel be justified, and shall glory;* as he was *delivered* into the hands of justice and death *for their offences*, to make satisfaction for them, so he was *raised again for their justification;* and when he was raised, he was justified, acquitted, and discharged himself from all the sins of his people, imputed to him, having satisfied for them; and then they were justified in him, Isa. xlv. 25. Rom. iv. 25. 1 Tim. iii. 16.

4. As Christ has wrought out a righteousness for his people, so he actually puts it upon them, clothes them with it; says the church, *He hath covered me with the robe of righteousness:* he is that Angel of the Lord before whom Joshua was brought, and accused by Satan; and to whom he himself said, *I will clothe thee with change of raiment,* Isa. lxi. 10. Zech. iii. 4.

5. As it is to faith the righteousness of Christ is revealed, and by faith it is received, hence believers are said to be justified by faith; so this faith, as well as righteousness, is of Christ; as he is the object of it, *Ye believe in God, believe also in me;* so he is the *author* and *finisher* of it, John xiv. 1. Heb. xii. 2.

Thirdly, The holy Spirit of God, the third Person, has also a concern in the justification of sinners.

1. He convinces men of righteousness, of their want of righteousness; of the weakness, imperfection, and insufficiency of their own righteousness, that they have none that can be called a righteousness; and that unless they have a better righteousness than that, they will never enter into the kingdom of heaven, John xvi. 8.

2. He brings near the righteousness of Christ; not only externally, in the ministry of the word; but internally, by the illumination of his grace; this is one of the things of Christ he takes and shews to souls enlightened by him; he shews them the fulness, glory, and suitableness of the righteousness of Christ, how perfect it is, how adequate to all the demands of law and justice, and how suitable to them; to cover their naked souls, to secure them from condemnation and death, to justify them before God, and render them acceptable in his sight, and entitle them to eternal life.

3. He works faith in convinced and enlightened persons, to look at the righteousness of Christ, and take a view of its glories and excellencies; to approve of it, desire it, and to lay hold on it, and receive it as their justifying righteousness. Such a faith is of the operation of God, of the Spirit of God; it is what he works in the saints, and enables them to exercise it; hence he is called, *the Spirit of faith,* Col. ii. 13. 2 Cor. iv. 13.

4. He bears witness to their spirits, that they are interested in the righteousness of Christ, and are justified by it; and he pronounces the sentence of justification in their consciences, or declares them justified, in the name of Christ, and on account of his righteousness; and which is the meaning of their being justified *in the name of the Lord Jesus, and by the Spirit of our God,* 1 Cor. vi. 11.

III. The objects of justification; and they are the elect. *Who shall lay any thing to the charge of God's elect? It is God that justifieth!* that is, the elect, Rom. viii. 33. for who else can be meant?

1. Elect men, and not elect angels; for though there are elect angels, and these are holy, just, and righteous; and so may be declared to be what they are, just and righteous, and in that sense justified; yet, since they never laboured under the suspicion of a crime, nor were ever chargeable with any, they cannot, in a strict sense, be said to be justified. But elect men, who are sinners in Adam, as chosen in Christ their Head, are reckoned righteous; for justification is a branch of election, in which the elect are reckoned as righteous, through the righteousness of Christ; and these being the objects of justification, shew the eternity of that act, since election was from the beginning, and before the foundation of the world; and the specialty of it, since the elect are a special and peculiar people; and the security of it, for it is certain, being closely connected with predestination, whom God predestinates, he calls and justifies; and its being a security from wrath and condemnation; for whom he justifies he glorifies, Rom. viii. 30.

2. Redeemed ones are the objects of justification; all that are chosen are redeemed; and all that are redeemed are justified; justification proceeds upon redemption; *Being justified freely by his grace, through the redemption that is in Christ Jesus,* Rom. iii. 24. by which they are redeemed from all their iniquities, and from all the curses of the law due unto them, and so are acquitted and discharged.

3. Pardoned ones; for all that are chosen and redeemed are pardoned, and those are justified: the chosen are pardoned; for the Lord says, *I will pardon them whom I reserve*, Jer. l. 20. that is, whom he has reserved for himself by the act of election; and the redeemed are pardoned; for forgiveness of sin is a branch of redemption; *In whom we have redemption, through his blood, the forgiveness of sin*, Eph. i. 7. and those whose sins are forgiven, they are justified, Rom. iv. 6, 7.

4. Hence it appears, that the objects of justification are not all men; for all men are not chosen; they are only a remnant, according to the election of grace: nor are all men redeemed; for those that are redeemed, are redeemed from among men, and out of every kindred, tongue, people, and nation: nor are all pardoned; for there are some whose sins go beforehand to judgment, and are never forgiven: nor do all men believe; faith is peculiar to God's elect: nor are all men saved from wrath, as they would be, if justified by the blood of Christ; some will go into everlasting punishment, when the righteous shall go into everlasting life: and so all are not justified; though there is an *all* that are justified, even all the seed and offspring of Christ, the seed of Israel, on whom the gift of righteousness comes to justification of life, Isa. xlv. 25. Rom. v. 18.

5. Yet they are many, Isa. liii. 11. Rom. v. 19. for whom Christ gave his life a ransom; and whose blood was shed for the remission of their sins; those are said to be many, Matt. xx. 28. and xxvi. 28.

6. The objects of justification are described as sinners, and ungodly; *sinners*, Gal. ii. 17. *ungodly*, Rom. iv. 5. So they are, in their unregenerate state: but when converted, they are described as believers in Christ; for the righteousness of Christ is *unto all, and upon all them that believe*; it is applied unto them, and put upon them; and they have a comfortable sense and perception of their justification by it; they *believe in Jesus Christ, that they might be justified by the faith of Christ*; by Christ, the object of faith, and through believing in him, have a comfortable view of their justification before God, and acceptance with him; hence it is said, that *by him all that believe are justified*, openly and manifestly, and have the testimony and comfort of it within themselves; and these may be said to be *justified by faith*; by Christ, and his righteousness received by faith, Rom. v. 1. and iii. 22. Gal. ii. 16. Acts xiii. 39. and such are not nominal believers, who only have a notional, historical faith, or who only profess to believe, as Simon Magus did; but who, *with the heart, believe unto righteousness*; who truly and heartily believe in the righteousness of Christ for their justification before God; and such shall never come into condemnation, Rom. x. 10. John v. 24.

IV. The charges, or sins, such are justified from. *Who shall lay any thing to the charge of God's elect? It is God that justifieth*, Rom. viii. 33. from all charges, all that may be truly brought against them, all criminal charges they are chargeable with.

1. They are chargeable with original sin, the sin of the first man; they were, seminally, in his loins, when he ate the forbidden-fruit; as Levi was in the loins of Abraham, when he paid tithes to Melchizedek: they were federally in him, as their covenant-head and representative, and sinning in him, they became chargeable therewith; and judgment so far proceeded against them, as to bring them under the sentence of condemnation and death; but God justifies and acquits them from that offence, through the gift of his Son's righteousness, which comes unto them to justification of life; and he frees them from the charge of that disobedience by which they were made sinners, through the imputation of Christ's obedience to them, Rom. v. 12, 18, 19.

2. They are chargeable with impurity of nature, and a want of original righteousness; which Adam, by sinning, lost, and all his posterity are without it; they are conceived in sin, and bring an impure nature into the world with them; which is the case of all, even of God's elect. The law requires purity and holiness of nature, and charges with the want of it; but God justifies from this charge, through the imputation of the holiness of Christ's human nature to them, which is a branch of their justification; and is thought, by some divines, to be *the law of the Spirit of life* in him, which *frees from the law of sin and death;* and who is made, to his people, *sanctification* and righteousness; and was typified by the high-priest, having an inscription on his forehead, *Holiness to the Lord*, Rom. viii. 2. 1 Cor. i. 30. Exod. xxviii. 36.

3. They are chargeable with actual sins, before conversion, and those many, and some very heinous; and yet God justifies from them all; as Saul was chargeable with blasphemy, persecution, and doing injury to others; but obtained pardoning mercy, and a justifying righteousness: the Corinthians were guilty of some of the blackest crimes, and most enormous sins, yet were justified, in the name of the Lord Jesus, and by the Spirit of our God: the apostles, and others, before conversion, were disobedient, serving divers lusts and pleasures; and yet were justified, by the grace of God, and made heirs, according to the hope of eternal life, 1 Tim. i. 13. 1 Cor. vi. 9, 10, 11. Tit. iii. 3, 7.

4. They are chargeable with a multitude of sins, after conversion; with many revoltings, and sometimes with great backslidings; their failings and infirmities, errors and mistakes, are innumerable; yet all are forgiven, and they are cleansed and justified from them, James iii. 2. Psalm xix. 12. Hos. xiv. 4.

5. They are justified from all their sins, of whatsoever kind, that they can be charged with; for they that believe in Christ, *are justified from all things*, from all sins, from all criminal charges; God forgives all their trespasses, for Christ's sake, and his blood cleanses from all sin, Acts xiii. 39. Col. ii. 13. 1 John i. 7.

6. They are justified by the righteousness of Christ, *from all things, from which they could not be justified by the law of Moses;* for there were some sins which the law made no provision of sacrifice for, as adultery and murder; such therefore that *despised* Moses' law, by breaking it in such instances, *died without mercy;* but God justifies from all such sins, as well as others, through the righteousness of Christ, Acts xiii. 39. Heb. x. 28. and ix. 15, 26.

7. God justifies his elect from all charges brought against them, from what quarter soever, and whether true or false: do they bring charges against themselves, as they often do? conscience, which is as a thousand witnesses, accuses and condemns them; but though their hearts and consciences condemn them, God is greater than their hearts, and knows all things; what provisions he has made for them in covenant, what a righteousness his Son has wrought out for their justification; and though as on one hand, if a good man knows nothing by himself, yet he is not hereby justified; so on the other, though he knows much by himself and against himself, yet God clears him from all. Do saints bring charges one against another, sometimes rightly, and sometimes wrongly, whether privately or publicly; and do not forgive one another, as they should do, since God, for Christ's sake, forgives them? yet God forgives all, and clears from all charges, true or false. Does the world bring charges against them, as they frequently do, even speak all manner of evil of them falsely, for Christ's sake, as Tertullus the orator, against the apostle Paul? yet every tongue that riseth up in judgment against them, God will condemn; for their *righteousness is of me, saith the Lord;* plainly suggesting, that he would justify and acquit them from all, Isa. liv. 17. Does Satan go about the earth to pick up charges against the people of God, and then accuse them to him, as he did Job, whence he is called, *the accuser of the brethren?* Jehovah repels his charges, and rebukes him for them; an instance of this we have in the vision of Zechariah, chap. iii. 1—4. In a word, whatever charges the law of God brings against the elect, which is broken by them, and for which it accuses, pronounces guilty, curses and condemns; and whatever charges the justice of God can produce against them, the mouth of the one, and of the other, is stopped by the righteousness of Christ; by which the one is honoured and magnified; and the other is satisfied and well-pleased; and so a full justification from all charges takes place, and God is just, while he is the justifier of him that believes in Jesus.

V. The matter and form of justification, the righteousness of Christ imputed: the matter of justification, or that for the sake of which a sinner is justified, is the righteousness of Christ; the form and manner in which it is made over to such an one, and becomes his, is by imputation.

First, The matter of justification, the righteousness of Christ; and every thing else must be removed from it, and denied of it. As,

1*st,* A man's own righteousness, or his obedience to the law; this is expressly denied to be that by which a sinner can be justified; *By the deeds of the law, there shall no flesh be justified in his sight,* in the sight of God; that is, by works done in obedience to the law; and which is meant, not of the ceremonial, but the moral law; that law by which is the knowledge of sin, and which pronounces a man guilty of it before God, and stops his mouth, as the context shews; and is opposed to grace, which the ceremonial law is not, being of grace, given to relieve, under a sense of sin, by pointing to the Saviour, and his propitiatory sacrifice; and hence this conclusion is drawn, *Therefore we conclude, that a man is justified by faith;* by Christ and his righteousness, the object of faith; *without the works of the law* being joined to Christ, and his righteousness, or considered as any part of a justifying righteousness, Rom. iii. 20, 28. And to the same purpose are the words of the apostle, in Gal. ii. 16. The reasons why a man's own righteousness cannot be the matter of his justification before God, are,

1. Because it is imperfect, and the law will not admit of an imperfect righteousness for justification; it requires perfect sinless obedience; and not any thing short of that will it allow to be a righteousness; *It shall be our righteousness,* says Moses, *if we observe to do all these commandments, before the Lord our God, as he hath commanded us,* Deut. vi. 25. so that if there is any failure, either in the matter or manner of obedience, it is no righteousness; and such obedience and righteousness, men, since the fall, were never capable of; the people of Israel, in general, followed after the law of righteousness; but did not attain to it, seeking it not by faith in Christ, in whom it is only found; but, as it were, by the works of the law, in which there is a deficiency, and so no righteousness: and those among them who made the largest pretensions to righteousness, fell short of it, as the Scribes and Pharisees; insomuch, that if a man's righteousness does not exceed theirs, he cannot enter into the kingdom of heaven; nay, even the works of the truly just and good, are not perfect; *There is not a just man upon earth, that doeth good and sinneth not,* Eccles. vii. 20. hence good men, sensible of the insufficiency of their own righteousness, decline and deprecate entering into judgment with God upon that foot, acknowledging the impurity and imperfection of their obedience; on account of which, they know they could not be just with God, Job ix. 2, 3, 20, 32. Psalm cxliii. 2. Isa. lxiv. 6.——2. If justification was by the works of men, it could not be by grace; for grace and works are opposed, and cannot consist together in the business of justification; for if it is of grace, then not of works; but justification is by grace, and therefore not by works; *Being justified freely by his grace,* Rom. iii. 24. not only by grace, but freely by it; or by grace that is altogether free; and, indeed, as Austin says, it would not be grace if it was not so, or was any ways clogged with the works of men.——3. If justification was by man's obedience, it would not be by a righteousness without works, and that imputed, as it is; if it is by a man's own righteousness, then not by a righteousness without works, for that consists entirely of works; and if a man's own, then not imputed; whereas, the blessedness of justification, lies in the imputation of a righteousness without works, Rom. iv. 6.——4. If justification could be by men's obedience to the law, then there would have been no need of the righteousness of Christ, nor of his coming into the world to work out one; it would have been an unnecessary thing for God to send his Son, that the righteousness of the law might be fulfilled in us, by him, if we could have fulfilled it ourselves; and not only his life, and the obedience of it, would have been useless, but his death also; for, as the apostle argues, *If righteousness came by the law, then Christ is dead in vain,* Gal. ii. 21.——5. If justification was by the works of men, boasting would be encouraged; whereas, God's design in the whole scheme of salvation, and so in this branch of it, is to prevent it, lest any man should boast; *Where is boasting then? It is excluded. By what law? of works? Nay, but by the law of faith;* that is, not by the doctrine of justification, by the works of men, that would establish boasting; but by the doctrine of justification by faith in the righteousness of Christ, which leaves no room for it, Rom. iii. 27.

2dly, Nor is man's obedience to the gospel, as to a new and milder law, the matter of his justification before God. It was a notion, that some years ago obtained, that a relaxation of the law, and the severities of it, has been obtained by Christ; and a new law, a remedial law, a law of milder terms, has been introduced by him, which is the gospel; the terms of which are, faith, repentance, and new obedience; and though these are imperfect, yet being sincere, they are accepted of by God, in the room of a perfect righteousness. But every article of this scheme is wrong; for, ——1. The law is not relaxed, nor any of its severities abated; there is no alteration made in it; neither with respect to its precepts, nor its penalty; it requires the same holy, just, and good things, it ever did;

Christ came not to destroy it, but to fulfil it: nor is the sanction of it removed; though it is not made for, or does not lie against, a righteous man; yet it is made for, and lies against, the sinner and transgressor; and as it has the same commanding, so the same condemning power, to them that are under it; it accuses, pronounces guilty, condemns, and curses, even such who continue not in all things to observe it.——2. Nor is the gospel a new law; there is nothing in it that looks like a law; it has no commands in it, but all promises; it is a pure declaration of grace and salvation by Christ; therefore called, the gospel of the grace of God, and the gospel of our salvation.——3. Nor are faith, repentance, and new obedience, the terms of it, and required by it, as conditions of men's acceptance with God; faith and repentance, as doctrines, are gospel-doctrines, and parts of the gospel-ministry; and as graces, are not terms and conditions required in it, to be performed by men of themselves; they are blessings of grace, declared in it, and are gifts of grace bestowed on men; faith is the gift of God, and repentance is a grant from him; and both they, and new and spiritual obedience, are provided for in the covenant of grace, Ezek. xxxvi. 26, 27.——4. If these were terms and conditions, required of men, in the gospel, to be performed by them, in order to their acceptance with God, the gospel would not be a remedial law; nor these milder terms than those of the old law; for it was easier for Adam, in a state of innocence, to have kept the whole law, than it is for man, in his fallen state, to repent and believe in Christ, and perform new and spiritual obedience of himself; till God takes away the stony heart, and gives an heart of flesh, and gives grace, as well as time and space, to repent, men never will nor can repent of their sins: and faith is not of a man's self; no man can come to Christ, that is, believe in him, unless it be given to him, and the Father draws him; and without Christ, his Spirit and grace, a man cannot do any good thing.——5. Nor is it true, that God will accept of an imperfect righteousness in the room of a perfect one: nor can any thing more highly reflect upon the justice and truth of God, who is the judge of all the earth, and will do right, and whose judgment is according to truth, and can never account that a righteousness which is not one.

3*dly*, Nor is a profession of religion even of the best religion, the christian religion, the matter of justification before God; men may have a form of godliness without the power of it; they may submit to the ordinances of Christ, baptism, and the Lord's Supper, and attend every duty of religion, and yet be far from righteousness: and even if a profession of religion was taken up upon right principles, on a good foundation, and held and maintained in an honorable manner, and even though a man may be ever so sincere in it, it is not the matter of his justification. For,

4*thly*, Sincerity itself, in any religion, even in the best religion, is not a justifying righteousness. There may be sincerity in a bad religion, as well as in a good one; a man may be sincerely wrong, as well as sincerely right; may be a sincere Pagan, a sincere Papist, and a sincere Mahometan, as well as a sincere Christian; yea, a man may be a sincere blasphemer of Christ, and a sincere persecutor of his followers, as the apostle Paul was, before conversion, and as the persecutors of Christ's disciples, Acts xxvi. 9. John xvi. 2. and taking sincerity in the best sense, as a grace of the Spirit of God, which accompanies all other graces, and denominates faith unfeigned, hope without hypocrisy, and love without dissimulation; it belongs to sanctification, and not justification; and is not the whole, nor any part of justifying righteousness.

5*thly*, Nor faith, the το *credere*, or act of believing; this is, by some, said to be imputed for righteousness; but is not so; for,——1. Faith, as a man's act, is his own; and is called *his* faith, *thy* faith, and *my* faith, Hab. ii. 5. Matt. ix. 22. and xv. 28. James ii. 18. whereas, the righteousness by which a man is justified, is not his own, but another's, and therefore not faith.—— 2. Faith is imperfect; it is so in the greatest believers; the disciples of Christ saw need to pray, Lord, *increase our faith!* whereas, a righteousness to justify must be perfect; nothing else can be accounted a righteousness.——3. Faith is not everlasting; as to its use; is only for the present life; it will be changed into vision: but the righteousness by which sinners are justified before God, and which was brought in by Christ for that purpose, is *everlasting righteousness*, Dan. ix. 24.——4. Faith and righteousness are manifestly distinguished; *The righteousness of God is revealed from faith to faith;* and therefore faith cannot be that righteousness. *With the heart man* believeth unto righteousness; and therefore righteousness must be a distinct thing from faith; which *righteousness is unto all, and upon all them believe;* and therefore must be different from that faith with which they believe, Rom. i. 17. and x. 10. and iii. 22.——5. Something else, and not faith, is said to be that by which men are made righteous, and justified; as *the obedience of one,* Jesus Christ, by which *many are made righteous;* and the blood of Christ; *being justified by his blood,* Rom. v. 9, 19. Now faith is neither the one nor the other; and though men are said to be *justified by faith,* yet not as an act of men; for then they would be justified by works, contrary to express scripture; nor by it as a grace of the Spirit in men; for this would confound justification and sanctification together; but by the object of it, Christ, and his righteousness, apprehended, received, and embraced by faith. And though believers are said to be justified by faith, yet faith is never said to justify them.——6. The passages produced to establish this notion, that faith is a man's righteousness, are insufficient; *Abraham believed God, and it was counted to him for righteousness,* Rom. iv. 3. And again ver. 5. *His faith is counted for righteousness.* And in ver. 9. *We say, that faith was reckoned to Abraham for righteousness.* Now this cannot be understood of the act of Abraham's faith; but of the object of it, or that which he believed in, the righteousness of Christ, which God imputes, without works, ver. 6. and that this must be the sense is clear, from this one single consideration, that the same *it* which was imputed to Abraham for righteousness, is imputed to all those who believe in God, who raised up Christ from the dead, ver. 22, 23, 24. Now supposing Abraham's faith was imputed to him for a justifying righteousness; it cannot reasonably be thought that it should be imputed also for righteousness to all that believe in all succeeding ages.

6*thly,* Nor is the whole of sanctification the matter of justification; these two are distinct things, and not to be confounded; the one is a work of grace within men, the other an act of God's grace towards and upon men; the one is imperfect, the other perfect; the one is carried on gradually, the other done at once.

But the sole matter of justification, or that for the sake of which a sinner is justified before God, is the righteousness of Christ, and which is,

1. Not his essential righteousness, as God; the righteousness by which men are justified is the righteousness of God, which was wrought out by Christ, who is God as well as man; but it is not that righteousness which is essential to him as God; he that is their righteousness is Jehovah, but the righteousness by which he is Jehovah, or which belongs to him as such, is not their righteousness, as Osiander dreamed; for this would be to deify them.

2. Nor his righteousness, integrity, and fidelity, which he exercised in the discharge of his mediatorial office; that was personal and respected himself, and not relative to others; he was faithful to him that appointed him to that office, and he did his work in so upright a manner, that he obtained the character of God's. *righteous servant,* Isa. xi. 5. and liii. 11. but though it is a righteousness he wrought out as mediator, which is imputed for justification, yet it is not his mediatorial righteousness, or the righteousness of his office, or that by which he shewed the discharge of it.

3. Nor does it consist of all the actions and works he did here on earth, nor of what he is doing in heaven; it wholly consists of those he wrought in his state of humiliation here on earth, yet not all of these; not his extraordinary and miraculous works, these were proofs of his Deity, and of his Messiahship; they were done and recorded to engage men to believe in him, and in his righteousness; but were no ingredients, as one observes,[3] in that righteousness on which they were to believe. Nor is his work in heaven, appearing for his people there, interceding for them, and preparing mansions of glory for them, any part of the righteousness wrought out for them, and imputed to them. But,

4. What he did and suffered in their nature on earth, and in their room and stead, and as their substitute and representative, commonly called his active and passive obedience; to which may be added the purity and holiness of his nature, and which altogether made up the $\delta\iota\kappa\alpha\iota\omega\mu\alpha$ $\tau\upsilon$ $\nu o\mu\upsilon$, *the righteousness of the law,* which was fulfilled by him, as their head and representative, Rom. viii. 4. for whatever the law required is necessary to a sinner's justification before God; and that requires of

---

[3] Dr. Goodwin, his Works, vol. 3. par. 3. p 336.

sinners more than it did of man in innocence. Man was created with a pure and holy nature, conformable to the pure and holy law of God; and it was incumbent on him to continue so, and to yield in it perfect and sinless obedience; and in failure thereof he was threatened with death; and now having sinned, whereby his nature is vitiated and corrupted, and his obedience become faulty and imperfect, suffering the penalty of the law is required; and all this is requisite to the justification of a sinner, purity of nature, perfection of obedience, and sufferings of death; all which meet in Christ, the representative of his people, in whom they are justified.——(1.) Holiness of nature: some consider this only as a qualification for his office, and the due performance of it in human nature; whereby he was capable of yielding sinless obedience to the law, and was qualified as an high-priest to offer himself a spotless sacrifice, and to be a proper advocate for sinners, being Jesus Christ the righteous; but this not only fitted him for his work, but made him suitable to us, *Such an high-priest became us, who is holy, harmless;* the law required an holy nature in conformity to it; it is wanting in us, it is found in Christ, *who is of God made to us sanctification;* see more of this under the *fourth head.*—— (2.) The obedience of Christ's life, commonly called his active obedience, which was sinless and perfect; his whole life was in perfect conformity to the law, and was a continued series of holiness and obedience; the holiness of his nature appeared in all his actions, throughout his whole state of humiliation, from his birth to his death; in all which he was the representative of his people; what he did, he did in their room and stead, and therefore was reckoned as if done by them, and is imputed to them as their righteousness: there are some divines[4] who exclude the active obedience of Christ from being any part of the righteousness by which men are justified; they allow it is a condition requisite in him as mediator, qualifying him for his office; but deny that it is the matter of justification, or that it is imputed and reckoned for righteousness to men. They suppose that Christ was obliged to this obedience for himself as a creature, and that it is unnecessary to his people, because his sufferings and death are sufficient for their justification. But, 1. Though the human nature of Christ being a creature, and so considered, was subject to a law, and obliged to obedience; yet it was not obliged to a course of obedience in such a low, mean, and suffering state, being entitled to glory and happiness from the moment of its union to the Son of God; this was voluntary: besides, the human nature being taken into personal union with the Son of God, the person of Christ, who was not subject to the law, but was above it, and Lord of it, it was an act of his will to submit to it, and a wonderful instance of his condescension it was; moreover, as Christ being made of a woman, and was made under the law, he was made both for the sake of his people; he became man for their sake, *to us*, or *for us a child is born*, Isa. ix. 6. and for their sake he became subject to the law, that he might yield obedience to it in their room and stead, and that he might redeem them from the curse of it; and this was the kind and gracious design of his divine Father in sending him in the likeness of sinful flesh, that he might both obey and suffer for them, that so the whole righteousness of the law might be fulfilled in them, Gal. iv. 4. Rom. viii. 3, 4.——2. Without the active obedience of Christ, the law would not be satisfied, the language of which is *Do and live;* and unless its precepts are obeyed, as well as its penalty endured, it cannot be satisfied; and unless it is satisfied, there can be no justification by it; Christ, as a surety, in the room and stead of his people, must both obey the precepts of the law and bear its penalty; his submitting to the one, without conforming to the other, is not sufficient; one debt is not paid by another; his paying off the debt of punishment, did not exempt from obedience; as the paying off the debt of obedience, did not exempt from punishment: Christ did not satisfy the whole law by either of them separately, but by both conjunctly; by his sufferings and death he satisfied the threatenings, the sanction of the law, but not the precepts of it thereby; and by his active obedience he satisfied the preceptive part of the law, but not the penal part; but by both, he satisfied the whole of the law, and made it honourable.——3. It is by a righteousness that men are justified, and that is the righteousness of Christ; now righteousness, strictly speaking, lies in doing, in actual obedience to the commands of the law, *This shall be our righteousness, if we observe to do, &c.* Deut. vi. 25.

---

[4] Wendelin, Piscator, Pareus, Lubbertus, Forbes, and others.

Christ's righteousness lay in doing, not in suffering; "all righteousness, as one says,[5] is either an habit or an act; but sufferings are neither, and therefore not righteousness; no man is righteous because he is punished; if so, the devils and damned in hell would be righteous in proportion to their punishment; the more severe their punishment, and the more grievous their torments, the greater their righteousness must be; if there is any righteousness in punishment, it must be in the punisher, and not in the punished." If therefore men are justified by the righteousness of Christ imputed to them, it must be by his active obedience, and not merely by his sufferings and death; because these, though they free from death, yet, strictly speaking, do not make men righteous.——4. It is expressly said, that *by the obedience of one shall many be made righteous*, Rom. v. 19. which cannot be meant of the sufferings and death of Christ; because, properly speaking, they are not his obedience, but the effect of it; besides, the antithesis in the text determines the sense of the words; for if by one man's actual disobedience, which was the case, many were made sinners, so by the rule of opposition, by one man's actual obedience, which is Christ's, many are made righteous, or justified.——5. The reward of life is not promised to suffering, but to doing; the law says, *Do this and live;* it promises life, not to him that suffers the penalty, but to him that obeys the precept; "there never was a law, as an excellent divine observes,[6] even among men, either promising or declaring a reward due to the criminal, because he had undergone the punishment of his crimes." Christ's sufferings and death being satisfactory to the comminatory or threatening part of the law, are reckoned to us for justification, that so we may be freed and discharged from the curse of it, and from hell and wrath to come; but as they do not constitute us righteous, they do not entitle us to eternal life; but the active obedience or righteousness of Christ being imputed to us, is *unto justification of life,* or is what gives the title to eternal life.——(3.) Nevertheless the sufferings and death of Christ, or what is commonly called his passive obedience, are requisite to our justification before God. Passive obedience is a phrase that may be objected to, as not accurate, being a seeming contradiction in terms; suffering and obedience convey different ideas, and belong to different classes; suffering belongs to the predicament or class of passion, obedience to that of action; yet as Christ's sufferings flow from his obedience, and were the effect of his submission to his Father's will, with respect to which he said, *Not my will but thine be done;* and as he was obedient throughout his life, in all the actions and in all the sufferings of it, even to the moment of his death; and was also obedient in death, laying down his life at the command received from his father; *For though a Son, yet learned he obedience by the things he suffered;* and was even active in his sufferings; he laid down his life of himself, he poured out his soul unto death, and gave himself an offering, and a sacrifice for sin; considering these things, the phrase, passive obedience, may be admitted of; especially as it is well known what is meant by it, the voluntary sufferings and death of Christ, which are most certainly ingredients in the justification of a sinner.

It may be asked, if Christ was the representative of his people in his active obedience, which constitutes them just or righteous, and is their justification of life, or what entitles to eternal life, what need was there of his sufferings and death? to which it may be answered, that it was necessary that Christ, as the surety and representative of his people, should satisfy the law in every thing it could require of them, both as creatures, and as sinful creatures. As creatures, the law could require of them purity of nature, and perfect obedience to it, which were in their first parents, but were lost by them, and are wanting in them; as sinful creatures, it could require of them to endure the penalty of it. Christ now as the surety of his people, represented them as creatures, in the purity of his nature and in the perfection of his life, or in his active obedience; and presented that to the law for them which it could require of them as creatures: and as it is certain he represented them in his sufferings and death, hence he is said to die for them, that is, in their room and stead, and they to be crucified and buried with him; in these he represented them as sinful creatures, and bore the penalty or curse of the law; and in both obediences

---

[5] Molinæus apud Maccov. Loc. Commun. c. 69. p. 613.

[6] Dr. Goodwin, ut supra, p. 338.

he satisfied the whole of it; and as by the one they are freed from death the sanction of the law, so by the other they are entitled to life, and by both Christ is the fulfilling end of the law for righteousness unto them. For that the sufferings and death of Christ, as well as his active obedience, are requisite to the complete justification of a sinner, appears,——1. That without these the law would not be satisfied, and all its demands answered; and unless it is satisfied, there can be no justification by it; and it cannot be satisfied unless its penalty is endured; for,—— 2. The law, in case of disobedience to it, threatened with death, and death is the just wages and due demerit of sin; and therefore this must be endured, either by the sinner or a surety for him, or else he cannot be discharged by the law.——3. The justification of a sinner is expressly ascribed to the blood of Christ, which is put for the whole of his sufferings and death, Rom. v. 9.——4. Justification proceeds upon redemption, *being justified freely by his grace, through the redemption that is in Christ Jesus*, Rom. iii. 24. now redemption is by the blood of Christ, and through his sufferings and death, Eph. i. 7. 1 Pet. iii. 18, 19. Rev. v. 9.——5. It is upon the foot of Christ's satisfaction that justification takes place, and satisfaction is made by Christ's doing and suffering all the law requires; and so as by his obedience, likewise by his blood and death, to which it is more frequently ascribed, peace is made by his blood, reconciliation by his death, atonement and expiation by his sacrifice, which is of a sweet smelling savour to God, Col. i. 20. Rom. v. 10. Heb. ix. 26. Eph. v. 2. ——6. The complete justification of a sinner, does not seem to be finished by Christ until his resurrection, after his obedience and sufferings of death; for he *was delivered for our offences, and was raised again for our justification*, Rom. iv. 25. In short, the righteousness by which we are justified, as Dr. Ames[7] says, is not to be sought for in different operations of Christ, but arises from his whole obedience both active and passive; which is both satisfactory and meritorious, and frees from condemnation and death, and adjudges and entitles to eternal life; even as one and the same disobedience of Adam, stripped us of original righteousness, and rendered us obnoxious to condemnation. So much for the matter of justification.

Secondly, The form of it, is imputation; or the manner in which the righteousness of Christ is made over to a sinner, and it becomes his, is by imputing it to him; *Even as David describeth the blessedness of the man unto whom God imputeth righteousness without works*, Rom. iv. 6. The words used both in Hebrew and Greek, חשב and λογιζομαι, ελλογεω, &c. signify, to reckon, repute, estimate, attribute, and place something to the account of another:[8] as when the apostle said to Philemon, concerning Onesimus, *If he hath wronged thee, or oweth thee ought, put that on my account,* τυτο εμοι ελλογει, let it be reckoned, or imputed to me. So when God is said to impute the righteousness of Christ to any, the sense is, that he reckons it as theirs, being wrought out for them, and accounts them righteous by it, as though they had performed it in their own persons: and that it is by the righteousness of Christ, imputed to his people, that they are justified, is clear, when it is observed,——1. That those whom God justifies, are, in themselves, ungodly; for God *justifieth the ungodly*, Rom. iv. 5. if ungodly, then without a righteousness; and if without a righteousness, then, if they are justified, it must be by a righteousness imputed to them, or placed to their account; which can be no other than the righteousness of Christ.—— 2. They that are justified, are justified either by an inherent, or by an imputed righteousness: not by an inherent one, for that is imperfect, and so not justifying; and if not by an inherent righteousness, then it must be by one imputed to them, for there remains no other.——3. The righteousness by which any are justified, is the righteousness of another, and not their own, even the righteousness of Christ; *Not having on mine own righteousness*, says the apostle, Phil. iii. 9. Now the righteousness of another, cannot be made a man's, or he be justified by it, any other way than by an imputation of it to him.—— 4. The same way that Adam's sin became the sin of his posterity, or they were made sinners by it, the same way Christ's righteousness becomes his people's, or they are made righteous by it. Now the former is

---

[7] Medulla Theolog. 1. 1. c. 20. s. 13. et. c. 27. s. 27.

[8] חשב putavit, imputavit, reputavit, æstimavit, Buxtorf. λογιζομαι, æstimo, reputo, item imputo, et alicujus veluti rationibus infero, tribuo, Scapula.

by imputation; and so the latter; *As by one man's disobedience many were made sinners;* that is, by the imputation of it to them; *so by the obedience of One shall many be made righteous;* that is, by placing it to their account, Rom. v. 19.—— 5. The same way that the sins of Christ's people became his, his righteousness becomes theirs. Now their sins became Christ's by imputation only; the Father laid them on him, or made them to meet upon him, imputed them to him, placed them to his account; and he took them upon him, and looked upon himself as answerable to justice for them; and so, in the same way, his righteousness is made over to, and put upon his people; *For he who knew no sin, was made sin for us,* by imputation, *that we might be made the righteousness of God in him;* accounted righteous in him, through his righteousness imputed, 2 Cor. v. 21. Now there are several things which are said of this imputed righteousness of Christ, which serve greatly to recommend it, and set forth the excellency of it; as,——(1.) That it is called *the righteousness of God,* Rom. i. 17. and iii. 22. being wrought by Christ, who is God as well as man; approved and accepted of by God, and freely imputed by him to believers, as their justifying righteousness.——(2.) It is called, *the righteousness of One,* Rom. v. 18. of one of the Persons in the Trinity, the Son of God; of him, who, though he has two natures united in him, is but one Person, and who is the one common Head to all his seed; and though his obedience, or righteousness, serves for many, it is *the obedience of One,* Rom. v. 19. and therefore they are justified, not partly by their own obedience, and partly by Christ's, but by his only.——(3.) It is called, *the righteousness of the law,* Rom. viii. 4. being wrought by Christ in conformity to the law; so that this righteousness is a legal righteousness, as performed by Christ, being every way commensurate to the demands of it; though evangelical, as made over to his people, and revealed in the gospel; for it is manifested without the law, though witnessed to by law and prophets.—— (4.) It is called, *the righteousness of faith,* Rom. iv. 13. not that faith is righteousness, or imputed for it, or is the matter of a justifying righteousness, or any part of it; but because the righteousness of Christ is revealed to faith, and that lays hold on it, receives it, rejoices in it, and boasts of it.——(5.) It is called, *the gift of righteousness,* and *the free gift,* and *the gift by grace,* Rom. v. 15, 16, 17. because freely wrought out by Christ, and freely imputed by God the Father; and faith is freely given to receive and embrace it.——(6.) It is called, *a robe of righteousness,* a garment down to the feet, which covers the whole mystical body of Christ, Isa. lxi. 10. Rev. i. 13. it is signified by gold of Ophir, clothing of wrought gold, and raiment of needle work; setting forth the preciousness of it, Psalm xlv. 9, 13, 14. It is said to be change of raiment, and the wedding-garment, Zech. iii. 4. Matt. xxii. 12. yea, the *best robe,* Luke xv. 22. a better robe than Adam had in Eden, or the angels in heaven; theirs, at best, being but the righteousness of a creature, and that loseable, as the event shewed; but Christ's righteousness is the righteousness of God, and an everlasting one; it may be rendered, the *first robe,*[9] being first in designation, and in the provision of the covenant of grace; though Adam's robe of righteousness was first in wear and use.

VI. The effects of justification by the righteousness of Christ may be next considered, which are as follow.——1. An entire freedom from all penal evils, in this life and in that which is to come. Justified ones are not freed from all evils; they have their evil things now, as Lazarus had, but they are not brought upon them by way of punishment; afflictions are evils in themselves, being not joyous but grievous; but then they are not penal ones; they are fatherly chastisements, they are fruits and evidences of the love of God to them, and not of his vindictive wrath, Rev. iii. 19. 1 Cor. xi. 32. death was threatened as a punishment for sin, and is the just demerit of it, and as such is inflicted on unrighteous ones, but is no penal evil to justified ones; it is their privilege and not their punishment, 1 Cor. iii. 22. Rev. xiv. 13. and therefore their death is desirable, even by wicked men, as it was by Balaam: nor will any penal evil befal the justified ones after death; for *being now justified* by his (Christ's) *blood, they shall be saved from wrath through him;* from wrath to come, the vengeance of eternal fire: should any penal evil be inflicted on them here or hereafter, it would highly reflect upon the justice of God, in punishing twice for the

---

[9] την γολην την πρωτην, stolam primam, Vulg. Lat. Arias Montanus.

same offences, once in their surety, and again in themselves; since the chastisement, or punishment of their sins has been laid on Christ, and he has endured it; and therefore it would be a lessening of the value of Christ's satisfaction, as if it was not made to full content, should punishment be inflicted in any degree upon those for whom it is made; and it would be contrary to the gospel-declaration, that they that believe in Christ are justified, and shall not enter into condemnation.——2. Peace with God is another fruit and effect of justification; being *justified by faith, we have peace with God*, Rom. v. 1. peace with God is made by the blood of Christ, and reconciliation by his death; and besides that, there is a peace of conscience which is had in a way of believing, and through a comfortable sense and perception of an interest in the righteousness of Christ, the effect of which is peace and quietness, Isa. xxxii. 17.——3. Access to God through Christ; for having a comfortable view by faith of interest in the righteousness of Christ unto justification, it follows, *by whom also we have access by faith into this grace wherein we stand*, Rom. v. 2. access to God as the God of grace, to him as on a throne of grace, to all the blessings of grace which come from God through Christ; and through the blood and righteousness of Christ justified ones have great freedom, boldness and confidence, to go to God, and present their supplication to him for what they want; not for their righteousness-sake, but in their requests making mention of the righteousness of Christ, and only pleading the worth and virtue of that.——4. Acceptance with God through Christ follows upon justification by his righteousness; there can be no acceptance with God upon the foot of a man's own righteousness, which cannot render him acceptable to God; but through the righteousness of Christ there is an acceptance both of persons and services; first of persons and then of services; as God had respect to Abel, and so to his offering, and accepted it; so he has respect to the persons of his justified ones, as considered in Christ; he has respect to him, and is well-pleased with him, and with all that are in him; they are accepted of God in the beloved, being clothed with the robe of his righteousness, and the garments of his salvation; and their services being done in the strength of Christ, and through faith in him, and to the glory of God by him, and their spiritual sacrifices being offered up by him their great high-priest, they become acceptable to God through him.——5. The well-being of God's people here and hereafter depends upon their justification, and is a consequent of it; *Say ye to the righteous*, one that is justified by the righteousness of Christ, *that it shall be well with him*, Isa. iii. 10. it is well with the justified ones in life; be it with them as it may, all is well with them and for the best; all things work together for their good, adversity and prosperity; what they have of worldly things, though but little, Psalm xxxvii. 16. Prov. xv. 16, 17. are blessings to them: it is well with such an one at death, he has hope in it, and rejoices in hope of the glory of God; peace is the end of the perfect and upright man, who is perfectly righteous through the righteousness of Christ imputed to him; and it is well with him at judgment, he has a righteousness that will answer for him in that time to come; and he shall have an abundant entrance into the everlasting kingdom and glory of our Lord Jesus Christ; and it will be well with him to all eternity; he that is righteous will then be righteous still, and ever continue so, and shall go into everlasting life.——6. Glorying, or boasting, is another effect of justification; not in a man's self, in his own righteousness; not of his duties, services, and performance; nor of blessings of goodness enjoyed through his own merit; nor of heaven and happiness, as his own acquisition; all such boasting is excluded, by the doctrine of justification by faith in the righteousness of Christ; but such as are justified in Christ, glory of him in whom they are justified; and glory in this, that he is *of God, made to them righteousness*, Isa. xlv. 25. 1 Cor. i. 30.——7. Justified ones have an undoubted title, to eternal life; hence justification by Christ's righteousness is called, *justification of life*, because it entitles to it; and such are *made heirs, according to the hope of eternal life;* are heirs of the inheritance, incorruptible and undefiled, and reserved in the heavens, and shall be possessed of it, Rom. v. 18. Tit. iii. 7. For,——8. Certainty of salvation may be concluded from justification; such as are justified, shall most assuredly be *saved from wrath;* there is an inseparable connection between justification and glorification; *Whom he justified, them he also glorified*, Rom. v. 9. and viii. 30.

VII. The properties of justification.——1. It is an act of God's grace, of pure grace, without any consideration of merit, worthiness, and works of men; grace is the moving cause of it, as has been already observed; it was according to the purpose and grace of God, that he resolved upon the justification of any of the sons of men; *The scripture foreseeing that God would justify the heathen through faith,* Gal. iii. 8. the scripture foresaw, or predicted, the justification of them; because God, of his sovereign grace and good-will, determined on it; grace set wisdom at work to find out a proper way and method of making men just with God, which could never have been found out by men or angels; and having found out a way to impute their sins, not to themselves, but to Christ, and to impute his righteousness to them; he was *gracious, and said, Deliver them from going down to the pit.* Grace put him on calling Christ to be their surety, to bring in an everlasting righteousness for them; and it was grace in Christ to accept the call, and say, *Lo, I come to do thy will!* one part of which was, to work out a righteousness for his people; and it was grace in God to send his Son to obey, suffer, and die for them, in their nature, that the righteousness of the law might be fulfilled in them; and it was grace in him to accept of that righteousness as if done by them, and to impute it to them freely without works, and to give them faith to lay hold upon it for themselves; and it appears the more to be an act of grace, in that they are *ungodly* whom God justifies, sinners, even some, the chief of sinners, Rom. iv. 5. 1 Cor. vi. 11.——2. It is an act of justice, as well as of grace: God is righteous in all his ways and works, and so in this; the law being perfectly fulfilled by Christ, the surety, both with respect to precept and penalty; justice is fully satisfied, and so God is *just, and the justifier of him that believeth in Jesus,* Rom. iii. 26.——3. It is universal, as to persons, sins, and punishment: as to persons, all the seed of Israel are justified; that is, all the elect of God and seed of Christ; as there was an *all* on whom judgment came to condemnation, through the offence of the first Adam, even all his natural posterity; so there is an *all* on whom the free gift by the righteousness of Christ comes, to the justification of life; even all the children of God, and offspring of Christ, the second Adam, whose righteousness is *unto all,* and *upon all* them that believe, Isa. xlv. 25. Rom. v. 18. and iii. 22. And with respect to sins, they that are justified, are justified from all sins whatever; Christ has redeemed his people from all their iniquities; all are forgiven for his sake; his blood cleanses from all, and his righteousness clears and acquits them of all: and as to punishment, they are entirely secure from it, even to the least degree; they are saved from wrath; they are secure from all condemnation; they are delivered from the curse of the law; nor shall they be hurt by the second death, the wages of sin; it shall not have any power at all over them: the whole righteousness of Christ is imputed to them; a whole Christ is made to them righteousness; and in such a manner, that they are made the righteousness of God in him; and they are complete in him, are perfectly comely through his comeliness put upon them, a perfection of beauty, all fair, and without spot.——4. It is an individual act, done at once, and admits of no degrees; the sins of God's elect were altogether and at once laid on Christ, and satisfaction for them was made by him at once; he removed the iniquity of his people in one day, and by one sacrifice put away sin for ever; all sins were pardoned at once, upon this sacrifice offered, and satisfaction made; and the righteousness of Christ was accepted of, and imputed to his people at once. The sense of justification, indeed, admits of degrees; *The righteousness of God is revealed from faith to faith;* from one degree of faith to another; from a lesser, and lower degree of it, to an higher; it is gradually that faith rises to a full assurance of interest in it, so that a man knows with certainty, that he is and shall be justified; the manifestations of it are various and different, at different times; but the act itself, as in God, is always the same, perfect and complete. Indeed, there are fresh declarations and repetitions of it, the sentence of it was first conceived in the divine mind from all eternity; it was virtually pronounced on the elect in Christ, their representative, at his resurrection from the dead; and it is afresh pronounced in the conscience of a believer, by the Spirit, and he bearing testimony to it; and it will be again notified at the general judgment, before angels and men; but justification, as an act of God, is but one, and done at once, and admits of no degrees· and is not carried on in a gradual, progressive way, as sanctification is.——5. It is equal to all, or all are alike justified, that are justified; the price of redemption, on which justification proceeds, is the same, the precious blood of Christ; even as the ransom-price, and atonement-money paid for the children of Israel, was the same, an half-shekel for the rich and for the poor: and it is the same righteousness of Christ that is imputed to one as to another; it is a garment down to the feet, and covers the whole mystical body, the lowest and meanest members of it, as well as the more principal; it is unto all, and upon all them that believe; there is no difference, they have all the same righteousness, and the same precious faith, though not to the same degree yet the weakest believer is as much justified, as the strongest believer; and so the greatest, as well as the smallest sinner, though one may be justified from more sins than another, having committed more; yet one is not more justified than the other; though one man may have more faith, and more sanctifying grace than another, yet no man has more righteousness, or a more justifying righteousness than another.——6. It is irreversible, and an unalterable act; it is according to the immutable purpose and grace of God, which can never be frustrated; it is part of that grace given, and one of those spiritual blessings wherewith the elect were blessed in Christ before the world began; it is one of those things which God does; and are for ever. Neither the righteousness by which they are justified, nor the faith by which they receive the justifying righteousness from the Lord, ever fail. The righteousness is an everlasting righteousness; and faith fails not; Christ is the author and finisher of it. Though a righteous man falls, he never falls from his righteousness: a man that is only seemingly and outwardly righteous, may turn away from his own righteousness, and go into a course of sin, and die; but one that is truly righteous, through the righteousness of Christ, can never turn and fall from that, nor shall ever enter into condemnation; but shall be eternally saved and glorified.—— 7. Though by the act of justification, persons are freed from sin, and from obligation to punishment for it, sin is not thereby taken out of them. They are, indeed, so freed from it, that God sees no iniquity in them, to condemn them for it; he sees all the sins of his people in the article of providence, and chastises for them; but in the article of justification he sees none in them; they are acquitted, discharged, and justified from all; yet sin dwells in them, as it did in the apostle Paul, who, undoubtedly, was a justified person; yea, *There is not a just man upon earth;* one that is truly righteous, in an evangelic sense, *that doth good and sinneth not*, Eccles. vii. 20.—— 8. Through justification by the righteousness of Christ, neither the law is made void and of none effect, nor is the performance of good works discouraged. The Law is not made void; *Do we make void the law through faith?* that is, through the doctrine of justification by faith in the righteousness of Christ; *God forbid! yea, we establish the law;* by presenting to it a righteousness every way commensurate to its demands, by which it is magnified and made honourable: nor does this doctrine discourage duty, but animates to it; and is to be constantly preached for this end, *That they which have believed in God, might be careful to maintain good works*, Tit. iii. 7, 8.

CHAP. IX.

OF ADOPTION.

SOME think that adoption is a part and branch of justification, and included in it; since that part of justification which lies in the imputation of the righteousness of Christ entitles to eternal life, hence called, *the justification of life*, as adoption does; so that the children of God may be said to have a twofold title to eternal life; the one by the free grace of God making them sons, which entitles them to it; the other by justification in a legal way, and confirms the former, and opens a way for it; or that it may appear to be founded on justice as well as grace: the learned Dr. Ames[1] seems to have a respect to both these. And such that are justified by the grace of God, through the righteousness of Christ, are *heirs* of it, as adopted ones be; *if children, then heirs*, Rom. v. 18. Tit. iii. 7. Rom. viii. 17. Some consider adoption as the effect of justification; and Junius calls it, *via adoptionis*, the way to adoption: it is

---

[1] Hinc omnes fideles duplici quasi titulo vitam æternam expectant, titulo nempe redemptionis, quem habent ex justificatione, et titulo quasi filationis quem habent ex adoptione, Ames. Medulla, Theol. 1. 1. c 28. s. 7.

certain, they have a close connection with each other, and agree in their author, causes, and objects; the *white stone* of absolution, or justification, and the *new name* of adoption, go together in the gift of Christ to the overcomer, Rev. ii. 17. Though I am of opinion they are distinct blessings of grace, and so to be considered : adoption is a distinct thing from either justification or pardon. A subject may be acquitted by his sovereign from charges laid against him; and a criminal, convicted and condemned, may be pardoned, yet does not become his son; if adopted, and taken into his family, it must be by a distinct and fresh act of royal favour.

I have treated already, in book ii. chap. 5. of adoption as an immanent act of the divine will, which was in God from eternity; hence the elect of God were not only predestinated to the adoption of children, to the blessing itself, openly and actually to enjoy it in time, and to the inheritance adopted to ; but this blessing itself was provided and bestowed in the everlasting covenant of grace, in which the elect of God had not only the promise of this relation, but were in it given to Christ, under this relation and character, Eph. i. 5. 2 Cor. vi. 18. Heb. ii. 13. hence they are spoken of as the children of God and Christ, previous to the incarnation of Christ, and to his sufferings and death ; as well as to the mission of the Spirit into their hearts, as the Spirit of regeneration and adoption, Heb. ii. 14. John xi. 52. Gal. iv. 6. I shall therefore now consider it as openly bestowed upon believing in Christ, and as manifested, applied, and evidenced by the Spirit of God. And,

1. Shall consider, in what sense believers are the sons of God ; which is by adoption, and the nature of that : they are not the sons of God in so high a sense as Christ is, who is God's own Son, his proper Son, his only begotten Son ; which cannot be said either of angels or men; for as *to which of the angels*, so to which of the sons of men *said God at any time, Thou art my son, this day have I begotten thee ?* Nor in the sense that their fellow-creatures are, whether angels or men, who are the sons of God by creation, as the former, so the latter; for they are all *his offspring :* nor in the sense that magistrates be, who are so by office, and, on that account, called *the children of the most High*, being his representatives : nor as professors of religion, who are called the sons of God, in distinction from the children of men ; but by adoption; hence we read of the *adoption of children*, these are predestinated unto, and which they receive, through redemption by Christ, and of which the Spirit of God is the witness; hence called the Spirit of *adoption :* and even the inheritance to which they are entitled, bears the name of *adoption*, Eph. i. 5. Gal. iv. 5. Rom. viii. 15, 23. There is a civil and a religious adoption. A civil adoption, and which obtained among all nations ; among the Egyptians, so Moses was adopted by Pharaoh's daughter ; and among the Hebrews, so Esther by Mordecai ; and it obtained much among the Romans, to which, as used by them, the allusion is in the New Testament, in a religious sense; it is sometimes used of the whole people of the Jews, to whom belonged *the adoption*, Rom. ix. 4. and at other times of some special and particular persons, both among Jews and Gentiles ; for of the former all were *not the children of God;* and of the latter, if they were believers in Christ, they were Abraham's spiritual seed, *and heirs according to the promise*, Rom. ix. 7, 8. Gal. iii. 26, 29. Between civil and spiritual adoption, in some things there is an agreement, and in some things a difference.

First, In some things they agree.——
1. In the name and thing, υιοθεσια, a putting among the children ; so spiritual adoption is called, Jer. iii. 19. or putting, or taking, one for a son, who was not so by nature and birth ; which is the case of adoption by special grace; it is of such who are, *by nature, children of wrath*, and *aliens from the commonwealth of Israel ;* and taking these from the family of the world, to which they originally belonged, into the family of God, and household of faith, Eph. ii. 3, 12, 19.——2. As civil adoption is of one to an inheritance who has no legal right to it; so is special and spiritual adoption. None, in a civil sense, are adopted, but to an inheritance of which they are made heirs; and so such who are adopted in a spiritual sense, are adopted to an inheritance incorruptible, undefiled, and eternal; and as the one are adopted to an inheritance they had no natural right unto, nor any legal claim upon ; so the other are such who have sinned, and come short of the eternal inheritance, and can make no legal pretension to it by works of the law, Rom. iv. 14. Gal. iii. 18.——3. Civil adoption is the voluntary act of the adopter. Among

the Romans, when a man adopted one for his son, they both appeared before a proper magistrate, and the adopter declared his will and pleasure to adopt the person presented, he consenting to it. Special and spiritual adoption is an act of the sovereign good-will and pleasure of God, who has predestinated his to the adoption of children, by Jesus Christ, to himself, according to the *good pleasure of his will;* it is a pure act of his grace to make them his sons and heirs, and to give them the kingdom, the inheritance, even eternal life, which is the free gift of God, through Christ, Eph. i. 5. Luke xii. 32. Rom. vi. 23.——4. In civil adoption the adopted took and bore the name of the adopter: so the adopted sons of God have a new name, which the mouth of the Lord their God names; a new, famous, and excellent name, which no man knoweth, saving he that receives it; a name better than that of sons and daughters of the greatest earthly potentate; a name by which they are called the sons and daughters of the Lord God Almighty, Isa. lxii. 2. and lvi. 5. Rev. ii. 17. 1 John iii. 1.—— 5. Such who are adopted in a civil sense are taken into the family of the adopter, and make a part of it; and stand in the relation, not of servants, but sons; so those who are adopted of God, are taken into that family, which is named of him in heaven and in earth, and are of his household; in which they are not as servants, nor merely as friends, but as the children of God and household of faith, Eph. iii. 15, 19. John xv. 15, 16. Gal. iii. 26. and vi. 10.——6. Persons adopted in a civil sense, as they are considered as children, they are provided for as such; provision is made for their education, their food, their clothing, their protection, and attendance, and for an inheritance and portion for them: all the children of God, his adopted ones, they are taught of God, by his Spirit, his ministers, his word and ordinances; they are trained up in the school of the church, and under the ministry of the word, and are instructed by the preaching of the gospel, and by precepts, promises, and providences; as for food, they are continually supplied with what is suitable for them, the sincere milk of the word for babes, and meat for strong men; they are fed with hidden manna, with marrow and fatness, with the finest of the wheat, with the richest dainties of the gospel-feast: as for their clothing, it is change of raiment, clothing of wrought gold, raiment of needlework, a robe of righteousness, and garments of salvation; fine linen, clean and white, which is the righteousness of the saints: for their protection, they have angels to wait upon them and guard them, who encamp about them, to preserve them from their enemies, and have the care and charge of them, to keep them in their ways; yea, they are kept by the Lord himself, as the apple of his eye, being his dear sons and pleasant children: and the inheritance he has prepared for them, of which they are heirs, is among the saints in light; is incorruptible, undefiled, never fading, and eternal, and is even a kingdom and glory.——7. Such as are adopted by men, come under the power, and are at the command of the adopter, and are under obligation to perform all the duties of a son to a parent; as to honour, reverence, and obey, and be subject to his will in all things. All which are due from the adopted sons of God, to him, their heavenly Father; honour is what God claims as his due from his children; *a son honoureth his father; if I then be a father, where is mine honour?* Mal. i. 6. obedience to all his commands highly becomes, and is obligatory on them; they ought to be obedient children, and imitate God in all his imitable perfections, particularly in holiness, benevolence, kindness, and goodness; and even should be subject to his corrections and chastisements, which are not merely for his pleasure, but for their profit and good, 1 Pet. i. 14, 15, 16. Eph. v. 1. Matt. v. 45, 48. Luke vi. 35, 36. Heb. xii. 9, 10.

Secondly, In some things civil and spiritual adoption differ.——1. Civil adoption could not be done without the consent of the adopted, his will was necessary to it. Among the Romans the adopter, and the person to be adopted, came before a proper magistrate, and in his presence, the adopter asked the person to be adopted, whether he was willing to be his son; and he answered, I am willing; and so the thing was agreed, and finished. But in spiritual adoption, though the believer, when he comes to be acquainted with the privilege of adoption he is favoured with, and is highly delighted and pleased with it, and admires and adores the grace that has brought him into the relation; yet his will and consent were not necessary to the constitution of the act of adoption; it may be said of that as of every other blessing of grace, that *it is not of him that willeth;* such was the grace of God that he did not wait for the will of the creature to complete this act, but previous to it put him among the children; and such is his sovereign power, that he had an uncontrollable right to take whom he would, and make his sons and daughters; and such the influence and efficacy of his grace, as to make them willing in the day of his power to acknowledge the relation with the greatest wonder and thankfulness, and to behave according to it.———2. Civil adoption was allowed of, and provided for the relief and comfort of such who had no children, and to supply that defect in nature; but in spiritual adoption this reason does not appear; God did not adopt any of the sons of men for want of a Son and heir; he had one, and in a higher class of sonship than creatures can be; more excellent and divine, and suitable to the divine nature; his own proper Son, begotten of him, was as one brought up with him, and his daily delight; the dear Son of his love, in whom he was well pleased; and who always did the things that were pleasing to him, and who inherited all his perfections and glory.———3. In civil adoption there are generally some causes and reasons in the adopted which influence and move the adopter to take the step he does. There are two instances of adoption in scripture, the one of Moses, the other of Esther; in both there were some things that wrought upon the adopters to do what they did. Moses was a goodly child, exceeding fair, and lovely to look upon, which, with other things, moved the daughter of Pharaoh to take him up out of the water, to take care of him, and adopt him for her son; Esther was also a fair and beautiful maid, and besides, was related to Mordecai, which were the reasons why he took her to be his daughter: but in divine adoption, there is nothing in the adopted that could move the adopter to bestow such a favour; no worth nor worthiness, no love nor loveliness, nothing attracting in them; children of wrath by nature, as others; transgressors from the womb, and rebels against God. There were so many objections to their adoption, and so many arguments against it, and none for it in themselves, that the Lord is represented as making a difficulty of it, and saying, *How shall I put them among the children?* Jer. iii. 19. such blackmoors and Ethiopians as these are? so abominable and so disobedient, enemies in their minds by wicked works, hateful and hating one another?———4. In civil adoption, the adopter, though he takes one into his family, and makes him his son and heir, and gives him the name and title of a son, and a right to an inheritance designed for him; he cannot give him the nature of a son, nor qualifications fitting him for the use and enjoyment of the estate he is adopted to; he cannot give him a suitable disposition and temper of mind, nor communicate goodness, wisdom, and prudence for the management of it; he may turn out a fool, or a prodigal: but the divine adopter makes his sons partakers of the divine nature, and makes them meet for the inheritance with the saints in light.——— 5. Persons adopted in a civil sense, cannot enjoy the inheritance whilst the adoptive father is living, not till after his death: but in spiritual adoption, the adopted enjoy the inheritance, though their father is the everlasting and ever-living God; and Christ, the first-born, lives for ever, with whom they are joint-heirs.———6. In some cases civil adoption might be made null and void;[2] as among the Romans, when against the right of the pontifex, and without the decree of the college; but spiritual adoption is never made void on any account.

There is a difference also between adoption and regeneration, though divines usually confound these two together. They both have the same author; the same God and Father adopts and regenerates; they flow from the same love and grace; and the same persons that are adopted are regenerated; and they are adopted and begotten again unto the same inheritance: but adoption is before regeneration; the one is an act of God's will in eternity, the other is an act and work of his grace in time; the one is the cause, the other the effect; men are not adopted because regenerated, which would seem unnecessary; but they are regenerated because adopted; *because ye are sons, God hath sent forth the Spirit of his Son into your hearts;* to regenerate, to sanctify, and testify their adoption, Gal. iv. 6. regeneration is the fruit and effect of adoption, and the evidence of it, John i. 12, 13. adoption gives the name of sons, and a title to the inheritance; and regeneration gives the nature of sons, and a meetness for the inheritance.

II. The causes of adoption. *First,* The efficient cause, God; none can adopt any into the family of God, but God himself;

---

[2] Alex. ab Alex. Genial. Dier. l. 2. c. 8.

none can put any among the children of God, but he himself; none but he can do it, who says, *I will be his God, and he shall be my Son*, Rev. xxi. 7. God, Father, Son, and Spirit, are concerned in the affair of adoption.——1. God the Father; *What manner of love the Father hath bestowed upon us;* the Father of Christ, the one God and Father of us all; *that we should be called the sons of God*, 1 John iii. 2. The God and Father of Christ, who blessed and chose his people in him, he predestinated them to the adoption of children by him; both to the grace of adoption, and to the inheritance they are adopted to, and obtain in Christ, in virtue thereof, Eph. i. 3, 4, 5, 11. he also predestinated them *to be conformed to the image of his Son, that he might be the first-born among many brethren;* he set him up as the pattern of their sonship, that as he partook of their nature, they should be partakers of the divine nature; and that as he was a Son and Heir of all things, they should be likewise; and which will more manifestly be seen when they shall appear to be what they are, as sons, and be like unto him, Rom. viii. 29. 1 John iii. 2. Besides, God the Father has not only determined upon their adoption, and all things relative to it; but he has provided this blessing in covenant for them, and secured it there; this is one of the *all things* in which *it is ordered* and sure; it is one of the spiritual blessings of the covenant, which he has blessed his people with in Christ; which covenant runs thus; *I will be a Father unto you, and ye shall be my sons and daughters, saith the Lord Almighty*, 2 Cor. vi. 18. yea, the act of adoption itself, or putting among the children, is his act; for though he says, *How shall I put thee among the children?* there being no difference between them and others by nature, they are as bad and as black as others; yet he did do it.—— 2. The Son of God has a concern in adoption; and there are several connections and relations he stands in to his people, which serve greatly to illustrate and confirm it. There is an union between them, a very near and mysterious one, John xvii. 21. and from this union flow all the blessings of grace to the saints; they are first of God in Christ, and then he is every thing to them, and they have every thing through him to make them comfortable and happy; and particularly, he and they being one, his God is their God, and his Father is their Father; he is a Son, and they are sons; he is an Heir, and they are joint heirs with him. There is a marriage relation between Christ and his people; he has betrothed them to himself in righteousness, and that for ever; he is their husband, and they are his spouse and bride; and as when a man marries a king's daughter, he is his son-in-law, as David was to Saul; so one that marries a king's son becomes his daughter: and thus the Church being married to Christ, the Son of God, becomes the King's daughter, Psalm xlv. 13. through the incarnation of Christ, he not only became the *goel*, the near kinsman, but even a brother to those whose flesh and blood he partook of; and because he and they are *of one*, of one and the same nature, *he is not ashamed to call them brethren;* and if his brethren, then, as he is the Son of God, they must be sons of God too: and through the redemption wrought out by him, they come *to receive the adoption* of children, the blessing before prepared for them, in the purpose and covenant of God; yea, the actual donation of the blessing of adoption is bestowed by Christ, for *as many as received him, to them gave he power to become the sons of God*, John i. 12. It is *the Son who makes free;* that is, by making them children; for the children only are free; not servants, John viii. 36.——3. The Spirit of God has also a concern in adoption; he is the author of regeneration; which, though it is not adoption, it is the evidence of it; the sons of God are described as *born of God*, John i. 13. and this spiritual birth, which makes men appear to be the sons of God, is owing to the Spirit of God; for *except a man be born of water and of the Spirit*, that is, of the grace of the Spirit, comparable to water, *he cannot enter into the kingdom of God*, John iii. 5. It is by faith in Christ that men receive the adoption of children; hence believers are said to be *the children of God by faith in Christ Jesus;* this receives and claims the privilege and blessing; which faith is of the operation of the Spirit of God, who is therefore called *the Spirit of faith*, Gal. iii. 26. 2 Cor. iv. 13. Moreover, it is the Spirit who witnesses the truth of adoption; he bears witness to the spirits of believers that they are the children of God; they receiving him as the Spirit of adoption, who is sent into their hearts for that purpose; *for because ye are sons, God hath sent forth the Spirit of his Son into your hearts, crying, Abba, Father*, Rom. viii. 15, 16. Gal. iv. 6. to all which may be added, that the several operations of the

Spirit on the souls of men, such as his leadings and teachings, confirm unto them the truth of their sonship; *for as many as are led by the Spirit of God, they are the sons of God*, Rom. viii. 14. who are led out of themselves, and off of themselves, to Christ and his righteousness; who are led into all truth as it is in Jesus, and to the fulness of Christ; and who are led through him, the Mediator, by the Spirit, unto God, as their Father; and which Spirit is given, and abides, as an *earnest in their hearts*; even *the earnest of the inheritance* they are adopted to, *until the redemption of the purchased possession*, 2 Cor. v. 5. Eph. i. 14.

Secondly, The moving cause of adoption, is the love, grace, free favour, and goodwill of God. There was nothing in the creature that could move him to it; no agreeable disposition in them, no amiableness in their persons, nor any thing engaging in their conduct and behaviour; but all the reverse, as before observed: wherefore, considering these things, the apostle breaks forth in this pathetic expression, *What manner of love the Father has bestowed upon us, that we should be called the sons of God*, 1 John iii. 1. in which he points out the source and spring of this blessing of grace, the amazing love of God.

III. The objects of adoption. And they are such who are the objects of the love of God; for since adoption flows from the love of God, such who are the children of God must be interested in it; and they are *dear children*, strongly interested in his affections, like Ephraim, dear sons and pleasant children, whom God loves dearly, and loves with a love of complacency and delight; they are the chosen of God; for such that are chosen of God in Christ, they are predestinated to the adoption of children by him; hence sons before calling. They are also redeemed from among men, out of every kindred, tongue, people, and nation, being the children of God scattered abroad, Christ came to gather together; and who, through redemption by him, receive the adoption of children, previously provided for them; though, in their nature-state, they are rebellious children, children that are corrupt, and that are corrupters; children of wrath by nature, as others, and in no wise better than others; but are only openly and manifestly the children of God, when they commence believers in Christ: till then they cannot be called the children of God by themselves, or by others; till then they have no claim to the blessing, nor have they the power, the privilege, the dignity, and honour, to become the sons of God. These are the characters of the adopted ones, both secretly and openly.

IV. The nature and excellency of this privilege.——1. It is an act of surprising and distinguished grace; it is an act of God's free grace to predestinate to the adoption of children; it is part of the grace of the covenant, and of the grace given in Christ before the world began; it is owing to the grace of God that Christ was sent to redeem any of the sons of men, that they might receive the adoption of children: it is an instance of grace in God to send his Spirit to manifest it, and bear witness of it; and every one that has seen his own sinfulness and vileness by nature, must say, that if he is a child of God, it is by the grace of God: and it is an act of marvellous grace, 1 John iii. 1. considering all things; and it will appear so, when the adopter and the adopted are put in a contrast; the adopter is the King of kings and Lord of lords, the most high God; hence these his children are called, *the children of the Highest*; and they are, by nature, in the lowest and meanest circumstances that can be imagined; lost and undone, poor and miserable, beggars and bankrupts, the foolish things of this world, and things that are not; and yet such God is pleased to adopt and take into his family: and it is an act of distinguishing grace, both with respect to angels and men; for they are men, the posterity of fallen Adam, that become the sons of God; and not angels, who are ministering spirits, or servants, but not sons; and of men, not all, only some, are the children of God; who are distinguished from the world who are not so, and who know not them that are the children of God, 1 John iii. 1.——2. It is a blessing of grace, which exceeds other blessings; as redemption, pardon, justification, and sanctification; a man may be redeemed out of a state of slavery by a king's ransom, may be pardoned by his prince, though he has been a rebel and traitor to him, and may be acquitted from high crimes laid to his charge, and yet not be a king's son; if adopted, and taken into his family, it must be by another and distinct act of royal favour. And it is more to be a son than to be a saint, as Zanchy[3] observes; who

---

[3] Comment. in Eph. i. 5.

thinks, that to be predestinated to the adoption of children, is something over and above, and what exceeds being chosen to be holy, and without blame: to which may be added, that angels are saints, or holy ones, even perfectly holy; *he came with ten thousands of his saints*, Deut. xxxiii. 2. but they are not sons, at least in the sense that some of the sons of men are.——3. It is a blessing of grace, which makes men exceeding honourable. David observed, that it was *no light thing to be a king's son-in-law;* it certainly cannot be, to be a son of the King of kings; the name of a son of God is a new name, a renowned and excellent one; a name which no man knows the grandeur and dignity of, but he that receives it; it makes a man more honourable than Adam was in his state of honour, and than the angels are in their high estate in heaven; since, though these are sons, yet only by creation, not by adoption, as saints are.——4. It brings men into the highest connections, alliances, relations, and offices; such are not only the sons and daughters of the Lord God Almighty; but they are the brethren of Christ, the Son of God, are fellow citizens with the saints, and of the household of God; yea, they become kings and priests unto God. ——5. The inheritance they are adopted to, exceeds all others: it is a most comprehensive one, it includes all things; *he that overcometh shall inherit all things;* the ground and foundation of which, lies in the relation between God and such persons, as follows; *and I will be his God, and he shall be my son*, Rev. xxi. 7. all things are theirs, civil, ecclesiastic, spiritual, and eternal; they are heirs of the grace of life, and possess the blessings of it; and they are heirs of everlasting salvation, and shall certainly enjoy it, 1 Cor. iii. 22, 23. 1 Pet. iii. 7. Heb. i. 14. yea, they are heirs *of God* himself; he is their portion, and their exceeding great reward, both in this life and that to come; they, in some sort or other, enjoy the benefit of all the perfections of God, and of his purposes, promises and providences; the heavenly state, particularly, is their inheritance, which is sometimes called *glory, substance*, and the *inheritance of the saints in light*, Prov. iii. 35. and viii. 21. Col. i. 12. and has such epithets given it, as show it to be superior to all other inheritances, 1 Pet. i. 4.—— 6. All other inheritances are subject to corruption, and have pollution written upon them, are fading things, and liable to be lost, and often are; but this is an incorruptible crown, a crown of glory, that fadeth not away; a crown of righteousness laid up in heaven, in the covenant of grace, and in the hands of Christ, the Surety of it; and who is the saints feoffee in trust, and so it is sure to all the seed.——
7. Adoption is a blessing and privilege that always continues. The love of God, which is the source of it, always remains; predestination, which gives birth to it, is the purpose of God, that stands sure, which is never revoked nor repented of; and therefore adoption is one of those gifts of grace of his, which are without repentance; the covenant of grace, in which it is secured, is sure, can never be broken, nor will ever be removed; union with Christ is indissoluble, the bond of which is everlasting love; the marriage knot can never be untied; saints are members of his body, and one spirit with him; and the relation between them as husband and wife, as children and brethren, will ever remain. The Spirit, as a Spirit of adoption, abides for ever; and he is the never-failing earnest of the heavenly inheritance, and by whom, the saints are sealed up to the day of redemption: the children of God may be corrected for their faults, and chastised by their heavenly Father; but never turned out of doors, nor disinherited, much less unchilded, which is impossible; the son abides in the house for ever; and such that are sons are never more servants; once a child of God and always so, John viii. 35. Gal. iv. 7. such who are the sons of God, may judge themselves unworthy of the relation, as the prodigal did; and who proposed within himself to desire his father to make him one of his hired servants; but he was not suffered to ask it, because it was what could not be done, Luke xv. 19, 21. yea, they may conclude they are not the sons of God; because they may imagine their spots are not the spots of God's children, and yet they are in such a relation in which they shall always continue.

V. The effects of adoption.——1. A share in the pity, compassion, and care of God, their heavenly Father; who, as a father pities his children, so he pities them that fear him, and reverence him as their Father; in all their afflictions he is afflicted, and sympathizes with them, and delivers them out of all their troubles; when they are in want of whatsoever kind, and particularly of food, he supplies them, and for which they are encouraged to ask it of him, as children of their parents; so our Lord reasons, *If a son*, &c. Luke xi. 11, 12, 13. ——2. Access to God with boldness; they can come to him as children to a father, use freedom with him, tell him all their complaints and wants, and come boldly to the throne of grace, and ask grace and mercy to help them in their times of need. ——3. Conformity to the image of Christ, the first-born among many brethren; which is begun in this life, and will be perfected in that to come; when the sons of God shall be like him, and see him as he is.—— 4. The Spirit of adoption, given to testify their sonship to them; for *because they are sons, God sends forth the Spirit of his Son into their hearts, crying, Abba, Father*, Gal. iv. 6.——5. Heirship; for *if children, then heirs, heirs of God, and joint-heirs with Christ*, Rom. viii. 17. heirs of the grace of life, heirs of a kingdom, of an inheritance most glorious, to which they are entitled, and for which they are made meet by the grace of God.

CHAP. X.

OF THE LIBERTY OF THE SONS OF GOD.

AMONG the several effects, or privileges of adoption, *liberty* is one, and a principal one; and requires to be treated of particularly and distinctly. *Then are the children free*, as our Lord says in another case; such are so, who are made free by him; *If the Son shall make you free, ye shall be free indeed*, John viii. 36. And as it is the Son that makes free, they are sons only who are made free. Freedom is the fruit and effect of sonship, and follows upon it; *Wherefore thou art no more a servant, but a son; and if a son, then an heir of God, through Christ*, Gal. iv. 6, 7. sonship and servitude, a son and a servant, are opposed to each other, and a spirit of adoption and a spirit of bondage; where the one is, the other is not, John viii. 35. Rom. viii. 15. hence this liberty is called, *the glorious liberty of the children of God*, Rom. viii. 21. being proper and peculiar to them; and is twofold, a liberty of grace, and a liberty of glory; the one is enjoyed in this life, and the other in that to come.

First, The liberty of grace; which lies, ——1. In a freedom from sin, Satan, and the law.——(1.) From sin; it is a liberty not to sin, but from it; liberty to sin is licentiousness, and cannot be that liberty wherewith Christ makes free; for it is contrary to his nature, who loves righteousness and hates iniquity; to his gospel, the truth of which makes free, for that is a doctrine according to godliness; and contrary to the Spirit of Christ, who, as he is a free Spirit, so he is the Spirit of holiness; and contrary to the principle of grace in the saints, and is confuted and condemned by the holy lives of the children of God in all ages: but it is a freedom from sin; not from the being of it; for the most eminent saints that have been in the world, have not been free from the indwelling of sin, and acts of it; but from the guilt of it, through the blood and righteousness of Christ applied to them; and from condemnation by it, as well as from the dominion of it, through the grace of God in conversion; when, though sin has reigned in them, in a very powerful and tyrannical manner; yet shall no more have dominion over them, because not under the law, but under grace, Rom. vi. 14, 17, 18.——(2.) From the power of Satan, who has usurped a dominion over the sons of men, and leads them captive at his will, until the Spirit of God comes and dispossesses him, and turns men from the power of Satan to God, and translates them from the power of darkness into the kingdom of his dear Son; when they are no more slaves and vassals to him, nor do his works and lusts; but the will of their heavenly Father: though they are not freed from his temptations, which the best of men have been beset with; yet they are not overcome by them, nor shall be destroyed through them.——(3.) From the law, and the bondage of it. From the moral law, as a covenant of works, obliging to work for life; but not from it as a rule of life, walk, and conversation; from it as the ministration of Moses; but not from it as in the hands of Christ: from it, so as not to be obliged to seek for justification by it, which is not to be had by the works of it; and from the curses and condemnation of it, Christ being made a curse for them; and from the rigorous exaction of it, requiring perfect and sinless obedience; and from that bondage of spirit, which, for want of it, it leads into: and from the ceremonial law, as a sign of guilt, that handwriting of ordinances being taken away, and nailed to the cross of Christ; and as a type of Christ, and its ordinances, as shadows of good things to come; which are all done away, Christ, the substance, being come; and as a severe, rigid school-master, as it was, till Christ, the object of faith, came; and as a partition-wall between Jew and Gentile, which is now broken down, and all are one in Christ: and from the judicial law, so far as any of the statutes of it were peculiar to the Jewish nation; but such as are founded on nature, reason, justice, and equity, are still binding. Nor are the sons of God, by their christian liberty, freed from the laws of nations, which are not contrary to religion and conscience; subjection to civil magistrates is not inconsistent with christian liberty; and which is inculcated by the apostles, in their epistles to the churches, and others, Rom. xiii. 1—4. Tit. iii. 1. 1 Pet. ii. 13, 14.——2. Christian liberty consists in a freedom from all traditions of men; such as those of the Pharisees, among the Jews, which were before the times of Christ, and were risen to a very great bulk in his time; and which were imposed as a heavy burden on the consciences of men, and by which the word and commandments of God were transgressed, and made of none effect, Matt. xv. 1—6. and such as among heathens, heretics, and false teachers, which the apostle exhorts to beware of, and not conform unto; which he calls philosophy and vain deceit, the tradition of men, the rudiments of the world; ordinances and commandments of men, which forbid the touching, tasting, and handling of some things, Col. ii. 8, 20—23. and such as the unwritten traditions of the Papists, respecting their hierarchy, doctrines, and practices, which have no foundation in the word of God; as the several orders, offices, and sacraments, not to be found in scripture, the doctrines of transubstantiation, purgatory, &c. rites and customs, as the observance of fasts and festivals, on certain days, and at certain times of the year; baptism of infants, signing with the sign of the cross, &c. such like things christian liberty sets us free from, and our consciences are not bound to pay any regard to them.——3. Christian liberty lies in the free use of the creatures, which God has provided for food and nourishment, and which were granted to men originally, without any distinction; for though there was very early a distinction of creatures into clean and unclean, with respect to sacrifice, yet not with respect to food, until the Levitical law took place, which made the use of some creatures unlawful; but now, under the gospel-dispensation, we are at full liberty to eat of every kind, that is fit, proper, and convenient for food: as Peter, by the vision, was taught to call nothing common and unclean; so we may be persuaded, with the apostle Paul, that there is nothing common and unclean of itself; but that every creature of God is good, and nothing to be refused, if it be received with thanksgiving; and provided it is used with moderation, and not indulged to excess, to luxury and intemperance; or used as an occasion to the flesh, to pamper that, and fulfil the lusts of it, Acts x. 14, 15. Rom. xiv. 14. 1 Tim. iv. 3, 4. The injunction by the synod at Jerusalem, to abstain from blood, and things strangled, was only *pro tempore*, for the peace of the churches, till things could be settled in them, between Jews and Gentiles, to mutual satisfaction.—— 4. Another part of christian liberty respects things indifferent; things which are neither commanded nor forbidden of God, and which may be used and abstained from at pleasure; and which in the first times of the gospel, chiefly concerned the eating, or not eating, some certain things, Rom. xiv. 2, 3. which might be made use of by those who thought fit to use them, provided they did it in faith; for if they made use of them, doubting whether they should or no, they sinned, Rom. xiv. 22, 23. and that they did not lay a stumbling-block in the way of weak christians, and so offend, grieve, and wound them, and destroy their peace, Rom. xiv. 13, 15, 20, 21. 1 Cor. viii. 9—13. and such that abstained from the use of them, were not to reckon it as a point of merit, thereby obtaining the favour of God, and the remission of their sins, and becoming more holy and more perfect; nor as a part of religious worship, and as necessary for the peace of conscience, and continuance in the divine favour; for the *kingdom of God*, true, real religion, and godliness, *is not meat and drink*; it does not lie in what a man eats or drinks, or wears, provided moderation, decency, and circumstances, are attended to, Rom. xiv. 17. and care should be taken, on the one hand, lest such things should be reckoned indifferent, which are not indifferent, and so any precept, or ordinance of God, be neglected; and on the other hand, such as are indifferent, should not be imposed as necessary, which may lead to superstition and will-worship.——5. Christian liberty lies in the use of gospel-ordinances, which God has enjoined; it is a privilege to come to mount Zion, the city of the living God; to have a place and a name in the church of Christ; to be of the family and household of God, and partake of the provisions which are there made for spiritual refreshment. Subjection to gospel-ordinances is not contrary to christian liberty; but accords with it, and, indeed, is a part of it; but to be subject to the ordinances and commandments of men is contrary to it; but not subjection to the ordinances of God. Carnal men may reckon them bonds and cords, and be for breaking and casting them away; but spiritual men account them their privileges, and receive Christ's *yoke* as *easy*, and his *burden* as *light*; and they yield subjection to them, not with a mercenary and servile spirit, but under the influence, and by the assistance, of the Spirit of God, who is a free Spirit; they act from a principle of love; they love the house and worship of God, his word and ordinances, and in love observe them, John xiv. 15, 21, 23. Christian liberty does not lie in a neglect of Gospel-ordinances, or in an attendance on them at will and pleasure; men are not to come into a church, and go out when they please, or attend an ordinance now and then, or when they think well: this is not liberty, but licentiousness. The ordinances of Christ, particularly the supper, are perpetual things, to be observed frequently and constantly, unto the second coming of Christ; and it is both well-pleasing to God, to keep the ordinances, as they were delivered; and it is profitable to the saints; since these are for the perfecting of the saints, for the edifying of the body of Christ, till they come to be perfect men, and arrive to the measure of the stature of the fulness of Christ.——6. Christian liberty lies in worshipping God according to his word, and the dictates of conscience, without the fear of men, which indulged to, brings a snare, and leads to idolatry, superstition, and will-worship: though christians are obliged to regard the laws of men, respecting civil matters, yet not what regard religion and conscience, and are contrary thereunto; by such they are not bound, but should serve God rather than men; as the cases of the three companions of Daniel, of Daniel himself, and of the apostles, and of the martyrs and confessors in all ages, shew; who chose rather to suffer imprisonment, confiscation of goods, and death itself, than part with this branch of christian liberty, to serve God, according to his word, and that light which they had in it. Nor does it become rulers and governors to infringe this liberty of theirs.——7. Another glorious part of christian liberty is freedom of access to God, through Christ the Mediator, under the influence of the blessed Spirit, Eph. ii. 18. this is a great privilege the sons of God have, that they can come to God as their Father; not as on a throne of justice, requiring at their hands satisfaction for their sins; but as on a throne of grace, communicating pardoning grace and mercy, and all supplies of grace to them, as the God of all grace; and this access they have through Christ, the Mediator between God and man, through his blood, righteousness, and sacrifice; and by the Spirit, who is a Spirit of grace and supplication, under whose influence saints can pour out their souls to God with great freedom, and make known their requests to him with thankfulness.——8. It also lies in a freedom from the fear of death, both corporal and eternal; Christ, through his incarnation, sufferings, and death, has delivered them, who, through fear of death, were all their lifetime subject to bondage: death, as formidable as it is, is no king of terrors to them; in a view of interest in Christ, and in the exercise of faith, and hope of being for ever with him, they choose to depart; knowing, that to die is gain; and in a prospect of death and eternity, can sit and sing, and say, *O death, where is thy sting! O grave, where is thy victory!* And as to an eternal death, they are comfortably assured, they shall not be hurt by it; that shall have no power over them, though it is the just desert of sin; yet being justified by Christ, and having access, through him, into a state of grace, they rejoice in hope of the glory of God; and being made spiritually alive, they believe they shall never die, neither a spiritual nor an eternal death.

Secondly, The liberty of glory, or that which the sons of God will be possessed of, in the world to come; and this will be entirely perfect; the soul, in its separate state, will be perfectly free from sin, be with the spirits of just men made perfect; free from all corruption and defilement, from the very being of sin, and any consequences of it; from all unbelief, doubts, fears, and distresses of mind; from all evil thoughts and vain desires; and from all the temptations of Satan: and at the resurrection their bodies will be no more subject to pains, griefs, disorders, and diseases of any kind; but be entirely free from corruption, and mortality, and dea and be, both in soul and body, perfectly pure and holy, and live for ever in the enjoyment of God, and in the company of angels and saints; and be in no danger of ever being brought into bondage in any sense: and as this state is called the *adoption*, so it may be said to be the *glorious liberty of the children of God*, Rom. viii. 21, 23.

The author, or *efficient cause*, of this liberty, is Christ; it is a liberty with which Christ has made his people free, Gal. v. 1. it is of his procuring, he has obtained it with the price of his blood, by which he has redeemed them from sin, Satan, and the law: and it is of his proclaiming; for he was anointed with the holy Spirit, to proclaim liberty to the captives, and the opening of the prison to them that are bound; and it is by his Spirit that they are put into the possession of it, who is a Spirit of liberty, being the Spirit of adoption, and so opposed to the Spirit of bondage; and Christ is the author and finisher of faith, by which they receive this privilege; so that it may be truly called, as it sometimes is, by divines, *Christian liberty;* both from Christ the author of it, and from the subjects of it, Christians, such as truly believe in Christ.

The *instrumental cause*, or the means by which liberty is conveyed to the sons of God, is the word of God, the truth of the gospel; which is not only a proclamation of this liberty, made by Christ, the great Prophet, in the church, and by his apostles and ministering servants; and was prefigured by the jubilee trumpet, which proclaimed liberty throughout the land; but is the means, attended with the Spirit and power of God, of freeing souls from the bondage they are in by nature, and when first under a work of the law; *ye shall know the truth, and the truth shall make you free,* John viii. 32. and the clearer knowledge men have of the gospel, and the truths of it; and the more they are evangelized, or cast into a gospel mould by it, the farther off they are from a spirit of bondage again to fear. So that this liberty may be rightly called *gospel liberty;* which, though not restrained entirely to the gospel dispensation, yet is more peculiar to that; since the saints under the former dispensation were as children in bondage, under the elements of the world, the law which gendered to bondage, and brought upon them that servile bondage spirit which prevailed in them.

Both from the nature of this liberty, and from the influence the Spirit of God has in it, it may be, with great propriety, called *spiritual liberty;* as well as from its having its seat in the spirits, or souls of men; and may be distinguished from corporal liberty, and from civil liberty. Nor does it at all interfere with the latter; it does not dissolve the ties, obligations, connections, and dependencies of men, one with, and on, another; nor free from subjection to parents, masters, and civil magistrates. It is in its nature, pure, holy, and spiritual; it is not a liberty to sin, as has been observed; but a liberty from sin. It is a real liberty, and not a shadow, an appearance of one; *If the Son make you free, ye shall be free indeed:* and it is perpetual; such who are once made free, shall never more be servants, or come into a state of bondage; they shall never be disfranchised, or lose their freedom; and the fruits and effects of it are, peace, joy, and comfort, and a capacity and disposition of worshipping and serving the Lord, in the most spiritual, evangelical, and acceptable manner!

CHAP. XI.

OF REGENERATION.

REGENERATION follows adoption, being the evidence of it; regeneration describes the persons who have received the power to become the sons of God, John i. 12, 13. and though these are distinct things, yet they are closely connected together; where the one is, the other is also, as to enjoyment and experience; and they bear a similarity to each other. Regeneration may be considered either more largely, and then it includes with it effectual-calling, conversion, and sanctification; or more strictly, and then it designs the first principle of grace infused into the soul; which makes it a fit object of effectual vocation, a proper subject of conversion, and is the source and spring of that holiness which is gradually carried on in sanctification, and perfected in heaven. Concerning regeneration, the following things may be enquired into.

I. What regeneration is, or what is meant by it, the nature of it; which is so mysterious, unknown, and unaccountable to a natural man, as it was to Nicodemus, though a master in Israel; now it may be the better understood by observing the phrases and terms by which it is expressed.

———1. It is expressed by being *born again*, which regeneration properly signifies; see John iii. 3, 7. 1 Pet. i. 3, 23. and this supposes a prior birth, a first birth, to which regeneration is the second; and which may receive some light by observing the contrast between the two births, they being the reverse of each other: the first birth is of sinful parents, and in their image; the second birth is of God, and in his image; the first birth is of corruptible, the second birth of incorruptible seed; the first birth is in sin, the second birth is in holiness and righteousness; by the first birth, men are polluted and unclean, by the second birth they become holy and commence saints; the first birth is of the flesh and is carnal, the second birth is of the Spirit and is spiritual, and makes men spiritual men; by the first birth men are foolish and unwise, being born like a wild ass's colt; by the second birth they become knowing and wise unto salvation; by the first birth they are slaves to sin and the lusts of the flesh, are home-born slaves; by the second birth they become Christ's free men; from their first birth they are transgressors, and go on in a course of sin, till stopped by grace; in the second birth they cease to commit sin, to go on in a course of sinning, but live a life of holiness; yea, he that is born of God cannot sin; by the first birth men are children of wrath, and under tokens of divine displeasure; at the second birth they appear to be the objects of the love of God; regeneration being the fruit and effect of it, and gives evidence of it; a time of life is a time of open love.———2. It is called a being *born from above*, for so the phrase in John iii. 3, 7. may be rendered; the apostle James says in general, that *every good and every perfect gift is from above;* and regeneration being such a gift, must be from above; and indeed he particularly instances in it, for it follows, *of his own will begat he us with the word of truth*, James i. 17, 18. The author of this birth is from above; those that are born again are born of God their Father who is in heaven; the grace given in regeneration is from above, John iii. 27. truth in the inward part, and wisdom in the hidden part, or the grace of God in the heart produced in regeneration, is that *wisdom that is from above*, James iii. 17. such that are born again, as they are of high and noble birth, they are partakers of the heavenly and high calling of God in Christ Jesus, and shall most certainly possess it, 1 Pet. i. 3, 4. Heb. iii. 1. Phil. iii. 14.———3. It is commonly called the *new birth*, and with great propriety; since the washing of regeneration and the renewing of the Holy Ghost, are joined together as meaning the same thing; and what is produced in regeneration is called the new creature, and the new man; and those who are born again are said to be new born babes, Tit. iii. 5. 2 Cor. v. 17. Eph. iv. 24. 1 Pet. ii. 2. it is a new man, in distinction from the old man, or the principle of corrupt nature, which is as old as a man is; but the principle of grace infused in regeneration is quite new; it is something *de novo*, anew implanted in the heart, which never was before in human nature, no not in Adam in his state of innocence; it is not a working upon the old principles of nature, nor a working them up to an higher pitch; it is not an improvement of them, nor a repairing of the broken, ruined image of God in man. But it is altogether a new work; it is called a creature, being a work of almighty power; and a new creature, and a new man, consisting of various parts, and these all new: there are in it a *new heart*, and a *new spirit*, a new understanding, to know and understand things, never known nor understood before; a new heart, to know God; not as the God of nature and providence; but as the God of Grace, God in Christ, God in a Mediator; the love of God in him, the covenant of grace, and the blessings of it made with him; Christ, and the fulness of grace in him, pardon of sin through his blood, justification by his righteousness, atonement by his sacrifice, and acceptance with God through him, and complete salvation by him; things which Adam knew nothing of in Paradise: in this new heart are new desires after these objects, to know more of them, new affections, which are placed upon them, new delights in them, and new joys, which arise from them, Ezek. xxxvi. 26. 1 John v. 20. 1 Cor. ii. 9. In this new man, are *new eyes* to see with; to some God does not give eyes to see divine and spiritual things; but to regenerated ones he does; they have a seeing eye, made by the Lord, Deut. xxix. 4. Prov. xx. 12. by which they see their lost state and condition by nature, the exceeding sinfulness of sin, their own inability to make atonement by any thing that can be done by them; the insufficiency of their own righteousness; their impotence to every good work

and want of strength to help themselves out of the state and condition in which they are, and the need they are in of the blood, righteousness, and sacrifice of Christ, and of salvation by him. They have the eye of faith, by which they behold the glories of Christ's Person, the fulness of his grace, the excellency of his righteousness, the virtue of his blood and sacrifice, and the suitableness and completeness of his salvation : and regeneration, in this view of it, is no other than spiritual light in the understanding. Moreover, in the new man are *new ears* to hear with ; all have not ears to hear ; some have, and they have them from the Lord, and blessed are they ! Rev. ii. 11. Deut. xxix. 4. Prov. xx. 12. Matt. xiii. 16, 17. they hear the word in a manner they never heard before ; they hear it so as to understand it, and receive the love of it ; so as to distinguish the voice of Christ in it, from the voice of a stranger ; so as to feel it work effectually in them, and become the power of God unto salvation to them ; they know the joyful sound, and rejoice to hear it. The new man has also *new hands*, to handle and to work with ; the hand of faith, to receive Christ as the Saviour and Redeemer, to lay hold on him for life and salvation, to embrace him, hold him fast, and not let him go ; to handle him, the Word of life, and receive from him grace for grace ; and they have hands to work with, and do work from better principles, and to better purposes than before. And they have *new feet* to walk with, to flee to Christ, the City of refuge ; to walk by faith in him ; and to walk on in him, as they have received him ; to run with cheerfulness the ways of his commandments ; to follow hard after him, and to follow on to know him ; and even to run, and not be weary, and to walk, and not faint.——
4. Regeneration is expressed by being *quickened*. As there is a quickening time in natural generation ; so there is in regeneration ; *You hath he quickened*, Eph. ii. 1. Previous to regeneration, men are dead whilst they live ; though corporally alive, are morally dead, dead in a moral sense, as to spiritual things, in all the powers and faculties of their souls ; they have no more knowledge of them, affection for them, will to them, or power to perform them, than a dead man has with respect to things natural ; but in regeneration, a principle of spiritual life is infused ; that is a time of life when the Lord speaks life into them, and produces it in them. Christ is the resurrection and life unto them, or raises them from a death of sin to a life of grace ; and the spirit of life, from Christ, enters into them. Regeneration is a passing from death to life ; it is a principle of spiritual life implanted in the heart ; in consequence of which, a man breathes, in a spiritual sense ; where there is breath, there is life. God breathed into Adam the breath of life, and he became a living soul, or a living person, and breathed again : so the Spirit of God breathes on dry bones, and they live, and breathe again. Prayer is the spiritual breath of a regenerate man ; *Behold, he prayeth !* is observed of Saul, when regenerated ; who, just before, had been breathing out threatenings and slaughter against the disciples of Christ. A regenerate man breathes in prayer to God, and pants after him ; after more knowledge of him in Christ, after communion with him, after the discoveries of his love ; particularly after pardoning grace and mercy : and sometimes these breathings and desires are only expressed by sighs and groans, yet these are a sign of life ; if a man groans, it is plain he is alive. There are, in a regenerated man, which shews that he is made alive, cravings after spiritual food : as soon as an infant is born, its shews motions for its mother's milk, after the breast ; so new-born babes desire the sincere milk of the word, that they may grow thereby. They have their spiritual senses exercised about spiritual objects ; they have what answer to the senses in animal life, their seeing and hearing, as before observed, and also their feeling ; they feel the burden of sin on their consciences ; the workings of the Spirit of God in their hearts ; as well as handle Christ, the Word of life ; which makes it a plain case that they are alive ; a dead man feels nothing. They have a spiritual taste, a gust for spiritual things ; the word of Christ is sweeter to their taste than honey, or the honey-comb ; they sit under his shadow with pleasure, and his fruit, the blessings of his grace, are sweet unto their taste ; they taste that the Lord is gracious, and invite others to taste and see also how good he is ; they savour the things which be of God, and not of men ; Christ, and his grace, are savoury to them ; his robe of righteousness, and garments of salvation, smell delightfully as myrrh, &c. Cant. i. 3. Psalm xlv. 8. and these spiritual senses, and the exercise of them in them, shew them to be alive, or born again ; such persons live a life of

faith; they live by faith; not upon it, but on Christ, the object of it; and they grow up into him their Head, from whom they receive nourishment; and so increase with the increase of God; which is an evidence of life. In a word, they live a new and another life than they did before; not to themselves, nor to the lusts of men; but to God, and to Christ who died for them, and rose again; they walk in newness of life.——5. Regeneration is signified by *Christ being formed in the heart*, Gal. iv. 19. his image is enstamped in regeneration; not the image of the first Adam, but of the second Adam; for the new man is after the image of him who has anew created it, which is the image of Christ; to be conformed to which God's elect are predestinated, and which takes place in regeneration, Rom. viii. 29. Col. iii. 10. The graces of Christ, as faith, and hope, and love, are wrought in the hearts of regenerate persons, and soon appear there; yea, Christ himself lives in them; *Not I*, says the apostle, *but Christ lives in me;* he dwells by faith there; Christ, and the believer, mutually dwell in each other.—— 6. Regeneration is said to be *a partaking of the divine nature*, 2 Pet. i. 4. not of the nature of God essentially considered: a creature cannot partake of the divine essence, or have that communicated to it; this would be to deify men; the divine perfections, many of them, are utterly incommunicable, as eternity, immensity, &c. nor of the divine nature, or of it in such sense as Christ is a partaker of it, by the personal, or hypostatical union of the two natures in him; so that the fulness of the Godhead dwells bodily in him. But in regeneration there is that wrought in the soul, which bears a resemblance to the divine nature, in spirituality, holiness, goodness, kindness, &c. and therefore is so called. ——7. There are also several terms, or words, by which the grace of regeneration is expressed; as by *grace* itself; not as that signifies the love and favour of God towards his people, or the blessings of grace bestowed upon them; but internal grace, the work of grace in the heart; and which consists of the various graces of the Spirit implanted there; as faith, hope, and love: such as are begotten again, are begotten to a lively hope, and have it, and believe in the Son of God; and love him that begot, and him that is begotten, 1 Pet. i. 3, 1 John v. 1. It is called *spirit*, John iii. 6. from its author, the Spirit of God; and from its seat, the spirit of man; and from its nature, which is spiritual, and denominates men spiritual men. It is also signified by *seed*, 1 John iii. 9. *Whosoever is born of God—his seed remaineth in him;* which is the principle of grace infused in regeneration; and as seed contains in it virtually, all that after proceeds from it, the blade, stalk, ear, and full corn in the ear; so the first principle of grace implanted in the heart, seminally contains all the grace which afterwards appears, and all the fruits, effects, acts, and exercises of it.

II. The springs and causes of regeneration; efficient, moving, meritorious, and instrumental.

First, The efficient cause of it; who is not man, but God.

1*st,* Not man; he cannot regenerate himself; his case, and the nature of the thing itself, shew it; and it is indeed denied of him.——1. The case in which men before regeneration are, plainly shews that it is not, and cannot be of themselves; they are quite ignorant of the thing itself. Regeneration is one, and a principal one, of the things of the Spirit of God, and which a natural man cannot discern and understand; let him have what share he may of natural knowledge; as Nicodemus, a master in Israel, and yet said, how can these things be? and a man cannot be the author of that of which he has no knowledge: nor do men, previous to regeneration, see any need of it; as those who think themselves whole, see no need of a physician, nor make use of any; and who reckon themselves rich, and stand in need of nothing; as not of righteousness, so not of repentance; and if not of repentance, then not of regeneration. And whatsoever notion they may have of it, from what others say concerning it; they have no inclination, nor desire, nor will to it, till God works in them both to will and to do; the bias of their minds is another way; yea, their carnal minds are enmity to it; they mock at it, and count it all dream and enthusiasm. And had they any disposition of mind to it, which they have not, they have no power to effect it; they can do nothing, not the least thing of a spiritual kind; and much less perform such a work as this: this is not by might or power of men, but by the Spirit of the Lord of hosts; to all which may be added, and which makes it impracticable, is, that men are dead in trespasses and sins; and can no more quicken themselves than a dead man can;

as soon might Lazarus have raised himself from the dead, and the dry bones in Ezekiel's vision, have quickened themselves and lived.——2. The nature of the work clearly shews that it is not in the power of men to do it; it is represented as a *creation;* it is called a new creature, the workmanship of God created in Christ, the new man after God, created in righteousness. Now creation is a work of almighty Power; a creature cannot create the least thing, not a fly, as soon might he create a world; and as soon may a man create a world out of nothing, as create a clean heart, and renew a right spirit within him. It is spoken of as a *ressurrection* from the dead; and as soon might dead bodies quicken themselves, as men, dead in sin, raise themselves up to a spiritual life; this requires a power equal to that which raised Christ from the dead; and is done by the same. Its very name, *regeneration*, shews the nature of it; and clearly suggests, that it is out of the power of man to effect it: as men contribute nothing to their first birth, so neither to the second; as no man generates himself, so neither can he regenerate himself; as an infant is passive in its natural generation, and has no concern in it; so passive is a man in his spiritual generation, and is no more assisting in it. It is an *implantation* of that grace in the hearts of men, which was not there before; faith is one part of it, said to be *not of ourselves*, but the gift of God; and hope is another, which men are without, whilst in a state of unregeneracy; and love is of such a nature, that if a man would give all he has for it, it would utterly be contemned; it is a maxim that will hold, *nil dat quod non habet*, nothing can give that which it has not: a man destitute of grace, cannot give grace, neither to himself nor to another. This work lies in taking away *the heart of stone*, and giving an *heart of flesh;* even *a new heart* and *a new spirit:* and none can do this but He who sits upon the throne and says, *Behold, I make all things new*. To say no more, it is a *transforming* of men by the renewing of their minds, making them other men than they were before, as Saul was, and more so; the change of an Ethiopian's skin, and of the leopard's spots, is not greater, nor so great, as the change of a man's heart and nature; and which, indeed, is not a change of the old man, or corruption of nature, which remains the same; but the production of the new man, or of a new principle, which was not before.——3. Regeneration is expressly denied to be of men; it is said to *be not of blood*, the blood of circumcision, *which availeth not any thing; but a new creature* is of avail, when that is not; nor of the blood of ancestors, of of the best of men, the most holy and most eminent for grace; the blood of such may run in the veins of men, and yet they be destitute of regenerating grace; as was the case of the Jews, of multitudes of them, who boasted of being of Abraham's seed, and of his blood: none need value themselves upon their blood on any account, and much less on a religious one; since all nations of the earth are made of one man's blood, and that is tainted with sin, and conveys corruption; sin is propagated that way, but not grace: nor are men born *of the will of the flesh*, which is carnal and corrupt; impotent to that which is good, and enmity to it: regeneration is not of him that willeth; God, of his own will, begets men again, and not of theirs: nor are they born of the *will of men*, of the greatest and best of men, who are regenerated persons themselves; these, of their will, cannot convey regenerating grace to others, if they could, a good master would regenerate every servant in his family; a good parent would regenerate every child of his; and a minister of the gospel would regenerate all that sit under his ministry; they can only pray and use the means; God only can do the work. Wherefore,

2*dly*, The efficient cause of regeneration is God only; hence we so often read, *which were born of God*, and *whosoever and whatsoever is born of God*, John i. 13. 1 John iii. 9. and v. 1, 4. and this is true of God, Father, Son, and Spirit, who have each a concern in regeneration.——1. God the Father, who is the Father of Christ; he as such begets men again according to his abundant mercy, 1 Pet. i. 3. and as the Father of lights, of his own sovereign will and pleasure, regenerates with the word of truth; and as light was one of the first things in the old creation, so in the new creation, or regeneration, light is the first thing sprung in the heart by the Father and fountain of light, James i. 17, 18. and as the Father of men by adoption, he regenerates; it is of him they are born again, who is their covenant God and Father in Christ; he has chosen them unto holiness, of which regeneration is the root, seed, and principle; he has predestinated them to be conformed to the image of his Son, which is done in regeneration; and it is by the washing of regeneration, and renewing of the Holy Ghost, which he sheds abundantly through Christ the Saviour, that he saves his elect ones.——2. God the Son has also a concern in regeneration, and so great a concern, that they who are born again are said to be *born of him*, that is, Christ; for no other is spoken of in the context, 1 John ii. 29. he is the *resurrection and the life;* the author of the spiritual resurrection to a spiritual life, which is no other than regeneration; he quickens whom he will, as the Father does; and it is through his powerful voice in the gospel, that the dead in sin hear and live; it is his Spirit which is sent down into the hearts of his people, as to bear witness to their adoption, so to regenerate them; his grace is given to them, yea he himself is formed in them; his image is enstamped upon them; and it is by virtue of his resurrection that *they are begotten* to a lively hope of the heavenly inheritance, John xi. 25. and v. 21, 25. Gal. iv. 6, 19. 1 Pet. i. 3, 4.—— 3. The holy Spirit of God is the author of regeneration, and to him it is ascribed by our Lord; *Except a man be born of water and of the Spirit,* John iii. 5. by *water,* is not meant the ordinance of water-baptism, that is never expressed by water only, without some other word with it in the text or context which determines the sense; nor is regeneration by it; Simon Magus was baptized, but not regenerated: regeneration ought to precede baptism; faith and repentance, which are graces given in regeneration, are required previous to baptism; nor is water-baptism absolutely necessary to salvation; whereas without regeneration, no man can neither see nor enter into the kingdom of heaven; but the grace of the Spirit is meant by water, so called from its cleansing and purifying use, as it has to do with the blood of Jesus, hence called the washing of regeneration; of this grace the Spirit is the author, whence it bears his name, is called *Spirit;* it is the renewing of the Holy Ghost, or the new creature is his workmanship; quickening grace is from him; it is the Spirit that quickens and gives life, and frees from the law of sin and death, Tit. iii. 5. John iii. 6. and vi. 63.

Secondly, The impulsive, or moving cause, is the free grace, love and mercy of God; *God, who is rich in mercy, for his great love wherewith he loved us hath quickened us,* Eph. ii. 4, 5. Regeneration, as it is a time of life when men are quickened, it is *a time of love,* of open love; it springs from love, which moves mercy to exert itself in this way; it is *according to his abundant mercy God hath begotten us again unto a lively hope,* 1 Pet. i. 3. and this was sovereign grace and mercy, not excited by any motives or conditions in men, or by any preparatory works in them; what were there in the three thousand, some of whom had been concerned in the death of Christ, converted under Peter's sermon? what were in the jailor, who had just before used the apostles in a cruel manner? what was there in Saul, the blasphemer, persecutor, and injurious person, between these characters and his obtaining mercy? no, it is not according to the will and works of men that they are regenerated, but God, *of his own will begat he us,* James i. 18. his own sovereign will and pleasure; and this grace and mercy is *abundant;* it is richly and plentifully displayed; it is *exceeding abundant,* it flows and overflows; there is a pleonasm, a redundancy of it, 1 Tim. i. 14. and to this, as a moving cause, regeneration is owing.

Thirdly, The resurrection of Christ from the dead is the virtual or procuring cause of it; there is a *power* or virtue in Christ's resurrection, which has an influence on many things; as on our justification, for which he rose again, so on our regeneration; for men are said to be *begotten again unto a lively hope by the resurrection of Christ from the dead,* 1 Pet. i. 3. and which also may be considered as the exemplary cause of it; for as there is a planting together *in the likeness of his death,* so *in the likeness of his resurrection from the dead;* as Christ's resurrection was a declaration of his being the Son of God, so regeneration is an evidence of interest in the adoption of children; and as the resurrection of Christ was by the mighty power of God, so is the regeneration and quickening of a dead sinner; and as Christ's resurrection was his first step to his glorification, so is regeneration to seeing and entering into the kingdom of God.

Fourthly, The instrumental cause of regeneration, if it may be so called, are the word of God, and the ministers of it; hence regenerate persons are said to be *born again by the word of God, which liveth and abideth for ever,* 1 Pet. i. 23. and again, *of his own will begat he us with the word of truth,* Jam. i. 18. unless by the Word, in these passages, should be meant the Eternal Logos, or essential Word of God, Christ Jesus, since Λογος is used in both places; though ministers of the gospel are not only represented as ministers and instruments by whom others believe, but as spiritual fathers; *though you have ten thousand instructors in Christ*, says the apostle to the Corinthians, 1 Cor. iv. 15. *yet have ye not many fathers, for in Christ Jesus I have begotten you through the gospel;* so he speaks of his son Onesimus, whom he had *begotten in his bonds*, Philem. ver. 10. yet this instrumentality of the word in regeneration seems not so agreeable to the principle of grace implanted in the soul in regeneration, and to be understood with respect to that; since that is done by immediate infusion, and is represented as a creation; and now as God made no use of any instrument in the first and old creation, so neither does it seem so agreeable that he should use any in the new creation: wherefore this is rather to be understood of the exertion of the principle of grace, and the drawing it forth into act and exercise; which is excited and encouraged by the ministry of the word, by which it appears that a man is born again; so the three thousand first converts, and the jailor, were first regenerated, or had the principle of grace wrought in their souls by the Spirit of God, and then were directed and encouraged by the ministry of the apostles to repent and believe in Christ; whereby it became manifest that they were born again. Though after all it seems plain, that the ministry of the word is the vehicle in which the Spirit of God conveys himself and his grace into the hearts of men; which is done when the word comes not in word only, but in power, and in the Holy Ghost; and works effectually, and is the power of God unto salvation; then faith comes by hearing, and ministers are instruments by whom, at least, men are encouraged to believe: *received ye the Spirit*, says the apostle, *by the works of the law, or by the hearing of faith?* Gal. iii. 2. that is, by the preaching of the law, or by the preaching of the gospel? by the latter, no doubt.

III. The subjects of regeneration are next to be inquired into, or who they are God is pleased to bestow this grace upon. These are men, and not angels; good angels have no need of regeneration; they are holy angels, and continue in that state of holiness in which they were created, and are confirmed therein; they have no need of it to make them meet for heaven, they are there already; they are the angels of heaven, and always behold the face of our heavenly Father there: as for the evil angels, none of them ever had, nor ever will have any share in regenerating grace; they believe indeed, but they have not the faith of regenerate ones, or that faith which worketh by love; they believe there is a God, but they do not, nor can they love him; they believe he is, and tremble at his wrath; they have no hope as regenerate ones have, but live in black despair, and ever will. They are men God regenerates, and not brutes, nor stocks nor stones; these are not subjects capable of regeneration; God could raise up children out of these, but it is not his way and work; they are rational creatures he thus operates upon, and he treats them as such in the ministry of his word; though he is represented as dealing otherwise by the adversaries of the grace of God: but though they are men, and men only, whom God regenerates, yet not all men; all men have not faith, and hope, and love; they are a kind of first fruits of his creatures, whom of his own will he begets with the word of truth; they are such who are called out and separated from the rest of the world; they are such who are the peculiar objects of his love; for regeneration is the fruit and effect of love, and the evidence of it; they are such whom God has predestinated to be conformed to the image of his Son, in which image they are created in regeneration; those whom the apostle speaks of as *begotten again unto a lively hope*, are first described as *elect according to the foreknowledge of God*, 1 Pet. i. 2, 3. and they are such who are redeemed by Christ, for they that are chosen in him, have redemption through his blood; and those are quickened by his Spirit and grace, when dead in trespasses and sins, for such is their state and condition before they are born again; they are such who are the sons of God by adopting grace, who because they are sons, the Spirit of God is sent into them, as to witness their adoption, so to regenerate them, which gives evidence of it; and thus they become openly the children of God by faith in Christ Jesus. Let it be farther observed, that though the chief and principal seat of regeneration is the spirit or soul of man, yet it extends its influence to the body and the members thereof; whereby they are restrained from the lusts of the flesh, as to yield a ready, constant, and universal obedience to them; or so as to *yield* their *members as instru-*

ments *of unrighteousness unto sin;* but, on the contrary are so under the power of the reigning principle of grace implanted in them in regeneration, that they, *through the Spirit, mortify the deeds of the body, and live,* Rom. vi. 12, 13. and viii. 13.

IV. The effects of regeneration, or the ends to be answered, and which are answered by it, and which shew the importance and necessity of it.———1. A principal effect of it; or, if you will, a concomitant of it, is a participation of every grace of the Spirit. Regenerate ones have not only the promise of life made to them, but they have the grace of life given them; they live a new life, and walk in newness of life: they partake of the grace of spiritual light; before, their understandings were darkened; but now they are enlightened by the Spirit of wisdom and revelation, in the knowledge of divine things; they were before, darkness itself; but now are made light in the Lord. In regeneration is laid the beginning of sanctification, which is carried on till completed, without which no man shall see the Lord; for the new man is created in righteousness and true holiness; the principle of holiness is then formed, from whence holy actions spring. The grace of repentance then appears; the stony, hard, obdurate, and impenitent heart being taken away, and an heart of flesh, susceptible of divine impressions, being given; on which follow, a sense of sin, sorrow for it after a godly sort, and repentance unto life and unto salvation, which is not to be repented of: faith in Christ, which is not of a man's self, but the gift of God, and the operation of the Spirit of God, is now given and brought into exercise; which being an effect, is an evidence of regeneration; for *whosoever believeth that Jesus is the Christ,* and especially that believes in Christ, as his Saviour and Redeemer, *is born of God,* 1 John v. 1. and such have hope of eternal life by Christ; whilst unregenerate men are without hope, without a true, solid, and well-grounded hope; but in regeneration, they are begotten to a *lively hope,* and have it; a good hope, through grace, founded upon the person, blood, and righteousness of Christ, which is of use to them both in life and death. Regenerated persons have their *hearts circumcised,* which is but another phrase for regenerating grace, *to love the Lord their God with all their heart and soul,* Deut. xxx. 6. and though before, their carnal minds were enmity to God, and all that is good; now they love him, and all that belong to him, his word, worship, ordinances, and people; and by this it is known, that they *have passed from death to life,* which is no other than regeneration, *because they love the brethren,* 1 John iii. 14. In short, regenerate persons are partakers of all the fruits of the Spirit; of all other graces, besides those mentioned; as humility, patience, self-denial, and resignation to the will of God. And they are blessed with such measures of grace and spiritual strength, as to be able to resist sin and Satan, and to overcome the world, and every spiritual enemy; *For whatsoever is born of God, overcometh the world,* the god of it, the men in it, and the lusts thereof; *Whosoever is born of God, sinneth not,* does not live in sin, nor is he overcome by it; *but he that is begotten of God, keepeth himself* from Satan, and his temptations, from being overcome with them; *and that wicked one toucheth him not:* being clothed with the whole armour of God, which he has skill to wield; he keeps him off, and at bay, so that he cannot come in with him; he holds up the shield of faith to him, whereby he quenches all his fiery darts, 1 John v. 4, 18.

———2. Knowledge, and actual enjoyment of the several blessings of grace, follow upon regeneration. The covenant of grace is *ordered in all things,* and is full of all spiritual blessings; and a grant of all the blessings of grace was made to Christ, and to the elect in him, before the world began, and they were secretly blessed with them in him as early; but then till the Spirit of God is sent down into their hearts in regeneration, to make known unto them the things which God has freely given them, they are strangers to them, and have no knowledge of them, cannot claim their interest in them, nor are they actually possessed of them. They are loved of God with an everlasting love; but then the first open display of it to them is in regeneration, when God draws them with loving kindness to himself, as a fruit and effect, and so an evidence of his ancient love to them. They are chosen in Christ before the foundation of the world; but this is not known by them till the gospel comes, not in word only, but in power, and in the Holy Ghost; working powerfully in them, regenerating, quickening, and sanctifying them; when that holiness to which they are chosen, is implanted, and that image of Christ, to which they are predestinated, is enstamped:

there is an union with Christ, which election in him gives; and there is a legal union between him and the elect, as between a surety and debtor, in virtue of suretiship engagements for them; and there is a mystical union, as between head and members; and a conjugal one, as between man and wife: but before regeneration there is no vital union, or such an union as between vine and branches, by which they actually receive life, and grace, and nourishment, and bear, and bring forth fruit. They are the sons of God by predestination; and in covenant, the adoption of children belongs unto them; but this does not appear till regeneration takes place, when they receive in person the power and privilege of it, and are manifestly the sons of God by faith in Christ. Justification was a sentence conceived in the mind of God from eternity; was pronounced on Christ, and his people in him, when he rose from the dead; but is not known to those interested in it, till the Spirit of God reveals the righteousness of Christ from faith to faith, and pronounces upon it the sentence of justification in the conscience of the believer; until he is born again, he has no knowledge of this blessing, no comfortable perception of it; nor can he claim his interest in it, nor have that peace and joy which flow from it. And now it is that an awakened sinner has the application of pardoning grace and mercy; for though pardon of sin is provided in covenant, and the blood of Christ is shed for it, and he is exalted to give it; yet it is not actually given, applied, and enjoyed, until repentance is given also; for they are both in Christ's gift together; and when also it is that God blesses his people with peace, with peace of conscience, flowing from the blood, righteousness, and sacrifice of Christ.——3. Another effect of regeneration is, a fitness and capacity for the performance of good works. In regeneration, men are *created in Christ Jesus unto good works;* and by their new creation, become fit for, and capable of, performing them; the new man is formed in them *unto righteousness and true holiness,* to the acts and exercises of righteousness and holiness, Eph. ii. 10. and iv. 24. such who are born again, are *sanctified and meet for the Master's use, and prepared unto every good work,* 2 Tim. ii. 21. whereas, an unregenerate man is *to every good work reprobate;* he has neither will nor power to perform that which is good, till God *works in him both to will and to do.* The principal ingredients in good works are wanting in them, wherefore they cannot be acceptable to God; and, indeed, *without faith,* as these are without it, *it is impossible to please God;* nor can they that are *in the flesh,* who are carnal and unregenerate, *please God;* that is, do those things which are pleasing to him, Heb. xi. 6. Rom viii. 8. without the Spirit of God, and the grace and strength of Christ, nothing of this kind can be performed; wherefore God has promised to put his *Spirit* in his people, which he does in regeneration, to *cause them to walk in his statutes, and to keep his judgments, and do them*: so though they can do nothing of themselves, yet, through the Spirit, grace, and strength of Christ, they can do all things, Ezek. xxxvi. 27. Phil. iv. 13. to which they must be referred; even a very heathen could say, "Whatever good thing thou dost, ascribe it to God."[1]——4. Regeneration gives a meetness for the kingdom of God; without this, no man can see, nor enter into it, John iii. 3, 5. whether, by *the kingdom of God* is meant, a gospel-church-state, and a participation of the privileges and ordinances of it, or the ultimate state of glory and happiness: the former may be meant, into which publicans and harlots went before the Pharisees; and which they would neither enter into themselves, nor suffer others to go in who were entering; and a removal of which from them, Christ threatens them with, Matt. xxiii. 13. and xxi. 31, 43. Unregenerate men may indeed, in a sense, see and enter into this kingdom of God; they may attend the word, and embrace the truths of it, make a profession of faith, submit to gospel ordinances, and become members of a gospel church; this they may do in fact, but not of right; they are such as do not come in at the right door, Christ, and true faith in him; but climb up another way, and are thieves and robbers; hypocrites in Zion, tares in Christ's field, and foolish virgins among the wise; to whom the kingdom of God is compared. Unregenerate men have not the proper qualifications for the church of God, and the ordinances of it; these particularly, are faith and repentance; these are required to a person's admission to baptism, Matt. iii. 2, 8. Acts ii. 38. and viii. 12, 37. and so to

---

[1] τι αν αγαθον πραττης εις θεους ανατεμπε, Bias apud Laert. 1. 1. in vita ejus.

the ordinance of the Lord's Supper; *Let a man examine himself, and so let him eat*, 1 Cor. xi. 28. whether he has true repentance towards God, and faith in our Lord Jesus Christ; and if such a man, devoid of these, which attend or flow from regeneration, gets admitted to these ordinances, and into a church state, of what avail is it to him here or hereafter? what does it signify now to have the form of godliness, without the power? a name to live, and yet be dead? or hereafter; for *what is the hope of the hypocrite?* of what use is it to him? *though he hath gained* the name of a professor, of a religious man, and a place in the house of God, *when God takes away his soul*, these will be of no service to him? Though it may be the ultimate state of glory may be meant by the kingdom of God, in the above passages; as in 1 Cor. vi. 9. Luke xii. 32. Matt. xxv. 34. An unregenerate man has no apparent right unto it; nor meetness for it. The proper right unto it lies in adoption; *If children, then heirs*. But this right, so founded, does not appear till a man is born again, which is the evidence of adoption; nor can he be meet and fit for it, without this grace of God regenerating, quickening, and sanctifying; for without holiness no man shall see the Lord; and nothing shall enter into the heavenly state that defiles or makes an abomination; but when men are born again, they are heirs apparent to the heavenly inheritance; they are rich in faith, and heirs of a kingdom; and are meet to be partakers of the inheritance with the saints in light.

V. The properties of regeneration; and which may serve to throw more light on the nature of it.——1. Regeneration is a passive work, or rather, men are passive in it; as they must needs be, in the first infusion and implantation of grace, and the quickening of them; even as passive as the first matter created was, out of which all things were made; and as a dead man, when raised from the dead is; or as the dry bones in Ezekiel's vision were, while the Spirit of God breathed upon them, and then they became active; and as infants are in the natural generation of them; for men no more contribute to their spiritual birth, than infants do to their natural birth; all this appears from regeneration being a creation, a resurrection from the dead, and a being begotten and born again.——2. It is an irresistible act of God's grace; no more resistance can be made unto it, than there could be in the first matter to its creation; or in a dead man to his resurrection; or in an infant to its generation. Regeneration is of the will of God, which cannot be resisted; the Spirit, in regeneration, is like *the wind*, which *bloweth where it listeth*, and none can hinder it; *so is every one that is born of the Spirit*, John iii. 8. it is done by the power of God, which is uncontrollable; whatever aversion, contrariety, and opposition there may be in the corrupt nature of men unto it, that is soon and easily overcome by the power of divine grace; when the stony heart is taken away, and an heart of flesh is given. When God works, nothing can let; an unwilling people are made willing in the day of his power; high thoughts, reasonings, and imaginations of the carnal mind, are cast down by him.——3. It is an act that is instantaneously done, at once; it is not like sanctification it gives rise to; which is but a begun work, and is carried on gradually; faith grows, hope and love abound more and more, and spiritual light and knowledge increase by degrees, till they come to the perfect day: but regeneration is at once; as an infant in nature is generated at once, and is also born at once, and not by degrees; so it is in spiritual generation; one man cannot be said to be more regenerated than another, though he may be more sanctified; and the same man cannot be said to be more regenerated at one time than at another.——4. As it is done at once, so it is perfect; some persons speak of a regenerate and an unregenerate part in men; and that they are partly regenerate and partly unregenerate. I must confess I do not understand this; since regeneration is a new creature, and perfect in its kind. There are, indeed, two principles in a man that is born again; a principle of corrupt nature, and a principle of grace; the one is called the old man, and the other the new: the whole old man is unregenerate, no part in him is regenerated; he remains untouched, and is just the same he was, only deprived of his power and dominion; and the new man is wholly regenerate, no unregenerate part in him; there is no sin in him, nor done by him, he cannot commit sin; *the king's daughter is all glorious within*: a man-child, as soon as born, having all its limbs, is a perfect man, as to parts, though these are not at their full growth and bigness, as they will be, if it lives: so the new man is a perfect man at once, as to parts, though as yet not arrived to the measure of the stature of the fulness of Christ.––––5. The grace of regeneration can never be lost; once regenerated, and always so; one that is born in a spiritual sense, can never be unborn again; for he cannot die a spiritual death; he is born of incorruptible and immortal seed; he is born of water and of the Spirit, or of the grace of the Spirit, which is as a well of living water in him, springing up unto everlasting life: and all such who are begotten again unto a lively hope of a glorious inheritance, are kept by the power of God, through faith unto salvation, 1 Pet. i. 3, 4, 5, 23. To which may be added, ––––6. An adjunct which always accompanies regeneration, a spiritual warfare between the old and the new man, the principle of sin, and the principle of grace; the flesh lusting against the spirit, and the spirit against the flesh; the law in the members warring against the law of the mind; which are, as it were, a company of two armies engaged in war with each other, which always issues in a victory on the side of the new creature; for *whatsoever is born of God overcometh the world*, and sin and Satan, and every enemy, and is more than a conqueror over all, through Christ.

CHAP. XII.

OF EFFECTUAL CALLING.

Though effectual calling may be distinguished from regeneration, taken more strictly, for the first infusion and implantation of grace in the heart; yet it is closely connected with it, and the consideration of it naturally follows upon it. It is, with great propriety, said to be *effectual* calling, to distinguish it from another calling, which is not effectual; at least, which is not attended with any salutary effect to the persons called with it; of which more hereafter. Concerning effectual calling, the following things may be observed.

I. What it is, and the nature of it. It is not of a civil kind, of which there are various sorts; as a call to an office in state; so Saul and David were chosen and called to take upon them the government of the people of Israel: likewise a call to do some particular service, which God has appointed men to do; so Bezaleel was called and qualified to devise and do some curious work for the tabernacle, and to teach and direct others in it: so the Medes and Persians were sanctified, or set apart by the Lord, and called by him to the destruction of Babylon; and Cyrus was raised up, and called from a far country, to let the captive Jews go free. Indeed, every ordinary occupation, employment, and business of life, men are brought up in, and exercise, is a calling, and a calling of God; hence the apostle says, *Let every man abide in the same calling wherein he is called*, 1 Cor. vii. 20, 24. But the calling now to be treated of is of a religious kind; and of which also there are various sorts; as a call to an ecclesiastical office, whether extraordinary or ordinary; so Aaron and his sons were called to officiate in the priesthood; for *no man taketh this honour to himself, but he that is called of God, as was Aaron*, Heb. v. 4. so the twelve disciples of Christ were called to apostleship; and Paul, *a servant of Christ*, is said to be *called to be an apostle*, Rom. i. 1. and ordinary ministers of the word, are set apart and called by the Lord, and by his churches, to the work of the ministry they are put into. There is likewise an universal call of all men, to serve and worship the one true and living God; this call is made by the light of nature, displayed in the works of creation, which demonstrate the Being of God; and by the law of nature, written on the hearts of all men; and by the works of providence, and the bounties of it, which all have a share in, and in which God leaves not himself without a witness; and by all which men are called upon, and directed to seek after God, to worship him, and glorify him as God. And besides this, there is a more special and particular call of men, and not so general, and is either external or internal; the *external* call is by the ministry of the word; by the ministry of the prophets under the Old Testament; and of John the Baptist, the forerunner of Christ, and of Christ himself in human nature, and of his apostles under the New; and of all succeeding ministers in all ages. The *internal* call is by the Spirit and grace of God to the hearts and consciences of men; these two sometimes go together, but not always; some are externally called, and not internally called; and of those that are internally called, some are called by and through the ministry of the word, and some without it; though, for the most part, men are called by it; and because it is usually so, and this external call is a matter of moment and importance, it is necessary to be a little more large and explicit upon it. And,

First, This may be considered either as a call to saints, to such who have a work of grace already begun in them; and to such it is a call, not only to the means of grace, but to partake of the blessings of grace; to come as thirsty persons, eagerly desirous of spiritual things, *to the waters*, the ordinances, and drink at them; to *buy wine and milk*, spiritual blessings, signified hereby, without *money, and without price*, these being to be had freely: and these are also called as labouring under a sense of sin, and under a spirit of bondage, to *come* to Christ for *rest*, peace, pardon, life, and salvation, Isa. lv. 1. Matt. xi. 28. and these in and by the ministry of the word, are called, excited, and encouraged to the exercise of evangelical graces, wrought in them, and bestowed upon them; as repentance, faith, hope, love, and every other; such were the three thousand converts under Peter's sermon, and the jailor, who were under a previous work of the Spirit of God, when they were called and encouraged to repent and believe in Christ, Acts ii. 37, 38. and xvi. 29, 30, 31. and these are also called, and urged, and pressed, in and by the ministry of the word, to a constant attendance on ordinances, and not to forsake the assembly of the saints, and to a diligent performance of every religious duty, and to be ready to every good work in general: or this external call may be considered, as a call of sinners in a state of nature and unregeneracy; but then it is not a call to them to regenerate and convert themselves, of which there is no instance; and which is the pure work of the Spirit of God: nor to make their peace with God, which they cannot make by any thing they can do; and which is only made by the blood of Christ: nor to get an interest in Christ, which is not got, but given: nor to the exercise of evangelical grace, which they have not, and therefore can never exercise: nor to any spiritual vital acts, which they are incapable of, being natural men, and dead in trespasses and sins. Nor is the gospel-ministry an offer of Christ, and of his grace and salvation by him, which are not in the power of the ministers of it to give, nor of carnal men to receive; the gospel is not an offer, but a preaching of Christ crucified, a proclamation of the unsearchable riches of his grace, of peace, pardon, righteousness, and life, and salvation by him. Yet there is something in which the ministry of the word, and the call by it, have to do with unregenerate sinners: they may be, and should be called upon, to perform the natural duties of religion; to a natural faith, to give credit to divine revelation, to believe the external report of the gospel, which not to do, is the sin of the deists; to repent of sin committed, which even the light of nature dictates; and God, in his word, commands all men every where to repent; to pray to God for forgiveness, as Simon Magus was directed by the apostle; and to pray to God for daily mercies that are needed, is a natural and moral duty; as well as to give him praise, and return thanks for mercies received, which all men that have breath are under obligation to do. They may, and should be called upon to attend the outward means of grace, and to make use of them; to read the holy scriptures, which have been the means of the conversion of some; to hear the word, and wait on the ministry of it, which may be blessed unto them, for the effectual calling of them. And it is a part of the ministry of the word to lay before men their fallen, miserable, lost, and undone estate by nature; to open to them the nature of sin, its pollution and guilt, and the sad consequences of it; to inform them of their incapacity to make atonement for it; and of their impotence and inability to do what is spiritually good; and of the insufficiency of their own righteousness to justify them in the sight of God: and they are to be made acquainted, that salvation is alone by Christ, and not otherways; and the fulness, freeness, and suitableness of this salvation, are to be preached before them; and the whole to be left to the Spirit of God, to make application of it as he shall think fit.

Secondly, This external call by the ministry is not universal, nor ever was: under the former dispensation, God sent his word unto Jacob and his statutes unto Israel; as for other nations, they knew them not; God overlooked the heathens in their times of ignorance for hundreds of years together, and sent no prophet nor minister unto them, to acquaint them with his mind and will, and lead them into the knowledge of divine things. When the gospel dispensation took place, the apostles of Christ were forbid, by their first commission, to go to the Gentiles, or to any of the cities of the Samaritans; and though, upon Christ's resurrection from the dead, their commission was enlarged, and they were sent to preach to all nations of the world; yet before they could reach to the extent of their commission, multitudes must be dead, to whom the gospel call, or the sound of it, never reached. To say nothing of the new world, or America, supposed not then to be discovered; in succeeding ages, many parts of the world have been without the preaching of the word, and are at this day; and, indeed, it is confined to a very small part of it; and where it is, though many may be externally called by it, yet few are chosen, and internally called by the Spirit and grace of God: and as this call is of many who are not chosen, so of many who are not sanctified, or that are not called with an holy calling; and so of many who are not saved; for it is to some the savour of death unto death.

Thirdly, The external call is frequently rejected, and for the most part, and by the greater number of those that hear it; *I have called, and ye have refused; I have spread out my hands all the day unto a rebellious people;* and to these it must be useless, as to any salutary effects; many that are called and invited to attend the gospel ministry refuse to come; such were they that were bidden and called to the marriage feast; but they made light of it, and some went to their farms, and others to their merchandise; such were the Scribes and Pharisees, who would neither go into the kingdom of heaven themselves, nor suffer others that were entering to go in, but shut it up against them; that is, would neither attend the ministry of Christ and his apostles themselves, nor suffer others, but discouraged them from it, by their reproaches, threats, and persecutions, as our Lord complains, Matt. xxiii. 13, 37. Others that attend the ministry of the word, do it in a careless and negligent manner, not minding what they hear, but like leaking vessels, let it slip, or run out; or stop their ears to the voice of the charmer, charming ever so wisely; many that hear have an aversion to what they hear; the gospel is an hard saying to them, foolishness to some, and a stumbling-block to others; some mock and scoff at it, as the Athenians did; and others, as the Jews, contradict and blaspheme it, putting it away from them, judging themselves unworthy of eternal life; and therefore it is no wonder it becomes of no saving effect to either of these sort of persons: and, indeed, it is always insufficient and ineffectual of itself unto real conversion, without the powerful and efficacious grace of God; when God goes forth with his ministers, working with them, then work is done, but not otherwise; when the hand of the Lord is upon them, or his power attends their ministry, many believe and turn to the Lord; but unless his arm is revealed, the report of the gospel will not be believed, nor the call of it be attended to. Yet,

Fourthly, The external ministry of the word, or the outward call by it, is not in vain; it has its usefulness, and various ends are answered by it. All things are for the elect's sake, and particularly the ministration of the gospel, which to them is the savour of life unto life; as it is the will of God that his chosen people, and others, should promiscuously dwell together, so he sends his gospel to them in general, and by it takes out a people for his name; calls them by his grace effectually, out of the world, and separates them from the men of it, to be a peculiar people to himself; and the rest are thereby left inexcusable; for if the light of nature leaves men so, much more the light of the gospel; the condemnation of men is aggravated by it; inasmuch, as though they are surrounded with light, they love darkness rather than light. Moreover, by the external ministry of the word, many, though not effectually called, become more civilized and more moral in their conversation; are reformed, as to their outward manners; and through a speculative knowledge of the gospel, escape the grosser pollutions of the world: and others are brought by it to a temporary faith, to believe for awhile, to embrace the gospel notionally, to submit to the ordinances of it, make a profession of religion, by which means they become serviceable to support the interest of it. So that it comports with the wisdom of God that there should be such an outward call of many who are not internally called: nor is he to be charged for it with dissimulation and insincerity; since by it he declares what is his good, perfect, and acceptable will, and what would be grateful and well-pleasing to him was it complied with and done. Should it be said, that that is called for and required which man has not power to perform; be it so, which yet may be questioned, it should be observed, that though man by sin has lost his power to comply with the will of God by an obedience to it; God has not lost his power, right, and authority to command. Wherefore, when the ministry of the word is slighted, and the gospel call rejected, it is most righteously resented by the Lord; see Prov. i. 24—28. and such are justly punished with everlasting destruction by him, 1 Pet. iv. 17. 2 Thess. i. 8, 9.

The *internal* call is next to be considered, which is sometimes immediately, and without the ministry of the word; as seems to be the case of the disciples of Christ, of the apostle Paul, and of Zaccheus, and others: and sometimes mediately by the word; for faith comes by hearing, and hearing by the word; so the three thousand under Peter's sermon, and those in the family of Cornelius, on whom the holy Spirit fell while the apostle was preaching; and this is the ordinary way in which God calls men by his grace; and which call is, ——1. Out of great and gross darkness, into marvellous and surprising light, 1 Pet. ii. 9. God's elect, whilst in a state of nature, are in a state of darkness and ignorance; they are in the dark about God, his perfections, purposes, counsels, and methods of grace; about themselves, the state and condition they are in; about sin, the nature of it, and its sad consequences; about the Person of Christ, his offices, and the way of salvation by him; about the Spirit, his work and operations on the souls of men; and about the scriptures, and the doctrines of the gospel contained in them: but in effectual calling, the eyes of their understandings are opened and enlightened, and they are made light in the Lord. When the apostle Paul was called by grace, a light surrounded him, as an emblem of that internal light which was sprung in him; and after that there fell from his eyes, as it had been scales, as a token of the removal of his former darkness and ignorance: as God, in the first creation, commanded light to shine out of darkness; so in the new creation, and at effectual calling, he irradiates the minds of his called ones with a divine light, in which they see light; see what sin is, what an evil thing it is, and the exceeding sinfulness of it; see themselves lost and undone by it, and just ready to perish; see their incapacity to save themselves, and the insufficiency of their own righteousness to justify them before God; see the glory, fulness, and grace of Christ, the completeness and suitableness of him as a Saviour; and see the truths and promises of the gospel, the great doctrines of it, in another light than they did before; so as to understand them, receive the love of them, believe them with the heart, and distinguish them from those that differ, and rejoice at them, as bringing good-news and glad-tidings of good things. ——2. The internal call, is a call of men out of bondage, out of worse than Egyptian bondage, into liberty, even the glorious liberty of the children of God; *Brethren, ye have been called unto liberty*, Gal. v. 13. whilst in a state of nature, they are, as they were by nature, home-born slaves, slaves to their sinful lusts and pleasures, and are brought into bondage by them, and held under the power of them, as in a prison; but in effectual vocation, the fetters and shackles of sin are broken off, and the prison-doors opened, and they are bid to go forth and shew themselves; they become free from the tyranny of sin, and sin has no more dominion over them: in their state before calling, they are under the power and influence of Satan, the strong man armed, who keeps possession of them, by whom they are kept in bondage, and led captive by him at his will; but when effectually called, they are taken out of his hands, and are turned from the power of Satan unto God, and are delivered from the power of darkness, and are translated into the kingdom of God's dear Son, where they are Christ's free-men. Whilst they are seeking righteousness and life by the works of the law, they are brought into bondage, for that genders to bondage, and brings on a spirit of bondage upon those that are under it; but in effectual calling they are delivered from it, by the Spirit of God, as a free Spirit; and are called to stand fast in the liberty with which Christ has made them free, and not be entangled again with the yoke of bondage; they are called and allowed to make use of a liberty of access to God, through Christ, by one Spirit, and to enjoy all the privileges of the gospel, and the immunities of a gospel church-state, being fellow-citizens with the saints, and of the household of God.—— 3. The internal call, is a call of persons from fellowship with the men of the world, to fellowship with Christ; *God is faithful, by whom ye were called unto the fellowship of Christ Jesus our Lord*, 1 Cor. i. 9. it is like that of the call of Christ to his church, Cant. iv. 8. *Come with me from Lebanon, &c.* a call to forsake the vanities, pleasures, and profits of the world, and the company of the men of it, and go along with him, and enjoy communion with him: as Abraham was called out of his country, from his kindred, and his father's house; so saints are called to forsake their own people, and their father's house; to relinquish the society of their former companions, and to have no fellowship with ungodly men: not that they are to have no civil correspondence, commerce, and society with the men of the world; for then, as the apostle says, they must needs go out of it; but not to join with them in superstitious worship, in acts of idolatry, in a false religion, and in the observance of the commandments of men; nor in any sinful, profane, and immoral practices; and as much as may be, should shun and avoid all unnecessary company, and conversation with them; for evil communications corrupt good manners; and it is a grief to the people of God, to be obliged to dwell among them, and with them, as it was to Lot, to Isaac and Rebekah, to David, Isaiah, and others: the people of God, in effectual vocation, are called to better company, to communion with God, Father, Son, and Spirit; to fellowship with one another; to converse with saints, the excellent in the earth, in whom is all their delight.———4. Such as are effectually called by the Spirit and grace of God, are called to peace; *God hath called us to peace*, 1 Cor. vii. 15. to internal peace, to peace of mind and conscience; which men, in a state of nature, are strangers to; for *there is no peace to the wicked:* but God calls his people to it, and blesses them with it; with a peace which passes all understanding; with peace in the midst of the tribulations of the world; with a peace which the world can neither give nor take away; and which arises from the blood and righteousness of Christ, and is part of that kingdom of God which is within them, into which they are brought at effectual vocation. They are likewise called to peace among themselves, and with all men as much as possible; *Let the peace of God rule in your hearts, to the which also ye are called in one body*, Col. iii. 15.———5. They are called out of a state of unholiness and sinfulness, into a state of holiness and righteousness; for being created anew in righteousness and true holiness, and created in Christ Jesus to good works, they are called to the exercise of them; to live holily, soberly, righteously, and godly, in this present evil world; *God hath not called us unto uncleanness, but unto holiness*, 1 Thess. iv. 7. and *hath called us to glory and virtue*, 2 Pet. i. 3. to glorious acts of virtue and goodness, becoming the nature of their call, and of him that has called them; *As he which hath called you is holy, &c.* 1 Pet. i. 15. ———6. The internal call is a call of persons *into the grace of Christ*, Gal. i. 6. into the gospel of the grace of Christ, as appears by what follows, to receive it, embrace it, profess it, and stand fast in it; and into the fulness of grace in Christ, to receive out of it, to be strong in it, to exercise faith on it; and to the blessings of grace in his hands, and which are given forth by him; to lay hold upon them, take them to themselves, and claim their interest in them; all being theirs, they being Christ's, his chosen, redeemed, and called ones; and by whom they have access into the state of grace in which they stand.———7. It is a call of them to a state of happiness and bliss in another world; *Who hath called you unto his kingdom and glory*, 1 Thess. ii. 12. to a glory, which is a kingdom; to possess a kingdom of grace now, which cannot be removed; and to inherit the kingdom of glory hereafter, which is an everlasting one; to a glory which is given to Christ; *To the obtaining of the glory of the Lord Jesus Christ*, 2 Thess. ii. 14. see John xvii. 22. Col. iii. 4. and to *eternal glory by Christ Jesus*, 1 Pet. v. 10. and to *lay hold on eternal life*, 1 Tim. vi. 12. and to an eternal inheritance; and *they which are called, receive the promise of it*, and shall certainly enjoy it; having a meetness for it, through the grace of God, and a right unto it, through the righteousness of Christ, 1 Pet. i. 3, 4. Heb. ix. 15. and they are all *called in one hope of their calling*, Eph. iv. 4. to partake of the same inheritance with the saints in light; and to enjoy the same blessed hope laid up for them in heaven; and for which hope of righteousness they wait by faith, through the holy Spirit.

II. The author and causes of effectual calling, efficient, impulsive, instrumental, and final.———1. The efficient cause is God; *Walk worthy of God, who hath called you; God hath not called us unto uncleanness, but unto holiness*, 1 Thess. ii. 12. and iv. 7. see 2 Tim. i. 8, 9. Sometimes it is ascribed to God personally, to the three divine Persons in the Godhead, to Father, Son, and Spirit; to the Father, when he is said to call by his grace, and reveal his Son; and to call unto the fellowship of his Son; and to call men by Jesus Christ, Gal. i. 15, 16. 1 Cor. i. 9. 1 Pet. v. 10. in which places, God that calls, is distinguished from his Son Jesus Christ. Sometimes calling is ascribed to the Son; so Wisdom, the eternal Logos, Word, and Son of God, is represented as calling both externally and internally, Prov. i. 20. &c. and viii. 1—4. and saints are said to be *the called of Jesus Christ*, whom he has a property in, as called ones, being efficiently called by him. And sometimes it is ascribed to the holy Spirit; *There is one body and one Spirit, even as ye are called in one hope of your calling;* that is, by the one Spirit, the holy Spirit of God; and to him are owing that illumination, and that freedom from bondage, and that fellowship with Christ, which make a principal part of what men in effectual vocation are called into; and it is he that leads to peace and holiness, and into the grace of Christ, and encourages to hope and wait for glory: so that effectual calling is a divine work, and not human.——2. The impulsive, or moving cause of effectual calling, are not the works of men, but the sovereign will, pleasure, purpose, and grace of God; as in 2 Tim. i. 9.——(1.) The works of men are not the moving or impulsive cause of their being called of God; for those must be either such as are done before calling, or after it: not before calling; for works done then are not properly good works; they are not subjectively good; the doers of them are not good men; and a man must be a good man, before he can perform good works; and though some works done by bad men, may have the shew and appearance of good, and be materially, or as to the matter of them, good actions; yet are not such circumstantially: the requisites and circumstances of a good work, being wanting in them; as not being done according to the will of God, and in obedience to it; nor in faith, and so sin; nor proceeding from a principle of love to God, nor directed to his glory: and such works can never be moving causes of men's being called. Nor can good works after calling be such; for they are fruits and effects of effectual vocation; and therefore cannot be ranked among the causes of it. Men, in and by effectual calling, are sanctified, and become meet for their Master's use, and ready to every good work.——(2.) The sovereign will, pleasure, and purpose of God, is what moves and determines him to call, by his grace, any of the sons of men: not their wills; for *it is not of him that willeth*, but of his own good will and pleasure; they that are called, are *called according to his purpose*, Rom. viii. 28. he has, in his eternal purpose, fixed upon the particular persons whom he will call, and the time when he will call them; for there is a time for every purpose, and so for this, called the time of life and of love; and the place where they shall be called; in this and that place; as at Corinth, Philippi, &c. the means and occasion of their calling, with the several circumstances thereof, are all according to a divine purpose; and shew that the whole is owing to the sovereign will and pleasure of God, who does all things after the counsel of his own will.——(3.) The free grace of God, in a sovereign, distinguishing way and manner, may truly be said to be the grand, impulsive, moving cause of effectual vocation; to this the apostle ascribed his own; *And called me by his grace:* that is, of his pure grace, and according to it. God, as the God of all grace, calls men to grace and glory by Christ; and an abundance of grace is displayed in vocation; yea, the first open display of grace, and discovery of love, to a sinner himself, is then made; then is he drawn with loving kindness, as a fruit and evidence of everlasting love; and therefore the time of calling, is called a time of love, Jer. xxxi. 3. Ezek. xvi. 8. and it being of some particular persons, and not of all, shews it to be the effect of distinguishing grace, and of sovereign good-will; and, indeed, nothing out of God could move him to such an act as this; and as his grace is his own, he may call by it, and to it, and bestow it on whom he pleases.——3. The instrumental cause, or rather means of effectual vocation, is the ministry of the word. Sometimes, indeed, it is brought about by some remarkable providence, and without the word; but generally it is by it; *Faith comes by hearing, and hearing by the word of God.* Christ stands in the gospel-ministry, at the door of men's hearts, and knocks and calls; and having the key of the house of David, he opens the heart by his power and grace, and lets himself in; and in this way, and by this means, the Spirit, and his graces, are received; men are called both to grace and glory by the gospel, Gal. i. 6. 2 Thess. ii. 14.——4. The final causes, or rather the ends of effectual vocation, which are subordinate and ultimate: the subordinate end, is the salvation of God's elect, that they may possess the blessings of grace, and eternal glory; to both which they are called. And the ultimate end is the glory of the grace of God; for this end God forms his people in regeneration and effectual vocation; namely, to shew forth his praise: and this end is answered, in part, in this life, they ascribing all they have, and expect to have, solely to the free grace of God; and it will be consummately answered in the world to come, when all their work will be praise; attributing the whole of their salvation to the sovereign will and pleasure, grace and goodness, of God.

III. The subjects of effectual vocation, or who they are whom God calls by his grace.———1. They are such whom God has chosen to grace and glory; *Whom he did predestinate, them he also called*, Rom. viii. 30. Election and vocation are of equal extent; the objects are the same, neither more nor fewer; they that were chosen from eternity, are called in time; and they that are called in time, were chosen in Christ before the foundation of the world; the *vessels of mercy afore prepared unto glory*, are explained and described by such *whom God hath called; not of the Jews only, but also of the Gentiles*, Rom. ix. 23, 24. ———2. They are such who are in Christ, and secured in him; for they are *called according to grace given them in Christ Jesus before the world began;* and as grace was given them in him so early, they themselves, in some sense, must then have a being in him; which they have, through being chosen in him, and thereby coming into his hands, they are secured and preserved in him, in consequence of which they are called by grace; thus stands the order of things, as put by the apostle Jude, ver. 1. *To them that are sanctified by God the Father;* that is, set apart by him in eternal election; *and preserved in Christ Jesus*, being put into his hands by that act of grace; *and called in virtue of the foregoing acts of grace.*——— 3. They are such who are redeemed by Christ; vocation, follows redemption, and is the certain consequent of it; *I have redeemed thee; I have called thee by thy name; thou art mine*, Isa. xliii. 1. Election, redemption, and vocation, are of the same persons; those whom God has chosen in Christ, are redeemed by Christ; and those who are chosen and redeemed, are, sooner or later, called; and the reason of their being called, is because they are redeemed; *I will hiss for them, and gather them; for I have redeemed them*, Zech. x. 8.———4. Those that are called, are, for the most part either the meanest, or the vilest, among men; the meanest, as to their outward circumstances; *Not many mighty, not many noble are called;* and the meanest, as to their internal capacities; *Not many wise men after the flesh;* the things of the gospel, and of the grace of God, are *hid from the wise and prudent, and revealed to babes,* 1 Cor. i. 26. James ii. 5. Matt. xi. 25. and oftentimes some of the worst and vilest of sinners are called by grace; publicans and harlots went into the kingdom of God, when scribes and pharisees did not; attended the ministry of the word, and were called by it, when they were not; and Christ came, as he himself says, *not to call the righteous, but sinners to repentance*, Matt. xxi. 31, 32. and ix. 13. see 1 Cor. vi. 11.

IV. The properties of effectual calling; which may lead more clearly and fully into the nature of it; though they may be, in general, collected from what has been observed.———1. It is a fruit of the love of God; because he has loved them with an everlasting love, therefore *with loving kindness he draws* them to himself, and to his Son, in effectual vocation, Jer. xxxi. 3. and as it is only of as many as the Lord our God thinks fit to call, it appears to be an act of special and distinguishing grace; it is of special and particular persons, by special grace, and to the special blessings of it.———2. It is an act of efficacious and irresistable grace. The external call may be, and often is, resisted and rejected; but when God calls internally by his Spirit and grace, it is always effectual, and can never be resisted, so as to be ineffectual; for when God works, none can let or hinder; men dead in trespasses and sins, rise out of their graves of sin, and live, at his all-commanding voice; even as Lazarus came forth out of his grave at the call of Christ; nor could that call be resisted; and even the same power that was exerted in raising Christ himself from the dead, is displayed in the effectual vocation of a sinner, Eph. i. 18, 19, 20.———3. This call is an *holy calling*, 2 Tim. i. 9. the author of it is the holy God; holy in his nature, and in all his ways and works, and in this; *As he that has called you is holy*, 1 Pet. i. 15. and the means by which they are called are holy; whether by reading the scriptures, which has been sometimes the case, they are styled the *holy scriptures;* or whether the first awakenings to a serious concern about divine things, are by the law; that *commandment is holy, just, and good;* or whether by the pure gospel of Christ; that is a *doctrine according to godliness*, and teaches to live an holy life and conversation: and as in effectual vocation, it appears that principles of grace and holiness are wrought in men; so by it they are called to the exercise of holiness and virtue, and of the performance of every good work; they are called into a state of holiness here, and to enjoy an incorruptible and undefiled inheritance hereafter, Rom. i. 7. 1 Thess. iv. 7. 2 Pet. i. 3.——4. It is an high calling, Phil. iii. 14. he that calls is the high and lofty One, who dwells in the high and holy place; and in and by calling grace, he raises men from the dunghill, and sets them among princes, that they may inherit the throne of glory; however poor they may be with respect to the things of this world, yet by effectual calling they become rich in faith, and heirs of a kingdom, and of an inheritance reserved for them in the highest heavens, to which they will be admitted. Wherefore,——5. This call is styled an *heavenly calling*, Heb. iii. 1. it is a call out of this earthly country, to seek a better country, even an heavenly one; and those that are called have their citizenship in heaven, and are free denisons of it; and shall enjoy the hope, the hoped for blessedness laid up for them there. For,—— 6. This is one of the gifts of God's special grace, and that *calling* of his, which is without *repentance*, Rom. xi. 29. it is unchangeable, irreversible, and irrevocable; such shall be preserved safe to the kingdom and glory of God, to which they are called, and shall most certainly enjoy it; for *faithful is he that has called them, who also will do it*, 1 Thess. v. 23, 24. wherefore such are most happy persons; for they may be comfortably assured of their election; for *whom he did predestinate, them he also called*: election and vocation are put together; the one as the fruit, effect, and evidence, of the other, 2 Pet. i. 10. and election is to be known by the internal call of the Spirit, through the ministry of the word, 1 Thess. i. 4, 5. and they may also be comfortably assured of their justification; for *whom he called, them he also justified;* and such may conclude themselves safe from all charges, from all condemnation, and from wrath to come: and they may most certainly expect eternal glory; for whom God calls and justifies, *them he also glorifies:* between calling-grace and eternal happiness, there is a sure and an inseparable connection.

CHAP. XIII.

OF CONVERSION.

CONVERSION, though it may seem, in some respects, to fall in with regeneration and effectual vocation, yet may be distinguished from them both. Regeneration is the sole act of God; conversion consists both of God's act upon men, in turning them, and of acts done by men under the influence of converting grace; they turn, being turned. Regeneration is the motion of God towards and upon the heart of a sinner; conversion is the motion of a sinner towards God, as one [1] expresses it. In regeneration men are wholly passive, as they also are in the first moment of conversion; but by it become active: it is therefore sometimes expressed passively; *ye are returned*, or converted, 1 Pet. ii. 25. and sometimes actively; *a great number believed, and turned to the Lord*, Acts xi. 21. and *when it*, the body of the people of the Jews, *shall turn to the Lord*, which has respect to their conversion in the latter day, 2 Cor. iii. 16. Effectual vocation is the *call* of men out of darkness to light; and conversion answers to that call, and is the actual *turning* of men from the one to the other; so that, with propriety, conversion may be considered as distinct from regeneration and effectual vocation. Concerning which may be observed,

First, What conversion is, and wherein it lies. The conversion to be treated of is not,——1. An external one, or what lies only in an outward reformation of life and manners, such as that of the Ninevites; for this may be where internal conversion is not, as in the Scribes and Pharisees; and is what persons may depart from, and return to their former course of life again; and where it is right and genuine, it is the fruit and effect of true conversion, but not that itself.——2. Nor is it a mere doctrinal one, or a conversion from false notions before imbibed, to a set of doctrines and truths which are according to the Scriptures; so men of old were converted from Judaism and Heathenism to Christianity: but not all that were so converted in a doctrinal sense, were true and real converts; some had the form of godliness without the power of it, had a name to live, and be called Christians, but were dead, and so

---

[1] Charnock.

not converted; thus the recovery of professors of religion from errors fallen into, to the acknowledgment of the truth, is called a conversion of them, James v. 19, 20.

―――3. Nor the restoration of the people of God from backslidings to which they are subject, when they are in a very affecting and importunate manner called upon to return to the Lord, Jer. iii. 12, 14, 22. Hos. xiv. 1―4. so Peter, when he fell through temptation, and denied his Lord, and was recovered from it by a look from Christ, it is called his conversion, Luke xxii. 32. But, 4. The conversion under consideration is a true, real, internal work of God upon the souls of men; there is a counterfeit of it, or there is that in some men who are not really converted, which is somewhat similar to that which is always found in those that are truly converted; as, a sense of sin, and an acknowledgment of it; an apprehension of the divine displeasure at it; great distress about it, a sorrow for it, humiliation on account of it, and an abstinence from it; and something that bears a resemblance to each of these may be found in unconverted persons; though their concern about sin is chiefly for the evil that comes by it, or like to come by it, and not for the evil that is in it; so in converted persons there is, sooner or later, light into the gospel and the doctrines of it; particularly the doctrine of salvation by Christ, which yield relief and comfort to them under a sense of sin, and encourage faith and hope in God; and there is something like this to be observed in some who are not truly converted, who are said to be *enlightened*, that is, in a notional and doctrinal way; and to *taste* the good word of God, though it is only in a superficial manner; and *to receive* it *with joy*, with a flash of natural affection, which lasts for a while; and to believe it with a temporary faith, historically, and become subject to the ordinances; but yet in all this there is no heart-work, whereas true genuine conversion lies,―――(1.) In the turn of the heart to God; of the thoughts of the heart, which are only evil, and that continually; and about evil things, not about God, and the things of God; *God is not in all their thoughts*, nor in any of the thoughts of wicked men; but when converted, their thoughts are about their state and condition by nature, about their souls, and the eternal welfare of them; and about God, and the methods of his grace in the salvation of men: it is a turn of the *desires* of the heart, which before were after vain, carnal, worldly, sinful lusts and pleasures; but now after God and communion with him, after Christ and salvation by him, after the Spirit and the things of the Spirit: it is a turn of the *affections* of the heart, which before were *inordinate*, and ran in a wrong channel; before they were fleshly, after the things of the world, the lust of the flesh, the lust of the eye, and the pride of life: but now they are checked, and turned towards God, their hearts being circumcised to love him; and whom they love with their whole hearts and souls, because he first loved them; though before, their carnal minds were enmity to him; and towards Christ, whom they now love affectionately, fervently, superlatively, and sincerely; and towards the saints, who are now the excellent in the earth, in whose conversation is all their delight, though before hateful to them; and towards the word, worship, and ordinances of God, which they take pleasure in attending on, though before a weariness to them. Conversion is a turn of the *mind* from carnal things to spiritual ones, and from earthly things to heavenly ones: yea it is a turn of the *will*, which before conversion is in a very bad state, is stubborn and inflexible, biassed to and bent upon that which is evil, and averse to all that is good; but in conversion, God *works in* men *both to will and to do of his good pleasure;* he gives them another will, or however a turn to their will, so that of an unwilling people, they are made a willing people in the day of his power on them; whereas they were unwilling to come to Christ for salvation, and take him alone to be their Saviour; *ye will not come unto me, that ye might have life,* says Christ, John v. 40. that is, ye have no will to come to me at all for life and salvation; they chose rather to go anywhere than to him for it; but now they are willing to be saved by him, and resolve to have no other Saviour but him; yea though he slay them they will trust in him, and say he shall be our salvation; and though before, they went about to establish their own righteousness, and did not and would not submit to the righteousness of Christ; now their stout hearts, which were far from righteousness, are brought down, and they become willing to be found in Christ, and in his righteousness only; and inasmuch as before, they would not have Christ to reign over them, and chose not to be subject to his laws and ordinances, now they are ready to acknowledge him as their king and governor, and turn their feet to his testimonies, and esteem his precepts concerning all things to be right.——(2.) Conversion lies in a man's being turned from darkness to light; the apostle says, he was sent by Christ to the Gentiles, as a minister of the gospel, *to turn them from darkness to light*, Acts xxvi. 18. that is, to be the instrument or means of their conversion, by preaching the gospel to them. In this, conversion may seem to coincide with effectual vocation; but it may be observed, that effectual vocation is a call to, but conversion is a turning of, men from darkness to light; God not only calls unto light, but turns them to light in every sense; to God who is light itself, and in whom is no darkness at all; to Christ, who is the light of the world; to the gospel, which is the great light that shines on men who sit in darkness; and to the light of grace, which is a shining light, that shines more and more unto the perfect day. ——(3.) Conversion lies in the turning of men *from the power of Satan unto God*, as in the above place, Acts xxvi. 18. Satan has great power over men in an unconverted state, his seat is in their hearts, which are the palace in which he rules; he works effectually with great power and energy in the children of disobedience, by stirring up their lusts and corruptions, suggesting evil things to their minds, and tempting them to them; he does all he can to keep them in their native blindness and ignorance, and to increase it, and to prevent them from hearing the gospel, and from its being beneficial to them, lest the light of it should shine into their minds; he captivates them, and leads them captive at his will; and they are willingly led by him, the lusts of their father they will do; but now in conversion they are turned from his power; he is dispossessed of them, and his armour taken from him in which he trusted; the prey is taken out of the hands of the mighty, and the lawful captive is delivered; men are translated from the power of darkness into the kingdom of God's dear Son; and though they are not freed from his temptations, yet they have grace sufficient given them to bear up under them, till it is the pleasure of God to save them from them, who will shortly bruise him under them; and as they are in conversion turned from him, they are turned to God; who before were without him, and alienated from the life of him, and strangers to him; but now they are turned to the knowledge of him, to love to him, to faith in him, and to communion with him.——(4.) Conversion lies in turning men from idols to serve the living God; not merely from idols of silver and gold, of wood and stone, as formerly, but from the idols of a man's own heart, his lusts and corruptions; with respect to which, the language of a converted sinner is, *What have I to do any more with idols?* this is a blessing bestowed in conversion, *Unto you first, God having raised up his Son Jesus, sent him to bless you, in turning away every one of you from his iniquities.* In redemption, Christ turns away iniquities from his people by bearing them and making satisfaction for them; and in conversion, he by his Spirit and grace turns them from their iniquities; he turns them from the love of them to an hatred of them, even of vain thoughts, as well as of sinful actions; from the service and drudgery of them to the service of righteousness; from the power and dominion of them and subjection to them, and from a course of living in them to a life of holiness; and from the paths of sin to the paths of truth and uprightness.——(5.) Conversion lies in turning men from their own righteousness to the righteousness of Christ; not from doing works of righteousness, for such converted persons are most fit for, and most capable of, and are under the greatest obligations to perform; but from depending upon them for justification before God and acceptance with him; in order to which they must be convinced by the Spirit of God of the insufficiency of their own righteousness to justify them, being imperfect; and of the necessity, perfection, and fulness of Christ's righteousness, which being turned unto, they receive, embrace, lay hold on, and plead as their justifying righteousness before God; and this requires more than human teachings: for though ministers are said to *turn many to righteousness*, that is, to the righteousness of Christ, yet only instrumentally, and as the means of it, through preaching the gospel, in which there is a revelation of it; for God is the efficient cause of the turn of them to it; for though the gospel is the ministration of it, yet it is the Lord that must bring it near to stout-hearted ones far from righteousness, and make them willing to submit unto it, and to be desirous of being found in it; for men naturally do not care to part with their own righteousness; it is their own, and what they have been a long time and with great labour rearing up, and to have it demolished, they cannot bear it; they would fain hold it fast, and lean upon it, though it shall not stand; it is their idol, in which they place their trust and confidence, and to take this away from them is to take away their god; as Micah said, when his idol was stolen from him, *Ye have taken away my gods, and what have I more?* Wherefore the conversion of a self-righteous person is more rare and difficult than the conversion of a profligate sinner; hence our Lord says to the Scribes and Pharisees, that *the publicans and harlots go into the kingdom of God before them;* and that he himself *came not to call the righteous, but sinners to repentance,* Matt. xxi. 31. and ix. 13.——(6.) Conversion lies in a man's turning to the Lord actively, under the influence of divine grace; and by this phrase it is often expressed in scripture, as in Isa. x. 21. Acts xi. 21. 2 Cor. iii. 16. men being thoroughly convinced that there is salvation in no other but in Christ, that it is in vain to expect it elsewhere; after they have made many inquiries and searches to no purpose, turn to the Lord Jesus Christ, and look to him alone for salvation; being apprized of their danger, they turn as they are directed, encouraged and enabled, to Christ the strong-hold, where they are safe from all danger, and from every enemy; being made sensible of the insufficiency of their own righteousness, and of the suitableness of the righteousness of Christ for them, they turn to him as the Lord their righteousness, in whom all the seed of Israel are justified and shall glory; and being fully satisfied with the equity of the laws, rules, and ordinances of Christ, they turn to him as their Lord and Lawgiver, and submit to his commands, renouncing all other lords and their dominion over them; and though in their nature-state they are like sheep going astray, in conversion they are returned to Christ, as the great Shepherd and bishop of souls: the parable of seeking and finding, and bringing home the lost sheep, is a fit representation of the conversion of a sinner. Christ's people are his sheep before conversion, but they are lost sheep, straying in the wilderness; and as sheep never return to the fold, shepherd and pasture of themselves, unless looked up and are returned; so neither do they, till they are sought for and found, and brought home by Christ, the proprietor of them, with joy; and the parables following, represent the same thing; as that of the lost piece of silver, for finding which the woman lights a candle and sweeps the house, and searches every corner till she finds it, which gives her joy; this sets forth the high esteem and value the elect are in with Christ, comparable to silver, yea to fine gold and precious stones; and the passiveness of men in first conversion, who no more contribute to it than the piece of silver to its being found; and the means and methods made use of in conversion, the light of the gospel ministry, and the stir and bustle on that occasion: so the parable of the prodigal son, and his return to his father, is expressive of the same; his manner of living before his return, is a lively picture of the state of unconverted men, living in their lusts, and pursuing the desires of the flesh and of the mind; in his return there are all the symptoms of a true and real conversion; as a sense of his starving, famishing and perishing state by nature; his coming to his right mind, his sense of sin, confession of it, and repentance for it; his faith and hope of meeting with a favourable reception by his father, which encouraged him to return, and which he met with; see Isa. lv. 7.

Secondly, The causes of conversion, efficient, moving, and instrumental.

1st, The efficient cause, which is not man but God. 1. Not man, it is neither by the power nor will of man.——(1.) Not by the power of man; what is said of the conversion or turning of the Jews from their captivity, is true of the conversion of a sinner, that it is *not by might nor by power,* that is not of man, *but by my Spirit, as saith the Lord of hosts,* Zech. iv. 6. Men are dead in a moral sense whilst unconverted, they are *dead in trespasses and sins,* which are the cause of their death; and their very living in them is no other than a moral death; nor can they quicken themselves, and unless they are quickened they cannot be converted; and being in a moral sense dead, they are *strengthless;* they are not only *weak through the flesh,* the corruption of nature, but they are *without strength;* without any strength at all to perform that which is good, and much less a work of so great importance as their own conversion; they have not the command of themselves, nor any power over their hearts, the thoughts, desires, and affections of them; they cannot check them and control them at pleasure; they cannot think any thing as of themselves, much less think a good thought; they cannot turn the streams of their desires and affections to proper objects; they cannot move their minds, nor bend their wills, even to that which is to their own advantage. Conversion is such an alteration in a man as is not in his power to effect: it is like that of an Ethiopian changing his skin, and a leopard his spots; such things are never heard of, as a blackmoor becoming white, and a leopard becoming clear of his spots; and as unlikely is it that a man should convert himself, Jer. xiii. 23. a tree must first be made good, so as to bring forth good fruit; *Make the tree good*, says our Lord; but the tree cannot make itself good; another hand must be employed about it, to engraft it, cultivate and improve it; a thorn-bush cannot turn itself, into a vine-tree, and so bring forth grapes; nor a thistle into a fig-tree, to bring forth figs; but as soon may these things be done, as a man to convert himself and bring forth the good fruits of righteousness, Matt. xii. 33. and vii. 16, 17, 18. Conversion is the motion of the soul towards God; but as this cannot be in a dead man, and unless he is quickened, so not unless he is drawn by efficacious grace; wherefore God, in conversion, draws men with loving kindness to himself; and, with the cords of love, to his Son; for *no man*, says Christ, *can come unto me, except the Father, which hath sent me, draw him*, John vi. 44. and even converted persons themselves are so sensible of this, that they pray, as the church did, *Draw me, we will run after thee*, Cant. i. 4. the thing speaks for itself, and shows that it cannot be done by the power of man; for it is no other than a *creation*, which requires creation-power to effect it, which a creature has not; for if the restoration, or conversion, of a backslidden saint is a creation, and requires the power of the Creator to do it; of which David, when backslidden, was sensible, and therefore prayed, *Create in me a clean heart, O God!* then much more is the first conversion of a sinner, and requires like power: it is a resurrection from the dead, and is not to be effected but by the exceeding greatness of God's power, even such as was put forth in raising Christ from the dead, Eph. i. 19.——(2.) Nor is conversion owing to the will of men; the will of man, before conversion, is in a bad state, it chooses its own ways, and delights in its abominations; it is in high pursuit after the desires of the flesh and of the mind; it is resolved to go after its lovers, its lusts, which feed its appetite, and furnish with things agreeable to the carnal mind; the will is become a slave to carnal lusts and pleasures; though the natural liberty of the will is not lost by sin, it can freely will natural things, as to eat or drink, sit, or stand, or walk, at pleasure; yet its moral liberty is lost, it is shackled with the fetters of sinful lusts, by which it is overcome and brought into bondage; and notwithstanding its boasted liberty, it is an home-born slave; and therefore Luther rightly called it *servum arbitrium*: man has no will to that which is good till God works it in him, and of unwilling makes him willing in the day of his power: he has no will to come to Christ, to be saved by him; nor to submit to his righteousness; nor to be subject to his laws and ordinances, until such a will is worked in him by efficacious grace. Conversion is denied to be of the will of men; as the whole of salvation is *not of him that willeth*; so this part of it in particular, regeneration, with which conversion, in the first moment of it, agrees, *is not of the will of the flesh, nor of the will of man, but of God*, Rom. ix. 16. John i. 13.

But it may be said, if conversion is not in the power and will of men, to what purpose are such exhortations as these; *Repent, and turn yourselves from all your transgressions; turn yourselves, and* and again, *Repent ye therefore, and be converted?* Ezek. xviii. 30, 32. Acts iii. 19. to which it may be replied, That these passages have no respect to spiritual and internal conversion, but to an external reformation of life and manners. In the first instance, the Jews were then in a state of captivity, which was a kind of death, as sometimes sore afflictions are said to be, 2 Cor. i. 10. and into which they were brought through their sins: now the Lord declares, that he took no pleasure in this their uncomfortable state and condition; it was more desirable to him, and therefore he exhorts them to it, to reform from their evil practices; then they would be returned from their captivity, and live comfortably in their own land, as they had formerly done. But what has this to do with the spiritual and internal conversion of a sinner unto God? With respect to the latter case, the Jews were threatened with the destruction of their city and nation, for their rejection of Jesus the Messiah, and other sins they were guilty of; and now the apostle advises those to whom he directs his discourse, to relinquish their wrong notions of Christ, and repent of their ill usage of him and his followers, and of their other sins, in an external way, that so they might escape the calamities coming upon their nation and people. But supposing these, and such like exhortations, respected internal conversion of the heart to God; such exhortations may be only designed to shew men the necessity of such conversion in order to salvation; as our Lord said, *Except ye be converted, ye shall not enter into the kingdom of heaven;* and when men are convinced of this, they will soon be sensible of their impotence to convert themselves, and will pray, as Ephraim did, *Turn thou me, and I shall be turned,* immediately and effectually; for,——2. God only is the author and efficient cause of conversion. He that made man's heart, and formed the spirit of man within him, he only can turn their hearts, and frame and mould their spirits, as he pleases; the heart of a king, and so of every other man, is in the hand of the Lord, and he can turn them as the rivers of water are turned; he, and he only, can give a check unto, and turn the thoughts, desires, and affections of the heart into another channel, and the mind and will to other objects; he can remove the stubbornness of the will, and bend it at his pleasure, and make it pliable and conformable to his own will; he can take away the hardness of the heart, though it is like an adamant stone, he can make it soft, and susceptible of the best impressions; he can break the rocky heart in pieces; yea, take away the stony heart, and give an heart of flesh; as he can take what he pleases out of it, so he can put into it what he will, as he does in conversion, his laws, the fear of him, and his Spirit; he can and does draw them, by the powerful influence of his grace upon them to himself and to his Son; and this he does without forcing their wills; he sweetly allures, by his grace, to come to Christ and his ordinances; he powerfully persuades Japhet to dwell in the tents of Shem; he makes his people willing, in the day of his power, to do what they had before no will nor inclination to; and yet they act most freely; the manslayer did not more willingly flee to a city of refuge, to shelter him from the avenger of blood, than a sinner, sensible of his danger, flees to Christ for refuge, and lays hold on the hope set before him.

The power of divine grace, put forth in conversion, is irresistible; that is, so irresistible, as that a stop cannot be put to the work, and that become of no effect, through opposition made unto it from within and from without. Conversion is according to the will of God, his will of purpose which can never be frustrated; *Who hath resisted his will?* his counsel shall stand, and he will do all his pleasure; it is wrought by his almighty power; the work of faith, which is a principal part of the work of conversion, is begun, carried on, and performed with power; nor can a sinner any more resist, so as to make of none effect, the power of God in conversion, than Lazarus could resist the power of Christ in calling him out of his grave. If it was in the power of the will of men to hinder the work of conversion, so as that it should not take place, when it is the design of God it should; then God might be disappointed of his end, which must not be said; for there is no counsel nor might against him; whatever devices may be in a man's heart, the counsels of God can never be disappointed; when God has purposed to convert a sinner, who can disannul it? and when his mighty hand of grace is stretched out, to put that purpose into execution, who can turn it back? when he works in any way, and so in this, there is none can let. Besides, if conversion was to stand or fall according to the will of men; or if that had the turning point in man's conversion, it would rather be ascribed to the will of men than to the will of God; and it would not be true what is said, *It is not of him that willeth:* yea, as the will of men then would have the greatest stroke in conversion, in answer to that question, *Who maketh thee to differ from another?* it might be said, as it has been said, by a proud and haughty free-willer, Grevinchovius, I have made myself to differ.

To all this may be objected the words of Christ; *How often would I have gathered thy children together, and ye would not!* Matt. xxiii. 37. but it should be observed, that this gathering is not to be understood of conversion; but of attendance on the ministry of the word under John the Baptist, Christ himself, and his apostles; to which Christ had affectionately and importunately exhorted them; which, had it been regarded, would have preserved them from the vengeance coming upon Jerusalem: and it should also be observed, that they are not the same persons whom Christ would have gathered, and those of whom he says, *and ye would not;* by whom are meant, the rulers and governors of the people, who would not suffer them to attend the gospel ministry, but threatened them with putting them out of the synagogue if they did; see ver. 13.

2*dly,* The moving, or impulsive cause of conversion, is the love, grace, mercy, favour, and good-will of God; the same as are the moving cause of regeneration and effectual calling, and not the merits of men; for what is there in men before conversion, to move God to take such a step in their favour? see 1 Cor. vi. 9, 10, 11. Eph. ii. 2, 3, 4.

3*dly,* The instrumental cause, or means of conversion, is usually the ministry of the word; sometimes, indeed, it is wrought without the word, by some remarkable awakening providence or another, and sometimes by reading the scriptures; but, for the most part, it is through the preaching of the word; hence ministers are said to *turn many to righteousness;* and the apostle Paul says, he was sent by Christ into the Gentile world, to *turn men from darkness to light, and from the power of Satan to God;* and this is done both by the preaching of the law and of the gospel; *the law of the Lord is perfect, converting the soul,* Psalm xix. 7. though perhaps not the law, strictly taken, but the whole doctrine of the word is there meant; however, the preaching of the law is made use of by the Spirit of God to convince of sin; for *by the law is the knowledge of sin;* and by means of it, when it enters into the heart and conscience, under his influence, sin is made to appear exceeding sinful, and the soul is filled with great distress on account of it; for the *law worketh wrath;* though some take this to be rather preparatory to conversion than conversion itself, which may be better ascribed to the gospel; and, indeed, the receiving of the Spirit, and his graces, and particularly faith, are attributed to the preaching of the gospel, and not to the law, as the means thereof; *Received ye the Spirit by the works of the law?* that is, by preaching the doctrine of obedience to it; *or by the hearing of faith?* that is, by the doctrine of the gospel, preaching faith in Christ; which is therefore called *the word of faith,* and by which it comes; for *faith comes by hearing, and hearing by the word of God,* Gal. iii. 2. Rom. x. 8, 17. but then the preaching of the word of the gospel is not sufficient of itself to produce the work of conversion in the heart; men may hear it, and not be converted by it; nor receive any benefit, profit, and advantage through it; if it comes in word only, and not with the demonstration of the Spirit, and of power; and when it is accompanied with the power of God, or is made the power of God unto salvation, even then it is only an instrument, and not an efficient; for *who is Paul, or who is Apollos, but ministers,* or instruments, *by whom ye believed?* 1 Cor. iii. 5.

Thirdly, The subjects of conversion; these are not all men, for all, in fact, are not converted; nor does it appear to be the design and purpose of God to convert all men; nor does he give sufficient grace to all men to convert themselves if they will; for he does not so much as give to all men the means of grace, the outward ministry of the word: this was not vouchsafed to the Gentiles for hundreds of years before the coming of Christ; and since, millions have never been favoured with it; nor are multitudes at this day; and those who have the scripture to read, to many it is a sealed book, and to all, unless opened by the Spirit of God; and to whom the gospel is preached, it is hid, unless it is given them to know the mysteries of the kingdom, which is not the case of all; the persons converted are the *elect* of God, both among Jews and Gentiles: in the first ages of the gospel, many among the Gentiles were converted, and churches formed of them; and ever since there has been conversions among them, and even to this day, and in the latter day an abundance of them will be converted; and when the fulness of the Gentiles is brought in, then the Jews, of whom only now and then one are converted, they will be all as a nation, born again, converted and saved. They are *redeemed* ones who are converted; and the reason why they are converted is, because they are redeemed; *I will hiss for them,* by the ministry of the word, and *gather them,* which is another phrase for conversion, *because I have redeemed them,* Zech. x. 8. they whom God converts, are the same persons for whom he has provided forgiveness of sins in the covenant of his grace, and an eternal inheritance in his divine purpose; for the apostle says, he was sent by Christ *to turn men unto God, that they may receive the forgiveness of sins, and inheritance among them which are sanctified by faith in Christ,* Acts xxvi. 18. In a word, they are described as *sinners: Sinners shall be converted unto thee*, Psalm li. 13. sinners by nature and by practice, and some of them the worst and chief of sinners; and therefore the wonderful grace of God is the more displayed in their conversion, 1 Cor. vi. 11. 1 Tim. i. 3, 14, 15.

CHAP. XIV.

OF SANCTIFICATION.

THE foundation of *sanctification* is laid in *regeneration;* as it is a holy principle, it is first formed in that; the new creature, or new man, is created in righteousness and true holiness; and it appears in *effectual vocation*, which is an *holy calling;* and is to be seen in conversion, which is a turning of men *from their iniquities:* and that holiness which is begun in regeneration, and is manifest in effectual calling and conversion, is carried on in sanctification, which is a gradual and progressive work, and issues and is finished in glorification; so that it may, with propriety, be distinguished from regeneration, effectual calling, and conversion, and be separately treated of.

There is a sanctification which is more peculiarly ascribed to God the Father; and which is no other than his eternal election of men to it: under the law, persons and things separated and devoted to holy uses, are said to be *sanctified;* hence those who are set apart by God for his use and service, and are chosen by him to holiness here and hereafter, are said *to be sanctified by God the Father*, Jude ver. 1. There is a sanctification also that is more peculiar to Christ the Son of God; not only as he is the representative of his people, and is *holiness to the Lord* for them; which the high-priest had upon his forehead, who was a type of him, and the representative of Israel; and as he has the whole stock of grace and holiness in his hands, which is communicated to the saints as is necessary; and as the holiness of his human nature, is, with his active and passive obedience, imputed to their justification, and so makes a part of that; hence he is said to be made to them *sanctification*, 1 Cor. i. 30. but as the expiation of their sins is made by his blood and sacrifice; this is called a sanctification of them; *Jesus, that he might sanctify the people with his blood, suffered without the gate,* Heb. xiii. 12. But there is another sanctification, which is more peculiar to the Holy Spirit of God, and is called *the sanctification of the Spirit*, 2 Thess. ii. 13. 1 Pet. ii. 2. and this is the sanctification to be treated of. Concerning which may be enquired,

First, What it is, and the nature of it. It is something that is *holy*, both in its principle and in its actings; and is superior to any thing that can come from man, or be performed by him of himself. It does not lie in a conformity to the light of nature, and the dictates of it; nor is it what may go by the name of *moral virtue*, which was exercised by some of the heathen philosophers to a very great degree, and yet they had not a grain of holiness in them; but were full of the lusts of envy, ambition, pride, revenge, &c. nor does it lie in a bare, external conformity to the law of God; or in an *outward reformation* of life and manners; this appeared in the Pharisees, to a great degree, who were pure in their own eyes, and thought themselves holier than others, and disdained them, and yet their hearts were full of all manner of impurity. Nor is what is called *restraining grace*, sanctification; persons may be restrained by the injunctions of parents and masters, by the laws of magistrates, and by the ministry of the word, from the grosser sins of life; and be preserved, by the providence of God from the pollutions of the world, and yet not be sanctified. Nor are *gifts*, ordinary or extraordinary, sanctifying grace; Judas Iscariot, no doubt, had both, the ordinary gifts of a preacher, and the extraordinary gifts of an apostle, and yet not a holy man. Gifts are not grace; a man may have all gifts, and all knowledge, and speak with the tongue of men and angels, and not have grace; there may be a silver tongue, where there is an unsanctified heart! Nor is sanctification a restoration of the lost image of Adam, or a reparation and an amendment of that image marred by the sin of man; or a new vamping up the old principles of nature: but it is something entirely new; a new creature, a new man, a new heart, and a new spirit; and the conformity of a man to another image, even to the image of the second Adam, the Son of God.

Some make sanctification to lie in the deposition, or putting off, of the old man, and in the putting on of the new man. This has a foundation in the word of God, Eph. iv. 22, 24. and belongs to sanctification, and may be admitted, if understood of the actings of it, as these are, which suppose a previous principle from which they arise. By the *old man,* is meant corrupt nature; which is as old as a man is in whom it is, and which he brings into the world with him; and by the putting of it off, is not meant the removal of it from him; for it continues with him, even with a sanctified person, as long as he is in the world; nor any change in the nature of it, which always remains the same; much less a destruction of it, which will not be till this earthly house is dissolved: but a dispossession of it, of its power, a displacing it from its throne, so as not to yield obedience to the lusts of it; nor walk according to the dictates of it; nor have the conversation according to it. By the *new man*, is meant the new principle of grace and holiness, wrought in the soul in regeneration: and by the *putting on* of that, the exercise of the several graces of which it consists; see Col. iii. 12, 13.

Others distinguish sanctification, into *vivification* and *mortification:* and both these are to be observed in sanctification. Sanctification, as a principle, is a holy, living principle, infused; by which a man that was dead in trespasses and sins, is quickened; and from whence flow living acts; such as living by faith on Christ; walking in newness of life; living soberly, righteously, and godly: all which belong to sanctification. And there is such a thing as mortification; not in a literal and natural sense, of the body, by fasting, scourging, &c. Nor is it the abolition of the body of sin, by the sacrifice of Christ; nor the destruction of the principle and being of sin in regenerate and sanctified persons; for though they do not live in sin, yet sin lives in them, and is sometimes very active and powerful: but the weakening of the power of sin, and a mortification of the deeds of the body, and of the members on earth; so that a course of sin is not lived in, but men are dead unto it; and to which the Spirit of God, and his grace, are necessary, Col. iii. 5. Rom. viii. 13. But leaving these things, I shall more particularly consider sanctification as an holy principle, and the holy actings of it.

1*st*, As an holy principle. The first rise of which is in regeneration; there it is first formed, as before observed. And this is no other than the good work of grace begun in the hearts of regenerate ones. It is a *work*, not of men; for as regeneration is not of the will of men; nor conversion by might or power of men; so neither is sanctification; none can say, *I have made my heart clean*, or have sanctified myself; it is the work of God; *We are his workmanship*, and a curious piece of workmanship sanctification is; too curious for a creature to perform; it is done *in the name* of the Lord Jesus, and *by the Spirit of our God*. It is a *good* work; the efficient cause is good, God himself; the moving cause good, his love, grace, kindness, and good-will; the matter good, some good thing towards the Lord God of Israel; the instrumental cause or means, the good word of God: and it is good in its effects; it makes a man a good man, and fits him for the performance of good works, and is the source of them. It is commonly called *a work of grace*, and with great propriety; since it flows from the free, sovereign, and abundant grace of God in Christ; and is an implantation of all grace in the heart. And in scripture it is called *the work of faith*, because faith is a principal part of it; and in the exercise of which, sanctification much lies; hence saints are said to be *sanctified by faith, which is in Christ*, Acts xxvi. 18. It is an internal work; it is a work *begun in* the soul, which the Spirit of God works in the hearts of his people, by putting the fear of God, and every other grace, there; hence it goes by various names, which shew it to be something within a man, and not any thing external; see Rom. ii. 28, 29. It is called *the inward man, and the hidden man of the heart*, which has its place there, and is not obvious to every one, Rom. vii. 22. 1 Pet. iii. 4. and not only from the author of it, the Spirit of God; and from the nature of it, being spiritual, and conversant with spiritual things; but from the seat and subject of it, the spirit or soul of man; it is called *spirit*, being wrought in the soul by the Spirit of God, John iii. 6. It has also the name of *seed*, which sometimes signifies the word; which being cast into the heart, and taking place there, becomes the *engrafted word;* and sometimes grace itself, which is like seed sown in the earth, which lies hid in it awhile, and then springs and grows up, a man knows not how; and this is that *seed* which remains in the heart of believers, and is never lost, 1 John iii. 9. Sometimes it is compared to a *root*, which lies under ground, is not seen, and is the cause of fruit being brought forth upwards; and may be what Job calls, *the root of the matter* in him; and which the stony-ground hearers being without, withered, and came to nothing, Job xix. 28. Matt. xiii. 21. It is called, *truth in the* inward parts; which is expressive of the integrity and uprightness of the heart, of a true and right spirit created there, and of the truth and reality of grace and holiness, or true holiness, in which the new man is created, Psalm l. 6, 10. Eph. iv. 24. Once more, it is signified by *oil in the vessel* of the heart, had with the *lamp* of an external profession, Matt. xxv. 4. by *oil* is meant grace, so called for its illuminating nature, grace is spiritual light in the understanding; and for its suppling, softening nature, it takes off the hardness of the heart, and the stubbornness of the will; and because it will not mix with other liquids, as grace will not mix with sin; and which is had, held, and retained in the heart, as in a vessel; and from which the lamp of profession is distinct, which is more visible. I proceed,

2*dly*, To consider sanctification in its holy actings.———1. With respect to God; which appear in the disposition of the mind, the motions of the heart Godwards, and in the behaviour and conduct of a saint before him, and with regard unto him; and which become manifest,———(1.) In a holy reverence of him, on account of his nature, perfections, works, and blessings of goodness. In an unsanctified man, there is no fear of God before his eyes; but where a principle of grace and holiness is wrought, the fear of God soon appears; it is the beginning of wisdom; and is one of the first things that appear in a regenerate man; he cannot do what he before did, and others do; *so did not I, because of the fear of God*, said Nehemiah, chap. v. 15. such an one will serve the Lord with reverence and godly fear.———(2.) Sanctification shews itself in love to God, and delight in him. An unsanctified man cannot love God, who is pure and holy; nor take any delight in him, in his word, his ways, and worship; *The carnal mind is enmity to God*, and desires him to depart from him, and chooses not the knowledge of his ways; nay, one that has taken on him the mask of religion, and is not sincere, can have no true affection for God, nor pleasure in the things of God. Job says of the hypocrite, *Will he delight himself in the Almighty? will he always call upon God?* No, he will not, Job xxvii. 10. But in regeneration and sanctification, the Lord *circumcises* the heart, or regenerates and sanctifies it, *to love the Lord with all the heart and with all the soul!* that is, sincerely and cordially.———
(3.) It appears in submission to the will of God in all things, even in the most adverse dispensations of providence; as the instances of Aaron, Eli, David, and others shew; who murmured not, nor complained, but were still and quiet, and resigned to the divine will, under some severe rebukes of providence. Much of sanctification lies in the conformity of our wills to the will of God. That holy man Bishop Usher said of it, "Sanctification is nothing less than for a man to be brought to an entire resignation of his will to the will of God, and to live in the offering up of his soul continually in the flames of love, as a whole burnt-offering to Christ."———(4.) It is to be seen in religious exercies, and in acts of devotion to God, and in the exercise of grace in them; as in an affectionate attendance on the ministry of the word, and administration of ordinances; and in fervent prayer, which is the breath of a sanctified soul towards God. Holiness only appears in these things, or is real, when grace is in exercise in them; for otherwise, there may be an outward performance of them, and yet no true holiness.———(5.) The holy actings of sanctification may be discerned in the earnest pantings and eager desires of the soul after communion with God, both in private and public; when a soul cannot be content with ordinances without enjoying God in them; when it pants after him, as the hart pants after the water-brooks; and when without him, seeks every where for him, till it finds him, and then exults in its fellowship with the Father, and his Son Jesus Christ.———(6.) A soul that is sanctified by the Spirit of God, seeks the glory of God in all he does, whether in things civil or religious : one that is unsanctified, and only makes a show of religion, and of good works, he does all to be seen of men, and seeks his own glory therein; whatever show of devotion and holiness may be made by such persons, there is not a grain of holiness in them. Whereas he that seeks the glory of God in all, *the same is true*, hearty and sincere, a real saint *and no unrighteousness is in him*, no insincerity and dissimulation, John vii. 18.

2. Sanctification discovers itself in its holy actings, with respect to Christ.———(1.) In applying to him for cleansing; as in a view of its guilt, it applies to his blood for pardon; and to his righteousness for justification: so under a sight and sense of its pollution, and of the spreading leprosy of sin all over it; it goes to him as the leper did, saying, *Lord, if thou wilt, thou canst*

make me clean! and such deal with his blood for the purification of their souls, as well as for the remission of their sins; and have their hearts purified by faith in it.——(2.) In subjection to him, as King of saints; they not only receive him as their Prophet, to teach and instruct them, and embrace his doctrines; and as their Priest, by whose sacrifice their sins are expiated; but as their King, to whose laws and ordinances they cheerfully submit; esteeming his precepts, concerning all things, to be right, none of his commandments grievous; but, from a principle of love to him, keep and observe them.——(3.) In setting him always before them, as an example to copy after; being desirous of walking even as he walked; both in the exercise of the graces of faith, love, patience, humility, &c. and in the discharge of duty.——(4.) In a desire of a greater degree of conformity to the image of Christ, which is what they are predestinated unto; which first appears in regeneration, and is increased by every believing view of Christ and his glory, and will be completed in the future state; hence sanctified souls desire to be with Christ, that they might be perfectly like him, as well as see him as he is.

3. Sanctification is discovered in its actings, with respect to the Holy Spirit.—— (1.) In minding, savouring, and relishing, the things of the Spirit of God. *They that are after the flesh,* carnal, unregenerate, unsanctified ones, *mind the things of the flesh,* carnal and sensual lusts and pleasures; *but they that are after the Spirit,* who are regenerated and sanctified by the Spirit of God, *mind the things of the Spirit,* which he reveals, recommends, and directs to; these they savour, relish, highly value, and esteem, Rom. viii. 5.——(2.) In walking after the dictates, directions, leadings, and teachings of the Spirit; so sanctified persons are described as such *who walk not after the flesh, but after the Spirit,* Rom. viii. 1.——(3.) In a desire and carefulness not to grieve the holy Spirit of God, by whom they have their present grace and experience, joy and comfort, and by whom they are sealed to the day of redemption, by any disagreeable behaviour to him, to one another, and in the world, Eph. iv. 30. ——(4.) In a desire *to live and walk in the Spirit;* to live in a spiritual manner, under his influence, to exercise every grace, and abound therein, through his power; to perform every duty by his assistance; and to wait, through him, for the hope of righteousness by faith. Gal. v. 5, 25. Rom. xii. 11. and xv. 13.

4. The holy actings of sanctification are apparent with respect to sin.——(1.) In approving, loving, and delighting in the law of God, which forbids it, and condemns for it. An unsanctified man cannot brook the law of God on this account; he is not subjected to it; nor can he be, without efficacious grace exerted on him; he despises it, and casts it behind his back: whereas, a man sanctified by the Spirit of God, approves of the law of God, as holy, just, and good, and loves it exceedingly; *How love I thy law!* says David; and he delights in it, after the inward man, and serves it with his mind and Spirit, Psalm cxix. 97. Rom. vii. 12, 22, 25.——(2.) In a dislike of sin, and a displicency at it; it is displeasing to him, as it is contrary to the holy nature of God, a breach of his righteous law, and is in its own nature exceeding sinful, as well as disagreeable in its effects and consequences.——(3.) In a loathing sin, and in an abhorrence of it. An unsanctified man chooses his own ways, and delights in his abominations; he takes pleasure in committing sin himself, and in those that do it; sin is a sweet morsel, which he rolls in his mouth, and keeps under his tongue; but one that has the principle and grace of holiness, loaths his sin, and himself for it; and, with Job, abhors himself, and repents in dust and ashes.——(4.) In an hatred of sin; unholy persons, hate the good and love the evil; but an holy man, loves righteousness and hates iniquity: such that love the Lord, cannot but hate evil; it being so extremely opposite to him; he hates, not only sinful actions, and even what he himself does, though he would not do them, but vain thoughts also, Rom. vii. 15. Psalm cxix. 113.——(5.) In an opposition to sin: a sanctified man, not only does not make provision for the flesh, to fulfil the lusts of it; does not regard it in his heart, so as to encourage, nourish, and cherish, it; but he acts the part of an antagonist to it, *striving against sin; the spirit lusteth against the flesh;* grace opposes sin, upon the first motion of it, and temptation to it; he has that principle within him that argues thus, *How can I do this great wickedness, and sin against God?*——(6.) In an abstinence from it, even from every appearance of it, a passing by the ways of it, and avoiding every avenue that leads to it, as being what wars against the soul, and is dangerous and

hurtful to it. The grace of God implanted in the heart, as well as displayed in the word, *teaches to deny ungodliness and worldly lusts*, Tit. ii. 11, 12.——(7.) Sanctification appears in lamenting sin, in deploring the corruption of nature, bewailing indwelling-sin, as well as all sinful actions, of thought, word, and deed; sanctified persons are like doves of the valley, every one mourning for his own iniquities, and for those of others, and the sad effects of them.—— (8.) In earnest desires to be wholly freed from sin; uneasy that vain thoughts should so long lodge within them, weary of a body of sin and death, they groan under the burden of it, and cry, O wretched men that we are! who shall deliver us from it? they long to be with Christ, and to be in heaven; for this reason greatly, among others, that they be entirely free from sin, and be perfectly holy.

Now can such actings in the mind, and in life, spring from nature? must they not arise from a principle of holiness in the heart? can there be such reverence of God, love to him, resignation to his will, affectionate and fervent devotion to him, desires of communion with him, and a concern in all things for his glory, without a supernatural principle of grace and holiness in the soul? Is it possible, that an unsanctified man should ever apply to Christ for cleansing, be subject to him as King, be desirous of walking as he walked, and of being wrought up to a conformity to him? or be concerned to mind the things of the Spirit, and to walk after the Spirit, and to live in him, and be careful not to grieve him? can there be such actings in the mind concerning sin, as to love the law, which forbids it; to dislike sin, abhor it, and hate it; engage in an opposition to it, abstain from it, lament it, and earnestly desire to be rid of it; can these be the produce of nature? or be without being internally sanctified by the Spirit of God?

Secondly, The subjects of sanctification are next to be enquired into; who they are that are sanctified, and what of them.

1*st*, Who are sanctified? not all men; all men are unholy, and need sanctification; but all are not made holy; some are filthy, and remain filthy still.—— 1. They are the elect of God; and all of them, whom God chose in eternity, he sanctifies in time; those who are a chosen generation, become an holy people; whom God chose, he chose to holiness, as an end which is always answered, and he chose them through sanctification, as a means in order to a further end, salvation; conformity to the image of the son of God, in which sanctification lies, is what the chosen are predestinated unto; and, in consequence of their predestination, are made partakers of it. Faith, which is a part of sanctification, flows from electing grace, and is insured by it; as many as are ordained to eternal life believe, and are everlastingly glorified, which is their perfect sanctification.——2. They are the redeemed ones; the subjects of election, redemption, and sanctification, are the same persons. In order, they are first chosen, then redeemed, and then sanctified; those who are chosen by the Father, and redeemed by the Son, are sanctified by the Spirit. One end of Christ's redemption of them, was to sanctify and purify them, a peculiar people to himself, zealous of good works; and that they being dead to sin, and that to them, through his sacrifice for sin, they might live unto righteousness; hence of the same persons it is said, *They shall call them the holy people, the redeemed of the Lord!* Isa. lxii. 12.

2*dly*, What of those persons is sanctified? The whole of them; *The God of peace sanctify you wholly;* that is, as next explained, in soul, body, and spirit, 1 Thess. v. 23.——1. The soul, or spirit, is the principal seat, or subject of sanctification, in all the powers and faculties of it; *Be renewed in the spirit of your minds*, Eph. iv. 23. It is the heart into which the fear of God is put, and which is circumcised to love the Lord, and which is purified by faith; it is the understanding that is enlightened, to discern holy and spiritual things; and so to mind them, approve of them, and gaze at them, with wonder and delight: the will is bowed to the will of God, and made willing in the day of his power, to serve him, as well as to be saved by him; and which is resigned to all the dispensations of divine providence: the affections are made spiritual, holy and heavenly; from whence springs a cheerful obedience to the commands of God and Christ: and the mind and conscience, which were defiled with sin, are purged from dead works to serve the living God. ——2. The body also is influenced by sanctifying grace. As, though the heart is the principal seat of sin, out of which all manner of wickedness flows, and spreads itself, not only over the powers and faculties of the soul, but also over the members of the body; so that there is no part nor place clean: thus, though the soul is the principal seat of sanctification, yet it diffuses its influence, as over all the powers of the soul, so over all the members of the body; its sensual appetite and carnal lusts are checked and restrained by sanctifying grace; so that sin reigns not in our mortal bodies, as to obey the lusts thereof, and to yield our members, as instruments of unrighteousness, unto sin, Rom. vi. 12, 13.

Thirdly, The causes of sanctification, by whom it is effected, from whence it springs, and by what means it is carried on, and at last finished.———1. The efficient cause is God, Father, Son, and Spirit. Sometimes it is ascribed to the Father, the God of all grace, who will make us perfect, perfectly holy; the very God of peace, with whom we have peace, through Christ, will sanctify us wholly; the Father, on whom we call, the Father of Christ, and of us, says, *Be ye holy, as I am holy*, and who only can make us so, 1 Pet. i. 15, 16. and v. 10. 1 Thess. v. 23. And Christ is not only our sanctification, but our sanctifier; *He that sanctifieth* is Christ, *and they who are sanctified* are his chosen and redeemed ones; and these *are all of one*, Heb. ii. 11. of one and of the same nature; he partakes of their nature, and they are made partakers of his; all that holiness which they have, they have from him; from that fulness of it which is in him. Though this work of sanctification is more commonly ascribed to the holy Spirit, who is therefore called, *the Spirit of holiness;* not only from his own nature, but from his being the author of holiness in the hearts of God's people, and which is therefore called *the sanctification of the Spirit;* it is he that begins, and carries on, and finishes this work; every grace is from him, faith, hope, and love, and every other; and which are supported and maintained, and drawn forth into exercise, and brought to perfection by him.———2. The moving cause, is the grace and good-will of God; the same grace which moved God to choose any to holiness, moves him to work it in them: the same grace which moved him to send his Son into the world to redeem men, moves him to send his Spirit into their hearts to sanctify them: the same great love, and abundant mercy that moves him to regenerate and quicken them, moves him to sanctify them; as of his own good-will he begets them again, it is of his own good-will that he sanctifies them; *This is the will of God*, not only his will of precept, and his approving will; but the purpose and counsel of his will, what flows from his sovereign will; *Even your sanctification*, 1 Thess. iv. 3. The state and condition of the people of God, before their sanctification, clearly shews that it must arise, not from any merit or motive in them; but from the free-favour and good will of God, 1 Cor. vi. 9, 10, 11.———3. The instrumental cause, or means, is the word of God; both the written word, the scriptures, which are holy scriptures; the author holy, the matter holy, and, when attended with a divine power and influence, are the means of making men holy, and of fitting and furnishing them for every good work; and also the word preached, when accompanied with the same power; *Faith comes by hearing*, and is increased thereby; the doctrines of the gospel are according to godliness; and with a divine blessing, influence both the heart and life to godliness and holiness; the ordinances are made and continued, for the perfecting of the saints, for the carrying on, and perfecting the work of holiness in them; and various providences of God, even afflictive ones, are designed of God, and are means, in his hand, of making his people more and more *partakers of his holiness*, Heb. xii. 10. of this use afflictions were to holy David, Psalm cxix. 67, 71.

Fourthly, The adjuncts or properties of sanctification.———1*st*, It is imperfect in the present state, though it will most certainly be made perfect; where the work is begun it will be performed: sanctification in Christ is perfect, but sanctification in the saints themselves is imperfect; it is perfect with respect to parts, but not with respect to degrees. Sanctification, as a principle, which is the new creature, or new man, has all his parts; though these are not grown up to the measure of the fulness of the stature of Christ, as they will do; where there is one grace, there is every grace, though none perfect; there is a comparative perfection in the saints, when compared with what they themselves once were, and others are; and when compared even with other saints, for one saint may have a greater degree of grace and holiness than another; *let us therefore, as many as be perfect;* and yet the greatest of those was not absolutely perfect, even the apostle himself, who so said, Phil. iii. 12, 17. all the saints may be said to be perfect, as perfection denotes sincerity and truth; so their faith, though imperfect, is unfeigned; their hope is without hypocrisy, and their love without dissimulation; but otherwise, sanctification in the best of men is imperfect; this appears,——1. From the continual wants of the saints; they are always *poor and needy*, as David says of himself; which could not be true of him as to things temporal, but as to things spiritual: the best of saints continually stand in need of more grace to oppose sin, resist temptations, perform duty, and persevere in faith and holiness; the grace of God is sufficient for them, but then that must be daily communicated to them; God has promised to supply, and he does supply all their need, as it returns upon them; but then it cannot be said that they are *perfect and entire, wanting nothing;* since they are continually in want of more grace.——2. This appears from their disclaiming perfection in themselves, and their desires after it. Job, David, the apostle Paul, and others, have in express words declared they were not perfect, nor thought themselves so, but far from it; and yet expressed strong desires after it, which shewed they had it not; the apostle Paul has fully set forth both in those words of his, *Not as though I had already attained, either were already perfect, &c.* Phil. iii. 12, 13, 14.——3. That sanctification is imperfect, is abundantly manifest from indwelling sin in the saints, and the sad effects of it; the apostle Paul speaks of *sin dwelling in him*, Rom. vii. 18, 19. and the apostle John says, *if we say we have no sin, we deceive ourselves*, 1 John i. 8. and the experience of the saints in all ages testifies the same: this is clear from their ingenuous confessions of sin, such as made by Jacob, David, Isaiah, Daniel, and others; from their groans and complaints under the weight of sin, as an heavy burden, too heavy to bear; from the continual war in them between flesh and spirit, the law in their members and the law in their minds; from their prayers for the manifestation of the pardon of their sins, and for cleansing from them, and to be kept from the commission of them; from the many slips and falls which the best are subject to in one way or another; and from backwardness to duty, remissness in it, and that coldness and lukewarmness which too often attend it. ——4. This is also evident from the several parts of sanctification, and the several graces of which it consists, being imperfect. Faith is imperfect; there are deficiencies in faith to be made up; the best of saints have had them, and their failings in the exercise of that grace have been manifest, as in Abraham, Peter, and others; and they have been sensible of their imperfection in it, as the apostles of Christ were, when they said, *Lord increase our faith*, or *add* to it, Luke xvii. 5. hope sometimes is so low as that it seems to be *perished from the Lord*, and only the mouth is put in the dust with an *if so be there may be hope*, Lam. iii. 18, 29. Love, however warm and fervent at first, remits and abates; its ardour is left, though that is not lost; the love of many waxes cold. Spiritual, experimental, sanctified knowledge is but in part, and will remain so until that which is perfect is come.

2dly, Though sanctification is imperfect, it is progressive, it is going on gradually till it comes to perfection; this is clear from the characters of the saints, who are first as little children, infants new-born; are in a state of childhood, and by degrees become to be young men, strong and robust, and overcome the evil one, and at length are fathers in Christ, 1 John ii. 13, 14. and from the similies by which the work of grace is illustrated; as that in general by seed sown in the earth, which springs up first the blade, then the ear, after that the full corn in the ear; and faith in particular by a grain of mustard-seed, which when first sown is small, the least of all seeds, but when it grows up, it becomes greater than all herbs, and shoots out great branches, Mark iv. 28, 31, 32. so spiritual light and knowledge at first is very dim and obscure, like the sight that the man had whose eyes Christ opened; first he saw men like trees walking, and after that all things clearly; so the path of the just is as the shining light, that shineth more and more unto the perfect day, Mark viii. 23, 24. Prov. iv. 18. there is such a thing as growing in grace, in the grace of faith, and abounding in hope and love, and increasing in the knowledge of divine things; which there would be no room for, if sanctification was perfect. Yet,

3dly, Though it is imperfect, it will certainly be perfected; grace in the soul is a well of living water, springing up unto everlasting life; it is always running to, and will issue in eternal life: it is *certain*, from election and redemption, the ends whereof would not be answered, if this was not completed; and from its being the work of the Holy Spirit, who having begun it, will finish it; he is a rock, and his work is perfect; having undertook it, he will not leave it till it is done; and when he works, none can let; he will perfect that which concerneth his saints, and will fulfil the good pleasure of his will in them, and the work of faith, with power.

4*thly*, Sanctification is absolutely *necessary* to salvation. It is necessary for many things; it is necessary to the saints, as an evidence of their election and redemption; this is the closing work of grace, and is the evidence of all that goes before. It is necessary to church-fellowship, to the communion of saints in a social manner. Members of churches are described as holy brethren, saints, and faithful in Christ Jesus, and none are meet to be admitted among them but such who are so; for *what fellowship hath righteousness with unrighteousness? &c.* 2 Cor. vi. 14, 15, 16. Sanctification is necessary as a meetness for heaven; for the inheritance of the saints in light; without regeneration, in which sanctification is begun, no man shall see, nor enter into the kingdom of God. It is absolutely necessary for the beatific-vision of God in a future state; *Without holiness no man shall see the Lord;* but being possessed of that, shall see him, and enjoy uninterrupted communion with him for ever, Heb. xii. 14. Matt. v. 8. Psalm xvii. 15. To say no more, it is necessary for the work of heaven, which is singing songs of praise, songs of electing, redeeming, regenerating, calling, and persevering grace; how can unholy persons join with the saints in such work and service as this? yea, it would be irksome and disagreeable to themselves, could they be admitted to it, and were capable of it; neither of which can be allowed.

CHAP. XV.

OF THE PERSEVERANCE OF THE SAINTS.

THE doctrine of the saints' final perseverance in grace to glory is next to be considered; which is, that those who are truly regenerated, effectually called, and really converted, and internally sanctified by the Spirit and grace of God, shall persevere in grace to the end, and shall be everlastingly saved; or shall never finally and totally fall, so as to perish everlastingly. This truth may be confirmed,

I. From various passages of scripture, which clearly hold it forth and assert it; it is written as with a sunbeam in the sacred writings; to give the whole compass of the proof of it, which they will admit, would be to transcribe great part of the Bible. I shall only therefore select some passages, both out of the Old and New Testament, which fully express it. And shall begin,

First, With Job, chap. xvii. 9. *The righteous also shall hold on his way; and he that hath clean hands shall be stronger and stronger.* By the righteous man is meant one that is made truly righteous, by the righteousness of Christ imputed to him, and which he receives by faith; in consequence of which he lives soberly and righteously; and by his *way* is meant, Christ *the way;* in whom he walks as he has received him, as the Lord his Righteousness. And it is promised, he *shall hold on* in this his way; which is opposed to going back, turning aside, and standing still; if he went back, or apostatized, or turned either to the right-hand or the left, or was at a full stop, he could not be said to go on; and if he goes on he must persevere; and though he meets with discouragements in the way, from sin, and Satan, and the world, yet he goes on; and though he may slip, and slide, and stumble, and even fall; yet as the traveller, when this is his case, gets up again and pursues his journey; so the believer rises again in the strength of Christ, in whom he walks, and in the exercise of faith and repentance; and still goes on his way, rejoicing in Christ his righteousness and strength; and to which his going on is owing, and not to his own conduct, power, and strength. As *hands* are an emblem of action, by *clean hands* are meant, a holy, upright walk and conversation, arising from an inward principle of grace in the heart; as appears by comparing Psalm xv. 1, 2. with Psalm xxiv. 3, 4. and such a man who walks uprightly, and works righteousness, though he may have but little strength, yet he has some, which is here supposed; and as he wants more, to resist temptations, oppose corruptions, exercise grace, and perform duty, he shall have more, be stronger and stronger, as here promised; God will, and does, *give power to the faint, and to them that have no might he increaseth strength, and renews their strength, so that they shall run and not be weary, and they shall walk and not faint,* and consequently persevere to the end; yea, the *way* of the Lord itself is *strength* unto them; as they walk in it, they become stronger and stronger, and go *from strength to strength,* till they appear before God in Zion above, Isa. xl. 29, 31. Prov. x. 29. Psa. lxxxiv. 5, 6, 7. Now if the righteous shall hold on his way, he must persevere; and if the good man shall be stronger and stronger, he must endure to the end, and be saved; or otherwise, he would become weaker and weaker, until he had no strength at all; and then how would this promise be fulfilled?

Secondly, Another passage of scripture, proving the saints final perseverance, is in Psalm xciv. 14. *For the Lord will not cast off his people, &c.* the Lord's people are his special and peculiar people, whom he has loved, chosen, redeemed, and called, his *fore-known people;* these he never casts off, casts out, nor casts away, Rom. xi. 2. though he may seem to do so; and they may think he has, when he does not immediately arise for their help in distress; and when he withdraws his presence, or afflicts them, or suffers them to be afflicted by others, which seems to be their case in this Psalm; and for their comfort these words are said; see ver. 5, 6, 12, 13. Psalm xliv. 9, 23, 24, and lxxxviii. 14. yet, in reality, God does not cast off, at least for ever, as unbelief sometimes suggests; he never casts them off, nor casts them out from being in his sight; for they are engraven on the palms of his hands; nor from being on his heart, for they are set as a seal there; nor from a place in his house, for being sons they always abide there; and whoever casts them off, or casts out their names as evil, he never will; so far from it, that he takes the utmost delight and complacency in them; grants them nearness to himself, and expresses the strongest affection for them, and takes the greatest care of them, even as the apple of his eye: and these are his *inheritance*, which he will never *forsake*, though he may seem to forsake them for a little while, yet he never does, finally and totally; he has promised he will not, and he is faithful who has promised; he never forsakes their persons, neither in youth nor in old age; nor the work of his hands on them, but fulfils the good pleasure of his goodness in them, and the work of faith with power; and for this reason he will not forsake them, because they are his inheritance, which he has chosen, his jewels, and his peculiar treasure; and therefore will never lose them: if, therefore, he will not cast off his people for ever, nor utterly forsake them, then they shall persevere to the end, and be saved, and not everlastingly perish.

Thirdly, This doctrine may be concluded from Psalm cxxv. 1, 2. the persons described are such who *trust in the Lord*, and not in the creature, nor in creature-services; that trust in him at all times, and for all things; for temporal and spiritual blessings; for grace and glory: these are *like mount Zion*, for many things, but especially for its immoveableness; for those, like that, *cannot be removed:* not from the love of God, in which they are rooted and grounded; nor from the covenant of grace, which is as immoveable as hills and mountains, yea, more so; they may be removed, but that cannot be removed; nor the Lord's covenant-people out of it; nor out of the hands of Christ, out of whose hands none can pluck; nor off of him, the foundation, on which they are laid, which is a sure and everlasting one; nor out of a state of grace, in which they stand; neither of sanctification, which is connected with life everlasting; nor of justification, for those who have passed from death to life, shall never enter into condemnation. These, like mount Zion, *abide for ever;* they abide on the heart of God, in the hands of Christ, on him the sure-foundation laid in Zion; in the house of God, and in the family of his people. And what makes their safety and security appear still the greater, is, that as Jerusalem was encompassed with mountains, which were a natural and strong fortification to it; so *the Lord is round about his people, even for ever;* he surrounds them with his love, encompasses them with his favours, as with a shield, guards them by his special providence, and watches over them night and day, lest any hurt them; and keeps them by his power as in a garrison, through faith unto salvation. And if all these things are true of them, as they most certainly are, then they shall finally persevere in grace, and be eternally saved.

Fourthly, This truth will receive further proof from Jer. xxxii. 40. *And I will make an everlasting covenant with them, &c.* In which words are more proofs than one of the saints' final perseverance. This may be concluded,——1. From the perpetuity of the covenant made with them; which is not a covenant of works, promising life on doing; then their perseverance would be precarious; but of grace, sovereign and free; and so is a better covenant, and established on better promises, which are absolute and unconditional, not depending on any thing to be performed by them; but which runs thus, *I will*, and *they shall; a* covenant *ordered in all things*, not one thing wanting in it, conducive to the welfare and happiness of the saints; in all spiritual blessings, for time and eternity, in both grace and glory, which are eternally secured in it, and therefore said to be *sure;* its blessings are the sure mercies of David; its promises yea and amen, in Christ; and the whole is ratified and confirmed by the blood of Christ, and sure to all the spiritual seed, to all interested in it; a covenant not made with them as considered by themselves, but with Christ, as their head, and with them in him; and it is kept, and stands fast with him for evermore. It is an *everlasting* covenant, flows from everlasting love, and founded on an everlasting purpose; consists of promises, which God, that cannot lie, made before the world began; and of grace, and blessings of grace, given in Christ so early, who was set up as the Mediator of it from everlasting, from the beginning, or ever the earth was; and the covenant-ones, with all their grace, were put into his hands; all which shew the certainty of their perseverance; for as God knew so early, when he took them into covenant, and provided for them, what they would be, even transgressors from the womb, and do as evil as they could; and yet this hindered not his taking them into covenant; then it may be depended upon, that none of these things shall ever throw them out of it, for it abides to everlasting; God that made it, has commanded it for ever; he will never break it; it shall never be antiquated and made void, by another covenant succeeding it; its blessings are irreversible, and its promises are always fulfilled; its grace is sufficient for the saints under all their temptations, trials, and exercises, to bear them up, and bear them through time to eternity: covenant-interest always continues; he that is their covenant-God, will be their God and guide even unto death, and through it, to the world beyond the grave; and therefore they shall most certainly persevere, and be saved.——2. This may be confirmed from the promise made in the covenant, that God will *not turn away from them to do them good!* he may withdraw his gracious presence, and return again, which shews that he does not turn away from them for ever; he never turns from his affections to them, which are unalterably fixed on them; nor from his kind purposes concerning them; for he is in *one mind*, and none can turn him: nor from his gracious promises to them; for he is not a man, that he should lie or repent; but what he has said, he will do, and not alter the thing that is gone out of his lips: nor from his gifts bestowed on them, which are without repentance, and which he never revokes, or calls in again; and he continues to do them good, both in things temporal and spiritual, as they stand in need of them; he has laid up much good for them in covenant, and in the hands of his Son; and he has bestowed much good upon them, given himself to them to be their portion and exceeding great reward; his Son, and all things with him; the holy Spirit, and his graces; and continues the supplies of his grace, and carries on his good work in them, and makes all things to work together for their good ——3. This is further strengthened by what follows; *I will put my fear in their hearts, that they shall not depart from me;* not that they shall cease to sin; every sin being, in a sense, a departure from his precepts, and his judgments, Dan. ix. 5. Nor that they shall not revolt and backslide from God, to which they are prone; and which backslidings are partial departures from him; but then these do not break the relation between God and them, as of father, and children, of husband and wife: and besides, he heals their backslidings, and still loves them freely, Jer. iii. 14. Hos. xiv. 4. but they do not wickedly depart from him; as David says, Psalm xviii. 22. purposely, obstinately, and with an evil intent, and finally and totally. They do not depart from the word of faith they have received; this, when it has once a place in their hearts, and becomes the engrafted word, and they have a true experience of, can never be utterly departed from, through the sleight of them who lie in wait to deceive: nor from the worship, ordinances, and people of God; having set their hand to the plough, they neither turn back nor look back, so as entirely to leave the good ways, and good people of God; and this the fear of God, put into their hearts, guards them against, and influences them to the contrary, Neh. v. 15. Now if God will not turn away from his people, and will continue to do them good; if he so influences their hearts with his fear that they shall not depart from him, then they shall certainly persevere to the end, and be saved.

Fifthly, Another passage of scripture, which clearly expresses this truth, is in John x. 28. *I give unto them eternal life, and they shall never perish, neither shall any man pluck them out of my hand!* These words are spoken of the sheep of Christ, which he has a property in, whom the Father has given to him, and he has laid down his life for; whom he knows and calls by name, and they follow him in paths he directs them to: now to these he gives *eternal life*, which he has in his hands, and a right to bestow; and which he does give to all his chosen, redeemed, and called ones; and if he gives them eternal life, they must live for ever, or it would not be an eternal life he gives them; they can never die the second death, or be hurt by it; but must persevere in a life of grace, till they come to a life of glory; and if Christ says, *they shall never perish*, who dare say they may or shall perish? though they were lost in Adam, with the rest of mankind, yet they were preserved in Christ, and saved by him, who came to seek and to save that which was lost; and though in their nature-state they seem ready to perish, and see themselves to be in such a condition, and therefore apply to Christ, and say, *Lord, save us, we perish!* yet they never shall really perish; for he is able and willing to save all that come to him; nor will he cast out any that are given him, as the sheep in the text are; and though when called by grace, they are liable to many slips and falls; to spiritual decays and declensions; to loss of comfort and peace, and in that sense to perishings, 1 Cor. viii. 11. and to fears of perishing finally; and to faintings and sinkings of spirit; yet they shall never fail and sink under their burdens, and be lost; and though they die as other men, in which sense the righteous are said to perish, Eccles. vii. 15. Isa. lvii. 1. yet they shall not perish eternally, as the wicked will, who will go into everlasting punishment, when these shall go into eternal life. Besides, they are *in the hands* of Christ, and can never be plucked from thence; being put there by his Father, through his act of choosing them in him, as an instance of his love to them, and care of them, and for their security: and which is expressive of their being in his possession, at his dispose, under his guidance, care and protection, and therefore must be safe; nor is it in the power of any man, either by force to pluck them, or by fraud to draw them out of Christ's hands; not the most violent persecutor, by the most cruel methods he can practice; nor the most cunning and artful false teacher, by all the wiles and sophistry he is master of; nor τις, *any one*, man or devil; Satan with all his principalities and powers, can never force any one from Christ; nor with all his stratagems, can draw any one from him: and if they are in his hands, who is not only the mighty Saviour, and mighty Mediator, who has all power in heaven and in earth, but is the Lord God Almighty; are in his hands, which made the heavens and the earth; and which hold and uphold all things in being, and who is the Governor of the universe; then they shall never totally and finally fall away, or perish everlastingly.

Sixthly, The words of Christ in his prayer to his Father, are another proof of the preservation of his people by him; and of their final perseverance through that, John xvii. 12. *While I was with them in the world, I kept them in thy name; those that thou gavest me I have kept, and none of them is lost, but the son of perdition, that the scripture might be fulfilled;* the persons spoken of, though primarily and more immediately the apostles of Christ, yet not they only; they were not the only persons given to Christ out of the world, and who stand opposed to the world, as these do, ver. 6, 9. nor are the words spoken of them as apostles, but as given to him by an act of special grace, as united to him, members of him, and believers in him; and as such, preserved by him: and if the preservation of them as such was secured to them, by being thus given to him, why may not the preservation of all other true believers in him be equally as sure and certain? Nor is this said of their preservation from a temporal death; and that this might be fulfilled, he requested what he did, chap. xvii. 8, 9. but as the other things Christ speaks of, and prays for in this chapter, are all of a spiritual kind; such as sanctification, union, eternal glory; it is most reasonable to suppose, that this was of the same kind. Besides, if preservation from temporal death is meant, the sense would be, *Those that thou gavest me I have kept* from a temporal death, *and none of them is lost* by a temporal death, *but the son of perdition*, he is lost by a temporal death: which last was not true; Judas was not, at this time, lost in such sense; he had not yet betrayed Christ, and it was after his condemnation that he went and destroyed himself. To which may be added, that as Christ had kept those that were given him, he prays his Father would keep them in like manner, ver. 11. now if he prayed they might be kept from a temporal death, he was not heard, and yet he is always heard; for as for his disciples, they all died a violent death, suffered martyrdom for his sake; though they were all, in a spiritual sense, preserved to his kingdom and glory, as all true believers will be. Moreover, as it was from *evil* that he desires his Father would keep them, it was the same which he kept them from, namely, from the evil of the world; not from suffering reproaches, afflictions, and persecutions in it; for such he has given all his followers reason to expect; but from sinking under them, and being overcome by them, so as to drop their profession of him; and from the evil one, Satan, under whose influence the world is; and from the evil of sin in the world. The time of Christ keeping those that were given him, *while I was with them in the world;* the expression does not imply, that he was not then in the world when he said these words, for he was, though the time of his departure was at hand; nor that he should be no longer with them when removed out of it; for though he would not be with them, as to his bodily presence, yet with respect to his spiritual, powerful, and all-preserving presence, he would be with them still, and with all his people, to the end of the world : nor does the expression imply, that Christ's keeping those that were given him was confined to the time he was in the world as to the flesh; for at his death he did not *deliver up the kingdom to the Father,* or the care and charge of his elect; this will not be done till his second coming; when he will say, *Lo, I, and the children,* even all the children, *thou hast given me;* till then, all the elect remain under the care and keeping of Christ. The manner in which he keeps them is in his Father's *name,* in the name of the Majesty of his God; in which he stands and feeds them, as Mediator, through a delegated power and authority committed to him as such; and in his gospel, and the doctrines of it, called his *name,* ver. 6. in the faith of the gospel, and in the profession of it, so as not to relinquish either; and, indeed, so as to be *lost,* no, not one of them, that is, to be eternally lost; for it is both his own will, and the will of his Father, that not one of those who truly believe in him, no not the least of them, should ever perish, Matt. xviii. 14. John vi. 39, 40. and whereas it may be said, there is an instance in the text of one that was given to Christ who perished, Judas. The answer is, that though Judas was given to Christ, and chosen by him as an apostle, yet was not given to him by an act of his Father's special grace; nor was he chosen in him, and by him, and united to him, and a member of him, as the rest were; nor does it appear, from all accounts of him, that he ever was a partaker of the true grace of God; and so no instance of the apostasy of a real saint. Judas stands distinguished from the rest of the apostles, in the choice of Christ; *I speak not of you all ; I know whom I have chosen,* that is, to eternal life; for otherwise, Judas was chosen as an apostle with the rest; *Have I not chosen ye twelve, and one of you is a devil?* John xiii. 18. and vi. 70. and as here, *a son of perdition;* and was never considered as an object of his, or his Father's love, and so was left to that perdition to which he was appointed, *that the scripture might be fulfilled,* which foretold it; and the particle *but* is not exceptive, but adversative; and does not imply, that he was one of those given to Christ to be kept, but the contrary.

Seventhly, When the apostle says of God, 1 Cor. i. 8, 9. *Who shall confirm you to the end, that ye may be blameless in the day of our Lord Jesus Christ; faithful is God,* &c. to do it; with other passages of the same kind, 1 Cor. x. 13. 1 Thess. iii. 13. and v. 23, 24. 2 Thess. iii. 3. These are so many proofs of the saints' final perseverance. The blessing itself promised and assured is confirmation, or establishment, in Christ; in faith in Christ, in the grace of faith, and in the doctrine of faith, and in holiness: the author of it is God; though ministers may be instruments of establishing the saints; God is the efficient; he has promised it; and he, as the God of all grace, is able to do it, and will; *He which establisheth us with you in Christ—is God,* 2 Cor. i. 21. see 1 Pet. v. 10. and the duration of it is *to the end;* not for a short time, but to the end of life; so that such shall endure to the end, or finally persevere; yea, so confirmed are they, that they shall be *unblameable at,* and be *preserved blameless to the coming of our Lord Jesus;* though not in themselves, yet in him, who will then present them to himself glorious, and without spot; and to his Father faultless, before the presence of his glory, with exceeding joy. And to do all this, the faithfulness of God is engaged, which is observed in the several passages; and which faithfulness of his he will never suffer to fail; and therefore the confirmation, and the preservation of the saints to the end, even to the coming of Christ, are sure and certain; and their final perseverance in grace to glory, out of all doubt.

Eighthly, It is said of those who are *elect*, and are *begotten again*, that they *are kept by the power of God, through faith, unto salvation*, 1 Pet. i. 5. they are kept in the love of God, in the covenant of grace, in the hands of Christ, and on his heart; in him, the strong hold, and on him, the foundation; in a state of grace, both of sanctification and of justification; and in the paths of truth and holiness: they are kept from Satan, not from his temptations, but from destruction by him; and from false teachers, and their errors, from being carried away with them, and finally deceived by them: and from sin, not from the indwelling of it in the hearts of believers; nor from all acts of sin in their conversation; but from the dominion, power, and tyranny of it; and from a final and total falling away through it. The means by which they are kept is, *the power of God*, which is as a fortress to them, inexpugnable; where they are φρουρμενοι, kept, as in a garrison, as the word signifies, and so are safe and secure; there being no might or power of men or devils, that can withstand, break through, or weaken the power of God. Likewise they are kept, *through faith*, in the power of God, and in the person and grace of Christ; through faith looking to Christ, living upon him, and leaning on him; through that faith which overcomes the world, and every spiritual enemy; and through the views it has of eternal glory; and so the believer endures, as seeing what is invisible: and what they are kept unto, is *salvation*; the full possession of that salvation which Christ is the author of, and they are heirs of; and which shall be completely enjoyed in a future state; to which, and till they come into it, their perseverance is certain. There are many other passages of scripture, which might be produced in proof of this doctrine; but these are sufficient. I pass on,

II. To observe those arguments in proof of the saints' final perseverance, taken from various sacred and divine things. As,

First, From the perfections of God; whatever is agreeable to them, and made necessary by them, must be true; and whatever is contrary to them, and reflects dishonour on them, must be false. The doctrine of the saints' final perseverance is agreeable to, and become necessary by them, and therefore must be true; but the contrary to it, that of the apostasy of real saints, so as to perish everlastingly, is repugnant to them, and reflects dishonour on them, and therefore must be false. The perfections of God, which are manifestly displayed in the doctrine of the saints' final perseverance, and by which it is confirmed, are the following.——1. The immutability of God. God is unchangeable; this is asserted by himself, *I am the Lord; I change not*: and he himself drew this inference from it, *Therefore ye sons of Jacob are not consumed;* ye that are Israelites indeed perish not, nor ever shall; and after God himself, we may safely draw the same conclusion: if they are consumed, or perish everlastingly, he must change in his love to them, which he never does, but rests in it; and in his purposes and designs concerning them. And those whom he has appointed to salvation, he must consign over to damnation; and his promises of grace made to them, and his blessings of grace bestowed on them, must be reversed; and yet he will not alter the thing that is gone out of his lips, nor change his mind; for he is *of one mind, and who can turn him?* The doctrine of the saints' final perseverance asserts the unchangeableness of God, and does honour to it; but the contrary doctrine makes him changeable in his nature, will, and grace, and reflects dishonour on him, with whom there is no *variableness nor shadow of turning*, Mal. iii. 6. Job. xxiii. 13. James i. 17.——2. The wisdom of God appears in this doctrine; and whose wisdom is seen in all his works of nature, providence, and grace; and is very conspicuous in the salvation of his people; which it would not be, should they perish. No wise man, who has an end in view, but will devise and make use of proper means; and will, if in his power, make those means effectual to attain the end, or he will not act a wise part. The end which God has in view, and has fixed, with respect to his people, is the salvation of them; and it can never be consistent with his wisdom to appoint insufficient means, or not to make those means effectual, which it is in his power to do; which must be the case, if any of those he has appointed to salvation should perish. Now as he has fixed the end, salvation, he has provided his Son to be the author of it, by his obedience, sufferings, and death; and has appointed as means to the enjoyment of this salvation, the sanctification of the Spirit, and the belief of the truth; for which purpose he sends his Spirit to sanctify them, and work faith in them, whereby these means become effectual, and the end is answered; and so the wisdom of God is highly displayed and glorified. But where would be his wisdom to appoint men to salvation, and not save them at last? to send his Son to redeem them, and they be never the better for it? and to send his Spirit into them, to begin a good work of grace, and not finish it? But this is not the case, he has put the work of redemption into the hands of his Son, who has completed it; and assigned the work of sanctification, in its beginning, progress, and issue, to the divine Spirit, who is equal to it, and will perform it: and throughout the whole, God abounds towards his people in all wisdom and prudence.——3. The power of God is greatly concerned in this affair. Such who are elect, according to the foreknowledge of God, and are regenerated by his grace, are *kept by his power to salvation,* so that they shall never perish, but be everlastingly saved. Not only salvation is appointed as walls and bulwarks to them, which is a sufficient security; but God himself is a wall of fire about them; and no enemy can possibly break through such walls, bulwarks, and fortifications, to destroy them. God is all powerful, his power is irresistible, nothing can withstand it, nor overcome it; nothing in earth and hell is a match for it. And this power of his can never be weakened, nor his hand shortened, that he cannot save; which must be the case, if any of those kept by his power perish. ——4. The goodness, grace, and mercy of God, confirm this truth. *The mercy of God is from everlasting to everlasting, upon them that fear him;* which it would not be, should any of those that truly fear him perish; *His compassions fail not;* which they would, should any of his be consumed; but because of his tender mercies they are not consumed: nor can it be thought that that God, who is *gracious and merciful, abundant in goodness and truth;* who has, of his *abundant mercy, begotten again his elect;* and because he is *rich in mercy,* and for his *great love* to them, has *quickened* them when *dead in trespasses and sins;* will, after all this, suffer them to fall, so as to perish everlastingly; no, *the Lord will perfect that which concerneth* them, his work of grace upon them, and the whole salvation of them: the reason is, *Thy mercy, O Lord, endures for ever!* and then follows a prayer of faith; *Forsake not the work of thine own hands!* which God never will, Psalm cxxxviii. 8.——5. The justice of God makes the perseverance of the saints necessary. God is righteous in all his ways and works, and so in the work of salvation. He is a just God, and a Saviour; his justice is, and must be glorified, in the salvation of men, as the other attributes of his; and it is through Christ's making satisfaction for sin, and bringing in everlasting righteousness. And can it be imagined, that God should accept of the righteousness of his Son, and express a well-pleasedness in it, because by it his law is magnified and made honourable; that he should impute it to his people, and give them faith to receive it, and plead it as their justifying righteousness; and yet, after all, suffer them to perish? Nay, where could be his justice, to punish those for whose sins Christ has made satisfaction, and God himself has discharged upon it? It is not consistent with the justice of God to punish sin twice; once in the surety, and again in those he has redeemed; which must be the case, if any for whom Christ suffered should perish eternally; for to perish eternally is the same as to be punished with everlasting destruction.——6. The faithfulness of God secures the final perseverance of the saints; God is faithful to his counsels, to his covenant; and to his promises concerning their salvation, and will never suffer his faithfulness to fail; which must fail if they perish. But God is faithful, who has called them by his grace, and will confirm them to the end; will not suffer them to be tempted above what they are able to bear; will establish them, and keep them from evil; and will preserve them blameless to the coming of Christ; faithful is he who has promised, who also will do it.

Secondly, The final perseverance of the saints may be concluded from the purposes and decrees of God; which are infrustrable, and are always accomplished; *The Lord of hosts hath purposed, and who shall disannul it?* or make it void, and of no effect? *and his hand is stretched out,* to execute his purposes, *and who shall turn it back* from doing the thing he is resolved on? as he has *thought, so shall it come to pass;* and as he has *purposed, it shall stand,* Isa. xiv. 24, 27. though there may be a thousand devices in the hearts of men and devils, they can never counteract, nor undermine the decrees of God. His *counsel shall* stand, every purpose of his, and particularly his *purpose according to election;* which stands not upon the foot of *works,* but upon the will *of him that calls,* which is unalterable and irreversible. *The election hath obtained,* or the elect, in all ages, have obtained righteousness, life, and salvation; it is not possible they should be deceived; nor can any charge be laid against them by law or justice, and therefore must be saved. Election is an ordination of men to eternal life, and therefore they shall never die the second death; it is an appointment of them to salvation, and therefore they shall be saved; they are chosen to obtain the glory of Christ, through sanctification of the Spirit, and belief of the truth; and accordingly they are sanctified by the Spirit, and do believe in Christ, who is the truth, and shall be glorified; for between their predestination and glorification, there is an inseparable connection; *Whom he did predestinate—them he also glorified,* Rom. ix. 12, 13. and xi. 7. and viii. 30.

Thirdly, The argument in favour of the saints' final perseverance, receives great strength from the promises of God, which are sure, and are all yea and amen in Christ, and are always fulfilled; not one of the good things God has promised has ever failed; and many are his promises, as has been observed, concerning the perseverance of his people; as that they shall hold on their way, and be stronger and stronger; that he will not turn away from them; and they shall never depart from him; with a multitude of others; and, in general, he has promised, he will never leave nor forsake them: and therefore it is impossible they should perish; for then his promises and his faithfulness in them would be of none effect; which ought not to be said.

Fourthly, This truth may be further confirmed from the gracious acts of God, flowing from his everlasting and unchangeable love. The love of God to his people is an everlasting love, which it would not be should they perish; for none can perish and remain the objects of his love: but his love always remains, it is never taken away, nor does it ever depart, nor can there be any separation from it; and consequently those interested in it can never be finally and totally lost: and there are many acts of grace arising from this love, which show it; not to take notice of the act of election before observed, which secures their salvation; nor the covenant of grace, from the perpetuity of which this point has been argued; nor the act of putting the elect into Christ's hands, from whence they can never be plucked; there are several others which ascertain the same thing; two or three of which I shall mention.——
1. The adoption of the children of God into his family; by which he takes them for his sons and daughters; which is a wonderful instance of his love, 1 John iii. 1. now to this they are predestinated according to the good pleasure of his will; and this predestination and appointment of them to adoption, is his will to adopt them; and his will to adopt them, is the adoption of them; this is what is called a putting them among the children, Jer. iii. 19. and whom God puts among the children, and accounts as such, it is not in the power of men or devils to put them out; nor can they put out themselves, should they even desire it, or express their contentment to be no longer sons, but to be servants; it is impracticable and not to be admitted, as the case of the prodigal shews, Luke xv. 19, 21. The blessing is bestowed in the covenant of grace, and is irreversible; Christ by his redemption has made way for the reception of it, which makes his redemption a plenteous one, this with other blessings of grace, being included in it; and to them that receive him, and believe in him, he gives a power to become the sons of God; his Spirit witnesses to theirs that they are so, and by faith it becomes manifest. Now between sonship and heirship there is a close connection: *if a son, no more a servant* of sin and Satan, and the world, but *an heir of God through Christ; if children, then heirs, heirs of God, and joint-heirs with Christ;* Gal. iv. 7. Rom. viii. 17. and can a child of God become a child of the devil? shall an heir of heaven be seen in the flames of hell? or shall one that is a joint-heir with Christ, come short of the incorruptible inheritance? no, that is reserved for them, and they are kept to that by the power of God.——2. Justification is another act of God's free grace, and the fruit of his ancient love, Rom. iii. 24. and v. 17. the sentence is pronounced in the mind of God by himself, and none can reverse it; it is God that justifies, and who shall condemn? such as are justified by him, can never come into condemnation and everlastingly perish; otherwise how could he be just, and the justifier of him that believes in Jesus; if, after all, notwithstand-

ing his imputation of the righteousness of his Son to them, and the justification of them by it, and their reception of it by faith, they should be condemned? or how would Christ's righteousness be an everlasting righteousness and answer for his people in a time to come, should they be condemned with the world and excluded from the kingdom of heaven? or how would this righteousness of his be unto justification of life? or what would signify their being made heirs of eternal life through it? or of what avail would their title to it by it, be unto them, if after all they perish eternally? But the connection between justification and glorification is inseparable; *whom he justified them he also glorified,* Rom. viii. 30. and most certain it is, that the righteous, who are justified by Christ's righteousness, shall go into everlasting life, when the wicked will go into eternal punishment, Matt. xxv. 46.——3. Pardon of sin is another act of the riches of divine grace, and flows from unmerited and distinguishing love. Those whom God forgives for Christ's sake, on account of his blood shed for the remission of their sins, and upon the foot of satisfaction made for them by him, he forgives all their iniquities; not one sin is left unforgiven; and if so, how can they be destroyed or perish everlastingly? Is it possible that a man should go to hell with a full and free pardon of all his sins in his hands? Was ever any man executed, having received the king's pardon? and especially can it be thought that any whom the King of kings has pardoned, whose acts can never be made void, should yet suffer everlasting punishment for sin? no, when *the iniquity of Israel shall be sought for, and there shall be none* to be laid to their charge, being cleared of all; and *the sins of Judah, and they shall not be found,* nor any bill on account of them be found against them, and that for this reason; *for I will pardon them whom I reserve,* that is, for himself; and if reserved for himself, being fully pardoned by his grace, they shall be preserved from everlasting destruction.

Fifthly, The saints' final perseverance in grace to glory, and security from ruin and destruction, may be concluded from the love of Christ to them, his interest in them, and theirs in him. Christ's love to them was from everlasting, his delights were with those sons of men before the world was, and from it nothing can separate them; *having loved his own, which were in the world, he loves them to the end,* John. xiii. 1. to the end of their lives, and to all eternity; and therefore they can never perish. And they are not only the objects of his love, dear unto him, but they are his *care* and *charge,* who are committed to him to be kept by him; and he has undertook the care of them, has eternal life to give them, and does give it to them, and they shall never perish, but have it; yea, they have it already, a right unto it and earnest of it; and as they are his Father's *gift* to him, to be preserved by him, so they are the *purchase* of his blood, the flock he has purchased with it, and he will not lose one of them; should he, so far his blood would be shed for nought, and his death be in vain. They are *members* of his body, and can never be separated from it; should they, even the least member of them, his body, the church, would not be *the fulness of him that filleth all in all;* if any one member in a natural body should be wanting, even the least, it would not be a complete body; and this would be the case of Christ's mystical body, should any member in it perish; but as sure as Christ the head lives, so sure shall every member of his body live also, and never die. They are his *children,* his spiritual seed and offspring, to whom he stands in the relation of an *everlasting Father;* these are a *seed* that it is promised he shall *see* and enjoy for ever, and that they shall *endure for ever;* nor shall any one of them be missing at the great day; but Christ will present them to his Father complete and safe, who gave them to him, saying, *Lo, I, and the children thou hast given me!* They are his *spouse* and bride, whom he has betrothed to himself in loving-kindness, and that for ever, to whom he stands in the relation of an *husband;* and between whom there is a conjugal and indissoluble union; whom he has so loved as to give himself for, to sanctify and cleanse, and make them spotless and glorious in his sight; and after all the cost and pains he has been at to make her so, can it be thought he will suffer this choice one, and beloved spouse of his, or any of them that make up this spiritual body, to perish eternally? They are his *portion, and the lot of his inheritance,* his Father has given him, and he is well-pleased with; they are his *jewels,* and he will never lose any of them; they are a crown of glory, and a royal diadem in his hand; his Hephzibah, in whom he delights; his Beulah, to whom he is married, and he will employ all his power in the preservation and security of them. They are on him the *foundation* laid in Zion, which is sure and everlasting; on which all those who are laid are safe, and from whence they can never be removed by all the winds, and waves, storms and tempests, raised by sin, Satan, and the world; they are built upon a rock immoveable, against which the gates of hell cannot prevail. They are interested in the *intercession* of Christ, which is always prevalent; for he is always heard; and he ever lives to make intercession for them; not only for all the necessary supplies of grace, for grace to help them in time of need; but for their eternal glorification, John xvii. 24. Lastly, Christ is making *preparations* in heaven for them; he is gone beforehand, and entered into heaven as their forerunner, and in their name to take possession for them; he is gone to prepare a place, and fit up mansions of glory for them; and has promised to come and take them to himself, that where he is they may be also, John xiv. 2, 3. And are these mansions preparing in vain? and shall these seats and dwelling-places be empty of those for whom they are designed, or any of them? this would be the case should any perish for whom Christ is gone to prepare a place.

Sixthly, A further proof of this doctrine may be taken from the work of grace, and the nature of it; and from the Spirit's concern in it, as the author of it, in those in whom it is wrought. Grace is an incorruptible seed, that never dies; it always remains, and is the reason why those in whom it is, shall not sin unto death, or so sin as to die eternally: it is a well of living water, springing up unto eternal life; grace and glory are inseparably connected; to whom God gives the one, he assuredly gives the other. The several particular graces of which the work consists, are abiding ones, as faith, hope, and love, 1 Cor. xiii. 13. Faith ever remains; it is more precious than gold that perisheth; and for that reason, among others, because it perishes not, when gold does. Christ who is the author, is the finisher of it; though it may sometimes seem as if it would fail, it shall not fail, through his powerful and prevalent mediation; he that truly believes in Christ, shall be most certainly saved by him, if there is any truth in the gospel of Christ. *Hope*, though a lowly grace, is a lively one; however, is always a living one, and is an anchor sure and stedfast; and is of great use to the saint under all his trials and afflictions in life, and will continue with him till death; *For the righteous hath hope in his death;* nor will it ever make *ashamed*, because it never disappoints, nor is disappointed. *Love*, though it sometimes waxes cold, and the first love may be left, though not lost; it is of such a nature, that all the floods of afflictions, persecution, and temptations, can never quench. The church in darkness, and without the presence of Christ, and sight of him, could even then describe him as the Person *whom her soul loved*. Peter, though he fell so grievously, through the temptations of Satan, yet did not lose his love to Christ; but upon first meeting with him, when asked the question, and that repeated again and again, declared he did love him; yea, he appeals to him, as the omniscient God, that he knew he loved him. The Spirit of God is the author of this work of grace; it is he who begins it, and will perform it, till the day of Christ, and finish what he has begun. He has his residence in the hearts of the Lord's people, and dwells in them, as in his temple; nor does he ever utterly depart from them; he is given to abide with them, and he does. Yea he is given as the earnest and pledge of their glorious inheritance; and having such an earnest, can they doubt or have any reason to doubt, of their full enjoyment of it, since by him, they are sealed unto the day of redemption? In a word, the glory of the three divine Persons is concerned in the final perseverance of the saints; for should they, or any of them perish, where would be the glory of the Father in choosing them to salvation? and the glory of the Son in redeeming them? and the glory of the Spirit in the sanctification of them? respecting them their glory would be lost, should they come short of heaven and happiness; but since the doctrine of the saints' final perseverance is bound together with this threefold cord, which cannot be broken, the certainty of it may be depended upon. I proceed,

III. To answer to, and remove the objections made, to this doctrine.

First, From some passages of scripture which may seem to be contrary unto it; or, however, are brought to disprove it.

1. The first passage of scripture, and which is usually set in the front of those that are brought against the saints' final perseverance, is Ezek. xviii. 24. *But when the righteous turneth away from his righteousness*, &c. from whence it is concluded,

that a man may be truly just and good, and yet become a very wicked man, and die in his sins, and perish everlastingly. ——(1.) The scope of the chapter should be attended to; which is to vindicate the justice of God in the dispensations of his providence towards the people of Israel; they had a proverb much in use among them, *The fathers have eaten sour grapes, and the children's teeth are set on edge:* the meaning of which was, their fathers have sinned, and they their children were punished for their sins; upon which they charged the ways of God with inequality and injustice. In answer to which, the Lord says, that whereas all souls were his, as the soul of the father, so the soul of the son, it was the soul that sinned that should die, or be punished with one temporal calamity or another; that if a man was a just man, and behaved well, he should live comfortably and happily in the land; if not, he should die, as to civil enjoyment in it, and be removed from it; for,——(2.) This chapter, and the context of it, only relate to the land of Israel, and to the house of Israel, the inhabitants of it; who, when first put into the possession of it, had a law given them; and according to their obedience, or disobedience to it, they were to live in the land, or be driven out of it; for they held their tenure by their obedience; if they were willing to serve the Lord, and keep his statues, and be obedient to them, then they should eat the good of the land and enjoy the benefits of it, Isa. i. 19. but if they were disobedient, they were to be exiled from it, and be captives in another land; which was now their case, and of which they complained. And, ——(3.) By the *righteous man* in the text is not meant one truly righteous; no man is truly righteous by the works of the law in the sight of God, these being imperfect; but he that is made righteous, by the perfect obedience and righteousness of Christ imputed to him, and received by faith. But there is not a word in the text, nor context, of the obedience and righteousness of Christ, which is an *everlasting righteousness;* from which no man that has it can turn, so as to die and perish eternally; for then it would not be everlasting: nor can a man that has true faith in this righteousness, or that lives by faith upon it, *commit iniquity;* that is, live a sinful course of life, make a trade of sinning, addict himself wholly to it; for such a man is a servant of sin, a slave to it, and of the devil; which can never be said of a truly just and good man; for though there is not a just man that doth good and sinneth not, yet he doth not sin at such a rate as this; the *seed* of grace remains in him, and he cannot sin, as to do *all the abominations* the wicked man does. Nor can he die spiritually and eternally; the just man lives by faith upon that righteousness by which he becomes just; he lives by the faith of the Son of God; and he that lives and believes in Christ shall never die spiritually; and the righteousness of Christ is upon him, *unto justification of life,* and entitles him to eternal life; and therefore he shall never be hurt by the second death; he shall never come into condemnation; but being righteous, shall be *righteous still,* and evermore so. But this is to be understood of one that only seemed to be a righteous man, was so in the sight of others, and in his own account, but not really so; one that reckoned himself righteous by his *own righteousness,* and *trusted* in that; see chap. xxxiii. 13. a righteousness that consisted of a few external, moral performances; as appears from ver. 5—9. and from such a righteousness, or course of living, a man may turn, and give up himself to all manner of wickedness; and become like the dog and the swine in the proverb; when it would have been better if such a man had not known the way of righteousness, than after to have turned from the holy commandment delivered to him. ——(4.) The death here spoken of, and in other passages in this chapter; as in ver. 23, 31, 32. is not an eternal death, or the death of the soul and body in hell; for this was now upon them, of which they were complaining, imagining it was for their fathers' sins; but of some severe judgment, or sore calamity, or some great affliction, which is called a *death;* as in Exod. x. 17, 2 Cor. i. 10. and xi. 23. so here the exile of the Jews from their native country, and captivity in a foreign land, which was a civil death, is here so called; wherefore no argument can be formed from hence, to prove the saints' perishing eternally. And,——(5.) After all, the words are only a supposition; *When,* or *if, a righteous man, turn from his righteousness;* and a supposition puts nothing in being, proves nothing, is no instance of matter of fact; and all that can be concluded from the whole is, that a just man may sin, and be afflicted for sin, which he may, and yet be everlastingly saved.

2. Another passage of scripture brought against the saints' final perseverance, and to prove their falling from grace, is the case of the stony ground hearer; who is said to *hear the word, and anon with joy receiveth it; yet hath he not root in himself, but dureth for a while; for when tribulation or persecution ariseth because of the word, by and by he is offended*, Matt. xiii. 20, 21. Or as in Luke viii. 13. *Which for a while believe, and in time of temptation fall away.* But it should be observed,——(1.) That those persons thus described, were not truly good and gracious persons; for though the seed, or word fell upon them, they were a rock, stony ground still; they were yet in a state of nature, no change or alteration in them; their hearts were as hard as an adamant-stone; the stony-heart was not taken away from them, nor an heart of flesh given them; otherwise the word would have had a place in them, took root in them, would have sprung up, and brought forth fruit.——(2.) And though they received the word with *joy*, this is what a wicked man, a very wicked man, may do; and Herod did, who heard John *gladly*, though he afterwards took off his head; such a man may receive the word with a flash of natural affection, and be pleased with it; being so far enlightened, as to see the truth, the harmony of it, and some interesting things in it, he may flatter himself he shall share in; so that this joy arises only from a principle of self-love: such do not receive it as the Thessalonians did, *in much affliction, with joy of the Holy Ghost;* having been either in great distress of soul, on account of sin, when the gospel of peace and pardon coming to them, was joyfully received as good news and glad tidings; or though they were reproached and persecuted for hearing, receiving, and professing the gospel, they rejoiced at it, and abode by it: but so did not these stony ground hearers; for when tribulation or persecution arose because of the word, they were offended and gone; their joy was the joy of the hypocrite, which is but for a moment.——(3.) The faith they had was but *for a while*, as it is expressed, Luke viii. 13. it was a temporary faith, like that of Simon Magus, who, though he professed to believe, was in the gall of bitterness, and bond of iniquity; their faith was not the faith of God's elect; for that stands sure, upon the same footing as electing grace itself does, from whence it springs; it was not that faith which is the gift of God; for his gifts of grace are without repentance, and are never revoked, but always abide: not that faith which is the operation of God; for that is maintained and performed with power; not that faith of which Christ is the author; for of that he is the finisher; and though it is sometimes low and languid, he prays for it that it fail not.——(4.) Those persons had no root in themselves, and therefore withered; they had not *the root of the matter* in them, as Job calls it, the truth of grace; they were not rooted in the love of God, nor in Christ, and had not the grace of God rooted in them; otherwise they would have been fruitful and established; for *the root of the righteous yieldeth fruit*, and is not moved, Prov. xii. 3, 12.——(5.) Those persons are manifestly distinguished from the *good ground*, into which the seed was received, ver. 23. and from an *honest and good heart*, in which they that heard the word kept it, Luke viii. 15. and so were not truly good and gracious persons, on whom the good work of grace was begun; were not trees made good, and so they brought forth no good fruit: wherefore the withering and falling away of those, are no proofs and instances of the saints' so falling as to perish everlastingly.

3. Another passage of scripture produced to invalidate the doctrine of the saints' final perseverance, is in John xv. 2, 6. *Every branch in me that beareth not fruit he taketh away; if a man abide not in me he is cast forth as a branch, and is withered, and men gather them, and cast them into the fire, and they are burned.* From whence it is inferred, that men may be branches in Christ, the true vine, and yet so fall as to perish everlastingly. Now it should be observed, that there is a twofold being in Christ, and two sorts of branches in him.——(1.) There are some who are truly and really in him through the grace of God; not only secretly by electing grace, being chosen in him; but by powerful and efficacious grace in effectual calling; who are created in Christ, and are new creatures in him, and have a vital union with him, and become fruitful by him: these are rooted and built up in him, and are established in the faith of him; and shall never be rooted up, but always have an abiding in him; and these are fruit-bearing branches in him; all their fruit is from him, and they are filled with it by him; and continue so even in old age, to the end of life; being under the constant

care and culture of Christ's Father, the Husbandman, who purges and prunes them by his word, and by his Spirit, so that they bring forth much fruit, whereby he is glorified.——(2.) There are others who are in him only by profession; which must be supposed of many of the members of external visible churches, which are said to be *in Christ*, Gal. i. 21. 1 Thess. i. 1. who, in a judgment of charity, are said to be so; though it cannot be thought that every individual member of them were really in Christ, only by profession; and such as these not being truly engrafted into him, though they have a place in his churches; being destitute of the true grace of God, are unfruitful, and wither in their profession; and fall into immoral practices, or unsound principles, and are cast out of the churches; and at last, like withered branches or chaff, are burnt with unquenchable fire. But what is this to real saints, or true believers in Christ? or what proof of their falling and perishing everlastingly?

4. Another instance of saints' falling from grace, is that of the broken branches from the olive-tree; and the threatening of such who are grafted into it with being cut off, if they continue not in goodness, Rom. xi. 17—22. From whence it is observed, that such who are grafted in the good olive tree, the spiritual and invisible church, may, nevertheless, so fall from God as to perish everlastingly. But,——(1.) By the good olive-tree is not meant the spiritual and invisible church; that general assembly and church of the first-born whose names are written in heaven; which consists only of elect men; and whose number will neither be increased nor diminished; that church which Christ gave himself for, to sanctify, and does sanctify; and whom he will present to himself a glorious church, not one missing; that church of which he is the head, and that his body and the fulness of him, which it would not be, should any member thereof perish. But,—— (2.) This olive-tree is to be understood of the outward gospel-church state, or the outward visible church, under the gospel-dispensation; the national church of the Jews, which is compared to an olive-tree, Jer. xi. 16. being abolished, and its branches broken off and scattered, a gospel-church-state was set up in Judea; and therefore called their *own olive-tree*. Now out of this, the broken branches, or the unbelieving Jews, were left; not admitted into the church at Jerusalem, nor elsewhere in Judea: and when there was a coalition of believing Jews and Gentiles, which were first made at Antioch, these were left out. So that,——(3.) Those who are signified by the broken branches, were never true believers in Christ; but because of their unbelief in him, and rejection of him, were broken off, and were never engrafted into, but left out of the gospel-church; these were such who did not belong to the election of grace among the Jews; but were the rest, that were blinded; and so no instances of the falling away of true believers.——(4.) Though those who are grafted in, are threatened to be cut off, in case they continued not *in goodness*; meaning, not the goodness, grace, and love of God; but the goodness of the good olive, the gospel-church; not abiding in the ordinances of it, and walking worthy of them, in which they were, then they should be cut off; not from the grace and favour of God, nor from an interest in Christ; but from the church, and the privileges of it; and who might be grafted in again, being restored by repentance; which is sometimes the case, and will be the case of the natural branches, the Jews; who when they are converted, and brought to believe in Christ, will be grafted into their own good olive, and then *all* Israel shall be saved, ver. 25, 26.

5. The passage of the apostle Paul concerning himself, is wrested to such a purpose; *I keep under my body, and bring it into subjection; lest that by any means, when I have preached to others, I myself should be a cast-a-way*, 1 Cor. ix. 27. The word αδοκιμος is not to be rendered *reprobate*, as it sometimes is; nor to be understood of such an one as opposed to an elect person; for an elect person, as the apostle was, for he includes himself among such, Eph. i. 4. can never be a reprobate in such a sense; for elect persons always obtain righteousness, life, and eternal salvation; though the faith of nominal professors may be subverted, theirs cannot; the foundation stands sure on which they are; and those who are predestinated, or ordained unto eternal life, as they believe, so they shall be glorified, and never be treated as non-elect. The apostle could never fear that he should be a cast-a-way in such a sense as to perish everlastingly; he knew Christ, in whom he had believed, to be an able and complete Saviour, and that he was his Saviour, and would keep what he had committed to him; he knew

his interest in the everlasting love of God, and was persuaded nothing should separate him from it: he instances in himself, as a proof that God had not cast away his people, whom he foreknew, Rom. xi. 1, 2. see chap. viii. 38, 39. 2 Tim. i. 12. But as the Greek word used, signifies *disapproved*, the sense of the apostle seems to be this, that he was careful not to indulge to sensual gratifications; but to keep his body under a due decorum and in subjection to proper rules; and not yield the members of it as instruments of unrighteousness; lest whilst he preached the gospel of the grace of God to others, he might stand reproved himself, and be disapproved by men, and his ministry become contemptible and useless; see 2 Cor. vi. 3. And the fears and jealousies of the saints over themselves, are not inconsistent with their perseverance in grace, much less disprove it; but are means of their perseverance in it.

6. When the apostle says, *Whosoever of you are justified by the law, ye are fallen from grace*, Gal. v. 4. it is not meant of falling from the grace, favour, and love of God in his heart; for that is everlasting and unchangeable, as immoveable as hills and mountains, and more so; they may depart, but the loving-kindness of God to his people never will depart; there is nothing in heaven, earth, or hell, that can separate from that; and consequently there can be no falling from it: nor of falling from the grace of God wrought in their hearts; for that is an incorruptible seed, which never dies, is never lost, but always remains: but of falling from the doctrine of grace; and particularly that glorious doctrine of free justification by the righteousness of Christ, without the deeds of the law; which some of the Galatians who had formerly embraced it, fell from, seeking for justification by the works of the law. And in like sense are we to understand other similar passages; as when the apostle beseeches *not to receive the grace of God in vain*, 2 Cor. vi. 1. the love and favour of God cannot be received in vain, being shed abroad in the heart by the Spirit of God; nor the grace of God implanted in the heart, which is an abiding seed there; but the doctrine of grace, when it is either dropped, or denied, or turned into lasciviousness, and men walk unbecoming their profession of it: and so in Heb. xii. 15. *Looking diligently, lest any man fail of the grace of God;* depart from the gospel, and drop his profession of it, or walk as does not become it. Once more,

7. What the apostle says of Hymeneus and Alexander, is produced as a proof of the apostasy of real saints; *holding faith and a good conscience; which some having put away, concerning faith have made shipwreck; of whom is Hymeneus and Alexander,* 1 Tim. i. 19. But,——(1.) It does not appear that these men were ever truly good men; of Hymeneus it is said, that he was a vain babbler, and increased to more and more ungodliness: and of Alexander, who is supposed to be the same with Alexander the coppersmith, that he did the apostle much evil by reproaching and persecuting him; by hindering him in his ministry as much as in him lay, and withstanding and contradicting his doctrines; and so can be no instances of true believers falling from grace; see 2 Tim. ii. 16, 17, 18. and iv. 14, 15.——(2.) Nor is it manifest that they ever had a good conscience; putting it away does not suppose it: persons may put away that with disdain and contempt, as the word here used signifies, which they never received and had, though presented to them: so the Jews put away the gospel from them, which they never embraced, but despised, contradicted, and blasphemed, Acts xiii. 45, 46. where the same word is used as here: and so here, when these found the gospel required men should exercise a good conscience, void of offence to God and men; they disliked it, and put it away, and chose rather to relinquish the gospel, than to be obliged by it to exercise such a conscience. Besides,——(3.) Persons may have a conscience good in some sense, in an external shew, and as it may appear by their outward behaviour among men in general, and with respect to some particular facts; or in comparison of what they may afterwards appear to have: and yet not have a conscience purged by the blood of Christ; or have their evil hearts sprinkled from an evil conscience, and so have a pure conscience. It is said, even of the heathens, that their consciences bore them witness of their actions, accusing of some, and excusing others: and the apostle Paul, before conversion, is said to live in *all good conscience;* when, as yet, he had not the grace of God, Rom. ii. 14, 15. Acts xxiii. 1. ——(4.) The faith these men made shipwreck of, was not the grace of faith they never had, but the doctrine of faith

which they had professed; for this phrase, *concerning the faith*, is only used of the doctrine of faith, Acts xxiv. 24. and the particular doctrine made shipwreck of, and which particularly Hymeneus erred concerning, was the doctrine of the resurrection of the dead, which he said was passed already, 2 Tim. ii. 18.——(5.) Supposing the grace of faith was meant, the phrase of making shipwreck of it, is not strong enough to express the entire loss of it; since a person may be shipwrecked and not lost; the apostle Paul *thrice* suffered shipwreck, and yet was saved each time. Besides, as there is a true and unfeigned faith; so there is a feigned and counterfeit faith, which may be in men who have no true grace, and may be shipwrecked so as to be lost; and such an instance is no proof of the saints' falling from grace.

8. Another passage usually brought to prove the apostasy of real saints, and against their final perseverance, is Heb. vi. 4, 5, 6. But,——(1.) The persons here spoken of, are distinguished from the believing Hebrews, who are compared to the earth that drinks in the rain that comes frequently on it, and brings forth herbs fit for use, and receives the blessing of God; when these are compared to the earth that bears thorns and briers, is rejected, is nigh unto cursing, and its end is to be burnt, ver. 7, 8. and then adds, with respect to the saints he writes to, *But beloved, we are persuaded better things of you, and things that accompany salvation, though we thus speak*, ver. 9. and goes on to take notice of their work and labour of love; and to excite them to diligence and industry; and encourages them, by the promises made unto them, and the immutability of them, and by the firm hope that God has given them; and by the glorious forerunner, who was entered into heaven for them.—— (2.) Admitting true believers are meant, the words are only conditional; *if they fall away*; and are but a supposition of it, and prove no matter of fact, that ever any did fall away; and at most, only express the danger of their falling; as there may be, through the power of indwelling sin, the force of temptations, and the frowns and flatteries of the world; and the difficulty of restoring them from a partial fall; a total and final one being prevented by the power and grace of God.——(3.) The words are, in some versions, so rendered, as to assert the impossibility of their falling; so the Syriac version, *it is impossible they should sin again;* as to die spiritually, and lose the grace of God, and stand in need of a new work of grace upon them; which would require the crucifying of Christ again, and a re-exposing him to open shame; things impossible to be done, and so the former; which sense agrees with the words of the apostle, 1 John iii. 9. *and he cannot sin, because he is born of God*: and this is confirmed by the Arabic version; and according to these versions, the several other things mentioned, are connected with the word *impossible;* as that they should be renewed again to repentance; and that they should crucify the Son of God afresh, and put him to open shame.——(4.) There is nothing said of them that is peculiar to believers; not a word of their faith in Christ; nor of their being begotten again to a lively hope; nor of their being sanctified by the Spirit of God; nor of their being justified by the righteousness of Christ; nor of their being the sons of God by faith in Christ; nor of their being sealed by the Holy Spirit of God; nor of their being made meet to be partakers of the heavenly inheritance.——(5.) What is said of them are what may be found in persons destitute of the grace of God. As,——1. That they were *enlightened;* the Syriac and Ethiopic versions render it, *baptized;* and it will not be denied, that some such, as Simon Magus, may totally and finally fall away. But not to insist on this sense, there are two sorts of enlightened persons: some are savingly enlightened by the Spirit of God to see their lost state and condition, and salvation by Christ, and their interest in it, and who shall never perish; others are only enlightened into the doctrines of the gospel; though some to such a degree as to be able to preach them to others; and yet be strangers to the true grace of God: and when such fall away, they are no proofs nor instances of the apostasy of real saints.——2. That they *tasted of the heavenly gift;* whether by it is meant the gift of a justifying righteousness, or of remission of sins, or of eternal life; men destitute of the grace of God may have some speculative notions about them, and desires after them, arising from a principle of self-love: or if Christ, the gift of God himself, is meant, *tasting* may stand opposed to *eating* his flesh and *drinking* his blood; which is proper to true believers, who feed upon him and are nourished by him; while hypocrites and formal professors only *taste* of him, have a superficial knowledge of him,

and gust for him.———3. That they *were made partakers of the Holy Ghost;* not of the Person of the Spirit, and of his indwelling in their hearts, as in his temple, and as the earnest of the heavenly inheritance; nor of his grace, as implanted in them, which are connected with eternal life: but of his gifts, whether ordinary or extraordinary, both of which Judas was made a partaker, and yet devoid of true grace.———
4. That they *tasted the good word of God;* had a superficial knowledge of it, had the bare form, without the power of it; were pleased with it for a while, as Herod was with the ministry of John the Baptist; and Christ's hearers were with his doctrines at first, though they presently sought to kill him.———5. That they tasted also *the powers of the world to come;* meaning either the miracles and mighty works done in the former part of the gospel dispensation; which some were able to perform, who were not true believers in Christ, as Judas and others; see Matt. vii. 22, 23. or the joys and glories of heaven; which natural men may have some self-pleasing notions of, and desires after, as Balaam had, Numb. xxiii. 10. Now when such persons as these, fall away from a profession of religion, and into sin, they are no instances of true believers falling from real grace.

9. Another scripture brought as a proof of falling from grace, is Heb. x. 26, 29. *For if we sin wilfully,* &c. From whence it is inferred, that one that has the knowledge of the truth, may in such sort sin as that there remains no sacrifice for it; and one that is sanctified by the blood of the covenant may so fall away as to perish everlastingly. But, 1. These words are not said of true believers; for though the persons described are such who,———(1.) Had knowledge of the truth; yet whether we understand this of Christ, who is the truth; or of the gospel, the word of truth, and of the several truths in it; as salvation by Christ, justification by his righteousness, &c. persons may have a notional and not a saving knowledge of these things; the devils know much of Christ, and so do many natural men; yea, the apostle says, men may have *all knowledge,* or knowledge of all truths, that which is notional and speculative; and *all faith,* which is historical, and yet be without grace, 1 Cor. xiii. 2.———(2.) Though said to be *sanctified by the blood of the covenant,* this is not to be understood of the expiation of their sins, and of their justification from them by the blood of Christ; for such are most certainly saved from wrath to come, and shall never enter into condemnation or perish eternally; but of their profession of their being thus sanctified; they were thought to be so by themselves and others, when they really were not; and by their profession of religion were externally sanctified and separated from others, submitting to baptism, and partaking of the Lord's Supper; when they outwardly ate the bread and drank of the cup, the external symbol of the blood of the New Testament, or covenant, though they did not spiritually discern the body and blood of Christ, but counted these symbols as *common* things. Though after all, it is the *Son of God* himself that is intended, and not the apostate; for the immediate antecedent to the relative *he,* is the *Son of God;* who was sanctified, or set apart, by the blood and sacrifice of himself, for the discharge of the other part of his priestly office, his intercession for his people in heaven; which is mentioned as an aggravation of the sin of such a person, who counted his blood an unholy thing.———
2. The sins ascribed to the persons spoken of, are such as are never committed by true believers; such as, (1.) To *sin wilfully,* after the knowledge of the truth is received; for this is not to be understood of common infirmities, or of grosser sins, which may be voluntarily committed by the saints after regeneration, as were by Lot, David, and others; but of a denial of that great and fundamental truth of the gospel, the atonement of sin by the blood, sacrifice, and death of Christ, after a man has known it and professed it: this is never done by one that has tasted that the Lord is gracious, and to whom his blood is precious; nor can it be. Peter denied his Master, and that he knew him; but he did not deny him to be his Saviour; nor deny the virtue of his blood and sacrifice for the atonement of sin; when, and by whom, this is done knowingly and wilfully, there *remains no more,* there is no other *sacrifice for sin;* and therefore such a man must be eternally lost.———(2.) To *tread under foot the Son of God;* doing as much as in them lies to strip him of his equality with God, and to reduce him to the class of a mere creature and deny him to be the eternal Son of God: this can never be done by such who have once believed, and are *sure* that he is *the Son of the living God;* for

whosoever denieth the Son, the same hath not the Father; he denies both the one and the other; and in effect says that there are neither, 1 John ii. 22, 23. he is *antichrist.* ———(3.) To *count the blood of the covenant an unholy* or *common thing;* as if it was the blood of a mere man, when it is the *blood of Jesus Christ his Son,* the Son of God, *which cleanses from all sin;* that blood with which the church of God is purchased; that blood by which it is redeemed from sin, Satan, and the law; that blood by which the covenant of grace is ratified and confirmed; and by virtue of which the covenant ones are delivered from their captive state.———(4.) To *do despite unto the Spirit of grace,* who has been a Spirit of grace and supplication to them; such who have had such an experience of him, can never do despite unto him, treat him with malice, scorn, and contempt; deny his divine Person, and his special operations of grace; nor deny him to be the Spirit of grace, and reproach him as such; true believers in Christ, who have been sanctified and sealed by him, can never do such things as these.———3. Truly sanctified persons are distinguished from the apostates, whose custom had been to forsake the assemblies of the saints, ver. 25. and the apostle declares for himself, and other true believers who were just men, and lived by faith, that they were not of the number of such men, and to be ranked with them, ver. 38, 39. So that these apostates are no instances of true believers falling from grace.

10. The passage just referred to, though it makes clearly for the doctrine of the saints' final perseverance, is brought as an objection to it, Heb. x. 38. *Now the just shall live by faith; but if any man draw back, my soul shall have no pleasure in him.* From whence it is inferred, that those who live by faith, and are justified persons, may not endure to the end, may draw back to perdition, and everlastingly perish. But, ———(1.) He that is truly a just man can never die spiritually and eternally; *Whosoever liveth and believeth in me,* says Christ, John xi. 26. *shall never die: believest thou this?* It ought to be believed: and if such shall never die, they cannot perish everlastingly; a believer in Christ, and justified by him, can never be condemned; *he hath everlasting life, and shall not come into condemnation, but is passed from death to life;* and therefore shall be eternally saved and glorified, John v. 24. ———(2.) The just man, and he that draws back, are not the same; as is clear from the next verse; *but we are not of them that draw back unto perdition; but of them that believe to the saving of the soul.* There are two sorts of persons mentioned; one that were πιϛιως, *of faith,* that had true faith in Christ, and lived by faith on him, and did not draw back to perdition, but went on believing till saved; of this number were the apostle, and every truly just and righteous man included in the word *we;* the other were υποϛολης, of the *withdrawing,* or separation, who forsook the assembly of the saints, ver. 25. withdrew from their society and communion, and apostatized from the ways and worship of God: by which distinction it appears, that those that truly believe do not draw back to perdition; but continue in the faith of Christ, and in the true worship of God, and are everlastingly saved; and that those that drew back to perdition were not of the faith, or true believers in Christ, nor ever just ones that lived by faith; and so their apostasy is no proof of the falling away of true believers as to perish everlastingly.———(3.) The passage in Heb. ii. 4. which is referred to, plainly shews who the man is that draws back, as opposed to the just man that lives by faith: he is one whose *soul is lifted up, and is not upright in him;* one that is proud and haughty, and is lifted up with a vain conceit of his own righteousness, in which he trusts; to which he betakes himself, as to a tower and fortified place, as the word used signifies, and imagines himself safe; and whose heart is not right with God nor humble before God; and that such a man should withdraw himself from the communion of the saints and apostatize, is not to be wondered at.———(4.) God's taking *no pleasure in him that draws back,* does not intimate that he took pleasure in him before his drawing back; since it is not said, *my soul shall have no more,* or *no further pleasure in him;* but, *shall have no pleasure in him;* which does not necessarily suppose that he had any pleasure in him before; but that he should have none in him hereafter. Besides, such who are the objects of God's delight and pleasure, are always so; he *rests in his love towards them, and joys over them with singing,* Zeph. iii. 17. see Psalm cxlix. 4. Rom. viii. 38.

11. To the doctrine of the saints' final perseverance, is objected the passage in 2 Pet. ii. 20, 21, 22. But there is nothing said in those words which shew that the persons spoken of were true believers;

but the reverse.————(1.) The knowledge they had of the Lord and Saviour Jesus Christ, was not a spiritual, experimental, saving knowledge of him; for then they would have followed on to have known him, and to have known more of him, and it would have issued in eternal life, Hos. vi. 3. John xvii. 3. but it was only a speculative notional knowledge of him, such as devils and Christless persons may have.————(2.) *Escaping the pollutions of the world* through it, designs no other than an external reformation of life and manners, joined with an outward conformity to the commands and ordinances of Christ, and an outward walk for a time in the ways of religion, they professed a knowledge and liking of.————(3.) Nor does it appear that they ever were any other than dogs and swine; and therefore when they apostatized, it was only a returning to their former state, and they only appeared to be what they always were; their case seems to be the same that is observed by Christ, Matt. xii. 43, 44, 45.

12. The falling away of real believers is argued, and their perseverance objected to, from various exhortations, cautions, &c. given unto them. As,————(1.) When he that thinks he stands, is exhorted *to take heed lest he fall,* 1 Cor. x. 12. but supposing a true believer is here meant, which yet is not clear and certain, since it is one ο δοκων, who *seemeth* to himself, and others *to stand;* but admitting it, the exhortation is not superfluous; since, though he cannot finally and totally fall away, yet inasmuch as he may so fall as that God may be dishonoured by it, the doctrines and ways of Christ spoken evil of, the Spirit of God grieved, weak believers stumbled, and the hands of the wicked strengthened, and a man's own peace and comfort broken; there is a good reason why he should take care of falling; for though there is no danger of his perishing eternally; yet if he falls to the breaking of his bones, and wounding his own soul, it behoves him to take heed lest he fall.————(2.) When believers are cautioned *to take heed, lest there be in them an evil heart of unbelief, in departing from the living God,* Heb. iii. 12. it shews that believers ought to be upon their guard against the sin of unbelief, to expose which is the design of the words; since it is a sin which easily besets good men, bereaves their souls of much comfort, and God of much glory; and therefore believers should be careful of giving way to it and encouraging it, since it leads to a partial departure from Christ, the living God; though God has put his *fear* into the hearts of such persons, *that they shall not depart from him* finally and totally.————(3.) When the apostle Peter exhorts those he wrote to, who had obtained like precious faith with him, to *beware, lest being led away with the error of the wicked, they should fall from their own stedfastness,* 2 Pet. iii. 17. his meaning is not, as though there was a possibility of their falling from the *precious* grace of *faith* they had *obtained;* but from some degree of the steady exercise of it; or rather from their stedfast adherence to the doctrine of faith, through the sleight and cunning of men who lay in wait to deceive; who might be able to stagger them, though they could not finally and totally deceive them; and therefore it became them to be upon their guard against them.————(4.) When the apostle John exhorts, saying, *Look to yourselves, that ye lose not those things which we have wrought,* 2 John, ver. 8. he speaks not of what the Spirit of God had wrought in them, as if that could be lost; nor even of what they themselves had wrought, under the influence of divine grace; but what *we,* the ministers of the gospel, had wrought, by teaching and instructing them, lest their labour in the ministry among them should be in vain, they giving heed to the doctrines of deceivers, mentioned both before and after, ver. 7, 9, 10.————(5.) And when the apostle Jude says, *Keep yourselves in the love of God,* ver. 21. it is not to be understood of the love which God has in his heart towards his people, an interest in which can never be lost, and from which there is no separation; but rather of the love which they bear to him, the fervour of which sometimes abates; and therefore they should make use of all means to maintain, increase, and inflame it, in themselves and others; *keep εαυτους one another,* in it, by the means directed to in the preceding verse; or it may chiefly respect, love, peace, and concord among themselves; called *the love of God,* as it is *the peace of God,* Col. iii. 15. which is of him, taught by him, and he calls unto; and so is of the same import with Eph. iv. 3.   Or, admitting that the love of God, in the first sense, is meant; it may design exercise of faith on it, meditation upon it, a constant keeping of it in view, in order to preserve themselves, by the love of God, from Satan's temptations, the snares of the world, and

the lusts of the flesh; against complying with which, the love of God, shown in what he has done for his people, is a strong argument, Gen. xxxix. 9. and that the apostle could have no thought of the possibility of the saints' falling totally and finally, appears from what he says of Christ with respect to them, ver. 24. *Now unto Him that is able to keep you from falling*, &c. And in like manner other cautions and exhortations, similar to these, may be understood; and it should be observed, that such cautions and exhortations as these are used and blessed as means of the perseverance of the saints, and are not to be improved against the doctrine of it.

Secondly, Objections are raised against the doctrine of the saints' final perseverance from the sins and falls of persons eminent for faith and holiness; as Noah, Lot, David, Solomon, Peter, and others. But these are no proofs of their final and total falling away. As to Noah and Lot, though guilty of great sins, they have after this the character of truly good and righteous men. As for David, though by his fall his bones were broken, and the joy of his salvation was taken from him, and grace lay some time unexercised by him; yet the Spirit of God was not taken from him, as appears from his own words, when most sensible of his case, Psalm li. 11, 12. As for Solomon, though his backsliding was great, attended with aggravated circumstances, yet not total, see 1 Kings xi. 4, 6. nor final, as to perish everlastingly; which would have been contrary to the promise of God, that his mercy should not depart from him, 2 Sam. vii. 14, 15. Besides, he was restored by repentance; and the book of Ecclesiastes was penned by him in his old age, as an acknowledgment and retractation of his former follies; and some persons, after his death, are spoken of with commendation, for walking in the way of Solomon, as well as in the way of David, 2 Chron. xi. 17. As for Peter, his fall was not total, Christ prayed for him, that his faith failed not; nor final, for he was quickly restored by repentance. And these several instances are recorded in scripture, not as instances of final and total apostasy, but of the weakness of the best of men in themselves; and for our caution and instruction, *to take heed lest we fall*. Demas is sometimes mentioned as an instance of apostasy; who, very probably, was a good man, since he is mentioned with such who were so, Col. iv. 14. Philem. ver. 24. and what the apostle says of him, that he had *forsaken him, having loved this present world*, is not sufficient to prove him an apostate, any more than Mark's departure from the apostle Paul, and others at Pamphylia; nor his too much love of the world, which is to be observed in many, otherwise good and valuable men, would prove them to be so. As for Hymeneus, Alexander, and Philetus, they do not appear to have been good men, as before observed; and so no instances of the apostasy of real saints.

Thirdly, Some ill consequences, supposed to follow the doctrine of the saints' final perseverance, are urged against it. As,——(1.) That it tends to make persons secure and indifferent, as to the use of means to preserve them from sin and apostasy. But this is not true in fact, any more than in other cases similar to it; but is rather an encouragement to the use of them: Joshua, though he was assured that not a man should be able to stand before him, but all his enemies should be conquered by him; this did not make him secure, nor hinder him from taking all the proper precautions against his enemies; and of making use of all means to obtain a victory over them. Hezekiah, though he was assured of his restoration from his disorder; yet this did not hinder him, nor the prophet, who assured him of it, from making use of proper means for the cure of it; and though the apostle Paul had a certainty of the saving of the lives of all that were in the ship, yet he directed them to the proper means of their preservation; and told them, that except they abode in the ship they could not be saved; and taking this his advice, though shipwrecked, they all came safe to shore.——(2.) It is said, that this doctrine gives encouragement to indulge to sin, and to commit such gross sins as Lot, David, and others; upon an opinion that they are the children of God; and upon a presumption, that they cannot so fall as to perish everlastingly. To which it may be replied, that such sins mentioned, committed without repentance towards God, and faith in the blood and sacrifice of Christ, those who are guilty of them shall not inherit the kingdom of God; but, according to the law, die without mercy; and even those good men who did commit such sins, though they had true faith, and genuine repentance, their sins were so displeasing to God, and resented by him, that he visited their transgressions with a rod, and their iniquities with stripes;

2 P

though his loving-kindness was not taken away from them. And the above instances of sin are recorded, not to encourage sin; but to caution against it; and to shew the weakness of the best of men, and to set forth the pardoning grace and mercy of God to such offenders; in order to relieve souls distressed with sin, and to give them hope of the pardon of it. And whatsoever ill use such persons may make of these instances, who have only an *opinion* of their being the children of God; such who are really so by faith in Christ, neither can nor will make such an use of them.——(3.) It is objected, that this doctrine lessens the force of the prohibitions of sin, and of exhortations to avoid it; and of motives offered to persevere in righteousness and holiness. But these prohibitions of sin, and motives to holiness, are used by the Spirit of God as means of perseverance; and so they are considered by good men. And it would be absurd and irrational to judge otherwise; for can a man believe he shall persevere to the end, and yet indulge himself in sin, as if he was resolved not to persevere? for there cannot be stronger motives to holiness and righteousness, than the absolute and unconditional promises of God to his people; and the firm assurance given them of their being the children of God, and the redeemed of the Lamb; see 2 Cor. vi. 18. and vii. 1. 1 Pet. i. 17, 18, 19.——(4.) Whereas we argue, that the doctrine of the saints' apostasy, obstructs the peace and comfort of believers; it is objected to that of their perseverance, that it is not therefore true, because it is comfortable to carnal minds, which are opposite to the doctrine according to godliness. To which it may be answered, that our argument does not proceed upon the comfortableness of the doctrine we plead for; but upon the uncomfortableness of the opposite to it; for though a doctrine may not be true which is seemingly comfortable to a carnal mind; yet that doctrine is certainly not true, which is really uncomfortable to a sanctified heart; or which manifestly breaks in upon the true peace and comfort of a believer; as the doctrine of the saints' apostasy does; since the whole scripture, and all the doctrines of it, are calculated for the comfort, as well as for the instruction and edification of the saints; and though their perseverance does not depend upon their comfort; for if they believe not, and are without comfort, God is faithful to his counsel, covenant and promises, and will preserve and save them. However, this is certain, that the doctrine of the saints' falling away from grace finally and totally, is a very uncomfortable one, and therefore to be rejected.

A BODY OF DOCTRINAL DIVINITY.

BOOK VII.

OF THE FINAL STATE OF MEN.

CHAP. I.

OF THE DEATH OF THE BODY.

THE death to be treated of, is not the death of the soul, which dies not, as will be seen hereafter; nor the moral or spiritual death, which has been discoursed of elsewhere; nor the death of the soul and body in hell, the second and eternal death; but the death of the body, in a strict and proper sense. The things to be enquired into, are, What death is? who the subjects of it? what the causes of it, and its properties?

First, What death is. To say what it is, is difficult; we know nothing of it practically and experimentally, though there are continual instances of it before our eyes; our friends and relations, who have gone through this dark passage, have not returned to us to tell us what they met with in it; nor what they felt when the parting stroke was given; nor what they were surprised into at once. We know nothing of death but in theory; it is defined by some a cessation of the motion of the heart, and of the circulation of the blood, and of the flow of the animal spirits occasioned by some defects in the organs and fluids of the body: no doubt such a cessation follows upon death, and such the effects of it; but what it is, is chiefly to be known from the scripture, by which we learn, ——1. That it is a disunion of the soul and body, the two constituent parts of man; the one consists of flesh, blood and bones, of arteries, veins, nerves, &c. and goes by the general name of *flesh;* and the other is a spiritual substance, immaterial and immortal, and consists of several powers and faculties, as the understanding, will, and affections, and goes by the name of *spirit;* see Matt. xxvi. 41. between these two there is a nexus, or bond, which unites them together; though what that is, none can tell; this puzzles all philosophy, to say by what bands and ligaments, things of such a different nature as matter and spirit be, should be coupled and fastened together. Now death is a dissolution of this union, a separation of those two parts in man.[1] The *body without the spirit,* χωρις, separate from it, *is dead,* James ii. 26. when that is removed, the body is left a lifeless lump of clay.——2. It is a dissolving this earthly house of our tabernacle, 2 Cor. v. 1. the body is compared to a tabernacle, as is the body of Christ, of Peter and others, Heb. viii. 2. 2 Pet. i. 13. 2 Cor. v. 4. in allusion either to military tents or tabernacles, pitched by soldiers when they encamp; or to those of shepherds, which were removed from place to place, for the sake of pasturage for their flocks, by which the brevity of human life is expressed,

---

[1] So Plato says, "Death, as it seems to me, is nothing else than διαλυσις της ψυχης και τȣ σωματος απ' αλληλοιν, a dissolution (of those two things) soul and body from one another," Gorgias, p. 357. and elsewhere, says he, "is not this called death, λυσις και χωρισμος ψυχης απο σωματος, the solution and separation of the soul from the body?" Phædo, p. 51. Ed. Fiein.

Isa. xxxviii. 12. such tents or tabernacles were commonly made of hair-cloth, stretched upon and fastened to stakes with cords or pins, as allusions to them shew, Isa. xxxiii. 20. and liv. 2. and the body and its several parts are fastened together with various cords; we read of a *silver cord*, which is loosed at death, Eccl. xii. 6. which, whether it means the bond of union between the soul and body in general, or some particular part and ligament of the body about which interpreters are not agreed, is not easy to say. However, besides what compacts the joints together, there are certain fibres or small cords, like threads, by which those parts are fastened on which life mostly depends; there are certain valves of the veins through which the blood is discharged into the heart, which are fastened to the sides of the ventricles of it with many tendinous fibres to secure them when they are shut; which fibres are fastened to some protuberances or *pins* of the sides of the heart: now in case one of these valves should be out of order, and unfit to perform its function; yea if one of these little fibres which are fastened to them should *break*, or be either too short or too long to do their service, the tabernacle would fall down at once: on such slender things hangs the life of every man, even of the greatest monarch upon the throne, as well as of the meanest peasant.[2] Now death is a pulling up the stakes of this tabernacle, the body; a loosening and breaking its cords; and unpinning it, a taking it down as it were by parts, and laying it aside for a time.————3. It is signified by a departure out of this world to another: so the death of Christ and some others is expressed in such language, John xiii. 1. Luke ii. 29. Phil. i. 23. 2 Tim. iv. 7. it is like going from one house to another: with the saints, it is a departure from their earthly house to an house not made with hands, eternal in the heavens; from houses of clay which have their foundation in the dust, to everlasting habitations, to mansions in Christ's Father's house. It is like loosing from the port, as the sailor's phrase is; see Acts xiii. 3. and xxvii. 13. and xxviii. 11. and launching into the ocean, and sailing to another port; the port loosed or departed from at death, is this world, which some loose from willingly, others not so; the port or haven to which saints are bound, is heaven, the heavenly and better country, to which desired haven they arrive at death, and by death. Death is the ship or boat which wafts them over to the shores of eternity. The heathens had by tradition, notions somewhat similar to these, though more coarse; for who has not heard of the Elysian fields, the Stygian lake, and old Charon's boat? by which are represented death's wafting men over the black lake to fields of pleasure. But these images stand in a more beautiful light in the sacred pages; where the saints are represented as quietly wafted over the swellings of Jordan to the land of Canaan, a land of rest and pleasure. ————4. Death is expressed by going the way of all the earth; so said Joshua when about to die, *Behold this day I am going the way of all the earth*, Josh. xxiii. 14. and so said David, 1 Kings ii. 2. it is a *going;* so Christ describes his death, Luke xxii. 22. it is a going a journey, to a man's long home; it is a going from *hence*, from this world, and a going *whither* we shall not return any more to this world, to be and live in it as formerly; it is going to an invisible state, to the world of spirits, of which we now have but little knowledge, and very imperfect conceptions; see Psalm xxxix. 13. Job x. 21, 22. the way lies through a dark valley, but God is the guide of his people through it; he is not only their guide unto death, but through it safe to glory; and this is the way all men go and must go; it is a common track,[3] a beaten path, and yet unknown by us; all must tread it, none can avoid it.———— 5. Death is called, a returning to the dust and earth of which the body is formed, Eccl. xii. 7. the body is originally made of earth and dust; and whilst it is in life, it is nothing but dust and ashes, as Abraham confessed he was; and when it dies, it turns to dust, Gen. iii. 19. the body at death is turned into corruption, rottenness, and dust; it is interred in the earth, and mixes with it, and becomes that; which is an humbling consideration to proud man, who if he looks back to his original, it is dust; if he considers himself in the present life, he is no other than a heap of dust; and if he looks forward to his last end, it will be the dust of death; his honour, in every view of himself, is laid in the dust; and this shews the knowledge and power

---

[2] See Nieuwentyt's Religious Philosopher, vol. 1. contempl. 6. s. 7. 8. p. 77, 78, 79.

[3] ———— omnes una manet nox, et calcanda semel via lethi, Horat.

CHAP. I. OF THE DEATH OF THE BODY.

of God in raising the dead, who knows where their dust lies, and will collect it together, and raise it up at the last day.—— 6. Death is frequently expressed by sleeping, Dan. xii. 2. John xi. 11. 1 Thess. iv. 14. and is so called, because sleep is an image and representation of death;[4] in sleep the senses are locked up and are useless for a time, as in death a man is wholly deprived of them; sleep is but for a short time, and so is death; after sleep a man rises, and being refreshed by it is more fit for labour; so is death to the saints; it is a rest unto them; and they will rise in the morning of the resurrection, fresh, lively, and active, and more fit for divine and spiritual exercises.

Secondly, Who are the subjects of death. Not *angels*, for they being simple, uncompounded, incorporeal, and immaterial, are incapable of death; they *die not*, Luke xx. 36. but *men*, even all men, a few only excepted, as Enoch and Elijah, under the Old Testament; the one was translated that he should not see death, the other was taken up to heaven soul and body in a chariot and horses of fire; and those saints that will be found alive at Christ's second coming, who will not die but be changed: otherwise all men die; all *flesh is grass*, every man is withering, mortal, dying, and dies: all have sinned, and so death comes upon all men.——1. Persons of every sex, male and female; of every age, young and old; small and great; some die in infancy, who have not sinned after the similitude of Adam's transgression; some in childhood, others in youth; some in the prime of their days, and in their full strength; and some in old age, and those that live the longest yet die, as Methuselah the oldest man did. Look over the account of the antediluvian Patriarchs, Gen. v. there it may be observed, that at the close of the account of each it is said, *he died;* such an one lived eight hundred years and odd, and *he died;* and such an one lived nine hundred years and odd, and *he died.*——2. Of every rank and class and condition in life, high and low, rich and poor; kings die as well as their subjects: Job wishes he had died as soon as born, then he had been with kings and counsellors of the earth, and with princes whose houses had been filled with gold and silver: riches cannot keep off nor buy off the stroke of death, nor deliver from it; the rich and the poor meet together in the grave, where they are upon an equal foot.——3. Persons of every character among men; it may be seen and observed in instances without number, that wise men die, and also the fool and brutish person; yea often so it is, that a wise man dies as a fool dies; Solomon, the wisest of men, died. Learning, in all its branches and in its highest pitch, cannot secure from dying; men learned and unlearned, die. ——4. Persons of every character in the sight of God, wicked men and good men; the wickedness of the wicked, of those who are the most addicted and abandoned to it, such as have made a covenant with death and with hell, are at an agreement, as they imagine; such covenant and agreement will not stand, nor be of any avail unto them to protect them from death; though they put away the evil day far from them, it will come upon them suddenly, whilst they are crying peace, peace, and promise themselves a long life of prosperity: and good men, they die also, *The prophets, do they live for ever?* they do not, Zech. i. 5. merciful and righteous men are often taken away in mercy from the evil to come; true believers in Christ, such who live and belive in him, or have a living faith on him, shall never die a spiritual death, nor the second death; but they die a corporal one, even though Christ has died for them, and by dying has satisfied for sin, and abolished death. Yet,——5. Their death is different from that of wicked men; they die in Christ, in union to him, and so are secure from condemnation; they die in faith of being for ever with him; they die in hope of eternal life; and their end is different from others: the end of a perfect and upright man is peace; he departs in peace, he receives the end of his faith, even the salvation of his soul; when the wicked man goes into everlasting punishment, he goes into everlasting life. ——6. The reason of which is, death is abolished as a penal evil, though it was threatened as such for sin, and is inflicted as such on some; yet being bore by Christ as a penalty, in the room and stead of his people, it ceases to be so to them; the sting of it, which is sin, is taken away by Christ; the curse of it is removed, Christ being made a curse for them; death is become a blessing to them, for blessed are they that die in Christ; and hence it is desirable by them, and there is good

---

[4] Stulte, quid est somnus, gelidæ nisi mortis imago? Ovid.

reason for it; since it puts an end to sin and sorrow, enters into the joy of the Lord, and fulfils it.

Thirdly, The causes of death, on what account it comes upon men, and to whom and what it is to be ascribed.

1*st*, The efficient cause is God, who is the sovereign disposer of life and death; it is he that gives life and breath, and all things to his creatures; life is a favour granted by him to men, and he upholds their souls in life; and since he is the author, giver, and supporter of life, he may with propriety be called the God of their lives; and he that gives life has only a right to take it away; and he is a sovereign being, and may do it at his pleasure; and he has particularly expressed his sovereignty in this instance, saying, *I kill, and I make alive*, Deut. xxxii. 39. see 1 Sam. ii. 6. he is God the Lord, to whom belong the *issues from death*; or rather, the issues to it, the ways which lead to it, and issue in it; for as the poet says,[5] it has a thousand ways to come upon men, attack and dispatch them.——1. No man has a right to take away his own life, nor the life of another; Christ, the Prince of life, who had the human nature united to his divine Person, had power to dispose of his human life, to lay it down, and take it up again; which none besides has: suicide, of all the kinds of murder, is the most unnatural and execrable; it has been committed by wicked men; as Saul, Judas, &c. Samson is no instance of it; what he did, was not with an intention to destroy his own life, but the lives of the enemies of God, and of his people, in doing which his own life fell a sacrifice; and was done in a devout and pious manner, praying unto God: and besides, he acted not as a private man, but as a civil magistrate, and judge in Israel. And whatever may be charitably hoped of some persons, who have been left to destroy themselves, care should be taken not to encourage, nor give any countenance to so sinful a practice. Nor ought any man to take away the life of another; since the life of man was neither to be taken away by another, in the heat of passion and wrath, or for sordid and sinister ends to obtain their property. God made a law, and it was one of the first he made after the flood, that *He that shed man's blood, by man should his blood be shed*, Gen. ix. 6. that is, by the order of the civil magistrate; and a person convicted of this capital crime, ought not to be pardoned; the law is express and peremptory. And though this sin may be ever so privately committed, yet, generally speaking, it is discovered, and is punished in this life; and it is sure to meet with its reward in the world to come; such sinners are always reckoned among those who shall not inherit the kingdom of God; but shall have their portion in the lake which burns with fire, which is the second death; unless the grace of God is displayed in giving them repentance and remission of sin.——2. Satan, though he is said *to have the power of death*, Heb. ii. 14. yet this is not to be understood as if he had a power and right to inflict death at pleasure on men; for if so, such is his malice and rooted enmity to men, that the race of mankind would have been extinct long ago. The case of Job shews that he lies under the restraint of God in this matter: he may have been by divine permission, in some instances, the executioner of death to the enemies of God, and to such who have given up themselves to him, and sold themselves to work wickedness. He was the introducer of sin into the world, the cause of death; and both are the works of the devil, which Christ came to destroy, and has destroyed; and Satan, because of his concern in the ruin of our first parents, by his temptations, and so of all mankind, he is said to be a *murderer from the beginning*, John viii. 44.——3. Death of right is of God only; it is he who threatened with it in case of sin; and made it the sanction of his law. Death, whenever he comes and attacks men, it is by a commission from God. He is sometimes represented as a person coming up at our windows, and into our palaces and houses, like a bailiff to arrest men; and sometimes as on horseback and armed, and power given him to kill men with various sorts of judgments, as famine, pestilence, sword, and wild beasts; see Jer. ix. 21. Rev. vi. 8. and whatever are the means of the death of men, whether extraordinary or ordinary, they are all of God, and under his direction; every disorder, disease, and sickness, are servants sent by him to execute his pleasure; insomuch that death is frequently spoken of as his act, and as inflicted by him; it is expressed by taking men away; by taking away their life or soul; by gathering the breath and spirit of men to

---

[5] Mille viæ lethi. Lucan.

himself; by prevailing against man, and causing him to pass away; and by changing his countenance, and sending him away, Job. xxvii. 8. and xxxii. 22. and xxxiv.14. and xiv. 20.——4. Death is by his appointment; it is the statute-law of heaven, Heb. ix. 27. The grave is the house appointed for all men living, Job xxx. 23. All things leading to death, and which issue in it, are under a divine appointment. All afflictions, diseases, and disorders, are of God; these are not fortuitous events, that come by chance, or spring out of the dust; but come by the appointment of God, to bring about the dissolution by death: all the circumstances of it are according to the determinate counsel and will of God; as what death, and by what event, a man shall die; and the manner of his death, and the place where; for though we are told where we were born, and know where we now live; yet no man knows where he shall die; none but God knows this, who has determined the times before appointed, and the bounds of men's habitations, where they shall live, and where they shall die. The time of a man's death is appointed by God; for there is a time for every purpose of God, for the execution of it : *A time to be born, and a time to die*, Eccles. iii. 1, 2. there is an appointed time for man on earth, when he shall come into the world, how long he shall continue in it, and when he shall go out of it; and before this time no man dies. The Jews sought to lay hold on Christ, to take away his life, but they could not, because his hour was not come; and the same holds good of every man. Nor can any live longer than the appointed time; *The time drew nigh that Israel must die*, Gen. xlvii. 29. there was a time fixed for it, and that was at hand, when he must die, and there was no going beyond it. Says Job, of man, *his days are determined, the number of his months are with thee; thou hast appointed his bounds that he cannot pass*, Job xiv. 5. a man cannot lengthen out his days, nor another for him; no man *can add one cubit unto his stature*, or rather, *to his age*, Matt. vi. 27. The days of men are compared to an hand breadth, Psalm xxxix. 5. and to this hand breadth, not a cubit, nor indeed any measure at all, can be added, with all the thought, care, and means, that can be made use of; physicians, in this respect, are physicians of no value; they cannot prolong the life of men; they may make life a little more easy and comfortable while it lasts; but they cannot protract it one moment : nor can men that abound with wealth and riches, give to God a ransom for themselves and others, that they should *still live for ever, and see no corruption*, Psalm xlix. 6—9.

There are several things objected to this; but are what have been mostly answered already; as that Hezekiah had fifteen years added to his days; and some men not living out half their days, and dying before their time,[6] Psalm lv. 23. Eccles. vii. 17. As for the objection taken from the insignificancy and uselessness of means, and temptations to lay them aside, if things are so, that no man can live longer, nor die sooner, than the appointed time: it should be known, that in general, with respect to things civil or sacred, the means are equally appointed as the end, and to be used in order to it; this appears in the case of Hezekiah; though the decree was express and peremptory, that fifteen years should be certainly added to his days; yet the prophet that brought the message from the Lord, and the King that received it, both agreed to have a plaister of figs laid upon his boil, for the recovery of his health, and the continuance of his life, Isa. xxxviii. 21. see also Acts xxvii. 31.

2*dly*, The procuring or meritorious cause of death, is sin; it was threatened in case of sin; and when sin entered the world, death came in by it; it is the wages and demerit of sin; *The body is dead because of sin ;* it is become mortal, and dies, on account of it, Rom. v. 12. and vi. 23. and viii. 10. Man was originally made an immortal creature; the soul, in its own nature, is such, being immaterial; and though the body is composed of matter, and such as was capable of being reduced and resolved into the elements of which it was made, for sin; yet it was gifted by God with immortality; and had man continued in his state of innocence, this gift would have remained with him; for the death of the body is not the fruit and effect of nature, as say the Socinians;[7] but of sin; for if man would have died, according to the course of nature, whether he had sinned or no; to what purpose was the threatening, *In the day thou eatest thereof thou shalt surely die*, if he would and must have died, whether he

---

[6] See book 3. chap. 4. p. 296.
[7] Socinus de Servatore, par. 3. c. 8. p. 208. et de Statu primi Hominis, p. 276. et Prælection. Theolog. c. 1.

ate or no? But it was through sinning that he became mortal, like the beasts, and perish or die, as they do. Otherwise man would have continued immortal; and, by means directed to, would have been supported in his present life, without dying, or any fears of it; or would have been translated to an higher kind of life, for evermore.

3dly, The instrumental causes, or means of death, are various; or which, and who, are employed in the execution of it. Angels are sometimes made use of to inflict it; thus an angel in one night, slew in the Assyrian camp, an hundred fourscore and five thousand, 2 Kings xix. 35. Multitudes are cut off by the sword of justice, in the hand of the civil magistrate, and that by the order and appointment of God. God has his four judgments, sword, famine, pestilence, and wild beasts, by which sometimes great havoc is made among men; the ordinary means by which death is instrumentally brought about, are disorders and distempers of the body; which operate sometimes in a quicker, and sometimes in a slower way; yet sooner or later they are the cause of men's drawing to the grave, and their life to the destroyers.

Fourthly, The properties of death, which serve to lead into the nature, power, and use of death.——1. It is but *once; It is appointed unto men once to die*, Heb. ix. 27. Ordinarily men die but once; they do not soon return to life again, and then die again; they go by death whither they shall not return to their houses, and families, and friends again, and to their business in life, as before; when they die, they lie down in the grave, and rise not till the heavens be no more; that is, until the second coming of Christ, when the heavens shall pass away; or until the resurrection-morn, which will be when Christ himself shall descend from heaven to judge the world, from whose face the heaven and earth shall flee away; see Job. vii. 10. and x. 21. and xiv. 10, 11, 12. There have been some instances in which men have died, and have been raised again to a mortal life, as it should seem, and then have died again; otherwise it is not easy to say, how Christ could be called the first-born from the dead, if any were raised before him to an immortal life, never to die more; since some were raised before; as the *son* of the widow of Sarepta, by Elijah; and the son of the Shunamite, by Elisha; and the man that revived upon touching the prophet's bones: and also others by Christ himself; as Jairus's daughter, the widow of Nain's son, and Lazarus; of whom it is particularly observed, that after his resurrection he sat at table as a guest, at supper-time, to eat and drink; which supposes the life he was raised to was a mortal one, and that he was supported in the manner mortals are, and died again, John xii. 2. But commonly men die but once, as Christ the Saviour did.——2. Death is certain; it is certain by the appointment of God, which cannot be frustrated; Israel must die, and so must every man; though the time when, is very uncertain; the Son of man comes in an hour men know not of; therefore they should be ready, and watching, and waiting for him. Nothing is more certain than death, as all experience in all ages testify; and yet nothing more uncertain than the time when a man shall die.—— 3. Death is mighty, powerful, and irresistible; what is stronger than death? No man has power over his spirit, to retain the spirit one moment, when it is called for: when God says, this night thy soul is required of thee, it must be given up: there is no resisting nor withstanding; when it is said, *The Master is come, and calleth for thee*, thou must go; when death comes and calls for a man, he must go with him; strugglings and intreaties are to no purpose.——4. Death is insatiable; it is one of those things that is never satisfied; and the grave, which follows it, is another, Hab. ii. 5. Prov. xxx. 16. though it has been glutting itself from the beginning of the world, it is as greedy of its prey as ever; and though it sometimes makes such a carnage of men, as in a battle, that thousands are slain in one day, and great numbers in a short time, by famine and pestilence, yet it never has enough.——5. Death is necessary; not only by the appointment of God, which must be accomplished; but for the truth of God, in his threatening with it, in case of sin; and for the justice of God on sinners, which requires it: and besides, it is also necessary to the saints, for their good; that they may be free from indwelling sin and corruption, which they cannot be as long as they are in this tabernacle; this earthly house, in which the spreading leprosy of sin is, must be pulled down, ere a thorough riddance can be made of it; it is necessary to deliver the saints from all the troubles of this life, and to introduce them into the joy of their Lord. Wherefore, ——6. Though death is formidable to nature, and to natural men; yet it is desirable by good men; they seek their dismission from hence by it; they choose rather to depart, and to be with Christ, which is much better than a continuance in a life of sin and sorrow; they are willing rather to be absent from the body, that they might be present with the Lord.

CHAP. II.

OF THE IMMORTALITY OF THE SOUL.

Though the body dies, yet when it dies, the soul dies not; it survives the body, and not only lives after it, but lives for ever, it never dies: though the body without the soul is dead, yet the soul without the body is not dead; when the body returns to the earth and dust, from whence it sprung, the soul returns to God, the immediate author and giver of it: the body may be killed by men, but not the soul; no man has any power over that, none but God that made it: the soul is immortal, it is not capable of death, that is, in a natural and proper sense; it is capable of dying, in a figurative sense; a moral or spiritual death; which is brought on by sin; but this lies not in a deprivation of the powers and faculties of it; but of its moral rectitude, righteousness, and holiness; and it is capable of an eternal death, which is the destruction of it in hell; that is, not a destruction of its substance, but of its peace, joy, and happiness for ever.

When it is said, the soul is immortal, it must be understood, that it is so in its nature; and is not liable to death, either from anything within itself or without it: but not that it has such an immortality as God himself has, *who only hath immortality;* he has it of himself: angels, and the souls of men, have their immortality of him, who has made them immaterial and immortal spirits; his immortality is without beginning, and any prior cause of it; theirs has a beginning from God, the first cause of them: his is independent; theirs depends on him, in whom they live, and move, and have their being. That the soul of man is immortal may be proved,

First, From the consideration of the soul itself, its original, nature, powers, and faculties.

1*st,* From the original of it; it is not of men; it is not *ex traduce,* or by generation from parents, as has been proved elsewhere; *What is born of the flesh, is flesh;* and is not only carnal and sinful, but frail and mortal; *All flesh is grass,* withering, decaying, and corruptible, as that is: but the spirit, or soul, is of God; it is the very breath of God; and has a similarity to him, particularly in immortality; *God breathed into man the breath of life, and he became a living soul,* immortal and never dying, Gen. ii. 7. Elihu says, Job xxxiii. 4. *The breath of the Almighty hath given me life,* a life that will never end: as the first man was made, so are his posterity; his body was formed out of the dust; and then a living, immortal soul was breathed into it: so the body of every man is first formed, and then the soul is created in it; hence God is described, as he that *formeth the spirit of man within him,* Zech. xii. 1. and as God is the former of the souls of men, so he is the supporter of them; he *upholds their souls in life;* as they have their being and their life from him, it is maintained by him; the souls of men are not dependent on their bodies, and therefore die not when they do: as they are independent of them in their operations, can think, reason, discourse, will, and nill without them; so they are in their being, and can exist and subsist without them. The most malicious and cruel persecutors can only kill the body; and after that, *they have no more that they can do;* they cannot kill the soul, Luke xii. 4. they cannot pursue that any further; that returns to God that gave it; he could, indeed annihilate it, if he would; but that he does not do, neither the souls of good men, who, after death, are under the altar, calling for vengeance on their persecutors; nor the souls of bad men, who are in perpetual torment; their worm of conscience never dies, but is always torturing them; and the fire of divine wrath in them is never quenched, of which they are always sensible, and therefore must be immortal, and never die; or else that *fire,* and its *burnings,* would not be *everlasting,* as they are said to be.

2*dly,* The immortality of the soul may be proved from the nature of the soul; which is,——1. Spiritual, of the same nature with angels, who are made *spirits,* spiritual substances, and so die not; and such are the souls of men, Heb. xii. 9, 23. Now as the souls of men are of the same nature with angels, and they die not, it may be concluded that the souls of men are immortal, and die not, Psalm civ. 4. Luke xx. 36. 1 Cor. ii. 11.——2. The soul of man is simple, unmixed, and uncompounded :[1] it is not composed of flesh, and blood, and bones, arteries, veins, &c. as the body ; a spirit has none of these ; not flesh, which may be torn to pieces ; nor blood, which may be let out and shed, and life expire ; nor bones, which may be broken, and be the occasion of death ; nor arteries and veins, which may be cut through, and life cease : nor is it, as the body, made up of the four elements, fire, water, earth, and air, and capable of being resolved into the same again.——3. It is immaterial, it is not composed of matter and form, nor is it a material form, educed out of the power of matter, as the souls of brutes, which die, go downward, and return to the earth ; matter is destitute of motion, and cannot move itself ; whereas the soul of man, being moved, can move itself ; as it appears by its thoughts, reasonings, and discourses ; this was Plato's argument[2] for the immortality of the soul,[3] that it can move the body at pleasure, or influence to any action, as to walk, sit, &c. Matter is incapable of thought, reasoning, and discoursing, willing and nilling, as the soul is. Matter is divisible, discerptible, may be cut to pieces ; not so the soul ; it is out of the reach of every slaughtering weapon ; the sharp arrow cannot penetrate into it, nor the glittering spear pierce it, nor the two-edged sword divide it ; none of these, nor any other of the same nature can touch it.——4. The soul has no contrary qualities, which, when one is predominant, threatens with destruction ; it is neither hot nor cold ; neither moist nor dry ; neither hard nor tender : it has no heat in it, which may, as in the body, be increased to such a degree, as in burning fevers, to dry it up like a potsherd, and consume it : nor such moisture, which may rise, abound, and overflow it, as in a dropsy, and drown the fabric : nor has it any such tender part which will not bear a blow, but be fatal to it : nor so hard as not to bend, and become pliable to proper uses, and endanger the machine.——5. The soul of man is made after the image, and in the likeness of God ; which chiefly consists in that it bears a resemblance to the divine nature, being the breath of God ; it has a likeness to him, and particularly in its immortality ; and this is given by Alcmæon [4] as an argument of it ; and so Plato,[5] the soul is most like to that which is divine, immortal, intelligible, uniform, indissoluble, and always the same.

3*dly*, The immortality of the soul may be proved from the powers and faculties of it, its understanding and will.——1. Its understanding. *There is a spirit*, or soul, *in man*, as Elihu says, Job xxxii. 8. *And the inspiration of the Almighty giveth them understanding ;* an intellective power and faculty of understanding things, which distinguishes men from the brutes that perish, the horse, the mule, &c. which have no understanding ; it is by this, God teaches men more than the beasts of the earth, and makes them wiser than the fowls of heaven, Psalm xxxii. 9. Job. xxxv. 11.—— (1.) The understanding of man can take in, and has knowledge of things spiritual, and incorporeal, immaterial, incorruptible, and eternal ; which it would not be capable of, if it was not of the same nature itself ; the images of these things would not be impressed on it, nor would it be susceptible of them : it can reflect on its own thoughts and reasonings, and knows the things within itself, which none but God and that know ; it has knowledge of angels, their nature, offices, and services ; it has knowledge of God himself, [6] of his nature, perfections, ways, and works: nor is it any objection to it, that it has knowledge of corporeal things, and therefore must be corporeal too, since these are things below it, and therefore within its reach ; whereas spiritual, incorporeal, and immaterial substances, would be above it, and not within its compass, unless it was a spiritual, immortal, and immaterial substance also ; thus God and angels know corporeal and material things, though they are incoporeal and immaterial.——(2.) The soul of man has knowledge of eternity itself ; though it may be observed, there is great difference in its apprehension of an eternity past, and of that which is to come : when it considers

---

[1] Vid. Aristot. de Anima, 1 1. c. 5. et 1. 2. c. 1. Cicero. Tuscul. Quæst. 1. 1. Non aliquid mixtum, non concretum ex elementis. Sed purum, æternum, quodque omne est tabe solutum. &c. Aonius Palearius de Immortal. Anim. 1. 2. 1. 89. Ed. Amster. 1690.
[2] Vid. Phædro, p. 1221.
[3] Animum autem hominis per se semper moveri, quia sit ad cogitandum mobilis, &c. Lactant. Divin. Institut. Epitome, c. 10.

[4] Apud Aristot. de Anima, 1. 1. c. 2. vid Laert. 1. 8. in vita ejus.
[5] In Phædone, p. 60, 61.
[6] This is used as an argument of the soul's immortality by Sallustius, de Diis, c. 8. and so by Lactantius, Divin. Institut. Epitome, c. 10. illud autem maximum argumentum immortalitatis, quod Deum solus homo agnoscit.

the former, it is soon at a loss, and at a full stop, is obliged to return, and cannot go on; it is like a bird that attempts to soar aloft, and take flights it is not used nor equal to, it flutters and hangs its wing, and is forced to descend. But when the soul fixes its thoughts on an eternity to come, how readily does it apprehend how that shall proceed without end! with what pleasure does it roll over millions of ages in it! The reason of this difference is, because the soul itself is not from eternity, but has a beginning; whereas it will endure to eternity, and have no end. There is, Cicero says,[7] though he knows not how it is, inherent in the minds of men, a sort of an *augurium*, soothsaying, divination, or foresight of future ages; and which chiefly and most easily appears in the greatest minds, and in the most exalted geniuses. There is in men a natural notion of futurity, a desire after it, and an expectation of it; which are things not in vain implanted in them; and would not appear if the soul was not immortal; it has knowledge of things past, present, and future; which proves its immortality.[8]——(3.) The knowledge which the mind and understanding of man has of things in the present state, is very imperfect, through the brevity of life; and therefore it may be reasonably concluded, that there is a future state, in which the soul will exist, and its knowledge of things be more perfect: it has been a constant and continual complaint of the sons of learning and science, *ars longa, vita brevis;* art is long, and life is short; man has not time enough to cultivate the knowledge he is capable of. It has been said,[9] that it would require a man's whole lifetime, and that not sufficient, to get a thorough knowledge of that single mineral, *antimony:* let a man employ all his time and studies in any one branch of literature, any particular art or science, or language, yet would his knowledge be imperfect, and room would be left for those that come after him to improve upon him: arts and sciences have been cultivating many thousands of years, and in some ages great improvements have been made, and especially in later ones; and yet there is room for farther improvements still: the knowledge of the best things, which good men have, as of God, of Christ, and of the mysteries of grace, is now very imperfect; those that know most, know but *in part*, and *see through a glass darkly:* but there is a state in which their souls will exist, when they shall see God face to face, see him as he is, and know as they are known; when their minds will be employed on more noble and interesting subjects than now, and have perfect knowledge of them.—— (4.) The knowledge the mind of man has of things now, is not in proportion to the powers that he is possessed of. How many are there that die in infancy, and as soon as they are born, whose reasoning powers are never called forth into act and exercise? and how many die in childhood and youth, before these powers ripen, and are brought to any maturity? and how many are there that even live a long life, and yet, either through want of education, or through their situation, circumstances, and employment in life, have not their faculties exercised in proportion to the capacities they are endowed with? Now can it be thought that these powers are bestowed upon them in vain? There must be then an after-state, in which the soul exists, when its powers will be employed in greater things, and to nobler ends and uses.——(5.) Let a man know ever so much in this present life, he is desirous of knowing more; let his acquisitions of knowledge be ever so large, after a life of studious search and enquiry, he is not satisfied, he still wants to know more; and what he has arrived unto, is only to know this, that he knows but little: now this desire of knowledge is not implanted in man, by the author of nature, in vain; wherefore the soul must remain after death, when it will arrive to a more perfect knowledge of things; this was the argument Socrates used, to prove to his scholars the immortality of the soul. But with respect to truly good men, the argument receives farther strength; they that know most of God, of Christ, and of divine things; they desire to know more, they follow on to know, they make use of all means to increase their spiritual knowledge, and after all, find it imperfect; and therefore are unsatisfied, and long after a future state, when all darkness and imperfection will be removed, and they shall see all things clearly. Now these gracious and earnest desires are not implanted in vain by the

---

[7] Tuscul. Quæst. 1. 1.
[8] Ut qui præterita teneat, præsentia comprehendat, futura prospiciat, multarumque rerum et artium scientiam complectatur, immortalem esse, Lactantius ut supra. An potest esse mortalis qui immortalem desiderat? Ibid.
[9] Basilius Valentinus apud Boyle's Nat. Hist. p. 13.

God of all grace, as they would be, if the soul was not immortal.

2. The will of man is another faculty of the soul, the object and actings of which shew it to be immortal.——(1.) The will has for its object universal good. It naturally desires complete happiness, which some place in one thing and some in another, but it is not perfectly enjoyed by any; some place it in riches, but find themselves mistaken in them, nor do they give the satisfaction expected from them; some in the gratification of carnal pleasures, but these soon pall and perish with the using, and new ones are sought after; some in enjoying posts of honour, and in the applause of men; but these depend, the one on the pleasure of princes, by whom they are set in high places, and which become slippery ones; the other on popular breath, which is as variable as the wind; some place it in wisdom, knowledge, learning, and science; which, as they are not only imperfect, but attract the envy of others, and, as Solomon says, are *vexation of spirit*, and cause grief and sorrow, Eccl. i. 17, 18. now there must be a future state, in which true happiness will be attained, at least by some, or else the actings of the will about it will be in vain.—— (2.) God is the *summum bonum*, the chief good, the will of man rightly pitches upon, nor can it be satisfied with any thing less; good men choose him as their portion; and which is the foundation of their faith, hope, love, peace, and joy; but then he is not perfectly enjoyed as such in this life; their faith and expectations are, that he will be their portion for ever; nor will they be fully satisfied until they enjoy him as such in another world; wherefore in order to this, the soul must remain after death and be immortal.——(3.) The will has its desires, and which desires, even the best, are not satisfied in this life; whatever it has, it is desirous of more, it is never satisfied; its desires of knowledge, as we have seen, are not gratified to the full; nor its desires after happiness in general, nor even after God himself, the chief good, of whom the truly good man says, *Whom have I in heaven but thee? and there is none upon earth that I desire besides thee*, Psalm lxxiii. 25. which desires, unless there is a future state in which the soul exists after death and is immortal, are not fully satisfied, and so far in vain.——(4.) The actions of the will are free, not forced by any creature; no creature has any power over it, to force it nor destroy it; its acts are independent of the body, it can operate without it in willing, nilling, choosing, and refusing; and it can subsist and live without, and when that is dead.——(5.) The will is not weakened, nor indeed any of the powers and faculties of the soul, impaired by sickness and approaching death; though the *outward man perish the inward man is renewed day by day*; how clear is the understanding! how active and vigorous the will, when on the verge of eternity! as appears by its willingness or unwillingness to die, to be freed from present pains and agonies, either by a restoration to health, or by a removal by death; particularly by a good man's choosing rather to depart and be with Christ, and even by his longing to be gone, saying, *Come, Lord Jesus, come quickly;* yea, when the body is become speechless and near expiring, the faculties of the soul are in exercise; a man understands clearly what his friends about him say, and can by a sign, by the lifting up of his hand, signify his faith, hope, joy, and comfort; all which shew that the soul sickens not with the body, nor becomes languid as the body does, nor dies with it, though it may be cramped by it.

Secondly, The immortality of the soul may be proved from the light of nature and reason.——1. From the consent of all nations. Cicero says,[10] that as we know by nature that there is a God, so we judge, by the consent of all nations, that souls remain after death, and are immortal; and in every thing, he says,[11] the consent of all nations is to be reckoned the law of nature: so Seneca[12] calls it a public persuasion, or belief; and observes, that the consent of men, either fearing hell, or worshipping God, is of no small moment to persuade unto it. This was, no doubt, the original belief of men, discoverable by the light of nature; but as that became more dim, and men more degenerate, they lost sight of truths, and of this among the rest. Thales the Milesian, who lived about six hundred years before Christ, is said[13] to be the first who taught it; though others say[14] Pherecydes was the first who asserted it,

---

[10] Tuscul. Quæst. 1. 1.
[11] Ibid.
[12] Ep. 117.

[13] Laert. in vita Thaletis, Suidas in voce Θαλης.
[14] Cicero. Tusc. Quæst. 1. 1.

who was cotemporary with him: some ascribe the first knowledge of it to the Chaldæans and Indian magi,[15] and others to the Egyptians;[16] who, it may be, received it from Abraham; and from them Plato had it. However, it has been embraced by the wisest among the heathens; by the best of their philosophers, as Pythagoras,[17] Socrates, Plato, Seneca, Cicero,[18] and others; and by the best of their poets, as Homer, Phocylides, Virgil, Ovid, &c. and though denied by some, these were such that were of the worst sect of them; and though by some among the Jews, as by the Sadducees, yet these were but few, and the most irreligious sect among them. Indeed, this doctrine has been received, not only among the more religious sects of the heathens; as the Brachmans[19] among the Indians, and the Druids[20] with us, and among the more civilized nations; but among the more savage and ignorant, even the wild Greenlanders;[21] as appears by the accounts lately published concerning them. ——2. This may be concluded from an extinction of man, soul and body, being abhorrent to man, as it is said to be to the people last-mentioned: the death of the body, though nature is reluctant to it, yet in many instances there has been a voluntary and cheerful submission to it; many good men have not loved their lives unto death, to serve their country; others have not counted their lives dear to themselves, but have freely parted with them for the sake of religion and truth; and others have chose rather to depart this life and to be with Christ; death to them has been more eligible than life; but a total extinction, to have no being at all, nature starts at! which must be the case if the soul dies with the body.——3. It may be argued from the natural desire in men to be religious, in some way or another; this is so natural to men, that some have chose rather to define man a religious than a rational animal. All nations have had their gods they worshipped; professed some religion or another, and have kept up some kind of worship; even the most blind and ignorant, barbarous and savage: but why are they concerned to worship God, and be solicitous about religion, if there is no future state, and the soul remains not after death, but that it perishes with the body? There is nothing can be a greater damp to religion and morality, than the disbelief of the immortality of the soul; for then one may encourage another in all vicious practices; and say, *Let us eat and drink, for to-morrow we shall die*, and it will be all over with us! nothing more discourages virtue, and encourages vice. Yet,——4. There is a consciousness of sinning in men; guilt arises in their consciences on account of sin: even in the very heathens there is *a conscience bearing witness* to their actions, good or bad; and *their thoughts, the meanwhile, accusing, or else excusing one another,* on account of them: from whence arise fears of the displeasure and wrath of incensed Deity and of divine judgment; all which show that there is a future state, in which souls remain immortal, and are accountable to God for their actions. And which still more appears,——5. Not only from the stings of conscience, but from the horrors and terrors, dread, trembling and panic fears, wicked men are sometimes seized with, as Felix was, on hearing of judgment to come: and if these fears, as some say, were the effect of education, which could not be the case of Felix and many others, it is strange that these fears should be so general and extensive as they are; and more strange, that none have been able to shake them off entirely; and stranger still, that those who have run the greatest lengths in infidelity and atheism should not be able to free themselves from them. These things not only show that there is a divine Being, to whom men are accountable for their actions; but that there is a future state after death, in which men exist, when they shall be either in happiness or in misery.——6. The belief of this may be further argued, from the providence of God concerned in the distribution and disposal of things in this life, which is oftentimes very unequal; wicked

---

[15] Pausanias in Messenicis, p. 277.
[16] Herodot. Euterpe sive, 1. 2 c. 123.
[17] Who says that το φρονιμον, that which is capable of prudence, is immortal, Laert. in vita ejus. Vid. Plutarch. de Placitis Philosoph. 1. 4. c. 7. Some indeed, as the Stoic philosophers, spake of it but doubtfully and confusedly; and as Minutius Felix, in Octav. p. 37. says, corruptaa et dimidiata fide; they rather conjectured they remained after death, but could not say how long; some thought they went into other bodies.
[18] Cicero in Tusculanis, quamvis dubitanter, tamen sensit summum homini bonum non nisi post mortem contingere, Lactant. Institut. 1. 7. c. 10.
[19] Strabo Geograph. 1. 15. p. 490.
[20] Ibid. 1. 4. p. 136. Cæsar. 1. 6. s. 13.
[21] Crantz's History of Greenland, vol. 1. b. 3. c. 5. p. 201.

men prosper, and enjoy a large portion of ease and plenty; and good men are greatly afflicted with a variety of troubles, which has been sometimes a sore temptation to good men, and difficult to them to account for; as it was to Asaph and Jeremiah, Psalm lxxiii. 2, 3, 12, 13, 14. Jer. xii. 1, 2. which difficulty can only be solved by the supposition of a future state, the immortality of the soul, and its existing after death; when such who have been wicked, and in their lifetime received good things, and good men evil things, the latter will have their comforts, and the former their torments; otherwise good men, if they were to have hope in this life only, they would be of all men the most miserable, Luke xvi. 25. 1 Cor. xv. 19. Wherefore,——7. The immortality of the soul may be concluded from the justice of God; who is the Judge of all the earth, who will do right; for righteous is the Lord, though his judgments are not so manifest in this life: it is a righteous thing with God to render tribulation to them that trouble his people and to fulfil the promises he makes to his saints; at present, the justice, faithfulness, and veracity of God, are not so clearly seen in bestowing favours and blessings on good men, according to his promises; and in punishing wicked men, according to his threatenings: it seems therefore reasonable to believe that the souls of men are immortal, and that their bodies shall rise from the dead; and that there shall be a future state, in which good men will be happy and wicked men miserable.——8. It seems not agreeable to the wisdom of God to create man in his image and likeness, and give him dominion over the whole brute creation, and constitute him lord over all; make the beasts of the field, the fowls of the air, and the fishes of the sea, for his sake and use, and yet he and they should have the same exit; the one die and perish, and be totally extinct as the other: this does not comport with the wisdom of God. But,——9. Between the spirits of men and those of brutes, there is a difference; the one at death go *upwards* to God that made them, and gave them to men, and live for ever, either in a state of bliss or woe; and the other go *downward to the earth*, and die, and live no more, Eccles. iii. 21.——10. If the soul is not immortal, but dies with the body, the brutes in many things, have the advantage of men; and their state and condition in this life is, in many respects, superior to theirs; they are not so weak and helpless at first coming into the world as men are, and who are so for a long time; nor subject to so many diseases as they are; in some the senses are quicker than in men, and they have more pleasure in the exercise of them; as in their sight, hearing, taste, and smell; some animals excel men in one or other of these: the brutes have no fearful apprehensions of danger beforehand; and when in any, their only concern is, for the present to get clear of it; and when it is over they are in no dread of its return: they know nothing of death, are in no expectation of it, nor fear about it; but men know that they must die, and expect it; and through fear of it, are subject to bondage, and attended with great anxieties, and therefore if the soul dies with the body, their present condition is worse than that of brutes.

Thirdly, The immortality of the soul, may be proved from the sacred Scriptures; both from plain and express passages of scripture; as from Eccles. xii. 7. where, when the body returns to the dust, the soul, or *spirit*, is said to *return to God that gave it*. And likewise from Matt. x. 28. *Fear not them which kill the body, but are not able to kill the soul*, which is incapable of being put to death; otherwise such is the malice of the persecutors of good men, that they would not spare it any more than the body; but having killed the body, *after that*, as Luke says, *have no more that they can do*, the soul being out of their reach, Luke xii. 4. This is to be proved from scripture doctrines and from scripture instances.

1*st*, From scripture doctrines; as from the doctrine of God's love to his people, which is everlasting, Jer. xxxi. 3. But this would not be true of it, if the souls of God's beloved died; then there would be no objects of this love, and so not everlasting; hence it would follow, that death can, and does, *separate* from the love of God, contrary to the apostle's firm persuasion, Rom. viii. 38, 39. And from the doctrine of eternal election; which is of the persons of God's people, both with respect to soul and body; and by it they are *ordained to eternal life*, Acts xiii. 48. But if the soul dies with the body, and is not immortal, how will God's elect possess eternal life and eternal glory they are chosen to? and consequently if they do not, the purpose of God, according to election, does not stand sure. Also from the covenant of grace, which is said to be an *everlasting covenant*, 2 Sam. xxiii. 5. But it is well known, that as in all covenants there are confederates, and if one of the parties covenanting, dies, the covenant is at an end ; and if God's elect, with whom the covenant of grace is made, should become extinct, soul and body, the covenant would not be an everlasting one. The argument used by Christ, to prove the resurrection of the dead, from covenant interest, Matt. xxii. 31, 32. Luke xx. 38. equally proves, or rather more clearly, the immortality of the soul ; and Menasseh Ben Israel,[22] makes use of the same scripture to prove it, and argues from it much in the same manner Christ does. And particularly the immortality of the soul may be concluded from the grand promise of eternal life, in the covenant made before the world began, Tit. i. 2. 1 John ii. 25. But how can this promise be fulfilled, if the souls of those to whom it is made, are not immortal ? It may be argued from the doctrine of adoption, another blessing in the covenant; by virtue of which saints are heirs of an eternal inheritance ; but how can the relation of sons subsist, which adoption gives, and the inheritance adopted to be enjoyed, if the soul dies with the body ? And the same may be evinced from the doctrine of regeneration ; in virtue of which men are begotten again to a lively hope of a glorious inheritance ; which yet can never be possessed if the soul is not immortal. The same may be concluded from the doctrine of sanctification, every branch of which has eternal life connected with it ; as knowledge of God in Christ, faith in Christ, and hope of eternal glory ; but if the soul is not immortal, in which these graces are, they will not only fail themselves, but the glory and happiness annexed unto them will not be attained. Likewise it may be argued from the doctrine of Christ respecting his work, the blessings of grace by him, and the services and benefits further to be expected from him ; as the redemption of the soul by the blood of Christ, which must be shed in vain : nor can it be called eternal redemption, if the soul is not immortal; nor will the saints' union to Christ be an indissoluble one ; nor they enjoy that life which justification by his righteousness entitles to ; nor his intercession and preparations for them in heaven be of any service to them : the second coming of Christ, with all his saints, and the resurrection of their bodies at his coming, shew that their souls live in a separate state before the resurrection, or they could not be said to come with him ; and that they will be alive at the resurrection, or to what purpose will their bodies be raised ? The doctrine of the judgment, whether particular or general, is a proof of the soul's immortality ; for if that dies with the body, there is nothing remains after death on which judgment can pass. Moreover, the doctrine of future rewards and punishments confirms this truth ; for if the soul is not immortal, a good man cannot be rewarded in a way of grace, or enjoy happiness in consequence of his piety, since there will be no subject of it remaining ; nor a wicked man be punished for his sins, for the same reason ; yea, it will lie in the power of a wicked man both to prevent the happiness of the one and the punishment of the other ; since it is in his power to take away his own animal life, and so put himself out of the power of God to inflict punishment upon him, if his soul survives not ; and so likewise to take away the life of a good man, and deprive him of any further and future happiness ; all which does not comport with the wisdom, justice, and goodness of God ; and therefore it may be concluded the soul survives, that it may be the subject of reward or punishment.[23] It is an observation of Hierocles,[24] that a wicked man would not have the soul to be immortal, that he may not endure punishment, and therefore prevents the Judge decreeing it, by inflicting death on himself ; and so Plato[25] observes, that if death is the dissolution of the whole (soul and body) it would be gain to the wicked to die, since they would be free from all evil, soul and body.

2dly, The immortality of the soul may be proved from scripture instances ; as from the cases of Enoch and Elijah, who were translated, soul and body, that they should not see death ; as not in their bodies, so not in their souls, which must be immortal, and so the souls of others ; for of what different nature can their souls be

---

[22] De Resurrectione Mort. l. 1 c. 10. s. 6.
[23] This Dr. Watts calls a moral argument for the immortality of the soul ; see his Miscellaneous Thoughts, in vol. iv. N° 75. p. 594.
[24] In Carmin. Pythagor. p. 165.
[25] In Phædone. p. 80. Ed. Ficin.

supposed to be? and from the instances of the patriarchs, Abraham, Isaac, and Jacob, who died, and yet after death were living, even in the times of Christ, as he argues in a place before referred to; and this was the case of all the old testament saints, who died in the faith of the heavenly city and country, and now possess it; and also from the spirits in prison, in the times of the apostle Peter, who were disobedient to the warnings of Noah; and from the resurrection of some particular persons; who after death, were raised and lived again, their souls, which died not, being returned to them, 1 Kings xvii. 21, 22. and from the souls under the altar, whose bodies were killed, but their souls were not, but were expostulating with God about taking vengeance on their perscutors, Rev. vi. 9, 10. and from the instances of persons committing their spirits, or souls to God at death; which shows that they believed their souls would survive their bodies, and therefore they committed them to the care of God, Psalm xxxi. 5. Luke xxiii. 46. Acts vii. 59. 1 Pet. iv. 19. Lastly, all such scriptures which speak of the joys of heaven and of the torments of hell, as to be enjoyed or endured by men after death, prove the immortality of the soul; as that good men, when they die, are received into everlasting habitations, and the souls of wicked men go into everlasting punishment, and therefore must remain immortal, or they could not be subjects either of joy or misery; and this the parable of the rich man and beggar, plainly declares; for though a parable, yet as every parable has its scope, which ought to be attended to, so has this; which is to represent the different state and condition of the souls of good men and wicked men after death, when the one are happy and the other miserable, and therefore the souls of both must be immortal.

There are some objections made to the immortality of the soul; taken, 1*st*, From reason. As,———1. That what has a beginning has an end. But this is not always true; angels have a beginning but not an end, they die not; and since the souls of men are spiritual, immaterial substances, as they are, it may be concluded, as before observed, that they die not also.——— 2. The powers of the soul are said to decay as the body decays; but this is only true of the powers of the sensitive soul, or part of man; not of the rational soul; not of the faculties of the understanding and will; for these, as we have seen, are clear, active, and vigorous, in the article of death.——— 3. When a man dies, nothing is seen to go out of him but his breath, which vanishes away: but it is no wonder the soul should not be seen at its departure, since being a spirit, incorporeal and immaterial, it is invisible; and as for the breath that goes out of a man, that cannot be the soul, which cannot be imagined to be the subject of thought, understanding and will.——— 4. Some will have it, that this is only a contrivance of men in power, a piece of state policy to keep men in awe and to their duty. But those men who contrived it were either bad men or good men: bad men would be unconcerned about ways and means to serve the cause of religion and virtue they have an aversion to; and good men would never make use of a known lie, and of hypocrisy, to serve such purposes. Besides, if this was the case, how comes it to be such a general belief in which all nations agree, and is so manifest by the light of nature?

There are other objections, which are taken from scripture. As,———1. From such scriptures which threaten the soul with death in case of sin; so the first man was threatened with death of soul and body should he eat of the forbidden fruit, Gen. ii. 17. and it is expressly said, *the soul that sins, that shall die,* Ezek. xviii. 4. To which may be replied: that there are various sorts of death; there is a spiritual or moral death, which took place in Adam as soon as he sinned; and is in all his posterity by nature; in which sense they are dead in their souls whilst alive in their bodies; it is a being *dead in trespasses and sins;* and lies, not in the substance of the soul, but in the qualities of it; in the loss of the image of God, as consisting of righteousness and holiness. And there is an eternal death, the destruction of both body and soul in hell; but this lies not in the destruction of the being of either, but in the misery of both: and there is a natural death, such as of the body, which the soul is not capable of; and if it was, it would put an end to the second death, called an eternal one; for then it would not exist, so as to be sent into everlasting fire, and to endure the vengeance of it, or undergo eternal punishment.———2. From what is said of man, Psalm lxxviii. 39. that he is but *flesh, a wind that passeth away and cometh not again:* but this is said of man with respect to his body, which is *flesh,* frail and mortal; and of the breath of his body, which is in his nostrils; a wind, a vapour, which appears for a little time, and then vanishes away; all expressive of the brevity of the bodily life of man.——3. From Psalm cxlvi. 4. *His breath goeth forth, he returneth to the earth:* which signifies the same as before, and relates to the body, which returns to the earth, from whence it came: but it follows, in which the strength of the objection lies, *in that very day,* in which the breath of his body ceases, and the body returns to the dust, that is, dies, his *thoughts perish;* and now, since the soul is, by some, defined a thinking substance, and the thoughts of it perish at death, then that must cease to be. But the meaning is, not that at the death of the body the soul ceases to think; but that all its former thoughts, schemes, projects, and purposes, concerning either civil or religious things, are then at an end, and cannot be carried into execution; as Job says, having death in view, as just at hand, *My days are past; my purposes are broken off; even the thoughts of my heart!* so that he could not perform what he had thought of, devised, and determined on, Job xvii. 11.——4. From the likeness of the spirits of brutes and of men, Eccles. iii. 19, 20. But then Solomon either in these words, personates an atheistical man; or, if he speaks his own sense, he must be understood of the sensitive part of man, which he has in common with other animals; and it is plain he speaks of that part of man which is of the dust and returns to it again, that is, the body, and of the breath of that; and in the next verse clearly observes the difference between the spirits of brutes and the rational souls of men, the one going upwards to God, and the other downward to the earth at death. ——5. The immortality of the soul is objected to, from such passages which speak of man's going at death from whence he shall not return; and as if it was not known where he was, Job x. 21. and xiv. 10. But these are to be understood of his returning to his house, and former manner of living, and employment of life, chap. vii. 10. And when it is asked, *Where is he* when he dies? it is easily answered, His body is returned to the dust, and is laid in the grave; and his soul is gone to God, and is either in bliss or woe.—— 6. From those places which speak of the dead as *not;* Rachel was weeping for her children, because they *were not,* Jer. xxxi. 15. But this cannot be meant of non-existence, either of soul or body; for the body, though reduced to dust, yet is, and is something; and the soul, that is either in heaven or in hell.

CHAP. III.

OF THE SEPARATE STATE OF THE SOUL UNTIL THE RESURRECTION, AND ITS EMPLOYMENT IN THAT STATE.

THAT the soul exists in a future state, after the death of the body, has been abundantly proved in the preceding chapter; and the business of this is to shew, that the soul, immediately after death, enters into a state of happiness or woe, in which it continues until the resurrection of the body: and that during that interval, it is not in a state of insensibility and inactivity; but that it is employed in various exercises; and what its employment is, will be pointed at.

First, That as soon as the body is dead, the soul immediately enters into a separate state of happiness or misery. The wise man, after a description of death, and the symptoms of it, in a most beautiful and striking manner; adds, *Then shall the dust return to the earth;* the body, composed of dust and earth, at death, returns to its original dust and earth, and is interred in it, where it sleeps until the resurrection; and *the spirit,* or soul, which is a spiritual, immaterial, and immortal substance, *shall return,* even immediately, as soon as the body is become a lifeless lump of clay, *unto God that gave it;* the former of the spirit of man within him, the giver of it to the sons of men, to whom it returns as soon as it leaves the body, as to the original proprietor of it; and to whom it is accountable for all actions done in the body; being summoned and gathered by him, or carried by angels to him; when a particular, personal judgment passes upon it; for *after this,* that is, death, comes *judgment;* that at once takes place; though the general judgment will not be until the resurrection of the dead; and according to the sentence passed on the soul, at its particular judgment, is it disposed of. The souls of the wicked are sent down to hell, and cast into it; to this prison they are committed, there to remain to the judgment of the great day; this has been the case from the beginning of the world, witness the spirits in prison, who were disobedient in the times of Noah; the wicked of all nations in the world, in all ages, as asserted by David; and that without respect to persons, rich or poor; the rich wicked man died, and in hell lift up his eyes, according to the parable of our Lord, 1 Pet. iii. 19. Psalm ix. 17. Luke xvi. 22. And the souls of good men return to God at death, are retained by him, into whose hands, at death, they commit them; and are immediately admitted into his presence, and fulness of joy there; and so remain until the second coming of Christ, when he will bring them with him, raise their bodies, and re-unite souls and bodies; and when in both, they shall be for ever with him: and whereas the immediate state of the wicked after death, is but sparingly spoken of in scripture; but that of good men more plentifully, the proof of the latter will be chiefly attended to, and which may be taken,

1*st*, From Eccles. iv. 2. where the saints dead, are preferred to living ones.——1. By the *dead* are meant the righteous dead; for though the righteousness of Christ, from which they are denominated righteous, delivers them from eternal death, yet not from a corporal one; *The righteous man perishes*, or dies, as others do; though his death is different from the death of others, and is attended with happy circumstances; hence Balaam desired to die the death of *the righteous*, Numb. xxiii. 10.——2. By the *living*, are meant saints in the present state, who are distressed with a body of sin and death, and groan being burdened with it; are harrassed by the temptations of Satan, with which they are sorely grieved; are exercised with a variety of afflictions, from different quarters, and on different accounts; meet with various tribulations in the world, and are greatly oppressed with the persecutions of men, as in ver. 1. which makes their present state uncomfortable at times. Now,—— 3. The righteous dead are delivered from all these; they are freed from sin, and are out of the reach of Satan's temptations, and of the persecutions and oppressions of men. And,——4. Are in a state of fellowship with God, and Christ, and with angels and glorified saints, in heaven, and so happy, and in a state preferable to living saints. But,——5. If this was not the case, if they were in a state of insensibility, and without the enjoyment of the divine presence; they would not be happier than, nor so happy, as living saints, with all their sorrows, arising from within and from without; for they have their intervals of joy, peace, and comfort; have the love of God shed abroad in their hearts, by the Spirit, at times; and are indulged with fellowship with the Father, and his Son Jesus Christ: and besides, they have comfortable fellowship with the saints, in the word and ordinances; with whom they go to the house of God in company, and are there greatly delighted and refreshed: the tabernacles of the Lord are amiable and lovely; a day in his courts is better than a thousand elsewhere. Wisdom's ways are ways of pleasantness, and her paths, paths of peace; and therefore they are happier than the righteous dead, if they are not in the divine Presence, and sensibly enjoying that, until the resurrection.

2*dly*, From Isa. lvii. 1, 2. *The righteous perisheth, &c.*——1. By the *righteous* and *merciful*, are meant such as are truly made so by the righteousness of Christ, and live righteously under a sense of such grace, and who have obtained pardoning mercy of God, and shew mercy to others; the same with the good man, the godly, and the faithful, elsewhere, Mic. vii. 2. Psalm xii. 1.——2. The death of such is meant by their *perishing*, and being *taken away;* for persons so described can never perish eternally, only as to the outward man, and the transitory things of this world; out of which they are taken by death, and to God himself. And,——3. As soon as they are taken from hence, they are at once in a state of happiness; being not only taken from evil to come, from public judgments and calamities coming upon a nation; or from the evil of sin, and of error, by which they might have been ensnared and distressed; all which is a kind of negative happiness; but they have, besides this, at death, a real and positive happiness, which they are at once possessed of; signified by the following things, ——(1.) They *enter into peace:* are not only freed from sorrow, disturbance, and distress, on any account whatever; but they are put into the possession of a peace which passeth all understanding, and can never be interrupted; they enter into it as into an house, where they are to dwell; and upon a land where there is no pricking brier nor grieving thorn.——(2.) They *rest in their beds;* not only their bodies rest in their graves, where their rest together is in the dust; but their souls in the bosom of Abraham, in the arms of Jesus; where they rest from all their toil and labour; and have continual and never ceasing communion with all the heavenly inhabitants.——(3.) They *walk* in their *uprightness;* they *walk*, and so are not in a state of insensibility and inactivity; they have *places* given them to *walk among those that stand by*, to take their turns, and converse with angels and glorified saints; and with them they walk clothed in white, because worthy, through the worthiness of Christ; in the righteousness of Christ, the fine linen, clean and white; and in spotless purity and holiness; and in the shining robes of bliss and glory.

3*dly*, From Luke xvi. 22, 23. *And it came to pass that the beggar died, &c.* The scope of this parable, as observed in the preceding chapter, is to be attended to; which is to set forth the immediate state of men after death, whether good men or bad men; for though it may have a principal respect to Christ, and to the Pharisees of his times, yet holds true of all good men, the members of Christ; and of all wicked men, whether under a guise of religion, or openly profane.——1. The beggar, the good man, upon his death, is represented as under the care and convoy of angels, and by them seated in Abraham's bosom, a phrase used by the Jews, expressive of the heavenly happiness; in allusion to a feast, at which, according to the custom of the Jews, the guests lay upon beds, or couches, about the table; so that he who lay below another, and next to him, leaned, as it were, on his breast, and lay in his bosom; and this denotes the intimate communion of the saints with each other, in the enjoyment of God. ——3. The rich and wicked man, he is said, upon his death, to be *in hell*, where he lift up his eyes, and saw the poor good man in great felicity and comfort, whom he had treated with neglect and contempt; which served to aggravate his misery; and where he found himself surrounded with the flames of hell, and filled with inward torments and horrors of mind.——3. The state of both these is summed up in a few words, ver. 25. *But now he is comforted, and thou art tormented;* even now, immediately after the death of both. And,—— 4. That this respects the intermediate state between the death of the body, and the resurrection of it, is clear, from what the wicked man petitioned, on the behalf of his brethren in his father's house, in the state of the living, and having the means, the law and the prophets; only he thought, if one sent from the dead to them, it would strike them with greater conviction; when he was told, they would not be persuaded, though *one rose from the dead;* which shews the parable respects the state of men before the resurrection, and as taking place immediately upon death.

4*thly*, From Luke xxiii. 43. *And Jesus said unto him,* the penitent thief, then suffering death; *verily I say unto thee,* which being thus solemnly affirmed might be depended on, *to-day thou shalt be with me in paradise,* in heaven! for,——1. By paradise is meant the third heaven, into which the apostle Paul was caught, 2 Cor. xii. 2, 4. the seat of the divine Majesty, and the dwelling-place of angels and glorified saints; so called in allusion to the garden of Eden, that earthly paradise, for the delight, pleasure, and happiness of it. ——2. Hither Christ himself, as soon as he expired on the cross, went; not into *limbus patrum*, to deliver the old testament-saints from thence; nor into the prison of hell, to preach to, and convert the spirits there, as say the papists, upon the mistaken sense of 1 Pet. iii. 19. but into heaven itself, having commended his spirit, or soul, into the hands of his divine Father, by whom it was received. And,—— 3. The happiness promised the thief, upon his request to him, to remember him in his kingdom, is, that he should be with him in paradise; should enjoy all the happiness of that place, and his presence in it, in which the happiness of it lay. And,—— 4. He assures him, that this happiness he should enjoy immediately, that very day; *This day thou shalt be with me, &c.* to put the stop after *to-day*, and read it as connected with what goes before, *I say unto thee to-day*, is a mere shift, and gives a most trifling and jejune sense of the words.

5*thly*, From 2 Cor. v. 1—8. *For we know that if our earthly house of this tabernacle were dissolved, we have a building of God, an house not made with hands, eternal in the heavens.* In which may be observed, ——1. That death is signified by a dissolution of the earthly body; that is called a tabernacle, or tent, set up for a while, and then taken down; and an *earthly house*, an house of clay, formed out of the earth, which has its foundation in the dust; and death is an analysis, or resolution of it, into earth and dust again.——2. Heaven is represented as another house of a different nature, not made with the hands of men; but what God is the maker and builder of; and it is not on earth, but in heaven; is eternal, will continue for ever; it consists of many mansions and apartments, prepared by Christ for his people.—— 3. Into which they are at once removed, when dislodged from their earthly house, the body; *We know, that if,* or *when our earthly house, &c.* when we are warned out of that, we have another house immediately to be admitted into; saints are not, at death, turned adrift, as Adam, when drove out of Eden; nor are they without any certain dwelling-place, as sometimes the apostles were; they have an house ready for them to go into; as soon as they are ordered out of one, there is another prepared to receive them.——4. This is no conjecture, but a certain thing; *We know,* from the provision God has made of it, from the preparations of Christ for it, from the right and title Christ's righteousness gives unto it, from the security of it in him, and from the testimony of the Spirit.—— 5. After which there are strong desires in the saints; they groan in the present tabernacle, being burdened, longing for a deliverance from it, and admittance into their other house in heaven; being willing to quit the body, that they might enjoy the presence of God; which they would not be so pressingly desirous of, if they knew they should not be introduced into it immediately.——6. But of this they have an earnest, even the Spirit of God; and therefore are quite confident, being wrought up by him for this self-same thing, by his power and grace, that when they are removed from hence they shall be with the Lord.——7. And this will be as soon as they are absent from the body, as they are at death, they shall be present with the Lord, and enjoy communion with him.

6thly, From Phil. i. 21, 23. *For to me to live is Christ, and to die is gain——for I am in a strait betwixt two, having a desire to depart, and to be with Christ, which is far better!* From whence it appears,—— 1. That the apostle believed, that upon his departure out of this world, by death, he should be immediately with Christ, and enjoy communion with him; which would be a real gain unto him, and be preferable to his continuance in this life, there being nothing here that could be a counterbalance to it. Or otherwise,——2. If he had not believed this, his immediate admission into the presence of Christ, and enjoyment of eternal happiness, he could never have considered death as gain unto him; for he must have been a loser by it; since in his present state, notwithstanding all his fatigue and labour, his sorrows and his sufferings, yet he had communion with God, the presence of Christ, the teachings and leadings of the divine Spirit, much pleasure and success in his work, being the happy instrument of converting sinners, and comforting saints; all which he would be deprived of, if at death he entered into a state of insensibility and inactivity. Nor, ——3. Would he have been at a loss what choice to have made, whether to live or die; whether to depart out of the world, or to continue in it; he could have easily discerned, that it was his interest to abide in the flesh, or in the present state, in which he received much good for himself, and did much for others; whereas, if he was not to enter upon a state of happiness until the resurrection, but remain inactive and useless; it certainly was much more eligible to continue as he was. For,—— 4. Most certain it is, that it would have been better for the churches of Christ, for the interest of religion, and for the glory of God, if he had remained on earth to this day, and so on to the second coming of Christ, than to be sleeping in his grave, receiving no benefit to himself, nor being of any use to others.

7thly, From Rev. xiv. 13. *Blessed are the dead which die in the Lord, &c.*——1. By *the dead that die in the Lord,* are not meant merely, or only, the martyrs of Jesus, who die for the sake of Christ, and his gospel; but all the saints who die in union with Christ, in faith in him, as the only Saviour and Redeemer; in hope of eternal life by him; and in expectation of being for ever with him; and whose faith, hope, and expectation, will not fail, nor be disappointed.——2. Truly good men are blessed now; they are blessed who trust in the Lord, and make him their hope; they are happy who dwell in his house, enjoy his ordinances, and are employed in his service; who walk in his ways, and keep his commandments: but they are much more blessed at death; which would not be their case, if they did not immediately enter into the presence of Christ, and into the joy of the Lord. And,—— 3. This is the blessedness intended here; for it commences *from henceforth,* from the instant of their death; and which is confirmed by the testimony of the Spirit; *Yea, saith the Spirit;* he says, they are blessed from that time; which blessedness,—— 4. Lies in a *rest from their labours;* not merely in a rest from the labours of their bodies, much less in a cessation from the spiritual exercises of their souls; but in inward everlasting peace, joy, and comfort; and in *their works following them*, not only what they had done as witnesses of the truth of grace, but what they were to do, and be employed in, until the coming of Christ; which leads to consider the proof that may be given,

Secondly, That the souls of men, when separated from their bodies by death, are not in a state of insensibility and inactivity. There are some, who, though they do not deny the immortality of the soul, yet think it sleeps with the body until the resurrection; and this was the firm opinion of Socinus, as he himself says,[1] that the soul of man, after this life, does not so subsist of itself, as to be sensible either of rewards or punishments; or, indeed, as to be capable of perceiving those things; and the same is held by some Arminian writers.[2] But in opposition to this notion, and some that Calvin calls Catabaptists, and who go by the name of soul-sleepers with us,[3]

1*st*, I shall endeavour to prove, that the soul is operative, and in a state of action, when separate from the body; and that insensibility is not to be concluded from the absence of the body. For,

1. The soul can and does operate without the use of bodily organs in its present state, and in many things stands in no need of them; the rational soul thinks, discourses, and reasons without the use of them; its powers and faculties, the understanding and will, need them not; the will is directed and guided by the understanding; and the understanding has to do with objects in the consideration of which bodily organs are no ways assisting; as in the consideration of God, his nature and perfections; of angels and spirits, and their nature; and of a man's own spirit, and the things of it, which it penetrates into without the help of any of the instruments of the body: it can consider of things past long ago, and of things very remote and at a great distance; and such objects as are presented to it by the senses, it reasons about them without making use of any of the organs of the body; and if it can operate without the body, it can exist without it; for since it is independent of it in its operations, it is independent of it in its being; and as it can exist without it, it can act in that separate state of existence without it: wherefore since it dies not with the body, it is not affected as to its operations by the absence of it, nor at death becomes insensible as that is.———2. The case of persons in raptures, ecstacies and trances, when the body is senseless and inactive, and as if it was dead, and yet the soul is active and attentive, and capable of receiving things communicated to it, shews most clearly the soul can operate without the body; and if in this state, much more in a more perfect one. The apostle John was in the spirit, in an ecstacy, when he saw and heard the various things recorded in the Book of the revelation: the case of the apostle Paul is very remarkable, a particular account of which he gives, though not knowing whether in the body or out of it, 2 Cor. xii. 2—4. now though the apostle was not certain whether his soul was in his body or not, during his rapture; yet this appears most certain, that it was his sentiment that a soul out of the body is capable of seeing such things as he did; or otherwise it would have been no difficulty with him to have determined whether he was in or out of the body; for if he could not hear and see such things as he did out of the body, then he must without all doubt be in the body when he heard and saw them; but his way of speaking clearly shews that he thought his soul was capable of attending to these things, though it might be out of it; and if this is the same with the trance recorded in Acts xxii. 17—21. as some think, it appears that while he was in it, and his body lay senseless and inactive, his soul had a sight of Christ, and a conversation with him, and received a mission from him to the Gentiles. Now if the soul is not in a state of insensibility when the body sometimes now is, there is no reason to believe it is in such a state when the body is dead and separated from it; since the body in an ecstacy is of no more use to it, nor the organs of it, than if it was dead.———3. The soul, freed from the body, must be more capable of exercising its powers and faculties, and be more active than when in it;

---

[1] Socin. Epist. 5. ad Volkelium inter opera ejus, tom. 1. p. 454.
[2] Vid. Peltii. Harmon. Remonstrant. et Socin. art. 22. paragraph. 2. p. 258.

[3] Calvin, Assertio non dormire sed vivere, &c. fol. 51.

especially, as it is corrupted with sin, and incumbered with it, which is a clog and hinderance in the performance of spiritual duties; it cannot attend to it as it would; *the spirit is willing but the flesh is weak;* but when it is separated from the body, and is joined to the spirits of just men made perfect, it must be much more capable of serving God with greater activity, spirituality, joy, and pleasure.———4. The soul separate from the body is most like unto the angels, and its state, condition, and employment, greatly resemble theirs. Now nothing is more foreign to angels, than insensibility and inactivity, who always behold the face of God, stand ready to do his commandments, hearkening to the voice of his word; and no sooner do they receive orders from him, but they do his pleasure; they are continually before the throne of God, praising his name, and celebrating his perfections.———5. If the souls of believers after death are in a state of insensibility and inactivity, their case would be much worse than that of the living, as has been observed; since in the present state, amidst all their evil things, they enjoy much good, receive much from God, and have much spiritual peace and joy in the exercise of grace; whereas there is a stop put to all this, and an entire cessation from it, if upon death they enter into a state of insensibility and inactivity; particularly it would have been much more happy for the apostle Paul to have stayed on earth, and continued here till Christ came again; and more to the advantage of the churches of Christ, than to be where he is, if insensible and inactive; here he might have made use of his great talents, exercised his graces, had much communion with God, and been of great service in the interest of Christ, in which he would have found a real pleasure, but now deprived of all, if the above is his case.———6. If the souls of truly gracious persons are, upon their departure from hence, insensible and inactive, what is become of the work of grace upon their souls? in what condition is it, and must that be? there must be a full stop to it, and to the exercise of it, and that for a long season; where is growth in grace, where no grace is to be seen? and when it might have been expected it would be in its full perfection, does not appear at all?⁴ How does this *well of water spring up into everlasting life,* when it does not spring at all, but the streams of it cease to flow? what a chasm must there be between grace and glory, when the scriptures represent them as closely and inseparably connected together? grace is the beginning of glory, and glory is the finishing and perfection of grace, and in which there is no interruption.———7. The proof that has been given of souls separate from the body entering immediately into a state of happiness or misery, is also an abundant proof of their sensibility; when either they enter into the presence of God, are with Christ, and feel unutterable pleasure and delight; or are in inexpressible torments under the lighting down of the arm of God's wrath and indignation upon them. I proceed,

2dly, To take notice of what is urged in favour of the insensibility of souls upon their departure.

1. All such passages of scripture are urged, which speak of persons *sleeping* when they die; as of sleeping with their fathers, and of sleeping in the dust of the earth, phrases frequently to be met with in the Old Testament; and of Christ being the first-fruits of those that slept, and of sleeping in Jesus; and of some not sleeping, which are used in the New Testament, 2 Sam. vii. 12. 1 Kings i. 21. Job. vii. 22. Dan. xii. 2. 1 Cor. xv. 18, 51. 1 Thess. iv. 14. But,

(1.) By sleep in all these passages, death itself is meant. It was a way of speaking much used in the eastern countries, and is expressive of the death of the body, and of that only; so to *sleep with the fathers,* is to die as they did, and to be buried with them; and to *sleep in the dust,* is, being dead, to be laid in the grave, to be interred in the dust of the earth; and to *sleep in Jesus,* is to die in the Lord. When Christ said, *our friend Lazarus sleepeth,* he meant that he was dead; and when the apostle Paul says, *we shall not all sleep,* he designs nothing else but that we shall not all die; for those who are alive at Christ's coming will be changed; the reason why death is expressed by sleep is, because sleep is the image of death, it locks up the senses, gives rest to the weary body, is but for a time, and then it awakes again.———(2.) Death being designed by those expressions, if they prove anything in this controversy they prove too much; for if they prove that the

---

⁴ Isti non solum opus Dei ad tempus intermittunt, sed etiam extinguunt, Calvin. Assertio non dormire sed vivere, &c. fol. 18. 2.

soul sleeps with the body, they would prove that the soul dies with it, since by sleep is meant no other than death.——(3.) No mention is made of the soul in any of these passages; it is not said of that, neither that it sleeps nor dies; the passages only respect the body; it is that only which at death is gathered to the fathers, and buried in the graves of ancestors; and which sleeps in the dust, or is buried in the dust of the earth; the sleep of which stands opposed to the change that will pass on the bodies of living saints at the coming of Christ.——(4.) Sleep is only of the body,[5] and, according, to the philosopher, is a passion that belongs to the sensitive part, a kind of a band and immoveableness of it, so that it cannot operate; and says it only belongs to animals that have a brain, or something analogous to it;[6] it is defined "a cessation of the external senses from operation, the vapours filling the nerves and the sensory passages, and so hinder the influx of the animal spirits.[7] But what is all this to the soul, an immaterial and incorporeal substance, which has no brain, nor nerves, nor sensory passages, nor animal spirits? and therefore sleep has no place in it, and cannot be predicated of it.——(5.) When the body is asleep the soul is awake and active, as appears in abundance of instances, in dreams and visions of the night, when deep sleep falls upon men, and is capable of attending to what is suggested to it, and of receiving instruction; see Job iv. 12—17. and xxxiii. 15, 16. it understands and perceives, devises, and contrives, reasons and discourses, chooses and refuses, grieves and rejoices, hopes and fears, loves and hates, and the like; it can take in hints, admonitions, advice, and directions from God, or angels sent by him; as in some not good men, as Abimelech, Laban, Balaam, &c. and others truly good men, as Jacob, Daniel, Joseph, &c. whose souls, when their bodies were asleep, were capable of attending to them, and receiving them, and acted according to them.

2. The advocates for the insensibility and inactivity of the soul after death, urge such scriptures which represent the happiness of the saints, and the misery of the wicked, as not taking place until the last day, the end of the world, the resurrection of the dead, and the day of judgment, when the wicked shall go into everlasting punishment, and the righteous into life eternal, Luke xiv. 14. 1 Thess. iv. 16, 18. 2 Tim. iv. 8. Col. iii. 3, 4. Matt. xi. 22, 24. and xiii. 40, 41, 47, 50. and xxv. 46. Rev. xx. 12, 15. to which may be replied, that though they are represented as then happy or miserable, it is no where said that they are not happy nor miserable before that time; nor that they are insensible of any happiness or misery, but the contrary. Besides there is a twofold state of the righteous and the wicked after death, respecting their happiness and their misery; the one is inchoate or but begun at death; the other is full, consummate, and perfect, at the resurrection and judgment; now it is of the latter, these scriptures speak, and not of the former; and it is allowed, the righteous will not be in the full possession of happiness until the last day, when their bodies will be raised and united to their souls, and both together enter into the full joy of their Lord; nor will the wicked receive the full measure of their punishment until the resurrection and the judgment are over, when both soul and body shall be cast into hell; just as it is with the devils, they are not yet in full torment, though cast down to hell, and are reserved to the judgment of the great day; but then they are not in a state of insensibility, they feel distress and anguish now, and tremble at their future doom; so the wicked, they are not insensible of their misery now, and of what they are to endure: and both righteous and wicked, upon death, enter immediately into a state of happiness or misery; the righteous are happy from the time of their death, and as soon as absent from the body are present with the Lord; and the wicked are no sooner dead, but in hell they lift up their eyes; though neither the one is in complete happiness, nor the other in full misery, yet both sensible of their present case, and what they shall be in hereafter.

3. They improve all such places to their advantage, which speak of those in the grave, and in the state of the dead, as incapable of praising God, Psalm xxx. 9. and lxxxviii. 10, 11. and cxv. 17, 18. Isa. xxxviii. 18. to which it may be answered, (1.) Not to observe that Calvin [8] interprets

---

[5] Anaxagoras et Leucippus apud Plutarch. de Placitis Philosoph. 1. 5. c. 25.
[6] Aristot. de Somno, c. 1. et c. 7. et de part. animal. 1. 2. c. 7.
[7] Conimbricenses apud Burgersdicii Philosoph. Natural. disp. 22. s. 13. vide Suidam in voce ὑπνος.
[8] Assertio, &c. ut supra, fol. 44, &c.

the passages, of the damned in hell under the wrath of God, and a sense of it. These scriptures speak only of the body, which is dust originally, and returns to the dust at death, and is buried in the dust, and whilst in such a state cannot praise God; *Shall the dust praise thee?* it is the body which only dies, and goes down to the pit, and is laid in the grave, and which, whilst there, cannot be employed in praising God, *Shall the dead arise and praise thee?* &c. but then this hinders not but that their souls may and do praise God, in the manner as angels do, with whom they are sometimes joined in the book of Revelation; and are represented 'as with them, glorifying God, praising his name, singing hallelujahs, ascribing *salvation to him that sits upon the throne, and to the Lamb for ever and ever,* Rev. vii. 9—12.——(2.) These passages only respect praising God before men, and in the church militant, as is done by saints now in the land of the living; but then notwithstanding, the souls of departed saints may and do praise the Lord in the church triumphant, and with the hundred and forty four thousand on mount Zion, and before an innumerable company of angels and spirits of just men made perfect, to whom they are come; and therefore such passages are no proof of the insensibility and inactivity of separate souls.

4. They argue from souls being deprived of thought and memory at death, that therefore they must be in a state of insensibility. As for thought, that passage is urged in Psalm cxlvi. 4. *in that very day*, that is, in which man returns to his earth, or dies, *his thoughts perish;* but these, as has been observed, do not design thoughts in general, but purposes, schemes, and plans, the effect of thought, which come to nothing at death, and are never carried into execution; and though the thoughts, particularly of good men, are not employed about the same things as when on earth, about worldly things, yet they are employed about spiritual and heavenly ones; and can, with pleasure and gratitude, remember the great and good things God did for them in life; yea, even the memories of wicked men are rubbed up after death; *Son, remember that thou in thy lifetime receivedst thy good things, &c.* Luke xvi. 25. And *that worm that dies not,* is no other than consciousness of guilt contracted, and the memory of past sins committed in life, which torture the separate soul after death, Mark ix. 44. Should it be urged, that a person, when asleep, is destitute of thought, especially when in a deep sleep; who, upon awaking, cannot remember any thing he has thought of: this doth not carry in it sufficient conviction, that the mind is then destitute of thought; for how often is it that a man, when awake, cannot remember what he thought of the last minute? it is owned, that in dreams the soul thinks, but then the man is asleep, and shews that sleep and thought are not incompatible: besides, when deep sleep falls upon man, the soul is capable of attending to what is suggested to it, and receiving instruction thereby; as some passages in Job, before mentioned, shew. And after all, it should be proved, that the soul is asleep when the body is; and particularly, when separate from it, ere any argument from hence can be brought to prove the soul is deprived of thought by it; and is in a state of insensibility.

5. It is observed, that it is said of the *dead*, that they *know not any thing,* Eccles. ix. 5. But this is to be understood of the things of this world; they do not know the affairs of it, what is done or doing in it, no, not the condition and circumstances of their own families they have left behind; they do not know whether their sons come to honour or to disgrace; whether they are in prosperous or in adverse circumstances, Job. xiv. 21. But then they know the things of the other world, in which they are; they know God, and Christ, and the holy angels, and the spirits of just men made perfect, and the happiness of these and of themselves; they know even as they are known: yea, wicked men know and feel the lashes of an accusing, torturing conscience, the pains of hell, and the wrath of God, the fire that is not quenched; and so are not in a state of insensibility. I go on,

Thirdly, to point out the work and employment of separate souls, especially of good men, after the death of the body, until the resurrection of it: and here I shall not give a scope to fancy and conjecture, which may lead persons to say many things doubtful and uncertain; and since the scriptures are sparing in the account they give of this matter, I shall content myself with just observing some few things which may be gathered from thence; and which may suggest unto us the work they are employed in; for it cannot be thought that they are idle and unemployed in the happy state in which they are. And,

1st, It need not be doubted, but that

they are employed in celebrating and adoring the perfections of God; since this is the work of their kindred spirits, the angels, with whom they are now associated; they are constantly employed, in ascribing glory to God, Rev. vii. 11, 12. see also v. 11, 12. so holy souls adore the perfections of God's holiness, to which they bear some resemblance, and are thankful at the remembrance of it; and the almighty power of God, of which they have had experience in this life, and in bringing them to the happy state they are now in; and the wisdom of God displayed in the works of nature, providence, and grace, of which they have now a clearer understanding; and the grace, mercy, and love of God, which appear in every branch of their salvation; and the faithfulness of God to his counsels, covenant, and promises; to dwell on these subjects will be no inconsiderable part of their employment.

2*dly*, They are also employed in beholding God in Christ, and the glory of Christ; being pure in heart, and perfect in holiness, they see God with the eyes of their understanding; behold him for themselves, and not another, as their covenant God and Father in Christ; and his glory as displayed in the Person of Christ; and have as much knowledge of him as creatures are capable of; and solace and delight themselves in the views of him, and in communion with him: and though they see not Christ with the eyes of their bodies, as they will after the resurrection; yet with the eyes of their minds they gaze upon and wonder at those glories and excellencies they see in him; and this is the end of Christ's intercession for them, that they be with him where he is, and behold his glory, John xvii. 24.

3*dly*, They are likewise employed in the exercise of various graces: it is commonly said of faith, hope, and love, that they are travelling graces, which accompany saints in this life; but cease, as to their exercise, at death, especially the two former; the latter is indeed allowed to continue after death: but faith is usually said to be changed for sight, and hope for fruition; which, in some respects, and in part, is true; yet I see not why faith and hope may not be thought to have their use, and to be in exercise after death, and especially in the separate state, until the resurrection: it can scarcely be doubted, that separate souls firmly *believe* the resurrection of their bodies, that they will be raised again, and re-united to their souls; and as that will add to their happiness, it cannot but be desired by them; and as it is what is at present unseen, unenjoyed, and is future, it must be the object of *hope*, about which that grace must be conversant, until it is brought to pass; and thus as Christ *rested in hope* of the resurrection of his body, Psalm xvi. 9. so the souls of saints in heaven rest in hope of the resurrection of theirs; and may be truly said to *wait for the redemption of the body*. Some think Job has respect to this, when he says, *All the days of my appointed time will I wait till my change come;* meaning, not his change by death, though that is a truth, but his change at the resurrection, when Christ will change the vile bodies of his people, and fashion them like to his glorious one. Yea, *patience*, rest, and quietness, are to be, and are exercised by souls in their separate state: to the souls under the altar it is said, *that they should rest yet for a little season, until their fellow-servants also, and their brethren that should be killed, as they were, should be fulfilled;* that is, be easy, quiet, and patient, till that time comes, and this is done, Rev. vi. 11. And as for *love*, there is no doubt but it will be in its highest act and exercise.

4*thly*, They are also employed in serving God; so those that come out of great tribulation are said to be *before the throne of God, and to serve him day and night in his temple*, Rev. vii. 14, 15. not by preaching, and hearing, and attending on the word and ordinances; yet there are duties which are performed in this state; if not prayer, yet most certainly praise, in the highest perfection: I see not why prayer may not be allowed to the church triumphant and its members, though not for themselves, yet for the church militant and its members, that they may be delivered from their present evils; and that the justice of God might be glorified in taking vengeance on their enemies; and that they may shortly join the general assembly; something like this is ascribed to the souls under the altar, who are represented as expostulating with God after this manner, *And they cried with a loud voice, saying, How long, O Lord, holy and true, dost thou not judge and avenge our blood on them that dwell on the earth?* Rev. vi. 10. and, indeed, what is the earnest wish and desire of separate souls, after the resurrection of their bodies and their reunion to them, but prayer, that so it might be? however, praise is their grand employment, their principal business, in which they are continually engaged; these ransomed ones come to Zion with songs, and there they sing them; the songs of electing, redeeming, calling, and persevering grace, ascribing glory to the Father, that has chosen them in Christ; and to the Son, who has redeemed them to God by his blood; and to the Spirit, who has regenerated, sanctified, and called them; and to all Three, for the preservation of them to the kingdom and glory of God.

5*thly*, Much of the employment of souls in this separate state, lies in converse with angels and the spirits of just men made perfect. Angels have some way or other of conversing with each other; we read of the *tongue of angels*; not that they speak any particular language, and with an articulate voice; but they have speech among themselves, which they understand; they can communicate their thoughts to one another, and be happy in their mutual converse; see Dan. viii. 13. and xii. 5, 6, 7. and angels can convey their sense to the spirits of men; and the spirits of men can communicate theirs to them; such an intercourse between angels and the souls of men has been carried on in dreams and visions, even in this imperfect state; and much more are they capable of conversing together in a more perfect one. The souls of men in the separate state, are distinguishable from one another; and there are ways and means, no doubt, of knowing one from another; thus the soul of Abraham may be known from the soul of Isaac; and the soul of Isaac from the soul of Abraham; and the soul of Jacob from both: and as the saints will know one another in heaven,[9] one part of their happiness will lie in conversing together about divine and heavenly things; and, indeed, about what they have had experience of, both in providence and grace, whilst they dwelt in their bodies on earth.

CHAP. IV.

OF THE RESURRECTION OF THE BODY.

Though the immortality of the soul may be known by the light of nature, yet not the resurrection of the body; the one arises from the nature of the soul itself; but the other does not arise from the constitution of the body, but depends upon the sovereign will and power of God: now the will and purpose of God, or what he has determined to do, is secret, and cannot be discovered by the light of nature, and is only known by divine revelation. It might be known by the light of nature, that God can raise the dead if he will, because he is Almighty, and nothing is impossible to him; though it has been asserted by some heathen writers, that it cannot be done by God himself: one says,[1] it is not in the power of God to raise the dead; and says another,[2] it seems to me, that no one can make one that is dead to live again: which is false; since by the light of nature, and the works of nature, are known the eternal power and Godhead, or that God is eternal and infinitely powerful. Indeed, it cannot be known by the light of nature, that God will raise the dead; this is of pure revelation: hence heathens, destitute of it, had no knowledge of the resurrection of the body: that that was mortal they all agreed; and that the soul was immortal, the wiser part of them especially, affirmed; but that the body, when dead, should be raised to life again, this, Tertullian says,[3] was denied by every sect of the philosophers. Those, the most refined among them, and who pretended to a greater degree of knowledge than others, as the philosophers of Athens, were so ignorant of this doctrine, that, as some think,[4] they took Jesus, and Ἀναςασις, the word used by the apostle Paul for the resurrection, when preaching to them, to be the names of some strange deities they had never heard of before; and therefore said, *He seemeth to be a setter forth of strange gods*, Acts xvii. 18. The heathens had no faith in this doctrine, nor hope of it; and therefore are sometimes described as without *hope*, Eph. ii. 12. 1 Thess. iv. 13, 14. that is of the resurrection of the body, neither of their own nor of their deceased relations;[5] and this may be rather thought to be, at least part of the sense of the apostle in these passages; since in his defence before Felix and Agrippa, he represents the resurrection of the dead as the object of the hope of the Jewish fathers, Acts xxiv. 15. and xxvi. 6, 7, 8. Yea, the Gentiles, not content

---

[9] See a Sermon of mine, called, "The glorious State of the Saints in Heaven," p. 34, 35.
[1] Plin Nat. Hist. l. 2. c. 7.
[2] Palæphat. de Incredib. p. 56.

[3] De Præscript. Hæret. c. 2.
[4] Chrysostom. et Oecumen. in Act. 17.
[5] αγιλπιςοι, τι θανοντις. Theocrit. Idyll. 4.

with barely denying this doctrine, have treated it with the utmost scorn, calling it a dream, fancy, and madness,[6] an old wives' fable;[7] as abominable and detestable;[8] and of all the tenets of the Christians, it was held in the utmost contempt by Julian the apostate;[9] the abettors of it were always accounted by the heathens vain, trifling, babbling fellows,[10] as the apostle Paul was by the Athenian philosophers of the Epicurean and Stoic sects,[11] Acts xvii 18, 32. it was so contrary to the reasonings of the unenlightened Gentiles, that they judged it quite incredible, and pronounced it beyond all belief of rational creatures; hence, says the apostle Paul, when before Festus the Roman governor, and king Agrippa, a Sadducee, why should it be thought a thing *incredible with you that God should raise the dead?* as it seems it was,[12] Acts xxvi. 8.

Some have thought the Gentiles had knowledge of the resurrection of the dead, which they conclude from some notions of theirs, which seem to bear some semblance to it, as is thought; as that the soul after death has a perfect human shape, and all the same parts, external and internal, the body has; that they both have an equal duration after death; that there is a transmigration of souls into other bodies, especially human; that man may be translated, soul and body, to heaven, of which they give instances; which, perhaps, take rise from the translations of Enoch and Elijah, communicated by some tradition or another; and particularly, that after certain periods and revolutions, when the stars and planets are in the same configuration and aspect to one another they formerly had, the same men shall appear in the world, and the same things in succession be done in it as formerly have been.[13] But I must confess, I cannot see any likeness between any of these notions, and the Christian doctrine of the resurrection of the dead; and at most and best, they are only hints borrowed from the Jews and their writings; or are the broken remains of some tradition, received from their ancestors, originally founded on divine revelation; so Plato[14] seems to speak of it, as an ancient tradition, that the dead shall live again. Likewise the belief of this doctrine among the pagans is argued from their account of future punishments; as of Aridæus, and other tyrants, having corporal punishments inflicted on them; of Sisyphus, Ixion, Tantalus, and others; which may arise from the above notion of the soul having the same parts with the body. Some passages are also produced out of the heathen writers, in favour of this doctrine; as some Greek verses of Phocylides, whose poem, perhaps, is the work of a Christian, or of some Jewish writer; and the opinion of the Persian *magi*, that men shall live again; which they doubtless had from Zoroastres, their founder, said to be originally a Jew, and a servant of one of the prophets. Some particular persons are mentioned as raised from the dead to life; the most remarkable of which is the case of one Er Pamphilius, who after he had been dead twelve days, revived on the funeral pile; and which seems to be credited by Plato:[15] but if such stories as these can be believed, why should the doctrine of the resurrection be judged incredible?[16]

But though the doctrine of the resurrection is above reason, it is not contrary to it; though it is out of the reach of the light of nature to discover it, yet being revealed, it is not repugnant to it; it is entirely agreeable to the perfections of God, knowable by it, and is no contradiction to them; for considering the omnipotence of God, with whom nothing is impossible, it is what may be: and though there are some things which argue imperfection and weakness, and imply a contradiction, which God cannot do; yet the resurrection of the dead is not an instance of either; it is no contradiction, that dust formed out of nothing, and of it a body made, and this reduced to dust again, that this dust should again form the body it once constituted: and this can be no instance of imperfection and weakness; but a most glorious instance of almighty power: and if God could, out of

---

[6] Plin. Nat. Hist. l. 7. c. 55.
[7] Cæcil. in Minut. Fel. Octav. p. 10.
[8] Celsus in Origen. contr. ibid. p. 240.
[9] Cyril. Alex. contr. Julian. l. 7.
[10] Tatian. contr. Græcos Orat. p. 146.
[11] Antoninus the emperor, of this sect, says, "When men are dead they exist no more, but are entirely extinct," De Seipso, l. 12. c. 5.
[12] The Indians of North America used to say when this doctrine was mentioned, "I shall never believe it," Mather's History of New England, b. 3. p. 192. though the inhabitants of Virginia and Louisiana are said to believe it; but perhaps this is a mistake. See Hody's Resurrection, p. 45, 46, 49.
[13] Of these notions of the heathens, see Hody's Resurrection of the same body, p. 3, &c. and Gale's Court of the Gentiles, par. 1. b. 3. c. 7. p. 81, 82. and par. 2. b. 2. c. 8. p. 189.
[14] In Phædone, p. 53—55 et in Philebo, p. 536.
[15] De Republ. l. 10. p. 761.
[16] See more of these things in Serms. on the Resurrec. s. 1. p. 5, 6, &c.

the dust of the earth, form the body of a man at first, and infuse into it a living and reasonable soul; then much more must he be able to raise a dead body, the matter and substance of which now is, though in different forms and shapes; and reunite it to its soul, which still has a real existence: and considering the omniscience of God, who knows all things, it is not impossible nor improbable that the dead should be raised; since he knows all the particles of matter, bodies are composed of; and when dissolved and transmuted into ten thousand forms, knows where they are all lodged, whether in the earth, air, or sea; and his all-discerning eye can distinguish those which belong to one body from those of another, and his almighty hand can gather and unite them, what are necessary, and range them in their due place and order. Nor is it beneath or unworthy of God to raise the dead; for if it is not unworthy of him to make a body out of the dust of the earth, which became subject to infirmities, corruption, and death; it cannot be unworthy of him to raise weak, inglorious, corruptible bodies, as they are when laid in the grave, powerful, glorious, and incorruptible. Nor is it inconsistent with the goodness of God; for by this he does no injury to any of his creatures; neither to those that are raised, nor to others, rational or irrational. Not to the angels; for the children of the resurrection will be like unto them: nor to the brute creation, who will not be; and who, if they were, would not suffer by it: nor will any injury be done to those that are raised, neither to the righteous nor to the wicked, since both will then receive a recompense for the deeds done in the body, whether good or evil. Some such like reasonings as these are used by that ancient and learned apologist, Athenagoras.[17] Besides, the justice of God seems to make it necessary that the bodies both of the righteous and the wicked should be raised; that being united to their souls, they may partake with them of the glory and happiness provided for the one, and they are made meet for; and of the punishment justly inflicted on the other; having been partners together either in sufferings or in sins.

However, the doctrine of the resurrection is most certainly a doctrine of pure revelation; the Jews were first peculiarly favoured with it; having *the oracles of God committed* to them, in which this doctrine is clearly revealed; and yet there were some among them who disbelieved it; as the Sadducees, who *erred, not knowing the scriptures*, which assert it; *nor the power of God*, which can effect it: and of the same sentiment were the Hemerobaptists:[18] and the Essenes:[19] also the Pharisees, at least some of them, held the Pythagorean notion of the transmigration of souls into other bodies:[20] but it is more surprising, that since Christ has abolished death, by his own resurrection from the dead, and by the gospel brought to clearer light this doctrine of the resurrection; that some very early, who bore the Christian name, should deny it; as some in the church at Corinth, and Hymenæus and Philetus, 1 Cor. xv. 12. 2 Tim. ii. 18. who were followed by Simon Magus, Saturninus, Basilides, Carpocrates, Valentinus, and others, too numerous to recite: and of late is rejected by Socinians and Quakers. Nevertheless, since it is a doctrine of such great importance, on which all other doctrines of the gospel depend, as well as the faith, hope, and comfort of the saints, 1 Cor. xv. 13—19. it should be held fast, abode by, and defended to the uttermost. The resurrection to be treated of, is not a figurative one; neither civil, like that of the Jews' restoration from captivity, represented by a resurrection, Ezek. xxxvii. nor spiritual, as the resurrection of the soul from the death of sin to a life of grace: but the resurrection of the body, in a literal sense, the quickening of mortal bodies; and not a particular resurrection, or a resurrection of particular persons; of which there are instances both in the Old and New Testament; but the universal resurrection; the resurrection of men, both just and unjust; of which,

I. I shall give proof from the sacred writings. It appears to have been the faith of the saints in all ages, according to the scripture account of them. It was the faith of Abraham, the father of the faithful, Heb. xi. 19. Rom. iv. 17—20. and of Joseph, as appears by the orders he gave concerning his bones, and his carefulness about the interment of them, Heb. xi. 22. and of Moses, in celebrating the divine perfections, in his song, Deut. xxxii. 39. with which words the mother of the seven

---

[17] De Resurrectione, p. 49. 5. See serm. 1 on the Resurrection, p. 11, 12, &c. where these things are more enlarged on.

[18] Epist. contr. Hæres. l. 1. hæres. 17.
[19] Joseph. de Bello Jud. l. 2. c. 8. s. 11.
[20] Ibid. s. 14. et Antiq. l. 18. c. 1. s. 3.

CHAP. IV.   OF THE RESURRECTION OF THE BODY.

brethren, who suffered martyrdom in the times of the Maccabees, animated them while suffering;[21] and of Hannah, in her song, expressed in much the same language, and more explicit, 1 Sam. ii. 6. This was the faith of Job, which he expresses, not only in the famous text hereafter to be considered, chap. xix. 25—27. but also in chap. xiv. 12, 14, 15. And likewise of David, who not only speaks of the resurrection of Christ, when personating him, Psalm xvi. 10. but in his last words, where he expresses his strong faith of his complete salvation, of soul and body, in the everlasting covenant, 2 Sam. xxv. 1. 5. And also of Isaiah, and other prophets, who speak of the resurrection of Christ, and his people with him; which they either expressly make mention of, or allude unto, when they foretel figurative resurrections, Isa. xxvi. 19. Hos. vi. 1, 2. Ezek. xxxvii. 11—14. Dan. xii. 2. This was the faith of those who suffered martyrdom in the times of the Maccabees, who refused deliverance that they might obtain *a better resurrection*, even the resurrection of the just, Heb. xi. 35. see 2 Maccab. vi. 26. and vii. 11. And this was the faith of the Jewish fathers and of all the old testament saints, Acts xxvi. 6, 7, 8. Heb. xi. 13. This was the faith of Christ and his apostles, as declared in the writings of the New Testament; to give the whole compass of the proof of this would be to transcribe a very considerable part of them. The doctrine of the resurrection of the dead will admit of proof from scripture types, as the deliverance of Isaac from death; from whence Abraham received him in a figure: the budding and blossoming of Aaron's dry rod, thought by some to be an emblem of it: the reviving of the dry bones in Ezekiel's vision; but especially Jonah's lying three days and three nights in the whale's belly, and his deliverance from it. However, if God could save Isaac when so near death; cause a dry rod to bud, blossom, and bring forth almonds; make dry bones to live; and deliver Jonah out of the whale's belly, it need not be questioned that God can raise the dead. To which may be added, the several instances of particular persons raised from the dead; as the widow of Sarepta's son, by Elijah; the child of the Shunamite, by Elisha; and the man cast into his sepulchre on the touch of his bones; those who came out of their graves at our Lord's resurrection, and who were raised by him in his life-time; as the daughter of Jairus, the widow of Nain's son, and Lazarus; Dorcas by Peter; and Eutychus by the apostle Paul: and if these particular resurrections are to be credited, as doubtless they are, then the resurrection of all the dead need not be thought incredible. But this doctrine may be further proved,

First, From express passages of scripture. As,——1. From Gen. iii. 15. which gives the first intimation of the Messiah and his work, which was to bruise the serpent's head, to destroy the devil and all his works; among which, death, the effect of sin, is a principal one. This, Christ has abolished in himself by raising himself from the dead; and will abolish it in his members, and even in all men, by the resurrection of them at the last day; when, and not before, all that is meant in the above passage will be accomplished, 1 Cor. xv. 21, 54.——2. From Exod. iii. 6. produced by Christ himself in proof of this doctrine; *As touching the resurrection of the dead,* says he, *have you not read that which was spoken to you by God; saying, I am the God of Abraham, the God of Isaac, and the God of Jacob; God is not the God of the dead but of the living?* Matt. xxii. 31, 32. Let it be observed, that it is not said, *I was,* or *will be;* but, *I am the God of Abraham,* &c. which, as it relates to covenant interest, respects a covenant in being, and an abiding one, even the covenant of grace; which is concerned, not only with the souls of men, but their bodies also, their whole persons; wherefore as the souls of the above patriarchs now live with God, who is the God of the living only, in the enjoyment of the promised good; it is necessary their bodies should be raised from the dead, that, with their souls, they may enjoy the everlasting glory and happiness promised in the covenant; or otherwise, it would not appear to be ordered in all things and sure.——3. From Job xix. 25, &c. *I know that my Redeemer liveth,* &c. None of the Jewish writers,[22] indeed, understood these words of a real, but of a figurative resurrection; and suppose, a deliverance from his afflicted state, and a restoration of him to his former health, honour, and happiness, is meant; in which sense they have been followed by some

---

[21] Joseph. de Maccabæis, s. 10.

[22] Vid. Menasseh Ben Israel de Resurrect. l. 1. c. 3. s. 6.

learned Christian interpreters;[23] at which the Socinians[24] have greedily catched: but Job's restoration is not expressed by such phrases as are here used; see chap. xlii. 10, 12. and against this sense may be observed, that Job was so far from any faith, hope, and expectation of such a restoration, that he utterly despaired of it; see chap. vi. 11. and vii. 7, 8. and x. 20. and xvi. 22. and xvii. 1, 14, 15. and even he expresses the same in this very chapter, ver. 10, 11. Besides, something of greater moment seems to be meant, as the solemn preface shews; *O that my words were now written!* &c. and what he had in view appears to be future, at a great distance, after death, the consumption of his body by worms, and was his comfort under his afflictions; and was an answer to what Bildad said, chap. xviii. 12, 13, 14. and the vision, with the eyes of his body he expected, is not suited to any state in this life; but rather to the state after the resurrection, when the saints shall see God in Christ, and Christ in the flesh, with the eyes of the body. To which may be added, Job speaks of the awful judgment, between which and death there must be a resurrection from the dead, ver. 29. Upon the whole, it is an observation of an ancient writer,[25] "No one since Christ speaks so plainly of the resurrection as this man did before Christ." Though Spinosa,[26] foolishly says, the sense of the text is confused, disturbed, and obscure.——4. From Isa. xxvi. 19. *Thy dead men shall live,* &c. which words are an answer to the prophet's complaint, ver. 14. *They are dead, they shall not live,* &c. and which answer is made by the Messiah, to whom the characters given, ver. 4, 12, 13. agree; assuring the prophet, that his people, though dead, should live again, either at the time of his resurrection, or in virtue of it; for the words are literally true of Christ's resurrection and of theirs by him; *With my dead body shall they arise,* as many of the saints did, at his resurrection; or, *as my dead body,* after the exemplar of it; or, *as sure as my dead body;* Christ's resurrection being the pledge of his people's; and the following phrases confirm this sense; *Awake, ye that dwell in the dust,* &c. see Dan. xii. 2. *Thy dew is the dew of herbs,* compared with Isa. lxvi. 14. *The earth shall cast forth her dead;* see Rev. xx. 13. The Jews[27] refer this prophecy to the resurrection of the dead.——5. From Dan. xii. 2. *And many of them that sleep in the dust of the earth shall awake;* which is generally understood of the resurrection of the dead, both by Jewish and Christian interpreters; only Grotius, after Porphyry the heathen, interprets the passage of the return of some of the Jews to their cities and habitations, after the generals of Antiochus were cut off: but surely this return was not of any of them *to everlasting shame and contempt,* but the reverse; nor of any of them *to everlasting life,* seeing they are all since dead: nor is it true that the Jewish doctors, from that time, shone illustriously; but, on the contrary, their light in divine things became dim, and they taught not the doctrines of the scriptures but the traditions of men. On the other hand, the whole agrees with the resurrection of the dead, as described by our Lord, John v. 28, 29. And when the bodies of the saints will be raised in incorruption, power, and glory, they will shine like the sun in the kingdom of their Father. Besides these, there are other passages of scripture referred to by the apostle, in 1 Cor. xv. 54, 55. as proofs of this doctrine; as Isa. xxv. 8. Hos. xiii. 14. which will have their full accomplishment at the general resurrection. The passages out of the New Testament are too numerous to recite, and so plain as to need no explanation; and many of them will be made use of in other parts of this subject.

Secondly, This truth may be proved from various doctrines contained in the scripture; as from the doctrine of election, which is of the persons of men, souls and bodies, unto everlasting happiness; and therefore their bodies must be raised, that they, united to their souls, may enjoy that happiness, or the end will not be attained: from the gift of the same to Christ, and who was charged, when given to him, to lose none, but raise them up again at the last day; which must be done, or his trust not discharged, nor his father's will be fulfilled: from their union to Christ; whose *bodies are members of him,* and a part of his mystical body, by virtue of which union they will be raised; or else he must lose a constituent part of those who are his mystical body and his fulness; from the

---

[23] Calvin. Mercer, &c.
[24] Enjedinus, p. 51. Volkel. de Relig. ver. 1. 3. c. 11. p. 59, 60.
[25] Hieron. ad Pammach. tom. 2. p. 59. 1.
[26] Philosoph. S. S. Script c. 8. p. 102.
[27] Aben Ezra et Kimchi in loc. T. Bab. Sanhedrin, fol. 90. 2.

redemption of them by Christ, which is both of soul and body; both are bought with the price of Christ's blood, and therefore their bodies must be raised from the dead, or Christ must lose part of his purchase: also from the sanctification of the same persons, in soul and body, by the Spirit of God, in whose bodies he dwells, as in his temple; and therefore, unless raised, he will lose that which he has taken possession of as his dwelling-place, and a considerable part of his glory as a sanctifier. Moreover, the general judgment, which is a most certain thing, requires the resurrection of the dead, as necessary to it: nor will the happiness of the saints be complete, nor the misery of the wicked proportionate to their crimes, without the resurrection of their bodies; but the grand and principal argument used by the apostle, 1 Cor. xv. in proof of this doctrine, with so much strength, is the resurrection of Christ. To which may be added, that there will be need of and uses for some of the members of the body in heaven; as the eye, to see Christ in the flesh, and one another; the ear, to hear the everlasting songs of praise; and the tongue, to sing them: as well as we read of men being cast into hell with two eyes, two hands, and two feet; yea, even the whole body. Nor may it be improper to observe, the translations of Enoch and Elijah, soul and body to heaven; and the saints that rose at our Lord's resurrection, and went to heaven in their risen bodies; and the saints who will be alive at Christ's coming, and be caught up into the air to meet him, and be for ever with him. Now it is not probable that some saints should be in heaven with their bodies and others without them; and therefore a general resurrection must be asserted and allowed.[28] I proceed,

II. To consider the subjects of the resurrection, who they are, and what that is of them that shall be raised.

First, Who they are that shall be raised; not the angels, who die not, and therefore cannot be the subjects of the resurrection; nor the brute creatures, as say the Mahometans [29] and some Jewish doctors; [30] since they have no immortal spirits for their bodies to be raised and united to; nor would they be of any use, nor is there any service for them in a future state. Only men shall rise from the dead, and not all of them; some have been translated, that they should not see death, and so cannot be said to rise from the dead; and others will be alive at Christ's coming, and will be changed, but not die; which change cannot be called a resurrection. But all the dead, all that are in their graves, whether in the earth or sea, shall rise and come forth, and those whether righteous or wicked; the resurrection of both is strongly asserted by Christ, John v. 28, 29. and by the apostle Paul, Acts xxiv. 15. The distribution of the persons to be raised are of these two sorts, the just and the unjust; that the just, or righteous ones, will be raised from the dead there can be no doubt; since the resurrection of the saints is called *the resurrection of the just* from them, Luke xiv. 14. it being peculiar to them; and *the first resurrection*, Rev. xx. 6. because they will rise first; and *the better resurrection*, Heb. xi. 35. being better than that of the wicked; and of which only some are counted worthy, Luke xx. 35. and is what the apostle Paul desired to attain unto, Phil. iii. 11. called ἐξανάστασις, *a resurrection out from* the dead, the wicked dead. The arguments before used to prove the resurrection in general, being such as chiefly regard the resurrection of the just, the proof of this need not be further enlarged on. But the resurrection of the wicked, being denied by some of the Jewish writers, in which they have been followed by the Socinians, though they care not to speak out their minds fully; and to which the Remonstrants and Arminians have shown a good liking; it will be necessary to confirm this. The arguments of the one and the other against the resurrection of the wicked are taken,

1. From reason: they reason from the mercy of God, that if he will not eternally save them, yet surely it cannot be thought that he will raise them from the dead merely to torment them; it will be enough to be deprived of happiness in heaven. The answer to which is, that though God is naturally and essentially merciful, yet the displays of his mercy to his creatures are according to his sovereign will and pleasure, Rom. ix. 15. Isa. xxvii. 11. Besides, he

---

[28] Of the proof from scripture passages and doctrines more largely, see my Sermons on the Resurrection, serm. 1. p. 17—30.
[29] Pocock, Specim. Hist. Arab. p. 145. et Not.
Miscel. in Port. Mosis. c. 7. p. 269. Reland. de Relig. Moham. I. 1. p. 53, 54.
[30] Drus. Observ. 1. 4. c 6.

is just as well as merciful; and it is necessary from the justice of God, as will be observed hereafter, that the bodies of the wicked be raised, not merely to be tormented, but that his justice might be glorified in the righteous punishment of them. They further argue, that Christ is the meritorious cause of the resurrection; and since he has merited nothing for the wicked or reprobate, they shall not be raised. The answer to which is, that Christ is the meritorious cause of the resurrection of life, but not of the resurrection of damnation; the saints will rise to life by virtue of union to Christ, through his merit, and the power of his resurrection: not so the wicked; they will rise, not through his merit, and by virtue of union to him, but by his almighty power. They also urge, at least some, that the wicked die an eternal death, and therefore rise not from the dead; which they think is a contradiction: but it should be observed, that eternal death, which is the second death, in distinction from the death of the body, and is a casting of both body and soul into hell, is not inconsistent with the resurrection of the body; yea, it requires that: and though corporal death is one part of the punishment of sin, which punishment is perpetual; nor is it removed by the resurrection of the wicked, since their bodies will be raised in such a state as to bear eternal punishment.[31]

2. There are other arguments and objections against the resurrection of the wicked, taken from various passages of scripture, as from Psalm i. 5. *Therefore the ungodly shall not stand in judgment;* which words are rendered in the Septuagint and Vulgate Latin versions, *Shall not rise again in judgment;* but admitting these versions were agreeable to the Hebrew text, as they are not; it will not follow that the wicked shall not rise again from the dead, but shall not rise, again so as to appear in the congregation of the righteous at the day of judgment, as in the next clause; for they will not rise when the righteous do, at the first resurrection, the resurrection of the just; besides, the word used does not intend the resurrection of the wicked, but their standing before God in a judicial sense, when raised; and the meaning is, they shall not stand before him with confidence, nor be able to justify themselves and vindicate their cause, and so must fall and not stand in judgment. Another scripture made use of is in Isa. xxvi. 14. *They are deceased, they shall not rise:* which must be understood either of those wicked lords who had formerly dominion over the people of Israel, but now dead, and should not rise again and live on this earth to tyrannize over them; or of the people of Israel themselves, and of the death of great numbers of them; and express the prophet's complaint of their present state, and of his distrust of their revival and restoration from it: and it may be also of their future resurrection, to which there is an answer ver. 19. as has been observed; and considered either way, cannot support an argument against the resurrection of the wicked. The words of the prophet Daniel, chap. xii. 2. before observed, though a plain proof of the resurrection of the dead, both righteous and wicked, yet are improved by some against the resurrection of the wicked; since not *all* but *many* are said to awake, and those many are only a few, and those only the righteous Israelites: to which may be replied, the *many* may be understood universally, as in Rom. v. 19. and in other places;[32] or in a comparative sense with respect to the few that shall be alive when the dead are raised; or rather distributively, many shall awake to everlasting life, and many to everlasting shame and contempt; and besides may respect the different times of rising, many at the first resurrection to the former, and the rest a thousand years after to the latter. Many can never design a few; as the Israelites were the fewest of all people, especially the righteous among them; and even the righteous of all nations are but few in comparison of the rest; besides the prophet speaks of some awaking to everlasting shame and contempt, which can only be understood of the wicked; so that the prophecy is a clear proof of their resurrection. Others object that passage in Eccles. vii. 1. *Better is the day of death, than the day of one's birth;* since if the wicked rise again, it must be worse with them at death than at their birth; but the words are not spoken of the wicked or reprobate, who, it would have been better if they had never been born, or had died upon their birth, than to have lived to aggravate their condemnation by a continuance in sin, and with whom it will be worse at death; but of the righteous, who

---

[31] See Sermon 2. on the Resurrection, p. 40, &c.
[32] Vid. Aug. de Civ. Dei, l. 20. c. 23. who instances in Gen. xvii. 5. compared with Gen. xxii. 18.

die in the Lord, and are blessed in their death, being freed from sin and sorrow, and are with Christ; which is far better than coming into, and continuing in a troublesome world. Even the words of the apostle, in 1 Thess. iv. 16. *The dead in Christ shall rise first*, are urged by some against the resurrection of the wicked; since such that die in Christ are only believers in him, and therefore they, and not the wicked, shall rise: the answer is, that though the apostle is speaking only of those that die in Christ, true believers in him; yet not here, nor any where else, is it said, that these only rise. Besides, the apostle says of these, that they shall rise first; which supposes, that others shall rise afterwards, who have no claim to this character; a first resurrection of believers in Christ, supposes a second resurrection of those who are not such.[33] But that the wicked shall rise, is not only to be proved from express passages of scripture, before observed, Dan. xii. 2. John v. 28, 29. Acts xxiv. 15. but also from reason; as from the justice of God, which requires, that sins committed in and by the body, as most sins are, should be punished in the body; that being not only an accessary, but a partner with the soul in sinning, and an instrument by which sin is committed, and so deserving of punishment: and whereas the wicked do not receive in this life the full reward of punishment in their bodies; it seems necessary from the justice of God, that their bodies should be raised, that with their souls they may receive their full recompense of reward. Besides, it may be concluded from the general judgment; when some will be *cast into the lake of fire*, Rev. xx. 12, 15. which must be understood of the wicked; and if all must *appear before the judgment seat of Christ*, to receive for what has been done in the body, then the wicked must appear there, that they may receive for the bad things they have done in the body; to which appearance and reception, there must be a resurrection of them from the dead. The scriptural account of the punishments and torments of the wicked, manifestly supposes a resurrection of their bodies, signified by outer darkness, weeping, wailing, and gnashing of teeth; by a furnace and lake of fire and brimstone, and by being cast into it, with two eyes, hands, and feet; and be these metaphorical and proverbial speeches, there must be something literally true, to which they refer. Besides, Christ exhorts his disciples, *to fear him, who is able to destroy body and soul in hell*, Matt. x. 28. To which may be added, that this notion that the wicked rise not, must have a tendency to licentiousness, to take off all restraints from wicked men, and embolden them in a vicious course of life, according to 1 Cor. xv. 32. From all which it may be concluded, there will be a resurrection of the wicked, as well as of the righteous;[34] indeed there will be a difference between the resurrection of the one and of the other; the righteous will rise first, at the appearance of Christ; the wicked not till a thousand years after: saints will rise by virtue of union to Christ; the wicked merely by his power; their resurrection will differ in their adjuncts; though the bodies of the wicked will be raised immortal, and in such a state as to bear perpetual punishment, yet will not be clothed with glory; whereas the bodies of the saints will not only be raised immortal and incorruptible, but powerful, spiritual, and glorious, even fashioned like to the glorious body of Christ. The end will be different also; the one will rise to everlasting life; the other to everlasting shame and contempt; hence the one is called the resurrection of life, and the other the resurrection of damnation. I go on,

Secondly, To enquire, what of men shall be raised? Man consists of two parts, soul and body. It is not the soul that is raised, for that dies not. There were some christians in Arabia,[35] who held, that the soul dies with the body, and at the resurrection revives, and returns to its own body; but that is an immaterial and immortal substance, as has been proved in a former chapter; but it is the body which dies, that shall be raised from the dead; it is that only that is mortal, and shall be quickened; it is that only which is laid in the grave, and shall come forth from thence; it is that which sleeps in the dust of the earth, and shall be awakened from thence; for

1. The body is not annihilated, or reduced to nothing at death, as say the Socinians;[36] which is contrary to reason and

---

[33] See Sermon 2. p. 36—40.
[34] Ibid. p. 33, &c.
[35] Euseb. Eccl. Hist. 1. 6. c. 37. Aug. de Hæres. c. 83. Isidor. Orig. 1. 8. c. 5. so Hobbes's Leviathan, c. 38, 44.
[36] Vid. Calov. Socinism. Profligat. s 10. art. 1. controv. 1. p. 1017.

scripture; at death there is a disunion of soul and body; but neither are reduced to nothing; the body returns to the earth, and the soul to God that gave it; and though the body after death passes under many changes and alterations, yet the matter and substance of it will remain in some form or another:[37] death is sometimes expressed by returning to dust; but then dust is something; and by seeing corruption; but that supposes something in being, which is corrupted, matter and substance still remaining; but annihilation leaves nothing: and by sowing seed in the earth, which rots; by pulling down a house; and putting off a tabernacle. But seed sown, though it dies and rots, it does not lose its being, nor its nature; but being quickened, in due time, it buds, and puts forth its seminal virtue; and so a house pulled down, and a tabernacle unpinned, the matter and substance, and the several parts of them, remain. And if the body was reduced to nothing at death, Christ would lose part of his purchase, and the Spirit his dwelling-place, 1 Cor. vi. 15, 19, 20. To which may be added, if this was the case, the resurrection would not be a resurrection, but the creation of a new body. As for those scriptures which speak of the dead as *not*, Jer. xxxi. 15. the meaning is, not that they do not exist; but they are not where they formerly dwelt, having their former possessions and friends; but they are somewhere; their souls are either in heaven or in hell; and their bodies in the grave: and when the apostle says, *Meats for the belly, and the belly for meats; but God shall destroy both it and them;* the sense is, not that the body, or any part of it, as the belly, should be destroyed, as to its substance, but as to its use, in receiving food to supply the natural wants of the body, as now; though it will be necessary as a constituent part, and for the ornament of it.

2. The body, at the resurrection, will not be a new, aërial, and celestial body, as Origen and others thought; or a spiritual one, as to its nature and substance. It will be different from what it is now, as to its qualities, but not as to its substance; when the apostle compares it to seed sown in the earth, which is *not the body that shall be*, 1 Cor. xv. 37, 38. he designs not a difference of substance, but of qualities; such as is between the seed sown, and the plant that springs from it; which differ not in their specific nature, but in some circumstances and accidents; as the difference in the risen body lies in incorruption, glory, power, and spirituality, ver. 42, 43, 44. The same comparison is made of Christ's body, John xii. 24. and yet it was not a spiritual body, when raised, as to substance, but consisted of flesh and bones, as before, Luke xxiv. 39. and such will be the bodies of the saints; and though the body will be raised a spiritual one, as the apostle affirms, yet it will not be changed into a spirit, and lose its former nature; but will be subject and subservient to the soul or spirit; be employed in spiritual services, and delight in spiritual objects; and will not be supported in a natural way, and by natural means, but be like the angels, Luke xx. 36. and though it will consist of flesh and blood, yet be neither sinful, nor frail and mortal; which is the sense of 1 Cor. xv. 50. but pure and holy, incorruptible, and immortal, ver. 53. If the body was a new, aërial, celestial body, different in substance from what it is, it would not be a resurrection, but a creation; nor would it be consistent with the justice of God, that such new, created bodies, which never sinned, should be everlastingly punished; nor can such be said to be truly human bodies, that are without flesh and blood; nor such to be men, who are incorporeal; nor can the same persons who have sinned, be said to be punished; nor the same who are redeemed be glorified, unless the same body is raised. Wherefore,

3. It may be proved, that the same body that now is, will be raised from the dead; this is fully expressed by Job, chap. xix. 26, 27. who firmly believed, that *this body* of his, which would be destroyed by worms, should be raised again; and in that very *flesh* of his he should see God incarnate, and that with the self-same *eyes* he had, and not another's; and which is as strongly asserted by the apostle Paul, 1 Cor. xv. 53, 54. *This mortal must put on immortality; this corruption, must put on incorruption;* pointing to the present mortal and corruptible body he then had; and which is confirmed by what follows; *So when this corruption, &c.* which would not be true if another, and not the same body was raised: and elsewhere he says, that Christ will change *our vile body;* but if

---

[37] Nil enim est quod perire funditus possit, &c. Servius in Virgil. Georgic, 1, 4, p, 334.

not the same body, but another, it will not be *our* vile body that will be fashioned like to the body of Christ. For the further confirmation of this, let the following things be observed.———1. The notation of the word *resurrection;* which signifies a raising up again that which is fallen;[38] by death the body falls, 2 Sam. iii. 38. John xii. 24. now if another, and not the same body, is raised, which fell, it will not be a resurrection; but a creation.———2. The figurative phrases, by which it is expressed, shew it; as by quickening seed sown; and by awakening out of sleep: now as it is the same seed that is sown and dies, which springs up, and appears in stalk, blade, and ear, as to nature and substance, though with some additional circumstances; so it is the same body that dies, is quickened and raised, though with additional glories and excellencies; the same IT that is sown in corruption; the same IT that is sown in dishonour; the same IT that is sown in weakness; the same IT that is sown a natural body, is raised in incorruption, in glory, in power, and a spiritual body; or there is no meaning in the apostle's words, 1 Cor. xv. 42. 43, 44. and as it is the same body that sleeps that is awaked out of it in a literal sense; it is the same body that falls asleep by death, which will be awaked and rise at the resurrection.———3. The places from whence the dead will be raised, and be summoned to deliver them, prove the same; our Lord says, *All that are in the graves shall come forth;*[39] Now what of men are laid in the grave but their bodies? and what else can be thought to come forth from thence? and what but the same bodies that were laid there? the sea, death, and the grave, are said to deliver up the dead in them, which must be the same that are buried in the earth and sea; for what else can such expressions design?———4. The translations of Enoch and Elijah, were in the very same bodies they had when on earth; the bodies of the saints, which arose out of their graves, when opened at Christ's resurrection, were the same that were laid in them; the bodies of the living saints, at Christ's coming, which will then be changed, will be the same they had before that change: now it is not reasonable to suppose, that some of the saints in heaven should have the same bodies they had on earth, and others not.———5. The resurrection of Christ's body is a proof of this truth; since he rose from the dead with the same body he suffered on the cross, and was laid in the grave; as appears from the print of the nails in his hands and feet, seen by Thomas after his resurrection: nor was it an aërial nor spiritual body, as to its substance, since it consisted of flesh and bones, which a spirit does not, and might be felt and handled, John xx. 25, 27. Luke xxiv. 39, 40. Now Christ's resurrection is the exemplar of the saints; according to which their *vile* bodies, and so surely not new, spiritual, and celestial ones, will be fashioned. Nor can it be reasonably thought that Christ, who partook of the same flesh and blood with the children, should be raised and glorified in the same body, and not they in theirs, for whose sake he assumed his.———6. It seems quite necessary from the justice of God that not others, but the same bodies Christ has purchased, the Spirit has sanctified, and which have suffered for the sake of Christ, should be glorified; and that those, and not others, should be punished, that have sinned against God, blasphemed the name of Christ, and persecuted his saints.———7. This may be concluded from the veracity of God, in his purposes, promises, and threatenings; for if the good things he has appointed for, and promised to his people, are not bestowed upon the same persons; and the punishment threatened is not inflicted on the same persons, where is his veracity? and how they can be the same persons, without having the same bodies, is not easy to understand.———8. It would be a disappointment to the saints, who are waiting for the redemption of their bodies, if not the same, but others, should be given them.———9. If the same bodies are not raised, the ends of the resurrection will not appear clearly to be answered; as the glorifying the grace of God in the salvation of his people; and of his justice, in the damnation of the wicked; or how shall every one receive in his body for what he has done, either good or evil, if the same bodies are not raised which have done those things?———10. If the christian doctrine of the resurrection of the dead is

---

[38] Sic et resurrectionis vocabulum non aliam rem vindicat, quam quæ cecidit, Tertull, ad v. Marcion, 1, 5. c. 9.

[39] See a trifling criticism of Mr. Locke's on this text exposed in Serm. 2. on the Resurrection, p. 62, 63.

not of the same body, it seems to be no other nor better, than the old Pythagorean notion of the transmigration of souls into other bodies. The objections to the identity of the risen body, will be considered hereafter. I go on,

III. To observe the causes of this stupendous affair.——1. The efficient cause is God: a creature is not equal to it; it is always ascribed to God, Rom. iv. 17. 2 Cor. i. 9. it is a work of almighty power; and being a work *ad extra*, is common to the three divine Persons. As the resurrection of Christ is frequently attributed to God the Father, so is the resurrection of the saints, 1 Cor. vi. 14. 2 Cor. iv. 14. Christ, as God, is a co-efficient cause of it; both of his own and of theirs, John v. 22. of his own, John ii. 19. Rom. i. 4. and of theirs: he has the keys of the grave, and can open it at his pleasure; and at his commanding voice the dead shall come forth; and he will change the vile bodies of his saints, and fashion them like his own, Rev. i. 18. John v. 28. Phil. iii. 21. The Spirit of God also will have a concern in this affair, Rom. viii. 11.——2. Christ, as the Mediator, is the meritorious cause of it; it will be in virtue of his death and resurrection, which is the earnest and pledge of it; as sure as he is risen, so sure shall his people rise; he is the first-fruits of those that sleep: and, as man, he is the exemplar of it; the bodies of the saints will be raised like his, incorruptible, immortal, powerful, and glorious.——3. The instrumental cause, or means, the voice of Christ, and the sound of a trumpet; the same with the voice of the arch-angel, and the trump of God, John v. 28. 1 Thess. iv. 16. 1 Cor. xv. 52. But whether this voice will be an articulate voice, like that at the grave of Lazarus; or be a violent clap of thunder, called the voice of God, Psalm xxix. and whether this trumpet will be blown by angels, and the shout made, be the shout of all the angels, is not easy to say.——4. The final cause, is the glory of the grace and mercy of God, in the complete salvation of his people, soul and body; and of his justice, in the punishment of the wicked, soul and body, John v. 29.

As to the time of the resurrection, it cannot be exactly fixed; nor does it become us curiously to enquire into it, any more than into the time of the kingdom and the hour of judgment, Acts i. 6, 7. Matt. xxiv. 36. in general, it is said to be at *the last day*, John vi. 39, 40, 44, 54. and xi. 24. at the last day of the present world; at the coming of Christ, they that are his will arise; when he shall descend from heaven, the dead in him will rise first; when the present earth shall be burnt up, and a new one formed, in which the saints will reign with Christ a thousand years; at the close of which the wicked dead will be raised, 1 Cor. xv. 23. 1 Thess. iv. 16. Rev. xx. 5.

IV. There are many objections made to this great and glorious doctrine; the principal of which will be attended to.

1. That maxim, or aphorism, is sometimes alledged; *a privatione ad habitum non datur regressus;* from a total destruction of any being, there is no restoration of it to its former state and condition: this may be true of things according to the common course of nature, and by the power of nature; yet will not hold good of what may be done in an uncommon and extraordinary way, and by the power of God. Besides, the bodies of men at death are not totally destroyed, in any way whatever, with respect to their matter or substance; whether reduced to ashes by fire; or cast into the sea, and devoured by fishes; or interred in the earth, and crumbled into dust; yet they are in being, and are something; out of which, it is not impossible, they may be raised by the power of God.

2. It is objected, that the body is dissolved into so many, and such small particles, and these scattered about, and at a great distance, and united to other bodies; that these should be distinguished, and separated from those to which they are united; and be gathered together, and replaced in their proper order; and that they should meet in their proper places in the body, as if it was with choice and judgment, seems incredible, if not impossible. But, as it has been already observed, considering the omnipotence and omniscience of God, who knows where every particle of matter lies, and can collect and range them together in proper order, the resurrection cannot be thought neither incredible nor impossible. Besides, it has been observed by some, that particles as numerous and more minute, as those of light be, are governed by, and subject to, certain fixed laws, when they seem to be in the greatest disorder; and may be separated from others, and be collected in *camera obscura*, in a dark chamber, into the exact image of

a man; and then what impossibility is there, that the parts of a body, though dispersed, and mingled among others, should be brought together again, and compose the same body; any more than the particles of light do the figure of it, after so many mixtures with, and percussions against other particles?[40] And it is further observed, that the parts of which the visible body is composed, were as much scattered over the whole earth, more than five thousand years ago, as they will be many years after death, or at the end of the world; and so not more impossible in this case, than at first to collect the parts so dispersed, and to bring them into order. And moreover, let the bones of a skeleton, or the wheels and parts of a watch, be jumbled and thrown together in the utmost disorder; yet a good anatomist can put all the bones of a skeleton, and a good watchmaker all the wheels and pieces of a watch, into the same structure again, so as to compose the very same skeleton and watch; and of infinitely more wisdom and power, is the great Artificer of all possessed, to put the human body, though its parts lie ever so dispersed, and in disorder, into the same structure again.[41] And as to the union of the particles of the body, with other bodies, and the difficulty of the separation of them, those that are well versed in chymistry, are able to produce innumerable examples of things that adhere and unite closely with one another, which are yet easily separated, by the addition of a third.[42] And as to the distance of the parts of the body, and the unlikelihood of their meeting at the same places of the body to which they belong, as if they acted with choice and judgment; it is observed, that the loadstone will draw iron when at a distance from it; and that the heavenly bodies, which are at a great and almost immeasurable distance, are subject to a law that brings them towards each other; and such is the virtue of the loadstone, that let iron, lead, salt, and stone, be reduced to a powder, and mixed together, and hold the loadstone to it, it will draw the iron only, and as it were by free choice out of this composition, leaving all the rest of the bodies untouched.[43] And surely then, the great Alchymist of the world, and he who is the Author of the loadstone, and has given it the virtue it has, is capable of doing as great, and greater things, than these; he can gather together the particles of the dissolved body, though ever so distant and dispersed, and separate and distinguish them from other bodies they have been united to, and put them in their proper place, in their own body.

3. The various changes and alterations the body undergoes are objected to the same body being raised; it is observed, that in the space of seven years all the particles of the body are changed; some lost and others got; and it seems impracticable that the same body should be raised, since its particles are not the same in youth as in old age, nor when emaciated as in better circumstances; and therefore being raised according to which it may, it cannot be the same. It may be observed, that though the body has not always the same fleeting particles, which are continually changing, as the fluids are, yet it always has the same solids and constituent parts; and so a man may always be said to have the same body and to be the same man; it is the same body that is born that dies, and the same that dies that shall rise again; the several alterations and changes it undergoes, with respect to tallness and largeness, fatness or leanness, do not destroy the identity of the body. Moreover, it is not requisite that all the particles of matter of which the body of a man has been composed, throughout his lifetime, should be collected, to constitute the risen body; it is enough that all the *necessary* ones should be collected and united together; otherwise it must rise in a gigantic form. It is a good distinction made by a learned writer,[44] of an *own* or *proper* body, and of a *visible* one; the visible body consists both of fluids and of solids; the former of which change and alter, according to difference of years, of constitutions, and other circumstances; but the latter continue the same an *own* or *proper* body, consists almost only of solids; as of skin, bones, nerves, tendons, cartilages, arteries, and veins; which continue the same from infancy to the age of maturity, and so on, excepting the strength and size of them;

---

[40] Nieuwentyt's Religious Philosopher, vol. 3. contempl. 28. s. 5. p. 1041, 1042. Ed. 4th.
[41] Ibid. s. 3. p. 1037. et. s. 5. p. 1040.
[42] Ibid. s. 7. p. 1046. see contempl. 29. p. 1078, 1079.
[43] Ibid. s. 9, 10. p. 1048, 1049.
[44] Nieuwentyt's Religious Philosopher, vol. 3. contempl. 28. s. 20—23. p 1058, &c.

and so sufficient to denominate the same body, notwithstanding the change of the fluids, and of the flying off and accession of the fleeting particles. And as every animal, so man, has a first principle, or *stamen*, which contains the whole own body; and which, in growth, is expanded or unfolded, and clothed as it were, and filled up with other particles continually; so that it is enough if this *stamen* is preserved, and at the resurrection unfolded and filled up, either with the same matter that belonged to it before, or with such other matter as it shall please God to constitute the same body; let one die, as it may, when a child, or full grown, or with a loss of a leg or an arm, or with any defect; since all will be filled up in the expanded *stamen*, as observed.[45]

4. The grossness, and gravity of bodies, are objected, as rendering them unfit to dwell in such a place as heaven, all fluid, and purely ethereal. As for the grossness of raised bodies, they will not be so gross as may be imagined, or as they now are; though they will not be changed into spirits, as to substance; they will be spiritual bodies, in the sense before explained; they will be greatly refined and spiritualized: and will not be supported in such a gross manner as with food, drink, &c. as now; and will be light, agile, and powerful, and capable of breathing in a purer air. As to the gravity of them, a learned man observes,[46] "There is no such thing as gravity in regions purely ethereal, which are above the reach and activity of particular orbs; there is no high and low in such places; our bodies will be there sustained, as the globe of the earth, and the several celestial orbs, are now sustained in the *air* and *ether*." And he further observes, that perhaps, after all, our heaven will be nothing but an heaven upon earth; or some glorious solid orb, created on purpose for us, in those immense regions which we call heaven; and he says, this is no new opinion, but embraced by many of the ancients: and certain it is, that the raised saints will, quickly after their resurrection, inhabit a new earth for a thousand years, prepared for them. As for the objection, taken from the impurity of bodies, and their unworthiness and unfitness to be united to souls; and their being a prison and a burden to them; and so would make the condition of souls worse: these are only heathenish notions, and cannot affect the minds of christians, and require no answer. But,

5. There is another objection, of more importance, which must be removed; which is taken from human bodies being eaten by men, either through necessity, as in distressed cases; or of choice, as by cannibals, or man-eaters; whereby the flesh of one man is turned into the flesh of another; and one human body becomes a part of another; and so there cannot be a distinct resurrection of each of these bodies, with the proper parts belonging to them. In answer to which, there is no need to say, as an ancient learned apologist[47] seems to do, that the substance of one man's body, when eaten by another, does not turn to nourishment, nor become the flesh of the other that eats it; it being not designed by providence for food; since it is certain men have been nourished by it, as when in distress, as well as otherwise: let it be observed, that it is a very small part of the food a man takes into his body, which turns to nourishment; not above the fiftieth part of it, according to the accurate Sanctorius:[48] and daily experience teaches, that what we use for food, belongs only to the *visible* body of an animal, and the fluids and juices thereof; and not its solid parts, its bones and nerves: nor is a cannibal, or man-eater, nourished with withered and dried bones, and with nerves and membranes, divested of their juices;[49] and so is nourished, not with the *own proper* body; but only with the *visible* one, and the fluids thereof. Besides, the nourishment of the bodies of men, is without their will and knowledge, and entirely depends upon the will and pleasure of God; in whose power it is to hinder that no one essential particle of a body should belong to another, through nourishment by it, and that even after a natural manner, there is no impossibility in it, since by numberless chymical experiments, as further observed, it will appear, that though a body has the property of uniting itself to another, yet it can be hindered by the addition of a third, and by other ways too, from doing the same;[50] and

---

[45] Ibid. s. 24, 25, 28. p. 1063, &c.
[46] Hody's Resurrection of the same Body asserted, p. 205.
[47] Athenagoras de Resurrectione, p. 44, 48.

[48] In Hody, p. 186.
[49] Nieuwentyt ut supra, s. 33. p. 1072, 1073.
[50] Ibid, s. 11. p. 1051, 1052.

God, who has promised to raise the bodies of all men, will take care that nothing relating to nourishment should hinder the performance of it; and that the particles of one man's body shall never so become the particles of another, as that the resurrection of either should thereby be rendered impossible.[51] And it is observed by a learned writer, that if even a cannibal, during his whole life, had fed upon nothing but the matter of the visible bodies of men, and it had only pleased God to hinder the *stamina* of all those whom he had devoured from being converted into food; but that they should have passed through his body, with other excrementitious matter; what impossibility is there that the particular *stamen* of each person (supposed to be his *own proper* body) should be separated from thence, and be filled up again by other proper matter? Thus likewise, may the *stamen* of the cannibal himself remain alone, without any of its expanding fluids, and be filled up with others at the resurrection; and he accordingly may rise likewise in his *own* body.—To conclude, adds he, since the *own* body must be considered abstractly from any humours and juices; and since all that serves for the food and nourishment of a man-eater, must only be divided from the *visible* body of the person devoured; it is plain, that although a cannibal had devoured hundreds of *visible* bodies of other men; it would likewise happen, according to the common course of nature, that the solid particles, divested of all their juices, or the *own* bodies of the devoured persons, would be discharged, or cast out, unmingled with those of the devourer; and consequently, that each of them might appear separate and entire, at the time of its resurrection.[52] So that upon the whole, there can be nothing in the above objections, to a rational man, who believes the power, promise, and providence of God.

To conclude, this doctrine appears to be of great importance and usefulness, and therefore to be abode by. It is one of the articles of the creed of the ancient Jews; it is reckoned among the first principles of the doctrine of Christ; it is a fundamental article of the christian faith. The resurrection of Christ stands and falls with it; the whole gospel is connected with it, and depends on it, 1 Cor. xv. 13—17. without this, there is no expectation of a future and better state, ver. 18, 19. practical religion greatly depends on the truth and belief of it. It has been observed,[53] that the opposers of it have always been bad livers; it is a natural consequence, what the apostle observes of the denial of it, ver. 32. Whereas, a firm belief of it, promotes a studious concern of a holy life and conversation, as may be observed in the experience and practice of the apostle Paul, Acts xxiv. 15, 16. It is very useful to instruct in various things. It serves to enlarge our views of the divine perfections; as of the omnipotence and omniscience of God, of his holiness and justice, of his immutability in his counsels and purposes, and of his faithfulness in his promises and threatenings. It teaches us to think highly of Christ, as God over all, and as possessed of all divine perfection, since he has so great a concern in it; and serves to endear the Spirit of God, and teach us not to grieve him, by whom we are sealed to the day of the redemption of our bodies. And it may be a means of encouraging our faith and trust in God, in the greatest straits and difficulties, as being able to deliver out of them, Rom. iv. 17. 2 Cor. i. 9, 10. And it may direct us to a due and proper care of our bodies, whilst living, that they are not abused through avarice or intemperance; and to provide or give orders for the decent interment of them after death. This doctrine affords much comfort; hence, in the Syriac version of John xi. 24. it is called, *the consolation at the last day*. It may be of great use to support saints under the loss of near relations, 1 Thess. iv. 13, 14. and under their various trials and afflictions, and under present diseases and disorders of body; from all which they will be freed at the resurrection; and in the views of death, and of the changes the body will undergo after death; and yet, after all rise again, and see God, and enjoy the company of angels and saints, Job xix. 26, 27.

CHAP. V.

OF THE SECOND COMING OF CHRIST, AND HIS PERSONAL APPEARANCE.

THE personal appearance of Christ will

---

[51] Hody ut supra, p. 185, 186.
[52] Vid. Nieuwentyt, ut supra, s. 29. p. 1067, 1068, et s. 33. p. 1073.
[53] Nemo enim tam carnaliter vivit, quam qui negant carnis resurrectionem, Tertull. de Resurrectione, c. 11.

be before the resurrection of the just, which is the first resurrection; that will be at the coming of Christ, which might properly have been treated of before that resurrection; but that I chose to lay before the reader in one connected view, the separate state of the soul after the death of the body, until the resurrection, and the resurrection of it: and for the same reason I have treated of the doctrine of the resurrection in both its branches together, of the just, and of the unjust; though the one will be a thousand years before the other; and many events will intervene between them; as the conflagration of the world, the making of the new heavens and the new earth, and the dwelling and reigning of Christ with his saints therein, and the binding of Satan during that time; all which will follow the personal appearance of Christ, and will be treated of after that, in their order.

There have been various appearances of Christ already; many in an human form before his incarnation, as a presage and pledge of it; but his principal appearance, and what may be called his *first* appearance and coming, was at his incarnation; there were several appearances of him to his disciples after his resurrection, and to Stephen, and to the apostle Paul, after his ascension; and there was a coming of him in his kingdom and power sometime after to take vengeance on the Jewish nation for their rejection of him, and the persecution of his followers. There is now an appearance of Christ in heaven as the advocate of his people; and there is a spiritual appearance of him at conversion, and in after-visits of his love, and communion with him; and in the latter day there will be a great appearance of Christ in a spiritual manner, or a coming of him by the effusion of his Spirit upon his people, when his spiritual reign will take place, elsewhere treated of; after which will be the personal appearance of Christ to reign in a still more glorious manner. Hence his appearance and kingdom are joined together, when he will judge both quick and dead, 2 Tim. iv. 1. and this will be attended with great glory, and is called his *glorious appearing*, Tit. ii. 13. and in distinction from his first coming and appearance at his incarnation, it is called his *second*, Heb. ix. 28. which will now be treated of,

I. By giving the proof of the certainty of it, that Christ will most surely appear personally to judge the world, and reign with his people; which may be most firmly believed, depended upon, and looked for; and this will appear,

First, From what the patriarchs before and after the flood have said of it; for so early has it been spoken of, as may be observed from the prophecy of Enoch, the seventh from Adam, recorded by the apostle Jude, ver. 14, 15. *Saying, Behold, the Lord cometh with ten thousand of his saints to execute judgment upon all;* which prophecy, whether it was written or not, is not certain, nor how the apostle came by it, whether by tradition, as the apostle Paul had the names of the magicians of Egypt, or by divine revelation; however, it is made authentic by the spirit of God, and is to be depended on as fact; and is to be understood, not of the first, but of the second coming of Christ, as appears by his attendants, *ten thousands of his saints;* such and such a number of them were not with him when he came in the flesh, but his second coming will be *with all his saints*, 1 Thess. iii. 13. and by the work he is to do, *to execute judgment on all,* and to convince of and punish wicked men for their words and works; see Eccl. xii. 14. John iii. 17. Job also declared his faith, that Christ his living Redeemer should *stand at the latter day on the earth,* that is, the latter or last day of the present world; since it is connected with the resurrection of the dead he believed in, and the future judgment, Job xix. 25, 26, 27, 29. Also David the patriarch, as he is called, Acts ii. 29. speaks of the coming of Christ to judge the earth and world, and the people of it with righteousness; and which is repeated to denote the certainty of it, Psalm xcvi. 13. and xcviii. 9.

Secondly, The certainty of Christ's second coming and personal appearance may be confirmed from what the prophets have said concerning it; for it has been *spoken of by the mouth of* them *all,* Acts iii. 21. and though the prophecies greatly respect his spiritual reign, yet are intermixed with many things concerning his personal coming and appearance; and it requires skill and care, being attended with some difficulty, to distinguish and separate the one from the other; and besides these, there are some which chiefly and plainly respect his personal appearance and kingdom; as, 1. The prophecy in Dan. vii. 13, 14. where, after the destruction of Antichrist and the Antichristian states in the spiritual reign, signified by the slaying and burning of the *fourth beast*, follows in a natural order the coming of the *Son of man* to take possession of his kingdom ; Christ said to be *like* one, either in conformity to the language of the former visions, his kingdom being humane, gentle, just, and wise, as well as powerful, and not beastly, as the others ; or because he was not yet become man ; or rather the *as* or *like* is not an *as* of similitude but of certainty, as in Matt. xiv. 5. John i. 14. Phil. ii. 7. and being described as coming *with the clouds of heaven*, fixes it to his second and personal coming, which is always so described, Matt. xxiv. 30. and xxvi. 64. Rev. i. 7. The *Ancient of days* he is said to come to, is God the Father, the eternal God ; they that brought him near him are either the saints, who hasten his coming by their prayers ; or the angels ; or it may be impersonally read, and *he was brought ;* which denotes the august and magnificent manner in which he will be personally and visibly put into the possession of his kingdom and dominion ; which will have a *glory* beyond all expression, and will be *everlasting ;* it will never be succeeded by another ; and though Christ's personal reign on earth will be but a thousand years, yet his whole reign, personal and spiritual, will be of a long duration, and which in scripture is called *everlasting*, Gen. xvii. 8. Lev. xvi. 34. Besides, this kingdom, when delivered up, will not cease, but will be connected with, and issue in the ultimate glory, in which Christ will reign with his saints for ever.———2. Another prophecy in Dan. xii. 1, 2, 3. respects the second and personal coming of Christ ; for he is meant by Michael, who is *as God*, as his name signifies, equal to him ; the *great prince*, the prince of the kings of the earth, and the head of all principalities and powers. *Who standeth for the children of Daniel's people ;* meaning the election of grace among the Jews, on whose behalf Christ will stand at the time of their conversion in the latter day ; previous to which it will be a time of great trouble ; both to the saints, when will be the slaying of the witnesses ; and to the antichristian states, when the vials will be poured out upon them, which will bring on the spiritual reign ; after which will be the personal coming of Christ, here implied, since the resurrection of the dead will follow, and when such will be rewarded in the kingdom of Christ, who have been eminently serviceable in his interest ; and the rest of the chapter is taken up about the time when these things shall be.———3. The prophecy in Zech. xiv. 4, 5. respects the second and personal coming of Christ ; since *all the saints* will come with him, and descend with him on earth ; when his feet shall stand on the mount of Olives, and when Christ will be king over all the earth, ver. 10. and the saints will be in a sinless state, ver. 20, 21. though there are some things which respect the spiritual reign of Christ, and a time of distress previous to it, ver. 1, 2, 3, 6, 7, 8. ———4. The prophecy in Mal. iv. 1—3. respects not the first, but the second coming of Christ, when the day of the Lord shall *burn like an oven ;* the elements shall melt with fervent heat, and the earth and all that therein is shall be burnt up ; and *all the wicked* shall perish in the conflagration ; be burnt up *like stubble*, and be properly *ashes under the soles of the feet* of them that fear the Lord : to whom it will be a glorious day, on whom the sun of righteousness shall arise, ver. 4.

Thirdly, The certainty of Christ's second and personal coming to reign on earth, may be evinced from several sayings and parables delivered by him. Not to omit the petition directed to, in the prayer commonly called the *Lord's Prayer ; Thy kingdom come*, connected with another, *thy will be done on earth as it is done in heaven ;* the sense of which is, that the kingdom of God might come, and so come, that the will of God might be done by men on earth, as it is done by the angels in heaven ; which petition, though it has been put up thousands of times, has never yet been fulfilled, nor never can be but in a perfect state ; and there will be no such on earth till the resurrection-state takes place, and Christ personally appears in his kingdom and glory.

1st, The answer of Christ to the question of his disciples, *What shall be the sign of thy coming, and of the end of the world ?* Matt. xxiv. 3. given in the following part of the chapter, seems to respect the second and personal coming of Christ ; for though it is so expressed as that it may be applied to his coming in his kingdom and power to destroy the Jewish nation, and so to be the end of their world, church and state ; yet what is said of that, and of the signs of it, may be considered as types, symbols, and emblems of, and to have a farther accomplishment in the second coming of Christ, and the end of the present world ; whose coming will be like lightning, swift, sudden, at an unawares, and local and visible ; for *then shall appear the sign of the son of man in heaven,* ver. 27, 30. that is, the son of man himself, as the sign of Jonas is Jonas himself; who will personally appear in the lower heaven, so as to be seen by all the tribes of the earth, who shall mourn on that account: and *they shall see the son of man coming in the clouds of heaven;* which, as has been before observed, is a distinguishing and peculiar characteristic of the second coming of Christ; which will be *with power,* seen in raising the dead, burning the world, binding Satan, making new heavens and a new earth, and setting up his glorious kingdom in it; and so *with great glory,* his own, his Father's, and that of the holy angels; and then he will *send his angels with a great sound of a trumpet,* ver. 31. and with such an one, and with his angels shall he descend in person from heaven, 1 Thess. iv. 16. 2 Thess. i. 7. and those he will employ to *gather together his elect from the four winds, from one end of heaven to the other;* that is, the raised saints, who will rise at this time in the several parts of the world where they died and were buried; and whom the angels shall collect together, and bring with the living saints changed, to Christ in the air, where he will be seen. But of *the day and hour* of Christ's coming, *knoweth no man, no not the angels in heaven,* ver. 36. Moreover the coming of the son of man will be *like the days of Noah* for carnality, sensuality, and security, ver. 37, &c. which agrees with the accounts other scriptures give; as that it will be like that of a thief in the night, sudden and at unawares; and that when persons are crying peace, peace, great pleasure and happiness, sudden destruction comes upon them; and therefore, since the son of man comes in an hour unthought of, persons ought to be *ready* for it, ver. 44. for nothing is more certain than death, the coming of Christ, and the judgment-day.

2dly, The parables in Matt. xxv. all respect the second coming of Christ. The parable of the wise and foolish virgins, describes the state of the church under the gospel-dispensation, as consisting of true believers, and formal professors, and their different behaviour, until the coming of Christ; when the door will be shut, the door of the word and ordinances; for after the spiritual reign, and in the millennium-state, they will be no more administered, and Christ, and his gospel, will be no more preached; and so no more a door of faith and hope for sinners. Before the personal coming of Christ, all the virgins, both wise and foolish, will be asleep, unconcerned about his coming, off of their watch and guard, and in no expectation of it; and having little faith about it, *When the Son of man cometh, shall he find faith on the earth?* To this state answers the Laodicean church-state, lukewarm, indifferent, and regardless of divine things; which will bring on, and issue in the last judgment of the people, as its name signifies. Christ, in this parable, is all along represented as a bridegroom, and as such he shall come, ver. 1, 5, 6, 10. when the church, his bride, will be made ready, and come down from God out of heaven, as a bride adorned for her husband; when she, the bride, the Lamb's wife, having the glory of God upon her, shall dwell with him in the new Jerusalem-state; which is the marriage-chamber they that are ready shall enter into with him.

The parable of the talents, in the same chapter, respects the same time, and describes our Lord's giving gifts to men, upon his ascension to heaven, and since; to some more, and others less, of which they make a different improvement: and also his *coming* again, after a long time, and reckoning with them; which will be done when he personally appears; and who will, in the resurrection-state, distribute honours and rewards to his servants, according as they have made use of the talents committed to them.

The chapter is closed with an account of the Son of man coming in his glory, and all the holy angels with him, and sitting on the throne of his glory, summoning all nations before him, and separating the good from the bad, and passing the definitive sentence on each, and executing it.

3dly, The parable of the nobleman, in Luke xix. 12, &c. is similar to that of the talents, in Matt. xxv. By the nobleman is meant Christ, who is of noble extract indeed; as the Son of God, he is the only begotten of the Father; as man, he sprung from the Jewish ancestors, Abraham, Isaac, and Jacob, and from a race of kings of the line of David. By the *far country* he went into, heaven is designed; which is the better country, a land afar off, from whence Christ came at his incarnation, and whither he went after his ascension, and where he will remain till his second coming. His end in going thither, was *to receive for himself a kingdom;* to take open possession of a kingdom that was appointed for him; and which he did in some sort, at his ascension, when he was made, or declared, Lord and Christ; and more fully will, in the spiritual reign, when the kingdoms of this world shall become his; but most openly, clearly, and plainly, at his personal appearing and kingdom ; which will be the time of his return, when he will appear manifestly instated in it, and possessed of it ; and then will he call his servants to an account for the monies he committed to them, to make use of in his absence ; and according to the use it shall appear they have made of them, they will be rewarded in the millennium-state, signified by giving them authority over more or fewer cities.

4thly, The words of Christ in John xiv. 2, 3. cannot well be neglected ; *In my Father's house are many mansions ; I go to prepare a place for you, and I will come again, and receive you unto myself.* By Christ's *Father's house*, is meant heaven, the house not made with hands, eternal in the heavens ; in which there are *many mansions*, dwelling, resting-places for the *many sons*, he, the great Captain of their salvation, must, and will bring to glory; and hither Christ is gone, as the forerunner, both to take possession of heaven for them, and to prepare it for their reception of it ; for though it is a kingdom prepared from the foundation of the world, in the purpose, council, and covenant of God ; yet Christ is further preparing, and fitting it for them, by his personal presence, and powerful mediation, whilst they are preparing and working up for the self-same thing, by his Spirit within them ; and when they are all gathered in, and made ready, he will come again in person, and raise their bodies, and re-unite their souls to them, and take them, soul and body, to himself, to be with him where he is, first in the millennium-state, and then in the ultimate glory.

Fourthly, That Christ will come personally on earth a second time, may be most certainly concluded from the words of the angels, in Acts i. 11. at the ascension of Christ to heaven ; *This same Jesus which is taken up from you into heaven, shall so come in like manner as ye have seen him go into heaven.* The angels reproved the apostles, that they stood gazing at Jesus, as he went up to heaven, being desirous of seeing the last of him, as if they were never to see him any more ; whereas he would come again from heaven, in like manner as they saw him go thither : as he ascended in person, in his human nature, united to his divine person, as the Son of God ; so he should descend in person, in the same human nature thus united; *The Lord himself shall descend from heaven:* and as his ascension to heaven was visible, he was seen of angels, and by the apostles ; so his descent from thence will be visible ; *Every eye shall see him;* not a few only, as then, but all : and as a cloud received him out of their sight, when he went to heaven; so when he comes again, he will come in the clouds of heaven : and as he was attended by angels, who escorted him through the regions of the air ; so he will be revealed from heaven, with his mighty angels : and though no mention is made in this narrative, of his ascension with a shout, and the sound of a trumpet attending it ; yet, as it was foretold in prophecy and type, no doubt is to be made of it ; *God is gone up with a shout, the Lord with the sound of a trumpet !* Psalm xlvii. 5. and certain it is, he will descend in such manner; *The Lord himself shall descend from heaven with a shout, with the voice of the arch-angel, and with the trump of God !* 1 Thess. iv. 16. and as his ascent was from the mount of Olives, ver. 12. it is very probable his descent will be on that very spot ; since it is said, that when the Lord shall come with all his saints, *his feet shall stand in that day on the mount of Olives,* Zech. xiv. 4, 5.

Fifthly, The second coming and appearance of Christ, may be confirmed from various passages in the sermons, discourses, and epistles of the apostles. And,——
1. From the words of Peter, Acts iii. 19, 20, 21. From whence it appears, that there was then to come, and still is to come, *a time of the restitution of all things ;* which cannot be understood of the gospel-dispensation, called the time of *reformation ;* for that had taken place already ; nor of the restitution of the brute creatures to their paradisaical estate, of which some interpret Isa. xi. 6, 9. Rom. viii. 19—23. for which I can see no need nor use of, in a perfect state, as these times will be ; nor of the restitution of gospel-doctrines, ordinances, discipline, and worship, to their former purity and perfection, which will be accomplished in the spiritual reign ; but of the restitution of all the bodies of the saints, a resurrection of them from the dead, and a restoration of them to their souls ; and of the renovation of the world, which will be at the second coming of Christ: and when the time fixed for it is come, then will God *send Jesus Christ* from heaven, where he now is, and where he will be

retained till that time, and then he will descend from thence, when the saints in their resurrection-state shall be judged; and though their sins are already *blotted out* by the blood of Christ, and for his sake; and a comfortable application of it is made to the consciences of all penitent and converted persons; yet there will be then a public blotting of them out, or a declaration that they are blotted out, never to be seen nor read more; which will be done before angels and men; and then it will be *a time of refreshing* indeed, *from the presence of the Lord;* for the tabernacle of God will now be with men, and he will dwell with them; and there shall be no more sorrow and weeping, crying and pain, Rev. xxi. 3, 4.

―――2. There are various passages, in which express mention is made of the coming of Christ; of his appearing a second time, unto the salvation of his people; of their waiting for his coming, looking for, and hastening unto it, and loving it, Heb. ix. 28. 1 Cor. i. 7. Tit. ii. 13. 2 Pet. iii. 12. 2 Tim. iv. 8. and of what the saints shall be, and shall have then; that they shall appear in glory with Christ, and shall be like him, and shall have grace given them, and a crown of glory likewise; and shall be the joy and crown of rejoicing of Christ's ministers, Col. iii. 4. 1 John iii. 2. 1 Pet. i. 13. and v. 4. 2 Tim. iv. 8. 1 Thess. ii. 19. and also of what shall then be done by Christ; all the saints shall be brought with him; the dead in him shall be raised, and both quick and dead be judged; and the counsels of all hearts shall be made manifest, 1 Thess. iii. 13. and iv. 14, 16. 2 Tim. iv. 1. 1 Cor. iv. 5.―――3. In all those places in which mention is made of *that day*, that famous, that well-known day, so much spoken of and expected, 2 Tim. i. 12, 18. and iv. 8. and of the day of the Lord, 1 Thess. v. 2. 2 Pet. iii. 10. and of the day of the Lord Jesus, 1 Cor. i. 8. and v. 5. 2 Cor. i. 14. Phil. i. 6. and of the day of redemption, Eph. iv. 30. the time of Christ's second coming, and personal appearance, is meant; which will be sudden, and at an unawares, like a thief in the night; till which time the saints commit themselves into his hands; and when the work of grace, in its utmost extent and influence on soul and body, will be completed, and they will be unblameable before him, and their bodies redeemed from mortality, corruption, and death.

Sixthly, In the book of the Revelation, frequent mention is made of the visible, quick, and speedy coming of Christ, and of what shall be then done by him; as in chap. i. 7. and iii. 11. and xxii. 7, 12, 20. and in particular of his descent from heaven, for the binding of Satan the space of a thousand years, chap. xx. 1, 2, 3. where he is described by his office, an *Angel*, not a created, but the uncreated one; nor is it unusual for Christ to be called an Angel; he is that Angel who appeared to Moses in the bush; and who went before the children of Israel in the wilderness; and who is called *the Angel of God's presence*, and the Angel, or *Messenger, of the covenant*: and he is described by his descent *from heaven*, whither he went at his ascension, and where he is now retained, and from whence he will come at the last day; and by what he had in his hand, a *key* and a *great chain;* a key to open the bottomless pit, to put Satan into it, and shut him up therein; and who so proper to have this key, as he who has *the keys of hell and death?* chap. i. 18. and a great chain to bind him therewith; and which will be greater, though shorter, than what he is now held with; and with which he will be bound faster and closer, and laid under greater restraints than he now is; so that he shall not be able to do the hurt and mischief, and practise the deceit among the nations he now does, by instilling evil principles into them, and stirring them up to evil practices; and so will he remain bound, shut up, and sealed, for the space of a thousand years.

II. The locality of Christ's second coming and personal appearance; or the place from whence he will come, and where he will appear.―――1. The place from whence he will come; heaven, the third heaven, where he now is in human nature, into which he was received at his ascension; and where he will continue till his second coming, and from thence he will then be revealed; he will descend from heaven to earth; he came down from heaven to earth at his incarnation; but that his coming was not local, not by change of place, which cannot agree with him as the omnipresent God; but by assumption of nature: but as his ascent to heaven in human nature, having assumed it, and done his work in it, which he came about, was local, by change of place from earth to heaven; so when he comes again from heaven to earth, it will be local, by change of place, which his human nature is capable of.―――2. The place whither he shall come, is the earth; for, as Job says, he shall stand on the earth in the latter-day; though he shall not descend upon it at once: when he appears from the third heaven, he shall descend into the air, and there stay some time, until the dead saints are raised, and the living ones changed; and both brought unto him there; and till the new earth is made and prepared for him and them; when he and they will come down from heaven to earth, and they shall reign with him on it a thousand years; and he shall reign before his ancients gloriously.

III. The visibility of Christ's personal appearance; he will appear in human nature, visible to all; the sign of the Son of man, that is, the Son of man himself, shall appear in heaven, in the air; and *every eye shall see him*, all the inhabitants of the earth: such will be the agility of his glorious body, that he will swiftly move from one end of the heaven to the other, like lightning, to which his coming is compared, Matt. xxiv. 27. so that he will be seen by all the tribes, kindreds, and nations of the earth: he will be seen by all good men, by the living saints, that will be changed; by the dead, who will be raised, and both caught up together to meet him in the air; when he appears, they shall appear with him, and see him as he is; and he will be seen by them in the millennium state, and throughout the whole of it; for he will reign *before his ancients*, in the sight of them, in a glorious manner; and then, as Job says, when they shall both stand together upon the earth, in their flesh, and with their fleshly eyes shall they see God in human nature, and that for themselves, and not another: and he will be seen by bad men; by all the wicked living on earth, at his first appearance, who will wail and mourn because of him, fearing his wrath and vengeance they justly deserve; and when they, even the greatest personages among them, shall flee, and call to the rocks and mountains to fall on them, and hide them from his face, terrible to them. And at the end of a thousand years, when they will be all raised, they will see him as their Judge on a throne of glory, and stand before him, small and great, and tremble at the sight of him, as the devils also will.

IV. The glory of Christ's second coming. His first coming was in a very low, mean, and abject manner, without observation, pomp and splendour; but his second coming will be in *great glory*, Matt. xxiv. 30. Luke ix. 26. and therefore is, with great propriety, called, *The glorious appearing of the great God!* Tit. ii. 13.

1*st*, Christ will come in the *glory of his Father;* this is sometimes said alone, and when no mention is made of his own glory with it, Matt. xvi. 27. Mark viii. 38. the glory of the Father, and the glory of Christ, as the only begotten of the Father, are the same; the same is the glory of him that begat, and the glory of him that is begotten; Christ is the brightness of his Father's glory, and the express image of his person; having the same nature and perfections, and so the same glory, with which he shall now appear: or by his Father's glory may be meant, the glory he promised him in covenant, on doing the work of redemption and salvation of men, proposed to him, and to which he agreed; wherefore when he came the first time, when he had finished his work, he pleaded the promised reward, John xvii. 4, 5. and which promised glory took place, first upon the resurrection of Christ from the dead; for *God raised him from the dead, and gave him glory;* and at his ascension he *highly exalted him, and gave him a name above every name;* and now by faith we see him *crowned with glory and honour!* and thus glorified, exalted, and crowned, will he come a second time. Besides, he will come as a Judge, to which office he is appointed by his Father; under whom, as such he will act; and will therefore come with a commission from him, and clothed with authority by him; for he hath *given him authority to execute judgment also, because he is the Son of man;* that Son of man whom the Father has appointed to judge the world in righteousness; and so will come with the power, pomp, and majesty of a judge; and shall sit on a *throne of glory,* with thousands and ten-thousands ministering unto him, called *a great white throne; great,* suitable to the greatness of his person and office; and *white,* to denote the purity, uprightness, and righteousness of his proceedings.

2*dly*, He will come *in his own glory:* this is sometimes also spoken of singly; and no mention made of his Father's glory, Matt. xxv. 31. And this his own glory, in which he will come, is twofold.——
1. He will come in the glory of his divine nature, and the perfections of it, as a divine Person, as God over all. At first he came as a man; and because he appeared so mean, was taken by the Jews to be a mere man, as he still is by many; but

when he comes a second time, his appearing will be the appearing of *the great God, the most high God*; and so his coming is called, *the coming of the day of God*, Tit. ii. 13. 2 Pet. iii. 12. see Zech. xiv. 5. his divine perfections will be very illustriously displayed, particularly his omnipotence; upon his coming, voices will be heard in heaven, the church, loud proclamations made; *The Lord God omnipotent reigneth!* Rev. xix. 6. he will come *with power*, with almighty power; which will appear by raising his dead saints, and changing his living ones; by burning the world, the heavens and the earth, and making all things new; by summoning all nations before him, setting them in their proper posture and distance, passing the decisive sentence, and carrying it into execution; especially on the wicked, who will be *punished with everlasting destruction from the presence of the Lord, and from the glory of his power*, 2 Thess. i. 9. Also his omniscience will be clearly discerned; he will let all the churches, and all the world know, that he is he who searcheth the reins and hearts, and who needs no testimony from men; for he knows what is in men, and is done by them; for he will bring to light the hidden things of darkness, and every secret thing into judgment; and neither men nor things shall escape his all-seeing eye. Likewise the glory of his holiness and justice will be very conspicuous; he will appear as the Judge of the whole earth, who will do right, and will truly claim the character of a *righteous Judge;* and his judgment be *righteous judgment;* and, as in all his other offices, so in the execution of this, *righteousness will be the girdle of his loins, and faithfulness the girdle of his reins.* There will be also large displays of grace and mercy, made at the appearance of Christ; hence saints are exhorted, *to hope to the end for the grace that is to be brought unto them, at the revelation of Jesus Christ;* and to *look for the mercy of our Lord Jesus Christ, unto eternal life!* 1 Pet. i. 13. Jude ver. 21. see 2 Tim. i. 16, 18.——2. Christ will come in the glory of his human nature. The apostle takes notice of this remarkable circumstance, which will attend the second coming and appearance of Christ, that it will be *without sin*, the disgrace of human nature, Heb. ix. 28. The human nature of Christ, when first assumed by him, was without sin, without original sin, the taint and contagion of corrupt nature, which is in all the ordinary descendents of Adam; hence it is called, the *holy thing;* and throughout his whole life it was free from all actual transgressions; no act of sin was ever committed by him: but then he was not without the appearance of sin; though his flesh was not sinful flesh, yet he was *sent in the likeness of sinful flesh;* being born of a sinful woman, brought up among sinful men, and conversed with some of the chief of them in life, and was numbered among transgressors at his death: and moreover, he had all the sins of his people imputed to him; he was *made sin* by imputation, who knew none; he bore all the sins of his people, and the punishment due to them, in his body on the tree; but having thereby made satisfaction for them, upon his resurrection from the dead, he was discharged, acquitted, and justified: so that when he comes a second time, he will appear as without sin inherent in him he never had, and without sin done by him he never did; so without sin imputed to him, this being satisfied for by him, and he discharged from it. Likewise, whereas he bore our sorrows, and carried our griefs, and was attended with the sinless infirmities of our nature, and was at last crucified through weakness; now he will appear without any such; as hunger, thirst, weariness, and pain; and whereas, what with one thing and another, his visage was more marred than any man's, and his form than the sons of men; now his body is become a glorious one; of the glory of which his transfiguration on the Mount was an emblem, when his face did shine as the sun: and if the righteous, whose bodies will be fashioned like to Christ's glorious body, shall shine as the sun in the kingdom of their Father, with what lustre and splendour will Christ appear in his glorified body?

3dly, Christ will come in the glory of his holy angels; this circumstance is always observed in the account of his glorious coming. This will add to the glory and solemnity of the day. So kings, when they go abroad, are attended by their guards, not only for their safety, but for the glory of their majesty; and thus, when God descended on mount Sinai, to give the law to Israel, he came with ten thousand of his saints, his holy ones, the holy angels: and when Christ ascended on high, his chariots were twenty thousand, even thousands of angels; and when he shall descend from heaven, he will be revealed from thence with his mighty angels: nor will they be only used for the glory of his Majesty; but they will be employed by him in certain services; as to gather out of his kingdom all things that offend, to bind the tares in bundles and cast them into the furnace of fire; and to collect together from the four winds, the saints raised from the dead, in the several parts of the world, and bring them to Christ, to meet him in the air, and come along with him.

V. The time of Christ's second coming and personal appearance, may next be enquired into; but to put a stop to enquiries of this kind, at least a boundary to them, it should be observed what our Lord says; *Of that day and hour knoweth no man, no not the angels; but my Father only*, Matt. xxiv. 36. Another evangelist has it; *Neither the Son*, that is, as man; the human nature of Christ not being possessed of divine perfections, and so not of omniscience: to *know the times and seasons* of Christ's personal appearance and kingdom, is not for us; these the *Father has put in his own power*, and keeps them secret there, Acts i. 6, 7. Some good men, in the last age, fixed the time of Christ's second coming, of his personal reign, and the millennium; in which being mistaken, it has brought the doctrine into disgrace, and great neglect: their mistake arose greatly from their confounding the spiritual and personal reign of Christ; as if they commenced together; namely, upon the destruction of antichrist, pope, and Turk; the calling of the Jews, and the large conversions of the Gentiles; whereas there is a distant space between the one and the other, and which is entirely unknown; the spiritual reign, indeed, will take place upon the above events, and there are dates given of them; namely, of the reign of antichrist, the witnesses prophesying in sackcloth, the holy city being given to the Gentiles to be trodden under foot, and the church in the wilderness; and the dates of these are the same, forty-two months, or one thousand two hundred and sixty days, which are alike; for forty-two months, reckoning thirty days in a month, as was the usual reckoning, are just one thousand two hundred and sixty days, and which design so many years; so that these things took place, go on, and will end together; see Rev. xi. 2, 3. and xii. 6. and xiii. 5. Now these dates are given to exercise the minds, the study, and diligence of men; and though men good and learned, have hitherto been mistaken in fixing the end of these dates, arising from the difficulty of knowing the time of their commencement, this should not discourage a modest and humble enquiry into them; for, for what end else are these dates given? could we find out the time when antichrist began his reign, the end of it could easily be fixed to a year. There is a hint given of his first appearance in 2 Thess. ii. 6, 7, 8. *Now ye know, what withholdeth that he* (antichrist before described) *might be revealed in his time; for the mystery of iniquity doth already work*; it was not only in embryo, but was got to some bigness, and was busy and operative, though secret and hidden; *only he who now letteth will let, until he be taken out of the way, and then shall that wicked one be revealed*, the man of sin, or antichrist: now that which let, seems to be rightly interpreted by many, of the Roman emperor, who stood in the way of the bishop of Rome, appearing in that pomp and power he was thirsting after; and which seemed to bid fair to be fulfilling, when Augustulus, the last of the emperors, delivered up the empire to Odoacer, a king of the Goths; and the seat of the empire was removed from Rome to Ravenna, whereby way was made for the bishop of Rome to take his seat, and appear in the grandeur he was aiming at. Now this seemed to be a probable æra to begin the reign of antichrist; and as this was in the year four hundred and seventy-six, if one thousand two hundred and sixty years are added thereunto, the fall of antichrist must have happened in the year one thousand seven hundred and thirty-six; this some learned men were very confident of, particularly Lloyd, bishop of Worcester, a great calculator of times, affirmed, that all the devils in hell could not support the pope of Rome, longer than one thousand seven hundred and thirty-six. But we have lived to see him mistaken; more than thirty years have since passed, yet the popish antichrist is still in his seat; though his civil power has been weakened, and still is weakening; so that it might be hoped, he will, ere long, come to his end. Nor should we be altogether discouraged from searching into the date of his reign: there is another æra which bids fair to be the beginning of it; and that is, when the emperor Phocas gave the grant of universal bishop to the pope of Rome; and this was done in the year six hundred and six: and the rather this date should be attended to, since within a little time after, Mahomet, the eastern antichrist, arose; so that as they appeared about the same time, and go on together, they will end together. Now if to the above date are added one thousand two hundred and sixty years, the end of antichrist's reign will fall in the year one thousand eight hundred and sixty-six: according to this computation, antichrist has almost an hundred years more to reign; and if the date of his reign is to be taken from his arriving to a greater degree of pride and power, or from the year six hundred and sixty-six, which is the number of the beast, Rev. xiii. 18. it will be protracted still longer. It may be observed, that the dates in Daniel xii. 11, 12. and in the Revelation, somewhat differ; they are larger in the former; instead of one thousand two hundred and sixty days, as in the latter, it is one thousand two hundred and ninety days; thirty days, that is, thirty years, more; which, after the fall of antichrist, may be taken up in the conversion of the Jews, and the settlement of them in their own land: and the date is still further increased in the next verse; *Blessed is he that waiteth, and cometh to the thousand three hundred and thirty-five days;* which make forty-five days, or years, more; and which may be employed in the destruction of the Ottoman empire; and in the spread of the gospel through the whole world; and therefore happy will he be that comes to this date; these will be happy, halcyon days indeed! But now supposing these dates could be settled with any precision, as they cannot, until more light is thrown upon them, which perhaps may be, when nearer their accomplishment; yet the time of the second coming, and personal appearance of Christ, and of the millennium, or thousand years reign upon it, cannot be known hereby; because the spiritual reign of Christ, will only take place upon the above events; and how long that will last, none can say: nor have we any chronological dates, nor hints, concerning the duration of it; only the Philadelphian church-state, in which it will be; but as that is not yet begun, so neither do we know when it will; nor when it will end: and after that, there will be another state of lukewarmness, drowsiness, and carnal security; which the Laodicean church-state will bring on, and will continue till Christ's personal appearance; for such will be the state of things when the Son of man comes; which will be like the times of Noah and Lot; and how long this state will last cannot be said; unless the *seven months,* allowed for the burial of Gog and his multitude, Ezek. xxxix. 12. can be thought to be the duration of this state;[1] which, if understood of prophetic time, takes in a compass of two hundred and ten years; but this is uncertain. So that it seems practicable and impossible, to know the time of the second coming of Christ; and therefore it must be vain and needless, if not criminal, to enquire into it. However, it is known to God, who has appointed a day in which he will judge the world by Christ; and as there was a set time for his first coming into the world, so there is for his second coming; and God in his own appointed time will send him, shew him, and set him forth. And it is often said by our Lord in the book of the Revelation, that he would *come quickly*, chap. iii. 11. and xxii. 7, 12, 20. to quicken saints to an expectation of it; and yet it is seemingly deferred, to try the faith and patience of saints, and to render the wicked inexcusable: but the chief reason is what the apostle gives, 2 Pet. iii. 9. that *the Lord is long-suffering to us-ward,* the beloved of the Lord, ver. 8. the elect of God he wrote unto; *not willing that any* of those his beloved and chosen ones *should perish, but that all should come to repentance;* and when they are all brought to repentance towards God, and to faith in Christ, he will stay no longer, *but the day of the Lord will come* immediately.

VI. The signs of Christ's appearance and kingdom. The more remote ones are such as Christ gives in answer to the question of the apostles to him; *What shall be the sign of thy coming, and of the end of the world?* whether they meant his second coming, or his coming to destroy Jerusalem, and the end of the Jewish world, church and state, Christ gave them signs which answer to both; the destruction of Jerusalem being a presage and emblem of the destruction of the world at the second coming of Christ; such as wars and rumours of wars, famines, pestilences, and earthquakes; persecutions of good men, false teachers, the preaching of the gospel throughout the world: all which had an

---

[1] See Rudd's Essay on the Millennium, p. 16, 363.

accomplishment before the coming of Christ to destroy Jerusalem: and they have been fulfilling again and again in all ages since; and perhaps will be more frequent before the destruction of the world at the second coming of Christ. The more near signs, or what will more nearly precede Christ's second and personal coming, are the spiritual reign, and what will introduce that? the destruction of antichrist, the call of the Jews, and numerous conversions of Gentiles, through the general spread of the gospel; and after that, great coolness and indifference in religion, and great defection in faith and practice. But after all, it seems as if there would be an uncertainty of it until the sign of the Son of man, which is himself, as before observed, appears in the heavens; for the Son of man will come in an hour unthought of by good men; and as a thief in the night to wicked men; suddenly and at an unawares; and to both wise and foolish professors, whilst they are slumbering and sleeping.

VII. The ends to be answered by the second and personal coming of Christ——1. The putting of the saints into the full possession of salvation, Heb. ix. 28. Christ's first coming into the world was to work out the salvation of his people; this he has obtained, he is become the author of it, and which is published in the gospel; and an application of it is made to particular persons, by the Spirit of God, at conversion; but the full enjoyment of it is yet to come, Rom. xiii. 11. to which saints are kept by the power of God; and of which they are now heirs, and when Christ shall appear he will put them into the possession of their inheritance, Matt. xxv. 34.——2. The destruction of all his and our enemies; all wicked men, the beast and false prophet, and Satan, who will be cast by Christ into the lake which burns with fire and brimstone; even all those who would not have him to reign over them: and by all this, the ultimate end of all, the glory of God, will be answered; the glory of his divine perfections, in the salvation of his people, and in the destruction of the wicked; and the glorification of Christ in all them that believe, 2 Thess. i. 10.

CHAP. VI.

OF THE CONFLAGRATION OF THE UNIVERSE.

THE effects of Christ's second coming and personal appearance are many; as the resurrection of the just, of which we have treated at large already; and the burning of the world, and making new heavens and a new earth, and the reign of Christ there with his saints a thousand years; and then the general judgment: of all which in their order. And to begin with the universal conflagration; which is strongly and fully expressed by the apostle Peter, 2 Pet. iii. 10, 12. where he says, *the elements shall melt with fervent heat; the earth also, and the works that are therein, shall be burnt up:* which is to be understood of the burning of the whole sublunary and visible world; signified by the heavens and the earth, taken in a literal and not in a figurative sense.

1*st*, Not figuratively, as some[1] interpret them, of the Jewish church, and of the Mosaic elements, the ceremonial laws, and the abolition of them; and who suppose, that the *new heavens* and the *new earth*, in a following verse, design the evangelical church state, or gospel dispensation, which took place upon the removal of the former. But, 1. Though the civil state of the Jews is sometimes expressed by the heavens and the earth, and the removing of it by the shaking of them, Heb. xii. 26, 27. and sometimes by the *world*, at the end of which Christ came, and upon whose apostles, the ends of it were, Heb. ix. 26. 1 Cor. x. 11. yet the Jewish church is never called the world; for, in opposition to that, the Gentiles are called the world; the name of church the Jews took to themselves, that of the world they gave to the Gentiles, Rom. xi. 12, 15. hence the love of Christ in dying for the Gentiles, is expressed by this phrase, John iii. 16. 1 John ii. 2.——2. Though the commandments of the ceremonial law are called elements or rudiments, in allusion to the elements or rudiments of a language, to which children are put to learn; under which the Jews were whilst children; and whilst under the law, as a schoolmaster, Gal. iv. 3, 9. Col. ii. 20. yet they are never so called, in allusion to the elements, which belong to the system of

---

[1] Lightfoot's Works, vol. ii. p. 626, 1074. And Owen. Theologoumena, 1. 3. c. 1. p. 153.

the natural world, such as air and earth, which are only capable of being burnt; for surely the burning of a few papers or parchments of the law cannot be meant here.
—— 3. The abrogation of the ceremonial law is expressed by other phrases usually; as by the fleeing away of shadows, the breaking down the middle wall of partition, the abolishing of the law of commandments, and a disannulling of it; but never by burning, melting, and dissolving.——
4. The Mosaic elements or the ceremonial law and its precepts, were already abolished when Peter wrote this epistle; these had their end in Christ, and were done away at his death; signified by the rending of the temple-vail asunder; and Peter knew this, who was the first to whom it was made known, by letting down before him a sheet, in a visionary way, with all kind of creatures in it, which he was bid to slay and eat; and from whence he learnt that now nothing was to be reckoned common and unclean, that law which made the distinction being abrogated; whereas the melting of the elements was a future thing in his time, and is yet so. And likewise,
—— 5. The new heavens and the new earth, if by them are meant the evangelic state, or gospel church-state; that also had already taken place, and Peter was an instrument in the forming of it; he had the keys of the kingdom of heaven given him, and opened the door of faith by preaching the gospel to Jews and Gentiles; and on the day of Pentecost three thousand were converted and baptized, and added to the church, which was the first gospel church in Jerusalem; and therefore this was not a state to be looked for as to be in future time. But,

2*dly*, The words are to be understood literally; yet not of a partial burning of some particular place or city; not of the burning of Jerusalem, the city and temple, and inhabitants of it; which is the sense some[2] put upon them; and which some take into the former sense, and so make a motley sense of them, partly figurative and partly literal; but such a sense of the words cannot be admitted; for,—— 1. This would not afford a sufficient answer to the objection to the promise of Christ's coming, taken from the continuation of all things in the same situation as they were from the creation, ver. 4. for what change in the system of the universe would the burning of a single city, and of a temple in it, make? Changes and revolutions in single states, kingdoms, and cities, had been frequent, and these objectors could not be ignorant of them: but nothing less than such a change as was made by the flood, could strengthen the answer to the objection and serve to remove it. Wherefore,——
2. The destruction here spoken of is of equal extent with the destruction of the world by the flood; as the world, the whole world that then was, was overflowed by the flood and perished; so the heavens and the earth which are now, will be dissolved and burnt by fire; and nothing short of such a dissolution of the whole frame of nature can answer such a description. Besides, it may be further observed, as it has been,[3]—— 3. That the apostle's quoting a passage in ver. 8. from Psalm xc. 4. seems to suppose, that the time of Christ's coming might be then a thousand years off, as in fact it was, and much more, and yet be a short time with God, and might be spoken of as such; but to make mention of a thousand years must seem very improper, with respect to an event that was not twenty years to come; and which Christ had assured would be in that generation, Matt. xxiii. 36, 38, 39. and xxiv. 3, 34.—— 4. No such events as here mentioned happened at the destruction of Jerusalem and the burning of the temple; as the passing away of the heavens with a great noise, a fervent heat in them, to the liquefaction of the elements; with the burning of the earth and all works in it; for even the land of Judea itself was not thus burnt up, with the cities, towns, villages, and inhabitants of them, and all things in them.—— 5. Nor was this destruction so desirable a thing as to be looked for with pleasure, and the coming of Christ to effect it, to be hastened to, as in ver. 12. whereas Christ's coming to judge the quick and dead, at his appearing and kingdom, will be glorious, and is to be looked for and loved. To say no more,—— 6. The destruction here prophesied of, is expressly said to be at the day of judgment, against which day the heavens and the earth are reserved unto fire, ver. 7. so that, upon the whole, nothing else can be meant but the general conflagration of the world by fire in a literal sense. The nature and extent of this burning, will be more particularly considered after we have proved that such a

---

[2] Hammond in Loc.

[3] See Ray's Dissolution of the World, p. 244, 245.

conflagration is possible and probable, yea, certain; as will appear,

First, From partial burnings; which may be considered as types, emblems, and presages of the universal burning; as,——
1. The burning of Sodom and Gomorrah, and the cities of the plain; which were set forth for *an example of suffering the vengeance of eternal fire;* and why not then be considered as an emblem of the burning of the world at the last day? These cities were destroyed by fire which came down from heaven; and on a day, when in the morning there was no appearance nor likelihood of it; a fine, bright, sunshine morning, Gen. xix. 23, 24. and when the inhabitants of it were thoughtless and secure, and indulging themselves in pleasures; and thus, says our Lord, *shall it be in the day when the Son of man is revealed,* that is, in flaming fire, to take vengeance on the wicked, Luke xvii. 28, 29, 30. and if God could destroy these cities, and all in them, by fire from heaven, what should hinder but that he can destroy the whole world in like manner?——2. The destruction of Jerusalem, and the burning of the temple, were emblems of the destruction of the world by fire: hence in answer to the question, put by the disciples of Christ unto him, *What shall be the sign of thy coming, and of the end of the world?* Matt. xxiv. 3. our Lord gives such as were common, both to the destruction of Jerusalem, near at hand, and of the whole world, at the end of it, the one being typical of the other: and so these signs had a double accomplishment; first in the destruction of Jerusalem, and then in the final dissolution of the world. And so the destruction of the Jews, is sometimes expressed in such language as suits with the destruction of the whole world; particularly in Deut. xxxii. 22. *For a fire is kindled in my anger,* &c. And, indeed, this conflagration here spoken of, may be thought to reach further than the land of Judea, though that seems principally designed; even other parts of the earth, and to terminate in the destruction of the whole world; and so Justin Martyr[4] interprets it of the general conflagration. And though Jerusalem and the temple were not burnt by fire from heaven, yet the hand of God was so manifest therein, that Titus, the heathen emperor himself, could observe it; who strove, by all possible means, to prevent the burning of the temple, but could not do it; for God, as the historian observes, had adjudged it to the fire;[5] as, indeed, it was; our Lord foretold the burning of the city by the Romans, Matt. xxii. 6. and the burning of the temple is prophesied of in Zech. xi. 1. there called Lebanon, because built of the cedars of Lebanon.——3. The burning of the beast, of antichrist, and of the antichristian states. The judgment which will issue in that, is described in such manner as if the last and the great day of judgment was intended, and the dissolution of all things at hand; yet nothing else follows upon it, but the body of the beast being destroyed and committed to the burning flame, Dan. vii. 9, 10, 11. and the destruction of Idumæa, which seems to be a type of Rome and of the antichristian states, is expressed in such language as agrees very well with the dissolution and burning of the whole world, Isa. xxxiv. 4, 5, 6, 9, 10. of the burning of Rome, see Rev. xviii. 8—18.——4. The destruction of Gog and Magog, or the Turk, will be by fire; which will be at the beginning of the spiritual reign of Christ; and when the Jews are converted, and returned to their own land, which will irritate the Turk to bring his armies against them, the Lord will *rain upon him an overflowing rain, and great hailstones, fire and brimstone,* Ezek. xxxviii. 22. this is said of Gog; and the like is said of Magog, chap. xxxix. 6. *And I will send a fire on Magog:* these are different from the Gog and Magog in Rev. xx. 8, 9. who are no other than all the wicked dead raised; whereas these are the Turks; and they will appear at a different time; the one at the beginning of the spiritual reign of Christ, as before observed; and the other at the end of the personal reign of Christ, or the millennium; and so the fire that comes down from heaven on the one, is of a different nature from that which comes on the other; the one is a material fire, the other the wrath of God. Now these several partial burnings, as they are types and presages of the universal burning of the world, so they at least make that possible and probable.

Secondly, The probability of the universal conflagration, may be argued from the preparations in nature which are made and making for it; for the apostle says, that *the heavens and the earth which are now,* which are now in being, *are by the same word,* the word of God, *kept in store,* as a

---

[4] Apolog. 2. p. 93.

[5] Josephus de Bello Jud. l. 6. c. 4. s. 5, 6.

treasure, and are treasured up among the stores of vengeance, *reserved unto fire ;* for which preparations are making in them, *against the day of judgment, and perdition of ungodly men,* when it will break forth and destroy the universe and all things in it. Preparations are making in the earth for this general burning. Not to take notice of the central fire, supposed by some to be in the midst of the earth, since it is doubtful whether there is such a thing or not ; it is certain there are various *volcanos,* or burning mountains, in different parts of the world ; besides Mount Etna, in Sicily,[6] which has been burning for many ages, as also has Vesuvius, near Naples ; and the island of Strombilo, in the sea, which lies between them both, and is thought to have a communication with them under the bottom of the sea; and Lipara, near Sicily : and so far north as Iceland, there are three burning mountains ; one of them called Hecla, which oftentimes rages no less than Etna, vomiting out prodigious stones, with a terrible noise; besides hot springs in abundance. In the East Indies, in the island of Java, not far from the town Panacura, a mountain broke out in 1586, for the first time ; discharging such quantities of burning brimstone, that above ten thousand persons in the country round about were destroyed. The mount Gonnapi, in one of the islands of Banda, in the same year, which had been burning seventeen years, broke from the rest, throwing out a most dreadful quantity of burning matter, and great red-hot stones, &c. There is another mountain on the island of Sumatra, which smokes and flames just like Etna. The earth, in the Molucca islands, casts out fire in several places; as in Sorea and Celebes ; especially a mountain in Ternata. In one of the Moorish islands, sixty leagues from those of the Molucca, there happens very often earthquakes, with eruptions of fire and ashes. In Japan, and the islands about it, there are many little, and one great burning mountain ; nay, it is said,[7] there are eight *volcanos* in Japan, besides many hot springs. In Tandaja one of the Philippine islands, are found many small fire-mountains ; and one in the island Marindica, not far from them. The like are found in North America, in the province of Nicaragua. And in South America, in Peru, among those mountains that make the ridge of the Cordillera, near the city Arequipa, there flames a mountain continually. There is likewise one near the valley Mullahalo, which being opened by fire, casts out great stones. There are also several burning mountains in the district that lies on the east side of the river Jeniscea, in the country of the Tongesi, some weeks' journey from the river Oby, according to the relation of the Muscovites ; as also near another water called Besida. Near the island Santorini, no longer ago than the year 1707, sprung up a new island from the bottom of the sea ; in which, about the end of August that year, the subterraneous fires, after a terrible rumbling, burst out with such a violent noise as if six or seven pieces of cannon were discharged at once ; and frequently a great quantity of ashes, glowing stones, and huge pieces of burning rocks, have been tossed into the air with such a force, that they have been carried seven miles before they had dropped into the sea![8] Strabo[9] reports somewhat similar to this, as done near this place some hundreds of years ago. Nor is our island free from symptoms and appearances of subterraneous fires ; for by what are the hot waters at Bath and Bristol occasioned, but by them, by which they are heated ? Besides, there are eruptions of fire in some places in other parts of the land.[10] And by the above accounts it appears, that not only there have been burning mountains in ages past, in some places, even thousands of years ago ; but that new ones, in later times, have broke out : so that the preparation for the general burning of the world is still carried on and is increasing; and which may seem to portend its being near. And there is not only a preparation making in the earth, but in the heavens also, where there is great store of materials fit for this purpose

---

[6] Pliny speaks of the burning of Etna in his time, and says of it, that nature not only raged in it, but that it threatened and denounced the burning of the world; and he makes mention of several places then always burning, as in Phaselis, Lycia, Bactria, Media, Persia, Ethiopia, Babylonia, &c. Nat. Hist. 1. 2. c. 106, 107.

[7] Philosoph. Transact. abridged, vol. 3. p. 621.

[8] See Nieuwentyt's Religious Philosopher, vol. 2. contempl. 21. s. 18. p. 621, 622. Philosophical Transact. abridged, vol. 2. p. 391—394. and vol. 5. part 2. p. 196, &c.

[9] Geograph. 1. 1. p. 39. vide Justin. e Trogo, 1. 30. c. 4.

[10] Of a burning spring at Brosely in Shropshire; see Philosophical Transactions abridged, vol. 4. part 2. p. 195.

CHAP. VI.   OF THE CONFLAGRATION OF THE UNIVERSE.   629

provided; witness the fiery meteors in them, the blazing comets, which sometimes appear, and are always in being, though not always seen by us; also those vast bodies of light and fire, the sun and stars, to be made use of on occasion; and the vast quantities of matter which occasion such dreadful thunders and lightnings, which, in some parts of the world, are almost continual, and from which they are scarce ever free. Now when these things are considered, the general conflagration of the world will seem neither impossible nor improbable; but rather it may be wondered at, and thought a miracle, that the earth has not been destroyed by fire long ago. Let the atheist, the infidel, the profane and careless sinner tremble at this. Pliny,[11] the heathen, observing the many fires in the earth and in the heavens, and how easily fire is kindled by holding concave glasses to the sun, says, "It exceeds all miracles, that one day should pass and all things not put into a conflagration!"

Thirdly, What may make the doctrine of the universal conflagration probable, is, that it has been believed in all ages, and by all sorts of persons. Josephus[12] says, that Adam foretold the destruction of all things, at one time by the force of fire; and at another time by the violence and multitude of water; and therefore the posterity of Seth built two pillars, one of brick and the other of stone, on which they inscribed their inventions; that if that of brick was destroyed by the force of showers of rain, that of stone remaining, would shew to men what was written on the brick: from hence, or, however, from an early tradition, this notion of the burning of the world has been received and embraced by various nations, both Jews and Gentiles: as for the Jews, they might have it, not only from tradition, but might conclude it from the word of God, as they do; who say,[13] that though God has sworn he will not bring a flood of water on the world, yet he will bring a flood of fire; as it is said, Isa. lxvi. 16. *For by fire will the Lord plead*, or judge; hence they speak of the wicked being judged with two sorts of judgments, by water and by fire:[14] and this same tradition got among the Gentiles, and was received by them; as by the Indians,[15] the inhabitants of Siam and Pegu, the Egyptians, the Chaldæans, and the ancient Gauls and Britons, and the Druids among them.[16] And it has been embraced by poets and philosophers, Greek and Latin. Lactantius[17] quotes a prophecy of one of the sybils, that as God formerly destroyed the world with a flood, so he would hereafter destroy mankind for their wickedness by burning. Justin Martyr[18] observes, that the sybil, Hystaspes (the Persian) and the Stoics, assert, that corruptible things shall be destroyed by fire. Orpheus, that very ancient poet, as quoted by Plato,[19] affirmed, that in the sixth generation, the world, κατακαυσται, (so it should be read) shall be burnt; and Sophocles, as quoted by Justin,[20] and Clemens of Alexandria,[21] speaks of this burning. The verses of Ovid,[22] concerning this matter, and so of Lucan,[23] are well known. The philosophers make frequent mention of it; Empedocles[24] says, there shall be sometime a change of the world into the substance of fire. And Heraclitus taught,[25] that as all things are of fire, all shall be resolved into it again: and that as the world was generated out of fire, in a course of years the whole world shall be burnt again; and so say Hippasus,[26] and Phurnutus;[27] and Zeno[28] expresses himself almost in the words of Peter, that the elements shall be destroyed, or corrupted, by a fiery eruption; and Plato,[29] in so many words, says, in length of time, or, as some read it, in a short time, there will be a destruction of the things on the earth by much fire. And it is the observation of many writers, that the Stoic philosophers held an εκπυρωσις, or conflagration of the world by fire; Epictetus[30] speaks of it; and so does Seneca,[31]

---

[11] Ut supra, c. 107.
[12] Antiq. 1. 1. c. 2. s. 3.
[13] T. Bab. Zebachim, fol. 116. 1.
[14] Zohar in Gen. fol. 50. 4. et 51. 1.
[15] Ross's View of all Religions, p. 51, 52.
[16] Strabo, 1. 4. p. 136.
[17] De Ira Dei, c. 23.
[18] Apol. 2. p. 66.
[19] In Philebo, p. 406. vid Plutarch. de Oracul. Defect. p. 415.
[20] De Monarchia, p. 105.
[21] Stromat. 1. 5. p. 606.
[22] Esse quoque in fatis, &c. Metamorph. 1. 1. fab. 7.
[23] Pharsalia, 1. 7. v. 812, &c.
[24] Apud Clem. Alex. Stromat. 1. 5. p. 599.
[25] Laert. 1. 9. in Vita Heracliti. vid. Hesychium de Philosoph. p. 35.
[26] Plutarch. de Placit. Philosoph. 1. 1. p. 877.
[27] De Natura Deorum, p. 39.
[28] Laert, 1. 7. in Vita Zenonis.
[29] In Timæo, p. 1043.
[30] Arrian. Epictet. 1. 3. c. 13.
[31] Nat. Quæst. 1. 3. c. 13. vid. Consolat. ad Marciam, c. 26.

who says, that fire is the *exitus* of the world; nay, Minutius Felix [32] asserts, that this was not only the constant opinion of the Stoics; but that the same was the sentiment of the Epicureans, concerning the conflagration of the elements, and the ruin of the world; and it has been observed, that of all the heretics under the Christian name, none have risen up who have denied the dissolution of the world by fire. Now that men of different nations, and ages, and sentiments, should agree in this, makes it probable that so it may be: but we have a more sure word of prophecy, which makes this matter certain to us Christians. Wherefore,

Fourthly, That the world, and all things in it, shall at last be consumed by fire, may be concluded from the sacred scriptures. And,

1*st,* From Psalm l. 3. *Our God shall come,* &c. By *our God,* is meant Christ, *Immanuel, God with us;* called *the mighty God,* ver. 1. and is one of his names, Isa. ix. 6. who, as at his first coming, came out of Zion, ver. 2. so he will when he comes again, Joel iii. 16. of which second coming these words are to be understood; as appears by his order to gather his saints to him, ver. 5. which order will be given to his angels, to gather his elect from the four winds, when raised from the dead, at his coming, Matt. xxiv. 30. and by his appearing under the character of a Judge, ver. 6. to judge his people, ver. 4. and even all the inhabitants of the earth, who will be called from one end of it to the other, ver. 1. and be judged in righteousness; and so the Targum applies the text to the judgment of the great day,[33] when he will *not keep silence.* His descent from heaven will be with a shout, with the voice of the archangel, and the trump of God; when his voice will be heard from the rising of the sun to the going down of it; and reach the dead in their graves, who will hear it and come forth; and then a *fire shall devour before him,* and consume all in the way, dissolve the heavens, melt the elements and burn the earth, and all in it, and be *tempestuous round about him;* which agrees with Peter's account of the conflagration, that the heavens shall pass away with a *great noise,* ροιζηδον, like that of a storm and tempest; and now in a literal sense, will the Lord rain upon the wicked fire and brimstone, and *an horrible tempest!* Psalm xi. 6.

2*dly,* From Psalm xcvii. 3, 4, 5. *A fire goeth before him,* to make way for him, by destroying every thing combustible; *and burneth up his enemies round about,* who would not have him to reign over them, reject him as a Saviour, despise his gospel, and submit not to his ordinances; so the fire with which the world shall be burnt, is *for the perdition of ungodly men,* all the wicked inhabitants of the earth; it will leave none: *his lightnings lightened the world;* such dreadful thunder and lightning will be in the heavens, that the coruscations thereof will blaze all over the world; the sight of which will be so awful and tremendous, that *the earth,* the inhabitants of it, will *see and tremble,* fearing the flashes of it will consume them: *the hills melted like wax* before the fire, *at the presence of the Lord, at the presence of the Lord of the whole earth;* who will now come to judge the world with righteousness, and the people with equity; as at the close of the preceding Psalm, with which this is connected; when *righteousness and judgment* will be *the habitation of his throne,* and he will sit on his throne judging righteously; when he will come in the *clouds* of heaven, and be surrounded with them, ver. 2. and when he will take to himself his great power and *reign,* which will cause joy and gladness to his people, ver. 1. for his judging of quick and dead, will be at his appearing and kingdom, 2 Tim. iv. 1. for all these things go together; Christ's appearance in the clouds, taking possession of his kingdom, the judgment of quick and dead, and the burning of his enemies.

3*dly,* From Isa. xxiv. which is a prophecy, not of the destruction of a single state and kingdom, but of the whole world; as appears from ver. 1, 3, 4, 19, 20. and which is expressed by a *dissolution* of it, and by *burning the inhabitants* thereof, ver. 19, 6. and is spoken of as what will immediately precede the personal and glorious reign of Christ, ver. 23.

4*thly,* From Isa. lxvi. 15, 16. *For behold the Lord will come with fire,* &c. which perfectly agrees with the account of Christ's coming to burn the world, and take vengeance on the wicked, given in the New Testament, 2 Thess. i. 7, 8. 2 Pet. iii. 10. *For by fire, and by his sword,* which proceeds out of his mouth, *will the Lord plead with all flesh,* with all mankind, or *judge* them;

---

[32] Octav. p. 37.

[33] So Austin de Civ. Dei, l. 20. c. 24.

CHAP. VI.   OF THE CONFLAGRATION OF THE UNIVERSE.   631

for of Christ's coming to judgment must this be understood; for the judgment is universal. In the former part of the chapter are various prophecies concerning the spiritual reign of Christ, the conversion of the Jews, and a large addition to the church from among the Gentiles, and of the great peace and prosperity of it, ver. 7—13. an hint is given of the resurrection of the dead, ver. 14. *Your bones shall flourish like an herb;*[34] compare with it chap. xxvi. 19. which will be at Christ's second coming; and after this, mention is made *of the new heavens and the new earth,* ver. 22. which will succeed the old heavens and earth that will perish in the conflagration of the universe.

5*thly,* From the various passages in the minor prophets; particularly in Nahum i. 3, 4, 5. for though the prophecy is concerning the destruction of Nineveh, yet God is described as what he will appear to be, and by what he will do at the dissolution of all things; *the Lord hath his way in the whirlwind and in the storm;* and in such an one the heavens will pass away, according to the apostle Peter: *And the clouds are the dust of his feet;* in these the Lord of the whole earth, the Son of man, will come to judgment. *He rebuketh the sea, and maketh it dry, and drieth up all the rivers;* which yet was never done; but will be done at the conflagration of the world; hence John says, *The first heaven, and the first earth, were passed away, and there was no more sea,* Rev. xxi. 1. being dried up at the general burning. *Bashan languisheth, and Carmel, and the flower of Lebanon languisheth;* the trees, herbs, and flowers, which covered and adorned these mountains, being all consumed by the fire; *and the hills melt, and the earth is burnt at his presence; yea, the world and all that dwell therein!* than which nothing can more fitly agree with the description the apostle Peter gives of the dissolution of all things, 2 Pet. iii. 10.

Some passages in Zeph. i. 2, 3, 18. seem to look this way; for though the destruction of the land of Judea is particularly threatened; yet they seem to have a further view, even to all the nations and kingdoms of the whole world, and to all the earth, which shall be devoured with the fire of God's jealousy, chap. iii. 8. and the time of it is called, *the great day of the Lord,* ver. 14. the day of judgment, the judgment of the great day, as that is called in the New Testament; against which the fire that shall burn the world is reserved, Jude ver. 6. 2 Pet. iii. 7. but especially the prophecy in Mal. iv. 1, 2, 3. in the ultimate completion of it, may be thought to respect the general conflagration; for though it may be applied to the destruction of Jerusalem, and the Jews in it, and to Christ's coming to take vengeance on them, yet only as a type and emblem of this; *for behold, the day cometh that shall burn as an oven;* the day of the Lord, as Peter expresses it, which will burn like an oven indeed, with great fury and fierceness; so that the heavens shall pass away, the elements melt, and the earth, and all therein, be burnt up; and *all the proud,* the despisers of Christ and his gospel, *and all that do wickedly, shall be stubble;* fit for such an oven, and which the fire will soon and easily consume; *and shall burn them up, that it shall leave them neither root nor branch;* not one wicked man will escape the conflagration, all will be burnt in it; yet the wicked only; for the righteous dead, who will then be raised, and the living saints, who will be changed, will be caught up together into the clouds, to meet the Lord in the air; and will be carried up far enough to be out of the reach of the devouring flames; and these are they who are meant by such that fear the Lord, to whom *the Sun of righteousness shall arise;* Christ shall appear to them as bright and as glorious, as comfortable and delightful, as the sun; and arise on them *with healing in his wings;* so that they, the inhabitants of the new heavens and the new earth, which will now be formed, *shall not say, I am sick;* these will be the times of refreshing from the presence of the Lord, and *the wicked shall be ashes under the soles of their feet:* which words will be literally fulfilled; for the wicked being burnt, and their ashes mixed with that matter which shall form the new earth, and be interred in it, the saints that dwell on it, will, in a literal sense, tread on them; and they will be, not as ashes, but really ashes, under the soles of their feet.

It will be needless to take notice of passages in the New Testament; since the famous one in Peter, which so fully asserts, and so clearly describes the conflagration, has been throughly considered, and its sense established; and the text in 2 Thess. i. 7, 8. has been often quoted, or referred to; only

---

[34] Ubi Resurrectionem Corporum Strinxit. Aug. de Civ. Dei. 1. 20. c. 21.

it may be proper to take notice of what our Lord says shall be at the end of the world, at the dissolution of it, and which plainly suggests it shall be by fire; that *as the tares are gathered and burnt in the fire, so shall it be at the end of the world;* the wicked shall be gathered and separated from the righteous, and be cast into a furnace of fire; and such the world will be when destroyed by fire, and all the wicked in it, Matt. xiii. 40, 41, 42, 49, 50. Proof being thus given of the general conflagration, I proceed,

Fifthly, To answer some queries relative to it; as with what sort of fire the world will be burnt? what the extent of this burning? and whether the earth will be destroyed by it as to its substance, or only as to its qualities?

1st, With what sort of fire the world will be burnt? Not with fire taken in a figurative, but in a literal sense; not with metaphorical, but material fire. Fire is sometimes taken figuratively for the wrath of God, whose fury is poured forth like fire, Nahum i. 5. see Psalm xviii. 8. and lxxix. 5. But though the burning of the world will be the effect of God's wrath against sinners for their sins, yet that will be executed by means of material fire: the world will be burnt with such fire as will come from heaven, and break forth out of the earth; with such fire from heaven by which Sodom and Gomorrah, and the cities of the plain were destroyed; with which Aaron's two sons were consumed; with which the two hundred and fifty men of Korah's company were destroyed; with which the two captains, and their fifties, perished, who came to take the prophet Elijah; of the same sort with that which fell on Job's sheep, and the servants that kept them, and killed them; and such as very often flashes from heaven, and destroys houses, buildings, men, and cattle: and such fire as breaks out of the earth, of which various instances have been given, in volcanos, and other eruptions; and like that which the historian[35] speaks of, which many hundreds of years ago broke out of the earth in Germany, and burnt towns, villages, and fields every where, and was with great difficulty extinguished. So that the world will be destroyed by fire much in the same manner as it was by water: the flood was brought upon it partly by the windows of heaven being opened above, which let down rain; and partly by the fountains of the great deep being broke up below, which sent forth great quantities of water; and both meeting together, drowned the world: so the stores of fire in the heavens being opened, and great quantities issuing out of the bowels of the earth, these joining together will set the whole world on fire, heavens and earth, and bring on their speedy dissolution. Some have thought the stars will have a great influence in this affair. Berosus, an ancient writer, says,[36] that it will be according to the course of the stars; and that all earthly things will be burnt up, when all the stars shall meet in Cancer: and one Serarius,[37] in the last century, because of the conjunction of all the planets in Sagittarius, a fiery sign, conjectured that the burning of the world was near; and Mr. Whiston,[38] of the present age, fancied the world will be burnt by the near approach of a comet to it; so the Brahmins.[39] But for such conjectures there is no foundation; the manner seems to be as before described. This fire will be but temporary, it will last but for a time; how long the world will be burning cannot be known; fire usually makes quick dispatch, and consumes presently; and so it is to be distinguished from that fire in which the wicked will be tormented, that is called everlasting fire, fire which cannot be quenched, the smoke of which ascends for ever and ever, Matt. xxv. 41. Mark ix. 44. Rev. xiv. 10, 11.

2dly, What will be the extent of this burning? or how far, and to what will it reach? To the heavens, the elements, the earth, and all the works in it.———1. To the heavens; not to the third heaven, into which the apostle Paul was caught up, and heard and saw what it was not lawful to utter; for this is the throne of God, the habitation of angels and glorified saints, and now the residence of the glorious body of Christ; but the fire will not reach the palace of Jehovah; nor at all annoy any of his courtiers and friends: it is a question, whether it will reach the starry-heaven, or at all affect the luminaries of the sun, moon, and stars; for though the city of the perfect saints, the inhabitants of the new heavens and earth, will stand in no need of the sun and moon to enlighten them,

---

[35] Tacit. Annal. l. 13. c. 57.
[36] Apud Senecæ Nat. Quæst. l. 3. c. 29.
[37] Apud Heidegger. Dissert. 24. de Signis Cœlest. s. 8.

[38] New Theory of the Earth, b. 4. c. 5.
[39] Bedang, ch. 1. apud Dow's Hist. of Hindostan.

CHAP. VI. OF THE CONFLAGRATION OF THE UNIVERSE.

it does not follow that these then will not be; but rather it is implied, that they will be, though the saints will not need them. Things that are durable, are said sometimes to endure, as the sun, and moon, and stars, for ever and ever; and it seems as if these will be always continued, as monuments of the power, wisdom, and goodness of God. But it will be the airy heaven,[40] that will be the subject of the conflagration, the atmosphere about us, the surrounding air, and the meteors in it. Some have thought this burning will reach no farther than the waters of the flood did, which covered the highest hills, and it may be reached fifteen cubits higher; but that is no certain rule to go by: however, as the fowls of the heaven or air, were destroyed by that, so they will by this, Gen. vii. 23. Zeph. i. 3.——2. To the earth, and all the works that are in it; to the whole terraqueous globe, both land and sea: it may seem a difficulty, how that part of the globe which contains such vast quantities of water, as are in the main ocean, in other seas, and in the rivers, should be consumed hereby; yet this will be none, when the omnipotence of God is considered, and what the prophet says of him with respect to this affair; *He rebuketh the sea, and maketh it dry, and drieth up all the rivers,* Nahum. i. 4. which will be the case, as represented to John in a vision, who saw the first heaven and earth pass away, and new ones succeed; and *there was no more sea,* that being dried up; see Amos vii. 4. This fire will reach to all the living creatures in the earth, land, and sea, the works of God's hands: as the fowls of the air, so the fishes of the sea, and " the cattle on a thousand hills;" all the beasts of the field, and all men found on the earth; all the wicked of the earth, who will be all burnt up root and branch, not one will escape. This fire is reserved for the perdition of ungodly men. It will extend to all the works of nature, mountains, hills, and rocks, metals and minerals in the bowels of them, and all that cover and ornament them, trees, herbs, plants, and flowers; for as the prophets says in the above place, *Bashan languisheth, and Carmel and the flower of Lebanon languisheth,* being stripped of all their glory; the same will be true of all other mountains and hills: It will consume all the works of art, towers, palaces, and stately buildings, which it was thought would have continued for ever; all the utensils and instruments of various manufactories; and all the curious things wrought by the hands of men. Likewise all literary works, the archives and records of kingdoms, states, and cities; the treaties, covenants, and agreements of princes; compacts between men; bonds, bills, deeds of conveyance of right to estates, lands, possessions, and inheritances; all the writings of men, good and bad: all that good men have wrote for the use of the church, which will be continued to this time, will now be destroyed, there being no further need of them, and use for them. Some think that moral works and actions are included, and that these are the works that will be burnt up, and this the fire the apostle speaks of in 1 Cor. iii. 13, 14, 15. but such works are not the subjects of fire; nor is it such fire the world will be destroyed with that is there meant: the *day* that shall declare every man's work, is the bright day of the gospel, in the spiritual reign of Christ; the light of which will be as the light of seven days, when the people of God, ministers and others, will see eye to eye; every truth will be seen in its true light, and be easily distinguished from error: and the *fire* designs the gospel, which will then burn bright and clear, and burn up every thing contrary to it; and so by *works* are meant doctrines, some comparable to gold, silver, and precious stones, which will bear the test of this day, and the fire; and others like wood, hay, and stubble, which will not be able to stand before them: and it should be observed, that the apostle is speaking of good men and ministers, who were on the foundation themselves, and laid the foundation, Christ, ministerially; but laid different things on this foundation, some very good, others good for nothing, and a mixture of both; which, when the day, the time spoken of comes, will be declared and distinguished; such as will abide the scrutiny and test, shall be rewarded in the kingdom-state; but such as will not, will be condemned, as not agreeable to the word, though the ministers of them, as to their persons, shall be saved, being on the foundation, Christ.

Here let it be observed, for the comfort of the saints, that there are many things which will escape the general conflagration; as the *book of life,* in which the names of God's elect are written; the *covenant of grace,* which contains the *magna*

---

[40] So Augustin. de Civ. Dei, l. 20. c. 18, 24.

charta of their salvation; the *word of God*, as it is the engrafted word in their hearts; their *title*, to the heavenly inheritance; the *inheritance itself*, which is incorruptible, and reserved in the heavens: nor shall they *themselves* be destroyed in it; the wicked will be all burnt in it, not one will escape that will then be found on the earth: but as for the saints, the dead bodies of all who have died from the beginning of the world will be raised, and their souls being brought by Christ along with him, will be reunited to them; and they, with the living saints then on earth, who will be changed, shall be caught up together into the clouds, to meet the Lord in the air; and shall be carried up high enough, and be with him out of the reach of this fire;[41] so that it may be said of them, as of Daniel's three companions in the furnace, that not an hair of their heads shall be singed, nor the smell of fire pass upon their garments.

3dly, The next query is, whether the earth shall be dissolved by fire, as to its substance, or only as to its qualities? There are persons of great note on both sides of the question; and the arguments of each are not despicable; but I rather incline to the latter, that the world will only be destroyed with respect to its qualities; those who are for the destruction of the world as to the substance of it, argue both from reason and scripture.——1. From reason: they urge, that as the world was made out of nothing, it shall be reduced to nothing again. But this reasoning will not hold good; for there are some beings which are produced out of nothing, which shall not be annihilated; as angels, and the souls of men, neither of which are formed out of any pre-existent matter, but out of nothing; and so being immaterial, are immortal, and shall never die, nor be reduced to nothing. They argue also, that there will be no farther use of the world hereafter, and of the things of it; and as God does nothing in vain, therefore it will not be continued any longer, as to its substance, men ceasing to be upon it, for whose use it was made. But it is more than we are able to say, that it will be of no use hereafter; there are some things that will be in a future state, that we are not able to assign the uses of; as some parts of the human body, when that shall be raised, as no doubt it will be, with all its parts, some of which are not suited to a state in which there will be no eating nor drinking, nor marrying, nor giving in marriage; yet be raised with the rest, both for the perfection of the body and the ornament of it: and besides, if for nothing else, this world, as to the substance, may be continued as a standing monument of the power, wisdom, and goodness of God; to which may be added, that there will be men to inhabit it, even all the righteous ones, at least for the space of a thousand years. It is farther observed, that God usually proceeds from things less perfect, to things more perfect; and so from things temporal to things spiritual and eternal. To which may be replied, that this will be the case, by renewing the earth as to its qualities; it will become more perfect, and be suitable to men in a perfect state, and whose bodies will be raised spiritual and immortal.——2. They also argue from scripture; as even from the text in 2 Pet. iii. 10. and observe, that the heavens are said to pass away, the elements to melt, the earth, and all therein, burnt up; which they judge, can intend no other than a substantial destruction of the world. But the phrases are not strong enough[42] to support this; the heavens may pass away into another state and form, as the fashion of the world will, and yet not be dissolved as to their substance: things may be melted, as wax, and other things; which, though they lose their form, do not lose their being; and things being burnt, may be reduced to ashes, yet not annihilated; ashes are something. They urge the text in Psalm cii. 26. *They*, the heavens, *shall perish, but thou shalt endure; they all shall wax old as a garment, as a vesture thou shalt change them, and they shall be changed*. But those on the other side of the question, urge the same text in favour of their sentiment; since the perishing of the heavens, is explained by changing them; and all change does not suppose a destruction of substance; and a garment that is waxed old, may be refitted, and put into a new form, and be for more and after use; and besides, the author of the epistle

---

[41] Futuros eos esse in superioribus partibus, quo ita non ascendit flamma illius incendii, Aug. de Civ. Dei, 1. 20. c. 18.

[42] Sed puto quod præterit, transit, transibunt, aliquando mitius dicta sunt quam peribunt, Aug. de Civ. Dei, 1. 20. c. 24. Mutatione namque rerum, non omnino interitu transibit hic mundus ——figura ergo præterit, non natura, ibid. c. 14.

CHAP. VI.   OF THE CONFLAGRATION OF THE UNIVERSE.   635

to the Hebrews, interprets this change by a folding up of a vesture, which is done in order to be laid up, and made use of hereafter. A similar place is produced by them, in Isa. li. 6. *The heavens shall vanish away like smoke;* but then smoke is something, and that vanishes into air, and that air is something; *And the earth shall wax old like a garment;* but that, as before observed, may be fitted up in another manner, and be for the better; *And they that dwell therein shall die in like manner:* but if the heavens and the earth perish in like manner as men do, they do not perish as to their substance, neither with respect to body nor soul; the body, at death, returns to the earth and dust, from whence it was, and the soul to God that gave it. They instance also in Isa. lxv. 17. *Behold, I create new heavens and a new earth;* and therefore the old heavens and earth must be destroyed, as to their substance, since the new ones are not formed out of them, but are created; and creation is a production of things out of nothing. But it may be observed, that the word *create* does not always so signify; but sometimes only the renovation of what already is; as in Psalm li. 10. They likewise make use of all those scriptures which speak of the heavens, and the earth, and the world, passing away, Matt. v. 18. and xxiv. 35. 1 John ii. 17. in what sense they may be said to pass away, as in 2 Pet. iii. 10. has been observed already. The first of those scriptures only says, *till heaven and earth pass,* which will never be; and so not one jot or tittle of the law shall pass till all be fulfilled: the other indeed asserts, that *heaven and earth shall pass away;* but then the sense may be only comparatively, that sooner shall heaven and earth pass away, as they never shall, than that *Christ's words shall pass away:* the last of them refers to the fashion of the world, and the lusts in it, which shall pass away, and have no place in the new earth; in which, not worldly and sinful lusts, only righteousness shall dwell. All such passages of scripture, likewise, which speak of *the end of the world,* are brought into this argument: but these, some of them, have only reference to the end of the Jewish state; as 1 Cor. x. 11. Heb. ix. 26. and others only refer to the present state of things in the world; but not to the destruction of it; as Matt. xxviii. 20. and such passages which only respect the mutability of the things of this world, and the temporary enjoyment of them, can be of no use in this controversy; as Heb. xiii. 14. 2 Cor. iv. 18. So likewise, when the Angel sware *that time shall be no more,* it can be understood only of antichristian time, or of the time of the reign of antichrist; of the holy city being trodden under foot by the Gentiles; of the witnesses prophesying in sackcloth; and of the church being in the wilderness; which will be finished at the period referred to: but then all time, in every sense, is not then to be no longer; for not only after that, but after the first resurrection, and the general conflagration, there will be a time of a thousand years at least, in which the saints will dwell with Christ on earth.

Those who suppose that the world will be only destroyed, as to the qualities of it, argue also from reason and scripture.

1. From reason: they observe that the old world which perished by the flood, was not destroyed as to its substance; for after the waters were removed from off the earth, Noah, with his family, and all the creatures with him in the ark, went out of it upon the earth; and he built an altar on it, and sacrificed; and he and his sons repeopled the earth. And in like manner, the earth will not be destroyed by fire, as to its substance; but renewed, so as to be inhabited again. They farther observe, that man, who is a microcosm, a little world, a world in miniature, when he perishes by death, it is not a destruction of him as to his substance, neither of soul nor body, as before observed. Besides, if God meant to annihilate the world, he would not make use of fire; for fire, though it divides and separates the parts of matter, it does not destroy it; it purges, purifies, and refines: but does not reduce the substance of anything to nothing. Besides, bodies raised, must have a place to be in, to stand before God in, at judgment: and to be either in a state of happiness or misery afterwards; for which there would be no place found, if the world, as to the substance of it, was dissolved.

2. They likewise produce passages of scripture, and argue from them, against the substantial destruction of the world, and for the change of it only, as to qualities. That the earth, as to the matter and substance of it, shall always abide, they urge Psalm civ. 5. and Eccles. i. 4. They argue from some of the places brought by others for the utter destruction of the

world; as Psalm cii. 26. Isa. li. 6. on the former of which they observe, with Jerom on the place, that the words do not express the utter destruction of the world, but a change of it for the better: and on the latter, that the words suggest, that the heavens and the earth will perish in like manner as men do at death; which is not a destruction of their being, but a change of them into another form and state. They reason from all those scriptures which speak of a new heaven and a new earth; that these signify renewed ones, not new as to substance, but quality: as a new heart, and a new spirit, do not design a new soul of man, new powers and faculties; but a renewing of the same as to qualities. They observe what the apostle says, *The fashion of this world passeth away*, 1 Cor. vii. 31. the scheme, the figure, and form of it, in its present situation; not the matter and substance of it. And they farther observe, that the state of the world at this time, is expressed by a *regeneration* of it, Matt. xix. 28. and by a *restitution of all things*, Acts iii. 21. which signify a forming and restoring them to a more pure and glorious state. I take no notice of Rom. viii. 19, &c. commonly made use of on this subject, because I think it belongs to something else,[43] and to another time; and from the whole, those on this side the question conclude, that the dissolution of the world by fire, will be only a purging, purifying, and refining it, as to its form and quality, and a removing from it every thing included in the curse, which the sin of man brought upon it; and so will become an habitation fit for the second Adam, and his holy, spiritual, and perfect offspring. But of this more in the following chapter.

CHAP. VII.

OF THE NEW HEAVENS AND EARTH, AND THE INHABITANTS OF THEM.

We have seen the world laid in ashes; and now we shall take a view of it as rising out of them. The eastern people had a tale, or fable, concerning a bird, called the *phoenix*; which many writers, both Heathen, Jewish, and Christian, have taken notice of;[1] concerning which they say, there is but one of them in the world at a time; that it is very long-lived, according to some it lives a thousand years; and when its end draws near, it makes itself a bed of spices, and seats itself on it, and by some means or other fire takes it, and it is burnt to ashes in it; from whence springs a worm, or egg, and from thence another *phoenix*: this some take to be an emblem of the resurrection; but it rather seems to be a fable, devised by the Indians, or Arabians, to transmit to posterity their traditional doctrine of the conflagration, and renovation of the world. The heathens had some notion of good men dwelling in pure and beautiful habitations on earth; so Plato says,[2] it was the opinion of the Stoics,[3] that at a certain determined time the whole world would be burnt; so that it would immediately be beautified and adorned again, and exist as it was before, perfectly beautiful. This is more clearly revealed in the sacred scriptures; and as the apostle Peter fully expresses the former, as we have seen, so he strongly asserts the latter, and his faith, hope, and expectation of it: nevertheless, though the heavens and the earth shall be burnt up, *we* believers, we christians, favoured with a divine revelation, *look for*, believe and expect, *new heavens and a new earth*, in the room of the former, consumed by fire, *wherein dwelleth righteousness*, righteous persons, and they only, 2 Pet. iii. 13. The promise of this referred to, is in Isa. lxv. 17. which is introduced with a *Behold*, as being something extraordinary and wonderful, and worthy of attention; *For behold, I create new heavens and a new earth, &c.* which being obscure in itself, is explained by the apostle: and what makes prophesies respecting the last times, so difficult of interpretation, is, their being mixed; some things in the context belonging to the spiritual, and others to the personal reign of Christ, which is the case here: however, the passage itself,[4] most certainly belongs to a perfect state, in which righteousness will dwell, as Peter says; and entirely agrees with John's account of the inhabitants of the new heavens and the new earth; who represents the new Jerusalem as coming down from

---

[43] See my Exposition of Rom. viii. 19, &c.
[1] Vid. Texelii Phoenix.
[2] In Phædone, p. 84.
[3] Aristot. apud Euseb. Evangel. Præpar. 1. 15. c. 14. Numenius in ibid. c. 18. Philo, quod mundus sit incorrupt. p. 940.
[4] Aben Ezra observes, that it respects the world to come, and is not in connection with the context, and is a truth that is alone by itself.

heaven, to dwell on the new earth, where the tabernacle of God will be with men; and he will shew himself to be their God, and them to be his people; and so it will be a time of great joy and gladness; and in Isaiah it is said, *Behold, I create Jerusalem a rejoicing, and her people a joy!* John says, in this state *there shall be no more sorrow nor crying*; which entirely agrees with the prophet, who says, *The voice of weeping shall be no more heard in her, nor the voice of crying!* which cannot be said of any state of the church in the present earth; and is only true of its perfect state in the new heavens and the new earth. The things to be enquired into are, what these new heavens and earth be, and who the inhabitants of them.

I. What are meant by the new heavens and the new earth in the above passages? these are to be understood not in a figurative, but in a literal sense.

First, Not in a figurative sense; 1. Not of the gospel church-state, or the gospel dispensation, in which indeed old things passed away, and all things became new; the former covenant waxed old and vanished away; the old Jewish church-state was abolished, and a new church-state set up; the ordinances of the former dispensation were removed, and new ones appointed: but then, as observed in the preceding chapter, this state had taken place before the apostle Peter wrote his epistle; and therefore he could never speak of the new heavens and new earth in this sense as future; nor say, that he and others were looking for them when they were already in being; and so likewise before the apostle John had his vision of them. John the Baptist and Christ began their ministry with saying, *the kingdom of heaven* was *at hand*, the gospel dispensation was just ushering in; yea our Lord afterwards says, the kingdom of God was among the Jews, though it came not with observation, and was weak and obscure: but after his death and resurrection, when he gave his disciples a commission to preach the gospel to all the world, and furnished them with gifts and abilities for it, and they accordingly preached it everywhere with success; then it plainly appeared that the gospel-church-state had commenced: besides, the gospel-church-state, even in the first and purest ages of it, was not so perfect as the state of things will be in the new heavens and new earth, in which none but righteous persons, and such as are perfectly righteous, will dwell; for into the new Jerusalem the seat of which will be the new heavens, and new earth, none shall enter that defiles or makes an abomination or a lie; whereas in the gospel-church-state, there always was, is, and will be, a mixture, of true believers and carnal professors; look into the first churches at Jerusalem, Antioch, Galatia, Corinth, &c. and you will find persons either of bad principles or of bad practices complained of. Moreover, in the new Jerusalem state, which will have its seat in the new heavens and new earth, there will be no temple, no worship, in the manner that now is in the gospel-church-state; no ministry of the word, nor administration of ordinances; the Lamb will be the temple and the light thereof; to which may be added, that in that state there will be no more death, sorrow, and crying: but death did not cease when the gospel-church-state took place, it has continued ever since, and is the last enemy that shall be destroyed; the putting men to death for the sake of Christ and his gospel began very early, in the first times of the gospel, both in Judea and in the Gentile world; and continued under Rome pagan and papal, and more or less to this day. Other things might be observed which shew that the new heavens and the new earth cannot be understood of this state; and for the same reasons they cannot be understood of the times of Constantine and following ones, at least for some of the above reasons.——2. Nor of the state of the Jews at the time of their conversion; for though there will be a new face of things then with respect to them; they will quit their old notions of the Messiah, and relinquish their old laws, customs, and modes of worship; and embrace the gospel, and submit to the ordinances of it, and join themselves to gospel churches, or be formed upon the same plan with them; and be called by a new name, which the mouth of the Lord shall name. But then this will be before the new heavens and the new earth are formed; the conversion of the Jews is designed in Rev. xix. 7, 8. and is what will introduce, or be a part of the spiritual reign; but the vision of the new heavens and the new earth is in chap. xxi. which respects a more glorious state of the church, and the personal reign of Christ in it.——3. Nor of the spiritual reign of Christ, which will be in the present earth and not in the new one; and in which will be the ministry of the word and ordinances: the everlasting gospel will be preached to all nations, by means of which the earth will be filled with the knowledge of the Lord, and gospel churches be planted everywhere, and gospel worship be carried on as now, only with greater purity; but in the new Jerusalem state, the seat of which will be the new heavens and the new earth, there will be nothing of this kind, as before observed; and though there will be then a great degree of spirituality and holiness, yet it will not be so perfect a state as that will be in the new heavens and the new earth; in which there will be only righteous persons, nothing that defileth, only the holy city, having the glory of God upon her, will dwell in them. But in the spiritual reign, the church will not be quite clear of hypocrites and nominal professors, and will sink into lukewarmness and indifference, into spiritual pride and carnality, even into a Laodicean state.——4. Nor of the heavenly state, or the ultimate glory; for these new heavens and earth are distinct from the third heaven, the seat of that. The new Jerusalem, the inhabitants of it, are said to come down out of heaven to reside upon the new earth; where the tabernacle of God will be with them, which denotes a moveable state, as a tabernacle is a moveable thing, and so distinct from the fixed state of the saints in the ultimate glory. The camp of the saints, and the holy and beloved city, are represented as on earth, even at the end of the thousand years. Rev. xx. 9. But,

Secondly, The new heavens and new earth are to be understood in a literal sense of the natural heavens and earth. It is a rule to be observed, that a literal sense is not to be departed from without necessity. Now there is no necessity, nothing that obliges to depart from such a sense here; it does not contradict any other passage of scripture; it is not contrary to the perfections of God, his wisdom, power, and goodness, yea these are displayed therein; nor is it to the disadvantage but to the advantage of his people, to have such new heavens and earth made for them to dwell in, in their raised state; and as there is no necessity to depart from the literal sense, there seems to be a necessity to abide by it; since the phrase, *heaven and earth*, are used by the apostle Peter in 2 Pet. iii. frequently, and always literally of the sublunary world, the natural heavens and earth; as when he says, the heavens and the earth that were of old, that were created in the beginning, are that world that was overflowed with a flood and perished; and that the same heavens and earth are reserved to fire against the day of judgment, when the one will pass away and be dissolved, and the other be burnt up; now as these can be understood in no other than in a literal sense, so the new heavens and the earth he speaks of in the room of these, can be meant of no other, to keep up the sense of the apostle uniform and of a piece; only these renewed, not as to their substance, or made entirely new, but as to their qualities.

1*st*, then, The *new heavens* must be interpreted of the airy heavens, and of a new air in them: we have seen that the heavens that shall be set on fire, and be liquefied and dissolved by it, are not the starry heavens, but the airy heavens only; which will be purged, purified, and refined by fire, and become a new air; and Aben Ezra interprets the new heavens in Isa. lxv. 17. of a good air, an healthful and salubrious one; and such will the new heavens be when purged by fire; they will be clear of all noxious vapours and exhalations, be free from all unhealthful fogs, mists and meteors, watery and fiery, such as are enumerated in Psalm cxlviii. 8. God has his treasures of hail, snow, &c. in the air, Job. xxxviii. 22, 23. but the new heavens will be clear of all these; no storms of hail, no stores of snow, no blustering storms and tempests, no coruscations and flashes of lightning, nor peals of thunder; nothing of this kind will be heard or seen, but a pure, serene, and tranquil air, quite suited to the bodies of raised saints;[5] for none else will inhabit the new earth, whose bodies will be incorruptible and spiritual. Moreover the air will now be cleared of devils, which have their residence in it: the devil is called *the prince of the power of the air*, of the posse of devils which dwell in the air; and he and his principalities and powers are *spiritual wickednesses in high or heavenly places* in the air above us, Eph. ii. 2. and vi. 12. and it has been the sentiment both

---

[5] Atque ipsa substantia (mundi) eas qualitates habebit, quæ corporibus immortalibus mirabili mutatione conveniant, ut scilicet mundus in melius innovatus aperte accommodetur hominibus etiam carne in melius innovatis, Aug. de. Civ. Dei. 1. 20. c. 16.

of Jews and heathens, that the air is full of demons; and which is not at all improbable; for when they were cast out of the third heaven, their first habitation, they fell into the air; where they are, at least at times, until their full torment; and here they are hovering over our heads, watching all opportunities to tempt, disturb, and distress the sons of men: but when Christ shall come in the clouds, and be met by his saints in the air, he will clear the air of all the devils in it; he will lay hold of Satan, the prince of them, and of the whole body of them under him, and bind them, and cast them into the abyss, the bottomless pit; so that they shall not be able to stir, nor give the least molestation to the saints for the space of a thousand years; and then, instead of being over their heads, they will be bruised under their feet.

2dly, The *new earth* will be an earth refined and renewed, and restored to its paradisaical estate; or as it was before the fall, free from the curse which came upon it on that account. But now the curse will be removed, and it shall no more bring forth thorns and thistles, nor require labour and pains to cultivate it; nor will there be any difficulty about a livelihood from it, which will not be wanted; it shall be as before the fall, when the whole of it was a paradise, and one part of it more especially so: and hence in that state, of which the new heavens and new earth will be the seat, figures are taken from thence to describe that; as a river of water of life proceeding from the throne of God and the Lamb; and a tree of life in the midst of the new Jerusalem, bearing all manner of fruit every month, and its leaves for the healing of the nations, Rev. xxii. 1, 2. and as the earth, before the fall, was subject to the first man, and all things in it, Psalm viii. 6, 7, 8. so this new earth will be to the second Adam; at his first coming, though Lord of all, yet in the present earth he had not where to lay his head; and now he is crowned with glory and honour, yet we see not all things put under him; but *the world to come*, or *the habitable earth*, which is future, and is not put in subjection to angels, will be put in subjection to him; so that where he was once in the form of a servant, and suffered much, he will now reign as a King, and a triumphant Conqueror. And it must be but reasonable, that since he hath redeemed his people from the curse of the law, being made a curse for them, that every degree of that curse should be removed, which, as yet is not, from the earth: and particularly, it is but reasonable, that when the second Adam, and his seed, come to enjoy the earth alone, that it should be free from the curse, the redemption from which he is the author of, and that for them; and accordingly so it will be in that state; *there shall be no more curse*, Rev. xxii. 3.

II. The inhabitants of the new heavens and the new earth are next to be considered. When God had made the first earth, and which was made by him to be inhabited, there were at first but *two* whom he created to dwell upon it; and when it was destroyed by the flood, and recovered from that deluge, there were but *eight* persons preserved in the ark to repeople it. But when the new heavens and new earth are formed, there will be enow to stock them at once. It may be asked from whence will they be had, since the air will be cleared of devils, and all wicked men will be burnt up with the earth; so that there will not be a devil in the air, nor a wicked man upon the earth; and who shall then inhabit them? Let it be observed, that Christ will bring with him the souls of all his saints, of all the chosen people that have been from the beginning of the world, whose bodies he will then raise, and reunite them to their souls; and the living saints that will be found on the earth when he shall come, will be changed, and caught up with the raised ones, to meet the Lord in the air, where they will abide till the earth is fit for them; and then they will be let down, millions and millions of them, even the whole general assembly and church of the first born, whose names are written in heaven, and will fill the earth at once. And these are described,

First, By the name of *righteousness* itself; *wherein*, in the new heavens and earth, *dwelleth righteousness*, 2 Pet. iii. 13. that is, righteous persons, the abstract for the concrete; a like phrase see in Isa. i. 21. and designs such to whom Christ is made righteousness, and they are made the righteousness of God in him; as Christ, the husband of the church, is called, *the Lord our Righteousness*; so she, by virtue of a marriage-union to him, is called by the same name, Jer. xxiii. 6. and xxxiii. 16. and this denotes such persons as are truly righteous; not in appearance only, but really; and not in the sight of men, but in the sight of God: and who are thoroughly righteous in every sense; who have the righteousness of

Christ imputed to them, and are created in righteousness and true holiness; are inherently holy and righteous, and that perfectly: and it designs such only; not a sinner, not a wicked man, nor an hypocrite, will be among them; and this is confirmed by other scriptures; particularly Isa. lx. 21. *Thy people shall be all righteous; they shall inherit the land for ever;* and though the former part of this prophecy respects the spiritual reign of Christ in the present earth; yet the latter part of it belongs to the perfect state of the church, the new Jerusalem-state, in the new earth; as appears by comparing ver. 19. with Rev. xxi. 23. Again in Psalm xxxvii. 29. *The righteous shall inherit the land, and dwell therein for ever;* not the present earth, which the saints have not by inheritance, and much less for ever; and it is but a small part of it they enjoy in any sense. Besides, this respects something future; it is not said they *do*, but *shall* inherit it. There are other characters in the same Psalm, descriptive of the inhabitants of the new heavens and the new earth, as in ver. 9. *Those that wait upon the Lord shall inherit the earth,* when the wicked will be cut off, as they will be at the general conflagration; and those who wait on the Lord, are the same with the apostle Peter, and others, who looked for new heavens and a new earth, and waited on the Lord for the fulfilment of his promise; and in ver. 11. *The meek shall inherit the earth:* the same is asserted by Christ, Matt. v. 5. these are opposed to proud and haughty sinners, and design the followers of the meek and lowly Jesus, who have but a very small share in the present earth: it is your proud, bold, blustering sort of men who share the earth among them; as for the meek-spirited saints, it is as much as they can do to get a livelihood in it; but they shall inherit the new heavens and the new earth.

Secondly, The inhabitants of which are the palm-bearing company in Rev. vii. 9. for this vision is synchronal, or cotemporary, with that of the new heavens and the new earth, the seat of the new Jerusalem, the church of God, consisting of all the elect, and respects the same time and things; as appears by comparing ver. 15. of that chapter with chap. xxi. 3. and xxii. 3. and ver. 16, 17. with chap. xxi. 4. the same persons are described by their number, ver. 9. *which no man could number;* who, though but a few in comparison of others, are a great number considered by themselves; and though numbered by God and Christ, cannot be numbered by men: and by their origin and descent, being *of all nations, kindreds, people, and tongues;* chosen, redeemed, and called out of all; and will be collected together at the coming of Christ: and by their position, standing *before the throne, and before the Lamb;* the throne of the Lamb, placed in the new Jerusalem, before which they will stand without fault, behold his glory, and enjoy his presence: and by their habit and gesture, *clothed with white robes, and palms in their hands;* appearing now as kings and priests; who, as such, shall reign with Christ on the new earth, being now not only clothed with the robe of his righteousness, but with the shining robes of immortality and bliss: and the *palms* in their hands is not so much expressive of their past uprightness and integrity, and of their having borne up under all their pressures and afflictions; but chiefly of their now victory over all their enemies: also they are described by their ascription of salvation to God and the Lamb, even their temporal salvation, and especially their spiritual and eternal salvation; to God, as the contriver of it, and to Christ the Lamb, as the procuring cause and author of it; in which they will be joined by all the angels around them, as guardians of them, ministering spirits to them, and fellow-worshippers with them; who will then ascribe a sevenfold praise to God, ver. 10, 11, 12. And some discourse passing between one of the elders about the throne, and John, occasioned a further description of the same persons, ver. 13, 14. by their being *come out of great tribulation;* which may signify, not only the afflictions of every individual of this great number; but more especially the public troubles of the saints, as a body, in the several periods of time; both of the old testament saints, and particularly of the new testament saints, under Rome pagan and papal, to the end of the reign of antichrist; and may have special respect to the last struggle of the beast, and the slaying of the witnesses. But now all will be at an end, and their *robes washed, and made white in the blood of the Lamb,* and so pure, without spot or blemish: and they are further described, by their constant service of God, *day and night,* that is continually; for there will be no night in this state: and their service will lie, not in an attendance on the word and ordinances; but in praising God, adoring his perfections, admiring his works of providence and grace, and ascribing the glory of salvation to him: *And he that sitteth upon the throne shall dwell among them*, the tabernacle of God being now with men on earth; *and they shall hunger no more, neither thirst any more;* neither in a literal sense, which is sometimes the case now; nor in a mystical sense, after the word and ordinances, they will have no need of; nor have any uneasy desires after spiritual things, which will now be enjoyed in plenty; *nor shall the sun light on them, nor any heat;* neither the sun of persecution, nor the heat of Satan's fiery darts, nor of any fiery affliction: the reason of all this happiness is, *the Lamb which is in the midst of the throne shall feed them;* not by his ministers, word, and ordinances, as now; but with the discoveries of his love, will feast them at his table, and cause them to drink new wine in his kingdom; *and shall lead them to living fountains of water*, to the river of the water of life, the everlasting love of the three Persons; *and God shall wipe away all tears from their eyes;* and there shall be no more tears on account of indwelling sin, Satan's temptations, divine desertions, and any trouble and affliction; but being come to the new Jerusalem, everlasting joy shall be upon them, sorrow and sighing shall flee away. These are the persons, and this will be the happy case of the inhabitants of the new heavens and the new earth.

Thirdly, A further account is given of those inhabitants in Rev. xxi. 1, 2. &c. after John had a vision of the new heavens and the new earth, the former being passed away; he had a sight of those that were to dwell in them; and by the account, they appear to be persons not in a mortal and sinful state, but in an immortal and perfect one. They are called *the holy city, and new Jerusalem*, by which the church is meant; but not as in any state on this present earth, and in the present circumstances of things; a state so glorious, pure, and holy, as this is represented, can never be expected here. Mortal men, dwelling in houses of clay, would never be able to bear such a glory as the church is said to have on her, ver. 11. and following; nor be so pure and holy as this new Jerusalem, so as to have nothing defiling, nor that commits iniquity in it, ver. 27. and yet it cannot be meant of it as in heaven; since it is said to descend from thence, ver. 2, 10. nor can the kings of the earth, in any sense, be said to bring their honour and glory, and that of the nations, into heaven, ver. 24, 26. But it designs a state in the new earth, and under the new heavens, where the tabernacle of God will be, ver. 1, 2, 3. and we find the camp of the saints, the beloved city, the same with the holy city here upon the earth, that is, the new earth, chap. xx. 9. even after the first resurrection, and even after the millennium. Now this church, called the holy city, is no other than the church of the first-born, the whole body of the elect, and the same with the palm-bearing company, and the church consisting of them.

The inhabitants of the new heavens and the new earth are here described under the names of *the holy city* and *new Jerusalem;* a *city*, as consisting of the whole family of God, who are fellow-citizens with the saints, and of the household of God; a *holy* one, as made up of persons perfectly holy, in spirit, soul, and body, and entirely free from sin; called Jerusalem, though in a state superior to the church under the gospel dispensation, called by that name; and even to it in the Philadelphian state, in the spiritual reign; since it is promised to the overcomer in that state, as something greater, and yet to come, that he should be a pillar, and have the name of the new Jerusalem written on him, Rev. iii. 12. which signifies the vision of peace, and fitly expresses that state, in which peace of every kind, in its utmost perfection, shall be enjoyed, the Prince of peace, Christ, being, with his people; and called *new*, because the seat of this church will be the new heavens and new earth; all which shews, that the inhabitants will be in a perfect state of holiness and peace. And they are further described by their *descent from heaven;* which designs, not their original, as regenerate persons; but their local descent with Christ; when he comes, the souls of all his saints will come with him; their bodies will be raised and united to them; and with the living saints, be caught up to meet him in the air, from whence they will descend with him on the new earth, and dwell on it with him, their head and husband; hence said to be *the bride, the Lamb's wife;* which intend not individuals, nor particular churches of Jews or Gentiles; but the whole body of the elect, given to Christ, and espoused by him; who will now be *prepared and adorned for her husband*, being all gathered in, and their number completed; and adorned, not only with the grace of God, and righteousness of Christ, but with the glorious robes of immortality and bliss; and so fit for Christ their head. And it will be the church and her members, thus prepared and ornamented, who will, with Christ, inhabit the new earth; for now *the tabernacle of God will be with men* on the new earth; which being for a determined time, a thousand years, his being with them is signified by a tabernacle, which is moveable; which is further explained; *he will dwell with them, in person*, for the space of time mentioned. *God himself shall be with them; Immanuel*, God with us, God in our nature; *and they shall be his people*, owned by him as such; and he *be their God;* which covenant interest may be claimed, as being out of all question. The inhabitants of the new earth are moreover described by their freedom from all evils, ver. 4. *God shall wipe away all tears from their eyes;* which is said of the palm-bearing company, chap. vii. 17. which shew them to be the same with those; the words are taken from Isa. xxv. 8. and refer to the resurrection state, when *death shall be swallowed up in victory; and there shall be no more death*, not even corporal death; for this is said of risen saints; *neither sorrow nor crying*, on account of disorders and diseases of body, loss of friends, &c. which will all be at an end; *neither shall there be any more pain; of body*, or mind; *for the former things are past away;* the old world, its lusts, temptations, and snares; all troubles from within and from without; from persecutors and false friends; which shews that those inhabitants will not be in a sinful and mortal state: yea, they are described, as *having the glory of God upon them*, ver. 11. upon their bodies being raised, and fashioned like to the glorious body of Christ, and upon their souls being perfect in grace, righteousness, and holiness; and the light, glory, lustre, and splendour of this church and her members, the inhabitants of the new earth, are expressed in such language in the following part of the chapter, that no adequate ideas can be formed thereof; and describe such a state as can never be imagined will be in the present world: and those inhabitants are again described by their holiness and purity, ver. 27. in such a manner, as shew them to be in a sinless state. To which may be added, the provision to regale those inhabitants, suitable to their state, is described in chap. xxii. 1, 2. as in the paradisaical earth, particularly in that spot of it, the garden of Eden, there was a river for delight and use, and a tree of life in the midst of it, for the preservation of health, and the continuance of life; so in this city, in the new earth, will be a river and tree of life, and, for ought I see to the contrary, in a literal sense; only, they will be emblematical, as the other might be in Eden; for here will be no need of corporal food, only of entertainment for the mind. Here will be a river, an emblem of the everlasting love of God, clear and free from all motives and conditions in men, arising purely from the sovereignty of God; which, for its abundance, will be a river to swim in, and not to be passed over; and will yield inexpressible pleasure in this city and its inhabitants: and there will be a tree of life in the midst of the street of this city, bearing monthly all kind of fruit, and its leaves of an healing nature; an emblem of Christ, the tree of life, Prov. iii. 18. Rev. ii. 7. and of all spiritual blessings to be continually enjoyed from him, in great variety, and with great pleasure. And though there will be no diseases of body and mind in that state; yet as the tree of life in Eden was for the preservation of the life and health of Adam, had he continued in his state of innocence; so the healing leaves of this tree may denote that every thing in Christ will contribute to the comfort, health, and happiness of the saints. Moreover, the happiness of those inhabitants is expressed by a variety, which shews it to be an accumulated happiness, a perfect one; *there shall be no more curse;* none upon the new earth, and its inhabitants; nor any accursed person or thing in it; *but the throne of God and the Lamb shall be in it*, the seat of his glorious majesty, who will reign as King here; *and his servants shall serve him;* both the ministering angels and his saints, especially the latter; *and his name shall be in their foreheads;* by which it will appear they are his people and servants, as if his name was written there; *and there shall be no more night;* either in a literal sense, or rather figurative, meaning no night of ignorance and error, of darkness and desertion, and of affliction of any kind; *and they need no candle, neither light of the sun;* neither artificial nor natural light; *for the Lord God giveth them light*, what vastly exceeds either; *and they shall reign for ever and ever;* first with Christ on the new earth, for a thousand years, next to be considered, and then in heaven to all eternity.

CHAP. VIII.

OF THE MILLENNIUM, OR PERSONAL REIGN OF CHRIST WITH THE SAINTS ON THE NEW EARTH A THOUSAND YEARS.

I HAVE treated already of the kingly office of Christ, as executed by him in various dispensations, particularly under the gospel dispensation, book v. chap. 13. and have observed, there are two branches of it yet to come; one called the *spiritual*, the other the *personal reign;* the former has been considered, and this is a proper place to treat of the latter; which I shall do by shewing,

I. That Christ will have a special, peculiar, glorious, and visible kingdom, in which he will reign personally on earth.——1. I call it a special, peculiar kingdom, different from other kingdoms of Christ; from the kingdom of nature and providence, which lies in the government of this world; which he, as God, has an equal right to with his Father; but when this kingdom will take place, this present world will be at an end: and from his spiritual kingdom, which belongs to him as Mediator; which rule he has exercised in the hearts of his people from the beginning of the world; and which has been, under the gospel dispensation, more large and manifest; and will be more so in the latter day, when his spiritual reign will take place; but this is different from that.——2. It will be very glorious and visible; Christ's kingdom in the spiritual reign, will be very glorious, when all the glorious things spoken of it, will be fulfilled; and it will be very visible, when exalted above all the mountains and hills, the kingdoms of this world: but this will be more so, since Christ will be in it; not only by his Spirit, and the effusions of his grace, but he will personally appear in all his glory, and reign gloriously before his ancients; hence his *appearing* and *kingdom,* are put together, as cotemporary, 2 Tim. iv. 1. he in person will appear, and his tabernacle be with men on earth.——3. This kingdom will be after all the enemies of Christ, and of his people, are removed out of the way. In his spiritual reign antichrist will be destroyed, *with the Spirit,* or breath of Christ, his gospel; and with *the brightness of his coming,* that clear light which will attend his coming, by the effusion of his Spirit;[1] which will be with such spiritual efficacy, as to dispel all darkness, Pagan, Papal, and Mahometan; and cause an universal reception of the gospel; which will open the way for the christian princes, to carry their victorious arms every where, and seize upon, and possess all the antichristian states; and in this order things lie in the prophecy of Daniel, chap. vii. where, after the vision of the *fourth beast,* of the judgment of it, of the slaying it, and burning its body, the Roman empire, and the remains of it, in antichrist, and the antichristian states; Daniel had a vision of Christ, the Son of man, coming in the clouds of heaven, and having an universal kingdom given him, which will not be succeeded by any other. And in the same order things lie in the book of the Revelation, chap. xix. where the beast, antichrist, and the kings of the earth, the antichristian princes, are represented as gathering together, to make war with Christ, described as an illustrious Warrior; when the beast and false prophet, antichrist, in both his civil and ecclesiastic characters, are taken and destroyed, and the rest slain, by the sword of Christ's mouth: all which will be done, with the ruin of the Turk, the eastern antichrist, at the beginning of the spiritual reign: but still there will remain a most potent enemy, Satan, with his principalities and powers; wherefore, in chap. xx. an angel descends from heaven, who is no other than Christ, who will then personally descend from thence; described as having a great chain, and a key in his hand; the one to bind Satan and all his angels; the other to open the bottomless pit, and cast them in it, and lock it up; that they may neither deceive the nations, nor disturb the saints for the space of a thousand years.[2] And all enemies being thus out of the way, follows the account of the Millennium, or personal reign of Christ.——4. This glorious and visible kingdom of Christ, will not take place till after the resurrection of the just, and the renovation of the world.[3] As soon

---

[1] So the author of Onus Ecclesiæ, published A. D. 1524. vid. Heidegger Dissert. 23. de Chiliasmo, s. 8.

[2] See p. 620.

[3] This is the sense of the ancient writers concerning the millennium; as of Papias, a hearer of the apostle John, and a companion of Polycarp, Euseb. Eccl. Hist. 1. 3. c. 39. and of Justin Martyr, and the orthodox christians in his time, Dialog. cum Trypho, p. 307. and of Irenæus, adv. Hæres. 1. 5. c. 20, 32. and of Apollinarius, Hieron, Catalog. Script. Eccles. c. 28. and of Tertullian, contr.

as Christ personally appears, the dead in him will rise first; this is the first resurrection, which they that have a part in shall reign with Christ a thousand years, as appears from the above place in the Revelation referred unto. These *children of the resurrection*, as Christ calls them, Luke xx. 35, 36. and who will be worthy of *that world*, the new world, in which Christ and they will reign, will be like the angels, die no more; nor will they eat and drink, in a corporal sense ; nor marry, and be given in marriage ; carnal appetites will not be indulged ; nor carnal pleasures enjoyed : in this state, nothing but pure, refined, spiritual pleasures, will be had, suited to the bodies and souls of men, united in the resurrection state. Our Lord, indeed, speaks of his disciples eating and drinking at his table, in his kingdom ; and of his drinking new wine in his Father's kingdom, which is the same, Luke xxii. 30. Matt. xxvi. 29. but then all this is to be understood of divine repasts, of spiritual joys and pleasures, they shall then partake of. The Jews, it seems, had very carnal notions of the kingdom of God, of a great affluence of meats and drinks in it, and of rich and delicious living ; hence a certain person said, *Blessed is he that shall eat bread in the kingdom of God!* Luke xiv. 15. meaning, that shall live deliciously there. And such gross and carnal conceptions, some that have borne the christian name, have entertained of the millennium, as well ancient[4] as modern writers, at least, as represented by their adversaries ; and therefore it has been objected to them, as if their nötion savoured more of a Turkish paradise, than of a kingdom of Christ; and which has brought disgrace upon the doctrine of the kingdom, and given disgust to pious and spiritual minds; as it did to Austin,[5] who had some light into it, and owned, that could it be restrained to spiritual delights and pleasures, it might be allowed : but now the manner in which I conceive it, clears it from such absurdities, and represents it as quite unclogged, and free from such an objection. All the prophesies of temporal blessings in the latter day, as length of life, a numerous offspring of the people of God, plenty of corporal food, an affluence of wealth and riches, will have their accomplishment in the spiritual reign, or latter day glory; when there will be such an effusion of the Spirit of God, as will be a counterbalance to such terrene enjoyments, that they will not do the hurt they would in the present circumstances of things ; and even then, when the influences of the Spirit shall go off, and be withdrawn, that state will gradually sink into lukewarmness, pride, self-conceit, and carnality, Rev. iii. 15, 16, 17. But nothing of this kind will appear in the millennium.——5. This kingdom of Christ will be bounded by two resurrections ; by the first resurrection, or the resurrection of the just, at which it will begin ; and by the second resurrection, or the resurrection of the wicked, at which it will end, or nearly ; for it is expressly said, that *the rest of the dead*, that is, the wicked, *lived not again until the thousand years were finished :* now in the interval between the resurrection of the one, and the resurrection of the other, will be the millennium, or thousand years' reign of Christ and his people together.——6. This kingdom will be before the general judgment, especially of the wicked. There is a particular judgment that passes on every man at death ; *After death, judgment!* and there will be a virtual judgment immediately upon the appearance of Christ, who will come to judge both *quick* and *dead*. Dead saints will be raised, and living saints changed, and both be with Christ ; which will be virtually pronouncing them righteous ; and as for the wicked, their bodies will be burnt in the conflagration of the earth, and their souls will be shut up with Satan and his angels in the bottomless pit ; which will be virtually pronouncing them guilty : but the formal judgment will proceed afterwards. Indeed, in the thousand years' reign, will be the judgment of the saints, as will be seen hereafter; and some time after the close of the millennium, will come on the general judgment of the wicked ; for John, after he had given an account of the former, Rev. xx. relates a vision of the latter.——7. This glorious, visible kingdom of Christ, will be on earth, and not in heaven ; and so is distinct from the kingdom of heaven, or the ultimate glory : the souls of the martyrs, and others, said to

---

Marcion, l. 3. c. 24. and of Lactantius, Instit. 1. 7. c. 14, 24. and of Victorinus Pictaviensis, vid. Hieron. ut supra. and of Sulpicius Severus, Hieron. in Ezek. 36. fol. 235. I.

[4] Vid. Euseb. Ec. Hist. l. 7. c. 24, 25. Hieron. in Esaiam, c. 66. fol. 120. D. et Dionysium apud ib. proem. in Esaiam, com. 18. fol. 112. L.
[5] De Civitate Dei, l. 20. c. 7.

reign with Christ a thousand years, cannot be understood of their reigning with him in heaven; for so they had reigned with him from the time of the death of their bodies; and was their reigning with him in heaven meant, there would have been no need of binding Satan and his angels, and shutting them up in the bottomless pit; as not to deceive the nations, so not to molest them; since being in heaven, they were out of their reach, and could not be disturbed by them: but it is on earth they are to reign with Christ; of which the living creatures, and four-and-twenty elders, the representatives of gospel-churches, and the redeemed of the Lamb, express their strong faith; *And hast made us unto our God kings and priests, and we shall reign on the earth;* meaning, no doubt, in the millennium; for they speak of it as future, saying, not *we do*, but *we shall reign on earth;* and that the millennium reign will be there, is clear, since the Gog and Magog army, at the end of the thousand years, are said to go up *on the breadth of the earth, and compass the camp of the saints about, and the beloved city;* the same with the saints before described as reigning with Christ, which therefore must be on the earth; and the same with the holy city John saw descending from God out of heaven, that is, on earth, with whom his tabernacle is said to be, and he to dwell with them, Rev. xx. 4, 6, 8, 9. and xxi. 2, 3. But then this kingdom will not be upon this present earth, or upon this earth in its present circumstances; the present heavens and earth will be burnt up before this kingdom takes place: this world is not good enough for the second Adam, and his saints, to dwell in; the curse must be removed from it, and it must be refined, and new fitted up, for such inhabitants; and all the wicked of it be no more in it, as unfit to dwell where such persons do. Christ's kingdom is not of this world, nor never will be. This has been the mistake of many, fancying that the millennium will be in the present earth; which have given the adversaries of this doctrine an occasion to object unto it; as subversive of civil government, and as encouraging sedition and rebellion in commonwealths, and as giving just umbrage to the kings and princes of the earth, and to all civil magistrates. And, indeed, in the last century, in this nation, there were a set of men, called *fifth monarchy-men*, and who were levellers, and riotous persons, were for pulling down civil magistracy, and all order of civil government, and setting up what they called a kingdom of Christ; which brought the doctrine of the millennium into great contempt, and under which it has much lain ever since. But putting it upon the footing I have, that this kingdom will not be in the present earth, the kings of it have nothing to fear from it; it will not interfere with theirs; civil government will not be hurt by it; for it will not be till that is no more, and the world itself at an end; and so can give no encouragement and countenance to persons of a riotous and seditious disposition. Indeed, in the spiritual reign, the dominion under the whole heaven, will be given to the people of the saints of the most High, which will last to the end of the world: but then there will be no alteration made in the order of civil government, much less will that be destroyed; it will only be translated into other hands; only christian princes shall possess it; there will be no more pagan princes, nor papal kings, nor mahometan emperors; only such who are not only nominal, but truly christian princes, according to Psalm lxxii. 10, 11. Isa. xlix. 23. and lx. 3, 10, 16. But as for the personal reign of Christ with his saints, that will be on the new earth, wherein will *dwell righteousness*, and that only; that is, Christ, who is the Lord, the Righteousness of his people; and they who are made righteous by him, 2 Pet. iii. 13. so the new heavens and new earth John had a vision of, are, according to the vision, the seat of the new *Jerusalem*, or church of God, and of Christ, who will there tabernacle with them, Rev. xxi. 1, 2, 3. and then the Lord will be King over all the earth; there will be no other; there will be one Lord, and his name one, Zech. xiv. 9.

Having explained the nature of Christ's kingdom, I shall proceed to give the proof that there will be such a glorious, visible kingdom of Christ on earth: this proof, as it depends on prophesies of future things, cannot be expected to be so full and clear in all respects, as a proof may be of things past or present; the prophesies respecting the first coming of Christ, doubtless, did not appear so clear and plain before their fulfilment, as since: so the prophesies of the second coming of Christ, and of his kingdom, may not be so evident as they will be, the nearer is the approach of it; or as when it will be. Besides, the prophesies of the Old Testament are delivered in very general, concise, and comprehensive terms; and sometimes include both his first and second coming, and things that intervene between them; and therefore it should be no objection to a proof of Christ's second coming and kingdom, that there are some things in the context which respect his first coming; and others which respect the spiritual reign; but these are to be separated, and distinctly considered; and what belongs to the one, should be applied to that; and what belongs to another, should be appropriated to that. Now the proof of this point, may be taken from various passages in the Psalms, in the Prophets, and in the books of the New Testament.

1*st*, From some passages in the Psalms; and to begin with the xlvth Psalm, which was made *concerning the King*, the King Messiah, who is called *the King*, by way of eminence, the famous King; and who is described as a divine Person, as God, whose throne is for ever and ever; and as graceful, and full of grace, as Man and Mediator; and as a most potent Prince, riding in great majesty, and as a triumphant conqueror. And though some things said of him may agree with the conquests of his grace, in the first and after ages of christianity; yet they will have their full accomplishment at his second coming, when all his enemies shall be subdued by him. His court is represented in the Psalm as a very brilliant one; some in it have the name of queen, others are called honourable women, or maids of honour; and among those, kings' daughters, and others the rich among the people; which may respect the different degrees of honour among the saints, in the resurrection and kingdom state, which will only obtain them; not in the ultimate glory. The glory and purity of the church are strongly expressed; the *queen* is said to be at the King's right-hand, *in gold of Ophir*, her clothing of massy gold; which agrees with the new Jerusalem, on the new earth, a city of pure gold. The King's daughter, the same, is said to be *all glorious within*, being perfectly pure and holy; such as the new Jerusalem will be, into which nothing sinful, defiling, and abominable, shall enter. The church is also, in the Psalm, represented as introduced into the King's presence, in a magnificent manner, *in raiment of needle work*, as well as in *clothing of wrought gold;* which fitly agrees with the kingdom state, in which Christ will present his church to himself a glorious church, being as a bride adorned for her husband; not only having on the robe of his righteousness, but the shining garments of immortality and bliss. Moreover, at this time he will make his people *princes in all the earth;* which shews that this his kingdom will be on earth, and agrees with the faith and expectation of his saints, that as they are made by him *kings and priests unto God*, they shall *reign on earth*.

I take no notice of Psalm lxxii. for though it relates to Christ and his kingdom, yet to that branch of it, his spiritual reign, and expresses the prosperity, peace, glory, extensiveness, and duration of it. But Psalm xcvi. must not be overlooked; which begins, *The Lord reigneth, let the earth rejoice!* which shews that the Psalm respects the kingdom of Christ on earth; and which will take place at his coming to judge the world, as appears by its connection with the last verse of the preceding Psalm; and which coming of his, as hereafter described, will be in the clouds of heaven, and with flames of fire, as has been observed in a preceding chapter. The cxlvth Psalm treats of the kingdom of Christ, and the glory of it, and represents the saints as speaking to one another of it; of its glory, majesty, and duration, ver. 11, 12, 13. which can suit no state so well as this; in which the saints will be employed in converse with each other, about the glory of their King, the glory of his coming to his kingdom, of his glorious acts done by him in it, and of the glorious things they enjoy therein.

2*dly*, From various passages in the prophets: and,——1. From Isa. xxiv. 23. *Then the moon shall be confounded, &c.* this glorious reign will take place after the punishment of the *kings of the earth upon the earth*, ver. 21. by whom may be meant the beast and the false prophet, with the kings of the earth, the antichristian kings; who will make war with the Lamb, and be overcome and slain by him, Rev. xvii. 14. and xix. 20, 21. and whose army may be called *the host of the high ones, that are on high;* being in high places, and in great power and dignity; and may be also very well applied to Satan, and his principalities and powers, those *spiritual wickednesses in high places;* and what is said in ver. 22. of the shutting of them up and confining them as in a prison, and then after many days visiting them, very aptly agrees with the binding of Satan and his angels, and the shutting of them up in the bottomless pit; and then after a thousand years letting them loose for a short time, which will issue in their everlasting punishment; see Rev. xx. 2, 3. Moreover this reign will not take place until the utter dissolution of the earth, when it shall fall and not rise again in the form it now is, ver. 19, 20. the person reigning is *the Lord of hosts*, the Lord of the armies of the heavens, the angels, and of the inhabitants of the earth, the greatest among them; who is King of kings and Lord of lords; all which is true of Christ, who reigns now in the kingdom of providence as God, and the Creator of all things; and in the kingdom of grace, as Mediator in the hearts of his people; and in his churches, where he will reign more illustriously in the latter day; but this is still a more glorious reign that is here spoken of: the place where he will reign is in Zion and Jerusalem, which may be literally understood of that spot of ground where those cities were, which may be the chief residence of Christ in this his kingdom; or mystically of that Zion where he and the one hundred and forty-four thousand, having his Father's name on their foreheads, stood; and the new Jerusalem, that will come down from heaven, among whom his tabernacle will be, Rev. xiv. 1. and xxi. 2, 3. The persons *before* whom, and in whose sight he will reign, for this kingdom will be visible, are *his ancients;* not his ancient people the Jews only, but all his elect, that have been from the beginning of the world; Adam, Abel, Noah, Abraham, Isaac, and Jacob, the prophets of the Old Testament, and the apostles of the New; and the four-and-twenty elders, the representatives of gospel churches; and even all those ancient ones whom God has loved with an everlasting love, chosen in Christ before the foundation of the world, called the *ancient people,* Isa. xliv. 7. with these Christ will reign *gloriously,* or *in glory;* he will appear in glory, in the glory of his deity, and in the glory of his human nature, and in the glory of his kingly office; and such will be his lustre and splendour, that the *sun* and *moon* will be *ashamed* and *confounded;* they will blush and withdraw their light, as it were, or that will not be comparable to his; and that city the new Jerusalem, where he will reign, will stand in no need of their light, for the Lamb will be the light of it, Rev. xxi. 23.——2. With this agrees another prophecy in Isa. xxx. 26. *Moreover the light of the moon shall be as the light of the sun, &c.* this prophecy will not be fulfilled until *the day of the great slaughter is over,* the great slaughter of the antichristian kings, captains, and mighty men; which carnage of them is called the supper of the great God, to which the fowls of the air are invited to prey upon, Rev. xix. 17, 18. *when the towers fall,* when the city of Babylon or Rome, with its towers, and the cities of the nations, of the antichristian nations, with their towers, will fall, Rev. xvi. 19. nor will it be fully accomplished until *the name of the Lord,* or the Lord himself, comes *with the flame of a devouring fire,* to burn up the world, and all things in it, ver. 27, 30. and so must respect the second coming of Christ, which will be from heaven with flames of fire: and another criterion of the fulfilment of this prophecy is, that it will be when the Lord will *bind* up and *heal* the *wounds* of *his people;* that is, forgive their iniquities, which in the kingdom state will be publicly and completely done; the sins of God's people will be so fully blotted out, that they shall not be seen by themselves, nor by others, any more; see Acts iii. 19—21. and though great will be the light and knowledge of men in the spiritual reign, the first branch of Christ's kingdom; yet this sevenfold light, which is expressive of a perfection of it, best agrees with that state, the light whereof exceeds that of the sun and moon; and when the Lord shall be the everlasting light of his people, and their God their glory, Isa. lx. 19, 20. a prophecy which respects the same thing. ——3. There is another prophecy which seems to belong to this glorious kingdom of Christ on earth in Jer. xxiii. 5, 6. *Behold, the days come, saith the Lord, that I will raise unto David a righteous branch, &c.* there can be no doubt but Christ is here meant, who is the Lord our righteousness, the author of righteousness to his people; he is the man whose name is the Branch, and is raised up to David as such, and a righteous one he is; a King that shall reign in righteousness, and so prosper as to be king over all the earth; and on the earth this his reign will be, since it is *in the earth* he will execute judgment and justice: and though his saints, who are meant by Judah and Israel, are always safe under his protection, being in his hands, and kept by his power; yet what state or period can be named wherein they will dwell in more safety, and in such freedom from the oppression and molestation of their enemies, as in the millennium? when all their enemies will be no more,

and even Satan and his angels will be bound and shut up in the bottomless pit for a thousand years, and so during that time can give them no disturbance.——
4. There are some passages in Ezekiel which seem to have respect to this kingdom state; as in chap. xxi. 27. *I will overturn, overturn, overturn it, and it shall be no more until he come, whose right it is, and I will give it him;* which may be understood not only of the overturnings in the Jewish state before the first coming of Christ, but also of the overturnings of empires before his second coming; and being expressed three times, may denote the overturning of the Pagan, Papal, and Mahometan empires, which when overturned will be no more: and after Christ will come, who is heir of all things, and by the designation of his Father, will be king over all the earth. In chap. xlviii. there is a prophecy of a city, the dimensions of which are such as cannot agree with any city on earth literally taken; but must be understood either of the gospel-church-state; or it may be rather of the city of the new Jerusalem, described in Rev. xxi. in which Christ will reign, and his saints with him, in a most glorious manner; and the rather this may be meant, since the name of the city is *Jehovah shammah,* the Lord is there, Ezek. xlviii. 35. and in the new Jerusalem will be the tabernacle of Christ with men on earth, where he is said to be with his saints, and dwell with them, Rev. xxi. 3.——5. There are some prophecies in Daniel which respect the kingdom of Christ, as in chap. ii. the image Nebuchadnezzar saw in his dream, is explained by Daniel as an emblem of the four monarchies, Babylonian, Persian, Grecian, and Roman; and in ver. 44. it is said, *In the days of these kings, shall the God of heaven set up a kingdom, &c.* that is, after these kings have reigned, and their kingdoms are ended, as Junius[6] interprets it; for this kingdom could not be set up in the days of them all, since their kingdoms were successive. Nebuchadnezzar also saw in his dream, *a stone cut out without hands, which smote the image, and became a great mountain, and filled the whole earth;* which must be understood of Christ, both in his human nature, which is a tabernacle not made with hands; and which God pitched, and not man; and in his kingdom, which was very small in its first beginning, but by degrees increased, and will still more increase, and become a great mountain, a mighty kingdom, and fill the whole earth, and so jostle out all other kingdoms: this will be, in part, fulfilled in the spiritual reign of Christ, when the kingdoms of this world shall become his; but most completely in the millennium, when he shall be King over all the earth. There is a prophecy of the same kind in chap. vii. where Daniel had a vision of four beasts coming up out of the sea; which design the same four monarchies rising up successively in the world: and after this, he had a vision of a judicial process, issuing in the slaying of the fourth beast, the destruction of the Roman monarchy; and the burning of the body of the beast, the remains of that monarchy, antichrist, and the antichristian states: after which he has a vision of Christ, the Son of man, coming in the clouds of heaven; and so it must respect the second coming of Christ, and of his then having a dominion, and glorious kingdom given him, which is an everlasting one, that is, which shall not be left to another people, as in chap. ii. nor be succeeded by another kingdom; but shall continue until the kingdom of heaven, or the ultimate glory, takes place; and this kingdom will not be *in* heaven, but *under the whole heaven;* as in ver. 27.——
6. There is a passage which has been frequently referred to, and belongs to this kingdom state, in Zech. xiv. 9. *And the Lord shall be king over all the earth; in that day shall there be one Lord, and his name one.* This kingdom will be on earth; and will be when there is no other; and when the homage and worship paid to Christ, this King, will be universally the same. And though there may be some passages in this chapter which belong to the spiritual reign, the first branch of Christ's kingdom; yet there are others, as well as this, which can only agree with his personal reign, upon his second coming; for it is expressly said, *The Lord my God shall come, and all the saints with thee;* which will be fulfilled, and not before, when Christ shall descend from heaven, and bring all his saints with him, 1 Thess. iii. 13. and iv. 14, 16. And this reign of Christ over all the earth, will be when the saints are in a perfect state; and so not before his second coming, and the resurrection of the just. Holiness will now be

---

[6] So the Hebrew particle ב sometimes signifies; see Noldius.

so universal, that, proverbially speaking, it will be written on *the bells of the horses;* and every member in the new Jerusalem-church-state, into which nothing defiling shall enter, meant by *every pot in Jerusalem and Judah, shall be holiness to the Lord,* or be completely holy; and there shall be *no Canaanite,* neither a profane sinner, nor a carnal professor, *in the house* and church of God; nor any sinful lust in any of its inhabitants.

3dly, The proof of this glorious kingdom of Christ, may be given from various passages in the New Testament; and, ——1. From Matt. vi. 10. *Thy kingdom come; thy will be done in earth, as it is in heaven.* To this, as a proof, it may be objected, at first sight, that this is the kingdom of the Father; since it is *Our Father which art in heaven,* the petitions are directed to. To which it may be replied, that the same kingdom may be called, the kingdom of the Father, and the kingdom of Christ, as it is certain this kingdom we are treating of is so called; as appears by comparing Matt. xxvi. 29. with Luke xxii. 30. And there is a good reason to be given for it; because this kingdom is a kingdom which the Father had appointed to Christ, and which will be given him by him, Luke xxii. 29. Dan. vii. 14. and for the same reason the Father calls him his King, because appointed and set by him as king over his holy hill of Zion, Psalm ii. 6. this kingdom may be called his. Now this is a kingdom yet to come, and is prayed for as being future; and so can design neither the kingdom of providence nor the kingdom of grace, nor the gospel-dispensation; and though it may include the spiritual reign, the first branch of Christ's kingdom, yet will not be fulfilled in that; since it respects a perfect state, when the will of God will be done on earth by men, as it is in heaven by the angels; the saints, in the kingdom-state, will serve Christ their king constantly and incessantly, and so perfectly; and this will be a kingdom on earth, where the will of God will be perfectly done, as it is in heaven, and so is a distinct state from that. To all which may be added, that the coming of this kingdom is to be prayed for;[7] not only the first branch of it, in the spiritual reign, as in Isa. lxii. 6, 7. but the second coming of Christ, to take possession of his kingdom personally, saying, *Come, Lord Jesus, come quickly!* and this may, and should be a prayer of faith; for since he has directed his people to pray daily for the coming of this kingdom, it may be assured that it certainly will come; for Christ would not direct his saints to pray for that which never will be.——2. From Matt. xx. 21, 22, 23. *Then came to him the mother of Zebedee's children, desiring that her two sons may sit the one on Christ's right-hand, and the other on the left, in his kingdom.* The same request is made by the two sons themselves, Mark x. 35—40. Now though these petitioners were tinctured with the national notion of the Messiah setting up a temporal kingdom on earth, at the time of his first coming; and with which all the apostles seem, more or less, tinctured, until the spirit was poured down upon them on the day of Pentecost; yet our Lord does not deny, but rather owns, there would be a kingdom of his, in which distinctions of honour would be made, and peculiar privileges, and marks of respect, bestowed on some; but that these would only be given to such for whom they were prepared by his Father: he blames them for their pride and ambition, in affecting to have pre-eminence above their brethren; and suggests, that their petition was an unseasonable one; it was not a time to think of, and expect honours and preferments, they being now in a suffering-state, and must expect sufferings for his sake; yea, that he himself must drink of a bitter cup, and be baptized with a bloody baptism, before he entered into his kingdom and glory; and this would also be their case: this glorious kingdom of Christ, and honours in it, are not to be expected in a militant suffering state; the saints must suffer with Christ first, before they reign and are glorified together with him; the crown of righteousness will not be given, till the good fight of faith is fought; and not before the glorious appearing of Christ, and only to them that love that: this cannot be understood of the kingdom of heaven, or a kingdom there, because there is no sitting at Christ's right-hand there; he is set down indeed in his Father's throne, and sits at his right hand, where no creatures, angels nor men, are admitted; but in the kingdom-state, he will have a throne distinct from his Father, in which his saints

---

[7] It is a rule with the Jews, that every blessing or prayer, in which there is no mention of God and his kingdom, is no blessing or prayer, Maimon. Hilchot, Beracot, c. 1. s. 5.

will sit with him, Rev. iii. 21. on his right and left; and in which state will be thrones, whereon some will sit, being distinguished from others, with some marks of honour and esteem ; for such there will be in this kingdom of Christ, though what they will be is not easy to say; they are signified by one being a ruler over ten cities, and another a ruler over five cities ; which is not to be understood literally, but of some posts of honour, and distinctive marks of respect some will have ; for as one star differs from another star in glory, so will be the resurrection of the dead; or such a distinction be in the resurrection-state—in this glorious kingdom of Christ. In Mark x. 37. instead of, *In thy kingdom*, it is, *In thy glory.*——3. From Luke i. 32, 33. *The Lord God shall give unto him the throne of his father David; and he shall reign over the house of Jacob for ever; and of his kingdom there shall be no end!* These words were spoken by the angel to the virgin, concerning her son, who should be *great*, and be called, *the son of the Highest;* and which respects him, not in his incarnate state on earth, for then he appeared, not *great*, but mean ; and his kingdom was not with observation : but hereafter, in the latter day, when his name should be great among the Gentiles, from the rising of the sun to the going down of the same, Mal. i. 11. and especially at his second coming, which will be with power and great glory ; and he will appear, as the *Son of the Highest*, as the great God, and our Saviour ; and whereas he was the Son of David, according to the flesh, it is foretold, that he should have the throne of his father David, not literally, but mystically; which will have its accomplishment, in part, at the conversion of the Jews in the last day, when they shall seek the Lord their God, and David their king, the true Messiah, and yield subjection to him ; but more fully when all the elect of God are gathered in, both Jews and Gentiles, over whom he will reign, even over the house of Jacob, that Jacob, the Lord has chosen for himself; and this his kingdom will be for ever; it will not give way to, nor be succeeded by another ; in the same sense as in the prophecy of Daniel, it is said to be an everlasting kingdom ; there will be no end of it ; for when Christ has reigned with his people on earth a thousand years, he will reign with them, and they with him, in heaven, to all eternity ; see Mic. iv. 7. ——4. From Luke xxii. 29, 30. *As my father hath appointed unto me a kingdom, &c.* Here is a special and peculiar kingdom of Christ, which he calls, *my kingdom;* and which he has by the designation and appointment of his Father ; and which was yet to come, as well as that he appointed to his followers ; in which kingdom there will be a *table*, at which all Christ's people will sit, and eat and drink ; not corporally, but spiritually, and shall feed upon a divine repast, suited to their resurrection state; for at this table shall sit Abraham, Isaac, and Jacob, and multitudes from divers parts, and who have lived in the several periods of time ; and here will be *thrones* placed, on which the saints shall sit ; for they will now be *kings and priests unto God*, and shall reign as such, and have judgment given them, and on some distinct honours will be conferred.——5. From Luke xxiii. 42, 43. *And he said unto Jesus, Lord, remember me when thou comest into thy kingdom!* The light and faith the penitent thief had in the kingdom of Christ, and in his future coming to it, were very great ; for though Christ appeared now very mean and despicable, suffering a shameful death, and lying under the greatest reproach and ignominy ; yet he believed that he would come again, and take possession of a kingdom that belonged to him ; and desires that he might be remembered by him at his appearing and kingdom ; to which an answer is returned ; *And Jesus said unto him, verily I say unto thee, to-day shalt thou be with me in paradise* : signifying, that he should not stay so long without partaking of his favours ; for that day he should be with him in the third heaven, and continue with him till his second coming ; and then he, with all his saints, should come with him, and share in the glories of his kingdom.——6. From Acts i. 6. *Lord, wilt thou at this time restore the kingdom unto Israel?* The sceptre, according to ancient prophecy, was now departed from Judah, and Judea was become a province to the Roman empire ; now the Jews had a notion, that when the Messiah came, he would restore the kingdom, and redeem them from the Roman yoke, and make them a happy people, as to temporal things; and with this notion, the disciples themselves were tinctured ; and as they believed that Jesus was the Messiah, they had raised expectations of this matter ; but when he was dead, their hopes seem to be almost quite gone, Luke xxiv. 21. but Christ being raised from the dead, their hopes revived: and it was a notion that prevailed with the Jews, and does to this day, that the coming of the king Messiah, to deliver them, and the resurrection of the dead, will be at the same time: and, indeed, Christ's personal reign will take place after the resurrection of the just. And now there having been a resurrection of many of the saints, Matt. xxvii. 52, 53. and especially Christ himself being risen, and also had spoken to his disciples of things, pertaining to the kingdom of God, ver. 3. they might hope that this was the time the kingdom would be restored. Now though they had very obscure and carnal notions of the kingdom; yet Christ does not deny that there would be a kingdom hereafter he should enjoy, and which should be restored to Israel; only blames them for their curiosity in enquiring into the time of it, ver. 7. and which shews that this kingdom will not be till Christ comes to judge the quick and dead, which time none knows but the Father only, Matt. xxiv. 36. and exactly agrees with this passage.——7. From 2 Tim. iv. 1. *I charge thee therefore before God, and the Lord Jesus Christ, who shall judge the quick and dead at his appearing, and his kingdom.* This appearing of Christ cannot be meant of his first appearing in human nature, that was past, this future; that was not to judge the world, this will be; nor did his kingdom then appear, now it will: but of his appearing a second time to those that look for him, Heb. ix. 28. and then his personal reign, and glorious kingdom will take place, he now personally appearing in his glory; and when he will judge both quick and dead, will virtually judge, as has been before observed, the dead and living saints, by raising the one and changing the other, when he shall descend from heaven, and thus appear; and the wicked also, by burning their bodies in the general conflagration which now will be, and by shutting up their souls with Satan, in the bottomless pit. And moreover, the actual judgment, both of the righteous and the wicked, will follow on this appearing of his kingdom; the judgment of the saints will be at the beginning of it, and in it, and the judgment of the wicked at the end of it.——8. From Heb. ii. 5. *For unto the angels hath he not put in subjection the world to come, whereof we speak;* though the *world to come,* may be understood of the gospel-dispensation the apostle had been speaking of in the preceding verses, in distinction from the legal, or Jewish dispensation, angels had a concern in; whereas they have none in the ministry of the gospel. And the Jewish dispensation is sometimes called *the world,* the end of which fell upon the times of Christ and his apostles, Heb. ix. 26. 1 Cor. x. 11. and with respect to which, the gospel-dispensation may be called *the world to come,* it being usual with the Jews, to call the days of the Messiah by this name; which may take in the whole time between the first and second coming of Christ. But though the apostle may have respect to what he was speaking of in the preceding verses, yet so as to include what he was going on to speak of in the following verses, concerning the second Adam's world; for the proof of which he refers to the eighth Psalm; which is spoken, not of the first Adam, not even in his state of innocence; the name of the Lord was not then so excellent in all the earth as it has been since, and especially will be; nor were there then babes and sucklings, out of whose mouth strength, or praise, could be ordained; nor was Satan, the enemy and avenger, stilled, he soon got the advantage over Adam; nor could Adam be called then Enosh, a frail mortal man, as that word is thought to signify; nor was he a son of man; nor were the works of God's hands so universally put under him as is said, not the angels: but Christ, the second Adam, is meant, with whom every thing agrees; though, as yet, all things, in the fullest sense, are not in subjection to him, nor will be, till his second coming, till after the binding of Satan, and the resurrection of the dead; and then the last enemy, death, will be destroyed, and his glorious kingdom take place, which angels will have no concern in; they will be employed at the beginning of it, in gathering together the risen saints; and at the end of it, in casting the wicked into hell; but not in the kingdom itself; nor will they be needed. Moreover, this world to come, seems to include the new world, the new heavens, and the new earth, the apostle Peter speaks of; for his beloved brother Paul, he says, had wrote and spoke of those to the same persons the apostle Peter wrote unto; now he wrote to the converted Jews, scattered abroad in divers places, and therefore must refer to the epistle to the Hebrews, written by the apostle Paul; and where, in that epistle, can he be thought to speak of this new world, the heavens and the earth, but in this passage under consideration? and which may be very well rendered, as it is by Dr. Burnet,[8] *the habitable earth to come;* which will be the seat of Christ's personal reign.

I take no notice now of the proof from the passages Rev. v. 10. and xx. 4, 5, 6. which are very express, because I have already made mention of them, and shall have occasion to make more use of them; though Socinus[9] thinks this kingdom cannot be proved from chap. xx. since the whole place, he says, must be taken and explained in an allegorical way; but he owns, but should he be asked, what is the allegorical interpretation of it, he is not ashamed to confess his ignorance of it. But that it is to be taken in a literal sense, will appear hereafter. I go on,

II. To shew, that in this glorious, visible, and personal reign of Christ, all the saints will have a share; they will *reign with him,* Rev. xx. 4, 6. I shall not dwell long on the proof of this; because those scriptures which speak of Christ's kingdom, give plain and clear hints of the reign of his saints in it.

1*st,* There are various passages of scripture, which give plain intimations of the reign of the saints with Christ in his kingdom; these are they which he will then *make princes in all the earth,* Psalm xlv. 16. these however mean in their original, are, through his grace, set among princes, and shall inherit the throne of glory; and these princes are altogether kings; and being such, shall reign with Christ on earth; for when he, the King, shall *reign in righteousness,* these are the *princes* that shall *rule in judgment,* Isa. xxxii. 1. In the same prophecy of Daniel, which speaks of the kingdom that shall be given to Christ, upon his coming in the clouds of heaven, chap. vii. 14. it is also said, ver. 27. *And the kingdom, and the dominion, and the greatness of the kingdom;* all which is expressive of a glorious kingdom *under the whole heaven;* and so not a kingdom in heaven, but under it, on earth, and which will extend to all the earth. Such a kingdom *shall be given to the people of the saints of the most High;* to the people and saints of Christ, who is Jehovah, the most High in all the earth; such a kingdom they never had yet, nor never will have, till the son of man comes in the clouds of heaven; *Whose kingdom is an everlasting kingdom, and all dominion shall serve and obey him:* which shews, that this kingdom is of the same nature, extent, and duration, with Christ's, ver. 14. and in which the saints will share with him. Brenius[10] thinks, that by one *like the Son of man,* ver. 13. is not meant Christ personally, but his glorious kingdom in the latter-day; that as the four preceding monarchies are represented by beasts, for their fierceness, cruelty and tyranny; his by a man, for the mildness, gentleness, lenity, and humanity of it: and that coming in the clouds of heaven, denotes the divine and heavenly original of it, not rising out of the sea, or earth, as the other kingdoms: and he supposes the Son of man, and the people of the saints of the most High, ver. 27. to be the same to whom the dominion will be given. There is a passage in Micah, chap. iv. 7, 8. which plainly intimates, that when Christ reigns, his church and people shall reign also; *The Lord shall reign over them in mount Zion, from henceforth even for ever;* to which reference seems to be had by the angel, in Luke i. 32. and then it follows; *And thou, O tower of the flock, the stronghold of the daughter of Zion;* which may be understood of Christ, the tower and strong-hold of his people: *Unto thee shall it come, even the first dominion;* he shall have the first, the chief, the principal share in this reign; yet also, *the kingdom shall come to the daughter of Jerusalem,* the church of God, the new Jerusalem, the holy city of the saints. Our Lord tells his disciples, *That ye which have followed me,* who had embraced him as the Messiah, and received his doctrines, and submitted to his ordinances: here should be a stop, and then another clause begin;—*in the regeneration;* meaning, not the grace of regeneration, or the new-birth; but a new state of things, the resurrection state:[11] the word παλιγγενεσια, is used by Greek writers, both philosophers and the christian fathers,[12] for the renovation of the world; and the Syriac version of it here, is, *in the new world,* that is, the new heavens and the new earth, the apostle Peter speaks of; in which new

---

[8] Theory of the Earth, vol. 2. b. 4. chap. 2, p. 198.
[9] Opera, tom. 2. contra Chiliastas, p. 458, 460.
[10] Not. in Dan. vii. 13. et de regno Eccl. glorioso, c. 2. fol. 11.

[11] Austin says, without doubt the resurrection of the dead is meant, De Civ. Dei, l. 20. c. 5.
[12] Antoninus de Seipso, l. 11. f. 1. Euseb. Præpar. Evangel. l. 15. c. 19. Basil. de Creat. Orat. 1. Epiphan. contr. Hæres. l. 1. Tom. 3. hær. 37.

state, *the Son of man shall sit on the throne of his glory*, reign in it before his ancients gloriously; and then *also*, adds he, *ye shall sit upon twelve thrones, judging the twelve tribes of Israel;* should have posts and places of honour in the church of God, Matt. xix. 28. similar to this, is what Christ says to them in Luke xxii. 29, 30. that as his Father had appointed him a kingdom, so he appointed one to them, in which they should *eat and drink at his table, and sit on thrones, &c.* which is expressive of great nearness to him, communion with him in his kingdom, and of great honour conferred upon them. The saying of Christ, in Luke xx. 35. refers to this state; where he speaks of some that *shall be counted worthy to obtain that world, and the resurrection from the dead;* by which is meant the world to come, in distinction from this present world, ver. 34. even the new world, the apostle Peter's new heavens and new earth, which will take place upon the resurrection of the dead; and they that are worthy of the first resurrection, through the grace of Christ, those shall obtain, possess, inherit, and dwell in the new world, and reign with Christ in it. The kingdom to be restored to Israel, Acts i. 6. which Christ seems to allow will be, is what will be restored and given to the mystical Israel, even the whole Israel of God, all his elect, consisting of Jews and Gentiles. When the apostle Paul speaks of saints that suffer with Christ, being *glorified together*, Rom. viii. 17. he elsewhere expresses, by their *reigning with him*, 2 Tim. ii. 12. and to this reigning together with Christ, he may well be thought to have respect in 1 Cor. iv. 8. *Ye have reigned as kings without us;* treating him, and his fellow ministers, with some degree of contempt, as if they were below them, and they stood in no need of them: and adds, *I would to God that you did reign*, in the best sense, and in the highest degree, even with Christ, in his personal reign; *that we also might reign with you;* in which state the saints will all reign together. Once more, Christ promises, Rev. iii. 21. *To him that overcometh, will I grant to sit with me on my throne; even as I also overcame, and am set down with my Father in his throne:* this promise will be made good to every overcomer; to every one that is made more than a conqueror through Christ; and will be fulfilled in the kingdom-state, when he will have a throne of his own; now he sits on his Father's throne with him; then he will sit on his own throne, and this will be large enough for all his saints to sit upon with him; which is as strongly expressive of reigning with him, as words can possibly be. To all which may be added, the relations and characters the saints bear in scripture, which will strengthen the proof of their sharing with Christ in the glories of his kingdom. They are, and will then appear to be, *the children of God, being the children of the resurrection*, Luke xx. 36. as Christ was declared to be the Son of God by his resurrection from the dead; so they will be declared also to be the sons of God, by their resurrection from the dead; *And if children, then heirs; heirs of God, and joint-heirs with Christ,* Rom. viii. 17. Christ is heir of all things, and they are joint-heirs with him; he is heir of the world, and the world is theirs, Christ being theirs; not the present world, in which they have but a small share; but the world to come, the new world, the world that Abraham was heir of, through the righteousness of faith; as are also all his spiritual seed, even they that are Christ's; and these are heirs according to the promise, and shall inherit the new earth, and reign with Christ in it. The church and people of God, stand in the relation of a bride to Christ, being espoused to him; hence as he is king, the church is queen; and not only stands at his right-hand in gold of Ophir, but sits on the same throne with him; and as she bears the same name with him, Jer. xxiii. 5, 6. and xxxiii. 16. she shares in his honour, dignity, and glory. The saints have the character of kings, being made so by Christ to God; and they have the regalia of kings, have thrones to sit on, crowns on their heads, and shall not want a kingdom; being kings, they shall reign on earth, and reign with Christ there, Rev. i. 6. and iii. 21. and iv. 4. and v. 10. and xx. 4.

2*dly*, All the saints will share in the glories of Christ's kingdom; though some will have distinguished honours, yet all will reign with Christ. Some think only the martyrs will rise first, and reign; and, according to the opinion of some, not on earth neither; but shall ascend to heaven, and reign there, whilst the other saints, during the millennium, are on earth; and which is grounded on a passage in Rev. xx. 4. *And I saw thrones, and they sat upon them, and judgment was given unto them,* those next described; *and I saw the* *souls of them that were beheaded for the witness of Jesus, and for the word of God—and they lived and reigned with Christ a thousand years.* That these were martyrs, no doubt is to be made; they suffered death for the testimony they bore to Jesus and his gospel; and by the manner of their death, beheading, it appears that such are designed who suffered under the persecutions of the Roman pagan emperors, this being a Roman punishment; hence the axe used to be carried before the Roman magistrates; and this one sort of death is put for all others that christians, in those times, were put to: and these souls seem to be the same with those in Rev. vi. 9, 10. such, indeed, who have been slain in the cause of Christ, shall *live*, that is, live again; their bodies shall be raised and united to their souls, and *reign with Christ* in their whole person, body, and soul: but not a word is here said, or elsewhere, of their ascension to heaven, and reigning there; but, on the contrary, those who are said to dwell with Christ, and he with them, are said to come down from God out of heaven, Rev. xxi. 2, 3. and that there should be two sorts of persons in the millennium, one in heaven and the other on earth; or, as others imagine, that there shall be on earth some in an immortal, perfect state, and others in a mortal and imperfect one; some having the word and ordinances among them, and others not, are mere chimeras, for which there is no foundation: and what communion can saints have with each other, who are either at such a distance from one another, or in such different circumstances? and as to the martyrs, it is certain, there are others besides them who shall live and reign with Christ a thousand years: and who are mentioned in the same text; for it follows, *And which had not worshipped the beast, neither his image; neither had received his mark upon their foreheads, or in their hands; and they*, as well as the martyrs before described, *lived and reigned with Christ a thousand years;* these are not represented as sufferers for Christ, only as confessors and professors of his name; who bore their testimony against the papacy, in every shape of it, and did not yield unto it, neither by word nor deed; and may include all such persons, who, in every age and period of time, abstain from all corrupt worship, false doctrines, and ordinances of men. The reason why such who suffered under Rome pagan, and those who submitted not to Rome papal, are particularly pointed at and described, is, because the book of the Revelation is chiefly concerned with the state of the church, from the resurrection of Christ to his second coming. Otherwise, all the old testament saints, as well as new, will have a part in the first resurrection, and share in the millennium reign; even all the saints that have been from the beginning of the world, now are, or shall be, to the end of it; for,——1. All the saints will come with Christ, who have departed this life, when he comes a second time; this is asserted both in the Old and New Testament, Zech. xiv. 5. 1 Thess. iii. 13. and iv. 14.——2. All that are Christ's shall rise from the dead at his coming, 1 Cor. xv. 23. and, in consequence of their resurrection, shall reign with him. Now all the people of God, from the beginning of the world to the end of it, all true believers in Christ, are his, belong to him; he has an interest in them, and they in him; and when he comes a second time, they will rise first; and having a part in the first resurrection, shall reign with Christ a thousand years, Rev. xx. 4, 6. ——3. All the elect of God, and the redeemed of the Lamb, are kings and priests; and being such, shall reign on earth; those that are a *chosen generation*, or who are *elect according to the fore-knowledge of God*, are a *royal priesthood*, or are kings and priests, 1 Pet. i. 2. and ii. 9. and all that are *redeemed by the blood* of the Lamb, *out of every kindred, tongue, people, and nation*, are *made unto God kings and priests*, and *shall reign on earth*, on the new earth, with Christ, a thousand years; even all of them, all that are chosen, all that are redeemed, Rev. v. 9, 10. and xx. 6.——4. The whole church of God, and the members of it, in every dispensation, shall have a share in the kingdom of Christ. Abraham, Isaac, and Jacob, and all the prophets, will have a seat in it, and multitudes from all parts of the world, and who have lived in different ages, shall come and sit down with them, Matt. viii. 11. Luke xi. 28, 29. The four-and-twenty elders, the representatives of the gospel church, under the New Testament dispensation, being redeemed out of every nation, and being kings and priests, declare their strong faith that they shall reign on earth; and accordingly, are sometimes represented as having on their heads crowns of gold, as well as clothed in white, the raiment of priests and princes, Rev. iv. 4. and v. 9, 10. In a word, the whole body of the elect, and redeemed of the Lamb, the church universal, consisting of all its members, not one wanting; and so a bride, completely prepared and adorned for her husband; even the holy city and new Jerusalem, will descend from God, out of heaven, on earth; and the tabernacle of God, of Immanuel, will be with them; and he will dwell and reign with them, and they with him, Rev. xxi. 2, 3. compared with chap. xx. 9.

3dly, In what sense the saints, even all the saints, will reign with Christ, may be next considered. This will not be after the manner of his spiritual reign among his saints; that is a reign *in* them, this a reigning *with* them, and of them with him. His reign of grace takes place at the conversion of men, when, as King, he sets up his throne in their hearts, and reigns there; and such a reign has been from the beginning of the world, as soon as the first man was called by grace; and has continued ever since, more or less, in every dispensation, and will continue until the last man is converted. Nor does this reign we are treating of, take place in the separate state of the soul in heaven, before the resurrection: that state is expressed, by a *being with Christ*, Luke xxiii. 42. 2 Cor. v. 8. Phil. i. 23. but never, as I remember, by *reigning with him*. This reign will not be until the resurrection, till soul and body are re-united; for there can be no proper reigning while the body is under the power of death and the grave, at least not fully and completely: the saints will first *live*, that is, live again in their bodies, have a part in the first resurrection, and then *reign with Christ*, soul and body, a thousand years, Rev. xx. 4, 6. And so,——1. This will be a reign *with Christ* personally and visibly; he will appear in person, and be visible by them; and they shall appear with him, in a most glorious manner, in soul and body; and will be *like him*, being glorified, and reigning together with him; and *shall see him as he is*, personally and visibly, in the glory of his person, as God-man, reigning before his ancients gloriously; see Col. iii. 4. 1 John iii. 2.——2. This reigning with Christ, implies some kind of share with him in the glories of his kingdom; hence *thrones* are said to be set for them to sit upon; and *judgment given them*, which denotes regal power to be exercised by them; yea, they are said to sit on the same throne with Christ, on *his throne*, and to *eat and drink at his table, in his kingdom*: all which expresses a great share of honour and dignity, and of large enjoyments; see Rev. xx. 4. and iii. 21. Luke xxii. 30.——3. This supposes dominion over all their enemies; as Christ will now have all enemies put under his feet, being subdued by him; so all enemies will be put under the feet of the saints, and they will have dominion over them. Sin will now be no more troublesome to them. Their power over sin, in the present state, is expressed rather negatively, by sin, *not having dominion over them*; than affirmatively, by their having dominion over sin; nay, they are sometimes so far from it, that they are brought *into captivity by it*: but now the struggle for dominion will be over, the warfare will be accomplished, and an entire victory obtained over sin, which will be no more. Satan, and his principalities and powers, though spoiled and bruised by Christ, and triumphed over by him, yet there is a wrestling and combat between the saints and them in the present life; and though the devil cannot devour and destroy them, yet he greatly disturbs and distresses them; but now he will be bruised under their feet also; when he, and his angels, shall be shut up in the bottomless pit, where they will remain during the thousand years. Christ and his saints shall reign together in the *world*, in which the saints have now so much tribulation; and the *wicked* men of it, from whom they meet with so much persecution, in one shape or another, shall be trodden down by them, and be ashes under the soles of their feet, their bodies being burnt up in the general conflagration; and their souls in no capacity to hurt or molest them, being shut up with Satan in the bottomless pit. The last enemy, *death*, will now be destroyed, being *swallowed up in victory*, by the resurrection of the dead; so that the risen saints, reigning with Christ, may say, *O death, where is thy sting? O grave, where is thy victory?* and, indeed of this, and every other enemy, they may say, *Thanks be to God, which giveth us the victory, through our Lord Jesus Christ!* 1 Cor. xv. 26, 54, 55, 57.

III. The description of the persons that shall thus reign with Christ, as given Re xx. 6.

First, They are such who have *part in the first resurrection;* which, what that is, must be enquired into.

1st, This cannot be understood of a spiritual resurrection, or of a resurrection from the death of sin to a life of grace, which men are made partakers of at regeneration; such a resurrection cannot be intended here; for,——1. As this was a vision of something future, that John saw, be it afterwards when it may, it could never be the first resurrection of this sort; since there had been thousands of instances of this, from the beginning of the world to the times of John; and therefore could be nothing uncommon, rare, and wonderful, to be shown him, if this was the case.—— 2. This can never be the first resurrection, with respect to the persons themselves raised; for they are such who had been raised in this sense before; since they are the souls of such who had suffered for Christ and his gospel, and had borne a testimony against antichrist in every shape; and had refused obedience to him by word or deed: and can it be thought that such persons had not been quickened by the grace of God; or were not raised from the death of sin, before they suffered for the sake of Christ, or professed his name? ——3. Persons once raised in this sense, never die again; nor stand in need of being raised a second time; he that lives, and believes in Christ, never dies a spiritual death; grace in him is immortal and incorruptible: and could this possibly be their case, it would not be the first, but a second resurrection.——4. There is no such resurrection after death. Those persons are represented in the vision, as having been slain for their faithful testimony; or as having departed this life, either under Rome pagan or papal; and as they stood in no need of such a resurrection, so if they had, they could not have had it; if a man dies in his sins, he remains in them; if he dies impenitent, and an unbeliever, so he continues; neither faith nor repentance, nor any grace, are given after death.—— 5. Persons who have been quickened in this sense, or have been spiritually raised from the death of sin, and have lived, never lived corporally a thousand years; not any of the saints in the patriarchal-state, partakers of a spiritual resurrection, even those that lived the longest, not Adam, nor Methuselah, lived to such an age; nor any afterwards to the times of John; nor any since; nor is there any reason to expect that any will in the present state.——

6. There will be none to be raised in this sense at the coming of Christ in the last day; the Jews will have been converted, and the fulness of the Gentiles brought in; all that God meant should come to repentance, will now have been brought to it; and when every one of them is effectually called, or, in other words, raised from a death of sin to a life of grace, then will the day of the Lord come, and the general conflagration take place, in which all the wicked of the earth will be burnt up; and the whole election of grace being gathered in, and the whole church of God completely prepared for Christ her husband, there will remain none to be the subjects of a spiritual resurrection.——7. If this living again before the reign, or at the beginning of the reign of the thousand years, is to be understood of a spiritual resurrection, then the living of the rest of the dead, that is, of the wicked, at the end of the thousand years, must be understood in the same sense, that they shall live a life of grace, being raised from the death of sin; for it is expressly said, *The rest of the dead lived not again until the thousand years were finished;* which supposes they will live when they are finished, and live in the same sense as they will who will live at the beginning of them; that is, a corporal life, being raised from the dead; not, surely, a spiritual one.

2*dly*, Nor is this first resurrection to be understood in a civil sense, of the resurrection of the martyrs, not in their own persons, but in their successors, or of a revival of the cause for which they suffered; which it is supposed [13] will be, when in the latter day the Jews will be converted, and the fulness of the Gentiles brought in; the conversion of the Jews being represented by a resurrection, by opening their graves, and bringing them out of them, and causing them to live, Ezek. xxxvii. 13, 14. and of which some [14] understand Dan. xii. 2. and by the apostle Paul called, *life from the dead*, Rom. xi. 15. But,——1. Though this may be called a resurrection, in a figurative sense, yet it is never called, *the first resurrection;* nor can it be called so, with any propriety; because there have been already revivals of the cause of the martyrs: there was a revival of the cause of them who suffered in the persecutions

---

[13] So Brenius in loc. et de Regno Eccl. Glorioso, c. 10. The Author of Theopolis, Whitby on the Millennium, Dr. Ridgley in his Body of Divinity, &c.

[14] Brightman in Dan. xii. 2.

of the pagan emperors, in the times of Constantine, when paganism was demolished throughout the Roman empire, and christianity got ground, and flourished every where; and there was a revival of the cause of the martyrs and confessors under Rome papal, at the time of the reformation; when whole nations, even many of the European nations, fell off from popery, and embraced the truths of the gospel; so that, admitting the time referred to may be called the revival of the cause of the martrys, it cannot be said to be the *first*, but rather the *third* resurrection. Besides, a first resurrection, supposes a second of the same kind. Now after the conversion of the Jews, and the great spread of the gospel among the Gentiles, what further reviving of the cause of Christ is there to be expected in the present state, that can be called a second resurrection?———2. Those that shall have part in the first resurrection, are expressly the same persons who really existed in the times of Rome pagan, and Rome papal, and not any successors of theirs, of whom the same things cannot be said as are of them; nor in the times referred to, will there be any persons similar, and answerable to the martyrs and confessors described; since there will be no antichrist to suffer from, nor to bear a testimony against; for the kingdoms of this world, both pagan, papal, and mahometan, will now become the kingdoms of Christ, and serve him.———3. The time of the conversion of the Jews, and of the Gentiles, will be over before this first resurrection takes place; and an account is given of those events in the book of the Revelation, before this resurrection and millennium-state. They are signified, partly, by the ascension of the witnesses to heaven; and partly by the kingdoms of this world becoming Christ's, chap. xi. 12, 15. and particularly, the conversion of the Jews, by the marriage of the Lamb being come, chap. xix. 7, 8, 9.———4. The resurrection of the cause of Christ, as in the conversion of the Jews, and the accession of the Gentiles, and this first resurrection, are assigned and belong to two different periods; the events relating to the Jews and Gentiles, will be upon the destruction of the Pope and Turk, at the sounding of the seventh trumpet, and the pouring out of the sixth and seventh vials, and when all the antichristian kings and states will be destroyed: but the events of the first resurrection, and the millennium, will be not only after the destruction of antichrist, but after the binding and shutting up of Satan and his angels, with the wicked in the bottomless pit, and after the burning of the world; and not before.———5. If the first resurrection could be understood of the revival of the cause of the martyrs, at the beginning of the millennium, it would follow, that there will also be a revival of it among the rest of the dead, or the wicked, at the end of it; since it is suggested, that they shall then live: but this is not only altogether improbable, but the reverse is the truth; for they will gather together in a body, and encompass the camp of the saints, the beloved city, with an intention to destroy it: it remains, therefore,

3*dly*, That this first resurrection is to be understood literally and properly, of a corporal one; for,———1. This resurrection is of such who died a corporal death, either a violent one, being slain for their testimony for Christ and the gospel; or in a natural way, not having given into antichristian principles and practices; and therefore their living again, or their resurrection, which is called the first, must be a corporal resurrection; for as is their death, so must be their resurrection from the dead. The souls slain, cannot be understood of such, distinctly considered; for they die not, and cannot be said to be raised again; but of the persons of men with respect to their bodies, which only die, and are the proper subjects of a resurrection; and which being raised, are united to their souls, and live; and so the whole person lives.———2. Of such a resurrection, is the living again of the wicked dead, at the end of the millennium; for as their living then cannot be interpreted, neither of a spiritual resurrection, nor of a civil one, it must be of a corporal one; and if theirs, who are the *rest* of the dead, is a corporal one, then those who lived before them, being raised from the dead, must be a corporal one likewise; for that one part of the dead should be raised, and live in one sense; and the rest be raised and live in another sense, is not reasonable to suppose.———3. It is a resurrection, which, by way of emphasis, is called, *the resurrection*, which some persons are *worthy* of, and others are not; or, *the resurrection which is out of*, or *from among the dead;* the wicked dead, leaving them to continue under the power of death for a longer time; and this is the resurrection the apostle was so desirous of attaining to, Phil. iii. 11. where he uses a different word, than what is commonly used of the resurrection; it being *a better resurrection*, Heb. xi. 35. the resurrection of the just, which is better than that of the wicked, being unto life, and *through Jesus*, Acts iv. 2. through union to him; and of which he is the example and first-fruits.——4. The resurrection in the text has a double article, which makes it the more emphatical, and points at what resurrection is meant, *The resurrection, the first;* that which is the first, with respect to the wicked, whose resurrection can be no other than corporal, and therefore this must be so too. And this may be confirmed by other passages of scripture; as by Psalm xlix. 14. *The upright shall have dominion over them*, the wicked; they rising first in the morning of the day of the resurrection; and the wicked in the evening, or at the end of that day: and especially by 1 Thess. iv. 16. *The dead in Christ shall rise first;* this can be understood of no other than a corporal resurrection, which will be at the second coming of Christ; nor of any other but of the saints who die in Christ, in union with him; and of their rising before the wicked, who die not in him, but in their sins; and not of their rising before the change of the living saints, as some think; for the resurrection of the dead in Christ, and the change of the living saints, will both be together, *in a moment, in the twinkling of an eye*, 1 Cor. xv. 52. and so not one before another. Nor are the several particular resurrections mentioned in scripture, any objection to the resurrection of the saints first;[15] since these were not a resurrection to an immortal life; and besides, would lie as strongly against Christ being the *first* that rose from the dead, Acts xxvi. 23. Nor is the resurrection of the saints, at the resurrection of Christ, any objection to it, Matt. xxvii. 52, 53. for whether or no they rose to an immortal life, is a question; and if they did, which is not improbable, theirs was only a presage and pledge of the general resurrection of the just, which is the first; and that of the wicked, the second.——5. Nor are the passages in Dan. xii. 2. and John v. 28, 29. to be objected to a first and second corporal resurrection, and to such a distance of time between them, as that of a thousand years; the resurrection of good and evil men being mentioned together, as if they were events that took place at the same time; since, in prophecies especially, as these are, things are often laid together, which are fulfilled separately, and at a distance from each other; as some concerning the first and second coming of Christ; and also concerning his spiritual and personal reign. Besides, these passages may be considered as perfectly agreeing with, and as expressive of this two-fold resurrection, as to the time thereof; thus the prophet Daniel says, *Many shall awake*, or rise from the dead; that is, *all;* but not at the same time, nor to the same end; *some* of these shall awake or arise, at the beginning of the thousand years, *to everlasting life;* and *some*, at the end of them, *to shame and everlasting contempt:* and so our Lord says in other passages; *The hour is coming;* the word ωϱα, does not always signify that part of time which is sometimes called an hour; but *time* in general, and a very long time too; see 1 John ii. 18. Rev. xvii. 12. and so here; *The time is coming*, the time of the millennium; within the compass of which *all that are in the graves shall hear his voice, and come forth; they that have done good, unto the resurrection of life*, at the beginning of the said hour, or time; *and they that have done evil unto the resurrection of damnation*, at the end of it.——6. The apostle John, when, in the context, speaking of the resurrection from the dead, says, *they lived*, that is, rose from the dead; *but the rest of the dead lived not again*, did not rise again from the dead till afterwards; speaks in the language of his nation; nothing is more common with the Jews, than to call a corporal resurrection תחיית המתים *the quickening of the dead*,[16] or causing them to live. And is agreeable to the sacred scriptures, Isa. xxvi. 19. Hos. vi. 2. Rom iv. 17. Now since only such who have part in the first resurrection, and which is a corporal one, will reign with Christ a thousand years; the millennium-reign will be a reign only of risen saints, in a perfect state, and who will not be in a mortal and sinful one; so that here will be no conversion-work, and so no need of the word and ordinances; and much less will there be an indulgence to carnal pleasures.

Secondly, Another part of the description of those that shall reign with Christ in the millennium, and which shews their happiness, is, *On such the second death hath*

---

[15] Theopolis, p 53.
[16] T. B. Sabbat, fol. 88. 2. Sotah, fol. 48. 2. et Sanhedrin, fol. 92. 1. Targum Hieros in Gen. 19. 26. et. in Gen. 25. 24.

no power : the phrase, *the second death,* is only used in the book of Revelation, and was common with the Jews, and what John was well acquainted with, and is frequently to be met with in their writings ;[17] what is meant by it, may be seen in Rev. xx. 14. and xxi. 8. and is no other than the punishment of body and soul in hell ; an eternal separation of both from God, and is called the *second* death, in distinction from the death of the body, which is the first death, and lies in a separation of the soul from the body : now to be free and secure from such a death, must be a great happiness ; and this all in the millennium-state will enjoy, and for evermore.

Thirdly, Those that will share in the millennium-reign with Christ, will be *priests of God and of Christ;* that is, made priests to God by Christ ; shall serve the Lord as the priests in the temple did ; draw nigh to him, and offer up the sacrifices of praise continually ; they will be a royal priesthood, both kings and priests ; as in Rev. i. 6. and v. 10. like Christ their head, who is a Priest on his throne ; and as his type, Melchizedek, who was king of Salem, and priest of the most high God : nor has it been unusual, in the nations of the earth, for men to be both kings and priests ;[18] and certain it is, that those in the millennium are priests, that shall reign as kings ; and the same word, in the Hebrew language, signifies both priests and princes.

Fourthly, Upon the whole, it is no wonder that they are pronounced *blessed* and *holy*: they must needs be *blessed,* since they will be always before the throne, and serve the Lord day and night, and hunger and thirst no more ; shall be free from evils of every kind, and from death in every shape, and of every sort ; and shall be in the perfect enjoyment of the presence of Christ. And they will be holy in body, being raised in purity, in incorruption, and in glory, like the glorious body of Christ ; and in soul, being perfectly sanctified, and entirely free from sin, from the being of it, and all defilement by it ; see Rev. xxi. 27.

IV. The continuance and duration of the reign of Christ and the saints together, which will be a *thousand years.* The things to be enquired into are, whether these years are to be understood definitely, or indefinitely? and whether they are past, or yet to come ?

First, Whether they are to be taken indefinitely, for an uncertain number; or definitely, for an exact, precise, determinate time literally.——1. One ancient writer[19] understands the words indefinitely, for a long time, even from the first coming of Christ to the end of the world ; a long time indeed! longer than the thousand years themselves ; for more than seven hundred years above a thousand, have run out already. Another,[20] indeed, interprets them of the ages of eternity, for which Psalm cv. 8. is quoted ; but whatever may be the sense of that text, it cannot be the sense of the millennium-reign, for that will have an end ; it is expressly said, *The rest of the dead lived not again till the thousand years were finished,* Rev. xx. 5. and of Christ's reign and kingdom in them, there will be an end, when he will deliver up the kingdom to the Father, 1 Cor. xv. 24. or else, as the same ancient writer thinks, the latter part of the last thousandth year of the world may be meant, a part being put for the whole. But however indefinitely this phrase may be sometimes so understood, as in 1 Sam. xviii. 7. Psalm xci. 7. it cannot be so taken in the passages relating to the binding of Satan, and the reign of Christ and his saints ; but must, ——2. Be interpreted definitely and literally, of a precise, determinate space of time ; better reasons for which cannot be well given, than are by a writer[21] in the last century, though not in the scheme of the personal reign of Christ a thousand years ; which are as follow,——(1.) Because when there is no necessity to take a scripture in a figurative sense, we are to receive it in the letter ; but neither the scope of the place, nor the analogy of faith, nor other scriptures, lay any such necessity upon us, so to take it.——(2.) Because this same space is so often repeated by the Spirit, to which we should take the more earnest heed, as matter of instruction and information (and so fix it on the mind the more strongly) for thrice it is said, Satan was bound a thousand years, and afterwards loosed, ver. 2, 3, 7. twice it is said, the saints shall reign a thousand years, ver. 4, 6. once that the rest of the dead

---

[17] Targ. Hieros. in Deut. 33. 6. et Tou. in Isa. 22. 14. et 65. 6, 15. et in Jer. 51. 39, 57. δευτερος θανατος is a phrase in Plutarch. de facie in luna, p. 942.

[18] Rex Anius, rex idem hominum Phoebique sacerdos, Virgil. Æneid. 1. 3. so the Roman emperors were called Pontifices.

[19] Ambros. in Apocalyps. c. 20. col. 473.

[20] Aug. de Civ. Dei, l. 20. c. 7.

[21] The Author of Theopolis, p. 43, 44.

lived not again till the thousand years were finished, ver. 5. in all six times.——(3.) The emphasis put upon the phrase. Pareus well observes, that in ver. 2, 6. the thousand years are without an article, χιλια ετη, *a thousand years;* but in the other places, *four* times, with an article, τα χιλια ετη, *these thousand years;* these emphatically, these precise thousand years. As if he should say, Satan's imprisonment shall continue a thousand years; the martyrs shall live and reign with Christ during these thousand years, and afterwards he shall be loosed.——(4.) The parts to which this number is applied, are so cemented together, as cause and effect, distinction and opposition, that they very much strengthen and prove that just account of a thousand years; namely, Satan is bound a thousand years, that he should not deceive the nations till the same thousand years be fulfilled; then the saints lived and reigned a thousand years with Christ, that same thousand years; but the rest of the dead lived not again until these thousand years were finished; whilst the holy ones, as their happiness, made priests of God and of Christ, reign with Christ a thousand years; to which may be added, that these thousand years are bounded both at the beginning and end: they are bounded by the binding of Satan at the beginning of them, and by loosing of him at the end of them, ver. 27. and they are bounded by two resurrections; by the first resurrection of the saints, and the reign of them with Christ upon it; and by the second resurrection, or the resurrection of the wicked, at the close thereof. The next enquiry is,

Secondly, Whether these thousand years are past or to come? To the solution of which, this observation is necessary, that the binding of Satan, and the reign of Christ, are cotemporary; that the same thousand years Satan is bound, Christ and his saints reign together; the thousand years of the one, and the thousand years of the other, run parallel with each other: and it is further to be observed, and what will contribute greatly to the settling of this point, and even to the decision of it, that by the binding of Satan is meant, an entire and absolute confinement of him, and of all his angels, in the bottomless pit; so that he and they will not be able *to deceive the nations* any more, till the thousand years are ended; that is, not be able to draw them into idolatry, to fill them with bad principles, and lead them into bad practices, and to stir them up to make war with the saints, and persecute them; and so by any, and all of these ways, deceive; during which time, the church and people of God must be in a state of purity and peace. Now if any such time can be shewn, in which the nations of the world, not any of them, were not so far under the influence and deception of Satan, as not to be drawn into idolatry; nor to embrace false doctrines, and go into evil practices; nor to be excited to persecute the saints, for the space of a thousand years; and that the church of Christ, during such a time, has been in a state of perfect purity and peace; free from being disturbed and distressed by idolaters, heretics, and persecutors; then may these thousand years be said to be past; but if this cannot be made to appear, then most certainly they are yet to come. Let us put this to the trial; which will be best done by considering the several epochas, or periods, from whence these thousand years have been dated. As,

1*st*, From the birth of Christ, who came to destroy the works of the devil, and before whom Satan fell as lightning from heaven; yet this falls short of the binding and casting him into the bottomless pit: whoever considers the state of the Gentile world when Christ came, being under the power of the god of this world, the nations thereof being left to walk in their own ways; nay, Christ forbad his disciples going into any of the cities of the Gentiles; nor had they a commission to preach the gospel to all nations, till after his resurrection from the dead; who, I say, that considers these things, can ever imagine that Satan was now bound? And if we look into the state of the Jewish nation and church, how sadly corrupted in their morals, being a wicked and an adulterous generation, and depraved in their religious sentiments; neglecting the word of God, and preferring the traditions of the elders to it; rejecting Christ, when he came to them with all the marks and characters of the true Messiah, and treating him with the utmost indignation and contempt; and were as our Lord says, *of* their *father the devil*, and his *lusts* they would *do;* there can be no reason to believe that Satan was now bound. His many attacks on the person and life of Christ shew the contrary; as his putting Herod on seeking the young child's life to destroy it, in his infancy; and to make that carnage of the infants in and about Bethlehem, he did; his tempting him in the wilderness, in the manner he did, which was bold, daring, and insolent; instigating the scribes and Pharisees to lay hands on him, and kill him; marching towards him as the prince of the world, and combating with him in the garden; and putting it into the heart of Judas to betray him; and stirring up the people of all sorts to be pressing to the Roman governor, for the crucifixion of him, and by which means he was brought to the dust of death. And though, indeed, Satan was dispossessed of the bodies of men, which possession shews he was not bound; yet when dispossessed he was not bound and cast into the bottomless pit, but was suffered to go and rove about where he pleased; and though Christ, by his death, destroyed Satan, who had the power of death, and spoiled his principalities and powers, and ruined his works; yet all this did not amount to a binding and confinement of his person in prison.

2*dly,* Others date these thousand years of Satan's binding from the resurrection of Christ; when it is true, Christ ascended on high, and led captivity captive, and poured down his Spirit upon his apostles, on the day of Pentecost, whereby they were wonderfully fitted to preach his gospel; and accordingly preached it with great success, both in Judea and in the Gentile world; but still Satan was not bound. Not in Judea; for in the first and purest christian church, he filled the hearts of Ananias and Sapphira to lie against the Holy Ghost. He stirred up the Jews to lay hold on the apostles, and put them in prison; and to stone Stephen the proto-martyr; he raised a violent persecution against the church at Jerusalem, and havock was made of it, and men and women hauled to prison; he put Herod upon killing James the brother of John, and committing Peter to prison. And whereas the ministers of the word went into other countries, preaching the gospel, the Jews, under the instigation of Satan, stirred up the people against them wherever they came; as at Antioch, Iconium, Lystra, Thessalonica, and other places; and what the christian-Hebrews suffered from them, may be seen in Heb. x. 32, 33. Nor was Satan bound in the Gentile world; for though the gospel made its way into divers countries and cities, to the conversion of many souls, and the forming of many churches; yet heathenism under the influence of the God of this world, was the prevailing religion every where; and the sect of the christians was every where spoken against; and the apostles and ministers of the word, were every where persecuted; bonds and imprisonment waited for them in all places; and all the apostles suffered death for the sake of the gospel; see the account the apostle gives of himself and others, in 1 Cor. iv. 9, 12, 13.

3*dly,* Others begin these thousand years of Satan's binding at the destruction of Jerusalem, which was very dreadful; in the siege of it eleven hundred thousand men perished;[22] and when such insurrections, intestine quarrels, seditions, murders, and scenes of iniquity were among the Jews themselves, Satan could never be thought to be bound then; and after it, though things took a different turn with the Jews, and in favour of the christians, in Judea and elsewhere; the Jews, though they had the same ill will to them, had not the same power against them; yet they themselves manifestly appeared to be under the deception of Satan, by their giving heed to false prophets, and false christs, which our Lord foretold would arise; witness Bar Cochab, a false messiah, who rose up in the times of Trajan, whom the Jews embracing, rebelled against the empire, which brought a war upon them in which fifty-eight thousand were slain;[23] and under the same deception by false messiahs, and under the same blindness and hardness of heart, and malice against Christ and his gospel, have they continued to this day. And as for the Gentile world, though the gospel got ground every where, and multitudes of souls were converted, and the Gentile oracles were struck dumb;[24] the temples almost desolate, and worship in them was intermitted;[25] yet Gentilism continued to be the prevailing religion throughout the Roman empire, till the times of Constantine, at the beginning of the fourth century; as appears by the persecutions of the christians by the Roman emperors: the first persecution was under Nero; this was indeed a little before the destruction of Jerusalem; the occasion of it was this, he himself set fire to the city of Rome, and then, under the instigation of

---

[22] Joseph. de Bello Jud. l. 6. c. 9. s. 3.
[23] Lampe Synops. Hist. Sacr. et Ecclesiast. l. 2. c. 3. p. 110.
[24] —— Delphis Oracula cessant, Juvenal. Satyr 6. v. 554.
[25] Plin. Epist. l. 10. ep. 97.

Satan, charged it upon the christians, whom he most inhumanly racked and tortured, and put to the most cruel deaths that could be invented.[26] The tenth and last persecution was under Dioclesian, a little before the times of Constantine; his æra was called by the Egyptians the æra of the martyrs;[27] the whole world was embrued with their blood; and the world was more exhausted of men thereby, than by any war, as the historian says;[28] it was the longest and most severe,[29] it lasted *ten* years; and perhaps, in allusion to the ten persecutions, or to the ten years of the last persecution, it is said in Rev. ii. 10. *The devil shall cast some of you into prison, and ye shall have tribulation ten days;* and if the devil cast the saints into prison, he himself could not be bound and cast into prison; nor could this be their reigning time; nay Dioclesian thought he had got an entire victory over the christians, and therefore set up pillars,[30] in some parts of the empire, signifying that the christian name was blotted out, and the superstition of Christ every where destroyed, as he called it; and the worship of the gods propagated; so far was Satan from being bound, that he triumphed over Christ and his cause: and that he could not be bound in this period of time, appears by the multitude of heathen deities worshipped; the number not only of heathen philosophers among the Greeks and Romans, but of the Magi in the east, and of the Druids in the west, and of the Brahmins among the Indians; also from the vile and false charges brought by the heathens under the influence of Satan against the christians, of idolatries, murders, incests, impurities, and unheard of crimes; which obliged their writers, as Justin Martyr, Tertullian, &c. to write apologies in the defence of them; to which may be added, the scoffs and flouts, the malice and blasphemy of the heathen writers against Christ and the christian religion, as Crescens, Lucian, Celsus and Porphyry: and if we look into the christian church in the three first centuries, how it was harassed and distressed with heretics and heresies, we shall soon be convinced that Satan was not bound, nor Christ's reign begun; to reckon up only the names of them from Simon Magus to Sabellius, would fill up a page; some denying the doctrine of the Trinity; some the distinct personality in the Deity; some the person of Christ, either his real humanity or his proper Deity, or divine Sonship; as vile a set of men now were, for corruption in doctrine and practice, as perhaps ever was, and may truly be called a *synagogue of Satan,* as they seem to be in Rev. ii. 9. in the times of these men therefore, the devil could never be said to be bound, when he had a synagogue of them.

4*thly,* Others begin the date of Satan's binding, and Christ's reigning, from the times of Constantine; and reckoning the thousand years from hence they will reach to the beginning of the fourteenth century. Those who go this way suppose the vision in Rev. xii. and that in chap. xx. to be the same, which cannot be; that in the former respects the imperial dragon, or the papal empire under the influence of Satan; the latter the person of the devil himself, with his angels; the former respects a battle in heaven, the latter a combat on earth; the former represents Satan as cast out of heaven on earth, the latter as cast out of the earth into the bottomless pit; the former says nothing of the binding and shutting up of Satan, the latter does; the former speaks of him after his casting down, as at liberty to go about in the earth and distress the nations, and annoy the church; but the latter as in such confinement as to be able to do neither: but that Satan could not be bound, nor the reign of Christ take place in the above period of time is manifest; for though upon Constantine's coming to the throne, and declaring himself a christian, the christian religion lift up its head, and flourished greatly with respect to numbers, wealth, riches, and grandeur, yet all its outward greatness in the issue ended in its ruin; and though heathenism was demolished throughout the empire, and pagan temples shut up,[31] yet pagan rites and ceremonies were introduced into the church, and gradually prevailed; and especially when the man of sin was revealed, so that the followers of antichrist go by the name of Gentiles, Rev. xi. 2. That the devil was not now bound, appears by the flood he cast out of his mouth to destroy the woman, the church, who was

---

[26] Sulpicii Severi Sacr. Hist. 1. 2. p. 96.
[27] Schmid. Compend. Hist. Ecclesiast. sec. 3. p. 116.
[28] Sulpicius, ut supra, p. 99, 100.
[29] Orosii Hist. 1. 7. c. 25.
[30] Gruter. Inscript. p. 280. apud Fabricii Salutar. Lux. Evangel. p. 157.
[31] Orosius, ibid. c. 28.

obliged to disappear and flee into the wilderness, the remnant of whose seed he persecuted, Rev. xii. 13—17. by which flood is meant either a flood of heresies, as those of the Arians, Nestorians, Eutychians, Macedonians, and Pelagians, which sadly infested and disturbed the churches; or a flood of persecution, particularly by the Arians, which was begun by Constantine himself; who, as the historian says,[32] exercised *vin persecutionis*, towards the latter end of his life, being imposed upon: and this was carried on with great violence by his sons, Constantius and Valens, who embraced that heresy; and in after times by some of the northern nations, who broke into the empire, and became Arians. In the reign of Julian, which, though but short, heathenism was in a great measure restored, and many diabolical arts were used by him to revive paganism, and extirpate christianity; the schools of the christians forbad, their temples shut up, and those of the heathens opened. These, with his attempt, in favour of the Jews, to rebuild the temple at Jerusalem, in spite of prophecy, and his outrageous blasphemies against the Galilean, as he used to call our Lord, plainly shew that Satan was not bound. The irruptions of the Goths and Vandals, and other northern nations, into the empire, and the destructions they made in church and state, is a full proof of this. Within this interval of time antichrist rose up, and manifestly appeared; whose coming was after the working of Satan, with all powers and signs, and lying wonders; whose followers give heed to seducing spirits, and doctrines of devils; and who worship devils, and idols of gold and silver; and whose reign is to continue one thousand two hundred and sixty days or years, and so not yet at an end: and whilst antichrist reigns, Christ's reign cannot take place, nor Satan be bound. Also much about the same time, that vile imposter Mahomet, under the instigation of the devil, arose; when the bottomless pit was opened, and then Satan surely could not lie bound in it; out of which came the smoke of the absurd Alkoran, which darkened the sun and moon, the light of great part of the world; and from whence came his locusts, the Saracens, which, for some centuries, greatly afflicted the christian empire, whose king was called Abaddon, and Apollyon, Rev. ix. 11. as did the Turks after them, whose empire was set up in the beginning of the fourteenth century, and continued to distress Europe till the latter end of the last. And now, so long as Mahometanism prevails over so large a part of the world as it does, the thousand years reign, and the binding of Satan, cannot be expected. To which may be added, the persecutions of the Waldenses and Albigenses, in the twelfth and thirteenth centuries, by the papal antichrist, and which have been exercised on them, even in the last century, in the valleys of Piedmont,[33] shew that Satan cannot be bound. And as to the state of heathenism, it will appear, by consulting the Magdeburgensian centuriators, that it has subsisted in various parts of the world, throughout all the centuries, from Constantine to the fourteenth century; and about the end of the fifteenth, when America was first discovered, in what state were the inhabitants of it? Idolators: yea, they worshipped the devil in some places in the West Indies;[34] as the inhabitants of the East Indies,[35] and others in North and South America: and how many nations and kingdoms, both in America and in the East Indies, are, at this day, under the power of heathenism? And it was a calculation made by some in the last century, that if the whole known world was divided into thirty equal parts, nineteen of them would be found idolatrous Gentiles.[36] Surely then Satan cannot be bound, so as not to deceive the nations.

5thly, Some begin the thousand years' reign, and the binding of Satan, at the reformation from popery; but whether the date is from Wickliff, John Huss, and Jerom of Prague, or from Luther; they all of them either suffered death, or met with great inhumanity and ill treatment, from the instruments of Satan, and therefore he could not be bound; and great numbers of their followers were persecuted unto death. Since the reformation, were the massacre in Paris, when ten thousand protestants were

---

[32] Sulpicius, ibid. p. 102. Socrat. Eccl. Hist. 1. 3. c. 11, 12.
[33] See Perrin's History of the Waldenses, and Morland's History of the evangelical Churches in the valley of Piedmont.
[34] P. Martyr de Angleria Decad 1. l. 9. Oviedo de Ind. Occident. c. 5.
[35] Vartomanni Navigat. 1. 5. c. 2. 23. et 16. 27. Ross's View of all Religions, p. 59. see p. 77, 79, 80, 88, 89
[36] Schmid. compend. Hist. Ecclesiast. sec. 17, p. 500.

murdered in one night, and seventy thousand in seven days time :[37] and the many martyrs burnt here in England, in queen Mary's reign; and the massacre in Ireland, in which two hundred thousand perished, all under an hellish influence; are clear demonstrations that Satan was not bound. Besides, though several nations, at the reformation, fell from popery, yet all did not, and some have revolted to it since; and whoever considers the great decline of religion in our day, the increase of popery, and the spread of errors and heresy among us, and the great profaneness and immorality that prevail, can never think that Satan is bound, or that the millennium is begun. Upon the whole, it must clearly appear, that there never as yet has been such a time, in which it could be said, that Satan had no power to deceive the nations, either by drawing them into idolatry, and other bad principles, or into persecuting practices; nor any time in which the church of Christ has been in a state of purity and peace, free from idolatry, heresy, and persecution; wherefore it may be strongly concluded, that Satan is not yet bound; and that Christ's kingdom is not yet come; nor are these things to be expected in the present state.

The spiritual reign in the latter-day bids fairest for it; and which, indeed, is a branch of Christ's kingdom, when both Pope and Turk will be destroyed; but then Satan will only be destroyed in his instruments, but not bound in his person. Besides, the spiritual and personal reign of Christ, though branches of his kingdom, belong to different periods; and will not both take place in the present state; the spiritual reign will be in the present earth, and of saints in a sinful, mortal state, and in the use of ordinances; but the millennium-reign will be on the new earth, and of saints in a risen perfect state, standing in no need of ordinances, as now. The millennium-reign will not be till after the first resurrection; and the first resurrection will not be till the second coming of Christ, when the dead in him shall rise first. The personal reign of Christ will not be till the new heavens and the new earth are made, which will be the seat of it; and these will not be till the present heavens and earth are dissolved and burnt up; and this conflagration will not be till Christ comes a second time. The reign of Christ with his saints, will not be till Satan is bound, as well as antichrist destroyed; and Satan will not be bound, till Christ, the mighty angel, descends from heaven to earth, which will not be till the end of the world.

V. I close all, with an answer to a few of the principal objections to the above scheme; and to two or three questions relative to the same.

1st, To objections. As,——1. It may be objected, to what purpose will Satan be bound a thousand years to prevent his deception of the nations, when there will be no nations to be deceived by him during that time, since the wicked will be all destroyed in the general conflagration; and the saints will be with Christ, out of the reach of temptation and seduction? I answer, this will not be the case at the first binding of Satan, which is the first thing Christ will do when he descends from heaven; first bind Satan, then raise the righteous dead, and change the living saints, and take both to himself; and then burn the world: but as the time between the binding of Satan, and the burning of the world, may be but short, I lay no stress on this. Let it be observed, that the same nations, Satan, by being bound, is prevented from deceiving any more, till the thousand years are ended, are those that will be deceived by him after his being loosed; as appears by comparing Rev. xx. 3. with ver. 8. and to prevent their being deceived by him, and put upon schemes to the disturbance of the saints, in their reign with Christ, he and they, that is, their separate spirits, will be shut up together in the bottomless pit; so that the one will be in a state of inactivity, and incapable of tempting and deceiving; and the other in a case and condition not susceptible of temptation and seduction; and both will have enough to do to grapple with their dreadful torments in this confined state; the one will not be at leisure to propose a mischievous scheme, nor the other to hearken to it; and Satan will full well know, that should he form a scheme, it would be impossible to put it in execution in their present circumstances. That the wicked, in an immortal state, are capable of being tempted and deceived by Satan, appears by a fact, after the loosing of him; for which reason it was necessary he should be bound during the thousand years: and that the saints, in an immortal state, are not exempt from

---

[37] Ibid. sec. 16. p. 462.

attempts upon them, by him and his emissaries, only when he is under absolute confinement, which made it necessary, during the said term of time ; and which will be his case after this affair is over, to all eternity.———2. That though the saints are said to reign with Christ a thousand years, Rev. xx. 4, 6. yet they are not there said to reign *on earth*. But it is elsewhere said, the meek shall inherit the *earth ;* and righteousness, or righteous men, shall dwell in the *new earth ;* and the redeemed of the Lamb, who are made kings and priests unto God, shall *reign on earth ;* and they are the same with the priests of God and Christ, that shall reign with him a thousand years. Besides, it appears from the context, that this reign will be on earth ; the angel that descends from heaven to bind Satan, descends on earth ; the binding of Satan will be on earth ; for there he deceived the nations before, and will after his loosing: the resurrection, and living again of the dead, will be on earth ; and so, in course, their reign with Christ there. Besides, they are manifestly the camp of the saints, the beloved city, the Gog and Magog-army will encompass, who will come up on the *breadth of the earth ;* and therefore the saints, the beloved city, must be on earth ; and who are no other than the holy city John saw come down from God out of heaven, that is on earth, where the tabernacle of God will be with them, Rev. xxi. 2, 3.———3. It is objected to the personal reign of Christ with the saints on earth, that they, by reason of the frailty of nature, will be unfit to converse with Christ, in his glorious human nature; but, like the apostles Paul and John, who, when he appeared to them, fell down at his feet, either trembling or as dead. But this objection proceeds upon a supposition, that the saints will then be in a sinful, mortal state ; which will not be the case ; but as their souls will be perfectly sanctified, so their bodies will be raised in incorruption, power, and glory, and fashioned like to the glorious body of Christ, and so fit to converse with him in it ; yea, more so than separate souls in heaven.———4. It is suggested, that for the saints to come down from heaven, and leave their happy state there, and dwell on earth, must be a diminishing of their happiness, and greatly detract from it. No such thing; for Christ will come with them ; all the saints will come with him, and dwell and reign with him ; and where he is, heaven is, happiness is. Did Moses and Elias lose any of their happiness when they came down from heaven, and conversed with Christ on the mount, at his transfiguration ? None at all. No more will the saints, by being and reigning with Christ on earth, in a more glorified state than he was then in : yea, so far from being lessened hereby, that the happiness of the saints will be increased ; their bodies will be raised, and united to their souls, they had been in expectation of, to complete their happiness : and this being now done, they will be more like to Christ, and more fit to converse with him. At the death of Christ, he committed his human spirit, or soul, to his Father, and it was that day in paradise ; on the third day, when he rose, his soul returned, re-entered, and was reunited to his body ; and after his resurrection, he continued on earth forty days, shewing himself to, and conversing with his disciples. During this time, was his soul less happy than before his resurrection ? yea, was it not more so ?———5. The bodies of the wicked lying in the earth till the thousand years are ended, may be objected to the purity of the new earth, and to the glory of the state of the saints upon it. The purification of it by fire, will, indeed, only affect the surrounding air, and the surface of the earth, or little more, and the figure of it, and its external qualities and circumstances ; and not the matter and substance of it, which will remain the same. And as for the bodies of the wicked, that will have been interred in it from the beginning of the world to the end of it, those will be long reduced to their original earth, and will be neither morally impure, nor naturally offensive; and if anything of the latter could be conceived of, the purifying fire may reach so far as entirely to remove that ; and as for the bodies of the wicked, which will be burnt to ashes at the conflagration, how those ashes, and the ruins of the whole world after the burning, will be disposed of, by the almighty power, and all-wise providence of God, it is not easy to say ; it is very probable they will be disposed of under ground : and this will be so far from detracting from the glorious inhabitation and reigning of the saints with Christ upon it, that it will greatly add to the glory of that triumphant reign ; for now all the wicked that ever were in the world, will be under the feet of the saints in the most literal sense ; now they will not only tread upon the wicked as ashes, but tread upon the very ashes of the wicked; and so the prophecy in Mal. iv. 3. will be literally fulfilled, which respects this very case.

2dly, To questions.——1. What will become of the new earth, after the thousand years of the reign of Christ and his saints on it are ended? whether it will be annihilated or not? My mind has been at an uncertainty about this matter; sometimes inclining one way, and sometimes another; because of the seeming different accounts of it in Isa. lxvi. 22. where it is said to *remain* before the Lord, and in Rev. xx. 11. where it is said to *flee away* from the face of the judge; as may be seen by my *notes* on both places, and by a *correction* at the end of the *fourth* volume on the Old Testament; but my last and present thoughts are, that it will continue for ever; and that the passage in Rev. xx. 11. is a rhetorical exaggeration of the glory and greatness of the judge, which appeared such to John in the vision, that the heavens and earth could not bear it, and therefore *seemed* to disappear; the phrase, *from whose face*, which is unusual, seems to suggest and confirm it. I am of opinion therefore, that the new earth will be a sort of an apartment to heaven, whither the saints will pass and repass at their pleasure; and which agrees with other scriptures, which speak of the saints dwelling on, and inheriting the earth for ever.[38]——
2. Who the Gog and Magog-army are, that shall encompass the camp of the saints, when the thousand years are ended? What makes an answer to this the more difficult is, that at the general conflagration of the present earth, all the wicked in it will be burnt up, and none but righteous persons will dwell in the new earth; it is to no purpose therefore, to think of Turks, Tartarians, Scythians, and other barbarous nations,[39] types of these; nor of any remains[40] of the wicked who escaped the general destruction, as supposed; nor of such frightened at the first appearance of Christ, who fled to the remotest parts, and now resume their courage, and come forth: it is a strange absurd notion of Dr. Burnet,[41] that these will be men born of the earth, generated from the slime of the ground, and the heat of the sun; and increasing and multiplying after the manner of men, by carnal propagation, after a thousand years will become very numerous, as the sand of the sea, and make the attack they are said to do. But there is no need to have recourse to so gross an expedient as this: the persons are at hand, and easy to be met with; they are *the rest of the dead*, the wicked, who live not till the thousand years are ended; and then will live, being raised from the dead, even all the wicked that have been from the beginning of the world; which accounts for their number being as the sand of the sea: and these rising where they died, and were buried, will be in and come from the four quarters of the world; and as they died enemies to Christ, and his saints, they will rise such; hell and the grave will make no change in them; and as they laid down with the *weapons of war, their swords under their heads*, they will be in a readiness, and rise with the same malicious and revengeful spirit; and though it will be a mad enterprise, to attack saints in an immortal state, who cannot die; and Christ, the King of kings, at the head of them; yet when it is considered, that they will rise as weak and feeble, as unable to resist temptation, and as capable of deception as ever; and what with being buoyed up with their own number, and the posse of devils at the head of them; and especially considering the desperateness of their case, and this their last struggle to deliver themselves from eternal ruin; it may not so much be wondered at, that they should engage in this strange undertaking,[42]——3. What the fire will be, which shall come down from heaven, and destroy the Gog and Magog-army? Not material fire; but the wrath and indignation of God, which will be let down into their consciences; and which will so terrify and dispirit them, that they will at once desist from their undertaking; like the builders of the tower of Babel, when the Lord not only confounded their language, but smote their

---

[38] The Stoic philosophers speak of the final resolution of all things into fire, into a liquid flame, or pure ether. Dr. Burnet was of opinion that the earth, after the last day of judgment, will be changed into the nature of a sun, or of a fixed star, and shine like them in the firmament, Theory of the Earth, b. 4. ch. 10. p. 317. Mr. Whiston thinks it will no longer be found among the planetary chorus, but probably become again a comet for the future ages of the world, New Theory, b. 4. ch. 5. p. 451.
[39] Vid. Hieron. in Ezek. 38. fol. 238. κ.
[40] Lactant. Institut. 1. 7. c. 24.
[41] Theory of the Earth, b. 4. ch. 10. p. 313.
[42] See my Exposition of Rev. xx. 8.

consciences for their impiety. The issue of all this will be, the casting of the devil and his angels into the lake of fire, where the beast and false prophet are; and the everlasting destruction of the wicked, soul and body, in the same, after the general judgment is over; which is the next thing to be considered.

CHAP. IX.

OF THE LAST AND GENERAL JUDGMENT.

WITH respect to the last and general judgment, the things to be considered are,

I. The proof of a general judgment: and it may be observed, that there will be a judgment of men in a future state; which is two-fold.——1. A particular one; and which passes upon particular persons immediately after death; and to which it is generally thought the apostle has respect in Heb. ix. 27. *But after this,* that is, death, *the judgment;* though if the words are to be connected with what follows, they may respect the judgment that will be at the second coming of Christ. However, it seems probable enough, if not certain, that whereas at death the body returns to the earth, and the spirit, or soul, to God who gave it, Eccles. xii. 7. that then it passes under a judgment, and is adjudged either to happiness or woe.——2. A general one, after the resurrection of the dead at the last day; and this is the judgment that proof is to be given of, and which may be given,

First, From reason: and it may be observed,——1. That the heathens, destitute of divine revelation, and who have had only the light of nature to guide them, have entertained notions of a future judgment; or, however, when suggested to them, have readily assented to it, and embraced it. When the apostle Paul preached to the wise philosophers at Athens, upon his discoursing about the resurrection, some mocked, and others more serious, said, they would hear him again of that matter, not being satisfied with what he had said concerning it: but though he had most plainly and fully expressed the doctrine of God's judging the world in righteousness, they did not in the least contradict that, nor make any objection to it.

The heathen writers sometimes speak of righteous judges in the infernal regions; as Æacus Rhadamanthus, and Minos, who judge the souls of the departed brought before them.[1] Sometimes they represent them as sitting in a meadow, where more ways than one meet, two of which lead, the one to tartarus, or hell, and the other to the island of the blessed,[2] or the Elysian fields; which, though but fables, have some truth couched in them. So it is storied of Er. Pamphilius, what he related after he was restored to life, having been twelve days dead; that he saw two chasms above, and two below, answering one another, between which the judges sat and judged men; and when they had judged them, the righteous on the right-hand they ordered to go upwards to heaven, and the wicked on the left-hand to go downward:[3] which is somewhat similar to the account in Matt. xxv. and it may be, that some of those things said by them, are only some broken remains of a tradition received from their ancestors; or what some got by travelling into the eastern countries, from the Jews, and their writings: and pretty remarkable is that expression of Plato;[4] "We ought always to believe the ancient and sacred words which declare unto us, that the soul is immortal, and has its judges, and will undergo very great judgments or punishments, when any one is separated from the body.——2. That there is a judgment to come, appears from the accusations of a natural conscience for sin, and from the fears and terrors men are possessed of, and cannot free themselves from; as witness the consternation and dread Belshazzar was thrown into on sight of the hand-writing upon the wall; which could not arise from the fear of any temporal evil coming upon him from men, but from a guilty conscience, and the apprehension he had of being called to an account by the divine being, for his impiety and wickedness; so Felix trembled when he heard the apostle Paul discourse of judgment to come; for the doctrine met with the light and conviction of his own conscience, which caused distress and terror.——3. The truth of a future judgment, may be argued from the justice of God, which requires it; for it is easy to observe, that the justice of God is not clearly displayed in the dispensation of

---

[1] Homer. Odyss. 4. v. 563, 564. et 11. v. 567, 568. Apollodorus de Deor. Orig. l. 3. p. 130, 184. Plato in Axiocho, 1308.
[2] Plato in Gorgias, p. 357.
[3] Plato de Republica. l. 10. p. 761.
[4] Epist. 7. p. 1283. Ed. Ficin.

things in the present state. Good men are afflicted, and evil men prosper; which has been a stumbling of saints, and an hardening of sinners: it seems reasonable to believe, that there will be a future state, when justice will take place, and the tables will be turned; and such who have had their evil things now, will have their good things; and such who have had their good things here, will have their evil ones hereafter; for it is a *righteous thing*, with God, to render tribulation to them that trouble his people, and to reward his saints according to his gracious promises.———4. This may be concluded from the relation men stand in to God, as creatures to a Creator. As God is their Creator, he has a right to give them a law; which he has, either written or unwritten; for the breach of which they are accountable to him; so that whether they have sinned without the written law, or in it, they will be judged accordingly; for every one must give an account of himself to God.———5. This may be reasoned from the judgments of God in this present life; and especially from the chastisements of good men, sometimes called a judging them, 1 Cor. xi. 32. from whence an argument may be framed in the words of the apostle; *If judgment begin at the house of God, &c.* 1 Pet. iv. 17. if the one are judged, most certainly the other will be.———6. The desires of the saints after it, implanted in their hearts by the spirit of God, furnish out an argument in favour of it; for however dreadful the thought of it is to Christless sinners, saints can look upon it, and for it, with pleasure; it is now their privilege, that they can *come to God the judge of all*, in the righteousness of Christ; as he is, through that, the justifier of him that believes in Jesus; and they know that the Lord, the righteous Judge, when he comes, will be their advocate and friend, and give them the crown of righteousness laid up for them; and therefore, in the view of this, most earnestly desire his coming to judgment; and importunately pray, saying, *Come, Lord Jesus, come quickly!* Now such desires are not implanted in vain.

Secondly, The truth of this doctrine will more fully appear from divine revelation. In Gen. iv. 8. in the Hebrew text, after these words, *And Cain talketh with Abel his brother;* there is a mark for a pause, as if something was wanting, and to be supplied; and which some ancient versions have supplied thus, *Let us go into the field;* but the Chaldee paraphrases add more, and give us an account of the conversation that passed between them in the field; how that Cain said to his brother, "There is no judgment, and there is no Judge, nor another world, &c." but Abel said, " There is a judgment, and there is a Judge, and another world, &c." upon which, Cain rose up and slew him. Now though this is not to be depended on, nor do I lay any stress upon it; and only observe it, to shew the sense of the ancient synagogue concerning this article; we have had a more sure word of prophecy to take heed unto, for our direction in this matter; and where this doctrine clearly appears; as, 1. In the prophecy of Enoch, the seventh from Adam, recorded in Jude, ver. 14, 15, which as it is to be understood of the second coming of Christ, since it will be with all his saints; so of his coming to judgment, which will be general; for he will then *execute judgment upon all;* and will judge men, both for their ungodly deeds, and for their hard speeches.———2. The character Abraham gives of Jehovah, as the *Judge of all the earth, who will do right,* Gen. xviii. 25. shews that there is a Judge, and that there will be a righteous judgment; and which is committed to the Son of God, who at this time appeared to Abraham in an human form, and was known by him.———3. It may be concluded from the faith of Job, in his living Redeemer, who believed he would stand on the earth in the latter-day, and raise the dead, and himself among the rest; and would have his friends know, that there was a judgment, which would then take place, Job. xix. 25, 26, 29.——— 4. Also from the declaration of Moses, in his song, *The Lord shall judge his people,* Deut. xxxii. 36. vindicate their cause, render tribulation to them who have troubled them, judge their persons, and introduce them into his glory.———5. Likewise from the song of Hannah; *The Lord shall judge the ends of the earth,* 1 Sam. ii. 10. even all the inhabitants of it, who have lived in the uttermost parts of it; and that by the Messiah, as is suggested; since it is added, *He shall give strength to his king, and exalt the horn of his anointed!*——— 6. From some passages in the Psalms; in which God calls to the heavens and earth to be witnesses of his judging his people; which will be, when he comes with a fire devouring before him, and he himself will be judge; when he will come to judge the world with righteousness, and the people with equity, Psalm l. 3, 4, 6. and xcvii. 13.

and xcviii. 9.——7. From others in the book of Ecclesiastes, where it is said, God will *judge the righteous and the wicked ;* and that though young men may indulge themselves in youthful follies and vanities, yet for those things they should be *brought to judgment ;* and into which *every work* shall be brought, whether *good or evil,* Eccles. iii. 17. and ix. 11. and xii. 14.——8. From various sayings of Christ, recorded by the evangelist ; as that whosoever should kill, would be *in danger of judgment ;* and he also that was angry with his brother without a cause; and when he exhorts men *not to judge,* lest they *be judged ;* and upbraids some cities where his mighty works were done, and they repented not; telling them, it would be more tolerable for Tyre and Sidon, Sodom and Gomorrah, *in the day of judgment,* than for them; and when he declares that every idle word must be given an account of in *the day of judgment ;* and affirms, that the men of Nineveh, and the queen of the South, will rise up *in judgment* against the wicked generation of the Jews, Matt. v. 21, 22. and vii. 1. and xi. 22, 24. and xii. 36, 41, 42.——9. From the sermons and epistles of the apostles, particularly the apostles Peter and Paul; the apostle Peter in Acts x. 42. 1 Pet. iv. 9. 2 Pet. ii. 9. the apostle Paul in Acts xvii. 31. and xxiv. 25. Rom. ii. 3, 5, 12, 16. and xiv. 10. 2 Cor. v. 10. 2 Tim. iv. 1, 8.——10. From Heb. vi. 2. where eternal *judgment* is mentioned as an article of a creed ; either of a christian creed, as is commonly thought ; or of a Jewish creed, to which I most incline ;[5] but understood either way, it is a proof of its being an article of faith to be embraced and professed.

To all which may be added, the partial descriptions of the judgment, which are separately given, and which, when laid together, give a complete view of the whole, and shew the judgment to be general. Thus for instance, the calling to account, the examination, trial, and judgment of persons in public work ; ministers of the word are apart made mention of in the parable of the talents ; who, when reckoned with by the Lord at his coming, he that had received five talents, and had gained five more, and he had that received two, and had gained other two, are commended as good and faithful servants, and rewarded with a rule over many things ; in a similar parable it is, with a rule over cities, in proportion to their gain : but he that received one talent, and made no use of it, is condemned as an unprofitable servant, Matt. xxv. 14—30. Luke xix. 15—26. The description of the judgment in Matt. xxv. 31—46. I take it, that it only refers to members of churches, professors of religion, good and bad ; for this account is only an explanation of the two preceding parables ; what is there delivered by way of parable, is here declared without one, which, in other places, is sometimes done by Christ : the first of the parables only concerns the wise and foolish virgins, professors of both characters, in the kingdom of heaven, or gospel church-state ; and the other only respects persons in a public character, in the same church-state, whether good or bad; and this account is of such who have belonged to the same flock, and have been folded together in the same church-state; only one were goats and the other sheep, but not known what they were; but now at the judgment it will be known, when the Lord shall judge between cattle and cattle, the sheep and the goats, and divide them from one another. Besides, what the wicked are upbraided with, shew that they were such who had dwelt among christians, and had been associates with them, and saw them in distress, and did not relieve them; but this cannot be said of multitudes who never heard of Christ, nor ever saw any of his people in distressed circumstances, and shewed them no pity ; and moreover, the sentence pronounced upon them, is the same which elsewhere it is said will be pronounced on such that have borne the christian name, yet bad men, either preachers of the word, or members of churches, Matt. vii. 22, 23. Luke xiii. 26, 27. I am aware what will be objected to all this, that it is said, that *all nations* shall be gathered before the Judge ; but then it should be observed, that the word *all* is frequently to be restrained, and taken in a limited sense, according to the subject treated of; as it must be here : for if what has been said is sufficient to prove, that only professors of religion are spoken of, then the sense must be, that professors in all nations of the world shall be summoned, and brought before the Judge. Likewise the text in Rev. xx. 12. seems only to respect the wicked ; the dead said to stand before God, are the wicked dead, the rest of the dead, who

[5] See my Exposition of Heb. vi. 1, 2.

lived not till the thousand years were ended, ver. 5. and are the same, who being raised, shall encompass the camp of the saints, the beloved city; but being defeated in their enterprise, shall be brought, and stand as criminals before God, the Judge of all, and be judged out of the books opened, according to their works: and what may further strengthen this sense, no other use, as appears, is made of the book of life; only that those whose names were not found in it, were cast into the lake of fire, which must be the wicked. However, putting all these descriptions together, they are a full proof of the general judgment, both of good and bad men, of men under every character and class, and of every age.

II. The next enquiry is, who the person is that shall be the Judge, preside in judgment, and carry on the judicial process to the end? God is, and will be Judge, and he only; hence we read of God the Judge of all, Heb. xii. 23. and of the judgment of God; and of the righteous judgment of God, Rom. ii. 3, 5. and John saw in a vision, the dead, small and great, stand before God, Rev. xx. 12. but not God the Father; *for the Father judgeth no man*, John v. 22. that is, no man separate and apart from his Son; nor in a visible form, for he never assumed any: but then he will judge the world by his Son, as he is expressly said to do, Acts xvii. 31. Rom. ii. 16. so that he is not excluded from a concern in the judgment; nor the Holy Spirit. The trine-une God will be the Judge, as to original authority, power, and right of judgment; but according to the economy settled between the three divine Persons among themselves, the work is assigned unto the Son, and is appropriate to him: hence we read of appearing and standing before the judgment-seat of Christ, and of the Lord Jesus Christ, who shall judge the quick and the dead, at his appearing and kingdom, Rom. xiv. 1. 2 Cor. v. 10. 2 Tim. iv. 1. this work belongs to him as Mediator, and is a part of his office as such; it is what is *committed* to him by the Father, and which he has an *authority* from him to *execute*, John v. 22, 27. it is what he was *appointed* to in the council and covenant of God, Acts x. 42. it is a branch of his kingly office, and therefore in the administration of it he is spoken of as a King; *then shall the King say to them on his right-hand, Come ye blessed*, &c. and when they shall say, Lord, when saw we thee so and so; *the King shall answer and say*, &c. Matt. xxv. 34, 40. Yea, Christ, by his death and resurrection, has obtained a right of dominion over all, as to be the judge of them; *for to this end Christ both died, and rose, and revived, that he might be the Lord both of the dead and living*, Rom. xiv. 9. that is, so as to judge both quick and dead, as the following verses shew. And accordingly, upon his resurrection from the dead, all power in heaven and earth were given to him as Mediator; and upon his ascension to heaven, he was made, or declared, Lord and Christ; and at his second coming, he will come as the Lord, the righteous Judge, with an acquired, as well as an allowed right to judge the world; and this office he will execute as God-man, in both his natures, human and divine, which are both necessary to the execution of it.

1. It is highly proper that the Judge of all the earth should be God. The work requires divine omniscience, infinite wisdom, almighty power, and strict justice and faithfulness; all which are to be found in Christ the Son of God. *Omniscience* is necessary to this work, which is proper to God; for all the works, words, and thoughts of men, must be known by him, in order to judge them; to know all the works, words, and thoughts, of only one man, for the space of sixty, seventy, or eighty years, is more than any mere creature can know; but what is even this knowledge to that of all the individuals throughout a kingdom and nation? and what is that to the knowledge of all the works, words, and thoughts, of the millions of individuals in all kingdoms and nations? and of those in every age of the world, from the beginning of the world to the end of it? Such knowledge is too wonderful for us to conceive of; yet this is in Christ, as God; who knows all persons and things, before whom every creature, and all things, are manifest, naked, and open; even before him with whom we have to do; or to whom we must give an account, as the words may be rendered. He is a discerner of the thoughts and intents of the heart; and needs not to be told any thing of man, for he knows all that is in him and done by him. Wisdom and sagacity are necessary to a judge. Solomon, by his judgment between the two harlots, becam every famous and respectable among his people; but a greater than Solomon is here: one who is the all-wise God, the wisdom of

God, in whom are hid all the treasures of wisdom and knowledge, and on whom the Spirit of knowledge and wisdom rests; a Judge whose head, and whose hairs, are white as wool, as white as snow, denoting his great gravity and wisdom; who is able, as it is necessary he should be, to distinguish between man and man; between that which has only the appearance of a good action, and that which is really such. *Almighty power* is likewise requisite in the Judge of the world, to do what must and will be done by him; as to raise the dead, summon all before him, and not only pronounce the decisive sentences on them, but carry them into execution; for which purpose he is said to come *with power*, as well as with great glory: and such an one is Christ, who is the mighty God, styled most mighty, yea, the Almighty. Strict *justice* and *faithfulness* are qualifications in a temporal judge, who is to execute true judgment; is not to be bribed, nor to respect persons; nor to pass sentence in a cause through favour and affection; and such a Judge, and one infinitely more so, is necessary to judge the world in righteousness and the people with equity; and such an one is Jesus Christ the righteous; and who will appear to be the Lord the righteous Judge, and his judgment to be just and true; for he will not judge according to the sight of his eyes, and the hearing of his ears; but with righteousness shall he judge, and reprove with equity; righteousness will be the girdle of his loins, and faithfulness the girdle of his reins, Isa. xi. 3, 4, 5.

2. That Christ should appear in human nature, when he comes to judge the world, is highly necessary; for God has appointed to judge the world by *that Man* whom he has ordained; so that Christ, as man, must be concerned in the judgment of the world; yea, the father has given him authority to execute it, *because he is the Son of man*, Act xvii. 31. John v. 27. because he has assumed human nature, and so can appear visibly in it, as it is proper a judge should be visible. The sight of a judge is very striking; it commands awe and reverence in all; it fills the criminal with terror, and the just man with pleasure: so Christ, the Judge, will come in such a visible manner, that every eye shall see him; he will appear to the joy of some, and to the shame and confusion of others. A judge usually appears, and it is proper he should, in some external pomp and splendour, in his habit, in his retinue, and attendants; and as placed on a seat, or throne, a bench of justice, with a court set around him: Christ, the Judge of all, will come in great splendour and glory, in the glory of his human nature visible, the rays of his divine nature beaming through it; attended by his mighty angels, and with a shout, the voice of the archangel, and the trump of God; a glorious great white throne will be prepared for him, on which he will be visibly placed, and thousands and ten thousands standing about him, and ministering unto him; it is proper he should appear in human nature, to deliver out, with an articulate voice to be heard, the sentences, both the one and the other; *Come ye blessed*, and *Go ye cursed!* Moreover, since he, as man, was arraigned at the bar of man, and stood before a judge, and was unjustly condemned by him, and dealt with injuriously by men; it seems highly proper, that when he comes as a Judge, he should come as man, and the tables be turned; and he that was his judge stand before him, and see the very man he used so ill, and receive his sentence from him; as well as all such who have spoken against him, his person, doctrines, and ordinances, and maltreated his people; and who will be obliged to confess, *that he is Lord, to the glory of God the Father*, Phil. ii. 11.

As for the concern of others in the judgment, angels or men, nothing is to be admitted, that derogates from the glory of the office of Christ, as Judge of the world. Angels will be no otherwise concerned, than as they will be attendants on him at his coming; be employed by him in gathering and bringing to him the elect, raised from the dead, in the several parts of the world, at the first resurrection; and in the binding up of the tares, the wicked, and casting them into hell, after the second resurrection, and final judgment. Approvers of the righteous judgement no doubt they will be; but as assisting and advising in it, as there will be no need of it, there is no reason to believe it: how far they may be evidences and witnesses in some cases, I will not say; since they are frequently in religious assemblies, and have been employed in many things in this lower world, and must be privy to many things done in it. As for the saints, there seems to be more that is said of them; as that thrones will be set for them, and judgment be given to them; the apostles are said to sit on twelve thrones, in the kingdom of Christ, and to judge men; and the apostle Paul says, that the saints shall judge the world; yea, judge angels, Rev. xx. 4.

Luke xxii. 36. 1 Cor. vi. 2, 3. not that the saints will be co-judges with Christ, and assistants to him in judgment; whatever may be said for them, as sitters by, and approvers of it, as no doubt they will be; and besides this, it is generally allowed, that they, as members of Christ, and as considered in him, their head, will judge the world; and also that their holy lives and conversation will rise up in judgment against their wicked neighbours and condemn them; as that of righteous Lot will rise up against the inhabitants of Sodom.

III. The persons that will be judged; angels and men: as to good angels, nothing is said of the judgment of them in scripture; nor does it seem probable, since they never sinned; were confirmed in their original state by the grace of Christ, and have always been in a fixed state of happiness, always beholding the face of God in heaven: how far their perfect obedience to God, and the faithful services they have performed to men, at his command, may be brought into judgment, to receive their just praise and commendation, I will not say. But as to the case of the evil angels, it is notorious that they will be judged; for if the saints shall judge angels, that is, evil ones, much more will Christ: these, indeed, as soon as they sinned, were cast down to hell, as into a prison; and as criminals are committed to prison, and laid in chains, until the assize, or session comes; so these are laid in chains of darkness, and reserved to the judgment of the great day, when they will receive their final sentence and enter into full punishment; in which it seems they are not as yet, 2 Pet. i. 4. Jude, ver. 6. Matt. viii. 29. But the judgment spoken of in scripture, chiefly concerns men, good and bad; for as the wise man says, *God shall judge the righteous and the wicked*, Eccles. iii. 17.

1. The righteous: and these shall be judged first alone; for *the ungodly shall not stand in the judgment* with them, *nor sinners in the congregation of the righteous*, and they will be first judged; not only according to the order of the words in Ecclesiastes, before mentioned, on which no stress is to be laid; but their judgment will be dispatched first, as represented in Matt. xxv. Besides, they will be raised first; *The dead in Christ will rise first;* even a thousand years before the rest; and it is not reasonable to suppose, that their judgment will not proceed; but be deferred until the rest are raised. Besides, Christ will *judge the quick and the dead*, the living saints changed, and the dead ones raised, *at his appearing and kingdom;* their judgment will be at the beginning of his kingdom, and be continued in it; and it will be proper that they should be judged first, that they may receive the distribution of rewards, made in the kingdom-state; though indeed, they may at once be put into the possession of distinguished favours, and have marks of respect, immediately, as soon as that state begins, and their judgment be brought on, to shew the justness of the distribution made to them. Moreover, since they are to judge the world, and to judge angels, it is necessary they should be first judged themselves.

Here would have been the proper place to consider the question, whether the sins of the righteous will be brought into judgment? but that I have given my thoughts of this in another place.[6] Thus much for the judgment of the righteous. Some have thought that Enoch and Elias, and so those who rose after the resurrection of Christ, and of whom it may be supposed, that they went with him at his ascension to heaven; that those will not come into judgment, since they have been so long in a state of perfection, both in soul and body, which will not be the case of the other righteous at the coming of Christ; but this I will not take upon me to determine.

2. The wicked will be judged; such who have indulged themselves in the gratification of sinful pleasures, and may have been so hardened in sin as to imagine they shall escape the judgment of God; yet they shall not, Eccles. iii. 17. and xi. 9. Rom. ii. 3, 4, 5. even all the wicked shall be judged. These are the *dead*, John saw stand before God, *small and great;* all the wicked dead from the beginning of the world to the end of it; who will not live again, or be raised from the dead, till after the thousand years are ended, Rev. xx. 5, 12. so that the judgment of those will not be till after the thousand years' reign of Christ and his saints, and after the second resurrection; after which, all the wicked being raised, shall be brought to judgment, *small and great;* that is, such as were so when they died, being either children or grown persons; though now as they will rise as persons in manhood, will so stand before

---

[6] Book 6. chap 7. p. 500.

God: or as high and low, rich and poor, kings and peasants; for now shall the rich and poor meet together, though not now distinguished as such; but having been such in their mortal state, shall not be exempted from the judgment of God: or as greater and lesser sinners, and accordingly shall receive their just punishment; for however it may be a question, whether there will be degrees in the ultimate glory; there is none concerning degrees of punishment; since it will be more tolerable for Tyre and Sidon, Sodom and Gomorrah, in the day of judgment, than for some cities where Christ preached and wrought his miracles, yet repented not nor believed in him.

I am aware, that there are some objections to be made to what has been said concerning the judgment of the righteous before the wicked; as,———1. That it seems to contradict the account given of the judgment of both, Matt. xxv. as appearing together, then separated and placed, the one at the right, and the other at the left-hand of Christ. To which it will be sufficient to answer, that in descriptions taken from men, and delivered after the manner of men, and in allusion to what is done among men, it is not to be expected that there should be an exact correspondence in every circumstance of them; the general design of them is what is to be attended to; and if that is answered, it is enough. Now the general design of this description is, to shew that both good and bad men will be judged; that they will be distinguished in judgment, and one will not be taken for the other; the nominal professor will be unmasked: and as for the position of them, at the right and left-hand of Christ, it cannot be understood of a natural position to the right and left; any more than in the petition of the two sons of Zebedee, to sit, the one at the right-hand, the other at the left-hand of Christ, in his kingdom. The allusion is to a sanhedrim, or court of judicature with the Jews; when, whom the judge absolved, he placed at his right-hand; and whom he condemned, he placed at his left. So that the whole of what is intended by this description is, that both sorts of persons shall be judged; that they shall be distinguished, and appear to be what they really are; that the one will be acquitted, and the other condemned, All which may as well be done by supposing the judgment of the one to precede the judgment of the other, as if together; and according to the description itself, the judgment of the righteous will be first dispatched.———2. It is objected, that this account of the judgment seems to make two days of judgment. Not at all: there will be but one day of judgment, though it will be a long one. We are not to imagine, that the day of judgment will be only a natural day, consisting of twenty-four hours: surely it cannot be thought, that all the affairs of kingdoms, states, and churches, and particular persons, from the beginning of the world to the end of it, which will be brought into judgment, and laid open there, will be huddled over in so short a space of time; when this judgment may well be supposed to be with the utmost precision and exactness. No, this day of the Lord will be a thousand years; and for which reason it may be called a *great day*, because of its great and long duration; as well as because of the great things done in it, and by a great Person; and may be also one reason why it is called *eternal judgment*, the word eternal, or everlasting, being sometimes used for a long time only, as this will be. The judgment of the righteous will proceed at the beginning of the thousand years, and continue in them; and during this time things will be preparing for the judgment of the wicked, at the close of them; and so things will go on successively till the whole is finished: as the resurrection of the just will be on the morning of this day, so will their judgment begin then; and as the resurrection of the wicked will be at the evening of this day, so likewise their judgment; and as the evening and the morning make but one day, so it will be in this case; there will be but one day of judgment.———3. Should it be further objected, that there seems no necessity for such a length of time to judge the world in, seeing Christ, the Judge, is omniscient, and knows all men and their works; and therefore can pass judgment upon them at once. I answer, if there is any thing in this objection, it lies as strongly against any formal judgment at all, whether of a shorter or longer space. Besides, the length of time is not taken, and the strict and accurate examination of things entered into, for the sake of the information of the Judge, but that all things might be made clear and plain to every man's conscience; and that it might be evidently seen, that the distribution of favours by the Judge, in the kingdom-state, is made to every one according to his works. God could have made the world at once, in a moment, but he thought fit to take six days in doing it, to shew the greatness of the work, his wisdom, and the counsel of his will in it; so when the affairs of the world, for six thousand years, and how much longer we know not, shall be called over, the Lord is pleased to take a thousand years for it, to shew his exactness and accuracy, strict justice and equity, with which all things shall be managed; and the rather, since the determination is for an eternity to come, in the final issue of things.——4. It may seem inconsistent to some, that the time of the saints reigning with Christ, and their being judged by him, should be together. That so it will be, seems most certain, since Christ will judge *the quick and the dead*, the living saints changed, and the dead saints raised, *at his appearing and kingdom;* when he shall appear and enter on his visible and glorious kingdom, and take his saints to reign with him; nor can I see any inconsistence in this; since the saints, while they are judging, will be in a sinless, perfect state, be like to Christ, both in soul and body, and shall enjoy his personal presence; so that their judgment will not in the least break in upon their felicity in reigning. Besides, they will not stand before the Judge as criminals, but as the favourites of heaven; and this judgment will not be of their persons, on which their final state depends; but of their works; and that it might appear, that the distribution of favours to them, in this kingdom-state, is just and equitable.

Before this head is dismissed, it may be proper briefly to observe, what of men will be brought into judgment.——1. All their works and actions, whether good or evil, Eccles. xii. 14. see also, 1 Tim. v. 24.——2. All the words of men, every hard speech against Christ and his people; yea, every idle word, and much more every profane and blasphemous expression, Jude, ver. 15. Matt. xii. 35, 36, 37. nay,——3. Every thought, good or bad; for there is *a book of remembrance* written, for those that *thought* on the name of the Lord, which are registered there, in order to be observed and taken notice of hereafter, Mal. iii. 16. *God will judge the secrets of men;* not only their secret works, but their secret thoughts, *by Jesus Christ, according to the gospel;* and the Lord the Judge will *bring to light the hidden things of darkness, and will make manifest the counsels of the heart,* Rom. ii. 16. 1 Cor. iv. 5.

IV. The rule of judgment, according to which it will proceed, and from whence the evidence will be taken, are certain *books opened*, Rev. xx. 12. the same is observed Dan. vii. 10. where the judgment of antichrist, the emblem of this judgment, is described; only there is no mention made of the other book, the book of life; because that only respected what will be done in this present life; but this respects the life to come, and the state of men in it.——1. The book of divine omniscience will be opened; Christ, the Judge, who is God over all, knows all persons; the *eyes* of his omniscience are *everywhere*, throughout the whole world, *beholding the evil and the good;* evil men and good men; evil actions and good actions; his eyes are upon *all the ways of men*, and he observes every step they take, and none can hide himself from him, who fills heaven and earth with his presence; and when he comes to judge the world, this book of his omniscience will be opened; he will let all the churches, and all the world know, that he it is who searches the hearts, and tries the reins of the children of men. What is unusual in human courts of judicature, for the judge upon the bench to become an evidence, and be a witness against the prisoner at the bar, will be the case now; *I will come near to you to judgment, saith the Lord, and I will be a swift witness against the sorcerers*, &c. Mal. iii. 5.——2. This book seems to be the same with the *book of remembrance*, in Mal. iii. 16. not that God needs any thing to assist and refresh his memory; he has a strong memory, to remember the sins which are written by him in his book, *with a pen of iron, and with the point of a diamond;* and what is written with an iron pen, or cut with a diamond, is not easily erased; great Babylon will come up in remembrance before God, with all her sins; and so will the sins of wicked men be remembered, be brought into judgment, and meet with their deserved punishment. Though the above book seems to be written for those only that fear the Lord, whose sins he remembers no more; but then he is not forgetful of their good works, which flow from his own grace; and even when they have been forgotten by them, they will be remembered by him, as appears from Matt. xxv. 37.——3. The book of the creatures, or creation, will be opened. Every creature of God is good and useful to men; but those which are given for use are often abused to gratify one carnal sensual lust or another; and which will be produced as witnesses against the sinner.——4. The book of providence will be opened. The providential goodness of God extends to all his creatures; and such who have despised the riches of his goodness bestowed upon them, which should have led them to repentance, and have abused the forbearance and long-suffering of God towards them, in his providence, will find that by the hardness and impenitence of their hearts, they have treasured up wrath against the day of wrath, and revelation of the righteous judgment of God; when the providential dealings of God with them shall be brought as an evidence against them, Rom. ii. 4, 5.——5. The book of the scriptures will be opened, both of law and gospel. The law of Moses will accuse those who have lived under the law, and been violators of it, and pronounce them guilty before God; they that have *sinned in the law shall be judged by the law;* nay, the Gentiles will *judge* them *who by the letter and circumcision transgress the law;* that is, will rise up in judgment against them, and condemn them, Rom. ii. 12, 27. Such who have lived under the gospel dispensation, and have neglected, despised, and rejected the gospel of Christ, will be judged according to it and by it; *The word,* says Christ, *that I have spoken, the same shall judge him* that rejects it *in the last day,* John xii. 48. *God,* says the apostle, *shall judge the secrets of men by Jesus Christ, according to my gospel,* Rom. ii. 16. and the grand rule in it, according to which judgment will proceed, is that in Mark xvi. 16. nay, even the law and light of nature will be a rule of judgment respecting those who have only had the benefit of that; *for as many as have sinned without law shall also perish without law.* Rom. ii. 12.——6. The book of conscience: in this are recorded the actions of men; and from thence are they to be brought forth upon occasion; and which either accuses or excuses for them, when it does its office; unless cauterized and seared, as it were, with a red-hot iron; and even such, in the day of judgment, will have their consciences awaked, and which will be as a thousand witnesses against them.——7. There is another book that will be opened; and that is *the book of life;* in which the names of some are written, which is the same as to be *written in heaven;* and means no other, than the ordination and appointment of them to eternal life in heaven. This is the Lamb's book of life, the book of eternal election, in which all the names of all the elect are written; and the use of this book in the day of judgment will be, that such whose names are found written in it, will be admitted into the new Jerusalem, the holy city, and partake of the privileges thereof, Rev. xxi. 27. and that such whose names are not found written in it; or, as it is expressed in Jude, ver. 4. who are *fore-written to this condemnation,* those shall be cast into the lake of fire, Rev. xx. 15.

Now the *dead* will be *judged out of those things which are written in the books, according to their works,* Rev. xx. 12. which must be understood of the *wicked* dead, when raised and brought to stand before God; who will have sentence pronounced upon them according to their wicked works; between which, and the punishment adjudged to, will be a just proportion; *the wages of sin is death;* eternal death is the just demerit of it: but as there is a difference in the sins of the wicked; some more, others fewer; some greater, others less; some more, and others less aggravated; their punishment will be proportioned to them, as will be seen in the next chapter: and so every one will be judged according to his works, in the most just and equitable manner. Indeed, good men also will be judged according to their works; but not adjudged to eternal life according to them; for there is no proportion between the best works of men, and eternal life; *eternal life is the free gift of God through Christ;* but upon the judgment of them, the distribution of rewards, or of peculiar and distinguished favours, more or less, in the kingdom-state, will be according to every man's works. This judgment out of the books, and according to works, is designed to shew with what accuracy and exactness, with what justice and equity, it will be executed, in allusion to statute-books in courts of judicature, to be referred unto in any case of difficulty.

V. The circumstances of the judgment, as to time and place.

First, The time of it; the particular judgment of men, or of particular persons in their souls, will be immediately after death; according to Heb. ix. 27. the general judgment, or the judgment of all men, in soul and body, will be after the resurrection; the judgment of the righteous, after the first resurrection; and the judgment of the wicked, after the second resurrection.

It is often spoken of in scripture as though it would be quickly, particularly in Rev. xxii. 7, 12, 20. to alarm men, and keep up a constant expectation of it. There is a *day appointed* for it, as may be reasonably thought; for if there is a *time to every purpose*, a time appointed to every thing done under the heavens, then certainly for a business of such moment, and of so great importance, as the general judgment is; and, indeed, this is expressly affirmed; *he hath appointed a day in which he will judge the world in righteousness*, Acts xvii. 31. the time of it is unknown to men, Matt. xxiv. 36. Acts i. 6, 7. hence the Judge is represented as coming *at an unawares*, as a thief in the night, at an hour unthought of; and therefore men should watch and pray, and be ready to meet him.

Secondly, The place. This is also uncertain. Some, because of some passages in Joel iii. 2, 12. have thought of the valley of Jehoshaphat; but no valley can be supposed large enough to hold all that will be judged at the day of judgment; nor does it appear from scripture that there ever was such a valley of such a name; nor does this seem to be the proper name of the valley, whatever valley is intended; in ver. 14. it is called, *the valley of decision;* it properly signifies, the judgment of the Lord, and so is applicable to any place where the Lord should judge the enemies of his people, and bring destruction upon them: and to me it seems to refer to the battle at Armageddon, where will be a great slaughter of the kings of the earth; which will make way for the latter-day-glory. The two more probable opinions are, that the judgment will be either in the air, or on the earth. Some think it will be in the air, because the Judge will come in the clouds of heaven, and the living saints will then be changed, and the dead saints raised; and both will be caught up together unto the clouds, to meet the Lord in the air. But I rather think it will be on earth; the judgment of the saints will be on the new earth, on which they will descend from the air with Christ; and which will be the seat of his reign with the saints, and of theirs with him; and which will be the time of their judging; and as for the wicked dead, who will live again after the thousand years are ended, they will come upon the breadth of the earth, where will be the camp of the saints, the beloved city, and encompass that; and being defeated in their design, they will be at once brought to judgment, and stand before God, the Judge of all and receive their sentence.

VI. The properties of this judgment, as may be gathered from what has been said about it, and from express passages of scripture.——1. It is *future*, yet to come: the apostle Paul reasoned before Felix, among other things, *of judgment to come*, Acts xxiv. 25. But because it seems to be deferred, and does not immediately take place, some have their hearts set in them to do evil, and put away this evil day far from them, as they reckon it, and put it very far away indeed, and fancy it will never be. But,——2. It is *certain ;* purpose and prophecy make it so : God has, in his purposes, appointed a day for it, and he will keep it; and his purpose is never disannulled. Enoch, the seventh from Adam, prophesied of it, as well as others ; and the word of prophecy is a sure one, and will certainly be fulfilled: therefore let young and old know, that for the things they have committed God will bring them into judgment, Eccles. xi. 9.——3. It will be *universal*, both as to persons and things. All men will be judged, sooner or later; in the morning, or in the evening of that day ; none shall escape it ; and all works will be brought into it, good or bad.——4. It will be a *righteous judgment ;* so it is called, Rom. ii. 5. The world will be judged in righteousness ; the Judge of all the earth will do right; Christ the Lord will be a righteous Judge, and his judgment just.——5. It will be the *last* judgment: it will be when the last trumpet shall sound, that the dead shall rise, in order to be judged ; and it will be at the last day, when the word of Christ, and Christ according to it shall judge men, 1 Cor. xv. 52. John xii. 48.——6. It is called *eternal judgment*, Heb. vi. 2. not only because it will be a long time about, as has been observed ; but because it will issue in the final state of men ; either in their everlasting destruction, or in their everlasting happiness, Matt. xxv. 46. which are next to be considered.

CHAP. X.

OF THE FINAL STATE OF THE WICKED IN HELL.

WHEN the judgment is finished, and the sentence pronounced, the wicked will go into *everlasting punishment*, Matt. xxv. 46. What that punishment will be, and the duration of it, are the things to be considered. With respect to the punishment itself, I shall,

First, Prove that there will be a state of punishment of wicked men in the future world. There is a punishment of the wicked in their souls, which takes place at death; as appears from the parable of the rich man, Luke xvi. 23. and there is a punishment of them in soul and body, after the resurrection, and the last judgment, see Rev. xx. 12, 15. which latter is the continuation and perfection of the former. And this will appear.——1. From the light of nature among the heathens; being owned and spoken of, not only by their poets, but by their philosophers, and those the more wise, grave, and serious among them. The poets, indeed, say many fabulous things of Pluto, the king of hell; of Rhadamanthus, and others as judges there; of Charon the ferry-man, and of the infernal rivers; yet under these fables, some truth lies disguised; nay, Tertullian,[1] charges the heathens with borrowing these things from the sacred writings; "When we speak of God as a Judge, and threaten men with hell-fire, we are laughed at; but, says he, the poets and the philosophers erect a tribunal in hell, and speak of a river of fire there: from whence, says he, I beseech you, have they such like things, but from our mysteries?" But not the poets only, but the more serious and wiser sort of the heathens, believed these things. Cæsar was reproved by Cato, for deriding punishments after death; as if there were neither joys nor torments beyond it, but that that puts an end to all.[2] Many of the philosophers[3] wrote of things done in *hades,* or hell; and Plato[4] denies that death is the last thing; but that the punishments of hell are the last; and says all the same things the poets do; yea, declares them to be rational, and not fables:[5] hence Arnobius,[6] an ancient defender of the christians against the heathens, says, "Dare ye deride us when we speak of hell, and of unquenchable fire, into which we know souls are cast? Does not your Plato say the same, in his book of the immortality of the soul? Does he not make mention of the rivers Acheron, Styx, Cocytus, and Periphlegeton, in which he asserts souls are rolled, plunged, and burnt?" Epicurus thought the punishment of hell to be a poetical figment. So Horace, who was an Epicurean, says,[7] *Mors ultima linea rerum est,* death is the last line of things. But Zeno the Stoic believed and taught, that the godly and ungodly will have different habitations; the one delightful, and the other uncomfortable.[8] Indeed, some of the Stoic philosophers[9] derided these things; but then it is thought they only meant the fables of the poets about them, since their founder, as now observed, believed and taught them. Hierocles, a Pythagorean and Platonic philosopher, speaks of εν αδυ κολαστηρια, *punishments in hell.*[10]——2. A state of punishment hereafter, appears from the impressions of guilt and wrath on the consciences of men now, for sins committed, being struck with the fear of a future judgment, and of punishment that shall follow; and which are observable in heathens themselves, whose consciences accuse, or excuse, one another; hence, as Cicero says,[11] "Every man's sins distress him; their evil thoughts and consciences terrify them; these, to the ungodly, are their daily and domestic furies, which haunt them day and night." Such may be observed in Cain, Pharaoh, Judas, and other wicked persons; in whom there was nothing but a fearful looking for of fiery indignation, which shall consume them in hell. And these are emblems, earnests, presages, and pledges of wrath to come. Yea, there is sometimes, some things in good men which bear a resemblance to this; and whilst they are under the sense of them, apprehend themselves as in a condition similar to it; as David, Heman the Ezrahite, and Jonah, Psalm cxvi. 3. and lxxxviii. 6, 7, 15, 16. Jonah ii. 2.——3. This may be argued from the justice of God. If there is a God, he must be believed to be just; and if there is a just God, there must be a future state of punishment; and, indeed, the disbelief of these commonly go together. It is certain there is a God; and it is as certain that

---

[1] Apolog. c. 47.
[2] Sallust. de Bell. Catilin. p. 28, 31.
[3] Heraclides Ponticus, Antisthenes, Democritus et Protagoras, vid. Laert. in eorum Vitis.
[4] De Legibus, l. 9. p. 948. et. l. 12. p. 994. et. in Phædone, p. 83, 84. in Axiocho, p. 1308.
[5] In Gorgia, p. 356.
[6] Adv. Gentes. l. 2. p. 67.
[7] Epist. L 1. ep. 16. v. 79.
[8] Lactant. Institut. 1. 7. c. 7.
[9] Senecæ Consolat. ad Marciam, c. 19. Arrian Epictet. 1. 3. c. 13.
[10] In Carmin. Pythagor. p. 165.
[11] Orat. 2. pro Roscio.

God is righteous in all his ways, and holy in all his works; and will render to every man according to his works. Now it is certain, that justice does not take place, or is not so manifestly displayed in this world; it seems, therefore, but just and reasonable, that there should be a change of things in a future state, when the saints will be comforted, and the wicked tormented: it is but a righteous thing with God to render tribulation to wicked men hereafter, who have had their flow of worldly happiness, and abused it. God is a God of vengeance, and he will shew it, and it is proper he should.——4. This is abundantly evident from divine revelation, from the books both of the Old and the New Testament. David says, *The wicked shall be turned into hell,* Psalm ix. 17. And our Lord speaks of some sins which make men in danger of hell-fire, and of the whole body being cast into hell for them; and of both body and soul being destroyed in hell, Matt. v. 22, 29, 30. and x. 28. But these, and such-like passages, will be considered hereafter.——5. This may be farther confirmed, from the examples of persons that already endure this punishment, at least in part; as the fallen angels, who, when they had sinned, were cast down from heaven, where was the first abode of them, to Tartarus, or hell, a place of darkness, where they are delivered into chains of darkness, and held by them; and though they may not be in full torments, yet they are not without them, and are reserved unto judgment, which, when over, they will be cast into the lake of fire and brimstone, 2 Pet. ii. 4. Rev. xx. 10. Another instance is, the men of the old world, who, by their sins, brought a flood upon it; and not only their bodies were destroyed by the flood, but the spirits, or souls of these men, who were disobedient in the times of Noah, were laid up *in prison,* that is, in the prison of hell, where they were when the apostle Peter wrote his epistle, 1 Pet. iii. 19, 20. these are, by some, thought to be meant by the *congregation of the Rephaim,* of the giants, in Prov. xxi. 16. The men of Sodom and Gomorrah, had not only their bodies and their substance burnt, in the conflagration of their cities; but their souls also are now suffering the vengeance of eternal fire, Jude, ver. 7. So Korah and his company, not only went down alive into the pit of the earth, that opening and closing upon them, but perished in their souls; since wicked men are said to *perish, in the gainsaying of Korah,* for the same sins, and in like manner, though not temporally and corporally; but in soul, and eternally, Jude ver. 11. The case of the wicked rich man, who lift up his eyes in hell, being in torment there, though it be a parable, relates to a fact, and ascertains the truth of it, and which yet some take to be an historical fact.

Secondly, I shall next consider the names, words, and phrases, by which the place and state of future punishment are expressed; which will still give a further proof of it, and lead more into the nature of it.

1st, The names of the place. I call it a place, and not a state only; though some speak of it only as such; but the scriptures make mention of it as a *place of torment,* Luke xvi. 28. and Judas is said to *go to his own place,* Acts i. 25. to which he was appointed, being the Son of perdition: and a place seems necessary, especially for bodies, as after the resurrection; though where it is, or will be, is hard to say: some make it to be the air; others the body of the sun; some the fixed stars; others the earth, either the centre, or the cavities of it, or under it; since the heaven is represented as high, and this as low; and sometimes called hell beneath, Job xi. 8. Prov. xv. 14. Isa. xiv. 9. But it should not be so much our concern to know where it is, as how to escape it, and that we come not into this place of torment, Luke xvi. 28.——1. It is called destruction, or Abaddon, which is the name of the king of the bottomless pit, Rev. ix. 11. which signifies a destroyer, and is rendered destruction in Job xxvi. 6. Prov. xxvii. 20. and xv. 11. where *hell and destruction* are mentioned together, as signifying the same thing, the one being explanative of the other. Indeed the grave, which the word used for hell sometimes signifies, is called the pit of destruction and corruption, because bodies laid in it corrupt and waste away; but here it seems to signify the place of the punishment of the wicked, where body and soul are destroyed with an everlasting destruction; which is not to be understood of an extinction of soul and body, as by the Epicureans and Socinians;[12] for this is

---

[12] Vid. Socin. in 1 ep. Johan. 2. 17. Oper. tom. 1. p. 178, et. Resp. alter ad Volanum, tom. 2, p. 392.

CHAP. X. OF THE FINAL STATE OF THE WICKED IN HELL. 679

contrary both to the immortality of the soul, which cannot be killed, and to the resurrection of the body, which, though it rises to damnation and everlasting contempt, yet dies not again; and to what purpose should it be raised, if it becomes immediately extinct? hell, or a state of punishment, follows upon death, and the resurrection, and is connected with them; it follows upon the death of the body; the rich man died, with respect to his body, and in hell he lift up his eyes; that is, he found his soul in torment, and therefore not extinct. And when the body is raised and united to the soul, and has passed the general judgment, and received its sentence, both will go into everlasting punishment; and therefore neither of them extinct. Besides, there would otherwise be no meaning in those words of Christ, *It had been good for that man if he had never been born*, Matt. xxvi. 24. since for a man to be extinct, or to be in a state of nonexistence, and not to be born, are the same; at least, if a man is extinct, it is as if he had never been born; and therefore no comparison can be made between them; nor better nor worse be said of them. But when hell, or the punishment of the wicked in it, is called destruction, it does not mean a destruction of the being of a person, but of all happiness to him; he is deprived of all, both in soul and body; no light of joy; but darkness, horror, and distress; nothing but indignation and wrath, tribulation and anguish.——2. Another name or word by which it is expressed, is Sheol, which is often rendered the *grave*; as in Gen. xlii. 38. and xliv. 31. and should be where it is sometimes translated *hell*, as in Psalm xvi. 10. yet in some places it seems as if it could not be understood of that, but of the state or place of punishment of the wicked; as in Psalm ix. 17. *The wicked shall be turned into hell*: now to be turned into the earth, or to be laid in the grave, is not peculiar to wicked men; it is the common lot of all, good and bad; it is the house appointed for all living, Job xxx. 23. but to be enveloped with all darkness, and consumed in a fire, not blown, and an horrible tempest rained on them, is the peculiar portion of wicked men from God, Job xx. 26, 29. Psalm xi. 6. Besides, the phrase being *turned* into it, denotes indignation, contempt, and shame; and is the same with the new-testament phrase, so often used, of being *cast into hell*, Matt. v. 29, 30. and viii. 12. so when this word is used of the adulterous woman, and her ways, that her steps take hold of hell, and her house is the way to it; and that her guests are in the depths of it, Prov. v. 5. and vii. 27. and ix. 18. to understand it of the grave, seems not to be strong enough, and to give too low a sense of it; and does not sufficiently express the danger persons are in through her; and into which they are brought: as well as it is not ascribing enough to the way of life, above to the wise, that it secures a person from the grave beneath; and which yet it does not; but rather that it delivers him from the punishment of hell, Prov. xv. 24. In like manner, when it is said of hardened and desperate sinners, that they with hell are at an agreement; they seem to outbrave, deride, and bid defiance to more than death and the grave; even to mock at hell, and its torments they give no credit to. It has its name, *Sheol*, from שאל because it asks and has, and is never satisfied; and applied, whether to the grave or hell, denotes the insatiableness thereof, Prov. xxvii. 20. and xxx. 16. Isa. v. 14. Hab. ii. 5.——3. Another name for hell is *Tophet*; which was a place in the valley of the son of Hinnom, where the Israelites burnt their sons and their daughters in the fire, sacrificing them to Molech; and that the cries of the infants might not be heard, to affect their parents, drums or tabrets were beat upon during the time; and from hence the place had the name of Tophet, *Toph* signifying a drum, or tabret; see Jer. vii. 31, 32. and this seems to be used of the place and state of the punishment of the wicked; *Tophet is ordained of old*, &c. Isa. xxx. 33. which the Targum interprets of hell, prepared from ages past for the sins of men; and which words, Calvin on the text, understands of the miserable condition, and extreme torments and punishments of the wicked; and, indeed, they seem fitly to describe them. *Tophet was ordained of old*, as hell is from eternity; and is that condemnation wicked men were of old ordained unto: it was *prepared for the king*; so everlasting fire is prepared for the devil and his angels, for the prince of devils, and all his subjects: it is made *deep and large*; so hell is the bottomless pit large enough to hold the whole posse of devils, and all the wicked, from the beginning to the end of the world. The *pile*, the fuel, for the fire, is much *wood*, wicked men, comparable to thorns and briers, straw and stubble, withered branches of vines, and dry trees; a fire *kindled,* and blown up by *the breath of the Lord,* at whose blast, and the breath of his nostrils, men perish and are consumed; a fire, not blown by men, but by the breath of the almighty; *like a stream of brimstone,* such as destroyed the cities of the plain.—— 4. From Gehinnon, the valley of Hinnom, where Tophet was, is the word used in the New Testament, γεεννα,[13] Matt. v. 22, 29, 30. Mark ix. 43, 45, 47. for the fire of hell; there, as just observed, children were burnt with fire, and sacrificed to Molech; which horrid custom the Israelites borrowed from their neighbours the Canaanites, or Phœnicians; and who carried it into their several colonies, and particularly to Carthage; where, as Diodorous Siculus relates,[14] the inhabitants had a statue of Saturn, the same with Molech, whose hands were put in such a position, that when children were put into them, they rolled down, and fell into a chasm, or ditch full of fire; a fit emblem of the fire of hell, often called in scripture a *lake of fire.*—— 5. Sometimes this place is called the deep abyss, or bottomless pit: the devils, when they came out of the man, in whom was a legion, besought Christ that he would not order them to go *into the deep,* which seems to be their place of full torment, since they deprecated going into it, Luke viii. 31. and is the same with the bottomless pit Abaddon is king of, and into which Satan, when bound, will be cast, Rev. ix. 1, 11. and xx. 3.—— 6. Another name it has in the New Testament, is *Hades,* which signifies an invisible state, a state of darkness. Some derive it from the word *Adamah,* earth,[15] from whence the first Adam; so that to go down to Hades, is no other than to return to the earth, from whence man was; and the word may signify the grave, in Rev. i. 18. and xx. 13, 14. but it cannot be so understood in Luke xvi. 23. when the rich man died, was buried, and his body laid in the earth, it is said, *in Hades, in hell he lift up his eyes;* which can never be meant of the grave; it is spoken of as distinct from that; and as elsewhere, it is said to be a place of torment; whereas the grave is a place of ease and rest; between this, and where Abraham and Lazarus were, was a gulf, that divided them from one another; whereas in the grave all lie promiscuously: so the gates of hell, in Matt. xvi. 18. must mean something else, and not the gates of the grave.—— 7. Another word by which it is expressed, is *Tartarus;* and this also but in one place, and comprehended in a verb there used, 2 Pet. ii. 4. *God spared not the angels that sinned;* but, ταρταρωσας, *cast them down to tartarus,* or hell: which word, though only used in this place, yet that with others, belonging to it, is to be met with frequently in heathen-writers, who speak of the Titans, and others, that rebelled against the gods, much in the same language as the apostle does of the angels, as bound and cast down to Tartarus; which they describe as a dark place, and as distant from the earth, as the earth is from heaven:[16] and, indeed, the story of the Titans seems to be hammered out of the scriptural account of the fallen angels; and so Plato[17] speaks of wicked men, guilty of capital crimes, as cast into Tartarus, or hell; and also of a place where three ways met, two of which leads, the one to the Islands of the blessed, the others to Tartarus.[18] Some derive this word from a Greek word, which signifies *to trouble,* it being a place of tribulation and anguish: and others from a Chaldean word, which signifies to *fall,* to subside, to go to the bottom,[19] as being a low, inferior place; hence called *hell from beneath.*

2dly, There are words and phrases by which the future punishment of the wicked is expressed; and which may serve to give a further account of the nature of it. And,—— 1. It is represented as a prison; so the fallen angels are said to be cast into hell, as into a prison, and where they lie in chains, and are reserved to the judgment of the great day. And the spirits that were disobedient in the days of Noah, are expressly said to *be in prison,* 2 Pet. i. 4. 1 Pet. iii. 19, 20. Wicked men are not

---

[13] Of some absurd derivations of this word, vid. Ruscam de inferno, 1. 1. c. 7. p. 22.
[14] Biblioth. 1. 20. p. 756.
[15] Vid. Sandford. de descensu Christi, 1. 1. s. 6. p. 8. et s. 25, p. 44.
[16] Apollodorus de Deor. Orig. 1. 1. p. 2. 4. Phurnutus de Nat. Deor. p. 11. 39. ειψο ες ταρταρον νεροντα, Homer. Iliad. 8. v. 13. Tartaro tenebricoso Hygin. fab. 146. vid. fab. 150.

[17] In Phædone, p. 84.
[18] In Gorgia, p. 357. vid. Virgil. Æneid. 6. v. 540, &c. Socrates apud Plutarch. de Consol. ad Apoll. p. 121.
[19] Tartari vox. Etymologo a ταρασσω deducitur—mihi origo Chaldaica, multo magis arridet, a themate, nempe דרד decidit, quo sensu Tartarus pro eo quod subsidit et fundum petit, accipitur. Windet. de vita functorum statu, p. 87.

CHAP. X.   OF THE FINAL STATE OF THE WICKED IN HELL.   681

only criminals, but debtors; and whereas they have not with which to pay their debts, and no surety to pay them for them, to prison they must go, till the uttermost farthing is paid, which never will be, Matt. v. 26. So Plato[20] speaks of Tartarus as a prison of just punishment; for those who have lived unrighteously and ungodly. ——2. It is spoken of as a state of darkness, *of blackness of darkness*, Jude, ver. 13. of the grossest, thickest darkness that can be conceived of; of *outer darkness*, Matt. viii. 12. those in it being without, shut out of the kingdom of light, the inheritance of the saints in light; and so like the darkness of the Egyptians, and such as might be felt; when the Israelites had light in all their dwellings; or, like the kingdom of the beast, said to be full of darkness: all which sets forth the very uncomfortable condition of the wicked, being without the light of God's countenance, and the joys of heaven.——3. It is set forth by *fire*, Matt. v. 21. than which nothing gives more pain, nor is more excruciating; by a *furnace of fire*, Matt. xiii. 42, 50. like that which Nebuchadnezzar caused to be heated seven times hotter than usual, for Daniel's three companions to be cast into, who refused to worship his image, than which nothing can be conceived of more dreadful; and by *a lake of fire*, and of *brimstone* also, which enrages the fire, and increases the strength of it, Rev. xx. 10, 15. and xxi. 8. in allusion to the sulphureous lake Asphaltites, where Sodom and Gomorrah stood: all which serve to give an idea of the wrath of God, poured out on the wicked like fire, and the quick sense they will have of it.——4. It is expressed by a *worm that never dies*, Mark ix. 44, 46, 48. see Isa. lxvi. 24. to die such a death as Herod did, to be eaten of worms, to have a man's flesh gnawn off of his bones by them till he dies, must be very dreadful, Acts xii. 23. but what is this to the continual gnawings of a guilty conscience; that *stimulus perpetuæ conscientiæ*, that sting of a perpetual conscience; or that perpetual sting of conscience Charite threatened Thrasyllus[21] with? This continued consciousness of guilt, and feeling of divine wrath for sin, are but faintly expressed by the heathens, by vultures feeding on the heart of Tytius in hell; or by a serpent eating out his liver, which grew again[22] as fast as eaten. ——5. This is what is called the second death, Rev. xxi. 8. of which good men shall not be hurt, and on whom it shall have no power, Rev. ii. 11. and xx. 6. but wicked men will ever abide under it, shall not become extinct, neither in soul nor body, though they may wish for it. This is death eternal, so called, not from a defect of life; nor from the quality of living, being always dying, yet never die.—— 6. A variety of phrases is used, to signify the terribleness of the future punishment of the wicked; as by tearing them in pieces, as a lion tears his prey; by cutting them asunder, in allusion to punishments of this kind, as Agag was hewed to pieces by Samuel; or to sacrifices, cut up when offered as victims; and by drowning men in perdition, which denotes the utter destruction of them; and by weeping, wailing, and gnashing of teeth, through grief, malice, and envy.——7. By the wrath of God, which comes upon the children of disobedience; by wrath to come, men are warned to flee from; and from which Christ only can deliver them; and by indignation and wrath on every soul of man that does evil. And this is what is chiefly intended by the several words and phrases before observed; and in a sense of which the future punishment of the wicked will greatly lie; as will appear by considering,

Thirdly, The species and sorts of that punishment; or the parts of which it consists, and wherein it lies: it is usually distinguished into *pœna damni*, punishment of loss; and *pœna sensus*, punishment of sense; nor is the distinction amiss, provided they are considered as together, and meeting in the same subject, as they do in the fallen angels; who sinning, were cast out of heaven, were driven from the presence of God, and so lost their original happiness; and were cast down to hell, and so punished with a sense of divine wrath: and both may be observed together in the sentence pronounced on the wicked at the general judgment; *Depart from me*, there is the punishment of loss; *ye cursed, into everlasting fire*, there is the punishment of sense; the one is the loss of the divine presence; the other a feeling of the curse of the law, and the wrath of God; and there cannot be the one without

---

[20] In Gorgia, p. 356, et Socrates apud Plutarch, de Consol. ad Apoll. p. 121.
[21] Apulei Metamorph. 1. 8. p. 114.
[22] Apollodorus de Deor. Orig. p. 10. Hygin. fab. 55.

the other: some have thought, that only the punishment of loss, but not of sense, will be sustained by devils, and wicked men, before the day of judgment; but though the devils may not be in full torment till then, yet not exempt from any, since they are cast down to hell; and as for wicked men, they are immediately after death in a state of pain, and under a sense of it, as the rich man in hell, *being in torment:* and others are of opinion, that such as die without actual sin, and are only guilty of original sin, shall only suffer the former, but not the latter. But as the scriptures say little of the case of such, it becomes us to say little also, and leave it to the wise and just Disposer of all things; yet if eternal death is the demerit of original sin, it is not easy to say how there can be one sort of punishment without the other; where there is a loss, there will be a sense of it, or else it is no punishment; and a sense of it will give pain; though as there are degrees of punishment of sin, as will be seen anon, it is reasonable to believe, the punishment of such will be comparatively a milder one, as Augustin expresses it: no doubt there were many such among the inhabitants of Sodom and Gomorrah, when those cities were destroyed; and yet the apostle says of them in general, that they were *suffering the vengeance of eternal fire*, Jude, ver. 7. But to proceed,

1*st*, There is the punishment of loss, which will consist of a privation of all good things. And,——1. Of God the chiefest good, as the enjoyment of God, is man's chief happiness; so a privation of that enjoyment is his greatest infelicity; the angels, when they sinned, and so Adam, when he sinned, were driven from the presence of God. And though wicked men desire not the presence of God, but say, depart from us, that is, this is the language of their lives and actions; yet when they come to be *punished with everlasting destruction from the presence of the Lord;* a great part of that destruction will lie in an eternal separation from it; it will be dreadful to them, as it was an aggravation of the punishment of Cain, and made it intolerable to him, though a wicked man; *From thy face shall I be hid!* so to be everlastingly banished from God, without any hope of his favour, will be dreadful: the words of an ancient writer [23] are, "Many men only fear hell-fire; but I say, the loss of that glory (the glory of God and of heaven) is much greater than hell, or the punishment of sense: if it cannot be proved by word, it is not to be wondered at; for we do not know the happiness of good things, till we clearly know the misery of evil things, from the privation of those good things."——2. Of Christ, the light, and life of men, the light of grace, and the light of glory, in whom all salvation is; as death is the privation of life in a natural sense, eternal death is a privation of eternal life in Christ; as blindness is a privation of sight, and darkness of light; so the judicial blindness and darkness of the infernal state is a privation of the sight of Christ, and of light, life, and salvation by him; as the happiness of glorified saints, will lie in beholding Christ, and seeing his glory; the miserable state of the wicked will lie in being eternally deprived of such a sight; and therefore this is always in the awful sentence pronounced on them by Christ; *Depart from me, ye cursed;* or *depart from me, ye workers of iniquity*, Matt. vii. 23. and xxv. 41. Luke xiii. 27. ——3. Of the grace, peace, and joy of the Holy Ghost, of which they are destitute now and will for ever be deprived of it; which will be in perfection in the kingdom of heaven; and instead of that, nothing but distress, anguish, and horror of mind; having no rest, no ease, nor peace, day and night, Rev. xiv. 11.——4. Of the company of angels and saints: they will be tormented in the presence of the angels, without receiving any benefit by them, or relief from them: they will be sensible of the happiness of the saints, which will aggravate their misery; they will not be able to come at them, and share with them in their bliss; nor have the least degree of consolation from them; the rich man saw Lazarus in the bosom of Abraham, but could not obtain one dip of the tip of his finger in water to cool his tongue. This seems to be the Tantalus of the heathens, or what they mean by Tantalus; a man athirst and hungry, standing up in water to his chin, and pleasant fruits just at his lips, and yet he not able to quench his thirst with the one, nor to satisfy his hunger with the other:[24] yea, they will not have the least pity shewn them by God, angels or men; God will

---

[23] Chrysostom. Homil. 47. ad pop. Antioch.
[24] Quærit aquas in aquis et poma fugacia captat Tantalus: hoc illi garrula lingua dedit. Ovid. Amor. eleg. 1. v. 43. Hygin. fab. 82.

CHAP. X.   OF THE FINAL STATE OF THE WICKED IN HELL.   683

mock at their destruction; angels will applaud his righteous judgment; and the holy apostles and prophets, and all the saints, will rejoice over them, as they will over Babylon, and at her destruction, because of the justice of God being glorified by it.
——5. Of the kingdom of heaven, from whence they will be excluded, and of the glories and joys of it, of which they will be for ever deprived; they will see the patriarchs and prophets, and all the saints, in the kingdom of God, and they themselves *thrust out;* the door will be *shut* upon them, and no entrance allowed them; they will be obliged to stand *without,* where dogs are; and will be *cast into outer darkness,* for ever deprived of the light of joy and comfort.

2dly, There is the punishment of sense, and which will lie both in body and soul; for both will be destroyed in hell, and be sensible of the fire of it.——1. The body: hence we often read of the whole body, and of the several members of it with it, being cast into hell, Matt. v. 29. 30. Mark ix. 43, 45, 47. now though these are proverbial, or parabolical phrases, yet they have a meaning in them, and have respect to corporal punishment, which will be endured in the body, some way or another. The body is subservient to the soul in the commission of sin; its members are yielded as instruments of unrighteousness; that little member the tongue, is a world of iniquity, defiles the whole body, and is productive of many evils; and it is but just therefore, that the body should have its share in the punishment of sin; and for this purpose is the resurrection of the body, that sinful men may receive the just demerit of their sinful actions done in their bodies. It is a question moved, Whether the fire of hell is a material fire? No doubt that it is not the only thing meant by it, nor the chief, which is the fire of the divine wrath, in which figurative sense it is often taken; though it seems to be sometimes taken in a proper sense, since it has those things ascribed to it which belong to fire properly so called; as smoke, flame, heat, &c. and, indeed, how the body can be affected with any other, is not easy to say, unless by sympathy with the soul, sustaining the fire of divine wrath; nor is it any objection, that the bodies of the wicked will be raised immortal, as never more to die; whereas they would be liable to be consumed, if cast into material fire. To which it may be answered, they may be preserved, by the power of God, from being consumed by it; as the three men in Nebuchadnezzar's furnace were preserved in the midst of it for their safety, so may wicked men be preserved in the furnace of fire for their punishment. And there are such things in nature which are not consumed by fire; as a sort of flax, and cloth made of it, cleansed by burning it; and a precious stone, set on fire, which is not to be quenched; for which reason both have the name of *asbestos,*[25] unquenchable: and there is a sort of fly, called *pyrausta,*[26] or the fire-fly, which lives in the fire. Besides, this fire may not be, as doubtless it is not, the same with our culinary fire; it may be, like that, excruciating, but not consuming; as we see with respect to lightning, or fire from heaven, which sometimes will scorch and burn, and yet not consume and destroy bodies, or reduce them to ashes; as in the case of Nadab and Abihu: but this is not very material to determine; since,——2. The soul will be filled with a sense of wrath, which will be poured forth on the wicked, and burn like fire, Psalm lxxix. 5. Nahum. i. 6. this is the fiery indignation which shall consume the adversaries of God and Christ in hell, Heb. x. 27. that indignation and wrath, tribulation and anguish, which will come upon every soul of man that does evil, Rom. ii. 8, 9. that fire which the breath of the Lord, like a stream of brimstone, will kindle, Isa. xxxi. 30. and which the body, by its near conjunction with the soul, will feel the effects of.

Fourthly, The degrees of this punishment; for it seems such there will be, since wicked men will be judged, and so punished, according to their evil works, whether more or fewer, greater or lesser. But then these cannot be understood of the punishment of loss; one cannot lose more nor less than another; all are equally excluded from the presence and communion of God and of Christ, and of the Spirit; and from the company of angels and saints, and from the kingdom of heaven and the

---

[25] Plin. Nat. Hist. l. 19. c. 1. et l. 37. c. 10. Strabo, l. 10. p. 307. Pancirol. rer. memorab. et Salmuth. in ibid. p. 16. vid. Philosoph. Transact. abridged, vol. 2. p. 552, &c. and vol. 4. par. 2. p. 282.
[26] Plin. l. 11. c. 36. vid. Philosoph. Transact. vol. 7. par. 2. p. 147.

glories of it: but can only be said of the punishment of sense; some are lesser sinners and others greater; some are only guilty of original sin, and not of actual transgressions, at least of very few, and so are deserving of a milder punishment only, as before observed; and of actual transgressions some are guilty of more, and of more heinous ones; see John xix. 11. and their guilt and punishment are in proportion to them; some are attended with greater aggravations, and so are deserving of a greater punishment; some are done in ignorance, and others against light and knowledge; one knows his master's will and does it not, and so deserves to be beaten with many stripes; and another knows it not, and yet does things worthy of stripes, and therefore to be beaten with few stripes, Luke xii. 47. Some have had the advantage of a written law, the law of Moses, as the Jews had, and this explained with the sanctions of it; when others, as the Gentiles, had only the light of nature and the law of it to guide them; and as both will be judged according to their different laws, so will they be punished in a different manner, Rom. ii. 12. Some have had the advantage of a preached gospel, and have despised it, and have been disobedient to it, which is an aggravation of their condemnation; so that it will be more tolerable for Tyre and Sidon, for Sodom and Gomorrah, than for them, Matt. xi. 20, 21. The scribes and pharisees who, against the clearest evidence, and the conviction of their own consciences, denied that Jesus was the Messiah, and blasphemed his miracles, which were proofs of it; and under a pretence of religion, devoured widows' houses, justly receive the greater damnation, Matt. xii. 25—32. and xxiii. 14. and those who have treated contumeliously the great doctrines of the gospel, respecting the person and blood of Christ; and the grace of the Spirit of Christ; of how much sorer punishment shall they be thought worthy, than those who have only broken the law of Moses? Heb. x. 28, 29. see 2 Thess. i. 9. 1 Pet. iv. 17. Some have been favoured with greater mercies in providence than others, and have abused them, and despised the goodness of God extended to them, and so have treasured up more wrath against the day of wrath; and having their good things here, will have their evil ones hereafter, with redoubled vengeance, Rom. ii. 4, 5. Luke xvi. 25.

II. What remains to be considered is, the duration of the punishment of the wicked in hell. It will always continue and never have an end, and is therefore called *everlasting punishment*, and *everlasting destruction*, Matt. xxv. 46. 2 Thess. i. 9. and this will admit of proof both from reason and revelation, from the light of nature, and from the sure word of prophecy. The heathens had not only knowledge of the future punishment of the wicked in hell, but of the eternal duration of it. Lucretius, the Epicurean philosopher, though he disbelieved it, bears a full testimony to the truth of it, even whilst he derides it; he wrote many years before the coming of Christ, so that what he says could not be derived from the writings of the New Testament, but from a more ancient tradition handed down among the Gentiles, time immemorial; he says,[27] that the fears of *eternal* punishment after death, and as what would never have an end, were the cause of all the troubles and miseries of human life; under the bondage of which men lay oppressed, until Epicurus, a man of Greece, rose up, and delivered men from those fears and fancies; so that, according to him, till the times of Epicurus, who lived more than two hundred years before Christ, this sentiment had always obtained among the heathens. And from the sacred scriptures the eternity of future punishment is abundantly evident; as,——1. From the punishment of the inhabitants of Sodom and Gomorrah, who were made an ensample to those that *after should live ungodly;* the destruction of those cities was an emblem of eternal punishment; they agree in the efficient cause of them, God; in the instruments, angels; in the matter and manner of the destruction, by fire and brimstone; in circumstances, suddenly, at an unawares; and in the nature of it, irreparable, and in a sense eternal; for those cities were reduced to such a state, as that they will not, nor can be restored again, and so a fit type of the everlasting punishment of sinners in hell; but more than this, the inhabitants of those cities are now *suffering the vengeance of eternal fire*, Jude, ver. 7. they are not only now suffering the vengeance, but the vengeance is eternal, and expressed by fire that is everlasting. ——2. From the sense and fears of sinners

---

[27] Æternas quoniam poenas in morte timendum, Lucret. de Rerum Natura, l. 1.

CHAP. X.   OF THE FINAL STATE OF THE WICKED IN HELL.   685

in Zion, expressed in Isa. xxxiii. 14. *The sinners in Zion are afraid; who among us shall dwell with everlasting burnings?* the Targum interprets this of the everlasting burnings of hell; and many christian interpreters,[28] of the wrath of God, and the tortures of a guilty conscience there; which are represented as what will endure for ever, and as intolerable; the desert which those sinners were conscious of, and that the outward form of religion would not deliver from them.——3. From the resurrection of the dead, and the issue of it, as described in Dan. xii. 2. *Some of whom awake to everlasting life, and some to everlasting contempt:* this two-fold resurrection is called, the one *the resurrection of life;* the other *the resurrection of damnation,* John v. 29. and as the life some are raised to, is everlasting life, the damnation that follows the resurrection of the other, must be everlasting damnation; here called, *everlasting contempt;* for such will be had in contempt for ever, by God, the holy angels, and good men: the word *everlasting* must have the same sense, and denote the same duration, with respect to the one as to the other.——4. From the sentence pronounced on the wicked, Matt. xxv. 41. to *depart into everlasting fire, prepared for the devil and his angels;* if the punishment of the devil and his angels will endure for ever, and have no end, then the punishment of the wicked will also endure for ever, without end, since the same punishment is prepared for the one as for the other; and which is here expressed by *everlasting fire;* and as elsewhere by *unquenchable fire,* by *fire that never shall be quenched,* Matt. iii. 12. Mark ix. 45. by *smoke of fire* and *torments, that ascendeth up for ever and ever,* Rev. xiv. 11. and by *blackness of darkness reserved for ever,* Jude, ver. 13. ——5. From the execution of the sentence, Matt. xxv. 46. *These shall go away into everlasting punishment;* as the happiness of the saints in heaven is everlasting, and there is no reason to believe it ever will have an end; so the punishment of the wicked in hell will be everlasting, and without end: the same word here rendered *everlasting,* is frequently used of the future life and happiness of the saints, John vi. 40, 47, 54. yea, it is used of it in this passage; for it follows, *but the righteous into life eternal:* now no reason can be given why the word in the one clause, which is the same, should be understood of an eternal duration, and in the other of a limited one. Besides, the opposition of the two states of the respective persons requires, that it should be understood in the same sense, and as of equal extent.——6. From the immortality of the soul. The soul of man, of every man, is immortal, and cannot die, or become extinct, as has been abundantly proved; if therefore it is immortal, and lives for ever, it must be for ever either happy or miserable; the souls of the righteous being immortal, shall be for ever happy; and the souls of the wicked, being so likewise, shall be always miserable: he that is unjust and filthy now, will be after death unjust and filthy still, and ever remain so, and therefore always unhappy and miserable, Rev. xxii. 11. ——7. From the parts of future punishment; the punishment of loss, and the punishment of sense. The loss of all good sustained will be irretrievable; and the sense of pain and torment will be constant, and without intermission; there will be no rest day nor night; the soul being immortal, the *worm* of conscience *dieth not,* but will be always gnawing, stinging, accusing, and upbraiding, and therefore the punishment will always endure.—— 8. From an incapacity of ever being relieved, through the use of means, the ministry of the word; or by a being brought to repentance; or by having sin pardoned, and satisfaction made for it; all which will be out of the question. The ministry of the word of peace and reconciliation will be no more; the door of the gospel will be shut; no place will be found for repentance; men will blaspheme God because of their pains, but not repent of their sins; there will be no remission of sin in the world to come; nor satisfaction to be made for sins; sinners cannot satisfy for them themselves by all that they endure; and there will be none to satisfy for them, for there will be no more offering for sin. ——9. From the impossibility of an escape, or a remove out of it. The place of torment is bounded by a great gulf, so that there is no passing from that to a state of happiness; which gulf is no other than the eternal and immutable decree of God, which can never be disannulled, but will remain fixed and unalterable. The heathens

---

[28] Supplicia hujus vitæ temporaria non explent emphasin phrasios ignis consumentis et focorum æternorum, Vitringa in loc.

themselves represent Hades and Tartarûs, by which they mean the same as hell, as so closely locked and shut up, that there is no return from thence;[29] and as strongly fortified with iron towers and gates, with walls and adamantine pillars,[30] as impregnable, and never to be broke through.——10. From the perfections of God: the veracity of God makes eternal punishment for sin necessary. He has threatened sin, the breach of his law, with eternal death; for such is the demerit of it; and his truth and faithfulness are engaged to fulfil the threatening, unless a compensation is made for sin committed. *Let God be true, and every man a liar!* The justice of God also requires it; not to punish sin, would not be doing justice to himself, and to the glory of his Majesty; it would be a denying himself, a concealing his perfections, and suffering his supreme authority over his creatures to be subject to contempt; his justice, and the honour of it, make it necessary that sin should be punished, either in the sinner, or in a surety for him: wherefore no satisfaction being made to justice, nor can there be any made in a future state, the punishment must continue for ever. It is pretended by some, as if it was contrary to the justice of God, that a transient, temporary action, as sin is, should be everlastingly punished. To which it may be replied, that though sin, as an action, is a transient one, yet the evil, the guilt, the demerit of sin continue, unless purged by the blood of Christ, and atoned for by his sacrifice. Besides, sin is continued to be committed in a future state, though not the same sorts of sins, some of them, as murders, adulteries, &c. yet blasphemy, malice, envy, and the like;[31] and therefore as they continue to be committed, it is but just that the wrath of God should remain upon them: moreover, though sin is a finite action, as an action, for nothing else can be done by a finite creature; yet it is, *objectively*, infinite, as committed against an infinite Being; and therefore is justly punished with the loss of an infinite good. And as the demerit of sin, as to the punishment of sense, cannot be inflicted *intensively* on a finite creature, that not being able to bear it; it is inflicted *extensively;* or is continued, *ad infinitum*, for ever. Nor is this contrary to the mercy and goodness of God; God is just, as well as merciful and good: and these attributes are not to be opposed to one another; justice must be satisfied, as well as grace, mercy, and goodness displayed; and besides, the displays of those, or the actings thereof, are according to the sovereign will and pleasure of God; and when men have despised his goodness in providence, and his grace and mercy held forth in the gospel, and in salvation by Christ; it can be no reproach to his mercy and goodness thus despised, to punish such with everlasting destruction, 2 Thess. i. 9.

CHAP. XI.

OF THE FINAL STATE OF THE SAINTS IN HEAVEN.

There is a state of happiness, which the spirits, or souls, of just men enter into immediately after the separation of them from the body; of which we have treated in a preceding chapter. But after the resurrection, which is of the saints unto everlasting life, and therefore is called the resurrection of life; and when the general judgment is over, and the invitation is given, *Come, ye blessed, &c.* then *the righteous* shall go *into life eternal*, soul and body, Matt. xxv. 34, 46. which is the state now to be considered. And, first, the state of happiness itself, and then the eternity of it.

I. The state of happiness the saints are possessed of after the resurrection, and general judgment, in soul and body, expressed in the passage above quoted, by *eternal life*, and very frequently elsewhere. But it is not animal life, which lies in the conjunction of soul and body, and a continuance of that for ever, which is meant by eternal life; for the wicked will live such a life upon the resurrection; for as there will be a resurrection of the just, so of the unjust; they will live again, and live for evermore; though their living will be no other than the second and eternal death; for they will be destroyed, both

---

Pausaniæ Eliac. sive 1. 5. p. 325. Plato in Phædone, p. 84.

[30] Homer. Iliad. 8. v. 15. Virgil. Æneid. 6. v. 548, &c.

[31] It is indeed denied by some that there is any sinning in hell, see Sandford vel Parker de descensu Christi, 1. 3. s. 96. p. 174, 175. Maccov. Theolog. Polemic. c. 23. qu. 26. though allowed by him in Distinct. Theolog. c. 22. s. 5. and is asserted by divines in general, as by Ames. Medulla l. 1. c. 16. s. 10, 11. Heidegger. Corpus Theolog. loc. 28. s. 113, et alii.

CHAP. XI. OF THE FINAL STATE OF THE SAINTS IN HEAVEN. 687

body and soul, in hell; not as to the substance of either, but as to the comfort and happiness of both; for it is not barely living, but living well, comfortably and happily, that is properly life; in which sense the word is used, Psalm xxii. 26. and such is the life the saints will live in heaven, in soul and body, in the enjoyment of God, as their covenant-God; and thrice happy are they that are in such a case; and in being with Christ! which is far better than to live in this world: and in having the communion of the holy Spirit, than which nothing can be more comfortable; and in the society of angels and saints; all which is most eligible and desirable. In treating on this state, I shall take much the same method as in the preceding chapter. I shall,

First, Prove that there will be a state of happiness of good men in the world to come; for *godliness has the promise of that life which is to come;* that is, of happiness in it. And this may be made to appear, in some respect,

1*st*, From the light of nature and reason; for though the kind of happiness is not to be discovered and demonstrated by it; yet some general notion of future happiness may be evinced from it.——1. A general notion of happiness after death, has obtained among the wiser sort of heathens, who have had only the light of nature to guide them; unless some general traditions transmitted to them, especially among those who have given any credit to the immortality of the soul. Hence they speak of the Elysian fields,[1] and islands of the blessed, as the seat and habitation of pious persons after death; and which they describe after a carnal and earthly manner; as grassy plains, and flowery meads; and as abounding with all manner of delicious fruits; and as in a most temperate climate, free of all wintry weather and blustering storms, and of scorching heat; and where they are fanned with gentle zephyrs, and delighted with flowing fountains and purling streams; and are continually regaling themselves with nectar and ambrosia. Though even their images of those things, Tertullian[2] thinks they have borrowed from the sacred writings, and the description of the heavenly state therein: "If, says he, we speak of paradise as a place of divine pleasantness, appointed for the reception of holy spirits——the Elysian fields seize upon and engross their faith." But those things are not only said by their poets,[3] but by their wise and grave philosophers; as Plato,[4] Plutarch,[5] Seneca,[6] and others.——
2. From a natural desire in mankind after happiness, and which is universal; and yet it is certain it is not attained in this present life, though eagerly sought for, in one way or another. Some seek for it in natural wisdom and knowledge; some in wealth and riches; others in the honours of the world, in fame and popular applause; and others in the gratification of sensual appetites and lusts; but is never found to satisfaction in either; and as abundantly appears from the first and second chapters of the book of Ecclesiastes. This is only found in God, the chiefest good; and that not to perfection in this life. Now either this desire of happiness is implanted in vain, which is not reasonable to suppose; or there must be a future state, in which this happiness will be enjoyed, at least by some of the individuals of human nature, even by all good men; who, at the resurrection, and not before, will be completely happy to full satisfaction; even when they shall awake in the likeness of God.——
3. From the unequal distribution of things in the present state; which makes the providences of God very intricate and perplexed, with difficulties not easy to be solved; and which cannot be solved without supposing a future state: here wicked men have a large portion of good things; and good men have a large share of evil things, afflictions, and distresses; and if their hope of happiness was bounded by this life, they would be of all men most miserable; especially such who are called to endure sharp and severe sufferings: but their hope extends beyond it; as it is reasonable it should; when, as they have suffered in the cause of goodness, truth, and righteousness, that they should be glorified together; and that their present momentary afflictions should work for them, as they do, an eternal weight of glory. But this more abundantly appears,

---

[1] These have their name from עלץ to rejoice, hence called læta arva et læti loci, in Virgil. Bochart. Canaan. 1. 1. c. 34. col. 600.
[2] Tertull. Apolog. c. 47.
[3] Homer. Odyss. 4 v. 563. vid Strabo Geograph. 1. 1. p. 2. et 1. 3. p. 103. Pindar Olymp. ode 2. Virgil. Æneid. 1. 5. v. 734. et 1. 6. v. 543, 638, &c. 743.
[4] In Gorgia, p. 356, 357. et. in Axiocho, p. 1308.
[5] De facie in ore lunæ, p. 942.
[6] Consol. ad Polybium, c. 28.

2*dly*, From divine revelation; by which life and immortality are brought to light; or an immortal life of happiness is set in the clearest light; and which may be strongly concluded,——1. From the promise of God concerning it. *This is the promise,* the grand and principal promise; and which includes and secures all the rest; *He*, that is, God, *hath promised us*, in the covenant of grace, and which lies in his word, *even eternal life*, 1 John ii. 25. which gives hope and assurance of it, and in which it issues: and this promise was made very early, even *before the world began*, and by God that *cannot lie*, and therefore to be depended on as sure and certain; and besides, it is in *Christ;* and not the promise only, but the thing itself, Tit. i. 2. 2 Tim. i. 1. 1 John v. 11. and in this lies the happiness of the saints, James i. 12.—— 2. From the predestination of men unto it; there are *vessels of mercy afore prepared* in the mind, and by the will of God, for this future *glory* and happiness; who are chosen *to the obtaining*, or to the enjoyment, *of the glory of Christ;* to behold his glory and appear with him in glory; who are *ordained to eternal life*, and therefore believe to the saving of their souls: and which act of the grace, and will of God, can never be frustrated and made void; for *whom he did predestinate—them he also glorified*, Rom. ix. 23. 2 Thess. ii. 14. Acts xiii. 48. Rom. viii. 30.——3. From the preparation of this happiness for them; this consists of things unseen and unheard of, and not to be conceived of by carnal minds, which God has *prepared* for them that love him, fear him, and wait for him; and which preparation was made in eternity; for it is a *kingdom prepared from the foundation of the world;* and which will only be given to, and will most certainly be given to, those for whom *it is prepared* of God, 1 Cor. ii. 9. Matt. xxv. 34. and xx. 23. ——4. From Christ's actual possession of it for his people, in their name; and from the preparation he is making of it for them; he is entered into heaven as the *forerunner* for them, and has taken possession of it in their name, as their head and representative; and in whom, as so considered, they are already set down in heavenly places, and shall be in person, most certainly, ere long; for he is gone before to *prepare a place* for them, in his Father's house in heaven, where are many mansions, by his intercession for them, which is always prevalent; and therefore he assures them, he will *come again*, and *receive them* to himself, *that where he is, they may be also*, partakers of his glory and happiness, Heb. vi. 20. Eph. ii. 6. John xiv. 2, 3.—— 5. From the effectual vocation of men to eternal life and happiness: *Lay hold on eternal life, whereunto thou art also called*, says the apostle Paul to Timothy; and to which happiness every man is called, who is called by grace: hence we read of the saints being called of God to *his kingdom and glory;* and of their being called *unto his eternal glory, by Jesus Christ*. Now between vocation and glorification there is an inseparable connection; *Whom he called—them he also glorified*, 1 Tim. vi. 12. 1 Thess. ii. 12. 1 Pet. v. 10. Rom. viii. 30.——6. From the grace of God implanted in the heart, and the earnest of the Spirit there. The grace of God, which is wrought in the heart in regeneration, is **a** *well of living water, springing up into everlasting life*, and issues in it; and the Spirit of God, in his operations on the souls of men, works them up *for that self-same thing*, eternal glory and happiness; and of which his indwelling also in them, is the earnest and pledge; for he is said to be *given* as an *earnest*, and to be *the earnest of the inheritance, until the redemption of the purchased possession;* that is, until all the purchased ones are redeemed from mortality, death, and the grave; and therefore as sure as they have the earnest, they shall enjoy the inheritance, which is eternal life, John iv. 14. 2 Cor. v. 5. Eph. ii. 14.—— 7. From the present experiences of the saints, from those foretastes they sometimes have of future glory and happiness; like the Israelites, they have some clusters of Canaan's grapes, some of the fruits of the good land by the way, as a specimen and pledge of what they shall enjoy when they come into that better country; they now receive the first-fruits of the Spirit, which encourage them to hope for the glorious harvest of the adoption of children: they now, at times, have communion with God in private, and also in public, in his house and ordinances, when they are as the gate and suburbs of heaven to them; and so, by inward felt experience know, from what they find in themselves, that there is something better, and more excellent for them in heaven.——8. From the desires of the saints after future happiness. They choose to be with Christ, as more eligible than to be here; they desire to be clothed upon, with their house from

CHAP. XI.   OF THE FINAL STATE OF THE SAINTS IN HEAVEN.   689

heaven, and are willing rather to be absent from the body, that they may be present with the Lord; and press towards the mark, for the prize of the high calling of God in Christ, Phil. i. 23. and iii. 14. 2 Cor. v. 2, 8. And now those desires in the hearts of the saints, are not formed by the Spirit of God in vain.——9. From the assurance of it some of the saints have had, both of the Old and of the New Testament; the patriarchs Abraham, Isaac, and Jacob, and others, all died in the faith of the better country they were seeking, and were desirous of; the psalmist Asaph expresses his strong faith of it, that *God would receive him to glory;* and the apostle Paul, in his own name, and in the name of other christians, says, *we know,* we are well assured, that *we have a building of God, an house not made with hands, eternal in the heavens,* Heb xi. 13. Psalm lxxiii. 24. 2 Cor. v. 1.
——10. This happiness is begun already in this life; in regeneration men pass from the death of sin, into a life of grace; and a life of grace, is the life of glory begun; he that believes in Christ hath *everlasting life;* is possessed of it in part, and has the earnest and the beginning of it; eternal life is founded in, and begins with the knowledge of God and Christ, John v. 24. and vi. 47. and xvii. 3.——Lastly, There are instances of saints already in heaven, and some in their bodies, as well as in their souls, as Enoch and Elijah; and, as it is highly probable, the saints that arose at Christ's resurrection, and went with him to heaven; see Luke xiii. 28. and xvi. 22. and as sure as they are there, all the rest of the saints will. I go on to consider,

Secondly, The names, phrases, and epithets, used of this happiness; which may serve to convey to us some ideas of the nature of it.

1*st,* The names by which it is called; both as a place and as a state. As a place, ——1. It is called *heaven;* for there this happiness lies, which is called the reward in heaven, the hope laid up in heaven, the inheritance reserved in heaven, and often the kingdom of heaven; and which is no other than the third heaven, where is the throne of God, whither Christ in human nature is gone, and there received, and is the habitation of the holy angels.——2. It goes by the name of *paradise,* in allusion to the garden of Eden, a place of pleasure and delight, 2 Cor. xii. 4. Luke xxiii. 43. in the midst of which, Christ, the tree of life, stands, laden with all manner of precious fruit, for the solace and delight of the blessed inhabitants; and where are fulness of joy, and pleasures for evermore, Rev. ii. 7. and xxii. 2. Psalm xvi. 11.——3. It is represented as a place of *light;* it is called the light of life; the inheritance of the saints in light; and needs no natural nor artificial light to illuminate it; where God and the Lamb are the light of it, and the angels of light dwell, John viii. 12. Col. i. 12. Rev. xxi. 23. and xxii. 5.—— 4. It is signified by an *house* to dwell in; an house not made with the hands of men, but is a building of God; in which there are many mansions, room enough for the many sons the great Captain of salvation will bring to glory, who is gone before them, to prepare them for them; even in his Father's house, 2 Cor. v. 1. John xiv. 2. ——5. It is said to be a *city,* a city of God's preparing, of which he is the builder and maker, and which has foundations firm and strong, and so is a continuing and lasting one, Heb. xi. 10, 16. and xiii. 14. and of this city the saints are now citizens; *our conversation,* ημων το πολιτευμα, *our citizenship is in heaven,* Phil. iii. 20.——6. It is called, *the better country,* Heb. xi. 16. better than this world or any country in it; better than the good land beyond Jordan, Canaan, the type of it: it is *the land that is very far off,* even in the highest heavens; the *land of uprightness,* where there is nothing but perfect purity and integrity, and where only upright persons dwell, Isa. xxxiii. 17. Psalm cxliii. 10. And as a state, it is sometimes called,——1. An *inheritance,* Acts xx. 32. and elsewhere, in allusion to the land of Canaan, distributed by lot for an inheritance to the children of Israel; or in allusion to inheritances among men, which are not acquired and purchased by them; but are bequeathed, or come to them by relations, and are transmitted from father to son; and so the heavenly glory is not obtained by the works of men, or is a purchase of theirs; but is bequeathed to them by their heavenly Father, and comes to them by his will and testament, upon, by, and through the death of the testator, Jesus Christ, Heb. ix. 15, 16. ——2. A *kingdom,* often called the kingdom of God, and the kingdom of heaven, of which the saints are heirs; and they are styled kings and princes, being possessed of the kingdom of grace, as they will be of the kingdom of glory; to which they are called, and which is prepared for them from the foundation of the world, and which it

2 Y

is their Father's good pleasure to give them, James ii. 5. Matt. xxv. 34. Luke xii. 32. ——3. A *crown;* a crown of righteousness and life, a crown of glory, that fades not away, an incorruptible one; which serves to set forth the grandeur of this state, 2 Tim. iv. 8. James i. 12. 1 Pet. v. 4. 1 Cor. ix. 25.——4. It is expressed by *glory* itself, Psalm lxxxiv. 11. and lxxiii. 24. as being exceeding glorious, beyond all conception and expression; it is said to be *a weight of glory,* 2 Cor. iv. 17. in allusion to the ponderous crowns of princes; it will lie in beholding the glory of Christ, in having a glory revealed in the saints, and in having a glory upon them, both in soul and body.——5. It has the name of *peace,* into which good men enter at death, Psalm xxxvii. 37. Isa. lvii. 2. there being nothing in this state to ruffle and disturb, but all tranquil, serene, and calm; no sin within, nor sinful men without: no sorrow and affliction; no pricking brier, nor grieving thorn, throughout the land. ——6. It is signified by a *rest,* which remains for the people of God, after this toilsome life is over, Heb. iv. 9. in allusion to the land of Canaan, a land of rest to the Israelites, after their weary travels in the wilderness; or to the Sabbath, the day of rest, this state being all day, and all Sabbath; a complete rest of body and soul, from all labours, troubles, and enemies whatever.——7. It is called *the joy of the Lord,* into which Christ's faithful servants will be invited to enter, Matt. xxv. 21, 23. a joy that can never be taken away from them, a fulness of joy, a joy unspeakable and full of glory.

2dly, There are various phrases also by which this happy state is expressed, and epithets used of it, which shew the happiness of it; as by being in *Abraham's bosom;* and sitting down as at a table and a feast, with him and others, expressive of the blessed communion of the saints, Luke xvi. 22. Matt. viii. 12. but more especially by being with Christ, and sitting with him on his throne, Phil. i. 23. Rev. iii. 21. and by being fed and led by him, to fountains of living waters, Rev. vii. 17. The various epithets of this state, besides what have been given, are worthy of notice. It is, as yet, an unseen happiness; it consists of things not seen at present; and which faith and hope are only concerned with; and saints have only some glimpse of it, which encourages to wait for it, 2 Cor. iv. 18. Heb. xi. 1. Rom. viii. 24, 25. It is future, it is yet to come; a glory that shall be revealed; grace that is to be brought at the revelation of Christ, and does not yet appear what it shall be: it is beyond all *compare;* the wealth and riches, the glories and grandeur of this world, are trifles to it; yea, the sufferings of the saints, their purest services, are not worthy to be compared with it, Rom. viii. 18. it is an *enduring substance,* a never-fading inheritance, a crown of glory that fades not away; the glory of this world passeth away; but this glory will never pass away; but of the eternity of it more hereafter. I proceed to shew,

Thirdly, The parts of this happiness, or wherein it will consist.

1st, In a freedom from all evils, both of soul and body; from all evils that affect the soul.——1. From the evil of evils, sin, which is exceeding evil in itself, and the cause of all evil: but in this happy state there will be an entire deliverance from it; even,—(1.) From all temptations to it, either from within or from without; glorified saints will have nothing within and about themselves, no sinful lust in their hearts to tempt, entice, and draw them away, as now; their souls being the spirits of just men made perfect; nothing in or about their bodies to incline and lead to sin, which are now vile, and have a world of iniquity in them; but then made like the glorious body of Christ: nor will they have any from without to solicit them to sin; not Satan, for he is cast out of heaven, and has not, nor ever will have, place there any more; nor wicked men, whose evil communications are very ensnaring and corrupting; but these will have no standing in the congregation of the righteous.—(2.) From the dominion of sin; it has not an entire dominion over the saints now, much less will it have any in heaven; nor will any attempts be made to bring them into captivity to it; nor will they be in any danger of it.— (3.) From the commission of it, and so from guilt through it: now none live without it, and daily need to have their garments washed in the blood of the Lamb; fresh guilt arises in their consciences, which must be removed the same way; but the saints will now be impeccable; not capable of sinning, as Adam was in innocence, and the angels before their confirmation; since the former sinned, and so did many of the latter. Yea,—(4.) The saints in heaven will be free from the very being

CHAP. XI. OF THE FINAL STATE OF THE SAINTS IN HEAVEN.

of sin; now it has a place, and dwells and operates in them; but then the Canaanite will be no more in the land.—(5.) They will be rid of an evil heart of unbelief, and be no more distressed with doubts and fears: now unbelief is a sin that easily besets them; and without are fightings, and within are fears; but then, as there will be no occasion to say to themselves, *Why art thou cast down, O my soul?* so neither will they hear such a rebuke, *Wherefore didst thou doubt, O thou of little faith!*—— 2. From the evil one, Satan and his temptations. Adam was not free from him in the garden of Eden; but saints will be in the paradise above: now he goes about like a roaring lion, terrifying and distressing; but then they will be out of the reach of his hideous noise, and where his fiery darts will never penetrate: he will be bound, and cast into the bottomless pit, during the saints' reign with Christ a thousand years; and though when they are ended, he will be let loose for a little while, yet he will be taken up again, and cast into the lake of fire and brimstone, where he will remain for ever, and never more be able to give the least molestation and disturbance.—— 3. From evil men. Whether profane sinners, with whose ungodly conversation they shall be no more vexed; as Lot, David, Isaiah, and other saints have been here; or violent persecutors, who here oppress them, and distress them, in person, in name, in body, and estate; but now will cease from troubling them, not being able to do them the least hurt, nor give them the least uneasiness; or hypocrites in Zion; there will be no more tares among the wheat, nor goats among the sheep, nor foolish virgins among the wise; they that offend, and do iniquity, will be gathered out of the kingdom of Christ.

This happiness will consist in a freedom from all bodily evils; or which affect the outward circumstances. No more penury, nor straitness, as to external things; no more want of food, of drink, and of clothing, which is sometimes now the lot of saints; they will hunger and thirst no more! there will be no more racking pains, nor loathsome diseases; no more sickness; no more death; nor will they be any more subject to disappointments from friends or others; nor to losses in the business of life; nor to loss of friends and relations by death; nor to anything that may mar their joy and pleasure.

2dly, This happy state will consist in the enjoyment of all that is good.——1. In the enjoyment of God himself, who is the chief good, who is the portion of his people now, and will be their portion for evermore; in enjoying communion with him, Father, Son, and Spirit, in the highest perfection, and without any interruption, and to all eternity; in the beatific vision of him, in beholding him as he is; not his nature and essence, so as to comprehend it; but they shall see him so as to have clearer, fuller, and more distinct apprehensions of his perfections and glory; especially his shining in and through Christ, the brightness of his glory, and the express image of his person.——2. In being with Christ, and beholding his glory, the glory of his divine Person, with the eyes of their understanding being more opened and enlarged; and the glory of his human nature with the eyes of their body; they shall see him in the flesh crowned with glory and honour, who was crowned with thorns, spit upon, buffeted, crucified, pierced, and wounded for them.——3. In having the company and society of angels, and of one another. They will now be come, in the fullest sense, to an innumerable company of angels; and will converse with them, and join with them in adoring the divine perfections, and blessing and praising God and the Lamb; they will then sit down with Abraham, Isaac, and Jacob, and other patriarchs, with the prophets, apostles, and all the saints in the kingdom of heaven; they will have communion with each other, though not in the same way and manner as now, in the use of ordinances, of which there will be then no need; yet there will be a social worship, in which they will be jointly concerned; in singing hallelujahs, and in ascriptions of blessing, glory, and praise, to the sacred and eternal Three. They will converse and discourse with each other about divine, spiritual, and heavenly things; in what language it is not easy to say; though *tongues* will *cease*, the multiplicity of languages now used, that jargon introduced at Babel or since; though some think every one will speak in his own language the wonderful things of God; but this is not probable, since then mutual converse would not be general; yet it is reasonable to suppose some one language will be used to employ the tongue; some have thought of the Hebrew language spoken in paradise, and by patriarchs, prophets, &c. but perhaps it may be a language more pure, more perfect, more elegant, and more refined, than ever was spoken by men on earth. It is also highly probable the saints will know one another personally; which seems necessary to their perfect happiness:[7] though they will know no man after the flesh: all natural relations and civil connections will now cease; and whether it will give any peculiar and superior pleasure, to see a relation or friend in this happy state, more than to see another saint, is a question not now to be resolved; as it will give no uneasiness that any relation or friend is missing there, which would mar their happiness. To all which may be added, the communion of the saints will be with the utmost peace and concord; they will dwell together in unity, in the highest perfection; there will be no jars nor discord among them; no envy and vexation among brethren; love will be arrived to its greatest pitch of vigour and glory, and continue so for ever. —— 4. This happiness will consist in perfect holiness. Sanctification will now be completed in soul and body; the soul, as before observed, will be entirely free from the very being of sin, as well as from any act of it; and from guilt and pollution, arising from it; and the body, though vile when lain in the grave, will, being raised, be like to the glorious body of Christ; and saints, both in soul and body, will be without fault before the throne, without any spot or stain of sin, or wrinkle or deformity, or any such thing; and so be perfectly fit for communion with God, with angels, and one another.—— 5. It will consist in the enjoyment of the greatest glory, both in soul and body, beyond all present conception and expression. There will be a glory revealed in the saints, which is beyond all comparison; and a glory put upon them that is inconceivable; a glory upon their souls, which lie in perfect purity in them, in having the righteousness of Christ upon them, and the shining robes of light and bliss: a glory upon their bodies, which will be raised glorious, powerful, spiritual, and incorruptible, and ever continue; as Christ will appear in glory, they will appear in glory with him, and be made like unto him. —— 6. From all which will arise the greatest joy and felicity; fulness of joy, joy unspeakable and full of glory! The redeemed of the Lord shall now be come to *Zion, with songs and everlasting joy upon their heads; they shall obtain joy and gladness, and sorrow and sighing shall flee away,* Isa. xxxv. 10.

Fourthly, It may be considered, whether there will be any degrees in the final happiness of the saints; or whether one saint will have a greater share of happiness than another. It appears, there will be degrees in the punishment of the wicked in hell; and some think there will be degrees in the happiness of the saints in heaven; and others not: and there are some things advanced on both sides not to be despised. Those who are for degrees of glory, do not think there will be any want of happiness in any, nor any uneasy desires after more; nor any envyings of others; nor do they suppose, with the Papists, that the distribution will be made according to the proper merit of men; but that the reward will be a reward of grace, and not of debt: yet, as it seems to incline to the popish notion and to have a look that way, it is not so agreeable; and besides, those passages of scripture which are usually brought to support it, as Dan. xii. 2. Matt. xxv. 14, &c. 1 Cor. xv. 40, 41, 42. belong to the kingdom-state, as we have seen, and not to the ultimate glory. The arguments against degrees in glory seem with me to preponderate. As,

1. That all the people of God are loved by him with the same love; they are not loved one sooner than another, for they are all loved with an everlasting love; nor one more than another: there are no degrees in the love of God, as in himself, though the manifestations of it may be more or less; yet the favour he bears to his own peculiar people is the same, and so always continues to the end, and to all eternity.

2. They are all chosen together in Christ, as not one before another, their election being together in Christ before the foundation of the world; so not one more than another: the election of one may be manifested before another, and be more clearly manifested to one than to another; but the act is the same; so is the glory they are chosen to.

3. They are equally interested in the same covenant of grace, which is an everlasting one; and the one were as early in it as the others; and are all alike blessed with the same spiritual blessings of it; and have the same grace given them in Christ before the world began, one as

[7] See a Sermon of mine, called, "The glorious State of the Saints in Heaven," p. 34, &c.

CHAP. XI.   OF THE FINAL STATE OF THE SAINTS IN HEAVEN.   693

another; and have all the same right to the exceeding great and precious promises of it.

4. They are all equally redeemed with the same price, which is the precious blood of Christ! 1 Cor. vi. 20. 1 Pet. i. 18, 19. and though they are redeemed out of every kindred, tongue, people, and nation, yet it is by the same blood, Rev. v. 9. as the half shekel for the ransom of the souls of the Israelites was the same for one as another, the rich did not give more, nor the poor less, Exod. xxx. 12—15. so the ransom-price for Christ's people is the same, which is himself, 1 Tim. ii. 6.

5. They are all justified by the same righteousness; it is unto all, and upon all them that believe; there is no difference between greater and lesser believers; though one may have more faith than another, that is, as to exercise; yet no man has more righteousness than another; and in every one it is the same precious faith as to its nature and object; it is by one and the same righteousness that all the seed of Israel, the spiritual seed of Christ, are justified; Christ's righteousness is a garment that reaches down to the feet, and covers the meanest member of his body as well as the greatest.

6. All are equally the sons of God, are predestinated to the same adoption of children; and which they receive through the redemption that is by Christ; and from whom they receive the same power, authority, and privilege to become the children of God, one as another; they are all the children of God by faith in Christ, and are fellow-citizens with the saints, and of the household of God; and being children, they are heirs, heirs of God, and joint-heirs with Christ; all alike so, they are all first-born ones, Heb. xii. 23.

7. They are all kings and priests unto God, made so by Christ; their office and dignity are alike; they are alike raised by his grace and favour, from a low estate, to sit among princes, and to inherit the same throne of glory.

8. The future glory and happiness of the saints is frequently expressed by words of the singular number; shewing, that though it belongs to more, it is the same to all, or that all have an equal right to and share in it; thus it is called, the inheritance of the saints in light; the inheritance reserved in heaven; a kingdom it is their Father's good pleasure to give them; a crown of righteousness laid up for them; and is signified by a penny given to the labourers alike, who came into the vineyard at different parts of the day, Col. i. 12. 1 Pet. i. 4. Luke xii. 32. 2 Tim. iv. 8. Matt. xx. 9, 10.

It is a question moved by some, whether there will not be an increase of the happiness of the saints in a future state, or some addition made unto it, and improvement of it, by fresh discoveries of the mysteries of grace and of providence, that may be gradually made, which may afford new pleasure and delight. This is not easy to determine; some are inclined to think there will be an increase, as in the angels, who desire to *look* more into the mysteries of grace, 1 Pet. i. 12. and have a greater knowledge of them, which may be an addition to their happiness. But it is not so certain that angels by nature are meant in the text referred to; but angels by office, ministers of the gospel: besides, the happiness of the good angels may not be as yet complete, until all the elect men are gathered in; as the punishment of the evil angels will not be full until the day of judgment: and if any addition is gradually made to the happiness of the saints in heaven, it must be imperfect until that addition is made, and must continue so till the last is made; which does not seem consistent with the perfection of their state. However, much may be said for the growing happiness of the saints onward in eternity; but the determination of this question must be left till we come into that state, when *we shall know even also as we are known.*

II. The eternity of this happiness is the next and the last thing to be considered, and which is essential to it; for let the happiness of men be what it may, yet if it is to have an end, though at a great distance, the thought of that will greatly spoil the pleasure of it; but this happiness will never have an end; as appears by its names.

1. By its being frequently called *eternal life, everlasting life,* a life that will never end. The present life has an end; let a man live ever so long he dies at last; it is said of Methuselah, the oldest man, that he lived so many years, *and he died;* but he that lives and believes in Christ *shall never die;* though he may die corporally, he shall not die spiritually and eternally, and therefore must be everlastingly happy.

2. It is a *glory,* and it is called *eternal glory,* an *eternal weight of glory,* a crown

of glory *that fadeth not away:* the glory of kings and kingdoms continues not long, but passes away, and so their happiness is temporal and transitory; but that of the saints endures for ever, 2 Cor. iv. 17. 1 Pet. v. 10.

3. It is an *house eternal in the heavens;* it consists of many rooms; there are many mansions, dwelling, abiding places for the saints in it; and those habitations are *everlasting habitations,* 2 Cor. v. 1. Luke xvi. 8. houses on earth may be consumed by fire, or be pulled down by violence, or decay through length of time; or a man may be turned out of house and home; but nothing of this kind can befal the dwelling-place of the saints in heaven, and them in that.

4. It is an *inheritance,* and an *eternal* one; an inheritance incorruptible and undefiled, and that fadeth not away, Heb. ix. 15. 1 Pet. v. 4. An inheritance on earth, a man may be dispossessed of by force or fraud; but an inheritance in heaven is *reserved* there, and so safe and secure; and is out of the reach of any to disturb the saints in their possession of it.

5. It is a *city,* and a *continuing* one; here the saints have none; but they seek one to come; a city which has foundations firm and sure, and can never be subverted, Heb. xi. 10. and xiii. 14. here cities of great antiquity and fame, of great strength and glory, are destroyed and come to nothing, and their memorial perishes with them; but this is a city that will endure to all eternity.

6. It is a *kingdom,* and an *everlasting* one, 2 Pet. i. 11. it is the kingdom of Christ, of which there will be no end; in it the saints will reign with him for ever and ever; his spiritual and mediatorial kingdom, when the end cometh, will be delivered up to the Father; the millennium kingdom will be at an end when the thousand years are expired; but the kingdom of heaven, or the ultimate state of glory, will never end.

7. It is a *country* in which the saints are not sojourners, as here, where they continue but for a while; and so a better country than this; for there they will for ever dwell as in their own native land, being born from above, and partakers of the heavenly calling.

8. It is expressed by *being with Christ,* and which will be *for ever;* and with which words the saints are directed to comfort themselves now, that they shall be *ever with the Lord!* Eternity infinitely adds to the happiness of this state.

9. The eternal purpose of God, which first gave birth to this state of happiness; the everlasting covenant of grace, in which it is secured; and the promise of it, made before the world began, confirm and ensure the everlasting continuance of it.

10. Were there any fears of its ever ending, it would not be perfect happiness; but as *perfect love casteth out fear,* so the full evidence that is given of the eternity of the saints' happiness, casts out all fear of its ever coming to an end: which, as it cannot be admitted, can never be an alloy unto it.

THE END OF THE BODY OF DOCTRINAL DIVINITY.

A TABLE OF TEXTS OF SCRIPTURE

EXPLAINED OR ILLUSTRATED

IN THIS BODY OF DIVINITY.

INTRODUCTION.

GENESIS.

Ch. Ver.	Page.
IV. 1, 25	xxxiii

ACTS.

Ch. Ver.	Page.
XVII. 2, 3	xxvii
XX. 21	xxvi

ROMANS.

Ch. Ver.	Page.
VI. 17	xxv
XII. 6	xxvi

2 TIMOTHY.

Ch. Ver.	Page.
I. 13	xxvi

HEBREWS.

Ch. Ver.	Page.
VI. 1, 2	xxiv

1 PETER.

Ch. Ver.	Page.
III. 21	xxxiv

GENESIS.

Ch. Ver.	Page.
I. 1	26, 131
I. 26	132, 269, 274
II. 2, 3	965
II. 8	309
II. 17	312
II. 19	311
III. 15	348
III. 21, 24	348
III. 22	133
IV. 3	967
IV. 25	349
VIII. 10, 11	967
VIII. 21	333
IX. 26, 27	351
XI. 7	133
XII. 7, 8	27
XIV. 18	27
XV. 2	28
XV. 6	351
XVI. 7	134
XVII. 1	27
XVIII. 2	134
XXII. 11	134
XXII. 18	435
XXXIII. 9, 11	790
XLIII. 9	240
XLVIII. 15, 16	134, 699

EXODUS.

Ch. Ver.	Page.
III. 2	134
III. 13, 14	29
VI. 3	28
XX. 2	991
XXXIII. 14, 15	131

LEVITICUS.

Ch. Ver.	Page.
X. 2	813

DEUTERONOMY.

Ch. Ver.	Page.
IV. 37	131
VI. 4	131
XVIII. 15, 18	424

1 SAMUEL.

Ch. Ver.	Page.
I. 3, 11	27
II. 3	59
III. 18	814

2 SAMUEL.

Ch. Ver.	Page.
XXIII. 2, 3	137
XXIII. 5	250

JOB.

Ch. Ver.	Page.
I. 6	967
X. 21	593
XIV. 10	593
XVII. 9	559
XIX. 25	605
XIX. 26, 27	610
XXXIII. 23	431
XXXVIII. 7	156, 262

PSALMS.

Ch. Ver.	Page.
I. 5	608
II. 7	154, 410
V. 5	100
XVI. 2, 3	120
XVI. 4	431
XVI. 10	406
XIX. 7	18
XXII. 15	407
XXXII. 1	494
XXXII. 2	494
XXXIII. 6	137
XXXIV. 10	117
XXXVII. 29	640
XLV.	646
XLVI. 10	812
XLVII. 5	415
L. 3	630
LI. 9	494
LI. 5	333
LXVIII. 4	29
LXVIII. 18	416
LXIX. 9	828
LXXII. 15	699
LXXII. 17	151
LXXVIII. 39	592
XCIV. 14	560
XCVI.	646
XCVII. 3, 4, 5	630
CII. 26	634
CX. 1	416
CXXV. 1, 2	560
CXXXIX. 7—10	43
CXXXIX. 16	221
CXLV. 9	191
CXLVI. 4	593
CXLVII. 5	41

PROVERBS.

Ch. Ver.	Page.
VIII. 22	155
VIII. 30	252
XVI. 4	196
XVI. 33	299
XIX. 2	705
XXII. 2	295

ECCLESIASTES.

Ch. Ver.	Page.
III. 19, 20	593
IV. 2	594
VII. 1	608
VII. 29	276
IX. 5	600
XII. 1	270

ISAIAH.

Ch. Ver.	Page.
VI. 2, 3	104
VI. 8	133
XI. 10	407
XXIV.	630
XXIV. 23	646
XXVI. 14	608
XXVI. 19	411, 606
XXVIII. 29	30
XXX. 26	647
XXX. 33	679
XLI. 21, 22, 23	134
XLII. 1	253
XLII. 6	226
XLIII. 13	49
XLIV. 22	494
XLV. 7	300
XLVIII. 16	138, 210

INDEX.

Ch. Ver.	Page.
XLIX. 5, 6	220, 252
LIII. 8	154
LIII. 9	407
LV. 3	411
LVII. 1, 2	594
LX. 21	640
LXIII. 7, 14	137
LXV. 17	636
LXVI. 15, 16	630

JEREMIAH.

Ch. Ver.	Page.
XX. 7	111
XXIII. 5, 6	647
XXXI. 15	593, 610
XXXII. 38	117
XXXII. 40	560

EZEKIEL.

Ch. Ver.	Page.
XVIII. 2, 3, 4	329
XVIII. 4	592
XVIII. 24	568
XXI. 27	648
XXXIX. 12	624
XLI. 18	307
XLVIII. 35	648

DANIEL.

Ch. Ver.	Page.
II. 44	648
IV. 17	132
VII.	648
VII. 8, 20, 26	450
VII. 13, 14	416
VII. 14	616, 652
IX. 27	361
XII. 1, 3	617
XII. 2	606, 608
XII. 11, 12	624

HOSEA.

Ch. Ver.	Page.
XIII. 14	415
VI. 7	312

JOEL.

Ch. Ver.	Page.
III. 2, 12	676

AMOS.

Ch. Ver.	Page.
III. 6	300

MICAH.

Ch. Ver.	Page.
II. 13	416
IV. 7, 8	652
V. 2	154
VI. 9	814

NAHUM.

Ch. Ver.	Page.
I. 3, 4, 5	631

ZEPHANIAH.

Ch. Ver.	Page.
I. 2, 3, 18	631

HAGGAI.

Ch. Ver.	Page.
II. 4, 5	138, 217
II. 6	362

ZECHARIAH.

Ch. Ver.	Page.
I. 11, 12, 13	433
III. 1, 4	433
VI. 13	211
XI. 4, 7	222

Ch. Ver.	Page.
XIV. 4, 5	617
XIV. 6, 7	448
XIV. 9	448, 648

MALACHI.

Ch. Ver.	Page.
I. 6	132
II. 5	216
III. 6	35, 564
IV. 1, 3	617
IV. 1, 2, 3	631

MATTHEW.

Ch. Ver.	Page.
III. 16, 17	139, 169
IV. 1, &c.	392
IV. 10	697
VI. 9	104
VI. 10	649
XIII. 4—8	935
XIII. 20, 21	570
XVIII. 15, 16, 17	892
XVIII. 17	888
XIX. 14	900
XIX. 17	92
XIX. 28	653
XX. 21, 22	649
XXIV. 3	617
XXV.	618
XXV. 10	780
XXVIII. 19	140, 901, 914

MARK.

Ch. Ver.	Page.
VI. 3	391
XII. 28, 30	126

LUKE.

Ch. Ver.	Page.
I. 32, 33	650
I. 32, 35	139, 150
II. 10, 11	467
IX. 26	621
XII. 50	912
XVI. 22, 23	595
XIX. 12	618
XX. 36	653
XXII. 29, 30	650
XXIII. 42, 43	595

JOHN.

Ch. Ver.	Page.
I. 7	468
I. 14	379, 389
I. 12, 13	202
I. 29	472
III. 13	387
III. 14, 15	356
III. 16	472
III. 36	98
IV. 22, 24	31
IV. 42	472
V. 17	172
V. 28, 29	611
VI. 32	355
VI. 38	384
IX. 2, 3	330
X. 28	561
X. 36	152
XI. 51, 52	202
XII. 32	468
XIV. 2, 3	619
XIV. 16	139
XIV. 23	134
XV. 2, 6	570

Ch. Ver.	Page.
XVII. 3	126
XVII. 4, 5	210
XVII. 12	568
XX. 23	315

ACTS.

Ch. Ver.	Page.
I. 6	650
I. 11	619
II. 37, 38	376
II. 37, 38, 41	900
III. 19, 21	619
VI. 3	884
XIII. 48	178
XIV. 23	867
XV. 10	901
XVI. 14, 15	902
XVI. 33	913
XVII. 25	121
XIX. 37	852
XXII. 16	913

ROMANS.

Ch. Ver.	Page.
III. 4	110
III. 25	489
III. 30	129
V. 5	760
V. 14	316
V. 18	469
V. 19	324
VIII. 5, 6	838
VIII. 29	189
VIII. 30	208
IX. 29	186
IX. 11, 13	101
XI. 17, 22	571
XI. 16	906
XI. 33	65
XIII. 1	984
XIII. 7	986
XIV. 15	474
XV. 5	89

1 CORINTHIANS.

Ch. Ver.	Page.
V. 3, 5	889
V. 7	355
VI. 11	209
VII. 14	907
VIII. 6	130
VIII. 12	474
IX. 27	571
X. 1, 2	912
X. 3, 4	355
X. 12	576
XI. 18, 20	22, 915
XIII.	771
XV. 24, 28	148
XV. 37, 38	610
XV. 42, 44	610
XV. 53, 54	610
XV. 47	384
XVI. 1, 2	971
XVI. 15	902

2 CORINTHIANS.

Ch. Ver.	Page.
I. 21, 22	140
V. 1, 8	595
V. 14, 15	470
V. 19	211, 473
XIII. 14	140

INDEX.

GALATIANS.

Ch. Ver.	Page.
I. 15	297
IV. 4	396
IV. 6	139, 202
IV. 8	30
V. 4	572

EPHESIANS.

Ch. Ver.	Page.
I. 4	180, 181, 186
I. 6	205
I. 7, 8	68
II. 2	308
II. 3	98
II. 4, 5	85
II. 18	698
IV. 11	863
V. 21, 29	973
V. 33	976
VI. 1	979
VI. 4	979
VI. 5	981
VI. 9	982

PHILIPPIANS.

Ch. Ver.	Page.
I. 21, 23	596
II. 6	30
II. 7, 8	395
II. 7	396
III. 10	415
IV. 11	788

COLLOSSIANS.

Ch. Ver.	Page.
I. 15, 16, 17	166
III. 20	978
III. 22, 23, 24	981

1 THESSALONIANS.

Ch. Ver.	Page.
IV. 3	187
IV. 16	609
V. 8	762
V. 12, 13	877

2 THESSALONIANS.

Ch. Ver.	Page.
II. 3, 8	450
II. 13	185, 187
II. 16	760

1 TIMOTHY.

Ch. Ver.	Page.
I. 16	90
I. 19	572
II. 1	944
II. 4	470
II. 5	130, 387
III. 1, 4, 5	864
III. 8—12	884
IV. 8	704
IV. 10	471
IV. 21	192
VI. 15, 16	52, 123

2 TIMOTHY.

Ch. Ver.	Page.
I. 9	297
II. 13	55
III. 16, 17	19, 20
IV. 1	651

TITUS.

Ch. Ver.	Page.
II. 11, 12	471
III. 1	985
III. 10	889

HEBREWS.

Ch. Ver.	Page.
I. 2	160
I. 3	146
II. 5	651
II. 9	471
II. 10	476
III. 12	576
III. 3, 4	966
IV. 8	356
IV. 14	153
V. 8	153, 234
VI. 19	761
VI. 4, 5, 6	573
VII. 22	237
VIII. 7, 8	363
VIII. 13	364
IX. 10	361
IX. 15	363
X. 26	574
X. 38	575
XI. 4	349, 432
XII. 1	813
XII. 23	853
XIII. 5	787
XIII. 7, 17, 18	873

JAMES.

Ch. Ver.	Page.
I. 4	818
III. 17	833

1 PETER.

Ch. Ver.	Page.
I. 1, 2	188
I. 3	761
I. 5	564
III. 20, 21	914

2 PETER.

Ch. Ver.	Page.
I. 4	30, 274
II. 1	474
II. 20, 22	575
III. 9	472
III. 10, 12	625
III. 13	636
III. 17	576

1 JOHN.

Ch. Ver.	Page.
I. 7	153
II. 2	473
III. 3	761
IV. 8, 16	78, 80
V. 7, 8	128, 135

2 JOHN.

Ver.	Page.
3	112
8	576

JUDE.

Ver.	Page.
4	194, 197
14, 15	616
21	576

REVELATION.

Ch. Ver.	Page.
I. 10	971
III. 14	165
IV. 11	119, 251
VII. 9	640
XI. 19	450
XII. 4	308
XIV. 13	596
XX. 1, 2, 3	620
XX. 4	653
XX. 5	659
XX. 12	674
XXI. 1, 2, &c	641

THE BAPTIST STANDARD BEARER, INC.
A non-profit, tax-exempt corporation
committed to the Publication & Preservation
of The Baptist Heritage.

SAMPLE TITLES FOR PUBLICATIONS AVAILABLE IN OUR VARIOUS SERIES:

THE BAPTIST *COMMENTARY* SERIES
Sample of authors/works in or near republication:
John Gill - *Exposition of the Old & New Testaments (9 & 18 Vol. Sets)*
   (Volumes from the 18 vol. set can be purchased individually)

THE BAPTIST *FAITH* SERIES:
Sample of authors/works in or near republication:
Abraham Booth - *The Reign of Grace*
Abraham Booth - *Paedobaptism Examined (3 Vols.)*
John Gill - *A Complete Body of Doctrinal Divinity*

THE BAPTIST *HISTORY* SERIES:
Sample of authors/works in or near republication:
Thomas Armitage - *A History of the Baptists (2 Vols.)*
Isaac Backus - *History of the New England Baptists (2 Vols.)*
William Cathcart - *The Baptist Encyclopaedia (3 Vols.)*
J. M. Cramp - *Baptist History*

THE BAPTIST *DISTINCTIVES* SERIES:
Sample of authors/works in or near republication:
Alexander Carson - *Ecclesiastical Polity of the New Testament Churches*
E.C. Dargan - *Ecclesiology: A Study of the Churches*
J. M. Frost - *Paedobaptism: Is It From Heaven?*
R. B. C. Howell - *The Evils of Infant Baptism*

THE *DISSENT & NONCONFORMITY* SERIES:
Sample of authors/works in or near republication:
Champlin Burrage - *The Early English Dissenters (2 Vols.)*
Franklin H. Littell - *The Anabaptist View of the Church*
Albert H. Newman - *History of Anti-Paedobaptism*
Walter Wilson - *History & Antiquities of the Dissenting Churches (4 Vols.)*

For a complete list of current authors/titles, visit our internet site at
www.standardbearer.com or write us at:

The Baptist Standard Bearer, Inc.
No. 1 Iron Oaks Drive • Paris, Arkansas 72855
Telephone: (501) 963-3831   Fax: (501) 963-8083
E-mail: baptist@arkansas.net
Internet: http://www.standardbearer.com

Specialists in Baptist Reprints and Rare Books

Thou hast given a *standard* to them that fear thee; that it may be displayed because of the truth. -- *Psalm 60:4*

www.ingramcontent.com/pod-product-compliance
Lightning Source LLC
Chambersburg PA
CBHW021347290426
44108CB00010B/146